Llywelyn ap Gruffudd

PRINCE OF WALES

Llywelyn ap Gruffudd

PRINCE OF WALES

J. Beverley Smith

UNIVERSITY OF WALES PRESS
CARDIFF
1998

© J. Beverley Smith, 1998

British Library Cataloguing-in-Publication Data
A catalogue record for this book is available from the British Library.

ISBN 0–7083–1474–0

All rights reserved. No part of this book may be reproduced, stored in a retrieval system, or transmitted, in any form or by any means, electronic, mechanical, photocopying, recording or otherwise, without clearance from the University of Wales Press, 6 Gwennyth Street, Cardiff, CF2 4YD.

The right of J. Beverley Smith to be identified as the author of this work has been asserted by him in accordance with the Copyright, Designs and Patents Act 1988.

Published with the financial support of the Arts Council of Wales

Typeset at University of Wales Press
Printed in Great Britain by Dinefwr Press, Llandybïe

Er cof am
Cecil a Hannah Smith

Contents

List of Genealogical Tables		viii
List of Maps		viii
Preface		ix
Abbreviations		xiii
1	Inheritance	1
2	Bryn Derwin	37
3	Supremacy	90
4	Rhyd Chwima	139
5	Lord of Snowdon	187
6	Prince of Wales	274
7	A Principality in Perplexity	338
8	Aberconwy	390
9	Contention and Conflict	451
10	Cilmeri	511
11	Epilogue	582
Genealogical Tables		607
Maps		610
Bibliography		615
Index		639

List of Genealogical Tables

Gwynedd   607
Powys   608
Deheubarth   609

List of Maps

Wales   610
Gwynedd   611
Powys   612
Deheubarth   613
The march of Wales   614

Preface

This volume has been written as a contribution to the study of a period of unique importance in the history of Wales. The policies pursued by the princes of the thirteenth century lend a coherence to the political history of the nation, and a significance to the course of Anglo-Welsh relations, hardly matched at any other time in the medieval centuries. The themes that suggest themselves for study in this period find their main focus in the person of Llywelyn ap Gruffudd, and a biographical study of the prince thereby becomes a means of approaching a historical record which, although still exceedingly sparse on several counts, provides a firm foundation for meaningful interpretation. A Welsh text, *Llywelyn ap Gruffudd, Tywysog Cymru*, published in 1986, was, rather surprisingly, the first attempt to make extensive use of the source materials in a study centred on the prince. The present volume is a new composition which, although it adheres to the plan and arguments of the first work, presents a somewhat enlarged discussion of several issues. The annotation, on occasion more extensive than I would wish, is in large part explained by the need to resolve matters raised in studying sources which, in many instances, have not hitherto been subjected to the critical examination they deserve, and it was often necessary to attend to problems of dating a document or to indicate the considerations which lie behind a statement made in the text.

I set out to write this book with a sense of great respect for the work of earlier scholars, both the authors of valuable historical discussions and those whose prodigious labours on the record sources have provided the edited texts on which so much medieval history is founded. My gratitude and admiration have deepened as this study progressed, and to a number of scholars I owe, besides the legacy of their written work, the great benefit of their kindness and generous encouragement. I owe to T. Jones Pierce and J. Goronwy Edwards, who guided my first efforts, both an inspiration and a discipline of enduring influence. I cherish the memory of my warm friendship with Hywel Emanuel, Glanville Jones, Thomas Jones, Gwyn Alfred Williams and Keith Williams-Jones, scholars of generous disposition and unbounded enthusiasm. My efforts have been eased by the comradeship of several

Preface

kindred spirits, whose names recur in the acknowledgements to be found in the pages that follow, among them D. J. Bowen, A. D. Carr, T. M. Charles-Edwards, R. R. Davies, E. B. Fryde, R. A. Griffiths, Daniel Huws, Richard Ireland, Dafydd Jenkins, Huw Pryce, Bryn Roberts, Llinos Beverley Smith, David Walker, R. F. Walker and Glanmor Williams. I have been greatly rewarded by contact with scholars engaged in major work in progress. A critical edition of the court poetry of the period of the princes has been completed at the Centre for Advanced Welsh and Celtic Studies of the University of Wales, and I am grateful for the many kindnesses I have received from R. Geraint Gruffydd and J. E. Caerwyn Williams and, among their colleagues, Nerys Ann Jones and Ann Parry Owen. J. P. Clancy graciously allowed me to draw upon his translations of the poetry addressed to the princes, and I am indebted to Ann Parry Owen for translations of poems not yet available in English. A. J. Taylor shared with me his unrivalled knowledge of the record sources and military architecture of the conquest, and it is a pleasure to record my appreciation of his friendship over many years. A work on the financial records of the period 1282-4 which he initiated is now being edited by R. F. Walker and Susan J. Davies, and it has been a privilege to be associated with this venture. An edition of the *acta* of the princes is being prepared under the direction of Huw Pryce to whom, along with Kary Maund and Charles Insley, I am grateful for the first-fruits of another important scholarly contribution.

In bringing my study to completion I have incurred a number of particular debts that I am delighted to acknowledge. Huw Pryce, Huw Ridgeway and R. F. Walker showed great kindness in reading several chapters and in giving me, by their perceptive comments, the benefit of their intimate knowledge of the period. The work was read by two readers appointed by the Welsh Arts Council and their reports, quite apart from ensuring the award of a generous grant towards the cost of publication, conveyed a number of valuable suggestions. Tomos Roberts enabled me to gain access to the Melville Richards collection of place-names and drew unstintingly on his own knowledge in that field. John Simpson kindly undertook an investigation by which his specialist knowledge could be applied to an understanding of the situation in which the English army suffered a calamity in the tidal flow of the Menai Straits. I was able to discuss a number of problems, to my great advantage, with Paul Brand and David Carpenter, and the help of a number of other scholars with particular issues is acknowledged in the volume. I have found unfailing courtesy and friendship in libraries and record repositories, and particular thanks are due to the staff of the Hugh Owen Library, the National Library of Wales and the Public Record Office.

In preparing the volume for publication Rosemary Mills valiantly bore the brunt of transforming my execrable manuscript into a word-processed text,

Preface

and I am also indebted to Delyth Fletcher and Gillian Parry. The maps were expertly prepared by Michael G. Jones to whom I am most grateful. I thank the University of Wales Press for undertaking publication, and I am especially indebted to the Director, Ned Thomas, and, for their great care in the production of the volume, to Susan Jenkins, Ceinwen Jones and those associated with them.

While the work was in its early stages I enjoyed tenure of the Sir John Rhŷs Visiting Fellowship of the University of Oxford, and I would like to acknowledge the hospitality and stimulating company of the Principal and Fellows of Jesus College, and especially that of my firm friend D. Ellis Evans. At the University of Wales Aberystwyth I had for many years a strong bond of friendship with my colleagues in the Department of Welsh History – Ieuan Gwynedd Jones, Llinos Beverley Smith, Brian Howells, Geraint Jenkins and John Davies – and I am grateful to them all for providing an extraordinarily friendly and supportive environment. Although this work was completed within a Department of History and Welsh History, I offer my volume in appreciation and encouragement of my colleagues' continued commitment to the history of Wales. My association with the Royal Commission on the Ancient and Historical Monuments of Wales has given me, together with the fellowship of Commissioners and staff, a fuller awareness of the way in which the Royal Commission, Cadw: Welsh Historic Monuments, the Welsh Archaeological Trusts and others are enriching our knowledge of the buildings and landscape that would have been known to those whose aspirations and anxieties are the subject of this volume.

The greatest debt of all is the one that I owe to my family. My wife, Llinos, besides the gift of knowledge selflessly shared, has given me, over many years, the love and encouragement that have sustained my efforts and brought me profound happiness. My sons Robert and Huw, remarkably tolerant of Llywelyn ap Gruffudd's intrusion into our family as they grew up, have even so ensured that both their father and the subject of his endeavours have been treated with due irreverence, and I am thankful to them for their lively support. All three will understand my wish to acknowledge one last debt of gratitude, to Gomer Smith for his constant and reassuring presence at my feet during the grim hours of solitude which are the lot of whoever embarks upon the task of writing a volume of inordinate length.

University of Wales Aberystwyth　　　　　　　　　　　　J. Beverley Smith
Michaelmas 1998

Abbreviations

AC	*Annales Cambriae*
AgHR	*Agricultural History Review*
AL	*Ancient Laws and Institutes of Wales*
AnnCestr	*Annales Cestrienses*
AnnDunst	'Annales Prioratus de Dunstaplia'
AnnOsney	'Annales Monasterii de Oseneia'
AnnTewk	'Annales Monasterii de Theokesberia'
AnnWav	'Annales Monasterii de Waverleia'
AnnWinch	'Annales Monasterii de Wintonia'
AnnWorc	'Annales Prioratus de Wigornia'
ArchCamb	*Archaeologia Cambrensis*
B	*Bulletin of the Board of Celtic Studies*
BIHR	*Bulletin of the Institute of Historical Research*
BL	British Library
Bracton	*Bracton on the Laws and Customs of England*
Breviate Annals	'Chronicle of the thirteenth century, MS Exchequer Domesday'
BS	*Brenhinedd y Saesson*
BT, Pen20	*Brut y Tywysogyon, Peniarth MS 20*
BT, Pen20Tr	*Brut y Tywysogyon, Peniarth MS 20 Version, Translation and Notes*
BT, RBH	*Brut y Tywysogyon, Red Book of Hergest Version*
CAC	*Calendar of Ancient Correspondence concerning Wales*
CAP	*Calendar of Ancient Petitions relating to Wales*
Cartae	*Cartae et Alia Munimenta . . . de Glamorgancia*
CCR	*Calendar of Close Rolls*
CChR	*Calendar of Charter Rolls*
CCW	*Calendar of Chancery Warrants, 1244–1326*
CFR	*Calendar of Fine Rolls*
Cheshire Pipe Rolls	*Cheshire in the Pipe Rolls, 1158–1301*
ChronBury	*Chronicle of Bury St Edmunds*
ChronPetroburg	*Chronicon Petroburgense*
ChronWykes	'Chronicon Thomae Wykes'
CIM	*Calendar of Miscellaneous Inquisitions*

Abbreviations

CIPM	*Calendar of Inquisitions Post Mortem*
CLibR	*Calendar of Liberate Rolls*
CMCS	*Cambridge Medieval Celtic Studies* to no. 25 (1993)/ *Cambrian Medieval Celtic Studies* from no. 26 (1993)
cmt	commote
Cotton, *HistAng*	*Bartholomaei de Cotton Historia Anglicana*
Councils	*Councils and Ecclesiastical Documents relating to Great Britain and Ireland*
Councils and Synods	*Councils and Synods with Other Documents relating to the English Church*
CPapL	*Calendar of Papal Letters*
CPR	*Calendar of Patent Rolls*
CR	*Close Rolls*
CRR	*Curia Regis Rolls*
ctf	cantref
CW	'Cronica de Wallia'
CWR	'Calendar of Welsh Rolls'
DamCol	*Damweiniau Colan*
DBM	*Documents of the Baronial Movement of Reform and Rebellion*
DipDoc	*Diplomatic Documents*
DNB	*Dictionary of National Biography*, 22 vols. (1908–9)
DWB	*Dictionary of Welsh Biography to 1940* (London, 1959)
EcHR	*The Economic History Review*
EHD	*English Historical Documents*
EHR	*The English Historical Review*
ExtAng	'The Extent of Anglesey'
ExtMer	'Extent of Merionethshire'
Flint Pleas	*Flint Pleas, 1283–1285*
FloresHist	*Flores Historiarum*
Foedera	*Foedera, Conventiones, Litterae, et Acta Publica*
GBF	*Gwaith Bleddyn Fardd*
GCBM	*Gwaith Cynddelw Brydydd Mawr*
GDB	*Gwaith Dafydd Benfras*
GirCamb, Op	*Giraldi Cambrensis Opera*
GlamCH	*Glamorgan County History*
GLlF	*Gwaith Llywelyn Fardd*
GLlLl	*Gwaith Llywarch ap Llywelyn*
GMB	*Gwaith Meilyr Brydydd a'i Ddisgynyddion*
Guisborough, Chronicle	*The Chronicle of Walter of Guisborough*
H	*Handlist of the Acts of the Native Welsh Rulers 1132–1283*
HGK	*Historia Gruffud vab Kenan*
HistCarm	*A History of Carmarthenshire*
HKW	R. A. Brown *et al.* (ed.), *The History of the King's Works: The Middle Ages*
HW	J. E. Lloyd, *A History of Wales* (1911)

Abbreviations

Inventory Angles	*An Inventory of the Ancient Monuments in Anglesey*
Inventory Caern	*An Inventory of the Ancient Monuments in Caernarvonshire*
Inventory Carm	*An Inventory of the Ancient Monuments in Carmarthenshire*
Inventory Glam	*An Inventory of the Ancient Monuments in Glamorgan*
Inventory Radn	*An Inventory of the Ancient Monuments in Radnorshire*
JFlintHS	*Journal of the Flintshire Historical Society*
JMerHRS	*Journal of the Merioneth Historical and Record Society*
Langtoft, *Chronicle*	*Chronicle of Pierre de Langtoft*
LHD	*The Laws of Hywel Dda, Law Texts from Medieval Wales*
LibEpist	*The Liber Epistolaris of Richard de Bury*
LlBleg	*Llyfr Blegywryd*
LlCol	*Llyfr Colan*
LlIor	*Llyfr Iorwerth*
LTWL	*The Latin Texts of the Welsh Laws*
LW	*Littere Wallie*
Mabinogion	*The Mabinogion*
MLSR	*The Merioneth Lay Subsidy Roll, 1292–3*
MonAng	*Monasticon Anglicanum*
MontColl	*Montgomery Collections. Journal of the Powysland Club*
MPW	*A Medieval Prince of Wales. The Life of Gruffudd ap Cynan*
NLW	*The National Library of Wales*
NLWJ	*The National Library of Wales Journal*
Owen, *Penbrokshire*	Owen, George, *The Description of Penbrokshire*
par	parish
Paris, *ChronMaj*	*Matthaei Parisiensis . . . Chronica Majora*
Paris, *HistAng*	*Matthaei Parisiensis . . . Historia Anglorum*
ParlWrits	*Parliamentary Writs*
PBA	*Proceedings of the British Academy*
PKM	*Pedeir Keinc y Mabinogi*
PR	*Patent Rolls*
PRO	Public Record Office
RC	*Registrum Vulgariter Nuncupatum: The Record of Caernarvon*
RCAHMW	Royal Commission on the Ancient and Historical Monuments of Wales
RegPontissara	*Registrum Johannis de Pontissara Episcopi Wintoniensis*
RegSwinfield	*Registrum Ricardi de Swinfield, Episcopi Herefordensis*
RG	*Rôles Gascons*
Rishanger, *Chronica*	William Rishanger, *Chronica et Annales*
Rishanger, *De Bellis*	William Rishanger, 'Chronica de duobus bellis'
RL	*Royal and Other Historical Letters . . . of the Reign of Henry III*
RotFin	*Excerpta e Rotulis Finium*
RotLittClaus	*Rotuli Litterarum Clausarum*
RotLittPat	*Rotuli Litterarum Patentium*
RotParl	*Rotuli Parliamentorum*
RotWall	*Rotulus Walliae*

Abbreviations

RPeck	*Registrum Epistolarum Fratris Johannis Peckham Archiepiscopi Cantuariensis*
RS	The Rolls Series
SC	*Studia Celtica*
SD	*Survey of the Honour of Denbigh, 1334*
SWMRS	*South Wales and Monmouthshire Record Society*
TAngAS	*Transactions of the Anglesey Antiquarian Society and Field Club*
TC	J. B. Smith, *Llywelyn ap Gruffudd, Tywysog Cymru*
TCaernHS	*Transactions of the Caernarvonshire Historical Society*
TDenbHS	*Transactions of the Denbighshire Historical Society*
Throne of Scotland	*Edward I and the Throne of Scotland 1290–1296*
THSC	*Transactions of the Honourable Society of Cymmrodorion*
TRadnS	*Transactions of the Radnorshire Society*
TreatyR	*Treaty Rolls*
Trevet, *Annales*	Nicholas Trevet, *Annales Sex Regum Anglie*
TRHS	*Transactions of the Royal Historical Society*
VCH	*Victoria County History*
Vegetius	*Flavius Vegetius Renatus, Epitoma Rei Militaris*
WAR	*The Welsh Assize Roll 1277–1284*
WHR	*Welsh History Review*
WML	*Welsh Medieval Law*
Wynn, *HGF*	Sir John Wynn, *The History of the Gwydir Family and Memoirs*

Titles not included in this list are abbreviated, where necessary, by author's surname and short title in a form (such as Altschul, *Clares*) which will be readily identified among the Secondary Works in the Bibliography at the end of the volume. Public Record Office Class Numbers (such as E101) are listed under 'Original Sources: Unpublished' in the Bibliography.

CHAPTER 1

Inheritance

ON Michaelmas day 1267 Llywelyn ap Gruffudd came before Henry III at Rhyd Chwima, the ford on the Severn a short distance from Montgomery castle. The ford of Montgomery had already become a recognized meeting place where proctors appointed by king and prince often met to resolve matters over which contention had risen on the frontiers between their lands. But the meeting between the king and the prince themselves had a particular significance. On that day Llywelyn did homage to Henry and swore fealty. No account of the event has survived but, if the two men followed the conventions which were well established among medieval nations, Llywelyn would have knelt before the king and placed his hands in his lord's hands and, when he had done homage in this way, he would have pronounced the solemn words which promised his fidelity in word and deed. Although the proceedings signified that Llywelyn had submitted himself to the king's lordship, they also served to elevate the prince. Henry had come to the frontier at Montgomery from Shrewsbury where members of his council had joined the prince's men in prolonged negotiations that ultimately led to a historic peace treaty. Ottobuono, the papal legate who conducted the later stages of the transactions, was able to present the outcome as an agreement which showed that the two nations, after prolonged conflict, had made peace with one another in a manner which brought credit upon both sides. Four days later, King Henry travelled the remaining distance to reach the furthermost part of his kingdom and complete the formalities which signified his wish to honour Llywelyn. In taking the prince's hands into his own the king recognized the special position that Llywelyn had won for himself by establishing his authority over an extensive part of Wales. For some years already Llywelyn had used the style 'prince of Wales' and, by the proceedings on the frontier between the kingdom of England and the principality of Wales, the king indicated his wish to confirm the prince's right to that exalted style.[1]

---

[1] Negotiations leading to a settlement and the completion of the formalities by the treaty of Montgomery are examined below, pp.173–86.

Inheritance

Llywelyn ap Gruffudd was the first prince in the history of Wales to secure the king of England's recognition of a title which implicitly proclaimed the unity of a large part of the country under the lordship of a single ruler, and securing Henry's acknowledgement that an extensive dominion was now vested in one person was a considerable achievement. For, though the prince who came to meet the king sprang from a royal lineage stretching back over centuries, the position which he formally secured in 1267 was entirely the result of his own endeavours. Only one man among the princes of Wales, namely his grandfather Llywelyn ap Iorwerth, or Llywelyn the Great, had ever achieved a comparable measure of unity. The nation's sense of identity may perhaps be traced to an early period in its history, but the idea of a single political structure embracing the various lands held under Welsh lordship was relatively new. Signs of an aspiration for political coherence may be discerned a little earlier, but the objective came to be a practical proposition only when Llywelyn ap Iorwerth, in the early years of the thirteenth century, was able to bring the princes of Wales together in a military alliance which gave birth to a form of political unity under his lordship. It was an altogether different matter, and still more difficult, to induce the king of England to tolerate a change in the internal organization of Wales which had such profound consequences for the relationship between Wales and England. Not even Llywelyn the Great had been able to surmount this difficulty. By his submission at Rhyd Chwima in 1267 Llywelyn ap Gruffudd registered an achievement which stood unique in the history of the nation. This volume attempts to trace the manner by which Llywelyn ap Gruffudd secured that triumph, to make an estimate of his achievement, and to understand how his success was subsequently reversed. A study of Llywelyn ap Gruffudd provides an opportunity to examine a period of momentous importance in the shaping of the nation's political destiny.

The prince's achievement was unique, but his endeavour was not without precedent and, in attempting to understand the objectives he set himself and the methods he employed, account needs to be taken of the efforts of his forebears. Particular notice has obviously to be given to Llywelyn ap Iorwerth, a predecessor to whom the grandson frequently referred in pursuing his own ends. Neither of the princes has gained the benefit of a modern historical assessment embodied in a substantial study specifically devoted to them, and much of our understanding necessarily stems from the considered and detailed chapters embodied in the work of John Edward Lloyd.[2] A

---

[2] J. E. Lloyd, *A History of Wales from the Earliest Times to the Edwardian Conquest* (London, 1911), ii, 587–693, 706–64 [*HW*]. His treatment of the first prince is much fuller than that of the second, and his discussion of Llywelyn ap Gruffudd ceases, in effect, in 1277, with barely five pages given to the critical course of events during the following five years.

Inheritance

reading of the *History of Wales* suggests that it was Llywelyn ap Iorwerth's achievement which the author considered to be the supreme accomplishment in the history of medieval Wales. He referred to the thirteenth century, it is true, as 'the age of the two Llywelyns', and he acknowledged the primacy which the second Llywelyn established in his time. But in his estimation it was, without doubt, Llywelyn the Great who revealed the subtle blending of the qualities of the statesman with the invincible spirit of a leader in war, who combined the gift of opportunism with the prescience which ensured that the princely interest was never placed in jeopardy, and who skilfully steered his dominion through the vicissitudes of the early years to the security of the period of his maturity. Despite a readiness to recognize the extent of his achievement, the qualities that he perceived in Llywelyn ap Gruffudd hardly matched those which had raised the grandfather above all other princes of the nation. In Lloyd's view the key to Llywelyn ap Gruffudd's success lay in fateful circumstances, and the prince possessed neither the judgement nor the instinctive prudence with which his grandfather was so well endowed. Although the second Llywelyn at the peak of his career won an elevated and recognized position which had eluded the first, and though in pursuing his objectives he trod a path already marked out by his predecessor, his triumph was still founded upon an uncertain basis, for so much depended on fickle fortune and transitory advantage. It is a view to which historical opinion may still afford some measure of assent, but one prince need not be diminished in order to respect another. Acknowledging the grandson's indebtedness to his grandfather's vision and capability does nothing to lessen the achievement of Llywelyn ap Gruffudd.[3] This study thus begins by identifying the essential features of Llywelyn ap Gruffudd's political endeavour and estimating the extent to which his objectives had entered into the calculations of the dynasty of Gwynedd in the preceding generations and particularly in the time of Llywelyn ap Iorwerth. Three themes may be readily recognized: the value the princes placed upon their patrimonial inheritance in Gwynedd and their concern for its integrity; their relationships with those who ruled in Powys and Deheubarth and the march of Wales, and particularly their quest for influence in those areas; and their constant concern for the persistently difficult relationship with the kingdom of England.

---

[3] Lloyd's work incurred some criticism when it first appeared for its inclination towards Llywelyn the Great (e.g. W. H. Jones, 'Llywelyn ap Gruffudd', *Y Beirniad*, 1 (1911), 123–7). T. F. Tout, *EHR*, 27 (1912), 131–5, in an appreciative review, remarked that the discussion of Llywelyn ap Gruffudd was cut short. Articles on Llywelyn ap Gruffudd were contributed by Tout, *DNB*, 12 (1909), 13–21; T. Jones Pierce, *DWB*, 597–8.

Inheritance

The record of their time shows that the princes were imbued with a consciousness of status which was closely bound up with their historical inheritance. It finds eloquent expression in a statement which Llywelyn ap Gruffudd made during his exchanges with Archbishop Pecham only a few weeks before his death in combat in 1282. Three features may be recognized: a memory of a royal lineage which could be traced back to the Trojan origins of the nation itself; a sense of territory; and a grasp of the legitimate and inherent nature of the status which the lineage maintained upon the patrimonial territory.[4] These perceptions may be sensed at a much earlier period in the history of the kingdom of Gwynedd and they are particularly relevant to the manner by which the lineage was able to extricate itself from the adversity in which it was placed in the Norman period.[5] There can be no doubt of the gravity of the challenge which confronted the Welsh dynasties in that period, and it could be portrayed as a conflict between one power which represented the virtues and superior capability of a society at the core of Latin Christendom and another less well endowed and a decidedly more fractious society upon its periphery.[6] Pecham's letters to Llywelyn ap Gruffudd reveal the extent to which the church could still view the nation that resisted the English crown as one which had need to be brought more securely within the Christian fold. Pecham was not the first to recognize characteristics in the Welsh which amounted to a flawed morality, and the image cultivated by contemporary commentators placed the nation among the more disadvantaged societies.[7] The fragmented nature of political authority, and the disability which arose from it, was perhaps a mark of ineptitude in the ordering of society. There can be no doubt that the fissile political configuration of Wales left the country exposed to alien intervention, but the precise nature of the contrast between Norman and Welsh capabilities might be considered more carefully. Military technology, and expertise in the deployment of military resources, counted for much, and the capacity of the Welsh rulers to adapt themselves to the specifically military needs which confronted them mattered immensely in containing and then reversing the Norman thrust within a generation of the first incursions. But this military effort was a facet of a decidedly political endeavour. The partial but crucial

---

[4] *RPeck*, ii, 469–71.

[5] Relations between Welsh and Normans, and among Welsh rulers, are afforded extensive recent study in R. R. Davies, *Conquest, Coexistence and Change: Wales 1063–1415* (Oxford, 1987), 24–107 [R. R. Davies, *CCC*].

[6] For the notion of core and periphery in Latin Christendom, R. Bartlett, *Gerald of Wales, 1146–1223* (Oxford, 1982), 158–77; idem, *The Making of Europe: Conquest, Colonization and Cultural Change, 950–1350* (London, 1993), 18–23.

[7] *RPeck*, ii, 435–7, 473–7. For Theodore of Bec's diatribe, *The Letters of John of Salisbury*, i, *The Early Letters (1153–61)*, ed. W. J. Millor, S. J. and H. E. Butler and C. N. L. Brooke (Edinburgh, 1955), 135–6.

recovery was the work of lineages engaged in salvaging their territories and restoring the power of Welsh kingship.

Attributes of this kingship remained an essential part of the political culture of the twelfth and thirteenth centuries. The poets who addressed Llywelyn ap Gruffudd or commemorated his death were quite sure of his royal inheritance and his royal quality. 'Gwir frenin Cymru, cymraisg ddoniau', proclaimed Llygad Gŵr, his prince a true king of Wales, of powerful qualities.[8] Symbols of royal status were cherished, notably the gold coronet (*aur dalaith*) to which poets referred, a relic which the conqueror of Wales was careful to preserve.[9] This royal status might be seen as a residual legacy of a gradually eroded pristine kingship. On the other hand, emphasis might reasonably be placed on the creative vigour by which the potentialities of Welsh kingship came to be realized only in a late era, when those who represented the ancient lineages had ceased to call themselves kings and their territories were not normally described as kingdoms. A calculated retention of the terminology of a royal antiquity was an essential part of the princes' armoury during their last tumultuous generations. The territory over which a prince exerted lordship might still be a *teyrnas*, the sphere of a king, in the language of a poet, a *regnum* in the parlance of a lawyer. Possession of a definable territory was a key attribute of kingship and one of enduring relevance. The lawyers' texts convey a keen sense of frontier that may, in one sense, be an admission of political fragmentation, but it may equally reflect a recognition that precise demarcation of political domains was a prerequisite of ordered society.[10] What lay beyond the frontier of *gwlad* or *patria* was the *gorwlad* or *aliena patria*; its raiding by the host might be sanctioned by custom, but the land beyond the frontier could equally be subject to reciprocal arrangements for the conduct of neighbourly relations including legal process. The frontier bounded a land which was a sphere of jurisdiction and an area where relationships between ruler and ruled were regulated by conventions which governed the rights and obligations of the one and the other. Crucially, too, the territory was the sphere from which the ruler drew the economic resources which sustained his power, and there can be no doubt that the demesnes associated with the princes' courts, and the fiscal obligations centred upon them, represented assets derived from the period of those

---

[8] *GBF*, 24. 155. References to the volumes containing critical texts of the poetry of the period of the princes, prepared at the Centre for Advanced Welsh and Celtic Studies, University of Wales (Cyfres Beirdd y Tywysogion), are to the number of the poem, followed, where appropriate, by line numbers. References to earlier editions, notably *Llawysgrif Hendregadredd*, ed. J. Morris-Jones and T. H. Parry-Williams (Cardiff, 1933), are given in the volumes cited.
[9] Below, pp. 29, 199, 332–3, 584.
[10] For the frontier, below, pp. 132–4.

Inheritance

of the lineage who, exercising stable authority over many generations, had called themselves kings.[11]

The image of kingship which emerges from the work of the twelfth-century court poets, Meilyr Brydydd, Gwalchmai ap Meilyr, Cynddelw Brydydd Mawr, or others, is one of men of lineage who bore responsibility for their territories in a manner appropriate to their royal status.[12] They had a capability for war, and the poets make much of this. Their territories were sometimes at war with one another but the historical record undoubtedly conveys the extent to which Norman intervention exacerbated conflict both between and within the territories.[13] It would be well to be wary lest the endemic strife of the period be seen as necessarily a testimony to an inherently violent society, endlessly indulging its heroic exultation in war. The military prowess of the kings was esteemed by the poets as a means of ensuring the security of the territories with which they were entrusted. The rulers were essentially concerned with the stability of the political order with which their royal status was inextricably linked. Welsh historical writing, represented in *Brut y Tywysogyon*, while preserving an account of daunting internal conflict, indicates in the same record of events, and in the encomia to the kings and princes, the value placed upon the cohesive power of rulers who governed their lands securely under God's grace. The manner by which the royal lineage of Gwynedd extricated itself from the adversity in which it found itself in the Norman period, as a result of both alien and native challenges, is the theme of the *History of Gruffudd ap Cynan*, a work which reveals a skilful blending of modes of thought characteristic of contemporary Latin writing with those conserved in the indigenous literary tradition. There is no better guide to the conceptual inheritance to which Llywelyn ap Gruffudd laid claim in the thirteenth century.[14]

Much as the historians of other nations elaborate upon the elevating qualities of the ancient lineages to which they belonged, the author of the *History* lays stress upon Gruffudd ap Cynan's honourable lineage. He, too, was 'of royal kin' and 'most eminent lineage' and stood on a par with con-

---

[11] Courts and demesnes are examined below, pp. 219–36.

[12] Poems to the major rulers include *GMB*, 3, 6, 7, 8; *GLlF*, 2, 18, 22, 24, 25; *GCBM*, i, 1, 2, 7, 8; *GCBM*, ii, 1–4, 6, 8–10, 13.

[13] Frequent reference is made in this study to the Latin annals in *Annales Cambriae* (*AC*) (citing, when necessary, the B or C texts), to the 'Cronica de Wallia' (*CW*), and to the Welsh texts of the chronicle, *Brut y Tywysogyon* (*BT, Pen20* and *BT, RBH*). The texts are examined in the introductions by Thomas Jones to *BT, Pen20Tr* and *BT, RBH;* K. Hughes, *Celtic Britain in the Early Middle Ages* (Woodbridge, 1980), 67–85. For the themes conveyed in the historical writings, J. B. Smith, *The Sense of History in Medieval Wales* (Aberystwyth, 1989), 6–14 [J. B. Smith, *SHMW*].

[14] Text and translation of the *Historia* in *HGK, MPW*.

temporary kings.[15] Describing Gruffudd's efforts to recover and rehabilitate the kingdom of Gwynedd he traces the troubled story of one who ultimately, after successive reverses, was able to establish his authority over a wide area of the historic territory and put his sons to complete the task: Môn and Arllechwedd, Arfon and Llŷn, Eifionydd and Ardudwy; Rhos and Rhufoniog, Dyffryn Clwyd and Tegeingl (the 'Four Cantreds' of Perfeddwlad), and Meirionnydd. It was a course which two of Gruffudd's distinguished descendants would pursue in due course. But if the main substance of the *History* is the tribulation encountered during the tortuous process by which the territory was restored to its furthermost boundaries, emphasis is constantly placed upon the rightfulness of the endeavour and the fact that the communities of the kingdom ultimately acknowledged Gruffudd's lordship. This outcome was not achieved at all swiftly, and the author makes no effort to conceal the fact that Gruffudd's problems stemmed not from Norman power alone but from the failure of the Welsh communities of Gwynedd to respond to his calls upon their loyalty. Gruffudd is likened to Judas Maccabeus in his resistance to foreign oppression, but the Antiochus represented by Hugh of Avranches, earl of Chester, was not his only adversary. Thus the defection of the men of Llŷn, which contributed to Gruffudd's defeat at Bron yr Erw, inspires a reflection that Judas Maccabeus, too, had suffered not from alien oppression alone but from betrayal on the part of the men of Israel themselves, for 'from the beginning there was treachery'.[16] Ultimately the men of the *cantrefi* of Gwynedd received Gruffudd 'as befitted their rightful lord'. The legitimacy of Gruffudd's rule is emphasized time and again, for he was truly their 'rightful lord', one who returned from exile 'to his own possession and his patrimony'.[17] The heroic endeavours of earlier years are vindicated in the rule of a righteous and pious king who brought stability to his kingdom and enabled its people to live in prosperity, and at peace with the king of England, under the kingship of one who ruled under God's protection. Beneath the panegyric the *History*, itself a composition which blends a conformity to a classical tradition with features of the native prose tales, conveys some important themes in the historical inheritance of indigenous Welsh kingship to which Llywelyn ap Gruffudd became the

---

[15] *HGK*, 1–5; *MPW*, 53–7. The *Historia* may be better appreciated if its themes and structure are studied alongside *Willelmi Malmesburiensis Monachi, De Gestis Regum Anglorum*, ed. W. Stubbs (RS, 1887–9) and *Guillaume de Poitiers, Histoire de Guillaume le Conquerant*, ed. R. Foreville (Paris, 1952). For its literary form, and the parallels to the *divisiones* characteristic of the work of Suetonius, J. B. Smith, *SHMW*, 6–7.

[16] *HGK*, 8–12, 28; *MPW*, 60–4, 79–80. For the appeal to the memory of the Maccabees, J. B. Smith, *SHMW*, 7 and n. 20; below, pp. 56, 282.

[17] *HGK*, 6–21; *MPW*, 59–74.

ultimate inheritor.¹⁸ Lineage, territory and status are inextricably intertwined. But before he was able to take possession of the territorial inheritance by which he could sustain the princely status with which his lineage had been endowed, Llywelyn ap Gruffudd had to surmount serious difficulties which will be recounted presently. No one bestowed an inheritance on Llywelyn: rather he took it to himself by force, and the significance of the decisive action he took at Bryn Derwin in 1255 cannot be understood unless account is taken of the question of the succession to princely inheritance, a vital aspect of the dynastic aspiration to which the evidence of the previous generations bears ample witness. The royal status depicted in the *History of Gruffudd ap Cynan* could be maintained only if the patrimonial territory remained undivided under the rule of a single representative of the lineage.

The need to ensure that the inheritance is conserved in its entirety from generation to generation may be counted among the abiding concerns of dynasties of the medieval West. A continuing attentiveness to the succession may be discerned in the kingdom of France and in its several principalities, and historical studies have recognized the care with which royal and noble lineages of many lands sought to ensure the integrity of the territory. Welsh kingdoms have often been envisaged very differently, deemed to be inexorably subject upon the death of a king, in accordance with the dictates of Welsh law, to equal division between his sons.[19] The Welsh lawbooks, of which several important texts derive from the thirteenth century, certainly deal in some detail with the manner in which an inheritance in land is divided.[20] These expositions of partible inheritance are concerned, however, not with succession to kingdoms but with the practice which applied to the lands of free proprietors. The lawyers' guidance on dynastic practice, the succession of kingdoms, is less explicit, but its indications are quite clear.[21] The provision for the succession has two complementary features.[22] In the lawyers' estimation there is but one heir to the throne, known in the Welsh texts as *edling* or *gwrthrychiad*, in the Latin texts as

---

[18] J. B. Smith, *SHMW*, 6–14; for the similarity to Aelred of Rievaulx's image of David I of Scotland, ibid., p. 7 and n. 21.

[19] The most important statement is the introduction by J. G. Edwards to *Littere Wallie* (*LW*, xxxvi–xxxvii); briefer notices in T. Jones Pierce, *Encyclopaedia Britannica* (1970 edn.), xxiii, 155; idem, *Chambers's Encyclopaedia* (1966 edn.), xiv, 384.

[20] Main references: *LTWL*, 132–5, 227–8, 387–9, 478–9; *LlIor*, 53–4; *LHD*, 98–100; *LlCol*, 35–6; *WML*, 50–2; *LlBleg*, 74–8. The legal literature is noticed below, p. 201.

[21] The theory and practice of Welsh succession are examined in J. B. Smith, 'Dynastic succession in medieval Wales', *B*, 33 (1986), 199–232; more briefly in idem, 'The succession to Welsh princely inheritance: the evidence reconsidered', in R. R. Davies (ed.), *The British Isles, 1100–1500: Comparisons, Contrasts and Connections* (Edinburgh, 1988), 64–81.

[22] J. B. Smith, 'Dynastic succession', 201–6.

Inheritance

heres or *successor*.²³ The single heir, who is accorded a place of particular honour at court, is raised from among the near kinsmen of the king who constitute the 'royal members' (*aelodau brenin, membra regis*). Designation is made by the ruling king, and the *edling* is the one 'to whom the king gives hope and expectation'. The kingdom is bestowed in its entirety upon a single heir and, according to a further provision, each of the other 'royal members' was provided with an estate so that thereafter his status was determined not by his membership of the royal kindred but in accordance with the status of the land bestowed upon him.²⁴ An apanage was thereby created within the bounds of the kingdom to be vested in the heir to the throne, allowing each of his near kinsmen maintenance and honourable status in a manner which in no way undermined the entirety or the integrity of the kingdom.

The theory of dynastic succession which may be elicited from the Welsh lawbooks reveals features closely comparable with practices consistently followed by the Capetian dynasty of France, whereby the heir to the throne is elevated as *rex designatus* and, more gradually, provision came to be made within the inheritance for other members of the lineage.²⁵ The testimony of the lawbooks, which can be informed by comparative study of the evidence for Ireland, indicates that the indivisibility of the royal inheritance was recognized, but that a multiple eligibility to the throne within the kindred left the succession indeterminate. Consistent adherence to a practice whereby a designation was made in each generation was conducive, however, to a more determinate patrilineal succession.²⁶ The lawyers' statements thus point to a

---

²³ *LTWL*, 110, 194, 277, 318, 437; *LlIor*, 2–3; *LHD*, 6–7; *WML*, 3–4; *LlBleg*, 4–5. For the terms *edling* and *gwrthrychiad*, D. A. Binchy, 'Some Celtic legal terms', *Celtica*, 3 (1956), 221–31; D. Dumville, 'The aetheling, a study in Anglo-Saxon constitutional history', *Anglo-Saxon England*, 8 (1979), 1–33. The present study is not concerned with the origin of the terms, nor the early development of the institutions to which they refer, but with their meaning in the period of the princes.

²⁴ *LTWL*, 238; *LlIor*, 3; *LHD*, 7.

²⁵ Among older studies see A. Luchaire, *Histoire des institutions monarchiques de la France sous les premiers Capétiens (987–1180)* (2nd edn. Paris, 1891), i, 60–87; among more recent works A. W. Lewis, 'Anticipatory association of the heir in early Capetian France', *American Historical Review*, 83 (1978), 906–27; idem, *Royal Succession in Capetian France: Studies on Familial Order and the State* (Cambridge, Mass., 1981), 44–77, 155–92. For the *rex designatus* in Scotland and the strengthening of royal government, see the introductions to *Regesta Regum Scottorum*, i, *The Acts of Malcolm IV, King of Scots, 1153–65*, ed. G. W. S. Barrow (Edinburgh, 1960); ii, *The Acts of William I, 1165–1214*, ed. G. W. S. Barrow and W. W. Scott (Edinburgh, 1971); G. W. S. Barrow, *Scotland and her Neighbours in the Middle Ages* (London, 1992), 45–66. For further references, and a consideration of Welsh succession in relation to *droit d'aînesse* and *parage*, J. B. Smith, 'Dynastic succession', 206–10.

²⁶ E. MacNeill, *Celtic Ireland* (Dublin, 1921), 114–43; D. A. Binchy, *Celtic and Anglo-Saxon Kingship* (Oxford, 1970), 24–7; idem, 'Irish history and Irish law, II', *Studia Hibernica*, 16 (1976), 37–42; G. Mac Niocaill, 'The "heir-designate" in early medieval Ireland', *The Irish Jurist*, NS, 3 (1968), 326–9; D. O'Corrain, 'Irish regnal succession, a reappraisal', *Studia Hibernica*, 11 (1971), 7–39.

conception of the succession which stands in marked contrast to the obligatory division of the kingdom often attributed to the law of Wales. Admittedly, study of each of the three major kingdoms of twelfth-century Wales provides evidence of fragmentation: Powys after Madog ap Maredudd in 1160, Gwynedd after Owain Gwynedd in 1170 and Deheubarth after Rhys ap Gruffudd in 1197. Each kingdom was sundered, and it might seem that the lawyers who sought to safeguard the principle of the indivisibility of the kingdom had laboured in vain. A distinction needs to be drawn, however, between division made by dynastic intent and that which was the result of a compromise made when the king's designation was frustrated, the heir designate's position challenged, and a contest waged in which no one among the contenders was able to secure an ascendancy. It is unquestionably the second alternative which commends itself if the manner in which each of the three kingdoms came to be divided is carefully considered.[27] The year 1160 saw the death of the king who, as the author of *Breuddwyd Rhonabwy* remembered, had ruled Powys in its entirety (*yn ei therfynau*) for a generation. But even more grievous for the kingdom than the death of the elderly Madog ap Maredudd was the killing of his son Llywelyn ap Madog within the year. Llywelyn may safely be identified as the heir to Powys, the person, in the words of the chronicler, 'in whom lay the hope of all Powys'.[28] He fell at an early stage in a conflict which saw Owain Cyfeiliog, a son of the elder brother of Madog ap Maredudd, use the apanage which he had been given in Cyfeiliog as a territorial basis from which he strove to win the succession for himself. Other contenders joined the fray. This was no squabble among the co-heirs of Madog ap Maredudd over their respective shares of the kingdom, but rather a conflict within the royal kindred to secure Powys in its entirety. The court poet Cynddelw Brydydd Mawr indicated quite clearly the dread significance of Llywelyn ap Madog's death: 'Marw Madog mawr im eilyw, / Lladd Llywelyn llwyr dilyw.' The death of Madog brought great distress, the killing of Llywelyn total destruction.[29] The poet's words reflect the chronicler's perception of the significance of Llywelyn's death in his comment upon the expectations centred upon the young man. They, in turn, echo the eternal hope to which an Irish lawyer had given expression several centuries earlier when he recognized in the *tánaise ríg* a person 'to whom the entire *túath* looked for kingship without strife'.[30] It was not in accordance with

---

[27] J. B. Smith, 'Dynastic succession', 210–15.

[28] *Breudwyd Ronabwy*, ed. M. Richards (Cardiff, 1948), 1; *Mabinogion*, 137; *BT, Pen20*, 107 ('yn yr hwnn yr oed gobeith holl Bowys'); *Pen20Tr*, 61–2; *RBH*, 140–1 ('y gwr a oed vnic obeith y holl wyr Powys').

[29] *GCBM*, i, 8, *englynion* commemorating Madog ap Maredudd and his son Llywelyn, quoting ll. 47–8.

[30] *Críth Gablach*, ed. D. A. Binchy (Dublin, 1941), 17 (ll. 434–5).

Inheritance

dynastic intent that Powys came to be sundered, nor Deheubarth. Rhys ap Gruffudd intended that his son Gruffudd ap Rhys should follow him in the rule of the kingdom, thereby designating a younger son who was born within marriage in preference to his eldest son, Maelgwn ap Rhys, who was not so. Rhys ap Gruffudd's will was frustrated by the violent reaction of the rejected bastard son. In this case again an apanage, bestowed to provide for one of the royal kindred not raised to be heir to the throne, came to be a power base in a conflict waged for twenty years until a partition left Deheubarth divided forever.[31]

By then Gwynedd, too, had endured a period of adversity which began shortly after the death of Owain Gwynedd when the eldest son, Hywel ab Owain Gwynedd, was struck down by his half-brothers Dafydd and Rhodri at the battle of Pentraeth. The division of Gwynedd was no part of Owain Gwynedd's purpose. He had maintained Gwynedd in its entirety, yielding nothing to his younger brother Cadwaladr except an apanage within the borders of his own kingdom, and eliminating Cunedda, the son of his elder brother Cadwallon. A king who could bring himself to castrate and blind a young man of his own kindred can hardly have intended anything for the future except that his kingdom should remain in its entirety under the secure rule of a single heir.[32] Which of his sons was the chosen successor is uncertain. The searing grief expressed in Peryf ap Cedifor's *englynion* commemorating Hywel ab Owain Gwynedd may reflect the close affinity of a foster brother but, on the other hand, the poet's reference to Hywel's 'irresistible claim' (*hawl diachor*) may provide a genuine indication of Owain Gwynedd's wishes for the future. It could well have been a matter of deep regret in the kingdom as a whole that the son of the mighty king of Gwynedd lay upon the battlefield: 'Bod mab brenin gwyn Gwynedd, / Yn gorwedd yn yr aerfa.'[33]

Hywel's death brought no end to the conflict and, no one among his kinsmen securing complete supremacy, Gwynedd became divided through the successive compromises made among those who contended for the inheritance.[34] The situation in the kingdom fluctuated, but remained essentially unchanged, until Llywelyn ap Iorwerth, a grandson of Owain Gwynedd, resolved the succession by force and declared anew the vital principle of the integrity of the Welsh kingdom. By 1201, when he swore an oath of fealty to King John, Llywelyn had established an irrefutable claim to be recognized, in succession to Owain Gwynedd and Gruffudd ap Cynan, as

---

[31] J. B. Smith, 'Dynastic succession', 212–13; idem, 'The "Cronica de Wallia" and the dynasty of Dinefwr', *B*, 20 (1962–4), 262–5.

[32] J. B. Smith, 'Dynastic succession', 213–15; idem, 'Owain Gwynedd', *TCaernHS*, 32 (1971), 8–17.

[33] *GLlF*, 21.

[34] *HW*, ii, 549–52, 564–5, 587–90, 612–13.

the rightful lord of his patrimony.³⁵ He styled himself 'prince of Gwynedd' (*princeps Northwallie*), ensuring that the idea of a principality (*principatus*) was henceforth reflected in the usage of official records. The territory of the principality was a Gwynedd extending from the Dyfi to the Dee, and it is the single heir to an integral royal estate who presents himself with assured authority in the early charters to the Cistercian houses of Aberconwy and Cymer.³⁶ The two documents provide a clear affirmation that a single jurisdiction extended over the *cantrefi* which appear as provinces (*provincia*) in the territorial entity between the two rivers. Within the territory, a kinsman of the prince, such as Hywel ap Gruffudd in Meirionnydd, might hold an estate as a tenant of the prince. He would be a former 'royal member' whose status was now determined by the land bestowed upon him, for all authority was vested in the prince unless it were delegated to another by his enfeoffment. Indigenous Welsh lordship was not inherent to *cantref* or *cwmwd* (commote); these were rather administrative organs by which the prince's authority was mediated throughout the land.³⁷ Llywelyn ap Iorwerth's assertion of power in Gwynedd brought, along with the resuscitation of the patrimonial territory, the restoration of the royal inheritance of the dynasty and its embodiment in the idea of a principality.

Llywelyn ap Iorwerth adhered to the traditional dynastic objective when he came to make provision for the succession to his inheritance by a formal ordinance in 1220.³⁸ He declared that it was his wish that his inheritance should descend to Dafydd, his son by his wife Joan, a daughter of King John. The significance of the ordinance lies in the fact that Llywelyn chose Dafydd as his heir in preference to Gruffudd, his elder son born by Tangwystl, a woman who had never been the prince's wedded wife. This was not the first occasion on which Llywelyn had set aside his first-born son. Even before the birth of Dafydd, in an acute crisis which he faced following John's intervention in Gwynedd in 1211, Llywelyn had to submit to the king's will and agree that, if

---

[35] *RotLittPat*, i, 8–9; *Foedera*, I, i, 84; for the idea of 'principality', below, pp. 281–5.

[36] *MonAng*, v, 672–4; *CChR*, iv, 267–9; *CPR, 1321–24*, 400; K. Williams-Jones, 'Llywelyn's charter to Cymer abbey in 1209', *JMerHRS*, 3 (1957–60), 45–78; *H*, 122, 123, 130 (this volume, K. L. Maund (ed.), *Handlist of the Acts of Native Welsh Rulers 1132–1283* (Cardiff, 1996), provides full details of sources and editions of the charters). For the prince's grants to Aberconwy, in two charters, below, pp. 205–6.

[37] For the *cwmwd*, or commote, as an entity in which lordship was inherent, J. G. Edwards, 'Sir John Edward Lloyd 1861–1947', *PBA*, 41 (1956), 323; idem, 'The Normans and the Welsh march', *PBA*, 42 (1957), 169–70; for the view expressed here, J. B. Smith, 'Dynastic succession', 216; below, pp. 193–6.

[38] J. B. Smith, 'Dynastic succession', 218–19. The text of the ordinance is in Vatican Library Reg. Vat 11; calendared versions, *Regesta Honorii Papae III*, ed. P. Pressutti (Rome, 1888–95), ii, 73; *CPapL*, i, 87, do not convey the substance in sufficient detail. A subsequent papal ordinance declared that Joan was a legitimate daughter of John (*Regesta Honorii Papae*, ii, 417; *CPapL*, i, 109); for a further submission to the papal court, below n. 87.

he died without an heir of his body by his wife, Gwynedd would fall to the king and Gruffudd would have only that which the king might choose to provide for him.[39] It is thus as a disinherited bastard son, that Gruffudd ap Llywelyn, the father of the prince who is the subject of this study, makes his first appearance in the historical record. Four years later Llywelyn was absolved from the severe terms imposed upon him in 1211 and he secured Gruffudd's release from the king's custody.[40] Even so, when the prince came to decide the future of his dominion for himself there was no change of fortune for Gruffudd. Dafydd ap Llywelyn was the younger son, but a son by a wedded wife who was a daughter of a king of England had a two-fold advantage over the son of Tangwystl. Gruffudd was an Ishmael, born of Llywelyn's concubine, a son neither by the prince's wife nor a daughter of the house of Anjou. Many historians have noticed the prince's ordinance and gathered that the effect of Llywelyn's decision was to deny Gruffudd that share of the inheritance which was due to him by Welsh law by adopting, for the first time in the history of the lineage, the principle that the inheritance should not be divided on the death of its ruler.[41] The words from the Book of Genesis quoted in the text might seem to justify this reading of Llywelyn's intention: 'in his country there was a despicable custom that the son of the handmaiden should be heir with the freeborn son, and illegitimate sons could possess the inheritance with the legitimate'. He now abolished a custom which stood at variance with the laws of God and man. But Llywelyn's enactment was not issued to establish any novel principle that the dominion should remain undivided. The principle of the indivisibility of the inheritance was already an essential feature of dynastic intent. The effect of the ordinance was to establish that, adhering to the practice of choosing a single heir, an illegitimate son could not be considered for the succession upon terms of parity with a legitimate son. Gruffudd was eliminated from consideration as a successor to Llywelyn because he was a bastard son. The prince's ordinance was concerned,

---

[39] The document, from PRO, E163/4/47, m. 6, is printed with discussion in J. B. Smith, 'Magna Carta and the charters of the Welsh princes', *EHR*, 99 (1984), 344–62. John's intervention is noticed below, n. 52.

[40] Gruffudd's imprisonment is not recorded in the Welsh chronicles but is noticed in a medieval chronology found in several MSS including NLW, Peniarth 32D, ff. 116^{r-v}; text in H. Llwyd, *Britannicae Descriptionis Commentariolum* (London, 1731), 141–64. For Gruffudd's release under the terms of Magna Carta, below, n. 58.

[41] E.g. *HW*, ii, 686–7; T. Jones Pierce, *Encyclopaedia Britannica* (1970 edn.), xxiii, 156; idem, *Chambers's Encyclopaedia* (1966 edn.), xiv, 384; idem, *DWB*, 317–18; F. M. Powicke, *King Henry III and the Lord Edward* (Oxford, 1947), ii, 630 [Powicke, *Henry III*]; idem, *The Thirteenth Century, 1216–1307* (Oxford, 1953), 393; M. Richter, 'David ap Llywelyn, the first prince of Wales', *WHR*, 5 (1970–1), 207–8; idem, 'The political and institutional background to national consciousness in medieval Wales', *Nationality and the Pursuit of National Independence*, Historical Studies, 11, ed. T. W. Moody (Belfast, 1978), 48–9, 52–3.

Inheritance

not with the bane of partible succession but with the burden of illegitimacy. Dafydd was chosen as *edling* in preference to Gruffudd.

Llywelyn undoubtedly appreciated that Gruffudd's response to this decision would be quite crucial and, as soon as Dafydd was designated heir, he made provision for Gruffudd in accordance with the established practices of his lineage. Gruffudd, a member of the royal kindred not granted the singular status of heir apparent, was given a broad estate in Meirionnydd and Ardudwy. He was conceded his apanage within the kingdom and was allowed to exercise lordship there as a tenant of his father, with a view to becoming, in due course, a tenant of his brother. Gruffudd would not stand for this, and it appears that the intemperate son created havoc throughout the territory granted to him in retaliation for his exclusion from the succession.[42] With four years' detention in the king's prison behind him Gruffudd now faced his father's wrath. He was deprived of the lands previously given to him, and, though father and son were then reconciled, renewed dissension led to an incarceration which was to last for six years.[43] Gruffudd's years were spent in virtually unrelieved tribulation, his children – Owain, Llywelyn, Dafydd, Rhodri, Gwladus and Margaret – spending their young years in painful awareness of the anguish of the rejected bastard son of the prince of Gwynedd. After the death of Llywelyn ap Iorwerth they witnessed a contest between Dafydd ap Llywelyn and Gruffudd ap Llywelyn which enabled the king of England to forego the pledge by which he had endorsed Dafydd's succession and, ostensibly embracing Gruffudd but doing nothing on his behalf, bring upon Gwynedd a new threat to its future.[44] Llywelyn ap Gruffudd's first triumph lay in his ability to lift the men of Gwynedd from the dire state in which they found themselves by the middle years of the thirteenth century, direct their minds to the long-established objectives of his lineage, and bring them to realize anew that Gwynedd's security could only be ensured if a single prince ruled an entire and integrated inheritance.

The vision of an entire Gwynedd was not the only inspiration which Llywelyn ap Gruffudd drew from his grandfather. Llywelyn ap Iorwerth fully intended that his heir should succeed, not only to his patrimonial dominion, but to the broader supremacy which he had come to establish, beyond the bounds of

---

[42] *BT, Pen20*, 182–3; *Pen20Tr*, 98; *RBH*, 220–1.

[43] *AnnCestr*, 54; *AC*, 80; *CW*, 38; *BT, Pen20*, 182–3, 194; *Pen20Tr*, 98–100, 103; *RBH*, 220–5, 232–3; *HW*, ii, 687.

[44] Llywelyn's wishes were endorsed on the king's behalf at a meeting with the king's council at Shrewsbury, 5 May 1220 (*RotLittClaus*, i, 436; *Foedera*, I, i, 159); for Dafydd's homage to Henry in 1229 and 1240 and the king's subsequent renunciation of his pledge, below, nn. 88, 100, 113.

Inheritance

Gwynedd, in the lands of the former kingdoms of Powys and Deheubarth. This was a major achievement and an entirely new departure in Welsh political history. At the end of the twelfth century Giraldus Cambrensis harboured no doubt that the main reason for the undoing of the Welsh was their stubborn refusal to submit themselves, as did other peoples that lived prosperously, to the dominion of a single king.[45] Ambivalences in the author's loyalties are no doubt reflected in the alternative prognoses which he embodied in the last pages of the Description of Wales. The nation could remain invincible; equally it could succumb to conquest, and much depended not only upon the king of England's commitment to purposeful military effort but upon his capacity to create dissension among the Welsh themselves and stir them up against one another.[46] Yet, apart from the influence of his conflicting loyalties, Giraldus's remarks may reflect the ideas current among those who, representing the values of the nations who formed the core of Latin Christendom, saw the peoples upon the peripheries much in the image of the barbarian.[47] Ordered political society was no part of their capability, and Wales could have counted among the lands which exemplified the political incapacity of the nations on the fringes of the Christian world. The historical record from the late eleventh century onward certainly indicates that, quite apart from the adversities in which the several political entities of Wales often found themselves, it was only rarely that their rulers had been brought together even in transitory military alliance, let alone anything better. Indeed, the cohesive political movement inaugurated under the leadership of Llywelyn ap Iorwerth early in the thirteenth century might reasonably be said to have had only one auspicious precedent. This was the alliance formed in the last years of Owain Gwynedd. At that time, the annalist somewhat grandiloquently relates, the whole of Gwynedd, Deheubarth and Powys joined together to cast off the Norman yoke, brought together in resistance to Henry II's attempt to reduce Wales by force.[48] Careful consideration of Henry's objectives and of the nature of the alliance formed against him might suggest a less graphic account and, in any case, the combined military effort proved short-lived. Yet, this brief period provides some indication of a desire, at least in Owain Gwynedd's province, for a more permanent association founded upon what might be portrayed as the historic supremacy of Gwynedd. One clear sign appears in Owain's decision to adopt a new style. It was from a position of strength at this time of

---

[45] *GirCamb, Op*, vi, 225 (*Descr*. II, ix); citation of book and chapter numbers of Itinerary (*Itin*.) and Description (*Descr*.) facilitates reference to translations.
[46] Ibid., 218–27 (*Descr*. II, viii, ix, x).
[47] Bartlett, *Gerald of Wales*, 158–77; above, n. 6.
[48] *AC*, 50: 'omnes Wallenses Norwallie, Suthwallie, Powysorum jugum Francorum unanimiter respuerunt'. For the campaign, P. Latimer, 'Henry II's campaign against the Welsh in 1165', *WHR*, 14 (1988–9), 523–52; *HW*, ii, 515–18; R. R. Davies, *CCC*, 52–3.

Inheritance

assertiveness that Owain ceased to present himself as 'king of Gwynedd', making a change from king to prince at his own will and not in response to prompting on the part of the king of England. The true nature of Owain's underlying political aspiration is suggested by the fact that he appears to have styled himself not prince of Gwynedd but 'prince of the Welsh' (*princeps Wallénsium*).[49] He was seeking something more than a combined, but necessarily short-lived, effort in war. These indications come, however, only at a late stage in the prince's career and, with his death, whatever hopes may have been cherished in Gwynedd that cohesive endeavour in war might be made permanent in a political association were completely shattered as Owain's kingdom came to be sundered into several parts. It fell to Llywelyn ap Iorwerth, when he had rehabilitated the kingdom, to breath new spirit into the aspiration for a wider supremacy.

Not that it could be said that Llywelyn won swift response to his initiatives in the early years of the thirteenth century. The lords of the fragmented territories of Powys and Deheubarth, for their part, saw his intervention in their lands as an unwelcome interference to be resisted with all their might, and their reaction was advantageous to John when, in 1211, he set about the subjugation of Gwynedd. There is, indeed, some resemblance between the circumstances of John's offensive in 1211 and Edward I's assault in 1282, for Gwynedd came perilously close to extinction early in the century.[50] The memory of the strong position which the crown established in Wales in the reign of John remained vivid in the time of Henry III, and a restoration of the situation created in the early years of the century became the crown's declared purpose in the period following the death of Llywelyn ap Iorwerth.[51] John penetrated Perfeddwlad and forced the Conwy to enter Snowdonia itself. In his extremity Llywelyn was constrained to acknowledge that further resistance was futile and, as the chronicler relates, he sent his wife to plead with her father on his behalf and assuage his anger. Severe terms were imposed on the prince even so. He faced the prospect of his dominion being ceded to the king at his death, if he had no heir by the king's daughter. Subjected to a severe punitive tribute, Llywelyn was confined to Gwynedd Uwch Conwy, yielding Perfeddwlad to the king forever, and he was deprived of any influence beyond its bounds.[52] But within

---

[49] J. B. Smith, 'Owain Gwynedd', 14–16; the change in style, and the difficulties faced in interpreting the texts, are noticed below, pp. 282–4.

[50] For comments on the similarity of the methods employed by the two kings, *The Great Roll of the Pipe for the Fourteenth Year of the Reign of King John*, ed. P. M. Barnes (London, Pipe Roll Society, NS, 30, 1954), xiv–xvii; W. L. Warren, *King John* (London, 1961), 197–200.

[51] Treaty of Gwerneigron, 1241, below, n. 118.

[52] *AC*, 67–8; *CW*, 34; *BT, Pen20*, 154–6; *Pen20Tr*, 85–6; *RBH*, 190–3; J. B. Smith, 'Magna Carta', 354–6, 361–2; R. R. Davies, *CCC*, 295–6. 'Gwynedd Uwch Conwy' describes Gwynedd west of the Conwy, including Môn (Anglesey), a land often termed Snowdonia in royal records; 'Gwynedd Is Conwy' could be used to describe the land east of the Conwy, but thirteenth-century practice suggests either 'Perfeddwlad' or 'the Four Cantreds'.

months of his mortification, availing himself of the reaction of the princes of Wales to the signs that John proposed to secure the crown's control upon them for all time, Llywelyn put himself at the head of a formidable alliance. In the lands where he had recently met resistance he now won active support, and the castles by which John had sought to consolidate his conquest were systematically erased. Within a year Llywelyn was able to respond positively to an invitation from Philip Augustus of France and declare his willingness to join the king in firm alliance. He did so as one who was able to speak for all the princes of Wales combined together in indissoluble union.[53] Llywelyn placed King Philip's letter in the aumbries of his church for safe-keeping, and put his seal to a document which indicated that a significant change in the political situation in the lands of the princes was now in train. Almost instantly, the dire version of Giraldus's prognosis gave way to the other.

The conflict of the reign of John became a crucible in which the princes forged a broad dominion founded on the supremacy of the lineage of Aberffraw. Unlike Owain Gwynedd, his grandson did not change his style but remained 'prince of Gwynedd' for some time.[54] There are other signs, however, that Llywelyn ap Iorwerth applied himself to nothing less than the task of transforming a war alliance into a political community. The new departure found a theoretical exposition in the lawyers' conception of Wales not as a land of three independent kingdoms but one with an internal unity and a new relationship with England. The existence of three historical kingdoms – Gwynedd, Powys and Deheubarth, ruled from the principal courts of Aberffraw, Mathrafal and Dinefwr – is still recognized, but one of the courts – Aberffraw – is accorded a supremacy over the others.[55] In a form of words with an implicit invocation of historical precedent, the king of Aberffraw is said to pay royal tribute (*mechdeyrn ddyled*) to the king of England when he receives his land from the king of England; and then all the kings of Wales should receive their lands from the king of Aberffraw and pay him royal

---

[53] *HW*, ii, 639–50; R. F. Treharne, 'The Franco-Welsh treaty of alliance in 1212', *B*, 18 (1958–60), 60–75; repr. idem, *Simon de Montfort and Baronial Reform*, ed. E. B. Fryde (London, 1986), 345–60; trans. *EHD*, III, 306–7. *HW*, ii, 638 includes reference to an entry in *BT, Pen20*, 158–9; *Pen20Tr*, 87; *RBH*, 194–5, which states that Innocent III released the princes from their allegiance to John; it would be best to discount the statement in the light of the evidence for England examined in C. R. Cheney, 'The alleged deposition of King John', in R. W. Hunt *et al.* (eds.), *Studies in Medieval History presented to Frederick Maurice Powicke* (Oxford, 1948), 100–16.

[54] Below, n. 86.

[55] Giraldus gives the three principal courts as Aberffraw for Gwynedd, Dinefwr for Deheubarth, but Pengwern for Powys; see *GirCamb. Op*, vi, 81, 169 (*Itin.* I, x; *Descr.* I, iv). The thirteenth-century lawbooks endorse Aberffraw and Dinefwr but their testimony to Mathrafal is slighter (*LTWL*, 316, 349, 435; *LlBleg*, 2, 3–4, 98–9; *DamCol*, 19); cf. H. Pryce, 'The evidence of written sources', in C. J. Arnold and J. W. Huggett, 'Excavations at Mathrafal, Powys, 1989', *MontColl*, 83 (1995), 61–5. For references in poetry and records, below, pp. 333, 336–7.

tribute.⁵⁶ The antiquity of the mode of expression hardly conceals the novelty of a theory which, propounding the idea that a royal tribute was paid by the one to the other, placed the lords of Wales in a position in which they were tenants of the prince of Aberffraw and he alone a tenant of the king of England. The theory involves recognition of the kingship of London, the ancient British inheritance, and the creation of the principality of Aberffraw in dependence upon it. Implicit in this pattern of relationships is the notion that authority is delegated by the crown of London to the prince who wears the coronet of Aberffraw, and by the prince of Aberffraw to the other lords of Wales. It is essentially a notion of enfeoffment, bearing the marks of contemporary practice and, though it is difficult to trace the origins of a concept such as this, the formulation may represent a response on the part of the lawyers of Gwynedd to Llywelyn ap Iorwerth's resolve to grasp the opportunity which presented itself during the traumatic conflicts of the reign of King John.⁵⁷

The practical effect of these changed political fortunes may be traced in the evidence of the years from 1212 onward. By 1215, in the wake of his co-operation with the English barons who opposed the king, and with his endeavours facilitated by mediation on the part of Archbishop Langton, Llywelyn secured the abrogation of the discomfiting agreement that he had been forced to make four years previously. Llywelyn's deliverance is embodied in Magna Carta and the conflict between king and prince was stayed for a while, but the charter hardly reflects the extent of the change which had by then been brought about in Wales.⁵⁸ Evidence of the following year suggests very strongly that the princes, now resorting to arms once more, were responding not to the demands of war alone but to specifically political needs as well. At a gathering of the princes of Wales before Llywelyn a partition was made of the lands of Deheubarth, resolving the discord that had rent the lineage for twenty years.⁵⁹ In time of war the princes were undertaking among themselves a responsibility of a kind which might normally have been reserved to the king of England. The manner by which Deheubarth was partitioned thus suggests that the lords of its several parts were accommodating themselves in a new political association. The precise nature of the bonds which now held the princes of Wales together may be recognized with some confidence, for there is an indication in the testimony of the chronicler that one of them, Gwenwynwyn ab Owain Cyfeiliog, lord of Powys Wenwynwyn, entered into a covenant with Llywelyn forged by homage and fealty.⁶⁰ If a

---

⁵⁶ *LTWL*, 207, 277, 437–8.
⁵⁷ *HW*, ii, 639–46.
⁵⁸ J. B. Smith, 'Magna Carta', 344–62; terms included release of Gruffudd.
⁵⁹ *CW*, 36; *BT, Pen20*, 169–70; *Pen20Tr*, 92; *RBH*, 206–7.
⁶⁰ *CW*, 36; *BT, Pen20*, 170–1; *Pen20Tr*, 92; *RBH*, 206–9.

bond of this kind was made in this instance it is likely that Llywelyn had entered into comparable agreements with each of the other princes allied with him in war. The leader in military alliance assumed the role of lord, his erstwhile allies were now his vassals. It was by virtue of these covenants that the political relationship envisaged by the lawyers, in the notion that royal tribute was due to the court of Aberffraw, came to be put to effect, unless, as has already been intimated, the lawyers' formulation was itself a response to the practical achievement now registered by Llywelyn ap Iorwerth.

The conflicts of the early years of the thirteenth century proved to be the means by which the princes came together, not for purposes of war alone, but to establish a political order. The supremacy of Aberffraw was acknowledged and a new structure created, not by military might, but by a unifying common will. Understandably, the crown was reluctant to concede that the princes were anything more than allies of Llywelyn, and he no more than their leader. This became clear early in 1218 when Llywelyn met the council of the young King Henry III as part of the process by which the realm was pacified after the civil war.[61] The changes in the internal relationships among the princes had important implications for their relations with the crown, considered presently, and the crown would not endorse those changes. The princes' objectives would evidently not be fulfilled at once, but they were not abandoned. Llywelyn's purposes were revealed in what emerges from his discussions with the king's council over the position of Maelienydd, a lordship in the central sector of the march of Wales.[62] For over a century or more its Welsh lineage had been resisting the power of successive members of the family of Mortimer. From their base at Wigmore the Mortimers had striven to extend their lordship over Maelienydd and raised their castle at Cymaron. They looked, too, for possession of the neighbouring lordship of Gwerthrynion and the intensity of the struggle is graphically reflected in Cynddelw Brydydd Mawr's elegy to Cadwallon ap Madog.[63] Their hold on these lands remained uncertain, even so, and it was not until the very end of the twelfth century that Roger Mortimer achieved a position where he could make a benefaction to the Cistercian monks of Cwm-hir in thanksgiving to God for his victory at Cymaron and in remembrance of the soldiers who had fallen in the campaign.[64] The final battle was still to be fought, and in the mean time the exiled young lords of Maelienydd were given refuge in Gwynedd by Llywelyn ap Iorwerth. The lineages of Aberffraw and Wigmore were thus engaged in the tortuous relationship which was to prove such a conspicuous

[61] Below, nn. 71–4.
[62] For this important region J. B. Smith, 'The middle march in the thirteenth century', *B*, 24 (1970–2), 77–93.
[63] *GCBM*, i, 21.
[64] B. G. Charles, 'An early charter of the abbey of Cwmhir', *TRadnS*, 40 (1970), 68–74.

feature of thirteenth-century political history. Llywelyn ap Gruffudd would wrestle with the Mortimers from the very earliest initiatives of his political career to the day on which he fell in battle, and it was the Mortimer claim to Maelienydd which exercised Llywelyn ap Iorwerth's mind in 1220. Emphasizing what had already been said during his negotiations with the king's council, Llywelyn insisted that it would be futile for Hugh Mortimer to attempt to remove its Welsh lords. Their homage belonged to his principality, and he would defend the land with the utmost vigour.[65] The letter provides the earliest known text in which the word 'principality' (*principatum*) is used to convey the idea of a broad political entity under the supremacy of Aberffraw. Formal recognition of this principality had evidently been broached in the discussions with the royal council, only to be postponed to an indefinite future. Llywelyn had not, even so, abandoned his determination to secure a settlement 'in justice and equity according to the status of Wales'.[66] His political objectives remained unchanged, and he was determined that in the fullness of time Gwynedd, Powys, Deheubarth and parts of the march would be incorporated in a wider principality. Llywelyn ap Gruffudd's second achievement, in the period of his ascendancy, would be to re-establish this broader unity.

It is clear that the endeavours of Llywelyn ap Iorwerth to secure the political unity of a wide area of Wales cannot be treated entirely separately from his concern with the relationship between Wales and England. The compulsions which brought Llywelyn ap Iorwerth and Llywelyn ap Gruffudd, each in turn in their years of supremacy, to seek the crown's recognition of the authority which they exercised in Wales may not be altogether easy to comprehend. Part of the explanation lies in the prominent place generally accorded to lordship, and the inter-relationship of lordships, in political associations. Part stems more specifically from the fact that, for several generations, political relationships in Wales had not been formulated in isolation from the English crown. Internal associations and the connection with the crown were, in effect, two facets of the same problem. The precedents whereby the crown dealt directly with the several, and increasingly numerous, seigniories of Wales were very firmly established. Any appreciable adjustment in Welsh relationships would need royal recognition, and the stability of any changed order would depend on royal consent. Recognition could not, even so, guarantee a prince the loyalty of the lords of Wales, as Llywelyn ap Gruffudd was to find in due

---

[65] *CAC*, 8–9; *RL*, i, 122–3.
[66] *RL*, i, 122–3 'in justitia et aequitate secundum statum Wallie'; for the phrase '*status Wallie*', below, pp. 291–2.

course, but without the imprimatur of the king of England the prospects for a viable political association among the lordships of Wales would remain uncertain. The changes brought about in the early thirteenth century meant the undoing of bonds which, for a very long time, had held every king or prince or lord, each one separately and directly, in fealty to the king of England.[67] They created a breach with a tradition deeply rooted in the experience of the two nations, and Llywelyn ap Gruffudd's strenuous efforts to resolve this problem would prove to be an important aspect of his political policy.[68]

The relationship with the crown had developed gradually and may have reached its definitive form in the reign of Henry II, for certainly by then it was established that the lords of Wales should do homage and fealty to the king.[69] The reference in the Four Branches of the Mabinogi to Manawydan's journey to Oxford to do homage to Caswallon may bear rather late overtones, but a bond of one kind or another had been forged for a considerable time.[70] By 1216, however, these links had been severed as the princes of Wales revoked their allegiance by making war against their king, and a new political unity came into being in their lands. Llywelyn recognized that the relationships made among themselves in conditions of conflict could not stand in perpetuity without the crown's consent, and he confronted the issue when, alone among the princes of Wales, he went to meet the king's council at Worcester in 1218. The meeting was part of the process by which, in accordance with the terms of the treaty of Lambeth the previous year, peace was restored in the realm of England after the turmoil of the civil war.[71] Llywelyn looked for nothing less than an acknowledgement on the king's part that it was now appropriate that the direct relationship between the crown and the lords of Wales be replaced by one in which he stood as an intermediary between the king and the princes of Wales. He sought the king's assent to what had been achieved in time of war. It is not difficult to envisage, however, that Henry's

---

[67] There are valuable surveys in Powicke, *Henry III*, ii, 618–85; idem, *Thirteenth Century*, 381–444; A. D. Carr, 'Anglo-Welsh relations, 1066–1282', in M. Jones and M. Vale (eds.), *England and her Neighbours, 1066–1453: Essays in Honour of Pierre Chaplais* (London, 1989), 121–38.

[68] Below, p. 116 *et seq*.

[69] W. L. Warren, *Henry II* (London, 1973), 162–9; Richter, 'National consciousness', 41–9. Each author rests heavily on Roger of Howden's comments on Henry II's arrangements with the Welsh rulers in 1177, but the evidence may not sustain the differentiation between the higher status said to be accorded to Dafydd ab Owain and Rhys ap Gruffudd as compared with the others. For Howden's texts, *Gesta Regis Henrici Secundi Benedicti Abbatis*, ed. W. Stubbs (RS, 1867), i, 162; *Chronica Rogeri de Hovedone*, ed. W. Stubbs (RS, 1868–71), ii, 133–4; discussion in J. B. Smith, 'Treftadaeth Deheubarth', in N. A. Jones and H. Pryce (eds.), *Yr Arglwydd Rhys* (Cardiff, 1996), 18–52, will be developed elsewhere.

[70] *PKM*, 50–1; *Mabinogion*, 42.

[71] J. B. Smith, 'The treaty of Lambeth, 1217', *EHR*, 94 (1979), 562–79. The treaty was made in September; Llywelyn was expected in November and came to Worcester in March 1218 (*PR, 1216–25*, 136; *Foedera*, I, i, 149–50).

councillors would be reluctant to yield anything to Llywelyn on a matter of such consequence while the king was under age. They were prepared to acknowledge his leadership and the influence which he exercised upon the princes but, in the carefully chosen term to which the chancery was to adhere thereafter, they were no more than his *inprisii*: they were his allies rather than his tenants; he was their leader, not their lord.[72] Resistance on the part of the council on this issue, quite apart from indicating an unwillingness to contemplate such a significant breach with traditional relationships, was dictated by the principle embodied in the treaty of Lambeth whereby it was agreed that those returning to the king's fealty should accept the *status quo ante bellum*.[73] It was on this basis that peace terms were offered to Llywelyn and Alexander II of Scotland. For Llywelyn the matters at issue concerned both territory, for extensive lands had been won from the marcher lords, and the new relationships which he had established with the princes. Entrusted with the custody of the royal castles of Cardigan and Carmarthen and the lands associated with them, he was now required to fulfil a pledge that he would make every effort to ensure that the conquered lands were restored and, quite crucially, bring the princes back into their old allegiance so that each of them did homage and fealty to the king as before.[74] The outcome of the negotiations at Worcester fell far short of Llywelyn's expectations. So soon after securing his supremacy Llywelyn was made an agent of the crown charged to return the princes of Wales to their ancient loyalties.[75]

This incongenial task was neither readily nor easily accomplished. Certainly, though some of the princes returned to the king's fealty quite soon, those of Deheubarth, who had shared their patrimony under the aegis of Prince Llywelyn in 1216, did so only with marked reluctance. Their unwillingness to go to the king and fulfil their obligations was noticed by the Welsh chronicler, and it is not difficult to understand their tardiness.[76] The patrimony divided between

---

[72] E.g. *RotLittClaus*, ii, 73, 83; *Foedera*, I, i, 229–30, 232; *PR, 1225–32*, 453.

[73] Cap. 10, *EHR*, 94 (1979), 577–8.

[74] *RotLittClaus*, i, 377–9; *PR, 1216–25*, 143; *Foedera*, I, i, 149–51.

[75] *HW*, ii, 653–4 has a different emphasis, conveying that, by the settlement at Worcester, Llywelyn secured terms 'which no doubt realised his highest expectations'. The records to which Lloyd refers do not support his conclusions, neither justifying his view that Llywelyn was confirmed in the possession of all his conquests, nor that he had no difficulty in getting the other princes to do homage to the king. W. Warrington, *The History of Wales* (London, 1786), ii, 42–7 has a more critical view, reflected in Gweirydd ap Rhys [R. J. Pryse], *Hanes y Brytaniaid a'r Cymry* (London, 1872–4), ii, 79–80. D. A. Carpenter, *The Minority of Henry III* (London, 1990), 74–7, conveys that Llywelyn's pretensions on the homage issue were resisted, but that in conceding him the custody of Powys Wenwynwyn and of the castles of Carmarthen and Cardigan the restoration of the *status quo* was not achieved. Llywelyn was, of course, granted custody rather than the lands and seisins envisaged in cap. 1 of the treaty of Lambeth.

[76] Llywelyn was expected to bring the princes to the king without delay and some of them came (*RotLittClaus*, i, 362; *PR, 1216–25*, 149–50, 155). *BT, Pen20*, 179; *Pen20Tr*, 96; *RBH*,

them in time of war consisted not only of the lands formerly held by Rhys ap Gruffudd but also several areas of Deheubarth, long since ceded to the marcher lords, that had been reappropriated by the princes during their recent campaigns. Rhys Gryg, in particular, would suffer a considerable diminution of his dominion, for he ruled from Dinefwr a lordship that included, not only Ystrad Tywi as it had been held by his father, but a territory broadened to include Cydweli and Gower, taken from their marcher lords, and Gwidigada, wrested from the king.[77] In his view these were lands to be colonized anew and retained for ever, the chronicler noting that the English had been driven out of Gower 'without ever hope of returning'.[78] Circumstances changed abruptly. The Welsh political community was rent as Llywelyn, who had only recently vested Gower in Rhys Gryg, now pressed him to respond to the demands made upon him and return to the king's fealty. Custodian of the castles of Carmarthen and Cardigan and responsible for the royal lands associated with them in south-west Wales by the agreement of 1218, Llywelyn was placed in an invidious position.[79] It is likely that it was during this crisis that Llywarch ap Llywelyn, a poet of Llywelyn's court, made his way to Dinefwr to address the recalcitrant lord of Ystrad Tywi, and that it was a poet in the role of mediator who composed the fine eulogy which recalls Rhys Gryg's triumphs on the battlefield during the forceful campaigns waged alongside the prince of Gwynedd.[80]

218–19, note that during the whole of 1219 Rhys ap Gruffudd alone among the princes of Deheubarth went, by Llywelyn's counsel, to do homage to the king. Carpenter, *Minority of Henry III*, 218–19, concludes that Llywelyn allowed only Rhys to do homage, but the evidence rather suggests resistance to Llywelyn's exhortations to do so.

[77] Cydweli, including Carnwyllion, was apportioned to Rhys Gryg at the partition of 1216, and probably Gwidigada also; Gower was given him after the campaign launched in 1217 upon Reginald de Braose's defection from those opposed to the crown. Maelgwn ap Rhys held Cemais, Emlyn, Cilgerran and possibly other lands in south-west Wales (*BT, Pen20*, 169, 176–7; *Pen20Tr*, 92, 95–6; *RBH*, 206–7, 214–15; *GlamCH*, iii, 221–3).

[78] *BT, Pen20*, 179; *Pen20Tr*, 96; *RBH*, 216–19.

[79] *RotLittClaus*, i, 378–9, 423.

[80] *GLILl*, 26, quoting ll. 15–22, trans. Ann Parry Owen: 'You shattered Carmarthen with hosts pressing upon the French, / And many a Frenchman put to flight; / And Swansea, a place of tumult, / With broken towers – and today there is peace! / And St Clears and the fine prosperous lands, / It is not English dwellers who possess it: / In Swansea, sturdy key of the English, / The wives are entirely widowed'. The poem reflects the situation that came to a head with Llywelyn's intervention in Ystrad Tywi in July 1220, but precise dating is difficult. If the poet's references (ll. 57–66) to conflict in Rhos, Haverford, Wiston and Narberth refer to the campaign of September 1220 (*AC*, 74; *BT, Pen20*, 181–2; *Pen20Tr*, 97–8; *RBH*, 220–1) mediation before Llywelyn's coming is not possible. But the chronicler does not state that Rhys participated in that campaign, and it is known that he had been wounded in a preceding skirmish at Carmarthen. The poet may refer to an earlier campaign by Rhys Gryg, possibly in alliance with Llywelyn in 1217. The structure of the poem, including its allusion to a prince of Gwynedd, is paralleled in Bleddyn Fardd's poem to Rhys Gryg's grandson, Rhys ap Maredudd, again composed perhaps with a mediating purpose, in 1277: *GBF*, 46 (comments by Rhian Andrews, pp. 540–1); below, p. 420, n. 113.

Inheritance

> Torraist Gaerfyrddin, torföedd – ar Ffrainc,
> Llawer Ffranc ar adwedd;
> Ac Abertawy, tref dyhedd,
> Tyrioedd briw – a heddiw neud hedd!
> A Saint Clêr a'r claer wyndiredd,
> Nid Saeson y maon a'i medd;
> Yn Abertawy, terrwyn allwedd – Lloegr,
> Neud llwyr weddw y gwragedd.

The *awdl* conveys, with the celebration of military prowess, an intimation of a wish for reconciliation between the two princes. Rhys Gryg's spirited resistance might be borne in mind when account is taken of the complex relationship between Llywelyn ap Gruffudd and Rhys's successors, Maredudd ap Rhys Gryg and Rhys ap Maredudd, which figures so prominently in the later course of events. The poet's entreaties were no more effective than the king's command and Llywelyn ap Iorwerth had to lead an army to Ystrad Tywi in the summer of 1220 and compel Rhys Gryg to accede to the terms which the prince had accepted at Worcester more than two years before.[81] He came to the castle of Dinefwr where the court had once possessed authority over Deheubarth in its entirety, but found it ruined as Rhys Gryg had dismantled the fortification in anticipation of his coming: 'olim famosum nunc autem ruinosum, ad quod tanquam ad caput Suthwallie pertinebat dignitates totius Suthwallie'.[82] Llywelyn went on to Carmarthen and an encounter in which Rhys Gryg was wounded, before 'the shield of Ystrad Tywi' succumbed to the pressure exerted upon him and agreed to do his homage to the king and swear fealty.[83] Llywelyn accomplished his mission, and the polity created in time of war was undone.

The years which followed Llywelyn's return to the king's fealty in 1218 were a troubled period as the prince tried to reconcile his responsibility as royal custodian and mediator with his natural inclination to maintain the position he had established by his forceful action in the preceding years.[84] While he

---

[81] *RotLittClaus*, i, 377; *Foedera*, I, i, 150.

[82] *CAC*, 24; *RL*, i, 176–7.

[83] The poet Philip Brydydd's description ('tarian Ystrad Tywi'), in one of two poems addressed to him (*GDB*, 11, 12). Carpenter, *Minority of Henry III*, 218 suggests that Llywelyn was acting in his own interests rather than the king's, and that his real object was the attack on Pembroke which followed. It is clear that Llywelyn was constrained to fulfil the terms to which he had agreed in 1218, thereby effectively dissolving the association formed in time of war. Llywelyn's motives at this time, to be considered more fully elsewhere, may have been influenced by his wish to secure royal support for his ordinance concerning the succession.

[84] Llywelyn's relations with the English government and the position in south-west Wales are considered in a valuable study, R. F. Walker, 'Hubert de Burgh and Wales, 1218–1232', *EHR*, 87 (1972), 465–94.

Inheritance

acted with some vigour in Ystrad Tywi in 1220, he did a good deal less than the English government required of him in returning the lands which had been taken from the marchers in the years of conflict. Urged to do so with necessary force, and promised military support if it were needed, the prince did not prove assiduous in restoring this aspect of the *status quo*. The marchers were, indeed, still liable to the prince's retribution, though the outcome, in one instance, proved decidedly counter-productive. His onslaught upon the lands of the lordship of Pembroke after his intervention in Ystrad Tywi provoked telling reaction on the part of William Marshal three years later. Unwilling to tolerate the territorial dispositions which Llywelyn had made to his disadvantage, Marshal recovered his own and, wresting the crown's possessions from Llywelyn, effectively discharged the prince from any responsibility as custodian of the king's interests in Deheubarth. He lost custody of Montgomery, which had also been granted to him at Worcester, and endured a largely self-inflicted reverse following his attack on Kinnerley in Shropshire. For some years thereafter he showed more restraint but he certainly maintained his power over a wide area, holding the lords of Powys Fadog and Deheubarth in an allegiance which greatly curtailed the king's authority in those regions. He maintained his hold, too, on Powys Wenwynwyn, placed in his custody for the minority of Gruffudd ap Gwenwynwyn.[85] Among marcher lands in his possession were Maelienydd, Gwerthrynion and, by his agreement with William de Braose for the marriage of the marcher's daughter with Dafydd ap Llywelyn, Builth. Powerful campaigns in the period 1228–34 enabled him to re-establish something of the supremacy he had first asserted in the reign of John, and the style he now adopted reflected the confidence which came with the triumphs of his successive offensives. The 'prince of Gwynedd' became 'prince of Aberffraw and lord of Snowdon', a style which evoked the concept of a wider unity under the aegis of his lineage.[86] Yet he still faced enormous difficulty in his efforts to secure the crown's recognition of his position, his problem underlined by the king's unwillingness to countenance his wish that his heir should inherit his broader authority. Llywelyn had secured the pope's confirmation of his ordinance designating Dafydd as his heir but the matter was not allowed to rest there. Some years later he wrote to the papal court again to convey that, at the instance of King Henry as he avowed, he had secured from the magnates of Wales an oath of fealty to his *primogenitus*. Pope Honorius duly bestowed his blessing upon the action taken on behalf of one whose parents, he recalled, had given him to the Roman

---

[85] R. F. Walker, 'Hubert de Burgh', *EHR*, 87 (1972), 473–92; *HW*, ii, 658–63; Carpenter, *Minority of Henry III*, 306–14; for Powys Wenwynwyn, *RotLittClaus*, i, 378; *Foedera*, I, i, 150–1.

[86] Chancery records point to a change of style between August 1230 and May 1231 (*CR, 1227–31*, 368; *PR, 1225–32*, 436).

church as an *alumnus,* and Dafydd had been received into the protection of the apostolic see.[87] Dafydd would later recall these exchanges – transactions that had made him a ward of the papal court – in an appeal for the pope's support that will be noticed presently. But his father's initiative in seeking papal support had no effect on the view of the succession taken at the English court. Henry had certainly recognized Dafydd as Llywelyn's heir in accordance with the prince's ordinance, but when Dafydd did homage to the king in 1229 Henry did no more than pledge his readiness to maintain the young man in those 'rights and privileges' which would come to him upon his father's death.[88] These were left entirely undefined and the devastating effect of this calculated ambiguity on the king's part would be appreciated when Henry came to offer his interpretation of their meaning upon Llywelyn's death. The prince's new style, despite its evocative connotations, still bore the mark of compromise. For Llywelyn, it was a title to be used in expectation of a full recognition of his position; for the king, the prince's position had no validity beyond armed might and, while chancery usage respected the prince's wish in regard to his style, the king would tolerate the situation it represented only for as long as it took to see it effaced.

Essential to the fulfilment of Llywelyn's aspirations was a treaty of peace which would properly reflect the position which he had achieved in his relations with the princes. The question of a peace treaty was undoubtedly raised from time to time. At the beginning of 1232, when successive campaigns had taken their toll and the king was constrained to admit that neither his military power nor ecclesiastical censure had been able to prevent Llywelyn from extending his influence over a wide area of the march, Henry conveyed his wish to negotiate a firm peace. He said so a second time in the autumn of the same year.[89] In 1234, following Llywelyn's alliance with Richard Marshal, earl of Pembroke, an association in resistance to the king which secured their control over a vast area of Wales and the march, the archbishop of Canterbury undertook the task of making a truce in the hope that it would lead to something better.[90] Archbishop Edmund, on the king's

---

[87] Vatican Library Reg. Vat. 11; transcript in BL, Add MS 15352, f. 323 (19 April 1226); brief calendar in *Regesta Honorii Papae,* ii, 417; *CPapL,* i, 109. The pope's letter was addressed to the bishops of Bangor, St Asaph and St David's; this suggests that the *magnates Wallie* who swore fealty were the princes of Wales, not simply the magnates of Gwynedd, and that Llywelyn's intimation that the fealty was sworn in response to Henry's *mandatum* needs to be read with caution. For Dafydd's later reference to his status as an *alumnus,* below, p. 52.

[88] *PR, 1225–32,* 269; *Foedera,* I, i, 196: 'de omnibus juribus et libertatibus que ipsum contingent post mortem ipsius Lewelini principis patris sui'.

[89] *PR, 1225–32,* 460, 466; *CPR, 1232–47,* 3; background in *HW,* ii, 673–82; Powicke, *Henry III,* i, 125–40.

[90] For the conflict in the march, Powicke, *Henry III,* i, 125–40; R. F. Walker, 'The supporters of Richard Marshal, earl of Pembroke, in the rebellion of 1233–34', *WHR,* 17 (1994–5), 41–65.

behalf, laboured in the hope of establishing nothing less than a firm peace with Llywelyn ('sub firma spe tractandi de pace inter nos et vos formanda et fortius firmandi').[91] Declarations of the king's readiness to negotiate with Llywelyn were prone to be made in times of difficulty, and there can be little doubt that the prince came to recognize that predilection for evasion with which his grandson would become so familiar as he in turn strove to secure Henry's recognition of the position he had won for himself. Whenever Welsh matters came to a head the crown had need to attend to more pressing concerns in Scotland or France, or in his own realm.[92] On the other hand, the evidence often suggests a hesitancy on Llywelyn ap Iorwerth's part, an instinctive wariness reflected in a tendency to dispatch proctors insufficiently empowered to resolve the matters at issue. It is difficult to divine the personal inclinations of one who, apart from a poet's eulogy or an annalist's commentary, is revealed only in a handful of letters written in his name. Alongside the heroic image bestowed upon him in the poets' work, there is the cunning (*versutia*) which one English chronicler recognized as a feature of his personality.[93] It was a quality which may have served him well as he steered a course among the countless obstacles created by princes of Wales, marcher lords, or king of England. Yet neither his heroism nor his cunning proved enough to enable him to reach his ultimate objective. Time ran out for Llywelyn, and the king emerged from the troubles that had encumbered him within his realm to find new confidence in his ability to adhere to the traditional tenets of royal policy. By 1237, when Llywelyn made his final bid to negotiate a definitive treaty with the king, it was clear that his strength had failed and that responsibility for his dominion was soon to be vested in his heir. These negotiations had no better result than those of earlier years, and Llywelyn the Great was to spend his last years under the uncertain conditions of truce rather than those of the firm peace that he had long sought.[94] Llywelyn ap Gruffudd's third achievement lay in his ability to secure the king's recognition of his supremacy, duly embodied in a treaty which established a new relationship between the kingdom of England and the principality of Wales.

* * * * *

[91] *CR, 1231–34*, 553, 564–5, 568–9; *CPR, 1232–47*, 41, 43, 55, 59; Paris, *ChronMaj*, iii, 290; C. H. Lawrence, *St Edmund of Abingdon* (Oxford, 1960), 130–8.

[92] E.g. *CR, 1234–37*, 541–2, 554.

[93] Walker, 'Hubert de Burgh', 473, quoting *FloresHist*, ii, 170: 'semper illaesus per suas versutias permansit'.

[94] The truce was renewed in 1236, 1237 and 1238 (*CR, 1234–37*, 526–7, 536–7, 541–2, 554; *CR, 1237–42*, 143; *CPR, 1232–47*, 153, 186, 225, 235; *Foedera*, I, i, 229, 232, 236). Lloyd, *HW*, ii, 680–2, has a different emphasis, seeing the conditions of truce as tantamount to a peace settlement which crowned the prince's long and triumphant career. For Llywelyn's failing health, possibly a paralytic stroke, Paris, *ChronMaj*, iii, 385; *FloresHist*, ii, 221.

Inheritance

In pursuing the themes raised for discussion in this chapter attention has not been focused upon particular episodes. Yet some of the crucial phases emerge reasonably clearly. Llywelyn ap Iorwerth found himself in desperate straits in 1211 when John was able not only to frustrate his ambitions for a broad supremacy, but to threaten the continued existence of the patrimonial dominion of Gwynedd. Constrained to disavow the only son of his body, Llywelyn was left to confront the prospect that at his death the patrimony would fall to the king by escheat.[95] He emerged from this exigency and by 1216 the cohesive influence of his hegemony augured the extension of his lordship over the lands of the princes and, conceivably, the forming of a new relationship with England. His initiative stayed in the years following the conflicts of the reign of John and then revived, he was in his later years still striving to turn the promise of his sustained efforts into conclusive achievement. Although he was not subject to military pressure, he was denied the agreement with the English crown that was vital for the stability and permanence of his broader sphere of influence. The difficulties that he encountered are made particularly clear in the evidence of the complex crisis which he faced in 1238, a matter especially pertinent to the present study because Llywelyn ap Gruffudd would have been old enough to be well aware of what was at stake. The young prince would doubtless have learned of earlier times of stress and exultation in Gwynedd. He would know of the perversity of princes and the severity of kings, of strenuous campaigns to Ceri or Caerleon or of unavailing embassies to royal councils in Worcester or Westminster. It is likely that he would have gathered much from those who joined him in the early years of his own enterprise in lordship. But he had a direct experience of the tense situation created by his father's unwillingness to conform to Llywelyn ap Iorwerth's provision for the future of his dominion. Llywelyn's decision to summon the lords of Wales to Strata Florida in 1238 to bind them anew in fidelity to Dafydd may reflect, not an assured progress towards the transmission to his heir of a secure principality, but the dire precariousness of the prince's provision for its future.[96] It appears that, in the event, the princes of Wales swore fealty without doing homage, an outcome which may reflect the king's ability to frustrate this last attempt on Llywelyn's part to proceed, without the king's consent, with a bid to bind the lords in a firm contractual obligation to his heir. Henry certainly made it perfectly clear

---

[95] Above, nn. 39, 52.

[96] The interpretation in *HW*, ii, 692–6, is reconsidered in G. A. Williams, 'The succession to Gwynedd, 1238–47', *B*, 20 (1962–4), 393–413, where consideration is given to the testimony of Matthew Paris, a contemporary and informed account, and an important source for the events preceding the death of Llywelyn ap Iorwerth and those of the following years; further reference, below, pp. 31–2, 34, 43, 47, 100; also Powicke, *Henry III*, ii, 630–5.

Inheritance

that the princes of Powys and Deheubarth should not, on any account, do homage to Dafydd ap Llywelyn.[97] If Llywelyn was gratified by something short of a finite engagement on the part of each of the princes it was his very last compromise. Without a binding agreement, and without the enforcing power to ensure adherence to the princes' pledge, it was virtually inevitable that the unity maintained under Llywelyn's supremacy would, in due course, be shattered. As the prince's strength failed him, and the definitive agreement with the king remained elusive, the twin pillars of his government were undermined, his authority over the princes destined to be dispelled at his death, and the succession to Gwynedd itself a matter of contention between the chosen heir and his bastard brother. On 11 April 1240 Llywelyn ap Iorwerth died, mourned and exalted by poet and chronicler, leaving Dafydd alone to face the crisis over his inheritance.[98]

The Tewkesbury chronicler provides an informed account of Dafydd ap Llywelyn's visit to the king's court at Gloucester six weeks later. Dafydd, he recounted, did homage wearing the coronet which was the mark of his princely status. The chronicler does not omit to record, however, that in return for his homage he was invested with no more territory than his father had held by right (*de iure*) and that he pledged his unreserved submission to the king's will.[99] The terms of the agreement made at Gloucester stand, at once, as an unintentional acknowledgement on the king's part of the extent of the personal supremacy that had been exercised by Llywelyn the Great and as a testimony to its fragility. Dafydd offered his homage for his right in Gwynedd (*pro iure suo Northwallie*) and for the lands that Gruffudd ap Gwenwynwyn and other barons of the king claimed against him as their right.[100] Predictably, and precisely as the Tewkesbury chronicler indicated, Dafydd was allowed to do homage for his right in Gwynedd and no more. The treaty formally recorded that the homage of the barons of Wales was conceded to the king, the text carrying an implicit admission that the previous position had been different from that which the king now laid down in clear terms. A number of decisions followed immediately, enabling Gruffudd ap Gwenwynwyn to take possession of his patrimony in Powys Wenwynwyn and

---

[97] The king's concern at what was afoot early in 1238 is reflected in the stream of letters issued from chancery, addressed to Llywelyn, Dafydd, the princes and the marcher lords (*CR, 1237–42*, 123–5). The Welsh chronicle records that the princes swore fealty to Dafydd (*AC*, 82; *CW*, 38; *BT, Pen20*, 197; *Pen20Tr*, 104; *RBH*, 234–5).

[98] *GDB*, 5 (Einion Wan), 27 (Dafydd Benfras); *AC*, 82–3; *CW*, 38; *BT, Pen20*, 197–8; *Pen20Tr*, 105; *RBH*, 236–7.

[99] *AnnTewk*, i, 115: 'dominus rex Anglie convocato magno colloquio apud Gloucestriam in Maio, accinxit David nepotem suum filium Lewelini gladio militari, et concessit ei omnes terras quas pater eius de jure tenuit, et ibidem portavit predictus David diadema minus, quod dicitur garlonde, insigne principatus Northwallie, per omnia tamen subiciens se regi Anglie'. For the coronet or *talaith*, below, pp. 199, 332–3, 584.

[100] *LW*, 5–6; Powicke, *Henry III*, ii, 631–2.

authorizing Ralph Mortimer to enforce his claims upon Maelienydd and Gwerthrynion.[101] Other matters not open to discussion while Llywelyn lived were made subject to arbitration. The ceding of the homage of the lords of Wales had immediate effect, for they did not tarry in making their way to Henry's court to be received as his vassals.

The lords' anxiety to register their fidelity to the king without delay is clearly indicated in chancery records of the summer of 1240.[102] Each had interests to safeguard, and the disintegration which followed so swiftly upon Llywelyn's death reflected something more than perverseness on their part, or mere inconstancy, or reaction against the order which had prevailed before. They looked to the future, following the needs of their baronial interests, searching for the security which their contractual relationship with their lord was intended to ensure. This concern provides, more than any other single factor, the key to an understanding of the cautious course which several of them were to take in the troubled period of Dafydd ap Llywelyn and the years which followed. They would maintain their wariness until Llywelyn ap Gruffudd, by word and deed, was able to convince them that, once more and in perpetuity this time, their concern for their security could be reconciled with the objectives of a prince of the lineage of Gwynedd in a new political unity. This would not be for some time, and the course charted by Gruffudd ap Madog, lord of Powys Fadog, illustrates the considerations which determined the allegiance of the Welsh princes in these years.[103] It cannot be said that Gruffudd, any more than his father before him, was as devious as successive members of the lineage of Powys Wenwynwyn – Gwenwynwyn and Gruffudd ap Gwenwynwyn – were in their relations with the princes of Gwynedd. At the same time, Gruffudd ap Madog can hardly be counted among the pillars of Welsh autonomy in the years following the death of Llywelyn ap Iorwerth. He lost no time in submitting to the king, impelled by dynastic considerations to seek the security which a relationship with the king was calculated to provide. He would not be drawn into any hazardous association with Dafydd ap Llywelyn. Gruffudd would safeguard his interests, and he would be vigilant that the crown should do nothing to undermine the indigenous law which obtained in his lordship. Particularly evident is his determination, as the eldest of several brothers, to ensure that the patrimony remained undivided and that, under his lordship, Castell Dinas

---

[101] G. A. Williams, 'Succession to Gwynedd', 398–9; J. B. Smith, 'Middle March', 82–4.
[102] The situation in Deheubarth is noticed in J. B. Smith, 'Cronica de Wallia', 266–9.
[103] *HW*, ii, 683–4, 697–701.

Inheritance

Brân should remain a symbol of the territorial integrity of Powys Fadog for another generation.[104] He adhered to his purpose with unflinching consistency throughout the troubled years, and he was not alone in his concern for seigniorial needs. Maredudd ap Rhys Gryg, who inherited only part of the territory of Rhys Gryg in Ystrad Tywi, was bent upon securing a broader dominion and availed himself of the opportunity afforded him upon the death of Llywelyn to take an initiative on his own account.[105] In Powys Fadog there was a determination to maintain a baronial inheritance in its entirety, in Ystrad Tywi an endeavour to reconstitute a similar inheritance but, in each case, the pursuit of seigniorial interests dictated swift submission to the English crown. With the heir to Llywelyn's patrimony unable to protect their interests, the princes lost the willpower to sustain the political order which the prince of Gwynedd had hitherto maintained. At Gloucester in the early summer of 1240 Dafydd ap Llywelyn virtually acknowledged the dissolution of the supremacy of Gwynedd, and the other princes, hastening to perform their services to the king, did likewise.

Dafydd's submission was made inevitable by the situation which confronted him in Gwynedd. Neither the king's demands upon him nor his desertion by the princes in any way affected his position in the territory where his father had exercised lordship *de iure*. Henry did nothing during 1240 to undermine his succession to that patrimony: he scrupulously fulfilled the promise made to Llywelyn twenty years earlier when the prince's ordinance for the succession was afforded royal confirmation; he might equally maintain that he had interpreted quite correctly his subsequent promise to maintain Dafydd in those 'rights and privileges' to which he would one day succeed.[106] For his part, Dafydd's main concern in 1240 was to make certain of Henry's adherence to his earlier undertakings and ensure that he was recognized as heir to Gwynedd. Dafydd's promptness in seeking the king was clearly a measure of his extremity, for there can be no doubt that his succession to Gwynedd was challenged by his brother Gruffudd. Matthew Paris's informed account, and his chronology, certainly carry some conviction, indicating Dafydd's imperative need to reach the king without delay

---

[104] G. A. Williams, 'Succession to Gwynedd', 400, 404–7; J. B. Smith, 'Dynastic succession', 227–8. Lloyd states that Powys Fadog was divided upon the death of Madog ap Gruffudd (1236), but it is certain that Gruffudd ap Madog secured a primacy by which he exercised control over the patrimony as a whole. Gruffudd's brothers were allied with Dafydd ap Llywelyn in 1241 (*CR, 1237–42*, 359–60); his relations with Llywelyn ap Gruffudd are noticed later.

[105] J. B. Smith, 'Cronica de Wallia', 266–9, notices Maredudd's prompt action, in association with Gilbert Marshal, earl of Pembroke, upon Llywelyn's death; for Maelgwn Fychan's subsequent need to adhere to the king, ibid., 267; G. A. Williams, 'Succession to Gwynedd', 398–9.

[106] For Henry's confirmation of the prince's ordinance, and the terms on which Dafydd did homage, *RotLittClaus*, i, 436; *PR, 1225–32*, 269; *Foedera*, I, i, 159, 196; above, nn. 44, 88.

Inheritance

so that, fortified by Henry's formal recognition, he could return to Gwynedd to confront his brother.[107] By the autumn, perhaps by treachery, he was able to capture Gruffudd and, with his challenger imprisoned, Dafydd was able to embark upon the task of consolidating his authority over the community of Gwynedd.[108] His subsequent reluctance to accede to the king's insistence that he fulfil his obligations under the treaty made at Gloucester, increasingly visible in the evidence from the autumn of that year, may reflect the confidence which he gained from the fact that Gruffudd and his son Owain were secured in Cricieth castle. Dafydd, who submitted so readily in the summer, proved increasingly intractable thereafter, notably in his failure, through procrastination and evasion, to facilitate the arbitration procedures envisaged in the treaty.[109] Nor had he abandoned every intention of bringing his influence to bear on matters beyond the confines of Gwynedd. When Ralph Mortimer moved to take possession of the lordships conceded to him by Henry he found that those who resisted him won the young prince's military support.[110] Dafydd may not have been in the least surprised that Henry III decided by the summer of 1241 to enforce a proper fulfilment of the obligations into which he had entered at Gloucester. But he would hardly have anticipated either the new terms which the king would now press upon him or the means to which the king would resort in order to achieve his objectives.

There is a strange irony in the fact that it was in this critical situation, as instruments by which the king might take disciplinary measures against the prince of Gwynedd, that members of Llywelyn ap Gruffudd's immediate family, other than Gruffudd ap Llywelyn himself and his eldest son Owain, make their first appearance in the historical record. With Gruffudd, once a captive of John and then of his father, now in his brother's prison, his wife took up his cause. At Easter, Senana had come to Henry III's court in an effort to persuade the king to secure her husband's release from Dafydd's prison. She maintained that he should be a tenant of the crown, but he was kept in captivity contrary to all justice.[111] Senana then met the king at Shrewsbury when he was on his way to Chester to lead his forces into

---

[107] Paris, *ChronMaj*, iii, 385; iv, 8, 47–8; *FloresHist*, ii, 221, 236. G. A. Williams, 'Succession to Gwynedd', 401–8, examines the disparity between Paris and the Welsh chronicle.

[108] Paris, *ChronMaj*, iv, 8, 47–8; Paris, *HistAng*, ii, 430; *AnnDunst*, 152; and, attributed to 1239, *AC*, 82; *CW*, 38; *BT, Pen20*, 197; *Pen20Tr*, 105; *RBH*, 234–7.

[109] G. A. Williams, 'Succession to Gwynedd', 398–9.

[110] Ibid. J. B. Smith, 'Middle march', 82–4, notes the submission of the men of Maelienydd and Gwerthrynion (*LW*, 54–8; *B*, 24 (1970–2), 89–93).

[111] *CRR*, xvi, no. 1595; for Senana, below, p. 37–9, 45.

Inheritance

Gwynedd, and she won a promise of the king's aid in securing Gruffudd's release. The document was sealed on 12 August 1241, thirty years to the day on which Llywelyn ap Iorwerth had sealed the document which compelled him to hand over Gruffudd ap Llywelyn to King John.[112] By his agreement with Senana King Henry agreed not only to secure Gruffudd's release but that his court should make a judgement, in accordance with Welsh law, in respect of the 'portion' of his father's patrimony which belonged to him but which his brother denied to him. For the very first time, as far as can be judged, the king declared his wish to divide Gwynedd into two parts. It became clear quite soon that the 'portion' which the king envisaged would not be an apanage within his brother's territory but that, on the contrary, Dafydd and Gruffudd would each hold his 'portion' as a tenant-in-chief of the crown. His object, in short, was to partition the patrimony into two parts and 'the custom of Wales' was invoked to justify the division of Gwynedd by a legal judgement of the king's court. This purpose was never fulfilled, but there is no doubting the ominous significance of the clause in the agreement between Senana and the king which conveyed this proposal, nor the similar clause soon to be embodied in the agreement made between Henry and Dafydd himself at Gwerneigron.[113] The king's intention was tantamount to a repudiation of an objective which had been an essential feature of the dynastic policy of the princes of Gwynedd ever since Gruffudd ap Cynan rehabilitated the kingdom after the depredations of the Norman period. That there were indigenous influences militating against the single succession there can be no doubt: a succession might be contested and ultimately resolved by a compromise which left the patrimony partitioned; the creation of apanages could lead to full and permanent separation; the fact that the apanages were themselves subject to partition might promote a trend towards partition. These factors tended to blur the distinction between those tenets that applied to seigniories and those, known to the lawyers as the practices of *cyfran*, that applied to ordinary proprietorial estates.[114] Even so, the crown's intervention in 1241 proved crucial, for it meant that a divisive interpretation of 'the custom of Wales' was applied to a major seigniory by the king's decision. Henry's action carried a threat not to Gwynedd alone but to the lordships of Wales in general. The 'custom of Wales' could hereafter be invoked to facilitate a continuing process of fragmentation as though the lordships were subject to an inexorable fate. Those who held by Welsh barony, their lands partitioned in each generation and their status in consequence progressively

---

[112] *LW*, 52–3; sureties given to the king on Senana's behalf, *LW*, 15, 19–20, 35.
[113] *LW*, 9–10.
[114] J. B. Smith, 'Dynastic succession', 221–2.

eroded, would be set upon a course leading irreversibly to the complete eradication of any seigniorial status.[115]

The dangers were recognized among the princes. Already confronted with his brothers' demands for a share of the inheritance but resolutely resolved to maintain the integrity of Powys Fadog, Gruffudd ap Madog had added reason to remain firmly in the king's fealty. This consideration was itself enough to ensure that he was at Shrewsbury on the decisive day in August 1241 when Henry made his agreement with Senana and found himself in the incongruous company of Ralph Mortimer and Maelgwn Fychan, Walter Clifford and Maredudd ap Robert, Roger of Mold and Gruffudd ap Gwenwynwyn.[116] The listing of these names together is itself a measure of Dafydd ap Llywelyn's extremity, as the king of England proceeded to summon the men of Wales to join him in his determined intention of doing justice to Gruffudd ap Llywelyn, accomplishing a diplomatic feat for which it would be difficult to find as fiendish a parallel in the whole history of Anglo-Welsh relations.[117] Before the end of the month Dafydd ap Llywelyn came before the king at Gwerneigron, on the banks of the Elwy in the *cantref* of Rhos, and made a submission which fully reflected his dire plight. He acknowledged that he was now called upon to hand over Gruffudd to the king, and that he was required to accept the judgement of the king's court in respect of the 'portion' of the patrimony which was due to his brother in accordance with Welsh custom or according to right (*ius*), as the king would decide. He had to yield the *cantref* of Tegeingl and agree that the lands that Llywelyn had seized in the reign of John should be restored to their lords. He promised anew that he would cede all homages that belonged to King John and that ought by right (*de iure*) to belong to King Henry. At Rhuddlan two days later he placed himself under ecclesiastical jurisdiction if he were ever to renounce his fealty to the crown, and acknowledged that breach of fealty would incur the forfeiture of the whole of his land.[118] Even then the transactions completed at

---

[115] Thus Henry took relief from *two* sons of Maredudd ap Cynan to ensure their succession to the lordship of Meirionnydd in 1241 (*RotFin*, i, 371). For the eventual results of successive divisions in a lordship such as Edeirnion, and the nature of 'Welsh barony' or *tir pennaeth*, A. D. Carr, 'The barons of Edeyrnion, 1282–1485', *JMerHRS*, 4 (1961–4), 187–93, 289–301; idem, 'An aristocracy in decline: the native Welsh lords after the Edwardian conquest', *WHR*, 5 (1970–1), 103–29.

[116] *LW*, 15, 19–20, 35, 52–3. For Gruffudd's power, prudence and friendship with the king, Paris, *ChronMaj*, iv, 150; his brothers' alliance with Dafydd is noticed above, n. 104.

[117] *CPR, 1232–47*, 256; G. A. Williams, 'Succession to Gwynedd', 400–1, 404–5.

[118] *LW*, 9–10, 12–13, 22 (Gwerneigron, 29 August; Rhuddlan, 31 August). The Patent Roll (C66/49, m. 1) has two texts: A, to which 'Liber A' (*LW*, 9–10; *Foedera*, I, i, 242) corresponds, except for the addition of a charter by which Dafydd pledges loyalty to the king and acknowledges that breach of faith would incur total forfeiture; B, struck through, to which a text in *ChronMaj*, iv, 322–3 corresponds, except that Paris has an additional clause recording, in a phraseology different from Text A, Dafydd's acknowledgment that, if he or his heirs rose against the king or acted contrary to the terms now agreed, he would

Inheritance

Gwerneigron and Rhuddlan were not enough. In London during the autumn, in a document which recited his submission in full excruciating detail, Dafydd had to make a new clear declaration that if he were ever to rebel against the king again and, crucially, if he were to die without heir of his body by his wife, his patrimony would be ceded to the king.[119] This was not the first time that the king of England had imposed the principle of escheat on a prince of Gwynedd, but the threat was no less real now than it had been when Llywelyn ap Iorwerth was burdened with the same undertaking.[120] His wife, Isabel de Braose, had not yet brought him either heir or heiress, and Dafydd returned to Gwynedd knowing that the continued existence of his dominion was once more put at risk.[121]

When Llywelyn ap Iorwerth accepted the humiliating terms which John decreed in 1211 it was incumbent upon him to entrust his son Gruffudd to the king's custody. By now a new prince ruled in Gwynedd and another king sat upon the throne of England, but in the summer of 1241 the same Gruffudd made his way to London.[122] His son Owain accompanied him, in accordance with the terms of the document to which Senana had agreed at Shrewsbury, but she had hardly anticipated that her husband and her first-born son would merely exchange captivity in Cricieth castle for confinement in the Tower of London. On the same occasion she had also pledged her readiness to hand over her two youngest sons as hostages for her good faith, though Dafydd and Rhodri were minors still in their mother's care.[123] Senana had one other son, her second-born son, of whom she made no mention in the document drawn up in the king's presence at Shrewsbury, and there is no ready explanation why his mother took no account of him. But it will be seen presently that the fact that Llywelyn ap Gruffudd was not named in that document probably means that this son of Gruffudd ap Llywelyn was already revealing the qualities which were to enable him to stand forth conspicuously as one of royal lineage with the attributes that made him a rightful lord of his people. He, like Llywelyn ap Iorwerth and Gruffudd ap Cynan, came to no better inheritance than an inherent capacity to inspire his fellow men to

---

forfeit his entire inheritance to the king and that he would be subject to excommunication and his land placed under interdict by four named English bishops; he further agreed that he would seek charters from the bishops of Bangor and St Asaph confirming that the ecclesiastical censures would be put to effect. Paris's inclusion of this text, and others relating to the transactions concerning Gruffudd ap Llywelyn in 1241 (*ChronMaj*, iv, 316–22) may well reflect Bishop Richard of Bangor's connection with St Albans mentioned later.

[119] *LW*, 10–11, 22–3 (London, 24 October).
[120] For the significance of the clause, Powicke, *Henry III*, ii, 633–4; cf. above, pp. 12–13.
[121] The list of hostages given to Henry, 2 December 1241, provides a striking reflection of the extent of Dafydd's subjugation (*CPR, 1232–47*, 267–8).
[122] Gruffudd was in the Tower of London by September 1241 (*CR, 1237–42*, 328; *CLibR*, ii, 70).
[123] *LW*, 52–3.

Inheritance

commit themselves in common endeavour with himself and to infuse them with the willpower to overcome changeful circumstances in resolute commitment to enduring purposes. It would be no easy task to re-establish the inheritance of Llywelyn the Great, reassert the broader supremacy, and forge ahead to win a formal recognition never known before. The origins of the new creative movements which were to achieve these objectives have to be sought in the decisions which Llywelyn ap Gruffudd was to take in the next years, when the government of Gwynedd was vested in his uncle, Dafydd ap Llywelyn, and when his father endured once more that captivity which was so much a part of his experience of being of princely lineage. With his father imprisoned, and he himself entirely without patrimony, Llywelyn ap Gruffudd securely established himself in the estimation of the community of the land of his forebears as a true heir to the inheritance of the principality of Gwynedd.

Chapter 2

Bryn Derwin

VERY little may be said of Llywelyn ap Gruffudd's early years. There is no record of the year of his birth, nor is it possible to say where he was born, and of his boyhood we have no more than may be gathered or imagined about the upbringing of the son of a prince whose years were so turbulent and so full of anguish. We have to be cautious even when considering who was the mother of the future prince of Wales. The most important surviving reference to Gruffudd ap Llywelyn's wife occurs in the document which records the terms of her agreement with Henry III in the summer of 1241, and we have already seen that, although Senana names three sons, there is no mention of Llywelyn.[1] If we were to give credence to the testimony of the Welsh genealogists we would have to accept that Llywelyn was not Senana's son, and we might be drawn to conclude that this explains why he is not named in the documents concerning her intervention on her husband's behalf. In the genealogies Llywelyn appears as a son of Rhunallt, who was, we are told, a daughter of the king of Man.[2] Llywelyn's lineage is, indeed, recorded in the late thirteenth-century volume Exeter Cathedral Library MS 3514. It traces the prince's lineage to its Trojan origins, through Camber son of Brutus, and to the biblical patriarchs, and it is an early genealogical remembrance whose significance will be noticed later.[3] But this manuscript, and others of

---

[1] *LW*, 52–3. The form normally found in records is 'Senana' (*LW*, 15, 19–20, 35, 52–3; *RC*, 252); 'Sauan' in *CRR*, xvi, no. 1595; 'Salente' in *Cheshire Pipe Rolls*, 77; 'Syna' is the form used by John Wynn (Wynn, *HGF*, 7, 9). *Issues of the Exchequer, Henry III–Henry VI*, ed. F. Devon (Record Commission, 1847), i, 29, records a payment to 'Friaute', wife of Gruffudd ap Llywelyn. For her lineage, P. C. Bartrum, *Welsh Genealogies, AD 300–1400* (Cardiff, 1974), 3. 454–5 [Bartrum, *WG*]; D. Stephenson, *The Governance of Gwynedd* (Cardiff, 1984), 115–19 [Stephenson, *GG*].

[2] E.g. NLW, Peniarth, 129; 131. The Man connection is cited in G. Broderick, 'Irish and Welsh strands in the genealogy of Godred Crovan', *The Journal of the Manx Museum*, 8 (1980), 34, 36 and nn. 34–5.

[3] For the genealogy, contained in the MS which provides the text of the 'Cronica de Wallia', D. E. Thornton, 'A neglected genealogy of Llywelyn ap Gruffudd', *CMCS*, 23 (1992), 9–23; the significance of an ascent through Camber son of Brutus is noticed in J. B. Smith, *SHMW*, 2, 14–15; cf. below, pp. 543–4.

comparatively early date, are concerned only with the prince's agnatic predecessors. The reference to Rhunallt, daughter of the king of Man, occurs in much later texts. Some indications of a connection between Wales and Man are, indeed, found in thirteenth-century sources. Bleddyn Fardd, in his elegy to Owain ap Gruffudd, conveys that the prince was of the lineage of the king of Man, but this was probably a recollection of a dynastic link made at a much earlier date.[4] In the eventful year 1241 itself, a person described as 'Godred, son of the king of Man' is found in association with Llywelyn ap Gruffudd, but his presence may perhaps be explained by political circumstances in the isle of Man, and it need not be a reflection of any dynastic connection in the thirteenth century.[5] Neither the recollection of an association between Aberffraw and Man, nor the presence of Godred in Llywelyn's company, provides any good reason to believe that Llywelyn's mother was the daughter of the king of Man; the genealogists' identification of Rhunallt as Llywelyn's mother stems from late sources and no reliance may be placed upon them in this respect. Contemporary record sources establish quite securely that Llywelyn, like Owain, his elder brother, and Dafydd and Rhodri, his younger brothers, was a son of Gruffudd ap Llywelyn and his wife Senana: she herself refers to Dafydd and Rhodri as her sons; she refers to 'Gruffudd her husband and her son Owain' and at a later date Owain and Llywelyn refer to their mother (*mater nostra*); and Dafydd is once named as Llywelyn's uterine brother.[6] There is no equally certain knowledge of Gruffudd's daughters, Gwladus and Margaret.[7] Record sources

---

[4] *GBF*, 48. 21: 'Hil gwrawl breiniawl brenin Manaw'. The preceding line refers to Owain's descent from Owain Gwynedd and this line could allude to Gruffudd ap Cynan who, according to the *Historia*, was a grandson, through his mother, of the king of Dublin and the island of Manaw. Gruffudd's line is also traced through Gwriad, grandfather of Rhodri Mawr, who was possibly asociated with Man (*HGK*, 1–2, 42, 47 and the sources cited; *MPW*, 53–4). For Rhodri ab Owain Gwynedd's marriage to a daughter of the king of Man, *HW*, ii, 588, 617; Broderick, 'Godred Govan', 35–6.

[5] J. B. Smith, 'The middle march in the thirteenth century', *B*, 24 (1970–2), 88–9, 92. Godred's presence in Wales may be connected with the troubles which followed Harold's succession to the throne of Man in 1237; the Man chronicle relates that Lauchlan, custodian of the kingdom, fled to Wales, taking his foster-son Godred Olafsson with him, but that both were drowned on the Welsh coast (*Chronicle of the Kings of Mann and the Isles*, ed. G. Broderick and B. Stowel (Edinburgh, 1973), 36–7, 76). There are problems still to be resolved, and I am grateful to Dr Sean Duffy, who kindly examined the evidence for possible solutions; it seems likely that the 'Godred son of the king of Man' named in 1241 was one who had, for whatever reason, fled from his own land.

[6] Senana refers to Dafydd and Rhodri as 'her sons' (*filios suos*) and to 'Gruffudd her husband and her son Owain' (*viro suo et Owyno filio suo*, *LW*, 52–3); if Owain were not her son the form *filio eius* would have been more likely. Owain and Llywelyn refer to lands 'which our mother held in dower' (*quas mater nostra habuerat pro dote*, *RL*, ii, 64–5); the agreement with the Scots in 1258 names Llywelyn and then Dafydd 'his uterine brother' (*fratre suo uterino*, *LW*, 184).

[7] Gwladus, who married Rhys Fychan (d. 1271) of Ystrad Tywi, is named at her death in 1261 as daughter of Gruffudd (*BT, Pen20*, 212; *Pen20Tr*, 112; *RBH*, 252). Margaret, not

establish beyond any doubt, however, that the four boys were sons of Gruffudd and Senana, and it is a pity that the genealogists, who so meticulously recorded the affiliations of a multitude of other men, failed to retain a memory of the name of Llywelyn ap Gruffudd's mother.[8] It appears from what follows that Llywelyn's name was omitted from the document of 1241 not because he was a son of someone other than Senana, but for other reasons explained by the events of that year. It is likely that he, like Owain, had already reached manhood, whereas Dafydd and Rhodri, though old enough to be given as hostages for their parents' good faith, were still young enough for the king to consent on humanitarian grounds to allow one of them to be set free. The two younger sons probably came of age after 1246, when Gwynedd was partitioned between Owain and Llywelyn without any provision being made for Dafydd and Rhodri. A great deal of uncertainty remains, but it would seem that Owain and Llywelyn were a good deal older than the others, and we would not be amiss if we were to place the birth of Owain and Llywelyn fairly early in the 1220s.[9]

These are not trivial matters, for one conclusion which may be safely drawn from the slender evidence is that the only one of Gruffudd ap Llywelyn's sons who was old enough to play a role in the political crisis of 1241, and who was not in captivity, was Llywelyn. Known royal documents make no reference to him for another four years, but we have two charters in Llywelyn's name which provide some record of his early political initiatives.[10] They belong to the period between Dafydd ap Llywelyn's submission to the king in 1241 and the sudden death of Gruffudd ap Llywelyn in 1244. These were the years of Gruffudd's last confinement, made captive in the Tower of London upon Dafydd ap Llywelyn's compliance with the terms of the engagement into which he had entered at Gwerneigron.[11] In theory, Gruffudd was placed in royal custody in order that the king might determine what portion of Gwynedd should come to him by hereditary right but, though the brothers did bring actions to the king's court, the issue of substance between them was

---

named in genealogies, is described as Llywelyn's sister in 1258 when the king was wary of the prince's intentions in arranging her marriage (*CPR, 1247–58*, 660); she married Madog ap Gruffudd (d. 1277) of Powys Fadog, and after his death, when she is again named as Llywelyn's sister, the prince mediated with the king on behalf of her sons, described as his nephews (*CCR, 1272–79*, 379; *CAC*, 93–4); for his concern and their ultimate fate, below, pp. 457, 520. The genealogies (Bartrum, *WG*, 3. 447) have Gwladus and another daughter of Gruffudd named Catrin, to whom there does not appear to be any reference in record sources.

[8] Llywelyn is recorded as a son of Senana, from record evidence, in Bartrum, *WG*, 3, 447.

[9] A. D. Carr, *Llywelyn ap Gruffydd* (Cardiff, 1982), 17, suggests that Owain and Llywelyn were probably born between 1225 and 1230; activity from as early as 1241 may point to slightly earlier dates.

[10] These are of earlier date than the charters noticed in *HW*, ii, 707, n. 76.

[11] *CR, 1237–42*, 328; *CLibR*, iii, 70.

never broached.¹² It seems that Henry and Dafydd reached an understanding, be it implicit or explicit, that the king would not enforce the partition of Gwynedd as long as Dafydd remained unswerving in his fidelity to the king. When Gruffudd ap Llywelyn fell from the height of the Tower of London on St David's Day 1244, Dafydd ap Llywelyn was released from the restraint which he had endured for three years. Declaring his determination to avenge his brother's death, he revealed his sense of relief that the bonds by which he had been constrained had now been severed. Henry soon realized that he faced a new challenge in Wales as Dafydd ap Llywelyn called the princes of Wales to arms once more, initiating a new conflict between Wales and England which was still to be resolved when the prince died early in 1246. But, if this represents the main sequence of events between 1241 and 1246, these years have another significance in that it was in this brief but crucial period that Llywelyn ap Gruffudd was able to establish the personal authority which, more than any other single factor, forced Henry III to acknowledge that, though Dafydd ap Llywelyn had died without heir, the annexation of Gwynedd was an objective still beyond his capability.¹³

Of the two charters in Llywelyn's name issued in this period only one is dated. It records that Llywelyn, at Llannerch in Dyffryn Clwyd on 27 September 1243, confirmed Einion ap Maredudd in his possession of land in that *cantref*.¹⁴ The deed itself may not be of any great importance, but it serves to show that Llywelyn had established lordship over at least part of Dyffryn Clwyd. It is not easy to see how he had been able to do so, but in this connection the testimony of John Wynn of Gwydir, to which reference will be made again, deserves some notice. He maintains that Llywelyn at this time held Perfeddwlad in spite of Dafydd ap Llywelyn and King Henry: he held Tegeingl, Dyffryn Clwyd, Rhos and Rhufoniog 'against his uncle Dafydd, having war on the one side with the king, on the other side with his uncle'.¹⁵ Llywelyn cannot in truth be said to have held these *cantrefi*. Under the terms of the treaty of Gwerneigron it had been provided that, of the four *cantrefi* of Perfeddwlad, the king would hold Tegeingl (Englefield) and, though no explicit grant of the remainder was made to Dafydd, the prince was allowed to

---

¹² *CRR*, xvii, nos. 97, 237, 2419; KB26/131, m. 1; 132, m. 14, actions brought by Dafydd and Gruffudd, each alleging that the other broke the king's peace. The illness that prevented Dafydd from appearing *coram rege* is noted later (n. 50).

¹³ For the main sequence of events, *HW*, ii, 694–706; G. A. Williams, 'The succession to Gwynedd, 1238–47', *B*, 20 (1962–4), 408–11; R. R. Davies, *CCC*, 300–3.

¹⁴ J. C. Davies, 'A grant by Llywelyn ap Gruffydd', *NLWJ*, 3 (1943–4), 158–62, from an original charter, NLW, Bachymbyd, 984; *H*, no. 145. For Einion ap Maredudd, below, n. 33.

¹⁵ Wynn, *HGF*, 10. Llywelyn is said to have held his court at Maesmynan (cmt Dogfeiling).

retain the lands west of the Conwy and, to the east of the river, the three *cantrefi* of Rhos, Rhufoniog and Dyffryn Clwyd. The evidence of Llywelyn's charter, however, suggests that John Wynn's statement embodies a kernel of truth and that there is reason to believe that Llywelyn had established himself in part of Perfeddwlad. It is thus likely that it was in Dyffryn Clwyd, part of the land between the Conwy and the Clwyd, that Llywelyn ap Gruffudd secured his first territorial lordship. It is conceivable that Henry III, despite the formal arrangements made in 1241, might not have been altogether averse to seeing Llywelyn established in what would otherwise have been a territory held by Dafydd ap Llywelyn. There might be some advantage to the king in seeing a son of Gruffudd ap Llywelyn in possession of a land from which he might pose a threat to the position of Dafydd, the prince whose power the king was most anxious to contain at this time. The presence of Richard, bishop of Bangor, among the witnesses to Llywelyn's charter would itself suggest, as we shall see, that Llywelyn was acting independently of the prince of Gwynedd, and the king could conceivably have connived in an initiative taken, quite possibly, in the critical year 1241.[16] Yet, though he might be prepared to countenance Llywelyn's presence within Perfeddwlad, it is unlikely that took any active part in bringing this about. By whatever means, Llywelyn established himself in a portion of Gwynedd, and by so doing he took some recompense for the fact that Henry had failed to provide for Gruffudd that 'portion' which had been formally promised by the terms of the agreement of 1241. When Senana, who received financial support from the crown, went to the Tower of London to visit her husband she could tell him that their son had secured a small part of the territory which the king, despite his promise to Gruffudd, still denied him.[17] Languishing from his long imprisonment, Gruffudd might have found encouragement in the knowledge that Llywelyn had secured a base which could prove useful in a struggle to secure a fair portion of the patrimony, perhaps rather more than that, if only he could contrive his release from the king's custody.

The other early charter to which Llywelyn is known to have put his seal is undated. It survives in a Mortimer cartulary along with several charters which record the submissions of a number of men of Gwerthrynion to Ralph Mortimer and, though the texts are undated, these may with reasonable confidence be attributed to the summer of 1241.[18] They testify to how the

---

[16] *LW*, 9–10. Llywelyn's position in Dyffryn Clwyd is instructively considered in Stephenson, *GG,* 229–32. When Gwenllian de Lacy brought an action in the *curia regis* for four vills in the *cantref* in 1241 she impleaded Dafydd ap Llywelyn (*CRR*, xvi, no. 1596), a fact that may be relevant to the question of the extent and status of Llywelyn's lordship.

[17] Senana was apparently permitted to visit her husband (Paris, *ChronMaj*, iv, 295); payments in *Issues of the Exchequer*, i, 29; *CLibR*, ii, 81; *Cheshire Pipe Rolls*, 71, 77.

[18] Two texts of the charter, from 'Liber Niger de Wigmore' (BL, Harley 1240, ff. 57, 58), in J. B. Smith, 'Middle march', 88–9, 92; *H*, no. 144.

marcher lineage finally established its power in Gwerthrynion and Maelienydd, but the particular charter which concerns us is invaluable for the light it throws on the first initiatives of Llywelyn ap Gruffudd. It is virtually certain that this charter, too, belongs to the summer of 1241.[19] During the summer months Mortimer was involved in the transactions by which Senana was able to secure Henry's promise that her husband, Gruffudd ap Llywelyn, and her son Owain, would be released from Dafydd's prison. Married to Gruffudd's sister Gwladus, Mortimer may have played a key role in formulating that agreement. He may, too, have been influenced by the attacks made upon his marcher lordships in 1241 by forces acting for Dafydd ap Llywelyn, unless those attacks were themselves motivated by Mortimer's animosity towards Dafydd.[20] In conflict with Dafydd, and supportive of Senana's endeavours on behalf of Gruffudd, Mortimer might well have been prepared to provide support for Llywelyn as a means of undermining Dafydd's authority, and he may even have provided a base within his lordships for dissentients from Gwynedd prepared to ally themselves with the one son of Gruffudd ap Llywelyn at liberty to do so. But if he were prepared to tolerate, even to promote, Llywelyn ap Gruffudd's endeavour to establish himself in Gwynedd he would insist on one crucial undertaking on the young prince's part. His concern for the future security of his marcher lordships is reflected in the charter in Llywelyn's name which was included in the cartulary in which the family muniments were ultimately set down. Mortimer obtained from Llywelyn ap Gruffudd an assurance that the prince, for himself and his heirs in perpetuity, surrendered all claim upon Gwerthrynion and Maelienydd.[21] In the summer of 1241, after an intermittent endeavour extending over a century and a half, the two lordships came to the possession of the Wigmore lineage and Ralph Mortimer was determined that they should remain so. It is a matter of considerable interest that, in the course of the vigorous action in which he was involved in the period following the death of Llywelyn the Great, Mortimer felt it necessary, or prudent, to extract from the prince's young grandson a solemn pledge that he would never venture to

---

[19] Neither place nor date are given in Llywelyn's charter nor in any of the Gwerthrynion charters; a date in the summer of 1241 is virtually certain in the case of the Gwerthrynion charters, mainly on account of their close affinity with the Maelienydd transactions, 14 August 1241 (J. B. Smith, 'Middle march', 82–4, 88–93; *LW*, 54–8). Llywelyn's charter is witnessed, from Mortimer's side, by five men (John Lestrange, Thomas Corbet, Brian de Brompton, Henry de Mortimer and Ralph de Arace) who also witnessed the Gwerthrynion charters; a sixth (Walter Clifford) was among those who, like Mortimer, provided a pledge for Senana on 12 August (*LW*, 52–3).

[20] *CR, 1237–42*, 359–60.

[21] Llywelyn, releasing to Mortimer and his wife Gwladus and their heirs forever all claim to the two lordships, pledged that he would respect their possession against all men, adding 'saving faith with the king of England' in one text but omitting the phrase in the other (*B*, 24 (1970–2), 88–9, 92). His subsequent annexations of the lordships are noticed later.

assert any claim upon those territories. Mortimer, with a close affinity to the lineage of Aberffraw and with his own interests to safeguard, clearly endorsed the course of action which brought Henry III to support the cause of the bastard son of Llywelyn ap Iorwerth, and support for Llywelyn ap Gruffudd could follow from this. Yet he may, too, have recognized the need to take Llywelyn seriously as a potential contender for power in native Wales. Mortimer's support for Gruffudd had to be linked with an insistence that his son should keep well clear of the Mortimer inheritance. For his part, and probably to his advantage at this stage, Llywelyn came to an arrangement with a lineage with which he was closely linked in kinship but one with which, as has been intimated already, he was to be embroiled in strenuous conflict from the time when he first asserted his power in the march until the very day on which he lost his life.

A foothold in the patrimony of Gwynedd and an acknowledgement of his forceful character: these conclusions are certainly indicated in the two charters in Llywelyn's name which belong to the years of acute crisis after 1240. The same documents also reveal evidence of the composition of the group of men associated with Llywelyn at this time. Those who witnessed the transaction at Llannerch included Richard, bishop of Bangor. It may seem surprising to find a person of such stature named in a charter issued by the prince at this early stage in his political enterprise. Bishop Richard can, of course, be counted among those who had been pledged in support of Gruffudd ap Llywelyn, and he proved a strenuous advocate on his behalf in the crisis in Gwynedd after the death of Llywelyn ap Iorwerth.[22] The facts that Dyffryn Clwyd, though situated to the east of the Conwy, formed a deanery of the bishopric of Bangor and that the prince's charter was dated at Llannerch, where the bishop possessed an estate, may indicate that Bishop Richard's solicitude for Gruffudd was extended to his son and that the young prince may have owed much to the bishop's protection.[23] Yet his espousal of Llywelyn's cause, if that be the case, would hardly be consistent with the king's formal dispositions for Gwynedd in 1241. The bishop had indeed been supportive of the measures by which Dafydd ap Llywelyn had been brought to submission but, once Dafydd had been received into the king's fealty, the bishop was bound by his own fealty to endorse the provisions made for the prince under the terms of his new engagements. More specifically, Dafydd

---

[22] G. A. Williams, 'Succession to Gwynedd', 401–6, 411–13, includes texts and a discussion of a partiality to Gruffudd in Paris, *ChronMaj*, iv, 8, 47–8, 148–51, which probably reflects the bishop's connection with St Albans noticed below, n. 83.

[23] Dyffryn Clwyd is shown to be a deanery of the bishopric of Bangor (which also included Ceinmeirch) in the valuation of church property in 1254 (*The Valuation of Norwich*, ed. W. E. Lunt (Oxford, 1926), 194); for the bishop's estate at Llannerch (par Llanfair Dyffryn Clwyd), *RC*, 113–15.

was required to acknowledge that, if he were to incur excommunication and interdict, the sentence would be carried out by the mandate of the bishops of Bangor and St Asaph and he placed himself under the guidance of the bishops, his counsellors, for the fulfilment of his obligations to the king.[24] This implicitly placed upon the bishops the responsibility of supporting Dafydd if he were to continue to abide by the terms of his undertakings to the king. But it appears that Bishop Richard had difficulty in coming to terms with the changed situation; and the prince, too, may have been unable to set aside his resentment at the bishop's role during the crisis over the succession. For whatever reason, Bishop Richard appears not to have returned to Bangor for some years. The deanery of Dyffryn Clwyd, where Llywelyn ap Gruffudd exercised lordship, may have been a haven for the bishop in the only part of the bishopric that he was able to visit. His presence at Llannerch in 1243 may thus reflect the constraints still placed upon him by his support of Gruffudd ap Llywelyn. His conduct in these years is intriguing, no less so the declaration made upon Dafydd's death which, explicitly acknowledging that his patrimony should fall to the crown, inevitably prejudiced his relations with Llywelyn whose cause, like that of his father, he had probably supported hitherto.[25]

Other names reflect something of the support which Llywelyn had secured among lay persons of some consequence in the community of Gwynedd. Iorwerth ap Gwrgunan and Tudur ap Madog represent early adherents who were to remain at the prince's side on the long march to Bryn Derwin and beyond.[26] A distinction may be made between them in one respect. Iorwerth's ancestral lands, though not in Dyffryn Clwyd, appear to have been in Perfeddwlad; Tudur's lands, on the other hand, appear to have been in Gwynedd Uwch Conwy, and his presence may reflect Llywelyn's ability to draw to his ranks men who, previously supporters of his father, joined the young prince in his first territorial lordship, even though their proprietorial interests lay in the area securely under Dafydd ap Llywelyn's authority. This possible distinction apart, the two reflect early adherences rewarded, or perhaps secured, by territorial endowments made to them by the young prince.[27] Both Iorwerth ap Gwrgunan and Tudur ap Madog were associated with Llywelyn in 1243, but Tudur is also named in the earlier charter, along

---

[24] Dafydd acknowledged the ecclesiastical censure that he would incur if he were to default upon the terms of his submission in 1241 in a clause additional to those in 'Liber A' (*LW*, 9–10) noticed earlier. On 24 October he placed himself under the guidance of the two bishops for his strict fulfilment of his obligations (*LW*, 10–12).

[25] Below, n. 80.

[26] E.g. *LW*, 77–8, 185; *CPR, 1232–47*, 461; *CPR, 1247–58*, 470; *CChR*, ii, 291, 460; Stephenson, *GG*, 98–100, 114–15, 216, 221.

[27] For these grants, J. B. Smith, 'Land endowments of the period of Llywelyn ap Gruffudd', *B*, 34 (1987), 150–64.

with another exceedingly important name, that of Einion ap Caradog. According to John Wynn, Einion was a brother of Senana whom he identifies as a daughter of Caradog ap Thomas ap Rhodri ab Owain Gwynedd, and there is every possibility that his testimony in this respect is perfectly accurate.[28] Einion ap Caradog, drawn from a lineage of princely origin but now assimilated to the upper echelons of the freemen of Gwynedd, represents an important accession of strength and possibly – as a maternal uncle of the young prince – a key influence in his early political initiatives.[29] Llywelyn's capacity to draw men of this measure of prestige into his ranks at this early stage may have been somewhat limited. It is clear from the surviving records that Dafydd ap Llywelyn had the support of very influential members of the leading lineages of Gwynedd. Conspicuous among them was Ednyfed Fychan who served as *distain*, or seneschal, to Dafydd as he had served Llywelyn ap Iorwerth. He was joined, and possibly succeeded in that office, by his son Tudur ab Ednyfed, and Einion Fychan was another capable minister active in Dafydd ap Llywelyn's service.[30] Yet it seems clear that loyalties were divided among the influential families, and that a lineage might even be divided within itself. This may have been true of the lineage of Ednyfed Fychan, for whereas Tudur ab Ednyfed was undoubtedly linked with Dafydd, his brother Gruffudd ab Ednyfed may have been a confidant of Llywelyn ap Gruffudd. Though his name does not appear in either of the two charters of 1241–3 his appearance in a prominent position in the prince's entourage by 1247 suggests an early adherence to Llywelyn which could, in turn, have stemmed from a previous identification with Gruffudd ap Llywelyn.[31] Many years later, in Dafydd Benfras's elegy to

---

[28] *B*, 24 (1972–4), 89, 92. Wynn, *HGF*, 9, says that 'some of our Welsh pedigrees say she [Senana] was the daughter of the King of Man, but this is an untruth. There are other most ancient records to the contrary verifying as here is laid down'. Her lineage is noticed above, n. 1.

[29] For his presence in Llywelyn's councils, *LW*, 4, 23, 44, 85, 97–9, 109, 185; *Councils*, i, 489–90, 505; cf. Stephenson, *GG*, 209–10. Petitions from his descendants concerning their lands in Llŷn, Eifionydd and Arfon are in *RC*, 220; *CAP*, 339, 454.

[30] *LW*, 5–6, 10, 18; *CPR, 1232–4*, 461; *CR, 1237–42*, 357; *CRR*, xvi, nos. 1595–6.

[31] He is the first witness to Llywelyn's charters, 1247, to Basingwerk and Iorwerth ap Gwrgunan (*CChR*, ii, 291; J. B. Smith, 'Land endowments', 155–6, 161–3; *H*, nos. 148, 149). G. Roberts, *Aspects of Welsh History* (Cardiff, 1969), 184–5, quoting L. Dwnn, *Heraldic Visitations of Wales*, ed. S. R. Meyrick (Llandovery, 1846), ii, 107, n. 7, citing a genealogical work by Sion Tudur, notes a traditional account of Gruffudd's estrangement from Llywelyn ap Iorwerth on account of an insult to Joan. A breach of this nature could be consistent with subsequent loyalty to Gruffudd ap Llywelyn and then to Llywelyn. But Gruffudd ab Ednyfed was at one with his brothers Tudur and Goronwy in giving hostages to the king in December 1241 (*CPR, 1232–47*, 267–8, 276). It would be best to treat the account which appears to stem from the MS of Sion Tudur with caution. What is certain, and more relevant, is that Gruffudd was identified with Llywelyn by 1247 and remained so until 1256; he probably died soon afterwards. An elegy by Dafydd Benfras (*GDB*, 33) is noticed later.

Gruffudd ap Ednyfed, there are intimations of a particularly close and trusting relationship which, taken along with the evident warmth of the poet's estimation of Gruffudd ap Llywelyn, might well have had its origins in the camaraderie of those, including the poet himself, who joined with Llywelyn ap Gruffudd in the troubled years after 1240.[32]

Yet all was not brave comradeship in arms by any means. The charter which he gave at Llannerch in 1243 shows that Llywelyn had already found that he had to come to terms with substantial figures, proprietors in his lordship in Dyffryn Clwyd, who were not necessarily his avid supporters. The charter to Einion ap Maredudd did not convey new lands but, granting him his lands in Dyffryn Clwyd in recognition of his 'liberty' (*libertas*), and doing so on terms which exempted him from all dues except military service, Llywelyn confirmed him in his possession of what he already held. The charter may be an indication of the prince's need to establish a relationship with one who was now, not altogether willingly perhaps, his tenant in that *cantref*. Certainly, Llywelyn encountered difficulty in his relations with Einion's son in later years.[33] Among the witnesses there were two other men, Cynfrig Sais and Gruffudd Gryg, who appear more prominently in years to come as servants of the crown in Perfeddwlad than adherents of Llywelyn.[34] Even by 1243 Llywelyn was no audacious youth, no *iuvenis* committed to intrepid adventure in company with a hardy band of adherents. Rather, with the aid of a number of persons of substance, he was already confronting the problems inherent in the exercise of lordship in the aftermath of serious political disturbance and

---

[32] *GDB*, 33. Dafydd Benfras composed an *awdl* addressed to 'Llywelyn' (*GDB*, 26), attributed to Llywelyn ap Iorwerth, but certain features, particularly some prophetic touches, suggest that it might have been addressed to Llywelyn ap Gruffudd. It is likely that this is the case and that the poem reflects the poet's wish, at an early date, to identify himself with the prince whose triumphs he was later to extol.

[33] *NLWJ*, 3 (1943–4), 158. Einion may have been an adherent of Llywelyn (Stephenson, *GG*, 232) but another interpretation commends itself. The family's status in Dyffryn Clwyd is underlined in a charter that Dafydd ap Gruffudd granted to his son Madog in 1260 (J. C. Davies, 'A grant by David ap Gruffydd', *NLWJ*, 3 (1943–4), 29–32, from NLW, Bachymbyd, 217; *H*, no. 151), made in consideration of Madog's 'ancient liberty and dignity' (*libertas et dignitas antiquas*) and including a fourth part of the right of patronage to Llanynys and Gyffylliog churches by virtue of Madog's position as lay *abad*. This is again in effect a confirmation of existing rights, though new lands were added at Llannerch and at Bryncelyn in Cafflogion. The release of his son Madog ab Einion from Llywelyn's prison was ordained by the treaty of Aberconwy, 1277, and his subsequent treatment incurred the king's censure (*LW*, 119; *CWR*, 173). Llywelyn may in 1243 have been trying to establish a relationship with a substantial lineage which was not partial to his authority then or ever again. For the lineage, A. D. Barrell and R. R. Davies, 'Land, lineage, and revolt in north-east Wales, 1243–1441: a case study', *CMCS*, 29 (1995), 27–51.

[34] Of the witnesses, Cynfrig Sais was also named among those who testified to Llywelyn's quitclaim to Mortimer (*B*, 24 (1970–2), 89, 92; but he and Gruffudd Gryg are found in royal service and favour later (*CPR, 1247–58*, 64, 113; *CLibR*, ii, 311; iii, 20, 57, 105; *Cheshire Pipe Rolls*, 88; Stephenson, *GG*, 232).

social division. The presence of these men underlines the possibility that at this period Llywelyn was not in overt resistance to the king.³⁵ The manner by which Llywelyn first established his authority is not easy to discern. Eventually, of course, the poets Dafydd Benfras and Llygad Gŵr would celebrate the triumph of Llywelyn ap Gruffudd, a prince who was a worthy heir to the powerful and royal qualities of Gruffudd ap Llywelyn, but his very earliest initiatives may have required careful political calculation. The testimony of these early years, slight though it may be, certainly suggests that there were some among his own family and the *nobiles* of Gwynedd who had already recognized the virtues with which the young prince was endowed, and had realized that he was one to whom the interests of the captive in the Tower of London could confidently be entrusted.

It is reasonable to ask whether Gruffudd ap Llywelyn's death in 1244 was the result of a precipitate action on his part, or whether it was the sad outcome of a long considered plan which went wrong. Gruffudd and those compatriots who shared his incarceration make an occasional fleeting appearance in records when arrangements were made for the simple needs of men in custody: fuel to heat their cells; winter clothes supplied by a king who, when making provision for his son, might remember the men in the Tower; and bed-clothes.³⁶ There are several references to bed-clothes, and we might well wonder if their delivery was entirely dictated by the prisoners' concern for warmth and cleanliness, or whether they were assiduously stock-piling the means of escape. They may have made more than one effort to get away, for less than a month before Gruffudd fell to his death the custodians of the Welsh prisoners were replaced because they had proved themselves worthless.³⁷ The crucial bid for freedom was made on St David's Day, not a day of unmixed joy in the experience of the Welsh nation. A make-shift rope was cast from an upper window, but the sheets and tapestries proved unequal to Gruffudd's weighty frame, and at dawn his broken body was found lying at the foot of the Tower.³⁸ Matthew Paris diligently recorded the event, once more conveying his singular sympathy with one to whom he consistently referred as the first-born (*primogenitus*) of Llywelyn ap Iorwerth. Dafydd Benfras, in an elegy with an intensity which may be a mark of close adherence,

---

³⁵ Stephenson, *GG*, 232.
³⁶ *CLibR*, ii, 70, 76, 93, 146–8, 160–1, 171, 189, 199; other prisoners, including Owain ap Gruffudd, are named in *CPR, 1232–47*, 432.
³⁷ *CR, 1242–47*, 159.
³⁸ *HW*, ii, 700–1, describes the tragedy in characteristic style.

saw the happening in London as a killing.[39] On the other hand a Welsh annalist could record that it was by ill-fate (*infortunio accidente*) that Gruffudd fell to his death and, not dwelling upon it, he proceeded at once to recount its consequences.[40] For now, Dafydd ap Llywelyn, moved by great anger, lost no time in summoning his men and the princes of the whole of Wales to a new encounter with the king of England.

The annalist's account that Dafydd won general support among the princes, with the exception of Gruffudd ap Gwenwynwyn and Gruffudd ap Madog, is reasonably well confirmed by documentary testimony.[41] It proved impossible to wean Gruffudd ap Gwenwynwyn from the only political association that he had known so far. Gruffudd ap Madog may have been more discomforted, for during the summer the king found it advisable to promise him that he would not introduce any new law in his land and that he would respect the indigenous rights and laws of Powys Fadog.[42] In a further highly significant reassurance, Henry told Gruffudd that he had no intention of denying him his right to the patrimony of Powys Fadog in its entirety, thereby touching upon a matter quite fundamental to an understanding of Gruffudd's political stance throughout the period between the death of Llywelyn ap Iorwerth and the triumphant assertion of power over native Wales by Llywelyn ap Gruffudd. These were important safeguards for Gruffudd but, no less essential for the retention of his loyalty, Henry provided both an annual subvention and further financial aid to enable him to withstand the offensive mounted by the alliance now gathered about Dafydd ap Llywelyn.[43] Gruffudd ap Gwenwynwyn secured comparable support. Among the princes of Deheubarth the response to Dafydd's call to arms was, if unequal, decidedly more vigorous, partly a reaction to a royal policy which had brought them within the orbit of a stricter administration based on a county organization.[44] Within weeks of the death of Gruffudd ap Llywelyn the king was well aware that he faced a new challenge over the greater part of Wales, but once more he knew that the heart of the problem lay in Gwynedd.

It would be easy, with the striking events in Wales as a whole, to overlook the extent of the change in Gwynedd during the course of 1244. While Gruffudd ap Llywelyn lived Henry III had wielded a corrective rod by which Dafydd might be chastized if need arose: the young prince had put his seal to

---

[39] Paris, *ChronMaj*, iv, 295–6; Paris, *HistAng*, ii, 482–3, with drawing of Gruffudd's fall in MS; *GDB*, 29. 33, 65, the poet using the words *lladd* (killing) and *llofrudd-dab* (murder).

[40] *AC(B)*, 84–5; *CW*, 39; *BT, Pen20*, 200; *Pen20Tr*, 106; *RBH*, 238–9. *AC(C)*, 84 (*sive dolo sive aliter ignoratur*), is less certain.

[41] *HW*, ii, 701–5.

[42] *CPR, 1232–47*, 430.

[43] Ibid.; J. B. Smith, 'Dynastic succession in medieval Wales', *B*, 33 (1986), 227–8. Gruffudd received an annual fee of £20 and other support (e.g. *Cheshire Pipe Rolls*, 77).

[44] Below, n. 101.

a document by which he solemnly recognized Gruffudd's hereditary right to a portion of Gwynedd. The king knew perfectly well that it would be extremely difficult to enforce a partition of the patrimony between the two princes, but if he wished to create division in Gwynedd he would achieve his objective much more readily by releasing Gruffudd, thus reanimating those old animosities and promoting the divisive influences from which the crown derived such considerable advantage in its dealings with the Welsh seigniories. Henry had, in fact, shown no inclination to create new conflict while Gruffudd lived, but the possibility of his envisaging an alternative course is rather more than a supposition. This consideration undoubtedly arose at court as soon as knowledge of Dafydd's rebellion was received. Gruffudd himself was dead, but his first-born son was still in custody. Henry soon sent Owain ap Gruffudd to Chester where he would remain in the keeping of John Lestrange, justice of Chester, until he might be used to further the king's purposes whenever circumstances were opportune.[45] Owain may not yet have achieved complete freedom, but he remained at hand with a view, in all probability, to his being sent into Gwynedd to draw support away from Dafydd ap Llywelyn at an appropriate time. Owain was given complete freedom in November. He was then sent to Westminster to declare his loyalty to the king, swearing fealty for two *cantrefi* which the king bestowed upon him, along with other lands due to him by hereditary right.[46] Precisely why the decision to release him was taken at this time is unclear, nor is there anything to suggest that the king provided him with the means to intervene in Gwynedd. It seems that Owain lingered under the king's protection for another fifteen months and that he did not go to Gwynedd until he heard of the death of Dafydd ap Llywelyn in February 1246. Matthew Paris says that, when he heard of his uncle's death, Owain fled like a hare to Wales.[47] By then it was too late to provide any real service to the crown, and it was rather late for him to seize any significant advantage for himself. The months Owain ap Gruffudd had spent at Chester proved to be of inestimable value in the political progression of Llywelyn ap Gruffudd.

The first reference to Llywelyn ap Gruffudd in chancery records occurs in a list of the lords of Wales who opposed the king in January 1245.[48] In the light of his career as a whole he might hardly be expected to be found anywhere except in the ranks of those who stood in armed resistance to the king of

---

[45] *CPR, 1232–47*, 432; *CLibR*, ii, 252 (15–16 July).

[46] *LW*, 15–16; *CPR, 1232–47*, 446, 462 (16–17 November); accommodation provided at Shotwick, co. Chester, with maintenance payments (*CPR, 1232–47*, 465; *CLibR*, ii, 15).

[47] Paris, *ChronMaj*, iv, 518. *AnnCestr*, 66, remarks that Owain made his way to Gwynedd during the week in which Dafydd died 'after having lived in the king's peace in Chester for a long time'.

[48] *CR, 1242–47*, 347–8; *Foedera*, I, i, 258.

England. But if the interpretation offered so far is correct, and Llywelyn had established himself in part of Perfeddwlad on his own initiative and possibly, as John Wynn states, contrary to the wishes of Dafydd and Henry alike, it seems clear that by the beginning of 1245 Llywelyn had made a crucially important decision. He had acknowledged that it was now incumbent upon him to throw in his lot with Dafydd, and, taking account of the animosities of recent years, this was a significant reappraisal of his position. Whether Llywelyn had been viewed by Henry as a means of withstanding Dafydd's new assertion of power we cannot tell. It is not inconceivable that Henry might have contemplated the possibility of deploying Llywelyn, as well as Owain, to Dafydd's discomfiture, but there is no knowledge of this and the king might have known from an early date that Llywelyn was unlikely to respond to overtures of that nature. Llywelyn's decision to join Dafydd may not, however, have been altogether the result of objective assessment. Royal forces advanced from Chester through Tegeingl to reach the castle of Degannwy in the *cantref* of Rhos. Control of the interior of Rhos and of Rhufoniog and Dyffryn Clwyd might have been much more difficult to achieve, but, even without securing the land for himself, Henry could well have made Llywelyn's position exceedingly difficult. Military pressure on Llywelyn, and the power of a persuasion exercised upon the prince's tenants by royal officers, might have taken their toll. Two of those who were evidently associated with him in 1243, Cynfrig Sais and Gruffudd Gryg, were in the king's service two years later, and Llywelyn may well have been unable to maintain his hold upon the allegiance of important figures among his own tenants. It is possible that Llywelyn had no choice but to join forces with Dafydd ap Llywelyn.[49] But whatever the impulses or compulsions which brought him to Dafydd's side, his presence signified that one of the sons of Gruffudd ap Llywelyn was prepared to forswear the dissensions of earlier years. Though he may have been forced to forgo his possessions in Perfeddwlad, he was now able to secure a foothold in Snowdonia that he would never yield.

Among those whom Dafydd ap Llywelyn, prince of Gwynedd, could count among his adherents, Llywelyn was the nearest to him in kinship, a proximity of immense significance should any misfortune befall Dafydd. This was, indeed, to be the case, though whether Dafydd's death in 1246 was the result of sudden or prolonged illness we cannot tell. We know that he had already suffered an illness which had caused him to lose his hair and the fingernails of hands and feet; he had told the king of his malady in explaining why he had been unable to come to Westminster to appear in the action *coram rege*

---

[49] For Cynfrig Sais and Gruffudd Gryg, above, n. 34.

between Gruffudd and himself.[50] There is no firm knowledge that Dafydd's capabilities were seriously impaired by an illness which left him with concurrent alopecia and onycholysis, and no reason to question whether he was capable of vigorous activity in the two years preceding his death. The historical record gives us no reason to doubt that he provided the main inspiration behind the sustained resistance of 1244–6. There is thus no indication that ill-health on Dafydd's part was a factor which had entered into Llywelyn's calculations in determining his political allegiance by 1245. Even so, a physical disability that Dafydd may have endured would have been an exceedingly important consideration in the minds of the prince's near kinsmen. Apart from any question of his physical state, Dafydd had no heir as yet, and, with no other close kinsman at his side, Llywelyn had every incentive to stand by. Moreover, renewed conflict with the king of England made identification with Dafydd ap Llywelyn a more palatable proposition. The consequences of Llywelyn's decision were profound. His adherence lent cohesion to a community which had been sorely divided and, in a situation fraught with difficulties, Llywelyn's readiness to renounce the divisive contentions of the past was no small advantage to Dafydd ap Llywelyn. By the end of 1245 Henry, as we shall see, would have to acknowledge that his military efforts were not likely to lead to any conclusive result; he concluded a truce, and the embassy that he received reflected the new unity in Gwynedd. Ednyfed Fychan, an elderly figure now, undertook one of his very last missions on behalf of the princes of the lineage of Gwynedd. He represented that part of the community which had kept faith with Llywelyn the Great's wishes for the future, and he had sustained the heir through the subsequent years of turmoil. But he was joined by Tudur ap Madog, an early and close adherent of Llywelyn ap Gruffudd, and one who may well have been among those once pledged to Gruffudd ap Llywelyn.[51] Those divisions belonged to the past, dispelled by Llywelyn ap Gruffudd's decision to identify himself with the prince who, rightly or wrongly, was heir to the patrimony of Gwynedd.

During the months in which he stood by the prince of Gwynedd, Llywelyn was constrained to tolerate an interpretation of recent history in which he would hardly have taken any great pleasure. As rebellion spread through a large part of Wales Dafydd seized the opportunity to break free from the

---

[50] Einion Fychan stated in 1242–3 that Dafydd was unable to appear on account of serious illness; at a further hearing in 1244 Dafydd stated that his illness had caused him to lose his hair and the fingernails of hands and feet (*CRR*, xvii nos. 97, 237). I am grateful to Dr John Hughes, Dr Emyr Wyn Jones, Dr W. J. Cynfab Roberts and Dr Iestyn Morgan Watkin for their guidance on the possible medical significance of this reference. Alopecia and onycholysis can occur together and may point to a tension-related illness liable to recur.

[51] *CPR, 1232–47*, 461.

shackles in which the king had placed him in 1241 with a bold appeal to Innocent IV.[52] Most of the story belongs to Matthew Paris, and the kernel of his account is that Dafydd sought to hold his dominion as a papal fief.[53] The essential substance is confirmed, however, in a letter of the papal court which conveys that Dafydd had argued that his parents had given him as an *alumnus,* a ward, to the church of Rome. It was on this account that he sought an absolution from the pledges that had been exacted from him under duress following his submission to the king. Dafydd, in short, was seeking the abrogation of the treaty of Gwerneigron. The prince's council may have shared the joy of an exultant moment when the papal letter raised a prospect that the king of England would be summoned to Caerwys and examined on the prince's behalf by the abbots of Aberconwy and Cymer.[54] Sober consideration of the circumstances in which his initial response was made would have suggested that Innocent was anxious to bring pressure to bear upon Henry to fulfil his financial obligations. For his part, Henry never intended to appear before the abbots, nor would he be represented; rather he put his emissaries to work at Rome and, when the pope secured the assurances he sought, Dafydd was told that he had erred in his appeal and that the papal court was no longer disposed to support his cause.[55] Henry's envoys had persuaded the pope that Dafydd, whose predecessors had for a very long time been vassals of the king of England, had falsely conveyed that his father had given him as an *alumnus* to the Roman church. Llywelyn ap Iorwerth had certainly made approaches to the Roman court and ensured first that Dafydd's designation as his heir was confirmed, and then that he was received as the pope's *alumnus* and taken into his protection. But Dafydd's interpretation of the implications of his position as a papal ward for his status in relation to the king of England reflects both his father's forethought and the audacious spirit that now prevailed at the prince's court.[56] Dafydd had sought nothing less than a position whereby he might hold his principality as a vassal of the pope, the frail thread which had once joined Gwynedd and Rome now woven into a bond of lordship. The authors of the appeal may have known that relationships of this kind had been forged elsewhere in Europe, and they may have had particular knowledge of the fact that the king of Man had once

---

[52] M. Richter, 'David ap Llywelyn, the first prince of Wales', *WHR*, 5 (1970–1), 208–18, provides a full discussion and documentation; reference is made here only to key texts.

[53] Paris, *ChronMaj*, iv, 323; Paris, *HistAng*, ii, 482–3.

[54] *Councils*, i, 470–1 (26 July 1244).

[55] Ibid., 471–2; *Foedera*, I, i, 255 (8 April 1245).

[56] For Llywelyn ap Iorwerth's overtures to the papal court, J. B. Smith, 'Dynastic succession', 218–19; in 1226 Honorius referred to the fealty sworn by the magnates of Wales to Dafydd: 'quem in alumnum quasi ecclesie Romane a parentibus nobis oblatum sub specialis apostolice sedis protectio ne suscepimus' (above, pp. 25–6). *Alumnus* may be rendered as 'foster-son' or 'ward', but 'ward' is probably appropriate in the present context.

placed his kingdom under papal protection.[57] Within a year of the initial overtures to Rome, the pope concurred with the view, expressed by Matthew Paris, that every Christian knew perfectly well that the prince of Wales was no more than a minor vassal of the king of England.[58]

It was during the course of the transactions with Rome, early in 1245, excommunicated by the archbishop of Canterbury and his dominion under interdict, that Dafydd used the style 'prince of Wales' in a letter to royal officers.[59] This is the only certain instance in which the form is known to have been used in records of this period, but it is unlikely to have been written in error and it is hardly an accident that it was used at this time. Gradually Henry came to realize the extent of the challenge with which he was faced in Wales, and it is in the text of a document which reflects the king's belated recognition of his difficulties that Llywelyn ap Gruffudd is named for the first time in a chancery record.[60] Hitherto the king had been unable to do more than support the two princes of Powys who remained faithful to him, and rely on the services of John Lestrange, who carried responsibility for the king's interests in north Wales by virtue of his office as justice of Chester.[61] No purposeful offensive had yet materialized, but preparations were made for a campaign in the summer of 1245. Tenants-in-chief in England were alerted, though Henry admitted to his justice in Ireland that they were less supportive than he would wish, and he clearly hoped for substantial assistance from the justice and the lords of Ireland.[62] The Welsh chronicler was convinced that the might of England and Ireland was gathered to subjugate Wales, but Henry's main effort was concentrated on Gwynedd, for there lay the strength of Wales and the 'conquest' to which he aspired.[63] His firmly declared objectives were commendable, but the delay in launching his offensive cost him dearly. John Lestrange's appeal for aid became more vociferous, remonstrating with the king that £10,000 would no longer be enough to accomplish what might earlier have been done for £1,000.[64] Even so, moving ahead of the main forces summoned to Chester, Lestrange secured Tegeingl and Henry was then able to advance through Rhos to Degannwy while forces from Ireland took

---

[57] Richter, 'David ap Llywelyn', 212, notes that Cadwgan, bishop of Bangor, was present when Reginald, king of Man, wrote to the pope; Godred, 'son of the king of Man', was in Wales in 1241 (above, n. 5).

[58] Paris, *ChronMaj*, iv, 324 (*vassalulum*).

[59] *CAC*, 49–50, probably January 1245. Henry called for ecclesiastical censure, 29 November 1244 (*CR, 1242–47*, 346).

[60] Above, n. 48.

[61] E.g. *CPR, 1232–47*, 427, 430–2; *CAC*, 10, 21–2.

[62] *CR, 1242–47*, 348–9.

[63] *BT, Pen20*, 201; *Pen20Tr*, 107; *RBH*, 238–9. Henry's call upon Ireland for aid 'to conquer the Welsh' is noticed in e.g. *Annals of Connacht (A.D. 1224–1544)*, ed. A. Martin Freeman (Dublin, 1944), 84–5.

[64] *CAC*, 21–2.

Anglesey.⁶⁵ His strategy was sound, and Edward could do no better when he came to Gwynedd in 1277, except that he made sure that his soldiers in Anglesey, rather than making destruction, would reap the harvest for themselves.⁶⁶ The king's forces at Degannwy certainly endured deprivation and the deployment there of 3,000 voracious Irish soldiers transferred from Anglesey exacerbated the difficulties encountered in the encampments above the Conwy estuary.⁶⁷ Efforts to secure adequate supplies were of no avail, and by early October Henry was prepared to arrange a truce with Dafydd ap Llywelyn. He made the first of the two difficult decisions which were to confront him at Degannwy and withdrew.⁶⁸

Historical judgement on the prince who failed to maintain the supremacy of Llywelyn ap Iorwerth has been unduly harsh. Heir to an exceedingly difficult inheritance, he had succumbed to overwhelming power in 1241; yet, five years later, he could be seen to have redeemed himself from his humiliating submission. The elegy composed by Dafydd Benfras upon Dafydd's death in 1246 may be more meaningful than it might appear. Just two years earlier the poet had commemorated Gruffudd ap Llywelyn in a poem vibrant with feeling, but his elegy to Dafydd was no less impassioned nor did he flinch from naming Dafydd as the rightful ruler of Gwynedd. The poet extols a prince who had proved a steadfast defender of his land, yielding nothing of Gwynedd to the crown of London. Entirely worthy of the lineage of kings to which he belonged, he had been one in whom his people rejoiced.

> Y llaw a gedwis erllynedd – adwy
> Yn Aberconwy cyn ei gorwedd.
> Ŵyr breenin Lloegr, llu teÿrnedd,
> Mab brenin Cymru, cymraisg fonedd
> Gŵr oedd a hanoedd, gorfoledd – gwerin,
> O iawn deÿrnllin y brenhinedd.⁶⁹

Far more than a poet's respectful observance of the elegiac proprieties, Dafydd Benfras's commemoration provides a vivid portrayal of the new resolve in the community of Gwynedd. The prince's nephew, Llywelyn ap

---

⁶⁵ *HW*, ii, 703–4.
⁶⁶ Below, pp. 427–30.
⁶⁷ *HW*, ii, 703–4, quoting Paris, *ChronMaj*, iv, 481–4.
⁶⁸ *CPR, 1232–47*, 461; *AnnCestr*, 64. Henry's withdrawal in 1257 is noticed later.
⁶⁹ *GDB*, 30. 75–80, trans Ann Parry Owen: 'The hand which last year held the breach / At Aberconwy until put to rest. / Grandson of the king of England, from a host of kings, / Son of the king of Wales, of steadfast lineage, / He was a man who sprang, great joy of the people, / From the true royal lineage of kings.' For his elegy to Gruffudd, *GDB*, 29; Dafydd is commemorated as 'the shield of Wales' in *AC(B)*, 85; *CW*, 39; *BT, Pen20*, 201; *Pen20Tr*, 107.

Gruffudd, was able to share in this as an active participant whose very presence was itself a cohering and invigorating influence.

Dafydd's death, at Aber on 25 February 1246, came within only a few months of Henry's retreat from Degannwy.[70] The alliance which he had forged among the princes of Wales soon fell apart, a tribute, perhaps, to his own ability to maintain a unity of purpose among men unequally committed to resistance. There had been signs of fissure even before he died. When he took charge of the king's lands in south-west Wales upon his return from Gascony, Nicholas de Molis was able to draw upon the resourcefulness he had had need to show in his dealings with the likes of Gaston de Béarn, but there was a fund of experience in the area itself. Those who had joined Nicholas FitzMartin to lead forces from the lordship of Pembroke to Ceredigion, at an earlier stage in the conflict, had had reason to believe that Maredudd ab Owain might be induced to withdraw from the princes' alliance if he could be supported in his dispute with Maelgwn Fychan. They recommended that Maredudd be received into the king's peace, for experience had shown that it was not easy to deal with the Welsh 'except through one of their own nation'.[71] A few days before Dafydd ap Llywelyn died, Molis sent detailed recommendations to Henry which, if implemented, would be enough to bring Maredudd back into the king's alliance. Molis scored a tangible success in Ystrad Tywi, where Rhys Mechyll and Maredudd ap Rhys Gryg proved responsive to his overtures.[72] Fortified by the support of these powerful lords of Deheubarth, and accompanied by Gruffudd ap Gwenwynwyn, Molis led 'the army of Dyfed' from Carmarthen through Ystrad Tywi and Ceredigion, forcing Maelgwn Fychan to flee to Gwynedd for protection.[73] Entering Meirionnydd and accepting the timely submission of Llywelyn ap Maredudd, Molis progressed without meeting any appreciable resistance right to Degannwy.[74] His advance demonstrated the complete

---

[70] *AnnCestr*, 64. Cause of death is unknown, and it is impossible to say whether it was connected with the illness he is known to have endured in 1242–3 (above, n. 50).

[71] *CAC*, 48; *RL*, i, 426–7: 'nisi sit per aliquem de lingua eorum propria'.

[72] *CPR, 1232–47*, 465, 470, 474, 479. Molis's negotiations with Maredudd ap Rhys Gryg are noteworthy in view of his similar initiative in 1257.

[73] *AC*, 86; *CW*, 39; *BT, Pen20*, 202; *Pen20Tr*, 107; *RBH*, 240–1; *CPR, 1232–47*, 485–8, 493. For the composition of the army, *LW*, 14, the document there attributed to 1241; the presence of the men named (including Maredudd ap Rhys Gryg, Maredudd ab Owain, Gilbert de Valle and Guy de Brian) and the submission of Llywelyn ap Maredudd, suggest that the document belongs to the time of the advance of the 'army of Dyfed', August–September 1246.

[74] *LW*, 14. Known as Llywelyn Fawr, he and his brother, Llywelyn ap Maredudd (Llywelyn Fychan), had paid £80 as a relief for Meirionnydd in 1241 (*RotFin*, i, 371). They supported Dafydd in 1245 (*CR, 1242–47*, 347–8; *Foedera*, I, i, 258). Llywelyn Fychan may have been dead by 1246; Llywelyn Fawr was succeeded by Maredudd ap Llywelyn (d. 1255), and then Llywelyn ap Maredudd, noticed below, pp. 91, 155–6, 216, 443.

collapse of the alliance which had formed around Dafydd ap Llywelyn, and opposition was now confined to Snowdonia.

By the time Nicholas de Molis had completed his advance Owain ap Gruffudd had finally left his secure haven at Chester for Gwynedd. With what measure of good grace he was received by his younger brother we cannot tell. It was a time of some anxiety. The Welsh annalist, writing at Strata Florida and faithfully recording the unhappy turn of events after the death of Dafydd, found solace in the fact that Gwynedd Uwch Conwy became the heartland of fierce resistance and a sanctuary for the disinherited. Maelgwn Fychan, forced to concede his territory to aliens, went to Owain and Llywelyn, sons of Gruffudd ap Llywelyn.[75] Hywel ap Maredudd, too, driven into exile from his lands in Glamorgan, found refuge in Gwynedd.[76] There, in the restricted confines of the land that was left to them, submitting themselves to the will of God, like the Maccabees of old, the young princes stood their ground in the mountains and wilderness. The invocation of those who, among the warriors of the Old Testament, are the prime exemplars of resistance to foreign oppression reflects both a recurring theme in Welsh historical writing and a clear realization of the stern challenges confronting the sons of Gruffudd ap Llywelyn.[77] They had problems among themselves, and we have no indication of what exactly lay behind the chronicler's brief notice that, on the advice of leading men of Gwynedd, the princes divided the territory between them into two halves.[78] The division may not, perhaps, have been accomplished at once, so critical was their situation. Beleaguered in Gwynedd Uwch Conwy, the previous year's harvest largely lost, their people faced a hardship made worse by the trade embargo imposed by the crown.[79] The princes faced a king who entirely denied their right to rule.

This was the import of a declaration which Richard, bishop of Bangor, issued at Windsor on 20 April 1246.[80] In a sternly worded statement, the bishop solemnly swore that, while he continued to hold the bishopric, he would maintain his fidelity to the king fully and unreservedly. He specifically undertook to do all in his power to bring the enemies of the king to his fealty and service. Richard acknowledged that Dafydd ap Llywelyn of his free will

---

[75] There is a close correspondence at this point between the texts of *AC(B)*, 85–6 and *CW*, 39–40; they provide a fuller and more spirited record than *BT, Pen20*, 201–2; *Pen20Tr*, 107; *RBH*, 238–41.

[76] Below, n. 105.

[77] J. B. Smith, *SHMW*, 6–10.

[78] *AC(B)*, 85–6; *CW*, 39; *BT, Pen20*, 201–2; *Pen20Tr*, 107; *RBH*, 240–1; for the partition, below, n. 113–20

[79] Paris, *ChronMaj*, iv, 647.

[80] *LW*, 21–2.

had conceded that, if he should die without an heir of his body, his entire patrimony should fall to the king. Dafydd had agreed, too, that if he ever were to rise against the king's peace his lands would suffer the same fate. The message was clear: on either count Gwynedd should legally be forfeited to the crown. The bishop had need to say so before he could hope to be allowed to return to his bishopric. He had spent the period of Dafydd's rule in exile and, on the day he made his declaration of the legal position of Gwynedd, he was granted a safe-conduct to return there.[81] Yet the statement he was induced to make at Windsor seriously jeopardized his chances of a return, for it effectively denied the sons of Gruffudd the right to rule their lands. Richard, in effect, renounced any allegiance he might have to the sons of the prince whose cause he had espoused with such conviction and at such cost to himself. The king would evidently not countenance any resort to the provision he had made in 1241, in his agreement with Senana, that there should be a judgement of his court concerning the portion of Gwynedd due to Gruffudd *and his heirs*.[82] He would not admit the sons to any such portion; that, at least, was the position that Henry wished to take for the present. There are a number of uncertainties in the evidence surrounding Bishop Richard but, whatever his inclinations may have been, he was constrained in the spring of 1246 to put the utmost pressure on the resistant princes.

The bishop may have found it difficult to exercise any direct influence in Gwynedd, for it was some years before he was able to establish a normal relationship with the princes and secure control over his diocese, finding sanctuary at the abbey of St Albans from the calamities which had befallen him.[83] The king was not, however, without the means of prevailing upon the princes, even though he did not resort to renewed conflict. During 1246 one Maredudd ap Richard appears as a claimant to lordship in Llŷn, the import of his bid being that he was, as a descendant of Cadwaladr ap Gruffudd ap Cynan, a member of the dynasty of Gwynedd.[84] An ally of Dafydd ap Llywelyn in 1245, Maredudd had subsequently submitted to the king and Henry, acknowledging his hereditary right, granted him lands in Llŷn by the

---

[81] *CPR, 1232–47*, 478.

[82] *LW*, 52–3.

[83] *HW*, ii, 744, based on Paris, *ChronMaj*, iv, 647; v, 288, 432, 608, which indicates the bishop's presence and may confirm that he made his home at St Albans for the next ten years 'with only occasional visits to Wales'. Francis Godwin (d. 1633) wrote that the bishop came to the abbey in 1248 along with his chaplain so that they might 'there breathe and rest themselves from those calamities wherewith they had been long affected'. Richard, along with Senana, was with Dafydd ap Gruffudd in 1252 (*RC*, 252). His association with Llywelyn from 1258 is considered later.

[84] For his lineage, Stephenson, *GG*, 148–51.

law and custom of Wales.⁸⁵ Maredudd represented a potentially divisive influence which Henry was eager to turn to his advantage, and Owain and Llywelyn recognized the threat to their position.⁸⁶ They had to come to terms, too, with the concern of those whose proprietorial interests would be endangered by any further prolongation of the war. Some of the most prominent, such as Tudur ab Ednyfed and Einion Fychan, had been captured during the conflict, and the conditions of their release required that they should not countenance the king's enemies. There were others, however, who had remained free, and whose territorial interests east and west of the Conwy made it imperative that the prince who exercised lordship over them in Snowdonia should do so in the king's fealty.⁸⁷ Owain and Llywelyn could not disregard the needs of powerful members of a community wherein deep divisions had only recently been repaired, and it is likely that those who had counselled the princes to share the rule of Gwynedd now advised them to make their peace with the king. Their need to divide the patrimony, if they had not already done so, and then to consolidate their lordship in their respective parts of it, underlined the brothers' need to come to terms with Henry. The heroic stand in the mountains and the wilderness was not enough. Henry was prepared to receive the prince's envoys in the summer of 1246; in the spring of the next year John de Grey, justice of Chester, was able to make a truce and, in accordance with the arrangements made on their behalf, Owain and Llywelyn came to meet the king at Woodstock. A treaty was sealed on 30 April 1247.⁸⁸

It might be reasonable to conclude that the treaty of Woodstock, and the situation in which it was agreed, marked the apogee of royal achievement in thirteenth-century Wales, short of the final conquest by Edward I.⁸⁹ The treaty impinged on the political future of Wales as a whole, but it specifically related to Gwynedd and in two particular respects: first, the territory itself, and, second, the status of its rulers. At Woodstock, formally pardoned for waging war upon the king and received into his grace, Owain ap Gruffudd and Llywelyn ap Gruffudd did homage. Each of them did so for an unnamed lordship consisting of what was left of North Wales after the king had

---

⁸⁵ Along with Ednyfed Fychan, Tudur ap Madog and Gruffudd ab Owain, Maredudd went to the king on Dafydd's behalf in October 1245 (*CPR, 1232–47*, 461). He was in the king's service by January 1247 when he was granted 'the land of Llŷn' (ibid., 480, 496, there wrongly described as 'Maredudd ap Rhys').

⁸⁶ *CAC*, 32–3; *RL*, ii, 64–6.

⁸⁷ *LW*, 30–1, 49–52; *CPR, 1232–47*, 496; submissions in 1241 are indicated in the list of hostages (*CPR, 1232–47*, 267–8).

⁸⁸ *CPR, 1232–47*, 480, 485, 498; *LW*, 7–8.

⁸⁹ The provisions of the treaty are examined in C. W. Lewis, 'The treaty of Woodstock, 1247: its background and significance', *WHR*, 2 (1964–5), 37–65.

annexed the portion he reserved for himself.⁹⁰ Perfeddwlad, the Four Cantreds, was surrendered in its entirety and for all time. Despite the fact that he had been forced to retreat from Gwynedd in 1245 with nothing to show for his efforts, Henry could now refer to the land between the Dee and the Conwy as 'the king's new conquest in Wales'.⁹¹ The castles of Diserth and Degannwy, two sites where building work continued, stood as symbols of his triumph and instruments for its maintenance. Meirionnydd was denied the princes by virtue of the statement, recalling those of 1240 and 1241, that the homage of the lords of Wales belonged to the king and to none other than him.⁹² Llywelyn ap Maredudd would rule it as a tenant-in-chief of the king. In the 'king's new conquest in Wales' royal government would be exercised directly over the community as an extension of the sphere of the justice of Chester. The territorial authority of the princes was severely curtailed. They were confined to Gwynedd Uwch Conwy, excluding Meirionnydd, a land coextensive with the territory to which Llywelyn ap Iorwerth had been confined upon his humiliation in 1211.

Even so, a portion of the patrimony remained in the possession of the lineage, and it might have been otherwise. The bishop of Bangor had recognized that, under the terms of Dafydd's treaty with the king, either the prince's death without heir or his rebellion against the crown would have been enough to spell the end of princely rule in Gwynedd.⁹³ Enforcing the king's right was a different matter, however, and the phraseology of the treaty of Woodstock, granting the princes the 'remainder of North Wales', after withholding his annexations, could not conceal the fact that the king had not secured possession of the land. The brothers had not yielded unconditionally. After his experience in 1245 Henry would have had no wish to contend for possession of Snowdonia by armed strength, and there would be little point in invoking the principle of escheat if he were not in a position to establish his right by a physical presence. Yet, if the annexation of Gwynedd was impossible, Henry could take encouragement from one consideration which found no explicit mention in the treaty but which mattered greatly for the future. By conceding the remainder of Gwynedd to the brothers, Henry placed his imprimatur on their decision to divide an already truncated land into two parts. The arrangement suited the king's purposes very well. The prognosis was still more encouraging, for Gruffudd ap Llywelyn had left not

---

⁹⁰ *LW*, 7–8. They were required to concede the four *cantrefi* of Rhos, Rhufoniog, Dyffryn Clwyd and Tegeingl (Englefield) 'which are called in the Welsh language Perfeddwlad', as well as Mold; they were granted 'the remainder of the whole of North Wales', excluding Meirionnydd. In this discussion the 'North Wales' of the records will be described as Gwynedd Uwch Conwy.
⁹¹ The term is noticed later.
⁹² *LW*, 8.
⁹³ *LW*, 10–12, 22–3.

two sons, but four. If Gwynedd were now divided into two parts by the current interpretation of 'the custom of Wales', there would soon be a further need to divide the land into three and four parts. The treaty of 1247 was by no means a finite statement of the distribution of land and authority in Gwynedd, and within five years the matter would be raised as Dafydd ap Gruffudd came to claim his portion. The battle of Bryn Derwin would be fought on this issue.[94] Although the treaty said nothing to this effect and, indeed, to the contrary, granted the remainder of north Wales to Owain and Llywelyn and their heirs, to be held of the king and his heirs in perpetuity, Henry knew that he could look forward to the division of the smaller Gwynedd into four parts in a short space of time. In another generation further division would probably follow, as long as the divisive interpretation of 'the custom of Wales' was faithfully respected. If Gwynedd had not been entirely annexed to the crown of England now, it would be a reasonable expectation that it would be fragmented to the point of complete extinction in due course.

Gwynedd was not the only territory where the crown's capacity to promote seigniorial fissure came to be revealed. The king had already taken the homage of two members of the lineage of Meirionnydd in 1241; a member of the lineage of Ceri did homage for half the lordship in 1248.[95] These are not the only instances. The 'custom of Wales' was already wreaking havoc among the Welsh seigniories and, with the disintegration of the territories, it was inevitable that indigenous lordship would be gradually undermined and the status of those who exercised lordship would be seriously impaired. Heirs to Welsh lordships now paid reliefs upon entry, reflecting a closer approximation to English baronial practice. This incident was not yet levied in the case of Gwynedd, but the king gave one clear sign of his determination to impose upon the princes an obligation which, more than any other, bears the mark of baronial obligation as it was recognized within the kingdom of England. It was laid down by treaty in 1247 that the brothers should fulfil a military obligation to the king as a condition of their tenure.[96] They did homage for a lordship to be held henceforth by military service. Already, after Gwerneigron, Henry had once tried to induce Dafydd ap Llywelyn in Gwynedd and Gruffudd ap Madog in Powys Fadog to raise forces for Gascony, but he had not been in a position to demand service. It is not known whether he was able to elicit any response to his request, and the forces then raised by John

---

[94] J. B. Smith, 'Dynastic succession', 222–3; below, pp. 68–73.

[95] *RotFin*, i, 371; ii, 37–8; *CIM*, i, nos. 76, 84; above, n. 74.

[96] *LW*, 7. The princes were required to provide at the king's command the service of 1,000 foot-soldiers and twenty-four horsemen at their costs, in Wales and the marches, when the king was on expedition there, and 500 foot-soldiers for service in England at the king's costs and at his command (C. W. Lewis, 'Treaty of Woodstock', 56–65).

Lestrange were probably recruited from that part of Perfeddwlad, namely Tegeingl, which was under royal lordship.[97] Now the lords of Gwynedd were placed under an obligation to provide a military quota specifically defined in a formal treaty.

These are not the only indications of the king's objectives, and the treaty needs to be seen, not solely as the specific consequence of the submission of the lords of Gwynedd, but as one among a number of ordinances and decisions which reflect royal intentions in these years. Henry's broad objectives have to be borne in mind in examining the provisions in the treaty of 1247 concerning the administration of justice, and particularly those which would apply to causes brought against Owain and Llywelyn for lands in Gwynedd.[98] It might appear as though the clause in question reflects what might reasonably be envisaged to have been the wishes of the princes themselves: if an action of this nature arose, they would be summoned to a place specified for them, either in Wales or the march, and they would have judgement according to the laws and customs of Wales. There appears to be an implicit assurance that they would be judged neither in a central royal court nor by English law. The princes thus appear to be placed in a decidedly better position than that in which Dafydd ap Llywelyn found himself when he had to accept that provision for Gruffudd would be made in the king's court and it would be for the king to decide whether or not the case should be tried by Welsh law.[99] The agreement of 1241 related, however, to one particular case and, though a judgement in the king's court on that issue might have important repercussions thereafter, the treaty of that year was specifically concerned with one issue, whereas in 1247 provision was made for what might prove to be a whole range of actions arising in Gwynedd. It could mean, at once, that Maredudd ap Richard could bring an action concerning his claims in Gwynedd, and in that case the right to determine the issue by Welsh law would not necessarily prove advantageous to Owain and Llywelyn, rather the opposite. They acknowledged their subjection to royal justice in this case, telling Henry that, though there were some who urged that Maredudd be dispossessed for his obduracy, they preferred to submit the matter to royal justice. If he brought an action before the king they were prepared to make satisfaction according to Welsh law.[100] The particular

---

[97] *CR, 1237–42*, 458, 498; *CR, 1242–47*, 76; *RG*, i, nos. 7, 10; *Cheshire Pipe Rolls*, 71.
[98] *LW*, 7–8.
[99] *LW*, 9.
[100] *CAC*, 32–3; *RL*, ii, 65 (October 1249–June 1250). In the full text the princes declare: 'parati sumus eidem secundum legem Wallie . . . satisfacere humiliter et devote'; this is calendared as a statement of their readiness 'to do justice' rather than an acknowledgment of their preparedness to submit to royal justice if Maredudd were to bring an action *coram rege*. This would reflect their treaty obligation of 1247. Maredudd received financial aid from the king, because he had lost his lands in Wales, from August 1248 (*CLibR*, iii, 198); gifts are recorded regularly until 1257 (*CLibR*, 277 *et passim*; iv, 22 *et passim*).

provisions embodied in the treaty of Woodstock reflect the much more general strengthening of royal influence in Wales which is perceptible during this decade. Owain and Llywelyn, and Llywelyn alone in due course, would be placed in a more complex and inhibiting situation than any in which Llywelyn ap Iorwerth had found himself. The fact that Llywelyn ap Gruffudd was eventually confronted with the exceptional ability of Edward I is only one element in the contrast between the political circumstances of the earlier and later parts of the thirteenth century. A number of factors in the synthesis of authority and power that Edward I came to represent had their origin in the course of action taken by his father, despite a major military reverse, in the decade following the death of Llywelyn ap Iorwerth. Thereafter the whole ambience of Anglo-Welsh relations changed.

Important features of the new trends are clearly revealed in Deheubarth after the death, first, of Llywelyn ap Iorwerth, who had exercised considerable influence in the province, and then the death (27 June 1241) of Gilbert Marshal, earl of Pembroke, who had held the castles of Carmarthen and Cardigan and the adjacent lands of the royal 'honor'. In Deheubarth the crown established a county organization.[101] The princes who exercised lordship in the commotes of Deheubarth, once the adherents of Llywelyn ap Iorwerth, were henceforth, more strictly than ever before, tenants-in-chief of the king. They and their men were made subject to the jurisdiction of the county courts of Carmarthen and Cardigan. The readiness of several of them to join Dafydd ap Llywelyn in 1244 may have been due, in part, to a reaction to their first experience of the rigour of the new royal administration. When they made their peace with the king two years later they could do no more than seek a guarantee that they would receive justice according to Welsh law, and they obediently acknowledged the jurisdiction of the county courts.[102] Henry made no comparable attempt to erect a county organization elsewhere and, though Perfeddwlad – 'the new conquest in Wales' – was the area most vulnerable to the imposition of new administrative organization, there is no indication there of radical structural change. English chroniclers' statements alleging the introduction of a county organization and English law, considered later, have to be treated cautiously. In contrast to Deheubarth, too, the roots of dissension there may be traced, not to the sensibilities of princes concerned that their jurisdiction would be undermined, but to the exactitude of the authority to which entire communities were subjected by royal officers.

---

[101] J. G. Edwards, 'The early history of the counties of Carmarthen and Cardigan', *EHR*, 31 (1916), 90–8; R. A. Griffiths, *The Principality of Wales in the Later Middle Ages: The Structure and Personnel of Government*, i, *South Wales, 1277–1536* (Cardiff, 1972), 1–2 [R. A. Griffiths, *PW*].

[102] J. B. Smith, 'The origins of the revolt of Rhys ap Maredudd', *B*, 21 (1964–6), 151–2.

Indications of increased royal intervention are revealed in other parts of Wales, including lands both of princes and marcher lords. Royal commissioners appointed to hear pleas in 1242 were charged to do justice both in Wales and the march and, though nothing tangible is known to have come of this initiative, those who exercised seigniorial authority in the march were alert to the need to safeguard their liberties.[103] The most significant case in the historical record of the period arose in the lordship of Glamorgan following determined action on the part of Richard de Clare, earl of Gloucester, in response to a conflict waged within his frontiers by two of his mesne lords, Hywel ap Maredudd and Richard Siward.[104] It was on this account that Hywel ap Maredudd, lord of Meisgyn, 'having been entirely dispossessed by the Clare earl', as the Welsh chronicler relates, sought refuge in Gwynedd and stayed there permanently as an adherent of Llywelyn ap Gruffudd.[105] His adversary brought an appeal to the king's court against a judgement given in the court of Glamorgan, prompting the earl into a defence of marcher liberty which presaged the arguments which the great magnates of the march were to use in their altercations with the crown in the later years of the century. The issue of whether marcher lord or king should have custody of the temporalities of the church of Llandaff during vacancy, though not resolved until later, was similarly broached in these years.[106] In the case of those lords of Wales who were of princely lineage sensitivities were inevitably heightened and, equally, the crown had need to be wary of the political repercussions which were likely in their lands when seigniorial interests were felt to be endangered. It has been noticed already that upon the outbreak of hostilities in 1244 Gruffudd ap Madog had secured reassurance from the king on matters which concerned him, the phraseology of Henry's reply suggesting that Gruffudd had expressed his disquiet with some conviction. He did not join forces with Dafydd ap Llywelyn, but his unswerving fidelity to the crown was accompanied by a close watchfulness of the king's intentions and a studious attention to the means by which his liberty was respected. Thus he secured, on a particular issue of legal procedure raised in an action *coram rege,* a decision of the king's council that a case could be resolved in accordance with the practices of Welsh law if both plaintiff and defendant were Welsh.[107] The award belongs to a period in which

---

[103] *CPR, 1232–47,* 272.

[104] M. Altschul, *A Baronial Family in Medieval England: The Clares, 1217–1314* (Baltimore, 1965), 69–73 [Altschul, *Clares*]; *GlamCH,* iii, 47–52; D. Crouch, 'The last adventure of Richard Siward', *Morgannwg,* 35 (1991), 7–30; text of proceedings in *Cartae,* iii, 547–55.

[105] *BT, Pen20,* 202; *Pen20Tr,* 107; *RBH,* 240–1; *LW,* 44, 185; *RL,* ii, 286.

[106] M. Howell, 'Regalian right in Wales and the march: the relation of theory to practice', *WHR,* 7 (1974–5), 284–6.

[107] *CPR, 1232–47,* 430; KB26/159, m. 1; summary in *WAR,* 15–16, does not convey the precise meaning of the text.

the evidence tends to reflect an extension of royal jurisdiction, and it was to this period that Edward I's searchers would turn first in their quest for precedents with a bearing on the conflict of laws of his reign. It might be well to be wary of attributing too much to the influence of theories of kingship upon Henry III, even in the best years of his reign, but there can be little doubt that in his dealings with Wales in these years he was able to establish precedents and practices which proved valuable to his successor in the fullness of time.[108] These were the trends in the years preceding the submission of the princes in 1247.

Owain ap Gruffudd and Llywelyn ap Gruffudd certainly had need to tread wearily within the limitations imposed by the treaty obligations into which they had entered. A letter which they addressed to the king, a rare instance of the two princes acting together, was phrased in terms which, while firmly stating their case, suggest a distinctly respectful caution.[109] They had left Woodstock with the knowledge that any breach of faith might incur total forfeiture, and the future would demand vigilance on their part. Above all else, they would need to stand together. The first joint act of which we have knowledge was one of symbolic significance for, within a year of their submission and in accordance with their wishes, the abbots of Aberconwy and Cymer were given the king's permission to remove the remains of their father, Gruffudd ap Llywelyn, from London to Aberconwy. He was laid to rest with Dafydd ap Llywelyn and Llywelyn ap Iorwerth. It is probable that it was on this occasion that Dafydd Benfras composed the elegy which, commemorating the three princes together, marked an acknowledgement that the tumults of the years of conflict were to be allowed to recede as the three were brought together in the precincts of the Cistercian abbey on the shore where the great river meets the sea.[110]

---

[108] The innovative nature of royal policy in these years is stressed in M. T. Clanchy, 'Did Henry III have a policy?', *History*, 53 (1968), 203–16; R. R. Davies, 'Kings, lords and liberties in the march of Wales, 1066–1272', *TRHS*, 5th Ser., 29 (1979), 41–61; for comments on the thrust of royal and marcher policies, idem, *Domination and Conquest: The Experience of Ireland, Scotland and Wales 1100–1300* (Cambridge, 1990), 88–108. In relation to royal policy D. A. Carpenter, *The Reign of Henry III* (London, 1996), 88, n. 62, is wary of 'absolutist' theory and expresses reservations regarding the view that the king pursued an 'assertive policy' in the march of Wales. Dr Huw Ridgeway makes the pertinent point that Henry's frailties may have been less exposed by the good fortune of there being several comital minorities as well as the Scottish minority. The end of the earldom of Chester brought an extension of royal territory which, through the association of Perfeddwlad with its administration, created problems in 1256 but proved to be an asset in the conflict of 1277.

[109] *CAC*, 32–3; *RL*, ii, 64–6.

[110] *BT, Pen20*, 204; *Pen20Tr*, 108; *RBH*, 242–3. The suggestion concerning the occasion of the composition is by J. Lloyd-Jones, 'The court poets of the Welsh princes', *PBA*, 34 (1948), 186; text in *GDB*, 31, quoting ll. 56–67, trans. Ann Parry Owen: 'Three of the finest warriors among warriors, / Three worthy men whom God has taken from among men, /

Bryn Derwin

Tri gorau dreigiau sy o'r dragon,
Tri gŵr a ddug Duw o'r dyniaddon,
Tri eres armes trachwres trychion,
Tri eraill ni eill oll eu deddfon,
Tri araf, pennaf penadurion,
Tri arwydd, hylwydd ar eu holion,
Tri arwr, eurdwr eurdorchogion,
Tri eryr yn wŷr ac yn weision,
(Tri chlwyf nad ydynt fal cynt Cynon!)
Tri chlau eu parau fal Peryddon,
Tri chlöyn pennyn penguchogion,
Tri chlo ar eu bro rhag bradogion.

The ruptures of earlier years were finally repaired, their presence at the abbey on this occasion an earnest of a new unity between the two princes who now shared responsibility for their patrimony, a pledge of their determination to resolve the difficult problems which confronted them in its government. How did the co-heirs of Gwynedd set about their task?

The document which embodied their agreement with the king contained no indication of the manner in which the brothers would share the rule of Gwynedd, though this does not necessarily mean that the arrangements had not been subject to the king's scrutiny. The text itself might even admit the possibility that the 'heirs to north Wales' maintained a joint lordship, and other records might give that impression.[111] Together they composed a letter to the crown recounting their grievances. They maintained that the justice of Chester had failed to respect the clause in the treaty of 1247 which was designed to safeguard the interests of those of the brothers' tenants who held land on either side of the Conwy; refusing to act until Maredudd ap Richard was given the lands which their mother held in dower, he denied them their right under the terms of the treaty.[112] For a brief moment we see the brothers acting as co-defenders of their common interest.

It appears, however, that the brothers had decided at an early date that joint lordship would be inappropriate and that the territory should be

---

Three astonishing men causing calamity for the fallen enemy by their fierceness, / Three whose deeds none others can match, / Three gentle men, finest of chieftains, / Three signal ones, swift to assert their rights, / Three heroes, a fine defence for gold-torqued warriors, / Three eagles as men and youths / (Three wounds I bear that they are now as was Cynon of yore!), / Three with spears swift like the flow of the river Peryddon, / Three with blades sharp upon helmeted men, / Three defenders of their land against traitors.'

[111] *LW*, 19, 160–1, a pledge of the fidelity of their brother Rhodri and an agreement with the princes of Ystrad Tywi considered later. Owain and Llywelyn were ordered in 1253 to prevent their men from interfering in the lands of the king of Man and the Isles (*Calendar of Documents relating to Scotland*, ed. J. Bain (London, 1881–8), i, no. 1917).

[112] *CAC*, 32–3; *RL*, ii, 64–6 (October 1249–June 1250).

partitioned between them. As we have seen, the chronicler records that Owain and Llywelyn, by counsel of wise men, 'divided the territory between them into two halves'. We cannot be certain how the division was made, nor on what basis an equitable arrangement was sought, but some indication of the distribution of lands may be gained from the scanty materials available for consideration.[113] Owain was evidently in a position to make grants of land in the commotes of Menai and Malltraeth in Anglesey, and as Llifon and Malltraeth formed the *cantref* of Aberffraw it would be reasonable to deduce that Owain, the eldest son, held the principal court of the dynasty at Aberffraw and the three commotes in the southern and western parts of the island.[114] Llywelyn's confirmation to the priory of Ynys Lannog (Priestholm) of the possession of lands in the commote of Dindaethwy suggests that he held this commote, along with Twrcelyn, where one of his early adherents, Iorwerth ap Gwrgunan, was endowed with land, and Talybolion.[115] On purely economic grounds a distribution such as this, giving Llywelyn the northern and eastern parts of the island, would be a fairly equitable arrangement.[116] It was one which provided both Owain and Llywelyn with access to the mainland from the commotes of Menai and Dindaethwy respectively.[117] The position on the mainland is much more difficult to discern. With regard to Owain, a document relating more specifically to Dafydd provides some indication of his possessions. Dafydd in 1252 exercised lordship in Cymydmaen, a commote in the *cantref* of Llŷn, and their association at a later date suggests that Dafydd had been granted that commote by Owain out of his original share.[118] This could mean that Owain, at first, held the *cantref* of Llŷn, namely the commotes of Cymydmaen, Cafflogion and Dinllaen and, in addition perhaps, the commote of Eifionydd. The circumstances surrounding the battle of Bryn Derwin are consistent with a division which would have placed Llŷn and Eifionydd in Owain's possession and Arfon Uwch Gwyrfai

---

[113] *AC*, 85–6; *CW*, 39; *BT, Pen20*, 201–2; *Pen20Tr*, 107; *RBH*, 240–1. Lloyd, *HW*, ii, 707, n. 76, is cautious on the distribution of lands. The account in *TC*, 63–4, differs in some details from that subsequently made in Stephenson, *GG*, 156–8, but there is substantial agreement.

[114] *MonAng*, iv, 582; *CChR*, ii, 460; *H*, no. 50. Stephenson, *GG*, 156, cites from *CIM*, ii, no. 538 a grant by Owain of lands in Malltraeth and Menai. Y Prydydd Bychan addresses Owain as 'the dragon of the court of Ffraw' (*dreic llys Ffraw, GBF*, 1. 24).

[115] *MonAng*, iv, 582; *CChR*, ii, 460; *H*, no. 147 (Ynys Lannog, or Priestholm); *RC*, 68 (Gwely Iorwerth ap Gwrgunan in Bodunod).

[116] Figures in T. Jones Pierce, *Medieval Welsh Society* (Cardiff, 1972), 118 [Pierce, *MWS*] 118, based on post-conquest documents, provide a means to an estimate of the comparative wealth of the Anglesey commotes, and are helpful also in relation to the division of lands on the mainland where there were marked disparities between upland and lowland areas.

[117] This distribution would correspond to the delimitation of the two Anglesey deaneries in the ecclesiastical valuation of 1254 in *Valuation of Norwich*, 192–6.

[118] *RC*, 252.

in Llywelyn's hands. The younger brother's grant to Basingwerk indicates that Penllyn was his, and the fact that the document was dated at Bangor suggests that Arfon Is Gwyrfai was part of his lordship.[119] There is, thus, some reason to believe that the whole of Arfon was in his possession. This would leave Ardudwy, a commote for which there is no information, and the *cantref* of Arllechwedd, namely Arllechwedd Uchaf, Arllechwedd Isaf and Nanconwy. Nanconwy was probably Llywelyn's land, for in 1247 he bestowed an estate in Cwmllannerch upon Iorwerth ap Gwrgunan, and it is likely that the whole of Arllechwedd was part of Llywelyn's portion.[120] The south-western and north-western division indicated in Anglesey may have been replicated on the mainland: Llŷn, Eifionydd and perhaps Ardudwy to Owain; Arfon, Arllechwedd and Penllyn to Llywelyn. Llywelyn's lands would then have been more extensive than those of Owain, but a distribution of this nature would have ensured a rough equality in economic value. Llywelyn had an advantage in that he took possession of the physical heartland of Gwynedd, an area already fortified by the stone castles of Dolwyddelan and Dolbadarn, and this could prove to be an asset in any struggle within the patrimony. If the fragmentary record reflects the broad nature of the partition of Gwynedd it suggests a somewhat comparable economic provision, but it is an arrangement which demonstrates the advantage which Llywelyn derived from his presence in Gwynedd, first alongside Dafydd ap Llywelyn and then briefly but crucially alone, while Owain, willingly or unwillingly, remained in the keeping of the king of England. Llywelyn established himself in the fastnesses of Snowdonia and no one would ever remove him.[121] If Owain had lingered in the king's protection of his free will, he was to find that his tardiness had cost him dearly.

It is not easy to discuss relations between Owain and Llywelyn during the brief period in which they shared the government of Gwynedd Uwch Conwy without allowing subsequent events to cast their shadow. Yet, when every care is taken, it is difficult to escape the conclusion that the instinct for resolute and decisive leadership belonged to Llywelyn rather than to Owain. This is the view suggested if two remarkable documents of the years 1250–1

---

[119] *CChR*, ii, 291; *H*, no. 148; cf. *HW*, ii, 707. Stephenson, *GG*, 157, 204, cites references to undated grants by Llywelyn (*H*, nos. 171–2) of land in Arfon Uwch Gwyrfai to Beddgelert priory.

[120] Text (J. B. Smith, 'Land endowments', 150–64), dated at Pennant Machno, 26 July 1247, is derived from a sixteenth-century source (E163/28/11); a grant by Llywelyn to Iorwerth would be consistent with his known early adherence and his descendants held land in Cwmllannerch and Penmachno in 1352 (*RC*, 9–11). The charter adds important evidence to that of two other charters of 1247, to Ynys Lannog and Basingwerk, including a list of witnesses.

[121] Hywel Foel, in a poem critical of Llywelyn, describes him as 'lord of Snowdonia' (*rhwyf Eryri*); below, n. 153.

are taken together. In the latter year Owain and Llywelyn made an agreement with Rhys Fychan and Maredudd ap Rhys Gryg of Ystrad Tywi by which each party pledged its resolve to stand together against all living men as though they were brothers in preserving for each his right and in recovering that which had been unjustly taken from them.[122] Considering this document by itself, it would be impossible to distinguish between the part likely to have been played by Owain and Llywelyn in negotiating the agreement, any more than it would be possible to recognize the respective roles of Rhys and Maredudd. But, during the previous year, a similar agreement had been forged between Llywelyn, acting alone, and Gruffudd ap Madog of Powys Fadog. Each one pledged, for as long as he lived, to be of one confederacy and union against all men, great or small, again in preserving for each his right and in recovering that which had been unjustly removed.[123] There can be little doubt that Llywelyn was the instigator of both agreements and it may be reasonably safe to conclude that it was in response to his initiative that Rhys Fychan and Maredudd ap Rhys Gryg came to Caernarfon in Arfon Is Gwyrfai, a commote which we have already concluded to have been in his possession, to put their seals to a document binding them in alliance with the heirs to Gwynedd. It is also likely that, though Owain presented his own grievances to the crown, the document in which the heirs to Gwynedd called upon the king to honour the pledges into which he had entered in the treaty of Woodstock, was a reflection of the forceful political attributes of the younger brother.[124] The evidence for the years after 1246, sparse though it may be, suggests that the division of authority in Gwynedd could not be expected to last for anything more than a brief while.

The arrangement commended to the princes by the wise men of Gwynedd in 1246 was brought to an end nine years later, though it was neither Owain nor Llywelyn who precipitated the change but the third brother, Dafydd ap Gruffudd. He is not known to have played any part in events before 1252, but in that year he is found presiding over proceedings by which the canons of the church of Aberdaron resolved a disagreement with the Austin canons of Bardsey.[125] We have a glimpse of a young prince, perhaps only recently come

---

[122] *LW*, 160–1; the situation in Ystrad Tywi is noticed later.

[123] *LW*, 148; Lloyd, letter to J. G. Edwards, 1941 (UW, Bangor, Library, J. E. Lloyd Papers, 318/51–2) maintained that the date, 20 November 1250, was 'far too early' and that 1257 was more likely; Edwards was inclined to agree that he might have been mistaken in accepting the date on the document. But the tenor of the document suggests the situation about 1251, and it lacks the features which might be expected in an agreement between Llywelyn and the lords of Wales *c*.1257–8.

[124] *CPR, 1247–58*, 432.

[125] *RC*, 252; for the record's relevance to the lands of Bardsey, Pierce, *MWS*, 391–407.

of age, and with his mother Senana still at hand, exercising lordship over Cymydmaen. This was the westerly commote of the *cantref* of Llŷn, where several of the *membra regis* of Gwynedd found themselves a share of the land of their fathers. Dafydd may initially have been associated with Llywelyn rather than Owain, for the name Dafydd ap Gruffudd appears first among those who witnessed Llywelyn's charter to Ynys Lannog in 1247.[126] But it would seem that it was by virtue of Owain's gift, rather than by Llywelyn's generosity, that Dafydd was able to exercise lordship over a small part of the patrimony. The chronicler states that Dafydd became captain of the household (*dux familia*) in Owain's service; he thereby occupied the position of *penteulu* which, according to the practices of his lineage, was reserved for a near kinsman of the ruler.[127] By 1252 he had evidently shown that he, no more than others of his kind, would not rest content with courtly office without territory, and he had secured lordship over Cymydmaen.[128] Owain presumably made provision for Dafydd out of the portion of Gwynedd which lay in his possession, but no comparable gift is known to have been made by Llywelyn. Lordship over Cymydmaen hardly satiated Dafydd's ambitions, and by 1253 he had taken his first steps towards securing what he would regard as an appropriate portion of the inheritance. During the summer the king arranged to receive Dafydd and his retinue when he came to do homage. This was a clear indication that the king was prepared to consider him, along with Owain and Llywelyn, as one of the heirs to Gwynedd. Dafydd did not come to court in time, for when he arrived the king had already sailed for Gascony. But though the young prince could do no more than swear fealty, his was no futile journey for his transactions with the council in September 1253 ensured that the crown endorsed his tenure of whatever part of Gwynedd he could secure for himself. The king had implicitly recognized that the territorial settlement ratified in 1247 had to be adjusted to accommodate the third of the four brothers. Owain and Llywelyn were told that Dafydd had sworn fealty for the portion due to him of the lands which had been held by Gruffudd ap Llywelyn and Dafydd ap Llywelyn.[129] His elder brothers were required to provide Dafydd with the portion due to him 'according to the custom of Wales'.[130]

---

[126] *CChR*, ii, 460.
[127] *CW*, 40; *LlIor*, 4; *LHD*, 8.
[128] *Breudwyt Ronabwy*, 1; *Mabinogion*, 137.
[129] *CPR, 1247–58*, 210; *CR, 1251–53*, 419 (29 September 1253): 'fecit regi fidelitatem de porcione ipsum contingente de terris que fuerunt predicti Griffini patris sui et David filii Lewelini avunculi sui in Wallia'. Dafydd's safe-conduct, 8 July, enabled him to come to the king or, if he were out of the realm, to the queen and Richard of Cornwall. Henry left for Gascony in early August and the letters of September were issued by the queen and Cornwall as regents. For the relevance of Henry's departure to the problems of Wales, below, n. 167.
[130] *CR, 1251–53*, 419; the king thereafter counted Dafydd, along with Owain and Llywelyn, as his tenant (e.g. *CR, 1253–54*, 110).

The king's council realized that Henry's pledge to Dafydd could create problems, for the letter communicating the council's decision told the justice of Chester to support and defend Dafydd 'without disturbing the king's land in Wales'.[131] Making provision for Dafydd, and thereby adjusting the territorial arrangements previously made by the two elder brothers and confirmed in principle by the treaty of Woodstock, could create difficulties in Gwynedd, but also beyond it. Though the king's decision had a direct bearing on the princes of Gwynedd alone, there were others who would be equally apprehensive of its wider implications. Gruffudd ap Madog would most certainly question the validity of the premise on which the decision was made, but he did not have to wait long before the king's council specifically applied the principle to Powys Fadog. Council insisted that he should, according to the custom of Wales, share his land with his co-heirs.[132] The justice of Chester was promptly authorized to proceed in Powys Fadog in accordance with that 'custom of Wales' which the king now cherished so tenderly. It would not be unreasonable to consider whether it was precisely this fear which, three years before, had brought Gruffudd and Llywelyn to pledge themselves to stand together to resist any attempt on the part of any man – be he great or small and to whatever nation he might belong – to undermine their rights. The phraseology admits the possibility that the two men were concerned, not only by a fear of attack from beyond their frontiers, but with a challenge which could arise within the lands and conceivably within the dynasties.[133] There can be no doubt that Gruffudd had been concerned, for many years, with the need to withstand the claims of his brothers to a share of the land of their father, Madog ap Gruffudd, in Powys Fadog. He may have been troubled, too, by claims put forward by kinsmen on the basis of their descent from earlier representatives of the dynasty, pleas which were certainly to be pressed years later when political conditions were more favourable to the prosecution of opportunist actions.[134] Owain and Llywelyn in Gwynedd already faced comparable claims from immediate and more distant kinsmen, and Llywelyn's agreement with Gruffudd ap Madog in 1250 may be, more than anything else, an affirmation of his resolve to withstand those claims. Nothing came of this declaration of mutual interest, but at the time when it was made, and for some years to come, Gruffudd ap Madog and Llywelyn ap Gruffudd were determined to resist, each within his territory, the partition which the king of England was urging upon them with such eagerness.

---

[131] *CR, 1251–53*, 419.

[132] Ibid., p. 511. The document refers to 'certain lands' (*quedam terre*) and there is no explicit reference to Powys Fadog, but it can only refer to that land or part of it.

[133] *LW*, 148.

[134] His brothers' claims are considered later. After 1277 an action was brought by the sons of Gruffudd Fychan, descendants of Iorwerth Goch ap Maredudd (*WAR*, 319, 324, 343).

In Gruffudd's case resistance to the king's demands meant adhering to the principle of undivided succession to which the king had given his assent a decade earlier when, needing support, he had assured Gruffudd that he would be maintained in his rule of Powys Fadog in its entirety.[135] In Gwynedd, on the other hand, the impetus for partition had already been created in 1241, and both Owain and Llywelyn had subsequently consented to the division of the patrimony. In the following years it is Llywelyn who stands forth conspicuously, first in incorrigible opposition to the further partition of the lordship, and then in a determination to restore the unity of the *regnum* by a forceful assertion of his power. For all we know, Owain may have cherished a hope that he, the first-born son, might be able to concentrate power over Gwynedd in his hands. We have no clear indication of such an aspiration, however, and on the more immediate issue as to whether Gwynedd would be made subject to a new partition to provide for Dafydd, it appears that Owain was prepared to accede to the proposal. He may have judged that it was only in alliance with Dafydd that he could possibly withstand a challenge from Llywelyn for possession of the whole inheritance. For Llywelyn the implications of his singular resistance were profound. He stood as the guardian of the interests of his dynasty, and his stand involved not only conflict with his brother but opposition to the king's overt wish to pursue his personal interest in this crucially important matter. By the beginning of 1254, at the latest, Llywelyn knew that the king was proceeding with his declared intention of securing for Dafydd the portion of the inheritance which he considered to be the prince's right. Llywelyn and Dafydd were informed that the king was sending to Chester by 26 April a commission consisting of Alan la Zusche, justice of Chester, John Lestrange, Gruffudd ap Gwenwynwyn and Gruffudd ap Madog. It was empowered to hear the disputes between the brothers, receiving each of the brothers' propositions against the other, and council would then do justice on the evidence presented to it.[136] Llywelyn and Dafydd were each told to ensure that they were present, or represented by their attorneys, to set out their charges, and each of them was warned to make sure that he did not disturb the king's realm or his land of Wales. The problem was evidently seen as a dispute between Llywelyn and Dafydd, but Owain was also told that if he wished to bring any charge against Llywelyn he should do so at the same time and he, too, was told to do nothing which would disturb the peace. Owain evidently made a submission to the king, but it is clear that

[135] J. B. Smith, 'Dynastic succession', 227; above, n. 42.
[136] *CR, 1253–54*, 109–10 (20 January 1254, given by the queen and Cornwall); *CPR, 1247–58*, 362. The hearing was envisaged as an opportunity for Llywelyn and Dafydd to set out their charges against one another ('ad propondendum que erga dictum fratrem vestrum in hac parte proponere volueritis'); Llywelyn subsequently indicated that he made proposals to the king towards a solution of the problem; below, pp. 86–9.

the main burden of responsibility was placed on Llywelyn.[137] The matter might at one point be presented as a dispute between Dafydd and Llywelyn; at another it might be between Owain and Llywelyn. But the essential issue was the same, and the cause of it was how – or whether – the land of Gwynedd should be redivided so as to provide for three, if not four, sons of Gruffudd ap Llywelyn. The bone of contention, as the Chester annalist put it, was the partition of lands.[138] What, if anything, the commission was able to report we cannot tell. There were some comings and goings between Llywelyn and the crown, and at the beginning of 1255 he was summoned to appear before the king.[139] In May a commission was appointed to determine the issues between Owain and Llywelyn, but before the appointed day the problems which had rent the dynasty of Gwynedd anew had been resolved by force.[140]

It is possible that the initial action was taken, not by Llywelyn, but by his brothers. This is certainly the testimony of chronicler and poet, who both convey that the opposing forces met in conflict at Bryn Derwin. According to the chronicler Llywelyn, trusting in God, faced the advance of Owain and Dafydd at the head of a mighty army.[141] The poet Llygad Gŵr conveys a similar interpretation of the conflict, commemorating the battle of Bryn Derwin as one in which Llywelyn repulsed a rash attack on the part of his kinsmen, his bravery in withstanding a shameless assault rewarded in triumph:

> Bryn Derwin! Clo byddin clodrydd!
> Ni bu edifar y dydd – y cyrchawdd
> Cyrch eofn esillydd.
> Gwelai wawr ar wŷr lluosydd
> Fel gŵr yn gwrthladd cywilydd,
> A welai Lewelyn, lewenydd – dragon,
> Yng nghymysg Arfon ac Eiddionydd.
> Nid oedd hawdd, llew aerflawdd lluydd,
> Ei dreisiaw ger Drws Daufynydd.[142]

---

[137] *CR, 1253–54*, 110; *CPR, 1247–58*, 432.

[138] *AnnCestr*, 70; conflict arose 'concerning the partition of lands' (*super terrarum participacione*).

[139] *CR, 1254–56*, 155; proposals which Llywelyn later said he had put to the king may have been presented at this time, but there is no evidence that he responded to the king's summons in person.

[140] *CPR, 1247–58*, 432 (10 May). Henry de la Mare, Geoffrey Langley and William de Wilton were to meet at Gresford three weeks after Midsummer (15 July).

[141] *AC*, 89–90; *CW*, 40; *BT, Pen20*, 207; *Pen20Tr*, 110; *RBH*, 246–7. Bryn Derwin is named as the site of the battle, *RBH*, 246–7; *BS*, 240–1; reference in the chronology in Llwyd, *Britannicae Descriptionis Commentariolum*, 162–3.

[142] *GBF*, 24. 94–102, trans. Ann Parry Owen: 'Bryn Derwin! He was the stay of a celebrated army! / There were no regrets the day he withstood / The shameless attack of his own stock; / He who saw Llywelyn, the jubilation of warriors, / On the borders of Arfon and Eifionydd, / Would see a lord over men in hosts / Like a man dispelling dishonour. / It was not easy, a lion in a host and fearsome in combat, / To vanquish him by Drws Daufynydd.'

Bryn Derwin

From the poet's precise account the site of the battle can be located near Bwlch Dau Fynydd, close by the boundary between Arfon and Eifionydd.[143] Conflict was brief and decisive. Owain and Dafydd may have established an initial advantage, but Llywelyn secured a convincing victory in this crucial encounter. Though historical and literary sources bear their remembrance of the battle, it cannot be accurately dated, but it is likely that Bryn Derwin was fought about the middle of June 1255. The king's council had heard about it by the twentieth of the month, and knew that Owain and Dafydd had been captured and that their lands were in Llywelyn's possession.[144] The crown understood that the victorious prince was already taking the homage of some of the king's tenants but, apart from urging the justice of Chester to support Gruffudd ap Madog in Powys Fadog if Llywelyn were to attack, the king's counsellors could do no more than record that the dispute to which the king had attended intermittently over a period of two years and more had now been resolved on the battlefield.

Triumph at Bryn Derwin gave Llywelyn the opportunity to establish his mastery over Gwynedd Uwch Conwy in its entirety. The king evidently feared that he would extend his power elsewhere, but Llywelyn's main concern, for the present, was to secure complete control over the lands that he had annexed at the expense of Owain and Dafydd. With regard to the fourth and youngest brother, Rhodri ap Gruffudd, we have no knowledge of any involvement in the conflict of 1255, nor in the disputes which led up to it. He may have been in no position to act. He had endured a period of captivity in his early years, for, along with Dafydd, his mother had given him as a hostage at the time of her agreement with Henry in 1241.[145] More relevant to the critical period in the contest for the patrimony, the appearance of one Rhodri ap Gruffudd as a hostage in royal custody in the years 1250–4 suggests that the youngest son of Gruffudd ap Llywelyn was confined once more, possibly as a pledge of faith for Llywelyn.[146] He was eventually to assert his hereditary

---

Bryn Derwin is recalled in the *awdl* that Gruffudd ap Maredudd ap Dafydd addressed to Owain ap Thomas ap Rhodri or Owain Lawgoch (*The Poetry in the Red Book of Hergest*, ed. J. G. Evans (Llanbedrog, 1911), col. 1313).

[143] *HW*, ii, 715 (SH459468, Bwlchderwyn).

[144] *CR, 1254–56*, 204 (letter to justice of Chester, by Cornwall and others at Woodstock, has a *teste ut supra* dating of 20 June, indicating a battle fought a few days earlier). The letter confirms *AC*, 89; *CW*, 40; *BT, Pen20*, 207; *Pen20Tr*, 110, that the two brothers were imprisoned and that *BT, RBH*, 246–7, is in error in stating otherwise (note in *BT, Pen20Tr*, 208).

[145] *LW*, 52–3; *Cheshire Pipe Rolls*, 77 (account 1242–5 showing imprisonment at Chester). In a document of 15 March 1248 (*LW*, 19) Owain and Llywelyn provided surety for the fidelity of Rhodri, who had been given as a hostage for the release of his father; he was released, along with Goronwy ap Heilin, 5 May 1248 (*CR, 1247–51*, 45).

[146] *Cheshire Pipe Rolls*, 98 (account indicating imprisonment 1250–4); Stephenson, *GG*, 160 notes a statement in a late thirteenth-century tract, considered later, that Rhodri was a hostage for Llywelyn.

right, if only to secure recompense for ceding it to Llywelyn. Whether he featured in Llywelyn's proposals 'concerning his brothers', considered presently, we cannot tell, nor is there any indication that the king was exercised by any concern that Rhodri had to be considered as a portioner in the patrimony on the same grounds as Dafydd. Rhodri may have been imprisoned by Llywelyn for a time, but he appears only fleetingly in the evidence until 1272, when he accepted a sum of a thousand marks from Llywelyn upon yielding his hereditary right to a share of the patrimony.[147] It was undoubtedly the assertiveness of the third brother, Dafydd, which proved to be the disturbing influence in the period up to 1255 and, from then until the very last crisis in the history of independent Wales, relations between Dafydd and Llywelyn would be crucial to the political fortunes of Gwynedd and Wales as a whole. But, in the aftermath of Bryn Derwin, Llywelyn's main concern was his elder brother.

Owain was the eldest son, a fact recalled by many in years to come, Matthew Paris and King Henry among them, who would well remember that Owain was the *primogenitus*.[148] Llywelyn was the second son, placed at a disadvantage to be overcome only by the elimination of the elder brother or by his perpetual imprisonment. Owain was imprisoned, adding to the years he had already spent in captivity a further confinement of twenty-two years' duration.[149] We must be wary of a literal reading of the words which refer to his captivity in chains. But we can be certain that his confinement took a form of restriction from which there was no escape, nor any easing of its severity. For the evidence which survives contains nothing to suggest that Owain was in any way unequal to the responsibilities of lordship, and it would be hazardous, while accepting that Llywelyn had proved to be the more forceful influence in the years before Bryn Derwin, to deduce that Owain suffered any disability or that he was unequal to the tasks of governing. There was nothing to deter the poets, Y Prydydd Bychan and Bleddyn Fardd, from employing the conventional eulogistic phraseology in extolling Owain's qualities. Y Prydydd Bychan, writing during the years when Owain exercised lordship, portrayed a man of valour, a ruler endowed with the virtues of those who had preceded him in the rule of the patrimony.[150] In his elegy, Bleddyn Fardd saw Owain as a worthy member of the lineage of Gruffudd ap Llywelyn and

---

[147] *CCR, 1272–79*, 506–7; *CWR*, 159; *LW*, xxxix, 85–6; *HW*, ii, 742, nn. 121–2; Powicke, *Henry III*, 637; Stephenson, *GG*, 159–60; A. D. Carr, *Owen of Wales: The End of the House of Gwynedd* (Cardiff, 1991), 3–6; below, pp. 440, 448.

[148] Paris, *ChronMaj*, v, 718, 727; *CR, 1261–64*, 142–3.

[149] Owain was released under the terms of the treaty of 1277 (*LW*, 119). According to John Leland (*The Itinerary in Wales of John Leland in or about the years 1536–1539*, ed. L. Toulmin Smith (London, 1906), 84), Owain was kept at the castle of Dolbadarn.

[150] *GBF*, 1. A man of Deheubarth, the poet's presence in Gwynedd may be related to Maelgwn Fychan's sojourn there.

Llywelyn ap Iorwerth, and he, too, saw the prince as a man sturdy in combat, a man of great valour, fearless in brandishing his shield: 'Hir ddewrllew traglew yn treiglaw – ysgwyd'.[151] Owain could be joined with Llywelyn and Dafydd in an elegy to the three sons of Gruffudd ap Llywelyn.[152] Much of what is said of Owain may be no more than literary convention but, at the very least, Owain's persona was not such as made conventional modes of eulogistic or elegiac address palpably inappropriate.

Firmer evidence of his capability is provided in two poems which Hywel Foel ap Griffri wrote while Owain was in captivity, compositions which provide striking testimony to the tensions in Gwynedd in the period after Bryn Derwin. The poet bewails his personal loss at Owain's confinement, an exile left without lord, without gifts, without the chief of warriors: 'Difro wyf heb rwyf, heb roddion / Heb Owain, hebawg cynreinon'. But he also expresses the devastating effect of the prince's absence upon his territory, the very earth left barren by his imprisonment: 'Diffrwythws daear o'i fod yng ngharchar'. If the first sentiment is a predictable affirmation of a poet's loyalty to his lord and the second no more than an adjustment to the circumstances of a lord's imprisonment of a motif frequently employed in elegiac verse, they nevertheless strike a note of deep sincerity in harmony with the more specific intimations which follow. His imprisonment at Llywelyn's hands was the only factor which prevented Owain from taking an honoured place in the pantheon of his dynasty, otherwise he could be counted among the defenders of his people. For Owain was, in truth, the protector of his people, formidable in war:

> Gŵr yn rhwym gan rwyf Eryri
> Gŵr, pai rhydd, fal Rhun fab Beli,
> Gŵr ni adai Loegr i losgi – ei derfyn.
> Gŵr o hil Merfyn, mawrfryd Benlli,
> Gŵr torfoedd, gŵr gwisgoedd gwisgi,
> Gŵr gwasgawd kiwdawd, cad weini,
> Gŵr cadarn cadoedd reoli.
> Gŵr cadwent, cedwis haeloni . . .
> Gwr nad oedd lyfrach nog Elifri.[153]

---

[151] *GBF*, 48.

[152] *GBF*, 54.

[153] *GBF*, 22, 23; B. F. Roberts, 'Dwy awdl Hywel Foel ap Griffri', *Bardos: Penodau ar y Traddodiad Barddol Cymreig a Cheltaidd*, ed. R. G. Gruffydd (Cardiff, 1982), 60–75; quoting ll. 9–16, 20, trans. Ann Parry Owen: 'A warrior made captive by the lord of Eryri, / A warrior, were he free, like Rhun fab Beli, / A warrior who would not allow England to burn his borders. / A warrior of the lineage of Merfyn, magnanimous like Beli, / A warrior of hosts, warrior of splendid armour, / A warrior protecting his people, ordering an army, / A steadfast warrior ruling his forces, / A warrior of battle, he maintained his generosity . . . / A warrior no more lacking in valour than Elifri.'

Expressions such as these may be the perennial ingredients of elegy, but it was an altogether different matter to set them out in poetry in Gwynedd when Owain was still alive and enduring captivity at his brother's hands. The poet reaches beyond panegyric convention to give voice to uncompromising criticism of Llywelyn for disinheriting his brother. If God had forgiven man the crucifixion of Christ, could not brother forgive brother? It belonged to God alone, and none other, to disinherit a man: 'Ni fedd namyn Duw ddigyfoethi – dyn'.

These are the reflections of a creative writer, and one who had, perhaps, a close personal attachment to the hapless prince. But it is perfectly conceivable that there were others in Gwynedd who shared his reaction to the harshness, even the injustice, of the manner in which Llywelyn – 'ruler of Snowdonia' – had dealt with his brother. Owain and Llywelyn had shared the rule of Gwynedd by the advice of the wise men of the land, and a period of nine years would have been enough to enable Owain to earn the loyalty of the community of his lordship. He had, indeed, stayed away from Gwynedd for an exceedingly long while, but he had subsequently exercised lordship within the land and had the opportunity to create a bond with some, at least, of those he ruled. Men such as Maredudd ap Iorwerth and his son Gruffudd may, perhaps, be representative of those in Gwynedd whose loyalty to Owain, founded on the prince's legitimate accession to lordship and assured by a bond of a personal nature, were discomforted by his expropriation.[154] And Owain was the eldest son. It may have been a consideration which mattered in the estimation of many and underscored their loyalty. However complete his military triumph may have been at Bryn Derwin, Llywelyn had no choice but to keep his elder brother in close confinement for ever.

The same considerations made it imperative that, after Bryn Derwin, Llywelyn should make sure that he had a secure hold upon the whole of the territory under his lordship, and this could not be done without securing the loyalty of those who had previously been tenants of the prince now condemned to imprisonment. For fifteen years Gwynedd had suffered grievously from its wounding variances. The loyalties of the men of Gwynedd had been torn by the contest between Dafydd ap Llywelyn and Gruffudd ap Llywelyn before changed circumstances, and war with England, enabled Dafydd to pull the community together again. The land and its people had then been shared, somewhat precariously perhaps, between Owain ap Gruffudd and Llywelyn

---

[154] Maredudd witnessed Owain's charter to Ynys Lannog, 1247 (*MonAng*, v, 582; *CChR*, ii, 460; *H*, no. 150). Stephenson, *GG*, 98, 110–12, 132–3, 217, identifies him as a member of the lineage of Llywarch ap Brân and traces its affiliations; he cites an inquisition of 1284 (*CIPM*, ii, no. 538) which tells that Maredudd's son, Gruffudd ap Maredudd, had been allied with Owain against Llywelyn and had been forced to leave for England, abandoning named lands which he had of the gift of Owain.

ap Gruffudd until dissension, and the conflict by which it was resolved, placed on Llywelyn the grave responsibility of demonstrating that the security and stability of the land could be ensured neither by respecting the equality of brothers, nor the primacy of an eldest son, but only by vesting its destiny in a person with the determination to prove that he, rather than any other of the lineage of Llywelyn the Great, had the personal qualities needed. It was less out of conviction, or legal precept, than from dire and regrettable necessity that the leading men of Gwynedd had counselled the division of the territory between the brothers. Even so, in assuming lordship over the whole of Gwynedd Uwch Conwy by force, Llywelyn ap Gruffudd faced a considerable responsibility within the land itself, quite apart from the possibility of a reaction on the part of the king of England. That the community could prove responsive to capable and honourable lordship can hardly be doubted. It was for Llywelyn to establish himself as a worthy prince of Gwynedd Uwch Conwy, and he was in no hurry to look beyond its frontiers. The men of Perfeddwlad, many of whom had been his tenants in his younger days, had to await their hour of liberation.

Llywelyn paused for sixteen months after Bryn Derwin, an interval all the more significant for the fact that, after forcing the Conwy towards the end of 1256 and establishing himself in Perfeddwlad, he moved immediately to establish the broader supremacy in Wales which the king was ultimately forced to recognize. The swiftness of these movements is undeniable, and it is little wonder that Llywelyn left his mark on the nation's memory as one whose success was due to a fusion of inspiration and opportunism. The advance into Perfeddwlad, accomplished in a matter of days, could be seen as testimony to these qualities, a decisive response to the deeply felt resentment in the area in the aftermath of the Lord Edward's visit. In any assessment of Llywelyn ap Gruffudd, however, heed has to be paid to the restraint which he revealed in the wake of his initial triumph in Gwynedd Uwch Conwy. His caution is all the more impressive for the fact that discontent had been gathering in Perfeddwlad for some time. After the two princes had conceded their right beyond the Conwy in 1247 the territory formed 'the king's new conquest in Wales' (*novus conquestus regis Wallie*), and it was administered as an extension of the sphere of authority of the justice of Chester.[155] Of the Four Cantreds, Tegeingl, which lay east of the Clwyd, was an area which could be brought under royal administration without undue difficulty. It had been

---

[155] For the use of the term, or slight variants of it, see e.g. *CR, 1251–53*, 365; *CR, 1254–56*, 301; *CPR, 1247–58*, 260, 365. Royal administration in Perfeddwlad is examined in A. J. Roderick, 'The Four Cantreds: a study in administration', *B*, 10 (1939–41), 246–56.

subject to extraneous influences for centuries and had seen extensive alien settlement even before the Norman intrusions. Tegeingl – the name Englefield itself reflecting its exposure on the Cheshire frontier – had come under royal control not in 1247 but six years earlier. Provision was made for its administration, partly under the terms of a charter which ensured that its community should receive justice under the law of Wales and, indeed, that the king's new tenants should be relieved of some of the financial impositions made in the time of Llywelyn ap Iorwerth.[156] The new castle of Diserth was not to prove to be any great asset to the crown, but Rhuddlan remained an important centre for a *cantref* which, relatively small and compact and in close proximity to Chester, was a manageable extension of royal administration beyond the frontier.[157]

Extending the crown's administration over the *cantrefi* of Rhos, Rhufoniog and Dyffryn Clwyd in 1247 created problems of an entirely different order. Royal control of the area in the period immediately preceding the treaty of Woodstock appears to have been rather uncertain, despite the intervention which military command made possible. It was only after the princes' formal cession of their rights in the Four Cantreds that Henry began to exercise any effective regulation.[158] In the commote of Creuddyn, in Rhos, above the estuary of the Conwy, stood the castle of Degannwy, its defences recently strengthened and its potential value to the crown increased by the founding of a borough.[159] Degannwy was the only stronghold between the Conwy and the Clwyd, but its strategic position was not altogether advantageous, its suitability as an administrative centre somewhat doubtful. Moreover, the king's attempt to promote commercial activity in the shadow of the defences met with little success. Burgage lands were apportioned in 1251, the burgesses offered privileges modelled on those of Chester, but the community was not to prosper. The settlers faced considerable difficulties, anything but eased by the attentions of the justice of Chester, Alan la Zusche, who was warned by the king to do nothing at variance with the privileges that the king had granted to the nascent borough. Within two years of its enfranchisement the intrepid entrepreneurs of Degannwy had departed in poverty.[160] The failure of this attempt to create a privileged and alien settlement in Rhos served, in

---

[156] *CChR*, i, 274–5.

[157] *HW*, ii, 699, n. 35; *HKW*, ii, 644–5. The king may have invested substantially in the nearby 'rock of Rhuddlan' (*CLibR*, ii, 129) but the town was supported and remained an important centre (*CPR, 1247–58*, 171; *CLibR*, ii, 69–70).

[158] Tudur ab Ednyfed and others were released from prison and did homage in September 1246, but they were granted their lands in the Four Cantreds only in May 1247 (*LW*, 50–2; *CPR, 1242–47*, 510).

[159] *HKW*, ii, 624–6; *Inventory Caern*, i, 152–5; L. Alcock, 'Excavations at Degannwy Castle, Caernarvonshire, 1961–6', *Archaeological Journal*, 124 (1967), 190–201.

[160] *CR, 1251–53*, 149, 365.

fact, to remove what could have proved to be a disturbing factor, as the tensions between the settlers and indigenous communities of Perfeddwlad would show in the period 1277–82. But sources of dissension were not entirely removed. There was continuing friction between the communities of the *cantrefi* and the officers who represented royal authority. Complaints from Perfeddwlad had begun to be registered at court in the time of John de Grey, who served as justice of Chester until 1250. They grew more strident under his successor, who was required to return to the crown, for the right to exercise his office, twice the amount levied upon Grey.[161] Within a year of his appointment the complaints of men of Tegeingl, Rhos, Rhufoniog and Dyffryn Clwyd against Alan la Zusche's rule were brought to the king's notice. It was alleged that he had introduced new customs contrary to the agreement made between king and community after the war. Henry expressed surprise that he should venture to do so and warned him not to impose laws nor levy dues other than those already established in the time of Llywelyn ap Iorwerth. He called for a meeting in the autumn of 1251, when the difficulties could be considered in the presence of Zusche and members of the community of the area. Zusche was duly warned again to respect the 'Welsh liberties and customs' under which the inhabitants had been governed at the time of their surrender. He was to do nothing at variance with the agreement (*forma pacis*) which had been made between king and community.[162]

The precise meaning of the king's repeated references to his agreement with the community is uncertain. The treaty of Woodstock contained no guarantees to the inhabitants of the Four Cantreds, for the king would in no circumstances admit that the princes had any concern for the well-being of the area, and there is no known charter, comparable to that which the men of Tegeingl had secured after 1241, embodying assurances for the communities of the other areas. It was in these other areas that his difficulties were largely encountered. Henry found it necessary to distinguish between the situation in Tegeingl and that which prevailed in the other three *cantrefi* of Rhos, Rhufoniog and Dyffryn Clwyd. Documents from chancery sometimes refer, indeed, not to the Four Cantreds, but to the problems confronting the king in the Three Cantreds.[163] In 1253, though the king had established another commission to examine the situation in the area, the community remained dissatisfied, and the justice was warned again to exercise restraint in his

---

[161] Grey's commission was renewed at a farm of 500 marks a year, 17 June 1249; Alan la Zusche's commission dated from 2 July 1250 at 1,000 marks (*CPR, 1247–58*, 35, 70, 151, 182; comment in Paris, *ChronMaj*, v, 227). The increase is partly explained by the exchequer's revised estimate of the value of the Four Cantreds added to the justice's bailiwick.

[162] *CR, 1247–51*, 541, 552; *CR, 1251–53*, 4.

[163] *CR, 1247–51*, 552; *CR, 1251–3*, 4, 465, 467, 483.

dealings with the men of the Three Cantreds.[164] Explicit instructions were issued that Zusche should deal with the community according to the law and custom hitherto used there. It was thought inappropriate to place the men of the Three Cantreds under compulsion to serve the king in Gascony, though Henry was able to secure the service of Welshmen from other parts of Wales without any obvious anxiety.

By 1253, well before he included Perfeddwlad among the lands granted to Edward, Henry had good reason to appreciate that he needed to tread warily in his dealings with the community of his new conquest in Wales. He had, indeed, responded to the appeals which reached him; he had urged restraint upon Alan la Zusche and had insisted on some specific measures: thus assarting in the woods of the proprietors was to be allowed, and the tallage initially levied on the Four Cantreds was converted into a cornage to be raised once a year as it had been in the time of Llywelyn ap Iorwerth.[165] Whether the king's decisions and exhortations were enough to ensure reasonably equitable lordship in Perfeddwlad is difficult to judge. Historical assessment of the extent to which blame for injustice can be apportioned between those in immediate charge and their more distant superiors is never easy; distinguishing between the one and the other was not necessarily any easier for those directly affected by whatever was done in the name of authority. When Alan la Zusche made the chauvinistic remark, reported by Matthew Paris, that the Welsh were obediently reconciled to English laws he was carrying treasure intended for the king's coffers at Westminster. The money he delivered may have been no more than was required of him by the terms of his engagement with the king, but it is impossible to know whether the income, coming partly from the earldom of Chester and partly from the Four Cantreds no doubt, had been raised in a just manner or not.[166] For his part, Henry may not have been averse to appropriating the benefit of an exacting administration exercised in his name as long as it did not arouse the wrath of the communities from where it was derived. But it was a fine balance and, though he may have been repeatedly exorted to exercise caution, his officer had not been removed from office. Henry's role is difficult to assess, no less so the effect of his departure for Gascony. Henry left the kingdom to attend to the situation created in the duchy by the sustained resistance of a formidable Gascon alliance, under the leadership of Gaston de Béarn, to the rule of the seneschal,

---

[164] *CR, 1251–3*, 465, 467, 483.

[165] *CR, 1247–51*, 552; *CR, 1251–3*, 4, 365; issues from a tallage and a fine to secure exemption from an aid in *Cheshire Pipe Rolls*, 99–100. It is possible that the tallage was required in addition to the farm of the Four Cantreds.

[166] Paris, *ChronMaj*, v, 288. It is not easy to measure the degree of disaffection and assess whether the mood, when Edward received his grant from Henry in 1254, was 'more one of post-war calm than pre-war tension' (M. Prestwich, *Edward I* (London, 1988), 16).

Simon de Montfort, earl of Leicester.[167] His departure coincided with the presentation of Dafydd ap Gruffudd's claim to be counted as an heir to the patrimony of Gwynedd, and the potentially disturbing implications of the decision made in the king's name were not recognized by those who shared responsibility in royal councils in the critical period which followed. The same period saw increased tension in Perfeddwlad and, with Henry and Edward preoccupied with Gascony for much of the time, it is not easy to deduce to whom the officers in the Four Cantreds were in fact responsible, still less to make any estimate of the care with which members of council dealt with the problems which festered there.

Three years after the king's departure for Gascony discontent in Perfeddwlad finally burst forth in rebellion. Llywelyn ap Gruffudd intervened in the area in response to the inhabitants' earnest appeal for their release from the yoke of alien oppression. That is the Welsh chronicler's interpretation of the course of events. Llywelyn answered the appeal of the noble men of the area who, again like the Maccabees of old, proclaimed that they would rather die in war for their freedom than suffer their subjection to servitude by aliens.[168] These are the words of the chronicler, not the men of Perfeddwlad but, though English chroniclers, too, offer their clear-cut views on the cause of the rebellion, documentary testimony to the state of affairs between 1253 and 1256 is extremely slight. There is certainly a fuller record for the earlier years of Henry's rule over his new conquest. The sparse references in later chancery sources could reflect an easing of the position in the area, or alternatively the lack of evidence may be due to the fact that, after he conceded lordship over the area to Edward in 1254, complaints of injustices may have been directed to that administration and left no mark in chancery documents.[169] On neither matter can we be certain, nor is it possible to make a precise estimate of the changes in personnel which followed from Henry's grant.[170] Alan la Zusche remained in charge for some time, probably until the autumn of 1255, but it is not certain to what extent he and his successor,

---

[167] For the coincidence of Gascon and Welsh problems, J. B. Smith, 'Adversaries of Edward I: Gaston de Béarn and Llywelyn ap Gruffudd', in C. Richmond and I. Harvey (eds.), *Recognitions: Essays in Honour of Edmund Fryde* (Aberystwyth, 1996), 55–88. Resistance to Montfort's oppressive rule and the forging of a Gascon alliance c.1248–53 are noticed ibid., 60–6.

[168] *AC*, 90; *BT*, *Pen20*, 208; *Pen20Tr*, 110; *RBH*, 246–7.

[169] Edward's grant was issued on 14 February 1254, confirmed on 11 October (*CPR, 1247–58*, 270; *Foedera*, I, i, 297; *RG*, i, no. 2374). In Wales it consisted of 'the king's conquest of Wales' (described as Rhuddlan, Diserth and Degannwy with the remainder of Perfeddwlad), the Three Castles (Grosmont, Skenfrith and White Castle), Carmarthen, Cardigan, Builth and Montgomery.

[170] For the degree of responsibility vested in Edward, J. R. Studd, 'The Lord Edward and King Henry III', *BIHR*, 50 (1977), 4–19; idem, 'The Lord Edward's lordship of Chester, 1254–72', *Transactions of the Historic Society of Lancashire and Cheshire*, 128 (1979), 1–25.

Gilbert Talbot, were by now acting in response to the directions of Geoffrey de Langley, steward of Edward's possessions as a whole.[171] Perfeddwlad was indeed initially omitted from Langley's sphere of authority, but we cannot tell for how long. Langley most certainly bore the brunt of the English chroniclers' criticism for the eventual outcome.[172] Matthew Paris, who could find little virtue in the heir to the throne, placed the responsibility squarely upon Edward's henchman, Geoffrey de Langley, insisting that the Welsh rose in defence of their land and the recognition of their law.[173] The Dunstable chronicler was more specific and, reporting a boastful assertion on the part of Langley not very different in sentiment from that pinned on Zusche by Paris, held that Edward's steward was confident that he had the Welsh in the palm of his hand, and that he could proceed to introduce shire and hundred and place the community under English law.[174] Record evidence reveals no administrative changes of that nature, nothing comparable to the reorganization which led to the setting up of a county organization in south-west Wales from 1241. Nor is there documentary testimony to any decision to amend the laws under which the men of the Four Cantreds were governed. The surviving evidence points more clearly to concern on the part of the community for the protection of indigenous law and custom in the period before 1254 rather than later. The English chroniclers' assertions need to be treated with caution.[175] It is possible, even so, that Langley, directly or in-

---

[171] Zusche was ordered to give seisin of the Four Cantreds to Edward in February 1254 (*CPR, 1247–58*, 272; *RG*, i, no. 2388), but, still justice of Chester, he was made custodian of Edward's lands in Chester and north Wales on 10 May 1254, at an unchanged farm of 1,000 marks. Langley served as chief steward of Edward's lands (e.g. *RG*, i, nos. 4486, 4544), with the exception of Chester and north Wales. Zusche was told on 16 September 1255 to convey provisions held in Perfeddwlad to Edward's bailiff, Gilbert Talbot, to whom instructions are subsequently given as justice of Chester (*CR, 1254–56*, 134, 264–5, 373–3).

[172] Geoffrey de Langley and William de Wilton, named by the chroniclers as men who bore responsibility for the Welsh rebellion, were associated with Henry de la Mare in a commission to determine contentions between Owain and Llywelyn, and Owain's complaints against Zusche, 10 May 1255, a commission aborted by the conflict at Bryn Derwin (*CPR, 1247–58*, 432). Wilton, who served in south-west Wales from a base in Edward's lordships in Gwent in September 1256 (SC6/1094/11), joined Lestrange on a mission to Llywelyn, also probably thwarted, in November 1256 (*CR, 1256–59*, 104). For Langley, whose involvement in the Four Cantreds is extremely difficult to establish from record sources, P. R. Coss, 'Sir Geoffrey de Langley and the crisis of the knightly class in thirteenth-century England', *Past and Present*, 68 (1975), 3–37; for Wilton, H. W. Ridgeway, 'The Lord Edward and the Provisions of Oxford (1258): a study in faction', in P. R. Coss and S. D. Lloyd (eds.), *Thirteenth Century England*, 1 (Woodbridge, 1986), 92–3.

[173] Paris, *ChronMaj*, v, 592–3; cf. ibid., 613.

[174] *AnnDunst*, 200–1. *AnnTewk*, 158, places the responsibility for the burdens borne by the Welsh on Langley and Wilton, attributing to Langley the imposition of what was in effect a poll tax.

[175] For historians' reliance on chroniclers' testimony, T. F. Tout, *The Collected Papers*, ii (Manchester, 1932–4), 8–9 [Tout, *CP*]; Studd, 'Lordship of Chester', 18; Prestwich, *Edward I*, 17.

directly, with or without conceiving or enacting any major departure in policy, increased the rigour of an administration which had already incurred deep resentment in the time of Alan la Zusche.[176] The months before the rising of 1256, like the immediate prelude to that of 1282, may have seen a marked intensification of the animosity in the area. Chancery records may provide no evidence of specific charges levied against Langley, but it emerges later that Edward's steward found it prudent to secure a pardon for any offences which he had committed in Wales, so that he would not be subject to any charge on account of the war there.[177] It is thus likely that the English chroniclers were not entirely wrong to attribute to Langley the prime responsibility for the rebellion, though their estimate of what precisely provoked the movement is more questionable.

The extent of Edward's responsibility is difficult to judge. Already in Gascony when he received his grant of the lands of his apanage, he remained abroad until November 1255.[178] In the summer of the next year, just four months before the rebellion, he visited Cheshire and the Four Cantreds, travelling as far as Diserth and Degannwy.[179] It was his first visit. The outbreak of the rebellion may reflect a failure to ensure that the officers in the area exercised the authority deputized to them in a proper manner, but to whom among the royal personages those officers were responsible is far from clear. The difficulties encountered in gauging the extent of the authority conceded to Edward by his father are generally recognized, and there is the further difficulty of identifying those who shared responsibility in the period when both Henry and Edward were abroad. For part of this time – when matters concerning both Gwynedd Is Conwy and Gwynedd Uwch Conwy needed attention – Queen Eleanor and Richard, earl of Cornwall, were regents of the realm. Important decisions in council, arising from Dafydd ap Gruffudd's claim to the patrimony, were issued under the authority of the queen and Cornwall.[180] In addition, the queen had a particular care for her son's interests, which was noticeable quite early, and she continued to exercise some supervision over the administration of his estates after the grant of 1254.

---

[176] Henry on 8 November 1255 found it necessary to admonish Gilbert Talbot for ejecting men from assarts which Zusche had allowed (*CR, 1254–56*, 372–3).

[177] *CPR, 1247–58*, 616. Paris, *ChronMaj*, v, 593, relates a rumour that Langley would have to pay for the expense that Edward incurred in the war in Wales.

[178] Edward returned to England on 18 November 1255. For his reputation in Gascony, Powicke, *Henry III*, i, 208 ff.; J. P. Trabut-Cussac, *L'Administration anglaise en Gascogne sous Henry III et Edouard I de 1254 à 1307* (Geneva, 1972), 7–15.

[179] *AC(B)*, 90, places Edward's visit to the Four Cantreds 'about 1 August'; *AnnCestr*, 72, records that he came to Chester on 17 July and left for Wales three days later, returning 3 August.

[180] E.g. *CR, 1251–53*, 419; *CR, 1253–54*, 109–10. Henry de la Mare was sent to Wales in June 1254 on business concerning Edward, as the queen before her departure from the realm had ordered *viva voce* (ibid., 76).

Her influence on the choice of Edward's officers may have been considerable, and may even have been fateful. For whatever reason, Geoffrey Langley was indebted to the queen's generosity, and the pardon he secured for whatever he had done in Wales was issued at the instance of the queen.[181] Edward may have been less than satisfied with the ministrations of his parents' nominees. Stephen Bauzan, who was to incur retribution for the manner in which he furthered Edward's interests in south-west Wales, was similarly favoured by the queen, who also remembered him after he met his death in royal service.[182] Each of the two men who, in north-east and south-west Wales, are most readily identified with the promotion of Edward's advantage found favour with the queen of England. Queen Eleanor's influence is not easy to measure, but it is conceivable that, far from simply making a polite gesture, Llywelyn may have reflected his estimate of the queen's clout when, in making his peace proposals in due course, he offered a substantial amount of money, not only to Henry and Edward, but to Queen Eleanor as well.[183] When Edward made his first visitation of his father's conquest in Wales in July and August 1256 he came to a land for which both his parents had some responsibility, despite Henry's inclination to regard the issues which led to rebellion as his son's concerns.[184] The view that Edward placed the yoke of servitude upon the Welsh more securely than ever before, and created intense enmity on that account, was expressed by the English chronicler who was the least disposed to find virtue in the heir to the throne.[185]

Four months after his visit, Edward's authority in Perfeddwlad was utterly destroyed. Whether his visit served to exacerbate the situation still further we cannot tell; a failure to provide redress for wrongs already committed may have been enough. It may be, as the Welsh chronicler indicates, that men of influence in the community resolved that they could endure no more. It could equally be that Llywelyn ap Gruffudd judged that the situation in the lands on either side of the Conwy made this an opportune moment to strike. In November 1256, no doubt acting with full knowledge of the state of affairs in Perfeddwlad, perhaps responding to the entreaties of its people, but undoubtedly guided by his own estimate of what was now appropriate for Gwynedd as

---

[181] E101/349/7; *CPR, 1247–58*, 616. For the fact that it was the queen who asked for Langley's pardon and the possibility that Edward blamed men such as Langley for the rebellion in Perfeddwlad, Ridgeway, 'Provisions of Oxford', 89–99.

[182] E101/349/12, m. 11; *CChR*, ii, 23; Bauzan was in Eleanor's service by 1251 and two years later is described on the queen's jewel roll as a knight of the Lord Edward. He was with the queen and Edward in England until he accompanied them to Gascony in May 1254. Bauzan's career is described by H. W. Ridgeway in the *New Dictionary of National Biography*; for his role in south-west Wales, below, pp. 92–3, 97–9.

[183] Below, pp. 122–3.

[184] *CR, 1256–59*, 107–8, 112; Paris, *ChronMaj*, v, 594, 596–8.

[185] *FloresHist*, ii, 416–17. The Welsh chroniclers' statements are less specific than those of England, but *AC(B)*, 90 notices the rebellion immediately after Edward's visit.

a whole, Llywelyn took his forces through the River Conwy. Accompanied by Maredudd ap Rhys Gryg, himself resentful of the action taken against him in Deheubarth in Edward's name, he entered Perfeddwlad to complete a decisive military enterprise. The speed and the completeness of the action suggests strongly that he did so with the assent, if not at the instance, of the community which had over a period of several years reported grievances which are, to some degree at least, recorded in the muniments of the royal chancery.[186]

The problems of Perfeddwlad, arising from the relations between the community and those who represented royal authority, were in large measure particular to that area, but they cannot be studied entirely in isolation from the stresses which were felt in Gwynedd Uwch Conwy. When Llywelyn's forces forded the Conwy they entered a land which had been an integral part of the patrimony of his predecessors, princes of Gwynedd, and he was later to stress the essential unity of the lands east and west of the river.[187] Llywelyn had himself entered into a formal engagement whereby he ceded all claims beyond the Conwy, but the treaty of 1247 acknowledged the difficulties implicit in establishing a political boundary along the river. Henry and the princes may have agreed upon the Conwy as a boundary, and had, indeed, agreed to divide the river itself between them, but they had to recognize that there were interests, and hence the possibility of problems, which traversed the frontier.[188] There were proprietors who had territorial stakes on both sides and who were thus tenants of both king and princes, and the problems which arose between these two spheres of authority were broached in the letter which, as we have seen, Owain and Llywelyn dispatched to the king a little later.[189] Even with the utmost goodwill on both sides there might be difficulties. From Henry's point of view it was especially important that princes beyond the Conwy had no pretext for interference on his side of the river, but his failure to ensure that his tenants in Perfeddwlad were governed in a manner which did not leave them alienated left him exposed to intercession, even intervention, on the part of the princes. Intervention became more likely when, in 1255, one prince had the better of the other, leaving Henry's settlement of north Wales impaired in one important respect. From that point onward it was evident, even more so than before, that any measure of misgovernance in Perfeddwlad could undermine that settlement as a whole and, in his exhortations to his officers to ensure that they did not provoke the

---

[186] Llywelyn advanced into Perfeddwlad at the beginning of November (*CR, 1256–59*, 107–8). *AnnCestr*, 73, says that Llywelyn released Dafydd about the feast of All Saints (1 November) and that they attacked Tegeingl; Paris, *ChronMaj*, v, 592, has a similar date. *AC(B)*, 90–1, states that he took possession of the land, with the exception of Diserth and Degannwy, 'within a week'.

[187] For the important statements of late 1282, below, pp. 189–90, 543–4.

[188] *LW*, 7–8; *CPR, 1232–47*, 501.

[189] *CAC*, 32–3; *RL*, ii, 64–6; above, n. 112.

community, Henry specifically warned that impositions should not be at variance with the terms of the agreement which the king had made with the Welsh. It has already been intimated that this may allude to an understanding with the men of Perfeddwlad of which we have no knowledge. But the essence of the king's instruction might equally have been the message that injustice on the párt of officers in that area was liable to disturb the broader settlement of which the treaty of Woodstock was the cornerstone. Apart, however, from the exploitation and the neglect which created the conditions for rebellion in Perfeddwlad, the king's council made a decision, already noticed, which has a further bearing on our understanding of the manner whereby he undermined the very stability that it was incumbent upon him to preserve.

This was the decision to take the homage of Dafydd ap Gruffudd and to consider Dafydd to be, along with Owain and Llywelyn, one of 'the heirs of North Wales'. The council's action could be seen to be a necessary consequence of the fact that in 1247 Henry had taken the homage of those of the heirs of north Wales who had by then come of age; those who were still under age, Dafydd and Rhodri, would be received into the king's fealty at the appropriate time. The decision made in 1253 in respect of Dafydd meant that three heirs, and a fourth no doubt in due course, would share the constricted territory of Gwynedd Uwch Conwy, facilitating a fragmentation of the land which Henry may have contemplated with some relish. Reflecting on the same prospect, the princes could well have envisaged an alternative solution which, while providing for the heirs of north Wales one by one, would obviate the stressful situation which would be created if new lordships were to be created in Gwynedd Uwch Conwy. Perfeddwlad – Gwynedd Is Conwy – remained under the king's lordship. A part of this land might reasonably be apportioned to the younger sons of Gruffudd ap Llywelyn. Llywelyn is known to have been engaged in transactions with the king before Bryn Derwin. Although we know nothing of the substance of any proposals made by Llywelyn, they may well have offered an alternative solution to that which the royal government commended.[190] It would not be unreasonable to postulate that Llywelyn had attempted to persuade the king to make provision for Dafydd ap Gruffudd in Perfeddwlad, and it might be remembered that, shortly before launching his campaign there, Llywelyn released Dafydd from captivity and that the younger brother joined him in the enterprise.[191] Dafydd may have been released with the specific intention of enabling him to participate in a campaign which, through common endeavour on their part, would secure precisely that provision beyond the

---

[190] *CAC*, 50–1; *RL*, ii, 312–14, considered more fully later, refers to the pleas (*querela*) he had submitted to the king before the Four Cantreds were granted to Edward.

[191] *AnnCestr*, 72; above, n. 186.

Bryn Derwin

Conwy that the king had not seen fit to make for his new tenant-in-chief. One of the grievances which Llywelyn enumerated was the king's decision to grant Edward the Four Cantreds 'making no mention of the prince's pleas'.[192] The estate which Llywelyn bestowed on Dafydd in the aftermath of the campaign consisted very largely of lands in Perfeddwlad, and it was in the same area that he found himself once more when he repaired to Llywelyn after a period in the king's fealty.[193]

There were further transactions at a later stage which tend to support the view that the prince was looking to Perfeddwlad for an alleviation of the consequences of King Henry's wish to provide for Dafydd, and perhaps Rhodri. In his letter to Richard of Cornwall, written after his advance into Perfeddwlad, Llywelyn referred to proposals which he had put to the king on what were clearly two occasions. The first was said to be before the grant of the Four Cantreds to Edward, and hence before Bryn Derwin, and concerned the proposition already considered. On a second occasion, according to his account, Llywelyn was prepared to 'offer' the Four Cantreds to the king if he were prepared to recognize the prince's lordship in the remainder of Gwynedd.[194] Llywelyn was in no position to 'offer' the land to the king of England until after 1256, but the phraseology may admit the possibility that the prince had been prepared to hold back from Perfeddwlad if Henry were to agree to make provision for Dafydd in that area. Llywelyn maintained that he had received no reply to his proposal and we cannot tell precisely when the proposal was made. However, a powerful delegation went to the king on Llywelyn's behalf in the summer of 1256, testimony to the fact that the prince had negotiated with the king, not only before Bryn Derwin, but afterwards as well, and that in both periods he had submitted proposals.[195] It may thus be pertinent to notice that, when the attack on the Four Cantreds was imminent, Henry hastened to get a message to Llywelyn so that they might discuss proposals (*oblata*) which the prince had put to him. It would be reasonable to conclude that John Lestrange was sent to Gwynedd when it dawned upon the king's council that Llywelyn was on the point of invading.[196] Though we have no means of knowing what the envoy was empowered to negotiate, it would

---

[192] *CAC*, 50–1; *RL*, ii, 312–14. This important letter was written to Cornwall in response to a missive from the earl conveyed by Dominican friars. It has been noticed already that Cornwall was regent of England during Henry's absence in Gascony, 1253–4, when Dafydd's claims in Gwynedd were the subject of exchanges between Llywelyn and the court.

[193] Below, pp. 154, 180–1, 374.

[194] *CAC*, 50–1; *RL*, ii, 312–14.

[195] *CPR, 1247–58*, 470: a delegation of Gruffudd ab Ednyfed Fychan, Cynwrig ab Ednyfed, Dafydd ab Einion and Iorwerth ap Gwrgunan.

[196] *CR, 1256–59*, 104 (2 November); Lestrange was to be accompanied by William de Wilton. The attack had occurred, or was known to be imminent, when the letter was issued.

be likely that he was sent to discuss matters of importance which the king had neglected to consider until the eleventh hour. They were, on the king's explicit admission, matters concerning his brothers on which Llywelyn had sent messengers on several occasions and submitted proposals.[197] No one would have greater cause to wonder at the king's ineptitude than Lestrange himself, who could recall Henry's failure to respond to successive requests for the resources to meet an earlier Welsh challenge, and would remember the harsh treatment meted out to the very men who had urged prudent action in good time.[198] In a subsequent letter which may have been written in sincerity but which might reasonably have been read with some scepticism, Henry expressed his surprise that Llywelyn, in whom among all the magnates of Wales he had particular confidence, should have attacked Edward's lands not only contrary to his fealty but despite the discussion (*proloquio*) which had proceeded between king and prince.[199] Whatever delegation of authority Henry had intended by the grant to Edward in 1254, and whatever Edward contributed to the calamitous outcome of events two years later, the king bore the ultimate responsibility. The need to ensure equitable and sensitive government in Perfeddwlad had been abundantly clear in the period before 1254, and the king was certainly responsible for the governance of north Wales as a whole. It was to king and council that Llywelyn addressed his successive requests for important policy decisions which would have a bearing on Gwynedd Uwch Conwy and Is Conwy alike, and he did so to no purpose. Once more, Henry had tarried too long.

In entering Perfeddwlad Llywelyn ap Gruffudd, on the one hand, acted in response to the need to relieve the community of the land from the harsh lordship which they had endured under the officers appointed by Henry and by Edward and in his name. When neither the king nor the heir to the throne was able to alleviate their difficulties, conflict became inevitable. On the other hand, Llywelyn responded to a fatal failure on the part of the king to give proper consideration to the difficulties confronting the dynasty of Gwynedd which the prince had tried to put to him in successive proposals. Bryn Derwin had not entirely resolved those problems, and Llywelyn was never to secure a complete solution, but the prince had sought the means by which, with the king's understanding, they might be alleviated. When Henry espoused Dafydd as an heir to Gwynedd, without providing for him in that part of Gwynedd which lay in the crown's possession, he undermined the stability of

---

[197] *CR, 1256–59*, 104: 'ad tractandum cum Lewelino filio Griffini super negociis fratres ipsius Lewelini contingentibus, de quibus idem Lewelinus nuncios suos ad regem frequenter destinavit et oblata per eos regi fecit'.

[198] Above, n. 64.

[199] *CR, 1256–59*, 107–8 (17 November); the sentiments are expressed again ibid., 112 (10 December).

the entire settlement he had achieved in north Wales. When he proceeded to invest Edward with the Four Cantreds he compounded his difficulties still more. Doing nothing either to ease the problems of the dynasty nor to ameliorate the misery of the communities of the Four Cantreds, he effectively placed Gwynedd in its entirety at Llywelyn's will. It was, as Llywelyn told Richard of Cornwall, by the advice of the magnates of Wales (*magnates Wallie*) that he went to Perfeddwlad, taking possession of a land which belonged to him and his heirs by right.[200] After Bryn Derwin he paused a while and, when the time and the circumstances were right, he forded the Conwy. He entered the land where, at a time of great anxiety in Gwynedd, he had first established lordship, and he went forth to restore the principality to its furthermost frontiers and take responsibility for the well-being of its people.

---

[200] Full text, *RL*, ii, 312–14, contains important features that cannot be gathered from the precis, *CAC*, 50–1, particularly the forceful phraseology of the last paragraph.

CHAPTER 3

Supremacy

VICTORY in Perfeddwlad was won swiftly and, exercising authority over Gwynedd in its entirety, Llywelyn ap Gruffudd stood poised for the advances which were to make 1257 a year of striking achievement. 'Llew Gwynedd, gwynfaith ardalau, / Llywiadr pobl Powys a'r Deau' – the poet Llygad Gŵr, in an exuberant celebration, recounted the triumphs by which the prince brought Gwynedd, Powys and Deheubarth into a new unity under his rule.[1] His successes during this year were secured largely through force of arms, and Llygad Gŵr was not the only poet to strike a militant note in addressing a powerful prince who stood conspicuously in the tradition of the defenders of his nation. Earlier in his life Dafydd Benfras had found inspiration in the great deeds of Llywelyn ap Iorwerth, writing in conscious emulation of the work in which Aneurin had extolled the warriors of an age that had already become, by the thirteenth century, a distant heroic era. Dafydd Benfras had then shared the tribulation which Gwynedd had endured after the death of its mighty prince, but now in his later years he could attune his verse to the new resurgence of princely power, rehearsing the events which brought Llywelyn ap Gruffudd to supremacy over the whole extent of the land from the Cheshire border to the lower reaches of Dyfed.[2] Nor were the poets of his own nation the only commentators to marvel at Llywelyn's triumph. Writing in the heart of England, the Dunstable chronicler sensed that the person he called the second Llywelyn was a prince most eminent among men and, sturdy in war, a man to whom the Welsh nation already adhered.[3] It would be a pity not to trace the course of events which brought poet and chronicler to commemorate the prince's achievements as he

---

[1] *GBF*, 24. 133–4.
[2] *GDB*, 24–7 (Llywelyn ap Iorwerth); 34–5 (Llywelyn ap Gruffudd). No. 34 is a brief eulogy, no. 35 is an extended celebration of the prince's ascendancy (*cynnydd*), enumerating his military triumphs.
[3] *AnnDunst*, 200: 'Lewelinus secundus, vir pulcherrimus, et bello strenuus, qui omnes Walenses quasi sibi conglutinatos'.

extended his authority from his patrimonial lands to become a power over the greater part of independent Wales. But, in offering an interpretation of this crucial phase in the prince's assertion of power, we need, too, to consider the problems which arose in the very hour of triumph as Llywelyn strove to reconcile his political aspirations with the continuing concern of the lords of Powys and Deheubarth for the traditional interests of their lineages. However forceful the power which inspired the poets' work, it was hardly possible for Llywelyn, any more than it had been so for his grandfather, to establish a broad authority unless he could create a will among the lords of Wales to commit themselves to binding ties of loyalty. Some of them were reluctant to be drawn from their fealty to the king of England, and the king was equally loathe to forgo that age-old allegiance which had hitherto been severed only briefly in the period of Llywelyn ap Iorwerth. After taking note of his early triumphs we shall need to pause and take account of the years in which Llywelyn exercised a marked restraint, evidently nurturing the hope that the king might be prevailed upon to recognize the position which the prince had won for himself, and that he might be able to transform an unstable truce into a lasting peace between the kingdom of England and a principality of Wales.

Early in December 1256, the whole of Perfeddwlad in his possession with the exception of Diserth and Degannwy, Llywelyn turned south to Meirionnydd. He may have hoped that its lord would see fit to join forces with him but Llywelyn ap Maredudd did not respond to the prince's call. Forced into exile he was constrained to commend himself to the king as one who had preferred fidelity to unfaithfulness and plead for support from the royal exchequer. He acknowledged, too, that it was only by the aid of God and the king of England that he could ever recover his patrimony.[4] Meirionnydd was brought under Llywelyn ap Gruffudd's direct lordship, giving him a dominion which extended from the Dee to the Dyfi. Llywelyn lost no time in fording the Dyfi to enter Deheubarth, and the alacrity with which he entered the southern province may have a particular explanation. Even before he had embarked on his campaign in Perfeddwlad, Llywelyn had secured the alliance of Maredudd ap Rhys Gryg, and it might be reasonably contended that it was the understanding between these two men that provided the impetus for the new unity forged in Wales during the course of the year 1257.[5] Their association may have had its origins in the period when each of

---

[4] *AC*, 88–9, 91; *BT, Pen20*, 206–8; *Pen20Tr*, 109–10; *RBH*, 244–7; *CAC*, 28–9; *RL*, ii, 123–4; *CLibR*, iv, 436, 472, 506. Llywelyn, who succeeded in 1255, was the son of Gwenllian, daughter of Maelgwn Fychan, who died at Llanfihangel Gelynrhod the previous year and was buried at Strata Florida; the annalist's interest in the marriage connection may help to explain his later reference to Llywelyn's death. For his son, J. G. Edwards, 'Madog ap Llywelyn, the Welsh leader in 1294–5', *B*, 13 (1948–50), 207–10.

[5] *AC*, 90–1; *BT, Pen20*, 208; *Pen20Tr*, 110; *RBH*, 246–7.

them was allied with Dafydd ap Llywelyn and, if the link was broken when the lords of Deheubarth were persuaded to return to the king's fealty in 1246, there were soon indications that Maredudd was becoming restive once more.[6] It would be safe to conclude that Llywelyn and Maredudd ap Rhys Gryg were the real authors of the compact of 1251 by which Llywelyn and Owain, from Gwynedd, and Maredudd and Rhys Fychan, from Ystrad Tywi, agreed to stand together against all living men as though they were brothers.[7] At that time they may have been primarily concerned to resist interference from outside, but their respective provinces were soon to witness severe internal conflict: within four years Owain ap Gruffudd found himself dispossessed and imprisoned by his brother; within another year Maredudd and Rhys Fychan were locked in vengeful contention.

The occasion for the dissension in Ystrad Tywi is not easy to discern, but it may have had its origins in the division of the patrimony of Rhys Gryg. Dinefwr and an extensive portion of Ystrad Tywi had come to the possession of Rhys Mechyll and then Rhys Fychan, son and grandson of Rhys Gryg. The remainder of Ystrad Tywi, a smaller portion centred on Dryslwyn, was held by Maredudd ap Rhys Gryg and inequality in the extent of the two estates may explain the subsequent discord. On the other hand, it is conceivable that Maredudd was bent upon something more than correcting an unequal partition of lands, for at an early date, promptly after the death of Llywelyn ap Iorwerth, Maredudd had made a bid to extend his possessions in Ystrad Tywi. He may, even then, have aspired to nothing less than the reconstitution of his father's patrimony, to be ruled from the ancestral court of Dinefwr.[8] Frustrated on that occasion he would try again and, whatever inspired the spirited agreement made between the four lords in 1251, it is evident that conflict soon erupted between Maredudd and Rhys Fychan. Maredudd was so worsted that he failed to maintain his hold even upon his own territory. He forfeited his inheritance, the chronicler remarks, through trickery (*cavillatio*) on the part of Rhys Fychan and the English. It would seem that Stephen Bauzan, the Lord Edward's officer in south-west Wales, was acting in the interests of Rhys Fychan when he brought substantial forces, mounted men and infantry, to Ystrad Tywi in September 1256.[9] This means that Edward's soldiers, drawn from his lordships throughout south Wales and from Ireland, were operating against Maredudd ap Rhys Gryg on

---

[6] J. B. Smith, 'The "Cronica de Wallia" and the dynasty of Dinefwr', *B*, 20 (1962–4), 268–70; idem, 'The origins of the revolt of Rhys ap Maredudd', *B*, 21 (1964–6), 151–2.

[7] *LW*, 160–1; above, pp. 67–8.

[8] J. B. Smith, 'Cronica de Wallia', 265–9. Rhys Gryg (d. 1233) had been succeeded by Rhys Mechyll (d. 1246), followed by his son Rhys Fychan (d. 1271).

[9] *AC*, 90–1; Bauzan's royal connections are noticed above, p. 84.

the very eve of Llywelyn ap Gruffudd's advance into Perfeddwlad.[10] In these highly disturbed conditions the agreement of 1251 became meaningful for two of the four princes who had put their seals to the document: in November 1256 Maredudd joined Llywelyn for the assault upon Perfeddwlad; a month later Llywelyn embarked with Maredudd upon a campaign in Deheubarth. Apart from any other objective, the movement had the specific purpose of restoring to Maredudd his patrimony in Ystrad Tywi. On their way, undoing everything which had been accomplished by Nicholas de Molis and 'the army of Dyfed' some years before, the army of Gwynedd took possession of the commote of Perfedd, the land about Llanbadarn Fawr administered by Edward's officers. By then, if not before, Maredudd ab Owain had come to appreciate where his duty and advantage lay. He met Llywelyn at Morfa Mawr on 5 December to establish a concord that was to remain unsullied while he lived. His adherence effectively ensured that Ceredigion was secured for the new alliance.[11] The army, growing in strength perhaps as it moved south, went directly to Ystrad Tywi. Maredudd ap Rhys Gryg was able to recover his territory and also took possession of the lands which had hitherto been held by Rhys Fychan. Neither Rhys Fychan's resort to royal support nor Stephen Bauzan's intervention had proved to be of any avail. Maredudd, enabled to govern an entire Ystrad Tywi from Dinefwr, reaped the handsome rewards of his adherence to Llywelyn ap Gruffudd. The chronicler duly relates that Llywelyn gave Rhys Fychan's lands to Maredudd 'keeping nothing for himself but fame and honour'.[12]

The accession of strength brought by the adherence of Maredudd ap Rhys Gryg and Maredudd ab Owain enabled Llywelyn to assert his power in a region where he had hitherto found little to encourage him. Gruffudd ap Madog of Powys Fadog, though he had entered into a sworn confederacy with Llywelyn in 1250, remained steadfast in his loyalty to the crown. It seems that Llywelyn, even before he entered the Four Cantreds, had been able to exercise some influence in Edeirnion and he may have drawn Gruffudd ap Madog's brother, Madog Fychan, into his alliance, but he does not appear to have made any appreciable headway in Powys Fadog. It is possible that,

[10] Substantial forces from Edward's lordships in Gwent were sent to the Llandovery area, September 1256 (A. J. Roderick and W. Rees, 'Ministers' accounts for the lordships of Abergavenny, Grosmont and White Castle, 1256–57', *SWMRS*, 3 (1954), 21–47). The forces' objectives are uncertain but there was conflict in Ystrad Tywi that summer, possibly due to an attempt by Rhys Fychan to secure by arms what he had sought by a plea *coram rege* in 1247, when he held that Maredudd had seized Llandovery and associated lands by the aid of the king's enemies (KB26/159, mm. 2d, 3). For forces from Ireland, below, nn. 30, 58.

[11] *AC*, 91; *BT*, *Pen20*, 208; *Pen20Tr*, 110; *RBH*, 246–7. Llywelyn is said to have given Maredudd ab Owain the portion of Ceredigion which belonged to Edward.

[12] *AC*, 91; *BT*, *RBH*, 246–9; inaccurately in *Pen20*, 208; *Pen20Tr*, 110; see note *Pen20Tr*, 209 for confusion between Builth and Ystrad Tywi.

having no reason to believe that Gruffudd would respect his earlier pledge, Llywelyn carried war to his lordship promptly after the annexation of Perfeddwlad, launching the attack that Henry III had feared immediately after Bryn Derwin.[13] Matthew Paris says so specifically, and conveys that Gruffudd ap Madog was forced to flee to England. The Welsh chronicler who, as we shall see, provides a graphic account of events in Deheubarth and Powys Wenwynwyn, makes no mention of Powys Fadog. Chancery records provide no certainty, but Gruffudd was compensated with land in England for losses that he had suffered in Wales, and the fact that Llywelyn was able to carry war to Kinnerley suggests that he had penetrated a part, if not the whole extent, of Powys Fadog.[14] He may, even so, have spared the territory the onslaught which he made on Powys Wenwynwyn. Llywelyn had no expectation of any response to whatever overtures he might make to Gruffudd ap Gwenwynwyn, only every anticipation of implacable opposition. So, early in 1257, with Maredudd ap Rhys and Maredudd ab Owain at his side, Llywelyn drove into Powys Wenwynwyn, reaching as far as Welshpool and setting fire to the town.[15] Gruffudd was forced to call to his aid the forces gathered under the Lord Edward's banner at Montgomery at the command of John Lestrange the younger and John FitzAlan. It was the prince's first confrontation with royal forces in that sector of the march which, perhaps more than any other, would come to represent the main arena of Anglo-Welsh conflict in this period. The English forces advanced westward and took up a position in the low-lying ground between the Severn and Berriew but, if the chronicler provides an objective account, they made an undignified retreat beyond the river without engaging the prince's forces in any a major encounter. Gruffudd ap Gwenwynwyn was able to retain possession of the castle of Welshpool and some of the adjacent lands, but much the greater part of his extensive lordship fell to Llywelyn's possession.[16] Further south, and possibly part of the triumphant campaign which he had waged in Deheubarth a little earlier, Llywelyn took possession of Gwerthrynion, abjuring his solemn pledge to Ralph Mortimer and initiating the struggle with Roger Mortimer that was to remain an important factor in Welsh political affairs for

---

[13] *LW*, 148; *CR, 1254–56*, 204. Paris, *ChronMaj*, v, 597, 613, conveys that Llywelyn attacked Powys Fadog immediately after taking Perfeddwlad; *HW*, ii, 719, accepts the account with caution. It appears that Owain ap Bleddyn, Madog Fychan and Gruffudd ap Iorwerth, all of Edeirnion, were in touch with Llywelyn and possibly in his fealty by July 1256 (*LW*, 35).

[14] *CIM*, no. 1059. Fears of an attack on the Shropshire border early in November may reflect the situation position in Powys Fadog.

[15] *AC*, 91–5; *BT, Pen20*, 208–9; *Pen20Tr*, 110–11; *RBH*, 246–51; *HW*, ii, 718–20. The attack was launched 'after Epiphany' (6 January 1257), leaving Gruffudd with some lands in the Severn valley and part of Caereinion. Pressure was maintained on Montgomery, with a further attack early in April (*AC*, 93).

[16] For Gruffudd's position thereafter, below, pp. 157–60.

the remainder of their lives. He took possession of the lordship of Builth and placed it in the custody of Maredudd ab Owain.[17] But if the lords of Deheubarth were engaged in Powys early in the year there was no undisturbed respite in their own lands. Stephen Bauzan activated the lords of the lordships on the fringes of Deheubarth, Nicholas FitzMartin of Cemais, Richard de Carew and Patrick de Chaworth of Cydweli among them, and not without good reason.[18] Before the end of February Llywelyn ap Gruffudd, in person it seems, returned to Deheubarth and launched an attack which carried his power into Cydweli and Carnwyllion and even into Gower, where he burned the castle of Swansea.[19] The chronicler's account of the discomfiture of the English inhabitants, and the subjection of the Welsh to the prince's power, graphically recalls the onslaught inflicted by Llywelyn ap Iorwerth in this area forty years before.

Even so, our knowledge of the prince's movements is incomplete, for neither chancery records nor the chroniclers of England provide anything like a comprehensive account of the far-flung conflicts of the winter of 1256–7, though in their several ways they convey something of the magnitude of the challenge which Llywelyn now represented. On the Welsh side we are largely dependent on the Strata Florida chronicler and, though his account of these events is unusually lengthy, it is only fortuitously, by means of what he gathered by way of the Cistercian agencies, that he was able to compile a record of the prince's activities. The incidents might not always be vital engagements, but they are indicative of the vigour of the conflict when, for instance, he recounts the attack which took Gwyn ap Madog and the men of Arwystli to Montgomery, then to withdraw and lure their pursuing enemies to their destruction near the grange of Gwern-y-go.[20] This was no major battle, perhaps one among a host of minor incidents in this period, but the memoir is instructive if only for the fact that major marcher positions can be seen to have come under pressure. It is pertinent, too, to notice that these positions were subjected to attack not simply by armies drawn from the distances of Gwynedd or Deheubarth, but by forces raised in areas close by and from among men, possibly tenants of lords opposed to Llywelyn, who were prepared to wage war in alliance with the prince and in his name. From the early months of 1257 Roger Mortimer, Humphrey de Bohun, Patrick de Chaworth and William de Valence were among those engaged in the march,

---

[17] *AC*, 91; *BT*, *Pen20*, 208–9; *Pen20Tr*, 110; *RBH*, 246–9.

[18] *AC*, 92, names them among those responsible for damages to the Cistercian house of Whitland, 5 February.

[19] *AC*, 92–3 (25 February); an attack on Gower, with the burning of Swansea and the submission of the Welsh of the lordship, is attributed in the Glamorgan annals in BL, Royal MS 6 Bxi, f. 108ᵛ to Rhys Fychan at an unspecified date; it would have followed his defection from the crown in early June, shortly before the battle of Cymerau, noticed later.

[20] *AC*, 95.

suggesting that pressure was exerted on an exceedingly broad front.[21] The Lord Edward, charged with responsibility for the defensive measures now urgently needed, was desperately short of funds. He was hampered, too, by a reluctance on the part of the marchers to come to his assistance, if we can accept the veracity of the account in which Matthew Paris was moved to a fulsome commendation of the virtues of the nation now galvanized in support of Prince Llywelyn ap Gruffudd.[22]

Llywelyn had evidently taken little heed of the king's exhortations, first issued when he heard of the prince's invasion of the Four Cantreds, that he should withhold from further conflict.[23] Writing again at the beginning of December, Henry referred to the prince's failure to reply, though he was aware that Llywelyn had written to the justice of Chester to the effect that, if he were to send messengers, he would be able to show that he had not transgressed against the king.[24] Llywelyn may well have conveyed that his quarrel was specifically one with Edward. The king, employing in successive letters a very similar phraseology, conveyed his astonishment that Llywelyn, in whom more than any other of the magnates of Wales he had had the utmost confidence, had resorted to violent action entirely at variance with the discussion (*proloquio*) which had been proceeding between them. Again and again Henry inadvertently acknowledged that he would have been well advised to consider the matters which Llywelyn had placed before him. He promised full justice for any wrong which Edward and his men had done to Llywelyn's men. He again urged Llywelyn to withdraw from the land he had invaded and, more realistically, he sent two Dominican friars with a view to opening a channel of communication between them. Llywelyn was once more prevailed upon to reply to his letter and, before the year was out, he sent letters to the king by the abbot of Basingwerk.[25]

He evidently conveyed his wish to reach an understanding with the king, and Henry assured him again that he would do justice on whatever matters troubled him. In due course Llywelyn would put new proposals to the king and place his whole emphasis on his wish for a genuine peace settlement, but not now. Writing in response to an initiative on the part of Richard of Cornwall, he conveyed that the proposals which he had once made, and which might have provided a basis for a settlement, were no longer on offer.

---

[21] By January 1257 Patrick de Chaworth, Humphrey de Bohun and Roger Mortimer were among those engaged in Wales (e.g. *CPR, 1247–58*, 538, 586); contingents were sent from Edward's lordships in Gwent to Brecon, Hay, Huntington and Radnor from 4 March (*SWMRS*, 3 (1954), 43).

[22] Paris, *ChronMaj*, v, 592–3, 597–8, 613–14, 633. Support for Edward is indicated in chancery enrolments, e.g. *CR, 1256–59*, 3, 35, 60, 128; *CLibR*, iv, 417, 419, 439.

[23] *CR, 1256–59*, 107–8 (17 November).

[24] Ibid., 112 (12 December).

[25] Ibid., 115 (Henry's letter, 2 January 1257).

There was no question now of yielding Perfeddwlad. His previous proposition, that he would hold back from Perfeddwlad if he were assured of possession of the remainder of Gwynedd, no longer stood. The proposals (*oblata*) put before the king in the period between Bryn Derwin and the invasion of Perfeddwlad were no longer negotiable. He would now negotiate for a permanent peace, or at the very least an extended truce, on the entirely new basis established by the dramatic extension of his power.[26] Courteous and earnest in its expression of his wish for a peaceful settlement, the letter addressed to Cornwall is the first in a series of important statements of his position. As yet he did not have sufficient incentive to bring hostilities to a close; he sensed the difficulties in which his opponents were placed and his earlier offers were withdrawn. Shortly before Easter 1257 Llywelyn returned to Gwynedd from Deheubarth, but after a brief interval he was waging war with renewed vigour on the whole front from Cardigan to Montgomery.[27] To men of an older generation the military movements of the winter of 1256–7 would have recalled those which had carried the power of Llywelyn ap Iorwerth to the furthermost parts of Wales. They brought a realization that the second Llywelyn was no less forceful than the first. When, in the early summer, a force under royal command was deployed in a major counter-offensive it met with a disaster which was known about far and wide and long remembered.

Forced into defensive measures along a wide front, the king was still able to sense that the extension of Llywelyn's power beyond the confines of Gwynedd had owed much to the understanding between Llywelyn and Maredudd ap Rhys Gryg. He would use every means to break this power and his first effort was a military venture in which substantial forces were deployed. It was designed to restore to Rhys Fychan the lands which he had been forced, by Llywelyn's intervention, to cede to Maredudd. The author of the plan was probably Stephen Bauzan who, after the reverse he had suffered in the area the previous year, had reasons of his own for a new campaign in Ystrad Tywi. Even so, Bauzan would not have embarked on a major enterprise without the

---

[26] *CAC*, 50–1; *RL*, ii, 312–14. This important letter is undated; the summer of 1267 suggested in *RL*, ii, 312–14, is unlikely; *HW*, ii, 720, n. 21, suggests March 1257, endorsed in *CAC*, 51; Powicke, *Thirteenth Century*, 401; N. Denholm-Young, *Richard of Cornwall* (Oxford, 1947), 89. There is a close resemblance between these proposals and those which the bishop of Bangor put to the king in the autumn of 1259, and the earl is known to have returned from Germany and to have been active January 1259–June 1260 (Denholm-Young, *Richard of Cornwall*, 98–103). But the tenor of the letter suggests a date soon after Llywelyn took Perfeddwlad. Paris, *ChronMaj*, v, 613, says that the earl communicated with Llywelyn after his election as king of Germany (January 1257), and Llywelyn sent envoys to him in February (*CPR, 1247–58*, 541). A date February–March 1257 seems very likely.

[27] *AC*, 93, states that Llywelyn made for home before Easter (8 April). Cornwall's departure for Germany may have occasioned a break in Llywelyn's diplomatic link with the court.

consent of Henry and Edward, and there can be no doubt that the catastrophe that occurred in Ystrad Tywi was a severe blow to the authority and prestige of the crown. Only rarely did it fall to the Welsh chronicler to describe a military triumph on the scale of the conflict he now recounted, and he made the most of his opportunity.[28] Prudently making his last will and testament before setting out, Stephen Bauzan left Carmarthen on 31 May 1257 and, after a day's march, the army came safely enough to the neighbourhood of Llandeilo Fawr and encamped.[29] During the night Maredudd ab Owain and Maredudd ap Rhys drew their forces about the encampment and, after the tumults of the hours of darkness, dawn brought a sustained attack as successive showers of arrows and lances descended on the invading army. Its leaders had to concede that they would not reach Dinefwr that day. By the following day Rhys Fychan, on whose account the whole venture had been launched, had slipped away from the royal army and made for Dinefwr alone. He was hardly welcome there, and his change of allegiance was to create a difficult problem which Llywelyn would soon have to deal with. But his decision created a more immediate contingency for his adversaries, and their forces included large contingents of Welshmen whose will for the fight may well have been undermined by Rhys Fychan's desertion. Facing a second day under sustained attack, the knights donned their armour once more, only to find, the chronicler relates, that they were no better than linen coverings, so fierce was the onslaught upon them. Conceding that advance to Dinefwr was no more possible now than on the previous day, the commanders resolved to make their way to Cardigan. Bauzan may have been hoping for aid from Cardigan, where men and supplies which Edward had ordered from Ireland were now being gathered.[30] Disaster befell the army soon after it set off. First, at Coed Llathen the force lost a great part of its supplies. Then, at Cymerau, about midday, the contending forces met in open conflict and the royal army suffered grievous losses. Three thousand men are said to have fallen. Most of

---

[28] *AC(B)*, 93–5; briefer notices in *AC(C)*, 91; *CW*, 40; *BT, Pen20*, 209; *Pen20Tr*, 111; *RBH*, 248–9. English notices include Paris, *ChronMaj*, v, 645–6; vi, 372–3; *FloresHist*, ii, 416–17; *AnnTewk*, 158; *AnnOsney*, 116–17. Commentaries in *HW*, ii, 720–1; J. E. Lloyd, 'The age of the native princes 400–1282 A.D.', in *A History of Carmarthenshire*, ed. J. E Lloyd (London, 1935–9), i, 188–9 [*HistCarm*].

[29] *PR, 1247–58*, 615.

[30] *AC(B)*, 94: *versus Kardigaun*. Lloyd, *HistCarm*, i, 189, states that the reference to Cardigan was 'a slip for Carmarthen' and that the army intended to return the way it had come, that is along the Tywi valley; but in the summer of 1257, certainly by July and possibly earlier, substantial supplies and forces from Ireland were assembled at Cardigan, where Bauzan had an estate (*LW*, 38–9, 46). There is every possibility that the leaders intended to make for Cardigan, as the chronicler states. This raises a question concerning the precise location of the conflict that ensued after the initial encounter at Llandeilo Fawr (see n. 32). For forces sent from Waterford, mainly to Cardigan, C. Macneill, 'Harris: Collectanea de Rebus Hibernicis', *Analecta Hibernica*, 6 (1934), 240–8; below, n. 58.

them were Welsh, but the chroniclers were in no doubt that this was a resounding Welsh victory.[31] The precise location of the conflict cannot be established with certainty.[32] But the battle of Cymerau was widely reported among the chroniclers of England and it was remembered for a long time in the Anglo-Norman lordships from which the king's army had largely been drawn.[33]

Llywelyn may well have been in Powys when the battle of Cymerau was fought, for it was reported that he had been in the area and put the castle of Bodyddon under siege before 22 May.[34] He lost no time in making for Deheubarth, and he did so for two reasons. On the one hand, he needed to maintain the impetus of the military movements in south-west Wales, and the several attacks recorded by the chronicler reflect his determination to maintain the pressure on the Anglo-Norman positions over a wide area from Cemais and Rhos in the west to Gower and Glamorgan.[35] On the other hand, Llywelyn came to Deheubarth to settle the political problems that had arisen once Rhys Fychan had deserted the king's army and sped for Dinefwr. His defection created consternation in the royal camp and brought immediate advantage to the king's opponents, but it created a dilemma for Llywelyn. This was perhaps the first major issue of contention to arise within the

---

[31] *AC(C)*, 91; *CW*, 40.

[32] Lloyd, *HW*, ii, 720 n. 23; *HistCarm*, i, 189, places the battle at the confluence of the Tywi and the Cothi in the parish of Llanegwad (SN501201); *Inventory Carm,* 159 in the parish of Llangathen (*c*.SN578232), but neither identification is certain, and I am grateful to Terry James and Heather James who kindly shared my concern with the difficulty. Egerton Phillimore, in George Owen, *The Description of Penbrokeshire*, ed. H. Owen (London, 1902–36), iv, 413–14, 430–2, accepting that the army was making for Cardigan, suggested a site at the confluences (*cymerau*) of Afon Ddulas, Afon Ddu and Nant Llwyd, two miles south-west of Talyllychau (SN645305). Phillimore's opinion deserves serious consideration, particularly in view of the possibility that, after the experience of the initial conflict, the English army was forced to make its way over the high ground north-west of Llandeilo Fawr and seek a route to the Teifi and thence to Cardigan. The matter could be resolved if either Cymerau or Coed Llathen could be securely identified.

[33] For the memory in Glamorgan, *GlamCH*, iii, 237. Lloyd, *B*, 7 (1933–5), 95–6 and *HistCarm*, i, 189, held that the battle is commemorated in a stanza in the Black Book of Carmarthen; this view is rejected in A. O. H. Jarman, 'Brwydr y Cymerau ac oed Llyfr Du Caerfyrddin', *B*, 14 (1950–2), 179–80; *Llyfr Du Caerfyrddin*, ed. idem (Cardiff, 1982), xxviii–xxix, 32, where it is argued that the line 'Ban llathery saesson y kimerev trin' (no. 17. 99) refers to a much earlier conflict.

[34] *AC*, 93, states that he put Bodyddon under siege 'before Pentecost' (27 May) This was probably Tomen-yr-allt, in Bodyddon, par Llanfyllin, cmt Mechain: D. J. C. King, *Castellorum Anglicanum* (London, 1983), 297–8 [King, *CA*]. Mechain was the lordship of Llywelyn Fychan, Owain and Maredudd, sons of Llywelyn ab Owain (*CCR, 1272–79,* 399, 434; *HW*, ii, 683, 709 n. 93), and the action may have been calculated to bring them to submission. They were allied by early 1258 (below, p. 113).

[35] For the capture of Nicholas FitzMartin of Cemais and Guy de Brian of Laugharne, *CPR, 1247–58,* 581, 601, 663; *CLibR*, iv, 436; FitzMartin may have been taken at Cymerau (*AnnTewk*, 158).

alliance forged under his leadership. Accommodating Rhys Fychan, the prince's nephew, in the Welsh alliance involved making territorial provision for him in Ystrad Tywi, and to do so would necessarily nullify the hegemony which Maredudd ap Rhys Gryg had recently secured. This, in turn, would inevitably imperil the understanding between Llywelyn and Maredudd on which the resurgence of Welsh political power was founded. *Brut y Tywysogyon* states that Llywelyn was able to effect a reconciliation between Maredudd and Rhys, and the campaign in south-west Wales was able to proceed. It was not long, however, before the chronicler acknowledged that the trust between Llywelyn and Maredudd had been irrevocably impaired.[36] After securing from Llywelyn precisely what he had long sought, Maredudd was required to forfeit his gains so that the prince could restore to Rhys Fychan his portion of the inheritance. Maredudd was left exposed to the advances of a king who knew full well, amidst the tribulations which had befallen him in Wales in recent months, that the lord of Dryslwyn was one who might now be weaned away from his adherence to Llywelyn. Although no part of Ystrad Tywi was now in the king's possession, Henry could promise that Maredudd would receive from him a broad estate the like of which he could no longer expect from Llywelyn.[37] The prince learned, so soon after asserting his authority over a wide sphere, how painfully difficult it was to reconcile the aspirations of the barons of Wales with his own, and it was especially hurtful to experience this harsh truth in his relations with one who, more perhaps than any other among his compatriots in the alliance, had in rich measure the qualities of a key member of a Welsh political community.

Yet these difficulties were not the matters which impressed themselves most forcibly upon those, in Wales and England alike, who recorded the course of events during this remarkable year. His triumphs in battle raised Llywelyn, in the estimation of the chronicler who wrote at Dunstable, to a position comparable with that of Llywelyn the Great: he was the second Llywelyn.[38] Matthew Paris similarly, in eloquent passages, remarked upon the great changes being brought about in Wales, doing so in the course of a commentary which blends eulogy of Llywelyn with severe strictures upon Edward.[39] The heir to the throne is portrayed as an irresponsible young man who attracted unruly scoundrels to his company. The crisis he faced in Wales was partly of his own making, for he had allowed too much liberty to

[36] *AC*, 95–7; *BT*, *Pen20*, 210; *Pen20Tr*, 248.

[37] The distribution of lands now made by Llywelyn may be reflected in the king's charters of October 1257 (below, n. 63).

[38] *AnnDunst*, 200.

[39] Paris, *ChronMaj*, v, 613–14, 639–40, 645–7; cf. *AnnTewk*, 158. Paris's remarks probably reflect the influence of Bishop Richard of Bangor, for whose presence at St Albans, noticed further, below, n. 105, see R. Vaughan, *Matthew Paris* (Cambridge, 1958), 12, 15.

Supremacy

unworthy officers. And, if his portrayal of Edward was decidedly uncomplimentary, he did not stop there, chastizing the English nation itself as a wretched people who placed their inheritance at risk and allowed themselves to be dominated by aliens. The Welsh were different. They, too, had known oppression by foreigners, but they knew that they sprang from the men of Troy, and they rose to defend their country and the lands which were their heritage from their ancestors. The oration which he wrote for Llywelyn dwells upon the theme of a nation pledged to the furtherance of a just cause: a virtuous people acting under the dispensation of Providence can withstand powers infinitely more potent than its own, and triumph over adversity: 'Let us stand together, for as long as we are undivided we shall remain invincible'. It was as though Paris had been moved to these sentiments by the ambiguous but inspired predictions which Giraldus Cambrensis embodied in the later chapters of the Description of Wales. It seemed as though the nation had found that one prince whom Giraldus had commended as the essential instrument of its salvation. In the judgement of the St Albans chronicler, the Welsh had forged a unity which had brought north and south together, something never seen before. Despite the rhetoric, and his preoccupation with his own anathemata, he was not entirely amiss in his estimation of the problems which confronted Henry III after the calamity in Ystrad Tywi.

News of the disaster reached King Henry by the middle of June. He realized that he had no choice but to intervene in Wales and do so with sufficient force. Henry would have been glad to have been spared the need to mount a major expedition, given the problems confronting him in England, especially his financial difficulties, and the strains felt within the royal council itself.[40] The problems posed by Llywelyn could enter into political discussion in various ways. The need for intervention in Wales might be cited as a reason for resisting royal expenditure, witness the argument used by the clergy of England in withstanding Henry's demands for payments to meet the costs of his involvement in the affairs of the kingdom of Sicily. Equally the danger from Wales could be used in advocating measures to improve the king's financial position, a reasoning to which a royal servant turned when, justifying the resumption of lands alienated from the king's demesne, he raised the

---

[40] For Henry's problems c.1257, R. F. Treharne, *The Baronial Plan of Reform, 1258–1263* (Manchester, 1932; repr. 1971), 55–63 [Treharne, *BPR*]; W. E. Lunt, *Financial Relations of the Papacy with England to 1327* (Cambridge, Mass., 1939), 269–90; Powicke, *Henry III*, i, 367–82; J. R. Maddicott, *Simon de Montfort* (Cambridge, 1994), 125–6, 139 [Maddicott, *Montfort*]; H. W. Ridgeway, 'Foreign favourites and Henry III's problems of patronage, 1247–58', *EHR*, 104 (1989), 590–610. For the costs to be faced in Wales in relation to the king's resources, Carpenter, *Reign of Henry III*, 123–6.

prospect of an attack from a neighbouring prince sufficiently powerful to threaten the overthrow of the entire realm.[41] The king's council had no relish for a campaign if other means of restraining the prince could be explored. But the exhortations to Llywelyn over the previous months had been of no avail and, within a few days of hearing the recent news from Wales, preparations for a campaign were taken in hand with a view to a muster at Chester on 8 August. The king first planned an assault on Gwynedd through Perfeddwlad, with a subsidiary expedition to Anglesey. He also made provision for the defence of the marches; Hamo Lestrange, Humphrey de Bohun and John FitzAlan were appointed to commands north and south of Montgomery, with other marchers in support. Significantly, and evidently the result of further deliberations in council, the king's army was then divided into two parts. One was directed to Chester as originally intended, but the other was sent to Deheubarth with a specific operational role to be fulfilled under the command of Richard de Clare, earl of Gloucester. The service of fifty tenants-in-chief (amounting to a hundred knights) was apportioned to Clare, and there can be no doubt that he was entirely responsible for the change of plan.[42] The chronology of the Welsh movements after Cymerau is not easy to establish but, apart from the attack on Cemais already noticed, the offensive was carried to the *cantref* of Rhos and the lordships of Narberth, Laugharne and Llansteffan. Gower had been attacked earlier in the year, and Rhys Fychan is credited with a new onslaught in which the town of Swansea was burned and virtually all the Welsh of the whole of the lordship brought into submission to the prince.[43] Llywelyn was certainly engaged in this area. The texts of *Brut y Tywysogyon* state that he took 'Llangeneu' or 'Llankynwch', a castle that can be identified as Llangynwyd.[44] Annals derived from Glamorgan confirm that Llangynwyd, the earl's castle in Tir Iarll, was taken, and they describe the circumstances in some detail. Clare, advancing from Cardiff, was at Llanbleddian when, on 13 July, Llywelyn, who had brought a great army to the neighbourhood of the Cistercian abbey of Margam, attacked Llangynwyd, killing twenty-four of the earl's men, and burned the castle.[45] Clare decided that he would advance no further in the king's cause

[41] 'Annales de Burton', *Annales Monastici*, i, ed. H. R. Luard (RS, 1864), 390–1; *DBM*, 90–2.
[42] *CR, 1256–59*, 137–41; Ridgeway, 'Foreign favourites', 139–41; enrolments have intimations of a campaign from late June, but writs of summons may have been issued earlier.
[43] *AC*, 95; *BT, Pen20*, 210; *Pen20Tr*, 111; *RBH*, 248–9; with valuable detail on Gower and Glamorgan in Royal MS 6 B.xi, f. 108ᵛ.
[44] *BT, Pen20*, 210; *Pen20Tr*, 111; *RBH*, 248–9; see note, *Pen20Tr*, 210.
[45] Royal 6 Bxi, f. 108ᵛ: 'venit Ricardus, comes Gloucestrie, apud Kayrd' cum multitudine armatorum. Et Lewelinus fuit cum magno excercitu iuxta abbathia de Margan. Tercio Id' Julii accessit Lewelinus apud Langunith et combussit castrum domini comitis et interfecit xxiiii homines comitis, domino comite existente cum magno excercitu apud Lanblethian'.

without adequate forces, and it was just five days later that, after a meeting of the royal council at Woodstock, it was resolved that a strong contingent should be placed at Gloucester's command in Glamorgan, Pembroke and elsewhere in south Wales.[46] He was allowed to draw upon the resources of Edward's lordships in Gwent, as well as the substantial aid which had already been summoned from Ireland.[47] The division of the royal force was a recognition of the extent of the power exercised by Llywelyn in Deheubarth and upon its confines during the preceding months, but the calculations may not have been entirely of a military nature.

Clare was probably aware that the deployment of sufficient forces in the southern areas could have a persuasive as well as a coercive purpose. He might well have recalled how, confronting Welsh resistance twenty years before, he had spent interminable weeks in the king's company at Degannwy, to little purpose, before Henry withdrew leaving Dafydd ap Llywelyn's resistance unbroken. Eventually the Welsh alliance was undermined by the initiative of Nicholas de Molis who, by power and persuasion, had brought the princes of Deheubarth back into the king's fealty and then led them on a march which took them to the confines of Snowdonia.[48] Molis was now recalled to fulfil this task in Deheubarth once more, and his appointment, so soon after it was decided to direct part of the king's army to Deheubarth, probably reflected Clare's influence.[49] Maredudd ap Rhys Gryg, who may have been a son of a daughter of the house of Clare, was known to be one who might now be drawn from his allegiance to Llywelyn. Affinity with Clare perhaps, and certainly respect for Molis, might do much to ease his path to the king's fealty, and his removal from the princes' ranks could serve to undermine the Welsh alliance.[50] The foreboding in Giraldus's assessment of the political propensities of the nation might seem to have a bearing on the calculations of those who advised the king, stressing as he did the advantages which would accrue to a conqueror who could 'divide their strength and create confusion among them'. By early August 1257 Clare was equipped

---

[46] *CR, 1256–59*, 139–41 (18 July).
[47] *SWMRS*, 3 (1954), 43 (from 7 July).
[48] Above, pp. 55–6.
[49] *CPR, 1247–58*, 570, 573.
[50] Rhys Gryg in 1219 married a daughter of 'the earl of Clare' (*BT, Pen20*, 180; *Pen20Tr*, 97; *RBH*, 218–19), that is a daughter of Richard de Clare, earl of Hertford (d. 1217). Maredudd, named as 'son and heir' in 1222 but not known to have acted on his own account for some years yet, may have been the son of that marriage (*Episcopal Acts and Cognate Documents relating to Welsh Dioceses 1066–1272*, ed. J. C. Davies (Cardiff, Historical Society of the Church in Wales, 1946–8), i, 352–3, from Statute Book of St David's, BL, Harl., 6280, ff. 40b–41). This would have made him a first cousin of Richard de Clare, earl of Gloucester. Clare and Molis had been engaged in negotiations with Maredudd during the conflict of 1244–6 (*CPR, 1232–47*, 431, 447, 465, 470, 474). For Maredudd's respect for Molis, below, n. 64.

with a force which gave him a range of choices in his dealings with the princes of Deheubarth: he could exert military strength to match the princes' capability in combat, or provide protection for those who could be persuaded to withdraw from the princes' alliance, or both. It had worked before, it would work with telling effect twenty years later, and it worked pretty well for Henry before the summer was out.

The presence of king and chancery in north Wales ensured that the campaign in that area proved to be the better documented. Forces were summoned for the octave of the feast of St Peter in Chains, and it was not the last time on which the feast – the first day of August – or the morrow of the feast or its octave was marked in the royal calendar for a muster against the king's Welsh opponents. Henry embarked upon the campaign only with the greatest reluctance, despite his call upon clergy and laymen alike for their commitment to the defence of the realm against those – *inimici, hostes, rebelles* – who presumed to oppose him. He waited at Chester for nineteen days and made an attempt to negotiate with Llywelyn; he endeavoured to divide his opponents, enticing Dafydd ap Gruffudd to forsake his brother's alliance. At the same time he raised hopes of great achievements, envisaging an outcome by which he would hold Anglesey and Perfeddwlad and dispose of the remainder of Gwynedd between Dafydd and Owain.[51] His hesitation was to no avail and, finding no good reason to do otherwise, he finally set out on a journey which, as he related in a disconsolate letter to Alphonso, king of Castile, took him to the furthermost bounds of his kingdom.[52] Using Diserth as a transit encampment, with his progress eased by the advances already made by John Lestrange, Henry came safely to Degannwy by 25 August. Fifteen days later, with nothing much happening, he sent the earl of Gloucester a letter which reflects the lack of resolve which impaired the entire campaign. The ships expected from Ireland and England had not arrived, so he would not proceed with the intended attack on Anglesey. It was only the first week in September but, lifting his eyes to the slopes of Snowdonia for signs of snow with rather more eagerness than he scanned the seas for the appearance of his ships, he already felt that winter was upon him.[53] The discomforting memories of Degannwy in 1245 preyed upon his mind. His troops did not endure the deprivation that they had seen on the previous occasion, but the king had not the willpower to proceed with his assault on Llywelyn's stronghold. He ensured that it was well understood that the decision to withdraw was made by council, and that Henry had every

---

[51] *CPR, 1232–47*, 573, 576, 600. Among those with Henry was Gruffudd ap Madog, whose chaplain appears to have been entrusted with the letter to Dafydd, subsequently torn up because he did not respond.
[52] *CR, 1256–59*, 152.
[53] Ibid., 90–1.

intention of coming back and taking possession of Anglesey next time.⁵⁴ By 8 September Llywelyn's men in Perfeddwlad saw the king's army begin its retreat from Degannwy, leaving the land in its entirety under his lordship. Presently, Llywelyn found that one who had hitherto remained faithful to the king, and served in the royal army on the recent campaign, was now forced to acknowledge that there was no virtue in maintaining his fidelity. No sooner had Henry crossed the Dee than Gruffudd ap Madog admitted that he could no longer expect the support and protection which a lord had reason to expect at a time of difficulty. After seventeen years of unflinching loyalty to the crown, the lord of Powys Fadog pledged himself to the second Llywelyn.⁵⁵

If there had been anything to ameliorate the king's discomfiture at Degannwy it was the news from Deheubarth, and he graciously acknowledged the success with which the earl of Gloucester and Nicholas de Molis had pursued their objectives in the area.⁵⁶ *Bene contenti sumus*: the king was well pleased with what he was told. His emissaries had had purposeful exchanges with Maredudd ap Rhys Gryg, and it was time to consider matters of detail. As part of the effort to bring him to the king's fealty it was agreed that, subject to the certainty of his fidelity, Maredudd should have two commotes, Gwynionydd and Perfedd, but he looked for something better than this.⁵⁷ He expected nothing less than the lordship he had enjoyed during that brief interlude between his triumphant return to Ystrad Tywi at the end of 1256 and the reversal of fortune that had followed the battle of Cymerau when Llywelyn decided to accommodate Rhys Fychan. It is difficult to know what pressures Clare and Molis were able to exert upon him, but though the evidence is fragmentary it seems that they were able to deploy substantial forces during late summer and early autumn. It is known, for instance, that in addition to the forces apportioned to Clare by the decision of the council at Woodstock a force of soldiers (*satellites*) had come from Ireland to Cardigan and served under the Lord Edward's constables.⁵⁸ The flow of men

---

⁵⁴ *CR, 1256–59*, 90–1; for Henry's later insistence that winter had curtailed the campaign and that he would return, ibid., 294 (14 March 1258).

⁵⁵ *AnnCestr*, 74; *BT, Pen20*, 210–11; *Pen20Tr*, 111; *RBH*, 250–1. For Henry's reaction *CPR, 1247–58*, 600, 627; *CR, 1256–59*, 201–2.

⁵⁶ *CR, 1256–59*, 90–1 (4 September 1257).

⁵⁷ Ibid.; *CPR, 1247–58*, 577 (4 September). Henry would not cede Mefennydd, held to be his demesne and not part of Maredudd ab Owain's lands, until it was certain that Maredudd ap Rhys would acquit himself well in the king's service.

⁵⁸ *Analecta Hibernica*, 6 (1934), 289–91. J. F. Lydon, 'Three Exchequer documents from the reign of Henry III', *Proceedings of the Royal Irish Academy*, 65 (1966–7), Section C, 1–27, has evidence that Henry and Edward drew heavily on the Dublin exchequer for the campaign, sending money to Chester and Cardigan, and that soldiers (*satellites*) and supplies of food were dispatched, largely to Cardigan, by early August. The numbers are uncertain; clothing for 1000 *satellites* was sent from Drogheda to Cardigan but it is not certain that all the soldiers clothed came from Ireland; but 500 horses and 700 *satellites* were sent in July and a further 400 in September. See also idem in A. Cosgrove (ed.), *Medieval Ireland, 1169–1534* (Oxford, 1987), 181–2.

and supplies from Ireland had been enough, if reliance can be placed on Matthew Paris's account, to induce Llywelyn to deploy some ships during the conflict of this year, and the main port which needed to be blockaded was Cardigan.[59] The delivery of resources into Cardigan was already in train when Stephen Bauzan made his fateful intervention in Ystrad Tywi at the end of May, and it is possible that he had intended to proceed from Dinefwr to link up with the forces being assembled at Cardigan.[60] The concentration of men and materials continued during the summer, and the close attention which Llywelyn gave to the situation in south-west Wales is readily understood. For his part, Edward placed some weight on the campaign in the hinterland of Cardigan and Carmarthen, and put his officers under strict orders to do their utmost to defend his marches in south-west Wales.[61] Part of his purpose was, no doubt, to provide protection for those lords of Deheubarth who might be prepared to desert the prince, a measure which would prove effective in the spring of 1277 when Llywelyn's position was undermined by the king's successful negotiations with the son of the prince with whom Molis and Clare were now negotiating.[62] By 18 October 1257 their endeavours were finally completed when Maredudd ap Rhys Gryg did homage to the king in London in the presence of the earl of Gloucester, Patrick de Chaworth and others who had been involved in the transactions in the area.[63] The terms agreed showed the value placed on Maredudd's adherence. He was granted his hereditary lands and those of Rhys Fychan, an estate commensurate with that he had held during his alliance with Llywelyn, with the exception of the commote of Gwidigada which the king considered to be part of the demesne associated with the castle of Carmarthen. This omission was made good by the grant of two commotes, Mabwynion and Gwynionydd, from among the lands of Maredudd ab Owain in Ceredigion. This document was no more than a scrap of parchment, for the king was in no position to give effect to his award, but it provides clear testimony to the dour determination of the man whom Llywelyn had sought to bind in alliance with himself. Maredudd had struck a hard bargain, and he had insisted upon a

[59] Paris, *ChronMaj*, v, 633.
[60] Above, n. 32.
[61] Lydon, 'Exchequer documents', 26–7.
[62] *AC*, 96–7; negotiations between Rhys ap Maredudd and Payn de Chaworth, 1277, below, pp. 418–22.
[63] Transactions embodied in three documents, 18 October: (*a*) receiving Maredudd into the king's peace and granting the commotes of Mabwynion and Gwynionydd (*LW*, 161–2); (*b*) pardoning Maredudd and others who had withdrawn their fealty and done homage to Maredudd; and providing assurance that no agreement would be made with Llywelyn until Rhys ap Maredudd was released, and that neither Maredudd ab Owain nor Rhys Fychan would be received into the king's peace without the counsel of Maredudd ap Rhys (*LW*, 170–1; *CPR, 1247–58*, 582); (*c*) conceding to Maredudd the lands he then held and those of Rhys Fychan, all specified (*LW*, 163–4; *CChR*, i, 475). Both (*a*) and (*c*) confirmed by Edward, 19 September 1265 (*LW*, 107, 163–4).

promise on the king's part that he should be allowed to enjoy the 'better lordship' that he had known when Nicholas de Molis had exercised responsibility in the area some years earlier.[64] It is difficult to be sure what exactly this might mean, but it would seem that Maredudd sought an assurance that he would be allowed to exercise lordship over his patrimony without interference on the king's part. Above all, he wanted to make certain that he would never again be exposed to anything like the intervention by which Stephen Bauzan had come to Ystrad Tywi with a view to bringing about his entire disinheritance. Entering into one engagement after another, Henry agreed that he would admit neither Rhys Fychan nor Maredudd ab Owain into his fealty without the agreement of Maredudd ap Rhys. If these concessions were ever implemented Maredudd would enjoy an incomparable seigniorial authority in Deheubarth.

The agreement reveals the essence of the problem that Llywelyn had to resolve in the aftermath of the battle of Cymerau if he was to transform an alliance of princes, pledged to go to war together, into a permanent political association. This was precisely the problem which Llywelyn ap Iorwerth had broached early in the thirteenth century. Just as the striking military movements of the previous months had been founded on the understanding between Llywelyn and Maredudd, so the undermining of that concord created an enormous obstacle in the way of fulfilling the political objective which Llywelyn had now set himself. There was no longer any trust between Llywelyn and Maredudd. At the time when he arranged the reconciliation between Maredudd and Rhys Fychan after Cymerau, Llywelyn had seen that he needed to take stringent precautions in his dealings with Maredudd. He had taken Maredudd's son as a hostage for his father's loyalty, so it was probably no surprise to Llywelyn that Maredudd should do homage to the king in the autumn. In the spring of 1258, however, Llywelyn and Maredudd formulated a new agreement. The document of 26 April 1258 in which it is embodied is the earliest surviving example of a formal agreement between Llywelyn and a prince who acknowledged his supremacy by doing homage, but it is probably far from typical of the engagements into which the prince entered in this period. Its most telling features are the undertakings into which Llywelyn was prepared to enter in order to secure Maredudd's homage, promises of an entirely negative nature: he agreed that he would never again imprison Maredudd or his son, nor take his son as a hostage, nor take possession of his castles.[65] Llywelyn, as we shall see again, placed himself

---

[64] *LW*, 170–1; calendar, *CPR, 1247–58*, 582, misreads at this point.

[65] *LW*, 168–9; Rhys ap Maredudd was imprisoned by October 1257 (*LW*, 171). This was the first of two interventions in Deheubarth noticed in *AC*, 95–6. The new agreement between Llywelyn and Maredudd was made on 26 April 1258, and the king maintained that Maredudd was in his fealty on 17 June (*CR, 1256–59*, 323–4).

under ecclesiastical censure if he were to fail to meet his engagements. The promises reflect the constraints placed upon him as he strove to retrieve Maredudd's fidelity, but it was to no avail. Maredudd's only purpose in formally identifying himself with Llywelyn anew was to get his son out of captivity, and he may well have told the king beforehand that this was the sole object of his subterfuge. By the summer of 1258 it was known to all that Maredudd was once more loyal to the crown, and the chronicler records the anger which his deviousness had aroused: he was a man whose infidelity had disturbed the whole of Wales (*per infidelitatem suam totam Wallie perturbavit*).[66]

Twice in the course of 1258 Llywelyn had to intervene in Deheubarth on Maredudd's account. On the first occasion he came in person and, with the support of 'all the men of Deheubarth', subjugated Maredudd's lands in Ystrad Tywi and pursued him to Cydweli where he evidently sought refuge with Patrick de Chaworth.[67] On the second occasion he entrusted the task to his brother Dafydd, 'a young man splendid in arms and powerful in cavalry', who called up Maredudd ab Owain and Rhys Fychan in support.[68] They encamped with a great army first at Maenordeifi and then at Cilgerran, where they got the better of their opponents in a fierce encounter with an army that Maredudd and Patrick de Chaworth gathered from Carmarthen and Cydweli, Pembroke and Rhos, Cardigan and Cemais. It was an action that the chronicler saw as a conflict between the Welsh and the English. Twice, at Carmarthen and then at Cilgerran, Maredudd had a narrow escape as he sought refuge with the English from the onslaught of men of his own nation, acting under the guiding hand of divine providence. Maredudd ap Rhys Gryg had now most certainly incurred the wrath of his countrymen, and we need search no further than the critical commentary of the Latin annalist to grasp the significance of Llywelyn's bid to establish and maintain a political ascendancy in the Wales of the princes.

In examining Llywelyn's achievements in this phase of his endeavour it would be quite wrong to envisage a relentless advance in which a forceful prince swept aside all resistance to his masterly authority. It fell to the poet alone to portray the sequence of events as triumphal progression to supremacy, for the

---

[66] *AC*, 97.
[67] *AC*, 95–6.
[68] *AC*, 96–7 (4 September 1258); *BT, Pen20*, 211; *Pen20Tr*, 111–12. *RBH*, 250–1, differs in that, when Dafydd and the princes went to parley with Maredudd, Chaworth fell upon his opponents and broke the truce. The accounts in *BT* texts are brief and lack the critical flavour of *AC(B)*; it is clear that the redactor of the Latin text on which the *Brut* is based has played down Maredudd's treacherous activity and the anger it aroused.

chronicler made no attempt to conceal the difficulties which arose even in the wake of the prince's initial campaign in Deheubarth. Llywelyn ap Iorwerth had found that it was impossible to win the support of the province without first resolving the dynastic rivalries by which it had been so sadly rent; a generation later Llywelyn ap Gruffudd, in the period of heroic resistance already recounted, had seen a military alliance crumble as the king exploited the anxieties of the heirs to the precarious patrimonies of the southern province. The prince had need of a more stable unity than an alliance formed for purposes of war alone, and once the king withdrew from Degannwy he applied himself to the task of forging a durable political structure. By the spring of 1258 the military alliance was transformed into a political unity, each of the princes who had hitherto acknowledged Llywelyn's leadership now bound in obligations which made him a vassal who recognized the prince's lordship. One text of *Brut y Tywysogyon* tells of a pact which the Welsh made to maintain loyalty and agreement together; the other tells of an assembly where the magnates of Wales gave an oath of allegiance to Llywelyn under pain of excommunication.[69] We may be certain that neither text does full justice to the transactions completed between Llywelyn and his fellow princes at a date probably early in 1258. In a document drawn up in March, noticed presently, he used the style 'prince of Wales' (*princeps Wallie*).[70] It was a sign that a new political association had been forged when those who had previously been his allies, sworn together in solemn undertakings to further their common purposes, now entered into engagements by which each acknowledged the prince's lordship by declaring his allegiance to him. Each was bound to him in homage and fealty. Llywelyn looked for nothing less than a contractual relationship of lord and vassal.

The next step would be to get the king of England to recognize the change brought about within the land by sealing a formal treaty with the prince, and quite soon Llywelyn would send an emissary to the king requesting that he be granted the homage of the magnates of Wales in the same manner as they had been held by his grandfather.[71] His appeal to history had no basis in reality, for Llywelyn ap Iorwerth had sought that treaty in vain, though we cannot judge whether this was how the relationship between king and prince in the earlier thirteenth century was perceived among those who now served Llywelyn ap Gruffudd.[72] What matters, however, is that his initiative

---

[69] *BT, Pen20*, 211; *Pen20Tr*, 111: 'all the Welsh made a pact together, and they gave an oath to maintain loyalty and agreement together under pain of excommunication upon whomsoever of them broke it'; *RBH*, 250–1· 'an assembly of the magnates of Wales gave an oath of allegiance to Llywelyn ap Gruffudd under pain of excommunication'.
[70] *LW*, 184.
[71] *CR, 1259–61*, 4–5 (1259); below, n. 124.
[72] Above, pp. 21–2, 26–7.

provides an unequivocal statement of his determination to secure a political relationship with the crown of England which reflected the unity now secured within the princes' lands by the bonds of homage and fealty. He had indeed gone a stage further than his grandfather in asserting, as prince of Wales, that the inner unity of those lands was already established. He did not persist with the style 'prince of Wales' for some time yet and, from the evidence we have, its use in 1258 was a singular instance.[73] But it is important to notice that in none of the surviving records of the next few years does he accord himself any other style: he was not 'prince of North Wales', nor 'prince of Aberffraw and lord of Snowdon'. It was preferable, as we shall notice again, not to use any style at all than compromise with one which signified something less than the position to which he aspired. Discretion might commend that he set his intended style aside while he persevered with his endeavour to secure a treaty by which his position in Wales, and its formal designation, would be duly conceded by the king of England. He persisted with his endeavours, as we shall see, for four years. That he should do so was equally a mark of his determination and his discretion. He was a son of Gruffudd ap Llywelyn, a grandson of Llywelyn ap Iorwerth.

Some indication of Llywelyn's authority, and of the new confidence in independent Wales, may be gathered from the document in which, for the present, Llywelyn made his singular use of the style 'prince of Wales'. It was an agreement made between Llywelyn and a number of the magnates of Wales on the one hand, and a group of Scottish magnates on the other.[74] The Scots who put their names to the document were bound together largely by their affinity with the Comyn family, whose considerable power in the realm had been diminished following Henry III's intervention in Scotland during the minority of Alexander III. They had subsequently retrieved something of their influence, but the document drawn up early in 1258, by the earls of Menteith, Buchan and Mar and others, still reflected some uncertainty on their part as the young king came increasingly to act on his own behalf. The main terms of the agreement were, indeed, firm and unambiguous: the two sides envisaged a treaty of alliance and friendship by which the king of Scotland would not enter into any agreement with the king of England, nor with the magnates of England and Scotland, unless they were bound in agreement with those of Wales who were party to the present treaty. The Welsh magnates had already put their seals to a document embodying the

---

[73] D. Stephenson, 'Llywelyn ap Gruffydd and the struggle for the principality of Wales, 1258–1282', *THSC*, 1983, 37–8, notes that Llywelyn did not use the style 'prince of Wales' again until late summer 1262. For the possible reasons, and subsequent adoption of the style 'prince of Wales and lord of Snowdon', below, pp. 145–6.

[74] *LW*, 184–6; calendared *Calendar of Documents relating to Scotland,* i, no. 2055; for the Scottish 'act of adherence', Powicke, *Henry III*, i, 381.

Supremacy

terms of the agreement, but the men of Scotland felt constrained to acknowledge that they could not bind their king. Though they would endeavour to persuade him to accept the terms of the agreement, they could offer no more than their willingness to abide by their engagement unless they were compelled to do otherwise.[75] The Scots evidently needed to be cautious and, though it is not easy to reconstruct the manner in which the agreement was negotiated, there is much to suggest that the initiative stemmed from the prince of Wales. The surviving evidence takes the form of a document by which the magnates of Scotland, on 18 March 1258, made an agreement of confederacy and friendship (*confederacio* and *amicicia*) with the Welsh magnates, each one making a pledge to the prince's emissary, Gwion of Bangor, and putting his seal to the cyrograph. The princes similarly made their pledge to Alan of Irvine, the Scots' emissary, and had almost certainly done so by the date of the document.[76] The transactions on the Welsh side may conceivably have been completed at the assembly where the magnates of Wales acknowledged Llywelyn's lordship.[77] It was the work of men who felt free to enter into a pact with the Scots without any reservation. On this occasion, contrary to what the respective political traditions of the two countries might lead us to expect, it was in Wales rather than in Scotland that the political initiative was conceived and unequivocally put into effect.

The names which appear in the text of the agreement with the Scots provide an indication of the composition of what might reasonably be regarded as the political community brought into being under Llywelyn's leadership.[78] First named was Llywelyn, prince of Wales, and second to him stood Dafydd ap Gruffudd, explicitly described as the prince's uterine brother. The king had tested Dafydd's loyalty the previous year but with no success as yet. The ranks included Gruffudd ap Madog, a late adherent but one who was to remain steadfast thereafter and, securing Powys Fadog, provided stability in an area of considerable strategic importance. One of Gruffudd's brothers, Madog Fychan was of the same persuasion and an early adherent to the

---

[75] The situation in Scotland is examined in D. E. R. Watt, 'The minority of Alexander III of Scotland', *TRHS*, 5th ser., 21 (1971), 1–23; A. Young, 'The political role of Walter Comyn, earl of Menteith, during the minority of Alexander III of Scotland', in K. J. Stringer (ed.), *Essays on the Nobility of Medieval Scotland* (Edinburgh, 1985), 131–49; idem, 'Noble families and political factions in the reign of Alexander III, 1249–1286', in N. H. Reid (ed.), *Scotland in the Reign of Alexander III, 1249–1286* (Edinburgh, 1990), 1–30; A. A. M. Duncan, *Scotland: The Making of the Kingdom* (Edinburgh, 1975), 562–74 [Duncan, *Scotland*]; Powicke, *Henry III*, i, 381–3.

[76] Alan de Irvine (Alanus de Yrewyn), apparently a Scots messenger in 1258, appears later in Llywelyn's service (*LW*, 150); after the prince's death, named as his former messenger, 'Alan' guided the king's men on their movements in Gwynedd (E101/351/9).

[77] *HW*, ii, 723, n. 42; this would mean that the assembly was held some time before 18 March 1258.

[78] *LW*, 184–5.

Supremacy

prince, but Hywel ap Madog remained faithful to the king and was to continue to claim his share of Powys Fadog until he finally conceded that it would avail him nothing and that he had better throw in his lot with his fellow princes.[79] Gruffudd ap Gwenwynwyn was not of the princes' fraternity, and he would spend several years more in the king's fealty before he joined his brother, probably a half-brother, Madog ap Gwenwynwyn, in Llywelyn's company.[80] Maredudd ap Rhys Gryg came from Ystrad Tywi, though his presence meant no more than that he was making a fleeting appearance in the prince's alliance before returning to his patrimony and the king's fealty.[81] His brother Hywel ap Rhys Gryg was not present on this occasion, but he received a grant of the commote of Mabelfyw from Llywelyn later in the year in return for his homage, and he would serve the prince with constancy to the very end.[82] From the same province came Rhys Fychan, one who owed everything he now held to the generous manner with which Llywelyn had dealt with him when he transferred his loyalty to the prince after manifestly failing to keep his solemn undertakings from some years earlier.[83] Maredudd ab Owain of Ceredigion had made an early and positive response to the prince's initiative in Deheubarth, contributing a great deal to the resurgence of the Welsh alliance, and he maintained a steadfast loyalty which made him in the estimation of the chronicler 'defender of all Deheubarth and counsellor of all Wales' and earned him the fulsome praise of Y Prydydd Bychan for his valour and discretion.[84] There was no representative of the lineage of Maelgwn ap Rhys among the princes named, but this may be explained by the fact that Maelgwn Fychan had died in 1257, following the death of his son Rhys ap Maelgwyn Fychan two years earlier. Maelgwn Fychan had been identified by the Latin annalist among those who took part in the early movements by which Wales began to win its release from the yoke of slavery that the English had imposed upon the land. Probably a young man himself, Rhys ap Maelgwn Fychan had left two sons, Llywelyn ap Rhys and Rhys Fychan, both of whom were probably too young to have participated in the

---

[79] *LW*, 35, indicating that Madog was associated with Llywelyn by July 1256. During the autumn of 1258 Henry was prepared to allow Hywel to make a bid to recover his lands in Wales, so long as he did so without infringing the truce (*CR, 1256–59*, 334); in 1262 the king was still hoping that Hywel would be able to wean Gruffudd away from the prince's alliance (*CR, 1261–64*, 142–3).

[80] Madog was allowed the commote of Mawddwy under the terms of the agreement with Llywelyn ap Gruffudd, 1263 (*LW*, 78).

[81] Above, pp. 105–8.

[82] *LW*, 45.

[83] Above, pp. 99–100.

[84] *BT, Pen20*, 216; *Pen20Tr*, 114; *GBF*, 8–12.

Supremacy

transactions of this year.⁸⁵ Owain ap Maredudd was a son of Maredudd ap Robert of Cydewain, 'eminent counsellor of Wales', and one whose adherence proved a considerable asset to Llywelyn when he campaigned in that key sector of the march in the neighbourhood of Montgomery.⁸⁶ The prince's strength in other areas neighbouring Powys is reflected in the presence of Llywelyn Fychan, Owain and Maredudd, sons of Llywelyn ab Owain, lords of Mechain, and Owain ap Bleddyn, Elise ap Iorwerth and Gruffudd ap Iorwerth, lords of Edeirnion and Dinmael.⁸⁷ Hywel ap Maredudd, exiled from Blaenau Morgannwg, could bring no accession of territorial power to Llywelyn, but he represented those early strivings in the fastnesses of Snowdonia which had eventually led to the creation of the powerful baronial association now centred on Llywelyn ap Gruffudd.

The new polity was founded on a solemn pledge of loyalty to Llywelyn on the part of men who represented the royal lineages of years gone by. Its future depended on their continued fidelity to one whom they formally recognized as their lord. Their constancy, in turn, depended upon Llywelyn's scrupulous fulfilment of his reciprocal obligations towards those who declared their loyalty to him. He had need, too, to maintain a strong personal authority and this depended a great deal upon the power he derived from the direct lordship which he exercised over Gwynedd. This was the land on whose economic resources he relied, and he drew heavily on the service of those who were men of some substance in its community. In the text of the agreement with the Scots the names of the princes, in effect the barons of the nascent principality of Wales, are followed by those of a number of others who, though not of princely stock, were still men of some consequence in the new political structure. They were representative of a group of men on whose constancy and competence the prince depended greatly. Drawn from the upper echelons of society in the prince's territorial lordship, they could, in a real sense, be counted among the magnates of Wales henceforth.⁸⁸ The presence of those named together in the document of the spring of 1258 testifies to the extent of Llywelyn's achievement in consolidating his position in the territory which formed the core of his wider principality. Tudur ap Madog, Iorwerth ap Gwrgunan and Einion ap Caradog were, as we have seen already, adherents associated with the prince from his initial assertion of lordship in

---

⁸⁵ Llywelyn died 1265; Rhys Fychan's fortunes 1277–83 are noticed later. The annalist at Strata Florida makes numerous references to the lineage, especially its links with Meirionnydd and Cydewain (e.g. *AC(B)*, 86, 89; *BT, Pen20*, 202, 206–7, 210, 215; *Pen20Tr*, 107, 109, 111, 114; *RBH*, 244–7, 250–1, 254–5).

⁸⁶ *BT, Pen20*, 201; *Pen20Tr*, 106; *RBH*, 238–9. Owain died 1261 and Cydewain was probably under Llywelyn's administration thereafter (*WAR*, 240–2, 254–6); he raised the castle of Dolforwyn there in 1273.

⁸⁷ *HW*, ii, 683, 709; above, n. 34.

⁸⁸ Stephenson, *GG*, 95–135, 205–21.

Supremacy

Perfeddwlad.[89] Goronwy ab Ednyfed Fychan, the prince's steward by now, and Einion Fychan were representative of those who had served Llywelyn the Great and remained faithful to Dafydd ap Llywelyn until they, too, identified themselves with Llywelyn ap Gruffudd.[90] The prince depended much upon the counsel of these men, and their active participation in day-to-day affairs and their unity of purpose under his direction was essential to the future of his dominion. A great deal rested upon the ability of the prince and his leading advisers to harmonize the demands of his direct lordship over Gwynedd with his indirect lordship over the broader territories. There was no prospect that this duality in the structure of the principality would be erased, nor much ameliorated, in the foreseeable future. In a little while the duality in Llywelyn's position would be expressed in the style he would employ in documents, but he was already in reality prince of Wales and lord of Snowdon.

Crucial to the promotion of the cohesion of the prince's territories, and the enhancement of his authority over them, were the senior churchmen. Relations between Llywelyn and the higher clergy were, in some instances, to prove stressful and, as his problems accumulated in the later years of his rule, his encounters with the bishops of Bangor and St Asaph were to be among his major difficulties.[91] Yet clerical and, specifically, episcopal support proved forthcoming and proved invaluable in the years in which he asserted his power. This was so despite the delicate issues which their canonical obedience to Canterbury, registered in the formal profession they made upon consecration, undoubtedly raised in the bishops' minds as they determined their relations with princes who were decidedly in breach of their fealty to the king of England.[92] Even the early confederations of 1250–1 were forged on the understanding that any breach of the solemn pledge into which the princes entered would incur ecclesiastical censure of excommunication and interdict, though their phraseology suggests that appeal to particular ecclesiastical persons could not yet be assured.[93] Once Llywelyn asserted a broader lordship, however, the documents recording his relations with fellow princes incorporated explicit statements that the terms agreed, or imposed by Llywelyn, came under an ecclesiastical censure liable to be imposed by the bishops of Bangor and St Asaph. These clauses were incorporated in the texts

---

[89] Above, pp. 44–5.

[90] Above, p. 45.

[91] Stephenson, *GG*, 171–81; relations with Anian of Bangor and Anian of St Asaph are considered later.

[92] Of the bishops of the northern dioceses from 1240, professions of obedience survive for Richard of Bangor, 1237, John of St Asaph, 1267, Anian of Bangor, 1267 and Anian II of St Asaph, 1268; not for Hywel ab Ednyfed of St Asaph (1240–2) or Einion [Anian I] of St Asaph (1249): *Canterbury Professions*, ed. M. Richter (London, Canterbury and York Society, 67, 1973), nos. 173, 209, 210, 214.

[93] *LW*, 148, 160–1.

of the agreements even though the authority exercised by Llywelyn had not won royal approval. When Llywelyn was, for the particular political reasons already considered, forced to provide guarantees to Maredudd ap Rhys Gryg in 1258 he placed himself under ecclesiastical censure if he were to fail to fulfil his undertakings, and the whole agreement was sealed by the two bishops and men of religion. When he later imposed severe terms on his recalcitrant tenant, Llywelyn was able to place Maredudd under the jurisdiction of the same bishops so that they could pronounce excommunication on Maredudd, his family and supporters and also commend the sentence to churchmen in the diocese of St David's.[94] At a later date, but still at a time when he was in breach of his fealty to the king, Llywelyn's agreement with Gruffudd ap Gwenwynwyn placed each of them under sentence of excommunication upon their persons and interdict upon their lands.[95] These were difficult relationships, and our knowledge of the agreements between Llywelyn and his more willing adherents is much more limited, but the terms on which Hywel ap Rhys Gryg did homage to Llywelyn suggests that a host of similar transactions were completed under the aegis of the ecclesiastical authority represented by the bishops of the two northern dioceses.[96]

The assent of the leading churchmen to his political initiatives was important in other connections also. The bishops themselves proved to be important intermediaries between the prince and the king of England, and their approbation and participation helped ensure that the prince won the active support of the church hierarchy as a whole. The aid of Cistercian abbots and the priors of houses of other orders was readily obtained, but that of the secular clergy, historically more difficult to secure, was certainly not lacking during the years which saw Llywelyn assert his power in defiance of the crown of England. Churchmen were moved to facilitate, however, not an imposition of princely will untempered by discretion, but a political process in which the prince had need to secure the consent of the lords of native Wales in the pursuit of an agreed objective. They were embarked on a momentous task which could be only partially fulfilled by military offensives against clearly recognizable opponents. The magnates of Wales may have shown greater confidence than their peers of Scotland at the beginning of 1258, but those of Wales had a great deal to accomplish before they could hope to put their dominion on a footing comparable with that of the realm of Scotland. Unlike the prince of Wales, Alexander III, now assuming full responsibility for his kingdom, could call upon a tradition of royal government already extending

---

[94] *LW*, 104–5, 168–9.
[95] *LW*, 79.
[96] *LW*, 45; further, below, pp. 287, 289–90.

over many generations. The situation in the two countries reflected a markedly different political tradition.[97]

Llywelyn ap Gruffudd, like his grandfather before him, had to start from a political position in many respects more closely comparable with that of Ireland than that of Scotland. Irish commentators, like those of Wales, were acutely aware of the divisions which frustrated the ambitions of those of their royal lineages who strove for a measure of political unity in the land. Yet, daunting though their political experience had been, the aspiration for an elusive unity had not been altogether lost, and it happened that, at precisely the time that Llywelyn asserted his supremacy over the Wales of the princes, the Lord Edward's officers were made aware that something was afoot in Ireland which might prove comparable to what was occurring in Wales.[98] Even as troops and supplies were being drawn from Ireland to provide for the royal forces in Wales, it became clear that the royal authorities there were confronted with new challenges on the frontiers of the royal lordship. Probably within only a few weeks of the formal occasion on which Llywelyn secured the allegiance of the princes of Wales, Brian O'Neill called the Irish kings to Cáeluisce to secure their recognition of the supremacy by which he sought the restoration of the kingship of Ireland.[99] For a while Henry III was certainly troubled at the presumption with which O'Neill elevated himself 'king of the kings of Ireland'.[100] The hopes centred on O'Neill's bid for power were soon shattered, and Henry and Edward may well have judged that the bonds which bound the magnates of Wales were likely to prove more durable. They had been confronted with a sequence of virulent military campaigns, and the alliances made for purposes of war were already being transformed into political relationships within the princes' lands. These were likely to have a far-reaching effect on the relationships between Wales and the crown of England. By the beginning of 1258, more firmly than ever before, Wales was pledged to the political fulfilment of its nationhood.

The historiography of Anglo-Welsh relations carries a firm impression that Llywelyn ap Iorwerth and Llywelyn ap Gruffudd, each in turn, derived immense benefit from the internal divisions which affected the realm of

---

[97] Contrasts with Scotland are considered below, pp. 274–9.

[98] Lydon, 'Exchequer documents', 18, 25, for writs (April 1258) relating to expenditure in Ulster, with comment on the situation confronting Edward; idem, in Cosgrove, *Medieval Ireland*, 244–9.

[99] G. H. Orpen, *Ireland under the Normans 1169–1333* (Oxford, 1911–20), iii, 272–3; K. Simms, 'The O Hanlons, the O Neills and the Anglo-Normans in thirteenth-century Armagh', *Seanchas ArdMhacha*, 9 (1978–9), 80–1; Cosgrove, *Medieval Ireland*, 244–9.

[100] *CR, 1259–61*, 64; Henry also feared Irish alliance with the Scots (*Calendar of Documents relating to Ireland*, ed. H. S. Sweetman (London, 1875–86), i, no. 652).

Supremacy

England in their time.[101] It is a view that can hardly be repudiated, though the precise effect of English dissensions on Welsh political fortunes needs to be appreciated. The troubles of the reign of John undoubtedly eased the path of Llywelyn ap Iorwerth to dominance in Wales. At critical stages in the princes' military initiatives the king was prevented from providing effective defensive measures; there was some understanding between the princes and disaffected English magnates and in the course of events which led to Magna Carta the princes' demands found an advocate in Archbishop Langton.[102] It might reasonably be concluded that the discords which troubled Henry III likewise proved advantageous to Llywelyn ap Gruffudd. Variances were appearing within the community of the realm before matters came to a head at Oxford in the early summer of 1258. The inadequacies of Henry's government were stressed in Matthew Paris's account of the previous year, when he drew his provocative contrast between the virtuous Welsh and the wretched English.[103] Yet it cannot be doubted that Llywelyn had already asserted his broad supremacy in Wales, and elicited a formal acknowledgement of his position from his fellow princes, well before the reformers carried their argument at the Oxford parliament. It could, indeed, be argued that the dissension in England thereafter proved more of a hindrance than a help to Llywelyn ap Gruffudd, as the tribulations in the realm accumulated, leaving the king unwilling or unable to attend to the essential matter which the prince urged upon him. By 1258 Llywelyn had gone a considerable way towards fulfilling the internal aspect of the political aspiration implicit in the jurists' conception of the supremacy vested in a king of Aberffraw. He knew, however, that any such internal reorientation of the princes' allegiance would be stabilized and safeguarded only if he could, at the same time, ensure that the aspiration was fulfilled in its external aspect as well. His search for an understanding with the crown on this issue provides the key to his activity in the period of nearly five years extending from the beginning of 1258 to the end of 1262.[104]

---

[101] J. E. Lloyd, *A History of Wales* (London, 1930), 25–7, refers to the advantage gained by Llywelyn ap Iorwerth from conflict in England in 1215, and describes how strife in England under Henry III 'once again crippled the power of the English realm'; for more specific references, *HW*, ii, 639–45, 722, 726–8.

[102] J. B. Smith, 'Magna Carta and the charters of the Welsh princes', *EHR*, 99 (1984), 345–50, 356–9.

[103] Above, n. 39.

[104] For the reform movement and subsequent conflict extensive reference is made to C. Bémont, *Simon de Montfort, Earl of Leicester, 1208–1265* (Oxford, 1930) [Bémont, *Montfort*], with reference to idem, *Simon de Montfort, Comte de Leicester* (Paris, 1884) [Bémont, *Montfort* (1884)] when necessary; Treharne, *BPR*; Powicke, *Henry III*, i, 377–502; *DBM*; Maddicott, *Montfort*, with other studies noticed later. T. F. Tout, 'Wales and the march in the Barons' Wars, 1258–67', *CP*, ii, 47–100, remains an important reference to be used with caution. It is a pleasure to acknowledge my indebtedness to historians of the University of Wales who have made substantial contributions in this field: R. F. Treharne, I. J. Sanders, F. R. Lewis, Alun Lewis and C. H. Knowles.

Supremacy

His overriding objective in his relations with England in these years was to secure definitive peace terms embodied in a formal treaty with the king. We have seen already that the vigorous pursuit of this aim was an essential feature of Llywelyn the Great's efforts in the period following his assertion of supremacy, though they were not successful. The experiences of the years following his death would have imprinted on Llywelyn ap Gruffudd's mind a realization that the stability of a principality of Wales could not possibly be ensured without agreement with the king of England. After the brief period of triumphal progress which so inspired poet and chronicler alike, Llywelyn had need to pause and seek the means of safeguarding his achievement. The historian, similarly, has to pause and consider the restraint which was as much a test of Llywelyn's capability as the forceful campaigns by which he had established his hegemony. Whenever Llywelyn went to war in the period now being considered he did so with one end in view: the exerting of pressure on Henry III to yield him the treaty which would secure the full peace essential to the security of the new polity. The difficulties confronting the English government could well be an enticement to further military action; they could also, perhaps, provide the prince with an opportunity to press for a political settlement. Matthew Paris, setting aside the rhetoric and reflecting the remarkable attentiveness to the affairs of Wales which characterizes his work, sensed that the Welsh prudently began to weigh future events. He now attributes to the prince not a new call to arms, but the astute counsel to his people that they take account of the fact that the kingdom of England was now in a disturbed state but that when peace returned the Welsh would be unable to withstand them.[105] It was a time to reach a political settlement. In the event, Llywelyn came to see that his search for a settlement was not made easier by the fact that Henry governed a divided kingdom.

In the spring of 1258 Henry tried to convince his kingdom that he wished to redeem his promise and return to Wales to complete the campaign which, by the decision of council, had been abandoned the previous year. He set a date, summoning forces to Chester by 17 June.[106] By early May it became clear that, in the period immediately preceding the campaign in Wales, Henry would be engaged in important transactions with the magnates of the realm at Oxford. But he insisted that he fully intended to proceed so as to deal with the problems created by Llywelyn's aggression. If it were God's will, he told Alexander of Scotland, it was his purpose to set out from the parliament at Oxford without delay to wage war on those who rebelled against him in

---

[105] Paris, *ChronMaj*, v, 727–8. Paris, again reflecting knowledge he owed to Bishop Richard of Bangor's presence at St Albans, reveals a perceptive awareness of the possibility of renewed internal dissension centred on Owain, Dafydd and Rhodri.

[106] *CR, 1256–59*, 294–7, 299; *CPR, 1247–58*, 627–33.

Wales.[107] It might appear from the record as though the lords who came armed to Oxford by 9 June did so with just that end in view, and there were certainly some among them who would have welcomed a campaign in Wales. William de Valence, lord of Pembroke, apart from his personal loyalty to Henry, had come to appreciate the extent of the problem in south-west Wales, as his forces, unable to dislodge their opponents, failed to reassert his authority in Cemais and Peuliniog.[108] Other magnates had other priorities at this time and their determination to resolve the discontent in the realm was to be reflected in the outcome of the deliberations at the Oxford parliament.[109] Simon de Montfort, earl of Leicester, opposed the proposal to go to war and his resistance incurred the charge of treachery, but though animosity to the king may have been particularly pronounced in his case, he was not alone. He was joined, in a declaration of mutual interest, by a group of magnates who included Richard de Clare.[110] Although he was exposed to renewed Welsh attacks Clare was disinclined to a new campaign, influenced both by his admission of the need for a reform of the king's government and his fear that, in the present state of the realm, the fiasco of the previous year might well be repeated. The outcome of the gathering of the magnates of the realm was not war in Wales but the formulation of a baronial reform programme in the Provisions of Oxford. Henry continued to insist upon his resolve to return to the conflict that had been stayed by the extraordinarily early winter but he invited Llywelyn to send proctors to Oxford.[111] Llywelyn explained that he was not able to attend in person but he empowered his envoys Anian, abbot of Aberconwy, and Madog ap Philip to act on his behalf. War had been averted, but Llywelyn looked for something better than a mere cessation of hostilities. Anian and Madog went to Oxford empowered to renew the truce

---

[107] *CR, 1256–59*, 310–11 (13 May); knights of Burgundy were to proceed from Oxford to Wales, 25 May, and preparations for war in Wales continued until 10 June (ibid., 231). By 2 May twenty-four men were to meet for the reform of the state of the realm (*DBM*, 75–7); by 13–19 May a *colloquium* or *parliamentum* was called to Oxford by 9 June (*CR, 1256–59*, 222, 223–4, 229).

[108] *AC*, 95; F. R. Lewis, 'William de Valence, *c*.1230–1296', *Aberystwyth Studies*, 13 (1934), 11–35; 14 (1936), 69–92; Carpenter, *Reign of Henry III*, 190–7. Dr Ridgeway suggests that Valence's rise to prominence in 1256–7 may be largely due to his position in relation to the need for a military response to Llywelyn's power.

[109] Treharne, *BPR*, 64–76; *DBM*, 96–112. Paris, *ChronMaj*, v, 677, 696, indicates a reluctance in England to contemplate a Welsh war in 1258.

[110] Paris, *ChronMaj*, v, 676–7, 688–90, cites the arguments and Valence's charges; cf. Carpenter, *Reign of Henry III*, 193–4.

[111] Bémont, *Montfort* (1884), 327–8; Altschul, *Clares*, 80–6; Maddicott, *Montfort*, 159–61. Henry's invitation is deduced from Llywelyn's letter, 31 May (*LW*, 29–30); precise date is unknown, but it was probably sent shortly after he wrote to Alexander, 13 May (*CR, 1256–59*, 310–11). A safe-conduct was issued for Llywelyn's envoys 2 June (*Foedera*, I, i, 372; *CPR, 1247–58*, 632).

(*treuga*) and to negotiate a peace (*pax*).[112] In view of the situation which prevailed at Oxford, Llywelyn may have hoped that the king would be prepared to enter into purposeful negotiations for more than a truce. The king's communications may have given him reason to believe that matters of some consequence could be considered. The outcome, however, was a truce. Paris says that Llywelyn would have paid heavily for a peace, but the king would have none of it. Henry would not have been alone in this, for, if Clare, Humphrey de Bohun, Roger Mortimer and the rest could not countenance a military solution at this stage, they would certainly not yield to Llywelyn any permanent recognition of his position. To the extent that the king recognized Llywelyn's possession (*seisina*) of the territories in his power, and agreed on arbitration procedures, the new provisions represented some advance upon the previous position.[113] Most of all, the terms of the truce show that Henry was constrained to acknowledge that any progress towards the regulation of the situation in Wales meant negotiating with Llywelyn. To this extent the prince had already won a position comparable to that which his grandfather had secured in the last decade of his life. Llywelyn ap Gruffudd's position in 1258 was, if not better, already on a par with that which Llywelyn ap Iorwerth secured by the truce made in 1234 and renewed thereafter. It provided Llywelyn ap Gruffudd with a basis for the sequence of truces that he would be granted in the following years. But, for the second Llywelyn, this was not nearly enough.

Llywelyn soon appreciated that the rifts in the community of the realm, which might ease the path of his military objectives, were likely to hinder his quest for terms which would ensure a permanent peace. By the summer of 1258 he knew that he had to negotiate with a king placed under the restraints exercised by the Council of Fifteen established by the Provisions of Oxford.[114] The Fifteen included several lords with territorial interests in the march and borderland of Wales – Richard de Clare, earl of Gloucester, Humphrey de Bohun, earl of Hereford, James Audley and Roger Mortimer – and they were unlikely to agree to any concession to the prince which might be damaging to themselves.[115] The deliberations at the Oxford parliament had shown that the reformers paid no heed to Llywelyn's objectives. In respect of Welsh issues it is clear that the circumstances in which the Provisions of Oxford came to be formulated were quite different from those which obtained at the making of

---

[112] *LW*, 29.

[113] *LW*, 27–8; *Foedera*, I, i, 372 (17 June); truce to remain in force 18 June 1259–1 August 1259. Envoys went to Oxford again by 28 June to arrange for the payments due under its terms (*LW*, 13–14). On 27 June, at Llywelyn's request, a meeting was arranged at the ford of Montgomery to deal with breaches of the truce (*CR, 1256–59*, 320).

[114] Treharne, *BPR*, 83–6; *DBM*, 96–113.

[115] For the marchers, below, pp. 140–3.

Magna Carta.[116] As far as the evidence shows, no mention of Llywelyn ap Gruffudd's submissions was made in any of the documents drawn up by the reformers. No one came to undertake any mediating role comparable to that of Stephen Langton earlier in the century. On the contrary, far from promoting Llywelyn's cause, it was likely that any embassy dispatched to the march to deal with the affairs of Wales would include some of those marchers who were understandably wary of the prince's threat to their position in the area. Thus in December 1258 the earl of Hereford, Roger Mortimer and James Audley were among those who went to the ford of Montgomery to meet Llywelyn's envoys and negotiate a prolongation of the truce made at Oxford and set up a procedure by which infractions of the truce might be corrected.[117] Matters of concern to the king and prince would be entrusted, on the king's behalf, to men who would often have their own interests to safeguard, their own grievances to set right.

It could still prove possible to secure some regulation of the troubled areas where Welsh and royal or marcher spheres met and merged, though the extent of the difficulty encountered might vary considerably. Those who were engaged in discussions at the end of 1258 were able to arrange for the resolution of some problems which had arisen on the Anglo-Welsh border. But there were troubles, too, in Deheubarth. Llywelyn alleged during the summer of 1258 that Patrick de Chaworth and Nicholas FitzMartin, constable of Carmarthen, had acted in a manner at variance with the truce made at Oxford in withdrawing Maredudd ap Rhys Gryg from the prince's fealty and then waging war together in Dyfed.[118] Henry insisted that Maredudd had returned to the king's fealty before the truce was made, but this was admitted by Llywelyn's envoy at the time, and hardly affected his complaint. By the end of the year the situation was reversed upon Maredudd's capture by Llywelyn. Following a meeting between the magnates and Llywelyn's envoys at the end of November the king appointed two arbitrators (*dictatores*), Trahaearn ap Hywel and Gwilym ap Gwrwared, to deal with infractions of the truce at a meeting with the prince's men at Abergwili, and they were specifically ordered to seek a means of bringing Maredudd back into the king's fealty.[119] This proved to be something more than the king's nominees could manage and Maredudd remained in detention until 1261. Convicted of treachery when he appeared before the prince's council, Maredudd made a submission in terms which reflect the strength of Llywelyn's position, though

---

[116] J. B. Smith, 'Magna Carta', 344–61.
[117] *CR, 1256–59*, 330, 466–7; *CPR, 1258–66*, 27, 34.
[118] *CR, 1256–59*, 323–4.
[119] Ibid., 466–7 (20 December); subsequent negotiations, 10 August 1259, ibid., 422–3.

even then he was to revert once more to the king's fealty.[120] There were clearly some matters which were not negotiable on Llywelyn's part, and equally so on that of the marchers. The presence of marchers on the delegations which the king sent to the ford of Montgomery was thus essential. They were there again in the summer of 1259: Mortimer, Bohun, Audley, John FitzAlan, Roger of Mold on this occasion.[121] Llywelyn himself was evidently anxious that these meetings be held and duly sent his representatives. He took care, however, to press, not just for corrections of infringements of the truce, but for a full peace between the king and himself. The king, though he was to issue a well-nigh ritual call for a summer campaign, appeared to take heed of his request. He told Llywelyn that he was sending magnates of his council and some of his liegemen (*fideles*) of the march to the ford of Montgomery. They would provide correction of infringements of the truce and discuss with Llywelyn the making of a peace between them ('ad tractandum vobiscum super pace inter nos et vos reformanda').[122] Llywelyn was told to be there on the appointed day in person, repeating an order of the previous autumn requiring the prince's personal attendance. Llywelyn is not known to have attended either meeting but, evidently hoping that matters of substance would be considered, he took care to send to the meeting (*parliamentum*) at the ford of Montgomery some of the major figures among his magnates: Dafydd ap Gruffudd, Rhys Fychan, and Gruffudd ap Madog were deputed to be there, along with Goronwy ab Ednyfed and other members of his immediate entourage.[123] Serious intent is indicated on both sides. However, the king was careful to ensure that, while his magnates were empowered to enter into discussions of the making of a peace between king and prince, any such exchanges should be reported to the king who would then take counsel with regard to what had transpired. In fact, nothing was accomplished beyond the prolongation, for another year, of the arrangements for the truce.

There was to be no swift resolution of the issues which he had raised but, indicating his wish to persist with his submissions to the king, Llywelyn sent a delegation to the king in the autumn of 1259 with important proposals. Headed by Bishop Richard of Bangor, the embassy conveyed the prince's unambiguous request for a peace agreement with the king of England and the heart of the matter was his submission that he might hold lands and homages in Wales as they had been held by Llywelyn ap Iorwerth ('pro pace et concordia cum rege optinenda et pro terris et homagiis Wallie de rege

---

[120] *AC*, 97; *LW*, 104–5. Maredudd's homage was granted to the king's son Edmund with the honour of Carmarthen in 1265, and was denied to Llywelyn in the treaty of 1267.

[121] *CPR, 1258–66*, 27.

[122] *CR, 1256–59*, 480 (13 May 1259); forces were summoned to Shrewsbury by 8 August, the octave of St Peter in Chains (ibid., 480–1, 12 June).

[123] *LW*, 15, 28 (22, 29 June 1259).

Supremacy

tenendis, prout Lewelinus avus euis tenuit').[124] Llywelyn declared his readiness to do homage to the king and swear fealty; he would marry a niece of the king; he would pay a sum of £11,000 to the king, £2,500 to the queen and £3,000 to Edward. These were no trifling sums, though it might be noticed that Llywelyn proposed that he should pay £200 a year for a period of eighty years. He would leave the king in possession of Prestatyn and Creuddyn, the commotes in which the castles of Diserth and Degannwy were situated; he would restore their lands to the marchers. Alternatively he would concede the king a truce for seven years, paying £100 a year. This is the fullest surviving text of the proposals made by Llywelyn in the period following his assertion of power. Though they date from the autumn of 1259 it is likely that they correspond closely to the proposals that he had submitted at the time of the Oxford parliament. They were probably much the same, too, as those which were to be submitted by Bishop Richard and others on several subsequent occasions.

These proposals represent Llywelyn ap Gruffudd's conception of what was involved in formal acknowledgement of the principality of Wales as it was formulated during the period of restraint which preceded the major offensives which he was to launch at the end of 1262. Their essence had been embodied in the letter to the earl of Cornwall, already noticed, which provides an early indication of the negotiating position adopted after he established his authority over the provinces of independent Wales.[125] He had offered a substantial sum of money to secure a permanent peace for himself and for all those who stood with him in peace and war. He insisted that the king would not find him amiss in fulfilling the service that he would undertake in return for royal recognition of his rights in Wales (*iura nostra in Wallia*). Llywelyn placed some emphasis on his rights and those of his predecessors. It was to restore those rights that he, with the agreement of all the magnates of Wales, had taken possession of the land where Edward had wrought destruction upon the prince's people. It is clear, from the proposals which Llywelyn then submitted to Henry, that what would in his estimation constitute a recognition of those rights was a concession on the part of the king of the homage of the lords of Wales. According to his interpretation of history, he sought no more than the restoration of the position which had existed under Llywelyn the Great. He urged his case persistently, and this might reasonably be seen as an interlude in Anglo-Welsh relations when it might, indeed, have been possible to establish an understanding with the monarchy by which authority over the provinces of Aberffraw, Mathrafal and Dinefwr could be formally vested in a Welsh prince. The rights (*iura*) which Llywelyn claimed at this

---

[124] Proposals are summarized in Henry's letter, 1 November (*CR,1259–61*, 4–5); bishop's safe-conduct 31 October (*CPR, 1258–61*, 57).

[125] *CAC*, 50–1; for the date, above, n. 26.

stage were entirely bound up with his lordship over the lands of those magnates who were men of the Welsh nation. When he failed to negotiate terms which would ensure him the dominion he envisaged, he was drawn to violate new frontiers and, extending his sway over other territories, he provoked animosities which ultimately served to undermine his authority in the very areas which mattered most to him. By 1267 Henry III was constrained to concede to Llywelyn a much broader authority than the prince could possibly have claimed at this time. It is not entirely futile to ponder whether it might have been better for the king, as well as for Llywelyn, if an agreement with the crown of England had been formulated in accordance with the proposals which the prince submitted in the period 1257-60 when he sought a peace treaty which would provide for himself and for those who, as he put it, stood with him in peace and war.

If Llywelyn laid any store by Bishop Richard's embassy in 1259 he would have been disappointed by Henry's reaction. Now, if not before, he began to know the frustration which Llywelyn ap Iorwerth had experienced in his efforts to secure stability in relations between Wales and England. The responses which Llywelyn elicited were closely comparable to the prevaricating missives which his grandfather had learnt to live with. It might be explained to him that some of the great magnates of his realm were absent, and the matters raised by Llywelyn could not possibly be resolved without them; or Henry had to sail for France; or other important matters concerning the realm needed urgent attention.[126] To bide time on this occasion, shortly before he went to Paris to do homage to Louis and ratify the treaty of Paris, the king empowered Bishop Peter of Hereford, the abbot of St Werbergh, Chester, and Roger of Mold, along with six of the arbitrators who habitually attended to infractions of the truce, to meet Llywelyn's representatives at Wepre. They were to adhere to a strict brief, limited to corrections of breaches of the truce. In confidence, the bishop and those with him were entrusted with the task of considering, with due discretion, both infractions of the truce and the making of peace. The intriguing marriage proposal made by Llywelyn, offering to marry a niece of the king, was also commended to the delegation's prudence. Anxious to ensure that hostilities be averted in his absence, Henry conceded that, if no other means suggested themselves, Llywelyn be allowed some trading concessions.[127] Far from entrusting the bishop with a clear authority by which he might make

---

[126] Circumstances in council at the time, e.g. the making of the provisions of Westminster by Edward and Montfort (October 1259), are noticed in Treharne, *BPR*, 159-64; Powicke, *Henry III*, 394-407; *DBM*, 18-21; Maddicott, *Montfort*, 184-6.

[127] *CR, 1259-61*, 4-5: emissaries, meeting at Wepre 1 December 1259, were to engage Llywelyn and his adherents in prudent and friendly discussion until the king's return. Nothing more is known of the marriage proposal ('quandam neptem regis libenter duceret in uxorem', ibid.); cf. Treharne, *BPR*, 194-5.

progress with matters of substance, Henry was concerned to engage Llywelyn in discussion until the king returned from abroad. Matters would then be considered in council. What might have been discussed in confidence and conducted with discretion at Wepre in December 1259 we cannot tell. It would seem, however, that in embarking upon a campaign in the march early in the new year Llywelyn was giving vent to his frustration at the failure to proceed with meaningful discussion and making a new attempt to bring pressure to bear on Henry III. The rifts which had become apparent in royal councils in 1259 had done nothing to ease Llywelyn's quest for a settlement. Edward, reversing a brief alliance with Gloucester, had pledged himself in aid and counsel of Montfort. But he and those associated with him – Henry of Almain, John de Warenne, Roger Leyburn, Hamo Lestrange, Roger Clifford – were likely to press for an even more vigorous resistance to Llywelyn's propositions than any that was likely to be provided by those members of council associated with Gloucester.[128] No faction in the royal council favoured any concession to Llywelyn beyond a truce which might hold off the Welsh threat in expectation of a concerted effort to repel his expansive incursions of the previous three years. By the end of 1259, while not deviating from the quest for a full peace, Llywelyn was prepared to look to a more forceful means of bringing his adversaries to serious negotiation.

In his first intervention in the march for some time, Llywelyn concentrated his attack on Builth. He had taken the lordship into his possession in 1257 and placed it in the custody of Maredudd ab Owain.[129] The castle had not been taken and Roger Mortimer, to whom Edward had granted custody, had been able to restore royal authority over a good deal of the lordship, if not over its whole extent. Builth was of obvious strategic importance to the crown and its possession would similarly be advantageous to Llywelyn, but there can be little doubt that his assault on the castle in January 1260 was dictated by his wish to induce the king to enter into purposeful discussion of the matters he had placed before him.[130] Henry was in France but he soon knew that

[128] Carpenter, *Reign of Henry III*, 241–52.
[129] For the lordship, D. Walker, 'The lordship of Builth in the middle ages', *Brycheiniog*, 20 (1982–3), 23–33; J. B. Smith, 'Llywelyn ap Gruffudd and the march of Wales', *Brycheiniog*, 20 (1982–3), 9–22; for the castle, *HKW*, i, 293–9; C. J. Spurgeon, 'Builth castle', *Brycheiniog*, 18 (1978–9), 47–59.
[130] *AC*, 97–8, dates the attack about the feast of St Hilary (13 January); *BT, Pen20*, 211–12; *Pen20Tr*, 112, immediately after Epiphany (6 January). The offensive had been launched before 7 January when council considered a letter from Roger Mortimer which, three days later, prompted an order to the lords to go to the march. No mention is made of Builth but, writing to Hugh Bigod, justiciar, from Luzarche, 26 January, Henry knew that Llywelyn had put the castle under siege on 9 January (*CR, 1259–61*, 23–4, 267–8). *AC*, 98, records that after Builth an attack was made on 'Dinbrec in Deved', possibly Tenby, by a strong force.

Llywelyn, his army equipped with siege engines, had put Builth under attack. He feared, too, that the prince was gathering his strength in Brecon and Netherwent to devastate the king's marches more widely. Henry argued that, in the light of the conflict in the march, it would be best to postpone the parliament scheduled to assemble upon his return to the kingdom. Perhaps with this in mind as much as anything else, he prepared for war.[131] At the same time he hastened to make arrangements for negotiations with Llywelyn. The bishop of Bangor had recently been with him for discussion of peace and truce, and the mission and its timing were both of some significance. They had arranged a day one month after Easter when properly empowered envoys would come to the king and the issues raised by the bishop could be considered. Henry, to sustain the truce and in hope of peace, and anxious to ensure that the bishop's efforts were not in vain, had secured Edward's agreement, and the consent of council, to the lifting of the embargo on trade between the lands of king and prince. Unrestricted trade, ensured at least until Whitsun, was a gesture of goodwill. The king wished it to be known that he would not necessarily consider the truce revoked by any particular infringement, but any breach should be corrected by the arbitrators (*dictatores*).[132] He made further provisions calculated to facilitate the arbitration procedures, and ensure that those concerned were able to act promptly whenever and wherever they were needed. Henry also provided that appropriate magnates, such as Roger Mortimer, were empowered to implement the decisions of the arbitrators.[133] Coming in the wake of a renewed Welsh offensive all this seemed promising, and the safe-conduct provided for Llywelyn's emissaries conveyed that they would come to discuss both truce and peace.[134]

During the months that followed, arbitrators made their way to Montgomery and Oswestry to deal with breaches of the truce involving Llywelyn and the king, or Edward, or Richard de Clare, or Roger Mortimer.[135] In accordance with the king's undertaking, too, Llywelyn sent his envoys to court to discuss the greater issues. Sadly, burdened by those arduous affairs concerning the realm which necessarily took precedence over those of Wales,

[131] Treharne, *BPR*, 219–23; Maddicott, *Montfort*, 193.
[132] *CR, 1259–61*, 30–1 (letter to sheriffs of border counties, 25 February).
[133] Arrangements are more explicit in a draft, *DipDoc*, i, no. 323, placed by the editor after 12 March 1261, that is at a date after the truce then made, itself a ratification of the truce of 22 August 1260 (*Foedera*, I, i, 404); close resemblance in substance and phraseology to the king's letter of 25 February 1260, particularly the king's wish for peace and his hope that the bishop's labours would not be in vain, suggest late February 1260.
[134] *CPR, 1258–66*, 65–6; *Foedera*, I, i, 394 (25 February 1260).
[135] *CR, 1259–61*, 162–3; *CPR, 1258–66*, 69–70. Mortimer's town of Knighton in Maelienydd was attacked in April by men of Cydewain and Ceri (*AC*, 98). The march was disturbed, too, by conflicts involving Gruffudd ap Gwenwynwyn, Thomas Corbet and others (*CR, 1259–61*, 49, 180–1; *CPR, 1258–66*, 184).

Henry could not attend to the prince's business.[136] Improvements to the arrangements for maintaining the truce were indeed made, but this was not enough. During the summer Llywelyn registered a telling success in the march which coincided with a renewed diplomatic initiative, and the synchronization of the two moves is striking. A mission headed by Bishop Richard made its way to Westminster, provided with the appropriate safe-conducts, in time for the session of parliament summoned for July.[137] Matters of considerable importance to the realm were to be considered, notably the charges brought by the king against Simon de Montfort which reflected their deep mutual animosity.[138] Roger Mortimer was specially summoned from the march, but on the very day on which he reached London, 17 July, Builth castle fell to Llywelyn's forces.[139] The chronicler conveys that the capture of the castle was facilitated by the susceptibility to bribery of some disaffected men among its English defenders but whatever the circumstances the Welsh forces had won a major success and the castle was promptly reduced to the ground. In this vigorous renewed effort Llywelyn, who was probably at Builth in person, was joined by Rhys Fychan, bringing the armed strength of Deheubarth, and by Owain ap Maredudd of Elfael. Owain's son, Madog, had been a captive of Llywelyn but his decision to adhere to the prince was rewarded with the release of his son and a gift of £300 from the prince's coffers.[140] Llywelyn's forces may have been engaged elsewhere as well, quite possibly in Clare's lordship of Glamorgan. But the main offensive was quite deliberately concentrated upon the royal stronghold of Builth, with precisely the same end in view as that which the prince had set himself at the beginning of the year.

Llywelyn's initiative, meticulously timed to coincide with the embassy undertaken on his behalf by Bishop Richard, brought a sequence of royal mandates which point to a royal council in serious disarray, though the various motivations reflected in the contradictory orders are exceedingly difficult to fathom. The first was predictable. On 22 July Henry wrote to Llywelyn expressing his astonishment that, at precisely the moment the bishop had come to him to arrange for the correction of infractions of the truce and for its extension, and even as those discussions were taking place, the prince should launch an attack on Builth. He was told to yield the castle at once to Philip le Bret whom the king was sending to him.[141] Llywelyn was, in

---

[136] *CPR, 1258–66*, 66, 69–70.
[137] *CPR, 1258–66*, 81, 83; *CR, 1259–61*, 184.
[138] Treharne, *BPR*, 220–43; Powicke, *Henry III*, ii, 415–17; *DBM*, 33–4; Maddicott, *Montfort*, 195–9.
[139] *AC*, 98–9; date confirmed in *CPR, 1258–66*, 85, which shows that Henry knew of the attack by 20 July; *HW*, ii, 716–7; Treharne, *BPR*, 242–4.
[140] *AC*, 98; *BT, Pen20*, 212; *Pen20Tr*, 112. Owain held Elfael Uwch Mynydd by 1248 (*CR, 1247–51*, 72, 113); for three other sons (Owain, Maredudd and Ifor), see *CR, 1264–68*, 496–7.
[141] *CR, 1259–61*, 184 (22 July).

Henry's reasonable estimation, in clear breach of the truce, but three days later the king announced that he and the bishop had arranged that the truce be extended for one month.[142] This was a good deal less than Llywelyn had hoped for when he sent Bishop Richard to Westminster, but it may have been a good deal more than some of the king's council could tolerate. On 1 August the king issued a call to arms, summoning his magnates to Chester and Shrewsbury by 8 September for a campaign in Wales. The cunning of his Welsh adversary, the same *versutia* which Henry had recognized as an attribute of the prince's grandfather, called for stern corrective measures ('ut dictorum rebellium nostrorum versucia adeo potenter reprimatur').[143] Simon de Montfort, earl of Leicester, would lead one army, Richard de Clare, earl of Gloucester, the other. The decision invites a range of speculative hypotheses; it might just be possible that the conflicting groups in council represented by the two earls had set aside their differences to ensure a concerted effort to withstand a renewal of the Welsh offensive, a prospect that had created considerable apprehension earlier in the year; Henry may have seen the Welsh peril as a means of diverting Montfort's energy to a sphere where it might be deployed to the benefit of the realm; it might be more convincingly argued that the Welsh campaign reflected particularly the wishes of the Lord Edward and that he was able to secure the support of his ally of late for a more vigorous response than their opponents in council were inclined to offer.[144] Certainly, on one particular matter relating to the crisis in Wales the differences in council were explicit: two days before the muster was announced Henry issued a declaration that Roger Mortimer, who had been summoned to Westminster at the king's specific command, was granted an exoneration of his responsibility for the loss of the castle. The declaration was made in the names of Henry and Edward, the chancery record carefully minuting the fact that the decision was made in the presence of a number of magnates and with their consent. The remission was then repudiated by Edward in the presence of council.[145] Edward is undoubtedly the one who suggests himself as the main advocate of a strong military response to Llywelyn's challenge, and he could be assured of Montfort's consent. Gloucester's position is difficult to establish. He appears to have been adversely affected by Llywelyn's recent offensive, a point made by the archbishop of Canterbury in calling upon the bishops of Wales to intercede with Llywelyn and, if they failed to get him to

---

[142] *CPR, 1258–66*, 83.
[143] *CR, 1259–61*, 191–4.
[144] Treharne, *BPR*, 242–3; Maddicott, *Montfort*, 199. Montfort's trial, on charges arising from his administration of Gascony, was suspended by the call to arms.
[145] *CPR, 1258–66*, 85; *Foedera*, I, i, 398; Powicke, *Henry III*, ii, 417; for further recrimination, below, n. 152.

release the castle of Builth, to put his lands under interdict.[146] Gloucester was, however, much the most powerful figure among those gathered about the king when, on 3 August, just two days after the summons to arms and his appointment to lead one of the two armies, the king issued new instructions of a distinctly different order.

By the terms of Henry's new mandates arbitrators were to go to the ford of Montgomery by 18 August so that amends could be made for the breaches of the truce in accordance with the arrangements made with the bishop of Bangor. Four days later magnates would be there to ensure the adherence of the king's men (*gens noster*) to the decisions reached by the arbitrators.[147] The new emphasis was reflected in further decisions by those who attended the king, first at Westminster and then at Windsor, after the dispersal of the magnates who had attended parliament. The bishop of Coventry and Lichfield, the prior of Wenlock, Humphrey de Bohun and Simon Passelowe would go to the ford of Montgomery to treat of peace with Llywelyn; these, with the addition of Roger Mortimer and James Audley, would consider the prolongation of the truce.[148] These orders went a good deal further than the king had envisaged only a few days earlier, when correction of breaches of the truce and their enforcement were the matters specified for discussion with Llywelyn's representatives. The decisions made during August, when Edward was at Chester preparing for war, evidently reflect the discordant influences at work in the king's council. Llywelyn maintained his representations, for while the king was at Windsor he received new documents from the prince. He was unable to discuss them with his council, but they were sent on to those empowered to go to the ford of Montgomery on the king's behalf.[149] That the decision to consider a renewed truce, even a peace, should come so soon after alerting the realm to war in Wales, itself a decision made abruptly after the king had agreed to a brief extension of the truce, can only be explained as a reflection of the divided views in council. The manner in which provision was made for negotiation with Llywelyn tends to confirm this view. The fact that Mortimer was named as one entrusted to speak of truce but not of peace may indicate an acknowledgement of his unwillingness to countenance any form of peace negotiation with Llywelyn. Mortimer may not have been alone in his disquiet. None of the magnates nominated to treat either of peace or truce were in fact associated with the outcome of the negotiations at the ford. Whatever its significance, the document which emerged from the *parliamentum* was linked only with the names of the prior of Wenlock, Thomas de Orreby, justice of Chester, and Simon Passelowe, a king's clerk, with the

---

[146] *CPR, 1258–66*, 103; *Councils*, i, 487–8; *Foedera*, I, i, 399–400.
[147] *CR, 1259–61*, 89.
[148] *CPR, 1258–66*, 88–9 (10 August).
[149] *CR, 1259–61*, 198 (8 August).

bishop of Bangor and the abbot of Aberconwy acting for Llywelyn.[150] Henry and Edward were both named in the text, but the chancery clerks who wrote the letters authorizing the king's representatives to go to Montgomery had been required to draw up two sets of documents, one including Edward's name and the other excluding him.[151] It was obviously doubtful at that stage whether Edward would consent to what was being done. The limited nature of the agreement may have satisfied Edward but it is far from certain that Henry was pleased with the outcome, any more than he had displayed consistency of purpose in the process leading up to it. Laying the blame for his losses in Wales, and specifically the loss of Builth, on his council, the king complained further that a truce which might have brought him a sum of 2,000 marks had been yielded for nothing.[152] The truce of 1260 was neither an unreserved expression of royal goodwill nor a measured expression of the considered judgement of the royal council.

War was averted and on 1 September, a week before the king's forces were due to assemble, Henry informed his tenants-in-chief and the sheriffs of England that, following the *parliamentum* at Montgomery, it was not, for the present, necessary to go to war.[153] It was not, however, for a mere renewal of the truce that Llywelyn had twice sent Bishop Richard to Westminster and twice sent his army to Builth. His military initiative had, indeed, proved the more rewarding. He had strengthened his position in a strategic quarter of the march. The castle of Builth was in his possession, and his hold upon the lordship a good deal more secure thereby. His offensive had brought Owain ap Maredudd of Elfael into his ranks, giving him control over Elfael Uwch Mynydd and enabling him to exert pressure on Elfael Is Mynydd, where the Tony family would now exercise a far more precarious hold.[154] More than this, his presence in Builth and Elfael strengthened Llywelyn's position in relation to Roger Mortimer. His embarrassment at the loss of Builth came after the loss to Llywelyn of his own Gwerthrynion, and now Maelienydd was

---

[150] *Foedera*, I, i, 404; below, n. 156.

[151] *CPR, 1258–66*, 88–9.

[152] For the document *c*.March–April 1261 enumerating the king's complaints against council, *DBM*, 213 (c. 2, text *a*), 233 (c. 21, text *b*); H. Ridgeway, 'King Henry III's grievances against the council in 1261: a new version and a letter describing political events', *Historical Research*, 61 (1988), 241 (c. 28, text *c*). Text *a* gives a general complaint concerning the king's disinheritance in Wales; *b* mentions Builth and the truce, *c* only the truce. Dr Ridgeway suggests that the projected campaign of 1260 had, probably at Gloucester's instigation, been the victim of the dissension in council between supporters of Gloucester and the coalition of Montfort and Edward (ibid., 232). He notes that the truce of August 1260 was not confirmed by the king until 12 March 1261 (*CPR, 1258–66*, 147; *Foedera*, I, i, 404). Henry issued an *inspeximus* and confirmation of the truce made at Montgomery on 21 May.

[153] *CR, 1259–61*, 200–1.

[154] Below, pp. 141, 183, 340.

Supremacy

left much more exposed. A new offensive in this area could leave Brecon at risk, too, as well as the lordships along the Wye and Usk valleys towards Hay and Abergavenny. All this proved true in the fullness of time, but there are good grounds to conclude that Llywelyn was concerned, for the present at least, not with further expansion but the consolidation of his position by formal recognition.[155] He had created consternation in royal councils, but it is doubtful whether, among the divided counsels of the summer of 1260, there were any who were genuinely concerned with making peace with the Welsh. It would be difficult to be certain that any faction in the fluid groupings in baronial ranks since the Provisions of Oxford had the will and the capacity to bring a quest for peace with Llywelyn on to the political agenda. Neither his resort to force, nor the cunning with which he went about his purposes, had enabled the prince to secure the objective he had set before him two years earlier.

The outcome of the negotiations provide, even so, the fullest surviving record of the arrangements made under conditions of truce in these years.[156] Agreement was based on the Oxford truce of 1258, prolonged now for a further two years until 24 June 1262. Under the terms newly agreed, king and prince were to retain the lands which were in their possession at that time. Detailed provisions were made concerning the supply of Diserth and Degannwy. The functions of the arbitrators called upon to rectify breaches of the truce were defined with a precision which reflects the importance of their role in maintaining the state of truce in accordance with the law and custom of the march. The removal of trade restrictions between England and Wales, conceded by the king in the emergency in which he found himself earlier in the year, was confirmed. All this amounted to a good deal less than Llywelyn would have wished, but the document incorporated several indications, perhaps clearer than in any previous instance, of the meaning of the truce. The king found it imperative to make practical arrangements which took account of Llywelyn's effective power. He had to acknowledge that in important respects Llywelyn now represented the interests of the Welsh people. In enabling the two countries to engage in unrestricted trade the king allowed movement between two peoples (*gentes*); in making provision for the regulation of criminal activity he had to acknowledge Llywelyn's responsibility for the actions of Welshmen. Llywelyn ap Gruffudd, Henry and the Lord Edward were the 'principal lords'; the prince's officers 'throughout the whole of Wales' and the magnates of his land were required to swear their adherence to the terms of the new agreement. The wording ensured that the

---

[155] The campaigns of 1262–3 are discussed later.
[156] Full text of the king's ratification of the truce, March 1261, in *Foedera*, I, i, 404, from the Patent Roll, C66/76, m. 14 (schedule); brief notice only in *CPR, 1258–66*, 147.

magnates were not seen to be Llywelyn's men, and the fact that those required to give their pledge would be selected by Henry and Edward confirmed their theoretical dependence upon the king.[157] The document, however, tacitly acknowledged the need to come to terms with the prince's position in relation to the magnates of Wales. Sealed by Henry and Edward on the one part and by Llywelyn and Dafydd on the other, the text registered a partial and belated royal admission of the supremacy which the prince had secured over a large part of the land peopled by communities who were of the Welsh nation. Llywelyn had won this measure of reward for his intervention in the march, on two occasions, during the course of 1260.

Friction in the march was not eliminated by any means and thereafter the arbitrators had fairly frequent recourse to Rhyd Chwima in an effort to maintain some order on the frontiers. Some of these men became well acquainted with the functions of the *parliamenta*, so often were they called upon.[158] On the king's side the names include John de Lingayn, Philip le Bret, Hywel ap Meurig, Hywel Fychan, Hywel ap Madog and Tudur ab Ednyfed, a list which itself conveys something of the political conditions in which these meetings were held. Of the men named, two were drawn from families which had settled in the march (and had Mortimer associations), two were from Welsh families in the area itself, and two were men of the princes' lands who were, at that time, in the king's service.[159] It is much more difficult to know who attended on Llywelyn's side, though his representatives were very probably drawn from leading lineages of his territories, and may have included men who were related to some of those who represented the king. On occasion meetings were held at places such as Wepre and Gresford, on the Cheshire frontier, but the great majority were held at Rhyd Chwima, the ford at Montgomery, where Henry III and Llywelyn were eventually to meet and complete the long peace process which the prince had been urging upon the

---

[157] Thus the clause requiring sworn assurance of the fulfilment of the truce: 'dominus Lewelinus suos ballivos per totam Walliam et etiam magnates partis sue, quos dominus rex et Edwardus filius suus, vel sui duxerint nominandos, jurare facient quod omnia predicta ... fideliter observabunt'.

[158] There are numerous references to the activity of arbitrators (*dictatores*), e.g. *CPR, 1258–66*, 45, 65–6, 69–70, 131; *CR, 1256–59*, 320, 422–3, 476; *CR, 1259–61*, 4–5, 162–3, 309; *CR, 1261–64*, 128, 135–7. On occasion, e.g. *CR, 1256–59*, 330, 466–7; *CPR, 1258–66*, 27, more powerful figures were sent to supervise the negotiations or deal with matters of particular importance.

[159] Lingayn and Bret had Mortimer associations and this was also true of Hywel ap Meurig, whose name will recur in this study; Hywel Fychan's links are less clear; Hywel ap Madog and Tudur ab Ednyfed later returned to the prince's service. Mortimer himself had a role in arbitration procedures, illustrated when letters to *dictatores* were addressed to him (*CR, 1259–61*, 162–3).

king for two decades.[160] These gatherings at the ford helped to establish the practice which made the *parliamentum* or *dies marchie* – the day of the march – an essential part of the experience of the lords and communities of the march of Wales for several generations to come.[161] There were other marches in Europe where comparable processes of arbitration, through institutions such as the *assize de la marche*, became an established practice. These marches were normally frontier areas placed between two polities which, at the very least, recognized one another's existence in a relatively stable relationship.[162] Yet this was hardly characteristic of the relationship between Wales and England in this period. When they came to the ford of Montgomery, or wherever they were directed, the arbitrators worked under conditions of truce rather than those of peace.[163]

To ensure that the truce was maintained, efforts were made to make the arbitration procedures work effectively. Early in 1260, following the first attack on Builth, those concerned with the correction of infractions of the truce were empowered to inquire into transgressions which might yet be committed and make awards at their discretion. They had authority to act, not only on particular matters deputed to them, but however often there was need. A single incident would not be allowed to invalidate the truce, if it were corrected by the arbitrators (*dictatores treugarum*) and appropriate amends made by the powers concerned. It was agreed by the king, and Llywelyn no doubt gave his assent, that Roger Mortimer and others should execute whatever the arbitrators agreed. Towards the end of 1260, in preparation for a meeting at Rhyd Chwima in the new year, Henry told Llywelyn that he was sending Mortimer and James Audley to execute the award (*dictum et*

---

[160] One Alexander of Montgomery held land in Montgomery on terms which required him to attend the king's *parliamenta* at the ford of Montgomery (*CIPM*, iii, no. 293). The ford was close by the site of the castle of Hen Domen and there is some archaeological evidence that the site was used in the thirteenth century after Henry III had built his new castle of Montgomery on another site in 1223 (P. Barker and R. Higham, *Hen Domen, Montgomery* (London, Royal Archaeological Institute, 1982), 20, 48–51, 93). The homage of 1267 at Montgomery is discussed later.

[161] J. B. Smith, 'The regulation of the frontier of Meirionnydd in the fifteenth century', *JMerHRS*, 5 (1965–6), 105–11; idem, 'Cydfodau o'r bymthegfed ganrif', *B*, 21 (1964–6), 309–24; 25 (1972–4), 128–34 (with texts of agreements between lordships); R. R. Davies, 'Frontier arrangements in fragmented societies: Ireland and Wales', in R. Bartlett and A. Mackay (eds.), *Medieval Frontier Societies* (Oxford, 1989), 77–100.

[162] J. Balon, 'L'Organisation judicaire des marches féodales', *Annales de la Société Archéologique de Namur*, 46 (1951), 5–72; the work of J.-F. Lemarignier is noticed below, p. 179, n. 153.

[163] Powicke, *Thirteenth Century*, 84–6, discussing relations between continental powers, held that a truce was not 'of necessity a fragile affair' and could secure stability under the rule of law; equally, Anglo-Welsh relations after 1267 might suggest that a formal treaty provided no guarantee of goodwill and stability. Yet it was only by securing a peace treaty that the existence of the political entity created in Wales could be formally recognized, and without recognition there could be no hope of stability.

consideracio) of the arbitrators and to make whatever distraints were necessary to secure observance of what had been agreed.[164] *Dictatores* and those empowered to enforce their *dicta* were duly informed of their responsibilities. Llywelyn in turn was asked to appoint arbitrators and ensure that he, too, sent men authorized to give effect to the awards made in accordance with practices which now constituted a 'form of truce' (*forma treugarum*).[165] The procedures of frontier regulation could no doubt be refined in accordance with the progress already made, but conditions in the march were inherently unstable. A state of abated conflict was very different from a state of peace.

If relatively peaceful conditions were maintained for the next two years, much was due to the restraint which characterized Llywelyn's conduct in this period. The image of a prince powerful in war should not efface the record of a person capable of exercising a marked restraint as he continued to seek a stable peace. He persevered with his efforts to urge his proposals upon the king and, from time to time, he was able to elicit encouraging intimations of the king's willingness to respond. During the course of 1261 Henry reasserted control over the government of England, and Llywelyn may have judged that the prospects for a solution were, at the very least, no worse than they had previously been. Sometime in the spring or early summer he sent his emissary Master Matthew to the king bearing proposals (*oblaciones*) for peace. The king received them, he told the prince, with favour (*benigne*). Of course, the king was not in a position to attend to the matter at that time, and Matthew made his way home.[166] Alan de Irvine, now working as a messenger for Llywelyn, stayed with the king for some time, but he was sent to his lord with a much more encouraging report.[167] Henry was anxious to emphasize that he had resumed royal power once more, responding to Llywelyn's approach more positively with an invitation to send representatives entrusted with power to arrange a peace ('ad tractandum efficacius de pace predicta, et qui potestatem habeant pacem illam nomine vestro firmandi').[168] Certainly acting in response to the king's message before the end of 1261, Llywelyn asked the king to name the day on which he could send envoys to him, so as to complete the negotiations concerning peace, a process upon which they were agreed.[169] Henry had to explain, however, that the negotiations could not proceed in the absence of his son Edward. He had been engaged in Gascony and day by day

---

[164] *CR, 1259–61*, 309.
[165] Ibid., 309–10.
[166] Ibid., 482 (8 July 1261).
[167] Ibid.; Llywelyn's messenger Alan, presumably Alan de Irvine, was sent back with a more positive response to the prince's letter.
[168] Ibid.
[169] *CR, 1261–64*, 100–1, undated letter from Llywelyn, cited in Henry's letter of 8 January 1262.

Supremacy

his father expected him to return. The king was not prepared to discuss peace in his absence and without his consent, lest anything done now might create difficulties in the future.[170] Llywelyn was assured that, as soon as Edward returned, or whenever the king had sure knowledge of his coming, he would be informed. He had to accept a further postponement of the negotiations, but this is the clearest indication in the surviving evidence that the king of England recognized that Llywelyn was in earnest in his wish to secure a better relationship between Wales and England than that of a conflict stayed. Henry went as far as to commend Llywelyn for his very creditable restraint in a period of turmoil in the kingdom.[171] He had looked for peace, the king acknowledged, when he might easily have been drawn to those who opposed the king in his kingdom. Llywelyn had resisted that temptation, and Henry commended him for his constancy.

Perhaps it was the king who was cunning now, but his generous reference to Llywelyn deserves notice and it may have been made with sincerity. There had certainly been a time when he was not free to exercise his will in matters of state, and at best he could not extricate himself entirely from the influence of those with power in the march who were present in the king's council. The marchers were not, as we shall see again, a naturally cohesive group. The extent of their resistance to Llywelyn's overtures might vary somewhat perhaps, but theirs was a decidedly negative influence. Not yet the most powerful of those either in the march or in council, but already revealing that combination of frontier interest and curial presence which he would reveal to good effect in latter years, Roger Mortimer was a key figure in dealings with Llywelyn.[172] He had endured discomfiture at the prince's hands. Apart from causing him acute embarrassment over the loss of Builth, Llywelyn had wrested one lordship from him at an early date. Llywelyn had subsequently sworn that he was ready to restore the marchers' lands as part of a peace settlement, but he was denied the opportunity to prove the sincerity of his propositions. He had, indeed, restored Cemais to Nicholas FitzMartin and released the noble prisoner from captivity – in return for a ransom, and perhaps a hefty one.[173] As far as we can tell, this was one of only a few instances of the kind, and the definitive peace which might have facilitated

---

[170] *CR, 1261–64*, 100–1.

[171] Ibid.: 'cum nuper de communi turbacione regni nostri suspicio haberatur, laudabiliter vos gessistis erga nos ac insuper sollicitastis nos de pace nobiscum ineunda, quamquam essetis in contrarium ut audivimus excitati'. Maddicott, *Montfort*, 212–13, following *HW*, ii, 729, suggests that Henry referred to recent baronial approaches to Llywelyn instigated by Montfort; the meaning is not clear, and the king may allude to Llywelyn's restraint at an earlier period, especially perhaps *c*.1258.

[172] Mortimer's part in the critical years 1262–7 and again in 1270–4 is examined later.

[173] FitzMartin and Guy de Brian were awarded £100 each towards their ransoms; FitzMartin was free by October 1258 (*CLibR*, iv, 436; *CPR, 1247–58*, 601, 653).

Supremacy

further and more important agreements of this nature remained elusive when, at the end of 1262, Llywelyn initiated a new period of intense conflict.

If kings and princes were inclined in later years to look back in regret for lost opportunities, both Henry and Llywelyn might have recalled one occasion in particular. This was that brief interval in the period following the king's resumption of personal control over the administration of the realm when the two of them had managed to maintain courteous and apparently well-disposed exchanges. England's adversity was Wales's opportunity: this is the notion which has permeated our conception of the political history of this period. Yet, if Llywelyn found any source of encouragement in his relations with the realm of England between 1258 and 1262, he found it, not in the period of the king's acute discomfiture, but from the early months of 1261 when Henry was able to re-establish something of his power to govern his kingdom and when his son was reconciled to him after the turbulent relations of recent years.[174] Sadly, the more promising exchanges between king and prince in 1261 brought no tangible result and, when the truce expired in the summer of the next year, the abbot of Aberconwy was able to negotiate no more than its extension for another two years.[175] Llywelyn's search for that definitive peace treaty had not been rewarded.

By the end of 1262 it was too late. In one view, the new military offensive which Llywelyn then launched was no more than an inevitable outcome of the conflict in the march which had been gathering momentum over several months.[176] More than before, the records speak not simply of unspecified frontier incidents but more damaging incursions by major figures such as Roger Mortimer and John Lestrange, who carried war into Powys Fadog.[177] In his letters to the king the prince now wrote not of peace but of the serious breaches of the truce by the powerful marchers, even by the justice of Chester. The actions of which he complained may have been retaliatory measures taken against Llywelyn. Henry certainly intimated that Llywelyn and his men were more to blame than were his own men. Yet it is not inconceivable that those who had most to lose from a peace settlement between king and prince, or who considered themselves likely to be adversely affected, would have been willing to resort to arms if renewed confrontation was the only way of staving off the prospect that Llywelyn's aggression over the previous years might be rewarded with royal recognition of his gains. Blame for frontier incidents is

---

[174] Treharne, *BPR*, 250–79; Powicke, *Henry III*, ii, 420–7, citing a letter to the pope (*CR, 1259–61*, 481–2) expressed in a tenor comparable to that addressed to Llywelyn.

[175] *LW*, 17–18 (4 May 1262). Dr Ridgeway notes that Mortimer, along with Edward and Gloucester, had opposed Henry's resumption of power in 1261 (*CPR, 1258–66*, 163, 195), and suggests that Henry avoided a settlement with Llywelyn as part of an attempt to win the magnates' support.

[176] *CR, 1261–64*, 128, 132–4, 172–3; *CPR, 1258–66*, 227.

[177] *CR, 1261–64*, 133–4 (24 August 1262).

Supremacy

extremely difficult to apportion, but it is clear that some of those very men who were entrusted with responsibility for the effective working of the 'form of truce' were themselves embroiled in combat. Viewed differently, the change that occurred by the end of 1262 reflected an acknowledgement on Llywelyn's part that, not only had the truce in the marches been grievously impaired, but that it had proved impossible to surmount the fundamental difficulties which stood in the way of a genuine settlement with the crown. The summer of 1262 brought some indication of a change of attitude on his part, an acknowledgement that after several years of perseverance he was making no headway in his dealings with King Henry. There were matters of greater concern than the frontier incidents, and serious discussion of these had not proved possible.

The underlying problems are revealed in a most telling manner by a letter which the king wrote shortly after he had landed in France during the summer of 1262.[178] His letter was inspired by a rumour that the prince was dead. It was known that Llywelyn had suffered an illness, possibly something serious, but the missive composed in the king's court at Amiens was no expression of royal felicitations with a princely neighbour at a time of illness, nor sympathy with those who might have been bereaved. Henry did not see fit to send the kind of message that was already part of the code of civilized practice in relations between the rulers of Christendom when one of their number endured sickness or bereavement. Llywelyn of Wales was never, at this time or any other, on a par with Alexander of Scotland, or Alphonso of Castile.[179] The one thing which occurred to Henry of England was that here was an opportunity which had to be grasped as soon as it was certain that Llywelyn was dead. If present tidings proved true, Wales's adversity had become England's opportunity. If it were certain that Llywelyn had been laid to rest with his forebears it would be time to proclaim that he had never been the true heir to Wales, and it followed that Dafydd ap Gruffudd, his younger brother, could not be a true heir. He possessed no right in Wales, especially since the first-born son was still alive. The king came at once to the matter which lay at the heart of the relationship between Wales and England: from the earliest times the homage of the lords of Wales belonged, by right, to the king and to none other. He called on the lords of the march to ensure that any attempt on Dafydd's part to assume authority would be frustrated, and that royal authority should be established.[180] The hegemony which Llywelyn had established would have to be undone, and the king knew exactly how to go about it: divide their strength and stir them up one against the other. As though he summoned up the memory of that renowned prescription, he put James Audley to warn his

---

[178] *CR, 1261–64*, 142–3 (letter to Philip Bassett, Amiens, 22 July 1262).
[179] Below, pp. 278–9.
[180] *CR, 1261–64*, 143: 'homagia nobilium Wallie ab antiquo iure ad nos debeant pertinere'.

brother-in-law, Gruffudd ap Madog, that it was now his duty to repudiate Dafydd ap Gruffudd and bring Powys Fadog back into the king's allegiance; his brother Hywel ap Madog, still a confidant of the king, would be urged to work to the same end. Henry knew that he had no need to take measures to ensure that Maredudd ap Rhys Gryg would not make any agreement with Dafydd. These were the names which first occurred to the king, and he could doubtless think of a few more. Roger Mortimer and the other marchers, told to ensure that alliances among the Welsh were dissolved, were warned to put themselves in readiness for a call to arms, the army summoned to Shrewsbury by the beginning of September.[181] Meantime, the king sought firm knowledge from Gruffudd ap Gwenwynwyn whether Llywelyn was alive or dead, and he may have been the person who first bruited the story abroad.[182]

This revealing evidence comes from the royal chancery itself, and the chroniclers of Wales make no mention of Llywelyn's illness nor the king's response. But there can be little doubt that, if that eloquent writer who recorded the stirring events of these years had taken note of the prince's malady, he would have interpreted Llywelyn's recovery as evidence of that mercy by which divine providence afforded its sure protection to the Welsh nation.[183] For Llywelyn was released from his sickness and recovered his power to show that he had not laboured in vain to bring the men of Wales to a unity which raised him to be prince of Aberffraw, Mathrafal and Dinefwr. After his triumphant assertion of power Llywelyn spent five years in a diligent quest for a firm peace with the king of England, but by the end of the fifth year the entire nation knew that it was once more a time for war.

---

[181] *CR, 1261–64*, 143–4.
[182] Gruffudd's letter to the king, *CAC*, 20.
[183] The chronicler's account of the providential care that raised Owain Gwynedd from sickness to renewed vigour (*BT, Pen20*, 94–5; *Pen20Tr*, 55; *RBH*, 122–5) comes irresistibly to mind.

CHAPTER 4

Rhyd Chwima

IT is impossible to be sure that Llywelyn ap Gruffudd ever knew what Henry III proposed for Wales in the summer of 1262 in the case of the prince's death. Nor are there any means of telling whether knowledge of the king's intentions influenced the prince's decision later that year to launch a major offensive in the march. If we were to rely entirely on *Brut y Tywysogyon* we would accept that the first initiatives owed nothing to Llywelyn, and that he simply responded to an eruption of conflict in the lordship of Maelienydd when men of that land attacked the castle of Cefnllys on the eve of St Andrew.[1] It is not inconceivable that the sequence of events was inaugurated in that way, for we can by no means discount the chronicler's reports that during the winter of 1262-3 the communities of several areas of the march chose, entirely of their own volition, to submit themselves to the prince's lordship. Much of this may be confirmed from English records. It is clear, even so, that formidable forces were deployed in Maelienydd from the first outbreak of hostilities, and it is more likely that the opening assaults on Roger Mortimer's lordship were the result of a decision made by Llywelyn himself. This new thrust needs to be considered in relation to what appears to have been a major change in his policy, and in the course of the discussion which follows a distinction will be made between two departures. First, the attack on Maelienydd launched a broad military offensive, sustained over a period of several months, by which Llywelyn extended his power to new areas of the march with a view, perhaps, to their incorporation in an extended principality. Second, the campaigns in the march led to co-operation with Simon de Montfort, earl of Leicester, and those associated with him, who transformed the baronial opposition to the king into a movement whose resort to force created civil war in England. The later phase of Llywelyn's association with the Montforts, in the years leading up to the war of 1277, has aroused considerable historical discussion and the course of action which the prince

[1] For the attack, below, n. 25.

pursued in that period will be considered at a later stage. But the initial phase in the relationship, between 1263 and 1265, has also provoked historians' critical comment. It was the prince's connection with Montfort in the earlier period which particularly moved William Stubbs to propound the view that the ultimate conquest of Wales did no more than exact an account for the doings of Welsh princes who, over a long time, 'had meddled in every English struggle, had fanned the flame of every expiring quarrel'.[2] The problems posed by Llywelyn's relations with Simon de Montfort will be considered in this chapter, but it has to be appreciated that when he went to war in the march at the end of 1262 Llywelyn could hardly have anticipated the change in the political situation in England which would follow Montfort's return from the continent in the spring of the following year.[3] Our first concern must therefore be the reasons which might have influenced Llywelyn's decision, late in 1262, to intervene in the march in such a forceful manner after the marked restraint which he had exercised for nearly five years.

The matter that needs to be noticed immediately is that the castle first attacked in the new offensive was one which belonged to Roger Mortimer. Cefnllys stood on a fine site, on the rocky ridge which rises above the Ieithon in the south-west portion of Maelienydd, and this stronghold was by now the main symbol of the power of the Mortimer dynasty in the march of Wales. We have noticed already that the family had settled at Wigmore in the Norman period and applied themselves to the conquest of the lands of Maelienydd and Gwerthrynion, their efforts focused on the castle of Cymaron. Similarly the Braose family had moved from their initial appropriation of Old Radnor into New Radnor and Elfael, and the castle of Colwyn in Elfael became another focus for the struggle in this area. Perhaps it is here, more than anywhere else, that the ferocity of the conflict upon the frontier between two peoples and two political traditions can be best appreciated. Maelienydd, Gwerthrynion, Elfael: these were the lordships which formed the core of the unstable area which may be conveniently termed the middle march of Wales.[4] It was initially the scene of a contest between, on the one hand, the Mortimer and Braose lineages and, on the other, the Welsh lords of the area itself. In the course of time, and with the changes in the distribution of power in Wales, the conflict in the march became part of a wider contest between the greater powers on each side. On occasion, admittedly, it was this area which drew these powers into conflict. Rhys ap Gruffudd, soon after his reconciliation with Henry II, found that it was extremely difficult to regulate

---

[2] W. Stubbs, *The Constitutional History of England* (4th edn., Oxford, 1896), ii, 112.
[3] Below, p. 156.
[4] J. B. Smith, 'The middle march in the thirteenth century', *B*, 24 (1970–2), 78–81; for Cymaron, *HKW*, ii, 624; King, *CA*, 407–8.

the area's affairs, for there was no certainty that any agreement between king and prince would do anything to mitigate the strife in the region itself. At the end of the twelfth century, supported from royal resources, Mortimer power was established at Cymaron and that of Braose at Colwyn once more, the marchers now convinced that they would never be removed again. However, as has been noticed already, Llywelyn ap Iorwerth came to provide succour for the Welsh lords of Maelienydd and to reaffirm their lordship over a patrimony that they would hold as tenants-in-chief of his principality. Neither Hugh Mortimer's power, nor a marriage between his brother Ralph and a daughter of Llywelyn, brought the lineage any benefit while the prince lived. Within a year of his death, however, Ralph Mortimer fulfilled his objective and, extinguishing every vestige of Welsh seigniory, brought Maelienydd and Gwerthrynion under his territorial lordship. The inheritance came to Roger Mortimer, to be enlarged by the appropriation of Radnor upon his marriage with one of the heirs of William de Braose.[5] In that portion of Maelienydd which forms a salient extending between Gwerthrynion and Elfael, almost to the frontier with Builth, stood the castle of Cefnllys, a symbol of Mortimer power and an instrument for its maintenance.[6] Yet by 1262 Cefnllys stood upon the furthermost frontier of the march. Gwerthrynion had fallen to Llywelyn in 1257; Builth had come to him at the king's expense and to Mortimer's discomfiture in 1260; in the same year the prince gained possession of Elfael Uwch Mynydd when Owain ap Maredudd came into his allegiance, leaving Elfael Is Mynydd exposed.[7] Before Llywelyn lay the other Mortimer lands, stretching from Maelienydd through Radnor to Wigmore, exposed now to his onslaught.

In dealing with the political history of thirteenth-century Wales, it is well-nigh inevitable that the interests of marcher lords and Welsh princes are seen to be pitched one against the other. It would, even so, be misleading to regard the lords of the march, any more than the Welsh princes, as an entirely homogeneous group motivated by common impulses. They varied greatly in their landed wealth and in the degree of their commitment to specifically marcher interests.[8] William de Valence, lord of Pembroke, possessed an

---

[5] *HW*, ii, 713.

[6] A. E. Brown, 'The castle, borough and park of Cefnllys', *TRadnS*, 42 (1972), 11–22; King, *CA*, 406–8, 411–12. Cymaron was the focus of Mortimer authority in the twelfth century, Cefnllys in the thirteenth; for Mortimer's castle of Dinbod, below, pp. 494, 521–2.

[7] Elfael Is Mynydd belonged to Roger de Tony (d. 1264); his tenants had submitted to Llywelyn early in 1263 (*CIM*, i, no. 1060; *CR, 1272–79*, 393; *CAC*, 17, 30), and the land was then administered by his officers (*LW*, 41–2; *CAC*, 53–4).

[8] The marchers' possessions are discussed in Altschul, *Clares*; *GlamCH*, iii; R. R. Davies, *Lordship and Society in the March of Wales, 1282–1400* (Oxford, 1978); idem, *CCC*; J. R. S. Phillips, *Aymer de Valence, Earl of Pembroke, 1307–1324: Baronial Politics in the Reign of Edward II* (Oxford, 1972); Ll. O. W. Smith, 'The lordships of Chirk and Oswestry, 1282–1415', Ph.D. thesis, University of London, 1970.

extensive estate in south-west Wales, part of a once wider complex which had enabled several of his predecessors, Marshal earls of Pembroke, to play a significant role in Welsh and marcher political history. In Glamorgan and Gwynllŵg in the south-east, first Richard de Clare, earl of Gloucester, and then Gilbert de Clare, held wide territories where marcher power was well entrenched and where its regality would be eloquently proclaimed in the later years of the century. By then considerable power was gathered, too, in the hands of Humphrey de Bohun, earl of Hereford, in the lordships of Huntington, Hay and, most of all, Brecon.[9] But if these were the greatest in landed wealth, and included those who were ultimately to be among the main protagonists of marcher rights, there were others who played an important role in marcher affairs in the last phases of Anglo-Welsh conflict. In the northern areas Henry III could call upon the services of Hamo Lestrange, lord of Knockin, and entrust him, like his father before him, with numerous responsibilities in the areas fronting Chester and Montgomery. James Audley may be included among these servants of the crown, though his estates lay just beyond the confines of the march. At Oswestry and Clun, within the march, John FitzAlan exercised a seigniorial authority, with its origins in the early years of Norman penetration, over areas of strategic importance fronting Shropshire. Close by the Herefordshire border Roger Clifford held the lordship of Clifford and, as a tenant of Bohun in the lordship of Brecon, the lordship of Cantref Selyf.[10] Men such as these, though not endowed with particularly extensive lordships, could prove to be considerable assets at times of crisis, and they were available to undertake the manifold tasks which the crown had need to see fulfilled both in normal conditions and those of warfare. If Valence was the best endowed of the lords of south-west Wales, the crown relied much more on the dutiful activity of men such as Patrick de Chaworth and then Payn de Chaworth, successively lords of Cydweli, Nicholas FitzMartin at Cemais or Guy de Brian at Laugharne. They took part in the king's wars and, investing in the building works evidenced in their castles, served the king's interests by strengthening their own positions.[11] The most well-endowed of the marchers possessed valuable estates in England which might bring them a place in the king's councils. These great magnates were in no sense 'lords of the march' and nothing else, nor was this necessarily the case with their lesser neighbours. It would be futile to regard the lords of

---

[9] Brecon came to Humphrey de Bohun (d. 1265), son of Humphrey de Bohun, earl of Hereford (d. 1275), by marriage to Eleanor de Braose; yielded to Llywelyn, 1263. Bohun lordship was reasserted by Humphrey de Bohun, earl of Hereford (d. 1298) in 1276–7.

[10] For lordships in Shropshire, or withdrawn from the county, including FitzAlan and Corbet lands, G. C. Baugh, 'The franchises', *Victoria County History: A History of Shropshire*, iii, ed. G. C. Baugh (Oxford, 1979), 34–42 [*VCH Shropshire*].

[11] Military activities and building works of these lords are noticed later.

the march as a group which revealed an unanimity of purpose during the period of baronial reform, and the references in contemporary sources to 'the marchers' had a particular connotation which will need to be noticed carefully.

If the marcher ranks were searched for one person who, more than anyone else, could be taken to represent the marcher interests of this period the choice would be likely to fall upon Roger Mortimer. Neither he nor his ancestors had been endowed with wide acres in the richer English counties. His antecedents in Normandy had themselves been men of the frontier, and in the second half of the thirteenth century Roger Mortimer stood impressively in the tradition of the sturdy characters portrayed by Ordericus Vitalis in the early years of the making of the march of Wales.[12] First established at the western extremity of the realm and then beyond its frontiers, the Mortimers might be seen to be far distant from the centres of English political concourse, but, as we have seen already, Roger was no mere frontier guardian isolated from affairs of government. Nor did his concern with interests in the march necessarily leave him inclined to opposition to the crown. It was not by reason of any conspicuous adherence to the cause of reform that he became a member of the Council of Fifteen. Thereafter he would enjoy neither entire good fortune nor undue prominence, let alone due recognition, but in the turmoil in the realm and the conflict in the march he would be a source of unflinching support for the monarchy. When political circumstances in the early months of 1263 gave birth to a group opposed to the king, often identified by contemporary commentators as the *marchiones*, Mortimer could not be counted among them. His was a position of singular isolation at that time, and in the constancy of his adherence to the needs of the crown and the interests of the march he stood alone.[13] Llywelyn ap Gruffudd was to realize, in years to come, the extent to which his intentions would be thwarted by the fact that Mortimer fulfilled a dual role as a power in the march of Wales and a strong influence in the government of England. It cannot be doubted, however, that even when he launched his attack on Cefnllys, or when he gave his approval to action already taken, Llywelyn already knew that he was contending with the most intransigent among his opponents. It was a strange fate which decreed that the ultimate conflict between the powers of Wales and the march would be a particularly gruelling contest between two grandsons of Llywelyn the Great.

---

[12] E.g. *Ordericus Vitalis Historia Ecclesiastica*, ed. M. Chibnall (Oxford, 1969–80), v, 24–6.

[13] For a historical recollection of Mortimer's predecessors, 'Wigmore Abbey Chronicle' in *MonAng*, VII, i, 348–50.

Rhyd Chwima

The attack on Mortimer's castle came after some months of increased tension over a wide area of the march. Hearing of the death of Richard de Clare soon after he arrived in France in July 1262, Henry was concerned to ensure the safety of Glamorgan. Humphrey de Bohun, earl of Hereford, to whom the king entrusted the safe-keeping of the lordship, took care to supply the earl's castles and put spies to work so he would be warned if any army were to move towards his borders.[14] No invasion of Glamorgan is known to have materialized but Llywelyn, for his part, complained that his lands were subject to attack from several marchers. Shortly before his departure Henry received a letter from Llywelyn complaining of attacks which Roger Mortimer and Hamo Lestrange had made on Powys Fadog contrary to the terms of the truce (*contra formam treugarum*).[15] Arbitrators were ordered to the ford of Montgomery by 24 July, with the earl of Hereford and James Audley empowered to give effect to their decisions. The meeting was not held, apparently because the earl was unwell and, disappointed by the king's failure to hold to the arrangements, Llywelyn wrote again. He vigorously complained, in particular, of new infringements on the part of John FitzAlan and other marchers. Philip Basset, the justiciar, by then in charge of royal administration at Westminster, suspected that Llywelyn was the more to blame for the disturbances and, presumably reflecting the king's wishes, alerted the marchers for military action as soon as Edward returned to the kingdom.[16] Even so, he urged John FitzAlan to exercise the utmost restraint and fixed a new date for a gathering of the arbitrators at the ford of Montgomery which the bishops of Norwich and Coventry and Lichfield, along with Hereford and Audley, would also attend.[17] He told Llywelyn that he would have been glad to name an earlier date but the fact that the magnates were engaged on other matters on the king's behalf made it impossible to do so.[18] Before they met Llywelyn felt bound to put his standpoint to the king once more, perhaps more strongly this time. Certainly his letter conveys an instructive indication of the strength of the prince's feelings in the weeks following his recovery from illness. Soon after Philip le Bret had been with him to make arrangements for the correction of breaches of the truce, and on the very day scheduled for a *parliamentum* with the justice of Chester, Powys Fadog had been subject to a new attack involving not only the sons of Hamo Lestrange and other marchers, but the royal justice himself. Llywelyn urged the king to

---

[14] *CR, 1261–64*, 141, 145; *CAC*, 37–8; *RL*, ii, 217–18; Altschul, *Clares*, 95–7. Clare's lands appear to have been attacked in 1260 (*CPR, 1258–66*, 103).

[15] *CR, 1261–64*, 128 (Llywelyn's letter cited by Henry, 8 June).

[16] Ibid., 132–3.

[17] Ibid., 133–4, letters to the bishops, the two magnates and, transmitted through Audley, to the *dictatores* (ibid., 136–7).

[18] Ibid., 135–6.

ensure that redress was made for the wrongs done to him lest he, for lack of justice, should be driven to seek vengeance.[19]

It may be significant that in this spirited letter, written in September 1262, Llywelyn styles himself, for the first time as far as the evidence indicates, as 'prince of Wales and lord of Snowdon'. He had, as we have seen, used the style 'prince of Wales', just once among surviving records, in the agreement with the magnates of Scotland in 1258.[20] Thereafter, for more than four years, he had used no style at all and, though full texts of his letters from this period are few, the examples are numerous enough to indicate the practice to which he adhered both in transactions with the crown and in dealing with others.[21] It is conceivable that the absence of the title 'prince of Wales' may be explained by a reluctance on the part of the other princes to acknowledge the legitimacy of the style.[22] Yet there can be no doubt of the extent of Llywelyn's power at this time. The documents from these years include a text of the severe terms imposed upon Maredudd ap Rhys Gryg upon his release from Llywelyn's prison and demonstrates the authority which the prince was capable of exercising over those from whom he had exacted declarations of allegiance.[23] In the same way, Henry's letters, prompted by the rumour of Llywelyn's death, are phrased in a manner tantamount to an acknowledgement that the prince was exercising a lordship over the magnates of Wales that had traditionally been vested in the crown. The absence of a title may rather reflect the prince's wish to withhold from any provocative assumption of the style that he hoped the king would bestow upon him when he secured the definitive peace treaty that he sought. His restraint in this respect is thus in complete accord with the thrust of his policy towards the crown in these years. The same calculations would make him eschew any style which failed to match his estimation of the status that was due to him. For the present he preferred to use no style at all. Up to the early months of 1262 Llywelyn was certainly pressing the king for the negotiations which, he fervently hoped, would secure that firm peace and bring the formal recognition which would be reflected in the concession of the style 'prince of Wales'. During the course of that year, however, he may have come to admit that he could have no real expectation

---

[19] *CAC*, 26; *RL*, ii, 218–19.

[20] *LW*, 184.

[21] Of letters to the king between 1258 and September 1262 not one is enrolled in full text (e.g. *CR, 1256–59*, 323–4, 422–3, 476; *CR, 1259–61*, 4–5, 198, 482; *CR, 1261–64*, 100–1, 128, 133–8); there are full texts in *LW*, 13–14, 15, 17, 27–9, 45, 97–8, 104–5. Early examples, 1262–5, of the form 'prince of Wales and lord of Snowdon', are found in *LW*, 58–9; *CAC*, 25–7; *CR, 1261–64*, 297; *RL*, ii, 284–7; *DipDoc*, i, nos. 400–1.

[22] D. Stephenson, 'Llywelyn ap Gruffydd and the struggle for the principality of Wales', *THSC*, 1983, 38, suspects that the abandonment of the title reflected hostility to Llywelyn's assertion of authority.

[23] Jurisdiction over the barons of the principality of Wales is examined below, pp. 285–90, 297–301.

that his wish for a peace settlement would be reciprocated in royal councils unless he were to exert greatly increased military pressure.[24] By the summer, if the substance of his letters is accurately reflected in the king's replies, he was concerned not so much with the quest for the definitive peace treaty but with the serious breaches of the truce for which he held the marchers responsible. It may be, of course, that he was confronted with sterner retaliatory measures on the part of the marchers. But there can be little doubt that, for whatever reason, there was a greatly heightened level of conflict on the frontiers, and he probably admitted that it would be futile to talk of peace in such disturbed conditions. Yet there may be a deeper reason, founded on a conviction that the king's prevarication, phrased though it might be in gracious terms, concealed a determination to yield nothing beyond a state of truce.

It is unlikely that Llywelyn had ever been entirely beguiled by the king's successive promises of negotiations to be held in the fullness of time, and his scepticism had surely deepened with each postponement. The king was never, as we have found already, an entirely free agent in matters which affected the magnates on whom he was necessarily dependent. Even though conditions in the realm were now easier than they had been before, and the constraints which may have inhibited the king in his dealings with Llywelyn had been somewhat relaxed, the marchers' interest in curtailing and reversing the prince's supremacy remained undiminished. The marchers' activity in 1262 may not have been entirely retaliatory, and Llywelyn may have suspected that their assaults upon his frontiers constituted a wilful endeavour to ensure that, even if the king might be inclined to a settlement with the prince, any such progress would be aborted by an upsurge of new conflict. However, the increased vigour which marks the letter that Llywelyn wrote in September 1262 might be explained if he had an inkling of the king's response to the prospect of his death. It is not impossible that Llywelyn came to know the tenor, even the detail, of the letters which Henry transmitted to chancery for circulation in the event of the rumours being confirmed. Whatever the reason, by the late summer of 1262 Llywelyn ap Gruffudd, prince of Wales and lord of Snowdon, gave notice that if he were denied justice with regard to the injuries done to him on his frontiers he might be forced to seek retribution. He had communicated his proposals to the king in successive submissions ever since the early summer of 1258. In the interval he had twice waged a limited campaign closely linked to his diplomatic initiatives, but these efforts had not yet worked to his advantage. He may have concluded, or he may have acknowledged the force of more militant arguments in his own ranks, that his objectives could only be secured, if at all, by a renewed and purposeful

---

[24] Henry's letter of 8 January 1262 (*CR, 1261–64*, 100–1) provides the last clear indication, before renewed conflict, that Llywelyn was pressing for a peace settlement.

offensive. This would be directed primarily, not at the king, but at those who could safely be identified as the main stumbling blocks to his endeavour to reach a settlement with the king. It was entirely predictable that the first to endure a new Welsh offensive was Roger Mortimer of Wigmore.

Whatever had afflicted Llywelyn in the summer, the movements which began with the assaults on Cefnllys and Bleddfa on 29 November gave a clear sign that the prince was restored to full vigour and, if he did not instigate the attack, he was able to bring considerable forces to the area with alacrity.[25] Time and again Hywel ap Meurig, constable of Cefnllys, had travelled to Rhyd Chwima to act as an arbitrator on the king's behalf, and he now endured a direct experience of an offensive which shattered the fragile accord of the years of truce. Llywelyn insisted that he had not broken the truce as regards the king but, while he was prepared to make amends if it were shown that he had in fact done so, he did nothing to disown the action taken in Maelienydd.[26] He maintained that Cefnllys was already in his possession when Mortimer, with the assistance of Humphrey de Bohun, arrived in an attempt to recover and fortify the castle. The marchers were, in fact, able to reach the site but they were surrounded by Llywelyn's forces and found themselves compelled to withdraw, and to do so with the prince's consent. In his account to Philip Basset Llywelyn held that he could have forced the marchers to an early surrender and, insisting that he was ready to make amends for every action contrary to the terms of the truce, he implored the king's council not be influenced by the complaints of his opponents until they heard his side of the argument. Llywelyn was neither vengeful on the battlefield nor uncompromising in the letters that he addressed to the crown. The essence of his message was the hope that the king could comprehend the problems of the march in a manner different from the standpoint of the lords of the area itself. He had struck Mortimer hard. After destroying Cefnllys and Bleddfa he captured Knucklas, Knighton and Presteigne. He took his power to the English border and, more pertinently perhaps, to the confines of the lordship of Wigmore.[27] In his letters to the king he would continue to reaffirm his quest for a firm peace and, however vigorous his action in Maelienydd had been, it would be unwise to conclude that he was now irrevocably committed to an all-out conflict throughout the march. He chose to attack the marcher power which, more than any other, frustrated his attempt to come to terms with the crown. It was Mortimer who endured the initial major onslaught, not

---

[25] *AC*, 100; *BT, Pen20*, 212–13; *Pen20Tr*, 112; *RBH*, 252–3, indicating initiative on the part of the men of Maelienydd. *AnnCestr*, 28, compresses these events and those of the following month.
[26] *CAC*, 26–7; *RL*, ii, 233.
[27] *AC*, 100: Mortimer and Bohun brought 'the flower of the youth of the whole march'; Llywelyn led 'all the magnates of Wales', and Knucklas fell 'in fear of the siege engines'.

Lestrange or FitzAlan or any other among the marchers who had attacked his territories. Nor is it certain that he attempted to gain advantage from the death of the earl of Gloucester by attacking Glamorgan, a possibility which had occurred to its custodian.[28] We are free to conclude that the effect of Llywelyn's action was simply to ensure that Mortimer was confirmed in his intransigent resistance to the prince's aspirations, but this would mean discounting the prince's ability to appreciate that the lord of Wigmore had already proved to be an incorrigible opponent. With Llywelyn's power extending to within a short distance of Wigmore, even Mortimer might be prepared to relent in his resistance to a negotiated settlement.

Henry was informed of the disturbances in the march by Philip Basset when he landed at Dover, safe and sound, *benedictus Dei*, on 20 December. The justiciar, however, did not know the full extent of the problem. As far as he knew at that stage Mortimer and Bohun were still under siege at Cefnllys and the king took comfort from fact that, at the very least, the marchers had recovered the castle. He would send forces to raise the siege at once; he took care to maintain the castles of Gwent and provided aid for the earl of Hereford's defence of Glamorgan. Beyond these immediate measures he summoned his forces to Hereford by 9 January, though he soon realized that the muster would have to be postponed for a month.[29] The letters which spurted out from chancery reveal the king's exasperation that he had once more to contend with trouble in the march. Only a few months earlier, in a letter to Alphonso of Castile, veritably brimming with confidence, Henry declined an offer of assistance in resisting his enemies in England and Wales, for his opponents in England had made their peace with him and the Welsh had made a new truce.[30] His irritation at the new turn in events is reflected in an angry letter to Edward, mournfully complaining that his son, who had promised to return from Gascony by Christmas, had still not arrived. The king's health did not permit him to go to Wales; in any case, he was growing old whereas his son was in the flower of youth.[31] Not long before, Edward had been commended for the admirable manner he had acquitted himself in the government of Gascony; he was now sorely chastized as an indolent and prodigal son. He was told to return at once to face his responsibilities in the march. Edward was not the only one to know the king's anger. Earlier in the year Llywelyn, too, had won commendation for his refusal to be drawn to those in conspiratorial opposition to the king of England. Now, conscious once more that new dissensions were festering in the realm, Henry conveyed

---

[28] Above, n. 14.
[29] *CR, 1261–64*, 191–2, 269–76; *CPR, 1258–66*, 238 (22–5 December); the campaign was postponed to 5 February.
[30] *CR, 1261–64*, 172–3 (16 August 1262).
[31] Ibid., 272–3.

his astonishment and annoyance that Llywelyn, whom he had taken to be a man of good faith, should renounce his fidelity and disregard the truce made between them. He was convinced that Llywelyn had responded to the instigation of certain men of the king's realm.[32] The king's remarks convey intriguing intimations of conspiracy theory, for rightly or wrongly he sensed that there was a connection between the encounters in the march and new discords in the realm. His suspicions were fed by a letter from Peter D'Aigueblanche, bishop of Hereford. He related that Llywelyn, 'prince of Wales in truth' in the prelate's prophetic words, had 300 horsemen and 30,000 troops in Maelienydd. The entire march was in terror as his forces carried war to the neighbourhood of Eardisley, Weobley and Wigmore. There were rumours of treachery, and he recounted that the escape of Mortimer and Bohun from Cefnllys gave grounds for the belief that there was an understanding between Llywelyn and the great powers of the march. Naturally, the bishop did not believe any such thing, but he could not resist the temptation to relate these tales to the king. Nor was he able to withhold the reports that there were some who had entered into discussions with their opponents and others who had sold their possessions and left the area. The bishop did no better. He urged the good citizens of Hereford to stand firm, and promptly departed.[33]

This was not the first occasion on which, amidst turmoil in the march, the hysteria of a critical hour proved conducive to suspicions of treachery.[34] The belief that there was understanding between Llywelyn and any of the marchers at this stage can hardly be sustained. On the other hand, there can be no doubt that Henry had sensed that there were divisions among the lords of the march.[35] His suspicions are borne out by the reports of two men, Peter de Montfort and John de Grey, who emerged from this crisis with their reputations in no way tarnished.[36] Montfort, sent to Abergavenny to take custody of the lordship, faced an extremely difficult situation early in 1263. Evidently maintaining the momentum of his offensive, Llywelyn now concentrated not on the area centred on Maelienydd but on the Usk valley.

---

[32] *CR, 1261–64*, 269: 'non mediocriter miramur et movemur eo maxime quod vix credere possumus quod homo bone fide contra fidelitatem et juramentum proprium talia acceptaret'; for similar expressions of the king's wonderment, *CR, 1256–59*, 107–8, 112. Henry told Edward (*CR, 1261–64*, 273) that Llywelyn was encouraged by 'certain men of the realm' ('set hoc de consilio et instinctu quorundam de regno nostro attemptare presumit').

[33] *CAC*, 15–16; *Foedera*, I, i, 423 (bishop's reply to Henry's letter, 26 December, *CR, 1261–64*, 271). For the bishop, who was concerned with the Welsh problem in 1259, W. N. Yates, 'Bishop Peter de Aquablanca, 1240–1268: a reconsideration', *Journal of Ecclesiastical History*, 22 (1971), 303–17.

[34] E.g. Paris, *ChronMaj*, iii, 159 (1228); v, 597–8, 676–7 (1257–8).

[35] *CR, 1261–64*, 278–9 (1 February 1263).

[36] For Montfort and Grey, Treharne, *BPR*, 75 *et passim*; *VCH Shropshire*, iii, 15–16, 31. Grey was appointed 1 February (*CR, 1261–64*, 278–9).

Montfort was able to report a Welsh attack on Llanfihangel Crucornau, indicating that the prince's forces had penetrated the lordship of Abergavenny.[37] The attack on this lordship posed, in turn, a threat to the Three Castles of Gwent, that is, the lordships of Grosmont, Skenfrith and White Castle.[38] Nor was this altogether the work of an army operating, at a great distance from its base, in alien territory. This was the essence of Montfort's message: all the men of the Welsh nation in the lordships of Brecon, Talgarth and Blaenllyfni, Elfael, Ystrad Yw, Tal-y-bont and Crughywel – in a word the Welsh to the confines of Abergavenny – had turned to Llywelyn. He feared that the men of Abergavenny would do the same. Of course, Montfort wished to impress upon the king the gravity of the situation confronting him, for he was desperately short of support. Yet these were not the words of a petrified bishop on the point of departure but of a soldier who stood his ground.

Peter de Montfort's account is confirmed by a report from John de Grey in which he relates that the Welsh of these areas had indeed forsaken their loyalty to the king and that Llywelyn ap Gruffudd had taken their homage.[39] These were, as Montfort put it, men 'of the Welsh language' (*de lingua Wallensica*), and both writers emphasize that they adhered to the prince entirely of their own will. The two commanders' letters entirely vindicate the account of *Brut y Tywysogyon* which records that it was at the request of the men of Brecon that Llywelyn came to that lordship and that, as in Maelienydd, he took their homage before he returned to Gwynedd.[40] It seems that Mortimer in Maelienydd and Bohun in Brecon witnessed a secession on the part of the men of these lordships, and their action may perhaps have reflected a discontent comparable with that which was to confront the heirs to these lordships at the end of the century when the power of the princes had long since been extinguished.[41] Llywelyn's power in the region now would

---

[37] *CAC*, 30; *RL*, ii, 230–1. Montfort refers 'to the vill of St Michael', that is Michaelston or Llanfihangel Crucornau in the northern part of Abergavenny, enclosed by Crughywel, Ewyas Lacy and the Three Castles.

[38] A. J. Taylor, 'White Castle in the thirteenth century: a reconsideration', *Medieval Archaeology*, 5 (1961), 169–75, notices the threat to Gwent. Henry appreciated the need to fortify the Three Castles and Monmouth in December 1262 (*CR, 1261–64*, 191).

[39] *CAC*, 17–18. Grey, indicating virtually the same areas as Montfort, specifies the lands of Humphrey de Bohun in Brecon; Reginald FitzPeter in Talgarth, Eglwys Iail (Llangynidr) and Blaenllyfni; Robert de Turberville in Crughywel; Robert Wafre in Tal-y-bont; Roger Pichard in Ystrad Yw (which would include Tretower); Roger de Tony in Elfael and Maud Longspée in Cantref Selyf.

[40] *BT, Pen20*, 213; *Pen20Tr*, 112–13: 'and he himself went, he and his host, to Brycheiniog, at the request of the leading men of Brycheiniog, to receive their homage'; *RBH*, 252–3.

[41] J. B. Smith, 'Edward II and the allegiance of Wales', *WHR*, 8 (1976–7), 142–3; R. R. Davies, *Lordship and Society*, 126–7, 165–6, 185–7. For relations between lord and community in a particularly instructive instance, Ll. B. Smith, 'The Arundel charters to the lordship of Chirk in the fourteenth century', *B*, 23 (1968–70), 153–66.

undoubtedly be greatly enhanced if he were able to secure the willing adherence of these communities. So the king had cause for real concern when his commanders reported both the massive switch of allegiance on the part of the communities of the area and the fact that the crown's power to resist Llywelyn was being undermined by disputes among his own men. Peter de Montfort found the lords of the area decidedly reluctant to support him, and the king had sensed that there were problems on this account even before he heard from his officer. He had been forced to appoint John de Grey to take charge of the defence of the area when the earl of Hereford, pleading ill health and the approach of Lent, asked to be relieved of his duties. Henry informed a number of magnates of the change in command, and urged them to reconcile their differences and provide Grey with the support he needed.[42] Grey had to make his own efforts to bring them together before setting out for Brecon, and he was even then forced to do so with only twelve knights. What exactly lay behind Hereford's wish to be relieved of his responsibility is not clear. He was the person on whom Henry had hitherto depended for overall command in this area of the march; he had recently been given a copy of the letter which was sent to Llywelyn, and he was entrusted with communicating with the prince on the king's behalf. Grey appears to have been given a task that, for whatever reason, Hereford felt unable to undertake.[43]

Grey was able to reach Brecon but, though he gathered that substantial forces drawn from the whole of Wales were concentrated in the vicinity, 180 barded horses and 10,000 foot according to his estimate, he made no engagement with them.[44] The Welsh forces had in fact been sent forward to the Usk at Abergavenny, and Grey moved back to lend assistance to Peter de Montfort, now severely hard-pressed. Montfort was convinced that Llywelyn was bent on crossing the Usk and attacking Gwent: Llywelyn sought nothing less than possession of Gwent.[45] This would be no easy task, but Llywelyn may have calculated that, quite apart from gaining possession, he might gain much from the devastation of an area which constituted such an important source of soldiery and supply. Substantial forces were committed, an army which was the pride of Wales. It was led by Goronwy ab Ednyfed, the prince's steward, and the presence of Maredudd ab Owain, Maredudd ap Rhys Gryg and Rhys Fychan indicated that the might of Deheubarth was at the prince's

---

[42] *CR, 1261–64*, 278–9 (1 February 1263), addressed to named magnates at Hereford and Ludlow.

[43] Henry wrote to Gloucester 22 December, urging him to secure quick response from Llywelyn. He expressed confidence in the earl's command on 24 January, but by 1 February Hereford had withdrawn from the fray. The king understood that he had done so 'on account of the approach of Lent and other difficulties (*impedimenta*) which you have' (ibid., 269–70, 276–9).

[44] *CAC*, 17–18.

[45] *CAC*, 52–3; *RL*, ii, 219–21.

service.⁴⁶ The forces had evidently approached the area from the west and occupied the moorland terrain in the western portion of the lordship as far as the Blorenge mountain. They pressed upon the Usk south of Abergavenny by 1 March and wrought destruction in the areas accessible to them. Two days later, supported by Grey and Roger Mortimer, whose stalwart service was warmly commended, Montfort was able to ford the river north of Abergavenny and attack the Welsh army on its flank.⁴⁷ The move was daring, its results decisive. The main body of the princes' army was forced to retreat up the slopes of the Blorenge and seek the safety of the mountainous tracts beyond. Unable to go in pursuit, the English commanders were, even so, able to inflict heavy losses on those who had been raiding and left themselves exposed. Montfort still felt that the Welsh would return and drive to the Wye and the Severn, but he and Grey clearly relished the reports they were able to send to the king. Whether Llywelyn was in the area when he heard of the destruction of the Welsh army is uncertain. Montfort specifically states that neither Llywelyn nor Dafydd were with the force deployed at Abergavenny and it is possible that circumstances in Gwynedd had by then caused Llywelyn to make a hasty return.⁴⁸

In tracing the course of the conflict in the march in the early months of 1263 it would be easy to lose sight of the fact that Llywelyn continued to press for negotiations and was anxious to stress that his quarrel lay with the marchers and not with the king himself. After the initial offensive in Maelienydd he had insisted that he wished to see the arbitrators put to work to correct breaches of the truce; he was anxious that the king be made aware of his side of the argument with the marchers.⁴⁹ Henry's summons for a Welsh campaign was in fact quickly followed by an order to Llywelyn to appear in person at the ford of Montgomery on 2 March. Maintaining that the notice was too short, and perhaps keen to press his advantage in the area between Brecon and

---

⁴⁶ Montfort names the leaders; Grey states that forces in the area were drawn from north, west and south Wales (*CAC*, 18, 52). The presence of Maredudd ap Rhys Gryg and Rhys Fychan may be noticed in the light of Maredudd's agreement of 1261 (*LW*, 104–5).

⁴⁷ The lordship straddled the Usk, its western portion consisting of high ground to which forces advancing from the west would have easy access, but a crossing south of the town of Abergavenny would have been fraught with danger. Montfort's report of an earlier attack on Llanfihangel Crucornau suggests that Welsh forces were then operating from the high ground to the north-west, a route which might have enabled them to reach the main portion of the lordship, and press upon the Three Castles, without the hazard of crossing the Usk. Grey's advance to Brecon, and Montfort's covering of that attack, may have induced the Welsh leaders to take a more southerly approach which involved forcing the river. It left them exposed to the outflanking movement that Montfort accomplished with devastating results.

⁴⁸ Knowledge of Dafydd ap Gruffudd's defection occurs a little later and is noticed presently.

⁴⁹ *CAC*, 26–7; *RL*, ii, 233.

Abergavenny, he asked for a postponement until after Easter.[50] On 1 March, when Peter de Montfort was withstanding the Welsh attack, Henry proposed that a meeting be held on 7 April and, as Llywelyn requested, that it be held at Oswestry. He asked Llywelyn to attend in person and, though there was no indication that anything more would be discussed than breaches of the truce, Henry was prepared to send members of his council fully empowered to deal with issues which might arise. He would urge his men to keep the peace meantime, and he expected Llywelyn to do likewise.[51] Once more Llywelyn found that divisions among the magnates, beneficial though they might be in impeding effective military action against him, were not to his real advantage. Henry certainly found that there was a conviction among the marchers that Llywelyn was extending his sway under the cover of a quest for a negotiated settlement of the problems of the march. The king's difficulty is reflected in the fact that, when he sent Philip le Bret to Llywelyn to arrange the meeting on which they had agreed, he instructed his messenger to ensure that he first secured the consent of Roger Mortimer and other lords, who had suffered from Llywelyn's attacks, to what the king proposed. Bret went to Mortimer and was kept at Radnor castle for eight days. Mortimer took possession of the letter, eventually yielding it, unwillingly and under compulsion, at a meeting convened by John de Grey at Hereford. It was only then that Grey was able to get a message to Llywelyn. The prince immediately informed the king of all this and explained that, as a result of Mortimer's perverse action, he had not received the king's instruction until 20 March.[52] Time was short but Llywelyn was still eager to attend the *parliamentum* proposed for Oswestry at his initial suggestion. Upon receiving Llywelyn's letter the king passed it to Edward, who had by then returned to England.[53] Along with the letter, the king transferred the whole problem confronting him in Wales to his son. Llywelyn was soon to appreciate the significance of that decision. There was no further mention of negotiation and contact with Llywelyn was broken forthwith. It was at this critical point in the spring of 1263 that Edward and Mortimer established the concord which proved so fateful thereafter.

Hitherto, theirs had hardly been an easy relationship, but from this point onward their understanding constituted an essential element in political

---

[50] Henry's order is known from Llywelyn's answer (*CAC*, 25–6; *Foedera*, I, i, 336). Edwards placed it January–February 1261 or 1262, but Henry's letter 1 March 1263 (*CR, 1261–64*, 293–4) is a reply to the prince's letter which can thus be safely dated February 1263.

[51] *CR, 1261–64*, 294–5: others consulted were Humphrey de Bohun, junior, John FitzAlan and Reginald FitzPeter; James Audley and Grey were informed and would be told of Llywelyn's reply.

[52] Ibid., 297; Llywelyn's letter is undated but he had written between 20 March, when he received Henry's letter, and 30 March, when Henry sent Edward the correspondence (ibid.).

[53] *HW*, ii, 731; Treharne, *BPR*, 299, adding *CAC*, 15, 19. He was at Hereford by 3 April, Shrewsbury 15 April.

relations in the realm and in the conflict in the march. If Llywelyn had driven to the Usk, and had intended to drive beyond the river, in an attempt to bring the king to serious negotiation – and there are good grounds for that conclusion – he came to appreciate that the opinion which ultimately prevailed in council was one which insisted that negotiations with Llywelyn would be tantamount to submission to his will. Entrusted with the responsibility of dealing with Llywelyn's challenge, Edward left for the march without delay and, in all probability, he sought an early meeting with Mortimer. His initial intention to wage a military campaign came to nothing, unless the prospect of war, coupled with Edward's promises, proved enough to induce Dafydd ap Gruffudd into the strange conclusion that this was an opportune time to forsake his brother.[54] He was granted Dyffryn Clwyd and Ceinmeirch, to be held until, by his labours and Edward's aid, he would be able to secure his inheritance in Gwynedd Uwch Conwy. But Edward was in no position to deliver these lands, nor the improved offer of Dyffryn Clwyd and Rhufoniog three months later.[55] Edward took counsel first at Hereford, where the agreement with Dafydd was made, and then at Ludlow. But no major military offensive was launched immediately. Edward left the confines of Wales and gave notice that he would embark on a campaign in August. There would be no more talk of peace and, once more, the feast of St Peter in Chains was marked in the royal calendar as the date for a new offensive in Wales. Nothing was to come of it, and the summer saw indeed the fall first of Diserth and then of Degannwy.[56] By then, moreover, the course of events in England had taken a new turn, following Simon de Montfort's return to England and the first alignment of the forces which would plunge the realm into violent conflict. Briefly, in the spring of 1263, Llywelyn ap Gruffudd, after once more pursuing his search for an understanding with the crown, faced the new threat posed by the uncompromising position taken by Edward and Mortimer, now joined in a forbidding alliance. Then he saw the political

---

[54] Edward had received Dafydd into his fealty by 3 April, the date of their agreement at Hereford (*CPR, 1258–66*, 261). Dafydd had thus defected before Edward's initiative in Wales, confirming *AnnCestr*, 82 ('after Easter', 1 April) and correcting *BT, Pen20*, 214; *Pen20Tr*, 113; *RBH*, 254–5 (that he departed after Edward returned to England). Dafydd had defected by the end of March at the latest. His motives for defecting at this time remain as uncertain as ever (*HW*, ii, 731). The Chester chronicler says that he wished 'to release his brother Owain'; it is difficult to fathom why he chose to depart when Llywelyn's power was increasing, unless he was opposed to the decision to launch a major offensive in the march.

[55] The initial grant was made on 3 April, confirmed 26 May, improved 8 July, with provision for Dafydd, pending delivery of the lands, in Hawarden and Shotwick. The territories now granted came to him in 1277 (C66/79, m. 9; C66/96, m. 4; *CPR, 1258–66*, 261; *CPR, 1272–81*, 231–2; *CWR*, 160).

[56] *CR, 1261–64*, 302–6 (25 May); forces summoned for the feast day of St Peter, 1 August. Diserth fell in early August, Degannwy in late September (*HW*, ii, 732–3). Negotiations led to a truce in September (*CPR, 1258–66*, 276, 280; *Foedera*, I, i, 433).

community of the realm of England rent by the dissensions which had so long threatened. How soon, in turn, the understanding between Llywelyn and Montfort materialized we cannot tell. If the chroniclers are to be believed we would need to accept that Llywelyn had, by the summer of 1263, joined together with well-nigh all the barons of England against Edward.[57] That would be to say too much, too soon. It is safer to trace the changing allegiances of those who exercised power in that part of the march in the neighbourhood of Montgomery which proved so vital, in peace and war alike, for so long.

It is clear that, apart from his activities in other sectors of the march early in 1263, Llywelyn pressed hard on Montgomery, where John Lestrange had custody of the royal lordship. He returned to an area which had seen conflict six years earlier, part of the effort that had enabled him to take possession of a major portion of Powys Wenwynwyn.[58] John Lestrange was himself discomforted for, after taking a strong force through Ceri to Cydewain, his soldiers suffered heavy losses as the Welsh fell upon them when, 'laden with spoil', they made their return.[59] By the spring Llywelyn was engaged in the area south of Montgomery centred on John FitzAlan's lordship of Clun.[60] The conflict is commemorated by the Welsh chronicler primarily as the place where, on 27 April, Llywelyn ap Maredudd, 'the flower of the youth of Wales', died in battle. He is undoubtedly the person whom Llywelyn had exiled from Meirionnydd in 1256, to be maintained for some years by gifts from the royal exchequer. The chronicler does not tell us explicitly in whose cause he fell, but the warmth of his tribute and the fact that royal subventions cannot be traced after the summer of 1262 suggest very strongly that he had by now revoked his fealty to the king.[61] He would thus have participated in a

---

[57] *AC*, 101; *BT, Pen20*, 214; *Pen20Tr*, 113, *RBH*, 254–5; Rishanger, *Chronica*, 13; Rishanger, *Chronicon De Bellis*, 151. *AnnCestr*, 84, says Diserth was besieged by Llywelyn and Gruffudd ap Madog by the command of the barons. Maddicott, *Montfort*, 228, accepts that Montfort allied with the Welsh immediately upon his return to England, but regards relations from 1263 to the summer of 1265 as a 'working partnership' (ibid., 337).

[58] Above, p. 94.

[59] *BT, Pen20*, 213–14; *Pen20Tr*, 113; *RBH*, 252–3.

[60] *AC*, 100; *BT, Pen20*, 213–14; *Pen20Tr*, 113; *RBH*, 252–3. John FitzAlan was named in March 1263 among those who had endured Llywelyn's attacks (*CR, 1261–64*, 294–5).

[61] *AC(B)*, 100, is the only reference to Llywelyn. It does not state on whose side he stood, but the generous sentiments, which may reflect the annalist's interest in a person with a marriage link to the lineage of Maelgwn Fychan, suggest that he fell fighting for the princes. He received exchequer payments up to June 1262 (*CLibR*, iv, 436, 472, 506; *CLibR*, v, 4, 50, 72, 102), but not afterwards, and there does not appear to be any record of gifts to his wife or sons until Madog ap Llywelyn received payments in 1277 (J. G. Edwards, 'Madog ap Llywelyn', *B*, 13 (1948–50), 209). Inquiry in 1308 established that Madog and his brother Dafydd received lands in Anglesey, at the prince's gift, on their father's death (*CIM*, ii, no. 49). The Llywelyn ap Maredudd who appears among Llywelyn ap Gruffudd's *fideles* in 1259 (*LW*, 28) is evidently not the former lord of Meirionnydd, who at that stage was still in receipt of royal favour.

campaign launched with a view to extending the power of the prince into the western portion of the lordship of Clun, known as Tempsiter or Dyffryn Tefeidiad, possession of which would take his authority to the furthermost bounds of the territory which maintained a community 'of the Welsh language'. It appears, even so, that Llywelyn suffered a reverse in Clun, and it is by no means certain that he secured possession of any part of the lordship at this stage.[62] The situation in the area was greatly complicated, however, and made advantageous to Llywelyn, by the intervention of a group of men whom the chroniclers of England identified as the 'marchers' (*marchiones*). For, just two days or so before the conflict in which Llywelyn ap Maredudd fell, Simon de Montfort landed in England to provide the impetus which transformed baronial opposition into armed rebellion.[63] Among the first to enlist in Montfort's alliance were the *marchiones*: Roger Clifford, John Giffard and Roger Leyburn were among the most conspicuous of them. They were hardly representative of the powers of the march of Wales, but they formed a group which vigorously attacked the possessions of those who were recognized adherents of the crown in the border counties of England. The estates of the bishop of Hereford were singled out for particular treatment.[64] Apparently part of the same movement, though perhaps of a slightly later date, John FitzAlan captured Bishop's Castle and wrought considerable damage in an episcopal estate only a short distance from his own lordship of Clun.[65] The person who had so recently resisted Llywelyn was now in opposition to the crown, and it is possible that he came to an understanding with the prince. Certainly, Llywelyn was later to claim that the lord of Clun had ceded Tempsiter to him by a formal deed.[66] The opposition mounted by John FitzAlan and the *marchiones* proved short-lived, for before the year was out Edward had been able to bring them back into the king's fealty to stand once

---

[62] *BT, Pen20*, 214; *Pen20Tr*, 113; *RBH*, 252–3. On Dyffryn Tefeidiad or Tempsiter, J. E. Lloyd, 'Border notes', *B*, 11 (1941–4), 53–4; *VCH Shropshire*, iii, 34–7; C. J. Spurgeon in L. Alcock *et al.*, 'Excavations at Castell Bryn Amlwg', *MontColl*, 60 (1967–8), 8–27. For the Welsh language on the frontier in this area, Llinos Beverley Smith, 'The Welsh language before 1536', in G. H. Jenkins (ed.), *The Welsh Language before the Industrial Revolution* (Cardiff, 1997), 16–19.

[63] Montfort returned *c*.25 April (Treharne, *BPR*, 301; Maddicott, *Montfort*, 222–3, quoting *AnnDunst*, 221); the battle at Clun was fought on 27 April.

[64] *HW*, ii, 731–2; Treharne, *BPR*, 301–3; Powicke, *Henry III*, ii, 435–9; Maddicott, *Montfort*, 220–3; see ibid., for the crown's alienation of this group, 1261–2, and new resentments created by Edward's mercenary army, as described by the Merton annalist in *FloresHist*, iii, 256; cf. Carpenter, *Reign of Henry III*, 270–2.

[65] *RegSwinfield*, 86 (5 July 1263).

[66] *CAC*, 86–7; Llywelyn's occupation of Teirtref Esgob, part of Bishop's Castle, is noticed later. The possibility that Llywelyn also came to an understanding with Hamo Lestrange, which might be suggested by a document in *LW*, 87, can be discounted for reasons given below, n. 174.

more alongside Roger Mortimer who, throughout the confused exchanges of these months, remained absolutely steadfast in his fidelity to the king.[67] The activities of this group has a further relevance in relation to an important decision made during this troubled summer by the lord of Powys Wenwynwyn.

Little mention has hitherto been made of Gruffudd ap Gwenwynwyn, who was later to do so much to undermine the supremacy of Llywelyn ap Gruffudd. He had chosen to lend his support to the crown in the conflicts of the two previous decades, frequently found acting in association with Gruffudd ap Madog of Powys Fadog. But, whereas his northern neighbour relented in his reluctance to join Llywelyn, not even Henry III's failure to re-establish his authority in Wales in 1257 had been enough to induce Gruffudd ap Gwenwynwyn to turn to Llywelyn and he remained denuded of the greater part of his inheritance.[68] His younger years spent under royal protection in England, married to Hawise Lestrange, and with a natural affinity to the barons of the realm among whom he had moved, no other political affiliation would have seemed in the least likely. But before the end of 1263, a year in which Dafydd ap Gruffudd switched to the king's allegiance, Gruffudd ap Gwenwynwyn turned to Llywelyn. The formal compact was made in December, but Gruffudd's decision was probably made during the summer which saw John FitzAlan and the *marchiones* in rebellion. It was almost certainly at this time of disturbance that Gruffudd set out to secure possession of Gorddwr, a land which lay across the Severn directly opposite that small part of Powys Wenwynwyn which remained in his possession. The name Gorddwr, indicating 'the land across the water', may itself reflect the fact that the land was once part of Powys, but for generations it had been in the hands of the family of Corbet and formed part of their lordship of Caus.[69] Gruffudd had for some years been trying to secure Gorddwr by a legal process against Thomas Corbet, not on grounds of any ancient right, but on the basis of his interpretation of territorial provision made when his father, Gwenwynwyn ab Owain Cyfeiliog, married a daughter of the Corbet lineage who was to be Gruffudd's mother. Gruffudd gained nothing from his prolonged legal action, and the issue of Gorddwr had already proved to be a source of disturbance.[70] Now, in the summer of 1263, evidently availing himself of the

---

[67] Treharne, *BPR*, 308–24. Maddicott, *Montfort*, 229–44, notices the baronial control of the government in the summer and autumn of 1263 and the defection of the *marchiones* to Edward. For a truce with Llywelyn in September, *CPR, 1258–66*, 276, 280; *Foedera*, I, i, 433.

[68] Above, pp. 48, 93–4, 105.

[69] J. E. Lloyd, 'Border notes', 48–50; *VCH Shropshire*, iii, 37–8.

[70] For disturbances and litigation between Thomas Corbet and Gruffudd ap Gwenwynwyn, see e.g. *CPR, 1247–58*, 438 (1255); *CPR, 1258–66*, 54 (1259); *The Roll of the Shropshire Eyre of 1256*, ed. A. Harding (London, Selden Society, 1981), xxvii–xxviii, 137–8.

confusion created when the *marchiones* attacked the royalists, but not yet perhaps in formal alliance with Llywelyn, Gruffudd ap Gwenwynwyn invaded Gorddwr, destroying the castle of Gwyddgrug, the stone structure which Corbet had raised on a rocky site near Nantcriba.[71] In September Gruffudd was told in a letter from chancery to restore to Corbet the castle of Gwyddgrug, and the land of Gorddwr and the territory between the rivers Camlad and Severn, that he had taken at the time of the disturbances (*turbaciones*) in the kingdom, undoubtedly a reference to the events in which the *marchiones* had played a conspicuous part.[72]

In Gorddwr, as in Clun, the power of a Welsh prince was extended to the boundary where two nations and two languages met. But this movement was not necessarily the result of any fundamental political conversion on the part of Gruffudd ap Gwenwynwyn. It stemmed, rather, from the circumstances in which some of Gruffudd's natural confederates, his brother-in-law Hamo Lestrange among them, ventured into armed action against their royalist adversaries.[73] When they returned to the king's allegiance Gruffudd found himself in a difficult predicament. Bereft of allies among his marcher associates he was confronted with a choice between alliance with Llywelyn and leaving himself exposed to further onslaught on the part of the prince. Certainly Gruffudd would find it impossible to retain possession of Gorddwr except in Llywelyn's alliance. Besides, much more important than Gorddwr were those valuable lands that had formed part of his patrimony but were now in Llywelyn's possession. When the rebellion of the *marchiones* came to an abrupt end the lord of Powys Wenwynwyn came to terms with the need to enter into a formal relationship with Llywelyn ap Gruffudd. It was by reason of dire necessity that Gruffudd ap Gwenwynwyn came into the political community of the principality of Wales. It is unlikely that he ever cherished his membership of the princes' fraternity in the period of ten years or so which

---

[71] Gwyddgrug castle is described in C. J. Spurgeon, 'Gwyddgrug castle (Forden) and the Gorddwr dispute in the thirteenth century', *MontColl*, 57 (1961–2), 125–36. The evidence, particularly the chancery letter, 16 September 1263 (*CR, 1261–64*, 265), is enough to establish the location of the castle of 'yr Wydgruc' (*BT, Pen20*, 214–15; *Pen20Tr*, 113; *RBH*, 254–5), a problem noted in *HW*, ii, 734, n. 90; *Pen20Tr*, 211.

[72] *CR, 1261–64*, 265. Gruffudd's attack is normally seen as a consequence of his alliance with Llywelyn formalized in December 1263 (e.g. Tout, *CP*, iii, 68; *HW*, ii, 734); this could be gathered from *AC*, 101, but the chancery letter indicates the summer of 1263 and the sequence of events, involving baronial opponents of the king, described in Treharne, *BPR*, 301–3; Powicke, *Henry III*, ii, 438–9. Llywelyn and Gruffudd may have come to an understanding some time before their formal agreement in December, and J. E. Lloyd, 'Border notes', 50, assumes that Gruffudd had submitted to Llywelyn in the summer. Distinction needs to be made between what appear to have been Gruffudd's initiatives then and the movements, probably early in 1264, involving both princes.

[73] Gruffudd's wife, Hawise, was a sister of Hamo Lestrange, who took part in the attacks made by the *marchiones* during the summer. Lestrange activities in the march are noticed in H. Lestrange, *Le Strange Records, 1100–1300* (London, 1916).

he spent in formal allegiance to Llywelyn before he committed himself to a conspiracy that contributed to the dissolution of the principality of Wales.

Agreement between Llywelyn and Gruffudd ap Gwenwynwyn was formalized at Ystumanner on 12 December 1263.[74] The document drawn up on that date is the best surviving example of a concord which established a relationship of lord and vassal in the principality of Wales. It first registered the fact that Gruffudd did homage to Llywelyn and swore fealty to him: 'the lord Gruffudd, of his free will, did homage for himself and his heirs and, placing his hand on holy objects (*sacrosancta*), swore fealty to the lord Llywelyn and his heirs'. These words might be included in an anthology of the diploma which registered the bonds by which medieval political relationships were formed, for there is a close verbal correspondence between the opening words of the present document and those of a host of comparable instruments from continental Europe. In similar accord with custom, the deed was sealed in the presence of magnates of the land, churchmen and laymen, but those who gathered together from Gwynedd and Powys on this occasion were witnesses to more than a formality. The document set out, secondly, a declaration of the obligations which lord and vassal recognized, and this was necessarily a statement that reflected the particular circumstances of the transaction. Gruffudd, in return for his homage, was granted and restored the possession of all his lands: Cyfeiliog, Mawddwy, Arwystli, Caereinion, Mochnant Uwch Rhaeadr, the land between Rhiw and Helyg, and Y Teirswydd, that is Deuddwr, Llannerch Hudol and Ystrad Marchell. These were largely lands which Llywelyn had wrested from him six years earlier, and their enumeration reflects both the severity of the measures then taken by Llywelyn and Gruffudd's implacable determination not to succumb to his power.[75] Yet not all the lands named had been yielded to Llywelyn, and the exceptions serve to underline the fact that the transactions at Ystumanner were concerned, not with the restoration of the lands of which he had previously been deprived, but with the vesting in Gruffudd, in return for his homage, of a baronial estate now deemed to be derived in its entirety from the prince of Wales. The significance of this aspect of the agreement will be considered later; more relevant now are the clauses which reflect the princes' immediate concerns. Lord and vassal were now pledged to stand together in peace and war. They no doubt hoped for eventual peace, but they prepared for war and agreed that, if one were to lose lands in war, the other, if he remained unaffected, would compensate for the losses. Llywelyn promised to provide a castle to ensure the safety of Gruffudd's family and possessions if he were ever to lose Welshpool. They did not dwell entirely on the possibility of

---

[74] *LW*, 77–80; the document is considered further below, pp. 287–9, 299–300.
[75] The chronicler indicates that few lands had been left in his possession in 1257.

adversity, for they looked eagerly for an opportunity to make new conquests by combined endeavour. Gruffudd was, after all, the son of a prince who had declared his wish 'to restore to the Welsh their original rights and their boundaries'.[76] This was precisely the objective which the two princes now agreed to set before themselves on the frontiers of Powys: the gains made to the north of the Camlad would come to Gruffudd, those south of the river to Llywelyn. It meant that Gruffudd would extend his power through Gorddwr to the very heart of Corbet's lordship of Caus, precisely the direction to which he had driven the previous summer, and they may have embarked upon a joint enterprise in this direction early in 1264.[77] Llywelyn would drive to Montgomery and beyond. It was possibly in the period following this agreement that Llywelyn carried his powers beyond Montgomery to take possession of Teirtref Esgob. This land, composed of the three vills of Muleton (Mellington), Aston and Chestroke (Castle Wright), was situated between the lordships of Montgomery and Clun and formed part of the bishop of Hereford's estate of Bishop's Castle.[78] If his advance had not been made earlier it is certain that Llywelyn now secured control of the western portion of Clun, his possession of this land of Tempsiter formally recognized perhaps by John FitzAlan.[79] Llywelyn's struggle for dominance in this sector of the march was undoubtedly facilitated by the disturbed conditions of the summer of 1263. However fortuitous Gruffudd ap Gwenwynwyn's adherence may have been, it proved an added source of strength as Llywelyn pressed upon the crucially important area around Montgomery. By the beginning of 1264 there was a prospect of a further extension of his power in the area. Such was the impression made upon a man of religion of the priory of Alberbury, situated close by Gorddwr itself, that he dated a charter concerning its lands to Candlemas 'in the year in which Llywelyn ap Gruffudd and Gruffudd ap Gwenwynwyn came together with a great army to destroy the marchers, and especially Roger Mortimer'.[80]

---

[76] *CW*, 31; *BT, Pen20*, 143; *Pen20Tr*, 79; *RBH*, 180–1.

[77] For Llywelyn's later possession of Gorddwr, recorded by jurors of Chirbury, Shropshire, 1274, *Rotuli Hundredorum*, ed. W. Illingworth and J. Caley (Record Commission, 1812–18), ii, 89–90, 113, and below, n. 174.

[78] The lands, said to belong to the bishop of Hereford's castle of Lydbury North, had been seized by Hamo Lestrange as belonging to the honour of Montgomery in the summer of 1263 (*RegSwinfield*, 86). Llywelyn's subsequent possession may be established from a group of seven letters, 1275–6, in *Registrum Thome de Cantilupo, Episcopi Herefordensis, 1275–1282*, ed. R. G. Griffiths and W. W. Capes (London, Canterbury and York Society, 1897), 9–11, 29–32, 42, 103–4; below, n. 173.

[79] *CAC*, 86–7; below, n. 173.

[80] Bodleian Library MS, DD All Souls, c. 1 (C. T. Martin, *Catalogue of the Archives of All Souls College* (London, 1877), 2, no. 12). Dr N. Auberin-Potter kindly identified the charter noticed in H. Owen and J. B. Blakeway, *A History of Shrewsbury* (Shrewsbury, 1825), i, 125–6, n. 4. The priory, a FitzWarin foundation, stood in the manor of Alberbury,

Rhyd Chwima

If the scribe at Alberbury had realized that the main objective of the Welsh forces was the destruction of the power of Roger Mortimer we may be certain that Simon de Montfort, too, had recognized the lord of Wigmore as a formidable adversary with whom he would have to contend. Whatever understanding may have been established between Llywelyn and Montfort – and we have no firm evidence of formal agreement for some time yet – the forces of the two men were collaborating in the march early in 1264.[81] In January the king and several of the great magnates of the realm had left the country for Amiens, where the king of France would make his arbitration award on the dissensions in the realm, with the administration entrusted to Richard, earl of Cornwall, at Windsor. Prompted particularly perhaps by a need to prevent Llywelyn from retaliating against Mortimer for the destruction he had wrought upon Montfort's estates in the march, but also aware that Llywelyn was in any case likely to resume his offensive, the king, shortly before his departure, had authorized Mortimer, James Audley and Hamo Lestrange to negotiate with the prince. He told Llywelyn to be at the ford of Montgomery by 13 January to meet the three magnates and discuss truce and peace, though his letter to the magnates indicated that he was more concerned to secure a truce until Easter.[82] It probably proved impossible to hold that meeting, and Cornwall made an effort to arrange another at the ford at a later date.[83] Soon afterwards, influenced perhaps by Edward's return from France and certainly by the deteriorating situation in the march, Cornwall acknowledged the need for sterner measures. Reacting, perhaps, to news of the award at Amiens, Montfort's forces were committed to action in the march in association with those of Llywelyn. Cornwall sensed that baronial forces had prepared to cross the Severn to join forces with Llywelyn and attack Mortimer's positions. Bridges were to be thrown down and boats destroyed and all possible measures taken to prevent the convergence of baronial and Welsh forces. But Cornwall found that it was too late to prevent the concerted attack on Radnor, directed

---

held by Fulk FitzWarin as a tenant of Thomas Corbet and a matter of contention between them (*Shropshire Eyre of 1256*, xxvii, 137–8). The text of the tale of Fulk FitzWarin, which may reflect the conflicts of this period, is in *Fouke le fitz Waryn*, ed. E. J. Hathaway *et al.* (Oxford, Anglo-Norman Text Society, 1975); discussion in E. A. Francis, 'The background of *Fulk fitz Warin*', in E. A. Francis (ed.), *Studies in Medieval French presented to Alfred Ewert* (Oxford, 1961), 322–7; M. D. Legge, *Anglo-Norman Literature and its Background* (Oxford, 1963), 171–4.

[81] Llywelyn made a truce with a government controlled by Montfort in August 1263, noticed already; apart from chroniclers' statements of alliance, there is no indication of formal concord.

[82] *CR, 1261–64*, 373 (24 December 1263). Mortimer is said to have attacked Montfort estates in co. Hereford in December 1263 (*FloresHist*, ii, 486; *AnnDunst*, 226).

[83] On 18 January Audley and Mortimer were told to be at the ford of Montgomery by 9 February to discuss peace and truce, but the letter suggests that the intention was a truce extending to Whitsun. Audley was to convey the letters to Llywelyn and receive his ratification of the truce (*CR, 1261–64*, 374).

by Llywelyn and Henry de Montfort, which so impressed itself on the scribe at Alberbury.[84] The earl had been responsible for the refortification of the castle following its destruction by Llywelyn the Great thirty years before and, considering the attention which Llywelyn ap Gruffudd had given to this area, it is somewhat surprising that his work at Radnor had been spared for so long.[85] Appreciating that the forces of Llywelyn and Montfort were working together, Edward now took direct responsibility for operations in the march, concentrating first on the lands of the only one of the marchers who now opposed him, namely Humphrey de Bohun. He attacked the castles of Huntington and Hay and forced his way to Brecon, putting the castle and the associated lands in the custody of Mortimer.[86] It was now a struggle between the forces of the crown and those of the English magnates and Welsh princes who worked in open collaboration.

Llywelyn had left himself exposed to the possibility of a counter-offensive on the part of the crown, and he would not have been surprised to know that the royal army was summoned to war by the spring. Someone in the king's service remembered the standard bearing the image of a dragon which had been taken to war in Wales before, and it was ordered that it be borne before the royal forces once more. Hardly a beneficent talisman in days gone by, the standard was not to embark on any royal progress in 1264. Henry faced confrontation in the heart of England and met with defeat at Lewes on 14 May 1264.[87] Henry and Edward, and the government of the realm, fell into Montfort's hands, and Llywelyn was left undisturbed. This is the gist of the Welsh chronicler's account of the year: the conflicts which led to the capture of Henry and his son took place in another land; the Welsh were left in peace by the English, with Llywelyn the prince of the entire country.[88] Llywelyn would appear to stand apart from the fray, and historians have commented upon his apparent inactivity during the course of the year and expressed the view that he missed a favourable opportunity to work in more purposeful cooperation with Montfort.[89] We can never be sure that the sources provide an

---

[84] *CR, 1261–64*, 374. *AC*, 101 indicates late 1263, but chancery documents establish early 1264.

[85] *AC(B)*, 79; *CW*, 37; *BT, Pen20*, 192; *Pen20Tr*, 102; *RBH*, 230–1.

[86] *AC*, 101; *FloresHist*, ii, 486; Rishanger, *Chronica*, 13; idem, *Chronicon De Bellis*, 20; Trevet, *Annales*, 254, each placing the advance after his opponents' attack on Radnor. In the Battle Chronicle, Bodleian Rawlinson MS B. 150 (Bémont, *Montfort* (1884), 379), the advance is placed after Montfort's agreement with Llywelyn in June 1265, but *HW*, ii, 737, n. 102, suggests confusion with events of early 1264. The Battle entry has a reference to Edward's advance to a new castle that Llywelyn had built in the lordship of Brecon, for which below, pp. 416–17.

[87] *CR, 1242–47*, 201; *CR, 1261–64*, 377–82; orders, 6–18 March 1264, for a muster at Oxford at the end of the month; cf. Powicke, *Henry III*, ii, 463–74.

[88] *BT, Pen20*, 215; *Pen20Tr*, 113–14; *RBH*, 254–5.

[89] Tout, *CP*, ii, 72, 80, 82, refers to the prince's 'masterly inactivity'; more accurate comment in *HW*, ii, 735.

adequate record of the course of events, but the evidence that we have serves to indicate that the year was by no means uneventful. Llywelyn may have been left alone, but he was not inactive. His year began with the attack on Radnor, alongside Montfort's forces. He maintained a presence on the border, inducing a complaint from Mortimer that the prince was preparing to attack his lands. The reply from the Montfort administration, while assuring Mortimer that Llywelyn had been told to desist, gave him no encouragement to resist but simply told him to ensure that he kept the peace.[90] Mortimer was soon, indeed, to be the object of a Montfort offensive, when the earl advanced to the borderland of Wales to break the power of those who, after effecting their escape from Lewes, undermined the agreement made in the wake of the battle. In July Montfort, in association with Llywelyn, moved through Hereford and Hay, and then Ludlow, and Richard's Castle, devastating Mortimer lands on their way to Montgomery. The chroniclers favourable to Montfort's cause did not omit to notice that he benefited greatly from Llywelyn's active support. The earl was in alliance (*amicitia*) with Llywelyn. It was an English and Welsh army which forced Mortimer, Audley and the others to submit at Montgomery.[91]

Before the year was out Montfort's opponents in the march were forced to submit a second time, following another expedition which did not go without substantial support from Wales. The earl came to Worcester to find the Severn bridges destroyed by the royalists in the hope that they could maintain their position to the west of the river but, traversing the Welsh frontier, Llywelyn was able to confront them and force a second submission.[92] Twice in the course of 1264 Llywelyn had intervened to good effect in the struggle between the earl and his opponents in the area where he encountered the most vigorous resistance. Yet on each occasion Montfort failed to drive home his advantage, and the waning of his cause may be traced from his successive failures to eradicate the opposition of the adversaries who withstood him in the march and borderland of Wales. On the second occasion, in accordance with the terms of an agreement of 12 December 1264, the royalists were required to withdraw from the realm for a whole year, and it was understood that they should depart for Ireland.[93] They never intended to do so, and Llywelyn may have been incensed that Montfort had allowed his opponents, and Mortimer in particular, to escape a second time. Henry and Edward

---

[90] *CR, 1261–64*, 387.
[91] *FloresHist*, ii, 498–9; Trevet, *Annales*, 261–2; Rishanger, *Chronica*, 30–1; idem, *Chronicon De Bellis*, 155–6.
[92] *FloresHist*, ii, 502–4. Bemont, *Montfort*, 227, compresses Montfort's two movements; see *HW*, ii, 735; Powicke, *Henry III*, ii, 476–7, 486–7; Maddicott, *Montfort*, 289–90, 307–8.
[93] *Foedera*, I, i, 449, 455; Powicke, *Henry III*, ii, 487–9.

might be held in captivity, but Mortimer was allowed to get away, and that escape was to prove decidedly damaging to the Montfort cause.

Both Llywelyn and Montfort no doubt recognized Mortimer's prime importance among their opponents. The *marchiones Wallie* to whom the chronicler might refer in the summer of 1264 may have had some affinity with the group which had acted briefly in opposition to the crown the previous year, but this was a new alliance which was to prove to be a key factor in the survival of the king's cause, and Mortimer was its focus.[94] Earl and prince may have acknowledged that combined endeavour to defeat the group centred on Mortimer was essential to their purposes, but whether they established any meaningful political concord during the period when Montfort exercised power in the realm is difficult to judge. The only agreement for which there is full documentary evidence is that which was formulated in June 1265 and is considered later. The papal court is known to have been troubled by Llywelyn's adherence to Montfort and wished to see it revoked, but it is not certain that Pope Clement had knowledge of any agreement preceding that which was made at that time.[95] The chroniclers certainly make numerous references to collaboration between the two men, and the Chester annalist refers particularly to a meeting early in 1265 when Llywelyn and Gruffudd ap Madog had discussions at Hawarden with Henry de Montfort.[96] This was an area where, especially after the earldom on Chester had been vested in Montfort, the interests of the two men met and where there might have been a need to define their respective spheres of authority. Discussions between the two parties may well have been concerned with specific issues of this nature and no more. Whether Llywelyn's broad political objectives were ever considered, quite apart from being endorsed, during the period of Montfort's effective power is thus uncertain. Chancery records contain only the slightest indications of any transactions whatsoever between the prince and the government of England in these months. The most substantial item is the administration's response to a complaint from Llywelyn concerning a dispute with the bishop of Bangor over their respective jurisdictions serious enough for the bishop to place the prince's chapel under interdict.[97] Llywelyn had seen fit to bring the matter to the government's notice, whereas he had previously preferred to resolve his differences with the bishop by arbitration

---

[94] For the *marchiones Wallie* (Mortimer, Audley, Roger Clifford, Roger Leyburn, Hamo Lestrange), *FloresHist*, ii, 498. Those identified in chancery records as Montfort's opponents include the same names, with John Lestrange, Fulk FitzWarin, Thomas Corbet, Peter Corbet, Robert de Tibetot (e.g. *CPR, 1258–66*, 332).

[95] *Foedera*, I, i, 461. This and other papal letters concerning the situation in the realm were dated at Perugia, 13 September; papal concern may have reflected known collaboration preceding formal agreement in June 1265.

[96] *HW*, ii, 735, from *AnnCestr*, 90; for Hawarden, below, nn. 114, 128–30, 171.

[97] *CR, 1264–68*, 117–18; cf. Stephenson, *GG*, 172–3.

Rhyd Chwima

within his dominions.⁹⁸ He may have had some confidence in Montfort's administration and the response he got was not unfavourable to him, but the matter was hardly central to his interests. There is no whit of evidence to suggest that his political aspirations were accorded any more sympathetic hearing in 1264–5 than they had been given by the baronial opposition in 1258–9.

It is indeed exceedingly difficult to recognize, amidst the evidence for confederacy in arms, the origins of the political association with the Montforts which proved so fateful for Llywelyn in years to come. By the mid-1270s Llywelyn had decided to marry Montfort's daughter, adding a new factor to those which already vitiated his relations with the crown and thereby contributing to the issues which led to war in 1277.⁹⁹ It is not impossible that, as the chroniclers aver, the plan to marry Eleanor de Montfort was agreed in Montfort's lifetime, and it could be expected that a marriage agreement of this nature would be formally recorded in a compact between the two men.¹⁰⁰ At the same time it would be fair to conclude that Llywelyn would not have pledged himself to marry Montfort's daughter unless there were reasonable expectation that the earl would be able to meet the demands that the prince would wish to enumerate in any agreement with the power which ruled the kingdom of England. Montfort exercised that power as a consequence of his victory at Lewes in the summer of 1264, but by the early months of the next year his power was diminishing, and the turning point was the earl's manifest failure to ensure that his opponents in the march abided by the terms of their submission. Even as early as February 1265 it was clear that the royalists were firmly in control of Shropshire and the adjacent march, certain of a strongpoint from which they could maintain their uncompromising resistance to Montfort and, while their power remained entrenched there, the solemn agreements made for the government of the realm during the summer following the battle of Lewes remained meaningless.¹⁰¹ Montfort made an attempt to galvanize the realm into a new belief in the agreement, and he recommended its terms to the king of Scotland and the lords of Ireland and Gascony. He may have recommended them to Llywelyn, too, but it is possible that the prince had by then lost faith in Montfort's ability to secure stable peace for the realm of England or for the principality of Wales. It was strange that, after a period of not inconsequential combination in arms, the offer of peace terms to Llywelyn was inspired by nothing better than a tacit admission

---

⁹⁸ *Councils*, i, 489–91; *LW*, 97–8 (29 April, 18 August 1261).

⁹⁹ Below, pp. 390–402.

¹⁰⁰ Trevet, *Annales*, 294; *AnnWinch*, 121; *The Chronicle of Melrose*, ed. A. O. Anderson and M. O. Anderson (London, 1936), 134–5.

¹⁰¹ For the 'form of peace' that Henry and Edward accepted, *DBM*, 294–301; Powicke, *Henry III*, ii, 474–9.

Rhyd Chwima

on Montfort's part that he had failed to break the power of the royalists in the march of Wales. The documents exchanged between Montfort and Llywelyn in June 1265 would have been much more meaningful had they been drawn up a year earlier, and Llywelyn's letters are not without an intimation that he was well aware that time was running out.

By then Montfort's position was critical and, if the denouement was to be enacted in the heart of England, some of Montfort's last desperate manœuvres were played out on the fringes of the principality of Wales. For Montfort this region was far from being a haven of support. On the contrary Mortimer and Roger Clifford held their ground in the march and provided a starting point for the rehabilitation of Henry III's kingship. Gilbert de Clare, earl of Gloucester, after some hesitation, deserted Montfort for the king, bringing the twin benefits of the political influence of a major English magnate and the strength that he drew from his broad territories in the Welsh march.[102] His switch in allegiance brought him into alliance with Mortimer, one collaborative occasion among a number of less cordial episodes which marked the uneasy relationship between the two men. It was, even so, one which was of considerable immediate value in that it provided Edward, when he escaped from Montfort's grasp at Hereford, with the basis of a formidable combination.[103] It was no accident that it was to Wigmore that Edward sped first, on his way to a meeting at Ludlow with Mortimer and Clare. The Welsh chronicler had no inclination to dwell at length on Edward's escape from prison by the stratagem of Roger Mortimer and his gathering of a mighty force for the campaign which would lead to triumph at Evesham, but it had the gist of the matter.[104] It was only in the wake of these decisive events that Montfort conveyed his wish to enter into the negotiations that led to the only agreement with Llywelyn of which there is historical record.[105]

The document drawn up by Montfort was issued in the name of King Henry, still held in captivity, and it carried the king's seal. Its terms reflect the objectives that Llywelyn had been seeking since 1258, and it included several of the provisions embodied in the treaty to which the king, no longer acting under duress, was to agree in 1267. But the agreements of 1265 and 1267 were made in very different circumstances, and the diplomas themselves reveal important contrasts. The terms of the agreement of 1267 were established by face-to-face negotiations between representatives of the principal parties and

---

[102] The chroniclers do not count Clare among the *marchiones* (e.g. *AnnWav*, 363). He left for the march, ostensibly to withstand Llywelyn, in February or March (ibid., 358).

[103] Powicke, *Henry III*, ii, 496–8; Altschul, *Clares*, 109. In May 1265 William de Valence and John de Warenne landed in Pembroke and advanced across south Wales (*CR, 1264–68*, 121–2; *FloresHist*, iii, 1–2, 264; *ChronWykes*, 165).

[104] *BT, Pen20*, 216; *Pen20Tr*, 114; *RBH*, 254–7.

[105] Tout, *CP*, ii, 77–82; *HW*, ii, 736–7; Powicke, *Henry III*, ii, 499–500; Maddicott, *Montfort*, 337–8.

were embodied in a single document. The negotiations with Montfort were conducted differently. On the one side, letters patent were granted by the king at Hereford; on the other side letters patent, in two documents, were given by Llywelyn at Pipton in the lordship of Cantref Selyf where Llywelyn was encamped.[106] This record was the outcome of a series of exchanges begun on 12 June when Simon de Montfort was formally empowered in the king's name to treat with Llywelyn concerning the discords which had arisen between king and prince.[107] During the following days a document was drawn up incorporating the results of negotiations which were concluded, presumably at Hereford, between representatives of the two sides. Their substance is contained in the king's letters patent dated at Hereford on 22 June, but the terms agreed had evidently been conveyed to Llywelyn at Pipton, and had been considered by prince and council, before the prince's letters patent were issued on 19 June. These letters registered the prince's acceptance of a financial commitment into which he was prepared to enter in return for the lands and rights which the king had granted and which had already been embodied in a written document.[108] This lends credence to a chronicler's statement that a document drawn up at Hereford was taken to the prince by Peter de Montfort, who then awaited the deliberations of the prince's council.[109] Letters written in the prince's name were conveyed to the royal court at Hereford where, three days later, the king issued the document enumerating the grants that he made to Llywelyn.[110] There is nothing to suggest that Llywelyn and Montfort came together either to discuss the terms of the agreement or to seal the final document, and it would be misleading to speak of a 'treaty of Pipton'. It may be significant that, even in formulating their only known formal agreement, the two men kept their distance.

It is the document given in the king's name that best conveys the substance of the agreement and, though dated later than the prince's letters, it must be taken first. For a fine of £20,000 the king granted Llywelyn the lordship of all the barons of Wales (*magnates Wallie*) along with the principality, to be held by Llywelyn and the heirs of his body. This is a form of words which, when contrasted with that of the treaty of 1267 (which refers only to Llywelyn and

---

[106] Text of document in the king's name in *Foedera*, I, i, 457, summary *CPR, 1258–66*, 433; those of Llywelyn in *DipDoc*, i, nos. 400, 401; *RL*, ii, 284–6, from C47/27/1, nos. 17, 18. These documents, dated 'in camp at Pipton' or 'at Pipton' ('in castris iuxta Pyperton' or 'apud Pipertone'), are among the most important of the original texts emanating from Llywelyn's court that have survived.

[107] *CPR, 1258–66*, 432.

[108] *DipDoc*, i, no. 400.

[109] *ChronWykes*, 168, erroneously placing the concession to Llywelyn after Montfort's advance into Wales.

[110] *Foedera*, I, i, 457. The dating of Llywelyn's letters on 19 June and those of the king on 22 June might seem to point to a different sequence of events, but Llywelyn refers to a text already available for consideration on the earlier date.

his heirs), defines the devolution of the principality in a manner consistent with the possibility that a marriage compact had been made, but there can be no certainty that this was so. Creating a new relationship between king and prince, their agreement provided that written engagements into which Llywelyn ap Gruffudd and Dafydd ap Llywelyn had entered, and which were not consonant with their rights and liberties, were now annulled. This ensured that the major treaties made in the period of royal supremacy following the death of Llywelyn ap Iorwerth were rescinded: Gloucester, Gwerneigron, Woodstock, all were now abrogated, and the king put aside all rancour against Llywelyn.[111] His seisin of the lands he now held was recognized and confirmed: Elfael Is Mynydd,[112] Ellesmere,[113] Hawarden[114] and Whittington[115] were the only lands named, but these were only the most recent of Llywelyn's annexations. These did not indicate the limit of his aspirations, for, in a particularly ironic clause of a document issued in the king's name, Montfort promised to assist the prince in the conquest of the remaining lands, still held by the common adversaries of prince and earl, that by right belonged to him or to his magnates, with Montgomery specifically mentioned. The entire document represented a yielding, in the king's name, on the issues on which Henry III, ever since he had assumed the responsibilities of kingship, had remained resolutely resistant in times of prosperity and exceedingly

[111] The text reads 'omnes obligationes litterales quas dictus princeps vel David filius Lewelini, predecessor suus, nobiscum fecerunt contra jura et libertates suas, omnino destruantur et pro infectis habeantur'. The calendar (*CPR, 1258–66*, 433) conveys that 'written bonds against their rights and liberties be destroyed'; it would probably be safe to take the *obligationes litterales* to be the major treaties of 1240, 1241 and 1247 considered earlier.

[112] For Elfael Is Mynydd, above, n. 7.

[113] Ellesmere was leased to Hamo Lestrange in December 1263, following his return to the king's fealty (*CPR, 1258–66*, 302); Llywelyn may have secured possession soon afterwards. Llywelyn ap Gruffudd Fychan's campaigns in Ellesmere and Whittington from Powys Fadog, commemorated by Llygad Gŵr (*GBF*, 28), probably occurred later and are considered with the events of 1282.

[114] Hawarden was of the inheritance of Roger of Mold (e.g. *CIM*, i, no. 1028); whether Llywelyn secured it by force or whether it was conceded by Montfort before the agreement of June 1265 is uncertain. For Llywelyn's concern with Hawarden later that year and its position under the treaty of 1267, below, nn. 128–30, 171.

[115] It was provided that Llywelyn should have lordship over Whittington so that the heir should do service to the prince in accordance with that which his predecessors had done to the prince's predecessors; any failure on the part of the heir would be set to right by the laws and customs of Wales. Fulk FitzWarin had fallen on the king's side at Lewes in 1264, leaving an heir under age. Llywelyn may have taken possession soon afterwards, a possibility that (along with the fact that Roger de Tony had also left a young heir) may explain the critical comment in a London chronicle (*Cronica Maiorum et Vicecomitum Londoniarum de Antiquis Legibus Liber*, ed. T. Stapleton (London, Camden Society, 34, 1846), 73–4 [*Chronica Maiorum*]) that the king through evil counsel yielded to Llywelyn the lands of persons too young to inherit their estates. The basis for Llywelyn's hereditary right in Whittington is not clear.

evasive in times of adversity. And these important concessions were made in perpetuity.

If, as seems likely, Peter de Montfort took with him to Pipton a full text of the document later enrolled, Llywelyn would have had his first sight of an instrument drawn up in the English chancery in which he was addressed as prince of Wales. His letters patent, in two separate instruments, are necessarily less informative than those of the king in that they were, essentially, limited to a statement of the prince's readiness to abide by what was required of him. He recognized that the principality of Wales was held of the king and he agreed to fulfil the services which his predecessors had done to the king and his predecessors. This was in accord with the tenor of the king's grant, though Llywelyn's reference to his predecessors as 'princes of Wales' and his repeated references to the 'principality of Wales' point to a keen awareness of the status now formally accorded to him. He promised to pay the £20,000 required of him and specified the dates on which the instalments would be paid and, again employing a rather self-conscious phraseology, indicated that his agreement was made with the counsel and consent of the magnates of his land and principality. Llywelyn remitted all rancour towards the men of the lands which Henry granted him, so that they could live there or depart in peace, each according to his will. He promised to maintain them in their rights, and to make amends if he acted in a manner inconsistent with the terms agreed. Reflecting present necessity urged upon him by Montfort, and reciprocating the promise of aid already made in the king's name, Llywelyn and his magnates swore that they would adhere to the ordinance for the release of the Lord Edward and would support, by armed force, the magnates pledged to bring pressure on those who infringed its terms.[116] The prince's promise to provide military aid against the marchers marks a last effort on the part of Montfort to pursue the quest for ordered government that had begun in the aftermath of the battle of Lewes.

Llywelyn sealed his instruments in the presence of the magnates of his principality and the list of names provides another glimpse of the group of men found in attendance upon him when great matters were considered: Gruffudd ap Gwenwynwyn, Gruffudd ap Madog and his brothers Hywel ap Madog and Madog Fychan, Rhys Fychan, Hywel ap Maredudd, Hywel ap Rhys Gryg and Owain ap Bleddyn are the princes named, with Goronwy ab

---

[116] For the main documents relevant to Llywelyn's undertaking, *DBM*, 46–54, 294–9, 309–14; *Foedera*, I, i, 451–2; Powicke, *Henry III*, ii, 467–90; Maddicott, *Montfort*, 284–9, 318–20. In the second of his letters patent Llywelyn promised that if Henry were to die before payments of the sums agreed were completed, or if the king were to go against 'the ordinance made in London', the prince would continue to make payments to Henry's heir or successor (*DipDoc*, i, no. 401). Maddicott, ibid., 338, observes that Montfort still envisaged the possibility of Edward's disinheritance.

Ednyfed the one person named from among the non-princely members of his entourage who would be in regular attendance.[117] With what measure of conviction prince and magnates agreed to accept the terms offered by Montfort we cannot tell. They may have had their doubts. Naturally unmentioned in the text, but apparently part of the understanding between prince and earl, Montfort is said to have given Llywelyn hostages in pledge of his adherence to the terms agreed, and Llywelyn sent them to the furthermost parts of his principality.[118] If this were indeed true it would spell the hollowness of the compact drawn up in the king's name. Those who gathered at Pipton probably appreciated to the full the fact that they were dealing with a crumbling power and they were surely sceptical of the prospect of any result of permanent significance. They may, too, have sensed that desperate measures on Montfort's part might arouse an animosity in England that would not serve Welsh interests well in changed political circumstances. Certainly there were English commentators who pronounced that what was done at Hereford was done by evil counsel, and that the earl's actions were dictated by the need to win support in his contest with Edward. No good had ever come from any agreement with the Welsh, only deceit and misunderstanding.[119] Others, less scathing but more perceptive, acknowledged that it was only in extremity that Montfort had come to terms with Llywelyn, and that the prince was simply endeavouring to re-establish the patrimony of his forebears, not to be blamed for seizing the opportunity to achieve his objectives.[120] The circumstances, even so, may well have placed Llywelyn in a dilemma, for a concord reached in these disturbed conditions would hardly provide the stable peace he sought. The tone of Llywelyn's letters suggest that the terms were agreed, not with any elation but with due caution, and that the prince's council may have concluded that it would be better to accept them than reject them, in the hope that, despite a possible adverse reaction in England, the agreement could become the basis for a new treaty forged with a king acting of his free will.

The document extending peace terms to Llywelyn was one of the very last acts of any consequence to be registered on the chancery rolls before Montfort's

---

[117] The prince's entourage is considered more fully, below, pp. 310–16, 328–9.

[118] Battle Chronicle (Bémont, *Montfort* (1884), 379): 'a comite ei traditis remotius in Cambriam transmissis'.

[119] *Chronica Maiorum*, 73–4; cf. *FloresHist*, iii, 258. The odium incurred by the agreement is reflected in the *Opusculum de nobili Simone de Monteforti* in its account of the sending of Montfort's foot to Llywelyn after the earl's death at Evesham (*Chronicle of Melrose*, 134–5).

[120] *AnnWav*, ii, 363; *ChronWykes*, 168.

Rhyd Chwima

power collapsed and ordered administration became impossible.[121] A few days later Montfort left Hereford, taking the king with him, and moved to the march of Wales. It might seem, as several chroniclers intimate, that he was making for the lands controlled by Llywelyn and a known source of support.[122] He took his forces, however, not upstream along the Wye towards Llywelyn's encampment, but downstream to Monmouth.[123] Montfort made for the Bristol Channel with a view to crossing to Bristol and securing the support which remained to him in southern England marshalled by his son Simon. He took Clare's castle at Usk and then, moving through Clare's lordship of Caerleon, reached the coast at Newport in the earl's lordship of Gwynllŵg. With Clare and Edward, after securing Gloucester, making a rapid advance through Usk in pursuit, and the ships by which he hoped to cross the Channel destroyed by Clare's action, Montfort was forced into a retreat. From Newport he made his way swiftly along a route which took him, east of the Usk, to Abergavenny and Hay. While his itinerary, traversing three Clare lordships, lends credence to the statements of several chroniclers that he wrought destruction in the earl's lands, the speed of his movements after his withdrawal from Newport suggests that the main onslaught would have been his attack on Usk on his way to the coast. His movements show that, contrary to the word of some chroniclers, he cannot have created havoc in Clare's lordship of Glamorgan. Nor is it by any means certain that at any point in his itinerary was he joined by Llywelyn. It remains possible that Llywelyn, in a simultaneous but independent movement, intervened in Glamorgan, where he is known to have established a presence, to Clare's considerable discomfiture, before the end of the following year.[124] Yet there is no clear indication of combined military effort. Again, while a large number of Welshmen fought, and many were killed, in the final encounter at Evesham, there is no certainty that Llywelyn committed forces to Montfort's

---

[121] Agreement with Llywelyn enrolled 22 June; there were no more entries on the Close Roll, entries on the Patent Roll only at Hereford, 23 July, and Monmouth, 25–8 July, before chancery came under new management after Evesham. For this period: Tout, *CP*, ii, 82–4; Bémont, *Montfort*, 239–41; *HW*, ii, 737 (each needing revision); Maddicott, *Montfort*, 338–9.

[122] *FloresHist*, ii, 486; iii, 3–4, 252; *AnnWav*, 362–3; *ChronWykes*, 166–8; Trevet, *Annales*, 265; Rishanger, *Chronica*, 34–5.

[123] Montfort's movements are noticed in D. Carpenter, *The Battles of Lewes and Evesham, 1264–65* (Keele, 1987), 38–9, using a roll of the king's oblations (E101/349/30). The roll shows the king at Monmouth, 28 June–3 July (a marginal indicating that Usk was attacked during those days); Newport, 4–8 July; Abergavenny 9–10 July; Hay 11–12 July; thence to Hereford.

[124] For Llywelyn's intervention, below, nn. 139–40.

cause in his last extremity.[125] The Welsh casualties may have been suffered by contingents recruited from the lands of Montfort's solitary ally among the marchers, Humphrey de Bohun, and Montfort certainly traversed Bohun's lordship of Hay. Bohun's firm resolve to remain at the head of the foot-soldiers, many of them Welsh, during the conflict at Evesham may reflect a loyalty to men of the lands of his inheritance.[126] For Montfort, the march of Wales proved to be no haven of security, but an inhospitable land through which he moved as rapidly as he could, leading an army portrayed by the chroniclers as a force in some distress.[127] From Hay he advanced to Hereford, then, crossing the Severn near Kempsey, went on to see the eclipse of his power and meet his own death at Evesham.

Llywelyn now knew that he and his fellow princes had no choice but to defend their principality by their own efforts, whatever force the government of a more united realm might be able to throw against them. The area of greatest concern lay in north-east Wales where the removal of Montfort's authority in Chester reopened the area to a reassertion of royal control, reflected in a grant of the county to Edward only ten days after Evesham. Llywelyn's activity was marked by the capture of the castle of Hawarden, his need to do so suggesting that Edward had succeeded in recovering the stronghold soon after his restoration to Chester.[128] Hawarden was promptly destroyed. Llywelyn preferred to rely for his defence on the castle of Ewloe. The castle's origins are uncertain but an attribution of the entire building to Llywelyn ap Gruffudd can probably be made with some confidence.[129] The precise circumstances in which Llywelyn built at Ewloe remain unclear but, though an early date following his annexation of Perfeddwlad in 1256 is possible, the construction may be better explained by the needs which confronted him on this frontier slightly later and particularly upon Edward's

---

[125] His ability to provide support might have been reduced if Edward and Clare, after retaking Usk, had proceeded to Hay and Huntingdon and even Brecon, a movement attributed by the Battle Chronicle to this time (Bémont, *Montfort* (1884), 379; Maddicott, *Montfort*, 339). This would need to be placed between the recapture of Usk, *c.*4 July, and their arrival at Worcester, *c.*25 July. This movement, as suggested in *HW*, ii, 737, n. 102 (above, n. 86), may be more credibly placed in 1264.

[126] For the Welsh foot-soldiers, see e.g. *FloresHist*, iii, 5; Rishanger, *Chronica*, 34–5; for Bohun at Evesham, D. C. Cox, 'The battle of Evesham in the Evesham chronicle', *Historical Research*, 62 (1989), 337–45.

[127] E.g. *ChronWykes*, 166–8; for the view that in the Welsh uplands Montfort was 'safe, under the protection of the prince of Wales', *HW*, ii, 737.

[128] *AnnWav*, 366; cf. *CPR, 1258–66*, 488–9. For Llywelyn's contact with Montfort's sons, *AnnWorc*, 456; *Foedera*, I, i, 461.

[129] W. J. Hemp, 'The castle of Ewloe and the Welsh castle plan', *Y Cymmrodor*, 39 (1928), 4–19; E. Neaverson, *Mediaeval Castles in North Wales* (London, 1947), 34–5; R. Avent, 'Castles of the Welsh princes', *Chateau Gaillaird*, 16 (1994), 11–20, with further references; below, p. 252, n. 288.

taking possession of Cheshire in the latter part of 1265.[130] If this were the case, appreciating that he would face difficulties if he attempted to retain the castle of Hawarden, Llywelyn would have chosen to establish a strongpoint upon a site, albeit not an ideal one, two miles to the north-west within the same lordship. Llywelyn was certainly energetically engaged on the Cheshire front at this time. An army led by Hamo Lestrange suffered a reverse in that area, and it was evidently in the aftermath of vigorous activity on Llywelyn's part that the crown agreed in November to a truce which was intended to hold good until Lent.[131] Two years more were to pass before Llywelyn had an opportunity to enter into peace negotiations and, in endeavouring to understand the difficulties which delayed the process, account has to be taken of the situation in England whose accurate comprehension was so important to Llywelyn himself.

When peace negotiations were eventually initiated in the late summer of 1267 they were attended, and eventually conducted, by the papal legate Cardinal Ottobuono.[132] He had been appointed legate *a latere* to England, Wales, Scotland and Ireland shortly before the battle of Evesham, and the charge laid upon him by Pope Clement reflected concern that rebellion in the realm should be ended and the king's authority fully restored.[133] Ottobuono set out from Rome to help bring Henry's opponents into allegiance to him once more, but the changed situation in England after Montfort's defeat did not by any means leave the legate absolved from any further mission. He was to fulfil an important role by his mediation between the estranged factions in the inevitably difficult circumstances which prevailed in the aftermath of civil war. In relation to Wales, too, Ottobuono's role proved different from what Pope Clement envisaged when he had insisted that Llywelyn's adherence to Montfort should be terminated and that the prince should submit himself to King Henry. The legate had been told to warn Llywelyn, under pain of excommunication, that he must abandon his alliance with Montfort, but the need to pursue that course was removed by Montfort's death. It was clear, even so, that Llywelyn would acknowledge the lordship of the king of England only on terms closely akin to those which had been agreed between

---

[130] J. E. Lloyd, 'Ewloe', *Y Cymmrodor*, 39 (1928), 1–3, 18–19, citing an inquisition of 1311 (Cest. 29/23, m. 48), indicates a construction soon after 1256, a view reflected in later work. This is not necessarily the conclusion to which the inquisition leads, and a later date may be preferable. For the demesne at Ewloe, where at least one letter of the prince is dated, below, pp. 221, 226.

[131] *Foedera*, I, i, 466; *CPR, 1258–66*, 512.

[132] R. Graham, 'Letters of Cardinal Ottoboni, 1265–68', *EHR*, 15 (1900), 87–120; Alun Lewis, 'The English activities of Cardinal Ottobuono, legate of the Holy See', MA thesis, University of Manchester, 1937, chs. 2–4; Powicke, *Henry III*, ii, 526–8; *Councils and Synods*, I, ii, 725–6.

[133] *Registres des Papes: Clement IV, 1265–1268*, 40–3; *Foedera*, I, i, 459–61.

Montfort and himself. The papal court saw that a settlement with Llywelyn would need to be negotiated and before the end of the year, responding to a call to arrange an agreement, Ottobuono indicated his wish to receive the prince's envoys.[134] A viable settlement required both an acknowledgement that Llywelyn's engagement with a king under duress had to be entirely abrogated, and a recognition that any new agreement had to incorporate much of the substance of that very compact. Ottobuono was eventually to preside over negotiations which produced a closely similar result, but the progress to the consummation of the peace process at the ford of Montgomery would be greatly hindered, not by difficulties encountered in Wales, but by the fact that issues concerning Wales could not be resolved in isolation from those of the realm of England. Ottobuono had to contend with deep differences within the community of the realm of England. He quickly came to recognize the implications of the relations between two men, Roger Mortimer and Gilbert de Clare, who were not only representative of two discordant views on how the difficulties created by civil war might be resolved but who also nurtured animosity towards one another. In addition, the position of each of these magnates both in the realm of England and the march of Wales could have an important bearing on the outcome of any deliberations on the issues which mattered to Llywelyn.[135]

Although they had been brought together in alliance with Edward in the early summer of 1265, the incompatibility of Mortimer and Clare came to be manifested in their attitude to the Montfortians who survived the battle of Evesham. Clare, though he seized extensive lands of defeated Montfort supporters in the aftermath of the conflict, had an affinity with the aspirations for reform which Mortimer never shared, and he came to show a concern for the rehabilitation for the Disinherited which Mortimer never admitted. Mortimer's fortitude and the losses he incurred in the conflict were certainly rewarded and recompensed in the ample grants that he received from among the Montfortian forfeitures. It was with the grant of the lands of Robert de Vere, earl of Oxford, that Mortimer could first relish the prospect of becoming a really substantial landowner in England and his personal interests inevitably influenced his attitude to the Disinherited as a whole.[136] Some who had been associated with him in the march of Wales, such as Roger Leyburn

---

[134] *Foedera*, I, i, 467; *CPR, 1258–66*, 521 (December 1265).

[135] Powicke, *Henry III*, ii, 503–50; Altschul, *Clares*, 110–21; *DBM*, 55–60; A. Lewis, 'Roger Leyburn and the pacification of England, 1265–7', *EHR*, 54 (1939), 193–214; C. H. Knowles, 'The resettlement of England after the Barons' War, 1264–67', *TRHS*, 5th ser., 32 (1982), 25–41.

[136] Altschul, *Clares*, 107–15, quoting *ChronWykes*, 164–5; Knowles, 'Resettlement of England', 26–32. Inquisition *post mortem* of Mortimer, 1282 (*CIPM*, ii, no. 446), is incomplete; for the family estates in a later period, G. A. Holmes, *The Estates of the Higher Nobility in Fourteenth-Century England* (Cambridge, 1957), 10–11.

and John Giffard, were more inclined to the conciliatory position taken by Clare, but with Mortimer and Roger Clifford remaining intransigent there was still an influence in the affairs of the realm reminiscent of that of the *marchiones* of 1264–5. These rifts did nothing to help Llywelyn, though he was not much troubled in the march. Mortimer's vain attempt to conquer Brecon in May 1266 may have been inspired by animosity towards Clare as much as a wish to strike a blow at the prince, for the lordship had been granted to Clare's custody when Humphrey de Bohun died of wounds received at Evesham in Montfort's cause.[137] Llywelyn may have been more concerned by the implications of Mortimer's implacable opposition to an accommodation with the Disinherited. The prince had indeed emerged from the conflict anything but dispossessed, but the solution of his problems was closely bound up with a resolution of those of Montfort's former supporters. Once more Llywelyn gained nothing from dissension within the realm of England. Mortimer was not among those who subscribed to the Dictum of Kenilworth in the autumn of 1266, a clear sign of his reluctance to countenance the rehabilitation of the Disinherited. Admittedly, Llywelyn's needs found no reflection in the Dictum of Kenilworth any more than in the Provisions of Oxford but, by withstanding negotiations which could lead to reconciliation in England, Mortimer stood opposed to a process which could also lead to an accommodation with Llywelyn. Ottobuono came to realize at an early stage that Mortimer's resistance was a factor with which he had to contend in England and Wales alike. When he communicated with Llywelyn in September 1266 his messenger took another letter to Mortimer and, though we have no knowledge of the substance of either communication, it is likely that the legate was attempting to contend with matters of concern to both men. It was at exactly this time that Mortimer left Kenilworth and returned in some anger to Wigmore. More than a year after Evesham, the prospects were hardly encouraging for the Montfortians in England or for Llywelyn in Wales, and Ottobuono's despondency may be sensed in one of his letters to Rome.[138]

Relations between Llywelyn and Mortimer after 1265 are difficult to establish, but there can be little doubt that the lord of Wigmore would not have exercised any influence that tended towards an accommodation with Llywelyn. It might thus seem that Llywelyn could have profited from an understanding with Clare, if his quest for a settlement favourable to the Montfortians was capable of being extended to an agreement with Llywelyn and the princes who had been Montfort's allies. Yet there is nothing to

---

[137] Altschul, *Clares*, 116–17; *HW*, ii, 738–9. Mortimer's defeat in Brecon is noticed in *AnnWav*, 370.

[138] *DBM*, 57–9, 316–36; Graham, 'Letters', 116–17.

suggest that Llywelyn developed an understanding with Clare, rather the contrary. Early in 1267 Clare stayed away from parliament and, according to the chroniclers, remained in Wales with a view to waging war in the marches. His concern with his marcher inheritance at this time will be more fully considered at a later stage in our discussion, when it will be found that Clare was, at this very time, combating an intrusion into his lordship of Glamorgan on the part of Llywelyn.[139] This explains the entry in *Brut y Tywysogyon* which relates that when, in the spring of 1267, Clare led an army to London to enforce his efforts on behalf of the Disinherited he did so after making a pact with Llywelyn. That pact, however, had nothing to do with any broad agreement on their political objectives but related, rather, to the conflict which had arisen between them in the uplands of Glamorgan by reason of the prince's armed presence in Senghennydd.[140] It is exceedingly difficult to understand why the prince remained entrenched in Clare's territory at a time when the earl was pressing vigorously for reconciliation in the realm in the teeth of Mortimer's unyielding resistance. It would seem that Llywelyn might have done better to exercise some prudence and stay his hand in his relations with an English magnate who might conceivably have done much to remove the obstacles which lay between Llywelyn and the fulfilment of his fundamental aspirations.

We may, of course, be denied important knowledge of Llywelyn's calculations, and we may be entirely mistaken in believing that Clare's care for the Disinherited might have been extended so as to prove beneficial to Llywelyn. It is perfectly possible that a proponent of reconciliation within the realm of England might still be implacably opposed to compromise with the Welsh prince, especially when that English magnate had major territorial interest in the march of Wales. It is possible, too, that conflict in the last stages of the war of 1265 remained a strong influence. The fact that Clare was, in the summer of 1266, granted possession of whatever lands of the Welsh supporters of Montfort and Llywelyn that he could conquer may point to a divergence in his English and marcher objectives, and it may be relevant to an understanding of the compulsions upon Llywelyn to maintain his hold upon the northern parts of Blaenau Morgannwg. Yet it remains the case that a settlement with Llywelyn could only be envisaged in the context of that settlement of England which was bound up with a resolution of the problem of the Disinherited. Each is best seen as part of the process by which a land wearied by prolonged conflict sought to put its dissensions behind it, and

---

[139] Powicke, *Henry III*, ii, 542–6; Altschul, *Clares*, 118; Knowles, 'Resettlement of England', 30–1.

[140] *BT, Pen20*, 217; *Pen20Tr*, 114; *RBH*, 256–7. In Tout, *CP*, ii, 88; *HW*, ii, 739, n. 112, it is suggested that prince and earl were acting in concert, but this was not so. The conflict in Glamorgan is examined fully below, pp. 339–48, 350–5.

Rhyd Chwima

Edward would eventually express the view that it was only by virtue of the difficult circumstances which then prevailed that his father had agreed to the peace settlement of 1267. These were two aspects of a charge given to Cardinal Ottobuono to which he devoted his efforts for the whole of two years. The chronology of the process leading to a settlement, first intimated early in 1267 when Henry authorized negotiations for a treaty of peace, accords with this view.[141] On 18 June 1267, after weeks of delay, Clare was satisfied that he had secured terms which did justice to the Disinherited and he agreed to withdraw his forces from London.[142] A few days later Henry confirmed the terms and the process which was to lead to negotiations with Llywelyn was set in motion at once. On 24 June Henry wrote to Llywelyn explaining that his dispute with Clare had prevented him from attending to the discussions on the date which Cardinal Ottobuono had arranged. Correct in so far as it went, the letter's real relevance lay in the fact that it marked the settlement of the issues arising from the civil war which had so exercised the earl of Gloucester. Henry was now free to turn to the matters which concerned the prince of Wales. He earnestly hoped for peace between them, something which would be to the benefit and honour of his kingdom. He proposed that they should meet at the ford of Montgomery on 2 August, and he expected a reply from Llywelyn by the hand of the abbot of Shrewsbury in three weeks.[143]

How much confidence Llywelyn felt able to place in Henry's letter is impossible to judge. He may well have felt that he had been through all this before, but he might equally have sensed that circumstances were now decidedly more propitious. His reply was evidently positive for, though there is no further record of contact between them, negotiations had commenced, at Shrewsbury rather than the ford of Montgomery, by 28 August. Henry had already arrived there and the following week, in a letter to the king of France, he related that negotiations were proceeding day by day.[144] Llywelyn and his adherents might still be described as the king's enemies but now, in such marked contrast to the situation on so many earlier occasions, the king of England was on the borders of Wales and he was telling the king of France that he had important business to transact in relation to Wales. The problems to be set aside now were those of Gascony. The problems of Wales took some time to resolve, and on 21 September Henry entrusted the making of an agreement to Ottobuono, indicating his readiness to ratify whatever the legate negotiated. Whether this was an indication that a treaty was in sight, or an

---

[141] *CPR, 1266–72*, 40; *Foedera*, I, i, 472 (21 February).
[142] Powicke, *Henry III*, ii, 546–7; Altschul, *Clares*, 118–19.
[143] *CR, 1264–68*, 374–5.
[144] *CChR*, ii, 79; *CR, 1264–68*, 386–8.

acknowledgement that the omens were not good, is difficult to judge.[145] The following days may have proved crucial, and Ottobuono was probably entirely justified when he conveyed to Pope Clement his great satisfaction that at long last king and prince had come to an understanding with one another.[146]

Cardinal Ottobuono had the pleasure of being able to announce that an agreement had been made, as the preamble to the treaty declares, to put an end to a conflict between the peoples of England and Wales which had been waged for a long time and caused suffering to each in turn.[147] God, it relates, sometimes suffers humanity to be troubled by the discord of war, and then by his will restores the harmony of peace, and now Henry and Llywelyn, rising above their dissensions, had made a firm agreement. The prince's case had been argued at Shrewsbury by Einion ap Caradog and Dafydd ab Einion, the first of these a confidant who had stood with the prince from the time of his very first political initiatives in the troubled period following the death of Llywelyn the Great. It may be imagined that the magnates of his council were at hand during a process that was undoubtedly seen as the consummation of the long quest for a negotiated settlement with King Henry. Who among the magnates of England accompanied the king we cannot tell in full, but his sons Edward and Edmund were with him, his nephew Henry of Almain, and John FitzAlan and Hamo Lestrange.[148] His immediate counsellors included Walter Merton, Godfrey Giffard (the chancellor), John de Chishull, Robert Walerand, John de la Lynde and Robert Aguillon.[149] When terms were agreed Walerand and Lynde swore on Henry's behalf, and Walerand was empowered to swear on Edward's behalf as well, and these men may have borne the brunt of the negotiations on the king's part.[150] Einion and Dafydd swore on Llywelyn's behalf, and the proceedings at Shrewsbury were completed on 25 September when the four proctors swore upon the Holy Scriptures that

---

[145] *CPR, 1266–72*, 111; *Foedera*, I, i, 473. Ottobuono was in Shrewsbury by 25 August; Welsh and English commentators saw him as the mediator who achieved a settlement (e.g. *FloresHist*, iii, 16).

[146] Graham, 'Letters', 118–19; commentary in Tout, *CP*, ii, 88–97; *HW*, ii, 739–41; Powicke, *Henry III*, ii, 546–7, 621, 637–42; Edwards, in *LW*, xliii–l; J. G. Edwards, *The Principality of Wales, 1267–1967: A Study in Constitutional History* (Caernarfon, 1969), 5–9.

[147] *LW*, 114.

[148] Owen and Blakeway, *History of Shrewsbury*, i, 129; *CPR, 1247–58*, 102–14, 156–7.

[149] *CR, 1264–68*, 331–43, 381–95. Walerand and Lynde are named in the text; for these and Merton, Giffard and Chishull, see *The Cartulary of Shrewsbury Abbey*, ed. Una Rees (Aberystwyth, 1975), i, 136–7.

[150] For the diplomatic conventions and the diploma, P. Chaplais, *Essays in Medieval Diplomacy and Administration* (London, 1981), i, 235–53. Neither the king nor his heir would swear an oath with a person who was not his peer; Geoffrey de Geneville and Robert Walerand had authority to swear on the king's behalf (*CPR, 1266–72*, 111); Walerand and Lynde in fact did so.

Rhyd Chwima

Henry, Edward and Llywelyn would abide by the terms of the treaty. The three 'principal lords' who had bound themselves, six years before, to maintain a truce were now pledged to maintain a stable peace. But the process of making that firm peace was not yet complete and the three 'principal lords' had not yet met face to face. Four days later, in the presence of Ottobuono, the king's sons and his counsellors, Llywelyn did homage to the king and swore fealty.[151] Llywelyn's acceptance of the terms and his homage and fealty to the king were registered in a document dated at Montgomery on 29 September, and the treaty is generally known by that name. It is probable that Llywelyn did homage and swore fealty, not in the castle of Montgomery but at Rhyd Chwima, the ford on the River Severn to which reference has been made so frequently during the course of this discussion.[152] The fact that these formal transactions were completed at the ford is all the more meaningful in the light of comparable instances of frontier homage in continental Europe. Indeed the document issued by Ottobuono, differing from the texts of previous agreements between the princes and the English crown, has a touch of the diplomatic practice of an agreement between two powers.[153] As part of these last formalities Llywelyn swore upon the Scriptures that he would abide by the terms of the treaty, and Hywel ap Madog, Goronwy ab Ednyfed, the prince's steward, Tudur ab Ednyfed, Einion ap Caradog, and Dafydd ab Einion swore to the same effect.[154] Henry and Edward put their seals to the

---

[151] *LW*, 4.

[152] In the text on the Charter Roll (C53/56, m. 2) Llywelyn's homage is dated at Shrewsbury rather than Montgomery (a point noticed by Charles Insley); consistent reference in the following years to the treaty made at Montgomery suggest that transactions were completed at Montgomery rather than at Shrewsbury. The precise location remains to be considered. A reference by Llywelyn ap Rhys and Hywel of Rhys of Ystrad Tywi in 1282 to the agreement (*forma pacis*) made by Henry and Llywelyn 'at Rhyd Chwima' appears to be the only direct evidence that formalities were completed at the ford of Montgomery rather than at the castle (*RegPeck*, ii, 452–3). *BT* texts say that peace was made at Montgomery (Castell Baldwin), and a chancery document shows that Llywelyn had a safe-conduct to come to Montgomery to do homage and fealty (*Foedera*, I, i, 473). Tout, *CP*, ii, 89, took this to mean that Llywelyn did homage 'at the impregnable castle of Montgomery'. He may be right, but numerous earlier arbitrations 'at the ford of Montgomery' suggest that the parties assembled at the crossing-point on the Severn beneath the old castle of Montgomery (Hen Domen). Henry had certainly prepared for a meeting at the ford in June 1267 (*CR, 1264–68*, 374–5), and it was there that Llywelyn would be expected to swear fealty in 1273. The evidence suggests that transactions were completed at Rhyd Chwima.

[153] For the significance of an act of homage on the frontier between two territories, J.-F. Lemarignier, *Recherches sur l'hommage en marche et les frontières féodales* (Lille, 1945), 1–8, 39–55, 73–125; cf. Powicke, *EHR*, 56 (1941), 493; idem, *Henry III*, ii, 646, for comparisons between Severn and Epte.

[154] The 'Grocion' that appears between Hywel ap Madog and Goronwy ab Ednyfed in 'Liber A' puzzled J. G. Edwards, in *LW*, 4–5, like Tout, *CP*, ii, 89, and J. E. Lloyd (UW, Bangor, J. E. Lloyd MSS, 318, 51–6). In the Charter Roll, the earliest surviving text (C53/56, m. 2), 'Groium' appears at the same point, and the two texts suggest scribal uncertainty over the name 'Goronwy'. It is unlikely that any name is missed between Hywel and Goronwy.

document embodying the terms of the agreement, and similarly Llywelyn, Einion ap Caradog and Dafydd ab Einion. We cannot tell whether the sealing was done at the ford or at the castle of Montgomery but, if Llywelyn went to the royal castle to complete these transactions, he had had the satisfaction of bringing the king of England to the frontier of his territory in a formal acknowledgement that he had conceded the prince the objective he had sought, in war and peace, for twelve years.

In the key clause of the treaty Henry declared his wish to honour the person of Llywelyn, and those who would come after him by hereditary right, and grant him and his heirs the principality of Wales, so that he would be called prince of Wales and his successors likewise.[155] Llywelyn's elevation was closely bound up with the grant to him of the homage and fealty of all the Welsh barons of Wales, made with the single exception of that of Maredudd ap Rhys Gryg.[156] This had been the exact purpose of the quest on which Bishop Richard had been dispatched nine years before, presenting the prince's case as a request for the restoration of the position which had existed in the time of Llywelyn the Great; the homage and fealty of the lords of Wales had been the essence of the matter placed before Earl Richard of Cornwall when Llywelyn sought a political settlement consonant with his rights (*iura*) in Wales.[157] Agreements previously made between Llywelyn and the king which were at variance with the terms of the new treaty were declared invalid, and acknowledgement of the prince's new status is reflected in their mutual pledge that they would not receive fugitives or enemies into one another's lands. Llywelyn would exercise untrammelled lordship in the territory now formally conceded to him, though his powers as immediate lord of his territorial lordship would be considerably greater than the indirect lordship he would exercise over the other lands, a distinction implicit in the style 'prince of Wales and lord of Snowdon' which Llywelyn continued to employ. Within the bounds of the principality of Wales he was required to fulfil just one obligation, namely to provide for his brother Dafydd, who had transferred his loyalty to the king in 1263. It was recorded that this requirement had been 'specially ordained', and it could well have been a matter of arduous negotiation at Shrewsbury.[158] The purport of the clause was to secure for Dafydd the restoration of the territory that he had held before his defection,

---

[155] *LW*, 2: 'dominus rex Anglie uolens prefati Lewelini magnificare personam et in eo ceteros honorare qui sibi hereditario iure succedent, ex mera sua liberalitate et gracia de uoluntate eciam et assensu domini Edwardi primogeniti sui dat et concedit prefato Lewelino et heredibus suis Wallie principatum, ut idem Lewelinus et heredes sui principes Wallie uocentur et sint: insuper fidelitatem et homagia omnium baronum Wallie Wallensium, ut dicti barones a prefatis principe et heredibus in capite teneant terras suas'.

[156] *LW*; for Maredudd below, n. 165.

[157] Above, pp. 96–7, 122–4.

[158] *LW*, 2–3.

and arrangements were made for the course of action to be adopted if Dafydd were not satisfied. Further provision would then be made by the decision of five named persons, each a member of the prince's council: Gruffudd ap Gwenwynwyn, Gruffudd ap Madog, Hywel ap Madog, Owain ap Bleddyn and Tudur ab Ednyfed. If Dafydd were still not satisfied justice would be done, according to the laws and customs of Wales, in the presence of one or two persons who would inform the king of the provision made. It was laid down that the whole matter should be resolved by Christmas, whatever the difficulties. This was clearly an intractable issue, and Dafydd had been at hand while it was considered at Shrewsbury, Edward perhaps respecting the promise made to Dafydd two years earlier that no peace would be made with Llywelyn without Dafydd's counsel. But its resolution was in effect placed in Llywelyn's hands.[159] Whatever would be done hereafter, Dafydd could expect no more than an estate within the frontiers of his brother's principality, and he had no alternative but to place himself under his jurisdiction.[160]

To secure this principality Llywelyn agreed to pay 25,000 marks, and he would need to pay a further sum of 5,000 marks if the king were ever to grant him the homage of Maredudd ap Rhyg Gryg. He was required to make an immediate payment of 1,000 marks with a further 4,000 marks by Christmas and thereafter 3,000 marks annually. He faced a very substantial financial obligation, and the strain of meeting the annual instalments of 3,000 marks – £2,000 – would be bound to tell. Yet Llywelyn had realized from the beginning that he would have to pay heavily for the elevated position that he sought. The sum now agreed (omitting the figure linked with the homage of Maredudd ap Rhys Gryg) was, in fact, smaller than that which he had been prepared to pay Montfort in 1265, though he incurred a much greater burden than he had envisaged in 1259 when he proposed that the substantial sum that he offered for a treaty of peace would be paid at an annual rate of £200 for eighty years.[161] The status of the prince of Wales was intimately bound up with the overlordship of the other Welsh lords of Wales for which he paid so substantially, and his conception of his status would find expression during the political discourse of the next years.[162] The constitutional position of the principality of Wales was not defined and the nearest approximation in royal ordinances is the reference in the Statute of Wales of 1284 to the position of 'the land of Wales' before its conquest. The land then transferred to royal

---

[159] Chancery records show that Dafydd was at Shrewsbury during the negotiations.
[160] For the significance of the clause, J. B. Smith, 'Dynastic succession in medieval Wales', *B*, 33 (1986), 222–4; its implementation is considered below, pp. 374–5.
[161] In 1265 he had agreed to pay 30,000 marks in ten annual instalments (*DipDoc*, i, no. 400; *RL*, ii, 284–5), leaving him with the same annual liability; for his offer in 1259, above, pp. 122–3.
[162] Below, pp. 291–2, 333–5.

lordship (*in proprietatis nostre dominium*) and annexed and united to the crown of the realm had previously been subject to the king 'by feudal right' (*iure feodali*).[163] The principality of Wales had, of course, been destroyed by 1277 and the ordinances of 1284 refer not to the principality but to 'the land of Wales'. But the entity recognized by the crown in the treaty of Montgomery was much the most extensive dominion ever established in 'the land of Wales' and held of the crown *iure feodali*. A sense of continuity with the principality of Llywelyn ap Gruffudd may be indicated by the investiture of Edward of Caernarfon in 1301, symbolized by ceremonial and reflected, along with the grant of the royal counties, in the overlordship of a number of marcher lands.[164] The status conferred on Llywelyn ap Gruffudd in 1267 marked a formal recognition which had eluded Llywelyn the Great despite the undoubted power which he had exercised. Llywelyn ap Gruffudd no doubt appreciated that there were manifold difficulties yet to be overcome in safeguarding the newly acquired status. But he and those joined with him during the struggles which had brought him to his present position may have felt confident that the recognition now secured would serve to consolidate the inner unity of Wales, an objective which, for several generations, had been intimately bound up with the endeavours of the dynasty of Gwynedd.

Apart from affording formal acknowledgement of Llywelyn's status, the treaty defined the territory of the principality conceded to him. Granted the services of the lords of Wales, with the one exception of Maredudd ap Rhys Gryg, he secured lordship over Powys and Deheubarth, save for that single estate.[165] In the estimation of the poet Llygad Gŵr, Llywelyn was already a prince possessed of the three coronets of the three principalities and the king of England now placed his imprimatur on the prince's broader sphere of authority.[166] There was no need to enumerate the constituent parts of these lands. Particular mention was made, even so, of the Four Cantreds of Perfeddwlad in a clause which made a formal cession of a territory once regarded as 'the king's new conquest of Wales'. The document records that Llywelyn, as a pledge of goodwill, agreed to restore to the king the lands taken in war, but important exceptions were made that permitted him to maintain his hold on Gwerthrynion, Builth and Brecon. Maelienydd was treated differently, and the wording of the relevant clause suggests that this, too, had been a matter of some difficulty at Shrewsbury. Mortimer was left free to build a castle in the lordship if he wished to venture to do so (*pro suo libito voluntatis*), but the castle – undoubtedly Cefnllys – and lordship would

---

[163] *Statutes of the Realm*, I, 55; J. G. Edwards, in *LW*, xlvii–l.
[164] J. G. Edwards, *Principality of Wales*, 8–11, 15–16, 31–4.
[165] In 1268 Maredudd held a barony of two commotes and a half of Edmund, earl of Lancaster (Marquess of Bath, Longleat, 268).
[166] *GDB*, 24.

be given to Llywelyn if he could establish his right (*ius*) to the land.[167] Provision for legal action was not limited to Maelienydd, for it was agreed that both the lands specifically granted to Llywelyn and those not conceded to him could be subject to legal process in accordance with the custom of the march. There was every possibility that he would face legal process brought by the marchers who had been forced to cede the territories specifically granted to Llywelyn; equally he might wish to prosecute his claims to lands, some of them conceded to him by the terms of his agreement with Montfort, for which the new treaty made no provision. But the position of Maelienydd was particularly intricate, with Llywelyn apparently in possession of the lordship and Mortimer having the right to fortify a castle within its bounds. Maelienydd and Cefnllys were inevitably a source of contention in years to come. Elfael, not mentioned in the treaty, may also have been a difficult case. Elfael Uwch Mynydd could be considered part of the principality for the fact that its lord had acknowledged Llywelyn's lordship; Elfael Is Mynydd had been held by Roger de Tony until his expropriation some years earlier, but after sealing the treaty Llywelyn was quick to lay claim to this lordship because, in his estimation, Is Mynydd, too, was of the inheritance of the lineage which ruled Uwch Mynydd. In the absence of a judicial verdict, Elfael Is Mynydd would be administered, with Gwerthrynion, Builth and Brecon, as though it were part of the land over which Llywelyn exercised territorial lordship.[168] Further north, Cydewain and Ceri, formerly the possessions of Welsh lineages, became part of the principality and were important territories, in the immediate vicinity of Montgomery, which Llywelyn would rule directly.[169] The lordship of Whittington was yielded to Llywelyn, unexpectedly perhaps, for though Llywelyn laid claim to it on historical grounds which found some acknowledgement in the text of the treaty, it probably represented a gain made in the period of the civil war.[170] Llywelyn specifically yielded only one territory, agreeing to restore Hawarden to Roger of Mold on condition that he would not build a castle there for sixty years. Ellesmere might be regarded as another concession on his part, for this lordship, like

---

[167] *LW*, 2.

[168] For Elfael, above, n. 7.

[169] Knighton was attacked by 'the lords of Ceri and Cydewain' in 1260 (*AC*, 98), the year preceding that of the death of Owain ap Maredudd, lord of Cydewain (*BT, Pen20*, 212; *Pen20Tr*, 112; *RBH*, 252–3). In litigation after 1277 his daughter Angharad claimed Cydewain as Owain's heir, stating that Llywelyn had taken possession immediately after his death (*WAR*, 241–2, 254–6, 286–7). It is certain that Cydewain formed part of Llywelyn's territorial lordship by 1267; in 1273 he built the castle of Dolforwyn 'in his own territory' there. It is difficult to determine who was the lord of Ceri who went to war in 1260; for the changes of the period 1241–50, J. B. Smith 'Middle march', 86–8, adding the petition of Owain ap Madog and Maredudd ap Madog in *CAP*, 61–2.

[170] Llywelyn was to have 'the service which his predecessors used to receive' for the castle and land of Whittington (*LW*, 2).

Hawarden and Whittington, was among the lands which Montfort had ceded two years before.[171] If Llywelyn had laid claim to any part of the lordship of Glamorgan, where he had already intervened, his arguments were not countenanced in the negotiations at Shrewsbury.[172] Nor did he win recognition of his hold, south of Montgomery, on Teirtref Esgob in Bishop's Castle nor Tempsiter in Clun, though he would continue to exert his authority there for some time.[173] He would in due course be found to hold other lands further north including, by the testimony of jurors of Shropshire in 1274, several vills which pertained to the honour of Montgomery and the whole of the land between the Camlad and the Severn, that is Gorddwr, which constituted a third of Peter Corbet's barony of Caus.[174] At the time the treaty was made Gorddwr was probably held by Gruffudd ap Gwenwynwyn, who was forced to yield the land to Llywelyn upon his breach with the prince in 1274 recounted later.[175] Gorddwr apart, Llywelyn already held more than the king was prepared to recognize, but his power over a wide territory, including several lands well beyond the bounds of the provinces of Gwynedd, Powys and Deheubarth, was formally acknowledged. In some of these far-flung lands he would exercise a direct lordship, and his power there could bring him substantial material resources, if the gain were not off-set by costs incurred in their defence. The principality was still far from being tantamount to the land

---

[171] Above, nn. 113, 114.

[172] Llywelyn's claims in Glamorgan are examined below, pp. 342–3.

[173] His occupation of Teirtref Esgob is noticed later; part of Clun was in Llywelyn's possession when John FitzAlan died in 1272 (*CIPM*, i, no. 812).

[174] *Rotuli Hundredorum*, ii, 89, 90, 113. The vills included Cilcewydd, Ackley and Llety Gynfarch in Gorddwr and land between the rivers which formed part of Corbet's barony. These and Chirbury are named in an undated document by which one Llywelyn ap Gruffudd acknowledged that he had received them from Hamo Lestrange, to be retained while he was in the Holy Land and restored upon his return (*LW*, 87). J. G. Edwards took this Llywelyn to be the prince and placed the deed before 1258. The transaction is more likely to date from 1270, shortly before Hamo's departure, and was probably executed by Llywelyn ap Gruffudd, son of Gruffudd ap Gwenwynwyn (R. Morgan, 'The territorial divisions of medieval Montgomeryshire', *MontColl*, 69 (1981), 9–44; 70 (1982), 11–39, following a suggestion by David Stephenson). This was one of several grants by Hamo to his brothers and his sister Hawise, wife of Gruffudd ap Gwenwynwyn (*CFR, 1272–1307*, 4, 21, 48; *CIM*, i, no. 966; R. W. Eyton, *Antiquities of Shropshire* (London, 1854–60), x, 274–5). Gruffudd ap Gwenwynwyn made other provision in Gorddwr (Buttington, Trewern and Hope) for his son Llywelyn, 1 March 1271, evidently part of the transactions involving Hamo and other members of the Lestrange family (*LW*, 132).

[175] Gorddwr, situated between Camlad and Severn, would have formed part of the conquests taken by Gruffudd ap Gwenwynwyn according to the agreement of 1263 (*LW*, 78). A part of Gorddwr, at least, was in Gruffudd's hands in 1270, and Llywelyn appears to have taken possession of the land as part of his stern dealings with Gruffudd in 1274 (*CPR, 1272–81*, 374; below, pp. 369–71, 373–4).

of Wales, but by 1267 Rhyd Chwima had become, more than ever before, a meeting ground between two nations and two political entities.[176]

Doubtless the negotiations completed under Ottobuono's guidance had had to skirt many problems, some of them reflected in the text of the agreement but others finding no mention there. The difficulties left unresolved, even created anew, by the treaty of Montgomery would be revealed during the following years. Llywelyn would hardly have harboured any illusion that the completion of the formal peace process represented a finite solution of his problems, and he was quick to register a statement of the issues on which he still sought satisfaction.[177] Henry and Edward, let alone the marchers discomforted by clauses which affected them directly, may have had misgivings set aside only for the overwhelming need to restore normality to the realm as a whole after prolonged and enervating discord. That the agreement provided at least an opportunity for sensible discourse is evident and the legate felt he could commend to the pope an agreement which brought credit to the two parties concerned. He could reasonably count the treaty of Montgomery among the major achievements of his mission in the realm of England. This was the third occasion on which the relationship between Wales and England had been considered under papal auspices and, if he were acquainted with the historical precedents, Ottobuono might have judged that, of the three, the arrangement in which he had been intimately concerned was the one with the best chance of securing a stable relationship between the two nations. In the course of the negotiations in which Guala and Pandulf had participated, Llywelyn the Great's power had been recognized, but no acknowledgement had been made of those internal political bonds which, had they been endorsed, would have created a new relationship between Wales and England two generations earlier. After the death of Llywelyn the legate Otto had taken part in the processes which had registered the removal of the hegemony which the crown had left unrecognized while the prince lived.[178] With the subsequent resuscitation of Welsh power a coherent Welsh political entity was created once more and its existence was finally recognized when Henry III and Llywelyn ap Gruffudd came together at the ford of Montgomery. It was a settlement which, even as it elevated Llywelyn, ensured that he was counted

---

[176] It would be wrong to accept the view of Tout, *CP*, ii, 92, that the treaty brought a final recognition of Llywelyn's natural right to lordship over all who spoke the Welsh language and who used the laws of Wales; see further, below, pp 331–2. For recent pertinent comment on the treaty, R. R. Davies, *CCC*, 314–17, 320–21; R. Frame, *The Political Development of the British Isles 1100–1400* (Oxford, 1990), 115–25.

[177] *CR, 1264–68*, 496.

[178] For Guala and Pandulph *c*.1218–20, R. F. Walker, 'Hubert de Burgh', *EHR*, 87 (1972), 468–73. By the treaty of Gloucester, 1240, lands formerly held by Llywelyn ap Iorwerth and now claimed by crown or magnates were remitted to a board of arbitrators led by Cardinal Otto (*LW*, 5–6).

among the king's vassals, and this was precisely what Ottobuono conveyed to Pope Clement. Long separated by discord Llywelyn, prince of Wales, a great and powerful magnate in the realm of England, had come to peace and reconciliation in an honourable concord.[179] Other commentators, in England and Wales alike, could agree that the legate's efforts had brought peace between king and prince and these, too, would give their assent to the legate's view that the prince of Wales stood among the greatest of the magnates of England.[180] Llywelyn ap Gruffudd turned from Rhyd Chwima at Michaelmas 1267 to face the dual responsibilities of prince of Wales and tenant-in-chief of the king of England.

---

[179] Graham, 'Letters', 118.

[180] *BT, Pen20,* 217–18; *Pen20Tr,* 115; *RBH,* 256–9; editor's note, *Pen20Tr,* 212–13; among English chronicles, *FloresHist,* iii, 16; Trevet, *Annales,* 272.

CHAPTER 5

Lord of Snowdon

JUST a few weeks before his death in battle, already hemmed in by the military might of Edward I, Llywelyn ap Gruffudd was offered terms which held out a prospect that he would be given an extensive estate in England if he were prepared to concede possession of Snowdonia to the king. In a dignified reply Llywelyn declined the offer made to him, insisting that Snowdonia, a barren land though it might be, was an integral part of his inheritance and he would on no account yield its possession to his adversary.[1] The letter is infused with the prince's sense of inheritance, even of his love for his patrimony, and it is not for the historian to deny to a prince of Wales what may well have been a sincere and deeply felt attachment to the land of his ancestors. More than a century before, Hywel ab Owain Gwynedd had combined a poet's gift of expression with a prince's instinctive love of his land.[2] Llywelyn ap Gruffudd, a prince of the same lineage, may have felt the same bond with a land which, for all the barrenness of so much of its mountainous extent, was a patrimonial territory which sustained him in body and spirit alike. His intransigent rejection of the terms offered him in the desperate situation in which he found himself by the autumn of 1282 may tell us something not only of princely hubris, but of an emotion which, deepened by his consciousness of his responsibility to his people, was intimately bound up with a sense of patrimony.

The lord's patrimony

The documents which record the transactions of the latter part of 1282 speak of the land or lordship of Snowdonia and the meaning of the term itself

---

[1] *RPeck*, ii, 470.
[2] *GLlF*, 6; trans. *Oxford Book of Welsh Verse in English*, ed. G. Jones (Oxford, 1977), 21–2.

deserves some notice. Snowdon (Yr Wyddfa) is, of course, the name of a high peak in a range of mountains known as Snowdonia (Eryri).³ First Llywelyn ap Iorwerth and then Llywelyn ap Gruffudd embodied the term 'lord of Snowdon' (*dominus Snowdonie*) in the style employed in formal documents.⁴ Clearly, the term indicated in this context is not the mountain range alone but the broader territory of which the massif formed the core. The extent of the land indicated in various documents by 'Snowdonia' still varied a good deal. The English crown used the term to denote the north-west part of Wales long before it came to define its delimits precisely, and to provide for its government, by the promulgation of the Statute of Wales in 1284.⁵ The name might signify the mainland of north-west Wales alone, or even part of that land, for in 1277 Edward outlined his arrangements for a narrowly circumscribed Snowdonia from which the adjacent lands (*valle*) of Anglesey, Llŷn and Penllyn could be distinguished. Similarly, those who drew up the surveys of the land in the aftermath of conquest were said to be concerned with the king's possessions in Snowdonia and Anglesey.⁶ In these connections Snowdonia meant, at best, the land which lay to the west of the River Conwy, but when Llywelyn ap Iorwerth, abandoning the style 'prince of Gwynedd' (*princeps Northwallie*), adopted the form 'prince of Aberffraw and lord of Snowdon' (*princeps Aberffraw et dominus Snowdonie*) he had intended that the second part of his title should indicate a wider territory. It embraced not only the land west of the Conwy, Gwynedd Uwch Conwy, but also the land which lay east of the river, Gwynedd Is Conwy, the land known, as we have seen, as Perfeddwlad or the Four Cantreds.⁷ The prince's style thus described his rule over the whole extent of the land between the Dee and the Dyfi over which he exercised immediate lordship. As 'prince of Aberffraw' he exercised a broader supremacy, never recognized by the English crown, over the remainder of Wales still under the rule of its princes. When Llywelyn ap Gruffudd came, by 1262, to adopt the style which he would use consistently thereafter he, too, chose two titles which reflected the dual nature of his power: he was prince of Wales and lord of Snowdon (*princeps Wallie et dominus Snowdonie*).⁸ On the one hand, he was prince of a broad principality of Wales, over which he exercised the authority, finally recognized by the king

---

³ I. Williams, 'Eryri', *B*, 4 (1927–9), 137–41; J. E. Lloyd, 'The mountains in history and legend', in R. C. Carr and G. A Lister (eds.), *The Mountains of Snowdonia* (London, 1948), 3–34.

⁴ 'Lord of Snowdonia' is perhaps the more accurate form, but J. E. Lloyd and J. G. Edwards have given currency to 'lord of Snowdon'.

⁵ *Statutes of the Realm*, i, 55.

⁶ *LW*, 103; E101/351/9.

⁷ Above, pp. 16, 25.

⁸ E.g. *CAC*, 28, 161–3; *LW*, 114. Llygad Gŵr refers to Llywelyn as *eryr Snawtwn*, 'eagle of Snowdon' (*GBF*, 24. 88).

of England, to be considered in the next chapter; on the other hand, he was lord of a Snowdonia envisaged in terms identical to those in which his grandfather had defined his position. It was a style that he used to the end of his life and his wife became, though only very briefly, princess of Wales and lady of Snowdon.[9] And in the last months of Welsh resistance in 1282–3, Dafydd ap Gruffudd adopted the style that his brother had used.[10] For each of the princes, the two-fold style reflects the broad distinction between their direct lordship in Gwynedd and their indirect lordship further afield.

These were not, of course, altogether accurate reflections of the princes' authority in the various parts of their dominions for, particularly in the case of Llywelyn ap Gruffudd, direct lordship came to be exercised in several areas beyond the limits of even the greater Snowdonia. Llywelyn may not have wished to elaborate too much upon the distinction suggested in the two elements in his style but rather to emphasize the unity of the broader *principatus* of Wales. This we can only surmise, for explicit references to the prince's conception of the status of the various parts of his principality are few, with nothing to suggest, for instance, differentiation between inheritance and acquisition.[11] In Llywelyn's exchanges with Archbishop Pecham in 1282 Snowdonia is said to be the prince's 'original inheritance' (*sua pristina hereditate*); he would never cede it to the king for it was part of the principality of Wales which he and his ancestors had held since the time of Brutus (*cum Snaudon sit de appenditiis principatus Wallie, quem ipse et antecessores sui tenuerunt a tempore Bruti*).[12] Snowdonia was the land where Llywelyn had first asserted power; it was the hereditary portion of his wide dominion, but the stress in the arguments of those desperate days lay on the territorial integrity of the principality of which Snowdonia was part.

The arguments were by then unreal, for it was only through the archbishop's intervention that the English assault on the last citadel of Welsh resistance had been held off. The conflict for the wider principality had been resolved in the king's favour and important parts of Snowdonia itself were already in the king's hands. Anglesey was lost and the king would tolerate no discussion of its future. The Four Cantreds had been brought within the king's power and in large part granted to some of the magnates who shared the task of conquest with the king.[13] Much more than Anglesey, the lands east of the Conwy – Perfeddwlad – had long been exposed to the ebb and flow of Anglo-Welsh conflict. Llywelyn was now arguing for the recovery of a land

---

[9] *RPeck*, 468–9; *CAC*, 75–6.
[10] *LW*, 74–5, 77.
[11] For the differentiation see e.g. J. C. Holt, 'Politics and property in early medieval England', *Past and Present*, 57 (1972), 3–52.
[12] *RPeck*, ii, 469–71.
[13] Below, pp. 526–30.

which, five years before, he had formally ceded to the king for all time. Yet this was the land in which he had first exercised lordship, then the land where he asserted power at a crucial stage in this thrust for a broad supremacy in Wales. His advance into the area and his subsequent withdrawal were recent events in its long history of changeful fortune. Topographically the easternmost of the Four Cantreds belonged to the Cheshire plains, and from an early period successive conquerors had left their mark upon it. Its name, Englefield or Tegeingl, and many a place-name within it, reflected the effect of successive colonizations.[14] The other three *cantrefi*, Rhos, Rhufoniog and Dyffryn Clwyd, though by no means immune to alien intervention, proved more difficult to control, and the problems which confronted Henry III in his 'new conquest in Wales' after 1247 have already been recounted.[15] These were to be key areas in the period after 1277, the experience of their communities quite crucial in creating the circumstances in which new conflict arose.[16] Llywelyn ap Gruffudd was greatly concerned at the end of 1282 by the suffering endured in Perfeddwlad and, though he might speak of the tribulation endured by the Welsh people in general, it is evident that he was troubled most by the situation which had arisen in that area. The complaints of the communities of Rhos and Rhufoniog were to figure prominently in the documents forwarded for the archbishop's consideration. Yet in the early years of his power Llywelyn had been constrained to make a distinction between the lands east and west of the Conwy, offering to hold back from Perfeddwlad if his position in the western part of Gwynedd could be assured.[17] When circumstances were more propitious he claimed the wider Gwynedd by hereditary right, but ironically the most eloquent statement of his right to Perfeddwlad as an integral part of his historical inheritance came during the course of the discussions conducted in the most difficult days in 1282. The Four Cantreds, he insisted, were indisputably and entirely part of his territory (*isti cantredi sunt de puro principis tenemento*), the assertion rounded off with another appeal to the legendary inheritance of the men of Troy.[18]

Though its topography was varied and the assets of its several parts might be unequal – upland pastures in Uwch Dulas or lowland areas in Llannerch – Perfeddwlad was an area valuable for its economic resources as for its manpower. Again, though the area might be exposed to extraneous political

---

[14] For Tegeingl, G. R. J. Jones, 'The portrayal of land settlement in Domesday Book', in J. C. Holt (ed.), *Domesday Studies* (Woodbridge, 1986), 190–2, 198–200; P. H. Sawyer and A. T. Thacker, 'Domesday survey', in *Victoria County History: A History of the County of Chester*, i, ed. B. E. Harries (Oxford, 1987), 335, 366–9.
[15] Above, pp. 77–84.
[16] Below, pp. 453–6, 464–5.
[17] Above, pp. 87–8.
[18] *RPeck*, ii, 469–71.

and cultural influences, Perfeddwlad proved to be a key area in Welsh resurgence at several critical periods. Llywelyn had benefited from the spirited response of its communities during his rise to power; their resort to arms was quite crucial in the spring of 1282. Nor was this the end of it. Madog ap Llywelyn and Owain Glyndŵr found that the capacity of these communities for armed resistance had not been spent in the last years of Llywelyn ap Gruffudd. The areas east and west of the Conwy were obviously joined in concerted resistance to English royal power at successive periods of difficulty, but their communities were bound together by other ties. By the thirteenth century there were numerous lineages with lands both in Gwynedd Uwch Conwy and Gwynedd Is Conwy, interests enhanced perhaps by a deliberate effort on the part of the princes to bind the communities together, not simply by common allegiance to their lord, but by their tenants' concern for their assets east and west of the river. The lineage of Edryd ap Marchudd was one which possessed extensive lands in Anglesey and in the *cantrefi* of Rhos and Rhufoniog in Perfeddwlad, estates that probably reflected endowments made by the princes in the twelfth and thirteenth centuries.[19] The settlement imposed on the princes in 1247 itself acknowledges that difficulties might arise from the fact that proprietors with lands on either side of the Conwy were subject to a different lordship.[20] That there were influences – political, social and cultural – which tended to the separation of Uwch Conwy and Is Conwy cannot be doubted, yet there were interests which tended to underpin Llywelyn ap Gruffudd's insistence that Perfeddwlad was an integral part of his inheritance. This chapter will be concerned with the nature of the lordship exercised in this broader Snowdonia and with the extent of the resources which facilitated, and perhaps served to curtail, the wider ambitions already described in this volume and more closely examined in the chapter that follows.

Historical understanding of the social arrangements of the prince's patrimony has to rest heavily on the documentary evidence of the post-conquest period, and the inquirer has to peer cautiously at the often uncertain images of a dark mirror. Immediately after the cessation of hostilities in 1283 Edward I ordered a detailed survey of his tenants' obligations and his rights. The movements of the surveyors can be traced in the very membranes which describe the dismantling of the king's camps and the withdrawal of his soldiers, but the results of their work survive only in part.[21] Of the extents completed by 1284, those for the new counties of Anglesey and Merioneth

---

[19] These lands are noticed at a later stage in the discussion.
[20] *LW*, 7–8; *CAC*, 32.
[21] Matthew, archdeacon of Anglesey, Guncelin de Badlesmere, Peter de Leek and Brother Llywelyn ap Gruffudd were engaged in making extents of Anglesey and other areas July–August 1283 (E101/351/9); for another commission, *CWR*, 274.

have survived, but there is no comparable survey of Caernarfon, though much of its detail can be deduced from the surviving account rolls.[22] By 1352 the fiscal obligations of the landholders of Anglesey and Caernarfon had been registered in a new and detailed survey, but there is no document for Merioneth and it is not certain that an extent of the county was made at that time.[23] Taken together, the extents and the account rolls for the counties provide sources invaluable for the study of pre-conquest tenurial and economic arrangements. Equally valuable are the records for what were by the end of the thirteenth century the marcher lordship of Dyffryn Clwyd, based on the *cantref* of that name, and the lordship of Denbigh, based on the *cantrefi* of Rhos and Rhufoniog. Dyffryn Clwyd possesses an incomparable series of court rolls, but no major fiscal survey and few account rolls.[24] The lordship of Denbigh, almost devoid of court records, has a number of account rolls and an exceptionally valuable extent drawn up in 1334.[25] Tegeingl, in the guise of the county of Flint, has a series of plea rolls and account rolls but again no extensive fiscal survey.[26] Further afield, beyond the Snowdonia of the princes, the extents of the lordships established in Powys Fadog – Chirk to the south, Bromfield and Yale to the north – provide further comparative evidence.[27] The task of eliciting even the main features of pre-conquest social and economic conditions is fraught with difficulty; and the lack of adequate quantitative evidence means that a range of issues remains largely unresolved. Even so, the sources of the post-conquest period, taken along with the juristic

---

[22] Extent of Merioneth, in *ExtMer*, 184–92; comment in Pierce, *MWS* (Cardiff, 1972), 107; extent of Anglesey in *ExtAng*, 3–25, bears the date 13 March 1294 and this is accepted in Pierce, *MWS*, 108–9, 121 n. 58; A. D. Carr, *Medieval Anglesey* (Llangefni, 1982), 51 *et passim* [Carr, *MAng*]. Stephenson, *GG*, 235–6, argues strongly that the correct date is 1284, and that a distinction can be made between the work of Richard de Abingdon and Prior Llywelyn. The case is strengthened by the certainty that the prior was engaged in making an extent in 1283 and in this study 1284 is the preferred date. Much of the detail of the Caernarfon extent may be gathered from the sheriffs' accounts 1301–51, especially SC6/1171/7; see Pierce, *MWS*, 107–8.

[23] *RC*, 1–116, for Anglesey and Caernarfon; *RC*, 261–92, for an early-fifteenth-century extent, probably 1415–20, of Merioneth. The Anglesey extent is translated in A. D. Carr, 'The extent of Anglesey, 1352', *TAngAS*, 1971–2, 150–272 [Carr, *Extent*].

[24] SC2/215/64–226/16; a substantial portion of the material was calendared in machine-readable form during the preparation of the Dyffryn Clwyd Court Roll Database 1294–1422 at University of Wales, Aberystwyth, 1991–5 (ESRC Award Nos. R000232548 and R000234070). The database is deposited in the ESRC Data Archive. List of tenants in R. I. Jack, 'The lordship of Dyffryn Clwyd in 1324', *TDenbHS*, 17 (1968), 7–53.

[25] *SD*; this text, *The Survey of the Honour of Denbigh, 1334*, is a key source to which frequent reference is made.

[26] Chester 30/1 *et seq*.; SC2/227/1 *et seq*.

[27] *The First Extent of Bromfield and Yale A.D. 1315*, ed. T. P. Ellis (London, 1924); *The Extent of Chirkland, 1391–1393*, ed. G. P. Jones (Liverpool, 1933); BL Add MS, 10,013. These sources have been used extensively in Llinos O. W. Smith, 'The lordships of Chirk and Oswestry, 1282–1415'; Michael Rogers, 'The Welsh marcher lordship of Bromfield and Yale, 1282–1485', Ph.D. thesis, University of Wales, 1992.

evidence of the thirteenth century, provide the means of making some estimate of the social organization of the land which sustained the political endeavours examined in this volume.[28] They provide, too, a basis for an estimate of the extent to which those endeavours created stresses within the prince's land. The importance of this issue is highlighted by a document drawn up at a gathering of representatives of the communities of the commotes of Gwynedd Uwch Conwy held at Nancall before Anian, bishop of Bangor, in the summer of 1283. It embodies a list of grievances against Llywelyn ap Gruffudd which, taken together, describe a harsh lordship exercised by a prince who made heavy demands upon his people.[29] The complaints were registered just as the surveyors were making the extents upon which the fiscal obligations of the king's tenants would be based, and caution needs to be exercised in using a document which may well reflect the concern of the communities that they might be burdened thereafter with obligations more onerous than they could reasonably bear. Yet the document, considered in greater detail at a later stage in the discussion, may well provide a reliable indication that the burdens borne by the communities of Gwynedd in the later years of Llywelyn ap Gruffudd were exceedingly heavy and that they had paid a high price for the fulfilment of their prince's political objectives and for his prolonged contention with the English crown.[30] Before considering the prince's sources of income and the means by which they were exploited, we need to consider the manner in which he ruled his territories and the nature of the power that he exercised over the communities under his immediate lordship.

The lord's authority

The main administrative divisions of the territory ruled by the lord of Snowdon – his *gwlad* or *regnum* in the language of the jurists – were the *cantref* and *cwmwd* or commote. The *cantref* was the older institution but the process by which the commote came to be, for most purposes, the key

---

[28] For the legal literature below, n. 70.

[29] Text and full discussion in Llinos B. Smith, 'The *gravamina* of the community of Gwynedd against Llywelyn ap Gruffudd', *B*, 31 (1984), 158–76 [Ll. B. Smith, '*Gravamina*']. The complaints were drawn up at Nancall, par Clynnog Fawr, 2 August 1283. Nancall was a grange of the abbey of Aberconwy; C. A. Gresham, *Eifionydd: A Study in Landownership from the Medieval Period to the Present Day* (Cardiff, 1973), 301–5; idem, 'The Aberconwy charter', *ArchCamb*, 94 (1939), 138–9; idem, 'The Aberconwy charter: further consideration', *B*, 30 (1982–3), 344–7. Gresham places Nancall in cmt Eifionydd, rather than Arfon Uwch Gwyrfai, in the medieval period. For the *gravamina*, below, pp. 255–60, 266–7, 271–2.

[30] These issues are considered later.

administrative district is not easy to establish.³¹ There may have been some variation, even within the boundaries of Gwynedd. The commotes of Anglesey or Llŷn may be of a comparatively early derivation explained by the fact that areas of arable production bore heavy populations which called for the development of more narrowly defined spheres of seigniorial administration. The commotes of Arfon or Meirionnydd, on the other hand, may be of later origin.³² In the Four Branches of the Mabinogi it is related that Math fab Mathonwy bestowed upon Lleu Llaw Gyffres the *cantref* of Dunoding 'that is nowadays called Eifionydd and Ardudwy', a remark which may be difficult to attribute to any particular period but one which at least conveys a memory of a process of change.³³ The *cantref* remained, even so, a convenient unit both of lordship and administration for some purposes. During the second half of the thirteenth century Dafydd ap Gruffudd was more than once vested with two *cantrefi* in Perfeddwlad – Rhufoniog and Dyffryn Clwyd – and not a cluster of commotes. After 1277 Goronwy ap Heilin was charged with responsibility for the *cantref* of Rhos as its *rhaglaw*, with another officer similarly entrusted with Tegeingl, the English crown in this respect probably adhering to earlier Welsh practice.³⁴ The communities of Uwch Conwy and Is Conwy were later required to enter into bonds by which they registered their pledge to maintain the peace and they did so *cantref* by *cantref*.³⁵ But it was the commote which was to be the main administrative entity of royal and marcher lands alike in the post-conquest period, and it seems likely that its functions were based upon practices already well-established in the preceding years. The commote has sometimes been seen as the source of inherent Welsh political power and thus as a political entity, but it can best be visualized as an administrative institution by which royal or seigniorial authority was mediated to the localities of a lordship.³⁶ Its boundaries were well-defined, and within those boundaries the lord's officers made his authority effective in a manner comparable to the functions exercised within similar institutions in

---

³¹ *HW*, i, 300 ff.; R. R. Davies, *CCC*, 20–3.

³² *ExtMer*, 184–7, for dues which are identical in the commotes of Tal-y-bont and Ystumanner, possibly reflecting a division of obligations once levied on the *cantref* of Meirionnydd as a whole and suggestive of late origin; but the correspondence could simply reflect the fact that the two commotes were for long periods under a single lordship. For the possibility of late origin cf. G. R. J. Jones, 'The models for organisation in Llyfr Iorwerth and Llyfr Cyfnerth', *B*, 39 (1992), 100–1.

³³ *PKM*, 84; *Mabinogion*, 68.

³⁴ *CCR, 1272–79*, 476, 563–4; *CWR*, 168, 189, 198; *CIM*, i, no. 1149.

³⁵ *LW*, 151–2, 154–7.

³⁶ J. G. Edwards, 'Sir John Edward Lloyd', *PBA*, 41 (1956), 319–27; idem, 'The Normans and the Welsh march', *PBA*, 42 (1957), 155–77; subsequent comment in R. R. Davies, 'Kings, lords and liberties in the march of Wales, 1066–1272', *TRHS*, 5th ser., 29 (1979), 42–52; J. B. Smith, 'Dynastic succession in medieval Wales', *B*, 33 (1986), 216; cf. above, p. 12.

England or Scotland or further afield.[37] The lawbooks emphasize the importance of the commote as a unit of jurisdiction, and its court was the place where justice was administered in the prince's name, with precise provisions made so as to enable the commote boundaries to be traversed when a legal action so required.[38] But the commote was also a focus for the fiscal and service obligations of the community to the lord and, increasingly perhaps, the means whereby the response or reaction to the prince's demands upon the community were formulated.

Within the commote the lord's authority was represented by officers charged with duties closely comparable to those entrusted to similar functionaries in other lands. According to the lawbooks it fell to the *maer* and *cynghellor* 'to organize the country and conduct its sessions'.[39] The local officials named in records, and who also appear in the lawbooks, are the *rhaglaw* and *rhingyll*. The *rhaglaw* was the superior officer, in some respects the successor to the *cynghellor* but with a more extensive responsibility. Termed in Latin sources *ballivus*, or bailiff, the Welsh title suggests a lieutenancy, and the prominence of this officer may reflect the development of a more clearly defined role as the prince's representative in the locality placed in his charge.[40] The *rhingyll*, who appears in the lawbooks as the servant of the *cynghellor*, was primarily perhaps a functionary of the courts of law, acting as steward of the commote court and bearing responsibility for distraints, but he was also, and perhaps increasingly, entrusted with fiscal duties within the commote.[41] These officers may have been the agencies by which the princes sought to impress their authority more firmly upon the free communities as opposed to the bond communities which were the particular charge of *maer*

---

[37] Parallels in J. E. A. Jolliffe, 'Northumbrian institutions', *EHR*, 41 (1926), 1–42; G. W. S. Barrow, *The Kingdom of the Scots* (London, 1973), 7–68. Relevant to comparative study is the use of *swydd* in marcher lordships such as Maelienydd (Swydd Buddugre, Swydd Dinieithon, Swydd Rhiwllallt), virtually as an alternative to *cwmwd*.

[38] J. B. Smith, 'Cydfodau o'r bymthegfed ganrif', *B*, 21 (1964–6), 309–24; 25 (1972–4), 128–34; R. R. Davies, 'Frontier arrangements in fragmented societies: Ireland and Wales', 94–8.

[39] *Lllor*, 61; *LHD*, 123–4. For *cynghellor*, D. Jenkins, '*Cynghellor* and chancellor', *B*, 27 (1976–8), 115–18.

[40] Stephenson, *GG*, 41–4. The terms 'deputy' and 'viceroy' are suggested in *LHD*, 377, for *rhaglaw*; it might be best to use the term 'bailiff' suggested by the *ballivus* of the Latin texts.

[41] *Lllor*, 17, 19, 45–8; *LHD*, 31, 34, 85–9; *LlCol*, 27; in the Latin texts he is termed *preco* (*LTWL*, 119–20, 206–7, 209, 243, 257, 324, 332, 347–8, 373), a term also used in record sources noticed later. 'Sergeant' is perhaps the best term, though 'beadle' and 'apparitor' are sometimes used; see Carr, *MAng*, 64–5; Stephenson, *GG*, 44–6; for south-west Wales, R. A. Griffiths, *Principality of Wales*, i, 60–3.

and *cynghellor*.⁴² There are, indeed, distinct indications of an antipathy to the *rhingyll* which may reflect the freemen's resistance to the imposition of a more rigorous authority.⁴³ When the area placed in the *rhaglaw*'s charge was at some distance from the prince's main territorial lordship, in marcher areas such as Builth and Elfael, Brecon and Gwerthrynion, the officer obviously had to be entrusted with the entire responsibility for its administration.⁴⁴ But even in Gwynedd the *rhaglaw* carried a wide responsibility, for he occupied the key position in the administration of justice and exercised a discretionary authority on the prince's behalf.⁴⁵ The evidence for his position in the *cantrefi* of Perfeddwlad is particularly instructive, demonstrating the duties of the *rhaglaw* in the provision of justice and in the supervision of officers concerned with the collection of revenue and the keeping of the peace. No single court roll or account roll survives to illustrate the working of the prince's administration, but, though we need to exercise due caution, we may surmise that the senior officers who took charge of the localities for king or marcher lord upon the cessation of hostilities fulfilled functions well established in the period of the princes. It is conceivable, too, that they implemented legal and fiscal directives which reflected the increasingly rigorous government imposed by the prince in the stressful decades of his period of supremacy. Of the extent of this pressure we cannot be sure, for the inclination of the communities to pose a contrast between the extractive policy pursued by Llywelyn ap Gruffudd and the less demanding rule of his grandfather is understandable. Llywelyn ap Iorwerth was not always presented in terms of total approbation, however, and it might be reasonable to postulate for the thirteenth century as a whole a gradually increasing stringency as the princes' officers imposed a more demanding seigniorial order.⁴⁶

---

⁴² Texts state that it was not right to impose on free districts, that is *maenolydd*, either *maer* or *cynghellor*, nor billeting except for 'the great circuit of the household every winter' (*kylch maur e teylu pob gayaf*, LlIor, 61; *LHD*, 123–4; *LlCol*, 40), and that there should be no circuit (*cylch*) by *maer* and *cynghellor* on free *maenolydd* (LlCol, 40). For the *maenol*, a district with fiscal liabilities subsequently assessed on the more narrowly delimited vill or township (*tref*), G. R. J. Jones, 'Post-Roman Wales', *The Agrarian History of England and Wales*, I, ii, ed. H. P. R. Finberg (Cambridge, 1972), 299–308 *et passim*; idem, 'Multiple estates and early settlement', in P. H. Sawyer (ed.), *Medieval Settlement: Continuity and Change* (London, 1976), 15–40.

⁴³ Below nn. 363–9.

⁴⁴ *LW*, 40–2; *CAC*, 53–4; J. B. Smith, 'The middle march in the thirteenth century', *B*, 24 (1970–2), 85–7.

⁴⁵ Stephenson, *GG*, 42–3, citing disputes between Llywelyn and the bishops of Bangor (1261) and St Asaph (1274) and the royal inquiry of 1281. The inquiry in Perfeddwlad (*CWR*, 195–201) refers to a decision of Goronwy ap Heilin, bailiff of Rhos, by which judgements were reached through the verdict of a jury rather than by traditional Welsh procedures. For Goronwy as *rhaglaw* of Rhos and Rhirid ap Madog as *rhaglaw* (*constabularius*) of Penllyn, *RPeck*, ii, 455; *MLSR*, lxxxi, 4; above, n. 34.

⁴⁶ Below, n. 372.

Lord of Snowdon

The fiscal obligations diligently recorded by the surveyors and accounting officers of the years following the conquest, taken along with those portrayed by the jurists, provide some basis for an examination of the nature of the prince's claims upon his tenantry and, in the absence of any extensive exposition from an earlier period, make it possible to attempt some estimate of the nature of the prince's authority itself. The power of the lord of Snowdon was not based on a changeless body of rights but was rather the product of a continuing interaction between the will of the lord and the tolerance of the community. The thrust of many earlier historical studies, with their varying degrees of emphasis upon the 'tribal' features of Welsh society, has tended to give the bonds of kinship a prominent role in social organization, often at the cost of some neglect of what may be termed regalian or seigniorial features. More recent studies have stressed the role of lordship in the workings of early medieval society, and a lordship based both on landownership and on personal bonds with both powerful and less powerful members of society.[47] Lordship had its military features, too. The lines of Llygad Gŵr depicting Llywelyn ap Gruffudd as 'the generous lord of golden sword' touched a theme which may be traced to the ultimate origins of lordship itself.[48] These differing strands cannot easily be disentangled. The image of a king accompanied by his military retinue, the *teulu*, stands prominently in both juristic and literary sources, and comprehends features besides the strictly military facets of his power. The leader of the retinue, the *penteulu* or *dux familie*, was a person highly esteemed at court, and the military power which he represented was one element in lordship.[49] This power was closely related to the claims which the 'superior lord' (*dominus superior*) might have upon the inhabitants of his territory, but it was still a power distinguishable from the mere exercise of might itself.[50]

Among the obligations of the tenants were those which sprang from the demands made by the king and his retinue during the course of their circuit (*cylch*) of his dominion. Those most clearly enumerated by the lawyers are the responsibilities, such as *dawnbwyd* and *dofreth*, which fell upon the

---

[47] D. Howells, 'The four exclusive possessions of a man', *SC*, 8–9 (1973–4), 48–67; D. Jenkins, 'Property interests in the classical Welsh law of women', in D. Jenkins and M. E. Owen (eds.), *The Welsh Law of Women* (Cardiff, 1980), 69–92; R. R. Davies, *CCC*, 56–68. Valuable for comparative study are D. O'Corrain, 'Nationality and kingship in pre-Norman Ireland', in T. W. Moody (ed.), *Nationality and the Pursuit of National Independence,* Historical Studies, 12 (Belfast, 1978), 1–35; P. Wormald, 'Celtic and Anglo-Saxon kingship: some further thoughts', in P. E. Szarmach (ed.), *Sources of Anglo-Saxon Culture* (Kalamazoo, 1986), 151–83.

[48] *GBF*, 24. 23.

[49] *LlIor*, 4–55; *LHD*, 8–11; Stephenson, *GG*, 15–16.

[50] Jolliffe, 'Northumbrian institutions', 40–1; R. R. Davies, *Lordship and Society*, 130–48.

bondmen.⁵¹ *Gwestfa*, the most conspicuous of the obligations borne by the freemen, is not as explicitly associated with the *cylch*, but it was in origin an obligation to provide hospitality for the king at the residences of the *optimates*, and one which evolved into an obligation, which the freemen shared with others, to provide for the needs of the king's hall, with an implicit expectation of the king's coming upon his circuit. Responsibilities towards the great circuit of the winter (*cylch mawr y gaeaf*) were met by bond and free alike.⁵² These obligations – *dawnbwyd, dofreth, gwestfa* – point to origins in circuit obligations of the dues variously described in the documents, often in minute detail, as the Latin *procuratio, pastus* or *potura*, or the Welsh *cylch* or *porthiant*. They are not confined to Gwynedd, and some of the most instructive evidence is drawn from Powys Fadog.⁵³ Nor is it difficult to find parallels well beyond the confines of Wales.⁵⁴ They are closely linked with the needs of an itinerant court, sometimes specifically linked with the prince, with his retinue or with a particular member of the retinue (*pastus principis, pastus famulie principis,* or *cylch rhaglaw*), and together they mark an acknowledgement of seigniorial claims upon society.⁵⁵ The obligations may, of course, have changed their nature over time: the circuit dues may not always bear the names found in the lawyers' texts, and the manner in which the obligations were met was certainly subject to change, notably in the commutation of a certain part of the renders from contributions in kind into money payments.⁵⁶ The extent of these changes will be considered presently. But whatever the form of payment, the fulfilment of these obligations was a mark of lordship: the various forms of *pastus* paid in the *cantrefi* of Rhos or Rhufoniog; the *porthiant* paid in those of Anglesey or Meirionnydd. Again the means by which liability was imposed or shared might vary: freemen's renders were frequently assessed not upon specific territorial entities but charged upon persons; bondmen's obligations might be determined not by the acreage tilled but by the number of ploughs or oxen in their possession.⁵⁷ It is evident, too, that, though the jurists' statements appear to limit the freemen's circuit

---

⁵¹ Stephenson, *GG*, 64–74; T. M. Charles-Edwards, *Early Irish and Welsh Kinship* (Oxford, 1993), 364–400.

⁵² For the 'great circuit of the household every winter', above, n. 42.

⁵³ *Extent of Chirkland*, xxiii–xxv, 5 *et passim*; T. P. Ellis, *Welsh Tribal Law and Custom in the Middle Ages* (Oxford, 1926), i, 305–17; R. R. Davies, *Lordship and Society*, 134–6; Ll. O. W. Smith, 'Lordships of Chirk and Oswestry', 225–33; Rogers, 'Bromfield and Yale', 140–2.

⁵⁴ E.g. W. Rees, 'Survivals of ancient Celtic custom in medieval England', in *Angles and Britons* (Cardiff, 1963), 148–68; Barrow, *Scotland and her Neighbours*, 135–47.

⁵⁵ D. Huw Owen, 'The lordship of Denbigh, 1282–1425', Ph.D. thesis, University of Wales, 1967, 9–18.

⁵⁶ Commutation is considered later; below, nn. 250–63.

⁵⁷ *SD*, 148, 222–3. In some cases *cylch* or *porthiant* was assessed according to wealth in chattels (*SD*, 47, 209; see below, n. 238).

obligations to those of the great *cylch* of the winter months, record evidence indicates that freemen were subject to a wide range of circuit renders.[58] The juristic and documentary evidence, taken together, bear the imprint of a personal lordship derived from an early period which was capable of adjustment and extension in response to a lord's demands, though those demands were necessarily reconciled with what his tenants could provide.

If the prince's power can be shown to have rested upon the claims already described, they were not the only rights by which his authority was exercised. The poets, understandably perhaps, brought forth the regality of the prince's status. His royal inheritance and royal qualities are extolled in the work of Llygad Gŵr at the height of Llywelyn's power, or by Bleddyn Fardd and Gruffudd ab yr Ynad Coch after his death.[59] Llywelyn was a man of royal lineage and, though his accession to power was not achieved by a natural succession even in Gwynedd, quite apart from any succession to the wider principality, he certainly came to the rule of a royal estate.[60] He was, for Gruffudd ab yr Ynad Coch, a lord of the right line to rule Aberffraw, and a gold coronet (*aur dalaith*) befitted him. The accoutrements of royalty borne by the prince of Wales came to him by virtue of his rule over his patrimony of Gwynedd, as did his custody of the holy relic of the Croes Naid. The jurists' work similarly stresses the regalian qualities of the prince's estate. Although the earliest of the surviving texts were written in the times of rulers who styled themselves princes, and though the texts often allude to lords (*arglwyddi*), they embody innumerable references to kings and, certainly in the Latin recensions, to kingdoms. Theirs is the ambience of *rex* and *regnum*. The designated heir to the ruler succeeds to a *regnum*, raised to the royal dignity (*regalis dignitas*) from among other members of the royal kindred (*membra regis*), and accorded a suitable place of honour at the royal court.[61]

The phraseology in which the prince's regality is expressed is often antiquated, perhaps deliberately so, witness the listing of those things which it was not right for a king to share with another person: gold treasure and silver, and buffalo horns, and clothing which had gold edgings. Again the jurists may offer a figurative expression of the prince's rights, notably the notion of 'the eight packhorses of the king' (*wyth pynfarch brenin*).[62] It is clear, even so, that they provide an account of readily recognized incidents of royal authority such as the sea or waste lands (*desertum regis*), relief or escheat.

---

[58] Eg. *SD*, 49–50.
[59] *GBF*, 24, 36, 50, 51; below, pp. 331–5.
[60] Below, pp. 275–6.
[61] E.g. *LTWL*, 110, 194, 207, 235, 277, 318, 437, corresponding to *LlIor*, 2–3; see J. B. Smith, 'Dynastic succession in medieval Wales', 201–2. *LlIor* has numerous references to *brenin*, but *brenhiniaeth* occurs only in relation to the kingship of Ynys Prydain.
[62] *LlIor*, 23; *LHD*, 40–1; *LTWL*, 135, 205, 377.

Beneath the rhetoric of the poets or the often picturesque depictions of the jurists we may detect the earthy concomitants of what may reasonably be termed a regality.[63] This is a quality better documented elsewhere than in twelfth- and thirteenth-century Wales, bound up with both the status and the material interest which the heirs to ancient kingdoms were careful to preserve.[64] Treasure trove and wrecks of the sea were attributes of an indigenous regality, and Llywelyn ap Gruffudd was greatly concerned for their protection.[65] These were, perhaps, less significant in material terms than emoluments derived from the pronounced emphasis placed on the king's rights in land. 'It is not right for any land to be kingless' was a principle firmly enunciated in the thirteenth century.[66] The ruler's concern in matters relating to the tenure of land is evident, for instance, in the practice of investiture. The law texts insist that a person entered legitimately only by virtue of a legal judgement or by a lord's investiture (*o estyn arglwydd*), a principle which points to the levying of a fee (*gobr*) upon entry into landed property.[67] The exaction of a fee upon succession to land ensured a seigniorial interest in what was originally, perhaps, an essentially kindred concern. The investiture fee (*gobrestyn*) was a form of relief (otherwise levied as *ebediw*) capable of extension into the field of wardship as well as being used to facilitate, at the cost of the appropriate premium, the succession of particular kinsmen to the estate of a proprietor.[68] Nor was the ruler's interest confined to various forms of succession. Somewhat elusive in our period, but possibly a source of increasing revenue, was the regulation of transactions in land. The care revealed by post-conquest rulers, in royal and marcher lands alike, to regulate

---

[63] The terms 'regality' and 'regalian' describe the functions and attributes of royal power and status indicated in twelfth- and thirteenth-century evidence, though in the period the term *regalitas* is used not by princes but by marcher lords wishing to describe the position of privilege which they conceived to be derived by conquest and not by delegation from the crown of England.

[64] Regalian qualities in the custom of lands north and south of the Pyrenees are noticed in J. B. Smith, 'Adversaries of Edward I: Gaston de Béarn and Llywelyn ap Gruffudd', 59–60.

[65] For treasure trove in medieval English law, G. F. Hill, *Treasure Trove in Law and Practice* (Oxford, 1936), 189–97. In 'Bracton' treasure trove and wreck (*thesaurus inventus* and *wreccum maris*) belong, by the *ius gentium*, to the crown and can be held by others only by grant from the crown (*Bracton*, ii, 58, 166–7). Welsh right to *thesaurus* or *eurgrawn* is best stated in *LTWL*, 126, 134, 199, 207, 283, 370–1; *WML*, 60 (brenhin bieu pop eurgrawn). References in *LlIor* and later texts in the same MS tradition are less explicit, but the prince's claims against the bishop of Bangor for treasure found on church land (*Councils*, i, 489–90) is noticed below. For wrecks, and references to the 'eight packhorses of the king', *LlIor*, 58; *LHD*, 112; *LlCol*, 37–8; *LTWL*, 389; *LlBleg*, 81–2; *RC*, 147; cf. Stephenson, *GG*, 80–1.

[66] *LlIor*, 54: 'ny dele un tyr bot yn dyurenhyn'; *LHD*, 101; *LlCol*, 36.

[67] *LlIor*, 57; *LHD*, 110; *LlCol*, 37.

[68] Stephenson, *GG*, 75–7, citations including *AL*, ii, 606–8, the fullest statement on *gobr* and *gobrestyn*. There appears to be an exercise of wardship in a late reference to Llywelyn's practice of taking *gobrestyn* from an heir to land (*CAP*, 335–6, 478).

land transactions may reflect a seigniorial interest already well established in the period of the princes and possibly a useful source of income.[69]

Law and jurisdiction

Many of the rights described already might reasonably be enumerated as attributes of the prince's lordship, sometimes enhanced by distinctly regalian qualities, and we shall later examine the income derived from his lordship over land as well as his exploitation of his own demesnes. His position in relation to the administration of justice, and the extent to which his jurisdiction was delegated to others, also affected his prestige and his prosperity. The law set out in the lawbooks is not the law of a royal lawgiver, despite the jurists' attempts to present the law of Wales as a law ordered, if not ordained, by one who had ruled as king albeit several centuries before.[70] Nor can we be sure that thirteenth-century society was entirely subject to a law administered by a judiciary controlled by the prince or to a law effectively enforced by the prince's coercive power. Justice was not achieved exclusively, perhaps not even mainly, by judgement in court. There was certainly a place for arbitration procedures which were themselves founded upon firm principles of Welsh law.[71] Judgement in court was only one of three means of dispute settlement noticed by the lawyers, who acknowledged the place of agreement between parties and arbitration in the making of just decisions.[72] The arbitral or equitable features of Welsh jurisprudence are very relevant to an understanding of the role of the *ynad* or *iudex* who occupies a key position in the judicial organization described in the texts which emanate from Gwynedd.[73]

---

[69] *LlIor*, 58; *LHD*, 114; *LlCol*, 38. Regulation of land transactions is examined in Llinos B. Smith, 'The gage and the land market in late medieval Wales', *EcHR*, 2nd ser., 29 (1976), 539–40.

[70] For the legal literature D. Jenkins, 'The lawbooks of medieval Wales', in R. Eales and D. Sullivan (eds.), *The Political Context of Law* (London, 1987), 1–15; T. M. Charles-Edwards, *The Welsh Laws* (Cardiff, 1989), and references cited.

[71] Llinos B. Smith, 'Disputes and settlements in medieval Wales: the role of arbitration', *EHR*, 106 (1991), 835–40.

[72] Ibid., quoting *LTWL*, 357. Arbitrative features in thirteenth-century inter-seigniorial disputes are noticed below, pp. 299–301.

[73] *Llyfr Iorwerth* and related texts give particular attention to the *ynad llys* (*iudex curie*, judge of the court, *LlIor*, 8–9; *LHD*, 16–17), but there are numerous references to the *ynad* other than the *ynad llys*. Dafydd Jenkins translates *ynad* as 'justice', reserving 'judge' as a translation of *brawdwr* (*LHD*, 393; D. Jenkins, 'A family of medieval Welsh lawyers', in D. Jenkins (ed.), *Celtic Law Papers Introductory to Welsh Medieval Law and Government* (Brussels, 1973), 128, n. 22). *Ynad* and *brawdwr* both correspond to the *iudex* of the Latin texts and it might be best to translate each as 'judge'. For the *ynad llys*, J. B. Smith, '*Ynad llys, brawdwr llys, iudex curie*', *The Welsh King and His Court*, ed. T. M. Charles-Edwards, M. E. Owen and P. Russell (in preparation).

The *ynad* of the legal literature represented by *Llyfr Iorwerth* betrays something of his origins as a jurist who, perhaps like the *brithem* of early Ireland, may have been capable of giving judgements or arbitraments which did not depend upon the powers of enforcement which came to be vested in the secular rulers of developed kingdoms.[74] Yet the same literature points to the development of a method of judicial provision in which the *ynad* gave judgement in the commote court, derived his authority to do so from the ruler, and gave judgements which were made in the name of the ruler and were enforced by his officers.[75] The procedure in a plea of land described in *Llyfr Iorwerth* provides for a judicial session on a day determined by the lord in a properly constituted commote court, held in the presence of the lord or his representative and the elders of the land, and administered by the lord's officers. The proceedings would be conducted by the *ynad*, who, possibly in association with other *ynaid*, heard the pleadings, and then gave judgement. We shall see that this was precisely the procedure by which Llywelyn ap Gruffudd sought to resolve the plea over Arwystli which he brought against Gruffudd ap Gwenwynwyn in the period between the wars of 1277 and 1282.[76] Edward I may have been reluctant to concede the suitability of this method of resolving that particular dispute, but the commission which he appointed in 1281 to examine the manner by which judgement was reached under Welsh law was concerned very largely with the role of the *ynad* in the legal procedures of Gwynedd.[77] The important place of judgement by the *ynad* in legal proceedings in thirteenth-century Gwynedd is clear, even though record evidence of court proceedings comes only from the post-conquest period.[78] Elsewhere, though testimony is slight, other means of reaching judgement may be detected. Documents from the early years of the century provide a record of proceedings before Maredudd ap Robert, lord of Cydewain, acting at the request of Llywelyn ap Iorwerth, in pleas heard in Arwystli. In one record reference is made to the participation of arbitrators

---

[74] *Ynad* may originally have meant jurist, one learned in the law (*LHD*, 393); for the *brithem*, F. Kelly, *A Guide to Early Irish Law* (Dublin, 1988), 51–6.

[75] Preparation and examination of the *ynad* within the legal profession, and investiture with the power of judgement by the lord, are described in *AL*, i, 216–18; *LlCol*, 14; *LHD*, 141–2; comment by D. Jenkins, *LlCol*, 86–7; *LHD*, 393.

[76] *LlIor*, 44–50; *LHD*, 83–91. T. M. Charles-Edwards, '*Cynghawsedd*: counting and pleading in medieval Welsh law', *B*, 33 (1986), 188–98, is a valuable study of court procedure; for the Arwystli case, below, pp. 470–89, 493–6, 504–5.

[77] *CWR*, 190–210; several *ynaid* gave evidence, *CWR*, 196, 199–200, among them Goronwy ap Philip, named in Llyfr Coch Asaph as 'judge of the secular court' (NLW, Peniarth 231, f. 79).

[78] Proceedings before Dafydd ap Gruffudd in Cymydmaen, 1252, include reference to circumstances in which an *ynad* would adjudge (*RC*, 252). Post-conquest evidence for north-east Wales is examined fully in R. R. Davies, 'The administration of law in medieval Wales: the role of the *ynad cwmwd* (*iudex patrie*)', in T. M. Charles-Edwards, M. E. Owen and D. B. Walters (eds.), *Lawyers and Laymen* (Cardiff, 1986), 258–73 [*LAL*].

(*datuerwer*) and in the other to upright men (*deduriht*), noble men (*obtimates*) and wise men (*sapientes*). There is no mention of *ynaid*, even though one of the wise men named, Cynyr ap Cadwgan, is known in legal literature as a jurist.[79] This extremely rare evidence from Arwystli provides an early indication that methods of reaching judgement may have varied considerably in the several provinces of Wales. By the later years of the century, while evidence of the important place of the *ynad* is strong in Gwynedd, collective judgement appears to have been well established in Powys and Deheubarth.[80] Practice might vary from one area to another, and there may have been significant change over time. It seems that even in Gwynedd, for all the resilience of native procedures, legal actions might be determined upon the verdict of a jury rather than by the pronouncement of an *ynad*. Certainly, evidence given by witnesses from Perfeddwlad during the inquiry into Welsh procedures in 1281 indicated that the princes themselves had promoted the use of the inquisition and the jury. Litigants were encouraged to adopt, alongside native practices, the English forms of procedure with which, through their experience in periods of royal administration, they may have become familiar. More generally, numerous witnesses, *ynaid* among them, maintained that the prince had the right to correct and amend the law or to amplify or abbreviate its provisions according to need.[81] But whatever the variation in legal practice from one area to another, and whatever changes might be introduced over a period of time, judgement in the commote court under the aegis of prince or lord was a normal feature of legal provision in independent Wales in the thirteenth century, though not by any means the sole method of resolving legal disputes. It is evident, too, that judicial processes were such as lent a prominent place to the princes' rights and to the functions of the princes' officers in conducting court proceedings and in the execution of judgement.

The almost total absence of judicial and financial records of the pre-conquest period makes it difficult to offer a meaningful estimate of the changes in legal procedures effected under the aegis of the princes and denies the historian any opportunity to assess the income which the prince derived from the justice done in his name. At the same time it can be reasonably envisaged that profits from criminal and civil actions were a source of remuneration in the thirteenth century, and it may have been one of increasing importance as the provision of justice became ever more closely

---

[79] *Charters of the Abbey of Ystrad Marchell*, ed. G. C. G. Thomas (Aberystwyth, 1997), nos. 64, 65; the litigation is discussed in D. Stephenson, *Thirteenth Century Welsh Law Courts* (Pamphlets on Welsh Law, Aberystwyth, 1980), 10–14. For Cynyr ap Cadwgan, R. R. Davies, 'Administration of law in medieval Wales', 264–5; Llywelyn asserted in 1281 that Cynyr's sons were *ynaid* in Arwystli (*CWR*, 195), though the veracity of a similar statement he made concerning Cyfeiliog was questioned at the time.

[80] For collective judgement, below, pp. 301–2, 484–5.

[81] *CWR*, 195–201; the use of the jury is considered further below, pp. 484–5.

linked with seigniorial power.[82] Llywelyn ap Gruffudd's assertion of the jurisdiction of his courts is made most explicitly, among the few surviving records, in the course of his arguments with the bishops of Bangor and St Asaph over the respective rights of secular and ecclesiastical courts. In these exchanges the prince was concerned with the courts of the localities and these, taken together, probably brought the greater emoluments.[83] There can be no doubt, however, that the thirteenth-century princes were also concerned with the development of the authority of their central court. The lawbooks accord the *ynad llys* (*iudex curie*), the judge of the court, a high status in the king's entourage. Yet the *ynad llys* appears to have no place outside the jurists' writings, an officer unknown in twelfth- and thirteenth-century records. Whereas several *ynaid*, judges in commote courts, are named in the evidence gathered by Edward I's commissioners in 1281, the *ynad llys* remains exceedingly elusive. It seems likely that the functions of the *ynad llys* were subsumed in those of the *distain* or *senescallus*, the officer who may be identified as the chief minister of the thirteenth-century princes.[84] Gwyn ab Ednywain and Ednyfed Fychan in the period of Llywelyn ap Iorwerth, or Goronwy ab Ednyfed and Tudur ab Ednyfed in that of his grandson, can be presumed to have exercised, along with their military and various other functions, a specifically judicial authority on the prince's behalf. Tudur ab Ednyfed, in the later years of Llywelyn ap Gruffudd's rule, appears on occasion as the prince's justice – *justiciarius domini principis* – and exercised an authority which extended, as we shall see, over the wider principality. Indeed the jurisdiction of the prince's council is revealed most clearly in contemporary records in relation to the prince's dealings with the magnates of his principality of Wales.[85] The strength of the prince's position depended a great deal on the effectiveness of his judicial authority in this wider sphere, but it rested, too, upon his authority in his territorial lordship of Gwynedd. The concentration in the lands of the *distain* of powers hitherto vested in the *penteulu* with regard to military duties and the *ynad llys* in relation to judicial affairs may be an indication of the manner in which the prince's authority was fortified during the course of the thirteenth century.[86] It would be inappropriate to claim too much for the courts of Gwynedd, certainly hazardous to envisage a rigid hierarchy of courts with, for instance, erroneous judgement in a commote court subject to correction in a high court (*uchel lys*) presided

---

[82] Stephenson, *GG*, 82–9, provides an admirable survey; for the growth of a more rigorous criminal law, Pierce, *MWS*, 304–6; Jenkins, *LHD*, xxx–xxxi.

[83] These arguments are examined in the course of this discussion.

[84] *LlIor*, 8–9; *LHD*, 16–17; J. B. Smith, '*Ynad llys*'.

[85] Stephenson, *GG*, 11–20; below, pp. 297–301, 303–4, 313–14, 328.

[86] The view that the *distain* supplanted the *penteulu* and that he appears as seneschal or constable (Pierce, *MWS*, 33–4) is modified in Stephenson, *GG*, 15–16, but evidence appears to point in that direction.

over by the prince's *justiciarius*. There is an intimation of a procedure of this nature in the legal writing, but we know nothing of its practical application.[87] Yet it would be invidious not to admit the likelihood that the needs which confronted the princes, and especially those which were accentuated in the later years of the thirteenth century, stimulated the development of a judicial order better capable of fulfilling the responsibilities of princely power and safeguarding its material interests. Its key institution was the council (*concilium*) of the prince of Gwynedd which became, as we shall see in the next chapter, the hub of the government of the principality of Wales and exercised, among its varied tasks, specifically judicial functions.[88] The prince's council, under the aegis of the prince himself, or representing his authority in the localities of his dominion, was an expression of the personal lordship and the regalian power which were joined in his authority.

The prince was not, even so, the sole provider of lordship even within the confines of his territorial lordship of Gwynedd. Whereas traditional historical interpretation may have tended to envisage relationships in the pre-conquest period in terms of tension between innovative seigniorial power and entrenched kindred interests, it is clear that seigniorial authority was capable of being shared, and the sharing of power could itself be a source of contention. The prince of Gwynedd certainly shared his lordship with both ecclesiastical and lay persons. Llywelyn's twelfth- and thirteenth-century predecessors had bestowed lands upon churches, monasteries and priories, the best documented being Llywelyn ap Iorwerth's grants to the Cistercian abbeys of Aberconwy and Cymer in which he made or confirmed concessions of land and jurisdiction.[89] The charter to Aberconwy, made in the first flush of the prince's triumphal assertion of power over 'the entire principality of Gwynedd', conveys privileges which reflect his willingness to yield, or to

---

[87] The notion of a 'high court' (*uchel lys*) is advanced in Pierce, *MWS*, 34. The procedures by which the judgement of an *ynad* might be challenged, described in *Llyfr Iorwerth*, do not indicate removal of the case to a court of higher authority; there is, however, an intimation to this effect in Latin B (*LTWL*, 212); see J. B. Smith, '*Ynad Llys*'. The '*uchel lys*' in the post-conquest lordships created in Powys Fadog (Chirk and Bromfield and Yale) was formed by a joint session of the courts of two commotes (*Extent of Chirkland*, 60; BL Add. MS 10,013, f. 8); there is no certainty that this practice had a pre-conquest origin. Procedure upon appeal is considered later.

[88] Below, pp. 309–16.

[89] *MonAng*, v, 458–9; 672–4; *RC*, 146–8; *CChR*, iv, 267–9; *CPR, 1321–24*, 400; K. Williams-Jones, 'Llywelyn's charter to Cymer Abbey in 1209', *JMerHRS*, 3 (1957–60), 54–9; *H*, nos. 122, 123, 130; Stephenson, *GG*, 199–201. The two charters in which Llywelyn ap Iorwerth's grants are recorded specify the privileges conceded to the abbey of Aberconwy in a degree of detail and in a terminology which would not be expected in gifts of a late twelfth-century date. It is accepted in this study that a charter was granted to the abbey by Llywelyn ap Iorwerth, probably in 1199, but the clauses concerning jurisdiction are not afforded any reference as a source for a consideration of the jurisdiction which was in the prince's gift. Charles Insley is engaged in a study of the charters.

admit that his predecessors had already yielded, seigniorial rights that he would normally seek to safeguard. Conceded immunity from the prince's courts and the exclusion of his officers, the monks were granted a number of specific rights such as wreck (*naufragium*). They enjoyed, too, the right, also conceded to Cymer, to recover cargoes wrecked by storms at sea, even though the goods might be cast on the prince's shores. No comparable indication of the jurisdiction conceded to other communities, ecclesiastical or religious, survives. Such evidence should not always be expected, certainly not in the case of the mendicant orders established in Gwynedd during the course of the thirteenth century. The Franciscan house at Llan-faes or the Dominican houses at Bangor and Rhuddlan probably won the prince's support, or at least their tolerance, but the prince's benefactions may well have been of limited extent, and the friars may have owed much to the more wealthy among the prince's tenants.[90] Moreover, jurisdictional privileges are unlikely to have been at issue in these cases. Of much more concern, among the institutions for which no comprehensive charters survive, were the rights exercised by the secular churches and by priories other than those of the mendicants. Llywelyn ap Gruffudd's relations with the bishops of the dioceses of Bangor and St Asaph proved strained, particularly in the years preceding the conflict of 1277, and a substantial documentary record of their disagreements survives and will be considered presently. More difficult to comprehend, but necessary as a background to the arguments with the bishops, and relevant in their own right, are the princes' relations with a wide range of churches, including those transferred to the reformed orders within the lordship of Snowdon.

In one of his early *acta* Llywelyn ap Gruffudd confirmed to the church of Ynys Lannog (Priestholm) the lands and privileges embodied in the *abadaeth* of Penmon, already granted by his predecessors, thereby recognizing the benefits enjoyed by a church which, like Bardsey, had been a *clas* refounded as a house of Augustinian canons.[91] Numerous other *clasau*, such as Clynnog Fawr, retained many of the characteristics of those indigenous collegiate churches long since endowed with lands over which their communities exercised a measure of jurisdiction. They included, too, the church of Dolgynwal, or Ysbyty Ifan, which, as a hospital of the Knights of St John, received the support of Llywelyn ap Iorwerth.[92] These churches may be taken

---

[90] G. Roberts, *Aspects of Welsh History*, 215–39.

[91] *MonAng*, iv, 581–2; *CChR*, ii, 460; *H*, no. 147; Stephenson, *GG*, 203; C. N. Johns, 'The Celtic monasteries of north Wales', *TCaernHS*, 21 (1960), 14–43.

[92] For Clynnog lands and privileges and those of the knights, *RC*, 26–34, 221–2, 257–8; Eyton, *Antiquities of Shropshire*, x, 247; *CPR, 1313–17*, 576; *H*, 134; W. Rees, *A History of the Order of St John of Jerusalem in Wales and the Welsh Border* (Cardiff, 1947), 63–4; Stephenson, *GG*, 202.

to represent the institutions to which the early texts of *Llyfr Iorwerth* refer in the course of their statement of the respective rights of king and church in *abatir* ('abbot land') and *tir ysbyty* ('hospital land').[93] The crux of the matter treated by the jurists is that 'no land shall be kingless': in respect of their temporal possessions these institutions were under the prince's jurisdiction. The prince was entitled to the fines of *dirwy* and *camlwrw* (imposed for greater and lesser offences respectively), and to jurisdiction over hosting and theft in the case of 'abbot land', and theft and fighting on 'hospital land'. Thus the *abadaeth* to which, in the case of Penmon, both Llywelyn ap Iorwerth and his grandson specifically referred, would have been subject to a shared jurisdiction, and the liberties which it embodied were derived from the prince. That 'bishop land', too, was subject to the prince's jurisdiction is indicated most clearly in one manuscript of *Llyfr Iorwerth* and in *Llyfr Colan* with the statement that the king reserved hosting and theft.[94] These texts may possibly indicate an extension of the prince's authority or, at least, a more explicit statement of its implications. Yet this would still point to the existence, before the period of Llywelyn ap Gruffudd, of a custom which, albeit only imperfectly reflected in the legal literature, defined the respective spheres of *regnum* and *sacerdotium*.[95] Spiritual matters, including sacrilege, usury and matrimonial questions, lay within the jurisdiction of the church and the province of canon law. But there were matters of temporal authority on which the church, be it headed by bishop, abbot or prior, could hold court (*cabidwl*) by their own law (*eu kyureyth ehun*), provided that it did not impede the king's law (*en lle na llesteyryoent kyureuth e brenhyn*).[96] Thus men under the lordship of an abbot or bishop who sought licence to sell or gage their lands would secure permission from those lords. The right to the regulation of land transactions may have brought remuneration to lay and ecclesiastical lord alike, and pecuniary interest was undoubtedly involved in a number of the matters on which controversy arose between prince and church in the period of Llywelyn ap Gruffudd. It evidently lay at the root of much of the debate over the respective jurisdictions of prince and church over lay tenants on church estates. Admittedly, documentary evidence of contention over the liberties claimed by churches which fall into the categories described by the

---

[93] H. Pryce, *Native Law and the Church in Medieval Wales* (Oxford, 1993), 204–33, 241–51 [Pryce, *NLC*], examines these issues, including 'abbot land' and 'hospital land' (*LlIor*, 54–5; *LHD*, 101).

[94] Pryce, *NLC*, 212–13. The additional clause appears in MS E, that is Peniarth MS 29, *Facsimile of the Chirk Codex of the Welsh Laws*, ed. J. G. Evans (Llanbedrog, 1909), 60.

[95] The earliest MSS of the texts represented by *Llyfr Iorwerth* and *Llyfr Colan* are attributed to the mid-thirteenth century and might reasonably be regarded as statements of legal learning in the period of Llywelyn ap Iorwerth; current estimates of their dates in D. Huws, 'Llyfrau Cymraeg 1250–1400', *NLWJ*, 28 (1993–4), 1–21.

[96] *LlIor*, 54–5; *LHD*, 101.

lawyers as 'abbot land' or 'hospital land' is difficult to find. In many cases, moreover, the *abadaeth* would have consisted of no more than the ordinary fiscal rights which are, perchance, portrayed in an arbitration, made by Dafydd ap Gruffudd as lord of Cymydmaen in 1252, between the Augustinian canons of Bardsey and those described as the secular canons and men of the *abadaeth* of the church of Aberdaron, representatives of a long-established *clas* community.[97] On the other hand, the jurisdiction exercised by the bishops of Bangor and St Asaph was more substantial and its relationship to that of the prince proved to be highly contentious. Compared with the episcopal estates found in many other lands, the territory vested in the two northern sees was not extensive, but within Gwynedd it constituted valuable assets and the bishops were among the prince's major tenants.[98] The evidence concerning relations between the prince and bishops provides the most instructive body of material surviving from the thirteenth century to reveal the conflicting jurisdictional interests found within the lordship of Snowdon and, indeed, is the most illuminating source of information on the prince's jurisdictional rights themselves.

An agreement made between Llywelyn ap Gruffudd and Bishop Richard of Bangor in the spring of 1261, following arbitration, attempted to clarify the spheres of lay and clerical jurisdiction (*regimen et sacerdotium*), particularly with regard to criminous clerks and lay tenants of the bishop.[99] In cases of treasure trove, for instance, whether the charges were laid against clerks or laymen, justice would be done in the secular court (*in curia seculari*); rights over wrecks cast up by the sea lay with the prince alone, an acknowledgement on the part of the bishop consistent with the tenets of the law texts. Correction of sacrilege belonged to the bishop. Violation of sanctuary, on the other hand, required the collaboration of secular and church authorities, and the particular matter addressed in the discussions would be resolved by a joint board of faithful men representing prince and bishop. In cases of rape, which offended government and priesthood alike (*regimen et sacerdotium*), justice would be done according to both laws (*secundum utramque legem*). There were circumstances in which fines would be shared between prince and

---

[97] *RC*, 252; Pierce, *MWS*, 391–407.

[98] Contentions between Llywelyn and the bishops are examined in G. Williams, *The Welsh Church from Conquest to Reformation* (Cardiff, 1962) 8–14; Owen E Jones, 'Llyfr Coch Asaph: a textual and historical study', MA thesis, University of Wales, 1968, ii, 94–112. For the episcopal estates, extent of bishop of Bangor's lands, 1306, in *RC*, 92–115, 231–7; *quo warranto* proceedings, 1348, *RC*, 133–8; NLW, Church in Wales Records, SA/MB/22, ff. 19–21, gives the issues of episcopal lands 1356–7 (O. E. Jones, 'Llyfr Coch Asaph', ii, 57–8).

[99] *Councils*, i, 489–91.

bishop.¹⁰⁰ The agreement, reached by a board of arbitrators consisting of the bishop of St Asaph, four friars and four members of the prince's council, marks a recognition that differences as well as uncertainties needed to be resolved, and it called for a sequence of meetings about territorial boundaries and matters of jurisdiction.¹⁰¹ Encroachment by the prince on episcopal rights is probably implied in some instances. The provision that young men under fourteen should not be liable for military service, nor made to compound for their service, probably reflects a wish to restrain the prince's demands upon lay tenants of the bishop. The prolonged absence of Bishop Richard from the diocese may itself have created a need both for clarification and for a stricter adherence to previously agreed procedures. Llywelyn may, too, have had his own good reasons for an accommodation with the bishop. After a long estrangement, Richard had recently been active in promoting the prince's cause in royal councils. His imprimatur on the agreements between the prince and the lords of Powys and Deheubarth, and his readiness to exercise ecclesiastical sanctions to buttress them, was vital, especially in view of the fact that the prince had not yet secured royal consent to these arrangements.¹⁰² The arbitration procedures may thus have been initiated in an accommodating, if still wary, spirit. The matter of shipwrecked goods was broached in terms of respectful criticism of the precedents established by Llywelyn ap Iorwerth and his successors; in the matter of stolen goods found in a clergyman's house the arbitrators drew, somewhat cautiously, on knowledge gained from their elders.¹⁰³ Yet the arbitration of 1261 may not have provided a sufficiently firm framework for the future. Problems remained to trouble Richard's successor, Bishop Anian, who had to contend with the stresses of the period of two major conflicts and the consequently heightened pressures on the relations between secular and ecclesiastical authorities.¹⁰⁴ Prince Llywelyn's main episcopal antagonist, however, would

---

¹⁰⁰ Apart from declarations of principle the document refers, in relation to treasure trove, to a case involving Ednyfed ap Hywel, who had been charged with unearthing treasure. The case would be heard in a bishop's court and if the charge was proved he would make satisfaction to the Lord Llywelyn according to the law of the land (*secundum legem patrie*, *Councils*, i, 489). For lawbook references to wreck, above, n. 65.

¹⁰¹ The text, Rhydyrarw 29 April 1261, appears to be based on an earlier agreement at Llandrillo; it was followed by an agreement over boundaries at Tal-y-llyn, and between Bodellog and Llanwnda (Rhydyrarw, 18 August, *LW*, 97–8). Each document was issued in the name of Bishop Anian of St Asaph, two Dominican friars of Bangor and two Franciscans of Llan-faes, and the laymen Goronwy ab Ednyfed, Tudur ab Ednyfed, Einion Fychan and Einion ap Caradog.

¹⁰² Richard's earlier relations with Llywelyn have been traced already; ecclesiastical support for the agreements between Llywelyn and the magnates of Wales is noticed, above, pp. 114–15; below, pp. 290–1.

¹⁰³ *Councils*, i, 489–91; the last matter concerned *cyfannedd* and *halacty*, for which *LlIor*, 76; *LHD*, 159; *LlCol*, 21.

¹⁰⁴ *CR, 1264–68*, 117; Stephenson, *GG*, 172–3.

be Bishop Anian of St Asaph who was consecrated, surely not without the prince's approval, in 1268. These exchanges provide an even better opportunity to appreciate the matters at issue in the light of the practice indicated in the legal literature.

The disputes which came to a head in the diocese of St Asaph undoubtedly reflect the pugnacity of the bishop and the tense political situation of these years.[105] First promulgated, as far as is known, in a document issued from a synod of canons, clerics and laymen in October 1274, and then greatly elaborated in the list of grievances drawn up at a second synod in December 1276, the charges against Llywelyn ap Gruffudd were numerous and varied.[106] Bishop Anian alleged the prince's intervention in some matters which, he insisted, lay entirely in the jurisdiction of the ecclesiastical courts. These included crimes committed in churchyards and consecrated places, and breaches of marriage law. More numerous, and difficult, were those matters where the spheres of secular and ecclesiastical jurisdiction met and merged. Llywelyn is alleged to have interfered in testamentary matters on three counts: that he prevented the bishop from making a will; that he refused to recognize the validity of wills made by laymen, except those made in sickness of which the testator died; and that he seized the goods of those who died intestate.[107] In protesting against Llywelyn's refusal to allow a bishop to make a will, and seizing the goods of a bishop who died, Anian certainly questioned the validity of a practice vouched for in the literature. When a bishop died, *Llyfr Iorwerth* avers, the king is entitled to all his goods (apart from church vestments and ornaments), for all goods without an owner are the king's waste (*diffaith brenin*).[108] A bishop's goods were potentially a source of profit to the prince, and both the prince's interest and the concern of the bishop to put matters to right are readily understood, as is the care of later incumbents of Welsh sees to ensure that they should be allowed to make wills in the manner customary in England.[109] Llywelyn's unwillingness to respect wills

---

[105] G. Williams, *Welsh Church*, 10–12; political circumstances are noticed below, pp. 377–82.

[106] Main documents, from 'Llyfr Coch Asaph' (Peniarth MS 231B), are: (a) investigation by clerks and laymen of liberties of the church, 19 October 1274 (*Councils*, i, 502–3; Peniarth MS 231B. 45–52); (b) thirteen articles drawn up later that year (*Councils*, 491–3; MS 39–42); (c) Llywelyn's letter to the archbishop of Canterbury, 25 May 1275 (*Councils*, 503–5; MS 71–4; *H*, no. 414); (d) twenty-nine articles drawn up by a synod of the church, 7 December 1276 (*Councils*, 511–16; MS 98–105); (e) Llywelyn's charter of liberties to the church of St Asaph, probably early 1277 (*Councils*, 519–21; MS 74–7; *H*, no. 153); below, pp. 377–82, 407–9.

[107] *Councils*, 512–13. Helen Chandler, 'The will in medieval Wales to 1540', M.Phil. thesis, University of Wales, 1991, 54–6, 97–107, examines intestacy and a bishop's testamentary capacity; Pryce, *NLC*, 112–27.

[108] *LlIor*, 54; *LHD*, 101.

[109] Anian of St Asaph's goods are listed in his will, 1288, in Canterbury Cathedral Archives, Dean and Chapter, Sede Vacante Scrap Book, II, 187; text in Chandler, 'Will in medieval Wales', 212–14; calendar in J. Fisher, 'Three Welsh wills', *ArchCamb*, 6th ser., 19 (1919), 186–7.

other than those made in mortal sickness raised a much wider issue on which there was probably a broad measure of discontent eventually reflected in the *gravamina* against him registered after his death.[110] His restrictive dictates on this count were linked with his insistence on the secular authority's right to the possessions of intestate tenants. This was a stance which incurred the displeasure of Archbishop Pecham who, taking issue with him on his actions in the diocese of Bangor, viewed the confiscation of the goods of intestates as a serious violation of the liberties of the church and asserted the exclusive jurisdiction of the church in testamentary matters.[111] The goods of intestates should fall to the ordinary who would supervise their administration. Llywelyn's appeal to the law of Hywel Dda was not to be countenanced by the archbishop, but there is no doubt that the prince's position was consonant with the concept of *marwdy* which was counted by the lawyers among the 'eight packhorses of the king', certainly to the extent that it comprehended cases in which sudden death had prevented the making of a will.[112] Anian's concern, however, may have been less with the non-canonical practice which incurred the archbishop's censure than with the fact that he was denied the bishop's right, which Welsh law allowed, to the moveable goods of lay tenants on the episcopal estates. His position was that of an immediate lord who claimed his right against an assertion of right on the part of a superior lord. This was a right which the bishops of the northern dioceses were to assert again after the conquest of Wales.[113] It was a concern which Anian shared, in Llywelyn's time, with lay tenants of the prince who were troubled by what they regarded as the prince's intrusion into this facet of their jurisdiction over their tenants.[114] In the political contingency in which he found himself by the beginning of 1277 Llywelyn ap Gruffudd was constrained, not only to yield on the broad principle of the church's jurisdiction in testamentary matters, but to make specific assurances that he would not impede the making of a will by his tenants of the diocese, nor take possession of the goods of tenants of the church who died intestate.[115] The concern which Pecham expressed two years later in relation to Bangor suggests, however, that the argument over jurisdiction and intestacy had by no means been fully resolved in the prince's lordship.

---

[110] Below, n. 318.

[111] *RPeck*, i, 77. For the position in England, F. Pollock and F. W. Maitland, *The History of English Law* (Cambridge, 1911; reissued 1968), ii, 356–63; M. M. Sheehan, *The Will in Medieval England* (Toronto, 1963), 162–76.

[112] *LlIor*, 23, 65–6; *LHD*, 40, 130–1; *LTWL*, 377. For *marwdy*, Chandler, 'Will in medieval Wales', 98–101; Pryce, *NLC*, 113–18.

[113] Ll. B. Smith, '*Gravamina*', 164–6.

[114] Ibid., 174–5 (cap. ix, xxix).

[115] *Councils*, i, 519–20.

More contentious still, and broaching matters of criminal jurisdiction which the prince might particularly wish to reserve to himself, were Anian's demands on the three issues of fighting, theft and homicide. On each issue reference may be made to the law texts which, indeed, indicate that the interests of both prince and church were involved. Thus a distinction is made between the manner in which a fine (*dirwy*) is imposed for fighting on the king's land and on the bishop's land: in the case of fighting between a king's man and a bishop's man on royal land the king took the fine of both offenders, whereas if it occurred on a bishop's land the fine was shared.[116] Broached in 1274 and elaborated two years later, the synod of St Asaph put the view that, in cases arising on royal land, half the fine should go to the bishop and, in cases of fighting on the bishop's land, the bishop and chapter took the entire fine. Llywelyn, it was maintained, took the entire fine in each case.[117] It is thus difficult to judge whether the prince, in the charter which he conceded to the bishop and chapter on the eve of war in 1277, was moved to restore the customary practice, or whether he was constrained by political circumstances to make an even more far-reaching concession. Whatever the explanation, he consented that, in offences for which two men of the prince and bishop were convicted, half the fine would go to the bishop for offences on the prince's land, and the whole fine for those committed on the bishop's land.[118] Theft, the second matter raised by Anian, was a matter of extended juristic exposition in which distinction was made between offences which incurred execution and those punished by fines. Theft (*lledrad*) on 'bishop land' was certainly included in *Llyfr Iorwerth*'s account of regalian right in its Peniarth 29 text, while *Llyfr Colan* more specifically describes the king's right to a thief and his goods.[119] Testimony from St Asaph in 1274 maintained, however, that when a person from the bishop's territory was punished for theft, bishop and chapter received half the correction up to a sum of £7.[120] Bishop and chapter saw their right, not as a concession on the part of the princes but rather the other way, for the bishop had once possessed gallows and with it a jurisdiction over theft, but ecclesiastical and secular lords had come to an agreement (*conventio*) by which the fine (*mulctus*) for minor offences was conceded to the church though, in the case of redemption from capital punishment (for which there is substantial evidence), half the price (*precium*) was apportioned to bishop and chapter.[121]

---

[116] *LTWL*, 228, 231; Pryce, *NLC*, 221–3.

[117] *Councils*, i, 492 (cap. 4); 513 (cap. 10). Sharing of fines is indicated in several cases, most of them of the period of Llywelyn ap Iorwerth, cited in 'Llyfr Coch Asaph' (O. E. Jones, 'Llyfr Coch Asaph', i, 172–7, from Peniarth 231B).

[118] *Councils*, i, 521.

[119] *LlIor*, 54; *LHD*, 101; *LlCol*, 36. Theft is treated at length in *LlIor*, 74–80; *LHD*, 156–69; *LlCol*, 20–4; see Pryce, *NLC*, 225–33.

[120] *Councils*, i, 491; for fines up to £7 see discussion of the *gravamina*, below, n. 314.

[121] *Councils*, i, 502–3.

Not that there was complete accord within the church on this issue, for one canon of St Asaph insisted that nothing of this should accrue to the bishop, for that was the price of blood (*precium sanguinis*). The canon's reservation prompts the possibility that the code of practice which governed offences involving the death penalty might reflect, not only an intrusive influence on the part of the prince, but a readiness on the part of the church, in response to canonical teaching, to yield to the secular power its jurisdiction in serious criminal offences which incurred the death penalty.[122] Claims against Llywelyn subsequently submitted by the church of St Asaph, in fact, fell short of the assertion into which the lone canon had entered his caveat when the issue had first been raised.[123] The jurisdiction of the prince's court was now admitted and the church sought only half the fines for theft. In the finite statement of the church's grievances in 1276, even so, the synod strenuously urged against Llywelyn his denial of ecclesiastical rights which old and agreed custom of the country decreed (*ex antiqua et approbata hactenus consuetudine patrie*).[124] Homicide was a third difficult issue and the text of *Llyfr Colan* explicitly includes the penalty for homicide (*cosb lladd celain*) among the matters on which the king's jurisdiction extended over 'bishop land'.[125] On the prince's right to the correction (*emenda*) incurred by homicide the church of St Asaph did not demur. The synod laid claim only to the goods of a tenant of the church who committed homicide on the bishop's land, but it did so to protest against Llywelyn's insistence on securing the homicide's goods as well as jurisdiction over his person.[126]

In the charter which Llywelyn ap Gruffudd granted to the church of St Asaph early in 1277 the prince conceded to the bishop the right to punish in the church court all those who transgressed on the bishop's lands, with the exception of those who committed homicide.[127] This particular clause, and the tenor of the document as a whole, reflects the dire straits in which the prince found himself at that stage. Whether the position established by his charter can be taken to constitute a restoration of a pristine code of practice that he had hitherto violated is less clear. Yet the charge that he had acted in a manner at variance with established custom reverberates through the evidence of his dispute with Bishop Anian: Llywelyn had acted contrary to the ordinances of

---

[122] Ibid., 503; Pryce, *NLC*, 230–1.
[123] *Councils*, i, 491–3.
[124] Ibid., 513 (cap. 9).
[125] *LlCol*, 36: 'o byt escoptyr ef a dyly eu lluyt a guyl uor, a cosb llat keleyn a dyeneydyau lleydyr a'y da'; Pryce, *NLC*, 213–14, 223–5.
[126] *Councils*, i, 492, 514 (cap. 8, 14).
[127] Ibid., 521; from Peniarth 231B. 77: 'transgressiones insuper in terris [MS curiis] episcopi perpetratas, nisi solum in casu homicidii, eidem episcopo facilitatem plenariam concedimus corrigendi'.

the Welsh princes. It can hardly be doubted that the church, not only the episcopal church but the secular church in general, enjoyed a body of privilege derived from an early period. The legal texts probably reflect long-established usage in their references to the *braint* or *dignitas* of the church.[128] There are, even so, clear intimations on all sides that the ecclesiastical privileges were ultimately derived from the princes and the kings who had preceded them. That recognition is implicit in Bishop Anian's reference to practice contrary to the the ordinances (*instituciones*) of earlier princes.[129] It pervades the law texts, well expressed in the passages which *Llyfr Iorwerth* devotes to ecclesiastical sanctuary. Upon the coming of a new king those who possessed ecclesiastical land would come and declare their privilege (*braint*) and their entitlement (*dylyed*) and, if the king consented, he would invest them with their privilege and their place of sanctuary (*noddfa*).[130] The *noddfa* was, in the jurists' view at least, derived from the king. Regulation of sanctuary still called for understanding between prince and church, and, as we have seen, an incident concerning sanctuary (*in refugio ecclesie*) in the diocese of Bangor was addressed in 1261 and referred to a joint board of arbitrators.[131] Implicit in the particular instance of sanctuary was the broad principle that church liberties and custom were derived from the royal power, a principle asserted unequivocally by Llywelyn ap Gruffudd in a letter to the archbishop of Canterbury, written at Abereiddon in 1275, which was prompted by Bishop Anian's initial complaints against him. Llywelyn insisted that, if the charters by which those liberties had been granted were shown to be inadequate, he was prepared to grant those liberties anew. He was prepared to initiate an inquiry to establish what needed to be put to rights. The material embodied in the lawbooks may then be taken to represent, albeit from the position of jurists depicting a broadly secular interest, some matters of principle and others of detail which may reflect the concord between *regnum* and *sacerdotium* as it stood in the time of Llywelyn ap Iorwerth. Much of the material may be of late twelfth- and thirteenth-century definition, and partly perhaps a product of the endeavours of that prince to safeguard and promote his interests, but partly due to the readiness on the part of the church to respond to canonical teaching and to subscribe to conventions agreed in the province of Canterbury. At the same time it is unlikely that the princes' early charters had embodied detailed statements of church privileges, and precise definitions of the respective

---

[128] For an important text relating to the privileges of the church of Llandaff, Wendy Davies, '*Braint Teilo*', *B*, 26 (1974–6), 123–37.

[129] *Councils*, i, 491.

[130] H. Pryce, 'Ecclesiastical sanctuary in thirteenth-century Welsh law', *Journal of Legal History*, 5/3 (1984), 1–13, discusses *nawdd*, with translation of passage on sanctuary from *LlIor*, 43–4; *LHD*, 81–3; cf. Pryce, *NLC*, 163–203.

[131] *Councils*, i, 490.

spheres of secular and ecclesiastical powers may have been the outcome, still less than complete perhaps, of interaction between them during the course of the thirteenth century.[132] What was agreed may have amounted neither to definitive statements nor immutable custom, but it was probably sufficiently coherent to be regarded as a norm which Llywelyn ap Gruffudd was subsequently deemed by the church to have violated. Some of his actions may have impinged upon matters of strictly spiritual jurisdiction for, though these were not the most prominent issues of contention, Llywelyn considered it prudent to begin his charter to St Asaph with an explicit admission that cases of testaments, matrimony, usury, tithes and sacrilege belonged entirely to the church courts (*ad forum ecclesie pleno iure*). There would be no hindering of confessions. The really contentious issues were those enumerated in the following articles, and they corresponded in large part to those which have already been recounted: interference over wills, rights over church tenants and the jurisdiction of church courts. There were concessions, too, on the seizure of moveable goods *sede vacante* and on procurations on churches.[133] Together they constituted the rights, liberties and customs that he now solemnly guaranteed. There can be little doubt that Llywelyn's relations with the bishops of Bangor and St Asaph reflect the pressures which he exerted upon his territorial lordship as a whole in the period leading up to 1277 as he strove to meet the extraordinary demands made upon his resources by the relentless pursuit of his political objectives. His letter to the archbishop in 1275 makes it clear that Bishop Anian had already impressed upon the primate the extent of the financial demands that Llywelyn was making upon the church.[134] Rights, liberties, customs: these had various connotations, but they were closely bound up with material interest. The disputes in the two dioceses provided the clearest evidence available to us from the fragmentary materials of the thirteenth century to illustrate the problems of jurisdiction which arose in the lordship of Snowdon, and the issues in contention are echoed in several clauses of the complaints against the defeated prince which were registered by secular communities, under the aegis of episcopal authority, in the summer of 1283.[135]

The extent to which Llywelyn ap Gruffudd shared jurisdiction with his lay tenants is extremely difficult to elicit from the surviving evidence. During the course of the twelfth and thirteenth centuries successive princes of Gwynedd

---

[132] Llywelyn's letter, ibid., 504; for the extent of written title, Pryce, *NLC*, 198, 239–40.
[133] *NLC*, 519–20. A strongly worded protection for the possessions of the monks of Ystrad Marchell, in which Anian authorized the excommunication of laity who committed injuries, is undated (*Charters of the Abbey of Ystrad Marchell*, no. 86); it is unclear at what lay persons the injunction was directed.
[134] Ibid., 505.
[135] Below, pp. 255–9.

certainly conceded estates to members of the dynasty. Thus Llywelyn ap Iorwerth, secure in his possession of the whole of Gwynedd, allowed his kinsman Hywel ap Gruffudd possession of Meirionnydd. No record of any transaction between the two men survives, but it is safe to surmise that whatever jurisdiction Hywel exercised in Meirionnydd was vested in him, not by reason of any inherent hereditary right, but by virtue of whatever status Llywelyn conferred upon him as one who held a dependency of the prince of Gwynedd.[136] Hywel's elegy, composed by Llywarch ap Llywelyn, commemorates him with due respect, and with some warmth, but in terms entirely appropriate to his standing as a vassal of Llywelyn.[137] Meirionnydd subsequently came to the lineage of Maredudd ap Cynan and was held from the crown until Llywelyn ap Gruffudd asserted his power over the whole of Gwynedd in 1256.[138] Whether Llywelyn ap Maredudd was at that point given an opportunity to become a feudatory of the prince of Gwynedd, or whether he was simply expelled from his lordship, we cannot tell. It is conceivable that Llywelyn ap Maredudd simply could not come to terms with the prospect of holding Meirionnydd as a fief within his kinsman's principality and made the departure which we have already noticed.[139] The fact that Llywelyn ap Gruffudd was prepared to tolerate the existence of a baronial estate of this nature within his dominion, or that he was constrained to accept its necessity, is indicated in his enfeoffment of his brother Dafydd ap Gruffudd with an estate in Perfeddwlad shortly after his annexation of the territory in 1256. Dafydd's subsequent defection, the problems which arose with regard to his position after his return to the prince's fealty, and his second defection may all point to his dissatisfaction with the extent of the lands conceded to him and nothing else. But Dafydd may also have been troubled by the degree of jurisdiction which he was allowed to exercise within those lands. We cannot tell whether problems arose over the respective jurisdictions of prince and mesne lord, or over the levying of taxes within the mesne lordship. It is, however, possible that postulating no more than a dispute over the extent of the territory which Dafydd was allowed entirely misconstrues the disaffection which underlies each of his two defections to the king of England.[140] We have

[136] Hywel secured possession by ousting his uncle Maredudd ap Cynan in 1202 (*BT, Pen20*, 147; *Pen20Tr*, 81; *RBH*, 184–5; HW, ii, 613, 622, 634, 647); his position as a feudatory of Llywelyn is implicit in the terms of the prince's submission in 1211 (J. B. Smith, 'Magna Carta and the charters of the Welsh princes', *EHR*, 99 (1984), 355; 361–2); for other members of the lineage for whom provision was made, J. B. Smith, 'Dynastic succession', 216–18.
[137] *GLlLl*, 13; see further, below, p. 289.
[138] J. B. Smith, 'Dynastic succession', 224–5; Stephenson, *GG*, 142–3.
[139] Above, p. 91.
[140] The creation of an estate for Dafydd, his defection and the restoration ordained by the treaty of Montgomery have been recounted; for subsequent difficulties over his estate, below, pp. 374–5.

no comparable evidence to guide us, for Llywelyn created no other estates within the confines of Gwynedd which approximated to baronies.[141] His relations with those who held baronies outside Gwynedd constitutes an altogether different matter and these are considered in the next chapter.[142]

Numerous grants of land were undoubtedly made, however, to favoured lineages among the freemen of Gwynedd, though we can deduce the manner by which they came into being only from the post-conquest extents. Many can be traced to the twelfth century and to the period of Llywelyn ap Iorwerth in the early thirteenth century. Evidently the grants were often extensive, they were invariably made in perpetuity, and they might be characterized by exoneration from dues and services and even exemption from military service. The lineage of Edryd ap Marchudd provides an instructive instance of generous early endowment in lands, lying both east and west of Conwy, which were subsequently enhanced by the bounteous grants which Llywelyn ap Iorwerth made to Ednyfed Fychan.[143] What became known as Wyrion Ednyfed tenure bore the hallmarks of privileged proprietorship.[144] This form of tenure stands out conspicuously in the fourteenth-century surveys of royal and marcher lands which depict the varying degrees of tenurial privilege vested in the proprietors. In each generation partible succession had taken its toll and many estates had been fragmented. But there were still a number of comparatively extensive estates vested in men who themselves had tenants, both bond and free, probably in some number. A few of these were subject to *quo warranto* inquiries: the estates of Hywel ap Goronwy at Penmynydd, Trecastell and Erddreiniog, of Llywelyn ap Goronwy Fychan at Trecastell and Gwredog, and of Ieuan ap Gruffudd at Tregarnedd and Dinorwig.[145] All were held under Wyrion Ednyfed tenure and in each case a steward held court on his lord's behalf. But the liberties exercised in these estates were of a very limited extent.[146] Again the descendants of Hwfa ap Cynddelw, an early beneficiary of the princes' largesse, shared the patronage of a 'portionary'

---

[141] He inherited a problem in Llŷn with the presence of Maredudd ap Richard, who appears to have held an extensive estate, before disappearing from view; above, pp. 57–8, 61.

[142] Below, pp. 285–301.

[143] D. H. Owen, 'Tenurial and economic developments in north Wales in the twelfth and thirteenth centuries', *WHR*, 6 (1972–3), 120–6, 133–4, 140, discusses this lineage and others, such as Rhawd Fychan, Marchweithian and Braint Hir, with references to earlier studies.

[144] G. Roberts, *Aspects of Welsh History*, 181–4; Carr, *MAng*, 72, 174, 203.

[145] Wyrion Ednyfed' tenure is well described in Trecastell (cmt Dindaethwy), 1352, when Hywel ap Goronwy and Tudur ap Goronwy rendered nothing in rent nor relief; one tenant 'de natura Werion Eden[eved]' went to war for the whole lineage (*sanguina*) of Ednyfed, at his own costs in the march of Wales and his lord's costs further afield (*RC*, 73); cf. Cororion (cmt Arllechwedd Uchaf) and Gwredog (cmt Twrcelyn, *RC*, 12–13, 69).

[146] Llywelyn ap Goronwy Fychan claimed his free court (*curia libera*) in Trecastell and was allowed to exercise his right as he claimed only cognizance of the pleas of his bondmen (*RC*, 168–9).

church and this might be seen as approximating to a seigniorial right, but otherwise their rights were exceedingly limited.[147] Even the best endowed of the freemen – the *nobiles* or *optimates* of the Latin sources, the *uchelwyr* of the Welsh texts – enjoyed what can best be described as proprietary rights. They were men nevertheless who belonged to lineages intensely protective of their interests, sensitive to any erosion of their position of privilege, and there is much to suggest that Llywelyn ap Gruffudd's position in the stressful years of the period leading up to 1277 was not made easy by the resentment and anxieties nurtured among members of this milieu in society. They might exercise an authority over tenants, both bondmen and freemen, which could be described in the law texts as lordship (*arglwyddiaeth*).[148] But the problems they encountered, and in turn posed for their prince, were of a tenurial rather than a franchisal nature.[149] The *nobiles* who, in the summer of 1283, expressed their disapproval of the manner in which they had been ruled by their late prince may be regarded as proprietors, their disaffection arising from the manner in which his rule had affected their proprietary rights. Extensive rights of jurisdiction were never at issue. To the extent that the lord of Snowdon shared his lordship at all, he may be said to have done so with the church, the monasteries and religious houses, but with a very few laymen. It enabled him to exercise a direct lordship over the vast majority of those who formed the communities of the commotes and *cantrefi* between the Dee and the Dyfi. It probably proved to be an increasingly exacting lordship, an authority which created a stressful relationship with proprietors who may have enjoyed a comparatively favoured position but who, rightly or wrongly, saw themselves exposed to the avarice of their prince. The numbers involved

---

[147] Rights claimed by the *lignages* of Hwfa ap Cynddelw and Llywarch ap Brân and their division among numerous heirs are reflected in *CAP*, 453; E315/166, f. 5a–b; *RC*, 246–8; cf. A. N. Palmer, 'The portionary churches of medieval north Wales', *ArchCamb*, 5th ser., 3 (1886), 175–209; Carr, *MAng*, 278–9. Hwfa ap Cynddelw lands were mainly concentrated at Conysiog (cmt Llifon), Llywarch ap Brân lands at Trellywarch (cmt Talybolion, *RC*, 51, 56 *et passim*; Pierce, *MWS*, 261–4; Carr, *MAng*, 152–5, 214–16).

[148] E.g. a freeman might exercise lordship (*arglwyddiaeth*) over his 'aliens' or advowry tenants (*alltudion*) even when they became proprietors (*priodorion*); see *LlIor*, 58; *LHD*, 114; *LlCol*, 38. The survey of Rhos and Rhufoniog (e.g. *SD*, 46–7) provides plenteous evidence of such tenancies. Llywelyn's denial to the freemen of the rights they previously exercised over advowry tenants (*homines advocationes*), thereby undermining their authority (*potestas*), was held against him in 1283, and there was similar concern over the rights of freemen to the goods of intestate tenants, especially bondmen (below, nn. 320, 328).

[149] D. Jenkins, 'Kings, lords and princes: the nomenclature of authority in thirteenth-century Wales', *B*, 26 (1974–6), 459, suggests an 'increasing importance of franchisal jurisdiction in thirteenth-century Gwynedd', showing that whereas in the Cyfnerth and Blegywryd texts (derived from Deheubarth) the ruler who enforces the law is normally, if not always, the king (*brenin*), in *LlIor* and even more clearly in *LlCol* he is often lord (*arglwydd*) in sections dealing with contract, criminal law and land law. This is an important matter; regrettably, it is difficult to find record evidence of extensive jurisdictions exercised in Gwynedd by others than the princes.

Lord of Snowdon

in overt political defection in 1277 may not have been large, and it might be easy to overstate its extent, but the defectors may conceivably have represented a broader disaffection. The problems which confronted Llywelyn in his relations with the communities of his lordship of Snowdon will be considered further when we have examined the manner in which he exploited the resources of that lordship and the extent to which his income is likely to have matched his expenditure.

The lord's courts and demesne lands

Llywelyn ap Gruffudd's allusion to the barrenness of his land is paralleled in numerous references in chronicles and other writings to the wilderness of Snowdonia or the rugged heights of Meirionnydd. The capacity of Gwynedd to sustain a relatively stable kingship had rested to some degree on the military advantages provided by its mountain massif, but it had depended more on the capacity of successive generations of rulers and ruled to manage its resources to the best possible advantage. This was a responsibility shared between the lord of Snowdon and his tenants, be those resources primarily arable or pastoral. The surviving documentary evidence, necessarily studied with an awareness of the nature of the landscape, reveals an economic order fashioned by the response of lord and proprietor to the potentiality and limitations of their varied terrain. Of the extent of that variation, both its broad and local contrasts, there can be no doubt, but its precise implications for the economy in the thirteenth century are less easy to judge. Estimates of the comparative wealth of various parts of Gwynedd have to be based on a very limited range of materials, and these are themselves exceedingly difficult to interpret and are derived almost entirely from the post-conquest period: the extents of various dates already noticed, account rolls unevenly distributed in time and area; estimates of ecclesiastical income and, though mainly helpful to a study of Merioneth, an assessment of the moveable property of the crown's tenants for 1292–3.[150] The broader contrasts in the nature of the terrain of Gwynedd are inevitably reflected in the evidence, but to make clear differentiations between entirely distinct economic modes would be unwise. Any distinction between 'arable' and 'pastoral' zones needs to be expressed in guarded terms. The capacity for grain production in Anglesey cannot be denied, and the alacrity with which Edward I dispatched

---

[150] K. Williams-Jones, in *MLSR*, lxviii–lxxxv; G. R. J. Jones, 'The impact of state policy on the rural landscape of Gwynedd in the thirteenth century', in H.-J. Nitz (ed.), *The Medieval and Early Modern Rural Landscape of Europe under the Impact of the Commercial Economy* (Göttingen, 1987), 16–20; both studies examine the assessments of movable wealth, 1292–3, and the valuations of clerical income, 1254, in *Valuation of Norwich*, 190–6, 467–73.

his reapers to the island in 1277 and again in 1282, careful not to destroy the crops but to reap them for the benefit of his own troops, reflects his awareness of the value of a resource which mattered immensely to the prince of Wales.[151] But evidence noticed later shows that the economy of the prince's demesnes on the island, and that of the proprietors likewise, was based not only on the production of grain (and a good part of it in wheat) but the rearing of cattle and, to a lesser extent, of sheep. In marked contrast, Merioneth was an area with a high proportion of its surface consisting of moorland where prince and proprietor would need to concentrate on stock-raising, with cattle again preponderating.[152] It is no matter of surprise that the king's officers were able to find herds of cattle in Penllyn and have them driven towards Rhuddlan, so that his soldiers were fed from a resource which had been carefully nourished to meet the needs of his opponents.[153] But if Penllyn was conspicuously a commote of pastoral farming, nearby Edeirnion was one which provided the means for a balanced exploitation of arable and pastoral resources. There Edward's men found a veritable lair, with a plenitude of corn and beasts stored up for the war needs of the defenders.[154] A comparatively densely populated commote with a noticeably high taxable capacity, Edeirnion was the richest commote in Merioneth, but the endeavour to maximize the arable and pastoral resources of a terrain of more limited potential may be demonstrated from the evidence for a commote such as Tal-y-bont. Where the documentary evidence is sufficient to provide any kind of basis for statistical study it points, as might be expected, to an endeavour to use the resources of the locality in the way most likely to yield the best results. In the following paragraphs we shall consider the prince's direct exploitation of his lands and then examine the manner in which he drew upon the resources generated by his tenants' husbandry.

Documentary sources derived from the period following the conquest provide, despite indications of a changing economic order, enough to corroborate the essentials of the lawbooks' depiction of the demesne exploitation which maintained a ruler's entourage. There is no doubt whatsoever that Llywelyn ap Gruffudd maintained a court which was itinerant for at least part of the year. The places where his letters and documents are dated are various. He can on occasion be found at a Cistercian grange. An important meeting of his council was held at the Cymer grange of Abereiddon in the summer of 1275, and Llywelyn appears to have favoured another of the abbey's granges

---

[151] Below, pp. 427–8, 526.
[152] These matters are examined below, pp. 231–4, 239–41.
[153] Edward's use of his opponents' cattle in time of war is noticed below, p. 428.
[154] *CAC*, 172; below, p. 246.

at Dinas Teleri.[155] Letters are dated, too, at the Aberconwy granges of Hafod-y-llan and Llanfair Rhyd Castell.[156] Llywelyn resided at some, at least, of his castles, certainly at Criciech and Dolwyddelan.[157] But the surviving material, though it is much too slight to provide the means of establishing the prince's itinerary, suggests that he relied mainly upon the resources of the courts which were the foci of commote jurisdiction and fiscal obligation and, particularly relevant in the present discussion, the centres of seigniorial exploitation. In Anglesey, apart from indications of his presence at Aberffraw, he is found at Penrhos in Twrcelyn, and Llan-faes in Dindaethwy.[158] On the mainland of Uwch Conwy he is known to have resided at Aber in Uwch Gwyrfai, Caernarfon in Is Gwyrfai, Nefyn in Dinllaen, Ystumgwern in Arudwy and at the courts of Tal-y-bont at Llanegryn and of Ystumanner, probably at Pennal.[159] In Perfeddwlad the evidence is slight, but the prince is found at Dinorben in Is Dulas, Dinbych in Is Aled, Clocaenog in Colion, and Sychdyn in Coleshill.[160] For some of those locations documentary evidence is meagre, but the arrangements at the centres for which the post-conquest materials provide the most helpful information make it possible to establish some knowledge of the prince's direct exploitation of the resources of his territory.

Whereas Llywelyn ap Iorwerth embodied the title 'prince of Aberffraw' in his style, Llywelyn ap Gruffudd decided differently, but the poets' references show that Aberffraw retained its emotive significance to the very end.[161] To what extent the ancient royal court remained an important centre of princely rule is less clear, nor can the post-conquest materials tell us with certainty

---

[155] *LW*, 32, 40, 44–5; *CAC*, 27–8, 75, 85–8. Abereiddon was at, or close by, the site of the present Hengwrt Uchaf (OS 800219) par. Llanfachreth, cmt Tal-y-bont (M. O. Griffith, 'Abereiddon and Esgaireiddon', *JMerHRS*, 9 (1981–4), 367–89). Dinas Teleri has not been identified; Peter Crew has noticed south-west of Craig y Dinas, near Dol-cyn-afon (SH795285), some field banks which could, he suggests, mark the site of the grange.

[156] *LW*, 25, 174–5; *CAC*, 95, 126–7, 161–2; Gresham, 'Aberconwy charter: further consideration', 323–4, 332–8, for Llanfair Rhyd Gastell and Nanhwynan, including Hafod-y-llan, also noticed below, n. 213.

[157] *LW*, 33, 43; *CAC*, 92–3; *RC*, 211.

[158] *LW*, 31, 33–5, 43; *CAC*, 75–6, 89–90, 111–12. For Llywelyn ap Iorwerth at Rhosyr and Dafydd ap Llywelyn at Cemais, *MonAng*, iv, 582; Stephenson, *GG*, 203; *H*, no. 140–1. For the location of the courts of Gwynedd Uwch Conwy, N. Johnstone, *Llys and Maerdref: An Investigation into the Location of the Royal Courts of the Princes of Gwynedd* (Bangor, Gwynedd Archaeological Trust, Report no. 167, 1995); idem, 'An investigation into the location of the royal courts of thirteenth-century Gwynedd', in N. Edwards (ed.), *Landscape and Settlement in Medieval Wales* (Oxford, 1997), 149–87.

[159] *LW*, 42–3, 45–6, 77–80, 160–1; *CAC*, 76–7, 84–5, 90–6, 163; *Councils*, i, 508. For Garthcelyn, below, pp. 233–4, 536, 543.

[160] *LW*, 26, 39–40; *CAC*, 28, 86, 94; *Registrum Thome de Cantilupo*, 9. Locations include Sychtyn, Sychtyn near Ewloe, Sychtyn near Mold as well as Mold; the prince's presence with his vice-chamberlain at Clocaenog suggests he had a court there.

[161] *GBF*, 24. 107; 36. 2, 36, 103; 48. 18; 51. 36; *Oxford Book of Welsh Verse*, ed. T. Parry (Oxford, 1962), 45–9; trans. *Oxford Book of Welsh Verse in English*, 31–3.

whether the classic form of demesne exploitation described in the lawbooks was maintained there. The lawyers' texts would lead us to expect, in association with the court, a bond township organized on manorial lines as a *tref gyfrif*. Direct exploitation of the demesne land (*tir bwrdd*) would be entrusted to the lord's officers, the land (*tir cyfrif*) apportioned to the bondmen shared equally (*per capita*) among the male tenants, with the obligations placed upon the township likewise shared among them.[162] A major *tref gyfrif* associated with a royal court, Aberffraw would be a *maerdref* with which other *tir cyfrif* townships might be linked in an integrated system of provisioning.[163] The extent made promptly upon the cessation of hostilities reveals several key features of this manorial structure. Demesne cultivation, with five carucates of arable (each probably of 60 acres), and *tir cyfrif* tenure are indicated both at Aberffraw and at the associated hamlets of Trecastell, Treberfedd and Dinllwydan along with tenants' circuit dues payable at the court. Additionally, Aberffraw had evidently been at the centre of a wider provisioning arrangement involving both bondmen and freemen.[164] Bondmen holding land, not in *tir cyfrif* tenure but in the *tir gwelyog* tenure which allowed them hereditary succession to their lands, fulfilled obligations centred on Aberffraw. Thus, among others, the bondmen of Tref Feibion Meurig in the commote of Llifon were obliged to maintain the walls about the *manerium* of Aberffraw and the fabric of hall and chamber, and were liable to circuit dues described as *potura* or *procuratio*.[165] In the same commote, among the freemen who contributed services, members of the well-endowed lineage of Hwfa ap Cynddelw were liable to contribute to work on the hall and chamber of Aberffraw and the circuit obligation of *cylch stalwyn*. The existence, in townships such as Rhosmor and Treberfedd, of both *tir cyfrif* and *tir gwelyog* bondmen indicates some degree of shift away from demesne cultivation and some amelioration of bond tenure in the two commotes of Malltraeth and Llifon which were linked with Aberffraw.[166] But the evidence suggests very

---

[162] *Tref gyfrif* is the 'reckoned land township'; *tir cyfrif* is the 'reckoned land'.

[163] *Tref gyfrif* features are indicated in e.g. *LlIor*, 54, 62–3; *LHD*, 100, 125–6; *LlCol*, 36, 40–1; commentaries include Pierce, *MWS*, 275–9; Carr, *MAng*, 30–5; G. R. J. Jones, 'The tribal system in Wales: a re-assessment in the light of settlement studies', *WHR*, 1 (1960–3), 119–22; idem, 'Field systems in north Wales', in A. R. H. Baker and R. A. Butlin (eds.), *Studies of Field Systems in the British Isles* (Cambridge, 1973), 434, 460–71; idem, 'Forms and patterns of medieval settlement in Welsh Wales', in D. Hooke (ed.) *Medieval Villages* (Oxford, University Committee for Archaeology, 1985), 158–63.

[164] Idem, 'The multiple estate: a model for tracing the inter-relationships of society, economy and habitat', in K. Biddick (ed.), *Archaeological Approaches to Medieval Europe* (Kalamazoo, 1984), 9–41. For *tir bwrdd*, idem, 'Models for organization', 110–16.

[165] *ExtAngl*, 8–9; *RC*, 54; Carr, *MAng*, 142–3.

[166] G. R. J. Jones, 'The distribution of medieval settlement in Anglesey', *TAngAS*, 1955, 81–4; idem, 'Rural settlement in Anglesey', in G. R. J. Jones and S. J. Eyre (eds.), *Geography as Human Ecology* (London, 1966), 211–14. For the elusive archaeology of Aberffraw, Johnstone, *Llys and Maerdref*, 17–22, and references cited. Timber from the hall

strongly that demesne exploitation had been an essential feature of the prince's economic management up to the eve of the final conquest, and that the needs of the court were also met, from the associated townships, by contributory services and dues fulfilled by bondmen under *tir gwelyog* as well as *tir cyfrif* conditions and by freemen.[167]

Comparable arrangements may be discerned at other Anglesey courts. At Penrhos the *maerdref* was the focus in the commote of Twrcelyn for the works of the *tir cyfrif* bondmen of Bodunod and Rhosmynach, and of members of free lineages in townships such as Llysdulas and Bodafon.[168] *Tir cyfrif* and *tir gwelyog* bondmen, and freemen too, in the commote of Talybolion contributed to works at Cemais, and similarly those of the commote of Menai did so at Rhosyr.[169] In the same way the procuration charges centred on the courts, which will be considered separately, were widely shared in the communities. Thus, in the several townships in Talybolion occupied by free *gwelyau*, circuit dues, such as *cylch stalwyn* and *cylch dyfrgwn*, are recorded as obligations linked to the need to provide for the needs of the prince's entourage at Cemais. The lands concerned may in some cases have been subtracted from what had previously been *tir cyfrif* townships worked directly for the princes. This had sometimes been done to the complete eradication of *tir cyfrif* conditions, as was the case in Mathafarn Eithaf or Mathafarn Wion, sometimes their partial removal, as in Bodynog, but the need to maintain the prince's court remained.[170] In the commote of Menai liabilities related to demesne cultivation borne by the bond tenants of the *maerdref* of Rhosyr were to some degree replicated not only in the *tir cyfrif* townships of Dinan and Hirdre-faig but in the bond *tir gwelyog* township of Treferwydd and in the free township of Trefioseth. During the last phase of the period of the princes the classic pattern of direct seigniorial exploitation of a central demesne manor at a *maerdref*, with subsidiary demesnes at other *tir cyfrif* townships, had been considerably modified both by changes in the status of some bond communities (making them contributors to the prince's needs by their fiscal obligations rather than mainly by their labour) and by ceding to freemen fractions of townships or entire townships. There was certainly some diminution in the extent of the land worked under *tir cyfrif* conditions. One effect was the loosening, though not the severing, of the links between the *maerdref* and its associated townships, another was change in the nature of

---

and other buildings formerly of the prince at Aberffraw ('de aula et aliis domibus quondam principis apud Aberffraw') was removed to Caernarfon castle in 1317 (SC6/1211/7; *HKW*, i, 386, n. 4; *Inventory Caern*, ii, 125).
[167] Bond hereditary tenure is described in Pierce, *MWS*, 274–6; Jones, 'Medieval settlement in Anglesey', 56–7.
[168] *ExtAng*, 13–14; *RC*, 65–72.
[169] *ExtAng*, 11–13, 17–21; *RC*, 56–65, 78–85.
[170] Instances are noticed later.

the *maerdref* itself. The appearance at Cemais and Penrhos, albeit in the extent of 1352, of bondmen described as *gwŷr mâl*, *gwŷr gwaith* and *gwŷr tir bwrdd* may point to the differentiation between monetary dues, contributory labour and demesne labour which can probably be attributed to changes in economic management undertaken by the princes.[171] A partial commutation of services and dues into money payments had been a feature of the process of change, probably for a considerable time.[172] At Llan-faes, the centre for the commote of Dindaethwy, the *maerdref* developed distinctly commercial, even urban, features which are considered presently.[173] The Anglesey evidence certainly points to processes of change in the seigniorial economy of the princes and some measure of breach with traditional modes, but there is still much to suggest a constant effort, possibly intensified in the later years of the princes' rule, to maximize the direct exploitation of the resources of the commotes.[174] It may well have been linked with an insistence, in certain connections, that fiscal obligations be met in kind rather than in money payments.[175] There is certainly much to suggest, from the evidence of the valuable grain-producing commotes of Anglesey, that the prince's itinerary was to a large extent determined by his need to avail himself of the economic resources of the demesnes associated with his courts, supplemented by his tenants' fiscal obligations which were similarly focused upon them. Courts such as Aberffraw and Cemais, where poets had addressed their royal patrons in the twelfth century, were still important centres of the prince's lordship a century later.[176] The substantial remains recently revealed by excavation at Rhosyr provide, for the first time, an indication of the arrangement and extent of the courts that Llywelyn ap Gruffudd visited upon his itinerary of his patrimonial lands.

The pattern which may be recognized in Anglesey, whereby the court was located at a main demesne whose resources were enhanced by those of associated contributory demesnes, may be traced elsewhere. Perfeddwlad, like Anglesey, included areas well suited to demesne cultivation on a comparatively substantial scale. The surveyor who made the extent of Rhos and Rhufoniog half a century after the conquest notes that his lord had 'of ancient

---

[171] *RC*, 63, 70; Carr, *Extent*, 210–15; Pierce, *MWS*, 278–9; Carr, *MAng*, 134–5, 138–41; Stephenson, *GG*, 59–60; Jones, 'Models for organisation', 114–15.

[172] Commutation is examined below, pp. 241–6.

[173] Below, pp. 243–4.

[174] Jones, 'Impact of state policy', 20, suspects increased exploitation at Cemais, Rhosyr and Penrhos before the conquest.

[175] Below, n. 261.

[176] References in poetry include *GMB*, 3, 8, 9; *GLlF*, 24, 27, 28; *GLlLl*, 4, 9, 17, 23, 25; *GCBM*, ii, 6.80; discussion in M. E. Owen, 'Literary convention and historical reality: the court in the Welsh poetry of the twelfth and thirteenth centuries', *Études Celtiques*, 22 (1992), 69–85. Edward I dated letters at Aberffraw, Penrhos and Rhosyr in 1283.

demesne' (*de veteri dominico*) only the manor (*manerium*) of Dinorben Fawr, and the features he described bore the unmistakable signs of a *maerdref* of the period of the princes.[177] There was by then no mention of the hall at which Prince Llewelyn would have been accommodated upon his coming to Rhos Is Dulas, but there were other buildings – two granges, a byre and a granary among them – which reflected the needs of demesne cultivation. There were then some 200 acres of arable in demesne, with 22 acres of meadow and 72 acres of pasture and some woodland. Direct exploitation of the demesne was maintained by hired labour, but the surveyor observed that in the time of the princes the *maerdref* of Dinorben Fawr had been worked by bondmen who performed services at the *manerium*.[178] Whether the use of hired labour and the concession of hereditary tenure to the bondmen were features of the period of the princes is uncertain, but what matters is that the evidence from 1334 describes several essential facets of the method of direct exploitation pursued by princes in the thirteenth century.[179] Dinorben Fawr had certainly been, too, the centre of a broader organization of bond services in the commote of Is Dulas, for ploughing and harrowing, as well as construction works at the *maerdref*, were shared by bond communities at Dinorben Fychan, Cegidog and Meifod. Detailed references to the agricultural obligations of the tenants of this commote provide the basis for conclusions which, in many other areas, have to be based on more residual indications of an economic order once based upon seigniorial exploitation of a central *maerdref* and associated demesnes.[180] The surveyor notes that in the case of the commote of Ceinmeirch the only demesne which the princes had possessed was Ystrad Owain. There, centred on a cluster of buildings comparable to those at Dinorben – two granges, a byre and a sheep-fold – was a *manerium* consisting of a demesne of 267 acres of arable and smaller areas of meadow and pasture.[181] Elsewhere in Rhos and Rhufoniog there were no lands in demesne, and the arrangements which had once been made at Dinbych and Cilcennis, probably the *maerdrefi* of Is Aled and Uwch Dulas,

---

[177] *SD*, 210.
[178] *SD*, 230–3; DL29/1/2 gives evidence of extensive demesne cultivation in 1304–5. For Llywelyn's presence, 1273, *CAC*, 86.
[179] *SD*, 232. Cultivation by the division of land into three 'seasons' (*seisona*) in 1334 may not reflect pre-conquest practice, and it is possible that the acreage in demesne may have been extended since the conquest. For a review of pre-conquest and post-conquest manors, Owen, 'Lordship of Denbigh', 209–27.
[180] *SD*, 222–9, 270; Owen, 'Tenurial developments', 118–19; G. R. J. Jones, 'The pattern of medieval settlement in the commote of Rhos Is Dulas and its antecedents', in W. Pinkwart (ed.), *Genetische Ansätze in der Kulturlandschaftsforschung* (Würzburg, 1983), 41–50; idem, 'Field systems of north Wales', 465–71; for possible continuity between the economy centred on the hill-fort of Dinorben and that of the *maerdref*, idem, 'Tribal system', 129–38.
[181] *SD*, 2–3, 44–6.

respectively, are barely traceable in the surviving record. The tenants of Is Aled, however, acknowledge that in the time of the princes bond and free tenants built and maintained at Dinbych a hall, an en suite chamber, a chapel and an enclosure about the prince's court.[182] In no case is the relationship of *maerdref* and associated demesnes as clear as it is in the case of Dinorben Fawr, nor can *tir cyfrif* tenure be readily identified. There were, even so, extensive bond settlements upon the coast, in townships such as Mochdre and Rhiw in Uwch Dulas, and along river valleys, in townships including Llech Talhaearn or Caledan in Uwch Aled or Segrwyd, Prior or Postyn in Ceinmeirch, where in the thirteenth century demesne cultivation may well have been organized in accordance with *tir cyfrif* precepts.[183] Beyond Rhos and Rhufoniog, in the commotes of the two *cantrefi* of Dyffryn Clwyd and Tegeingl, the princes' courts and the demesnes which sustained them remain more elusive. But even the tenuous evidence which we have for these areas suggests that the prince's presence at Clocaenog in the commote of Colion in Dyffryn Clwyd, or at Sychdyn in the commote of Coleshill in Tegeingl, or at Ewloe, reflects his wish to avail himself of the resources of areas of demesne production comparable to those which are better documented elsewhere.[184] The commotes of Gwynedd Is Conwy provide, moreover, not only testimony to the wish of the princes to maximize the resources of demesnes suited to agricultural production, but to their determination to use and develop the assets of the broad stretches of moorland, notably those of Mynydd Hiraethog, which were best suited to pasturage. It is a form of seigniorial investment which commends itself for particular notice in a study of the arrangements which may be discerned in the upland areas of Gwynedd Uwch Conwy.[185]

The mainland of Gwynedd Uwch Conwy was the hub of the prince's dominion and he made extensive use of its courts.[186] These were sustained by the same pattern of central *maerdref* demesne and ancillary demesnes as that

---

[182] *SD*, 52–7, 149, 275. Provision for construction of buildings (*domos*) is recorded in Ceinmeirch, Uwch Aled and Uwch Dulas (*SD*, 50, 209, 313), but with no indication of their location.

[183] *SD*, 7–9, 18–20, 25–7, 306–14; Owen, 'Tenurial developments', 119–20, notes, for instance, townships of 1,200 acres at Prion and 1,000 acres at Postyn.

[184] For Llywelyn's presence at Clocaenog and Sychtyn, above, n. 160. A cluster of customary tenants at Clocaenog in 1324 (Jack, 'Lordship of Dyffryn Clwyd', 50–3; court roll references, e.g. SC2/219/13, mm. 13, 28) possibly point to an earlier demesne; R. R. Davies, *Lordship and Society*, 108, notes in Dyffryn Clwyd seigniorial manors at Rhuthun, Llysfasi, Bathafarn, Maesmynan and possibly at Aberchwiler and Penbedw. At Ewloe there were 480 acres of arable in demesne in 1295 and it had a high taxation value (Jones, 'Impact of state policy', 20, from C145/55/2; E179/242/52).

[185] These features, and the opportunities for investment noticed by the surveyor, Hugh de Beckley, are noticed below, n. 208.

[186] Above, n. 159.

revealed in the areas already considered. Of the three commotes of Llŷn, Cymydmaen was centred at Neigwl, Cafflogion at Pwllheli and Dinllaen at Nefyn, the earliest surviving evidence indicating that bond and free communities in each commote were held liable to contribute to the maintenance of court buildings, a responsibility that was probably a residuary relic of what had previously been a wide range of communal responsibilities.[187] Similar arrangements may be discerned in Eifionydd, with the original focus probably located at Dolbenmaen, and in Arfon Is Gwyrfai and Arfon Uwch Gwyrfai.[188] In the case of Dinllaen, for instance, the resources of the *maerdref* at Nefyn were supplemented by those of other *tir cyfrif* townships at Trefgoed, Hirdref, Buan and Bleiddiog. The abandonment of demesne exploitation makes it impossible to judge either the extent or the precise nature of the prince's economic arrangements, but the renders for which the proprietors of these commotes were responsible and, in the case of Cafflogion, the survival of a detailed record of their possessions at the end of the thirteenth century, suggest very strongly that the demesnes were characterized by a close integration of crop and animal husbandry upon lands which carried a substantial bond population organized very largely under *tir cyfrif* conditions.[189]

A close integration of tillage and stock is suggested, too, in the southern commotes of Tal-y-bont and Ystumanner, Ardudwy and Penllyn. These were not conspicuously fertile lands, yet they counted among the prince's assets and were included in his itinerary. In Tal-y-bont, where the court was located at Llanegryn, and Ystumanner, probably centred at Pennal, provision was made for maintenance of buildings and the sustenance of prince and entourage.[190] For despite the fact that Castell y Bere was located in a position

---

[187] *RC*, 27–38.

[188] *RC*, 39–43. It is likely that services had earlier been centred at Dolbenmaen, the only *tref gyfrif* in Eifionydd in 1352; the concentration of services on Cricieth (*RC*, 39) may not have been a pre-conquest feature, though J. E. Lloyd, 'Medieval Eifionydd', *ArchCamb*, 6th ser., 5 (1905), 296–9, and T. Jones Pierce, quoted *TCaernHS*, 17 (1956), 24, n. 4, favoured a transfer of services to Cricieth before the conquest. For Dolbenmaen, Gresham, *Eifionydd*, 371–3; Johnstone, *Llys and Maerdref*, 35–6; its motte, *Inventory Caern*, II, 74. For Is Gwyrfai and Uwch Gwyrfai, below, n. 204.

[189] Below, pp. 239–41

[190] *ExtMer*, 184–91. The court of Tal-y-bont, where letters of the prince were dated in 1275, 1278–9 (*CAC*, 93; *Councils*, i, 508), was probably located close by the motte of Tomen Ddreiniog, Llanegryn (King, *CA*, 277). There were 2 carucates of arable in demesne in 1284 (*ExtMer*, 184–6). Letters were dated at Ystumanner in 1263, 1278–81 by Llywelyn and Eleanor (*LW*, 77–80; *CAC*, 76, 95–6). There was a demesne, and some commercial activity, at Tywyn, but the centre of the commote was probably at Pennal, where there were 3 carucates in demesne in 1284 (*ExtMer*, 186); for Pennal, G. R. J. Jones, 'Die Entwicklung der landlichen Besiedlung in Wales', *Zeitschrift für Agrargeschichte und Agrarosoziologie*, 10 (Frankfurt am Main, 1962), 191–4). An inquiry, 1308, concerning the court of Ystumanner (*CIM*, ii, 49) does not record its location.

central to the two commotes of Meirionnydd, and appears to have been provided with refinements suggestive of princely residence, the extents preserve a record of arrangements made in expectation of the prince's coming to the courts of the two commotes rather than to the castle, and Llywelyn can indeed be shown to have dated letters at Tal-y-bont and Ystumanner.[191] The arable in demesne, at the date of the earliest evidence, consisted of only a few carucates, with the lord's income derived very largely from the rents and renders of his tenants. These reflect a balance between arable and pasture, proportions that were probably reflected in the prince's demesne exploitation, and the resources of the land were enough to maintain a high valuation in the assessment made after the conquest. The arable lands in the environs of the courts and elsewhere were complemented by the *vaccaria*, or cattle farms, placed at some distance from the main demesne. In Tal-y-bont the pastures of Nancaw and Cefnteilo had been leased by 1284, and another three vaccaries capable of maintaining 120 cows between them were by then denuded of beasts, but the surveyor's intimation of the profit that might accrue to the king if he had his own beasts suggest that the prince had recently availed himself of this resource. In Ystumanner, too, the vaccaries had been leased, but they had evidently been important features of demesne exploitation here and in Ardudwy.[192]

The commote of Ardudwy was centred at Ystumgwern, and letters bearing either of these names can be assumed to have been written at the court, located in close proximity to the *maerdref*, whose hall was subsequently removed and reconstructed within the walls of the castle of Harlech.[193] Ardudwy was an extensive commote, with a marked contrast between its lowland and upland parts. The demesne at Ystumgwern was quite diminutive in 1284, the vast majority of the bondmen, who formed a substantial portion of the population of Ardudwy, holding their lands in *gafaelion* on terms similar to those conceded to the bondmen who held their lands in *gwelyau*.[194] The bond tenants of Llanengan, Llanaber and Llanddwywe, who owed suit at the mill of Ystumgwern, thereby fulfilled a vestige of what their predecessors

---

[191] E.g. obligations *de preconibus* in Tal-y-bont (*ExtMer*, 184) recall the passage *de iure preconibus* describing remuneration of the *rhingyll* in *LTWL*, 119, 209; cf. *LlIor*, 19; *LHD*, 34. Apart from a carucate of arable 'about the castle of Bere', a castle meadow and minor obligations 'which pertain to the castle', there is no reference in the extent to Castell y Bere.

[192] *ExtMer*, 185, 187. Llywelyn is described as *llew Nancoel, llurig Nancaw* ('lion of Nancoel, Nancaw's mail') in the elegy by Gruffudd ab yr Ynad Coch. Nancaw may be located at SH657094, less than 1 mile from Castell y Bere; Nancol, where there was a demesne (SH641273), is noticed presently.

[193] *LW*, 45–6 (Ystumgwern, 1281); *CAC*, 92 (Ardudwy, 1275–76). The hall, 18′ × 37′, was moved from Ystumgwern to Harlech (C. R. Peers, 'Harlech Castle', *THSC*, 1921–2, 63–82).

[194] *ExtMer*, 189–91; *RC*, 277–92; C. A. Gresham,'Ystumgwern and Prysor: medieval administrative districts of Ardudwy', *JMerHRS*, 10 (1985–9), 100–18, 221–6.

had once fulfilled as *tir cyfrif* tenants. The arrentation of these lands to be held in *gafaelion*, and the denoting of some tenants as *gwŷr mâl*, may have been made in the period of the princes to ensure profitable exploitation of the small and dispersed demesne lands of a somewhat unpropitious terrain. There are several indications of an intensive arable exploitation of the narrow coastal strip of Ardudwy where tillage was productive.[195] This was complemented by the demesne pastures, such as those at Nancol on the slopes of the Rhinog.[196] The prince's demesne thus embraced a lowland and upland terrain, with an opportunity for a short-distance transhumance which may have constituted a factor of some consequence in the economy of numerous areas of the lordship of Snowdon. Still more significant, perhaps, was the creation of foci for the exploitation of the moorland pastures in that terrain itself. A small demesne at Prysor marked the nucleus of an upland settlement, close by the castle built to protect the approach to Ardudwy from the east and with *gwŷr mâl* and other tenants holdings lands in *gafaelion*, linked with the vaccaries of Prysor itself, Bryn-coch, Y Feidiog and Glasynys.[197] In Ardudwy strategic needs intensified the search for the fullest possible exploitation of the land, whatever its potential might be. Beyond Ardudwy, in the commote of Penllyn, also included in the prince's itinerary, arable farming was limited in extent so that livestock, and more especially cattle production, was the mainstay of seigniorial and proprietorial economies alike. Arable resources were, even so, developed at Bala and at other demesnes at Penmaen, Crogen and elsewhere. Upland vaccaries, again denuded of their beasts during the conflict, along with heavy *porthiant* charges imposed upon bond and free tenants, had evidently contributed substantially to the prince's efforts to provide for his needs in peace and war.[198]

The princes' endeavours to fortify their position by enhancing the natural advantages of their mountain bastions are best represented by the stone-built castles of Dolwyddelan in Nanconwy and Dolbadarn in Is Gwyrfai.[199] Sited for strategic reasons, and thereby placed in areas of limited resources, these castles had need to be supplied by a commissariat provision which may have

---

[195] D. Hooke, 'Llanaber, a study in landscape development', *JMerHRS*, 7 (1973–6), 221–30; idem, 'The Ardudwy landscape', *JMerHRS*, 9 (1981–4), 246–52.

[196] *ExtMer*, 189.

[197] *ExtMer*, 189–90. For the castle at Prysor (SH758369), King *CA*, 276; C. A. Gresham and W. J. Hemp, 'Castell Prysor', *ArchCamb*, 100 (1949), 312–13; Avent, 'Castles of the Welsh princes', 12. Edward I was at Prysor in June–July 1284 (*LW*, 170; E101/359/9).

[198] *CAC*, 845, 93–4, letters dated Bala, 1274–7 and Penllyn, 1279. The extent records that 16 carucates in Penllyn had been wasted in war and vaccaries had been emptied (*ExtMer*, 187, 189); for cattle in the proprietors' economy, below, nn. 240–4.

[199] *Inventory Caern*, I, 80–2; II, 165–8; King, *CA*, 34; Avent, 'Castles', 14–15; idem, *Dolwyddelan Castle. Dolbadarn Castle* (Cardiff, 1994); C. J. Spurgeon, 'Dolbadarn: the castle', in P. Joyner (ed.), *Dolbadarn: Studies on a Theme* (Aberystwyth, 1990), 65–82.

involved carrying supplies over considerable distances.[200] Yet the utmost use was made of the assets of the immediate neighbourhood. Nanconwy, despite its essentially upland terrain, had a high percentage of bond townships. It was centred at Trefriw, a *maerdref* with a location which provided an opportunity for a modest commercial growth, to whose hall and court the services of the prince's tenants were directed.[201] Opportunities for grain production were limited, though references to cultivation at upland sites such as Bwlch-y-groes point to a determination to use the resources of the commote to the utmost, and renders of free and bond communities include corn as well as lactile products. The impressive feature of seigniorial effort, however, is the extent to which cattle were reared at vaccaries located on the upland pastures. In Gwydir there were vaccaries at Bryn-tyrch and Cwmclored, and close by Dolwyddelan a concentration of vaccaries at Penamnen, Bertheos, Gorddinan, Brynhalog, Coed-mawr, Hafod-boeth, Pen-rhiw and Llwynoron, together capable of sustaining 500 cows.[202] The development of the cattle farm, known either as a *vaccaria* or a *havotrie* in the earliest records, was a feature of the prince's provision in Arfon Is Gwyrfai, too, with extensive vaccaries in the vicinity of Dolbadarn and Llanfair Prysgol.[203] The commote centre was probably at Caernarfon, the surviving evidence providing a glimpse of the prince's manor (*manerium*), its court the focus for demesne cultivation of nine carrucates, with pastures and the services of bond and free tenants, and benefiting from tolls levied at its port.[204] It is possible that the association of the services of the free tenants of Rug and Llanfair Prysgol, and those of the bondmen of the *tir cyfrif* townships of Llanbeblig and Dinorwig, with the *manerium* of Dolbadarn was a feature of post-conquest arrange-

---

[200] G. R. J. Jones, 'The defences of Gwynedd in the thirteenth century', *TCaernHS*, 30 (1969), 38–9; idem, 'Impact of state policy', 11–15, 20–3.

[201] *RC*, 9–12; W. H. Waters, 'Account of the sheriff of Caernarvon for 1303–1304', *B*, 7 (1933–5), 144, 151.

[202] Waters, *B*, 7 (1933–5), 152–3; *RC*, 10–11; for their location at the upper reaches of Cwm Lledr, Jones, 'Impact of state policy', 22–3; E. Davies, 'Hendre and hafod in Caernarfonshire', *TCaernHS*, 40 (1979), 24–7).

[203] *RC*, 18–19 (Cwm Brwynog, Helfa-aelgarth, Maes-gwm, Hafod Dwythwch); *Inventory Caern*, II, 164, 170 (nos. 1143, 1144). Vaccaries were placed, too, in areas well removed from defensive zones, e.g. Bleiddiog and Gwnnws in Dinllaen.

[204] Documents indicate Llywelyn's presence at Caernarfon 1258, 1268, 1272, and an agreement in the names of Owain and Llywelyn was made there in 1251 (*LW*, 45, 58–9, 85–6, 160–1). An account for 1350–1 (SC6/1171/7 in T. Jones Pierce and J. Griffiths, 'Documents relating to the early history of the borough of Caernarvon', *B*, 9 (1937–9), 237–8) incorporates details from the lost extent and describes a *manerium* with lands at Llanbeblig, Penllan and Penygelli. For pre-conquest Caernarfon, *HKW*, i, 369–71; K. Williams-Jones, 'Caernarvon', in R. A. Griffiths (ed.), *Boroughs of Mediaeval Wales* (Cardiff, 1978), 73–5. The centre of Uwch Gwyrfai is uncertain; it may have been at Baladeulyn, which may be located in Dyffryn Nanlle at SH509532 (Johnstone, *Llys and Maerdref*, 23–4).

ments.[205] Dolbadarn does not, in fact, stand forth prominently in the evidence of the pre-conquest period. Dolwyddelan, on the other hand, may certainly be counted among the places where the prince and his entourage are found, and it appears that Llywelyn kept part of his treasure there. The concentration on the advance to Dolwyddelan on the part of Edward's forces in the weeks following Llywelyn ap Gruffudd's death testifies to his opponents' realization of the castle's importance in the prince's defensive calculations.[206]

The need to meet the demands of war is obvious, but it remains possible that the vaccary, or *hafod*, was developed on the high pastures of Snowdonia, not only as a source of food in times of conflict, but as a means of livestock production which could accrue to the prince's profit by marketing. Denuded of their stock in 1282–3 the vaccaries of Dolwyddelan were only partially replenished several years later, but elsewhere the custodian of the vaccaries of the county of Caernarfon could show a worthwhile income from the sale of bullocks and calves and skins, as well as cheese and butter.[207] Fifty years after the conquest a vaccary at Archwedlog in Rhufoniog Uwch Aled, by then part of the earl of Lincoln's lordship of Denbigh, was stocked with 240 beasts sustained by mountain pastures of over 300 acres, but there was a still greater potential. The surveyor observed that there were at Hafodelwy, in Rhos Is Aled, opportunities for the use of an extensive area capable of sustaining 120 beasts; another at Galchefed was remote from any settlement and could not therefore be leased, but, if it were enclosed by the lord, it was judged that it would provide for sixty breeding mares and their foals; yet another at Hafodlom in Ceinmeirch could support 200 beasts the year round.[208] In envisaging the potential of vaccary and stud alike, Hugh de Beckley may well have been pointing to the advantage which might be derived from precisely that form of seigniorial investment which the princes had made, both in Is Conwy and Uwch Conwy, on a substantial scale. It cannot be doubted that Llywelyn ap Gruffudd was driven by the economic compulsions of war, but he may also

---

[205] Llywelyn is said to have had nine bovates at Dolbadarn, but whether services of other townships had been linked to the castle is not clear from SC6/1171/7. The concentration of the services of the named vills upon Dolbadarn is certain only in 1352 (*RC*, 18–22), and Llanbeblig was certainly part of the manor of Caernarfon in 1283–4. No letters are known to have been dated at Dolbadarn by Llywelyn; those issued by Dafydd at Llanberis, May 1283, may indicate Dolbadarn (*LW*, 74–5, 77, 133; below, pp. 571–2, 576).

[206] *RC*, 211; *LW*, 43 (1278, 1281). Tudur, abbot of Valle Crucis, acknowledged receipt from Llywelyn of £8 in cash (*in pecunie numerata*) at Dolwyddelan, 1275 (*LW*, 33). For Llywelyn's treasure there, Ll. B. Smith, 'Gravamina', 174; its capture, 1283, below pp. 573–4.

[207] Waters, *B*, 7 (1933–5), 149–50, 152–3; J. Griffiths, 'Two early ministers' accounts for north Wales', *B*, 9 (1937–9), 62–3 (account of Rhirid ap Cadwgan, custodian of the vaccaries of co. Caernarfon, 1291–2); idem, 'Early accounts relating to North Wales *temp.* Edward I', *B*, 14 (1950–2), 302–12 (summary account of income from vaccaries 1289–90). Cistercian vaccaries are noticed below, n. 246.

[208] *SD*, 25, 152–3, 204; Hugh de Beckley, the surveyor, had joined a syndicate to lease the vaccaries of Archwedlog.

have appreciated the advantages to be gained from the resources of his upland pastures under normal conditions. He may have availed himself of these assets just as some of his contemporaries among the great magnates of northern England realized the benefits of an investment in vaccaries upon the shielings of their estates, designed not only to meet the requirements of their households but to produce profitable commodities for the market.[209] We have all too little knowledge of the commercial outlets of the lordship of Snowdon, but the prince's anxiety to get the king of England to remove the embargo on trade, which was inevitably imposed in times of conflict, suggests that he was concerned to ensure that essential commodities could be acquired and that he and his tenants could dispose of their own produce so that they could pay for the supplies they needed. Penllyn was perhaps the area least well endowed by nature, but the complaints registered with Archbishop Pecham in 1282 show that the prince's tenants and his officers in the commote were accustomed to sell their bullocks and the fruits of their labour in the market place at Oswestry. Rhirid ap Madog, the prince's *rhaglaw* in the commote, endured injustice there, one among several who were involved in cattle trading, and at least one of those who complained had been discomforted while acting on the prince's behalf (*in negotio domini principis*).[210] The products of a seigniorial vaccary would have been profitable merchandise, and the cattle may have been driven along routes well established by later times. The use of the term *havotria* as an alternative to *vaccaria* in the early documentary evidence serves to emphasize two features of the prince's economy which, however, represent a marked contrast from that of later centuries. The *hafod* appears to have been a cattle farm and not a sheep farm in the thirteenth century.[211] The *hafod* of that period, moreover, need not necessarily have played its main role as a facility in seasonal transhumance, for the *havotrie* and *vaccarie* were established as permanent means of exploiting the upland pasturages of the prince's territories.[212] The Cistercians' development of cattle farms, such as the group of some six *hafodydd* located upon their estates at Nanhwynan, was

---

[209] Seigniorial vaccaries in northern England are noticed in G. H. Tupling, *The Economic History of Rossendale* (Manchester, 1923), 17; E. Miller, 'Farming in northern England during the twelfth and thirteenth centuries', *Northern History*, 11 (1975), 12–13; A. J. L. Winchester, *Landscape and Society in Medieval Cumbria* (Edinburgh, 1987), 6–7, 42–3

[210] *RPeck*, ii, 455–8.

[211] Detailed studies, necessarily largely based on post-medieval evidence but with instructive earlier references, in E. Davies, 'Hendre and hafod in Merionneth', *TMerHRS*, 7 (1973–6), 13–27; idem, 'Hendre and hafod in Denbighshire', *TDenbHS*, 26 (1977), 49–72; idem, 'Hendre and hafod in Caernarfonshire', *TCaernHS*, 40 (1979), 17–46; idem, 'Hafod and lluest, the summering of cattle and upland settlement in Wales', *Folk Life*, 23 (1984–5), 77–96.

[212] Much detailed evidence is drawn from the extents of 1334 and 1352, but the immediate post-conquest extents suggest that these were features of the princes' economy.

a closely comparable enterprise.²¹³ The lands would probably have been enclosed, and shelter provided for the animals as well as for those who cared for them. The archaeology of the seigniorial vaccaries is yet to be properly explored.²¹⁴

The upland vaccaries may, perhaps, have been among the features of the princes' seigniorial economy which most attracted the interest of those who administered the land after the conquest. Demesne cultivation, on the other hand, was in most cases quickly abandoned though, in arrenting lands previously tilled on the lord's behalf, the new administrators may have been adhering to a trend already established before the conquest. Among the exceptions, where demesne exploitation was maintained, was the *manerium* associated with the court at Aber, which may have been an important residence among the courts included in the prince's itinerary.²¹⁵ The *maerdref* of the commote of Arllechwedd Uchaf, Aber was situated on the Menai Straits north of Bangor and directly opposite Llan-faes.²¹⁶ It stood, too, at the head of an ancient routeway which, traversing the Conwy at Gronant, the lowest point at which the river could be forded, led through Bwlch y Ddeufaen to the straits.²¹⁷ Aber was at the heart of the lordship of Snowdonia, yet located at a point from which the prince could have easy access to Anglesey and Perfeddwlad and to the southern parts of his lordship. Though documents dated at Aber are not numerous, it is known to have been the place where both Joan, wife of Llywelyn ap Iorwerth, and their son, Dafydd ap Llywelyn, died, and it was from there that Joan, and perhaps Eleanor, wife of Llywelyn ap Gruffudd, were taken for burial at the Franciscan house of Llan-faes.²¹⁸ Aber was almost certainly the court to which John Pecham made his way to conduct his discussions with Llywelyn in 1282. The only letter dated by Llywelyn in the course of the exchanges with

---

²¹³ Nanhwynan is noticed in Gresham, 'Aberconwy charter: further consideration', 332–8; E. Davies, 'Hendre and hafod in Caernarfonshire', 27–30. Nanhwynan *hafodydd* included Hafod-y-llan, possibly the *hafod* where Llywelyn dated a letter in 1281 (*LW*, 25), though two others of that name are noticed.

²¹⁴ For upland sites of uncertain date, often well above 1200′, with building foundations occasionally associated with enclosures, *Inventory Caern*, III, xc–xcv, with references.

²¹⁵ Letter, 1274 (*CAC*, 163); sureties for the fidelity of Gruffudd, son of Budrihossan, 1276 (*LW*, 42–3).The township has long been known as 'Abergwyngregyn', the form adopted in *TC*; medieval records consistently refer to 'Aber', and the earliest use of 'Abergwyngregyn' appears to be sixteenth-century (Leland, *Itinerary*, 79). It might be best to adhere to the medieval form.

²¹⁶ Aber, including the motte (SH656726), is surveyed in *Inventory Caern*, I, 2–18. Subsequent geophysical survey and excavation of an area adjacent to the motte revealed the foundations of a rectangular building (N. Johnstone, *Ty'n y Mwd, Aber, Archaeological Excavation* (Bangor, Gwynedd Archaeological Trust, report no. 86, 1994); idem, *Llys and Maerdref*, 13–16).

²¹⁷ *Inventory Caern*, I, lxxiiii–lxv; III, lxxxiv.

²¹⁸ *BT*, *Pen20*, 196, 201, 223; *Pen20Tr*, 104, 107, 117; *RBH*, 234–5, 238–41, 262–5.

the archbishop was addressed, in fact, not from Aber but from Garthcelyn. It may not have been securely identified as yet, but it was probably the site of a hall close by, if not within, the confines of the prince's manor of Aber.[219] It is certain that Aber was a *maerdref* where extensive demesne cultivation was maintained.[220] At the time of the earliest post-conquest evidence the demesne was worked by twenty-four bondmen whose labours were supplemented by the hired work of eleven cottars. Of the tenants' renders only a small part was paid in money (*in denariis*), the remainder required in wheat, barley and oats. Procuration charges were specifically related to the substantial obligation to provide for the prince's entourage. But in providing sustenance for the prince's court reliance was not placed entirely on the produce of the arable demesne and the bondmen's renders, for there were four vaccaries situated on the *ffriddoedd*, the resources of the fertile lowland about the *maerdref* thereby complemented by those of the uplands above Afon Anafon and Afon Rhaeadr.[221]

The only other bond settlement in Arllechwedd Uchaf was nearby at Wig and its tenants, as well as the free communities of other townships in the commote, contributed towards the maintenance of the hall at Aber known as *y tir hir* (the long house).[222] The same obligation was placed on the bond and free communities of Arllechwedd Isaf, the commote which, lying to the east of Aber, was reached by way of Bwlch y Ddeufaen. This might suggest that the area liable to provide for Aber had been broadened on account of the court's

---

[219] *RPeck*, ii, 468–9 (Garthcelyn, 11 November 1282). Claire Bray, Lambeth Palace Library, kindly confirmed that the 'Garthekevyn' of the printed text has been read in error for 'Garthkelyn'. The name Garthcelyn remains elusive, but Hafodcelyn has been identified in the Anafon valley, where the foundations of a group of round and long buildings with associated fields has been located just within the township of Bodsilin but in the parish of Aber (*Inventory Caern*, I, 7–16: nos. 13–66). One site (no. 31) was identified in W. Bezant Lowe, *The Heart of Northern Wales* (Llanfairfechan, 1912–27), ii, 43–8, as that of Llywelyn's hall, but the evidence may be insufficient for a firm conclusion. For references, 1806, by William Williams, Llandygái, to a farm 'Garthgelyn', see 'A Survey of the ancient and present state of the county of Caernarvon', *TCaernHS*, 33 (1972), 190–210; 34 (1973), 112–60: p. 151). See below, pp. 536, 543.

[220] Details in sheriff's accounts 1301, 1303–4 (SC6/1230/2; E101/57/11, in *B*, 7 (1933–5), 144) examined in T. Jones Pierce, 'Aber Gwyn Gregin', *TCaernHS*, 23 (1962), 37–43. Taking the commuted value of a day's work as 1*d*. (*B*, 7 (1933–5), 144), it could be calculated that the bondmen's works on the demesne lands had come to 576 days in winter and spring and 684 days in autumn, with a further 793 days contributed by cottars, whom Jones Pierce compared with the *gwŷr gwaith* at Penrhos and Cemais (above, p. 224).

[221] Four vaccaries were located 'on the ffridd near Aber' (Nantmawr, *Nanteraçadret*, Meuryn and *Nanheske*), *B*, 7 (1933–5), 152; 16 (1954–6), 116; *RC*, 138–40; for their location and possible link with material remains, Jones Pierce, 'Aber Gwyn Gregin', 412; *Inventory Caern*, I, nos, 39, 46; Gresham, *ArchCamb*, 106 (1957), 127.

[222] Duties at the prince's manor or *ad opus Tehyre* or *ad opus manerii de Aber vocatur Tehire*, 1352 (*RC*, 3–7, 8, 15) and earlier (*B*, 1 (1921–3), 272; 7 (1933–5), 143, 144; 14 (1950–2), 240). In 1304, in addition to the annual charge, the two commotes of Arllechwedd paid £30 for repairs at Aber (E101/485/49).

particular importance, but there can be no certainty that the arrangements described in the earliest records represent practice in the period of Llywelyn ap Gruffudd. The association of the tenants of Arllechwedd Isaf with Aber may rather have been a result of changes which followed the transfer of the abbey of Aberconwy to Maenan and the settlement at Gronant of the tenants displaced at Maenan.[223] On several grounds Gronant suggests itself as the location of the *maerdref* of the commote of Arllechwedd Isaf.[224] It was sited at the crossing of the Conwy, already noticed, where there was a motte closely similar to those at Aber and Dolbenmaen, and it is known to have been a bond township before it was conceded to the freemen of Maenan for whom Edward I had need to provide.[225] The services of the tenants of Arllechwedd Isaf may have been diverted to Aber as part of the reorganization undertaken after the conquest, and it is likely that the 'hall of Llywelyn' which was located within the walls of Conwy was not a prince's hall established within the precincts of the Cistercian abbey, but a building of timber construction removed there, perhaps from Gronant, when the new arrangements were being made, and building works had commenced, at Conwy.[226]

The surviving evidence relating to the several parts of the prince's lordship of Snowdon suggests that Llywelyn ap Gruffudd continued to use the courts whose economic mainstay had long been, and in some cases continued to be, the direct exploitation of the arable resources of the demesnes. The methods of economic management pursued by the prince were not changeless, even so, and some of the changes that may be detected have already been noticed. It

[223] CWR, 285–6, 290–1.
[224] C. A. Gresham, 'The commotal centre of Arllechwedd Isaf', *TCaernHS*, 40 (1979), 11–16.
[225] For the earthwork (SH785719), *Inventory Caern*, I, 27 (no. 114); III, cxliii. In 1352 it was recorded that there had been bond *gafaelion* at Gronant previously, not the *tir cyfrif* which would be expected at a commotal centre, but there was at least a recollection of bond tenure.
[226] *HKW*, i, 337–8, 343, 353; *Inventory Caern*, I, 57; III, cxliii; M. A. Mason, 'Llywelyn's Hall, Conwy', *TCaernHS*, 56 (1995), 11–35. The existence of 'the hall known as the hall of the prince' can be shown from 1286 (E101/485/28), and this has often been regarded as a hall of the prince which stood on the site before the king's building works began, possibly from the time of Llywelyn ap Iorwerth (*HKW*, i, 353; *ArchCamb*, 119 (1970), 5). There does not appear to be a single instance of a document of any prince dated at Aberconwy. The judicious wording of *Inventory Caern*, I, 57 'that a timber building stood on the site before work commenced on the walls', admits the possibility that the hall was constructed at the site in the early stages of the king's works. Timber structures, including the king's hall, were being assembled from the spring of 1283, sometimes said to be built 'in the abbey of Conwy' (E101/351/9). It is quite conceivable that a timber hall was moved from a neighbouring princely court to the abbey precincts, just as the hall of Ystumgwern was moved to Harlech, and the removal of a hall from Gronant would be a very strong possibility (Gresham, 'Arllechwedd', 16). It would then have been logical to transfer the maintenance obligations of the men of Arllechwedd Isaf to the court of Arllechwedd Uchaf at Aber. The hall was dismantled in 1316 and its timbers removed to Caernarfon (*CCR, 1313–18*, 267).

would appear that the resources exploited by *tir cyfrif* means were reduced by the arrentation of lands to both bond and free tenants. There were probably advantages to the prince in the releasing to bond tenants, thereafter liable to renders in kind and possibly in money, of those demesnes which might be of small extent and perhaps situated at some distance from the main manor. The change was accompanied, however, by an adjustment to the bond tenures by which lands previously managed by the princes' officers, and periodically apportioned to the bondmen, were thereafter held hereditarily in *gwelyau* and *gafaelion*.[227] These bond vills thereby lost one of the prime characteristics of the classic demesne manor, and their bondmen came to share with freemen the hereditary succession which was a cardinal feature of free tenure. It seems clear that the grants made to favoured laymen, already noticed, might involve the removal from the prince's direct management of well-sited and extensive *tir cyfrif* townships upon fiscal terms which saw a diminution in the prince's income. It was a process partially compensated, perhaps, by moving some of the bondmen previously deployed in those established townships to more marginal lands, thereby extending the area under cultivation.[228] The extent and chronology of changes such as these is difficult to deduce, but it is probable that by the late twelfth and early thirteenth centuries there had been some modification in the organization of bond townships (including an appreciable switch from direct to indirect exploitation), in the form in which fiscal obligations were required, and in the relative proportions of land vested in freemen and bondmen. The extent to which Llywelyn ap Gruffudd promoted further change in the directions suggested, or sought to arrest the process of change, is difficult to judge. He may have had precious little scope for change. He needed to ensure that there was no further erosion of his capacity to derive the utmost from the resources of his demesnes, and his economic management may well have been directed to ensuring that these valuable seigniorial assets were conserved in their traditional form. He laboured under considerable restraints, too, in relation to his income from indirect exploitation which needs to be considered in the next stage of our discussion. Any attempt to increase his revenue from these sources had to be made within the framework of fiscal obligations which carried the sanction of long practice. They were already met, it is safe to judge, partly in kind and partly in money, and reflected that same combination of tillage and pasturage which, as we have seen, was a feature of the prince's direct exploitation. Furthermore, these indirect issues were again to a considerable extent related to the needs of an itinerant court.

---

[227] For bond *tir gwelyog* lands, above, n. 167.
[228] G. R. J. Jones, 'Distribution of medieval settlement', 53–63.

Lord of Snowdon

The obligations of society

The dues levied for the support of the prince and his entourage have already been noticed briefly for the light which they shed on the nature of his authority. The *gwestfa, dawnbwyd* or *dofreth* of the lawbooks are matched in the documentary evidence by a wide range of renders whose names – *pastus principis, cylch rhaglaw, pastus famulie principis, cylch hebogyddion* and many more – record the obligations of bond and free to provide for the needs of the court upon its *cylch,* or circuit, of the prince's lordship.[229] These *porthiant* or procuration charges are ubiquitous in Gwynedd Uwch Conwy and Is Conwy, and as indicated earlier are closely comparable to those found in other parts of Wales, notably in Powys Fadog, and further afield. They are also substantial in relation to other payments. In Ardudwy, for instance, the monetary charges on those tenants of the commote whose lands lay outside the confines of the *manerium* of Ystumgwern were far outweighed by *porthiant*, with still further charges made for the support of the prince's groom and huntsmen; thus in the area linked with the *manerium* of Prysor procuration obligations in the form of renders of butter, pigs and cattle, and charges for the maintenance of horses and grooms, formed much the greater part of the tenants' obligations.[230] In Penllyn, similarly, comparable charges upon freemen were greater than the sum of the dues embodied under the heading of 'assessed rents' (*redditus assize*), and those imposed upon the bondmen, further increased by a levy of *maeroniaeth*, were also substantial in relation to other obligations.[231] These levies may have been increased by Llywelyn ap Gruffudd, for it was said in the locality after the conquest that, whereas Llywelyn ap Iorwerth and Dafydd ap Llywelyn had taken *potura* for 300 men once a year, but only when they came to hunt in the commote, Llywelyn ap Gruffudd had taken *potura* for 500 men each year whether he came or not.[232] Upon a very different terrain, procuration charges in Anglesey, levied upon both bond and free, were again a major item in the tenants' liability. The precise proportions varied but, for instance, the numbers of men and horses supported for one day in the commotes of Llifon and Malltraeth are given as 2,000 men and 300 horses, in Twrcelyn 850 men, 280 horses and 800 hounds, and in Menai 1,400 men and 550 horses, and these still did not reflect the full extent of the tenants' duties in this respect.[233] In Dindaethwy, though the details of the obligations are not enumerated, procuration charges were very substantial in relation to the rents and services embodied in the *redditus*

---

[229] *LlIor*, 60, 64; *LHD*, 121, 128; *LlCol*, 39, 41; Stephenson, *GG*, 64–7; above, pp. 197–9.
[230] *ExtMer*, 189–91.
[231] *ExtMer*, 187–9.
[232] *CIM*, i, 392.
[233] *ExtAng*, 8–11, 14–21, with *maeroniaeth* charges in some areas.

assize.²³⁴ In Anglesey generally, though the charges are expressed differently from one area to another, *porthiant* constituted a substantial portion of the total charge. In the extent for 1352 the values of the *porthiant* charges are not specified separately, but in recording the payment of *cylch stalwyn, cylch rhaglaw, cylch hebogyddion* or *cylch dyfrgwn*, and the composite *staurum principis*, the surveyor identifies rather more clearly than his predecessors the origin of the substantial levies made both in Anglesey and on the mainland of Gwynedd Uwch Conwy.²³⁵ The terminology studiously adhered to has a distinctly antique quality, and this is true also of the record of comparable charges in the extent of Rhos and Rhufoniog in Gwynedd Is Conwy in 1334. There the 'great circuit of the household' (*cylch mawr y teulu*) described in the lawbooks appears to be reflected in the *pastus principis* required of freemen and the *pastus famulie principis* imposed on bondmen. They were among a number of obligations – such as *pastus pen macwy* and *pastus gweision bychain* – which the surveyors evidently felt constrained to preserve in detail.²³⁶ Regarded as a proportion of the entire seigniorial income of the two *cantrefi* the procuration charges were not inordinately large, but they formed a significant part of the income which was derived from land, and the authorities were in no mind to consolidate these obligations in corporate sums. Rather, they took pains to maintain a remembrance of how, for instance, in the time of the princes, it had been customary to provide, for one day and one night, provender for a stallion and sustenance for a groom at the house of every free tenant if he had no sub-tenants, or at the house of each sub-tenant of the freemen, and at the house of each bondman.²³⁷ At the same time it was explained that *porthiant* fell as an integral charge on each commote and was levied upon the tenants according to their wealth in moveable goods (*catalla*) rather than in land.²³⁸ The surveyor's exegesis may not be altogether helpful, but his search for explanation in the period of the princes, no less than his care to maintain a minutely itemized account of the renders due to the lord, points to an enduring awareness of the importance of *porthiant* in the time of Llywelyn ap Gruffudd. There is a slight suggestion that procuration requirements were reflected also in purveyance impositions,

---

²³⁴ *ExtAng*, 4–5.

²³⁵ E.g. *RC*, 45–6, 51–3, 65–7, 74–5, 80–1; Carr, *Extent*, 172–6; Carr, *MAng*, 133–43. Early post-conquest evidence for Uwch Conwy is reflected in SC6/1171/7 (*B*, 6 (1931–3), 255–75), with substantial *potura* payments evident in Nanconwy and Uwch Gwyrfai, but less so in other areas.

²³⁶ *SD*, lxiii–lxvii, 7, *et passim*; Owen, 'Tenurial developments', 121–2; for the 'great circuit of the winter', above, n. 42.

²³⁷ The custumals for Ceinmeirch, Is Aled and Uwch Aled (*SD*, 46–7, 148–50, 208–9) are particularly informative.

²³⁸ *SD*, 47, 209.

for the surveyor records the obligations of the tenants of Rhufoniog to provide animals or produce for sale for the prince's bailiff at a fair price to meet his needs.[239]

The renders for which free and bond tenants were responsible, though not always specifically enumerated as procuration duties, reflect the extent to which the prince's charges upon the community were related to the need to provide support for the itinerant court additional to that which he drew from the produce of his demesnes. The varied nature of the obligations helps to illuminate the differing emphases in the manner in which the several parts of the prince's lordship were exploited. The prominence of renders revealing an emphasis on animal husbandry in what were distinctly upland areas contrasts with the grain renders which form more substantial proportions of the obligations of tenants in lowland areas. Yet the contrast is far from complete. Grain renders form part of the obligations of tenants in Penllyn or Ardudwy: flour, though milled from oats rather than wheat, was counted among the dues of the freemen of Penllyn Is Meloch; the bondmen of Prysor, in the moorland reaches of Ardudwy, had need to supply their crannogs of flour along with heavy obligations in pigs and cattle.[240] In the commotes of Malltraeth and Menai in Anglesey grain renders in wheat, oats and barley form a major part of the proprietors' dues but their obligations included delivery of butter and fowls, pigs and lambs.[241] A similar pattern of varied renders may be discerned in the commotes of Dinllaen, Cafflogion and Cymydmaen in Llŷn, and the detail which may be derived from the subsidy assessments of 1292–3 provides, in the case of Cafflogion and Malltraeth, a particularly clear picture of the proprietors' economy.[242] At Aberffraw in Malltraeth the high proportion of tenants in possession of draught animals points to extensive cultivation, but they also had substantial wealth in sheep and particularly in cattle.[243] Animal husbandry was evidently an essential feature of the economy of the commote. Even more instructive is the case of Cafflogion, where the needs of tillage are again reflected in the number of draught animals and a high productivity in cereals (wheat in several areas, but particularly oats), most notably in the townships of Bodfel, Llangïan, Marchros and Ystrad Geirch. The emphasis

---

[239] *SD*, 151. For the vexation caused in England in the late thirteenth century by purveyance, see citations below, n. 297.

[240] *ExtMer*, 187–91.

[241] *ExtAng*, 8–10, 17–20.

[242] Malltraeth: E101/242/49 (F. Seebohm, *The Tribal System in Wales* (2nd edn., London, 1904), App. 37–45); Cafflogion: E101/242/50B (T. Jones Pierce, 'Two early Caernarvonshire accounts', *B*, 5 (1929–31), 142–8). For the proprietors' economy, particularly as reflected in these sources, C. Thomas, 'Thirteenth-century farm economies in north Wales', *AgHR*, 16 (1968), 1–14; idem, 'Livestock numbers in medieval Gwynedd', *JMerHRS*, 7 (1973–6), 113–17; idem, 'Peasant agriculture in medieval Gwynedd', *FolkLife*, 13 (1975), 24–7.

[243] Idem, 'Farm economies', 3–9; Tables I–V.

on oats may reflect the physical conditions which prevailed even on the well-drained and fertile soils, but it equally reflects the relationship between cultivation and livestock. There was evidently some variation in the pattern of production within the area, with sheep-rearing profitably pursued in Marchros and Cilan but with a very substantial investment in cattle in the commote as a whole. Despite their substantially higher value per head, the number of cattle exceeded those of sheep in several townships such as Bodfel, Llangïan and Cae-hwsni.[244] Comparable information is not available for any other area but, though there may have been considerable diversity between the production of one area and another, the evidence from Cafflogion points to an intensive exploitation, in physically advantaged areas and in less favoured terrains, of animal and crop husbandry in a closely integrated economy.

The indications which we have of the proprietors' economy, largely conveyed by their renders to their lord, underline the conclusions reached on the evidence of the demesne economy that the efforts of prince and proprietors alike were directed to the exploitation of arable and pastoral resources in close combination. The antithesis between animal and crop husbandry needs to be moderated, but the nature of the pastoral activity itself has to be properly appreciated. Pig-rearing, which may be traced in lowland localities and was also an important part of seigniorial farming in upland locations such as Prysor, is a mark of a settled agricultural economy.[245] Nor can there be any doubt of the preponderant place of cattle in the economy. Sheep-rearing may not have been a major factor in the exploitation of upland pastures either in seigniorial or in proprietorial economies, but was reflected in limited investment made more particularly in lowland localities.[246] The importance of the seigniorial *hafod* (*havotria*) as a cattle farm rather than a sheep farm has already been noticed. Its role was not that of the *hafod* of seasonal transhumance of later centuries.[247] The lawbooks, of course, reflect

---

[244] Thomas, 'Farm economies', 7–10; tables IV–V for numbers of tenants possessing cattle and sheep, and numbers of animals; cf. idem, 'Peasant agriculture', 30–2; idem, 'Livestock numbers', 114–16. For valuations of a cow at 3*s.* 4*d.* and a sheep at 8*d.*, *MLSR*, xiv.

[245] For the villein's herd of pigs and herd of cows, *LlIor*, 22; *LHD*, 40.

[246] Estimates of the quantitative composition of farm stock are made in R. E. Hughes *et al.*, 'A review of the density and ratio of sheep and cattle in medieval Gwynedd', *JMerHRS*, 7 (1973–6), 373–83, and studies cited. Medieval evidence is slight and estimates need to be treated with caution. It is possible that the proportion of sheep to cattle increased from the late medieval centuries onward. Much of the earlier evidence is derived from Cistercian estates and even there the ratio of sheep to cattle is not marked, despite the possibility that sheep ratios were higher on their lands than on lay estates. For ratios indicated in the *Taxatio* of 1291 for Wales, R. A. Donkin, *The Cistercians: Studies in the Geography of Medieval England and Wales* (Toronto, 1978), 68–74, with vaccaries noticed for Aberconwy, Valle Crucis and Ystrad Marchell, ibid., 185–6. The most reliable evidence for lay estates is that of the subsidy rolls studied by Colin Thomas, above n. 242.

[247] Above, n. 211.

the fact that seasonal migration to upland pastures was a facet of the economy.[248] But, even then, the transhumance of the Rhinog or Carn Fadrun was not the transhumance of the Pyrenees. It was necessarily a short-distance movement which allowed the proprietors of Llanaber access to the pastures of Ardudwy or those of Llangïan the pastures of Llŷn. The emphasis in the lawbooks is decidedly upon the close inter-relationship of corn and livestock. Theirs is the economy of barn and byre, and this was so for prince and proprietor alike. The picture which emerges, albeit from late and tenuous documentary sources, is that of a seigniorial and proprietorial economy founded upon an intensive but necessarily regulated use of the land in an expedient integration of arable and pastoral resources.[249]

The form in which the prince exacted his dues from the proprietors, who shared with him the exploitation of the lordship of Snowdon, is an important part of his economic management. Part of what was due to the lords in the immediate post-conquest period is set out solely in cash terms, and part is described as a cash equivalent of renders in kind which are specifically enumerated. The question whether those distinctions represent the degree to which the process of commutation of renders in kind, or labour, into money payments had been taken before the conquest is not easy to resolve. In an important study of the documentary sources for Gwynedd Uwch Conwy T. Jones Pierce argued that the *redditus assize* ('assessed rent') recorded by the surveyors and accounting officers of the late thirteenth century reflected the cash payments which had been levied in the period of the princes. He sensed a deliberate intention on the part of the princes to promote the use of money, and this could be seen as a key feature of the innovative policies by which the social and economic order was modified to serve their political purposes.[250] *Redditus assize* could be seen as the equivalent of *twnc*, a term known to the jurists who compiled the law texts as a monetary composition of renders in kind.[251] Whereas in some areas beyond the confines of Gwynedd, notably in

---

[248] *LlIor*, 22, 60, 62, 91; *LHD*, 40, 121, 125, 190. Thus the lord should have his *maerdref* and shieling (*hafod-tir*); the *maer* had care both for ploughing and sowing, livestock and shielings (*hafodydd*); the bondman had cowhouse and barn, summer house and harvest house. Cf. G. R. J. Jones, 'Models for organisation', 110–11.

[249] C. Wickham, 'Pastoralism and underdevelopment in the early middle ages', *Settimane di studio del Centro italiano di studi sull'Alto medioevo*, 31 (1985), 401–51, includes valuable comment on the relationship of cultivation and pasturage in a rural economy, and the distinction between short-distance ('vertical') and long-distance ('horizontal') transhumance. These considerations have a bearing on the interpretation of archaeological remains and are reflected in the instructive report on an important site near Clynnog: R. S. Kelly, 'The excavation of a medieval farmstead at Cefn Graeanog, Clynnog, Gwynedd', *B*, 29 (1980–2), 859–87.

[250] Pierce, *MWS*, 103–25; comment in Stephenson, *GG*, 67–9. For recent discussion of commutation, P. J. Spufford, *Money and its Uses in Medieval Europe* (Cambridge, 1988).

[251] Pierce, *MWS*, 110–20; lawbook references include *LlIor*, 11, 60, 63, 64; *LHD*, 21, 121, 125, 128.

Powys Fadog, the monetary sums recorded had an irregularity which suggests a process of commutation by natural means, in Gwynedd the regularity of *twnc*, and an occasional specific equation of *redditus assize* and *twnc*, point to commutation along more systematic lines laid down by the princes as a matter of fiscal policy.[252] A nucleus of commuted renders in the form of *twnc* is a feature also of the fiscal obligations noted in Rhos and Rhufoniog studied by D. Huw Owen. There, however, two further consolidations of renders could be identified in *treth*, paid by freemen, and *ardreth*, paid by bondmen, each representing a second stage in a process of commutation and again attributable to the period of the princes.[253] In each area east and west of the Conwy free renders were subject to a higher degree of commutation than bond. In Uwch Conwy, moreover, the evidence pointed to a distinctly higher ratio of commutation to some areas than others, with the higher values tending to be a feature of the areas of extensive tillage, such as Anglesey, and a lower set revealed in what could be characterized as more pastoral areas such as Ardudwy and Penllyn.[254] A pattern of differentiation of this nature is less clearly discernible in Is Conwy, but the evidence from both areas might suggest a deliberate attempt on the part of the princes to promote the conversion of renders in kind into money payments, a policy pursued with greater vigour in those areas most responsive to such processes of change.[255]

The quantitative assessment which can be based on the evidence of the post-conquest materials may thus demonstrate that, whatever care is taken to qualify the distinction between crop and animal husbandry as alternative forms of agricultural production, a contrast between the economic potential of various parts of the prince's lands remains evident. Earlier discussion in this chapter has certainly been concerned with the nature of seigniorial and proprietorial endeavour rather than with any attempt to gauge its efficacy. The evidence of the lay subsidy assessment on moveable goods made in 1292-3 provides a means of assessing the comparative wealth of a group of commotes - Ardudwy, Penllyn, Tal-y-bont, Ystumanner and Edeirnion - which came to form the post-conquest county of Merioneth. A wide divergence in the wealth of different localities can be recognized in the marked contrasts between, in particular, the high valuation levels in Edeirnion and the much lower levels in Penllyn and Ardudwy.[256] At the same time, Tal-y-

---

[252] Pierce, *MWS*, 114-16; for Powys Fadog, Ll. O. W. Smith, 'Lordships of Chirk and Oswestry', 225-40; Rogers, 'Lordship of Bromfield and Yale', 127-35.

[253] D. H. Owen, 'Treth and ardreth: some aspects of commutation in north Wales in the thirteenth century', *B*, 25 (1972-4), 446-53; idem, 'Tenurial developments', 131-4; comment in Stephenson, *GG*, 69, n. 28.

[254] Pierce, *MWS*, 118-20.

[255] D. H. Owen, 'Tenurial developments', 132, detects higher ratios in the western areas of Rhos and Rhufoniog.

[256] Williams-Jones, in *MLSR*, lxviii-lxxx; G. R. J. Jones, 'Impact of state policy', 16-20.

bont and Ystumanner occupied an intermediate position, with areas within these commotes assessed at noticeably high valuations. A tax on the moveable possessions of tenants certainly provides one indication of the comparative prosperity of the localities and, if evidence comparable to that which survives for this group of commotes were available for Gwynedd as a whole, other marked contrasts would undoubtedly emerge. Commutation ratios may, therefore, reflect the constraints imposed upon the princes' policies in what might perhaps be regarded as their quest for a means of quickening the pace of economic change.

The princes may, even so, have been influenced by other considerations which could well be reflected in the dispositions of their demesnes and the renders of their tenants. These might, too, reflect not only the broad contrasts between the predominantly arable or pastoral areas already intimated but more localized considerations. It may be noticed that a particularly low ratio of commuted renders in Dindaethwy contrasts markedly with those of the remainder of Anglesey. Not only bond renders but those of freemen were made in kind, or were recently made in that form, and these were demonstrated in the weight of the *porthiant* charges already described.[257] These figures are particularly difficult to explain since the centre of the commote of Dindaethwy at Llan-faes had by the time of the conquest developed into one of the most flourishing commercial centres in Gwynedd. A *maerdref*, necessarily a nucleated settlement and a focus for the legal and financial administration of a commote, by its very nature had a potentiality for growth of a commercial nature, particularly if it were well placed in relation to routeways by land or sea. All this was conspicuously true of Llan-faes, a natural point of transit between the island and the mainland at Aber. Llan-faes gained the benefit of ferry tolls, the customs and tolls levied at its markets and fairs, and those levied on ships using its harbour. Tenants' holdings in the *maerdref*, as many as 120, are described in the extent as burgage lands.[258] It is not difficult to lend credence to the burgesses' subsequent assertion that they had enjoyed privileges at Llan-faes by virtue of the princes' charters (*per cartas principum*).[259] The income derived from the

---

[257] *ExtAng*, 4–7. Whereas in other commotes *porthiant* dues are enumerated one by one, in Dindaethwy they are given, along with *redditus assize* sums, as integral figures township by township. T. Jones Pierce argued that the procuration figures represented a statement of dues still rendered in kind at the conquest, and in this paragraph it is accepted that the two sets of totals in the Dindaethwy extent may reflect the monetary and non-monetary obligations as they stood at the conquest.

[258] *ExtAng*, 3–4; *B*, 9 (1937–9), 64–6, account for Llan-faes 1291–2; commentary in Pierce, *MWS*, 121–3, 279–81; Stephenson, *GG*, 79–80; Carr, *MAng*, 231–6.

[259] E. A. Lewis, *The Mediaeval Boroughs of Snowdonia* (London, 1912), 295; *CAP*, 82–3.

sources described in the extents may not have been enormous, but it points to the princes' regulation and, quite conceivably, an effort on their part to stimulate a commercial activity for which a monetary means of exchange was essential. The recent discovery at Llan-faes of a very large number of silver pennies provides a graphic reflection of the fact that this was indeed a thriving commercial centre where money circulated in some quantity from the late twelfth or early thirteenth century onward.[260] The retention of a high level of uncommuted dues in the commote of Dindaethwy, which formed the immediate hinterland of this thriving centre, is thus surprising. Search for explanation might reasonably lead to the conclusion that military needs in an area twice subject to invasion by English forces in Llywelyn's time dictated the retention of important sources of foodstuffs.[261] At the same time, and not necessarily at variance with the need to ensure preparedness for war, the more constant need to provide for the prince's court at Llan-faes, or conceivably across the straits at Aber, may have been reason enough to insist upon the fulfilment of fiscal obligations, not in money, but by the delivery of produce by free and bond in kind. There remains the further possibility, again readily reconciled with the considerations already postulated, that the prince had a specifically commercial interest in requiring produce in kind for disposal in the market.

The figures for Dindaethwy are not a singular aberration among those which relate to regions which generally reveal high levels of commutation. A similar pattern emerges in the case of Nefyn and the commote of Dinllaen. At Nefyn, too, the *maerdref* had developed into a commercial centre described in the earliest post-conquest records as a borough.[262] Its customs and tolls indicated a flourishing market economy. The large concentration of bond communities in Dinllaen were, however, heavily committed to renders in kind rather than money, and the fact that a similar emphasis may be discerned among free communities in the commote, and in those of Cafflogion and Cymydmaen, strengthens the possibility that the fiscal calculations of the princes, even in respect of areas of marked prosperity, may not necessarily have led to a comprehensive conversion to money payments.[263] The variations in the proportions of dues paid in money and in kind may not be altogether a reflection of the unpropitious nature of the land in some areas as compared

---

[260] E. Besly, 'Short-cross and other medieval coins from Llanfaes, Anglesey', *The British Numismatic Journal*, 65 (1995), 46–82. Finds 1991–4 amounted to 592 coins, the great majority short–cross (332) and long-cross (135). The short-cross coins, of the period 1180–1247, are of exceptional interest; see below, n. 269.

[261] Edward's invasions of Anglesey in 1272 and 1282 are examined later.

[262] Subsidy roll in *B*, 5 (1929–31), 54–71; commentary in Pierce, *MWS*, 122, 141–4; T. Jones Pierce, 'The old borough of Nefyn 1355–1882', *TCaernHS*, 18 (1957), 36–53.

[263] In the absence of an early extent for co. Caernarfon reference is made to details in sheriffs' accounts; above, n. 22.

with others. For whatever reason, Llywelyn ap Gruffudd appears to have retained both the capacity for food production by direct demesne management and the arrangements by which he received a substantial part of what was due to him from his tenants, not in money, but in commodities.

The continued fulfilment of fiscal obligations in kind was not, therefore, necessarily a mark of a retarded economy. Study of other lands, some of them by no means those of penurious societies, suggests that the process of change from *Naturalwirtschaft* to *Geldwirtschaft* could be susceptible to differing seigniorial need and convenience.[264] In the case of Gwynedd, even so, a broad trend in the direction of an increased use of money in major transactions can be safely postulated. Whereas the princes' obligations to the king of England had tended to be paid in cattle up to the early thirteenth century, they were offered or met in pounds sterling by the later years of the century. Llywelyn ap Iorwerth bought his peace with John by heavy renders in livestock; Llywelyn ap Gruffudd secured the treaty he so earnestly sought from Henry by the promise of sums payable in coins.[265] Prince Llywelyn's obligation to the king of England was one in a plethora of reasons why he had every incentive to promote the use of money, and one obvious course of action would be to insist that certain fiscal obligations were fulfilled in cash payments. Specific indications of commutation in the princes' lands in the thirteenth century are few, but they include firm evidence that military service could be substituted by a money payment and that fines in money were levied for the evasion of military duty. It was a matter which Llywelyn was alleged, after his death, to have exploited in an unfair manner.[266] On the other hand, there were considerations which tended towards a retention of renders in kind. One of the weapons used against the princes by kings of England was the trade embargo. Calls upon neighbouring communities in England to desist from trading were often accompanied by surveillance of frontier areas and the restrictions could have a decidedly unwelcome effect. In the early years of his rule Llywelyn ap Gruffudd revealed a keen wish to ensure that truces arranged with the king should include provision for the lifting of restrictions on trade. This was important, as has been suggested already, not only in order to secure vital commodities but to ensure that goods were sold. In times of full-scale conflict embargo could be enforced by blockade or, even worse, grain-producing or cattle-raising areas might be penetrated and harvests and stock removed. The wars of 1277 and 1282–3 provide clear instances of the severe measures of which Edward was capable in

---

[264] R. Lennard, *Rural England, 1086–1135* (Oxford, 1959), 139–41.
[265] *MLSR*, xvii; J. B. Smith, 'Magna Carta', 344, 362; the sums of money offered by Llywelyn from 1258 or paid by him from 1267 have been noticed earlier.
[266] *Councils*, i, 490, 493, 514; Ll. B. Smith, '*Gravamina*', 174 (VIII).

his efforts to exert pressure on his opponents.[267] A time of war, or the anticipation of war, called for stock-piling. The king's officers who came to Edeirnion during the conflict of 1282 were astonished at the abundance of corn stored in granges and the great number of beasts as well.[268] The discovery may reveal something of the prince's determination to ensure that Edward would be met with more than the obstacles of a difficult terrain fortified with properly defended positions, and that the defenders should be sustained by a co-ordinated means of production and distribution of the essentials for their sustenance. It was a purpose dictated by the cumulative experience of the men of Snowdon in resisting intervention in their land. There were some defensive measures which could be taken only in response to particular contingencies, tactical dispositions of forces obviously among them, but the provision of adequate supplies called for arrangements of a permanent nature geared to the needs of war. This, it has been intimated already, would be consistent with a wish to ensure that in normal conditions surplus commodities could be disposed of to the prince's profit. The retention of a proportion, indeed a substantial proportion, of dues in kind had one other critically important advantage. It was a means of withstanding those inflationary pressures which, though with fluctuating severity, were a factor in thirteenth-century economic conditions. It is quite conceivable that the *twnc* to which the jurists' texts bear testimony represents a commutation effected by the later years of the twelfth century or the early thirteenth century, and the coins discovered at Llan-faes suggest extensive use of money by that period. If commutation had been well advanced by then the value of the dues would have been severely eroded over the intervening years, and Llywelyn ap Gruffudd would have been grateful that a substantial part of what was owed to him by the tenants of his lordship was still payable in kind, and resolved that it should remain so.[269]

Discussion has necessarily concentrated on the nature rather than the extent of the prince's demands upon the communities of his patrimony and it has been largely concerned with his direct and indirect income from the land. His regalian or seigniorial rights, which have been noticed, afforded other sources of income: the regulation of succession to land, and possibly the custody of heirs, and some power to regulate alienation of land. Right of wreck and treasure trove were safeguarded, and they may have counted significantly

---

[267] Trade embargoes 1257–67 have been noticed already; in 1276–7 a blockade was imposed to deprive the prince of imports such as corn, wine, salt and iron (*CCR, 1272–79*, 410).

[268] *CAC*, 172.

[269] The short-cross coins from Llan-faes, indicating money circulation in the first half of the thirteenth century, have been noticed. For coinage in the law texts, especially the *ceiniog cyfraith* and *ceiniog cwta* ('legal penny' and 'short penny'), G. C. Boon, *Welsh Hoards, 1979–1981* (Cardiff, 1986), 60–2. Inflation and the problem of fixed income consequent upon alienation of demesnes are considered below, n. 333–7.

among incidental sources of revenue. His assiduous care for his rights in wreck and for the profits of the foreshore were indeed held against him after his death. Impossible to estimate, but conceivably of increasing value by the late thirteenth century, were the profits drawn from the administration of criminal law and from fines levied from litigants who sought the judgement of his court. The prince's care for the profits to be derived from justice is evident from his disputes with the bishops, and there can be no doubt that he would not fail to avail himself of the remuneration which lay within his jurisdiction.[270] There are occasional instances from the period of Llywelyn ap Gruffudd of the imposition of substantial fines for what may have been political or disciplinary reasons, notably that of £100 exacted from Rhys ap Gruffudd ab Ednyfed for contempt and disobedience at the court of Aberffraw.[271] Income to the lord was, of course, derived one way or another from individuals and communities who sustained an economic order largely based on cultivation and stock-raising. The prince was able to draw upon some sources of a commercial nature which may have augmented his income quite appreciably, but it is unlikely to have been more than a useful increment in a seigniorial economy essentially based on profits from land. The pursuit of his political objectives was not facilitated by any substantial new mercantile wealth, nor was he engaged in alliance with any new interest group within the society of his lordship. It is impossible to place a monetary value on the regalian rights noticed in this discussion, nor is it possible to know the extent to which mineral deposits were worked. The prince had need of iron production, but the manner by which his needs were met remains largely unexplored.[272] Nor is there knowledge that veins which carried silver were worked in this period. Certainly the prince's regalian rights are not known to have extended to providing his own minted coin. He did not share the advantages enjoyed by those of his milieu in the kingdom of France who exercised a *ius monete*, notably Gaston de Béarn, who reaped the benefits of his mint at Morlaàs.[273] The coins exacted from his tenants of the lordship of Snowdon, and those which he delivered in fulfilment of his obligations under the treaty of Montgomery, bore the imprint of the king of England.

---

[270] Stephenson, *GG*, 74–89; the prince's regalian rights have been noticed.

[271] *LW*, 31; relations with the prince from 1277 are noticed later; instances of the prince's dispensation of his *benevolentia* are cited in the next chapter.

[272] For iron-making, P. Crew and S. Crew, 'Medieval bloomeries in north-west Wales', in G. Magnusson (ed.), *The Importance of Ironmaking: Technical Innovation and Social Change* (Stockholm, 1995), 43–50, citing further references

[273] For *ius monete*, J. B. Smith, 'Adversaries of Edward I: Gaston de Béarn and Llywelyn ap Gruffudd', 58. The short-cross coins from Llan-faes were derived from fifteen mints and, after London and Canterbury, the largest number were minted at Rhuddlan (Besly, 'Short-cross coins', 53, 63–70). These coins are attributed to a period from 1205 to 1247, that is, with the exception of 1211–12 and 1241–7, to years when Rhuddlan was under the princes' power, a matter which calls for further consideration.

Lord of Snowdon

Income and expenditure

It has been intimated already that any attempt to estimate the prince's income would be a hazardous undertaking. Hardly a single item in that revenue can be quantified from the evidence of the period of Llywelyn ap Gruffudd, and estimates could only be, at best, precarious calculations based on the figures for the income of those who shared the rule of the prince's lands after the conquest. Some sources of revenue were more stable than others. The extents drawn up as soon as conflict subsided in 1283 were doubtless based on the customary obligations of the preceding period. The monetary obligations then recorded, and the monetary values attached to renders in kind enumerated in the extents, and reflected in account rolls, may have borne a fairly close relationship to what had been due to Llywelyn. Extents do not survive, however, for the whole of the lordship of Snowdon, and account rolls for the years immediately following the conquest are very few. New pressures exerted by new lords, or the exploitation of resources not hitherto tapped, might easily distort the figures as indications of pre-conquest income. The difficult questions which still remain over the extent and effect of post-conquest commutation create further difficulty. Yet the officers of the crown and the marcher lords were guardians of traditional seigniorial interests and were to a large extent the captives of the power that their masters had wrenched from their predecessors. Despite the difficulties in the way of establishing a basis for a calculation of the income of the several counties and lordships created in the former lordship of Snowdon, some attempt at an estimate needs to be made. It cannot be more than a calculation of the income derived by crown and marcher lords from those sources of income which were open to them and had also been available to the prince. No estimate can be made of advantages or disadvantages derived from an increased ratio of commuted services and dues, or from complete commutation into money payments. It would be best to exclude the profits of justice, variable year by year and possibly substantially different from those secured by the prince, and prudent to make no attempt at estimating extraordinary income. Calculations are limited to income from those sources which post-conquest lords would not have exploited in a significantly different way from the prince.[274]

The earliest figures available for Anglesey, Caernarfon and Merioneth, which together constituted an area virtually corresponding to Gwynedd

---

[274] Where calculations are based on accounts, the charge (*summa totalis recepte*) has been used as a base figure, from which arrears, profits of courts and, if necessary, income from boroughs have been subtracted. No estimates are included for Edeirnion and Dinmael, nor outlying areas such as Cydewain, nor lands such as Powys Wenwynwyn which came into Llywelyn's possession for brief periods. Income from these lands may have been off-set by the costs of security and defence, and realistic estimates are impossible.

Uwch Conwy, indicate an annual income of £1,200 at the time of the making of the extent: subsequent increments brought the aggregate sums by the early fourteenth century to nearly £1,600.[275] In Rhos and Rhufoniog, in the absence of a series of early account rolls, main reliance has to be placed on the valuation made in 1334, when the income of the five commotes which then formed the lordship of Denbigh came close to £1,000, but a figure of £1,200 is indicated by an account roll for 1304–5 which provides detailed figures for the income from the commotes and from demesne farming, and the latter figure (which excludes court profits) is preferred.[276] The accounts for Dyffryn Clwyd are few, and a valuation of 1308 suggests a figure, after normal adjustments, of £500.[277] If the prince's income from Tegeingl is reasonably reflected in the profits drawn from the county of Flint, calculations from early account rolls point to a figure, including Hope and Ewloe, of £260.[278] The figures would suggest that the prince's successors drew from an area roughly equivalent to the territorial lordship of Gwynedd a sum of approximately £3,000, or one nearer £3,500 if the increases recorded in the counties reflect already existing income which had not been reflected in the initial extents. No attempt is made to estimate profits from territorial lordships outside Gwynedd, and a deduction of a sum possibly even in excess of £1,000 would need to be made in respect of those years when Dafydd ap Gruffudd was vested with Rhufoniog and Dyffryn Clwyd, if Dafydd was allowed a normal degree of lordship in those lands.[279] These calculations, excluding court profits and making no

---

[275] Figures from the sheriffs' accounts 1291–2 (SC6/1227/2, *B*, 9 (1937–9), 50–70); 1304–5 (SC6/1211/2, *B*, 1 (1921–3), 256–75). Stephenson, *GG*, xxxv, n. 56, calculates that a sum of £1,000, the value of the estates in England offered to Llywelyn in 1282, does not fall far short of the total valuation put upon the rents and services due to the prince as indicated in the early post-conquest extents of Gwynedd Uwch Conwy.

[276] DL29/1/2. Sources of income in survey and account compare very closely. The figure from the account is reached by taking expected income from the commotes, minus court profits, and actual income from demesnes at Denbigh, Dinorben and Cilffwrn. Seven account rolls 1362–97 give incomes, before deductions for expenditure, between £776 and £1,194 at an average of £991 (D. H. Owen, 'Lordship of Denbigh', 179–201, 326–32); seigniorial pressures exerted in the later fourteenth century may not have produced figures to match those of a century earlier.

[277] Figure based on the extent at the death of Reginald de Grey (C134/3, no. 5), excluding court profits and 'easements' of the castle of Rhuthun assessed at £100. The valuation in 1323, excluding court profits, was £490 (C134/82, no. 9).

[278] SC6/771/1 (1301–2) *et seq.*; *Flintshire Ministers' Accounts 1301–1328*, ed. A. Jones (Flintshire Historical Society, no. 3, 1913), i *et seq*. Issues of the boroughs of Flint and Rhuddlan have been subtracted, except that a sum is included for Rhuddlan comparable to that for the vills of Caerwys and Coleshill but, at £10, slightly larger in view of the probable comparative prosperity of Rhuddlan. The vills of Ewloe and Hope were assessed at £41 and £20 respectively.

[279] The extent of Dafydd's estate after 1267 is unknown but it may have consisted of Rhufoniog and Dyffryn Clwyd. This would have made a substantial barony, with Rhufoniog valued in 1334 at about £750 and Dyffryn Clwyd in 1308 at about £500.

estimate of extraordinary levies, indicating a figure between £3,000 and £3,500 appear to come as close to an estimate of the prince's income as the sources allow.[280]

A sum of this nature, even when adjusted downward to take some account of factors which might tend to overestimate the revenues, place Llywelyn ap Gruffudd among the great magnates of the realm in terms of income. The Clare estates in England and Wales, with some income from Ireland, were valued at something between £4,500 and £5,000 in the period of the prince's adversary Gilbert de Clare, earl of Gloucester (d. 1295). Henry de Lacy, earl of Lincoln, appears to have drawn from his estates at the turn of the century an income exceeding £6,000.[281] These were probably exceptionally large baronial incomes. The estates of magnates such as John de Warenne, earl of Surrey, and Humphrey de Bohun, earl of Hereford, might be estimated at sums not greatly in excess of £2,000.[282] The lordship of Snowdon may have been a barren land, but it may have brought its lord an income not inconsiderable by comparison with that of the magnates of England.[283]

Estimates of income are more meaningful if they can be set beside some indication of expenditure, but in Llywelyn's case this would call for even more speculative calculation. The only major disbursement accurately quantified is the indemnity incurred by the treaty of Montgomery in 1267, by which Llywelyn was required to pay the king of England £2,000 a year for ten years. Llywelyn's conduct in this connection, the whole question of whether he was to refuse to pay on a point of principle or whether he found it difficult to raise

---

[280] Figures in J. Given, *State and Society in Medieval Europe: Gwynedd and Languedoc under Outside Rule* (Ithaca, NY, and London, 1990), 120–1 (table 3), give the revenue from the principality indicated by payments made by the chamberlain of north Wales to the London exchequer. They are of limited value in attempting to assess pre-conquest income. Williams-Jones, in *MLSR*, xviii, offers no calculation but indicates that he would not have expected the prince's income to have exceeded £4,500–£5,000; that may be a generous estimate, but if the figure were lower it would underline his argument that Llywelyn was under very severe financial constraints.

[281] Altschul, *Clares*, 203–5, calculates that the estates of Earl Gilbert (d. 1295) yielded £4,500–£5,000, the English estates yielding some £3,000–£3,500 and those of Wales and Ireland the remainder; the valuation of the estates of Earl Gilbert (d. 1314) at the partition of 1317 is put at £6,000–£6,500. J. F. Baldwin, 'The household administration of Henry de Lacy and Thomas of Lancaster', *EHR*, 42 (1927), 180–200, concludes from SC6/1/1, 2 (1295–6, 1304–5) that Lacy's ministers produced an annual income estimated at 10,000 marks.

[282] Late-thirteenth-century evidence is slight, but see Altschul, *Clares*, 205–6; S. Painter, *Studies in the History of the English Feudal Barony* (Baltimore, 1943), 173–7.

[283] Comparison with the king's income from the counties of England, excluding the very substantial yield of the customs and parliamentary taxes, is not entirely futile. Exchequer estimates in 1284 of the county farms paid by the sheriffs came to only £10,168 a year out of a total of £26,828: M. Mills, 'Exchequer agenda and estimates of revenue, Easter Term 1284', *EHR*, 40 (1925), 229–34; M. Prestwich, *War, Politics and Finance under Edward I* (London, 1972), 178–9 [Prestwich, *WPF*]; idem, *Edward I*, 242–3.

the money, is considered in a later chapter. But if our calculation of his income in any way approximates to Llywelyn's actual position, he was charged during these years with an annual obligation equal to a very substantial fraction of his total financial resources. This would have been particularly so in what proved to be the crucial years 1267–74, when Dafydd ap Gruffudd would have taken what was due to him by virtue of the lordship ceded to him. The extent of Llywelyn's obligation as a share of his total disposable income is a consideration which, taken by itself alone, lends support to the view, strenuously urged by Keith Williams-Jones, that Llywelyn 'grossly over-estimated his financial resources', and that his downfall in 1277 was partly the result of the 'overweening ambition and ill-conceived policies' which he had pursued.[284] It would be helpful, even so, if we could gain some impression, if not a calculation, of Llywelyn ap Gruffudd's level of expenditure apart from his owings to the crown. Sadly, we know little of his personal inclinations, of the lavishness or spareness of his spending upon his court, or of the extent to which the generosity which gratified the poets was such as made a significant drain upon his coffers. We cannot tell how many men and women served him, and we might be mistaken if we were to envisage the prince of Wales maintaining day by day a great host of courtiers in plenteous affluence. Later depictions of the royal or noble courts of Europe may be entirely inappropriate to the circumstances of a thirteenth-century prince of Gwynedd. The impression left by the contemporary record, taking due account of the poets' eulogy and elegy, is of a prince not conspicuously inclined to largesse or lavish patronage. The itinerary of his court, whatever the extent of his entourage, was evidently dictated by a need to live off the produce of his demesnes and minimize expenditure in hard currency. There were, of course, other reasons for movement, some of more serious concern than others. He no doubt shared his brother Dafydd's satisfaction in 'the solace of hunting', as is suggested in a letter which recounts difficulties which had arisen when, hunting in Meirionnydd, a stag was pursued to the king's land of Genau'r Glyn.[285] The prince was surely concerned to make his presence known over the whole extent of his lordship, but his itinerary was confined to Gwynedd and the fact that journeys beyond its confines appear to have been limited to military and other necessary purposes reflects his dependence on the resources of his patrimonial land.[286] The resources of Gwynedd bore the burden of the apparatus of the wider principality, and

[284] *MLSR*, xviii–xx.
[285] *CAC*, 88–9; for Dafydd's pleasure in hunting, *CAC*, 74.
[286] Journeys to Dolforwyn in 1274 and to the frontier in the same area in 1277 (a region in which he possessed the territorial lordship of Cydewain) are among those noticed in the chapters which follow, but they are not many and there is no indication that the prince made an itinerary of his broader principality.

those who transacted its business were supported from the prince's funds as ruler of Gwynedd. The court of the thirteenth-century princes was different, and perhaps less elaborate, than that depicted in the lawbooks, but it assumed new responsibilities and may have incurred substantially increased costs.

Llywelyn's dependence on the demesnes associated with the courts of his dominion has been examined already and it was concluded that the services of the bond and free communities was directed to the courts rather than to the castles which had been constructed within the ambit of some of the courts. The main investment in stone castles was made by Llywelyn ap Iorwerth in an impressive building programme which accounts for the building, or certainly for the main works, of Dolwyddelan, Dolbadarn, Castell y Bere and Cricieth.[287] It is possible that additional work at some of these sites was done by Llywelyn ap Gruffudd; he embarked upon major new works at Ewloe and Dolforwyn and he may have built Carndochan.[288] We cannot be certain that we know the full extent of the prince's building works, and Llywelyn may have undertaken building initiatives at other sites, such as those, well beyond the confines of Gwynedd, at Clun and Sennybridge.[289] For those he may have drawn upon the resources of the territories over which he extended his power, but, even though he benefited from the outlay of his grandfather in his own dominion, the existing castles of Gwynedd incurred recurrent charges and these may not have been borne from the customary services which were, from the evidence already cited, apparently still linked with the courts rather than the castles. References in the lawbooks to customary works upon *castra* appear to refer to the making of encampments rather than the building of castles.[290] Castle-building costs, even much of their maintenance, may have

---

[287] For problems in attribution, Avent, 'Castles', 12–16, with citations of earlier work.

[288] D. Renn and R. Avent, *Flint Castle. Ewloe Castle* (Cardiff, 1995), 5–8; Ewloe, above, pp. 172–3, Dolforwyn, below, p. 360; Carndochan (SH846306), west of Llanuwchllyn, is noticed in King, *CA*, 275; A. H. A. Hogg, 'Castell Carndochan', *JMerHS*, 2 (1953–6), 178–80.

[289] For a site in Nant Ffrangcon (SH 626660), possibly a fortification at Abercaseg visited by Edward I in 1284: *Inventory Caern*, I, 134; D. Hopewell, *Tŷ'n Tŵr, Bethesda, Archaeological Excavation* (Bangor, Gwynedd Archaeological Trust Report No. 96, 1993); for other works, above, pp. 156, 162; below, pp. 372, n. 118, 416–17.

[290] References to *gueyth kestyll ebrenhyn* (*LlIor*, 61, *LlCol*, 40) might suggest 'work on the king's castles' (*LHD*, 124), and correspond to the obligations of those who responsible for *castra regis* in *LTWL*, 137, 205, 377. While this duty might appear (*LlCol*, 170, n. 667) to differ from that in the Cyfnerth text (*WML*,57), which requires the building of encampments, there is a very close correspondence between Latin and Cyfnerth texts in that the bondman came with horse and axe, just as *LlIor* expects a man with an axe to make encampments for the king upon his hostings ('gur a buyall y wneythur lluesteu ydau en e lluyd', *LlIor*, 62; *LHD*, 125; *LlCol*, 40). Making *castra* probably meant making encampments (*castrametor*), and there are numerous references to the prince encamped (*in castris*) at places such as Pipton and Caerffili. In post-conquest documents building works are related to courts rather than castles, and the complaints of 1283 refer to the building of courts (*edificia curiarum*), not castles.

had to be stood from the coffers of his central treasury and it may have proved to be an expensive business. It is true that marcher lords, probably less well endowed than Llywelyn, managed not only to maintain their structures but to build imposing stone castles in that remarkable investment which occurred in the late thirteenth century. Clare building at Caerffili was somewhat exceptional in scale perhaps, but Mortimer building at Cefnllys and Dinbod, or Chaworth at Cydweli or Camville at Llansteffan or Brian at Laugharne demonstrate the capacity of the prince's marcher contemporaries to invest in substantial building.[291] Yet building works were only one facet of the charges placed on Llywelyn by the needs of war.

The degree to which Llywelyn was able to mobilize the military capability of his broader principality is considered in the next chapter. As lord of Gwynedd he could call upon the service due to him from the freemen, but to what extent these obligations sufficed is far from clear. The lawbooks point to a claim upon six weeks' service at the freeman's costs and thereafter at the prince's costs, an obligation (*lluyd* or *exercitus*) for which there is some endorsement in post-conquest sources.[292] The prince could conceivably arrange his offensive campaigns so as to avail himself of these obligations, but his defensive calendar was not within his power to determine. There were certainly times in the later years of his rule when he had need to match the king's ability to maintain forces in the field by the payment of wages. Quite apart from their wages, his soldiers needed to be supplied, sometimes at some distance from their own land. Llywelyn needed, too, if not the war-band, or the *teulu*, as depicted in the lawbooks, certainly a military force comparable to the household of his opponent, properly armed and equipped.[293] Horses equal to the needs of war were at a premium even in England, and, necessarily dependent on his own resources, Llywelyn was obliged to maintain studs capable of providing suitable beasts.[294] These needed the protection which was one of the significant factors in the cost of thirteenth-century warfare. Apart from the chroniclers' excitable estimates, there are reliable indications that Llywelyn was capable of deploying substantial numbers of barded

---

[291] R. Avent, 'The early development of three coastal castles', in H. James (ed.), *Sir Gâr, Studies in Carmarthenshire History* (Carmarthen, 1991), 167–88, with references to Cydweli, Llansteffan and Laugharne. Caerffili, Cefnllys and Dinbod are noticed below, pp. 352–3, 361–2, 494, 521–2.

[292] For *lluydd* and the principle of six weeks' service outside the king's country, *LlIor*, 61; *LHD*, 124; *LlCol*, 40; C. W. Lewis, 'The treaty of Woodstock, 1247: its background and significance', *WHR*, 2 (1964–5), 61–4; F. C. Suppe, *Military Institutions on the Welsh Marches: Shropshire AD 1066–1300* (Woodbridge, 1994), 125–30.

[293] The texts allow the king a retinue of thirty-six persons on horseback, the twenty-four officers of the court and twelve guests (*LlIor*, 2; *LHD*, 6; *LTWL*, 194), but give no indication of the size of his fighting force (*teulu*).

[294] For post-conquest references to studs and Llywelyn's generosity with foals from his studs, *SD*, 152–3, and below, n. 373.

horses, and he appears to have made use of siege engines in the campaigns in the march, though we have no means of knowing how elaborate those machines may have been.[295] The lawbooks' account of the right of the king to summon his host once a year – and only once – and their references to the mounted men who formed his retinue (*in comitiva sua*) describe a provision hardly adequate to meet what was required in the conflicts of the period of Llywelyn ap Gruffudd. Even the early campaigns of the years in which he asserted power in Wales were no doubt costly enterprises, not least in that they were not invariably successful. More expensive by far, and undoubtedly a strain upon the resources of the lands from which he could draw seigniorial income, were the measures by which he maintained the protection of his dominions in the period preceding the war of 1277, and their tenacious defence during its course. The principality of Wales, and particularly the territorial lordship of its prince, was among the many lands where, faced with sustained conflict in a period when the waging of war proved increasingly expensive, the political and social order was placed under intense strain.[296] The great powers of England and France were not immune to the effect of the costs of warfare, and Edward I was to be confronted with resistance on the part of the community of the realm sufficiently vigorous to force a humiliating concession on his part.[297] There can be no doubt that Llywelyn ap Gruffudd faced expenditure on a vastly greater scale than his predecessors, and there is nothing to suggest that he was able to meet increased demands from entirely new sources of revenue. To what extent the pressures exerted on the lord of Snowdon led to increased, and burdensome, impositions on the community is a matter of some consequence and one which has a particular bearing upon our estimate of Llywelyn's capacity to maintain himself in the crucial conflict with Edward I.[298]

---

[295] Opponents' estimates of the number of his barded horses in 1263 (*CAC*, 52–3; *RL*, ii, 219–30) were noticed earlier; other estimates include Paris, *ChronMaj*, iv, 614; *AnnTewk*, 167; *AC*, 98. References to siege engines include *RL*, ii, 150 (Builth, 1260); *AC*, 100 (Maelienydd, 1262); there were other sieges, such as that at Caerffili, where engines may have been used. It is impossible to tell whether they were e.g. the elaborate trebuchet or less cumbersome *perriere*, but construction and transport costs would have been involved in each case.

[296] P. Contamine, *War in the Middle Ages* (Oxford, 1984), 90–118; R. Bartlett, 'Technique militaire et pouvoir politique, 900–1300', *Annales: Economies, Societes, Civilizations,* 41 (1986), 1135–59; R. W. Kaeuper, *War, Justice and Public Order: England and France in the Later Middle Ages* (Oxford, 1988), 23–117.

[297] Important studies include E. Miller, 'War, taxation and the English economy in the late thirteenth and early fourteenth centuries', in J. M. Winter (ed.), *War and Economic Development* (Cambridge, 1975), 11–31; J. R. Maddicott, *The English Peasantry and the Demands of the Crown, 1294–1341* (Past and Present Supplement, 1, Oxford, 1975); E. B. Fryde, *Studies in Medieval Trade and Finance* (London, 1983), i, 824–60.

[298] Below, pp. 264–7.

Lord of Snowdon

Lord and community

The most explicit indication that Llywelyn ap Gruffudd's lordship was considered to be harsh and extortionate is contained in the statement of the grievances of the community against the defeated prince in the summer of 1283.[299] It has already been noticed that the representatives of the communities of Gwynedd Uwch Conwy gathered in the presence of the bishop of Bangor at a time when the fiscal obligations of the tenants to their new lord were being determined. The document agreed at Nancall may reflect an anxiety on the part of the communities that the impositions which they regarded as excessive would be perpetuated under the new dispensation. The charges against the prince are quite specific in some instances, more general in others. But taken together they reflect a wish to register the view that Llywelyn ap Gruffudd, in his effort to increase his revenue, had breached hitherto accepted practice. The communities of Gwynedd Uwch Conwy, like so many others in medieval societies, were aggrieved at the harshness and exactitude of officers and their increased numbers. They complain of the burden of a multitude of officers, for whereas in earlier times one officer sufficed there were now two or three. The men of Arfon were particularly troubled by the weight of princely rule which had been brought to bear upon them, for whereas before the time of Llywelyn ap Gruffudd there had been just one court and one bailiff (*ballivus*) with two sergeants (*precones*), their number had now doubled.[300] These officers were seen as the agents of an extractive taxation imposed by the prince. The most specific charge was that Llywelyn, as he prepared for war against the king, had imposed a tax of three pence on each great beast, and did so without consulting the people or securing their consent. Nor would he release anything from his treasure kept at Dolwyddelan and elsewhere.[301] The charge that tax was levied on cattle is in close accord with the testimony of Bishop Anian of St Asaph some years before, when he maintained that the prince had levied a tax of this nature on the pretext that he would pay the money to the king for the peace that they had made.[302] The basis on which impositions were assessed was a source of contention, the complainants intimating that they were disadvantaged by being taxed according to the number of their possessions rather than upon

---

[299] Ll. B. Smith '*Gravamina*', 158–76; MS source and the origins of the document are considered ibid. 158–62 and noticed above, n. 29. References in next paragraphs are to the numbered clauses of the document.
[300] XIV, XXIII; the terms are noticed in view of earlier discussion of *rhaglaw* and *rhingyll*.
[301] XIII; financial transactions and holding of treasure at Dolwyddelan, above, n. 206.
[302] *CAC*, 105.

their lands.³⁰³ The prince profited by allowing all manner of men to gather corn and sheep, and it was done violently and unjustly.³⁰⁴ During his time the measures of wine and grain and ale were increased, changes recalled, perhaps, in later references to 'Llywelyn's measures'.³⁰⁵ The butter obligations of the men of Eifionydd were doubled, and the annual charge (*census*) on those of Llŷn and Arllechwedd were also doubled.³⁰⁶ The prince increased the procuration charges made for the support of his entourage. The communities alluded particularly to the fact that, as the bondmen of Dindaethwy were unable to provide sufficient *porthiant,* freemen – *nobiles* – were compelled to do so. The specific charge is difficult to substantiate, but it has been noticed that the *porthiant* levied in Dindaethwy was substantial and that it fell not only on bondmen but on freemen.³⁰⁷ The prince's demands may well reflect his need to garrison an area which was shown to be vulnerable in the wars of 1277 and 1282. Military pressures were felt in increased demands upon those not serving upon expedition to provide support for soldiers (*satellites*) who were so deployed, and in the demand, never made before the time of Llywelyn, for the use of horses to fulfil carriage requirements and for their pasturing.³⁰⁸ The document speaks eloquently of the needs of war.

The prince's usurpation of lands was a vexed issue. He seized large and small lands without the consent of the heirs and created vaccaries there, or put the lands under the plough and brought himself profit in a way that no other prince had done.³⁰⁹ So it may well be that the extensive seigniorial exploitation of the pastures of Snowdonia may owe something, and perhaps something substantial, to Llywelyn ap Gruffudd himself. It was alleged, too, that he seized townships to his own use, or conceded them to others for service, and burdened the community with their dues. To place the dues of one township upon another was a great burden, the communities insisted, and their complaints have an affinity with the bishop of St Asaph's charges

---

³⁰³ XXIII; cf. *SD*, 47, 209 for evidence of dues assessed on goods in Ceinmeirch and Uwch Aled. Taxes on moveable property, an important feature of English taxation from 1290, had been remunerative from 1275, and Anian's report on Llywelyn's tax of 3*d.* on each head of cattle was made in September 1275. It is conceivable, but impossible to prove, that Llywelyn was influenced by English practice, considered in S. K. Mitchell, *Studies in Taxation under John and Henry III* (New Haven, 1914); G. L. Harriss, *King, Parliament, and Public Finance in Medieval England to 1369* (Oxford, 1975), 39 *et seq.*; bases of assessment are examined in J. F. Willard, *Parliamentary Taxation on Personal Property 1290–1334* (Cambridge, Mass., 1934).
³⁰⁴ II.
³⁰⁵ XVII; e.g. *cranoca Lewelini* (*ExtAng*, 24); 'mensura domini Lewelini nuper principis Wallie' (*RC*, 249).
³⁰⁶ XVIII, XX.
³⁰⁷ XXI; *ExtAng*, 4–5; above, n. 257.
³⁰⁸ VIII, XIX.
³⁰⁹ VI.

against Llywelyn for the seizure of church fees.[310] The prince appears, too, to have exercised rights of wardship over heirs in their minority, a charge which finds some corroboration years later.[311] Those rights which we have described as regalian were evidently exercised to the full, the complaints reflecting issues which stand prominently in the disputes between Llywelyn and the bishop. In cases of shipwreck, even when the goods were saved, if even one plank or a nail were broken, the prince would deprive the owner of all his goods. If a ship in harbour were to break its moorings and were found elsewhere, on land or at sea, the prince would confiscate the vessel.[312] The prince's rights on the foreshore, which are indeed vouched for in the lawbooks, were evidently asserted vigorously, for he would appropriate any animal drowned by flood or one which might fall from a cliff and be found on the foreshore.[313] How substantial were the prince's profits from justice we cannot tell, but it is clear that it was a source of income to which his officers did not fail to attend. There was evidently some discontent over the manner in which justice was done: among several clauses it was alleged that a person charged with bloodshed was not admitted to purgation (*ad purgandum*); a person charged with theft, and with no acquaintance with the law, was not allowed an advocate nor the services of a person knowledgeable in the law of Hywel Dda.[314] The message throughout the numerous clauses of this remarkable document is the rigorous and grasping nature of Llywelyn's rule, and the extent to which he had disowned the conventions which his predecessors had respected. No prince, nor king before him, the men of Gwynedd concluded, had inflicted injuries like these upon the people in times past, no one but Llywelyn, and they prayed God for remedy. Llywelyn ap Gruffudd was not altogether reprehensible, and those who enumerated the communities' grievances had the grace to acknowledge that their former prince had not been wholly ungenerous.[315] But their document stressed the severity of his lordship and the extent of his people's vexation.

The purpose of the document was to establish the fact that the prince's lordship had already affected the community at large: the Welsh community was greatly aggrieved (*communitas Wallie fuit multum aggravata*) it was proclaimed at one point.[316] Yet two observations need to be made. The

---

[310] V; *Councils*, i, 514–15; cf. *CPR, 1292–1301*, 75.

[311] X; *CAP*, 335–6.

[312] XXVIII, XXXII; for lawbook references and disputes with the bishop of Bangor over wreck, above, pp. 200, 208–9; later concern for wreck, below, pp. 502–4.

[313] XXXIII; for foreshore rights in law texts, *LlCol*, 37–8; Peniarth MS 32, f. 186.

[314] XI, XV, XXII, XXX, XXXIV. The reference (XXII) to the rough justice meted out to a poor man, who might be sentenced to death or subjected to a fine of £7, echoes a complaint from the diocese of St Asaph, 1276 (*Councils*, i, 491; above, n. 120).

[315] Below, pp. 271–2.

[316] III.

document was drawn up under ecclesiastical auspices and includes several clauses concerning matters on which there is known to have been contention between Llywelyn ap Gruffudd and the bishops in earlier years. The tribute raised on each head of cattle had first been reported by Anian of St Asaph; the issue of right to wreck had been broached by the bishop of Bangor, whose successor presided over the proceedings at Nancall. There were other issues which might have been of particular concern to the churchmen. The odium against the clerical fraternity with which Anian of St Asaph charged Llywelyn might be echoed in the allegation that the prince refused to accept clerics and religious as warrantors, a practice contrary to God and justice (*quod est contra Deum et iusticiam*). There may have been more at issue in this connection than animosity on Llywelyn's part, for a legal text maintains that priests or other men in orders were not entitled to warrant a title to stolen property, as their status as churchmen prevented them from submitting to secular law. The charges may have reflected current secular legal tenets.[317] The allegation in the document of 1283 that the prince interfered in wills made before a priest or a layman has a similarity to Anian of St Asaph's complaint, already noticed, that Llywelyn refused to admit wills unless they were made in sickness of which the testator died.[318] Bishop Anian had also, of course, complained of Llywelyn's refusal to allow him to make a will but the prince's attitude to testamentary matters was an issue of much more general concern.[319] It is evident that in the prince's lands the goods of intestates fell to their lord. The complaint made in 1283 that Llywelyn had usurped the rights of freemen to the goods of their tenants dying intestate implicitly recognized that lay persons exercised these rights.[320] They were carefully guarded by the prince's marcher successors in resistance to episcopal protest, but this was a matter on which Anian of St Asaph had already taken issue with Llywelyn.[321] Complaining that the goods of intestates were seized by the prince, Anian had been able to secure a promise that Llywelyn would not seize the goods of a vassal of the church who died intestate.[322] In confronting the same issue in the diocese of Bangor the bishop was able to call up the authority of Archbishop Pecham to lay down the canonical law that the disposal of the goods of

---

[317] XXVII; the articles of complaint against Llywelyn drawn up in the diocese of St Asaph, 1274, state that the prince acted *in odium clericorum* (*Councils*, i, 515); for the clause on warranty in *Damweiniau Colan. Llyfr y Damweiniau yn ôl Llawysgrif Peniarth 30*, ed. D. Jenkins (Aberystwyth, 1973), 54–5 (para. 472), see discussion of juridical capacity in Pryce, *NLC*, 137–8 and n. 21.
[318] XXIX; *Councils*, i, 513.
[319] Ibid., 512–13, 519–21.
[320] IX.
[321] Ll. B. Smith, '*Gravamina*', 165–6.
[322] *Councils*, i, 520.

intestates belonged to the administration of the ordinary.[323] The document drawn up at Nancall has something of the tenor of the arguments between the prince and the prelates and suggests that a degree of ecclesiastical interest and influence was brought to bear upon the process by which the grievances of the community came to be formulated.

The matters which are known to have exercised the churchmen were not altogether particular to the clerical fraternity but rather demonstrate that there were churchmen and laymen who needed to safeguard the interests which they shared by virtue of the authority which they exerted within the social order. This is a second matter which has a bearing on the making of the document drawn up at Nancall. Thirteenth-century society in Gwynedd was hardly one bound in solidarity, and it was not an undifferentiated society. The distinction between the interests of freemen and bondmen – *nobiles* and *ignobiles* – emerges clearly enough in 1283 in successive allegations: the status of *nobiles* was not respected as they came to be compelled to repair court buildings whereas others – *ignobiles* and *rustici* – had been accustomed to do so in the past;[324] procuration dues which had fallen upon bondmen were imposed on freemen;[325] whereas there had always been just two classes of men – *nobiles* and *ignobiles* – Llywelyn created a third class (*genus*) from a mixture of these two classes in an endeavour to further his purposes.[326] As an indication of precisely what had been amiss in the period of Llywelyn ap Gruffudd these clauses are not particularly helpful. Nor can they be safely evaluated with regard to the extent of the changes brought about in that period. For, if the references made in later extents to the building and procuration charged placed upon freemen really derive from the rule of Llywelyn, his influence on the social obligations of his free tenants had been truly profound. A degree of caution would be appropriate in these cases, and also when considering the possibility that the *gwŷr mâl*, *gwŷr gwaith* and *gwŷr tir bwrdd* identified in the extents reflect a differentiation into social groups which might accord with the notion of the third class of person attributed to Llywelyn.[327] At the same time the broad assertions in these clauses of the *gravamina* may provide an indication that men of substance in the community, men precisely like those who may be presumed to have come to Nancall from the several commotes of the prince's lordship, had been discontented with the manner in which they had been governed. It has been

---

[323] *RPeck*, i, 77; Ll. B. Smith, '*Gravamina*', 165–6.
[324] XVI; works contributed by freemen to the maintenance of court buildings are frequently recorded in the extents and have been noticed earlier.
[325] XXI; the clause refers particularly to Dindaethwy.
[326] IV: 'princeps accipiebat tertium genus de nobilibus et ignobilibus sibi usurpando quicquid emolumenti proveniret ab ipsis'.
[327] Citations above, n. 171.

suggested earlier that there is little to indicate that the princes of Gwynedd had yielded much in the way of franchisal rights to their tenants and that the more privileged orders in society occupied no more than a modest degree of tenurial advantage. Even so, those who submitted grievances voiced their concern that the power (*potestas*) of men over their advowry tenants had been undermined and, as indicated already, they spoke for *nobiles* who had enjoyed the goods of tenants, particularly bondmen, who died intestate.[328] The document was presented as a statement of the grievances of a community – the words *populus* and *communitas* were an essential part of the presentation – but its proctors were unable to conceal their concern for the particular discomfiture of those substantial persons within the community whose fidelity might depend on the extent to which their interests could be reconciled with those of the prince who exercised lordship over them.

There was in the late thirteenth century, as the document of the summer of 1283 conveys, a clear perception of the distinction between bond and free, but there were undoubtedly gradations within free society. There were men who, though not of princely status, still stood apart from those who might be regarded as peasant proprietors. Yet the better endowed were not without their anxieties, and these could indeed be underlined by the very status they sought to sustain. Irrespective of economic differentiation the free proprietors had a hereditary interest in their land; hereditability was the very essence of their proprietorship. It was, however, a hereditability bound up with partibility, a succession practice which, at least as it is depicted in the lawbooks, was a rigorous system which generation by generation brought a division of properties and the creation of new households.[329] To what extent, if at all, the rigour could be mitigated by the will of the lineages themselves we cannot tell, but there is much post-conquest evidence which suggests that in preceding generations estates had indeed been subject to a continuing fractionization and, on account of the manner in which lands were divided, an inexorably increasing intermingling of assets on the ground.[330] The broad economic effect of these processes is difficult to judge, but it is likely that Gwynedd could be counted among the lands which, though it probably shared in the

---

[328] III, IX.

[329] For partible succession in the lawbooks, *LlIor*, 53–4; *LHD*, 98–100; *LlCol*, 35–6; and references in J. B. Smith, 'Dynastic succession', 200, n. 3.

[330] Fragmentation and dispersal of holdings are examined in the studies of T. Jones Pierce, *MWS*, 48–55, 216–24, 236–7, 253–65, 340–2; G. R. J. Jones, 'Hereditary land: its effect on the evolution of field systems and settlement patterns in the Vale of Clwyd', in R. C. Eidt, K. N. Singh and R. P. B. Singh (eds.), *Man, Culture and Settlement* (New Delhi, 1977), 82–96; idem, 'Field systems in north Wales', 446–57; idem, 'Forms and patterns of medieval settlement', 156–8, 163–4. Late medieval inheritance, and the light it throws on earlier practice, is treated in Llinos Beverley Smith's forthcoming volume on the social history of the period.

growth in population characteristic of western lands in general, was inhibited in its capacity to sustain commensurate economic growth. It is reasonably clear that the social effect of an adherence to partible succession in a period of population growth could be profound as free lineages of comparatively affluent origins became increasingly reduced to the status of peasant proprietors. The effect in individual lineages, if in each generation they increased their numbers, could be severe, and the consequences would be felt particularly in those very lineages with pretensions to elevated status as they saw their proprietorial assets eroded and their endeavour to maintain stability constantly vitiated.[331]

The problems which may thus have confronted the more prominent among the freemen could well have an important bearing on their relations with the prince. The estates of lineages such as those of Hwfa ap Cynddelw or Edryd ap Marchudd appear to have been derived from endowments made by the princes, or perhaps early appropriations had been sanctioned by the princes' grace. But the economic viability of early endowments, or registrations, would diminish in each generation and create new demands upon the princes for replenishment which could only be met at the cost of a continuing diminution of their demesnes. Llywelyn ap Iorwerth appears to have been generous in his grants to favoured members' lineages which were, in many cases, already well-endowed. His seneschal, Ednyfed Fychan, received extensive lands which supplemented those which had come to him as one of the heirs of the lineage of Edryd ap Marchudd.[332] These lands, held as we have seen by what became known as Wyrion Ednyfed tenure, were held on particularly advantageous terms, but there were other instances of the prince's liberal patronage in the early thirteenth century. These may have been years of conspicuous princely largesse. There were, however, two considerations which created some difficulty by Llywelyn ap Gruffudd's early years. He came to power at a time when the demesnes had already been depleted by his predecessors' concessions. Alienations from the demesnes were extensive and they were permanent. Admittedly, the notion of a land conveyance other than outright alienation is well attested in the lawbooks in the form of the *prid* or

---

[331] For the inhibiting effect of partibility on the economy and its social implications in differing areas, see e.g. D. Herlihy, *The Social History of Italy and Western Europe, 700–1500* (London, 1978), ii, 23–41; L. Genicot, *L'Economie rurale namuroise au bas moyen âge* (Louvain, 1943–60), i, 77–82; ii, 7–62; F. R. H. Du Boulay, *The Lordship of Canterbury* (London, 1966), 146–9; K. Nicholls, 'Anglo-French Ireland and after', *Peritia*, 1 (1982), 371–81.

[332] In *SD*, 228 (Dinorben Fychan) favour extended to the lineage of Ednyfed Fychan is specifically attributed to Llywelyn ap Iorwerth. Grants are said to have been made, or can be deduced to have been made, to Ednyfed Fychan's grandfather, father and Ednyfed himself (e.g. *SD*, 303), and a process of continuing augmentation may be envisaged. For the extensive Wyrion Ednyfed lands, above, pp. 217–18.

gage transaction, most clearly enunciated in clauses which provide that both the sale and the gaging of land by proprietors were subject to the lord's regulation.[333] But there is nothing to suggest that the princes' grants were anything but outright conveyances. There is no indication in the post-conquest evidence on which reliance has to be placed that the prince's demesnes had been conveyed to proprietors on terms other than those which ensured permanent alienation and embodied hereditary right.[334] The princes made what were in effect grants of new tenures in fee which left the donor or his successors with no power of discretion and disposition in future years and constituted permanent depletions of the patrimony. Indeed, quite apart from alienations to freemen, the conversion of *tir cyfrif* demesne into *tir gwelyog* or *gafael* holdings for bondmen was tantamount to the creation of a hereditary right.[335] Patrimonial right was certainly the cardinal characteristic of the estates vested in the free tenants. The princes' grants were thus irreversible, for only if there were no heirs within a prescribed degree of consanguinity or in other exceptional circumstances would an estate revert to the prince.[336] The princes were affected by another material consideration. Alienation was made on fiscal terms which became increasingly favourable to the tenants. Some were, of course, made entirely free of rent from the beginning and the others were subject to fixed assessments which came to be, even if they were not so from the beginning, purely recognative payments. The choice confronting a thirteenth-century prince lay, it seems, between the direct management of the demesnes and the permanent ceding from those demesnes of estates whose remunerative value to the prince diminished as, exposed to a variable but still deleterious rate of inflation, he was left with decidedly dwindling assets.[337]

---

[333] *LlIor*, 58; *LHD*, 114; *LlCol*, 38; Ll. B. Smith, 'Gage and land market', 537–50.

[334] The extents have evidence of leasing for fixed terms and of land held at farm, but they do not provide any certainty that these had been features of pre-conquest practice. The position in Gwynedd in the thirteenth century appears to have been different from that of the English landlords whose options are described in e.g. Lennard, *Rural England*, 105–41.

[335] Bond land held in *gwelyau* or *gafaelion* was hereditary, and even tenants in *tir cyfrif* might be described as 'heirs' (e.g. the *heredes* of Botacho, *RC*, 34). The custumal of Rhos Uwch Dulas describes the payment of relief by freemen and bondmen upon entering their inheritance (*hereditas*) in virtually identical terms (*SD*, 313).

[336] *LlCol*, 17, specifies treachery to the lord (*brad arglwydd*), ambush (*cynllwyn*), and failure to meet fiscal obligations as reasons for loss of patrimony, with variant forms noted *LlCol*, 96.

[337] The princes were thus in a position very different from that of their counterparts in England who, confronted with the inflationary pressures of the late twelfth century, were able to recall lands previously leased and revert to direct exploitation. For inflation and economic management in England, P. D. A. Harvey, 'The English inflation of 1180–1220', *Past and Present*, 61 (1973), 3–30; E. Miller, 'England in the twelfth and thirteenth centuries: an economic contrast?', *EcHR*, 2nd ser., 24 (1971), 1–14; P. D. A. Harvey, 'The Pipe Rolls and the adoption of demesne farming in England', *EcHR*, 27 (1974), 345–59.

Lord of Snowdon

A second consideration arises from the fact that Llywelyn ap Gruffudd came to rule the lordship of Snowdon, not by undisputed hereditary succession but by the assertion of power which has been recounted earlier.[338] These circumstances made it imperative that he should retain the support of early adherents and earn the confidence of those whose fidelity was essential to his security and the well-being of his dominion. His political situation made it imprudent to halt the disposal of land entirely. Yet he laboured under severe restraints. The post-conquest extents which point to extensive endowments by Llywelyn ap Iorwerth and his predecessors suggest no comparable largesse on the part of his grandson. He evidently found it necessary, more especially in his early years, to draw upon the depleted resources of his demesnes to meet the calls, no doubt the strident demands, of his adherents and he was constrained to do so in accordance with traditional practice. In the two cases of Iorwerth ap Gwrgunan and Tudur ap Madog concessions were made to early supporters who belonged to established lineages in augmentation of their inherited properties.[339] Precisely in the way by which Llywelyn ap Iorwerth had furthered the interests of the Wyrion Ednyfed segment of the progeny of Edryd ap Marchudd, Llywelyn ap Gruffudd, albeit on a far less extensive scale and perhaps somewhat grudgingly, enlarged the territorial stakes of those to whom he was indebted. Iorwerth ap Gwrgunan, heir to a portion of Gwely Cyfnerth ap Rhufon in Is Aled, itself a fifth part of the greatly fragmented patrimony of the earliest known proprietors, received half the township of Cwmllannerch in Nanconwy.[340] It was not a generous grant, but it meant ceding part of the prince's demesne. A further grant of land which came to form Gwely Iorwerth ap Gwrgunan was made out of the prince's *tir cyfrif* township of Bodunod in Dindaethwy. Llywelyn drew on *tir cyfrif* demesnes in Penwynllys and Twrgarw, again in the commote of Dindaethwy, to provide for Tudur ap Madog in enhancement of the estate which had come to him as a parcenor in the inheritance of Cynddelw ap Iarddur, who had been favoured by Llywelyn ap Iorwerth.[341] Political necessity, rather than instinctive generosity, may have induced Llywelyn ap Gruffudd to convey to these two early confidants lands which, though not extensive, were granted upon terms of exceptional favour in accordance with the most liberal precedents established by his predecessors.

These were early and conspicuous adherents and, though it is not clear whether it was enough to retain their commitment to the prince's interests, they earned or exacted favourable treatment. How many more endowments

---

[338] Above, pp. 72–7.

[339] J. B. Smith, 'Land endowments of the period of Llywelyn ap Gruffudd', *B*, 34 (1987), 150–64.

[340] Ibid., 153–9, 162–3; Stephenson, *GG*, 114–15, 216.

[341] J. B. Smith, 'Land endowments', 155–6, 159; Stephenson, *GG*, 98–100, 112–13.

of this kind Llywelyn felt bound to make is difficult to judge, for direct indications of his gifts are rare and we depend largely on identifications which may be made among *gwely* or *gafael* names in the extents. But *gwely* and *gafael* affiliations are not always noted in connection with holdings derived from this period. Concessions by the prince may therefore remain concealed, explicit reference, such as that which we have to a holding at Bryncelyn in Cafflogion derived from a grant by Llywelyn (*de dono Lewelini principis*), being quite exceptional.[342] Llywelyn may thus have been induced to draw upon the resources of his land, and occasionally at least on the *tir cyfrif* demesnes, to favour deserving proprietors or those able to press their demands upon him. The grants do not appear to have been extensive, however, nor are they known to have been numerous, and we are left with an impression of the period of Llywelyn ap Gruffudd very different from that of his grandfather. Confronted with unprecedented financial obligations, and perhaps finding himself constrained by the legacy of the prodigality with which his predecessors had drawn upon the demesnes to secure the service and allegiance of important lineages, Llywelyn ap Gruffudd may have found it impossible to maintain any comparable degree of liberality, nor indeed to maintain that measure of largesse which he revealed in his early years. He might have been deemed to have failed to fulfil his part in the reciprocal obligations of lord and tenant by which loyalty was repaid with generosity. His situation, meeting increased commitments out of diminished assets, called for retrenchment. Land was at a premium, and he may well have found himself in the position of being unable to break with established practice and make non-hereditary grants of land and, more seriously perhaps, unable to secure adequate means of providing alternative remuneration in monetary form. We have no indication that Llywelyn ap Gruffudd was able to embark on any innovatory form of contractual lordship calculated to surmount the underlying difficulties with which he was burdened and provide for his adherents without prejudicing the future through permanent disposal of his territorial assets.[343]

The limitations on his power of giving may conceivably have affected his position in the increasingly stressful years after 1267. In these years the disaffected may have cherished the prospect, perhaps illusory, that the king of England would be an alternative and more bountiful provider of patronage. Relationships between the prince and his *nobiles* might be influenced by a whole range of considerations of which we have no knowledge.

[342] J. B. Smith, 'Land endowments', 159–62.

[343] The growth of 'contractual lordship', with a lessening of the prominence of grants in fee but a retention of the reciprocity of service and reward, is examined in S. C. Waugh, 'Tenure to contract: lordship and clientage in thirteenth-century England', *EHR*, 101 (1986), 814–19.

Disenchantment with their position in his entourage, dissent from the policies he might pursue or the manner in which they were pursued: there are countless possibilities of personal disillusion or animosity which might explain why men of substance might withhold their service, and even defect to the king of England. Still more difficult to fathom is the relationship between issues of a personal nature within the political community of Gwynedd and the broader issues affecting a wider social spectrum which have been broached already. Two instances, while far from resolving the problem, serve to illustrate the difficulties.

The lineage of Ednyfed Fychan could reasonably be judged to have provided, to a greater degree than any other, the continuity and stability within the community by which the prince's rule could be sustained. The succession of Goronwy ab Ednyfed and then Tudur ab Ednyfed to the position of seneschal which had been occupied for so long by their father, Ednyfed Fychan, will be noticed in the next chapter.[344] Contemporary estimates are indicated by the encomium upon Goronwy ab Ednyfed in *Brut y Tywysogyon* and in the elegy composed by Bleddyn Fardd.[345] Tudur ab Ednyfed, after a long period first in custody in England and then in the service of its king, returned to share in the prince's triumphs and in the responsibilities of the stressful period leading up to the conflict of 1277.[346] Their sons, Tudur ap Goronwy and Heilin ap Tudur, were both recipients of the prince's favour in his later years, and the historical perception of the lineages is one of fidelity and constancy.[347] With the lineage of Gruffudd ab Ednyfed perceptions are less clear. Certainly an early adherent, and possibly the prince's seneschal for a period, Gruffudd ab Ednyfed appears to have remained active in the prince's service until his death. The elegy composed by Dafydd Benfras portrays a man of unbreachable loyalty, the entire poem infused with a sense of fidelity which the memory evoked as he prayed for God's blessing upon his soul.[348]

At least one of Gruffudd's sons, as we shall see, was privy to Llywelyn's most inner counsels in the mid-1270s but this Dominican friar, Llywelyn ap Gruffudd, and his brother Rhys ap Gruffudd were to defect to the king during the course of the conflict of 1277.[349] Rhys's prominence in Edward's service thereafter suggests that he was of the stuff of which seneschals were made, but whether any personal disenchantment influenced his judgement, or

---

[344] G. Roberts, *Aspects of Welsh History*, 181–5; Stephenson, *GG*, 14–15, 102–4, 207–9, 213–14, 218–21; below, pp. 312–14.
[345] *BT, Pen20*, 218; *Pen20Tr*, 115; *GBF*, 45.
[346] Below, pp. 313–14, 328–9, 437–8.
[347] *RC*, 211, 217.
[348] J. B. Smith, 'Land endowments', 155–6; Stephenson, *GG*, 18, 104–5, 214–15; *GDB*, 33; below, p. 313.
[349] Below, pp. 430–2

whether he was moved by entirely different, and entirely honourable, considerations is impossible to judge. He may previously have had the benefit of the prince's favour, for Dinsylwy Rys could have been bestowed upon him in enhancement of the extensive lands which were in his possession, by virtue of his being of the progeny of Edryd ap Marchudd, in Dinorwig and Tregarnedd.[350] It may have proved to be an alienation of valuable *tir cyfrif* to no avail. Conditioned to expectations of continuing favour, the more affluent lineages might be discomforted if favour were withheld, but its dispensation brought no certainty of constant fidelity. Defection on the part of one of this milieu in society could have damaging repercussions. A rupture on personal grounds, or dissent from the prince's decisions on matters of policy, might bring men from the upper echelons of society to a position where they might join their disenchantment with the feelings of those in the community who, totally oblivious to the intrigues within the coterie in attendance upon the prince and unmindful of issues of policy, might still be resentful of those decisions on the prince's part which breached the conventions which had hitherto regulated relationships within the prince's lordship.

Associated with Rhys ap Gruffudd in the defection which will be considered presently, Gruffudd ap Iorwerth was of the lineage of Hwfa ap Cynddelw whose endowments in the twelfth century may have been made in augmentation of an estate of earlier origin.[351] Portioners in the church of Caergybi, successive members of the lineage exercised in this respect a privilege which went beyond the normal range of proprietorial rights.[352] But the relentlessly increasing number of men who shared their privilege in the church of Caergybi also shared the patrimonial lands, illustrating the problems which confronted the *nobiles* of even the best-endowed lineages. Despite his celebrated ancestry Gruffudd ap Iorwerth cannot be shown to have enjoyed a place of favour in the prince's entourage, and he might well be taken as a representative figure among the freemen of the late thirteenth century as the inheritance on which the status of his lineage was founded came to be eroded, though in varying degrees, in each generation.[353] Edward might seem to be an alternative source of favour and Gruffudd, too, another whose standing in society is reflected in a poet's praise, made his departure in the

---

[350] For Dinsylwy Rhys, *RC*, 72–3; J. B. Smith 'Land endowments', 155–6, 161–2.

[351] P. C. Bartrum, 'Hen lwythau Gwynedd a'r Mars', *NLWJ*, 12 (1961–2), 230–2; idem, *Welsh Genealogies* (Cardiff, 1974), iii, 515–18. Cynddelw ap Conws is placed *c*.1081 in *HGK*, 14; *MPW*, 67, and a *floruit c*.1130–70 is probably appropriate for Hwfa ap Cynddelw. Lands are noticed above, n. 147.

[352] Above, n. 147.

[353] The genealogy names five sons of Hwfa ap Cynddelw, each linked with a *gwely* in the extent of 1352, cmt Llifon (*RC*, 51); Mathwsalem is credited with one son; Maredudd ap Mathwsalem with two sons (Iorwerth and Gruffudd); Gruffudd ap Iorwerth left five sons, named in the extent and other sources.

critical summer of 1277.[354] Political reorientation could owe something, quite apart from the animosities engendered in court circles, to the economic problems of a broader social group. More may have been at work in 1277 than personal disillusionment among Llywelyn's leading adherents. The problems which were to be broached under the lordship of English king and marcher lords after the conquest may have been formulated to some degree in the period of the prince; matters concerning the succession to land and the alienation of land may have been part of an interaction between lord and community long before princely authority came to be extinguished.[355] What comes forth more clearly before the conquest, however, is less an impression that the community was troubled by issues which the prince had been unable to resolve than a sense that difficulties were created by the prince's departure from accepted custom. This was what was said at Nancall in 1283: Llywelyn had done things which no other prince had done except he alone (*quod nunquam aliquis princeps fecit nisi ipse solus*).[356] Llywelyn emerges as the grasping lord who had disowned the conventions governing relations between lord and community which his predecessors had respected, his purposes furthered by the odious ministrations of the hard men who served him. These were not the plaints of a thoroughly depressed peasantry, though Llywelyn was indeed charged with extending favour to the powerful among the *nobiles* at the expense of the less forceful. They were, rather, the complaints of those in society who were of sufficient status to exercise authority over other men. This was not, perhaps, reflected in extensive jurisdictional privilege, but it was enough to maintain that sense of position which was part of the established order that the prince was deemed to have undermined.

The veracity of the precise charges is difficult to estimate, no less the question whether the transactions at Nancall were an altogether exceptional set of proceedings. Negotiations between the seigniorial power and proctors for the community certainly came to be a feature of the era of conquest. Promptly upon the pacification of the conquered lands in 1283 king and marcher lords saw to the need to bind the communities of their territories in fidelity to the new authority exercised over them, and they sought suitable pledges from those who could bear responsibility for the community as a whole. The communities of each of the *cantrefi* of Gwynedd were gathered before the bishop of Bangor to pledge their loyalty and six of the best of them, upright and faithful *nobiles*, put their seals to a document which embodied the

---

[354] *GBF*, 56; circumstances of the defection are examined later.
[355] Post-conquest tensions and loyalties are considered, noticing the sons of Gruffudd ap Iorwerth, in J. B. Smith, 'Crown and community in the principality of North Wales in the reign of Henry Tudor', *WHR*, 3 (1966–7), 145–71; idem, 'Edward II and the allegiance of Wales', *WHR*, 8 (1976–7), 139–71.
[356] Ll. B. Smith, '*Gravamina*', 174 (VI).

solemn undertakings into which they had entered on behalf of the community. Similar arrangements were made in the marcher lands.[357] Thereafter negotiation between lord and community was a necessary part of the means by which the lands were governed. To what extent the procedures and the language of these transactions were already known to these communities we cannot be sure. It is by no means unlikely, however, that relations between rulers and ruled had already been to some degree regulated by comparable processes. Pertinent documentary evidence from the princes' territories is exceedingly sparse. Yet it is conceivable that those who, for instance, negotiated an agreement between the men of Tegeingl and Henry III upon his annexation of the *cantref* in 1241 were well versed in the needs of the community and practised in the task of formulating demands and grievances and presenting them to the ruler.[358] An acknowledgement of the need for understanding between lord and community can be sensed in the juristic literature. For though the redactions of the thirteenth century lay stress upon regalian rights, they are not without their intimations that limitations were placed upon the king's expectations of his community. He might summon his host for service beyond his frontiers.[359] But he could do so just once a year. On occasion the surviving literature conveys a more explicit recognition of the need to respect the rights of others than the ruler.

Amidst the profusion of twelfth-century eulogy of the princes, Cynddelw Brydydd Mawr composed a poem of extraordinary interest entitled 'Breintiau Gwŷr Powys' (the Privileges of the Men of Powys).[360] It stands apart from his other poems and offers a remarkable insight into problems of relationships between ruler and ruled which are extremely difficult to elucidate from the documentary evidence, even of a much later period, and barely broached in the voluminous eulogies of twelfth and thirteenth-century kings and princes. In more than one poem, indeed, Cynddelw touches upon the theme of the identity of purpose of prince and retinue, portraying the privileges enjoyed by the warriors as their reward for their valour in battle beside their prince.[361] In 'Breintiau Gwŷr Powys' the emphasis is entirely different, for in this poem Cynddelw extols the resistance of the freemen of Powys to the influences which threatened to diminish their privilege. The warriors of the kingdom had by their deeds enhanced royal rights, but it was now their duty to ensure that

---

[357] Below, p. 576.

[358] *CChR*, i, 274–5; a process of negotiation probably lay behind the charter granted by Henry III to the men of Englefield, 1242.

[359] *Lllor*, 61; *LHD*, 124; *LlCol*, 40.

[360] *GCBM*, i, 11. The argument in these paragraphs is presented more fully in J. B. Smith, 'Gwlad ac arglwydd', in M. E. Owen and B. F. Roberts (eds.), *Beirdd a Thywysogion: Barddoniaeth Llys yng Nghymru, Iwerddon a'r Alban* (Cardiff, 1996), 249–52.

[361] *GCBM*, i, 2, 8, 9, 10; 'Gwelygorddau Powys' is a particularly important text.

they took their share of those cherished rights.[362] The *cyneddfau* that were now at issue were not solely the rights that pertained to those of the war-band alone, however, but a body of attributes which belonged to the men of Powys – the freemen of Powys – as a whole. The poem was no less than a call to withstand oppression, and there were issues on which the poet was quite explicit: the unwelcome attentions of the *rhingyll* was one; the unwarranted imposition of circuit dues another.

> Cynneddf iwch, Bowys, ban wnaeth – awch gorsaf,
> Awch gorsedd na bai gaeth,
> Glyw gwyrthfawr, gwrthodwch – chwi etwaeth,
> Gwrthodes rhywyr, rhingyllaeth!
>
> Cynneddf i'r dreigiau, fegis dragon – berth
> Ni borthynt anneddfon,
> Yn eu byw, ar eu rhyw roddion
> Na rennid rhannau cynyddon.[363]

The matter of the poem has a distinct affinity with some of the key clauses of the document compiled at Nancall in Arfon a full century later.

Still more pertinent is the brief tract entitled 'Breintiau Arfon' (the Privileges of Arfon), embodied in the perfectly estimable thirteenth-century lawbook Peniarth 29.[364] The origins of 'Breintiau Arfon' are traced to an alarmingly distant era of British history, even though some of it was affirmed by the jurist Iorwerth ap Madog's recourse to authentic knowledge ('druy

---

[362] Both 'Gwelygorddau Powys' and 'Breintiau Gwŷr Powys' (*GCBM*, i, 10, 11) allude to the contribution made by the warriors of Powys to the historic victory at Meigen but, while the former stresses the identity of purpose and common interests of prince and retinue, the latter emphasizes the need for the men of Powys to take their share of the rewards of victory, specifically to ensure that they safeguard the rights enumerated as their fourteen *cyneddfau* ('qualities'). For the significance of Meigen, *GCBM*, i, 10. 4 n.; R. Bromwich, *Trioedd Ynys Prydein* (Cardiff, 1961), 151–2, 293–5; J. Rowland, *Early Welsh Saga Poetry* (Cambridge, 1990), 127–9, 446, 614.

[363] *GCBM*, i, 11, quoting ll. 53–60, trans Ann Parry Owen: 'Your peculiar quality, men of Powys, when it established your defence, / Is that your court would never be captive, / You powerful brave men, may you resist once more / the authority of the rhingyll like valiant men. / The peculiar quality of the warriors who are like fine heroes / Who do not tolerate wrong-doing, / Is that, during their lives, it was not on their kind of gifts / Was placed the responsibility of providing lodgings for huntsmen.'

[364] *Facsimile of the Chirk Codex*, f. 29–29ᵛ; 'The Laws of Hywel Dda: the Black Book of Chirk, Peniarth MS 29', ed. T. Lewis, *Zeitschrift für Celtische Philologie*, 20 (1936), 75–6; *AL*, i, 104–6; for the MS, mid-thirteenth-century, Huws, 'Llyfrau Cymraeg', 19; J. B. Smith, 'Gwlad ac arglwydd', 251, n. 64; recent detailed study in P. Russell, 'Scribal (in)competence in thirteenth-century north Wales: the orthography of the Black Book of Chirk (Peniarth MS 29)', *NLWJ*, 29 (1995–6), 129–76, especially pp. 130–4.

audurdaud e keuarhuidyt').³⁶⁵ But the material of this composition, too, has a bearing upon veritable historical experience. For neither would the men of Arfon tolerate the *rhingyll*, nor would they succumb to any demand for payment towards horses of guests or men on circuit.³⁶⁶ The bane of officers and the burden of the circuit were two of the three charges against Llywelyn ap Gruffudd specifically linked with the men of Arfon in 1283. The third charge, that the prince made bondmen of freemen, is echoed elsewhere in the document and has a consonance with the tenor of the statements of the privileges of Arfon and Powys alike.³⁶⁷ There can be no doubt that several specific clauses of the *gravamina* of 1283 may be linked with decisions made by Llywelyn ap Gruffudd. At the same time the material of historical relevance embodied in the antiquarian cast of 'Breintiau Arfon' suggests very strongly that the document compiled in 1283 gave expression to some issues of a fundamental nature which had been matters of disputation between the princes and their communities for a long time. Indications in the lawbooks that the exercise of regalian rights was tempered by a recognition of their limitations have been noticed already and there are, too, intriguing indications that regalian authority was much more securely imposed upon bond communities than upon those of the free.³⁶⁸ It is not difficult to envisage that the *rhingyll* – the 'messenger of great dread' ('cennad mawr ergryd') of the law text – would have incurred the odium suggested by 'Breintiau Arfon' and 'Breintiau Gwŷr Powys' if he were the officer whose ministrations had subjected the freemen to new or increased demands upon their services.³⁶⁹ In several other societies in contemporary Europe the limitations placed upon regalian or seigniorial power are more explicit. Certainly the lands north and south of the Pyrenees shared a legal culture in which relations between rulers and ruled are defined in redactions – notably the *fors de Béarn* – with clear reference to the constraints placed upon authority and the immunities

---

³⁶⁵ The legendary material, concerned with conflict between the men of Gwynedd and the Men of the North, is examined in Bromwich, *Trioedd Ynys Prydein*, 501–2; Rowland, *Early Welsh Saga Poetry*, 236–8; for Iorwerth ap Madog, D. Jenkins, 'Family of Welsh lawyers', 124–33.

³⁶⁶ The sixth and twelfth privileges of the *cantref* read: 'na bo righill endhi' (that there shall be no *rhingyll* therein); 'na thalher meirch guesteyon na guyr ar kilc' (that there shall be no payment for horses of guests nor for men on circuit).

³⁶⁷ Ll. B. Smith, '*Gravamina*', 174 (XXIIII, XXV, XXVI).

³⁶⁸ E.g. *LlIor*, 61; *LHD*, 123–4; *LlCol*, 39–40; above, n. 359.

³⁶⁹ The term is used in Lat A (*LTWL*, 119); for 'garw gychwedyl gwas y kygkellawr', *LlBleg*, 115.9–10; *LTWL*, 373. Despite the aversion of the men of Arfon to the *rhingyll*, the officer exercised his functions there after the conquest (*B*, 7 (1933–5), 147–8); *cylch rhaglaw* was payable by freemen in Arfon Is Gwyrfai and Uwch Gwyrfai, though *cylch* payments are less in evidence there than in several other areas (*RC*, 17–27). The vigilance of the freemen of Arfon is reflected in the protestations by which charges placed upon them were reduced (*RC*, 21, 24–5).

ensured for the communities subject to it.[370] It is unlikely that the provinces of Wales were altogether immune to these tensions in the period of their princes. At issue in Gwynedd in the second half of the thirteenth century were not only the impositions of an interventionist prince but the matter of an enduring argument over the demands which a prince might reasonably make upon the men of his land for the maintenance of the political order which he represented.

By the summer of 1283 not only was Llywelyn ap Gruffudd dead but the political order had itself been brought to an end, and the men who gathered at Nancall were already concerned with the circumstances in which they would find themselves under a new dispensation. The order was changed with a comprehensiveness and a finality never known before. Llywelyn ap Iorwerth had died in peace, his memory dutifully preserved as a prince who had shown sound justice to all, with love and in fear of God.[371] Even so, in that part of his patrimony which fell to the lordship of the king of England, swiftly upon his death the community had sought something short of a complete adherence to the practices which had obtained in his time.[372] They were certainly prepared to make a composition with the king by which, rather significantly, those living outside the demesnes were rid of the procuration charges and building obligations previously due to Llywelyn ap Iorwerth. Even then the community may not have been wholly enamoured of the exemplary rule of a beneficent prince. Forty years later the unparalleled pressures of the intervening years had left their mark, but the grievances against the vanquished prince were to some degree an expression of tensions created by antagonisms which lay deep in the experience of medieval Gwynedd. For those facing an uncertain future the virtue of an appeal to the position which had obtained under their late prince was obviously less compelling than it would have been if he were not also their last prince. Taken by itself the document compiled at Nancall may be read as a forthright condemnation of that prince, but it calls both for a broader historical perspective and a proper appreciation of the ambivalences of those now placed in an entirely new contingency.

Yet those who came to Nancall could not go their several ways and live in good conscience with a depiction of a prince entirely devoid of generosity. The men who recited his excessive greed felt bound to acknowledge that he was capable of a benign gesture. He might remit amercements, or provide foals from his stud for his freemen, or distribute beasts and money among old soldiers down on their luck. He was, too, capable of a generous deed on a

[370] J. C. Holt, *Magna Carta* (2nd edn., Cambridge, 1992), 78–81; J. B. Smith, 'Adversaries of Edward I: Gaston de Béarn and Llywelyn ap Gruffudd', 59–60.

[371] *AC*, 83: 'bonam justitiam secundum merita sua cum amore et timore Dei omnibus exhibebat'.

[372] *CChR*, i, 274–5.

Christmas Day.³⁷³ At the same time the testimony brought together before the bishop of Bangor suggests that Llywelyn, albeit as a consequence of the determined manner in which he had pursued his political vision, had stretched his resources to the utmost. When engaged in the direct exploitation of his demesnes he was able to exert his efforts as far as prudence in the use of the land and the energy of his bondmen allowed. He was, however, also dependent on the ability of the community at large to respond to heavy and, in some cases no doubt, novel demands. He may have forced his tenants beyond the threshold of tolerance determined by their own economic necessities. He pursued his political objectives at the cost, perhaps, of undermining the trust of the community he ruled in Gwynedd and alienating those upon whom he ultimately depended for the maintenance of his position. In the *gravamina* of 1283, at least, the communities managed to present themselves as the guardians of customary good practice who had been confronted with the innovative inclinations of their prince.

There were probably innovations which the prince might make, or to which he might give his consent, and earn the commendation of those he ruled. The evidence collected by the king's commissioners in Perfeddwlad in 1281 suggest that changes in legal practice, notably the use of the jury in determining legal actions, had been promoted by the prince and had won the consent of litigants.³⁷⁴ Nor did the initiative in departures from accepted practices necessarily lie entirely with the prince. The interaction between lord and community revealed in the years following the conquest, sometimes creating acute tension, sometimes ameliorated by compromise, had probably been a feature of earlier relations. But major conflict, and the need to be prepared for conflict, had doubtless created exceptional difficulty. That conflict had to be waged, too, with a major royal power which, for obvious historical reasons, could be seen both as a force to be resisted and as an alternative source of support for dissentient members of the community. The problems created by the existence of this alternative focus of loyalty to which the princes of Powys and Deheubarth might turn is a recurrent theme in this study, and it will be considered more particularly in the next chapter. This alternative was not without its relevance to the calculations of the men of Gwynedd. Powerful individuals and some communities had had their experience of royal government before Llywelyn ap Gruffudd asserted his power over the wider lordship of Snowdon and, all in all, it probably served him well in his bid for supremacy. Nor was its effect necessarily short-lived. Despite the stresses of later years, the community of his lordship showed remarkable resilience in two strenuous confrontations with the massive power

---

[373] Ll. B. Smith, '*Gravamina*', 174 (VI).
[374] *CWR*, 195–201.

of Edward I. The complaints lodged in 1283 certainly reflect the strains created within the prince's lordship, more particularly perhaps in the period leading up to the war of 1277, but they were made at the end of a prolonged struggle in which the resolve of the defenders had created much stress in the community of the realm of England. The historical record of the inner experience of the prince's lordship may provide the means to some understanding, but it hardly lends itself to assured verdicts.

Shortly after his death, according to contemporary chroniclers, an English poet and a Welsh poet each composed some verses to commemorate Llywelyn ap Gruffudd: 'defender of Gwynedd, and pattern for the future', declared the Welshman; 'despoiler of men and source of evil', was the view of the Englishman.[375] Is it possible for a historian to reconcile these views in a dispassionate assessment of the magnitude of Llywelyn's achievement and the depth of the calamity which was, to some degree, brought upon him by the manner in which he ruled his lands? In governing Snowdon Llywelyn employed to the utmost all that his status and authority placed within his reach. He claimed his regality and his lordship over men, his treasure and his grain. In pursuing his objectives he faced great difficulties, for the security of his dominion could be sought, let alone ensured, only at a vast cost. There could well have been many in the lordship of Snowdon in the later years of Llywelyn's rule who might have given their assent more readily to the feelings to which the English poet gave expression rather than the poet of their own nation as they bore the burden of sustaining his political endeavour.

---

[375] E.g. *AnnCestr*, 110; Rishanger, *Chronica*, 101.

CHAPTER 6

Prince of Wales

EARLY in the sixteenth century someone in English heraldic circles produced an imaginary depiction of the scene in parliament at Westminster as it might have been in the reign of Edward I. It shows a crowned king, sceptre in hand, upon his throne; seated at his right hand was Alexander, king of Scotland, and at his left hand Llywelyn, prince of Wales.[1] The scene is attributed to a parliament of 1278, but the portrayal in Thomas Wriothesley's manuscript has no historical veracity and there was no occasion when Alexander III and Llywelyn were present at an English parliament. The illustration does no more than reflect early Tudor interest in British history. But it provides a suggestive introduction to a chapter which, while mainly concerned with the internal arrangements of the principality of Wales and the means by which it was governed, also considers Llywelyn ap Gruffudd's position in relation to the world beyond his frontiers.[2]

Prince and principality

The portrait reflects the notion that there were in Britain in the reign of Edward I three persons who exercised an authority of a royal nature, but the idea that there was some similarity between the position of the king of Scotland and that of the prince of Wales in relation to the king of England is by no means derived solely from the historical consciousness of the Tudor period. The princes were themselves alert to the notion that their status was comparable to that of the king of Scotland. In a letter addressed to Henry III in 1224 Llywelyn ap Iorwerth maintained that the right (*libertas*) which he claimed in the particular matter at issue at that time, namely his power to

---

[1] Prestwich, *Edward I*, plate 14, from Royal Library, Windsor Castle, Wriothesley MS.
[2] T. D. Kendrick, *British Antiquity* (London, 1950), 33–44; S. Anglo, 'The *British History* in early Tudor propaganda', *Bulletin of the John Rylands Library*, 44 (1961), 17–48.

receive in his land a person outlawed from England, was no less than that of the king of Scotland.[3] Even so the prince made no general assertion of parity with Scotland, and the notion of a 'constitutional' equivalence between his principality and the realm of Alexander II of Scotland would be very difficult to substantiate. In due course Llywelyn ap Gruffudd was able to achieve, with the creation of the principality of Wales, a political edifice that had been no more than a declared but unrealized aspiration in the time of his grandfather. Its status was formally recognized by the crown of England. Henry III, in the treaty of Montgomery, indeed expressed his wish to 'honour the person of Llywelyn' (*uolens prefati Lewelini magnificare personam*), and it was at that point in Anglo-Welsh relations that the stature of the prince of Wales stood at its highest.[4] By the putative date of the pictorial representation in Wriothesley's manuscript Llywelyn had been reduced to a position which was, in terms of political authority, no match whatsoever for that of Alexander III. But, as we shall see in a moment, even when Llywelyn stood at the height of his power it would hardly have been realistic to place kingdom and principality on the same footing.[5]

Any conception of 'constitutional' status could only be a reflection of the political development of the two countries and, when they are considered side by side, the history of Wales and Scotland reveal marked contrasts, graphically illustrated in the differing early careers of the two contemporary rulers. Llywelyn would himself have known very well that Alexander III, while still a minor, had succeeded his father in the rule of his kingdom and, though his early years were not without their anxieties, the young heir was blessed with an unchallenged succession to an unbroken tradition of kingship. At his inauguration in 1249, in accordance with the custom of his dynasty, the *seanchaidh* came before the king and proclaimed a royal lineage going back to the furthermost reaches of the mythological memory of the kingdom.[6] Yet infinitely more important than the renown of any distant forebears were the achievements of Alexander's more recent predecessors in the twelfth century and the thirteenth. As he recited these names in turn the nation's remembrancer would evoke the memory of a line of kings which, from David I onward, even though there had been times of anxiety, had ruled the kingdom in a continuous succession and, generation by generation, consolidated its

---

[3] *CAC*, 24–5; *RL*, i, 229–30.
[4] *LW*, 2.
[5] Below, pp. 277–8.
[6] John de Fordun, *Chronica Gentis Scotorum*, ed. W. F. Skene (Edinburgh 1871–2), ii, 293–5; M. D. Legge, 'The inauguration of Alexander III', *Proceedings of the Society of Antiquaries of Scotland*, 80 (1945–6), 73–82; J. W. M. Bannerman, 'The king's poet and the inauguration of Alexander III', *Scottish Historical Review*, 69 (1989), 120–49; Duncan, *Scotland*, 555–6.

security.[7] Llywelyn's beginnings were very different, and his inheritance from earlier generations was quite unlike that of the king of Scotland. A poet from his land could undoubtedly trace his ancestry to a distant age and summon a memory that was part of the intellectual inheritance of the nation. But, as the second son of a prince who was himself a bastard to whom the inheritance had been denied, Llywelyn's inexorable lot was one of unrelenting endeavour, and few would have predicted the elevated status that he would eventually enjoy if it were not for the character that he demonstrated as he grappled with the enormous difficulties which confronted him.

> Cyfarchaf i Dduw, ddawn orfoledd
> Cynechrau doniau dinam fawredd,
> Cynyddu canu, canyd rhyfedd – dreth
> O draethawd gyfannedd
> I foli fy rhi, rhwyf Arllechwedd,
> Rhuddfoawg freiniawg o frenhinedd:[8]

the opening lines of Llygad Gŵr's salutation of Llywelyn ap Gruffudd's supremacy, in which he beseeches God's beneficence upon a composition addressed to a king born of a line of kings, strikes the keynote of an estimation in which the poet lays his stress upon the prince's inherent attributes. 'Gwir frenin Cymru, cymraisg ddoniau': he was truly king of Wales, one of steadfast qualities. Neither the poem composed by Llygad Gŵr, nor those of Dafydd Benfras, could possibly be taken to be the celebration of a formal inauguration by which an heir was able to proceed, in accordance with established custom, from his place of honour at court to the throne of the kingdom. Rather, Llywelyn owed his position to his personal disposition for he was, as Llygad Gŵr proclaimed, one with the matter of which kings are made: 'Llew breiniog, brenhinedd deithi', a privileged lion with the qualities of kings. The poet saw him, not simply as a worthy successor to those of his lineage who had ruled before him, but as one who inherited the fortitude shown by his father, Gruffudd ap Llywelyn, who had never been able to succeed to the rule of the patrimony. 'Hil Gruffudd, grymus gyneddfau': he was of the seed of Gruffudd, of powerful qualities. But to be born of a prince of forceful disposition did not make Llywelyn heir to a royal estate.

[7] See introductions to *Regesta Regum Scottorum*, i, *The Acts of Malcolm IV*; ii, *The Acts of William I*; also Barrow, *Scotland and her Neighbours*, 23–44.

[8] *GBF*, 24. 1–6, from the eulogy in five cantos composed, probably c.1257–8, in celebration of Llywelyn's triumphs; trans. Ann Parry Owen: 'I ask of God, glorious His grace, / The source of favours perfect in their splendour, / To enrich my singing, because it is not too splendid a tribute / By means of a delightful composition / To praise my king, my lord of Arllechwedd, / The red-ravaging noble one descended from kings.' Further lines from *GBF*, 24. 54, 141, 155.

Nor was it, in Llywelyn's case, simply a matter of overcoming problems of personal adversity or the transitory vicissitudes that came between him and the rule of an extensive and stable dominion. On the contrary, he was confronted with the unenviable task of re-establishing that dominion itself. The notion of the resuscitation of a dominion from its sorrows pervades the work of Dafydd Benfras, a poet who had known the triumphant years of Llywelyn ap Iorwerth, then the disintegration which followed, and lived long enough to witness the crucial stages in Llywelyn ap Gruffudd's advance to the supremacy which restored the hegemony of his lineage. Dafydd then celebrated the prince's progress (*cynnydd*) in a poem written shortly before he died, almost certainly in the prince's active service upon a campaign in Deheubarth, in joyous exuberance at the fulfilment of the promise of youth. 'Teyrnfab Gruffudd, teyrn ddadannudd / Teyrnas ddatgudd prudd y preiddia'. Far from merely maintaining a tradition of princely rule, Llywelyn re-established that authority itself.[9] Yet even when he had done so, and won recognition from the king of England, his position was far from one of parity with the king of Scotland. Alexander never did homage for the kingdom of Scotland, and, even if he had conformed to Edward I's wish that he should do so, his status in relation to the crown of England would have been no less elevated than the very highest status to which Llywelyn aspired, the position to which he acceded when he went to Rhyd Chwima to do his homage to Henry III. Alexander's constant concern in his dealings with the king of England was to ensure that he did not do homage for Scotland; Llywelyn's whole objective was to reach a position whereby he would be able to do homage for his wider dominion, and the contrast reflected the fundamental difference between the internal situation of Scotland and that of Wales.[10] The homage of the lords of Scotland to their king was part of the kingdom's corporate inheritance, but Llywelyn had need to establish his right to the homage of the lords of Wales. It was a contrast which put equality with Scotland beyond Llywelyn's grasp, and invocations of the notion of parity would carry no conviction. Llywelyn once urged the right of each of the lands under Edward's *imperium* to its own laws, but in the course of the argument,

---

[9] *GDB*, 34, 35; quoting 35. 27–9: 'Royal son of Gruffudd, royal redeemer of his patrimony, / The restorer of his lands, prudent in his raiding.' Eulogies and elegies of Llywelyn by Dafydd Benfras, Llygad Gŵr and Gruffudd ab yr Ynad Coch are published in scholarly critical editions in *GDB* and *GBF*; texts also in *Llywelyn y Beirdd*, ed. A. Llwyd (Swansea, 1984), 11–102, with further references to texts and translations below when citations are made. For authoritative discussion, J. E. Caerwyn Williams, *The Poets of the Welsh Princes* (Cardiff, 1994), with select bibliography; idem, *The Court Poet in Medieval Wales* (Lampeter, 1997).

[10] *Anglo-Scottish Relations 1174–1328*, ed. E. L. G. Stones (Oxford, 1970), xviii–xxxi, 76–82. For the arguments of the period of the Great Cause, *Throne of Scotland*, i, 113–17, 137–62; ii, 10 *et seq*.

putting Scotland, Ireland, Gascony, and Wales on a par with one another, he ventured upon a view which would have found no favour with the king and the community of the realm of Scotland.[11] More indicative of contemporary perceptions of the position of the two nations is the attitude of each to the legendary account of their origins embodied in the *Historia Regum Britanniae*. As we shall see, the Welsh were prepared to admit the superiority of the crown of England that was implicit in the primacy accorded to Locrinus over Camber, while the Scots would admit of no comparable status for Albanactus, preferring an entirely different interpretation of their beginnings.[12] It was a standpoint, vigorously maintained in the political exchanges of the later years of the century, which was already well established in Scottish tradition. The papal court, though its pronouncements might not be entirely consistent with one another, was inclined to endorse this view of the status of the realm of Scotland, and could do so quite eloquently.[13] The position of Wales was seen to be very different. The princes of Wales succeeded from time to time in eliciting encouraging responses to their submissions to Innocent III, or Innocent IV, or Gregory X.[14] But the evidence as a whole is consistent with the view that, whereas the kings of Scotland ruled a separate kingdom, the principality of Wales was part of the kingdom of England. Even when a papal legate conducted negotiations designed to establish peace between Wales and England, he was in fact charged with the restoration of peace within the confines of the realm of England.[15] Papal records implicitly endorse the view advanced by Edward I, when his envoys and those of Llywelyn competed for papal support during the critical period leading up to the war of 1277, that the prince of Wales was no more than one of the greatest among the other magnates of his kingdom.[16]

Even apart from the contrast in the 'constitutional' position of Wales and Scotland, contemporary evidence points to significant differences in their relations with other lands. By no means the least of them is the close affinity between the royal lineages of Scotland and England. Marriages between their royal dynasties were obviously no guarantee of peaceful relations between great powers, but letters exchanged between Henry III and his son-in-law who ruled in Scotland suggest a courteous and amicable relationship.[17] The gracious phraseology of the exchanges may do no more than reflect the

---

[11] Below, p. 475.
[12] J. B. Smith, *SHMW*, 14–16; below, nn. 232–3
[13] *Anglo-Scottish Relations*, xxii, xxviii–xxix, 28–36, 58, 162–74.
[14] G. Williams, *Welsh Church*, 10–11, 31; M. Richter, 'David ap Llywelyn, the first prince of Wales', *WHR*, 5 (1970–1), 205–19; below, pp. 374–5, 379–81, 387–9.
[15] Above, pp. 173–5, 177–9, 185–6.
[16] Below, p. 401.
[17] Powicke, *Thirteenth Century*, 588–9; Duncan, *Scotland*, 576–7.

protocol that royal lineages were careful to respect, and it would be well to remember the wariness with which the king and magnates of Scotland could regard the king of England. Even so, the correspondence between the two courts reveals a degree of trust. It remained so in the early years of Edward I and the two kings were no doubt sincere in acknowledging how personal grief might strengthen the bonds of friendship between them.[18] On occasion the civilities which marked the personal relations of the kings were reflected in letters dealing with practical problems, such as those which arose in regulating the frontier between the two kingdoms.[19] It is then easier to understand how Edward's assertion of superior lordship, and his determination to secure his objectives, proved so deeply disturbing. But Llywelyn knew little enough of the courtesies of the royal circles. The tone of the letters that dealt with the problems of the march of Wales is distinctly less cordial, and we have already seen that rumour of Llywelyn's death evoked in King Henry anything but a generous concern for the well-being of his principality or sympathy with his kin.[20] At an early stage of his dominance over the provinces of Wales Llywelyn conveyed his desire to marry someone of the king's affinity, and there was already some precedent for this in his dynasty. But, when he decided to marry a woman who was indeed a niece of the king, he did so under a pronounced political compulsion and he brought upon himself the king's great anger towards the Montfort lineage.[21] Edward proved civil enough in his relations with Eleanor herself, and after her marriage the prince's letters show rather more of the conventional courtesies.[22] Perhaps the familial connection was beginning to tell, but the princess of Wales had little opportunity to assuage the untrusting relationship between Llywelyn and Edward. There are only a few letters in her name to point to the role that she might have played in Anglo-Welsh relations, and even before she came to Wales the prince had been forced to yield the political position that he had to maintain in order to win a place in the royal fraternity. Llywelyn's name might appear in the elaborate genealogical chart that would include the royal family of England, and many of his magnates, and the royal family of Scotland.[23] He was a grandson of Llywelyn the Great, but he was not of the blood of Anjou, nor would his place on the chart be very meaningful.

The affinities and courtesies of royal and noble lineages may, of course, have little bearing on the course of political events, and it may be mistaken to

---

[18] E.g. *Anglo-Scottish Relations*, 84–6.
[19] *Foedera*, I, ii, 531.
[20] Above, pp. 137–8.
[21] Below, pp. 390–402.
[22] Letters of Eleanor, and Llywelyn in the same period, *CAC*, 75–7, 85–6, 93–6. Eleanor refers to the king's kindness at the time of her marriage, but for Llywelyn's later charge that Edward had deceived him even on the morning of his marriage, below, p. 501.
[23] Powicke, *Henry III*, ii, 711–12.

place any emphasis upon them. There can be no doubt, however, of the importance of the prince's relationship with the king of England: Llywelyn had no alternative to the king of England. He found nothing to compare with the opportunity that Gaston de Béarn was able to seize when, at different stages in a long and turbulent career, he was able to strengthen his resistance to oppressive government in Gascony by alliance with Castile or, availing himself of the overlordship exercised over the duchy by the king of France, making an appeal to the *parlement* of Paris.[24] There was no independent power with which Llywelyn could establish any helpful links. When he sought alliance beyond the confines of Wales he tended to look to the political opposition rather than to the established authority: his alliance with Scotland was forged, not with its royal administration, but with a baronial faction; in England he collaborated with the baronial opposition and even that association derived, not from the period of the movement for political reform, but only from the time when its leaders had to resort to armed conflict.[25] Unlike the king of Scotland, Llywelyn was unable to develop independent associations, or make marriage arrangements with continental countries such as France or Norway.[26] Of the thirteenth-century princes it was Llywelyn ap Iorwerth rather than Llywelyn ap Gruffudd who ventured most into the network of dynasties and political connections beyond his frontiers, though he was still left to rue the loneliness of his position, with his adversaries in positions of influence and no one to advocate his cause in the king's councils.[27] Llywelyn ap Gruffudd was not to marry a daughter of the king of England nor forge dynastic links in the march of Wales, nor was he honoured with a letter under the royal seal of the king of France that he might place for safe-keeping among his cherished objects in the aumbries of his church.[28] Llywelyn was a lonely figure in more than one sense. He admitted one obvious facet of his isolation in a letter to Gregory X. Of all those to head the Christian church in the thirteenth century it was probably Gregory who had the clearest understanding of the political aspirations of the princes of Wales, and he took account of them in making his decisions. Writing to him at a critical hour, Llywelyn acknowledged the disadvantage of the great distance and the great perils which lay between him and the papal court, and that it was impossible to send messengers across the seas without their being under

---

[24] Trabut-Cussac, *L'Administration anglaise en Gascogne*, 9–11; Powicke, *Henry III*, i, 227–36; idem, *Thirteenth Century*, 284–5; Prestwich, *Edward I*, 298–301; J. B. Smith, 'Adversaries of Edward I; Gaston de Béarn and Llywelyn ap Gruffudd', 61–2, 65–70, 74–7.

[25] Above, pp. 110–11, 161–70.

[26] E.g. R. Nicholson, 'The Franco-Scottish and Franco-Norwegian treaties of 1295', *SHR*, 38 (1959), 114–32; Duncan, *Scotland*, 580–2, 592.

[27] *CAC*, 8–9.

[28] Above, p. 17.

the surveillance of the king of England.²⁹ Nor were the king's calculations, in dealing with the prince of Wales, influenced by the possibility that his adversary, quite apart from having recourse to the aid of another power, might be useful in promoting royal interests, as Gaston de Béarn again was well placed to do in relation to Edward's diplomatic interests in Castile and Aragon. There would be no considerations such as these to mitigate Llywelyn's treatment at Edward's hands. The physical isolation was not the whole problem by any means. A part of the kingdom of England which tended, from time to time, to give him a spot of trouble: this was the image of Wales which European rulers such as Philip of France or Alphonso of Castile might gain from what they were told by Edward I, and Llywelyn would be able to do little to convince them otherwise.³⁰ Llywelyn might indeed have pledged himself from the beginning to be rid of the conflicting impulses revealed by a predecessor who tried to distance himself from the crown of England and at the same time felt bound to admit the disadvantage of his isolation. The grandson may have judged that true security could only be assured through the bonds that bound him in unity with men of his own nation. Even so, the task of forging those bonds was fraught with difficulty, and from a very early stage in his political experience it was clear that he had to tread warily as he sought to reconcile the internal needs of his dominion with the unavoidable necessity to establish an agreed relationship with the king of England.

The sense of a broad political unity encompassing the territories under Welsh lordship was embodied in the notion of a 'principality'. Llywelyn ap Iorwerth propounded the idea of a *principatus* of this nature early in the thirteenth century, and the same idea appears prominently in his grandson's political statements, not least in those that he made within only a few weeks of his death in 1282. It is not easy to trace the origins of the idea in Wales, and the Latin and Welsh versions of the term suggest two approaches which, while not mutually exclusive, need to be considered separately. The terms *princeps* and *principatus* are frequently found used in the plural, or as collective names, to describe medieval rulers and their realms. It happens that when Llywelyn ap Gruffudd was about to secure the king's recognition of his use of the term *princeps*, Aquinas wrote *De Regimine Principum*, one of several treatises in which theoretical writers, adopting a practice derived from antiquity, used the term *principes* for the rulers of kingdoms. Giraldus Cambrensis had adhered

---

[29] *LW*, 114–16.
[30] *CPR, 1247–58*, 567; *CCR, 1256–59*, 142; *CAC*, 56. For Llywelyn's wish that his proposals to Edward I be referred to the king of France, below, p. 411.

to the convention, as would William of Occam.[31] But it was unusual for an individual ruler, who might exercise the powers discussed in these theoretical works, to present himself as a *princeps*.[32] In France the ultimate origins of the authority shared between the king and the rulers of its provinces may perhaps be traced to a *princeps regni* in the early centuries.[33] Yet, by the central period of the middle ages, though the convenient collective term used by commentators might be *principes*, the individual ruler of Burgundy or Flanders, Gascony or Champagne is known as a *duc* or *comte*.[34] The most conspicuous exception has indeed a Welsh connection, for when Edward, son of Edward III, was made *princeps Aquitaine* in 1362 he was given a style that he already enjoyed as *princeps Wallie*. He did so by virtue of the crown's adherence to a practice established by Edward I in designating his son as *princeps Wallie* in what appears to have been a deliberate attempt to establish a link with the native principality that he had previously annexed.[35] It seems that those who ruled in independent Wales, when they assumed the title *princeps* or referred to their dominion as a *principatus*, adopted a practice that was somewhat exceptional among the Christian nations of the middle ages.

In trying to divine the meaning of 'prince' and 'principality', and establish the chronology by which the usage became established, the Welsh versions of the terms are certainly relevant. A *tywysog* was one who led his people, and we have already noticed how the scriptural allusions in *Brut y Tywysogyon*, and particularly the inclination to liken the princes of the nation to the leaders of the Maccabees, serve to underline the virtue of a person who led his people out of captivity.[36] It is not, however, along these lines that historians have generally sought to explain the change by which the kings (*brenhinoedd*, *reges*) of twelfth-century Wales decided to present themselves as princes

---

[31] 'De Regimine Principum', in Aquinas, *Selected Political Writings*, ed. A. P. D'Entreves (Oxford, 1959), 2–82; 'Liber De Principis Instructione', in *GirCamb, Op*, viii; Wilhelm von Ockham, *Briviloquium de Principatu Tyrannico*, ed. R. Scholz (Stuttgart, 1952).

[32] *Princeps* is, of course, used in addressing a king, e.g. letters of the king of Scotland or the archbishop of Canterbury to the king of England (*RL*, ii, 340; *Foedera*, I, ii, 531; *RPeck*, ii, 412, 432, 498, 523).

[33] From a vast range of literature, H. Wolfram, 'The shaping of the early medieval kingdom', *Viator, Medieval and Renaissance Studies*, 1 (1970), 1–20; idem, 'The shaping of the early medieval principality', *Viator*, 2 (1971), 35–51.

[34] E.g. J. Le Patourel, 'The king and the princes in fourteenth-century France', in J. R. Hale *et al.* (eds.), *Europe in the Late Middle Ages* (London, 1965), 155–83.

[35] For the investitures of 1301 and 1343, J. G. Edwards, *Principality of Wales*, 9–11; D. L. Evans, 'Some notes on the history of the principality of Wales in the time of the Black Prince (1343–1376)', *THSC*, 1925–6, 28–30.

[36] *AC*, 90; J. B. Smith, *SHMW*, 7–8; for comparative references, Barrow, *Scotland and her Neighbours*, 16–19; M. H. Keen, *Chivalry* (London, 1984), 119–22; J. Dunbabin, 'The Maccabees as exemplars in the tenth and eleventh centuries', in K. Walsh and D. Loud (eds.), *The Bible in the Medieval World* (Oxford, 1985), 31–41.

(*tywysogion, principes*). The change has rather been understood as a response to pressure from the English monarchy soon after it came to the strong hand of Henry II in 1154.[37] Sensing that the king insisted on a fuller recognition of his lordship, enacted now by homage and fealty and recorded in specific terms, historians have judged that the change in style marked an acknowledgement on the part of the rulers of Wales that they had need to present themselves in a less exalted manner than had been customary in earlier centuries. The king (*brenin, rex*) became a prince (*tywysog, princeps*), if not a lord (*arglwydd, dominus*). The evidence which survives hardly provides the means for any elaborate study of the Welsh princes' titles, and it might be unwise to attempt to emulate the studies undertaken for lands blessed with a fuller record.[38] Charter evidence is extremely scanty, with many of the most important exemplars of the rulers' gifts conserved only in texts derived from a period much later than that of the original transaction, and there cannot always be a certainty that the titles ascribed to the benefactors conform to practices at the time of the gift. Nor can we be sure that the styles employed by the texts of *Brut y Tywysogyon*, in their references to twelfth-century rulers, are anything more than embellishments made when the Latin text, on which the Welsh texts were based, was given its finite form.[39] They cannot be shown to have formed part of the original annalistic entry. Certainly the styles recorded in the surviving texts of the *annales* are noticeably fewer, and much more economical with the titular adornment, than those which enhance the texts of *Brut y Tywysogyon*. The most illuminating chink of light comes, in the last years of Owain Gwynedd, with the record of the correspondence between the prince and Thomas Becket, archbishop of Canterbury.[40] Considered in relation to Owain Gwynedd's formidable position in the mid-1160s the texts suggest that it was not in response to pressure on the part of the king of England that Owain changed his style. The change was made in anything but a state of crisis, nor was it intended to reflect a diminution in status. It seems rather that Owain made the change of his own volition in a period of strength, with a view to presenting himself as leader of his nation. In so far as the evidence of the letters may guide us, it appears that Owain did not cease to be king of Gwynedd in order to be prince of Gwynedd, but that he chose to present himself as 'prince of the Welsh' (*princeps Wallensium*). In his hour of triumph, with Henry foiled in his attempt to bring Wales into subjection by

---

[37] Pierce, *MWS*, 28–9; D. Jenkins, 'Kings, lords and princes: the nomenclature of authority in thirteenth-century Wales', *B*, 26 (1974–6), 451–62.

[38] For an application to Wales of work represented in H. Wolfram, *Intitulatio* (Mitteilungen des Instituts für Österreichische Geschichtsforschung, 21, 24, 1967–73), M. Richter, 'The political and institutional background to national consciousness in medieval Wales', 43–6.

[39] J. B. Smith, *SHMW*, 7–8, and references cited.

[40] *Councils*, i, 364–74; *Materials for the History of Thomas Becket*, ed. J. C. Robertson (RS, 1875–85), v, 48–9, 225–39.

force, Owain projected himself as the focus of a broader unity. Becket did not miss the significance of the change and, evidently disinclined to reciprocate, preferred to continue to address the ruler of Gwynedd as 'king' rather than as 'prince'.[41]

The evidence we have, slight though it be, suggests that the term *princeps* entered Welsh titular terminology as a result of Owain Gwynedd's determination to establish himself as nothing less than the leader of his nation, reflecting the circumstances in which, as the annalist observed, albeit rather grandly, all the Welsh of Gwynedd, Deheubarth and Powys with one accord cast off the Norman yoke. When Llywelyn ap Iorwerth came to power, exerting force over other members of the dynasty, he had need to ensure that the title he assumed reflected his power in a well-defined territory, and he presented himself early in the thirteenth century as 'prince of Gwynedd' (*princeps Northwallie*).[42] The style was territorialized and linked with the historic *regnum* of Gwynedd. But he was soon to revive the notion of a broader leadership. In the later years of his rule, using the style 'prince of Aberffraw and lord of Snowdon' (*princeps Aberffraw et dominus Snowdonie*), Llywelyn ap Iorwerth invoked anew that sense of broad leadership on the basis of the supremacy of Gwynedd that had already been adumbrated, very briefly, by Owain Gwynedd. The style reflects a blending of the notion of broad supremacy with the actuality of an immediate lordship over a defined territory: Aberffraw represented the leadership of the nation; Snowdon stood for the sphere of the prince's lordship, the land considered in the last chapter. The choice of style, even so, conveyed an implicit acknowledgement of the uneasy compromise inherent in Llywelyn ap Iorwerth's position. It was a compromise that Llywelyn ap Gruffudd would not wish to countenance. Assuming, as it seems, no style whatsoever in the immediate aftermath of Bryn Derwin, he used the style 'prince of Wales' briefly in 1258 though, if surviving records provide an accurate reflection of his practice, he did not persist with it. But then, coincident with a new phase of forceful action, following a prolonged and patient quest for a negotiated settlement with the crown, he adopted the style 'prince of Wales and lord of Snowdon' (*princeps Wallie et dominus Snowdonia*). He was to use this form consistently for the remainder of his life. In the style he now used the ideas of leadership and lordship were finally and definitively combined, the duality of his position

---

[41] *Councils*, i, 49: Becket refers to Owain, 'who calls himself prince (*qui se principem nominat*) . . . on account of this the king is greatly disturbed and offended'. Further textual study is essential; abbreviation of titles makes it difficult to determine the form intended in some instances, but revaluation of the evidence in its political context suggests an interpretation different from that hitherto accepted. For recent valuable study, H. Pryce, 'Owain Gwynedd and Louis VII: the Franco-Welsh diplomacy of the first prince of Wales', *WHR*, 19 (1998–9), 1–28.

[42] For the basis of this argument, above, pp. 11–12.

reflected in the two elements signifying his overlordship of the broader sphere and his immediate lordship of the narrower sphere, but each now a clearly defined territory. Even the broader sphere was a good deal less than the whole extent of Wales, but in 1267 king and prince accepted the suitability of a style which, at once, acknowledged and proclaimed a status unique in Welsh political history. If Llywelyn sought that status somewhat in isolation, the manner in which he did so reflects a capacity to draw on the experiences of his lineage over earlier generations and, to some degree as part of that inheritance, to gain the benefit of those precepts and practices of political action which were part of the broader experience of thirteenth-century nations. The blending of indigenous and extraneous influences is variously reflected in the matters considered in the discussion which follows.

Authority and allegiance

A pervasive theme in Llywelyn's political achievement is clearly the manner by which, establishing a relationship with the princes or lords of Wales that raised him to be their lord and made them his tenants, he created a polity of singular significance in the history of his nation. We have noticed already the statement in the lawbooks which conceived a pattern of relationships between the king of Aberffraw and the kings of Powys and Deheubarth. The jurists envisaged an association in which royal tribute (*mechdeyrn ddyled*) was paid to the king of Aberffraw by the other kings of Wales, and was paid to the king of England by the king of Aberffraw and by him alone.[43] It was suggested earlier that this theoretical formulation may have been stimulated by the supremacy established by Llywelyn ap Iorwerth in the early years of the century. The pattern conveyed in the jurists' work contains what may reasonably be termed 'feudal' features.[44] The heart of the matter, as far as this study is concerned, is that a lord was seen to be capable of bestowing land upon another person who thereby became his tenant, and that the bestowal and acceptance created a contractual relationship which placed specific obligations upon each of those who entered into the engagement. Certainly, in the jurists' construction, the giving and receiving of land was, no less than the payment of *mechdeyrn ddyled*, an essential feature of the relationship. It

---

[43] Law texts record that £63 was paid to the king in *syrhaed*, 'because that is the sum of the *mechdeyrn ddyled* that the king of Aberffraw ought to give to the king of London when he received his land from him; afterwards all the kings of Wales ought to receive their lands from him, that is from the king of Aberffraw, and give him their *mechdeyrn ddyled* and *ebediw* after death' (*LTWL*, 207; cf. *LTWL*, 277, 437–8; above, pp. 17–18.).

[44] In using the term 'feudal' account is taken of the arguments in S. Reynolds, *Fiefs and Vassals* (Oxford, 1994), 323–95 and the brief comment in Holt, *Magna Carta*, 127, n. 20. For the terminology, such as *vassallus*, *iure feodali*, see e.g. *LW*, *passim*.

need be none of our purpose to trace the origin of this relationship in Welsh society, but a study of Gwynedd suggests that tenurial bonds, in which the reciprocal duties of lord and tenant are fully recognized, were indeed derived from an early period.[45] Transactions in land were not necessarily part of the early contractual affiliation, but what is relevant to our purposes is that a relationship of this nature, in which land was a necessary ingredient, and was already well rooted in Welsh social arrangements, came to be used to create and stabilize the political relationships which traversed the well-established regalian or seigniorial frontiers. Homage was the essence of the contract, and it may be surmised that a process of establishing a bond between two political entities by means of homage was already at work in the period of Llywelyn the Great. *Brut y Tywysogyon* cites the homage which Gwenwynwyn ab Owain Cyfeiliog did to the prince of Gwynedd, a transaction confirmed by the giving of hostages and recorded in written documents.[46] The act of homage made one who had hitherto been an adherent of the prince thereafter his tenant, and made the erstwhile leader a lord. There is thus reason to believe that this bond was used for specifically political objectives in the time of Llywelyn ap Iorwerth, that he sought to ensure that his adherents (*inprisii*) of the years of conflict were recognized as his men, his vassals, in a stable political relationship. The concession of their homage would have been a keystone in the peace (*pax*) which he sought from the king in preference to the truce (*treuga*) that was all the king was prepared to concede. Never admitted while Llywelyn lived, the alacrity and pertinacity with which Henry III insisted, after the prince's death, that homage should thereafter be done to him alone was virtually a tacit retrospective acknowledgement that a different situation had prevailed before.[47] Record evidence of contractual bonds comes only in the period of Llywelyn ap Gruffudd. It is scanty enough even then, but it is sufficient to establish that, quite apart from the documentary evidence which demonstrates the centrality of the issue of homage in the argument between king and prince, the Welsh princes were availing themselves of those means of forging stable relationships that are reflected in the texts noticed by historians who have interpreted the feudal features of political relationships in contemporary Europe.[48] What can safely be said of the relations between Llywelyn ap Gruffudd and Gruffudd ap Gwenwynwyn or Maredudd ab Owain, Gruffudd ap Madog or Maredudd ap Rhys?

Regrettably, but perhaps inevitably, the instructive texts are those which record the prince's relationship with his more reluctant or recalcitrant vassals.

---

[45] Above, pp. 197–9.
[46] *CW*, 36; *BT*, *Pen20*, 170–1; *Pen20Tr*, 92; *RBH*, 206–9; above, pp. 18–19.
[47] Above, pp. 21–2, 26–7, 29–30.
[48] The reference is to studies in the tradition represented by F. L. Ganshof, *Feudalism* (London, 1952), 63–151; R. Boutruche, *Seigneurie et féodalité* (Paris, 1959–70), 190–204.

Indeed the sole text which records a contractual bond between Llywelyn and a truly loyal tenant is that in which Hywel ap Rhys Gryg declared that he had done homage to Llywelyn and sworn an oath of fealty for the commote of Mabelfyw which the prince bestowed upon him (*quas nobis liberaliter contulit*), and placed himself under the jurisdiction of the bishops of Bangor and St Asaph if he faltered in his allegiance.[49] This brief document drawn up in 1258 hardly provides any indication of the reciprocal obligations into which lord and tenant entered. The document which bears the closest resemblance to the diploma characteristic of continental *féodalité* is that in the form of a final concord made between Llywelyn and Gruffudd ap Gwenwynwyn when the lord of Powys Wenwynwyn came into the prince's allegiance in 1263.[50] It has two aspects. First it provides a brief statement of the fact that Gruffudd, of his own free will, did homage for himself and his heirs and touching holy objects (*tactis sacrosanctis*) swore fealty to Llywelyn. Homage was done and fealty sworn in the presence of magnates of Gwynedd and Powys, the transactions establishing between the two men a relationship of lord and vassal. We may gain a fuller understanding of the significance of the act which was performed, and the words uttered, if we turn to the fuller texts found among the muniments of other lands. We may be reasonably sure, for instance, that a form of words closely akin to those noted in 'Bracton' would have been perfectly familiar to the princes of Wales, and to men of ministerial rank such as Tudur ab Ednyfed or Gruffudd ap Gwên, who were present at Ystumanner on this occasion.[51] A number had been bound in fealty to the king in the course of the conflict of the period of Dafydd ap Llywelyn, quite apart from earlier occasions, and there were probably a large number of men of baronial or lesser rank who would have been familiar with the formal acts and the written declarations which effected the contractual obligation of which the prince's agreement with the lord of Powys Wenwynwyn is a rare exemplar.[52] We can safely postulate a close resemblance between these transactions and those more fully recorded in other lands.

In its second and fuller aspects the document defines the obligations upon which lord and vassal were agreed and, necessarily reflecting the particular circumstances in which the agreement was made, provides an illustration of the infinite variety in the obligations which may be found specified in documents of this nature even within the confines of a single country. F. M. Powicke, reflecting his particular awareness of English conditions, found the Welsh texts lacking in what he would regard as the essential qualities of a feudal relationship. If tenure by knight's service were taken to be the touchstone of

---

[49] *LW*, 45.
[50] *LW*, 77–80; political circumstances are noticed above, pp. 157–60.
[51] *Bracton*, ii, 225–43.
[52] E.g. *LW*, 49–52.

feudal quality it would be fair to conclude that the evidence from the principality of Wales would fall short of historians' expectations.[53] Evaluation of the Welsh evidence in its own right needs to take account both of the social relationships considered at an earlier stage of the discussion and of the nature of the political alliances of which the agreement between Prince Llywelyn and Gruffudd ap Gwenwynwyn is the prime instance. It might reasonably be taken, as Powicke intimates, to involve no more than a declaration of a pledge to joint campaigning resonant of 'the brotherhood of war'.[54] Features of the document of 1263 closely resemble the agreements which Llywelyn made at an earlier stage in his career as a means of establishing, not a relationship of lord and vassal, but a concord between persons who remained, for the present at least, of equal status. Such was the 'alliance and union' (*confederatio et unio*) on which Llywelyn ap Gruffudd and Gruffudd ap Madog agreed in 1250, and the 'friendship' (*amicitia*) that Llywelyn and Owain forged with the lords of Ystrad Tywi, Rhys Fychan and Maredudd ap Rhys, a year later.[55] *Confederatio, unio, amicitia*: these terms reflected the making of alliances which were capable of being developed into a relationship of lord and vassal, or which could equally exist quite apart from such a relationship.[56] Llywelyn's agreement with Gruffudd ap Gwenwynwyn reflects, as we have seen, the making of what was emphatically a relationship of lord and vassal. A matter of considerable relevance, it carries an explicit acknowledgement that the vassal received his lands by the lord's bestowal: Llywelyn 'gave and restored' (*concessit et restituit*) his lands to Gruffudd. Much of Gruffudd's lordship had in fact been in Llywelyn's possession as a consequence of the prince's seizure some years earlier and, in one sense, the prince now simply restored to Gruffudd what he had previously taken away from him.[57] But, in another sense, Llywelyn might be seen to be restoring to Gruffudd the lands which he had ceded to the prince as part of the transactions by which they established their new relationship. Certainly, the phraseology indicates that there was more to the agreement than the restoration of property which Llywelyn had once wrested from Gruffudd, and that in 'giving' and 'restoring' to Gruffudd

---

[53] Powicke, *Henry III*, ii, 619–20. For 'classic' English feudalism, F. M. Stenton, *The First Century of English Feudalism, 1066–1166* (Oxford, 1961); for Scottish features, Barrow, *Kingdom of the Scots*, 279–315; idem, *The Anglo-Norman Era in Scottish History* (Oxford, 1980), 118–44.

[54] Powicke, *Henry III*, ii, 620; precise agreements made in 1263 are noticed above, pp. 159–60.

[55] *LW*, 148, 160–1; for the circumstances in which Gruffudd ap Gwên agreed to return into union (*unitas*) with Llywelyn in 1278 (*LW*, 34–5), below, p. 317.

[56] Cf. K. B. McFarlane, 'An indenture of agreement between two English knights for mutual aid and counsel in peace and war, 5 December 1298', *BIHR*, 38 (1965), 200–10; P. S. Lewis, 'Of Breton *alliances* and other matters', in C. T. Allmand (ed.), *War, Literature and Politics in the Late Middle Ages* (Liverpool, 1976), 122–43; Gascon alliances in resistance to Montfort are noticed in J. B. Smith, 'Adversaries of Edward I', 61–4.

[57] Above, p. 159.

all his lands Llywelyn was exacting a recognition of the principle that Powys Wenwynwyn was now a lordship held by virtue of a bestowal on the part of the prince of Wales.

In the same manner, when he received Maredudd ap Rhys Gryg into 'his peace and goodwill' (*ad pacem et beneuolenciam suam*), Llywelyn 'restored' (*restituit*) the lands which had been in Maredudd's possession when he withdrew from the 'unity' (*unitas*) of the prince.[58] In this case, too, the lands had been in Llywelyn's possession, but if we had the text of the first agreement between the two men it might well have shown that the notion that Maredudd's lordship was in the prince's gift had already been accepted and embodied in the record of the transactions between them. The most important feature of the few surviving documents is the principle that the several lordships of Powys and Deheubarth, formed in what were once the kingdoms of those names, were now in the gift of the prince of Wales. We have no direct evidence of other transactions, but it would seem that this principle would have been reflected in agreements made between Llywelyn and those lords, such as Gruffudd ap Madog or Maredudd ab Owain, whose lands had not come into Llywelyn's possession by force but by virtue of their adherence to the prince. What we have in the few surviving documents is not a reflection of the prince's capacity for conquest, and a subsequent restoration of confiscated property, but rather an indication of the principle on which the community of the principality of Wales was founded. Nor was it a simple choice between giving or restoring the land to its lord and retaining it for himself, for Llywelyn took it upon himself to bestow upon others the lands which might be forfeited by an errant vassal. He certainly did so in the case of Maredudd ap Rhys Gryg, creating a lordship for Hywel ap Rhys Gryg in Mabelfyw and another for Maredudd ap Gruffudd in Hirfryn.[59] Principles and practices already well established within each of the provinces of Wales were now extended beyond the frontiers of a single province as part of the process of creating a wider dominion. Early in the century Hywel ap Gruffudd had secured Meirionnydd by virtue of the fact that he was of the lineage of Gwynedd, but it was by Llywelyn ap Iorwerth's consent that he retained his lordship, and he did so as a feudatory of the prince of Gwynedd. He may have done so on conditions of tenure carefully defined and formally recorded.[60] Adhering to precedents already acknowledged within his territorial lordship of Gwynedd and availing himself, too, as he indicated in a letter to the king, of the precedents established beyond its boundaries by his grandfather's relations with the lords of Powys and Deheubarth, Llywelyn ap

---

[58] *LW*, 104; the circumstances, 1261, are examined above, pp. 121–2.
[59] *LW*, 45; enfeoffment of Maredudd ap Gruffudd, below, pp. 345–7.
[60] Above, pp. 12, 216. His position would accord well with the holders of franchises envisaged in D. Jenkins, 'Kings, lords and princes', 451–62.

Gruffudd created bonds which traversed the historic frontiers of the princes' territories to create the broad political entity of the principality of Wales.

When Llywelyn ap Iorwerth first broached the issue of a principality early in the century he did so by virtue of the initiatives he had taken when he and the other princes of Wales were at war with the king of England. Similarly, Llywelyn ap Gruffudd's extension of his power beyond Gwynedd created a state of war by which he and those leagued with him revoked their fealty to the king. This did not prevent the bishops of the northern dioceses from placing their imprimatur upon the solemn agreements made between the princes. Again the evidence is confined to Llywelyn's agreements with his more difficult vassals, with the same exception of Hywel ap Rhys Gryg, who placed himself under the jurisdiction of the bishops of Bangor and St Asaph should he fail in his allegiance to the prince.[61] The bishops' sanction was something of greater moment when it was invoked in the agreements with Maredudd ap Rhys Gryg and Gruffudd ap Gwenwynwyn, and precise provisions reflect the particular circumstances in which the transactions were made. Necessarily treading warily in the way in which he dealt with Maredudd in 1258, Llywelyn placed himself under ecclesiastical sanction if he were to fail to fulfil his undertakings to Maredudd in return for his homage, and he renounced recourse to canon- and civil-law procedures if he should falter in that respect. The agreement was sealed by both bishops, a significant indication that Bishop Richard of Bangor, after a prolonged estrangement, was now prepared to countenance the greatly changed situation created by Llywelyn ap Gruffudd and, indeed, to put the prince's arguments for a recognition of his broad authority in Wales before the king's council.[62] Three years later, when Llywelyn was able to impose more stringent conditions upon Maredudd, the ecclesiastical penalties were directed specifically and solely to Maredudd. If he were to fail in his obligations to Llywelyn he would bring excommunication upon himself and his supporters, and the same bishops would seek to make the sentence effective in the diocese of St David's. It was Maredudd who was constrained to renounce recourse to canon- and civil-law procedures this time. The sanctions specified in the agreement between Llywelyn and Gruffudd ap Gwenwynwyn are expressed in more equal terms, for both princes placed themselves under the jurisdiction of the bishops and the abbots of Aberconwy and Ystrad Marchell, any one or more of whom were empowered to excommunicate the persons of Llywelyn or Gruffudd and place interdict upon their lands. Both princes, on this occasion, renounced any resort to canon and civil law in relation to the ecclesiastical

---

[61] *LW*, 45, 79, 105, 169.
[62] Stephenson, *GG*, 169–72; for renunciation of civil- and canon-law procedures, below, n. 200.

sanctions upon which they agreed. How effective these differing precepts might prove to be is a matter which may have been doubted even at the time they were put in writing, yet it was of some advantage to Llywelyn that, despite whatever disagreements there had been between prince and bishops, and notwithstanding the bishops' professions of obedience to Canterbury, they were prepared to lend their authority to these important agreements. They did so well in advance of the king's consent to what was done, and in the knowledge that the princes who entered into these pledges had effectively renounced their fealty to the king.[63]

The bishops may have been influenced by the fact that, however forceful Llywelyn's interventions in Powys and Deheubarth may have been, his relations with the lords of those provinces were expressed in the agreements into which they entered, in formal terms at least, of their free will. The contractual nature of the bonds made by the will of two lords ensured that each recognized his obligations to the other. 'Homage', it is said in 'Bracton', 'is contracted by the will of both, the lord and the tenant, and is to be dissolved by the contrary will of both'.[64] The emphasis on will (*voluntas*) is reflected in the documentary evidence of the principality, though it is indicated most clearly in texts which record the prince's wish to ensure that his tenant would not abandon his obligation against the will of his lord (*sine eius voluntate*).[65] The lord's responsibility is demonstrated in his duty to provide protection (*protectio*), and earlier discussion would suggest that this was by no means an idea suddenly grasped upon Llywelyn's assumption of elevated princely status. The main means of exercising protection was the lord's jurisdiction (*iurisdictio*), and one of the key issues which arises in examining the prince's government is the extent to which he was able to extend the authority which he possessed in Gwynedd, which has been examined already, to the provinces of his wider dominion. The nature of that authority can to some degree be elicited from the law texts, but suggestive indications may be gathered from the phraseology of the few documentary sources available for the study of the thirteenth century. Thus the records of Llywelyn ap Iorwerth's grants to the abbeys of Aberconwy and Cymer reflect his consciousness of his authority over the provinces (*provincia*) of his entire principality as he extends the benefit of his peace (*beneficium pacis*) and took them under his protection (*sub nostre protectio et defensione*), and gave them privileges which extended over the whole sphere of his authority (*potestas*).[66]

[63] Above, pp. 114–15.
[64] *Bracton*, ii, 228.
[65] *LW*, 26. For *voluntas*, J. E. A. Jolliffe, *Angevin Kingship* (London, 1955), 50–86; its place in Edward I's consciousness, J. B. Smith, 'Adversaries of Edward I', 74–7.
[66] *MonAng*, v, 458–9, 672–4; *RC*, 146–8; K. Williams-Jones, 'Llywelyn's charter to Cymer abbey in 1209', *JMerHRS*, 3 (1957–60), 54–9; *CChR*, iv, 267–9; *CPR, 1321–24*, 400; *H*, nos. 122, 123, 130.

The charters embody the language of an authority that stemmed from indigenous kingship and came to be embodied in the *status* of the principality visualized by Llywelyn ap Iorwerth or the *iura* claimed by Llywelyn ap Gruffudd. Finding the means of giving effect to that authority within the lordships which now became provinces in a still wider principality was not easy. Llywelyn ap Iorwerth made an early call upon the crown for a settlement of his relationship on terms consistent with 'the status of Wales' (*status Wallie*).[67] This was not forthcoming, nor are there any certain indications that he was able to proceed to create effective channels for his authority within the territories of the princes whom he held in his allegiance. It fell to Llywelyn ap Gruffudd to embark upon the task of ensuring that the *status* or the *iura* of the principality of Wales were expressed in a set of practical measures which made his authority effective over that principality as a whole. Llywelyn was able to devote barely twenty years to the task. We can hardly look for spectacular results in such a brief period, but it may be possible to detect the direction in which the prince endeavoured to take his broader principality. The matter may be addressed by considering his relations with the lords of Wales under the heads of military service, financial obligations and jurisdiction.

We have seen already that the agreements between the princes reflect a vivid consciousness of war. This is a feature of the agreement made between Llywelyn and Maredudd ap Rhys Gryg after their reconciliation in 1261. Maredudd agreed to ask Maredudd ab Owain if he wished to be at one with him in seeking his right and inheritance in Dyfed (*utrum velit esse unius consilii et auxilii cum ipso ad conquirendum ius et hereditatem suam in terra de Dyvet*), with provision for the division of the rewards of their efforts if the lord of Ceredigion agreed to take part.[68] The document points to a new resolve on the part of the princes to extend their frontiers in south-west Wales. We need, however, to distinguish between, on the one hand, those arrangements for joint campaigning which are indicated in this proposal and, on the other hand, provision to enable the prince of Wales to call upon his tenants for military aid, defensive as well as offensive, in the form of cavalry and infantry service. This was one source of military strength available to the king of England when he summoned forces for war in Wales and, although other forms of service were important under Edward I, it remained an appreciable factor in the king's capacity for war.[69] For his part, Llywelyn could call upon somewhat comparable service in Gwynedd and in the other lands where he

---

[67] *CAC*, 8–9; *RL*, i, 122–3; For *status*, G. Post, *Studies in Medieval Legal Thought* (Princeton, 1964), 19–23, 301–67.

[68] *LW*, 104–5.

[69] For the 'common army' of Scotland, G. W. S. Barrow, *Robert Bruce and the Community of the Realm of Scotland* (London, 1965), 122–3; Duncan, *Scotland*, 378–9.

exercised direct lordship.[70] But what service could the prince call upon from those lordships which lay beyond the bounds of his territorial lordship? The same agreement with Maredudd ap Rhys Gryg contains several informative clauses, for the feudatory's obligations are set down in clear terms.[71] First, Maredudd was bound to provide the service which Llywelyn required so as to withstand his enemies in Deheubarth; he was required to come in person with his whole strength (*cum toto posse suo*), without any reservation whatsoever, however often and wherever necessary. Second, Maredudd was bound to come, again in person, on expedition at Llywelyn's command, again with his whole strength, either along with the lords of Wales or along with any one of them, except with Rhys Fychan. He was not required to go on expedition in person with Rhys except when Llywelyn provided aid (*succursum*) from Gwynedd. Though he was not bound to go with Rhys Fychan he was nevertheless bound to send his forces with Rhys Fychan, if he were required to do so.

The clauses of the document of 1261 reveal the deep rift and continuing distrust between the two lords of Ystrad Tywi. They graphically reflect, too, the lasting effect of the estrangement between Maredudd and Llywelyn which arose from the favour that Llywelyn extended to Rhys Fychan upon his late adherence to the prince's alliance at the time of the battle of Cymerau. Drawn up after Maredudd's release from prison and in the form of a reconciliation (*composicio*) between them, the document, as a reflection of the military obligations of the prince's tenants, may be atypical of its genre. On the other hand, the stress on joint campaigning, which is a prime feature of the agreement, may reflect a practice common among the lords of Wales as a whole. Distinctions should not perhaps be made too finely on the basis of a single document, but Maredudd was required to participate with his lord, or with his fellow lords of Wales, or to supply his entire forces, in joint defence or joint campaigning rather than required to provide the prince of Wales with a specified amount of military service to be deployed at the prince's discretion. The arrangements made with Gruffudd ap Gwenwynwyn point to a similar conclusion. There is something of the nature of a call of the lord upon his tenant in Gruffudd's undertaking to join Llywelyn upon campaign (*tenetur venire in excercitum cum domino Lewelino*) whenever he was required to do so, unless his lands were obviously under imminent threat. Yet the document as a whole reflects an emphasis on their bonding together for joint campaigning, with an appropriate sharing of the spoils – gains north of the Camlad to the one and south of the river to the other – and on their mutual agreement to stand together and be 'of one war and of one peace' (*quod sint unius gwerre et*

---

[70] Above, p. 253.
[71] *LW*, 105.

unius pacis), neither entering into any confederacy without the other.[72] This was indeed the brotherhood of war, with Llywelyn no less than Gruffudd bound in specific obligations: if Gruffudd were under pressure of invasion, and Llywelyn were not, the prince would provide support for him rather than for other adherents (*pre omnibus aliis suis imprisiis*) if his need were the greater; if Gruffudd were to lose his castle of Welshpool in war Llywelyn would provide another for him until he recovered his own.

Joint pledges on the part of two men who might well be of equal status are blended with the explicit submission on the part of one, who was emphatically a tenant, to the command of another, who was his lord; a statement of confident assertiveness fused with an underlying lack of trust: these are the themes which suggest themselves in considering the military features of the surviving examples of agreements made among the princes of Wales. It is a great pity that we have no evidence whatsoever of the obligations recognized by those of the prince's tenants who were men of unquestioned constancy, such as Gruffudd ap Madog and Maredudd ab Owain. We have no impression of the tone or the phraseology of the documents in which their compacts were registered, but that such agreements were made there can be little doubt. These two barons occupied strategically important lands at the north-east and south-west extremities of the principality, and the lineages to which each belonged had had associations, including marriage alliances, with the marcher powers beyond their frontiers.[73] They had come to Llywelyn's alliance with differing degrees of alacrity. A clearly defined statement of their military obligations would have been essential. But their relations with Llywelyn were not fraught with anxieties comparable to those revealed in the relationships already noticed, and without some record of their agreements we can make only a partial estimate of the manner in which Llywelyn set about the task of availing himself of the resources of his principality so as to ensure its security, quite apart from any assessment of the degree to which he was successful in fulfilling that task. From what is available for study, we can hardly say that he was able to establish an ordered system of military service which ensured purposeful deployment of resources, and the impression left by the documents which we have from the period is that the prince's tenants had barely embarked on the work of girding themselves, by true collective action and deliberation, for the great necessity which was held in abeyance only too briefly.[74]

With so little evidence to consider, the question of whether the prince's tenants were bound in financial obligations to their lord can be considered at

---

[72] *LW*, 78–9.
[73] For the marriages of the lords of Powys Fadog and Ceredigion, below, pp. 304–5.
[74] For *magna necessitas*, the needs of war, below, pp. 295–7.

no great length. In its account of the implications of the relationship expressed in the notion of *mechdeyrn ddyled* the law text recounted that a specific sum was due to the king of England and it strongly suggested that, on the same principle, a monetary payment was due to the king of Aberffraw from the other kings of Wales: *mechdeyrn ddyled* was paid when the kings received their lands from the king of Aberffraw, and a relief (*ebediw*) was paid upon the death of a king. The references bear a resemblance to the practices which obtained within the individual seigniories of Wales – *cynasedd* or *gobrestyn* on the one hand, and *ebediw* on the other – and they suggest close parallels with practices much further afield.[75] We have nothing to suggest, however, that any obligation to make payments of this nature came to be embodied in the agreements between Llywelyn and his tenants beyond the boundaries of Gwynedd, nor is there any other evidence to indicate that such payments were made. More generally, there does not appear to be any intimation that Llywelyn levied a tax upon his tenants in his broader dominion, nor on their lordships, neither regularly nor occasionally. As far as can be judged, but always remembering the tenuous nature of the evidence, the entire financial burden of the principality fell upon the lands under Llywelyn's immediate lordship, even though a substantial part of the burden arose from the agreement that registered the king's consent to the extension of Llywelyn's authority over Powys and Deheubarth. Any attempt on Llywelyn's part to share that liability over those provinces might well have been resented, but equally the community of Gwynedd might well have rued the fact that they, and the communities of the other lordships under the prince's power in the march of Wales, had to stand the entire cost of the liability incurred by the prince of Wales by his treaty obligation to the crown. There is certainly nothing to suggest that any subjection to a financial obligation, incurred by the treaty of Montgomery or otherwise, counted among the considerations which brought the prince's tenants in Powys and Deheubarth to secede in 1277, but there is good reason to conclude that Llywelyn's own tenants, particularly those of Gwynedd, were put under some strain as they stood the whole responsibility for the prince's obligations to the king of England.[76]

A similar conclusion is indicated in relation to the great costs which Llywelyn incurred as he prepared for war. The necessity for a prince to secure the means of defending a country against attack was acknowledged throughout the Christian world. Aquinas called upon the words of the prophet to denounce the princes who were like wolves ravaging their prey, shedding

---

[75] These obligations of the prince's tenants in Gwynedd are noticed above, pp. 199–201.
[76] The burden upon the lordship of Snowdon has been examined already; the prince's financial obligations to the king are considered in the next chapter.

blood and destroying souls for their gain, but he did so in the course of a discussion which established the principle that it was just that a prince should ensure that he had sufficient means to withstand enemy attack. In an emergency it was right that his tenants should contribute whatever was needed to safeguard their common well-being.[77] The financial and military obligations of a prince's tenants were closely related to one another, and it can hardly be doubted that men of letters in the principality of Wales were perfectly well aware of the political and theological discourses which emphasized the duties of ruler and ruled to defend the *patria*, and unto death if need be.[78] The poet's references to the protection provided by the princes can often be distinguished from the conventional praise of their prowess in arms, and, shortly before his death, Llywelyn revealed his concern and his conscience for the safety of his people.[79] What is found wanting in the evidence available to us is an emphatic indication that the *patria* to be defended was conceived to be, not a particular lordship, but the principality of Wales as a whole. We lack sure knowledge that practical measures were taken to share the burdens which war, or the threat of war, brought in its train. We have no knowledge that the community of the principality of Wales, though never entirely free from military contingency, ever acknowledged its sense of *communis utilitas* by making monetary contributions to the prince's coffers. The fact that the prince's peregrination was confined to the lands over which he exercised immediate lordship may reflect his well-nigh total dependence on the resources of those lands. Be they demesne manors or Cistercian granges, the places where the prince invariably dated his letters were within the confines of his own areas of resource.[80] His journeys beyond these frontiers appear to have been occasional and largely dictated by military need. They cannot be seen to have been determined by that conjunction of need and advantage which was, in the experience of so many royal dynasties, inextricably linked with the functions of government. It was only in war, and very late in the day, that the principality of Wales even began to act in a manner which suggested some conception of common necessity. To the extent that it was achieved at all, over the extent of the principality as a whole, it was the product of desperate measures undertaken in the heat of conflict. We cannot show that the economic resources of the broader dominion were geared to the provision of properly co-ordinated means of resistance. The

---

[77] 'De Regimine Judaeorum', in Aquinas, *Selected Political Writings*, 90–2. The problems in practice are examined in Harriss, *King, Parliament, and Public Finance*, 32–74; for a wariness of too great an emphasis on the link between taxation and necessity, Prestwich, *Edward I*, 454–8.
[78] Post, *Medieval Legal Thought*, 435–53.
[79] Below, pp. 532–6, 543–4.
[80] Above, pp. 220–1.

trial of strength, which might have inspired a determination to achieve these means of protection, itself proved overwhelming. Unlike Robert Bruce and the community of the realm of Scotland, Llywelyn was denied the opportunity to turn the striving of the hour of crisis into a sustained and purposeful endeavour to stabilize a viable political entity.

The materials which relate to military service and financial obligations are exceedingly slight and allow for very limited conclusions. We have seen, however, that the lord's command (*mandatum domini*) finds its place in military organization, and something may be said with regard to the means by which Llywelyn endeavoured to extend his authority over the principality of Wales. His ultimate objectives have been deduced in the course of earlier discussion: to extend to the provinces of his wider sphere of authority a significant measure of that regalian or seigniorial power already exercised over his territorial lordship. An essential ingredient in any such process would be the extension of the prince's jurisdiction so that judgement might be dispersed in the courts of the principality in his name and enforced by his sanctions. Establishing an authority of this nature in Powys and Deheubarth would be a long-term objective, to be pursued not in one generation alone but through the sustained efforts of successive princes of his dynasty. A more immediate need, and one more readily resolved perhaps, would be to ensure that his baronial tenants who exercised lordship over these lands acted in a manner consistent with their solemn pledges. The men of learning, who would later reflect on the qualities which poets should hold in esteem when addressing their patrons, undoubtedly registered an abiding sense of acknowledged social values when they wrote that a man owed 'fidelity in word and deed and thought to his rightful lord'.[81] A lord, in turn, had a similar duty of fidelity to his lord. The pledge of fidelity was an essential element in the contractual relationship established by the bond of homage but, to be certain of that fidelity, the lord needed the means of dispensing justice in a manner consistent with the conventions of a civil society and adequate powers of enforcement. The documents that reflect the troubled relations between Llywelyn and Maredudd ap Rhys Gryg reveal that the prince had resorted to powers of judgement and enforcement. Their first encounter, following Maredudd's duplicitous defection, was probably marked by a somewhat scant regard on the part of Llywelyn to judicial procedure. In 1258, upon Maredudd's doing homage after returning to the prince's allegiance for what was to prove an exceedingly brief stay, Llywelyn promised that he would not imprison him again, nor would he imprison his

---

[81] *Gramadegau'r Penceirddiaid*, ed. G. J. Williams and E. J. Jones (Cardiff, 1934), 56.

son nor hold him as a hostage, neither would he take possession of his castles nor prevent him gaining access to the prince.[82] The purport of the document was to provide Maredudd with the guarantees that could create new confidence in the prince's wish to deal with him in an equitable manner, and the document does not provide any comprehensive statement of how their relationship thereafter would be regulated. Llywelyn went to some lengths to provide those assurances, to the extent of placing himself under ecclesiastical censure if he failed to fulfil his solemn undertakings.[83] He would have been concerned, above all else at that point, to ensure that Maredudd's disaffection should not become a matter of arbitrament at the court of the king of England. There was no indication, in this agreement, of the procedures which would need to be applied if Maredudd were to falter again. These were early days in the principality of Wales, when stress had need to be laid on the mutual respect of obligations, by prince and barons alike. They were still to establish the means of resolving more abiding problems than those which were dictated solely by the prince's inspired call to arms. The barons of the principality would certainly agree that the nexus between lord and tenant established by homage was such that the lord owed as much to the tenant as the tenant owed to the lord.[84] The practical implications of the dictum would still need to be agreed. More than anyone else it was Maredudd ap Rhys Gryg who revealed the intricate problems created by the prince's determination to interpose his authority between the barons of Wales and the king of England. Their tortuous relationship served to inculcate into the corporate consciousness of the new political community the need to ensure, in equal measure, rigorous adherence to the mutual obligations into which lord and tenant had entered and agreement upon the judicial processes by which any necessary correction might be made.

In the very next year, when it was clear that Maredudd had again been found wanting in fidelity, Llywelyn was determined to show that disloyalty on the part of one of his baronial tenants would incur the judgement of the fraternity which had brought the new polity into being. Left vulnerable on the previous occasion by his failure to proceed by judicial process, he now made sure that the great men of Wales (*nobiliores Wallie*) came together to take counsel. Maredudd was convicted of infidelity (*infidelitas*) and imprisoned.[85] We have only the annalist's word for this, but it is enough to establish that it was by judgement of his peers, barons of the principality of Wales, that Maredudd spent many months in prison, his lands in Llywelyn's possession.

[82] *LW*, 168–9.
[83] *LW*, 168–9; Llywelyn placed himself under the jurisdiction of the bishops of Bangor and St Asaph and abbots of Aberconwy and Bardsey.
[84] *Bracton*, ii, 228.
[85] *AC*, 97; above, pp. 121–2.

All this was directly contrary to the undertakings which Llywelyn had made the previous year, but he had made those promises in return for Maredudd's 'faithful homage', and that faith had been breached and the perfidy had been a matter on which a judicial process had now taken its course. The effect of the judgement is reflected in the new compact (*composicio*) made in 1261: there are no longer any vestiges of the unqualified promises which Llywelyn had previously made when he enumerated what he would not do again; the emphasis is placed on Maredudd's obligations, though he was not left denuded of safeguards.[86] His military obligations were, as we have seen, phrased in a way which respected his sensibilities. If he were charged with an offence and he confessed or was convicted, and if justice could be done by a levy upon his goods or lands according to the nature and magnitude of his offence in accordance with the decision of the prince's court and council, he should not be captured nor imprisoned nor be subject to assault upon his person. The undertakings are now inextricably linked with judicial process: if he were to offend again, Maredudd would be charged before Llywelyn and would be bound to come before him, and he would be subject to the decisions of Llywelyn's court and council; if he were to falter in his observance of the new agreement, and failed to come and receive justice, he would forfeit to Llywelyn his entire right to his inheritance in Deheubarth. He submitted himself to ecclesiastical censure, but he placed himself, too, in Llywelyn's peace and benevolence (*ad pacem et benevolentiam suam*). There was no longer any doubt that the lords of the principality of Wales were subject to the prince's jurisdiction, no question that any serious breach of faith on the part of any one of them would leave him liable to forfeiture and excommunication. They were no longer allies responding to the prince's leadership, but tenants who acknowledged his lordship.

The implications of the treatment meted out to Maredudd were probably clear to Gruffudd ap Gwenwynwyn when he came into the prince's allegiance.[87] For, if the military clauses reflect a firm commitment to joint campaigning in expectation of shared rewards, there are signs of wariness in the clause in which Gruffudd secured his lord's promise that he would not set out to magnify any charge against his tenant if it were not evident that it could be proven and that, if he were faced with a charge which would not be substantiated, Llywelyn would have to do right in respect of any injury due to him. But though the provisions embodied safeguards for Gruffudd in the event of unproven charges, and even proven charges, Llywelyn was not deterred from laying down that any offence with which Gruffudd was charged would be examined. If it were proved, appropriate redress (*condingna*

---

[86] *LW*, 104–5.
[87] *LW*, 77–80.

emenda) should be made by the judgement (*arbitrium*) of fifteen men, named laymen, churchmen and religious, almost every one of them drawn from among the men of Gwynedd. Eleven years later it became necessary, as we shall see, to proceed against Gruffudd for a serious breach of faith.[88] It may be a sign of Llywelyn's wish to tread warily at a time of great stress, and to be seen to proceed justly, that the case was examined, not by the men named in 1263, nor by men chosen on the principle adopted then, but by a board of eight arbiters (*arbitri*), four from Gwynedd and four from Powys.[89] But if the procedure adopted in 1274 reflects the prevailing political circumstances and the tendency to arbitrament which was a feature of judicial practice in Wales and the march, the decision reached by the arbiters placed Gruffudd and his son entirely in Llywelyn's grace and at his will, and there can be no doubt that the decision carried the full weight and authority of the prince's court. It was recorded at the same time that any action which might arise by reason of any person's assertion of right in the lands restored to Gruffudd would be determined in the prince's court, a clause whose significance will be considered presently. The main matter of concern, however, was the breach of fealty on the part of the lord of Powys Wenwynwyn. The prince's dealings with Gruffudd ap Gwenwynwyn and Maredudd ap Rhys Gryg demonstrate that, though the varied political circumstances in which the transactions were completed are duly reflected in the record, and though the prince's baronial tenants were sometimes able to insist on safeguards and assurances, Llywelyn was determined to establish that the bonds forged by homage and fealty meant submission to a lordship made effective through the unquestioned judicial authority of the prince's court. Proceedings in the prince's court could well have created resentment. It is doubtful whether the procedures adopted in Llywelyn's court invariably ensured that barons of Wales would receive a judgement of their peers. For, while Maredudd may have been convicted by 'the barons of Wales' in 1259, judgement upon Gruffudd four years later was reached by the arbitrament of men of non-baronial status, and there is no certainty that the prince's council then present included representatives of the barons of Wales capable of endorsing the judgement. When Llywelyn was

---

[88] *LW*, 108–10. A text of the process at Dolforwyn, 17 April 1274, is preserved in a transcript, 21 July 1278, validated by the abbot of Aberconwy and dean of Arllechwedd; for this recourse to Llywelyn's archives, below, p. 470.

[89] *LW*, 109: from Gwynedd, Tudur ab Ednyfed (the prince's justice), his brother Cynfrig ab Ednyfed, Einion ap Caradog, Dafydd ab Einion; from Powys, the prior of Strata Marcella, Adam ap Meurig (official of Powys), Gruffudd ap Gwên (Gruffudd ap Gwenwynwyn's justice) and Einion ab Ednyfed. The document is read ibid. as though Dafydd ab Einion were prior of Strata Marcella; the text needs a comma between the two names and another, *LW*, 77, to separate the prior and Cyfnerth ap Heilin. Only two laymen of Powys are named in 1274, Gruffudd ap Gwên of Cyfeiliog and Einion ab Ednyfed ap Sulien of Caereinion (*LW*, 110), for whom, D. Stephenson, 'The politics of Powys Wenwynwyn in the thirteenth century', *CMCS*, 7 (1984), 46–8; below, pp. 317, 369–71.

constrained, in difficult political circumstances on the eve of the war of 1277, to promise to do full justice to the barons of Wales by judgement of their peers he may well have pledged himself to a means of judgement that he had not hitherto always respected. In the aftermath of Gruffudd's conviction, for reasons that will be examined presently, Dafydd ap Gruffudd thought it best to evade proceedings against him in the prince's council altogether by a sudden departure from the principality of Wales.[90]

It would be an entirely different matter to argue that the prince was able to exercise an influence on the manner in which judicial proceedings were conducted in the courts of the constituent parts of the principality, or that he introduced his judges or his jurisdiction into those areas, or that their courts were made subject to the higher authority of the prince's court. These might well have proved to be long-term aims of successive princes of Wales, but Llywelyn's opportunities to pursue objectives such as these, or to move towards a uniform provision of justice in his name, were severely limited. Later evidence certainly reveals considerable variation in the practice of the courts held in the lands which had previously formed part of the principality. One important distinction, already noticed briefly, can be made in relation to the method by which judgement was given in the commote court. The indications given in lawbooks emanating from Gwynedd that judgement was given there by the professional judge, the *ynad* or *iudex*, is confirmed in documentary sources.[91] The law texts, even so, drew a distinction between the practice in Gwynedd and, as they aver, in Powys also, and that which prevailed in Deheubarth where collective judgement was given in the commote court. In Deheubarth, certainly by the late thirteenth century, judgement was vested in 'judges by privilege of land' (*brawdwyr o fraint tir, iudices per dignitatem terre*), normally described in documentary sources as suitors (*sectatores*).[92] There are good indications that in Powys, too, by then collective judgement was usual. Llywelyn ap Gruffudd's insistence, during legal disputations of the period 1277–82 considered later, that there were professional judges called *ynaid* in Arwystli and Cyfeiliog, might be taken as an indication of a desire on his part to extend the sphere of the judicial

---

[90] Llywelyn's promise in 1277 (*promittit . . . facere iusticiam baronibus Wallie . . . secundum iudicium parium eorum in Wallia*) in J. B. Smith, 'Offra principis Wallie domino regi', *B*, 21 (1964–6), 362–7, quoting text, p. 366; for the initial action of the prince's council in relation to Dafydd's offence, late 1274 (*a principis consilio fuerat increpatus*), *LW*, 136–8; Stephenson, *GG*, 7; below, p. 372.

[91] Above, pp. 201–3.

[92] *LTWL*, 324–55, 349–53; *LlBleg*, 15, 98–106, provide main textual references. Collective judgement is examined in S. Reynolds, *Kingdoms and Communities in Western Europe 900–1300* (Oxford, 1984), 23–34, 51–9; idem, 'Law and communities in Western Christendom, c.900–1140', *American Journal of Legal History*, 25 (1981), 213–21. Judgement under Welsh law will be examined in another study.

practice which prevailed in his territorial lordship and thereby promote his interests.[93] But the prince's statement has to be considered strictly in the context of the controversy in which it was made, and there is no suggestion in this evidence of any attempt, comparable to those which may be noticed in other lands, to extend his authority through judges empowered to do justice in his name.[94]

More pertinent as an indication of the prince's purposes may be his insistence, at the time of the process against Gruffudd ap Gwenwynwyn in 1274, that a person claiming a right (*ius*) to land in those territories which he restored to Gruffudd would need to prosecute his claim in the prince's court.[95] At the same time it was provided that if Gruffudd himself wished to bring a similar action he, too, should come to the prince's court and justice would be done to him there. The inclusion of these provisions may have been prompted by a particular issue. When Gruffudd had come to the prince's fealty in 1263 it had been agreed that enfeoffments in his lordship made by Llywelyn ap Iorwerth or Dafydd ap Llywelyn would remain undisturbed; those made by Llywelyn ap Gruffudd were left at the will of Gruffudd ap Gwenwynwyn. It is conceivable, as we shall notice again, that the princes of Gwynedd had made links with certain lineages in the community of Powys Wenwynwyn, perhaps introduced favoured tenants, and that the prince was concerned for the protection of these tenures in 1274.[96] Whatever the precise significance of the provision it appears reasonably clear that the prince was endeavouring to establish his judicial authority, at least in one particular connection, within a dependent seigniory of the principality of Wales. It might be an opportunistic indication of a more general objective that the prince would pursue as circumstances allowed. Firm indications to this effect from the period of Llywelyn are difficult to find, and post-conquest statements that might appear to point in this direction need to be treated with caution.[97] Even so, the evidence from Powys Wenwynwyn – drawn from one of the very few documents of its kind – may be indicative of a more general trend.

There are, then, as might be envisaged, clear indications that procedures in the courts of the several parts of the principality varied and no firm evidence of any significant effort to establish a uniform judicature. There is, however,

---

[93] *CWR*, 195; for the occasion in 1281, below, p. 484.

[94] R. C. van Caenegem, *Royal Writs in England from the Conquest to Glanvill* (London, Selden Society, 1959), 357–9, notices the various means of promoting change in judicial provision.

[95] *LW*, 109–10.

[96] *LW*, 78.

[97] E.g. the claim by the abbot of Strata Florida, 1293, that he and his predecessors had previously been impleaded only in the court of the prince of Wales by the prince's writ (S. W. Williams, *The Cistercian Abbey of Strata Florida* (London, 1889), App. xxxii, quoted in Stephenson, *GG*, 6, n. 24).

some suggestion of the prince's wish to intrude his jurisdiction into dependent seigniories in addition to establishing his authority over the lords of those seigniories in the manner indicated in the instances already examined. There is a further question as to whether the prince's court exercised a corrective and supervisory jurisdiction over the courts of the constituent seigniories. The main judicial institution was the commote court, which possessed a comprehensive jurisdiction and, it would seem, one of an exclusive nature. Documentary evidence that the prince's court was empowered to reverse erroneous decisions of the commote courts or to supervise the working of those courts does not appear to be forthcoming. The law texts of both Gwynedd and Deheubarth certainly provide some reference to the procedures by which an erroneous judgement, presumably given in a commote court, would be challenged and corrected, specifying both the penalty incurred by the erring judge and the recompense made to him if his judgement were vindicated.[98] There is little indication even so as to how it might be established that an erroneous judgement had been given, with the conspicuous exception of the procedure intimated in the Cotton Vespasian E.i text of Welsh law (Latin B). The text states that when an erroneous judgement by the judge of commote court (*iudex patrie*) was alleged, the judge of the court (*iudex curie*, that is the *ynad llys*) would, by the king's command, adjudge the plea.[99] This suggests that, in theoretical terms at least, the issue of whether a plea might be removed from a commote court to a court of higher authority was broached by thirteenth-century jurists. The textual evidence of this exceedingly important manuscript may point to the direction in which the prince's court was moving and it is conceivable that the provision adumbrated was intended to apply, not only to judgements made in the commote courts of the prince's territorial lordship of Gwynedd, but further afield as well.[100] The statement is couched in the terms of the juristic literature but it needs to be evaluated in the context of the changes indicated by the documentary evidence of the thirteenth century. The offices depicted in the 'law of the court' were re-ordered as arrangements in the prince's entourage were brought into closer conformity with contemporary royal and baronial administration.[101] One change has an obvious bearing on the procedure indicated in the Cotton Vespasian text. There is no trace in records of the *ynad llys*, the judicial officer depicted in the whole range of texts of the 'law of the court'. His duties were

---

[98] *LTWL*, 115, 198, 283, 324, 443; *LlIor*, 8–9; *LHD*, 17; *MWL*, 15–16; *LlBleg*, 17–18, 100–5.
[99] BL, Cotton MS. Vespasian E xi, described in *LTWL*, 172–3.
[100] *LTWL*, 212.
[101] The officers are examined in T. M. Charles-Edwards, M. E. Owen and P. Russell (eds.), *The Welsh King and his Court* (in preparation).

probably subsumed into those of the *distain*, the prince's leading minister.[102] It was the *distain* who presided over the prince's court and council in the absence of the prince, or at the prince's wish, whatever the nature of the matters transacted. He was in practice empowered to deal with whatever issue arose which needed judicial or any other form of decision. The extension of the prince's jurisdiction would be achieved, not by an edict to that effect, but by prescriptive means as the *distain* established precedents in response to specific needs. These could conceivably include consideration of a difficulty which might arise if injustice was alleged in a commote court; he would, as the redactor of the Vespasian text expressed it, act by the command of the king. The appearance of the *distain* of Gwynedd in the guise of 'the prince's justice' (*justiciarius domini principis*), even 'justice of Wales' (*justiciarius Wallie*), provides an indication of the direction of change in thirteenth-century Wales.[103]

In attempting to recognize the way in which the prince exercised his authority and extended its range it would be well, however, to take account of matters other than those already considered. Comparative study would suggest that a regalian authority such as that of a prince of Wales would seek to establish some regulation over the land transactions of the prince's tenants-in-chief and over the provisions that they might make for the succession to their inheritance. A vigilance over property dispositions which might affect the prince's interests could reasonably be envisaged, and there is some indication that this was so in the principality of Llywelyn ap Gruffudd. When Owain ap Maredudd bestowed the commote of Anhuniog in Ceredigion upon his wife Angharad in 1273, to provide for her needs in the future, he did so by a charter which reflected contemporary practices in England.[104] Adopting one of the two forms available under the common law of England, Owain's grant to Angharad 'in free marriage' (*in liberum maritagium*) took the form, not of the *dos rationabilis* that ensured a widow a third of the land of which her husband was enfeoffed, but the *dos nominata*, the specified dower described by 'Glanvill', by which land was assigned to the wife as a gift made at the church door.[105] The text is particularly noteworthy in the present connection because it includes a brief record that Llywelyn ap Gruffudd, prince of Wales, confirmed the deed and put his seal to it. It indicates that Llywelyn had begun to register those gifts by which seigniorial rights vested in a tenant-in-chief

[102] Stephenson, *GG*, 11–20; J. B. Smith, '*Ynad llys*'.
[103] *LW*, 26, 109; below, pp. 313–14, 328–9.
[104] J. B. Smith, 'Dower in thirteenth-century Wales: a grant of the commote of Anhuniog, 1273', *B*, 30 (1982–3), 348–55.
[105] *The Treatise on the Laws and Customs of the Realm of England commonly called Glanvill*, ed. G. D. G. Hall (London, 1965), 58–69. The document has a hybrid quality, with the term *liberum maritagium*, normally associated with marriage portion, used with reference to dower.

were transferred to another. Anhuniog, described as an 'entire commote' (*commotum integrum*), constituted a baronial estate of whose disposition the prince wished to make a record and thereby establish his right to regulation. The principle itself was not a novel one. Owain's father, Maredudd ab Owain, had obtained Henry III's consent when he made comparable provision a generation earlier.[106] On that occasion the deed was registered in chancery; exactly the same procedures were now taken at the prince's court. This, as far as is known, is the only charter that contains a specific reference to the prince's confirmation, but we can be certain that it was not the only document of its kind drawn up at this time. Evidence from Powys Fadog shows that arrangements which Gruffudd ap Madog and his sons made for Gruffudd's wife Emma in her widowhood were approved by Llywelyn 'who confirmed all grants' (*qui omnes donaciones confirmavit*).[107] Dower provision which involved the giving of land was not prescribed under Welsh law. Arrangements made *pro dote*, such as *cowyll* and *agweddi*, consisted of the provision of moveables rather than land and were akin to those which, in English law, would be expressed by dowry rather than by dower.[108] The lords of Ceredigion and Powys Fadog, marrying women from marcher families, had need to make arrangements in accordance with the practices of marcher lineages and these might impinge on the interests of the prince of Wales. These might not be part of the practice for which Cyfraith Hywel provided, but they came to be part of what was deemed appropriate under the law and custom of Wales.[109] The 'liberties' (*libertates*) conveyed by Owen ap Maredudd, which included the patronage of churches, constituted seigniorial rights; the clause in Gruffudd ap Madog's charter which stipulated that after Emma's death the *patria* of Maelor Saesneg would revert to Gruffudd and his heirs, and that it should never be removed from Welsh lordship, reflected the seigniorial interests, not of Gruffudd alone, but of Llywelyn, too.[110] Grants of this nature came under the prince's surveillance and indeed the prince was vigilant of the implications for himself of the marriages into which his barons might enter. His interests and those of his barons had to be reconciled with one another.

---

[106] *CPR, 1232–47*, 487.

[107] Text of charters, Seebohm, *Tribal System*, App. 103–5; inquisition, 1277, App., 102–3; see J. B. Smith, 'Dower', 350–2.

[108] J. B. Smith, 'Dower', 348–50; D. Jenkins, 'Property interests in the classical Welsh law of women', 76–85.

[109] For the marriages, J. B. Smith, 'Dower', 351–3. The jurors in Powys Fadog stated that 'by the custom of Wales' a Welshman could provide lands for his wife either before or after their marriage (Seebohm, *Tribal System*, App. 102–3); cf. assignments of dower by Maredudd ap Robert to Juliana de Lacy 'which she ought to have by the law and custom of Wales', 1252 (*CR, 1251–53*, 185); Rhys ap Maredudd to Ada de Hastings, 1285 (*CWR*, 303).

[110] Seebohm, *Tribal System*, 103; for Emma's surrender of the land to the king, 1278, *CWR*, 170–1; *CCR, 1272–79*, 513.

The provision made for Gruffudd ap Madog's wife in Powys Fadog was part of a fuller territorial disposition which touches the wider question of Llywelyn's attitude towards the succession to his baronial tenants' estates. In tracing the political processes which gave birth to the principality of Wales we have had reason to appreciate how much depended on Llywelyn's ability to reconcile the pursuit of his objectives with his barons' concern for their territorial interests. The several lords of Powys and Deheubarth were themselves heirs to once royal estates and were often motivated by concerns closely comparable to those of the princes of Gwynedd. The degree to which these lords, in the middle and later years of the thirteenth century, were able to preserve the integrity of their inheritances might vary considerably and, indeed, it is not always clear that this was the paramount objective.[111] The outcome of the succession to Welsh baronial estates differed greatly among those which occurred, in a clutch between 1265 and 1271, upon the death of Llywelyn ap Rhys ap Maelgwn and Maredudd ab Owain in Ceredigion, Maredudd ap Rhys Gryg and Rhys Fychan in Ystrad Tywi, and Gruffudd ap Madog in Powys Fadog.[112] It is not always clear whether the outcome was what the late lord had intended, even more difficult to judge what Llywelyn ap Gruffudd's attitude might have been and what action he might have taken to influence the devolution of the estate. Yet the prince could be affected by the outcome, and the succession to Powys Fadog in 1269 and the provision made rather later in Powys Wenwynwyn provide particularly instructive instances of the means by which the succession to a Welsh baronial estate might be resolved and the bearing that it might have on the interests of the principality as a whole.

Powys Wenwynwyn did not lose its lord during the years of Llywelyn ap Gruffudd's power but the arrangements which Gruffudd ap Gwenwynwyn made in 1278 for the succession to his lordship are certainly instructive. It fell to Edward, rather than Llywelyn, to register the important document which embodied Gruffudd's provision for the future, and the deed conforms closely to the forms of the instruments by which, in areas subject to the common law of England, the succession of an estate to specified heirs was ensured and provision made for contingencies that might arise in the future.[113] It is very likely, however, that the lord of Powys Wenwynwyn would not have made any different provision had he gone about the matter as a tenant of Llywelyn, nor is there good reason to believe that the form of the document would have been much different from that which came to be enrolled among chancery records. It does indeed appear that the arrangements were first made when

---

[111] J. B. Smith, 'Dynastic succession in medieval Wales', *B*, 33 (1986), 224–30.
[112] *BT, Pen20*, 215–19; *Pen20Tr*, 114–16; *RBH*, 254–9.
[113] *CWR*, 171–3; full text in *RotWall*, 37–9; *MontColl*, i, 124–5.

Gruffudd was in Llywelyn's fealty, for a document of 1270 embodied that part of the provision which applied to one of his sons and it is phrased in a manner which would have been perfectly acceptable at common law.[114] In the comprehensive statement of 1278 Gruffudd conveyed the inheritance to Owain ap Gruffudd, the eldest of six sons, but he ensured that each of the other five was provided with an estate within the eldest brother's lordship. It was specifically ordained that the brothers should hold their estates as tenants of Owain and do him homage; he alone, as lord of the fee (*feudum*), would fulfil the services done to the king from Powys Wenwynwyn. If a legal action arose between the brothers it would be determined in Owain's court, and it fell to his court to determine actions between the tenants of the brothers which could not be resolved in the courts of the brothers. Owain received by far the greater part of the lands, and this, along with the fact that the brothers' lands were scattered, must reflect Gruffudd's wish to ensure the continued existence of the estate in its entirety. If the deed, in its form and phraseology, had several of the features of common-law instruments, it would be quite wrong to conclude that it is testimony to the fact that, by ensuring the integrity of the inheritance in this way, Gruffudd was adopting the principles of English law.[115] He was no doubt attracted to the beneficence of that law, but there are good reasons for the view that the deed enrolled in chancery demonstrates the wish of a Welsh lord, proceeding in conformity with the procedures of the common law, to secure an objective well founded in the dynastic practice of his own dominion. Gruffudd's brother, Madog ap Gwenwynwyn, never enjoyed any better provision than that made for Owain ap Gruffudd's brothers in 1278. For when Gruffudd came to Llywelyn's fealty in 1263 Madog was given no more than the commote of Mawddwy, to be held for his lifetime as a tenant of Gruffudd.[116] Madog's share of the land of his fathers was no more than an apanage within his brother's lordship. The provisions made by Gruffudd ap Gwenwynwyn in 1278 were not necessarily at odds with 'the custom of Wales', and we can reasonably conclude that, if Llywelyn ap Gruffudd had maintained his authority over his powerful tenant, an identical provision would have been confirmed by the prince and duly registered in his archives. Such provision, vesting the lordship of Powys Wenwynwyn in the eldest son, but with territorial provision made within the lordship for each of the other sons, may indeed have been made under Llywelyn's lordship some years before.[117]

---

[114] *LW*, 132; witnessed by churchmen, religious and laymen of Powys Wenwynwyn; J. B. Smith, 'Dynastic succession', 226, n. 4.

[115] J. C. Davies, in *WAR*, 40; the deed is seen as a compromise between Welsh and English succession practice in R. Morgan, 'The barony of Powys, 1275–1360', *WHR*, 10 (1980–1), 1–42.

[116] *LW*, 78.

[117] J. B. Smith, 'Dynastic succession', 225–6.

Powys Fadog appears at first sight to present a marked contrast, for the charter in which Gruffudd ap Madog's sons confirmed the provision made for their mother was part of an arrangement which, whatever had been the intention of the late lord, led to the dismemberment of the lordship.[118] In the course of subsequent litigation one of the sons, Owain ap Gruffudd, held that the original provision, which had reflected the influence of Prince Llywelyn ap Gruffudd, apportioned to Madog ap Gruffudd (the eldest son) a larger share than was appropriate in accordance with the law and custom of the area.[119] The prince is stated to have taken possession of the patrimony and by his power assigned that extensive share to Madog. Llywelyn, who certainly authenticated the provision made for the widow, might well have had an even greater interest in the main transactions concerning the extensive and strategic lands of Powys Fadog. An unequal apportionment, whoever was responsible for its assignment, may well explain the decision of the second son Llywelyn ap Gruffudd ap Madog, or Llywelyn ap Gruffudd Fychan, to defect to the king in 1276, and it would certainly explain his subsequent insistence on an equal division of the property between Madog ap Gruffudd and himself.[120] It is conceivable, however, that the inequality of the partition reflected a wish on the part of Gruffudd ap Madog and Prince Llywelyn, acting in agreement with one another, that the eldest son Madog ap Gruffudd should inherit the greater part of the patrimony, and with it a measure of seigniorial control over the whole of the patrimony. Gruffudd's constant concern, for a whole generation, to maintain a single lordship over the inheritance in its entirety suggests that any provision he made for the future would reflect that same enduring objective.[121] It would not be unreasonable to postulate that what was envisaged at the demise of the lord of Castell Dinas Brân was not a partition of the patrimony, but a *parage* by which, while enabling each brother to secure a substantial estate, a greater share would be conveyed to the eldest son. He would be endowed with lordship over Powys Fadog in its entirety and ensure its integrity for another generation.[122]

---

[118] Distribution of lands may be traced from a legal action of 1278 (*WAR*, 247–8). There were four sons, Madog ap Gruffudd, Llywelyn ap Gruffudd (also named Llywelyn ap Gruffudd Fychan, the form used in this volume), Gruffudd Fychan and Owain ap Gruffudd.

[119] *WAR*, 247; Owain states that Madog had married Margaret, described as Llywelyn's niece (*neptem*); it has been noticed earlier that Margaret is elsewhere described as his sister; for his concern for her sons, his nephews, after 1277, *CAC*, 93–4; below, pp. 456–7.

[120] *LW*, 53–4; below, pp. 410–11, 423–4.

[121] Above, pp. 30–1, 34, 48, 70.

[122] Castell Dinas Brân was located in the portion conveyed to the eldest son. D. J. C. King, 'Two castles in northern Powys: Dinas Brân and Caergwrle', *ArchCamb*, 123 (1974), 113–39, suggests building at a date *c*.1270; historical evidence points to a date in the period of Gruffudd ap Madog (d. 1269).

Prince of Wales

Llywelyn ap Gruffudd hardly had the power to enforce his will in all cases such as this, and he could well have presided over arrangements which differed from one lordship to another. Nor can it be assumed that his needs dictated the same solution at every succession. Over the longer term a prince of Wales might have a great deal to gain from a process by which the lordships of Wales would be subject to continuing fragmentation.[123] Hindered by the studious reluctance of the lords of Powys and Deheubarth to cede anything of their inherent status, the prince had much to gain from the shattering of the territorial basis on which their regality was founded. It would enhance his opportunity to extend his influence within these lordships. The territorial and social cohesion of the wider principality would be affirmed, and the extension of the prince's jurisdiction over its constituent parts would be greatly facilitated. On the other hand, Llywelyn had to contend with more immediate problems of security, and he had every reason to maintain the stability of a strategic quarter as important as that of Powys Fadog. It would be unwise to conjecture on the basis of such a scanty record, better to do no more than take account of the indications that Llywelyn was vigilant of the descent of baronial estates in his principality and that he may have tried to influence decisions in a manner consistent with the interests of the polity as a whole. Others in his position did so, not least Edward I, whose dealings with some of his greatest magnates, though exceedingly difficult to interpret, point to a calculation of long-term dynastic interest.[124]

Court and council

Implicit in this discussion is the sense that the fulfilment of Llywelyn ap Gruffudd's wishes could in many cases be assured only with the consent of those who formed the community of the principality of Wales. The common interest of government and society was not a matter of theoretical exposition alone, and the fact that a process of reconciling various political interests in a single polity was set in motion within a Welsh framework during the thirteenth century is, perhaps more than anything else, the essential matter which needs to be appreciated in a biographical study of Llywelyn ap Gruffudd. He gathered the magnates of his land about him in his council, the key instrument in securing the unity of his principality and ensuring its effective government. It was the body which shared with the prince the responsibility for decisions made in his name, and the role of the 'court and

---

[123] J. B. Smith, 'Dynastic succession', 216–18.
[124] Powicke, *Henry III*, ii, 705–7, 732–3, 788–9; K. B. McFarlane, *The Nobility of Later Medieval England* (Oxford, 1973), 248–67.

council' in the exercise of his jurisdiction has been noticed already. It was seen by the king as a body with a recognized responsibility in respect of the prince's relations with the crown. Prince and council were held in shared responsibility for the fulfilment of the terms of the treaty of 1267, and members of his council were sworn to ensure implementation of the agreement negotiated ten years later.[125] Llywelyn himself on occasion indicated, as he did in times of great stress in 1277 and 1282, that decisions on matters relating to the crown would be resolved by the prince in association with his council, even to the extent of his being constrained by its decision.[126] The composition of the council was itself a reflection of the prince's political achievement and of his search for an ordered government of his dominion. When Llywelyn ap Iorwerth replied to King Philip's invitation to join him in forging an alliance between the principality of Gwynedd and the kingdom of France, he said that he had summoned the council of his magnates (*proceres*), and that, apart from this, he had also secured the unanimous consent of all the princes of Wales.[127] The distinction reflects the duality of his position in 1212: on the one hand lord of Gwynedd and, on the other, leader of a broader Welsh military alliance. The princes of the other provinces could not, at that stage at least, be counted among the members of his council. When Llywelyn ap Gruffudd came to assert his hegemony in 1258 the leading figures among the men of Gwynedd and the princes of Wales were joined together in the prince's council. As we have seen already, *Brut y Tywysogyon* records that an assembly of the magnates (*dylyedogion*) of Wales was held in that year, and the text of the agreement with the lords of Scotland, drawn up perhaps at the assembly mentioned by the chronicler, provides the first of several indications of the composition of the prince's council at a plenary session.[128]

The presence of the princes of Powys and Deheubarth, the baronial members, was probably an occasional occurrence, the prince attended more regularly by those from his patrimonial land who formed the council's ministerial core. The distinction between baronial and non-baronial members made in lists of those present on notable occasions has been instanced already. Protocol dictated that baronial members were named first, followed by the non-baronial names, with a fairly constant differentiation between the two groups.[129] The ministerial corps in the prince's service included men whose ancestral origins lay in the dynasty of Gwynedd, but in lists of those

---

[125] *LW*, 4, 121.

[126] J. B. Smith, 'Offra principis Wallie domino regi', 367; *RPeck*, ii, 468–71. For the council, Stephenson, *GG*, 6–10.

[127] R. F. Treharne, 'The Franco-Welsh treaty of alliance, 1212', *B*, 18 (1958–60), 74; idem, *Simon de Montfort*, 359; trans. *EHD*, iii, 306–7.

[128] *LW*, 184–5; above, pp. 109–13.

[129] E.g. *LW*, 99, 110, 184–5; *RL*, ii, 286; *DipDoc*, i, no. 400.

present in council they took their places among the non-baronial members. On the other hand, not all those included in the baronial ranks were men of territorial power. They included, for instance, Hywel ap Rhys Gryg and Hywel ap Maredudd, minor or disinherited members of princely dynasties who were probably in regular attendance upon the prince and loyal dependants upon him. Owain ap Bleddyn and his kinsmen, heirs to the increasingly dismembered lordships of Edeirnion, were placed among the baronial members, though they may have carried much less weight in council deliberations than the non-baronial members considered presently.[130] Men of the dynasty of Gwynedd, who might have retained the landed position that they held upon Llywelyn ap Gruffudd's assertion of power, would no doubt have been accorded a place consistent with baronial precedence had they remained in the prince's fealty. The one person to be afforded baronial status in fact was Dafydd ap Gruffudd. The prince's entourage may have included, quite often, men of lesser baronial rank from outside Gwynedd along with the ministerial group. Major baronial figures, such as Gruffudd ap Gwenwynwyn, Maredudd ab Owain, Gruffudd ap Madog and Maredudd ap Rhys Gryg were probably present less frequently, but they were undoubtedly called upon when important matters had to be resolved. Men of this standing would certainly have been summoned to participate in the decision of the 'court and council' of the Lord Llywelyn which, it was agreed in 1261, would need to be made if Maredudd ap Rhys Gryg were to falter once more in his allegiance to the prince.[131] They were gathered together at times when important political decisions had to be made, their deliberations sometimes made at a moment of triumph, sometimes in time of deep anxiety. They were present to consider Monfort's proposals in 1265; the surviving members were among those present when the prince's council conducted its deliberations on the proposals set out by Archbishop Pecham late in 1282. It seems, too, that barons of the principality might be with their prince at times other than those of full sessions of the council, and that was certainly true of Dafydd ap Gruffudd during the years when he was in his brother's allegiance.[132] Military or diplomatic responsibilities might be deputed to them: Dafydd ap Gruffudd and Gruffudd ap Gwenwynwyn were engaged in the armed conflict in Glamorgan and then in negotiation with the prince's opponents in that area; Gruffudd ap Madog and Rhys Fychan lent their weight to negotiations with representatives of the king at the ford of Montgomery, and instances of responsibilities delegated to the prince's baronial tenants could be

[130] *LW*, 99, 184–5.
[131] *LW*, 105.
[132] E.g. Bishop Anian of St Asaph and Dafydd ap Gruffudd were the two members of the council in attendance at a date in 1273 (*CAC*, 161–2).

multiplied.[133] Counted among these weighty figures were the bishops of the northern dioceses and the abbots of Cistercian houses. Bishop Richard of Bangor, racked by conflicting impulses in earlier years, came to terms with Llywelyn ap Gruffudd's assured lordship and assumed the responsibility of presenting Llywelyn's plea for a definitive settlement with the king. He persevered with his task, on several occasions lending his authority to delegations that otherwise consisted of men of ministerial rank who would perhaps have had the more intimate knowledge of the matters under discussion.[134] His successor at Bangor, Bishop Anian, and Bishop Anian of St Asaph, too, were among the prince's emissaries, despite the rifts which may have curtailed their presence at the prince's side.[135] Madog, abbot of Valle Crucis, when he travelled to the papal court on what were described as matters concerning his house in 1275, may well have had opportunity to explain the prince's position at that time of great anxiety, even if that were not the main purpose of his journey. He and Llywelyn, abbot of Cymer, certainly represented the Cistercian adherence to the prince which proved to be of considerable advantage in adversity.[136] It is clear that men such as these were, more than bearers of parchment or verbal messages, occasional participants at least in the deliberations by which the interests of the community of the principality were furthered and safeguarded.

In the surviving lists the non-baronial members of the prince's council follow those of the baronial figures and the distinction between them was almost invariably respected.[137] We have noticed already the significance of the names which came together as Llywelyn, in the wake of victory at Bryn Derwin, began to unify the community of Gwynedd after the divisions which had torn it apart in the preceding years. These were the men who came to bear the main responsibility for the conduct of business relating to the broader principality. It was from among these, laymen and clerics, that the prince drew the capability and the expertise in composing the letters which were sent to the court of the king of England and the court of Rome, and from their ranks came the envoys who travelled constantly on his behalf. The office which stands out most prominently in the record is that of the *distain.* The manner in which the *distain* absorbed, as it seems, the office of the *ynad llys* has already been recounted, and it may be that the responsibilities of the *distain* also

[133] *LW*, 28; *Cartae*, iii, 763–5; *CR, 1256–59*, 466; *CPR, 1258–88*, 27.
[134] Above, pp. 122–3, 126–30.
[135] Below, pp. 377–8, 409–10, 413.
[136] Circumstances at the time of his journey are considered later. For Cistercian support for Llywelyn, Pierce, *MWS*, 38, n. 27; F. G. Cowley, *The Monastic Order in South Wales, 1066–1349* (Cardiff, 1977), 209–12; below, pp. 379–81, 384–5.
[137] Owain ap Bleddyn's placing after Goronwy ab Ednyfed in the agreement with Montfort, 1265, is either an instance of a breach of the order of precedence or a sign of an assimilation of the lesser baronial and ministerial groups.

embraced the military duties traditionally associated with the *penteulu*.[138] Vested in Ednyfed Fychan for a long period during the rule of Llywelyn ap Iorwerth and Dafydd ap Llywelyn, the office, though not hereditary, was entrusted to successive members of the lineage.[139] It is possible that, in the early years of Llywelyn ap Gruffudd's rule, the responsibility was given to Gruffudd ab Ednyfed, an early and weighty adherent.[140] His sterling qualities are commemorated in an eulogy by Dafydd Benfras, who mourns the loss of a soul whose steadfast fidelity was matched by worthy deed: 'Enaid hir cywir cyfuch weithred', and commends a faithful companion to God's unassailable protection: 'Ceidwad nef, Ei nawdd ni thorrir / A'i cadwo, cydymaith cywir'. The fidelity he had maintained in companionship with the poet would be matched by loyalty to his lord.[141] By early 1258, perhaps shortly after the death of Gruffudd, the office was probably conveyed to Goronwy ab Ednyfed, who was *distain* during the decade which saw Llywelyn consolidate his hegemony over Powys and Deheubarth and secure the king's consent to his achievement. Goronwy earned the praise of chronicler and poet alike. In the estimation of the chronicler he was, not only eminent in arms and generous, but 'wise of counsel and true of deed' (*doeth ei gyngor a chywir ei weithred*); he was revered by Bleddyn Fardd, who valued his valour and liberality, but who was more deeply moved by his impregnable fidelity, for he was a pillar of the prince's dominion.

> Byth am walch rhwyddfalch rhy-n-doeth – trais galar
> Bu traws golofn cyfoeth,
> Arwr dŵr, erys dewrddoeth,
> Eurwawr, carueiddfawr coeth.[142]

Goronwy was succeeded by his brother Tudur ab Ednyfed, who returned to the prince's service after a prolonged exile, years when he was first held in captivity and then retained in royal service while his son Heilin remained a hostage for his fidelity.[143] These two sons of Ednyfed Fychan were at the

---

[138] Stephenson, *GG*, 11–20, offers cautious discussion of the roles of *penteulu* and *distain* in military matters. Record references are sparse, but Goronwy ab Ednyfed led the prince's forces in Gwent in 1263. For *distain* and *ynad llys*, above, n. 102.

[139] Stephenson, *GG*, 17–19.

[140] Ibid., 18, 104–5, 214; J. B. Smith, 'Land endowments of the period of Llywelyn ap Gruffudd', *B*, 34 (1987), 155–6, 161–2; idem, 'Gwlad ac arglwydd', 238; above, pp. 45–6.

[141] *GDB*, 33.

[142] *BT, Pen20*, 218; *Pen20Tr*, 115, more briefly *RBH*, 258–9; *GBF*, 47; Stephenson, *GG*, 14–18, 213.

[143] Heilin was released in February 1263; Tudur, who certainly served Llywelyn from later that year, is named as an arbitrator in the agreement between prince and bishop of Bangor, 29 April 1261 (*CPR, 1258–66*, 248; *LW*, 78; *Councils*, i, 489). Service to the crown from 1248 is indicated in chancery enrolments; service to the princes in Stephenson, *GG*, 13, 17–19, 218–21.

prince's side during his years of supremacy, and one of them shared his humiliation: Goronwy and Tudur both swore on the prince's behalf to the observance of the treaty of Montgomery; Tudur swore upon the soul of the prince due observance of the treaty of Aberconwy. The adherence of Ednyfed Fychan's lineage to Llywelyn ap Gruffudd was not, even so, marked by unexceptionable fidelity, a matter noticed at a later stage in our discussion.[144] But there can be no doubt that the achievements of Llywelyn ap Gruffudd owed a great deal to those who were associated with him as members of the ministerial group which centred on the *distain*. They fulfilled the new range of tasks entailed by the extension of the prince's authority to the principality of Wales as a whole, developing the necessary expertise, and represented their prince in negotiations with crown and marchers. During the course of the succession which has been described, the *distain* of Gwynedd became, as we shall see again, the justice of Wales.[145]

The men of Gwynedd listed with the *distain* were of diverse origins within the land. They included, as has been suggested already, men who could count princes and kings of Gwynedd among their ancestors. They may be regarded as instances of those whose status, in the jurists' parlance, was determined not by their predecessors' position as members of the royal lineage – *aelodau brenin, membra regis* – but by virtue of their proprietorial position.[146] They are best represented by Einion ap Caradog, undoubtedly a man of the lineage of Owain Gwynedd, who was an early adherent of Llywelyn ap Gruffudd and one whose long service was ultimately to bring him, by the summer 1267, the gratification of sharing the responsibility of negotiating the peace treaty that had hitherto proved so elusive.[147] Dafydd ab Einion, his companion during the exchanges at Shrewsbury, was a member of a family of non-princely origin closely associated with the dynasty over a long period. He was a son of Einion Fychan, servant of Llywelyn ap Iorwerth, Dafydd ap Llywelyn and Llywelyn ap Gruffudd, and was probably of the lineage of Einion ap Gwalchmai, Gwalchmai ap Meilyr, and Meilyr Brydydd. He would thus belong to a line which had provided ministers to serve the princes and poets to give voice to their aspirations and share their grief.[148] Drawn from the upper

---

[144] The succession after Tudur is uncertain; a possibility that Dafydd ab Einion was *distain* from 1278 is considered in Stephenson, *GG*, 107–8. Rhys ap Gruffudd ab Ednyfed's loyalties are noticed below, pp. 430–2, 444.

[145] Below, pp. 328–9.

[146] J. B. Smith, 'Dynastic succession', 205–6; Stephenson, *GG*, 115–19, 147–51.

[147] Stephenson, *GG*, 115–19, 209–10, 230–1; above, pp. 44–5, 178–80.

[148] Stephenson, *GG*, 106–10, 206–7, 210–12, includes a strong case, tentatively advanced in *TC*, 226–7, for the identification of Dafydd as a son of Einion Fychan and grandson of Einion ap Gwalchmai; for the poets Meilyr Brydydd, Gwalchmai ap Meilyr and Einion ap Gwalchmai, who addressed princes from Gruffudd ap Cynan to Llywelyn ap Iorwerth, see the texts and critical study in *GMB*, 6 *et seq.*

echelons of the *nobiles* of their communities, these men were part of a small corps whose names appear constantly in the prince's service. Their names are not normally linked with any particular office at court, and it is indeed difficult to estimate the degree to which functions were differentiated.[149] Little enough can be said of the prince's financial officers, for there are only occasional references to those who fulfilled the duties suggested in the lawbooks' accounts of the *gwas ystafell* or *camerarius*. The successors of the *offeiriad teulu*, the priest of the household associated with writing duties, are similarly elusive, though the prince's secretarial arrangements will be considered presently.[150] Apart from the *distain*, what emerges most clearly from the scant record is a group of confidants found serving as envoys, arbiters and participants in the negotiations which led to the agreements to which they often bore witness.

There were many occasions when, serving on delegations or arbitration panels, the prince's ministerial servants were associated with men of baronial standing. Protocol demanded, as has been noticed, that in formal documents precedence was accorded those of baronial status, even though the main responsibility for the practical fulfilment of the tasks undertaken may well have fallen to those of ministerial rank. Another distinction, implicit in earlier discussion, can be made by virtue of the fact that, whereas those of baronial rank were drawn from the principality at large, the non-baronial servants associated with the prince's court and council were probably drawn largely, or even exclusively, from among the men of Gwynedd. This was not necessarily so, of course, in the case of those who bore responsibility in the lordships which came under the prince's authority in the march of Wales. Few in number, the names which survive tend to be those of men drawn from the areas themselves. They included Ifor ap Gruffudd, the prince's bailiff of Elfael Is Mynydd, who ultimately transferred his loyalty to the powers of England and the march.[151] Another servant drawn from the area, Rhys ap Gruffudd, bailiff in Builth, could be counted among those who stood by the prince in his final conflict and fell beside him on the day he died.[152] The prince's servants normally appear to have fulfilled their responsibilities in the lands with which they were themselves associated and there is little evidence of deployment across established frontiers. There is not much to suggest that

---

[149] Stephenson, *GG*, 24–5.

[150] Financial organization is discussed ibid., 20–4, with cautious consideration of the suggestion that there was a financial department under a treasurer (Pierce, *MWS*, 33). The treasurer remains elusive, but a chamberlain with financial duties is indicated in lawbooks, and there are record references to a sub-treasurer and a treasury (*LW*, 39; Ll. B. Smith, '*Gravamina*', 174; above, pp. 231, 255).) Secretarial responsibilities are noticed later.

[151] Officers in Gwerthrynion. Elfael, Builth and Brecon are noticed in J. B. Smith, 'The middle march in the thirteenth century', *B*, 24 (1970–2), 85–7; below, p. 404.

[152] Below, pp. 404, n. 57, 565, n. 188.

Llywelyn ap Gruffudd was able to recruit ministers from the provinces of Powys and Deheubarth, or that he had any significant opportunity to dispatch his ministers to those lands. Over a longer span than that allowed to Llywelyn ap Gruffudd, a prince of Wales might well have increased ministerial activity across the seigniorial frontiers of his principality. His surveillance of land transactions, already considered, would be one pretext for the dispatch of officers to the seigniories of the principality and there may have been opportunities of which we have no knowledge. But these areas were formally linked with the prince by little more than the bonds which bound their lords in fealty to him. The sphere of his ministerial servants was essentially that of the patrimonial lands on which he depended for his sustenance and to whose courts he confined his peregrinations.

There were already, however, in Powys and Deheubarth men other than the lords of the several lordships of these provinces who had, in one way or another, connections with the prince of Wales. Members of Ednyfed Fychan's progeny, including Goronwy Fychan and Hywel ap Goronwy, sons of Goronwy ab Ednyfed, possessed lands in Ceredigion and Ystrad Tywi.[153] The prince of Wales would probably have been glad to see these cross-frontier connections multiplied, and there is some indication that such links were created during his time. Bonds created by enfeoffment might be particularly valuable, traversing seigniorial frontiers in a manner comparable to that by which the prince's predecessors had made endowments which ensured that there were among the *nobiles* of Gwynedd some with territorial assets which bridged the boundary between Uwch Conwy and Is Conwy.[154] Intruding the prince's influence by these means beyond the confines of the patrimonial lands of Gwynedd was much more difficult, but there is some indication that the thirteenth-century princes had been able to make enfeoffments in Powys Wenwynwyn.

It is perfectly conceivable that both Llywelyn ap Iorwerth and Llywelyn ap Gruffudd sought, during the periods in which they exercised direct lordship over the area, to introduce reliable adherents drawn from their own dominion.[155] On the other hand, they might equally have been anxious to cultivate alliances with collaborative lineages from within the community of Powys Wenwynwyn itself. The importance of associations of the one kind and

---

[153] A. D. Carr, 'An aristocracy in decline: the native Welsh lords after the Edwardian conquest', *WHR*, 5 (1970–1), 123; R. A. Griffiths, *PW*, i, 9–10. Goronwy Fychan and Hywel ap Goronwy held lands in Ceredigion 1278 (*CWR*, 175; *THSC*, 1895–6, 123, from SC6/1158/1).

[154] Stephenson, *GG*, 130–5.

[155] *LW*, 78; identifications remain uncertain. Stephenson, 'Politics of Powys Wenwynwyn', 46, notes that Gruffudd ap Rhodri and Bleddyn ap Meurig, servants of Llywelyn ap Iorwerth (idem, *GG*, 204, 215) were among witnesses to a charter of Gruffudd

the other would be clear in a situation such as that created in 1274 when Gruffudd ap Gwenwynwyn was convicted of a serious offence against the prince of Wales. The homage of twenty-five of Gruffudd's tenants was reserved by the prince and they were required to pledge themselves to remain faithful to him in the event of a further lapse on Gruffudd's part.[156] It might have been helpful for the prince if, in these circumstances, their number included men who owed their position in the lordship, or an improvement to their position there, to a prince of Gwynedd. On the other hand, it was important to Llywelyn that he should try to bind in allegiance to him a strong representation of those who were of recognized standing in the community of the area, quite apart from known adherents of the prince, still less *advenae* from Gwynedd.[157] There were indeed men of substance from the locality among the guarantors of Gruffudd's fealty. They included three men of the lineage of Goronwy ab Einion of Cyfeiliog, namely his sons Tudur ap Goronwy and Iorwerth ap Goronwy and his grandson Gruffudd ap Gwên, who served as justice of Gruffudd ap Gwenwynwyn.[158] It was not easy to maintain a grip on these men. On the eve of conflict two years later Llywelyn exacted pledges from several of them for the fidelity of Gruffudd Budr ei Hosan and his sons, who were evidently under suspicion, or worse.[159] But, within months, Gruffudd ap Gwenwynwyn, re-entering his lordship by the king's power, was able to call his tenants to their old allegiance and the prince of Wales was forced to imprison some of those who had previously pledged their loyalty.[160] After his humiliation Llywelyn ap Gruffudd made a bid to maintain a hold upon the allegiance of Gruffudd ap Gwên, but the transaction may be little more than a record of a form of words to which a captive might be persuaded to give his assent in order to secure his release.[161] The creation of bonds with the men of the dependent lordships might, over time, promote the cohesion of the principality as a whole. Yet, attempted for only a brief period, and pursued against the grain of local seigniorial power, it could hardly bring any tangible reward.

ap Llywelyn to Strata Marcella in 1226. This may point to a link with the prince in his rule of the lordship, but may not indicate enfeoffment there.

[156] *LW*, 110.

[157] Ednyfed ap Gruffudd ab Ednyfed is named in 1274, but there is no reason to believe that he was a son of Gruffudd ab Ednyfed Fychan. The Tudur ap Goronwy named is not of the lineage of Ednyfed Fychan but a son of Goronwy ab Einion of Cyfeiliog; he may be the 'official of Cyfeiliog' of that name who witnessed the provision made by Gruffudd ap Gwenwynwyn for his son Llywelyn in 1271 (*LW*, 132).

[158] *LW*, 99, 110; Bartrum, *WG*, iii. 578; iv. 831, 834. For Gruffudd ap Gwên and Einion ab Ednyfed ap Sulien, Stephenson, 'Politics of Powys Wenwynwyn', 46–8.

[159] *LW*, 42–3.

[160] Gruffudd ap Gwenwynwyn stated in litigation, 1278, that Einion ab Ednyfed and Einion ap Dafydd had been captured by Llywelyn in the war and were still imprisoned (*LW*, 110; *WAR*, 241).

[161] *LW*, 34–5; below, p. 495.

It would, however, be unwise to stress tenurial links to the exclusion of a more personal form of princely influence, and this could be secured both by willing adherence and by more compulsive means. When Llywelyn's loyal adherent, Hywel ap Rhys Gryg, entered into an undertaking to the prince, by which he provided security for the fidelity of men of the marcher areas in proximity to Deheubarth, he was joined by several others from among the freemen of the commotes of Ystrad Tywi.[162] They included Madog ab Arawdr, who was to provide stalwart support for the prince in the conflicts of the later years, and military commitment could be complemented by other means of identification with the prince. They were not tenants of the prince, yet in a document embodying their pledges, these sureties could refer to the prince as their lord. The connection with the prince of Wales might express an identity of interest, or it might reflect the imposition of his authority. The transactions in which Hywel ap Rhys Gryg and Madog ab Arawdr were involved were indeed concerned with the fidelity of those in his lordships whose loyalty was suspect, and the stringent measures taken by Llywelyn to secure his position by extracting pledges of allegiance will be considered presently.[163] These were not altogether the problems of marginal lands. It is clear that he took stern measures in response to what appears to have been a breach of trust on the part of Rhys ab Ednyfed, a prominent tenant within the patrimony of Gwynedd. One of Rhys's sureties felt bound to address Llywelyn in exceedingly effusive terms.[164] But neither these expressive acknowledgements of the prince's stature, nor the strict measures which evoked them, were confined to the prince's relations with tenants under his immediate dominion either in Gwynedd or in the march. It is evident that, certainly when set upon a corrective purpose, the prince could make a direct call upon the fidelity of a tenant of one of his own mesne lords. There is a distinctly submissive tone to the letters patent by which Owain ap Maredudd, addressing the prince in respectful terms, stood surety for the sum by which Hywel Fychan secured the prince's 'benevolence' (*benevolentia*) and permitted him to do homage to the prince and swear fealty, even though he was Owain's man.[165] A similar deference, and an even more pronounced effort to address Llywelyn in exalted terms, marks the letter in which Cynan ap Maredudd became surety for the payment by which Cadwgan, his foster-

---

[162] *LW*, 33–4.
[163] Below, n. 193.
[164] *LW*, 23, 24, 29: 'illustrissimo viro et honesto L[ewelino] . . . et a suo mandato nulatinus tegilire'. Rhys ab Ednyfed was among witnesses to the treaty with the magnates of Scotland, 1258 (*LW*, 185).
[165] *LW*, 24. There were three named Owain ap Maredudd: lords of Cydewain (d. 1261), Elfael (d. c.1260–7) and part of Ceredigion (d. 1275). It is difficult to judge who stood surety for Hywel Fychan, himself elusive; close similarity between this and the document cited next, involving another lord of Ceredigion, suggests that area c.1267–75.

Prince of Wales

son (*alumnus*), secured a remission of the prince's anger towards him.[166] Precisely what lies behind these transactions is unclear, nor is it possible to make any estimate of their incidence. But the few of which we have knowledge point to the rigour with which the prince of Wales could impose his authority, both in his own lands and in the lordships of his wider principality, if circumstances provided sufficient pretext. Disciplinary proceedings were not necessarily confined to tenants-in-chief such as Maredudd ap Rhys Gryg. The documents to which Hywel ap Rhys Gryg, Owain ap Maredudd and Cynan ap Maredudd put their names provide a glimpse of a forceful personal lordship made manifest both within the prince's territorial lordship and well beyond its frontiers.

The prince's acta

The surviving records of the transactions undertaken on the prince's behalf, or the letters written in his name, were the work of men whose names elude us. The writing of the documents was probably the work of scribes drawn from among the clerics. But a degree of literacy among laymen may reasonably be envisaged, for those whose names have entered our discussion of the activities of the prince's ministerial corps probably possessed a measure of the practical literacy that was increasingly a feature of the processes of government in the thirteenth century.[167] A tradition of lay literacy is represented in the learning of the jurists who composed the law texts, though they, too, have proved to be exceedingly elusive. Even the most conspicuous among them, Iorwerth ap Madog, who may be placed in the later years of Llywelyn ap Iorwerth, is known only from genealogical sources and the legal literature itself.[168] We have no more than a few names of practising lawyers, mainly those of the *ynaid* named in the evidence gathered for Edward I in the course of the inquiry of 1281.[169] Just as there is no trace of the *ynad llys* (the judge of the court) among the documentary records of the prince's government, so there is no record testimony to the actions of the *ynaid* in the commote courts or indeed otherwise. The men who appear in connection with legal proceedings as arbiters named to act on the prince's behalf cannot be shown to have

---

[166] *LW*, 34.

[167] M. T. Clanchy, *From Memory to Written Record: England 1066–1307* (London, 1979), 29–87, 258–65; evidence for Wales is studied in Llinos B. Smith, 'Inkhorn and spectacles: the impact of literacy in late medieval Wales', in H. Pryce (ed.), *Literacy in Medieval Celtic Societies* (Cambridge, 1998), 202–22.

[168] D. Jenkins, 'A family of Welsh lawyers', in D. Jenkins (ed.), *Celtic Law Papers* (Brussels, 1973), 121–33.

[169] *CWR*, 195–201.

included practising *ynaid*.¹⁷⁰ Yet legal learning and expertise was an essential part of the cultural ambience of the period. Taken together, the Latin and Welsh texts reflect a capacity, to which lay and clerical talents probably contributed, to combine indigenous learning and custom with precepts of canon law and civil law, too.¹⁷¹ The Cotton Vespasian Exi text (Latin B), already mentioned in this discussion, is a particularly instructive manuscript in several respects, not least in that it was evidently the work of a compiler at work at an ecclesiastical centre, able to draw on texts of Roman law, though perhaps transmitted through canon law, and a person at the same time sensitively attuned to the political inclinations of the thirteenth-century princes.¹⁷² The texts of *Llyfr Iorwerth* and *Llyfr Colan*, resonant of a robust native and secular learning, are not without their touches of Latinity.¹⁷³ The range of legal texts drawn from Gwynedd and Deheubarth, in Latin and Welsh, and the historical writings, too, point to a reservoir of literate skills, drawn in large measure, perhaps, from among those in clerical or monastic orders, which could be applied to other needs than the composition and preservation of texts.¹⁷⁴

By the period of Llywelyn ap Gruffudd, quite apart from the broad trend towards an extended use of written instruments, a particular need came to be created by the greatly intensified political and diplomatic activity generated by the prince's expansive policies. Precisely how these literate resources were employed to the prince's advantage is far from clear. In the antiquated phraseology of 'the law of the court' in *Llyfr Iorwerth*, it is the *offeiriad teulu* ('the priest of the household') who was entrusted with the secretarial functions of the royal court.¹⁷⁵ Constant in his attendance on the king, lodged with the other clerks (*ysgolheigion*) beside him, his emoluments include 4*d.* for every patent seal that the king gave for land. The details may be a little quaint, but they point to the *offeiriad teulu* as a precursor of the chancellor (*cancellarius*) who appears in records of the thirteenth century. The evidence for the chancellor is, in fact, fuller for the earlier years of the century than the later period, and the Master Instructus who is prominent in the records of the

---

¹⁷⁰ For arbiters, see e.g. the process against Gruffudd ap Gwenwynwyn (*LW*, 109).

¹⁷¹ For legal learning, Pryce, *NLC*, 22–30, with citations of earlier studies.

¹⁷² *LTWL*, 13–45, 172–268; for its particular interest in relation to the succession, J. B. Smith, 'Dynastic succession', 201, 205–6; above, pp. 8–9.

¹⁷³ Pryce, *NLC*, 26, with particular reference to *Llyfr Colan*. For Roman law, Emanuel, *LTWL*, 24–40; D. B. Walters, 'Roman and Romano-canonical law and procedure in Wales', *Recueil de mémoires et travaux publié par la société d'histoire du droit et des institutions des ancient pays de droit écrit*, 15 (Montpellier, 1991), 67–102; below, n. 200.

¹⁷⁴ Historical texts are noticed in J. B. Smith, *SHMW*, 3–11.

¹⁷⁵ *LlIor*, 5–6; *LHD*, 11–12. Lat. B (*LTWL*, 200) states that wherever *offeiriad teulu* (*sacerdos familie*), *distain* and *ynad llys* were together they maintained the dignity or authority of the court (*dignitates curie*, i.e., *braint y llys*) in the absence of the king.

period of Llywelyn ap Iorwerth is not matched by any comparable figure in the time of his grandson.[176] Nor is there, at any point in the course of the thirteenth century, a well-authenticated chancery, by that name or any other, nor any trace of an associated record repository, though by this period many lay magnates, including lords of the march of Wales, had developed the facilities for the writing of documents.[177] In the case of some magnate families a high proportion of the muniments which survive consists of charters.[178] It is a form of document which often prompts the question whether the parchments were written by scribes employed in the magnates' households or whether the magnates relied on scribes provided by the beneficiaries, but there can be little doubt that writing facilities were available to major magnates. Among the *acta* of the thirteenth-century princes charters are not represented in great numbers.[179] For the period of Llywelyn ap Gruffudd, indeed, charters are exceedingly few, and the chief interest of the *acta* of this period lies in the profusion of letters and various documents which reflect the prince's relations with his fellow princes and with the lay and ecclesiastical powers beyond his frontiers. By their very nature these documents, unlike charters that provided title to land or some other benefice, cannot be ascribed to the clerks of their recipients, and the need for adequate facilities for their production is evident. It is also obvious that, though many were straightforward documents requiring no great expertise, they included some that made greater demands upon those who composed them than the charters, whose forms and phraseology could to a large extent be culled from formularies. The term 'chancery' may not appear in documents emanating from the principality of Wales, and even the chancellor is elusive in the period of Llywelyn ap Gruffudd, but it is difficult to envisage how the prince's administration could have been maintained without the presence of a secretariat directed by a principal officer in constant attendance upon the prince. *Llyfr Iorwerth* points to the existence of precisely that kind of officer in

---

[176] Stephenson, *GG*, 28–39, 224–5. The need to distinguish between *cynghellor* and *cancellarius* is established in D. Jenkins, '*Cynghellor* and chancellor', *B*, 27 (1976–8), 115–18.

[177] Stephenson, *GG*, 26–8. For the march, Altschul, *Clares*, 267; J. C. Otway-Ruthven, 'The constitutional position of the great lordships of south Wales', *TRHS*, 5th ser., 8 (1958), 7–8. In the Braose charter of liberties to Gower, 1306, the chancery is mentioned in relation to availability of writs (*Cartae*, iii, 994); the use of the term chancery in the march may have been advanced by the growth of proceeedings by writ.

[178] Important collections of baronial muniments include *Charters of the Honour of Mowbray 1107–1191*, ed. D. E. Greenway (London, 1972); *Earldom of Gloucester Charters*, ed. R. B. Patterson (Oxford, 1973).

[179] Stephenson, *GG*, 199–204, lists twenty-nine charters of the thirteenth-century rulers of Gwynedd; *Handlist of the Acts of the Welsh Princes*, ed. K. L. Maund, has thirty-five charters for the same period, apart from references to lost charters. The known *acta* of Earl David of Huntingdon, 1152–1219, number ninety documents, of which there are texts of thirty-five, each one a charter making a grant or confirmation (K. J. Stringer, *Earl David of Huntingdon* (Edinburgh, 1985), 220–70).

the *offeiriad teulu*, one closely comparable, perhaps, to the 'principal chaplain' who may be noticed elsewhere in the late twelfth century and the thirteenth.[180]

Identification of those who might have served the prince in a secretarial capacity is difficult, and the scant evidence has to be treated with caution. For instance, in the period of Llywelyn ap Gruffudd successive abbots of Aberconwy appear in two distinct but possibly related roles. On several occasions, in the earlier years, Anian served as an envoy to the crown and witnessed agreements between Llywelyn and his barons; Maredudd, in the later years, appears to have had access to the prince's records and may have had charge of their custody.[181] Thus in 1278 Maredudd and Dafydd, dean of Arllechwedd, put their seals to a transcript of the process against Gruffudd ap Gwenwynwyn at Dolforwyn four years before. They did so in order that an authenticated record was available for proceedings before royal justices, their transcript sealed at Ardda, a grange of the abbey of Aberconwy in Nanconwy.[182] Maredudd was concerned, too, in transactions concerning Rhodri ap Gruffudd and with the record of those affairs.[183] Safe-keeping of documents 'in the aumbries of the church' is indicated in Llywelyn ap Iorwerth's letter to King Philip early in the century, noticed already, and it is possible that churches and monastic houses were used for this purpose throughout the period of the princes.[184] It is evident, too, and mentioned at several points in this volume, that churchmen and members of monastic or religious houses were constantly engaged as the prince's envoys. On occasion they did so in circumstances which suggest very strongly that, more than the bearers of letters, they possessed an intimate knowledge of the matters under discussion and that they may have been concerned in the production of the documents transmitted. They were sometimes senior dignitaries. Like Abbot Anian of Aberconwy, Bishop Richard of Bangor's role has been noticed already; Bishop Anian of St Asaph was also engaged as an envoy on the prince's behalf.[185] In the critical period preceding the outbreak of war in 1277 Bishop Anian of Bangor went to the king as Llywelyn's envoy, bearing a

---

[180] For a 'principal chaplain' with possible oversight of scribal work, Stringer, *Earl David of Huntingdon*, 151–5. Post-conquest evidence (e.g. *CWR*, 292) indicates that the position of *offeiriad teulu*, by then a benefice in the king's gift, was held by a churchman of Anglesey (H. Pryce, 'Offeiriad teulu', in Charles-Edwards (ed.), *The Welsh King and his Court*).

[181] Stephenson, *GG*, 33–4, 222, 224.

[182] *LW*, 108–10; for *Ardev*, Ardda or Ardda'r Mynaich, C. A. Gresham, 'The Aberconwy charter: further consideration', *B*, 30 (1982–3), 341–2; for the litigation that called for the transcript, below, pp. 470 *et seq.*

[183] *LW*, 42, 85; *CCR, 1272–79*, 506.

[184] Treharne, 'Franco-Welsh treaty', 74; idem, *Simon de Montfort*, 359; trans. *EHD*, iii, 306.

[185] *CAC*, 10 (envoy to the king concerning conflict with Clare and Bohun).

statement of the prince's proposals for peace. He was accompanied by Master Iorwerth, described as Llywelyn's clerk and vice-chancellor.[186] Given the apparent absence of any specific reference to a chancellor in the period of Llywelyn ap Gruffudd, and with only sparse reference to a vice-chancellor, the arrangements made for the secretarial needs of the prince are indeed difficult to deduce. It is, however, possible that the office of chancellor was vested in a senior clerical dignitary, with a vice-chancellor as the person effectively in charge of the clerks who fulfilled the secretarial duties. It seems that Llywelyn was able to draw on the resources of the church of Bangor, both clerics of the church of St Deiniol, at a higher and lower level, and others who held benefices in the diocese. There may well have been some, however, possibly in minor orders, who were closely attached to Llywelyn's court and dependent upon him. Such, it seems, were the two 'clerks of Llywelyn' to whom Archbishop Pecham refers, Madog ap Magister and William ap Daniel, whose names appear in the prince's service.[187] The prince's secretarial requirements called, if not for a chancery by that name, for the services of a group of clerks capable of attending to his needs upon his itinerary of his dominion and, probably, more than this a writing-office with a continuity in personnel and an established working practice, and with access to a repository for the records for which safe-keeping was essential. There would surely have been one person with responsibility for the duties fulfilled by the clerks, and it would be reasonable to conclude that he would have been charged with the custody of the prince's great seal to which, along with the privy seal, there are references throughout the period though, sadly, not a single impression of Llywelyn's seal appears to have survived.[188] So the depiction in *Llyfr Iorwerth* of a household chaplain with associated clerks identifies a service which had to be provided, to an ever-increasing extent, in the dominion of the thirteenth-century prince.

The letters composed for the prince are known very largely from English royal archives, though they have survived by several means. Many letters are known from enrolments made in chancery when the matters they contained were considered and a reply elicited. Chancery practices varied but it is only in a few cases that a full text of the prince's letter, as apart from a precis of the content, is conserved on the rolls. A number of letters survive in their original form in royal archives, though it is not always clear whether the text is that

---

[186] *CAC*, 87; for Master Iorwerth (Gervase), Stephenson, *GG*, 36–7, 224. Anian was also arbitrator in the dispute with Clare (*LW*, 101–2).

[187] *RPeck*, i, 125–6; Stephenson, *GG*, 38–9, 226, 228.

[188] For the thirteenth-century princes' seals, M. P. Siddons, *The Development of Welsh Heraldry* (Aberystwyth, 1991–3), i, 280–2; idem, 'Welsh equestrian seals', *NLWJ*, 23 (1983–4), 304–5; idem, 'Welsh seals in Paris', *B*, 29 (1980–2), 539–40; for Llywelyn ap Iorwerth's reference to his great seal and privy seal, *CAC*, 51; *RL*, i, 369; Llywelyn ap Gruffudd's privy seal, below, p. 552.

inscribed upon the parchment received from the prince or a transcript subsequently made in chancery.[189] A particularly valuable group of documents may have derived, in part at least, from the archives of the prince of Wales. Whereas there is some account of the removal of documents from Scotland to England, there appears to be no comparable indication of the removal of material from Wales, but there can be little doubt that Edward's officers located documents after the cessation of conflict and took care to preserve them.[190] The registers known as 'Liber A' and 'Liber B' in royal archives were products of an ordering and transcribing of records, largely of a diplomatic nature, undertaken in the later years of Edward I. They included materials relating to Scotland, Wales, Gascony, Norway, France and several other lands. 'Liber A' includes a substantial body of documents entitled 'Littere Wallie' and 'Scripta Wallie', transcribed from originals kept in large part in two receptacles, marked with drawings of a Welsh archer and a spearman, in an exchequer coffer.[191] The ultimate sources of these documents are probably various. A number, including the texts of the major Anglo-Welsh treaties of the thirteenth century, could well have had their origin among the royal muniments themselves. Particularly intriguing, however, is the source of an important group, consisting of rather more than fifty documents, extensively used during the course of this study, which conserves a record of the inner workings of the principality of Wales. They include records of transactions between Llywelyn and major figures among the Welsh barons and represent some of the key political agreements of the period.[192] Copies of some of these could well have passed to the crown officials before the collapse of the prince's power. Maredudd ap Rhys Gryg might well have transmitted a copy of the agreement of 1258, by which he was so sorely discomforted, at the time of its making. Others provide testimony of transactions, such as bonds and securities given to the prince by lesser figures, or on their behalf, embodying the strictures to which the likes of Rhys ab Ednyfed or Hywel Fychan were subjected.[193] Disquieted figures such as these might have preserved the evidence of the prince's severe lordship as a means of easing their progress into the king's fealty when the time was opportune, a chit of parchment that could be helpful in establishing their credentials as

---

[189] Letter in full text in a chancery enrolment, *CR, 1261–64*, 297; letters in original text or contemporary transcript from PRO Ancient Correspondence (SC1) are calendared in *CAC* (e.g. ibid., 84–96).

[190] *Anglo-Scottish Relations*, 150–3, 232–3.

[191] J. G. Edwards, in *LW*, xxvii–xxxiii; G. P. Cuttino, *English Diplomatic Administration, 1259–1339* (Oxford, 1940), 73–6; contents listed in M. S. Giuseppi, *A Guide to the Manuscripts preserved in the Public Record Office* (London, 1923–4), i, 211–12.

[192] *LW*, 77–80, 104–5, 168–9.

[193] *LW*, 23–4, 29, 34, already noticed; transactions concerning the fidelity of men of the prince's marcher lordships (*LW*, 24–6, 28, 30, 32–6, 40–2, 44) are considered later.

Prince of Wales

needful seekers of royal protection. There were numerous avenues by which the inner truths of the lands of Llywelyn ap Gruffudd might be transmitted to the crown's keeping. But among the documents lodged in the exchequer coffer when 'Liber A' came to be compiled there may have been a number that represented material salvaged from the archives of the prince of Wales.

In a study of thirteenth-century Welsh diplomatic practice the most instructive *acta* of the period of Llywelyn ap Gruffudd are, therefore, not the charters, which are very few in number, but the letters and other documents of which the group in 'Liber A' provide a kernel. The volume known as *Llyfr Coch Asaph*, the register of Archbishop Pecham and English chancery enrolments are among a number of other sources which provide further material from which some estimate of the *acta* of the prince may be made.[194] The total number of documents is not large and, with little opportunity to judge whether the formulae employed in the texts indicate routine production, it is difficult to estimate to what extent the thirteenth-century princes developed bureaucratic methods of government, reflected in marked growth in the use of written instruments, comparable with that which can be demonstrated in England or France. The instruments that survive are varied. A small but valuable group provides the texts of the covenants between the princes, and these certainly indicate a wish to extend the use of the written word to ensure that the prince's authority was secured in precise definitions of his tenants' obligations. Letters are numerous, many revealing no more than a capacity for precision and clarity on the part of those who wrote them, others composed so as to exert persuasion or to convey a forceful statement of the prince's viewpoint. The conspiracy upon Llywelyn ap Gruffudd's life, to be considered presently, produced not only a formal record of the process against Gruffudd ap Gwenwynwyn and his son, and their submission to the prince's will, but the more demanding composition of a letter sent in Llywelyn's name to the bishops of Bangor and St Asaph, when the full extent of the conspiracy was revealed, and another that the dean of Bangor later addressed to Archbishop Kilwardby.[195] The same grave matter is mentioned in the prince's letter to the prelates of England and another addressed to Pope Gregory X. This is a singular exemplar of what may have been a sequence of

---

[194] 'Llyfr Coch Asaph', a compilation of the muniments of the diocese derived from the episcopate of Llywelyn of Bromfield (1293–1314), including a number of important documents of earlier date, partially conserved in sixteenth- and seventeenth-century transcripts, notably NLW, Peniarth 231B, is described in D. L. Evans, 'Llyfr Coch Asaph', *NLWJ*, 4 (1945–6), 177–83; R. I. Jack, *Medieval Wales: The Sources of History* (London, 1972), 131–2; text and valuable discussion in O. E. Jones, 'Llyfr Coch Asaph'. A number of the important documents are in *Councils*, i, the normal source of reference in this study. Letters of Llywelyn, additional to those in the sources cited, may be found in e.g. *Registrum Thome de Cantilupo*; NLW MSS 13211, 13215.

[195] *LW*, 136–8, 174–5.

letters which elicited from the papal court several responses of great interest.[196] The prince's letters, and the activities of his envoys at Rome, in turn prompted Edward I to some carefully constructed statements by which he sought to convince the *curia* of the strength of his case. Llywelyn's written exchanges with Archbishop Pecham, late in 1282, again reflect a capacity among those in attendance upon him to construct a cogently reasoned argument enhanced by emotive touches as their author gives expression to Llywelyn's concern for the well-being of his people or calls upon the historical consciousness enshrined in the notion of the prince's descent from Camber, son of Brutus.[197] The documents may not survive in great numbers, but their range reflects, more than the regular work of competent scribes, the capabilities of men versed in epistolary styles and with a facility in Latin prose, and possessed of an intimate knowledge of the matters which confronted prince and council.

Distinct from the epistolary compositions among the *acta* of Llywelyn ap Gruffudd is a group of documents which bears what may broadly be termed notarial features. Specific references to notaries (*notarii*) are rare, and it is not clear what these, as distinct from mention of clerks (*clerici*), might signify.[198] Two notaries are named in the document by which Hywel ap Rhys Gryg acknowledged his obligations upon doing homage to the prince in 1258. Described as his letters patent obligatory (*hiis patentibus litteris nostris obligatoriis*), Hywel's instrument declares his acknowledgement that he would be subject to ecclesiastical censure if he were to default upon his fealty to the prince.[199] Several of the other documents of this genre among those conserved in 'Liber A' reveal distinct traces of a civil-law practice by which the efficacy of a covenant is safeguarded by the renunciation of the legal exceptions to which the parties might otherwise have recourse to frustrate the fulfilment of the obligation.[200] Renunciations in a form common among continental financial covenants are well reflected in transactions, in which the civil-law term *ypoteca* appears, by which the dean and chapter of St Asaph and the

---

[196] *LW*, 114–16; NLW MSS 13211, ff. 8–9; 13215, ff. 303–5.

[197] *RPeck*, ii, 437–40, 468–71; below, pp. 532–4, 543–5.

[198] John, notary of Llywelyn, is among witnesses to his grant to Ynys Lannog (*CChR*, ii, 460). A distinction needs to be drawn between the instruments drawn up by public notaries, such as those studied in C. R. Cheney, *Notaries Public in England in the Thirteenth and Fourteenth Centuries* (Oxford, 1972), or *Throne of Scotland*, ii, 77–9 (of which there are no known examples from Wales in the period of the princes), and those that are notarial to the extent that they may be attributed to writers skilled in canon or civil law, or to clerks with access to exemplars drawn up by men with canonist or civilian training.

[199] *LW*, 45.

[200] D. B. Walters, 'The renunciation of exceptions: Romano-canonical devices for limiting possible defences in thirteenth-century Welsh law-suits', *B*, 38 (1991), 119–28; idem, 'Roman and Romano-canonical law and procedure in Wales' (1991), 67–102.

abbot of Valle Crucis acknowledge debts to Llywelyn.[201] More interesting, however, are the instances in which civilian devices are employed to afforce agreements which are designed to ensure fidelity to a lord. The earliest among the Welsh documents in 'Liber A' are those by which Tudur ab Ednyfed and Einion Fychan renounce resort to canonical or civilian remedies upon their swearing fidelity to Henry III after their release from imprisonment in 1246.[202] The texts of these obligations would have been prepared by clerks in the service of Henry III, but the civil-law features which they reveal are soon found in transactions among the men of Wales themselves. When they made their agreements with the men of Ystrad Tywi in 1251 Owain ap Gruffudd and Llywelyn ap Gruffudd embodied in the document a renunciation of the *beneficium* of canon and civil law. In Llywelyn's agreement with Gruffudd ap Madog the previous year, however, the same provision is entered, along with a renunciation of the exception of excommunication, so as to ensure that neither party would seek to bring ecclesiastical censure upon the other as a means of evading the solemn promises made.[203] Most instructive of all are the exceptions, drawn from civilian practices, included in the instruments relating to Llywelyn's relations with Maredudd ap Rhys Gryg and Gruffudd ap Gwenwynwyn.[204] The precise use made of the devices reveal a capacity to vary the provisions in accordance with the need dictated by the political circumstances in which the agreement was made. In 1258, despite his supremacy over his fellow princes, Llywelyn found it necessary, as we have seen, to conciliate Maredudd and create new confidence in their relationship and he renounced resort to ecclesiastical and civil law. In the composition made in different circumstances in 1261 it was Maredudd who made the renunciation. An endeavour to create mutual confidence is indicated in the agreement between Llywelyn and Gruffudd ap Gwenwynwyn two years later when, by the terms of their final concord, they agreed that in certain circumstances excommunication and interdict should be brought upon either of them, and together they renounced resort to canon and civil law as a means of circumventing such sentence. The prince evidently had at his service men who, whether they were called notaries or not, had a knowledge of the practices and phraseology of canon and civil law. The clauses embodying the renunciations may, of course, be to some extent an expression of a wish to provide an embellishment of the documents, but there can be no doubt that these were important transactions designed to forge new relationships which were crucial to the fulfilment of the prince's purposes. The financial transactions mentioned earlier

---

[201] *LW*, 39–40.
[202] *LW*, 49–52.
[203] *LW*, 148, 160–1; these agreements are examined above, pp. 67–8.
[204] *LW*, 77–80, 104–5, 168–9; above, pp. 107–8, 121–2.

reflect the importation of what was already a conventional form. The variation in the forms used in the engagements among the princes, on the other hand, and their application to the particular circumstances which arose in the middle years of the century, indicate a capability on the part of those who composed the documents to meet the new needs created by the prince's political initiatives.

The men who did so may well have drawn upon those sources of canon- and civil-law learning which, to varying degrees as we have seen, are reflected in the law texts written in the thirteenth century. The jurists who wrote the texts may be exceedingly elusive figures, the practising lawyers difficult to link with the prince's ministerial entourage, but this handful of compacts drawn from record sources, and the letters already noticed, reflect a competence in the composition of legal and diplomatic documents necessary for the fulfilment of the prince's practical needs. Those immediately responsible probably had access to men of letters of a higher order. Bishop Anian of St Asaph is one who is judged to have been knowledgeable in civil and canon law, with books of canon law in his library and perhaps a text of the law of Wales.[205] He would, no doubt, have shared his knowledge of the two laws, which were matters of contention between the prince and himself, with others within the clerical fraternity. But the knowledge and expertise revealed in the practical documents which survive were not entirely a clerical preserve. Themselves bound to enter into pledges dictated to them under duress upon release from captivity, Tudur ab Ednyfed and Einion Fychan provided a timely conduit by which the practice of the royal court, and the products of its reserve of expertise, was brought to the prince's court. Retained in royal service for some years yet, Tudur ab Ednyfed eventually brought with him into the prince's service an experience which would have proved to be of some avail when, quite soon, he succeeded to the office of *distain* now, or on occasion at least, described as that of 'justice of the prince', even 'justice of Wales'.[206] Tudur ab Ednyfed or Goronwy ap Heilin, who came to share high responsibility in the prince's entourage, would have had an informed and precise perception of what was required of their clerical colleagues. This may not have been true of all those whose names appear prominently in the prince's service. Envoy to the court though he undoubtedly was, Iorwerth ap

---

[205] Anian's will included a bequest of all his works of canon law (*omnes libros meos iuris canonici*) to his nephew Ithel, canon of St Asaph (Canterbury Cathedral Archives, Dean and Chapter Sede Vacante, Scrap Book II, 187), and he may have possessed the Cotton Titus Dii text (MS B) of *Lllor* (*Report on MSS in the Welsh Language*, ed. J. G. Evans (HMC, 1898–1910), ii, 946). Sadly, the number of volumes known to have been housed in the medieval libraries of Wales, listed in N. R. Ker, *Medieval Libraries of Great Britain* (2nd edn. London, 1964; suppl, 1987), is very small.

[206] For 'justice of Wales', 'justice of the lord prince', and 'seneschal of Wales', *LW*, 26, 85, 109; the *justiciarius* of the text may be given as 'justiciar', but 'justice' is preferable.

Prince of Wales

Gwrgunan may have earned his place at the prince's side by a sturdy presence in the strenuous conflicts of the early years of the prince's quest for supremacy. This may do him injustice perhaps but, even if Iorwerth cannot be counted among them, it is clear that there were some among the prince's confidants who could respond to the need for the ministerial qualities that the creation of the principality of Wales, and its representation in lands beyond its frontiers, increasingly required.

Principality and nation

The matter which, perhaps more than anything else, lends coherence to the various objectives to which Llywelyn ap Gruffudd directed his resources was his endeavour to ensure the stability of his principality. The quest for stability is revealed in the government of his lordship of Snowdon and it mattered greatly to his wider dominion. It is a theme reflected in the alacrity with which, after his initial triumphant campaigning, he sought a stable relationship with the king of England. We shall need to consider to what extent the policies he pursued in his relations with the marcher lords after the treaty of Montgomery served to safeguard, or to undermine, the stability which was so crucial, and so difficult to secure. The march was a land where authority was fragmented, yet a land shared between lords who exercised formidable power; it was a land vested in lords of alien stock who were none the less claimants to an indigenous inheritance. In his relations with the marchers Llywelyn had need to steer a course of measured firmness and restraint. Perhaps it was only late in the day, when the principality had already been destroyed, that Llywelyn came to realize the emphasis that the lords of the march placed on the regality entrenched in their lordships, or to ponder the extent to which its exercise might be compatible with his own.[207] Indeed, their stress on their regality came to be expressed in its clearest terms only in the prince's last years, and he was not to live to see the confrontation it would engender in their relations with Edward I. Mortimer, Clare, Bohun: these are the names which matter, in this connection no less than in the course of Anglo-Welsh conflict that will be considered further in the chapters which follow. It may be that it was in this connection that Llywelyn's isolation left him most markedly disadvantaged. He is not known to have sought the links which Llywelyn ap Iorwerth made in the march, one particular aspect of the isolation noticed

---

[207] A more explicit and strident expression of marcher regality is noticeable from *c.*1280, marked, for example, in Gilbert de Clare's assertion of his rights in Glamorgan and Humphrey de Bohun's claim that the king's statutes had no place in his lands (J. B. Smith, 'The legal position of Wales in the middle ages', in A. Harding (ed.), *Law-making and Law-makers in British History* (London, 1980), 33–7; R. R. Davies, *Lordship and Society*, 257–61.

earlier. This may have been due to some extent to the fact that he did not have a progeny that he could deploy to his advantage in alliances with his marcher neighbours. Llywelyn sometimes laid emphasis on the fact that his objectives were founded on precedents established by his grandfather; he might equally have questioned the extent to which his predecessor's marcher connections had brought tangible rewards. How much benefit had he derived from the fact that Roger Mortimer was a son of a daughter of Llywelyn the Great? The son, not of a daughter of a king of England, nor the daughter of a marcher magnate, but of a woman of his own nation, Llywelyn came to political awareness when the uneasy compromises of the period of his grandfather may have been held in precious little regard. Llywelyn ap Gruffudd may have put his trust, by deliberate choice, on sturdy relationships to be forged within his own dominions.

Yet his assertiveness led him to anything but an isolationist position. Very quickly after securing his triumph in Powys and Deheubarth he came to seek, earnestly and persistently, a means of stabilizing his relations beyond his frontiers. It meant, more than anything else, securing that firm peace which had eluded his grandfather. Unable, during those long years of restraint, to secure an understanding with the king of England, he embarked on a course that led him to extend his frontiers beyond those which best defined the polity, based on the domains of Welsh princely lordship, to which he could most reasonably lay claim. To what extent Llywelyn and those joined with him deliberated upon the prospect of a different conception of a principality embracing the lands of those communities which were 'of the Welsh language' as a whole we cannot tell. Whatever his reasons for new aggression, his renewed and forceful offensives from the end of 1262 made it so much more difficult thereafter to secure a stable relationship with the marcher powers who shared with him a dominion over the land of Wales. His entry into the land of Gilbert de Clare in Glamorgan, an enterprise still to be recounted, compounded his difficulties enormously. Clare could not call upon the symbols and images of kingship, but he made a great deal of the regality which he saw as his inheritance in Wales. His powerful lordship stood virtually as a counterpoint to Llywelyn's own dominion. Clare, and each of the others who founded his power on marcher regality, raised their liberty (*libertas*) on the seigniorial rights which they asserted to be part of their inheritance. The lord of Glamorgan was able to display this power, somewhat ostentatiously perhaps, upon the king's coming to the lordship after the conquest of Wales.[208] Constructing his princedom on what were, in practical terms, closely similar regalian or seigniorial foundations, Llywelyn strove for a liberty with an altogether unique meaning.

[208] Trevet, *Annales*, 309; Altschul, *Clares*, 268–80; *GlamCH*, iii, 56–9, 67–72.

Prince of Wales

His most eloquent statements of its significance came, not from the period in which he dominated a wide area of Wales, but from the days of desperate resistance in Gwynedd Uwch Conwy a short time before he met his death.[209] The prince's statements of those difficult days, the most moving compositions fashioned by those who wrote the letters that appear in his name, bring forth more than a touch of that sense of liberty to which Robert Bruce would give expression in due course.[210] Yet at the time of his greatest power the liberty which he enjoyed as prince of Wales gave him something far short of a decisive influence on the fortunes of the Welsh nation as a whole. Principality and nation did not match. Llywelyn and those about him may have been racked by the inherent tension in the situation created by the disparity between *principatus* and *natio*. The expression given in his years of straitened circumstances after 1277 to ideas of *natio* and *patria* may, ironically but understandably, convey something of the aspirations shared within the fraternity of the principality of Wales in the earlier years of supremacy, but kept in check so that the prince could pursue what could realistically be extracted from the king of England by agreement. In the end his formidable opponent himself served to underline the incongruity in the prince's position in previous years when he steeled the people of England to a supreme effort to subjugate nothing less than the Welsh nation (*lingua Wallensica*).[211] Edward's words provide a striking reflection of the place of language in defining a medieval nation, even though the language itself might not be an issue in political argument. The English monarch's comment echoed that consciousness of the language – *yr iaith* – as a 'critical defining characteristic' of a historical experience that the Welsh nation shared with other European nations in the middle ages.[212] In the final struggle Edward sought to bring into submission to his dominion, not a principality, for that had already been destroyed without solving his problem, but a nation. While he pursued a viable political policy Llywelyn was constrained, not only by the extent of the resources he could muster, and the energies he could generate, but by his estimate of what the king of England and the marchers could tolerate. It has been argued earlier that his first diplomatic approaches to the king, made when his principality was delimited in close conformity to the frontiers of the lands under Welsh lordship, were those best calculated to secure the stability which he sought, and his extension of his frontiers both before and after the treaty of Montgomery created new animosities which proved to be destabilizing influences. The royal inheritance of the prince of Wales might

---

[209] Below, pp. 532–4, 543–4.
[210] Barrow, *Anglo-Norman Era*, 147–56; idem, *Scotland and her Neighbours*, 10.
[211] *Foedera*, I, ii, 630: BL, Cotton Cleopatra, iii, f. 76.
[212] See discussion of the significance of *iaith* and *anghyfiaith*, with European parallels, in Ll. B. Smith, 'The Welsh language before 1536', 38–9.

have found its most stable political expression in a land which fell within much narrower limits than the natural frontiers of a nation set apart by its language.

References to the symbols and rituals of that royal inheritance are sparse enough. After the conquest Edward took possession of a few material objects which had belonged to the prince. The matrix of his seal, and those of Eleanor his princess, and Dafydd ap Gruffudd, were unceremoniously melted down and the silver put to other use.[213] Llywelyn's coronet (*talaith*) was treated differently. This was the gold coronet which Gruffudd ab yr Ynad Coch, in the opening lines of his elegy, described as one which the prince was so eminently worthy to wear:

> Oer galon dan fron o fraw – allwynin
> Am frenin, dderwin ddôr Aberffraw,
> Aur dilyfn a delid o'i law,
> Aur dalaith oedd deilwng iddaw.[214]

The coronet was, the Westminster chronicle tells us, presented to the shrine of St Edward.[215] The *talaith* excited some interest in Scotland in 1292, during the debate about the succession to the throne; it was remembered that the prince of Wales had had a coronet (*garlandeche*), and that he was enthroned by a bishop (*e fust assis en se par evesque*).[216] Despite the fact that its royal tradition was so secure, there was no crowning in Scotland, though Alexander III had sought this attribute of royal status, and anointing too.[217] We hear little enough of this from Wales itself. The Tewkesbury chronicler, as we have seen, records that when Dafydd ap Llywelyn came before Henry III at

---

[213] The Jewels Roll, 1284, records the receipt into the wardrobe of the seals of Llywelyn, Eleanor and Dafydd and the making from the silver of a chalice that the king intended to bestow on the abbey of Vale Royal (A. J. Taylor, *Studies in Castles and Castle-Building* (London, 1985), 198–200 [Taylor, *SCCB*], from E101/351/12). Dr Taylor argues persuasively that this was the chalice, with a paten, discovered in Cwm-mynach, near Dolgellau, in 1890 (H. J. Owen, 'The romance of the chalice and paten of Cymer abbey', *JMerHRS*, 2 (1953–6), 181–90). Chalice and paten are in National Museum of Wales (Department of Art, 10.1). William de Farndon, goldsmith, acknowledged the receipt of 'the old money' of Llywelyn (£66 of clipped money, £57. 3s. 0d. in weight), from which he made 26 silver dishes for the king's use (E101/372/11, m. 4, reference by the kindness of Dr Susan Davies).

[214] *GBF*, 36. 1–4; *Oxford Book of Welsh Verse*, 45; trans. J. P. Clancy, *The Earliest Welsh Poetry* (London, 1970); *Oxford Book of Welsh Verse in English*, 31: 'Heart cold in the breast with terror, grieving / For a king, oak door, of Aberffraw. / Bright gold was bestowed by his hand, / A gold chaplet befitted him.'

[215] *FloresHist*, iii, 59; the 'golden coronet' was presented by Alfonso, heir apparent, in 1284 (J. G. Edwards, *Principality of Wales*, 10–11).

[216] *Throne of Scotland*, ii, 339–40.

[217] For the debate over coronation and anointing, Duncan, *Scotland*, 552–60; *Throne of Scotland*, 320, 327–9, 332–3.

Prince of Wales

Gloucester he wore the coronet which was the symbol of the principality of Gwynedd.[218] The gold object which passed into the possession of Edward I, even if it were the same circlet, represented by then something very different from that which Prince Dafydd's wearing had meant forty years before. Llygad Gŵr marked the change as he celebrated the triumphant progress of Llywelyn ap Gruffudd to the position in which he stood as the *taleithiog*, the crowned prince, of the courts of Aberffraw of Gwynedd, Dinefwr of Deheubarth and Mathrafal of Powys.[219] Edward took good care of this symbol of Welsh regality, as he did of the sacred relic of the Croes Naid, which had long been in the custody of the kings and princes of the now conquered land.[220]

The king's care for these material remains represents a recognition of the defeated prince's royal status that he would have been reluctant to concede while his adversary lived. The prince, as we have seen already, had himself laid stress upon his status – the *iura* or the *dignitates* to which he alludes in his letters – as an attribute of the political edifice which he brought into being. The essence of the political endeavour which lay behind the prince's sense of status was a fusion of a regality, derived from those who had preceded him in the rule of his patrimony, with the authority that he drew from the consent of those who acknowledged his lordship over his wider dominion. It is this fusion of authority which enables us to comprehend the principality of Wales as a polity, and those who formed its members as a political community. To conceive of the thirteenth-century principality of Wales in this way is not altogether an indulgence in historical construction. In the earliest known reference to the principality in its wider meaning Llywelyn ap Iorwerth declared his determination to secure a political order in justice and equity according to the status of Wales (*status Wallie*) in a letter which concerned his right to the allegiance of the lords of Wales; Llywelyn ap Gruffudd, writing to the very same effect, urging the king to grant him the homage of the lords of Wales, sought suitable recognition of the *iura* vested in himself and his predecessors, taking care to convey that he did so with the consent of all the lords of Wales.[221] He defended the *iura* of his principality in the years of supremacy, and the will to proceed in a manner consistent with the *iura* permeates his final pronouncements in 1282.[222] These privileges were derived from predecessors who had been kings, and the lawyers were studious in

---

[218] Above, p. 29.
[219] *GBF*, 24.105–20. The notion of the three principal courts has been noticed earlier. The memory lingered; in actions concerning the position of Arwystli in 1374 and 1397 a jury from Meirionnydd testified that the crown of Mathrafal and the lordship of Powys should be held under the crown of Aberffraw (E315/166, f. 10v.).
[220] For the Croes Naid, below, n. 227.
[221] Above, pp. 19–20, 122–4.
[222] *CAC*, 86, *RPeck*, ii, 469–71.

conveying the sense of kingship, the historians taking care to nourish a remembrance of a kingship reaching back to a distant past.[223] The status which all this entailed had in turn to be maintained by the consent of those who shared with the prince a lordship over the communities of those who were of the Welsh nation and when, for whatever reason, that consent was withdrawn or undermined the principality ceased to be.

But if the prince was acutely sensitive of the princely status bound up with the political order he established, his was a measured estimate of his position. He certainly never claimed to rule by divine ordination: unlike Gaston de Béarn in Gascony, Llywelyn never used the grace, *Dei gratia*, in his style.[224] Yet it would be a pity to miss the intimations of the princes' sense of divine protection. It was indeed by the grace of God (*per Dei gratiam*) that Llywelyn ap Iorwerth and his fellow princes combined to rid their country of the yoke of oppression. He called upon his conscience before God when compelled to withstand the power of the English king. Llywelyn ap Gruffudd did likewise in stressing his duty to stand by his people in their hour of need. Archbishop Pecham was quick to see how closely intertwined were the notions of the prince's status and his *conscientia*.[225] The law which Llywelyn ap Gruffudd vigorously proclaimed in his arguments with Edward as an attribute of Welsh nationhood was presented in the work of the jurists as a law given by a king who had ruled Wales by the grace of God. 'Dei gratia atque providentia rex Howel, qui cognominatur Da, totius Wallie principatu presidebat pacifice': these were the opening words of the text which, more clearly than any other, conveys the sense of the royal inheritance of the principality of Wales that Llywelyn ap Gruffudd was able to bring into being.[226] The image of the ruler who gave the law of Wales is that of a king seated on his throne, sceptre in hand. And if the lawyers emphasize that the law was given under the protection of God, so it was under the sanction of the Christian church that the lords of Wales enacted the everlasting covenants which bound the heirs to the kingdoms of Powys and Deheubarth in indissoluble allegiance to the prince of Wales. Those lords, taking each his oath of fealty touching holy relics, may have been privileged to swear upon the Croes Naid, that portion of

---

[223] The notion of sovereignty has found favour in studies of literary texts (e.g. G. Goetinck, *Peredur: A Study of the Welsh Tradition in the Grail Legends* (Cardiff, 1975); C. A. McKenna, 'The theme of sovereignty in Pwyll', *B*, 29 (1980–2), 35–52. In historical discussion of Wales it would be best to speak of kingship; expressions such as *sovereign seignurie* belong to relations between the great powers of England or France and Scotland or Gascony, matters broached in e.g. *Throne of Scotland*, i, 120–2, ii, 14–19; P. Chaplais, *Essays in Medieval Diplomacy*, V, 449–69.

[224] J. B. Smith, 'Adversaries of Edward I', 58–9.

[225] Treharne, 'Franco-Welsh treaty', 74–5; idem, *Simon de Montfort*, 359–60; trans. *EHD*, iii, 306–7; *CAC*, 8–9; *RPeck*, ii, 437–40, 465–6.

[226] *LTWL*, 193; the text is Latin B (Cotton Vesp. Bxi), whose particular interest has been noticed earlier.

the True Cross about which we know so little except that its transmission to Edward I was a sign that all Wales was cast to the ground.[227]

When Edward, writing to the papal court, referred to Llywelyn as 'one of the greatest among the other magnates of my kingdom' he said nothing to which the prince could take exception. At no stage did Llywelyn fail to acknowledge the supremacy of the English king. In the firmest of his pronouncements upon his status, even as he maintained that his rights as prince of Wales were entirely separate from those of the king's realm, he conceded that he held his principality under the king's royal power.[228] In his last statements, made in his final exchange of letters with Pecham, he made his appeal to history. It was an appeal to legendary history, to the matter of the *Historia* which describes the division of Britain after the death of Brutus, envisaging the principality of Wales as an inheritance from the time of Camber, son of Brutus.[229] His invocation of a distant past carries an implicit acknowledgement of the superiority of Locrinus, heir to England, over Camber, the heir to Wales, as the ultimate historical foundation for the relationship between Edward and himself.[230] Twice making his appeal to this particular passage of the *Historia*, each time he linked his allusion to the legendary history with a reference to the treaty that he had secured by negotiation with King Henry, through the mediation of the papal legate.[231] Legend and history were reconciled in a realistic reflection of the principle that had been fundamental to his political objectives from his first assertion of power. There is no suggestion in the surviving record that he had questioned the fact that he needed to reconcile his lordship over the principality of Wales with the formidable power of the kingship vested in the king of England. As heir to Camber he could lay claim to an ancient and royal inheritance, but his position carried an implicit acknowledgement of the supremacy of the crown of England. In Scotland those who, according to the interpretation offered in the *Historia Regum Britanniae*, were the heirs to Albanactus saw it differently. The Welsh, accommodating their political aspirations to the historical supremacy of the English crown, might come to terms with the *Historia*; the Scots, rejecting the Trojan origin in its entirety, withstood the political

---

[227] *FloresHist*, iii, 59; Rishanger, *Chronica*, 104. Discussion in E. Owen, 'The Croes Nawdd', *Y Cymmrodor*, 43 (1932), 1–18; T. H. Parry-Williams, 'Croes Naid', *Y Llinyn Arian* (Aberystwyth, 1947), 91–4; W. C. Tennant, 'Croes Naid', *NLWJ*, 7 (1951–2), 102–15; Taylor, *SCCB*, 283–4, 195 n. 18 For the presentation of the Croes Naid to Edward, below, pp. 580–1.

[228] *CAC*, 86.

[229] *RPeck*, ii, 469–71; *The Historia Regum Britanniae of Geoffrey of Monmouth*, ed. A. Griscom (London, 1929), 253 (ii. 1); Geoffrey of Monmouth, *The History of the Kings of Britain*, trans. L. Thorpe (London, 1966), 75; medieval Welsh text in *Brut Dingestow*, ed. H. Lewis (Cardiff, 1942), 21.

[230] J. B. Smith, *SHMW*, 1–2, 14–15.

[231] *RPeck*, ii, 469–71.

pretensions which made Edward I invoke the *Historia* as a means of promoting his claim to *sovereign seigneurie* over Scotland.[232] Appealing to the legend of Scota, daughter of Pharaoh, they drew upon a remembrance more consonant with the political aspiration that they were in a position to sustain.[233] The princes of Wales had to come to terms with a more constricting political tradition, but the course they had to pursue was fraught with difficulty. In endeavouring to give effect in Wales to the perfectly ordered scheme of government imagined in the heraldic depiction of the sixteenth century, prince and king would face great difficulty. Llywelyn may have turned from the ford of Montgomery with new resolve in the autumn of 1267, but he may still have been burdened by the knowledge that the new beginning intimated in the legate's trustful words had been wrested from the king of England only after prolonged conflict and persistent advocacy. The prospect for the stability he sought was greatly enhanced by a treaty which did honour to king and prince alike, but it could be ensured only by maintaining, on the part of prince and community, the judgement and restraint to match the inspired and forceful activity that the poet Llygad Gŵr celebrated upon the prince's triumph.[234]

> Terfysg aerllew glew, glod ganymddaith,
> Twrf toredwynt mawr uch môr diffaith;
> Taleithawg deifnawg dyfniaith – Aberffraw,
> Terrwyn anrheithiaw, rhuthr anolaith.
> Tylwyth ffrwyth, ffraethlym eu mawrwaith,
> Teilwng blwng blaengar fal goddaith;
> Taleithawg arfawg aerbaith – Dinefwr,
> Teilu huysgwr, ysgyfl anrhaith.

---

[232] For Edward's use of the Trojan legend, with emendations calculated to emphasize his superior lordship, *Throne of Scotland*, ii, 298–300.

[233] E. J. Cowan, 'Myth and identity in early medieval Scotland', *Scottish Historical Review*, 63 (1984), 111–35.

[234] These lines form the third canto in Llygad Gŵr's celebration of Llywelyn's supremacy in the Hendregadredd MS (*GBF*, 24.105–20; above, n. 8); trans. Ann Parry Owen: 'A brave battle-lion in tumult, fame's companion, / Charging with the uproar of a mighty gust of wind above a desolate sea. / The crowned one of Aberffraw, well-endowed and of profound words, / Brutal in his pillaging, unavoidable his onslaught. / The product of a blood-line, dexterous and swift their mighty battle, / Worthy, fierce and bold like a blazing fire, / The crowned one of Dinefwr, armed and wreaking destruction in battle, / Steadfast his host, the pillager of booty. / The flawless one, excellent his host of compatriots, / Handsome and proud bearing a battered and finely wrought lance; / The crowned one of Mathrafal, great are your boundaries, / Lord Llywelyn, the ruler of four nations. / He held his ground in battle (prominent was his course) / Against a foreign nation with an alien lament. / May the King of heaven of royal rule, / Stand by the splendid prince, battle-lord of the three provinces.

Prince of Wales

Telediw, gad gywiw gyfiaith,
Telaid balch â bylchlafn eurwaith;
Taleithawg Mathrafal, maith – yw dy derfyn,
Arglwydd Lywelyn, lyw pedeiriaith.
Sefis yn rhyfel (diymgel daith)
Rhag estrawn geneddl gŵyn anghyfiaith;
Sefid Brenin nef breiniawl gyfraith
Gan eurwawr aerbair y tair talaith.

CHAPTER 7

A Principality in Perplexity

ONLY ten years after Llywelyn ap Gruffudd had won formal recognition as prince of Wales his principality collapsed about him, leaving him to make peace with the king on grievously humiliating terms. The final *dénouement* of 1282, with its poignant blend of personal tragedy and political annihilation, may have made the deeper impression on Welsh historical consciousness, but the destruction of the political edifice that represented Llywelyn's unique achievement, and secured his singular position among the princes of his nation, was the result of the war of 1277. Llywelyn's behaviour between 1267 and 1277 has left historians perplexed and, in their endeavour to understand this critical period, many have sensed an ominous change in his political attitudes promptly upon Henry III's death in 1272. It seems as though the prince, as soon as Edward I came to the throne, began to prove intransigent, failing to pay the annual instalments of the indemnity imposed upon him by the terms of the peace of 1267 and refusing first to swear fealty to the king and then to do homage to him. In not fulfilling these obligations Llywelyn defaulted upon two undertakings which were key features of the treaty of Montgomery, 'the legal cornerstone of his whole position'.[1] Reneging in these important respects upon his duties as a vassal, he put the very existence of his principality at risk.[2] It cannot be doubted that relations between Edward and Llywelyn were central to the course of events leading to the destruction of the principality, but it would be hazardous to suggest that the war of 1277 stemmed from a fatal personal antagonism made manifest as soon as Edward came to the throne. To pursue this argument would be to discount numerous difficulties posed by the chronology of events in these years. During the first three years after the treaty of Montgomery, with Henry ageing and his powers failing, the heir to the throne was active in the

---

[1] J. G. Edwards, in *LW*, l–li.
[2] Tout, *CP*, ii, 97–100; idem, *Edward the First* (London, 1906), 107–8; idem, *The History of England 1216–1377* (London, 1905), 155–9; *HW*, ii, 754–9; J. G. Edwards, in *LW*, l–liiii; Frame, *British Isles*, 151–4.

A Principality in Perplexity

government of the kingdom, and there can be little doubt that Llywelyn dealt with a royal administration in which, certainly in relation to the problems of Wales, Edward exercised some considerable responsibility.[3] The historian needs to sense the atmosphere in which business was conducted between Llywelyn and Edward in this brief period. For then, in the summer of 1270, Edward left the kingdom and was away for four years: the last twenty-seven months of his father's reign and the first twenty-one months of his own reign. It was only in the summer of 1274 that Llywelyn began to deal with an administration directed by Edward as king of England. The phasing of the history of his relations with the royal administration thus has to be borne in mind, and the whole question of Llywelyn's intransigence in his dealings with Edward needs to be considered in relation to the intricate problems which he already faced by 1274. Not least among them are those which arose within the political community of his own principality. The crisis in which he found himself in his own lands by the time Edward returned to his kingdom will demand particular notice in this chapter, but the account needs to begin in the march of Wales during the months immediately following the making of the treaty of Montgomery. The historian, like the prince himself, needs to take account not only of Edward, but of the three powerful figures of Gilbert de Clare, Humphrey de Bohun, and Roger Mortimer.

Llywelyn came to an early realization that he would have to resort to arms to defend the position conceded to him by the treaty of Montgomery, but his first major conflict had its origins, not in any need to defend his frontier, but in his decision to extend his interests into Gilbert de Clare's lordship of Glamorgan.[4] This conflict was to demand his attention for a long time, and his efforts were to be entirely in vain. It is extremely difficult to understand why he chose to intervene in Clare's territory, but it is evident that he had entered Glamorgan some time before the making of the peace settlement of 1267. The earliest firm indication of conflict in this area comes at the beginning of that year when Clare entered the lordship of Senghennydd with an armed force. This was a lordship, in the upland of Blaenau Morgannwg, held by Gruffudd ap Rhys as a tenant of the lord of Glamorgan. Gruffudd was captured and imprisoned, and he was held at Clare's castle in Kilkenny.[5] But, if Clare's action is the earliest recorded incident, it seems likely that his decision to enter Senghennydd was made in response to an intervention in the

---

[3] Prestwich, *Edward I*, 61–5, for a circumspect view of Edward's role in these years.

[4] Altschul, *Clares*, 122–34; *GlamCH*, iii, 53–6; J. E. Lloyd, 'Llywelyn ap Gruffydd and the lordship of Glamorgan', *ArchCamb*, 6th ser., 13 (1913), 56–64.

[5] BL, Royal MS 6 Bxi, f. 109; Breviate Annals, 282 (two sets of Glamorgan annals, the second from PRO, Breviate of Domesday, E164/1). Each text records the capture of Gruffudd ap Rhys on the Saturday after Epiphany (8 January 1267); the king, in a letter to Llywelyn, 1 January 1268, says that Clare was then holding Gruffudd ap Rhys (*CR, 1264–68*, 496–7); for Gruffudd, below, n. 16.

area on the part of Llywelyn. Precisely when this might have occurred is impossible to determine. It is conceivable that Llywelyn seized an opportunity to enter Blaenau Morgannwg during the last weeks of Montfort's conflict with his opponents in the summer of 1265 when, as we have seen, Clare's lands were subject to attack from Montfort and possibly from Llywelyn as well. But if that were not the case it is highly likely that the prince had intervened there, and secured possession of a part of the territory, in the unusual circumstances which prevailed in this sector of the march during 1266.

Llywelyn might then have been influenced by one or more of several factors. From the spring of that year Glamorgan was in the king's hands by reason of an action brought *coram rege* by Gilbert de Clare over his mother's dower lands, and the prince may have decided to enter Glamorgan when its lord was not, as he might have imagined, in a position to provide for its defence.[6] There were, however, two possible sources of contention apart from Glamorgan. In the autumn of 1265 Clare had been granted custody of the lordship of Brecon and, though there is no firm evidence of this, it is possible that conflict arose then or later between its nominal custodian and the prince who exercised effective control over much, if not the whole extent, of the lordship. Furthermore, in the summer of 1266, perhaps in an attempt to assuage the earl's sensibilities over the fact that his estates were in royal custody, Henry granted him the right to hold whatever lands of the prince, and of the Welsh adherents of Montfort, he could conquer.[7] Whether Clare made any attempt to avail himself of this concession we cannot tell, but it might be noticed that, among charges levied towards the end of 1267, Llywelyn related that Clare had occupied and held the patrimony of the prince's barons in Elfael Is Mynydd, an action especially difficult to explain for which there appears to be no other testimony.[8] The course of events, the chronology of aggressive movements and retaliatory measures, is not easy to establish and it is thus virtually impossible to determine if Llywelyn's action in Glamorgan was provoked by a Clare initiative which might have been

---

[6] Altschul, *Clares*, 117; *GlamCH*, iii, 53–4. Glamorgan and Usk were taken into royal custody pending the settlement of the earl's action for the castles of Usk and Caerleon which his mother held in dower. Humphrey de Bohun, earl of Hereford, was appointed keeper on 30 April 1266 (*CPR, 1258–66*, 588).

[7] *CPR, 1258–66*, 495, 674.

[8] *CR, 1264–68*, 496. Clare was alleged by Llywelyn to have taken the lands of Owain, Maredudd and Ifor, sons of Owain ap Maredudd, to the manifest injury of king and prince. Llywelyn evidently took Elfael Is Mynydd to be, like Elfael Uwch Mynydd, a lordship held by Welsh barony; the king regarded Elfael Is Mynydd as the inheritance of Roger de Tony, after whose death in 1264 the land was taken into royal custody (*CIPM*, i, no. 588; *CPR, 1258–66*, 316, 435). It was not among the lordships granted to Llywelyn in 1267; when royal authority was restored in 1277 it was stated that Llywelyn had held the lordship to the exclusion of Tony's heir (*CCR, 1272–79*, 393).

made either on the basis of his custody of Brecon or in response to the king's invitation to conquer.[9] Despite the uncertainties, it seems safe to conclude that, certainly by the end of November 1266, when he was once more in possession of his lordship of Glamorgan, Clare had need to attend to the consequences of a Welsh advance into the northern parts of the lordship.[10] It has been suggested already that the pact made between the earl and prince early in the following year, noticed in *Brut y Tywysogyon*, was dictated by a wish on Clare's part to be relieved of the prince's pressure on Glamorgan while he brought the issue of the Disinherited to a head with his march on London.[11] He had already moved to counter Llywelyn's initiative by entering Senghennydd and removing Gruffudd ap Rhys. But as later evidence clearly reveals, Llywelyn remained well entrenched within Clare's frontiers, and the position in Glamorgan remained a matter of concern when the treaty of Montgomery was negotiated, for an order issued from chancery on the very day on which Llywelyn did homage to Henry III indicates that the king feared that there might be further trouble in Glamorgan.[12]

The king's anxiety at this time prompts a question concerning the position which Clare might have taken in relation to the settlement with Llywelyn. Admittedly, the extent to which the earl's opinions might have influenced royal counsels when the treaty was made is questionable, but his position as a major baron of the march made his attitude to the concessions won by Llywelyn a matter of some consequence for the future. It has been intimated earlier that his endeavours to promote a conciliatory approach to the problem of the Disinherited might conceivably have inclined him to favour a settlement with Llywelyn, and, for his own good reasons, he might have appreciated the advantages of an agreement which could stabilize the political situation in independent Wales and define the sphere of its prince. He might even have been prepared to commend the advantages of such a settlement to Mortimer. But even if the two marchers could reconcile themselves to the new order, there can be no doubt that, however strained their relations may have been in recent years and however sceptical each of them might have been of their ability to establish a harmonious relationship with one another, they would have been in full accord in their determination to contain Llywelyn within the well-defined territory accorded to him by the treaty of 1267. Moreover, each of them had a problem for which the treaty provided no clear

---

[9] Altschul, *Clares*, 118, notes that, without possession of Glamorgan, Clare was hardly in a position to take advantage of the king's licence to conquer. The lands beyond the frontiers of Brecon, such as Elfael Uwch Mynydd, might have provided opportunity for expansion if he were in effective custody of that lordship.
[10] *CR, 1264–68*, 264.
[11] Above, pp. 175–6.
[12] *CPR, 1266–72*, 113–14.

A Principality in Perplexity

solution: Mortimer would be anxious to deny Llywelyn possession of Maelienydd and Clare would be equally concerned to remove Llywelyn from Blaenau Morgannwg. No specific reference was made to the area in the treaty but, in the light of the alacrity with which Llywelyn raised the issue after the sealing of the treaty, Glamorgan may well have been a contentious issue during the course of the negotiations at Shrewsbury. In acting in a manner likely to ensure that Gilbert de Clare was brought to the ranks of those who would seek every opportunity to reverse his fortunes, and provoking one who was wont to stand apart from Mortimer on matters of policy in the realm of England, the prince of Wales made a decision with very costly implications.

Llywelyn may have intervened in Glamorgan in somewhat fortuitous circumstances, demonstrating perhaps that ability to grasp an opportunity with which historians have often credited him. Yet it is clear that there were influences at work which impelled him to advance his power further and further into marcher areas settled by communities of Welsh nationality. The uplands of Glamorgan were certainly among them. In entering Senghennydd he came to a lordship which bordered Meisgyn, once the patrimony of Hywel ap Maredudd who had joined him during the heroic days of the prince's early assertion of power in Snowdonia. Hywel's presence in the prince's entourage would have been a constant reminder of the fact that Blaenau Morgannwg sustained a Welsh community, and that its lords had in earlier years spontaneously allied themselves with Llywelyn ap Iorwerth.[13] At the same time, the evidence indicates that Llywelyn ap Iorwerth, after the cessation of hostilities, had been extremely circumspect when the lords of the upland areas endeavoured to transfer their allegiance from the Clare lord to the prince of Gwynedd.[14] Llywelyn ap Gruffudd, though he, too, had made an early intrusion into Glamorgan, had similarly acted with restraint during the years of truce about 1261–2 when, particularly after the death of Richard de Clare, circumstances would seem to have been propitious for a vigorous assertion of power in the area.[15] But, some time later, he decided otherwise and crossed the mountainous frontier between Brecon and Glamorgan. It became clear that he had come to Glamorgan, not to enhance his bargaining power, but to stay.

By the end of 1267, advancing his own interpretation of the treaty of Montgomery, he asserted that the homage of Gruffudd ap Rhys, as one of the Welsh barons of Wales, belonged to his principality.[16] For his part Gilbert de

---

[13] J. B. Smith. 'The lordship of Glamorgan', *Morgannwg*, 2 (1958), 28–34; Altschul, *Clares*, 66–75; *GlamCH*, iii, 47–53.

[14] *CR, 1231–34*, 590, 594–5.

[15] *Foedera*, I, i, 340–1, an undated document which probably belongs to a period of truce *c*.1261; an attack on Glamorgan was feared upon the death of Richard de Clare in 1262, but it does not appear to have materialized (*CAC*, 37–8; *RL*, ii, 217–18).

[16] *CR, 1264–68*, 496–7 (the king's reply, 1 January 1268).

Clare urged the king to insist that Llywelyn restore the territories that he had occupied unjustly and retained by force. The prince should desist from withdrawing men from the earl's allegiance and subjecting them to his lordship.[17] In his replies to prince and earl the king ventured no opinion on the conflicting claims but, in virtually identical phraseology, recommended that the two men should submit their differences to the processes of negotiation which were customary in the march. If these proved unsuccessful Henry would send a commission from his council to the march, empowered to do justice according to the terms of the peace of 1267. The king commended to prince and earl, as he did to Roger Mortimer in respect of other matters raised by Llywelyn, the arbitration procedures which were part of the custom of the march, but with provision for recourse to a judgement under royal jurisdiction if arbitration should fail. It was an incentive to both parties to settle their differences, but in his letter to Llywelyn, though not in his communication to Clare, the king raised one further possibility. As Gruffudd ap Rhys was 'of our Englishry' (*de Anglescheria nostra*), Llywelyn, if he so wished, could bring an action against the earl to the king's court (*coram rege*) over the matter of Gruffudd's imprisonment and receive justice according to the law and custom of the realm. Llywelyn might not be expected to be enamoured of the prospect of seeking justice *coram rege*, but the king's proposal may not have been entirely displeasing to him. However, the prospect of litigation on this issue in the king's court, and judgement by the law and custom of the realm, was one which Gilbert de Clare could not possibly countenance. Nor would he submit easily to a decision of a royal commission, not even a decision taken in accordance with the custom of the march. He had taken direct action in a matter that was, in his view, entirely within his jurisdiction. His decision early in 1268 to build a castle in Senghennydd Is Caeach, the southern commote of the lordship in contention, was a new pledge of his determination to act on his own behalf.[18]

The same resolve brought him, in the autumn of that year, to make an attempt to establish an understanding with Llywelyn, and it is not difficult to see what spurred him to do so at that particular time. By mid-September royal commissioners had gone to the ford of Montgomery to consider the disturbances in the march, and among them the problems in Glamorgan loomed large. Up to that point nothing had been accomplished in response to the first recommendation embodied in the king's letter at the beginning of the year. No arbitration had been arranged, nor, quite evidently, had the king's commissioners found it possible to give judgement in accordance with the

[17] *CR, 1264–68*, 497 (Clare's allegation is reflected in the king's letter).
[18] Royal MS 6 Bxi, f. xxx; Breviate Annals, 282, attribute the beginning of work on Caerffili to 11 April 1268, and note the capture of Gilbert son of Gilbert de Umfraville and others in hard fighting; for the castle, below, n. 51.

terms of the treaty of Montgomery. They now recommended that the contention in Glamorgan should be heard in the king's court five weeks later.[19] Clare acted swiftly. On 27 September, two weeks after the commissioners had deliberated at Montgomery, he met Llywelyn at Pontymynaich in Cantref Selyf. Both men recoiled from the prospect of a judgement *coram rege*. They remitted their dispute to a board of arbitrators, four from each side, scheduled to meet in the new year and deliberate day by day until an arbitrament was secured in accordance with justice.[20] If the arbitration produced no judgement, they would seek another way of resolving the issue, and only if that were to fail would they bring their dispute *coram rege*.[21] Meantime Clare would hold the commote of Senghennydd Is Caeach and Llywelyn would hold Senghennydd Uwch Caeach and the northern part of the commote of Meisgyn.

It appears that both lord of Glamorgan and prince of Gwynedd were anxious to resolve their differences without involving the king of England, though whether they shared this feeling to an equal degree is difficult to judge. Even so, the customs of the march were hardly famed for their effectiveness, and it is not difficult to appreciate that the matter at issue was not readily amenable to the compromise solutions or the mutual reparations to which the arbitration procedures were best suited. Certainly, in this instance, arbitration came to nothing, and eventually the king decided that the matter should be submitted to the judgement of the Lord Edward.[22] It may be that neither this proposal, nor the composition of the commission empowered to gather evidence, augured well for Llywelyn, but Llywelyn responded to the king's summons to a *parliamentum* at the ford of Montgomery in a gracious manner. It appears, indeed, that Edward's intervention at this difficult time served to

---

[19] *CPR, 1266–72*, 254; *Foedera*, I, i, 477. Commissioners were appointed on 17 August to go to the ford of Montgomery by 14 September; it was agreed that the dispute should be heard before the king in October (*LW*, 102).

[20] *LW*, 101–3; *Cartae*, ii, 693. Bishop Anian of Bangor, Goronwy ab Ednyfed, Tudur ab Ednyfed and Dafydd ab Einion were to act for Llywelyn, but Goronwy died before the appointed day; Clare was to be represented by John de St John, John de Braose, Roger of Leicester (papal chaplain) and Hervey de Borham. J. E. Lloyd identified Pontymynaich as a place near Gwenddwr in Cantref Selyf ('Llywelyn ap Gruffydd and the lordship of Glamorgan', 59). The arbitrators were to meet at 'Eadbryn', in Brecon but as yet unidentified.

[21] Altschul, *Clares*, 125–6; *GlamCH*, iii, 55, suggests that the parties were persuaded to negotiate, but the agreement indicates that they accepted arbitration so as to avoid recourse to the proceedings before the king which the commissioners had prescribed. The king in January 1268 had recommended arbitration and then, if necessary, judgement by a royal commission according to the custom of the march; by September, according to the agreement between the disputants, they were offered only judgement *coram rege*. They bought time by postponing process before the king from October 1268 to February 1269, and meantime sought arbitration. For the arbitration procedures Ll. B. Smith, 'Disputes and settlements in medieval Wales: the role of arbitration', *EHR*, 106 (1991), 840–1.

[22] The parties submitted to Edward's award (*CPR, 1266–72*, 205; *Cartae*, ii, 686–7).

establish some degree of understanding between the heir to the throne of England and the prince of Wales.[23] The two men met at the ford of Montgomery and Llywelyn found the discussions distinctly encouraging. Following the meeting Llywelyn sent an unusually cordial letter to the king, and Henry reciprocated by conveying his pleasure that the prince had found the meeting with Edward rewarding and his gratification at the amiability (*dilectio*) which Llywelyn had shown towards Edward and himself. Llywelyn, he related, was well pleased with the outcome of the negotiations.[24] Edward had now to leave for France to discuss the matter of the crusade to which he was pledged, and he could not meet Llywelyn at Chester in September as had previously been agreed between them. Still, anxious to maintain the momentum, Henry indicated his wish that discussions should proceed, and he invited Llywelyn to London on the occasion of the translation of the body of Edward the Confessor to its shrine in the great church of Westminster, a building on whose completion the king had set his heart for so long.[25] If it were to prove difficult for Llywelyn to come at that time Edward would go to Gresford during November. The civility of the exchanges of the summer of 1269 suggest that there was, at that stage, a prospect that perseverance and good faith on the part of the prince and the heir to the throne would enable them to resolve the difficult problems confronting them. There was some reason for hope that the two nations might yet be brought to the continuing accord that the papal legate had held in prospect when peace had been made two years before.

Perhaps the meeting at Rhyd Chwima brought little more than a promise of better relations still to be achieved, but it produced one specific decision on Edward's part that helps to explain both Llywelyn's gratification and Clare's anger. It concerned the allegiance of one who leaves a fleeting trail in the historical evidence, momentarily illustrating the perennial problems of the relations between kingdom, principality and march. It seems that Edward adjudged at the ford that it would be right to accede to Llywelyn's request for the homage of Maredudd ap Gruffudd for the commote of Machen in the lordship of Gwynllŵg and the commotes of Edeligion and Llebenydd in the lordship of Caerleon.[26] He came to this conclusion despite the fact that Gwynllŵg had always been part of the Clare inheritance and that Earl Gilbert had recently extended his authority in the southern march to embrace

---

[23] The commissioners were Roger de Somery of Dinas Powis, a tenant of the earl, and Hugh de Turberville, soon to be active in the reassertion of marcher power in Brecon. Henry proposed a meeting on 30 May; Llywelyn preferred 24 June, but was prepared to attend on the earlier date (*CPR, 1266–72*, 344; *Foedera*, I, i, 479; *CAC*, 28; *RL*, ii, 329–30).

[24] *CPR, 1266–72*, 385; *CR, 1268–72*, 72 (26 July 1269).

[25] For Edward's discussions in France, J. P. Trabut-Cussac, 'Le Financement de la croisade anglaise de 1270', *Bibliothèque de l'école de chartes*, 119 (1961), 113–40.

[26] *CPR, 1266–72*, 385.

Caerleon as well.[27] Maredudd ap Gruffudd's estates were not confined to those lands in Gwynllŵg and Caerleon, for by this time he also held the commote of Hirfryn in Ystrad Tywi. The fact that he did so may be an indication of Llywelyn's determination to get the better of Clare in Glamorgan and Gwent. For, although Maredudd was of the lineage of the princes of Deheubarth, Hirfryn had not come to him by any unbroken succession. After the death of his grandfather, Maredudd ap Rhys ap Gruffudd, in 1201, other members of the lineage had gained possession of his territories. It may be concluded with a fair degree of probability that it was by virtue of an enfeoffment by Llywelyn, almost certainly made shortly before 1269, that Maredudd ap Gruffudd secured a small part of the patrimony of his forebears to augment the estates which had come to him in Glamorgan and Gwent by his father's marriage with the heiress of those properties.[28] It is by no means inconceivable that Llywelyn had deliberately invested Maredudd with the status of a Welsh lord of Wales, and had taken his homage for the commote of Hirfryn, in order to support his efforts to get the king to allow Maredudd to be a tenant-in-chief of the prince of Wales, not only in Deheubarth, but in Gwynllŵg and Caerleon as well. Llywelyn maintained that Maredudd was a Welsh baron and ought to hold his lands of himself by Welsh right (*iure Wallensica*). Maredudd duly swore before Edward at the ford of Montgomery that he, like his ancestors, should hold his lands according to the custom of Wales (*secundum consuetudinem Wallie*) and the king in due course granted that he should be a tenant of Llywelyn.[29] In acceding to Llywelyn's wishes, not only did Edward revoke Clare's lordship over

---

[27] Altschul, *Clares*, 126–7.

[28] Maredudd ap Rhys ap Gruffudd died in 1201 in possession of Cantref Bychan (*BT, Pen20*, 146; *Pen20Tr*, 81; *RBH*, 184–5); Gruffudd ap Maredudd, whose marriage to Gwerful, daughter of Morgan ap Hywel (Bartrum, *WG*, iv. 758, 779), brought him lands in Gwynllŵg and Edeligion and Machen in Caerleon (*CIPM*, ii, no. 289), is not known to have held anything in Deheubarth. Maredudd ap Gruffudd, who died at his castle of Llandovery in 1270 and was buried in the chapter house of Strata Florida, was described as 'lord of Hirfryn' in Cantref Bychan (*BT, Pen20*, 219; *Pen20Tr*, 115; *RBH*, 258–9). The commote, held by Maredudd ap Rhys Gryg in 1257 but not in his hands in 1268 (*LW*, 163; Marquess of Bath, Longleat MS 268), was probably given by Llywelyn to Maredudd ap Gruffudd following one of Maredudd ap Rhys's defections. Maredudd ap Gruffudd's son, Morgan ap Maredudd, claimed his patrimony first from Llywelyn and then from the crown (*CIPM*, ii, no. 289; *WAR*, 268) but without success; he rose in rebellion in Glamorgan before becoming prominent in royal service (J. B. Smith, 'Edward II and the allegiance of Wales', *WHR*, 8 (1976–7), 142). Literary associations of his lineage in the fourteenth century are noticed, with references, in D. J. Bowen, 'Dafydd ap Gwilym a Morgannwg', *Llên Cymru*, 5 (1958–9), 164–73.

[29] *CPR, 1266–72*, 385, read in conjunction with the original roll C66/87, m. 9d. The king's concession to Maredudd that he should hold of Llywelyn contained the caveat that, if it were shown that Maredudd held any lands of the king, he should answer according to the law and custom of the realm; there was no mention of Clare's claim to lordship over Maredudd.

A Principality in Perplexity

Maredudd ap Gruffudd, but he established a precedent which might be invoked in relation to the main issue in the confrontation between Llywelyn and Gilbert, that is the homage of Gruffudd ap Rhys of Senghennydd.

It might have been too much to expect Llywelyn to attend the royal festivities at Westminster, but he may well have awaited a resumption of his discussions with Edward in eager expectation of further progress upon some of the issues which troubled him. He probably sensed that, for the moment, circumstances were propitious in that Edward, though hardly moved by magnanimity towards the principality of Wales, was manifestly influenced by the state of his relations with Gilbert de Clare. The latter's agreement in the summer of 1268 to take the Cross, and his willingness to participate in a crusade in which Edward would clearly be a leading figure, had been an indication of improved relations.[30] Yet, during the following year, there was renewed animosity between them.[31] The contentious issues, of which the situation in the march was one, were submitted to the arbitration of Earl Richard of Cornwall. His award, in May 1270, duly reflected Clare's wish that his dispute with Llywelyn should be resolved by the custom of the march.[32] Yet, quite apart from his concern for the protection of his territories against the prince of Wales, Clare was deeply resentful of Edward's handling of the marcher problems. His attitude was undoubtedly influenced by Edward's decision on the issue of Maredudd ap Gruffudd's allegiance and its further implications for his position in the march. It may be significant that the earl's conflict with Llywelyn had been included among the matters considered by the envoys of Louis IX upon their visit to the English court in the autumn of 1269, but it is possible that neither the surviving documents relating to these discussions nor Cornwall's award fully reflect the tensions between Edward and Gilbert on the marcher issues.[33] Clare's response to Cornwall's recommendations in the summer of 1270 reflects not only his concern at the threat from Llywelyn but his suspicions of Edward's

---

[30] For Edward's crusade, R. Röhricht, 'La Croisade du prince Edouard D'Angleterre, 1270–1274', *Archives de l'Orient latin*, 1 (1881), 617–32; S. Lloyd, 'The Lord Edward's crusade, 1270–72, its setting and significance', in J. B. Gillingham and J. C. Holt (eds.), *War and Government in the Middle Ages* (Woodbridge, 1984), 120–33; idem, *English Society and the Crusade, 1216–1307* (Oxford, 1988), 113–53; Prestwich, *Edward I*, 68–71.

[31] Powicke, *Henry III*, ii, 578–80; Altschul, *Clares*, 127–8; *Accounts of the Constables of Bristol Castle in the Thirteenth and Early Fourteenth Centuries*, ed. M. Sharpe (Bristol Records Society, 34, 1982), xxii–xxiii; S. Lloyd, 'Gilbert de Clare, Richard of Cornwall and the Lord Edward's crusade', *Nottingham Medieval Studies*, 30 (1986), 46–66.

[32] *Historical Papers and Letters from the Northern Registers*, ed. J. Raine (RS, 1873), 29; *The Register of Walter Giffard, Lord Archbishop of York, 1266–1279*, ed. W. Brown (London, Surtees Society, 109), 237–40. The award was probably made on 25 May 1270 and on the following day Henry appointed a commission to resolve the disputes in the march (*CPR, 1266–72*, 431).

[33] *CPR, 1266–72*, 369; Powicke, *Henry III*, ii, 578–80; S. Lloyd, 'Gilbert de Clare', 52–3.

intentions. It was a feeling which Cornwall, in turn, felt obliged to respect.[34] The ostensible marcher factor in Clare's wish to delay his departure from the realm was the need to provide for the security of his territories against further Welsh attack, and renewed pressure from Llywelyn by the autumn of 1270 was to give him reason enough to stay and protect his inheritance. Llywelyn's sustained offensive against him also gave Clare an opportunity to do everything in his power to ensure that nothing more was done at the English court to undermine his position in the march still further. He might even be able to secure a reversal of Edward's decision in relation to Maredudd ap Gruffudd, or at least render that decision ineffective. Llywelyn had seized his opportunity at the ford of Montgomery in the summer of 1269; Gilbert de Clare would seek to wrest that advantage from him at the earliest opportunity.

By the middle of August 1270 Edward had set out on the long journey which was to keep him away from the realm for four years, and it is not unreasonable to surmise that Llywelyn ap Gruffudd would have heard of his departure with considerable regret. Knowing that Edward would soon be leaving, Llywelyn sent an earnest appeal to the king and pressed him to attend to the problems which were gathering in the march.[35] Henry commended the prince's goodwill, but insisted that the matters at issue could not be determined while Edward was abroad, and Llywelyn knew exactly what this would mean. He knew well enough of the frustration of having issues that concerned him set aside while the king or the heir to the throne crossed the channel to France, or attended to matters of urgency in the kingdom itself. The new situation was infinitely more disconcerting, for it was generally known that Edward would be away for an extended period. Nothing of any account would ever be resolved, and the conflicts in the march were bound to escalate month by month. Already Edward's other recent preoccupations may have left Llywelyn somewhat daunted. It had been impossible to maintain the impetus created the previous year but, shortly before Edward left the kingdom, Llywelyn was given one more indication that, whatever his motives might be, he was a person capable of making firm decisions upon some of the issues that Llywelyn felt bound to urge upon the royal administration.

The matter resolved on the eve of Edward's departure was the question of the homage of Maredudd ap Rhys Gryg. It was doubtless in accordance with Maredudd's wishes that the king had retained his allegiance, alone among the Welsh barons of Wales, when the treaty of Montgomery had been negotiated.

---

[34] S. Lloyd, 'Gilbert de Clare', 55–60; and ibid., 64–6, for Clare's objections and Cornwall's replies.

[35] Henry sent a commission to Gresford by 9 June (*CPR, 1266–72,* 431); in response to a letter from Llywelyn, sent when he found that nothing had emerged from this meeting, Henry on 24 August arranged another gathering at the same place for 1 November (*CR, 1268–72,* 290–1).

It had been stipulated in the treaty that if the king were ever to concede Maredudd's homage it would cost the prince 5,000 marks but, though Llywelyn had moved with an alacrity which suggests a keen desire to obtain the homage, and had coupled his request with a firm promise to pay the required amount, Henry had rejected his appeal.[36] However, shortly before Edward left the kingdom the king relented, and did so in deference to his son's wishes. Edward's motives were not altogether altruistic, for he needed the money to support his great venture and he needed it quickly.[37] Robert Burnell, the Lord Edward's trusted clerk, was sent to Gwynedd with the relevant documents already prepared, though they were not to be conveyed to the prince until the agreed sum was handed over in its entirety. The terms were strictly cash on delivery.[38] It was a demanding transaction, and if the sum were to be paid as the king required it might well impose a strain on the resources of the prince's treasury. There is no certainty, however, that the money was paid and the transaction may not have been formally completed.[39] But, however great the price the crown had set and whatever brought Edward to urge his father to concede the homage, the king's letters were enough to enable Llywelyn to secure a final triumph over one who had proved to be, after an initial *rapport* that had augured so much, an incorrigible opponent. Exactly a year later the chronicler noticed the death at his castle of Dryslwyn of Maredudd ap Rhys Gryg, a brave and powerful man, whose body was borne to the Cistercian house of Whitland and given honourable burial in the great church, on the steps before the altar.[40] After the prolonged conflict between these two forceful men, Maredudd went to his grave a feudatory of Llywelyn. This last satisfaction, like the concession of the homage of Maredudd ap Gruffudd, came by dint of Edward's intervention. He now left the kingdom, and it was not long before the correspondence between prince and royal administration, which for a while had contained signs of growing confidence, slid gradually to a depth of distrust from which there would be no easy escape. Certainly, by the time Maredudd ap Rhys Gryg had been laid to

---

[36] *CR, 1264–68*, 497 (1 January 1268).

[37] Trabut-Cussac, 'Financement', 114–21; Prestwich, *Edward I*, 71–2.

[38] *CAC*, 209–10; *CPR, 1266–72*, 457 (30 August 1270); transactions included a release by Edmund, earl of Lancaster, the king's son, to whom the homage had been granted.

[39] The Patent Roll has an enrolment of Henry's confirmation of his grant of Maredudd's homage and an order to Maredudd to do homage to Llywelyn; the relevant documents were to be handed to Llywelyn when Burnell received the required sum (*CPR, 1266–72*, 457), but the enrolments provide no certainty that payment was made. In proposals made in 1277 Llywelyn promised to pay 5,000 marks due to the king for the homage of Rhys ap Maredudd, probably offering the money which had been expected but not received in 1270; the transactions may not have been formally completed in 1270, but subsequent records carry a tacit acknowledgement that Maredudd was a tenant of Llywelyn.

[40] These words reflect the phraseology of *BT, Pen20*, 219; *Pen20Tr*, 116, which is fuller, and more benevolent to Maredudd, than *RBH*, 258–9.

A Principality in Perplexity

rest, Llywelyn knew perfectly well that Edward's departure had placed him at a distinct disadvantage in his escalating confrontation with the powers of Clare and Bohun and Mortimer.

Llywelyn ap Gruffudd was now confronted with marcher power not only on the fringes of his principality, but in the innermost councils of the government of England. While Henry lived the administration of the realm remained, in theory at least, in the hands of those to whom the king entrusted the execution of royal authority. In practice, increasing power came to be exercised by those whom Edward had chosen to safeguard his interests in his absence. Richard, earl of Cornwall, took charge of Edward's children and shared the responsibility for the heir's estates with the churchmen Walter Giffard, archbishop of York, and Robert Burnell, and the laymen Philip Basset and Roger Mortimer.[41] Llywelyn had had dealings with Cornwall and Basset in earlier years, senior figures in whom he might have had some confidence, but neither was to survive the king. The only one of Edward's chosen laymen to see the end of King Henry's reign, and to receive the new king upon his return to the kingdom, was Roger Mortimer.[42] Although the king was dead before Llywelyn gave the clearest surviving indication of his awareness of Mortimer's influence in royal administration, it can hardly be doubted that he came to realize the extent of his adversary's power very soon after Edward's departure. More particularly, he was confronted with the fact that in Edward's absence Mortimer and Clare, despite the mutual antagonism of earlier years and their continued wariness, were brought to a closer understanding with one another if only by virtue of their common interest in retrieving their position in the march of Wales.

The early autumn of 1270 saw a marked change in relations between Llywelyn and the royal administration, and it was not altogether due to the prince's heightened offensive in the march. Writing in the summer, following the failure of a conference held at Gresford to produce any alleviation of his problems, Llywelyn again urged that action be taken with regard to the damages inflicted upon him.[43] He made particular reference on this occasion to injuries done to him by the men of Montgomery.[44] Henry's reply, four days after Edward left the kingdom, indicated that though there were serious difficulties to be resolved and could not be addressed immediately solutions would be sought. The dispatch of a commission to the march, arranged for early September, had to be postponed for two months, but meantime the

[41] Powicke, *Henry, III*, ii, 583–7; Prestwich, *Edward I*, 72–3.

[42] Bassett died in October 1271, Cornwall in April 1272. According to the arrangements originally made, Cornwall was to be succeeded by his son, Henry of Almain, but he had died in March 1271 in circumstances noticed below, pp. 391–2.

[43] The substance of Llywelyn's letter may be gathered from the king's reply, 24 August 1270 (*CR, 1268–72*, 290–1).

[44] Ibid.

issues raised by the prince would be considered at the parliament summoned for mid-October.[45] By then Llywelyn had written again and there was now a greater urgency to his missive. He was anxious to keep the peace with the king, and would continue to do so unless he were provoked into action by others. He pointed clearly to the likely source of provocation. Gilbert de Clare had gathered a great force to attack a land described as 'the prince's land of Morgannwg'.[46] Henry took heed, and Llywelyn's letter was undoubtedly one among the considerations which prompted the king to summon Clare to parliament. Clare, for his part, was no doubt glad of the opportunity to put his view of the conflict directly. The matter singled out by the king for transmission to Llywelyn, after consultation with the earl, was the position of Maredudd ap Gruffudd. Clare had complained that Maredudd had revoked his fealty and removed himself to the prince's allegiance. He proposed to launch an attack on Maredudd's castle, for it belonged, as he insisted, to his fee and not to Llywelyn's.[47] He was calling for nothing less than an abrogation of the decision made by the Lord Edward at the ford of Montgomery and subsequently endorsed by the king. The earl of Cornwall's award in May 1270 had respected Clare's concern for the marcher interests; now, in Edward's absence, Clare revealed what he really wanted to ensure. More than holding Llywelyn at bay, he wished to reverse Edward's award but, whatever happened in royal councils, he would make that decision null and void by direct action. Llywelyn's assessment that he was threatened with an attack from Clare is confirmed by the earl's admission of his intentions. But Clare alleged that Llywelyn, too, was prepared for war and that he had a bannered army poised for attack. On 13 October, the very day on which Clare put his case before council, the prince's army moved, with banners raised, to make the expected attack on the castle that Clare had built in Senghennydd Is Caeach.[48] The assault may have been made in retaliation

---

[45] Robert Walerand, previously authorized to go to the ford of Montgomery by 8 September, would not be able to do so until November. But Llywelyn was told to send envoys to the Westminster parliament in October and they would be informed of what the king proposed. The marcher issues, involving Clare and other barons, would be remitted to a commission of bishops and laymen who would meet at the ford on 2 November (*CR, 1268–72*, 290–1).

[46] Ibid., 234–5 (from Henry's letter, 16 October 1270). The king's letter was written two days after parliament had assembled.

[47] Ibid., 234. The text refers to *Mareducus Resy*, an error for Maredudd ap Gruffudd; chancery clerks had recently been writing documents concerning the homage of Maredudd ap Rhys Gryg, but he is not the person in question. Altschul, *Clares*, 125; *GlamCH*, iii, 54–5, says that *Mereducus Resy* was probably a brother of Gruffudd ap Rhys of Senghennydd and his nominal successor, but there is no other reference to a Maredudd ap Rhys of Senghennydd and such a person would not fit into the present context. Clare, it is said, threatened to attack the castle of *Mereducus Resy*; he did precisely that when he drove Maredudd ap Gruffudd from his lands in Caerleon.

[48] *Breviate Annals*, 282, provides a precise date, though it places the occurrence in an entry for 1269; *BT, Pen20*, 219, *Pen20Tr*, 115; *RBH*, 258–9, place it in October 1270.

A Principality in Perplexity

for an action by which Clare drove Maredudd ap Gruffudd from Edeligion and Llebenydd in Caerleon. Clare had evidently prepared for such action before he appeared at Westminster, but precisely when he struck we cannot tell.[49] Llywelyn's attack may equally have been a pre-emptive strike dictated, not simply by the situation in Glamorgan and Gwent, but by his judgement that the influences at work in the king's council were now distinctly unfavourable to him. It was, perhaps, some time before Mortimer became the dominant influence, but Llywelyn ap Gruffudd may already have judged that an identity of interest between Mortimer and Clare would be exceedingly damaging to the principality of Wales. Yet there can be no question that the danger to the principality had been compounded by his intervention in the southern march.

Llywelyn had by now committed himself to a very costly enterprise which diverted his attention when other problems began to gather about him. One by one the expensive months slipped by and nothing came of the successive attempts to get the opposing parties together in purposeful negotiations.[50] In the spring of 1271 Clare began to rebuild his castle in Senghennydd Is Caeach, initiating a building programme that was to make Caerffili an impressive monument to the capabilities of the great powers of the Welsh march.[51] By the

---

[49] Morgan ap Maredudd later maintained that his father had been ousted by Clare 'when Edward was in the Holy Land' (*CIPM*, ii, no. 289), and Edward had set out before the end of August 1270. Maredudd died in the second half of the year: on 19 October in *BT, Pen20*, 219; *Pen20Tr*, 115; 14 December in *RBH*, 258–9; a note in *Pen20Tr*, 213 explains the textual problem. The date of Maredudd's death does not therefore provide a conclusive indication of the date of the attack; but if Maredudd died on 19 October (which appears to be the more likely date on the textual evidence), and if Maredudd was still alive on the date of the attack, Clare's action would have been taken very soon after Llywelyn's attack on Caerffili on 13 October, if not before. Altschul, *Clares*, 129; *GlamCH*, iii, 55, concludes that Clare's attack on Maredudd's lordships occurred after the prince's attack on Caerffili, and in reaction to it, and this may well be correct.

[50] Attempts early in 1271 to arrange meetings at the ford of Montgomery appear to have come to nothing (*Cartae*, iii, 757–8; *CPR, 1266–72*, 581, 596). Llywelyn's representations produced a letter from the archbishop of York promising that persons named would be summoned to Wallingford on 7 June to consider the matters raised by the prince (*Historical Papers and Letters from Northern Registers*, 37–8). A meeting was arranged for Montgomery in late September, then postponed to October, when Llywelyn and Gilbert could present their case before magnates of the realm. Writing on 4 August, Henry referred to his impending visit to France and urged Llywelyn to act in a manner consonant with his obligations to his lord and to maintain peace in the marches (*Cartae*, iii, 759–60).

[51] W. Rees, *Caerphilly Castle and its Place in the Annals of Glamorgan* (Caerphilly, 1974); C. N. Johns, *Caerphilly Castle* (Cardiff, 1978); D. Renn, *Caerphilly Castle* (Cardiff, 1997); *GlamCH*, iii, 423–6; *HKW*, i, 231–2; *Inventory Glam*, III, ii, *The Later Castles*, no. LM 3. The origins of Castell Morgraig, built on the ridge of Cefn Onn, are difficult to trace. Its position, within the frontiers of Senghennydd and sited to withstand advance into the lordship from the south, suggest a castle of Welsh origin, possibly attributable to Gruffudd ap Rhys or to Llywelyn ap Gruffudd, or to the two of them acting in agreement, when the prince first intruded into the lordship. However, the surviving remains show that extensive use was made of Sutton stone, derived from the Vale of Glamorgan, material to which

autumn Llywelyn was threatening vengeance upon Clare and, declaring that he would destroy the earl's fortifications in three days, he unfurled his banner before the castle.[52] The king hurried to get two bishops to the scene, empowered to try to prevail upon Llywelyn to hold his hand and promising that the whole issue would be considered in earnest. Llywelyn was loath to agree to what was proposed.[53] It was only after some delay that Dafydd ap Gruffudd and Gruffudd ap Gwenwynwyn were able to put their seals to an agreement between their prince and the bishops which provided that the prince would raise the siege of Caerffili and wage no further war upon the earl of Gloucester. The castle would be placed in the bishops' custody while the issue was resolved at the ford of Montgomery in accordance with the custom of the march.[54] Regrettably Clare was not party to the agreement, and Llywelyn's suspicions seemed justified when, by a ruse, the lord of Glamorgan regained possession of his castle. King Henry, in failing health but sufficiently informed to be deeply troubled by the turn of events, fully appreciated that powerful men in his kingdom were threatening forceful action. He turned to his brother, Richard of Cornwall, in the hope that his standing and experience might prove of some avail in a crisis which, as the king himself conveyed, raised doubts over his own good faith.[55] Neither Henry nor Richard could withstand Clare's power, nor provide a credible solution, and the substance of the king's proposals to Llywelyn was essentially a restatement of his opponent's point of view.[56] Yet it is difficult to envisage what might have been done other than what Clare proposed: arbitration between earl and prince

---

neither Gruffudd nor Llywelyn could have had access. This consideration indicates that the structure, whose remains certainly bear the marks of Clare building, was built by Gilbert de Clare. There remains a possibility that Clare built on a site that had already been chosen by Gruffudd or Llywelyn, and where building had commenced, but that work there was then abandoned for the more extensive site chosen for the works at Caerffili. Castell Morgraig is described in *Inventory Glam.*, III, ii, *the Later Castles*, no. LM 9.

[52] *Cartae*, iii, 888–9; *CPR, 1266–72*, 583.

[53] *Cartae*, iii, 889: 'Lewelino ad hoc cum magna difficultate inducto'.

[54] Writs of 25 October empowering the bishops of Coventry and Worcester to take possession of the castles and secure Llywelyn's withdrawal, *Cartae*, iii, 760–2; *CPR, 1266–72*, 583; agreement between Llywelyn and the bishops, 1 November, *Cartae*, iii, 763–5, from C47/1/28.

[55] *Cartae*, iii, 888–9; there appears to have been prolonged and perhaps contentious discussion in council (ibid.; *CR, 1268–72*, 546–7; Powicke, *Henry*, III, ii, 581, n. 1).

[56] *CR, 1268–72*, 546–7; *RL*, ii, 342–3 (22 February). Clare, summoned before council, had offered explanations (*excusaciones*) that the king was unable to accept, but the outcome was virtually an endorsement of what Clare had proposed to council on 2 February (*CR, 1268–72*, 474). Llywelyn was required to come in person or send properly empowered envoys and Clare likewise. This was in accordance with Cornwall's recommendation that, as Clare and Llywelyn were vassals of the king, the matters at issue between them should be adjudged before the king, with the difference that it was now proposed that judgement should be given in accordance with the custom of the march (*Historical Papers and Letters from Northern Registers*, 27–30).

A Principality in Perplexity

without the involvement of the crown had been tried and had failed; action in the king's court was no more acceptable to the one than the other. The only other course possible, and this was what the king proposed, was to send to the ford of Montgomery a group of magnates, acceptable to both parties, empowered to resolve the issue in accordance with the treaty of 1267 and the custom of the march. During the months which followed, nothing came of this proposal, and before the end of October 1272, in what threatened to be a third autumnal crisis, Henry wrote to Llywelyn in terms which virtually admitted that he was washing his hands of the whole issue. Llywelyn pressed the urgency of the matter, sending letters to the king and dispatching Bishop Anian of St Asaph to explain his position. The king commended the manner in which the bishop had presented the prince's arguments, but Anian was unable to bring any encouraging message. Nor was the king able to suggest any way forward. In what reads as a valedictory letter he could offer Llywelyn nothing except the knowledge that his son, the prince's friend, was on his way back from the Holy Land.[57] The king himself planned to cross the channel to do homage to the king of France. It was a journey that Henry was not destined to make. Within three weeks the king of England was called to meet his Maker, his very last letter to the prince of Wales revealing that propensity to postponement which Llywelyn ap Gruffudd, like his grandfather before him, had recognized so often.[58] The prince of Wales had no choice but to await the return of his friend, Edward, king of England.

It was five years since Llywelyn had first claimed the homage of Gruffudd ap Rhys, more than that since he first intervened in Glamorgan, and he had absolutely nothing to show for the time he had given to this area nor for the strain upon his resources. It is conceivable that there were many among his tenants in the principality of Wales who questioned his judgement in contending with such a powerful marcher magnate upon a territory that had always been, without a shadow of doubt, part of the lordship of Glamorgan. Besides, it was patently beyond the confines of the principality delimited by the treaty of 1267. One cannot but imagine what thoughts passed through the minds of Dafydd ap Gruffudd and Gruffudd ap Gwenwynwyn, or what sentiments they might have shared, during the cold days and nights spent encamped on the moorlands of Senghennydd during what may well have been a winter of deepening discontent in the community of the principality of Wales.[59] It may not be entirely futile to ponder whether an understanding between Llywelyn ap Gruffudd and Gilbert de Clare might have served to stabilize the march as a whole, creating a situation in which political authority

---

[57] *CAC*, 10–11; *Cartae*, iii, 765–7 (30 October 1272).

[58] The meeting assigned to hear the prince's case was postponed from 29 October to 23 April 1273 when Edward would be present and the matter could be more readily resolved.

[59] *Cartae*, iii, 763–5; subsequent relations with the prince are considered later.

A Principality in Perplexity

over a very large part of Wales would have been shared between two powers, one founded upon the rights of Wales as they were represented in the principality of Wales, the other upon the marcher rights that Clare himself was to propound so eloquently in years to come. Llywelyn chose to pursue a different course, and the problems which confronted him in Blaenau Morgannwg arose entirely, as far as we can judge with confidence from the surviving evidence, from a wilful intervention justified only by a highly tendentious interpretation of the treaty of Montgomery. If he was to venture into this area at all, he needed to justify his decision by results, but the enterprise brought him no reward. And, as he persisted with a prolonged and futile contest, other problems arose which he was to find increasingly taxing. He ultimately abandoned the siege of Caerffili and withdrew, and he was unable to arrest that withdrawal until he stood on the frontiers of Snowdonia itself.

Llywelyn's retreat from Glamorgan may have been made imperative by the effect of Humphrey de Bohun's intervention in the lordship of Brecon. Bohun, who was to succeed his grandfather as earl of Hereford in 1275, was eventually to create an amalgam of English and marcher baronial power second only to that of Clare himself. In the last years of the century the two men would indeed be locked in fateful conflict in the march, but their early contests with Llywelyn may have brought them into advantageous collaboration. Clare yielded custody of the Bohun estates to the young heir in the summer of 1270, shortly before Edward's departure, and he may have done so entirely of his own volition with a view to encouraging Bohun to embark upon the recovery of Brecon.[60] He certainly had much to gain from a diversion of Llywelyn's resources to the defence of Brecon and, as the conflict with Clare dragged on, the prince came to include Bohun's name among his marcher opponents.[61] With a base in the march by virtue of his tenure of the lordships of Huntington and Hay, Bohun was in a position to exert pressure on Brecon. But the problems confronting Llywelyn in the lordship of Brecon and its environs did not arise entirely from the threat of an external attack by Bohun. There were two other important factors. Llywelyn's first assertion of power in the area in 1263 had been facilitated by the fact that the Welsh communities of the area had deserted their marcher lords.[62] His continued

---

[60] *CR, 1268–72*, 205–6 (5 July 1270); the marcher estates were the lordships of Hay and Huntington. Humphrey de Bohun (d. 1298) was given livery of the earldom on 26 October 1275.

[61] Specific references to Bohun occur from the autumn of 1272 (e.g. *CAC*, 10–11; *Cartae*, iii, 765–7); earlier mentions of unnamed marchers may have included him (e.g. *CR, 1268–72*, 211, 234; *Cartae*, iii, 759–60).

[62] Above, pp. 149–51.

A Principality in Perplexity

security there depended a great deal on their constant fidelity, a matter considered presently. But his prospect of being able to stabilize his position in the area would be greatly improved, too, if he were able to reach some understanding with the lesser lords of Brecon and its environs who had probably been ousted during that initial offensive. It was certainly not inconceivable that a prince of Wales might establish such a relationship with the Anglo-Norman lords of the march, more particularly those whose lands lay within the areas where the prince's authority had been formally recognized by treaty. Llywelyn ap Iorwerth may well have visualized a gradual process of accommodation of this nature when he sought marriage alliances with families such as that of Clifford, who held the lordship of Cantref Selyf within the confines of the lordship of Brecon.[63] John Giffard, who had recently secured a title to Cantref Selyf, did so by virtue of his marriage to a Clifford heiress who was a granddaughter of Llywelyn ap Iorwerth.[64] The prince's grandson had subsequently won the lordship of Brecon by force, but his position there was legitimized by the treaty of Montgomery and, if stable relationships could have been established within the lordship, John Giffard, holding an extensive estate centred on the castle of Bronllys, would have been one of his major tenants.[64] But whether Llywelyn was able to establish any understanding with Giffard is very doubtful, nor do we know whether the lord of Bronllys was even able to obtain possession of his estates.[65] There is uncertainty, too, with regard to those neighbouring lordships into which Llywelyn had intruded in 1263. The prince may conceivably have withdrawn his frontier to the lordship of Brecon, yielding possession of their estates to Reginald FitzPeter at Blaenllyfni, Hugh de Turberville at Crughywel and Roger Pichard at Tretower. But even if he did so he was unable to avert their wrath. When evidence first becomes available in 1273 we find that Turberville and FitzPeter were vigorously attacking Llywelyn's position in Brecon and

---

[63] For the tenurial position of Cantref Selyf, J. B. Smith, 'Marcher regality: *quo warranto* proceedings relating to Cantrefselyf in the lordship of Brecon, 1349', *B*, 28 (1978–80), 267–88.

[64] The marriage between Walter Clifford and Margaret, previously wife of John de Braose (d. 1232), may have been arranged in 1233 when the prince asserted power in the area in alliance with Richard Marshal and Clifford, who opposed the king (*HW*, ii, 678–80; R. F. Walker, 'The supporters of Richard Marshal, earl of Pembroke, in the rebellion of 1233–34', *WHR*, 17 (1994–5), 54–5).

[65] I. J. Sanders, *English Baronies* (Oxford, 1960), 116; R. R. Davies, *Lordship and Society*, 46, n. 41; Maud Clifford's first husband William Longspée died in 1263, and she held the lordship when Llywelyn entered Cantref Selyf in that year (*CAC*, 17); the date of her marriage to Giffard is uncertain, but it is likely that he had become lord of the fee in her right before Llywelyn withdrew from the area in 1277. Giffard, along with Roger de Clifford, was among the magnates sent to the ford of Montgomery to make a truce between Llywelyn and Bohun in the spring of 1274 (*CPR, 1272–81*, 48) and he was actively involved in Brecon and its neighbourhood in 1277.

were at that time cautioned by the royal administration for their eagerness to do battle with the prince of Wales.[66] They may have recovered their own possessions by then, at the latest, but they could still see the advantage to themselves if Bohun power was re-established in a major lordship which would provide a sturdy bastion between their lands and the principality of Wales. Llywelyn was clearly confronted, not simply with the determination of Humphrey de Bohun to establish his control over Brecon, but with the vigorous participation of other lords, from the lordship of Brecon and its neighbourhood, in a concerted endeavour to drive him out. It was a corporate effort to reverse the losses sustained a decade earlier, and Llywelyn's position in the area had to depend on a combination of military power and the continued allegiance of the Welsh communities of the lands under his direct lordship.

There are indications, however, that he was confronted with some degree of desertion on the part of his tenants in the lordship of Brecon and in several neighbouring areas. The relevant documents are not easy to interpret and the extent of the problem is not easy to judge, but it seems that the prince found it necessary to take measures to secure the fidelity of men of some substance in a community which, as it seemed at the time, had willingly adhered to him during his triumphant campaigns in the region. He had reason, for instance, to question the loyalty of Einion ap Rhys and Meurig ap Llywelyn of Brecon, and took hostages to secure their adherence. Our first indication of the prince's difficulties in this connection come towards the end of 1271 when the hostages were released and Einion and Meurig provided sureties from among the men of Deheubarth for their new pledge of loyalty.[67] There was evidently a problem in Brecon by 1271 and perhaps a little earlier. It may have been eased for a while but it was not to be entirely resolved, and it is not surprising to find these men among the leaders of the contingents raised in this sector of the march to serve the king in Gwynedd during the war of 1277.[68] Nor was the loyalty of the men of Brecon the only cause for concern, for Llywelyn was constrained to take similar action with regard to the loyalty of Iorwerth ap Llywelyn, probably a man of Builth, and Meurig ap Gruffudd of Elfael, and it

---

[66] *CCR, 1272–79*, 56 (13 September 1273); they were charged with giving aid to the castle of Humphrey de Bohun and to adjoining lands and besieging the castle. The order should be read in conjunction with the evidence considered below. For Turberville, M. Prestwich, *War, Politics and Finance under Edward I* (London, 1972), 49.

[67] *LW*, 28–9, 33–4, 126, documents dated at Rhyd-y-briw, 7 November 1271; those who provided surety for Einion and Meurig included Hywel ap Rhys Gryg and the sons of Madog ab Arawdr, who will be mentioned again. For the adherence of Einion ap Madog's descendants to Bohun, R. R. Davies, *Lordship and Society*, 225–6; for Rhyd-y-briw, below, pp. 416–17.

[68] Below, pp. 417, 429–30.

may well be that these things are seen only dimly and in part.[69] Imprisonment, the taking of hostages and sureties, the exacting of solemn pledges from the men of the area itself and from neighbouring Deheubarth: these are the measures to which the prince had to resort in his endeavour to retain the allegiance of the frontier communities on the furthermost reaches of his principality where he himself would ultimately meet his death.[70] When Llywelyn faced Humphrey de Bohun's attempt to reassert the authority of his lineage in the lordship of Brecon he had to contend not only with an external assault by Bohun and his fellow marchers, but with an internal disintegration of his power as well. In assessing the significance of the evidence, however, consideration has to be given not only to his eventual withdrawal from the area but to the resistance he maintained right up to the beginning of 1277.[71]

The lordship of Brecon also provides clear evidence of the influence which Roger Mortimer exerted in the realm after Henry III's death and its implications for Anglo-Welsh relations. It has been noticed already that, of those who had taken charge of the heir's interests in 1270, only Walter Giffard, Robert Burnell and Roger Mortimer survived the king. These then became the regents of the realm and, along with the chancellor, Walter Merton, were the persons most directly concerned with the conduct of royal business. It was not long before Llywelyn became aware of the power exerted by his old adversary in royal councils. Already indicated before the king's death, it was now more clearly revealed in documents emanating from chancery. It marked a distinct convergence of Mortimer, Bohun and Clare interests. By the summer of 1273 royal documents could refer to Brecon as 'the land of Humphrey de Bohun', and Llywelyn invoked royal stricture for a counter-offensive by which he sought to re-establish his control over a part of the lordship which had slipped from his grasp.[72] He would surely have been angered by a royal command which, urging him to hold his hand, warned him not to commit any action contrary to the terms of the treaty of Montgomery, when the lordship had been formally conceded to him by that same agreement. He might have been even more incensed had he known of an exchange of letters between Mortimer, on the one hand, and Burnell and Merton on the

---

[69] A document issued by the prince's major tenants and officers in Elfael, Builth and Gwerthrynion at Builth, 30 November 1271, testified that they had taken pledges for the release of Iorwerth ap Llywelyn from the prince's prison and for his fidelity in the prince's homage and service, with a further stipulation that he should provide his son as a hostage upon the prince's demand (*LW*, 40–1). In a group of four documents, one dated at Sychdyn near Mold, 7 December 1271 (*LW*, 24–6, 30, 35–6), Cynan ap Maredudd, Gruffudd ap Maredudd and Hywel ap Rhys Gryg made similar provision for the fidelity of Meurig ap Gruffudd of Elfael; see J. G. Edwards, in *LW*, xliv–xlv; further transactions for the release of a son of Hywel ap Meurig, 1276, below, p. 429.

[70] The prolonged conflict in the area has been noticed in earlier discussion.

[71] Below, p. 416.

[72] *CAC*, 57–8 (18 May 1273).

other, concerning the position of the lordship of Brecon. There is every indication that Mortimer had, in effect, recognized Bohun's claim to Brecon and was concerned only with the means by which he might be justified in deploying royal resources in support of the marcher's endeavour to recover the lordship. At Mortimer's request, Burnell and Merton turned to the text of the treaty of Montgomery and found that its terms indicated clearly that Brecon had been conveyed to Llywelyn. The two churchmen came to the view that it would not be expedient to defend the land by the king's command and by his power, for to do so would clearly infringe the treaty, unless it could be shown that Bohun had recovered the land by judicial process according to the custom of the march as the treaty had provided. But they proceeded to reason that, while the treaty of Montgomery had given Llywelyn seisin of the land of Brecon, he had never had seisin of Humphrey de Bohun's castles and it would be perfectly proper to defend the castles and provide effective aid for their defence. The distinction between castles and lands was, in this context, quite invidious, but it was an interpretation which suited Mortimer's purposes very well.[73] Llywelyn would have known nothing of this revealing correspondence, but the letters written to him in the king's name very early in the new reign would have indicated clearly enough that the regents had convinced themselves of the propriety of a course of action which would enable the lords of the march to gain royal support in their endeavour to recover marcher lands, even though they had been formally granted to the prince under the terms of the treaty of 1267 to which Edward himself had put his seal. Much more serious than his failure to secure the homage of Gruffudd ap Rhys, Llywelyn was now confronted with the prospect of losing a lordship which formed part of the principality for which he had done homage, and doing so by the forbidding combination of marcher aggression, disloyalty among some men of substance in the community itself, and royal intervention. Those representing royal authority might still urge restraint, but the surviving evidence indicates that Llywelyn had cause to be concerned at the influences being exerted on royal policy within a very few months of Edward's accession. He may have read the signs a good deal sooner. When, promptly upon Henry's death, he was summoned to Rhyd Chwima to swear fealty to Edward, he knew that the instruction emanated from an administration directed by men in whom he could have no confidence.[74] Rightly or wrongly, he could not bring himself to surmount the anger and the frustration he had increasingly felt during the king's last years. On the appointed day early in

---

[73] *CAC*, 57–8, 109–10; undated, the editor suggests early 1273. Powicke, *Henry III*, ii, 640, n. 3, says that the two clerics felt bound to explain the legal difficulties to their more 'headstrong' colleague; but Mortimer would probably have been content with a reasoning that served his purposes quite well.

[74] Edward succeeded on Henry's death, 16 November 1272.

A Principality in Perplexity

1273, in accordance with the order which they had received, the abbots of Dore and Haughmond went to the ford at daybreak and waited. They waited all day until nightfall, but Llywelyn neither came to the appointed place nor sent anyone there on his behalf.[75]

Of the letters addressed to him by the old dispensation of the new king, he was particularly irritated by a letter which ordered him not to proceed with the building of his castle at Dolforwyn. Appreciating that the strategic importance of this sector of the frontier called for a construction of a major stronghold, he decided to built a castle in Cydewain located upon an elevated site above the Severn a short distance from the ford of Montgomery.[76] He planned to establish a town and market in association with the castle and, to the extent that a new commercial enterprise could be seen to be damaging to the interests of Montgomery, he might have expected the king to oppose his plans.[77] But this was hardly the main reason for the royal administration's decision to forbid the building at Dolforwyn. Llywelyn was at Dinorben, in the *cantref* of Rhos, when he received the letter by the hand of the prior of Wenlock towards the end of June 1273. The prior was kept waiting for several days while Llywelyn's aides prepared a reply which stands among the most notable statements of his view of his status as prince of Wales.[78] The prince conveyed his conviction that the king himself knew nothing of this letter, and that it would never have been sent from chancery if the king were present in his kingdom. The king knew very well that the rights (*iura*) of his principality were entirely separate from the rights of the king's realm, though he held his principality under the king's royal power (*potestas*). He maintained that he and his predecessors had built castles and established markets without prohibition, and he implored the king not to listen to the evil suggestions of those who tried to influence the king's mind against him.

---

[75] Summons 29 November 1272 to swear fealty at the ford of Montgomery on 20 January, *CCR, 1272–79*, 2; report of the abbots, with confirmation of their testimony by Roger de Springhose, constable of Montgomery, *Foedera*, I, ii, 499.

[76] For Llywelyn's possession of Cydewain, above, p. 183.

[77] The king later vigorously opposed Gruffudd ap Gwenwynwyn's bid to establish a market at Welshpool on the grounds of its propinquity to Montgomery (*Select Cases concerning the Law Merchant*, ed. H. Hall (London, Selden Society, 1908–32), III, 140–2. Dolforwyn was rather nearer Montgomery than was Welshpool.

[78] *CAC*, 86, where the date of Llywelyn's letter (11 July [1273]) is considered in relation to the royal order, 23 June 1273 (*CCR, 1272–79*, 51; *Foedera*, I, ii, 504). The castle, named 'Abrunol' in the king's letter and 'Abermiwl' in the prince's reply, was Dolforwyn (J. E. Lloyd, 'Dolforwyn', *B*, 10 (1939–41), 306–9, and, for 'Bachyranelau', below, n. 112). An account of the castellan of 'the new castle above the Severn' commenced 3 April 1273 (*LW*, 23–4) and the editor concluded that building began on that date. For the structure, L. A. S. Butler, 'Dolforwyn castle, Montgomery, Powys, first report: the excavations, 1981–1986', *ArchCamb*, 138 (1989), 78–89; idem, 'Dolforwyn Castle, Montgomery, Powys, second report: the excavations, 1987–1994', *ArchCamb*, 144 (1995), 133–203, with further references.

A Principality in Perplexity

Despite its studied adherence to diplomatic conventions, Llywelyn's letter was plainly directed at Mortimer, as the author of the royal order. When the letter was written in his name Edward himself was journeying through the lands of his cousin Philip of Savoy, who did homage to him on a celebrated occasion at St George-d'Espéranche in the Viennois.[79] The king had an opportunity to see the land where Philip's builders were at work on a notable group of castles, Yverdon, Saillon and Chillon among them, whose architectural features would be reflected in the castles that the Savoyard craftsmen would later build in Wales, when Edward had humiliated the prince who now proclaimed the rights of his principality in such sonorous language.[80] At this distance from his kingdom, Edward would not have known what was sent out from chancery in his name from day to day, and in his absence the problems of the principality of Wales were gathering fast.[81] Nor had the forthright phraseology of Llywelyn's letter concerning Dolforwyn satiated his anger by any means. The issue rankled still, and a few days later a second letter, though this again adhered to diplomatic protocol, was clearly directed at Mortimer. Llywelyn took the initiative and complained that the building work that Mortimer had put in hand at the castle of Cefnllys in Maelienydd went far beyond the repair which, as Llywelyn maintained, had been envisaged in the treaty of Montgomery. He insisted that materials were being assembled for nothing less than the construction of a new stronghold, and that this would surely be built unless the work was stopped either by the king or by Llywelyn himself.[82] The position of Maelienydd was one of the most sensitive issues left unresolved in 1267 and, given the antagonism between the two men, the wording of the treaty in this connection boded ill for the future. Direct evidence that Llywelyn initiated proceedings to establish his right to Maelienydd, as the treaty provided, is slight. His statement, in the letter written from Mold, that he had hitherto been unable to obtain justice, may perhaps be a reference to deliberations at the ford of Montgomery of which

---

[79] Powicke, *Henry III*, ii, 612–13; Arnold J. Taylor, *Studies in Castles and Castle-Building* (London, 1985), 29 [Taylor, *SCCB*]; Prestwich, *Edward I*, 83–4. Edward received Philip's homage on 25 June 1273 (*Gascon Register A*, ed. G. P. Cuttino (London, 1975–6), ii, no. 115; *Foedera*, I, ii, 504).

[80] Taylor, *SCCB*, 1–43, 63–97. Edward was accompanied by several men who were to play a prominent part in his Welsh wars (ibid., 29).

[81] It is likely that the regents consulted the king after he came to France in the summer of 1273. He had reached Savoy by mid-June and Paris by mid-July; he then turned south to Gascony and arrived by mid-September.

[82] *CAC*, 94. The letter is dated 22 July, and the editor suggests 1273 or 1274. The earlier year is preferable, the letter a riposte to the king's letter on Dolforwyn. Llywelyn's letter of 11 July concerning Dolforwyn was dated at Dinorben and that concerning Cefnllys at Mold, a further indication, perhaps, that the letters belong to the same year. For the interest of Llywelyn's letter in relation to the surviving remains at Cefnllys, A. E. Brown, 'The castle, borough and park of Cefnllys', *TRadnS*, 12 (1972), 11–22.

we have no record. But the letter explicitly states that he had by no means ceased to assert his claim. Mortimer, for his part, had lost no time in providing for the security of Cefnllys, as he was perfectly entitled to do. The castle had been refortified even before the end of 1267, and Llywelyn's complaints against him at that time were to be matters for discussion (*interloquendum*) in accordance with the custom of the march.[83] Maelienydd was not Mortimer's only concern. Gwerthrynion was probably beyond his reach, but promptly upon the death of John FitzAlan, a few weeks after the making of the treaty of Montgomery, Mortimer had moved to protect the marcher interest in the lordship of Clun. Llywelyn thereupon asked the king to order Mortimer not to disturb his possession of Dyffryn Tefeidiad or Tempsiter, the western part of Clun that had been in his hands, possibly with John FitzAlan's acquiescence, for some years.[84] Mortimer remained vigilant of Llywelyn's interest in Clun.[85] But the main matter of contention was undoubtedly Cefnllys. Llywelyn would hardly have expected his letter to elicit any meaningful response, but it indicates his wish to assert his claims and his conviction that Mortimer's care for his own interests in the march militated against a proper discharge of his responsibilities in the kingdom as a whole. His concerns as a marcher and his responsibilities as regent of the realm were entirely incompatible with one another.

Mortimer's building work at Cefnllys may have been initiated before 1273 but, provoked by the marcher's intervention in the prince's work at Dolforwyn, Llywelyn now registered his mounting concern that the third of the powerful marcher triumvirate was preparing to contest possession of a vital area of the march. Clare, Bohun, Mortimer: it was the third of these who posed the greatest threat to the fragile state of equilibrium created in the march by the peace settlement of 1267. The issues now being raised were far

---

[83] Llywelyn's early representations over Maelienydd are reflected in Henry's reply 1 January 1268 (*CR, 1264–68*, 496). He had asserted a right (*ius*) to the land of Maelienydd which Mortimer possessed and where he had already built a castle. This was one of the matters, raised against Mortimer and Clare, which were to be the subject of negotiation and which, if there were no agreement, would be resolved by royal commissioners sent to the march to do justice. The précis of Llywelyn's letter conveys that, contrary to the indication given in the text of the treaty of 1267, Llywelyn was not in possession of Maelienydd, a fact which subsequent evidence tends to confirm, and that Mortimer's building work was already in progress. The work of which Llywelyn complained in 1273 may, as his letter suggests, represent more substantial work than before. For Mortimer building at Dinbod, also in Maelienydd, below, p. 494.

[84] John FitzAlan had died before 10 November 1267 (*Handbook of British Chronology*, 449, n. 2). In his letter to the king, reflected in *CR, 1264–68*, 496, Llywelyn urged that Mortimer be ordered not to disturb the prince's possession of Dyffryn Tefeidiad; this matter, too, was submitted to negotiation and then, if there were need, to judgement in the king's name. For a further allegation that Mortimer had seized the land, *CAC*, 86–7 (14 May 1276).

[85] *CAC*, 49.

A Principality in Perplexity

too intractable for the normal arbitration processes conducted at the ford of Montgomery. They demanded the more weighty deliberations by the custom of the march which, so often promised, so rarely came to pass. Llywelyn would continue to press for these discussions for, without them, the treaty on which so much depended would be put in jeopardy. No one would wish to admit that he repudiated the treaty, though indeed Llywelyn had warned that, though he wished to observe the treaty, he was not to be provoked by others.[86] The situation deteriorated year by year and, as those who held the responsibility for the kingdom of England awaited first the death of one king and then the return of another, unable to stem the conflict in the march but doing much to intensify its severity, they increasingly witnessed the creation of a situation very different from that which obtained when the treaty was made. Sooner or later the pledges into which king and prince had entered at that time would be devoid of meaning, and Llywelyn, no less than his adversaries, could be counted among the men of power whose actions disturbed the *status quo* even as their words continued to proclaim the validity of the agreement upon which it was founded.[87] The years which the king had spent overseas had seen the conflict which began in Glamorgan spread and intensify. His accession to the throne had not made a whit of difference, except to the extent that his absence allowed those who acted in his name to exercise their own judgement as to what the situation demanded. Llywelyn's intransigence hardly stemmed from his dealings with Edward, nor was it something which dated from Edward's accession. The prince's difficulty lay in the fact that he found it impossible to cast off his old anxieties with the death of the old ruler.

Whenever Edward returned to the realm, his regents would be able to relate that Llywelyn had failed to fulfil his duty of swearing fealty to the king, and that he had failed to pay the money which was due year by year under the terms of the treaty. In failing to go to the ford of Montgomery to swear fealty Llywelyn had made a symbolic remonstrance, and by the time the king returned to England he had made a stand, too, on the issue of the payments due on the indemnity. He insisted that he would pay the sum which was outstanding as soon as the king compelled the marchers to make amends for

---

[86] *CR, 1268–72*, 234–6.
[87] The situation invites reference to the doctrine *clausula rebus sic stantibus*, of later times, by which a treaty bound the parties only for as long as the situation which existed at the making still obtained. After 1267 each side continued to protest its adherence to the treaty and it was Edward, on the eve of conflict in 1277, who came closest to its repudiation when he expressed the view that it was only in difficult circumstances that the king of England had made peace with Llywelyn (*CAC*, 252–3; below, p. 407, n. 65.).

A Principality in Perplexity

their breaches of the agreement between them.[88] This second protestation, made in February 1274, might be taken as a further expression of the obdurate stance adopted by Llywelyn as soon as Edward had come to the throne. Historians have often seen Llywelyn's actions in this light and it has been argued that, while Henry lived, Llywelyn was able to raise all but a small amount of the enormous sum due to the crown, that he had the resources and the will to meet his obligation, and that his subsequent failure to do so reflected a change in his outlook.[89] But there is good reason to consider whether Llywelyn's failure to deliver the money was due, less to any desire to withhold payment on an issue of principle, than to the fact that he faced a financial crisis which made it difficult for him to meet his obligations. This is a possibility suggested by close examination of the dates of the payments made and of the precise sums handed over to the crown's officers.[90] Up until 1269 he made his payments promptly and paid each of the substantial sums required in its entirety. Between the date of the treaty and the end of 1269 Llywelyn had paid Henry III the enormous sum of 11,000 marks. The fact that he had been able to meet his obligations up to that date in full and with commendable promptitude is quite remarkable. But when it came to the payment due at the end of 1270 he failed to deliver on time. The money was conveyed later, reaching the royal coffers bit by bit. The two facts, taken together, may suggest that Llywelyn was by then under financial strain.[91] In addition, during August 1270 he had been required to find 5,000 marks to pay for the homage of Maredudd ap Rhys Gryg although there is no certainty that he actually made the payment. Maredudd's service was something that the prince had eagerly sought, and he had known since 1267 precisely what it

---

[88] *CAC*, 92–3; for the date, below, n. 97.

[89] J. G. Edwards, in *LW*, li–liii; Powicke, *Henry III*, ii, 638.

[90] Calculation is difficult (J. G. Edwards, in *LW*, li; Powicke, *Henry III*, ii, 638, n. 3), because acquittances in chancery enrolments, and sometimes in 'Liber A', are documents prepared for the attorneys sent to receive money from the prince and are not necessarily proof of payment. Records of actual payments (e.g. *LW*, 140, 150) provide only an incomplete record; for the total to the end of 1269, J. G. Edwards, in *LW*, li, n. 1.

[91] Of 3,000 marks due in December 1270, 2,000 marks were paid in two parts in April and May 1271 (*LW*, 140, 144, 150), leaving a deficit of 1,000 marks increased by 3,000 marks in December 1271. Of this, 250 marks was paid in January 1272, and probably more than this, for Reginald de Grey, in September 1273, states that only 2,000 were due to Poncius de la More by assignment on the part of Henry III, apart from the 3,000 marks due in December 1272 to Edward (*CAC*, 39). Llywelyn's calculations concur (*CAC*, 161–2), as do those of Edward, who found that by 1274 2,000 marks were due to the merchant and 6,000 marks to himself for 1272 and 1273 (*CPR, 1272–81*, 72). Llywelyn thus appears to have paid all but 2,000 of the immense sum of 17,000 marks payable between 1267 and 1271. These figures do not correspond to those given in *LW*, li, n. 1, but they point to the conclusion which Edwards acknowledges, and which needs a particular emphasis, that, for whatever reason, Llywelyn's failure to deliver the indemnity as required by the treaty dates, not from the first payment due to Edward in 1272, but from the last two due to Henry in 1270 and 1271.

would cost him if the king were ever to concede the homage.[92] If, indeed, Llywelyn had not paid the required sum it could well be an indication of his inability to raise money even for something he earnestly desired.

Llywelyn was confronted with this extraordinary charge at what was, and not for him alone, a particularly difficult time. Travelling to Gwynedd in the late summer of 1270 and returning to Westminster, probably without the hard currency which would have been a most useful contribution to Edward's crusade fund, Robert Burnell would have seen on all sides the saddening evidence of a failed harvest. The harvest failed again in 1271, causing a sharp rise in prices and a high mortality over wide areas of western Europe.[93] One of Burnell's colleagues in royal administration, Walter Giffard, explained the difficulties encountered in England in a letter to one of the king's proctors at Rome.[94] Llywelyn was not the only one to endure a cash-flow problem at this time, but his difficulties may have been particularly acute, quite apart from the money due for the homage of Maredudd ap Rhys, and his response to successive royal demands for payment of the sums due under the treaty of Montgomery is very revealing. In so far as the available evidence provides a guide, Llywelyn, for a considerable time yet, made no declaration whatsoever of his refusal to pay the king on an issue of principle. On the contrary, he made part payments and, with regard to the remainder, he offered successive excuses and made new promises. He insisted, in the autumn of 1273, that he had imposed a tax upon his lands to raise the money for the king, and he seems to have had resort to a similar measure a second time when he again linked his demands upon his people with his obligations to the king.[95] As late as the end of 1273 his response to the crown's requests continued to be

---

[92] The uncertainty over this payment is noticed above.

[93] D. L. Farmer, 'Some grain price movements in thirteenth-century England', *EcHR*, 2nd ser., 10 (1957–8), 207–20; idem, 'Some livestock price movements in thirteenth-century England', *EcHR*, 2nd ser., 22 (1969), 1–16. Grain prices certainly reveal fluctuations which point to adverse climatic conditions in the early 1270s. For 1270–2 see also M. M. Postan and J. Titow, 'Heriots and prices on Winchester manors', in M. M. Postan, *Essays on Medieval Agriculture and General Problems of the Medieval Economy* (Cambridge, 1973), 166–7.

[94] *Historical Papers and Letters from Northern Registers*, 39–40: 'caristia enim anni preteriti et presentis [1270–1] cum sterilitate terrarum nostrarum omnem exhaurit pecuniam'.

[95] *CCR, 1272–79*, 57. Bishop Anian of St Asaph stated that Llywelyn, on the pretext that peace had been made with the king, imposed a heavy tribute on his people; he did so 'after the king's recent withdrawal from the march', which suggests to the editor, *CAC*, 105, a date following Edward's withdrawal from Chester in September 1275. Powicke, *Henry III*, ii, 638, n. 3, suggests that another possible date would be after Edward's visit to Worcester in January 1277, when reference to a peace would be more meaningful since king and prince were not at war in 1275. A levy of 3d. on each animal is linked with the making of peace in the *gravamina* of 1283 (Ll. B. Smith, 'Gravamina', *B*, 31 (1984), 174, cap. XIII). A date in late 1275 is most likely.

phrased in evasive and delaying terms.[96] He may conceivably have been concealing his true purposes, but a prince so fastidious with regard to his dignity would hardly have wished to convey an impression of serious financial stringency, and his messages to the crown can hardly be taken to indicate anything other than the fact that he was in considerable difficulty. It was only in February 1274 that Llywelyn began to refuse the king's demands on principle: he then insisted that the money was available, ready to be handed to the king's agents, and he would do so as soon as the king fulfilled his obligations under the treaty made between them. If the king were to compel Clare and Bohun and the other marchers to restore the lands they had taken by force, Llywelyn would pay the money due without delay.[97] Coming at this late date, these words would have carried little conviction. Even before the old king had been put to rest, Mortimer and his associates in royal service might have read the signs that the power of the prince of Wales, who laid such great stress upon the rights of his principality, rested upon a financial basis that was palpably uncertain. They might have sensed that any unexpected demand upon his resources, or some severe disaster, could place him in extreme difficulty.[98] A failure of the harvest, war in Glamorgan and Brecon: misfortunes or miscalculations such as these could place a considerable burden upon the resources of a community which, at best, would not find it easy to sustain itself upon a terrain which Llywelyn himself was to describe as a barren land.

Edward I had moved on from Savoy to the environs of Paris by July 1273, but he judged that the state of affairs in Gascony was more pressing than anything related to him about the situation in the realm of England. He turned south to confront the recalcitrance, and then the armed rebellion, of Gaston de Béarn. Edward was forced into a campaign which took his forces deep into Béarn where, in the approaches to the Pyrenees, the castles of Orthez and Sauveterre and Salies were held against him and vigorous resistance offered at several locations. Gaston's submission early in the new

---

[96] *CCR, 1272–79*, 110 (30 November 1273); for reference to the king's demands, but no clear response, *CAC*, 161–2; *Foedera*, I, ii, 505 (3 September 1273), a letter dated at 'Rydgastell', that is Llanfair Rhyd Gastell, a grange of Aberconwy (C. A. Gresham, 'The Aberconwy charter: further consideration', *B*, 30 (1982–3), 321–6).

[97] *CAC*, 92–3; the letter, dated Monday after St Matthias, indicates late February; the editor gives strong reasons for 1274 rather than 1273, and the fact that Llywelyn was still offering excuses in late November 1273 supports the later date.

[98] Williams-Jones, in *MLSR*, xviii–xx, stresses Llywelyn's difficulties and argues that 'intention outran capacity'; Stephenson, *GG*, xxxiii–xxxv, argues that Llywelyn was capable of meeting his obligations had he wished to do so. The evidence considered in this paragraph, and that of the *gravamina* of 1283, support the view that Llywelyn's heavy commitments did impose severe strain on the resources of his territorial lordships. His letters to the king may reflect a genuine difficulty on his part in regard to a matter which he would have preferred to conceal.

A Principality in Perplexity

year brought no immediate resolution of the issues as the obdurate Gascon – resorting to a means of resistance denied to any prince of Wales – looked to the king of France for justice.[99] Edward's return, expected early in 1274, was still further delayed and it was only in August that he reached England.[100] He was no doubt soon fully informed of the recalcitrance of a feudatory who was to pose far greater problems than the lord of Béarn. The two main manifestations of Llywelyn ap Gruffudd's intransigence were his failure to make the payments due to the crown each year, already considered, and his failure to swear fealty to the king. With the king now present in his kingdom the obligation of fealty became a duty to do homage, and the two men would need to come face to face. Edward made no immediate demand upon Llywelyn to do homage, and the first call upon Llywelyn's presence was an invitation to attend to his coronation. He did not attend, and in failing to do so Llywelyn may have added something to the evidence which Mortimer and his colleagues could adduce to demonstrate the prince's estrangement.[101] The king of Scotland duly attended the coronation, but, as has been suggested already, Alexander's relations with the king of England were of a rather different order, and Edward may not have expected to find Llywelyn among the royals and nobles who gathered for the festivities at Westminster.[102] More important, for king and prince alike, was the letter which Edward issued early in November to summon Llywelyn to Shrewsbury a month later, on 2 December, to fulfil his duties as a vassal by doing homage to the king.[103]

It is conceivable that Llywelyn saw the meeting as a means whereby fundamental issues, set aside for so long, might be considered in purposeful discussion. He would have harboured no illusions about the prospects, but Llywelyn himself had sought a meeting with certain magnates of the realm at the ford of Montgomery in the spring of this year. It was a request which reflected a sustained effort to have something done about the injuries inflicted

---

[99] For Edward's journey to Gascony and his dealings with Gaston, Trabut-Cussac, *L'Administration anglaise en Gascogne*, 41–5; J. B. Smith, 'Adversaries of Edward I: Gaston de Béarn and Llywelyn ap Gruffudd', 68–70.

[100] Arrangements for Edward's coronation a week after Easter were being made in early February (*CCR, 1272–79*, 68). Edward's letter to Walter Giffard, Mortimer and Burnell, 18 February 1274 (*Select Cases in the Court of King's Bench*, ed. G. O. Sayles (London, Selden Society, 1936–71), II, cxxxi, from SC1/8/29, makes the arrangements necessary by his continued absence).

[101] *Foedera*, I, ii, 505; *CAC*, 161–2 (3 September 1273), a letter from Llywelyn to Reginald de Grey, includes a reference to an invitation to the king's coronation, at that point planned for April 1274. Llywelyn took note of the invitation and the demand for money and explained that he could not attend to these matters immediately as his brother Dafydd and the bishop of Bangor were the only members of his council who were with him.

[102] Prestwich, *Edward I*, 89–91; H. G. Richardson, 'The coronation of Edward I', *BIHR*, 15 (1937–8), 94–9.

[103] The summons was issued 3 November requiring Llywelyn's presence 2 December (*CCR, 1272–79*, 136; *Foedera*, I, ii, 518).

A Principality in Perplexity

upon him by the marchers in the encounters that continued month by month.[104] The royal administration appears to have taken the prince's approach seriously. The fact that one of those sent to the ford, William Bagod, set off shortly afterwards to see the king may suggest that Edward was informed of the substance of the discussions with Llywelyn. He may indeed have been told of other matters concerning the inner problems of the principality of Wales, to be considered presently, which the royal council might by then have known about.[105] Llywelyn was now called to meet the king at exceedingly short notice, especially when the date originally given him was brought forward by seven days to 25 November. Even so, it is evident that he had sent messengers to the king promptly upon receiving the summons, and Edward conveyed verbally to the prince's envoys his expectation that Llywelyn would be at Shrewsbury at the earlier date. It is impossible to know whether the king had reason to believe that Llywelyn did not intend to be present, or whether the prince was creating difficulties over his attendance. There is certainly nothing in the king's letters to suggest that he had any reason to question the prince's intention. We know only that a letter, written on 22 November, just three days before they were due to meet, conveyed that the king had suddenly suffered an abscess and that he would not therefore be able to meet Llywelyn as he had intended.[106] There is no means of knowing how serious the king's indisposition may have been. A year later Edward certainly endured an illness when the wounds he had received by an assassin's blade at Acre began to fester again, and on that occasion proceedings in parliament were cut short.[107] Chancery documents do not convey that the

---

[104] Arrangements were made for William Beauchamp, Roger de Clifford, William Bagod and Odo Hodnet to be at the ford of Montgomery for a meeting on 6 May (*CAC*, 55, 163; *CPR, 1272–81*, 47); Llywelyn was required to be there in person or to send emissaries fully empowered to determine the matters at issue.

[105] A journey by Bagod to the king is noted in the account of Stephen of Pencester, constable of Dover (Taylor, *SCCB*, 252). Pencester accounts for 1272–4 and the entry is not dated. Bagod is known, from the Liberate and Issue Rolls, to have been sent abroad on an important errand on two occasions in this period. The first was authorized by Merton, Giffard, and Burnell on 29 November 1272, nine days after the king's accession (C62/49; E403/20), the second on 15 June 1274 (C62/50, m. 5). From its place on Pencester's roll, that entry may well relate to the earlier journey. But the later entry in the Liberate Roll tends to confirm Dr Taylor's suspicion that Bagod may have been sent to the king to give a verbal report on the meeting at the ford of Montgomery. Bagod may also have had knowledge of the events at Dolforwyn the previous month examined in the paragraphs which follow.

[106] Edward's postponement was dated at King's Cliffe on 22 November (*CPR, 1272–81*, 72). He had received Llywelyn's messengers at Northampton, so the prince had received a summons dated 3 November and dispatched his envoys so as to reach the king before 17–18 November. Llywelyn had evidently acted swiftly. Edward now expected Llywelyn not on 2 December but, as he had informed the prince's envoys, a fortnight after Martinmas, that is on 25 November. If the new date had not been conveyed to Llywelyn before his messengers reached the king, the prince had been given very short notice of the change.

[107] *CCR, 1272–79*, 197–8; *ChronWykes*, 263; Prestwich, *Edward I*, 100–1.

conduct of government business was impaired in any comparable manner in 1274, but the imposthume of that year may have been due to the same cause and the king may have endured a similar malady.[108] The cancellation of the meeting may thus have been entirely due to the king's inability to attend, and it may be perverse to search the documents for any indication other than the fact that the king was unwell. Yet the exceedingly short notice first given, the fact that the meeting was even then brought forward, and its cancellation at such a very late stage, taken together, raise intriguing questions. Again, the king's movements in the days preceding his engagement with the prince are hardly suggestive of an intention to reach Shrewsbury in time for the meeting.[109] The questions posed by the evidence may not be readily answered, but they deserve to be carefully considered. Whatever his reasons, and despite his subsequent imputation that Llywelyn had failed to respond to his summons, it was Edward who withdrew from the projected meeting with Llywelyn. He did so, moreover, at a time of crisis in the history of the principality of Wales whose repercussions were to have a devastating effect on relations between king and prince.[110] What expectations or apprehensions the two men had harboured as they contemplated their meeting in 1274 we cannot tell, but there can be no doubt that, though the problems confronting them were already a great deal more difficult than they had been when they last met, the subsequent calls upon Llywelyn to fulfil his obligations to his lord were to be made in even more complex circumstances than those which prevailed in 1274.

Chancery documents for 1274 provide no inkling of the crisis that shook the community of the principality of Wales and so gravely affected relations between Llywelyn and Edward. The fullest account comes from a letter which the dean and chapter of Bangor addressed to the archbishop of Canterbury in the spring of 1276.[111] Much of the substance of the letter is, however,

---

[108] Chancery enrolments do not indicate any obvious disturbance of royal administration, but there was no great business in hand at that time comparable to the transactions in parliament in the following year when the king's personal attention was required and when his absence was bound to be reflected in the record.

[109] During the days immediately preceding the announcement of his illness Edward moved from Northampton to Fotheringay (18–21 November) and then to King's Cliffe (22 November), thus moving in a direction which took him further away from Shrewsbury. It might still have been possible for him to reach Shrewsbury by the revised date of 25 November, but the king's movements do not altogether inspire confidence in his intention to be there on the date he had given the prince. The letter cancelling the meeting was dated at King's Cliffe, on the day that he arrived there, leaving just three days for the messengers to reach Llywelyn. The whole matter is certainly intriguing.

[110] For the chronology of events, below, n. 121.

[111] *LW*, 136–8 (18 April 1276). The crisis is examined in *HW*, ii, 748–50; J. G. Edwards, in *LW*, liii–lv; Powicke, *Henry III*, ii, 642–4.

corroborated by two documents from the critical year itself and by an entry in *Brut y Tywysogyon*.[112] The dean's letter relates that Gruffudd ap Gwenwynwyn and his eldest son, Owain, plotted with Dafydd ap Gruffudd to kill Llywelyn. The conspirators had agreed that Dafydd should remain in his brother's entourage until 2 February 1274 when Owain would bring armed men by night to accomplish the deed, but a snowstorm on the night in question confounded their plans. From the evidence which survives Llywelyn is known to have taken action only several weeks later. *Brut y Tywysogyon* records that it was about Low Easter (*Y Pasg Bychan*), that is about 8 April, that Llywelyn came to Dolforwyn and, summoning Gruffudd ap Gwenwynwyn to him, charged him with infidelity and deceit.[113] Record evidence shows that the charges against Gruffudd, made in the presence of several magnates of the principality of Wales, were examined by a board of eight arbitrators, four from Gwynedd and four from Powys, each one of whom had witnessed the pledge of fealty which Gruffudd had made to Llywelyn eleven years previously.[114] Just as the magnates of the principality had gathered on that occasion, so they came together again, and it was by the authority of this assembly of the prince's council that the eight were entrusted with the examination of the evidence. Regrettably the document which records the judgement does not convey the substance of the action against Gruffudd, but it evidently proved to be enough to give the arbitrators grounds to recommend that Gruffudd and his son should place their lands at Llywelyn's will. For a second time Gruffudd ap Gwenwynwyn came upon bended knee before the prince of Wales. At Ystumanner, in more propitious circumstances in 1263, he had pledged his fidelity to Llywelyn and was formally endowed with extensive estates. Now, at Dolforwyn, put on trial and found guilty of the serious charges against him, Gruffudd pleaded that he might retain

---

[112] A record of the process against Gruffudd ap Gwenwynwyn and his son Owain, heard on 17 April 1274, exists in a transcript given under the seal of the abbot of Aberconwy and the dean of Arllechwedd at Arddau on 21 July 1278 (*LW*, 108–10), prepared in connection with a legal process over Arwystli and the land between the Dyfi and the Dulas brought before the king's justices in that year and considered later; a document embodying undertakings by Gruffudd and Owain is dated 18 April 1274 (*LW*, 98–9). The two documents were dated at 'Bachyranelau in Cydewain'; J. E. Lloyd, 'Dolforwyn', 307, suggests that this is another name for Dolforwyn, 'the new castle on the Severn'. Bachyranelau occurs once more in the same period (*LW*, 23–4).

[113] *BT, Pen20*, 220; *Pen20Tr*, 116; *RBH*, 260–1. J. G. Edwards, in *LW*, liii, n. 2, took *Y Pasg Bychan* to be Palm Sunday, attributing Llywelyn's coming to Dolforwyn to 25 March; Powicke, *Henry III*, ii, 641, n. 2, took it to be Pentecost, giving 20 May, but the lawbooks (*LlIor*, 40; *LHD*, 76; *LlCol*, 8) leave no doubt that *Y Pasg Bychan* (Low Easter, that is Low Sunday), fell a week after Easter. In 1274 it was on 8 April, a date consistent with the completion of the proceedings at Dolforwyn 17–18 April.

[114] *LW*, 77–80, 108–10; for the form of proceedings, Powicke, *Henry III*, ii, 642, n. 3.

Teirswydd (Deuddwr, Ystrad Marchell and Llannerch Hudol), Caereinion, Mawddwy, Mochnant Uwch Rhaeadr and part of Cyfeiliog. This meant, as the chronicler noticed, that he was forced to yield possession of Arwystli, the remainder of Cyfeiliog, and the townships between the Rhiw and the Helyg, lands which would later be the subject of prolonged litigation. Llywelyn also appears to have wrested Gorddwr from him at this time.[115] Gruffudd retained the greater part of his inheritance, but he was able to do so only by the prince's grace and under conditions defined in sufficient detail to ensure that, if he were ever again to falter in his allegiance to the prince, he would forfeit his entire inheritance in perpetuity. Owain, who would have married Dafydd's daughter and gained lordship over Ceri and Cydewain had the plot not been foiled, became a hostage in Llywelyn's hands. For further security Llywelyn took the homage of twenty-five men of the lands granted to Gruffudd and ensured that they swore to be faithful to the prince, and relinquish their homage to Gruffudd, if he were ever to break faith again. On the following day Gruffudd and Owain executed a document, witnessed by the magnates present, whereby they solemnly agreed that their lands should fall entirely to the prince if Owain were ever to seek to escape from the prince's custody, and they placed themselves under the ecclesiastical sanction of the four bishops of Wales.[116]

In the much changed political situation of a few years later Gruffudd maintained that, though he was without blame, the prince had deprived him of fourteen vills, driven him into exile and seized his eldest son.[117] But in the spring of 1274 he acknowledged his guilt in respect of the charges brought against him at that time. The conditions imposed upon him were stringent. Yet Llywelyn came away from Dolforwyn leaving the greater part of Powys Wenwynwyn in the possession of its lord, and the manner in which the prince dealt with the

---

[115] *BT, Pen20,* 220; *Pen20Tr,* 116; *RBH,* 260–1. Lands noted in document and chronicle, taken together, correspond to those for which Gruffudd did homage in 1263 (*LW,* 78). For Gorddwr, *CPR, 1272–81,* 374.

[116] *LW,* 98–9 (18 April 1274); in this case the authority of the bishops of St David's and Llandaff, as well as those of the northern dioceses, could be called upon.

[117] *CAC,* 79, an undated letter to Edward, attributed to 1274–8. It is evidently related to the litigation in which Gruffudd ap Gwenwynwyn asserted that Llywelyn had taken Arwystli, the land between Powys and Meirionnydd and the castle of Welshpool, and that he had been captured at Machynlleth and imprisoned; the prince had extracted from him a written agreement and inflicted other wrongs upon him ('quoddam scriptum convencionale inter eos confectum ab eo abstulit et alia enormia ei intulit', *WAR,* 241). J. C. Davies, in *WAR,* 130–1, n. 1, takes this document to be the agreement of 1263 (*LW,* 77–80), but J. G. Edwards, in *LW,* 99, using the text in *B,* 8 (1935–7), 250, correctly takes it to be that of 18 April 1274; for the plea, below, p. 472.

A Principality in Perplexity

matter at this stage is not easy to comprehend.[118] He may have held back from the possible consequences of more forceful action, but it is also conceivable that he had not yet fathomed the enormity of the conspiracy against him. When Maredudd ap Rhys Gryg was found guilty of infidelity in 1259 he had been entirely expropriated and imprisoned, and the fact that Gruffudd ap Gwenwynwyn was allowed to escape comparatively lightly in the spring of 1274 may indeed mean that Llywelyn did not appreciate the extent of the treachery and that all was not revealed for some months. There is some uncertainty, too, with regard to Dafydd ap Gruffudd's share in the conspiracy, and what knowledge Llywelyn might have had of it. Although, as we shall see, Llywelyn was aware of Dafydd's disaffection early in 1274, the surviving evidence suggests that it was only late in the year that Dafydd was confronted with action on the prince's part when he was summoned to Rhuddlan to answer charges made against him. Another day was given him to appear at Llanfor in Penllyn, and the fact that Dafydd was not kept in custody makes it highly doubtful whether Llywelyn, even at this stage, knew the whole truth about the treachery which, as it seems, had been hatched at the beginning of the year. Dafydd, knowing full well what the purpose of the conspirators had been, fled to England along with a following of armed men. It is possible that it was only then that all was revealed when Owain ap Gruffudd, of his own volition according to the surviving record, but perhaps under the persuasion of those who kept him in captivity if not in fear of his life, made a full confession to the bishop of Bangor.[119] This would seem to be the interpretation suggested by the surviving evidence, unless Llywelyn had indeed appreciated the threat to his person from the beginning but had chosen not to reveal the full extent of the treachery lest his opponents be given reason to believe that his position in the principality of Wales had been perilously undermined. It would be understandable that, on the eve of Edward's return to the kingdom, Llywelyn would wish to maintain an

---

[118] Llywelyn may have proceeded to Clun before leaving the area. Hywel ap Meurig, a servant of Mortimer, was aware that Llywelyn was expected in Cydewain 'to see his new castle'. He was well-informed on the expected length of the prince's stay and the provisioning, and understood that he would proceed to Clun to decide on the site of a new castle. Hywel also conveyed a rumour that Llywelyn would meet some of the great men of England, though he did not know whether this was for good or evil (*CAC*, 49, dated 'possibly March 1274', but in view of the correct dating of Low Easter it is more likely to have been early April). The meeting with the magnates is possibly that of early May already noticed. Hywel ap Meurig conveys nothing to indicate any awareness of the grave matters which were considered at Dolforwyn, but the watchfulness over Llywelyn's movements and his wish that Mortimer be informed is interesting. It is possible that Mortimer and the royal administration knew, at a very early date, exactly what was done at Dolforwyn.

[119] *LW*, 136–8 (15 April 1276). J. G. Edwards, in *LW*, lii–lv, in a careful examination of the evidence, took the view that up to the time of Dafydd's flight 'it was unlikely that Llywelyn can have known the full extent of the conspiracy'. This would appear to be a reasonable conclusion, though the possibility of concealment of the full extent of the conspiracy for political reasons should not be discounted.

impression of a prince in full command of his dominion. The evidence that survives admittedly suggests the more straightforward explanation that only towards the end of the year were the full facts revealed.

These sources still need to be used with some circumspection, not least in relation to the later stages of the prince's dealings with the conspirators. The dean's letter relates that late in 1274 the prince sent five of his men to Gruffudd ap Gwenwynwyn in the hope that he could be persuaded amicably to reconcile himself to Llywelyn either by removing all suspicion of treachery or by submission to the prince's will. The envoys were courteously received but, having placed his visitors under lock and key and raised the banner of war on the tower of Welshpool castle, Gruffudd fled by night and joined those who opposed the prince. Llywelyn made one further attempt to recall his vassal, but to no avail.[120] Gruffudd took residence in the town of Shrewsbury while Llywelyn, *Brut y Tywysogyon* avers, gathered the princes of all Wales to lay siege to the defector's castle. It was taken and burned and the prince took possession of his territory without opposition and placed it under his own officers. Whether that was the whole and unexceptional truth is impossible to judge, for another annalist, recording that Gruffudd fled to Edward's protection on account of persecution by the men of Gwynedd, may at least reflect a variant contemporary impression of the concluding stages of the remarkable events of 1274. It is pertinent to notice, too, that it was at this critical stage in his dealings with Gruffudd and Dafydd that arrangements were being made for Llywelyn's meeting with the king at Shrewsbury. If, as seems possible, it was only then that the true nature of the conspiracy was revealed and if, as is very likely, Edward was now fully aware of the extent of the prince's difficulties, a reluctance on the part of the king to take the homage of a feudatory whose power might be crumbling is readily understood.[121]

---

[120] *LW*, 136–8.

[121] *BT, Pen20*, 220–1; *Pen20Tr*, 116–17; *RBH*, 260–3. *AC*, 102 records that Gruffudd fled 'on account of the persecution of the North Welsh' (*propter persecutionem Northwalensium*). *BT* attributes the dispatch of the messengers to a date 'about the feast of Andrew the Apostle' (30 November). Stephenson, 'The politics of Powys Wenwynwyn', *CMCS*, 7 (1984), 39–61, quotes a document from 'Llyfr Coch Asaph' (NLW, Peniarth MS 231B) which appears to indicate that Madog ap Gruffudd was engaged on an expedition completed by 15 November, and makes the valuable suggestion that this was an action against Gruffudd ap Gwenwynwyn undertaken a good two weeks earlier than the date on which Llywelyn's envoys are said to have been sent to Welshpool castle. This might cast doubt on the accounts given in the dean of Bangor's letter and *BT* in so far as they relate to the last phase of Llywelyn's dealings with Gruffudd. It is less clear that the document in 'Llyfr Coch Asaph' provides sufficient grounds for a reconsideration of the whole matter of Llywelyn's dealings with Gruffudd or that the prince had been preparing from the spring of 1274 for Gruffudd's expulsion. We are left, even so, with a teasing possibility that broader political considerations, already intimated, may have influenced the manner in which Llywelyn treated the conspirators in the spring. Furthermore, if Llywelyn was engaged with Gruffudd by about 15 November, the king's decision on 22 November to postpone their meeting becomes even more intriguing.

A Principality in Perplexity

Whatever the truth of the matter, there is no doubt that before the year was out Edward I authorized the sheriff of Shropshire to allow Gruffudd ap Gwenwynwyn to live in peace in Shrewsbury.[122] But it soon became clear that neither Gruffudd ap Gwenwynwyn nor Dafydd ap Gruffudd had any intention to live in peace with the prince of Wales.

Dafydd ap Gruffudd's motives for treachery in 1274 are as difficult to comprehend as those which brought him to desert his brother in 1263 or venture into rebellion in 1282. After Bryn Derwin Llywelyn had placed some trust in him, and Dafydd had taken a position in the principality second only to that of Llywelyn himself. He then seceded, and the disaffection which he felt by 1274 may well have had its origins in the period preceding that first secession. Dafydd may never have been content with a provision which, 'specially ordained' though it might have been in 1267, brought him no certainty of any improvement upon the position in which he had found himself in the earlier period.[123] Under the arrangements made in 1267 Llywelyn had had to agree to restore to his brother the lands he had previously held, but it would be quite wrong to conclude that the provision embodied in the treaty of that year meant that Llywelyn had to accept the principle of partible succession.[124] Dafydd was given no more than an apanage in his brother's principality, and probably no more than he had possessed upon his defection. It is true that the treaty prescribed that fuller provision would be considered if Dafydd were not satisfied, and it was laid down that the arrangements should be made before the following Christmas. But there is no evidence that the brothers finalized any agreement before 1269 and, when the composition was eventually made, it gave Dafydd no more than he had possessed when he seceded to the king. Llywelyn received his brother into his fidelity once more and, undertaking not to imprison him, he gave him his protection and right of recourse to canon- and civil-law procedures.[125] The prince placed himself under the jurisdiction of the bishops of Bangor and St Asaph and accepted that the two prelates, or either of them, could declare him excommunicate if he failed to honour the agreement. The bishops, too, along with men acceptable to Llywelyn and Dafydd, were authorized to resolve any dispute which might arise between them. It was agreed further that the princes were free to seek papal approval of what had been agreed between them. The document provides striking testimony to the lack of trust which had characterized the brothers' relations hitherto, and further evidence suggests that new confidence between them was not readily established. The bishops were indeed called

[122] *CCR, 1272–79*, 142 (27 December 1274).
[123] Above, pp. 86–7, 111, 154, 180–1.
[124] J. B. Smith, 'Dynastic succession in medieval Wales', *B*, 33 (1986), 222–3.
[125] The text of the agreement from 'Llyfr Coch Asaph' (Peniarth MS 231B. 67–9) is dated at 'Abbereu' in 1269.

upon to exercise their power of arbitrament, and Llywelyn subsequently called on Pope Gregory X to confirm the 'interpretation and statement' which the bishops had provided in relation to matters, concerning lands and possessions, which the original agreement had left ambiguous.[126] The prince's envoy to the papal court was sent sometime before the midsummer of 1274, and Gregory's warranty, given on 18 August, proved helpful before the end of the year when Llywelyn sent the bishops a notable letter, carefully composed, explaining the course of action which he had taken with regard to the doings of Dafydd ap Gruffudd and Gruffudd ap Gwenwynwyn. Taking note of the bishops' mediation on behalf of the two vassals who had forfeited their fidelity to him, and enclosing a text of the pope's statement, Llywelyn insisted that he had adhered strictly to the terms of the agreement with Dafydd. His brother had brought tribulation upon himself by embarking upon such a desperate enterprise. He was equally confident in his justification of his handling of Gruffudd ap Gwenwynwyn, and he had made sure that the bishop of Bangor was present to hear what his son Owain had to reveal.[127] Llywelyn seems to have taken an exceedingly long time to get to the root of the matter, but by the end of 1274 he knew the whole truth and he was determined that the bishops should be informed of his side of the story in unequivocal terms.

It would be hazardous to venture an emphatic opinion as to whether Gruffudd ap Gwenwynwyn or Dafydd ap Gruffudd was the main instigator of the conspiracy of 1274. Several historians have tended to accept that Gruffudd was its main author, and this may have been the case.[128] He may well have harboured deep resentment against Llywelyn, and he may have been particularly incensed by the building of Dolforwyn in Cydewain, an enterprise on which the prince had embarked the previous year. That land was largely bounded by Gruffudd's lordship of Powys Wenwynwyn and he no doubt coveted the area for himself.[129] That apart, Llywelyn's determination to enhance his power in Cydewain would have been most unwelcome. Yet the evidence of the bishops' concern with Dafydd makes it possible to delve deeper into the significance of the conspiracy than would be the case if attention were concentrated on Gruffudd ap Gwenwynwyn.[130] Previous

---

[126] Gregory's reply, 18 August 1274 (*Foedera*, I, ii, 515, from SC/7/16/18).

[127] *LW*, 174–5 (20 December 1274).

[128] *HW*, ii, 748–9, describes Gruffudd's wife, Hawise Lestrange, and her son Owain as 'the moving spirits', but Gruffudd was party to the secret and their plan was 'to work on the jealousy of David', a view echoed in Powicke, *Henry III*, ii, 642; J. G. Edwards, in *LW*, liii–lv, ventures no opinion.

[129] Cydewain, as noticed already, would have come to Owain ap Gruffudd had Llywelyn been overthrown.

[130] R. Maud, 'David, the last prince of Wales', *THSC*, 1968, 51–2, argues that there is no certainty that Dafydd had any part in the conspiracy, a conclusion difficult to accept on the evidence put forward.

inclinations and affinities suggest that Gruffudd might be more readily envisaged as a seceder from the principality than as a pillar of an alternative regime under the power of Dafydd ap Gruffudd. No other person, in Powys or Deheubarth, enjoyed a territorial power equal to his, but Gruffudd would at best be a somewhat uneasy member of the community of a Welsh *principatus*. He had come to it late and in distinctly fortuitous circumstances. The ambivalences inevitably bred by the marginal location of his estates, and his associations with the English baronage, suggest that his natural tendency at a time of disenchantment would be to depart rather than to instigate rebellion.

With Dafydd, on the other hand, we have to comprehend matters which arose in the very heart of the principality and were of the essence of its existence. Admittedly, Dafydd had seceded in 1263 but, given Llywelyn's impregnable strength at that time, he could not conceivably have withstood his brother and he could give vent to his disaffection only by departing. Eleven years later he rose against Llywelyn with a view to replacing him, and there is every possibility that Dafydd was the true begetter of the conspiracy of 1274. It would be Dafydd who would be best able to assess the prospects for the overthrow of Llywelyn, and it was he who would have had most to gain from it. He might well have calculated that the circumstances were distinctly more propitious for rebellion than they had been about 1263. He would have been well aware of any sign of discontent in Gwynedd, and we have seen already that there is some evidence to suggest that, by the early 1270s, Llywelyn was placing heavy burdens upon the communities of his lordship at a time when they may well have been experiencing some economic difficulty.[131] Of course, these may be no more than indications of a community under pressure; resistance to Llywelyn's authority is an altogether different matter. It is not difficult, however, to envisage the perilous situation which might arise if Dafydd ap Gruffudd, moved by the personal grievance which he nurtured, were able to avail himself of a broad discontent engendered by oppressive governance on the part of his brother. Dafydd was certain of some support within Gwynedd; unless he, too, alienated those over whom he exercised lordship, he could expect a measure of fidelity, and we know that neither in 1263 nor in 1274 did he leave Gwynedd without an armed following.[132] He was assured of the nucleus of what could become a powerful movement. In the conditions which prevailed by the 1270s, a group of conspirators, bent on a challenge to Llywelyn's authority, might well have been convinced of their ability to succeed. The surviving evidence, *ex parte* though it may be, indicates that the conspirators sought nothing less than

[131] Above, pp. 255–67.
[132] *BT, RBH*, 254–5; *LW*, 136–8.

A Principality in Perplexity

Llywelyn's death. Associated with one another in the prince's service, spending time together, as they undoubtedly did in Glamorgan two winters earlier, they would have had ample opportunity to sense one another's inclinations and to establish their common interest in Llywelyn's removal. But, in all the conceivable circumstances which the evidence suggests, it is Dafydd ap Gruffudd who presents himself as the most obvious source of a conspiratorial initiative of this nature. How well-grounded his hope of success may have been is difficult to judge; the tenuous evidence allows no more than a surmise that there was a measure of discontent that might provide him with a possible source of support. But if evidence is scanty in this respect we have a rather better measure of the discontent felt by another of the prince's major tenants in Gwynedd, none other than one of the bishops who had arbitrated between Llywelyn and Dafydd. By the early months of 1274, if not before, the prince could regard Bishop Anian of St Asaph as an opponent not a whit less uncompromising than those who had conspired to kill him.[133]

Privilegiorum sedis suae vindex et assertor: Bishop Anian – Einion ab Ynyr of Nannau – established a reputation as a steadfast defender of the rights of his see, and in the course of his tenure of the episcopacy he found himself in conflict with both the prince of Wales and the king of England.[134] Elected to St Asaph in 1268, at a time when Llywelyn exercised lordship over much the greater part of the diocese, and almost certainly elevated with the prince's approval, Anian might seem to be a bishop with whom the ruler could establish good relations. During the early years of his episcopate he was found acting for Llywelyn and, along with the bishop of Bangor, was entrusted with matters of great responsibility with regard to relations between Llywelyn and

---

[133] For Bishop Anian's contentions with Llywelyn, R. C. Easterling, 'Anian of Nanneu', *JFlintHS*, 5 (1914–15), 9–30; T. Jones Pierce, 'Einion ab Ynyr (Anian II), bishop of St Asaph', *JFlintHS*, 17 (1957), 16–33; G. Williams, *Welsh Church*, 8–13; O. E. Jones, 'Llyfr Coch Asaph', II, 94–112.

[134] The phrase is from H. Wharton, *De Episcopis Londoniensis et Assavensis* (London, 1695), 330, inspired by the notice of Anian's death in 1293 in *BT, Pen20*, 229; *Pen20Tr*, 121. The chronicle refers to him as 'the Black Friar of Nannau'. Although some writers (e.g. J. E. Lloyd and T. Roberts, in *DWB*, 10–11, 680–1) have been wary of identifying him as a son of Ynyr ap Meurig, historical opinion tends to accept the testimony of Robert Vaughan (NLW, Peniarth MS. 287, ff. 385–6, 521) that he was a son of Ynyr ap Meurig and a brother of Ynyr Fychan, though he does not appear in the genealogies of the Nannau family (Bartrum, *WG*, i, 74). Vaughan's MS makes him a son of Gwerful, daughter of Madog ap Llywarch Goch; Madog was a brother of Tangwystl, grandmother of Llywelyn ap Gruffudd, and Anian and Llywelyn would thus have been second cousins. For Ynyr Fychan, *RC*, 230; K. Williams-Jones, in *MLSR*, lxxxv, lxxxviii. Anian's will (Canterbury Cathedral Archives, Dean and Chapter Sede Vacante Scrap Book, II, 187, calendared *ArchCamb*, 1919, 186–7; full text Chandler, 'Will in Medieval Wales', 212–14) includes a bequest to Brother Adam of Nannau, for whom, below, pp. 546, 554–5.

A Principality in Perplexity

Dafydd.[135] Anian probably realized from the beginning that the concordat between the brothers was fraught with problems, and that he might need to take decisions at variance with the wishes of Llywelyn. Disagreement between prince and bishop arose primarily, however, from a wide range of issues which concerned their respective jurisdictions and material interests. These have already been considered, but they are relevant to the present discussion as they constitute an important element among the complex problems which confronted Llywelyn in these years.[136] The charges levelled against the prince were calculated to establish that he acted in a manner contrary to the practice of his predecessors. There was probably some substance in the bishop's claims, and the experience of the period immediately preceding his consecration, when the temporalities of the bishopric were in the prince's hands, may have exacerbated resentment among the churchmen.[137] There is every indication that Llywelyn's exactions, as he strove to meet his heavy financial obligations, bore heavily upon the churchmen and the bishop's lay tenants, as they did upon his own men. An instruction which Llywelyn issued to the bailiffs of Perfeddwlad on 1 May 1269 would appear to have been drawn up in an attempt to resolve disagreements which had arisen within a year of Anian's election. It ordered his officers to respect the better customs (*consuetudines meliores*) hitherto observed between the predecessors of prince and bishop, but at the same time reserved for further enquiry what practices would be appropriate in lay fees. The bishop's prompt and pointed injunction that all customs (*consuetudines universas*) should be respected throughout his lordship and lay fees (*per totum dominium nostrum et feodum laycalem*) suggests very strongly that discord between prince and bishop was far from being resolved.[138] Llywelyn had little reason to hope that, as he put it, he would hear no more of this from the bishop. Nor was it altogether a matter of adhering or not adhering to established custom, for Anian was probably a good deal less tolerant than his predecessors had ever been of the traditional relationship between ecclesiastical and secular powers, and in this respect his natural combativeness may have been reinforced by some of the ordinances upon which the church of the province of Canterbury had recently agreed.[139] The

---

[135] E.g. *CAC*, 10–11; *LW*, 85; *CCR, 1272–79*, 506, and earlier discussion. Anian made his profession of obedience on 21 October 1268 and was consecrated by Archbishop Boniface on the same day (*Canterbury Professions*, no. 214: *Handbook of British Chronology*, 295).

[136] The issues are considered in detail, above, pp. 210–15.

[137] Wrongs inflicted by Llywelyn during the vacancy preceding Anian's appointment are recounted among the *gravamina* of 1276 (*Councils*, i, 512–13; Peniarth MS 231B. 98b–99a).

[138] *Councils*, i, 497–8; Peniarth MS 231B. 66b. Anian issued a text of Llywelyn's instruction to his bailiffs, dated Mold, 1 May 1269, in letters patent of his own dated at the same place in the same year.

[139] The testamentary jurisdiction of a bishop's court is one such matter; it was reflected in the constitutions of the London council over which Ottobuono presided in 1268 (*Synods and Councils*, I, ii, 764–5).

matters in dispute, varied and reflecting diverse influences, were publicly proclaimed in the autumn of 1274 when Anian, as has been noticed already, summoned a synod of churchmen and laymen of the diocese to assert the rights and liberties of the church of St Asaph. The resulting document, a precursor of the fuller statement which was to be drawn up two years later, reflected a set of complaints which had already been communicated to Canterbury and Rome.[140] They constituted the substance of a deep disagreement which could be counted among the serious problems to confront Llywelyn by the spring of 1274. It was on 17 March, shortly before Llywelyn set off for Dolforwyn to deal with Gruffudd ap Gwenwynwyn's treachery, that the abbots of seven Cistercian houses of the principality of Wales came together at Strata Florida to compose a notable letter addressed to Pope Gregory.[141] They were evidently moved to do so by Anian's communication to the pope, and possibly by the pope's reply. They implored the pope not to believe the charges that Bishop Anian had made against Llywelyn. No one from the Cistercian Order had ever made charges that the prince extorted procurations from the monasteries, and whoever had suggested this to the pope had most evidently spoken falsely. Strenuously denying the accusations, they affirmed that Llywelyn was by no means an oppressor of monasteries but that, to the contrary, in peace and war he had been a steadfast and distinguished defender of their Order, and every other Order, and of the churchmen of Wales.

The abbots' letter can hardly have been written entirely at the prince's behest and it probably reflects at least a degree of mutual interest. One of their number, the abbot of Valle Crucis, was himself involved in conflict with Anian over what the bishop, perhaps with good reason, regarded as the deleterious effect of the monastic appropriation of a number of churches in the diocese. Anian considered that parochial provision was entirely inadequate, and he could call upon the constitutions drawn up at the church council under Ottobuono's guidance to justify his concern.[142] Asserting a right of presentation, he appointed vicars to two of the appropriated churches at Llangollen and Wrexham. Upon the abbot's appeal to Rome, Pope Gregory appointed the abbot of the Premonstratensian house of Talyllychau as judge-delegate, and his arbitrament in favour of Valle Crucis prompted an appeal by Bishop Anian to the court of the province of Canterbury. Cited to appear at the provincial court, the abbot of Talyllychau refused to do so and, fortified by the support of Llywelyn ap Gruffudd, excommunicated Bishop Anian and

---

[140] *Councils*, ii, 502–3, 511–16; Peniarth MS 231B. 67a, 98b–99a.

[141] *Councils*, ii, 498–9; Peniarth MS 231B. 49b. The date suggests that Anian had appealed to Rome before the end of 1273.

[142] O. E. Jones, 'Llyfr Coch Asaph', II, 139–44, citing numerous references to appropriations in the text of the diocesan register; *Councils and Synods*, I, ii, 770–1.

A Principality in Perplexity

the vicars appointed to the churches in dispute.[143] The argument was protracted and when, in the summer of 1275, the abbot of Valle Crucis went to Rome to plead his cause, he secured financial support from a prince who could be assured that the abbot would be able to place the particular problems of his house in the context of the broader dispute between the bishop of St Asaph and himself.[144]

Madog of Valle Crucis may have proved a most useful emissary at a time of great need, and he may have remained at Rome for an extended period, but the substance of the complex issues confronting Llywelyn had evidently been conveyed to the papal court, and vigorously urged, during the previous year. Llywelyn's representatives elicited from Pope Gregory as many as three letters, all written on the same day, 18 August 1274, when the pope was attending the Council of Lyons. Writing to Llywelyn the pope conveyed his affirmation of the 'interpretation and declaration' which the bishops of Bangor and St Asaph had made of the prince's agreement with Dafydd.[145] The letter contains nothing to suggest that Llywelyn was dissatisfied with the bishops' action. He appears to have been concerned, rather, that the agreement and the bishops' subsequent action should be registered at the papal court, and his approach to Rome would appear to have been of a precautionary nature. He secured what he sought, namely papal endorsement of what had been agreed, along with a warning of the censure that would be incurred by whoever ventured to act in a manner contrary to the terms of the agreement. This could have implications for Llywelyn and Dafydd equally, but Llywelyn was evidently anxious to do everything which could possibly be done, save involving the crown of England, to ensure adherence to the concordat of 1269. There were other matters that concerned him, though their precise nature is not clear. He had evidently conveyed that, despite the danger to himself and his men occasioned by current conflict and division, they were summoned to receive justice in the court of Canterbury and were liable to be placed under excommunication and interdict. Whatever was involved, Gregory felt bound, in a second letter, to advise Robert Kilwardby, archbishop of Canterbury, who was himself present at the Council of Lyons, not to summon Llywelyn and his men to answer any charges anywhere except

---

[143] Peniarth MS 231B. 29–30, 49a, 71a, 81a–b. In several cases 'Llyfr Coch Asaph' provides only a summary reference and no full text survives.

[144] *LW*, 32; receipt for a loan of £20 by Llywelyn to the abbot and convent at a council at Abereiddon on 25 May 1275. Tudur, prior of the house, received a sum of £8 in August 'to expedite difficult negotiations concerning our house at the court of Rome', and another £12 in May 1276, when it is stated that the abbot, Madog, was engaged in negotiations at Rome; with the abbey seal in the abbot's possession at Rome the prior put his seal to the acknowledgement (*LW*, 33, 40). Cistercian journeys are noticed further, below, n. 157.

[145] *Councils*, i, 501–2; *Foedera*, I, ii, 515, from SC7/47/3.

A Principality in Perplexity

before the archbishop's commissioner in Wales.[146] He urged the archbishop, too, to exercise discretion before applying ecclesiastical censure in Wales. Gregory did not question the archbishop's jurisdiction, but his directive had potentially far-reaching implications for the efficacy of Canterbury's jurisdiction in the principality. It is likely that much more was involved than Llywelyn's part in the dispute between Anian and the abbot of Valle Crucis, and the pope's letter may have reflected a concern with some of the wider issues raised by Anian's complaints against the prince. This may not have been the pope's first communication to Llywelyn on this matter. At a later stage in their argument Anian referred to letters addressed by Gregory to Llywelyn on two occasions, when the prince was severely warned, under peril of ecclesiastical censure, to desist from actions which were contrary to the liberties of the church of St Asaph.[147] Anian may refer to documents of which there is now no record and Gregory's initial response to the troublous reports from Wales may conceivably have proved disconcerting to Llywelyn; the letter which the Cistercian abbots composed at Strata Florida may have itself been dictated by an urgent need to withstand the overtures which the prince's opponents had made to the court of Rome. Llywelyn, however, could take encouragement from Gregory's response to the representations he had been able to make by the summer of 1274. Gregory's understanding of his position, perhaps a fuller understanding than before, is reflected quite clearly in a third letter which he wrote at Lyons on 18 August. He strongly urged Edward I to adhere to the terms of the agreement made in 1267 under the mediation of Cardinal Ottobuono.[148] Llywelyn may have received, and no doubt deserved, a word of warning, but the letter to the king of England indicates the value to Llywelyn of a papal influence which served to fortify his position during those months of excruciating difficulty when he had need to withstand, on the one hand, the evil intrigues of those who planned to kill him and, on the other hand, the activities of the bishop who, albeit with a good measure of justice in his case, pressed his arguments with relentless vigour.

Pope Gregory's cautionary words from the Council of Lyons had little effect upon Anian. He proceeded to hold the synod where, in the autumn of 1274, his complaints against Llywelyn were given the first of two public promulgations. The matters embodied in the document reflected the difficulties that could arise in the relations between secular and church authorities. A number of comparable problems had been raised in the earlier dispute between Llywelyn and the bishop of Bangor and, while negotiations with Bishop Richard brought a degree of agreement, there were other issues still to be resolved with

[146] *Councils*, i, 500–1; *Foedera*, I, ii, 515, from SC7/16/24.
[147] *Councils*, i, 512; Peniarth MS 231B. 98b.
[148] SC7/47/3; the evidence entirely sustains the pertinent remarks in G. Williams, *Welsh Church*, 10–11, 31.

Richard's successor.[149] But if, in each diocese, there were problems of particular concern to the church authorities, the matters raised by the bishops were not, in every instance, altogether different from those which might be raised by a secular lord exposed to the prince's severe regime. And, of those tenants who held lands of Llywelyn in Gwynedd, the most conspicuous was Dafydd ap Gruffudd. It is not difficult to envisage that Anian and Dafydd found that they both endured something of the same rigour at the hands of the prince of Wales. What is known of Dafydd's concern for his position in Gwynedd might most obviously suggest dissatisfaction over the territorial extent of his lordship. But it is possible that Dafydd, like Anian, may also have been dissatisfied with the degree of jurisdiction allowed to him within the bounds of his territory and the extent to which the prince intervened in its administration. Llywelyn certainly considered that the bishop's rights and liberties were entirely derived from grants made by the prince's predecessors;[150] even more clearly Dafydd's position derived, not from any inherent right, but from the grants which Llywelyn had seen fit to make to him, first upon his adherence to the prince and then upon his return to the prince's allegiance following his defection. Bishop Anian, entrusted along with the bishop of Bangor with a solemn duty with regard to the agreement between the brothers, could not possibly have countenanced Dafydd's treacherous action in 1274. But both bishops, and perhaps Anian of St Asaph in particular, may have needed to be convinced of the truth of the matter, for they may have felt sympathy with the younger brother on the basis of some common experience. Certainly, Llywelyn took care to answer the bishops' criticism of his action with regard to Dafydd in a very carefully worded statement. He did so even though the bishop of Bangor had been present when Owain ap Gruffudd had made his crucial revelations.[151] The rigour of the prince's rule, imposed on laymen and churchmen, would have affected Dafydd and Anian alike, although we cannot be sure of the various elements in the concern felt by Anian, Dafydd and Gruffudd ap Gwenwynwyn. We can only visualize a convergence of resentments, harboured by men who could not all be brought to act together, perhaps, but who could appreciate the diverse problems which drove them to their various responses. Between them they placed Llywelyn in a position of extreme difficulty in 1274.

It was thus at a time of considerable stress in the principality of Wales that Llywelyn had received the king's summons to Shrewsbury to do homage. If he

---

[149] Later relations are considered below, pp. 480, 496.
[150] *Councils*, i, 504; Peniarth MS 231B. 61.
[151] *LW*, 174–5.

had failed to keep his appointment he would, no doubt, have had reason enough. Yet it was Edward who failed to keep to the arrangement.[152] In the circumstances, though there is nothing to suggest that Llywelyn had no intention of meeting the king, he may have been relieved that the encounter had been delayed, but this proved to be a fateful postponement. However fraught with difficulty Llywelyn's position proved to be in the summer and autumn of 1274, it would be unwise to assume that there was already an unbridgeable rift between Edward and Llywelyn. Even so, before the year was out, the two men who had conspired to put the prince to death had found refuge in England by the king's permission. The decision to allow them sanctuary in the king's realm made a fundamental difference to relations between king and prince. The escalation in the conflict in the march called for more purposeful measures than those to which the combatants had had recourse in the past, but these were not now the matters which the prince found the most perturbing.[153] The marchers remained a constant irritant, but now he was troubled more by the attacks made by Dafydd ap Gruffudd and Gruffudd ap Gwenwynwyn. Dafydd, pressing the king for support, asked for guidance as to how he could do most to damage Llywelyn.[154] The surviving evidence suggests that the prince's principal adversaries had no need to be told, and by the summer of 1275 the combatants were joined in strenuous conflict. This is made clear in a letter addressed to Edward from Abereiddon in May 1275, one of two important documents to emanate from a particularly important meeting of the prince's council, which indicates the main source of conflict at his time. Llywelyn told how the men of Gruffudd ap Gwenwynwyn had come from the safety of their retreat in Shropshire to attack Powys Wenwynwyn. They had come six times and audaciously sold the booty at the markets of Shrewsbury and Montgomery. One of the prince's men had been decapitated in public.[155] The account of these depredations was followed three days later by a letter, addressed to the archbishop of Canterbury, which provides the only surviving statement of the prince's response to the

---

[152] Above, n. 106.
[153] Letters in *CAC*, 11, 57, 60–1, reflect continuing conflict in frontier areas.
[154] *CAC*, 74; the letter is undated, but this communication may have brought Dafydd financial aid in January 1276 (*CCR, 1272–79*, 266). Dafydd had been attacking Llywelyn at an earlier date.
[155] *CAC*, 27–8 (22 May 1275); several of Llywelyn's letters are dated at the Cistercian granges of Cymer at Abereiddon and Dinas Teleri (*CAC*, 75, 85–7; *LW*, 44–5). They included Llywelyn's refutation of Bishop Anian's charges, the letter composed at Abereiddon in the parish of Llanfachreth, where it appears Bishop Anian was brought up, and only a short distance from Hengwrt, where Robert Vaughan was to transcribe the text of 'Llyfr Coch Asaph' and preserve a valuable record of the transactions in which Anian of Nannau was involved (D. L. Evans, 'Llyfr Coch Asaph', *NLWJ*, 5 (1945–6), 177–83; O. E. Jones, 'Llyfr Coch Asaph', I, ix–xiv).

complaints of Bishop Anian.[156] He emphatically refuted the charge that he denied the church its rights and privileges, or that he made exactions and procurations upon churchmen as he liked and without the bishop's consent. He most vigorously rejected the accusation that he had committed or tolerated acts of sacrilege. Llywelyn did no more than exercise those rights which, properly belonging to his dominion, the bishop had assumed to himself. These privileges belonged to himself and his ancestors, but he was willing to concede them if the bishop could produce charters, granted by the prince's ancestors, showing that the customs rightly belonged to the church. Anian had evidently proposed that the dispute should be submitted to the arbitration of Tudur ab Ednyfed and Einion ap Caradog, placing responsibility for the verdict on two of the prince's close confidants, or that they allow the truth of the matter to be determined by impartial inquiry and abide by the findings. Llywelyn was in no doubt that whatever rights Anian claimed were derived from the prince's predecessors, and this was an assertion of profound significance. But he earnestly sought an agreement with the bishop and he appealed to the archbishop not to believe too readily all that Anian told him, for he was convinced that the bishop was determined to do all in his power to damage his reputation.

The letter may well have made some impression upon the archbishop, and it may have some bearing upon his handling of the Welsh crisis during the following year. Certainly, those who gathered at Abereiddon would have been deeply troubled by the moral damage no less than the physical harm inflicted upon the prince by those who, for whatever reason, stood opposed to him. Letters were thus addressed not only to Edward but to Archbishop Kilwardby, and it may well be that it was agreed to send a new embassy to the papal court and that the abbot of Valle Crucis should be entrusted to convey, along with his account of the matter which particularly troubled him, a full exposition of the critical situation now confronting the prince of Wales.[157] The position in which the prince now found himself was infinitely more serious than it had been only a year before. He now knew the whole extent of the conspiracy against him and the king's response; he had a full measure of the influence which Anian exerted upon Canterbury. The tension is clearly reflected in the

---

[156] *Councils*, i, 503–5; Peniarth MS 231B. 61. It is possible that Llywelyn also wrote to Edward concerning the dispute with Anian at this time; the king's undated reply is in *CAC*, 61.

[157] In July 1274 the abbot of Cymer had been assisted with the expense of a journey to Citeaux (*LW*, 33); this may well have been his destination and he may have travelled on matters concerning the Order. But it would not have been difficult to combine the journey to Citeaux with a visit to Lyons where Gregory then was. It is evident that someone had gone to the papal court on Llywelyn's behalf in the summer of 1274. The possible employment of Cistercian emissaries is relevant in view of the difficulty of communication with Rome which Llywelyn mentioned in a letter to Gregory in 1275 (*LW*, 116).

letters from Abereiddon. It was only a few weeks later, on 24 June 1275, that Edward formally summoned Llywelyn to fulfil the duty that he was bound to perform before the king could consider the matters which the prince was anxious to put before him. He was called to Chester by 22 August to do homage to the king and swear fealty, and thereby do that which he, like other vassals of the king, was required to do by reason of the king's royal status.[158]

It is in the situation that came to a head in the summer of 1275, more than any other, that Llywelyn's political judgement is most open to question. Whereas in 1282 war was brought upon him by the precipitate action of his brother and others over whom he had no authority, during the years leading up to the conflict of 1277 he had full charge of the destiny of the polity which was so much the creation of his own vision and determination. The view that, in these years, he 'just fumbled his way to disaster' is not easy to set aside. The assessment offered by J. Goronwy Edwards turned largely on the prince's conduct in his relations with the king.[159] His relations with the barons of his principality in this period were grievously affected by the ruthless conspiracy against him on the part of two of their number, but it is difficult to judge whether his dealings with his barons at large were conducive to the retention of their confidence and loyalty. Moreover, while Llywelyn expressed a deep and sincere concern for the well-being of his people during the final stages of the ultimate struggle, and anxiety for their fate under alien rule, he none the less dragged them into the earlier conflict for reasons which had no bearing upon their needs. It was sad, and it stands as a severe judgement upon the creator of the principality of Wales, that so great and singular an achievement in the political history of the nation was put at risk by contention between king and prince over the fulfilment of the obligations of a feudal bond. The view of a prince overwhelmed by difficulty on several sides is one which recent historical study has served to emphasize, but it still leaves unanswered the question whether these very perplexities within the confines of his own dominion might reasonably have dictated a more accommodating position in his relations with Edward. His conduct in the period immediately preceding the outbreak of war is still to be examined, and they certainly indicate an earnest wish to seek a negotiated settlement, but much of the making of the conflict of 1277 belongs to the years already recounted. His predicament in the summer of 1275 and the course of action he took need to be noticed very carefully.

---

[158] *CCR, 1272–79*, 241. The king a little earlier (20 June) ordered Bogo de Knovill, sheriff of Shropshire, to be cautious and prudent in his relations with Llywelyn, but to make no amends for trespasses until Llywelyn had made satisfaction for damages (ibid.). Llywelyn was summoned for 22 August, but Edward gives the date as 26 August in a reference to this writ in 1276 (ibid., 359). Edward came to Macclesfield by 24 August and to Chester by 1 September.

[159] *LW*, lx–lxi.

A Principality in Perplexity

Llywelyn faced a clear choice between fulfilling his obligation to his lord and refusing to do so. He tarried a while and then made a decision not to be reversed until he was eventually forced to submit to the king and witness the utter destruction of the political edifice upon which he had set heart and mind in the years of endeavour and triumph. He made his decision in consultation with the men who formed the political community of the principality of Wales. *Brut y Tywysogyon* records that he called all the barons of Wales to him and by common counsel Llywelyn did not go to the king because the king harboured his fugitives, namely Dafydd ap Gruffudd and Gruffudd ap Gwenwynwyn.[160]

Viewed over the distance of several centuries the narrative of events which led to Llywelyn's humiliation reads like the saga of a man who laboured under an inexorable fate. In the years immediately following the formal recognition of his position in Wales he undoubtedly acted in a manner certain to incur enmity on the part of the marchers, and thereafter his problems accumulated on all sides. It is not easy to identify occasions when, by his own will, he might have stayed the drift to war, and it is difficult to distinguish the factors which contributed most to his downfall. Neither the death of Henry III nor Edward's return to the kingdom proved to be a single turning point. The conflict in the march, however much it protrudes in the historical evidence, was in itself hardly enough to create a conclusive rift between king and prince. The embers of old marcher animosities might flare up and subside again to eternity without bringing the two nations to war. If we seek a single catalyst we find it, not in any change in the government of the realm nor in any particular conflict in the march, but in the crisis created by what presents itself in the surviving record as the unfaithfulness of Dafydd ap Gruffudd and Gruffudd ap Gwenwynwyn. For though this was a matter which belonged to the internal affairs of the principality, it could not possibly be contained within its bounds. Nothing in the entire history of Wales provides a clearer instance of the inherent difficulty which confronted those who sought to insulate Welsh political affairs and resolve their problems in isolation from the king of England. It was this internal crisis which drew the other threads together in an intricate entanglement that Llywelyn was never to unravel. If he be judged to have failed his nation when he refused to do homage to Edward, it has to be acknowledged that, of the five summonses to do homage which came to hand, it was the one which summoned him to Chester by the month of August 1275 which was the crucial call. He made his decision in response to this summons after he had realized the true nature of the

---

[160] *BT, Pen20*, 222; *Pen20Tr*, 117; *RBH*, 262–3.

A Principality in Perplexity

conspiracy against him and when he had seen the frustrated conspirators use their sanctuary in England to damage him to the utmost of their ability. He was summoned three more times – to London by October 1275, to Winchester by January 1276, and to London by April 1276 – but Edward cannot have had any realistic expectation that Llywelyn would respond to any of these calls. They may indicate no more than Edward's wish to thicken the dossier on Llywelyn's contumacy in anticipation of a final judgement.[161]

By the late summer of 1275 Llywelyn had made his stand on principle, and he had made the most important statements of the reasons for his intransigence. There are two letters. The letter which he now sent Pope Gregory concentrated on the internal problems of the principality of Wales and Edward's reaction to the events which stemmed from them.[162] He mentions no marcher baron by name – no word of Clare or Bohun or Mortimer – nor is there any reference to the recurrent conflicts which had caused him to send his envoys to the ford of Montgomery or to London time and time again. It may be unreasonable to expect a letter to the Pope to contain a wholly comprehensive list of his grievances, but he could be expected to convey the essence of the matter. By now the essential issue was his disagreement with the king, a matter which sprang from Edward's decision to provide security and support for those of his vassals who had proved unfaithful. He conveyed his fears for his own safety, summoned to a place to which it was unsafe for him to go, among men who had plotted his death. These were men, he wrote in a second letter which conveyed the essentials of his case to the archbishops of Canterbury and York and the bishops of England, who shared the king's table and joined him in his council.[163] As an earnest of his sincerity he offered to swear fealty to the king in the presence of royal emissaries, leaving us to wonder whether he had a momentary regret that he had failed to go to the ford of Montgomery to meet those two monks on the appointed day at the beginning of 1273.

We are left to conjecture, too, whether the message which Llywelyn conveyed to the king, while he was expecting him at Chester in the summer of 1275, was phrased in entirely uncompromising terms. This is the impression conveyed by *Brut y Tywysogyon*, and it would be easy to visualize a prince, with the accord of his council, valorously defying the king from the fastnesses

---

[161] The successive summonses are noted by J. G. Edwards, in *LW*, lvi and below, n. 165.
[162] J. G. Edwards in *LW*, lvii–lviii, 114–16.
[163] This letter is dated at Tal-y-bont 6 October 1275. There are texts in NLW MSS, 13211, ff. 8–9; 13215, ff. 303–5, and an English translation in D. Powel, *The Historie of Cambria* (London, 1584, repr. Amsterdam and New York, 1969), 329–33; Warrington, *History of Wales*, ii, 569–71. It was addressed to the archbishops of Canterbury and York 'gathered in council in London'; there does not appear to be any other reference to an ecclesiastical council at this time, but parliament had been summoned for 13 October and it may have been to this occasion, when the prelates would be gathered together, that the letter refers.

A Principality in Perplexity

of Snowdonia. At variance with this view, we know that he sent Edward certain 'explanations' (*excusaciones*) while the king was at Chester, an indication that he was at least maintaining diplomatic contact with his lord during those critical days.[164] It is particularly instructive, too, to notice the place from which his letter to Pope Gregory was dispatched and the date on which it was given. Edward stayed at Chester and its environs until 11 September, when he left the city on his journey to London.[165] It was on that very day that Llywelyn dated his letter to Gregory, and he did so, not in the heart of his principality but at Treuddyn, on its furthermost border and within twelve miles of the city where Edward had been awaiting him.[166] Two weeks earlier he had been at Sychdyn, near Ewloe, again close by the frontier with the earldom of Chester, where he referred, in a letter to the bishop of Hereford, to the difficult negotiations in which he was engaged.[167] The letter written from Treuddyn was hardly the work of distant defiance, rather the composition of one who had earnestly hoped that Edward would have had the grace to traverse those few miles to the frontier between his kingdom and the principality of Wales. At no great distance from Treuddyn was Gresford, where it had been intended that they should meet during that hopeful summer before Edward left the realm, a place which, like the ford of Montgomery, had been a meeting-place for the envoys of king and prince on several occasions.[168] The impression of a prince hovering on the frontier gives us an entirely different conception of this decisive moment in Llywelyn's life. The *Brut* notes that Edward returned enraged to England and that Llywelyn returned to Wales, a remark which is more meaningful if we realize that the two men had gone almost to the borders of their territories. But they failed to meet, and thereafter the distance between them widened more and more.

---

[164] *CCR, 1272–79*, 359–61; *Foedera*, I, ii, 535–6.

[165] *CPR, 1272–81*, 104–5; on 10 September Edward sent Llywelyn a letter summoning him to London by 20 October and he set out upon his return journey on the following day, doing so 'in rage' (*BT*) and on account of the *contemptum* shown by the prince (*AnnCestr*, 102). There would be further summonses to Winchester by 10 January 1276, and to London by 26 April 1276 (*CCR, 1272–79*, 325; *Foedera*, I, ii, 535); the circumstances surrounding these further summonses are considered later.

[166] *Foedera*, I, ii, 528, gives the form as 'Treschyn', corrected to 'Trefchyn' in *LW*, 116; reference to 'Liber A' shows that it is equally possible to read 'Trefthyn', and there can be no doubt that the letter was dated at Treuddyn.

[167] *Registrum Thome de Cantilupo*, 9. Llywelyn promised to attend to the matter which concerned the bishop, the prince's occupation of three manors at Teirtref Esgob in the neighbourhood of Montgomery, by making an inquiry as soon as he had completed the difficult negotiations in which he was engaged (*expeditis arduis negociis quibus ad presens occupamur*).

[168] Edward refers, May 1275, to his going 'to the march' to receive Llywelyn's homage (*CAC*, 58); he was later to refer to his going 'to the furthermost frontiers of his kingdom' (below, p. 402).

A Principality in Perplexity

By now Llywelyn's solicitude for his status and for his personal safety were joined, and he would yield nothing on this two-fold concern. But, from the beginning, he appreciated the implications of his stand. Writing from Treuddyn, he conveyed that he foresaw a new conflict between the Welsh and English nations and a shattering of the peace that he had laboured so hard to secure. He recalled that the peace between Wales and England had been secured under the auspices of Pope Clement and by the mediation of Cardinal Ottobuono. In addressing the pope's successor, Gregory, he appealed to one who, as Tedaldo Visconti, had served Ottobuono during his period as papal legate in England. If he had been engaged in the kingdom at the time, Gregory could conceivably have been at the ford of Montgomery when Llywelyn did homage to Henry, and there can be no doubt that the person who now presided at the Holy See showed a remarkable perceptiveness in dealing with the matters which Llywelyn placed before him.[169] The prince of Wales was never in greater need of a sympathetic hearing at Rome than he was to be by the end of 1275 when news was broken of an enterprise which had been in the making for some time, and which, though never mentioned, may have been a matter of considerable relevance during the summer of that year. It arose from an initiative on Llywelyn's part which sprang from the deeply hurtful experience of realizing the true nature of the conspiracy against him. When Llywelyn next wrote to Rome, Gregory was dead, the first of four of the Vicars of Christ to die in the space of eighteen months. So it fell on others than Gregory to try to unravel the complex web in which the threads of the internal tribulations of the principality of Wales became intertwined with those which, drawn from the internal dissensions of the realm of England in the previous reign, had spread to the continent to trouble Edward on the long journey through Christendom and beyond. The new threat, necessarily left unmentioned in his letter to Gregory, was Llywelyn's decision to marry Eleanor de Montfort.

---

[169] For Tedaldo Visconti in England, L. Gatto, *Il Pontificato di Gregorio X, 1271–1276* (Rome, 1959), 44–6; for Pope Gregory, Powicke, *Henry III*, ii, 586 *et passim*; S. Runciman, *The Sicilian Vespers* (Cambridge, 1958), 148–70.

CHAPTER 8

Aberconwy

LYWELYN'S decision to marry Simon de Montfort's daughter was revealed in dramatic circumstances at the end of 1275. Eleanor was travelling from France to join the prince when she was detained at sea and taken into Edward's custody. She sailed in the company of her brother Amaury, and the king was jubilant at a capture which placed Montfort's son and daughter in his hands and revealed, hidden beneath the ship's boards, the arms and banner of the Montforts.[1] Edward had found evidence which entirely justified intervention in Wales, for Llywelyn's renewed involvement with the Montforts was a threat to the security of England. The fact that Llywelyn had failed to do homage and that he had not met his monetary obligations were matters of great concern, and Edward did not cease to make the most of these issues. But he would also urge his conviction that the prince's stratagem was calculated to revive the dissension which had rent the community of the realm in the troubled years of his father's reign. Though Edward, as we shall see, was anxious to stress that Eleanor's capture was entirely providential, there is much to suggest that her arrest on the high seas reflected the king's alertness to the activities of those of the Montfort progeny who were still at large in Europe. Neither the possible implications of Llywelyn's initiative, nor Edward's reaction can be properly understood unless account is taken of the doings of the Montforts who had been in dispersion since the civil war. The anger which this issue aroused in the king does much to explain the determination with which he proceeded to secure the supremacy formally registered when the prince of Wales submitted to his will at Aberconwy in the autumn of 1277.

Eleanor had spent the years since the civil war with her mother, the Countess Eleanor, in the seclusion of the Dominican nunnery at Montargis.[2]

---

[1] Chronicle accounts are noticed below.
[2] Bémont, *Montfort*, xxix–xxx, 41, 258–9. The two Eleanors are noticed in M. A. E. Green, *Lives of the Princesses of England* (London, 1849–55), ii, 148–69, 456–8; M. W. Labarge, *Simon de Montfort* (London, 1962), 259–73; Maddicott, *Montfort*, 38–44, 369–71.

390

The house was a Montfort foundation, and several members of the family had found their last resting-place within its precincts. But if the young Eleanor had been burdened by the memories which gathered about the tombstones of those of her ill-fated lineage, she would have found in her mother a spirited defender of her interests. Both mother and daughter might of late have been heartened, too, by the fact that, though the countess had seen only unrelenting anger on the part of her brother, Henry III, she had been given several indications of friendship on Edward's part. She may have been encouraged to believe that the bitterness of earlier years might gradually be assuaged. When Edward came to the environs of Paris in the summer of 1273 he conveyed his wish to set aside all rancour against the countess, and he received her into his peace and allowed her the income which accrued to her from her English estates.[3] This was a generous expression of his goodwill for, though the civil war had come to an end eight years before, it was only six months or so since Edward had sought to prosecute one of her sons for a beastly deed which might easily have aroused once more the enmities of the earlier conflict. The countess could hardly be held responsible for the actions of her sons; she may have known little enough about them, and Edward was not deterred from making a benevolent gesture to his elderly kinswoman. But, even so, during 1275, and probably before the countess's death in the spring of that year, the recent activities of her sons, Simon, Guy and Amaury, was very much on Edward's mind as he came to realize that the Montfort sanctuary at Montargis had been a meeting-place for a convergence of influences calculated to secure a new link between the lineage of Simon de Montfort and the principality of Wales. Edward's anxieties reflect the deep distress which he had felt following an earlier incident at Viterbo.

This was the foul murder of his cousin, Henry of Almain, by two sons of Montfort in the spring of 1271 when the crusaders were in southern Italy on their way to the Holy Land. Simon and Guy had both participated in the civil war alongside their father but, according to Edward's subsequent account, he had sent his cousin to intercede on his behalf and bring about a reconciliation with them. Edward was shocked to find that the brothers, in a sudden vengeful act, had struck his envoy dead in the precincts of the church of San

---

It has been suggested (e.g. *DNB*, xxxvii, 282), from Adam Marsh, *Monumenta Franciscana*, ed. J. S. Brewer and R. Howlett (RS, 1858–82), i, 293, that Eleanor was born at Kenilworth in 1252; Maddicott, *Montfort*, 43–4, suggests that the child born then was Richard and that Eleanor was probably born about 1258. According to *FloresHist*, ii, 16, she was an elegant young lady.

[3] SC1/7/91; text in Green, *Princesses of England*, ii, 456, a letter to Merton, 10 August 1273, at the instance of King Philip.

Silvestro at Viterbo.[4] He continued on his way, but he returned to Italy in 1273 determined that justice should be done for the murder. By then Simon was dead, but though he found it impossible to bring Guy before any secular court he was able to ensure that, following a process at Orvieto, he came under ecclesiastic censure. Despite the long delay since the act was committed, Edward made sure that it was denounced by Pope Gregory and the condemnation was duly made in decidedly forceful language.[5] Edward could do no more than leave Guy a discredited excommunicate, but he probably made a new resolve to be wary of the Montfort fraternity. He would maintain his surveillance not only over Guy de Montfort but Amaury de Montfort too. Amaury was in holy orders, he had taken no part in the conflict in England and could prove that he was nowhere near Viterbo when the murder was committed, but he had been prepared to put his intellectual ability and his training at the Schools of Padua at his brother's service during proceedings at Orvieto. He had vehemently argued his case until Pope Gregory had stayed his eloquence with firm words of his own.[6] Thereafter Edward would wish to make certain that Amaury should never set foot in England. But the king had travelled no further than Savoy when Amaury made an attempt to get into England in the company of Stephen Bersted, the exiled bishop of Chichester.[7] Amaury had chosen a worthy companion, a venerated figure who represented the virtues of the movement which had produced the Provisions of Oxford. Exiled by Ottobuono in the aftermath of the civil war, Bersted had subsequently been pardoned by Pope Gregory, and Edward was prepared to allow him to enter the kingdom. But it was one thing to allow a good churchman to return by the pope's permission; to allow him to take Simon de Montfort's son with him, and thereby conceivably threaten the security of the

---

[4] Bémont, *Montfort*, 265–7; Powicke, *Henry III*, ii, 606–9; idem, *Ways of Medieval Life and Thought* (London, 1949), 69–88; Maddicott, *Montfort*, 320–1. Evidence for Edward's sending of Henry upon a conciliatory errand is in Pope Gregory's recital of the case against Guy de Montfort in 1273 (*Foedera*, I, ii, 501–2). R. Studd, 'The marriage of Henry of Almain and Constance of Béarn', in P. R. Coss and S. D. Lloyd (eds.), *Thirteenth Century England*, 3 (Woodbridge, 1989), 161–79, enters a cautionary remark upon the propaganda value for Edward of this account of the killing, but notes the conciliatory efforts of Henry's father, Richard of Cornwall, on behalf of the Montforts after Evesham. The murder is often seen as an act of vengeance for Henry's desertion of Montfort but Dr Studd suggests, as another possible motive, the Montforts' resentment at Henry's intrusion into Gascony, where the family had long pursued territorial interests.

[5] *Registres des Papes: Gregoire X*, nos. 209–17, 220; *Foedera*, I, ii, 499–502. Edward and Gregory met at Orvieto 14 February 1273; Gregory issued his summons to Guy on 1 March and his denunciation a month later. For subsequent events, Powicke, *Henry III*, ii, 609–12.

[6] Bémont, *Montfort*, 260; idem, *Montfort* (1884), 365–7; *Registres des Papes: Gregoire X*, no. 218. Amaury is normally regarded as the fourth-born son; Maddicott, *Montfort*, 43, suggests he was the third son, older than Guy.

[7] *DNB*, ii, 371; Powicke, *Henry III*, ii, 459, n. 1, 469, 484, 528–9; Maddicott, *Montfort*, 265–6, 275, 279.

realm, was an altogether different matter. By the summer of 1273 the shores of England were being watched and ships were guarding the channel to ensure that Amaury de Montfort would not set foot in the kingdom. Amaury's movements on the continent were closely observed.[8] The king may not have been concerned with routine matters of government, or known anything of letters written in his name on issues such as the building of Dolforwyn, but there can be little doubt that the watch on the coasts was maintained at his express instructions.[9] He might be generous towards the elderly countess but he was determined that neither of her surviving sons – Amaury no more than Guy – would have any opportunity to interfere in the affairs of the realm of England.[10]

Among the chroniclers, Nicholas Trevet provides a particularly full account of the capture of Amaury and Eleanor at the end of 1275, and his interest may well reflect the part played by the Dominicans in the intriguing story which lies behind the event.[11] According to his narrative, the countess sent her daughter to Wales to marry Llywelyn, doing so in fulfilment of a promise made in her husband's lifetime, and entrusted the responsibility for her journey to her son Amaury. The countess had in fact died a full seven months before Eleanor sailed, but the chronicle's words deserve some notice.[12] Writing to Robert Kilwardby, archbishop of Canterbury, after the capture, Edward conveys that Eleanor had married Llywelyn 'by the advice of her relations and other of her friends', words which at least admit the possibility that the countess had a share in the negotiations over the marriage.[13] If this were so it would mean that Llywelyn had decided to marry Eleanor, and had put his preparations in hand, not later than the early months of 1275. A decision in the spring rather than the autumn would have

---

[8] The factual basis of the critical notice in *Chronica Maiorum*, 158–9, is confirmed in accounts of the constable of Dover 1272–4 (Taylor, *SCCB*, 249–56). Payments were made to two men who prepared a royal ship to guard the coast against the coming of the bishop and Amaury, to a crew who sailed to capture them, and to Richard Spaniel who went to Paris to keep watch on the movements of the two. The expenditure is authorized in the Liberate Roll for 1274–5, but neither source provides precise dates. The bishop's estates were taken into the king's custody 25 May 1273 (*CFR, 1272–1307*, 6) and a capture at a slightly earlier date is likely. Royal vigilance is noteworthy in view of matters discussed later.

[9] Above, pp. 360–1.

[10] In response to intercession by the king of France, Henry had set out in September 1267 the strict conditions on which Simon de Montfort the younger might return to England (*CR, 1264–68*, 387; *RL*, ii, 315).

[11] Trevet, *Annales*, 294.

[12] The countess died 13 April 1275 (*CFR, 1272–1307*, 44), a detail not available to Bémont, *Montfort*, 259; *HW*, ii, 756, n. 208. In June executors were allowed to attend to her affairs in England (*CCR, 1272–79*, 181), among them Nicholas de Waltham, for whom see below, n. 18.

[13] *LibEpist*, no. 85: 'per consilium parentum et aliorum amicorum suorum'.

an obvious meaning in the chronology of Anglo-Welsh relations, for Llywelyn would thus have decided to marry Simon de Montfort's daughter very soon after those who had tried to kill him had found refuge in England. The prince's action would demonstrate how deeply affected he had been both by the revelations of the latter part of 1274, the eventual unfolding of the plot to assassinate him, and by the king's readiness to provide a refuge for the conspirators.[14] This would mean, too, that Llywelyn had put the arrangements for the marriage in motion before he failed to respond to Edward's second call upon him to do homage, and this raises the question whether Edward, as he waited at Chester in the summer of 1275, already knew of the intrigues between Llywelyn and the Montforts. It is certain that he was keeping a close watch on Amaury de Montfort two years earlier, and he may have maintained his vigilance in the interval. There is every likelihood that Llywelyn, too, was under surveillance, for in his letter to Gregory he conveys that he did not find it easy to communicate with the papal court as the king was keeping watch on the seas.[15] It is thus possible that Edward, when he called upon Llywelyn to do homage at Chester, knew very well that something was afoot at Montargis. If he maintained vigilance on the coasts and the seas, the king would hardly have failed to ensure that he be told if detectably Welsh accents were heard in the environs of the Orléanais.

A new understanding between Llywelyn and the Montforts, of which the king may conceivably have been aware, may thus do much to explain the hardening of attitudes, on both sides, during the summer of 1275. Llywelyn's decision to marry Eleanor can probably be seen as part of his reaction to the flight of Dafydd ap Gruffudd and Gruffudd ap Gwenwynwyn to England and their reception by Edward I. Llywelyn had waited an exceedingly long time before he married. He had indicated his readiness to arrange a marriage with a lady of the royal family of England – a niece of the king – at an early date, and his agreements with Montfort in 1265 and with the king in 1267 both contained a clause which ensured the succession of the principality to his heirs. But it is still not altogether certain that his marriage to Eleanor was undertaken in fulfilment of an agreement with Montfort. Several chroniclers, Trevet among them, make specific statements that this was so.[16] It has been suggested already, however, that, in the precise circumstances in which the

---

[14] Above, pp. 371–4.
[15] *LW*, 116.
[16] Trevet, *Annales*, 294: 'sicut patre puellae vivente sub certis pactum conventum fuerat'; *AnnWinch*, 121; Rishanger, *Chronica*, 87. Bémont, *Montfort*, 260–1; Powicke, *Henry III*, ii, 647; Maddicott, *Montfort*, 325, accept that Eleanor had been 'betrothed' by her father to Llywelyn; *HW*, ii, 756, is circumspect: cf. above, pp. 165–8.

concordat of 1265 was made, it is more readily conceivable that Montfort had offered his daughter in marriage than that Llywelyn had accepted an offer. None the less, the fact that the agreement refers to 'the prince's heirs of his body' while the agreement of 1267 refers only to 'his heirs' might strengthen the supposition that the possibility of a marriage agreement had indeed been broached even if it had not been forged. But whatever had been agreed or contemplated in earlier years, Llywelyn finally decided to take a wife only at a very late date and in the immediate aftermath of a political crisis in which his very life had been imperilled. That he was deeply disturbed by what had occurred can hardly be questioned. His reaction, in turn, gave the king considerable cause for concern. In an early response to the news of Eleanor's capture Edward conveyed, along with his elation, his deep disquiet. What troubled him was not that Llywelyn had fulfilled a long-standing agreement with the Montforts but that the marriage was conceived as a means of creating new dissension in the realm. Writing to Robert Kilwardby he insisted that Eleanor was inspired by the belief that in the fullness of time she could, through the prince's power, spread the seed of malice which her father had conceived, something that she could not do on her own.[17] Deeply disturbed by Guy de Montfort's evil deed and suspecting that he had need to be wary of the manœuvres of Amaury de Montfort, he felt that the marriage with Llywelyn threatened the security of his kingdom. To what extent the theory of conspiracy in the realm was justified is impossible to tell. Later evidence alleged that Nicholas de Waltham, a canon of Lincoln who had acted as an executor of the will of the Countess Eleanor, had conspired with Guy de Montfort and Amaury de Montfort and Llywelyn ap Gruffudd. He had frequented the king's court and communicated information to those enemies of the king.[18] Edward certainly remained vigilant of the Montforts and, as we shall see, despite the vigorous efforts made by many on Amaury's behalf, he insisted that he should remain in prison. If Edward had left England generously inclined to conciliate the Montfort family, he had come home convinced that the remaining survivors of the brood could still prove damaging to him. In choosing to enter into marriage with this niece of Henry

---

[17] *LibEpist*, no. 85: 'quod de tali coniunctur a principi posset antiquum malicie seminarium quod pater suus conceperat, quod per se spargere non poterat . . . per huius principis potestatem'; there is a further reference to the evil of the Montforts in Edward's letters to Adrian, below n. 47.

[18] Allegations made before justices in eyre in Oxfordshire 1285 (*Oxford City Documents 1268–1665*, ed. J. E. T. Rogers (Oxford Historical Society, 1891), 204–5. Writing from Abereiddon, 10 October 1279, Eleanor states that Edward had not allowed Waltham to execute her mother's will (*Foedera*, I, ii, 576, from SC1/17/1, noticed briefly in *CAC*, 75).

III the prince made a decision with potentially profound implications for the future of his principality.[19]

By the beginning of 1276 Edward's suspicions had been entirely confirmed, but he did not wish to enlarge on his part in the outcome; he professed to attribute the capture on the high seas to the Will of God. With a touch of the phraseology he would use in the ordinances pronouncing the final annexation of Wales to the crown, he insisted that divine providence, which is infallible in its disposition, had unexpectedly placed Eleanor and her companions in his hands.[20] It can reasonably be suspected that it was not entirely by accident, nor under divine inspiration alone, that the sailors of Bristol captured the two ships near the Isles of Scilly, but that they were acting under Edward's instructions.[21] They were well rewarded for their work, and the messenger who brought the news without delay also earned his mead; more intriguing is the payment made to Thomas Larchdeacon for some commendable service done to the king, for this may substantiate a chronicler's statement that the Cornish knight had planned the capture.[22] Edward was still not at all sure that

---

[19] Contemporary interest is reflected in several chronicles. Guisborough later refers to the event as though it had been the main cause of the war of 1277 (Guisborough, *Chronicle*, 215). For historians' comment, Lloyd, *HW*, ii, 756–7; Bémont, *Montfort*, 260–1; Powicke, *Henry III*, ii, 647; J. G. Edwards, in *LW*, lx–lxi. J. E. Lloyd, 'Wales 1066–1485', *The Cambridge Medieval History*, 7 (Cambridge, 1932), 517, remarks that Llywelyn 'began by persistently refusing fealty and homage as though he hoped to revive the Barons' War and shake off finally the English overlordship, a scheme shadowed forth in his proposed marriage to Eleanor daughter of Earl Simon'.

[20] *LibEpist*, no. 85: 'divina prouidencia que in sua disposicione non fallitur' corresponds to the opening phrase in the preamble to the Statute of Wales (*Statutes of the Realm*, i, 55). Edward's letter to the pope, *TreatyR*, no. 134, has another reference to divine intervention, intimations reflected in chronicles (e.g. *FloresHist*, iii, 46).

[21] Edward states that the ships were captured 'on our seas' as they sailed 'near the prince's land' (*TreatyR*, no. 134). Bémont, *Montfort*, 260–1, says that they were captured 'not far from Bristol' and near the island of Sully on the coast of Glamorgan; cf. Powicke, *Henry III*, ii, 647. The task was done by ships of Bristol, and a capture 'near Bristol' is noted in *AnnWinch*, 121; *FloresHist*, iii, 46; continuation of Gervase of Canterbury, *Chronicles*, ii, 283. The majority of the chroniclers who comment in detail indicate a point near the Isles of Scilly and off the coast of Cornwall (Trevet, *Annales*, 294; Rishanger, *Chronica*, 87). Ships sailing from France would be more likely to set a course past the Isles of Scilly for the western promontories of Wales than enter the Bristol Channel, unless unfavourable winds had driven them off course, a possibility suggested by Edward (*TreatyR*, i, no. 134) and some chronicles, or if there were deception on the part of the sailors. There appears to be no support for the statement, *BT, Pen20*, 222; *Pen20Tr*, 117; *RBH*, 262–3, that the capture was made by merchants of Haverford (co. Pemb.).

[22] Payments *de dono nostro* of 220 marks to six named persons and the crews of four ships of Bristol (C62/52, mm. 3, 5; cf. *CPR, 1272–81*, 161). The money could have been paid in reward for a service done by accident, but it is indicated by Bartholemew Cotton (Cotton, *HistAng*, 153) that the capture was planned beforehand and that the sailors acted under the king's orders. *HW*, ii, 757, n. 211, quotes *Florentii Wigornensis Chronicon ex Chronicis*, ed. B. Thorpe (London, English Historical Society, 1848–9), 216, to the effect that Thomas the Archdeacon planned the capture; £20 was paid to him in May 1276 by the king's order, through the sheriff of Cornwall, for a particular task which he had undertaken in that area (*CCR, 1272–79*, 292).

he had quite fathomed the conspiracy. He told Kilwardby that Eleanor was accompanied by two Dominicans – two of the great men of Wales (*magnates Wallie*) – who were now in his custody.²³ The stratagem was said to be due to their ingenuity and, though the king was prepared to hand them over to the archbishop's keeping, he urged him to question them carefully and punish them. Apart from the two friars, the king was convinced that the marriage could not have been arranged without the connivance and counsel of many people and he was determined to get to the root of the matter. With the capture, and the telling evidence of the Montfort banner concealed in the ship, the king had cause for jubilation and the prince of Wales was dealt a cruel blow.²⁴

Llywelyn had come within an ace of fulfilling a purpose on which, whatever its origins, he appears to have set his mind during the period following the full revelation of the attempt on his life. To have brought Eleanor to Wales would have been a forceful retaliation upon the king who had given his protection to those who had conspired against him. His envoys had been able, almost to the last, to surmount the difficulties in the way of travel to and from the continent, and he had made sure that Eleanor de Montfort was his wedded wife before she left the safety of Montargis. *Brut y Tywysogyon* relates that the prince had taken Eleanor as his wife *trwy eiriau cynddrychol*, the expression 'by words of the present' reflecting, we may be sure, the use of the phrase *per verba de presenti* in the Latin original of the chronicle.²⁵ Pope John, in a letter to Edward I urging Eleanor's release, conveys Llywelyn's statement that he had taken Eleanor as his wife *per verba de presenti*, and implicitly acknowledges the completion of a consensual marriage.²⁶ Canon law fully endorsed a

---

²³ *LibEpist*, no. 85: 'duos fratres de ordine Predicatorum de maioribus parcium Wallie'; cf. Gervase of Canterbury, *Chronicles*, ii, 283–4; *ChronWykes*, 267; for captured French companions, *CPR, 1272–81*, 161–2.

²⁴ *TreatyR*, no. 134 (letter to Adrian, 8 August 1276): 'arma cum eis in navi predicta ad usum corporis sui, et vexilla cum insigniis armorum eiusdem patris sui'.

²⁵ *BT, Pen20*, 222: 'A'r Elenor hono a briodassei y tywyssawc drwy gynnyrcholyon eiryeu'; *RBH*, 262: 'A'r Elienor honno a gymerassei Lywelyn yn wreic priawt idaw trwy eireu kynndrychol'. The slightly variant phrases are translated 'through words uttered by proxy' (*Pen20Tr*, 117; *RBH*, 263), but this needs to be corrected. In citations in the files of *Geiriadur Prifysgol Cymru* 'cynddrychol' invariably means 'of the present'; a marriage 'trwy eiriau cynddrychol' was probably a term in frequent use.

²⁶ *Registres des Papes: Jean XXI*, no. 78: 'quam ipse dudum per verba de presenti sibi, prout asserit, disponsavit uxorem'. Calling upon Edward to set her free, the pope urged that her release would make physical union possible ('quod huiusmodi copula conjugalis fructum, auctore Domino, producere poterit'); the phraseology does not suggest that physical union was necessary for the completion of the marriage but rather that the pope endorsed a consensual union *per verba de presenti*.

marital bond made by the consent of the parties *per verba de presenti*.[27] The prince's consent would have been given by proxy, again in full conformity with the tenets of the church, and a marriage with Eleanor made by proxy (*per nuncios*) is indicated among some of the English chroniclers.[28] Others regard Eleanor at this time, not as the prince's wife but as his betrothed, her journey to Wales undertaken, as the Worcester annalist records, in order that she might marry the prince according to the practice of the church (*secundum formam ecclesie*), an intention duly fulfilled three years later upon her marriage at the cathedral church.[29] On that festive occasion Edward would give Eleanor in marriage to Llywelyn, his decision to do so a mark of his wish to establish that the marriage of his kinswoman was made with his consent.[30] He may have been loath to admit that Llywelyn and Eleanor were already man and wife at the time of her capture, but his letter to the archbishop indicates that, however reluctantly, he had accepted that a marriage had been made.[31] In chancery records Eleanor is sometimes described only as the daughter of Simon de Montfort or the king's kinswoman, sometimes the wife of Llywelyn, though it was only after the ceremony at Worcester that she became, in royal letters, princess of Wales.[32] But the prince of Wales had no doubts: it was his wedded wife, not his betrothed, whom Edward had

---

[27] Marriage *per verba de presenti*, expressing the parties' wish to create an indissoluble union with immediate effect, created a firm marriage bond; a declaration *per verba de futuro*, expressing a wish to create a union at a future date, had to be completed by sexual consummation: solemnization in church was not essential, nor priestly benediction: A. Esmein, *Le Mariage en droit canonique* (2nd edn., Paris, 1929–35), i, 119–24, 178–87; J. Dauvillier, *Le Mariage dans le droit classique de l'église* (Paris, 1933), 122–36; Pollock and Maitland, *History of English Law*, ii, 368–72; J. A. Brundage, *Law, Sex and Christian Society in Medieval Europe* (Chicago and London, 1987), 237, 262–8, 333–5, 351–5.

[28] Brundage, *Law*, 355, 436, 497–8. *AnnDunst*, 266; Cotton, *HistAng*, 153, refer to proctors (*nuncii*). For a marriage *per verba de presenti* contracted between Alfonso, son of Peter II of Aragon, and Isabella, daughter of Edward I, 1282, with Alfonso present and Isabella represented by her proctor, P. Chaplais, *English Medieval Diplomatic Practice*, part I, ii (London, 1982), no. 248.

[29] *AnnWorc*, 469–70 (1276): 'ut dictus Leulinus eam secundum formam ecclesie duceret in uxorem'; *AnnWinch*, 121: 'ut dicto Lewelino desponsaretur'.

[30] *BT* records the prince's marriage in 1276 and again in 1278 (*BT, Pen20*, 222–3, 226; *Pen20Tr*, 117, 119; *RBH*, 262–3, 266–9). Llywelyn later referred to an agreement made with Edward 'before mass on the day of his marriage' in 1278 (*in die desponsationis ante missam, RPeck*, ii, 443).

[31] *LibEpist*, no. 85: 'cum principe Wallie matrimonium contraxisse disposuit'. Writing 8 August 1276 Edward told the pope that Amaury was captured 'dum . . . predictam sororem suam de partibus Gallicanis ad principem duceret memoratum sibi matrimonialiter copulandum' (*TreatyR*, i, no. 134).

[32] E.g. *CWR*, 162–3, 170; *Foedera*, I, ii, 548–9, letters, 4 January 1278, which twice refer to Eleanor as the king's kinswoman, daughter of Simon de Montfort, but once adding that Llywelyn had married her (*quam ipse duxit in uxorem*). For Eleanor as princess of Wales, *CPR, 1272–81*, 306; *CPR, 1281–92*, 11; below, pp. 448–50, 503–4.

captured and kept in captivity. His wife's imprisonment was added to his list of grievances against the king.[33]

The circumstances in which the marriage was arranged reflect strong political compulsions. Nevertheless, in contracting a marriage the prince attended to fundamental dynastic needs which reached far beyond the present exigencies. He needed, not merely the means of raising the Montfort banner beside his own, but the heir without whom the future of the principality would be imperilled. Among his main lay adversaries there was hardly one who was denied an heir of his body: Edward, Dafydd ap Gruffudd, Roger Mortimer, Gruffudd ap Gwenwynwyn: each was blessed with a male heir.[34] No people was more conscious of lineage than his own, no princely lineage more aware of the link between dynastic succession and political stability. Why he had not looked to this fundamental need at an earlier date is one of the most puzzling questions posed by a study of his life. He finally did so in 1275 promptly upon a second desertion on the part of a younger brother who, while Llywelyn remained childless, would have been heir to the prince's inheritance and who may conceivably have been formally acknowledged to be so. An opportunity to bring Eleanor de Montfort from Montargis to Snowdonia would have brought him recompense for the wounding experience of the previous year when he had, as it seems, only slowly unravelled a plot which might have destroyed him while he was still without an heir of his body. Within so little of a triumph which would have given him cause for jubilation, his plans were thwarted.

Amaury de Montfort was detained briefly at Bristol and then taken to Corfe castle, to be held in what Edward described as private custody.[35] He could only regard it as strict captivity.[36] There he composed some writings which reflect his anguish at being, along with his sister, imprisoned upon suspicion and denied the opportunity to defend themselves.[37] He had to wait a

---

[33] He pleaded in 1276 for the release of 'his wife' (*CCR, 1272–79*, 360; *Foedera*, I, ii, 535).

[34] It should be remembered, even so, that Edward endured the death of his first-born son Henry in 1274, and he was to lose Alphonso in 1284; Dafydd's sons, Llywelyn and Owain, are noticed later.

[35] C62/52, mm. 3, 5; E372/121, m. 21, expenses for the custody of Amaury, Eleanor, two knights and others. Payments for Amaury and Eleanor were authorized from 21 January 1276 and for certain others from 25 January, but wages for two men employed at Bristol castle to guard the prisoners were paid from 1 January. It is thus possible that, as some chroniclers indicate, the ships were captured about Christmas 1275. Amaury was probably taken to Corfe on 1 February (E101/505/16; C62/52, mm.3, 5; /55, m.7). For the knights and others, *CPR, 1272–81*, 306.

[36] Letter to Adrian, 8 August 1276 (*TreatyR*, i, no. 135; *LibEpist*, no. 23).

[37] For Amaury's authorship of the treatise and confession in an autograph MS, Bodley MS Auct.D.4.13, ff.129–224, derived from his period at Corfe, L. E. Boyle, ' "*E cathena et carcare*", the imprisonment of Amaury de Montfort, 1276', in J. G. G. Alexander and M. T. Gibson (eds.), *Medieval Learning and Literature: Essays presented to Richard William Hunt*, (Oxford, 1976), 379–97; reprinted in L. E. Boyle, *Pastoral Care, Clerical Education and Canon Law, 1200–1400* (London, 1981), VII, 379–97.

long time for his freedom despite the fact that, as a clerk in holy orders and a papal chaplain, both the English clergy and the papacy interceded on his behalf. The bishops pressed that he be released into their custody, but Edward insisted that he would do so only if the churchmen were able to give sufficient security that no danger would come to the king or kingdom, or to the church itself.[38] Neither continued efforts on the part of the English church nor papal persuasions, first those of Adrian then of John, were enough to convince Edward that he could safely agree to Amaury's release.[39] It was only after the cessation of conflict between Edward and Llywelyn in 1277, when the king was reasonably satisfied that he had thwarted any intention on the part of the prince and the Montforts to foment dissension in the realm, that Amaury's lot was eased. Even then he was only released into the custody of the bishops.[40] In the period of better relations following the war pressure for a further measure of freedom was exerted from several quarters, Nicholas and then Martin indicating papal readiness to take responsibility for Amaury's conduct if he were allowed to leave England.[41] His sister, by then at liberty and united with the prince, wrote eloquent appeals on his behalf and Queen Margaret of France added her persuasions.[42] Llywelyn himself interceded on his behalf and sought the archbishop's permission to send a messenger to speak with Amaury.[43] Ironically, after vigorous intervention on the part of Archbishop Pecham and successive deliberations at church assemblies in the New Temple, it was only after new conflict had broken out in 1282 that Edward finally agreed to let his prisoner go.[44] The new Welsh war threatened to complicate

---

[38] *TreatyR*, no. 134; *LibEpist*, no. 23.

[39] *Registres des Papes: Jean XXI*, no. 79; *CPapL*, i, 452; *RPeck*, i, 297–8; *Councils and Synods*, II, ii, 823, from *AnnDunst*, 276.

[40] *CPR, 1272–81*, 253 (19 January 1278); *RPeck*, i, 231.

[41] *Registres des Papes: Nicholas III*, nos. 629–31; *Registres des Papes: Martin IV*, nos. 18, 19; *CPapL*, i, 461, 463; *Foedera*, I, ii, 577–8, 597–8; *LibEpist*, no. 523.

[42] *CAC*, 76; *Foedera*, I, ii, 587. Eleanor's letter, Ystumanner, 18 October, attributed to 1280 in *Foedera* and 1279–81 in *CAC*, would be 1279 if her appeal were written at the same time as her request that her mother's will be executed (*CAC*, 75; *Foedera*, I, ii, 576). This is likely as Queen Margaret of France, in one and the same letter, raises the issue of the will and conveys her hope that Edward would be merciful to Amaury, do him justice and receive him into his grace (*Lettres de rois, reines et autres personnages des cours de France et d'Angleterre tirées des archives de Londres par Brequigny*, ed. J. J. Champollion-Figeac (Paris, 1839–47), i, no. 198, from SC1/17, 127). The queen's letter, dated on a Monday after St Denis, was probably written 7 October 1279.

[43] In April 1280 Pecham, in a letter to Amaury's custodian, John of Somerset, indicated his agreement to a request from a servant of Llywelyn that he might speak to Amaury, but the archbishop was evidently concerned both about the danger involved and the attitude of the king; in August 1281 Pecham told Llywelyn that the pope had sent him a letter concerning Amaury's liberation. Llywelyn had evidently taken up Amaury's case with the archbishop (*RPeck*, i, 119, 137; *CPR, 1272–81*, 403).

[44] *RPeck*, i, 287–9; *Foedera*, I, ii, 601–2. Pecham wrote to Edward two days after a council of the province on 5 February 1282 (*Councils and Synods*, II, ii, 918–19).

the issue once more, and the king's anger towards Amaury had still not been assuaged nor his suspicions removed, but he was released on the strict condition that he should leave the kingdom and never return.[45] Amaury's long detention was a measure of the alarm, no less than the animosity, which was reflected in Edward's response to the train of events which culminated with the capture of the Montforts on their way to Wales.

In the period following the capture Edward was no more inclined to release Eleanor than her brother. The lady was transferred from Bristol to Windsor Castle, where she remained for nearly three years.[46] Eleanor was probably maintained in an honourable manner befitting a kinswoman of the king but her situation was, in her husband's view, none other than that of a prisoner. Llywelyn's decision to marry Eleanor became an important factor in Edward's endeavour to establish his rationale for intervention in Wales, his standpoint best revealed in two lengthy letters which he prepared to send to Pope Adrian during the summer following the capture.[47] Edward was well aware that he needed to provide a full exposition of his standpoint. Apart from the fact that Llywelyn's proctors were working assiduously at the papal court, Edward knew that in writing to Adrian he addressed one who, under the name of Ottobuono, had presided over the negotiations between the envoys of Henry and Llywelyn which had led to the historic treaty of peace in 1267. Adrian had intimate knowledge of the problems underlying the predicament in which king and prince were now placed; he knew the hopes sealed by a treaty that he had himself commended with such eloquent expression of his confidence in the prospect of lasting peace. The papal emissary had seen the transactions of 1267 as a means of bringing two peoples to peace; Edward, on the contrary, did not see his conflict with Llywelyn as a struggle between two political powers representing the interest of two distinct peoples. The prince was no more than one of the greatest among the other magnates of his kingdom – *unus de maioribus inter magnates alios regni nostri* – and the difficulties confronting the king in Wales were among internal problems of his kingdom to be resolved in accordance with his wishes. The new accord between Llywelyn and the Montforts had to be seen in this light. In forceful prose Edward recalled the turmoil which Simon de Montfort had created in

---

[45] A further council was held at the New Temple, 19–25 April; the archbishop refers to the new complications in a letter to Martin (*Councils and Synods,* II, ii, 921; *RPeck,* i, 325–7; *Foedera,* I, ii, 605). Amaury pledged that he would leave the kingdom and never return, and declared that he had never intended to stay in Wales nor impair the king's honour. He finally left 23 April, and repeated his oath never to return to the kingdom in the presence of papal emissaries at Arras, 6 May (*RPeck,* ii, 361–2; *Foedera,* I, ii, 607). For even later indications of Edward's wrath, provoked by continued truculence on Amaury's part as he sought the revocation of his father's excommunication, *TreatyR,* no. 144; *LibEpist,* no. 519.
[46] C62/52, mm.1, 3; 54, m.3; 56, m.3; C47/4/1, ff. 36v, 45v.
[47] *TreatyR,* nos. 134, 135, with draft of one letter in *CAC,* 64; *LibEpist,* no. 23.

the realm and the fact that Llywelyn had allied with him for purposes of war; he was convinced that if Eleanor were allowed to join Llywelyn some of Montfort's kinsmen outside the realm would seek to make common cause with allies within the realm and reopen old wounds. He referred specifically to Guy de Montfort and insisted that he would not release Amaury de Montfort – however much the church might bring pressure on him for the fact that his captive was in holy orders – unless he was completely assured that the realm would not be imperilled in any way. The link between Llywelyn and the Montforts was not the only point at issue, however. The prince's fidelity had been tried, and he had been found wanting. In precisely the same manner as the other lords of the realm were bound to do homage to the king, so Llywelyn had been summoned, as his vassal, to fulfil his duty of allegiance. To please Llywelyn, and in response to his explicit wish, the king had gone to Chester, to the furthermost frontiers of his kingdom, in expectation that the prince would come under safe-conduct to do his homage. Yet Llywelyn had not done so, nor had he responded to Archbishop Robert's subsequent intercession, but he had chosen to maintain his incorrigible stubbornness. Edward could not in all conscience endure his disobedience any longer; neither could he continue to ignore the entreaties of his people nor discount the bloodshed and the depredations which those who lived upon the frontiers endured day by day at the hands of Llywelyn's forces. The pope should not wonder if Edward were, at the appropriate time, to decide to apply his corrective hand according to justice and the decision of his court.

Llywelyn's formal condemnation was pronounced at an assembly of prelates and magnates in November 1276 and it would be still some months before the military campaign in Wales reached its height.[48] War might have been waged a good deal earlier, for it seems that Edward had intended to secure a declaration of Llywelyn's contumacy during the parliament held in May 1276. When Eleanor de Montfort had been captured Llywelyn had already received his fourth summons to do homage, a call to Winchester by 10 January 1276. Edward can hardly have expected him to be there, but the king was at Winchester on the appointed day and, when he was certain that Llywelyn did not intend to appear, he gave his final order to the prince to come and fulfil his services to the crown. He was called to Westminster by 26 April, and if he did not come the king would proceed to consider the matter at the parliament which would assemble soon afterwards.[49] Edward may at that stage have

---

[48] *CCR, 1272–79*, 359–60; *Foedera*, I, ii, 535–6.
[49] J. G. Edwards, in *LW*, lvi; payments to messengers carrying summonses to Llywelyn in *Cheshire Pipe Rolls*, 119. Parliament assembled on 3 May 1276.

contemplated a military campaign in the summer, in the mean time making an early start with preparatory movements in the marches. Even before parliament assembled in May, Llywelyn faced attacks on several fronts, not only in the eastern marches but on the borders of Deheubarth where Payn de Chaworth started campaigning in an area that had seen no major engagements since the prince's forces had registered those striking successes, notably the long remembered conflict at Cymerau, twenty years before.[50] Chaworth and his associates may have embarked on these initiatives in anticipation of an imminent declaration of war. It was clear to Llywelyn that storm clouds were gathering and, if he remained obdurate on the issue of homage, he did not neglect to set out his reasons for his unyielding stance.

Shortly before the final date given to him to do his homage the dean and chapter of Bangor sent Archbishop Robert Kilwardby their report on the conspiracy of 1274.[51] The timing was no accident, nor was it fortuitous that this communication was devoted entirely to an account of the conspiracy. No mention was made of the issue of homage, nor Eleanor's detention. It was evidently agreed that they should concentrate on a factual account of the matter which lay at the root of Llywelyn's decision that he would not do homage to the king and which, in all probability, explains his decision to marry Eleanor. The archbishop had already heard from Llywelyn during the previous autumn.[52] The prince evidently appreciated that he needed to continue to explain his position and, among much else, to withstand the pressure exerted by the bishop of St Asaph.[53] Early in 1276 he sent two Dominicans to seek the archbishop's mediation. Bearing letters from the prince, they asked specifically for the archbishop's intercession between the king and himself so that peace could be secured between them.[54] Himself a member of the Dominican Order, Archbishop Robert was no doubt furnished with one interpretation of the tribulations of the principality of Wales by the Dominican bishop of St Asaph and another by the friars of the same Order who came to him at Llywelyn's request. The division in the ranks of the Order of Preachers would have provided the archbishop with a measure of the problems now gathering. The Dominican envoys may well have returned to

---

[50] *CAC*, 86–7, 162–3.
[51] *LW*, 136–8 (18 April 1276).
[52] Letters from Abereiddon, May 1275, and Tal-y-bont, October (Councils, i, 503–5; Peniarth MS 231B, 61; NLW MSS 13211, ff. 8–9; 131215, ff. 303–5). For Kilwardby as archbishop, E. M. F. Sommer-Seckendorff, *Studies in the Life of Robert Kilwardby O.P.* (Rome, 1937), 67–129; W. A. Hinnebusch, *The Early English Friars Preachers* (Rome, 1951), 374–86 *et passim*; transactions with Llywelyn are noticed below.
[53] For the bishop's continued contact with Edward see e.g. his summons to Winchester by the date on which Llywelyn was expected to do homage (C62/52, m. 2; E372/120, m. 10r.).
[54] Kilwardby informed Edward, 9 March 1276, that Llywelyn, by the embassy of two Dominicans, had sought the archbishop's mediation (SC1/18/170; text in Sommer-Seckendorff, *Kilwardby*, 181).

Aberconwy

Llywelyn convinced that his case had need to be put still more strenuously than before. The report on the conspiracy of 1274 which the dean and chapter of Bangor addressed to the archbishop soon afterwards, with its clear intimation that he might be led to condemn the prince on the false testimony of the conspirators, may well have been prompted by what had transpired during his discussions with the friars.[55] Kilwardby may, however, have been sufficiently persuaded by the representations made on Llywelyn's behalf to urge the king to postpone the campaign and make one last attempt to secure peace. He won enough encouragement among prelates and magnates at the May parliament to induce the king to hold back from war, allow him to send his archdeacon to Llywelyn, and await an attempt at mediation.[56] The archbishop's envoy, William de Middleton, made his way to Llywelyn several times, but his mission was made more difficult, as the prince himself conveyed in letters to the archbishop, by the heightened conflict on the frontiers of the principality as the king's men and the marchers alike launched increasingly vigorous attacks. He insisted that he had commanded his men to exercise the utmost restraint and adduced evidence of the difficulties encountered by his officers in the march as they endeavoured to give effect to his wishes in areas such as Brecon, Elfael and Gwerthrynion. The peace to which he was still entirely committed, as he insisted, and the truces he had been able to make in some localities, were disturbed by the determined attacks of opponents bent on undermining the peace in Powys Fadog, in Deheubarth and in the marcher areas formally vested in his possession. Stressing again and again his earnest wish that peace be restored between the king and himself he called on Kilwardby, on whose efforts for peace he laid great store, to urge the king to compel the aggressors to desist from inflicting further damage.[57]

There can be no doubt that during the summer and autumn of 1276 the principality was placed under pressure over a wide front extending from Montgomery across the southern parts of Wales to Cardigan. Writing to the king directly, as well as to the archbishop, Llywelyn complained that lords of the march, men who preferred conflict to the peace of the realm, had penetrated his territory at several points and openly displayed the banners of war.[58] He named the most conspicuous among them: Roger Mortimer and Dafydd ap Gruffudd; Humphrey de Bohun and Gruffudd ap Gwenwynwyn. If the great lords of the march had for a while appeared less prominently in

---

[55] *LW*, 136–8 (18 April).

[56] *CCR, 1272–79*, 359–60; *Foedera*, I, ii, 535. For the emissary, Sommer-Seckendorff, *Kilwardby*, 116, n. 181; the termination of the negotiations is noticed later.

[57] *CAC*, 126–7, 162–3; full text in Sommer-Seckendorff, *Kilwardby*, 181–3 (letters 24 June, 15 July). A report by Rhys ap Gruffudd, recounting difficulties met by bailiffs in the marcher lordships in abiding by the prince's call for restraint (*CAC*, 53–4), may be the document to which Llywelyn refers on 15 July.

[58] *CAC*, 86–7, 126–7, 162–3 (14 May, 24 June, 15 July).

the record as king and prince argued their case, their activities came to loom large once more and in familiar theatres of conflict. Llywelyn's position in some of his more exposed territories was already being assailed as Mortimer, for instance, wrested Dyffryn Tefeidiad, or Tempsiter, from him. Dafydd ap Gruffudd in Powys Fadog and Payn de Chaworth in Deheubarth launched strong attacks on the lands of the prince's vassals. Llywelyn conveys his suspicion that his opponents were bent on pre-emptive action which would place them at greater advantage if the peace, for which the archbishop laboured, were to come about. Peace between king and prince was already something to be recovered rather than preserved, and in some crucially important areas resort had already been made to localized truces to maintain some semblance of order.[59] This was true of the areas facing Montgomery where Llywelyn had to maintain substantial forces. Here was a land of old confrontation, and when Llywelyn had first come to the area he had done so in a strenuous endeavour to extend his power to the furthermost bounds of the Welsh nation. It was very different now, his efforts necessarily concentrated not on expansion but on preventing the further contraction of his frontiers. It is likely that he had already been forced to cede some of his furthermost acquisitions, such as Teirtref Esgob, the bishop of Hereford's three manors of Castle Wright, Aston and Mellington, whose occupation had already brought upon him the archbishop's threat of severe spiritual censure.[60] Yet it was crucially important that he should maintain his position in the really vital positions in those areas, both for strategic reasons and for the symbolic significance of this historic meeting-ground upon the boundary between two nations and two political authorities. Matters of principle at issue between king and prince could no longer be separated from the military exigencies on the frontier. He could hardly sustain his argument with Edward, nor could he hope that his efforts to bring papal pressure to bear upon the king would be of some avail, unless he were to maintain his position in this quarter of his dominion.[61] He pressed upon the frontier at Montgomery with all his power and forced the royal commanders to send for reinforcements. Bogo de Knovill, in charge of the defence of the area between Montgomery and Oswestry, stressed the great strength of Llywelyn's forces in that sector

---

[59] A letter to Edward, dated Ardudwy 24 January in an unspecified year (*CAC*, 92), refers to a meeting at Montgomery between the king's men and his own and calls for the settling of disputes according to the custom of the march. J. G. Edwards suggests 1279; Powicke, *Henry III*, ii, 673, n. 2, prefers 1275–6 and the year is probably 1276. The method envisaged by Llywelyn may not be the mixed jury suggested ibid. but arbitration by *dictatores*; for *parliamenta* held at the ford of Montgomery 1274–5 and possibly later, below, n. 90.

[60] *Registrum Thome de Cantilupo*, 9–11, 29–32, one letter from Llywelyn (Sychdyn, 27 August 1275), three to Llywelyn from the bishop of Hereford, and one from Kilwardby.

[61] Edward's letter to Adrian, August 1276 (*TreatyR*, no. 135) refers to the activities of the prince's envoys in Rome.

and his urgent need for support in a situation which was neither one of peace nor war.[62] Llywelyn continued to press his case. In the autumn, with the archbishop's emissary admitting that his negotiations were proving of no avail, Llywelyn sent his proposals directly to the king.[63]

This document was considered by the king and council in November 1276: the prince would do homage at Oswestry or Montgomery if he were assured of a safe-conduct provided by the archbishop of Canterbury and the archdeacon, the bishop of Winchester, the earls of Cornwall, Norfolk and Gloucester and the Earl Warenne, and Roger Mortimer. He asked for two things: the king's confirmation of the peace of 1267 and the release of his wife Eleanor so that she might join him. In Edward's view the prince's proposals simply underlined the intransigence that he had already shown, and there was now no reason for further withholding a condemnation which might well have been issued in May. It might take another summer to bring Llywelyn to submission, but his denunciation could be issued forthwith and it was made in a formal declaration on 12 November. The crux of the matter was Llywelyn's failure to fulfil his obligations to his lord the king. Though summoned five times, he had failed to do homage. The archdeacon's mission had been authorized as a means of bringing the prince to acknowledge the need to fulfil his fundamental obligation; so long as he failed to do homage there could be no negotiation on any other matter. By the counsel of the prelates and magnates the king decided that Llywelyn's proposals could not be accepted, nor could the king admit his reasons for not doing homage. The king should not heed Llywelyn's submissions nor accept his explanations. The great men of the realm gave their consent to the view that the prince of Wales should henceforth be treated as a rebel and a disturber of the peace, and the magnates were given advance notice that they would be expected at Worcester in June 1277 unless their services were required at an earlier date. In the following weeks writs of summons were issued which predictably stressed the depredations which Llywelyn had inflicted on the king's lands and subjects in the marches, and Edward would continue to ensure that his reasons for taking action were clearly enunciated.[64] The heart of the matter was Llywelyn's failure to fulfil his duties as a vassal and his inability to respond to the

---

[62] *CAC*, 82 (attributed to November 1276). Knovill's arrangements for the defence of Montgomery and Oswestry are noticed later.

[63] There is no full text of the proposals, but they are summarized in the record of the proceedings on 12 November (*CCR, 1272–79*, 359–60; *Foedera*, I, ii, 535–6). The process against Llywelyn was recited before an assembly of 'magnates of the king's council, justices and others of the king's council', and prelates and other clerics. For the transactions, J. G. Edwards, in *LW*, lx; Powicke, *Henry III*, ii, 647.

[64] *ParlWrits*, i, 193–6. Llywelyn's depredations in the march are noted by the chroniclers, e.g. *AnnWav*, 387; *ChronWykes*, 271; *FloresHist*, iii, 47–8.

persuasions of the church. The king would proceed deliberately.[65] But the contest between Edward and Llywelyn had already developed into a war between England and Wales. By the beginning of 1277 Edward had written to Alphonso of Castile conveying his regret that he could not help him in his war with the Saracens because he had had to go to war, in his own territory, with the prince of Wales and the Welsh.[66] He had no choice but to direct his forces to Wales.

The solemn phraseology of Llywelyn's condemnation would not appear to admit of any further discussion. His explanations for his failure to fulfil his obligations to the king had been castigated as entirely frivolous. Llywelyn had failed to fulfil, unconditionally and without prevarication, the service to the king which it was his duty to perform before the king could enter into any discussion of the grievances that he might nurture with regard to the king's obligations under the treaty of Montgomery. It might seem that Edward would now wish to concentrate entirely on his plans for the prince's subjugation. Yet it is reasonable to ask whether Llywelyn, at this late hour, might still have been able to extricate himself from a conflict in which he would face an opponent of great ability who had infinitely greater resources at his command than a prince of Wales could possibly call upon. Could the man who had created the principality of Wales conceivably have saved it from destruction? There were still two avenues by which discussion could proceed. Llywelyn put further proposals directly to the king and he did so, as we shall see, not without encouragement from Edward himself. There was, too, a further intercession on the part of Archbishop Kilwardby which merits historical notice alongside the more celebrated intervention by Archbishop Pecham at a late stage in the conflict of 1282. Kilwardby, despite the failure of his sustained effort to intercede between king and prince during the previous months, cannot be said to have been precipitate in enacting the excommunication of Llywelyn and those associated with him. The archbishop had been present when Llywelyn had been formally condemned, along with a number of bishops including Anian of St Asaph. On the following day the bishops addressed a letter to Llywelyn.[67] He would no doubt have expected to be

---

[65] A statement of Edward's standpoint, justifying his decision to go to war, is in *CAC*, 252–3. Undated and unaddressed, it appears to belong to late 1276 or early 1277 and may be a draft of a communication to the papal court. Edward had been punctilious in doing his service to Philip III in 1273, despite the problems which remained over the treaty of 1259, but his homage to Philip IV in 1286 would be couched in a conditional form, dependent on the king of France fulfilling his part of the treaty (Chaplais, *Essays in Medieval Diplomacy*, III, 24–5).

[66] *TreatyR*, nos. 179–81 (of which nos. 179, 180 appear to be drafts); *Foedera*, I, ii, 540–1 (8 January 1277). Edward maintained that his expedition to Wales was one to which the pope was well disposed. For Edward's reluctance to be drawn into Alphonso's concerns with Navarre, Prestwich, *Edward I*, 315–16.

[67] *LW*, 94–5; *Foedera*, I, ii, 536–7; *Councils*, i, 510–11.

informed of his impending, if not immediate, excommunication. For the present, however, the bishops did no more than warn him that the church could now exercise its spiritual authority and declare him excommunicate, for reasons declared in canons of church councils, in accordance with recognized procedures.[68] Excommunication was withheld so that Llywelyn might have fifteen days, upon receiving the letter, to acknowledge his obligations to the king. After that, if the prince were to fail to respond, excommunication would proceed. However frustrating his envoy may have found his missions to Llywelyn, and whatever disappointment he may have felt that the prince had not been more responsive to his initiatives, the archbishop seemed to be anxious not only to maintain a scrupulous regard for canonical convention but to give Llywelyn a last opportunity to meet those obligations to his lord which the church was bound to enjoin upon him and which no Christian prince could ever deny. Whether this course of action commended itself to Bishop Anian of St Asaph we cannot tell, for whereas he was named among the bishops who were present at Llywelyn's condemnation, he is not named among those who gave their assent to the prelates' letter on the following day. It may be that he was not partial to the tenor of a letter which reflects the archbishop's instinctive wish to ensure that everything be done, consonant with respect for the king's authority, to avert conflict. What is certain is that Anian promptly left for his diocese and convened a synod of churchmen and laymen to draw up a full statement of their complaints against Llywelyn.[69] The material had been gathered together already, but Anian was determined to impress upon the archbishop once more the extent of the grievances which had prompted Pope Gregory, despite his tolerant response to Llywelyn's representations, to warn the prince that he could incur ecclesiastical censure if he were to fail to do justice for the wrongs which were alleged against him.[70] Anian made a public declaration of his case against Llywelyn within the bounds of the principality and conveyed them to Kilwardby so that, as it was pointedly expressed, he could take the appropriate corrective action.

The bishops of the province of Canterbury, reflecting perhaps the influence of their erudite archbishop, whose concern at the deteriorating relationship between Edward and Llywelyn is all the more noteworthy for his disinclination to involvement in the political affairs of the realm, preferred to wait a while. Although it may have been a pause calculated to do no more than give Llywelyn a short period in which he could declare his willingness to do his duty to the king, it was probably more than Anian would wish to concede to his lord and kinsman. In the event Llywelyn was given several weeks in which

---

[68] The letter refers to the *sententiae* of the Oxford council summoned by Stephen Langton in 1225 and subsequent church councils, for which *Councils and Synods*, II, i, 106 *et passim*.

[69] *Councils*, i, 511–16 (7 December 1276).

[70] Ibid., 512.

to save himself from ecclesiastical censure as the archbishop continued to seek a means of persuading him to relent. Kilwardby's influence may have played a part in prompting Llywelyn to yield on a number of issues that had created contention with the bishop of St Asaph. For it is certain that it was in this period of acute stress that Llywelyn put his seal to a document making important concessions to the bishop, dean and chapter.[71] But, as we shall see, there was no yielding on the crucial matters concerning his relations with the king that the archbishop earnestly enjoined upon him.

At the end of 1276 Bishop Anian may have felt that the archbishop was not the only one who tarried and that Edward himself, despite the apparent accord between them, was not in any hurry to apply the corrective hand.[72] The king's field commanders had been appointed and military operations had commenced, but despite the finality of the prince's condemnation Edward was still prepared to receive the prince's submissions. At a date, probably early in December 1276, certain 'petitions and offers' submitted by Llywelyn were considered by the prelates and magnates. These were found unacceptable, but the king was still prepared to consider proposals which the prince might wish to make if he were to do so before the end of January 1277.[73] It is known that Llywelyn communicated with the king on two further occasions, first in January, when he sent proposals borne by Bishop Anian of Bangor and Master Iorwerth, the prince's vice-chancellor, and then in February. He thus appears to have made as many as three submissions to the king after his formal denunciation in the autumn.[74] In a letter which accompanies the

[71] This important document (*Councils*, i, 519–21; Peniarth MS 231B. 74–7; *H*, no. 153) is undated, but it certainly belongs to the end of 1276 or the beginning of 1277. The bishop of Hereford, in an undated letter written at Leominster, refers to Llywelyn's recent restoration to the bishop of St Asaph of the liberties of the see; the bishop's itinerary shows that he was at Leominster on 11 January (*Registrum Thome de Cantilupo*, lxv, 42). For the dispute, G. Williams, *Welsh Church*, 11–12; O. E. Jones, 'Llyfr Coch Asaph', 97–112; above, pp. 210–15.

[72] For contact and the king's support, *CAC*, 61, 105; *CPR, 1272–81*, 112, 129; above, n. 53. Edward confirmed the liberties of St Asaph in November 1275, January 1276 and November 1277 (*CPR, 1272–81*, 112, 129, 235).

[73] In *TreatyR*, no. 152, an undated letter from Edward to Llywelyn, certain *peticiones et offra* recently submitted by the prince are said to have been considered *in parliamento nostro*. Llywelyn's letter from Aberalwen, 22 January 1277 (*CAC*, 87), quotes a letter from the king in a phraseology identical to that of the Treaty Roll, adding that the king's letter was written at Windsor, 9 December 1276. That letter could conceivably refer to the gathering on 12 November when, before Llywelyn's condemnation, proposals are known to have been considered; but it is possible that the proposals to which the king refers were embodied in a new document subsequently considered by another meeting of prelates and magnates. A month had elapsed since the condemnation and that text makes no reference to the king's readiness, declared on 9 December, to receive proposals which Llywelyn might make before the end of January 1277.

[74] *CAC*, 87, 91 (22 January, 21 February). Llywelyn's envoys were given a safe-conduct to come to the king on 14 January (*CPR, 1272–81*, 188), and it appears that it was then that Bishop Anian of Bangor and Master Iorwerth (Gervase) went to present the first of two sets of proposals made early in 1277 examined in the next paragraph.

second set of proposals, made in response to the archbishop's mediation, Llywelyn insisted upon his wish to demonstrate his fidelity to the king and give him the honour due to him; he protested that he was more loyal to the kingdom than those who incited Edward against him; he would be of greater service to the king than those who, even though they waged the king's war, sought their own advantage rather than the king's honour. Llywelyn vigorously protested his fidelity, but Edward would no doubt be more concerned with the precise content of any documents which the prince might convey to him. Two texts survive which enable us to make an estimate of the position which Llywelyn took at this late stage in his diplomatic exchanges with the king. Of these, one is quite brief, the other more lengthy.

In the shorter communication Llywelyn pleads that he might be received into the king's peace and friendship, and that he be given a safe-conduct to come and do homage to the king at an appropriate place in the march so that he might hold his principality under the king's authority. He would pay handsomely for the king's grace, as much as 11,000 marks in addition to his outstanding debts, making a total of 25,000 marks.[75] In the fuller statement Llywelyn again declared his readiness to do homage, either at Oswestry or Montgomery, under the safe-conduct of magnates of the realm.[76] He offered 6,000 marks for the confirmation of the peace and the release of his wife, 5,000 marks for the homage of Rhys ap Maredudd and whatever was owed the king already.[77] He described in detail what he was prepared to do to secure

---

[75] *DipDoc*, no. 411, attributed by the editor to a date prior to the treaty of Montgomery of 1267, reflects circumstances in late 1276 and early 1277. It seems impossible to determine whether it was the document sent in January 1277 or February, but the texts have a close affinity which suggests that they contain the two sets of proposals sent early in that year, unless one of them was the document submitted sometime before 9 December 1276 already considered.

[76] C47/27/2, no. 9, printed with discussion in J. B. Smith, 'Offra principis Wallie domino regi', *B*, 21 (1964–6), 362–7. The most specific indication of date is the reference to the defection of Llywelyn ap Gruffudd Fychan (Llywelyn ap Gruffudd ap Madog), noticed in a chancery enrolment of 26 December 1276 (*CPR, 1272–81*, 186). This points to a later date, although the defection may have been known to Llywelyn for some time. It is possible (*TreatyR*, i, 61, n. 1) that the document, which has sections entitled 'offers' and 'petitions', is the one which embodies the 'petitions and offers' known to have been submitted before 9 December. In his letter of February, however, Llywelyn uses the same term 'petitions and offers' to describe the submissions he was then making (*CAC*, 91). Llywelyn's reference to the war being waged in the march may be an allusion to the mounting conflict of the early weeks of 1277. The present document may best be attributed to early 1277, and perhaps to February in preference to January. The appearance of Henry de Lacy among those from whom Llywelyn sought a safe-conduct may point to a date after the earl, in late January, took up a command on the Montgomery front.

[77] It has been noted already that it would be difficult to understand why Llywelyn was required to pay 5,000 marks for the homage of the son of Maredudd ap Rhys Gryg if he had paid for Maredudd's homage in 1270; failure to pay that sum does not appear among the matters subsequently charged against Llywelyn, but the evidence points to the conclusion that it had not in fact been paid.

the king's peace: he would do justice to the barons of Wales in accordance with the terms of the peace and by judgement of their peers and he would do justice to the marcher lords. This provides a fuller statement of his promises than we have in any other document, but the clause concerning his safe-conduct demonstrates that, even in this extremity, he remained resolutely unyielding. Apart from the prelates, he insisted upon a safe-conduct guaranteed by the earls of Cornwall and Gloucester and the Earl Warenne, but if neither the first nor the second were able to be present he would ask for the presence of the earl of Lincoln and that three men be handed over to him as hostages for his safety: Roger Mortimer, Dafydd ap Gruffudd and Gruffudd ap Gwenwynwyn.[78] He explained why. The king had received Gruffudd ap Gwenwynwyn, and now Llywelyn ap Gruffudd of Madog of Powys Fadog; he had given them succour and taken their homage and he had permitted them to wage war upon him.[79] He kept the prince's wife in captivity and Llywelyn feared that he, too, would be imprisoned unless he came to the king under the safe-conduct that he specified. War was now being waged and it was no longer safe for him to come to do homage except under the conditions which he set out. He was prepared to place himself under the judgement of the king of France as to whether his proposals were reasonable or not, and he asked the king of England to reply to his proposals in a manner which had regard for his authority and status (*habito respectu ad facultates et statum principis*) and to stop the conflict in the march while negotiations took place.

Even at this time of crisis Llywelyn continued to convey that deep sense of status which had been a feature of his pronouncements in the years of supremacy following his triumph at Bryn Derwin. The more lengthy of the two documents now being considered is the fullest surviving statement of his standpoint since he wrote to Pope Gregory and the bishops of England in the autumn of 1275, and it shows that he was still greatly concerned over two issues which had troubled him at that time, that the king provided sanctuary for his most dangerous opponents and that he was summoned to do homage at a place to which he could not go without endangering his life. The new element which caused concern was the imprisonment of Eleanor, though, as we have seen, he had made an appeal for her release in the submission which had been considered in council in November. Llywelyn had striven to convince the papacy of the justice of his case and, after Innocent and Adrian had followed Gregory to the grave, he was able to persuade Pope John to urge the king to release her. The pope sent Edward a strongly worded letter pressing him to set her free. Was not the consummation by physical union of a

---

[78] Llywelyn made more stringent demands, with regard to his safe-conduct, than those which, at least on the testimony of the chancery record, he had made before his condemnation.

[79] For the effect of his defection, *LW*, 53–4; below, n. 129.

marriage made *per verba de presenti* in accordance with the will of God? What wrong could an innocent woman do? But the pope's entreaties would have no more influence on Edward than the prince's pleading.[80] He would not be moved on this issue. As for Llywelyn, his wife's captivity only served to confirm him in his obduracy and to heighten his concern for his own safety. He would do homage only on conditions which assured his protection. The document, unyielding in tone, provides the last substantial statement known to have emanated from the prince's court before the destruction of the principality of Wales.

By the time his emissaries had set off on their last efforts on his behalf, Llywelyn may well have doubted whether further appeal to the crown was likely to be of any avail. For his part, Edward, upon the expiry of the time set for the consideration of new proposals, was probably convinced that further negotiations would not be justified. By then, too, Llywelyn's excommunication had finally taken effect. On 10 February, following a further convocation of the clergy of Canterbury, the archbishop called upon the bishops of the province to proceed with the excommunication formally communicated to the prince by envoys specially sent to him fully three months earlier. Llywelyn was excommunicated by name (*nominatim*) and his supporters with him, unless they renounced their obduracy within a month. His land was put under interdict.[81] Kilwardby, writing to the archbishop of York later in the month, said that Llywelyn had failed to fulfil his duties to his lord and had created disturbance in the realm. He recounted his own efforts to intercede, and told how Llywelyn, heaping one offence upon another, scorned his attempts at reconciliation. The archbishop's mediation had been abruptly terminated.[82] His envoys had come to Llan-faes, where Llywelyn and his magnates were in court, but they were not admitted to his presence. Momentarily, we sense the

---

[80] *Registres des Papes: Jean XXI*, no. 78; J. B. Smith, 'Offra principis Wallie domino regi', 365, n. 6. Dispatched on 28 January 1277, John's letter would not have arrived while exchanges between king and prince were still continuing, but it shows that Llywelyn had persisted with his efforts at Rome. Ironically, the pope's appeal on Eleanor's behalf was written at Viterbo, where her brothers had committed the deed which left Edward so incensed.

[81] *Councils and Synods*, II, ii, 820–2, a letter of the archbishop of Canterbury, at the New Temple, requiring that the bishops of his province excommunicate Llywelyn *nominatim* along with his supporters. Those stated to have been present at this convocation were, with the archbishop, the bishops of London, Rochester, Bath, Hereford, Llandaff and St Asaph, and the proctors of the other bishops. Llywelyn's excommunication was pronounced on 10 February and the editor's note, *CAC*, 91–2, should be corrected. The letter of February 1277 makes no reference to the laying of interdict on the prince's lands, but the terms of the treaty of Aberconwy provide that the interdict should be lifted (*LW*, 119). The reference to Llywelyn's excommunication *nominatim* needs to be noted in view of the apparent lack of comparable evidence in 1282 (below, pp. 468, 515–16).

[82] On 27 February, at the king's request, Kilwardby called on the archbishop to secure the promulgation of the excommunication in his province (*LW*, 171–3; *Foedera*, II, ii, 541; *Councils*, i, 517–19).

tension and the anger at the prince's court in the critical months following his denunciation. Kilwardby could not conceal his disappointment that Llywelyn had failed to respond to his earnest endeavour to intercede, and that his patient and prolonged efforts had met only with wilful intransigence. Even so, the archbishop's efforts had not been entirely disregarded by any means for, even after his excommunication had been pronounced in convocation, Llywelyn conveyed that it was by his mediation that he submitted his last proposals to the king. Nor was he denied clerical sympathy within his dominions. In the early weeks of 1277 Llywelyn could still call upon the services of the bishop of Bangor on his behalf, and Anian set out upon his attempt to preserve the peace which his predecessor had sought by successive journeys to the king's court twenty years earlier.[83] His efforts were of no avail, but, unlike Anian of St Asaph, it does not appear that Anian of Bangor was at the New Temple when the excommunication was finally enacted. He could do no more to spare Llywelyn, even though he was his confessor, nor could he protect those of his diocese who, by their continued intransigence, shared the ecclesiastical censure which was now imposed upon their prince. The bishop acknowledged that, confronted with the inevitable choice between his love for the prince and his people and his duty to God and the church, he faced a deep crisis of conscience. He waited for some time and then, at last, he publicly excommunicated Llywelyn. Throughout the diocese of Bangor, like the rest of the provinces of Canterbury and York, bells were rung and candles were extinguished to proclaim that the prince of Wales had incurred the judgement of the church of Christ by his failure to fulfil the solemn duty to his lord which, in the estimation of the church, he was bound to respect. Bishop Anian celebrated mass in the church of St Deiniol at Bangor on the morning of Palm Sunday and then, under the stress of a strained conscience and in fear for his own safety, fled for his life.[84] Again like his predecessor in his time of anguish and peril, Bishop Anian found a retreat in the abbey of St Albans, and he may well have felt something of the despair which had brought Bishop Richard to the point where he implored his archbishop to release him from the burdens of his troubled pastorate. The bishop withdrew from his diocese, but there may have been many among his flock who, while harbouring no wish to leave the see, were deeply troubled by the inevitability of a major conflict. It is likely that those who had gathered at Llan-faes at the critical moment at the beginning of 1277 knew that their deliberations would prove to be of fateful consequence in the history of the political entity which they and their prince had laboured to build. Once more it was a time for war, and

---

[83] *CAC*, 87.
[84] *CAC*, 66; Palm Sunday fell on 21 March and the bishop, who was the prince's confessor, wrote to Edward from St Albans shortly afterwards.

it was already evident that powerful forces were gathering on the frontiers of the principality.

The war of 1277 was the greatest military undertaking to confront a king of England for many years, and it was the greatest challenge yet for which Edward had taken the main responsibility.[85] The king had gained valuable experience of warfare, some of it painfully instructive, but his conflict with Llywelyn was the first occasion on which he had taken supreme command of a major campaign. His experience, and perhaps the benefits of an inclination to a study of the methods of warfare suggested by his possession of the classical manual of Vegetius, could now be brought to bear on his confrontation with the prince of Wales.[86] In his first Welsh war Edward revealed many of the characteristics which were to emerge during his conduct of later campaigns, and his ability to organize his resources was amply demonstrated when his forces gathered at Chester for the assault on Gwynedd.[87] By then, it is true, a great deal had already been accomplished, largely by methods which were established features of Anglo-Welsh conflict. Three commanders who had been appointed towards the end of 1276 went to their respective posts: William Beauchamp, earl of Warwick, to Chester, Roger Mortimer to Montgomery and Payn de Chaworth to Carmarthen.[88] They were charged with the dismembering of the principality of Wales in advance of the greater gathering of the might of the realm of England scheduled for the summer of 1277.

---

[85] J. E. Morris, *The Welsh Wars of Edward I* (Oxford, 1901) [Morris, *WW*] remains a valuable study; among more recent works, Prestwich, *WPF*; Taylor, *SCCB*; and *HKW*, i, 293–330, reprinted as Arnold Taylor, *The Welsh Castles of Edward I* (London, 1986); and R. F. Walker, 'Edward I and the organization of war', *WHR*, 7 (1974–5), 357–65, are indispensable. For trends in the nature and recruitment of armed forces, Contamine, *War in the Middle Ages*, and M. R. Powicke, *Military Obligation in Medieval England* (Oxford, 1962). No attempt is made in this study to offer a thorough treatment of Edward's campaigns, nor to undertake the much more difficult task of studying Llywelyn's defensive measures; it concentrates on the political compulsions and predicaments of the two main contenders, and necessarily reflects to some degree the relationship between political and military influences.

[86] For an Anglo-French text of Vegetius' *Epitome de Re Militaris*, possibly prepared for Edward while on crusade, L. Thorpe, 'Mastre Richard, a thirteenth-century translator of the "De Re Militari" of Vegetius', *Scriptorium*, 6 (1952), 39–50; *Scriptorium*, 7 (1953), 120–1; M. D. Legge, 'The Lord Edward's Vegetius', *Scriptorium*, 7 (1953), 262–5; cf. Prestwich, *Edward I*, 123; below, pp. 419, 434, 526.

[87] It would be wrong, even so, to overestimate the extent of Edward's resources or the effectiveness of their deployment; see the considered remarks in Prestwich, *WPF*, 67 et passim; idem, *Edward I*, 170 et seq.

[88] *CPR, 1272–81*, 171. For Chaworth, Robert de Tibetot, Roger de Clifford, Luke de Tany and Geoffrey de Geneville, among the men who accompanied Edward to the east and who served with him in Wales, Powicke, *Henry III*, ii, 698–700; Prestwich, *WPF*, 42–3; idem, *Edward I*, 68–9; for the Savoyard contribution, below, n. 94.

Aberconwy

The main activity in the early part of the year was probably centred at Montgomery and it is the evidence from this sector which best exemplifies the strength and the composition of the forces confronting Llywelyn ap Gruffudd in the first stage of the campaign.[89] This theatre had already seen heavy fighting during the previous months, and Llywelyn is known to have spent some time with his army in the neighbourhood of Montgomery. Bogo de Knovill, as we have noticed already, took measures for the defence of the frontier between Montgomery and Oswestry, as well as maintaining contact with the prince. Early in 1277, when he appears to have given attention to the defence of an extensive stretch of the frontier, Llywelyn was in the Montgomery area again.[90] He had built Dolforwyn in an attempt to stabilize his position in this key strategic area, and his castle became the main objective of the royal forces summoned to this sector. Roger Mortimer was now able to draw on the services of the cavalry of the royal household and of the men of Shropshire and Herefordshire.[91] But the army was greatly augmented by a force of a hundred cavalry led by Henry de Lacy, earl of Lincoln. These were men in royal pay, and they remained in the field continuously for four months. With the household knights who, in this sector, probably came to something approaching fifty, and the infantry from the neighbouring counties, the king was evidently able to commit a formidable force to this part of the frontier.[92] It was in this strategic quarter that Llywelyn had his first experience of Edward's ability to put an army embodying substantial paid contingents in the field under competent commanders and keep it there until its task was completed. In his appeal to the king to halt the conflict in the march, conveyed in what was possibly one of his very last attempts to communicate with the king, Llywelyn would have been most acutely aware of the problems confronting him in the neighbourhood of Montgomery.[93]

It may be an indication of the ferocity of the conflict in this area that, though Dolforwyn was a strongpoint on which royal forces needed to concentrate their efforts, and though the castle was situated only a short distance from the frontier on the Severn, it was only in late March, several

---

[89] Morris, *WW*, 114 *et seq.*, from E101/3/11–21.

[90] Knovill, who describes the prince's great strength in the area (*CAC*, 82), was granted the costs of safeguarding Montgomery for fourteen weeks while Llywelyn was in the area with his army. Three *parliamenta* had been held at the ford of Montgomery in 1274–5 at which magnates and knights of co. Shropshire were present, and Knovill is known to have made two journeys to Llywelyn in 1275–6 (C62/52, m. 3; E372/121, m. 21). Llywelyn's presence, before Lincoln arrived at the end of January, is indicated in E101/3/11. Letters of the prince dated at Aberalwen in Edeirnion 22 January and in Englefield 21 February (*CAC*, 87, 91) suggest attention to frontier defence during these weeks.

[91] Morris, *WW*, 120–2. Prestwich, *WPF*, 50, notes the difficulty in distinguishing between household troops and other paid cavalry.

[92] Morris, *WW*, 120–1, mainly from E101/3/12.

[93] J. B. Smith, 'Offra principis Wallie domino regi', 367.

weeks after they had gathered on the frontier for the offensive, that the forces commanded by Mortimer, Lincoln and Otto de Grandson were able to put the castle under siege. Two weeks later the garrison yielded and the castle was placed in the custody of Gruffudd ap Gwenwynwyn.[94] By then Gruffudd had secured control of the areas adjacent to his castle of Welshpool – Deuddwr, Llannerch Hudol and Ystrad Marchell – and the surrender of the men of Arwystli enabled him to regain an important part of the interior of his lordship. Similarly, Peter Corbet took possession of Gorddwr.[95] During the later stages of the conflict in the sector centred on Dolforwyn royal forces had been augmented by a contingent from Abergavenny, previously the base for operations in the lordship of Brecon. Llywelyn had been placed under pressure in Brecon some years earlier, but his hold on at least part of the lordship had been maintained.[96] Substantial forces had to be sent from Abergavenny, probably in the early weeks of 1277, to enable Humphrey de Bohun to combat Welsh resistance 'in the lordship of Brecon'.[97] Two further advances were made in February and March, from the same base and again through the lordship of Brecon, to deal with resistance maintained by defenders in Deheubarth who were evidently determined to prevent any advance over the watershed between the Usk and the Tywi.[98] The second of the two expeditions is said to have moved through Brecon to Defynnog and Llywel to support Bohun and John Giffard, and it is possible that this expedition was confronted with strong resistance within the confines of the lordship of Brecon. Its focus could well have been a defensive position which may, with some degree of confidence, be attributed to Llywelyn ap Gruffudd. At Rhyd-y-briw, immediately north-west of Defynnog, are the remains of a masonry castle sited so as to withstand movements precisely akin to those which took royal forces through the lordship of Brecon into Deheubarth early in 1277.[99] Important transactions concerning the fidelity of the prince's

---

[94] *CAC*, 31, 123–4; *BT, Pen20*, 224; *Pen20Tr*, 118; *RBH*, 264–5. The garrison had agreed to yield the castle if it had not been relieved by that date (*CAC*, 30–1, a letter there attributed to Lacy but credited to Otto de Grandson in Taylor, *SCCB*, 212, n. 1; idem, 'Master Bertram, *ingeniator regis*', in C. Harper-Bill et al. (eds.), *Studies in Medieval History presented to R. Allen Brown* (London, 1989), 296, n. 41). For the Savoyards in Edward's service, C. L. Kingsford, 'Sir Otho de Grandison (1238–1328)', *TRHS*, 3rd ser., 3 (1909), 125–95; Taylor, *SCCB*, 209–27.

[95] *CAC*, 81 (Knovill to Edward); for Gorddwr, *CPR, 1272–81*, 374.

[96] Above, pp. 355–8.

[97] C62/52; payment to Henry de Bray, constable of Abergavenny, authorized 25 January.

[98] C62/52. A substantial force of cavalry and infantry was sent, 28 February, from Abergavenny to Brecon 'to attack the Welsh of Deheubarth our enemies', a second deployed from 17 March, advancing to Brecon, Defynnog and Llywel, and thence to Myddfai in Deheubarth.

[99] A thirteenth-century structure with an apsidal tower at Rhyd-y-briw (SN919283), close by Sennybridge, in the medieval parish of Defynnog, is noticed in D. J. C. King, 'The castles of Breconshire', *Brycheiniog*, 7 (1961), 80–1; idem, *CA*, i, 20; idem, 'Camlais and

tenants of Brecon had been completed at Rhyd-y-briw in 1271, and Einion ap Rhys may have made his new profession of loyalty to Llywelyn at a castle built by the prince himself.[100] Just as some of the prince's stalwart adherents in Deheubarth had been present at the negotiations calculated to secure the allegiance of the community of Brecon, so it is likely that men of the same area were deployed in a sustained effort to withstand royal and marcher advance into Deheubarth from the upper reaches of the Usk. By the middle of March resistance in this quarter had at last been extinguished, almost certainly by virtue of the convergence of the forces of Bohun and Giffard advancing from Brecon and those of Payn de Chaworth deployed, after an advance along the Tywi valley, in Cantref Bychan.[101]

Thereafter, forces from Abergavenny could be dispatched to Dolforwyn and, by the summer of 1277, Welsh contingents from the lordships of this sector of the march, several led by men whose loyalty to the prince had long been questioned, were deployed on the frontiers of Snowdonia.[102] Llywelyn had been unable to retain the allegiance of the marcher communities. The fact that his son was in the prince's hands did not deter Trahaearn ap Madog from defecting to the crown.[103] Nor did the same consideration influence Hywel ap Meurig, who remained, as we shall see again, a steadfast and active adherent

---

Sennybridge castles', *Brycheiniog*, 21 (1984–5), 9–11. King described the castle as 'probably Welsh', and later concluded that this, rather than Camlais castle, was the 'new castle' which was built by Llywelyn ap Gruffudd and destroyed by Edward in 1264 ('A castle of Llywelyn ap Gruffydd in Brycheiniog', *Brycheiniog*, 11 (1965), 151–3; *CA*, i, 17, 21; above, pp. 162, 172, n. 125). Camlais, which also stood in the medieval parish of Defynnog, appears from NLW, Penpont Supplementary MSS (a deed of 1358 cited by King, *Brycheiniog*, 21 (1984–5), 10) to have been built by Humphrey de Bohun (d. 1298) upon a site purchased from Trahaearn ap Hywel. Records of the advances made in 1277, with specific mention of Defynnog, tend to support the conclusion that Rhyd-y-briw was a castle built by Llywelyn, perhaps one that he and the princes of Deheubarth had agreed to construct, and to suggest that it was the focus for strenuous resistance in this strategically vital sector.

[100] Above, p. 357.

[101] These movements, and the important consequences of Giffard's taking of territories in Cantref Bychan, are examined in the next paragraphs.

[102] A contingent from Abergavenny was sent to Montgomery and Dolforwyn during a period of thirteen days from 28 March, to be at the command of Lincoln, Mortimer and Grandson; for the marcher contingents in Gwynedd in the summer of 1277, below, nn. 146–9.

[103] He stated that, after he had been in the prince's fealty, he came to the peace of Bohun and the king, but that when his son Madog attempted to do so he was captured and kept in captivity contrary to the terms of the peace between king and prince (*CAP*, 468). The 'form of peace' to which the undated petition refers is certainly the treaty of Aberconwy rather than Montgomery; Llywelyn agreed to release Madog ap Trahaearn under the terms of a document dated at Dolwyddelan in May 1278 (*LW*, 43). The petition thus belongs to November 1277–May 1278 rather than the earlier date suggested by the editor; below, p. 492.

of the marchers and the king.[104] What is surprising is that Llywelyn had been able to maintain his hold on Brecon and neighbouring areas for so long. For, despite whatever erosion there may have been of his support in the communities of these areas, it was only by reason of substantial royal support that Humphrey de Bohun was able to establish full control over the lordship of Brecon nearly four years after he had first challenged the prince's hold upon the area. But by the fall of Dolforwyn on 8 April Llywelyn had been forced into retreat from every one of the troublous lordships of the central sector of the march. Cydewain and Ceri, Elfael and Gwerthrynion, Brecon and Builth (where the king's building accounts begin on 3 May) could be added to Maelienydd and Dyffryn Tefeidiad, areas from which he had probably been forced to withdraw at an early stage in the conflict.[105] Gruffudd ap Gwenwynwyn was then able to establish full control over Powys Wenwynwyn. The fall of Dolforwyn marked the end of Llywelyn's power in the march of Wales. Edward had committed substantial forces to this crucial theatre, led by several of his key commanders – Roger Mortimer, Henry de Lacy, earl of Lincoln, Otto de Grandson – and supported by the artillery and engineering skills of the likes of Master Bertram.[106] Before the end of May Edward would be in a position to release the paid forces in his service and prepare to raise new contingents, many from the newly recovered lordships, for the major assault on Gwynedd. By then both Deheubarth and Powys Fadog had also been removed from Llywelyn ap Gruffudd's control.

If the course of events in the march had seen a realization of the fears of Llywelyn ap Gruffudd when he first had reason to question the fidelity of the men of Brecon and Elfael, so his reverses in Deuheubarth and Powys Fadog, too, were to a considerable degree the result of a crumbling of his authority in these areas. His supremacy had been founded on his ability to bring the Welsh lords of these areas into his allegiance, though with varying degrees of commitment, and his downfall reflected his inability to maintain their fidelity in the stressful situation in which he was placed in the spring and summer of

---

[104] Arrangements in 1271 concerning the fealty of certain men of the march have been examined already. Further transactions were completed in May 1276 to secure the release from Llywelyn's prison of John ap Hywel, son of Hywel ap Meurig (*LW*, 32–3, 41–2, 44). The process did not go smoothly, for Cadwgan, abbot of Cwm-hir, showed that he participated only in response to Hywel's request, while Madog ab Owain, lord of Elfael Uwch Mynydd, though named in one document, refused to be a pledge for John's fidelity, signs of a stressful situation.

[105] *BT, Pen20*, 223–4; *Pen20Tr*, 118; *RBH*, 264–5, records the ceding of Cydewain, Ceri, Gwerthrynion, Builth and Brecon in the entry for 1276 and the chronology is evidently imprecise. Elfael had fallen by January 1277 (*CPR, 1272–81*, 169, 191; *CIM*, i, no. 1060); accounts for Builth are noticed in *HKW*, i, 295; for Maelienydd and Dyffryn Tefeidiad (Tempsiter), areas from which Llywelyn was ejected by Roger Mortimer, *CCR, 1279–88*, 227, 260.

[106] For the siege-works at Dolforwyn, Taylor 'Master Bertram', 296.

1277. To grasp the real nature of the crisis in these areas account has to be taken of that combination of political persuasion and military power which Edward, not without precedents in the periods of his father and grandfather, put to good purpose. Edward might indeed have taken heed of the advice in his text of Vegetius that a prudent commander would do well to sow dissension among his adversaries, for no nation, however weakened, could be entirely ruined by its enemies unless its destruction were facilitated by their own distractions.[107] Since the early summer of 1276 Payn de Chaworth, with royal authorization, had been pressing upon the frontiers of Deheubarth, drawing upon the resources of the lordships of south-west Wales. Since the destruction wrought by Llywelyn in his campaigns of 1257 the lords of this area had consolidated their position, their investment marked in extensive building works at several castles. Chaworth himself at Cydweli, William de Camville at Llansteffan and Guy de Brian at Laugharne each completed extensive works at greatly strengthened strongholds of lordships which were themselves important sources of soldiery.[108] But by now Chaworth, like Roger Mortimer in the neighbourhood of Montgomery, was able to draw on the support of knights of the royal household and other knights paid for their services. He, too, was provided with foot soldiers paid by the crown.[109] These contingents, not large perhaps but still a viable military force, proved enough to enable Chaworth to penetrate Ystrad Tywi – a scene of past and subsequent disasters – and link up with the forces led by John Giffard which, as we have seen, drove into the area from the lordship of Brecon. But, besides their strictly military functions, these forces were a means of reinforcing the political pressures exerted upon the Welsh lords of the area. They ensured that those who might be prepared to secede to the king's fidelity would be given adequate protection, an essential feature of any attempt to create dissension among the king's adversaries.

These methods had been used to good effect in 1257 so as to secure Maredudd ap Rhys Gryg's defection, and these were precisely the means by which Edward won the submission of his son in the spring of 1277. Rhys ap Meredudd had come to his troubled inheritance six years before, nurturing

---

[107] *Flavius Vegetius Renatus: Epitoma Rei Militaris*, ed. L. F. Stelten (New York, 1990), Lib. III, 10: 'nulla enim quamuis minima natio potest ab aduersarios perdeleri nisi propriis simultatibus se ipsa consumpserint. Nam ciuile odium ad inimicorum perniciem praeceps est, ad utilitatem suae defensionis incautem'.

[108] Avent, 'Three coastal castles', *Sir Gâr*, 167–88, identifies an important building period at each of the three castles consistent with new investment following destruction in 1257 and includes reference to recent archaeological work.

[109] Chaworth's role and the support from the barons of west Wales and the king may be gathered from *CAC*, 55–6, 70–2, 87; *LW*, 36–7, 41, 48–9, 130–1, 196, 201; *ParlWrits*, i, 201–3; E101/3/13; Morris, *WW*, 116–24. In January 1277 John de Beauchamp was appointed to the custody of Carmarthen and Cardigan castles with a hundred cavalry in his service.

that same yearning for a wider dominion in Ystrad Tywi, and that same resentment towards Llywelyn, which his father had revealed. The pursuit of these ambitions had meant that Rhys himself had been placed in captivity as a surety for his father's uncertain loyalty.[110] In precisely the same way as Henry had seized the opportunity to wean Maredudd from his allegiance in 1257, Edward now sought to bring Rhys into his ranks, and by doing so he was to initiate a process which was to see Llywelyn's position in Ystrad Tywi and Ceredigion entirely undermined. Entrusting the task to Payn de Chaworth, Edward placed his trust in the son of the person who had lost his life fighting beside Maredudd ap Rhys Gryg in those enterprises which had aroused the nation's anger a generation before.

By Palm Sunday, 21 March, when the forces deployed by Mortimer and Lincoln were preparing the siege of Dolforwyn, Payn de Chaworth was able to report that Rhys ap Maredudd, as a result of diligent negotiation, had submitted and accepted terms which would enable him to be received into the king's fealty. Gruffudd ap Maredudd of Ceredigion had done likewise, and the two were expected to swear fealty on the day on which Chaworth wrote. He suggested that the princes had hesitated in fear that the king's army would not remain in the area very much longer and that they would be left without protection.[111] Chaworth was prepared to use the forces under his command to force the two princes to abide by their undertaking, and he called his captains together at the Cistercian abbey of Whitland for a council of war on the morrow of Easter. But he had no need to take further action in Ystrad Tywi. Within two weeks Rhys ap Maredudd came to Carmarthen to seal his agreement with the king in the presence of the lords who served with Chaworth.[112] The document now drawn up reflects the extent to which Llywelyn reaped the deep-rooted animosity due to his failure, in the aftermath of the triumph at Cymerau, to satisfy the aspirations of the powerful figure who had deserted him then and whose son abandoned him now. The objective of the lineage remained unchanged: the restitution of Cantref Mawr in its entirety, if not Ystrad Tywi as a whole, to be ruled from Dinefwr by a lord who would be a true heir to Rhys Gryg. It was a moment when political opportunity invoked a compelling sense of patrimony, and it was in the confidence inspired by the memory of the former unity of the province that Rhys ap Maredudd called for the fulfilment of the promise which Henry III had made to his father.[113] The son was given, in the event, no more than a new

[110] Above, pp. 107–8.
[111] *CAC*, 55–6, 71–2.
[112] *LW*, 36–7, 48 (11 April).
[113] J. B. Smith, 'The "Cronica de Wallia" and the dynasty of Dinefwr', *B*, 20 (1962–4), 272–82, suggests that the 'Cronica de Wallia' was compiled in the spring of 1277 and that it reflects Rhys's political aspirations at that time. For possible intercession by Bleddyn Fardd on Llywelyn's behalf, 1277, *GBF*, 46; above, p. 23, n. 80.

promise. Edward agreed that, if the castle of Dinefwr and the four commotes associated with it should fall to the king in war, Rhys's claim upon them would be given proper judicial consideration.

The implications of this agreement for Llywelyn's cause in Deheubarth are quite obvious. Rhys Wyndod, lord of Dinefwr and those four commotes, was put under heavy pressure to submit to the king's lordship. Chaworth had sufficient forces at his disposal to force him into submission if he did not come promptly, but Rhys Wyndod submitted with a minimum of delay. After just two weeks, implicitly acknowledging that he could not afford to maintain any further resistance and appreciating the threat to his entire position in Ystrad Tywi, Rhys Wyndod accepted terms by which, though he lost Dinefwr and two commotes, he was permitted to retain the remainder of his inheritance: Malláen and Caeo in Cantref Mawr and Hirfryn, Perfedd and Is Cennen in Cantref Bychan, but not the castles of Llandovery and Carreg Cennen.[114] Rhys ap Meredudd's hopes of extending his dominions in Ystrad Tywi at the expense of his kinsmen were not entirely fulfilled as yet, but he secured, to add to his castle of Dryslwyn and the commotes of Catheiniog and Mabudrud, his kinsmen's commotes of Maenordeilo and Mabelfyw.[115] His early secession had important consequences not only in Ystrad Tywi but in Ceredigion. Gruffudd ap Maredudd, heir to part of the patrimony of Maredudd ab Owain in Ceredigion, realized that he would expose himself to expropriation if he did not respond quickly to the king's persuasions. Twenty years earlier Henry III had held out to Maredudd ap Rhys Gryg the prospect that he might, in adherence to the king, enhance his position by the king's grant of the commotes of Gwynionydd and Mabwynion then held by Maredudd ab Owain.[116] These were still coveted by Rhys ap Maredudd, and he was told that, if he could persuade Gruffudd ap Maredudd to submit to the king, Gruffudd would be recompensed elsewhere.[117] Gruffudd was placed in a difficult dilemma. He was already negotiating with Chaworth by the middle of March but he evidently hesitated and during the following weeks the royal commander took a large force into Ceredigion and forced him into submission.[118] Chaworth wrested Mefennydd and Anhuniog from Gruffudd and

---

[114] *LW*, 49; *CPR, 1272–78*, 212. The castles of Cantref Bychan (Llandovery and Carreg Cennen) were ceded to the king (*LW*, 64; *CWR*, 163, 182, 236–7).

[115] Maenordeilo was in his possession in June 1280, though by then the king was seeking to arrange an exchange by which he could secure it; Mabelfyw was not among the commotes conveyed to Rhys ap Maredudd in 1282, so he may have received it in 1277 (*LW*, 165–6; *CWR*, 182, 185).

[116] *LW*, 161–2.

[117] *LW*, 37. Rhys persisted with his claim to the commotes in 1282–3 (*LW*, 159, 165).

[118] Chaworth had received Gruffudd into the king's peace, pending a formal agreement, by 21 March, but he still planned to proceed to the neighbourhood of Llanbadarn Fawr, with the greatest possible strength, on 5 April (*CAC*, 71).

his brother Cynan and took Perfedd from Rhys Fychan ap Rhys ap Maelgwn.[119] By the terms of their formal submission, early in May, Gruffudd and Cynan were required to relinquish those two commotes, and it is likely that Rhys Fychan ceded Perfedd as the price of his admission into the king's peace.[120] By Whitsun, 16 May, in the words of Chaworth's communication to the king, the greatest, strongest and most noble by birth in Deheubarth were on their way to Edward to submit themselves to his will: from Ystrad Tywi, Rhys ap Maredudd and Rhys Wyndod and, from Ceredigion, Rhys Fychan ap Rhys ap Maelgwn, Gruffudd ap Maredudd and Cynan ap Maredudd, taking their young nephew Llywelyn ab Owain (son of Owain ap Maredudd) along with them.[121] They duly did homage to Edward at Worcester.

The situation in Ceredigion remained unstable for some time and, partly to provide protection for the workmen gathered for the building of a castle in the area, Edmund, earl of Lancaster, the king's brother, and Chaworth were constrained to lead a large army there. They reached Llanbadarn Fawr on 25 July and decided upon a site on the north side of the estuary of the Rheidol where building promptly began.[122] The building works may have helped to create new disturbances as Rhys Fychan ap Rhys ap Maelgwn, despite his earlier submission to the king, fled to Llywelyn in Gwynedd, taking the men of Genau'r Glyn with him, the chronicler's statement to this effect substantiated by royal records.[123] There he joined Hywel ap Rhys Gryg and Llywelyn ap Rhys (a brother of Rhys Wyndod), to make Gwynedd once more a refuge for the disinherited as it had been in the days of heroic resistance thirty years before.[124] The subjugation of Deheubarth was now complete. By late September the earl of Lancaster and Chaworth felt free to leave Ceredigion, and the king was confident enough to allow the lords of Deheubarth to return to their lands.[125] The reassertion of the king's control over Deheubarth had taken a little time, but the expenditure on the campaigning had not been enormous and the king's ability to sow dissension among the prince's lieges had been a key factor in his achievement.

[119] *BT, Pen20*, 224; *Pen20Tr*, 118; *RBH*, 264–5.
[120] *LW*, 41 (2 May). Rhys Fychan surrendered on 24 April (*CPR, 1272–81*, 208), evidently in the wake of Chaworth's advance.
[121] *CAC*, 70–1 (Chaworth to Edward, 7 May); *BT, Pen20*, 224–5; *Pen20Tr*, 118; *RBH*, 264–7. The princes, named by the chronicler, did homage at Worcester 1 July. For the commotes held by the lords of Ceredigion, R. A. Griffiths, *PW*, i, 3–4.
[122] *AC*, 105, 'apud Llan Padarn'; *BT, Pen20*, 225; *Pen20Tr*, 118, 'built a castle at Aberystwyth'; *RBH*, 266–7, 'came to Llanbadarn and began to build the castle of Aberystwyth'; *HKW*, i, 299–308; Morris, *WW*, 136–8, from E101/3/20; *ParlWrits*, i, 209–13.
[123] *BT, Pen20*, 225; *Pen20Tr*, 119; *RBH*, 266–7 (7 August); Genau'r Glyn, Perfedd and Creuddyn were taken into the king's hands.
[124] For this group in the war of 1282–3, below, pp. 459–60, 571–2, 574, 576–7.
[125] *BT, Pen20*, 224–5; *Pen20Tr*, 118–19; *RBH*, 264–7.

Aberconwy

Uncertain loyalties among members of the princely lineages did much to undermine Llywelyn ap Gruffudd's position in Powys, too, though the situation differed greatly in the southern and northern lordships. In Powys Wenwynwyn, the problems which had erupted in 1274 stemmed from the uneasy relationship between Gruffudd ap Gwenwynwyn and Llywelyn and, following the former's early departure from the principality, he was able to participate in the action by which Llywelyn was repulsed. Though he was unable to improve upon his previous position in the area, the fall of Dolforwyn certainly enabled him to reassert an authority which secured his control over the whole of Powys Wenwynwyn, including Arwystli and the lands in Cyfeiliog that Llywelyn had previously denied him. In Powys Fadog there was no mischief comparable to that which had convulsed the principality of Wales in 1274, but the course of events three years later revealed the far-reaching effect of the king's ability to exploit internal dynastic dissension. Difficulties had arisen between the sons of Gruffudd ap Madog – Madog, Llywelyn, Owain and Gruffudd Fychan – over the disposition of territory made after their father's death in 1269.[126] The problems may simply have reflected an inequality in the partition by which, possibly through the prince's influence, Madog ap Gruffudd had received what his younger brothers regarded as an excessively large share. On the other hand, it is conceivable that Madog may have attempted to maintain something of the unity of that entire patrimony which, in the previous generation, had been centred on Castell Dinas Brân. There would be obvious advantage to Llywelyn if he could ensure that the greater part of a lordship of such strategic importance, if not the entire patrimony, were vested in a single lord. It may be pertinent, too, that Madog was married to Llywelyn's sister Margaret. The precise problems in Powys Fadog are not easy to identify, but by the end of 1276 they had proved sufficiently serious to cause the defection of the second son, Llywelyn ap Gruffudd ap Madog, or Llywelyn ap Gruffudd Fychan (the name by which he will be known in this discussion). This was, as we have seen, a matter to which Prince Llywelyn referred in one of the two sets of proposals submitted to the king early in 1277. His departure was undoubtedly caused by dissensions within the lineage of Powys Fadog, possibly exacerbated by the prince's intervention, and was spurred by the prospect of royal intervention in the area.[127]

By the spring of 1277 the earl of Warwick, with Dafydd ap Gruffudd beside him, pressed upon Powys Fadog with a royal force based on Chester.[128] The earl was able not only to exert the military power at his disposal, but to

---

[126] J. B. Smith, 'Dynastic succession in medieval Wales', *B*, 33 (1986), 228–9.
[127] Ibid. for the possibility of a *parage*, with the eldest son exercising seigniorial authority over the whole inheritance and his brothers holding their lands as his tenants.
[128] Morris, *WW*, 115–20. Dafydd was active in the vicinity of Chester before the end of 1276 (*CPR, 1272–81*, 186); for his anxieties, below, pp. 425–6.

exploit the political contingency created by the younger brother's defection. Madog ap Gruffudd was, in effect, forced to choose between submission to the king and disinheritance in favour of Llywelyn Gruffudd Fychan. The document recording the terms of Madog's submission reflects the devastating effect of these dissensions. An entirely new partition would be made between the portions of Madog and Llywelyn: Maelor would be given to one, Nanheudwy to the other, and the remainder would be shared equally between them. Castell Dinas Brân, hitherto the centre of the patrimony and the symbol of its unity, but now situated on the boundary between two clearly defined lordships, was liable to be finally destroyed.[129] The king would decide whether the castle should stand or whether it should be thrown down. It is perfectly evident that military defence of this crucial quarter was seriously undermined by dynastic discord. Resistance was in fact maintained at Castell Dinas Brân for some weeks after Madog's submission but who exactly was responsible for this continued stand is unclear, and it is possible that men loyal to Prince Llywelyn stood firm after the lords of Powys Fadog had abandoned the struggle. But on 10 May – a month after Madog ap Gruffudd's submission – the earl of Lincoln, his task at Montgomery now completed, gathered his army for an assault upon the stronghold high above the Dee. He then learned that the garrison had set fire to the castle and withdrawn. Two days later he saw it for himself and found that, despite the damage, the tower and walls were intact and he judged that there was 'no stronger castle in Wales, nor in England a greater'.[130]

The end of resistance at the key to Powys Fadog was another serious reverse for Llywelyn. Writing to Edward with an account of the progress made since the fall of Dolforwyn, Roger Mortimer was able to report the penetration of the furthermost reaches of Powys Wenwynwyn and Powys Fadog, listing Caereinion, Cyfeiliog, Mawddwy, Mechain, Cynllaith and Nanheudwy. He thus recorded the virtual completion of operations in the theatre for which he had held the main responsibility.[131] By the end of May the king was, as we have indicated already, in a position to release the forces he had employed since the beginning of the year, knowing that the broad principality of Wales had been destroyed by the combined effect of its internal dissensions and his purposeful military and political initiatives. He had been able to convince some of the most powerful among the lords of Wales that

---

[129] *LW*, 53–4, an agreement between Warwick and Dafydd, on the king's behalf, and Madog ap Gruffudd, 12 April 1277, the day after Rhys ap Maredudd's submission in Deheubarth.

[130] *CAC*, 83. Situated on the border between the lordship of Chirk and that of Bromfield and Yale, Castell Dinas Brân was abandoned; Roger Mortimer built a castle at Chirk, the Earl Warenne at Holt.

[131] SC1/21/188, for which see below, n. 155.

their interests were no longer at one with those of the prince of Wales. It was time for a return to the age-old loyalties of the Welsh lineages to the crown of England which had been disturbed only by the transitory ascendancies of the thirteenth-century princes of Gwynedd. Edward had already done a great deal more than apply his corrective hand so as to bring the prince of Wales to a state of obedience in which he would fulfil his duties as a vassal in respect of the princedom he had been granted ten years before. The principality of Wales had been dismembered, the prince's broader supremacy terminated, but Edward would not stop there. He could now gather his forces anew for that assault on Snowdonia on which he had set his mind for a long time. Llywelyn ap Gruffudd had need now to defend his position in the land over which he exercised immediate lordship.

When Edward came to Chester in the middle of July his mind was set on nothing less than the possession of Gwynedd in its entirety and the complete disinheritance of Llywelyn ap Gruffudd. His purposes are best revealed some weeks later when he issued a document which prescribed the territorial dispositions he envisaged for Gwynedd Uwch Conwy.[132] No mention was made of Gwynedd Is Conwy, the Four Cantreds of Perfeddwlad, for this would presumably be retained under the king's lordship. He was still to make a choice between two alternatives with regard to Gwynedd Uwch Conwy but, either way, the whole of that territory would be at the king's disposal. He would either divide Anglesey, Snowdonia, Llŷn and Penllyn between himself and Dafydd ap Gruffudd and Owain ap Gruffudd, or he would take Anglesey for himself and divide the remainder between Dafydd and Owain. Dafydd's truculent presence in the king's forces, and his acute sensitivity on matters which might affect his interests, may help explain why Edward found it necessary to declare his intentions at this stage.[133] The earl of Warwick had felt bound to report to the king that Dafydd was angry that his men were not paid as he judged was appropriate, insisting that their wages should be paid to him in a single sum, and urging their right to booty. Dafydd was perturbed, too, that others were pressing their claims for land in Wales, so much so that Warwick feared for his continued fidelity. Likewise, the fact that Madog ap Llywelyn was among those in the king's following, and in receipt of financial support, may explain why Edward acknowledged that, under the one arrangement or the other envisaged for Gwynedd Uwch Conwy, he would be prepared to consider any claim which might be made in respect of

---

[132] *LW*, 103–4; *Foedera*, I, ii, 544; brief entry in *CPR, 1272–81*, 225.
[133] *CAC*, 55, 66–8; payments to Dafydd are noticed later.

Meirionnydd.[134] He would do justice in this according to the law and custom of Wales. Pressure exerted by the expatriates may explain Edward's decision to declare his plans, but it is clear that the king was determined to maintain a secure hold on Gwynedd thereafter. The king reserved his right to retain, for reasons of security, any part of Snowdonia and make an appropriate exchange with Dafydd and Owain. He revealed a wariness lest he commit himself to a course of action which might see Dafydd too securely entrenched in the patrimonial heartland. The provisions in this document fell far short of what Dafydd would have wished, but there was no crumb of comfort for the prince of Wales. Llywelyn would know, if he were aware of this explicit if not definitive statement the king's intentions, that if he failed to withstand the assault on Gwynedd he would face complete disinheritance. The final incorporation of Gwynedd within the realm was now firmly fixed in the king's mind, his intentions clearly revealed in the proposal that Dafydd and Owain should be summoned to the king's parliaments in England (*ad parliamenta nostra in Anglia*) just as other earls and barons of the king were called upon to attend.[135] The monarchy's plans for Gwynedd had never been more clearly stated. Nor had there been more convincing evidence of its ability to fulfil its purposes than what was being displayed on the Chester front by the date on which this declaration of intent was made.

The document was issued at 'le Flynt near Basingwerk' on 23 August, when Dafydd was also granted the lordship of Hope, and by then, to a much greater degree than was the case in the early months of the year, the king's ability to launch a major military campaign was being revealed very clearly. He could draw on the resources of a land vastly richer than that on which Llywelyn had to depend. Nevertheless, countless royal campaigns in Wales had revealed the difficulties encountered in harnessing those resources for the needs of war. Time and again campaigns had been hampered, not so much by tactical ineptitude, but by a failure to maintain the supplies and the money for sustained military pressure. Edward's operations in the march and in Powys and Deheubarth had shown the advantages of being able to deploy cohorts of cavalry and infantry maintained from royal coffers for as long as they were needed in the field. To pay these forces, now greatly increased in number, Edward drew heavily on loans provided by the Italian banking houses, and credit finance became a new and crucial factor in the armed conflict between England and Wales.[136] Edward turned to the Riccardi of Lucca and a

---

[134] *LW*, 103–4; Madog is on more than one occasion described as 'lord of Meirionnydd' (E101/3/19; Wellcome Medical Historical Library MS 253).

[135] *LW*, 103–4.

[136] R. W. Kaeuper, 'The role of the Italian financiers in the Edwardian conquest of Wales', *WHR*, 6 (1972–3), 387–403; idem, *Bankers to the Crown: the Riccardi of Lucca and Edward I* (Princeton, 1973), 173–91; Prestwich, *Edward I*, 239–40. There are very important

substantial part of the costs of the war, a total expenditure estimated at about £23,000, was met from their advances. By early summer the Riccardi had been charged with providing a war fund, and their movements may be traced as they disposed of their moneys to pay, among innumerable expenses, the wages of the soldiers deployed first in Deheubarth and then, on a much larger scale, in the main theatre of conflict in Gwynedd.

Long before Edward reached Chester on 15 July the city had been filling, not only with soldiers, but with contingents of craftsmen and labourers. Within a week many of these had pitched their tents at the place on the banks of the Dee described as 'the camp near Basingwerk' and then, as we have seen, as 'le Flynt near Basingwerk'.[137] The Welsh chronicler noted that Edward 'fortified a court in Flint with huge ditches around it', and this was the place from which Edward governed the realm until he moved to Rhuddlan.[138] There, on the banks of the Clwyd, diggers from the Fenlands, recruited willingly or unwillingly into his service, gathered in some numbers. They began not only to prepare another court 'with ditches around it' and the site of a second major fortification, but to straighten the course of the river to ensure that the castle could be supported directly by sea.[139] It would take many months to complete the works at Rhuddlan and Flint, but it seems clear that from the beginning Edward was giving effect to a plan to establish two fortresses which would be the centres of a permanent royal lordship in Englefield. Staying only a few days at Rhuddlan, Edward moved on to Degannwy, to encamp once more in the defences above the estuary of the Conwy. There his father had fortified a castle which had been among the major strongholds of his kingdom until Llywelyn had destroyed the defences after a long siege.[140] Edward's memories of Degannwy would have been rather mixed, his estimate of the advantages of a stronghold at that site not altogether favourable, and there is nothing to suggest that he put any new work in hand there. He may, too, even during those early days, have peered across the estuary and realized anew the enormous difficulty of launching an assault upon Gwynedd Uwch Conwy from Degannwy. There were two tasks which he had to undertake without delay. His father had contemplated one of

suggestions of earlier date in E. B. Fryde and M. M. Fryde, 'Public credit, with special reference to north-west Europe', *Cambridge Economic History of Europe*, iii (1963), 456–7, which indicated the significance of the king's credit resources in Anglo-Welsh conflict. For support from Ireland, *CPR, 1272–81*, 209; *CCR, 1272–79*, 373. War costs are estimated in Morris, *WW*, 140–1; Tout, *Chapters*, ii, 112–13; Prestwich, *WPF*, 170; idem, *Edward I*, 182.

[137] J. G. Edwards, 'The building of Flint', *JFlintHS*, 12 (1951), 5–20; Taylor, *SCCB*, 165–72; *HKW*, i, 308–18; for the name 'le Flynt', ibid., 309, n. 6. The advance was made to 'the camp near Basingwerk' on or about 21 July; the accounts do not indicate that advance was delayed by resistance at the castle of Ewloe.
[138] *BT, Pen20*, 225; *Pen20Tr*, 118–19; *RBH*, 266–7.
[139] *HKW*, i, 318–27. For Edward's stay at Rhuddlan, ibid., 319, n. 6 and below, n. 175.
[140] E101/3/19.

them during those hesitant weeks spent at Degannwy twenty summers before, and Edward put that task in hand at once by obtaining the ships to secure the coast and carry an adequate contingent of soldiers to take possession of Anglesey. The king took care, too, as the Welsh chronicles remarked, that they reached the island in time to ensure that the king's reapers, summoned to the task in good numbers, would be able to deprive the defenders of their harvest.[141] Similarly, as his forces undertook their second major task and penetrated inland from their strongholds at Flint and Rhuddlan to secure the moorlands, they were able to gain possession of the cattle kept at the prince's vaccaries and drive them, sometimes even from the distances of Penllyn, to feed his soldiers. Flint and Rhuddlan were designed, not as stepping stones upon the direct campaign route from Chester to Degannwy, but as focal points for the occupation of the Four Cantreds in their entirety. A firm hold would be further assured by the building of another castle at Rhuthun in Dyffryn Clwyd.[142] Secure possession of the interior would make it possible for the king to force the Conwy upstream, but the assault on Uwch Conwy remained a major undertaking. It is not inconceivable that the king, even before he left Degannwy to return to Rhuddlan on 11 September, contemplated an outcome to the conflict substantially different from that envisaged in the document issued at Flint only a short time previously.

Even so, Llywelyn would have no reason to doubt that the king had any intention other than to subjugate his territory by military might. The prince would know, far more clearly than we can possibly know, of the ferocity of the conflict already being waged in Perfeddwlad. Our clearest testimony comes from the complaint which Bishop Anian made to his provincial, alleging that English forces had desecrated churches and churchyards, and inflicted damage on church property including the burning of an episcopal manor.[143] Anian of St Asaph spoke of sacrilege and rape. It was enough, along with the bishop's threat to excommunicate the offenders, to prompt Robert Kilwardby to issue an order to the earl of Warwick to ensure that nothing was tolerated which was in any way contrary to the purposes of the votive expedition (*expediccione votiva*) that had set out under ecclesiastical approbation. The campaign in Wales might have something of the quality of a sanctified mission, but Warwick was warned to ensure that he did not countenance any action which would not be witnessed in conflict waged in

---

[141] *BT, Pen20*, 225; *Pen20Tr*, 119; *RBH*, 266–7; E101/3/16, 19; E101/485/19; payments were made to 360 mowers and reapers among the forces under John de Vesci and Otto de Grandson and others of Edward's *familia* in Anglesey; transport costs in E101/3/15.

[142] Work on Rhuthun castle commenced in the summer of 1277 (*HKW*, i, 327–9) and probably continued until Dyffryn Clwyd was given to Dafydd ap Gruffudd on 10 October.

[143] *Councils*, i, 522–3 (Peniarth MS 231B, 55).

England.[144] Some of the most conspicuous among the prince's opponents – Bishop Anian and, for his own reasons, Dafydd ap Gruffudd – were by no means wholly enamoured of the way the king's campaign was proceeding. But, again, Llywelyn had no reason to question the king's resolve to ensure a military solution, nor to have any doubt concerning the strength of the forces waged against him.

From either end of Bwlch y Ddeufaen, the pass which traversed the high ground between the Conwy valley and the Menai Straits, Llywelyn ap Gruffudd could find ample evidence of the king's military capabilities. From the slopes above his court at Aber he could look across the Straits to Anglesey where Edward's soldiers were already well established, providing protection for those who reaped the harvest and, for all that Llywelyn knew, preparing for an attack upon the mainland. From the other end of the pass, on the slopes above the Conwy, the defenders could see the advance encampments of royal forces which, by the end of August, came to as many as 15,000 foot-soldiers and a commensurate number of mounted men.[145] The defenders would have been able to converse in their own language with a large number of their opponents, for a substantial proportion of the royal forces had been raised in the lordships of the march of Wales. There were contingents from Gwerthrynion and Maelienydd, Elfael and Builth, Radnor and Brecon. They were led by Hywel ap Meurig, one whom Llywelyn had long come to recognize as a resolute adherent of Roger Mortimer and his fellow marchers.[146] Llywelyn had imprisoned Hywel's son, only to concede in the end that neither this, nor any other pressure which might be imposed on the father, would do anything to deter him from adhering to the marchers and to the king whom he was now to serve in numerous capacities. Llywelyn knew some of Hywel's captains, too. The men of Brecon were led by Meurig ap Llywelyn, one of those whom Llywelyn had held in deep suspicion several years before.[147] Those of Elfael came with Ifor ap Gruffudd, to whom the prince had once entrusted the custody of the lordship, and taken his surety for the release of Hywel ap Meurig's son from prison.[148] Einion ap Madog, who was among the leaders of the Builth contingent, had served as Llywelyn's bailiff in

---

[144] The deeds alleged against the English soldiers would be 'omnino contraria expedicioni uotive [et] vestri negocii inchoatis'.

[145] Morris, *WW*, 131–2. This was the highest number to serve Edward at any one time during 1277; numbers fell substantially from early September.

[146] E101/3/11. There were 2,700 foot-soldiers led by twenty-six constables in addition to Hywel ap Meurig, described as the steward of the king, the earl of Hereford and Roger Mortimer. For the release of John ap Hywel ap Meurig, above, n. 104.

[147] Above, p. 357.

[148] The document of 1276 concerning the son's release was drawn up at Brynysgefyll, described as Ifor's *manerium* (*LW*, 41–2). For his subsequent association with the lord of Elfael, *Select Cases in the Court of King's Bench*, ii, 58.

Gwerthrynion.[149] Llywelyn had to come to terms with the fact that forces from lands which had so recently formed part of his principality were now gathering on the frontiers of Snowdonia for the decisive conflict, but neither this, nor the obvious fact that royal forces were now closing upon him, were the only factors which, by the early autumn, might have given him cause to consider his position and ultimately decide, like his grandfather before him, to submit to the will of the king of England.

The relevant and incontrovertible evidence is slight but enough to point to the fact that by the late summer of 1277 Llywelyn endured the anguish of a desertion on the part of some of his own men similar to one that he would face once more during the final conflict five years later. To lose the loyalty of his men in the march or in the provinces of Powys and Deheubarth was a grievous reverse; it was an altogether more serious matter to lose the fidelity of men of substance in his own patrimony in Gwynedd, and their defection was undoubtedly a key matter in his predicament as he faced his critical confrontation with Edward. There were ominous indications even before the king set off from Chester, when a document was drawn up which casts a shaft of cold light on the situation facing Llywelyn even in Gwynedd Uwch Conwy.[150] By an instrument drawn up on 21 July, Friar Llywelyn ap Gruffudd of the Dominican Order testified that he had interceded on behalf of three men of some consequence in Gwynedd, and counselled them to do homage to the king. Each was related to the friar, one of them being his brother, Rhys ap Gruffudd, and there is no doubt that Llywelyn and Rhys were sons of Gruffudd ab Ednyfed Fychan, an early adherent of Prince Llywelyn ap Gruffudd and a major figure in the most eminent lineage in thirteenth-century Gwynedd.[151] Evidence from a slightly later period indicates that there was a close association between the descendants of Ednyfed Fychan and the Dominican house at Bangor,[152] and Friar Llywelyn ap Gruffudd, who was its prior by 1277, played an altogether intriguing role in the events of these tumultuous years.[153] Two Dominicans, said to be drawn from among the *magnates* of Wales, were found in the ship which brought Eleanor de Montfort to Wales, and we have seen that Edward, probably rightly, concluded that members of the Order of Preachers had been deeply

---

[149] Einion had been among those who guaranteed the fidelity of Hywel ap Meurig's son (*LW*, 41–2); he was said in evidence recorded in 1343 to have been granted Hafod Fraith ('Haverod Vyreich') in Builth by Llywelyn (*ArchCamb, Original Documents*, 1877, clxxv).

[150] E30/1512 (21 July 1277), printed with commentary in J. B. Smith, 'Welsh Dominicans and the crisis of 1277', *B*, 22 (1966–8), 353–7.

[151] Above, pp. 45–6, 313–14.

[152] G. Roberts, *Aspects of Welsh History*, 226–8.

[153] Llywelyn's name may be added to those of the descendants of Ednyfed Fychan, ibid., 184–7, 227–8; Bartrum, *WG*, iv. 681. His role after the treaty of Aberconwy is noticed later; for his part in making the extents of Gwynedd, above, p. 191, n. 21.

involved in the negotiations by which the marriage had been arranged and completed.¹⁵⁴ The friars are not named at the time of the capture, but it is certain that Llywelyn ap Gruffudd, prior of Bangor, was one of Eleanor's companions on that fateful voyage.

This emerges from the letter which Roger Mortimer sent to Edward upon the completion of military operations in the Montgomery sector in the early summer of 1277. Evidently writing about the middle of May, Mortimer, as we have seen, was able to report the total collapse of Llywelyn's position, not only in the march but in Powys Wenwynwyn and Powys Fadog. He was able, too, to provide the king with vital information concerning three of Llywelyn's closest confidants.¹⁵⁵ Friar Llywelyn ap Gruffudd was by then ready to transfer his own allegiance to the king. Members of the religious orders were obviously affected by the conflicting influences peculiar to those in holy orders and, if Edward's request to the archbishop had been heeded, the two Welsh friars would have had to explain their position to Robert Kilwardby upon their coming into his custody at the beginning of 1276.¹⁵⁶ There is no reason to believe that Friar Llywelyn's loyalty to his prince was undermined at that stage; he may indeed have been one of the Dominicans who were sent as envoys to the archbishop three months later, and he may have remained active on the prince's behalf until the spring of 1277.¹⁵⁷ His breach with Llywelyn came by the intercession of Roger Mortimer, who recommended that the friar should go at once to the archbishop. Robert Kilwardby may well have impressed upon him where his duty lay in relation to a secular ruler whom the church had felt bound to excommunicate. But the pressures which brought the friar to the point of defection were not altogether those peculiar to a person in holy orders. Churchmen and men of religion were not a class apart from the laymen of the lineages to which they belonged for they were subject to the compulsions which affected their kinsmen and peers. Certainly, Mortimer was concerned to facilitate the defection, not of the Dominican

---

¹⁵⁴ Above, n. 23.

¹⁵⁵ The letter, SC1/21/188, is not in *CAC* and I owe a photographic copy and transcript of a good deal of a barely legible text to the kindness of Dr Arnold Taylor. The letter refers to the fall of lands, such as Caereinion, Cyfeiliog, Mochnant, Mawddwy, Cynllaith and Nanheudwy, not reported in letters sent by Mortimer, Lacy and Grandson immediately after the taking of Dolforwyn; probably written about mid-May, it prompted the safe-conduct for Rhys ap Gruffudd and Hywel ap Gruffudd, coming to the king's peace, 22 May (*CPR, 1272–81*, 211).

¹⁵⁶ Above, n. 24.

¹⁵⁷ The Dominican mission in March 1276 has been noticed. Friar Llywelyn and another Dominican were given safe-conducts to come to the king on 6 March 1277 (*CPR, 1272–81*, 197), after the prince's excommunication but fifteen days before Bishop Anian pronounced sentence in the diocese of Bangor. It is possible that the friars were then engaged on the prince's errand, and Mortimer's letter suggests defection about mid-May. Ifor ap Gruffudd, prior of Rhuddlan, possibly another envoy, also identified himself with the king (E101/3/19), cf. below, n. 177.

alone, but his brothers Rhys ap Gruffudd and Hywel ap Gruffudd as well. Nor were the laymen without their links with families of comparable status beyond the frontiers of the prince's domains and beyond the frontiers of Wales. Just as the princes had intermarried with baronial families of the march and further afield, so these non-princely lineages established similar alliances. In the document which he drew up at Chester the prior promised that his brother, Rhys ap Gruffudd, and two other kinsmen, should be provided with appropriate sustenance in accordance with the arrangements which the prior would make in association with Roger Lestrange, and he was Rhys ap Gruffudd's brother-in-law.[158] Several weeks evidently elapsed before the defection, first intimated to the king by Roger Mortimer, was completed by the transactions at Chester. Yet it is clear that, already by the middle of May, Mortimer was able to inform the king that key figures in an important lineage – 'le plus fort linguage de Wales' – were prepared to abandon their fealty to the prince even though they were among his closest confidants. The defectors may have had to await a favourable opportunity to make their escape from Gwynedd. In the event, Rhys ap Gruffudd was foiled in his purposes and imprisoned, but he was not the only one of his milieu to withdraw from the prince's service at this time of great stress.[159]

Associated with Rhys ap Gruffudd in the prior's document were two others, themselves described as kinsmen (*consanguines*) of the friar, who may be regarded as representative figures from among the upper echelons of society in Gwynedd in the period of the princes. Hywel ap Goronwy was a son of Goronwy ab Ednyfed who, 'wise in counsel and true in deed', had served as Llywelyn ap Gruffudd's seneschal, and he was thus a first cousin of the prior and Rhys ap Gruffudd.[160] Gruffudd ap Iorwerth belonged to a prominent Anglesey lineage descended from Hwfa ap Cynddelw, his tombstone being among the remains of the Dominican friary at Bangor.[161] It happens that among the comparatively few surviving poems addressed to members of

---

[158] *CWR*, 285.

[159] Under the terms of the treaty of Aberconwy Llywelyn was required to release him and restore the lands he had held when he negotiated his adherence to the king (*LW*, 119); for his activities after 1277, below pp. 445, 477.

[160] Restoration of lands to Tudur ap Goronwy, Goronwy Fychan and Hywel ap Goronwy, 12 September 1278 (*CWR*, 175) indicates that all three were sons of Goronwy ab Ednyfed; inclusion of Hywel (ibid.; SC6/1156/1, in *THSC*, 1895–6, 123) suggests that he may not have defected from Llywelyn. Hywel can be added to the sons of Goronwy in G. Roberts, *Aspects of Welsh History*, 184–7, 227–8. For Tudur ap Goronwy as a benefactor of the Dominican house, ibid., 227; J. B. Smith, 'Welsh Dominicans', 355–6.

[161] J. B. Smith, 'Welsh Dominicans', 354–5; idem, 'Edward II and the allegiance of Wales', *WHR*, 8 (1976–7), 144–5, 170–1. For the monument, C. A. Gresham, *Medieval Stone Carving in North Wales* (Cardiff, 1968), no. 45; *Inventory Caern*, II, no. 684. Gruffudd's lands have been noticed already.

the non-princely lineages of the thirteenth century there are two which commemorate the persons, Hywel ap Goronwy and Gruffudd ap Iorwerth, who sought to secede to the king in the company of Rhys ap Gruffudd. Each is the work of Bleddyn Fardd, who would eventually compose an elegy of exceptional finesse in memory of Llywelyn ap Gruffudd.[162] In the poet's estimation Hywel was 'a brave and generous one of the finest lineage'; it could not be doubted that Gruffudd ap Iorwerth was 'a chosen warrior renowned of honour'. But by the summer of 1277 these were virtues placed at the service of the king of England and, though these matters can be seen but darkly, the evidence suggests that, as he approached the confines of Gwynedd, Edward's support was not to be confined to that of disillusioned princes. Monetary gifts from the king are by no means confined to men of the status of Dafydd ap Gruffudd, or Llywelyn ap Gruffudd Fychan, or Madog ap Llywelyn. Rhys ap Gruffudd was unable to make his escape and was confined by the prince, but his brother Hywel ap Gruffudd, also commended to the king by Roger Mortimer, is found in royal service.[163] Gruffudd ap Iorwerth served in the war and was rewarded.[164] Names such as those of Cynfrig Sais, Tudur ap Gruffudd and Tudur Fychan may be added to the list of defectors. There were others who remained within the prince's power against their will, for Rhys ap Gruffudd and Iorwerth Foel were surely not the only seceders to endure the prince's wrath.[165] But, from the evidence relating to the humiliation of Prince Llywelyn ap Gruffudd, no piece is more intriguing than the brief entry which records that Edward I gave the sum of £20 for some service fulfilled by one named Gruffudd ab yr Ynad, who may be safely identified as the person who was to compose the magnificent elegy of Llywelyn ap Gruffudd.[166] We can only imagine what commendable service earned him such a substantial bounty from the royal coffers in the aftermath of the war of 1277.

---

[162] *GBF*, 47, 56.

[163] E101/3/19.

[164] More than one of this name appear in records but Gruffudd ap Iorwerth of the lineage of Hwfa ap Cynddelw, who went to the king's court early in 1278, was the person given land at Maenan for his good services in the war. The grant may have been made on account of his exclusion from his Anglesey lands, for Dafydd ap Gruffudd petitioned that Gruffudd might have his lands there restored, evidently hoping that Edward would bring pressure on Llywelyn. After the war of 1282–3 he was given land at Rhosmor in exchange for Maenan. He is probably the person who was bailiff of Maelor Saesneg in 1278 (Wellcome Medical Historical Library MS 253; *CWR*, 161, 164, 178, 183, 290; *CAC*, 74; *WAR*, 260–1).

[165] Iorwerth Foel of Aberffraw complained that Llywelyn took his revenge upon him after he joined the king (*RotParl*, i, 5; Carr, *MAng*, 53, 55, 95–6); for the case of Madog ab Einion, noticed presently, above, p. 46.

[166] E101/3/19: 'Gruffino Aberennard Wallico, de dono regis, xx li'. He may be identified as Gruffudd ab yr Ynad Coch, who composed the great elegy of Llywelyn ap Gruffudd.

Aberconwy

The considerable strength of the forces at his service, his knowledge that the prince could no longer depend on the loyalty of some of his men, and his siege of a prince's dominion already deprived of its more productive areas might suggest that Edward had no reason to do anything but persist with that intention to secure the total appropriation of Gwynedd Uwch Conwy that he had declared during the summer. Military assault might be difficult and might take time, but deprivation would gradually tell on the defenders. Edward had no need to turn to his Vegetius to appreciate that more often is an army destroyed by famine than by battle, that hunger is more cruel than the sword.[167] Contemporary commentators saw the war of 1277 as, more than anything else, a siege of Snowdonia which left its defenders in a dire state of starvation.[168] Yet the conflict was concluded not by a total submission on the part of Llywelyn and the consequential confiscation of his land, but through a negotiated settlement. By early November king and prince had agreed to a treaty which fell short of securing for Edward the objectives which, as it seems, he had set himself at the outset of his campaign in Gwynedd. The territorial provisions envisaged for Dafydd ap Gruffudd and his brother were obviously contingent upon the defeat of Llywelyn and the annexation of his territory. But on 10 October, a full month before agreement was reached between the two main protagonists, Edward issued a charter which pronounced that he was bestowing upon Dafydd ap Gruffudd two of the Four Cantreds.[169] The grant of Rhufoniog and Dyffryn Clwyd was in fact a reaffirmation of a concession which Edward had made to Dafydd when he had first defected in 1263.[170] At that time Edward was not in a position to give Dafydd possession of the lands, and his charter could be no more than a pledge of an undertaking to be fulfilled when circumstances allowed. But the charter of 1263 itself specifically acknowledged that the provision of an estate in the Four Cantreds was a measure taken so as to provide for Dafydd, and implicitly to retain his allegiance, until such time as he could obtain his due portion of Gwynedd Uwch Conwy. This was again the declared purpose of the charter issued in the autumn of 1277; the transaction was completed in expectation of a permanent provision by which Dafydd would be invested with a share of Gwynedd Uwch Conwy.

Yet the precise reason for making the grant remains to be considered, more particularly whether it was seen by Edward as a temporary expedient, made in anticipation of an early conquest of Gwynedd, or whether it was already envisaged as the only form of settlement which could conceivably be made for

---

[167] *Vegetius*, 69 [Liber III, 3]: 'saepius enim penuria quam pugna consumit exercitum et ferro saeuior fames est'.
[168] Cotton, *HistAng*, 155.
[169] *CPR, 1272–81*, 231–2.
[170] Above, p. 154.

the foreseeable future. It is clear that Dafydd was constantly vigilant of his interests and Edward had to draw upon the resources of his treasury to maintain him. He had given him the lordship of Hope, and helped him with the construction of the castle within its bounds at Caergwrle, but this was clearly not enough and substantial monetary payments continued to be made to him.[171] Dafydd was evidently an exceedingly prickly adherent, and we have seen already that the earl of Warwick had found it necessary to report the difficulties which had arisen during the course of the campaign. Dafydd would not easily set aside his suspicion that the king might bestow conquered territory upon members of the English baronage who aspired to lands in Wales and do so to the exclusion of his own claims.[172] The grant of the two *cantrefi* could conceivably have been made to placate the restive prince while the final appropriation of Gwynedd was still being sought, a concession soon to be superseded by a new provision in accord with Edward's declaration of the month of August. Alternatively, and much more likely, the king's decision in October might be taken to signify that he had by now decided that he would not proceed with the annexation of Gwynedd Uwch Conwy. The charter would thus stand as a means of satisfying Dafydd's demands until the king was given an opportunity, other than the present campaign, to secure possession of Gwynedd Uwch Conwy.

The forces deployed in north-west Wales, the incentives given to members of Llywelyn's entourage to defect, or the pressures exerted on them to do so, the continuing siege of the prince's narrowed dominion, all this might thus be diverted, not to an outright military solution, but a negotiated settlement. On purely military grounds a solution other than one secured by frontal assault might well be preferable on Edward's part. Indeed, ever since the early part of September, not long after the king had withdrawn from Degannwy, the ranks of his soldiers had been gradually thinned as more and more men were released from service; the military activities had possibly lessened even by the time the king's men had gathered the harvest in Anglesey. It is possible that Edward, like his father before him, had paused on the Conwy estuary and acknowledged that an assault on Snowdonia, with a force of soldiers properly paid and adequately supplied but inexperienced in combat, would certainly be expensive and might well be hazardous. He may even then have acknowledged that he could not be assured of an efficacious assault until he had the means, not only to occupy Anglesey and deprive the prince of its crops, but to attack the mainland from the island. The fact that he put preparations in

---

[171] Payments in E101/3/19; C62/53, m. 5; Wellcome Medical Historical Library MS 253; cf. *CAC*, 67–8. He was given Hope on 23 August and later aid for the building of Caergwrle (*CPR, 1272–81*, 227; Taylor, *SCCB*, 177–8; *HKW*, i, 330–2; King, 'Dinas Brân and Caergwrle', *ArchCamb*, 123 (1974), 117–18, 131–9; idem, *CA*, i, 151).
[172] Above, p. 425.

hand for this feature of his strategy at a very early stage of the war of 1282 may well suggest that he was by then determined to ensure that he had the means to a military advantage that he had found wanting in the earlier campaign.[173] His father's incompetence may account for much of the frustration endured by the armies who had tarried on the banks of the Conwy in the past, but Edward may have recognized that the defeat of Llywelyn in Snowdonia could prove an exceedingly expensive operation. The means to that end would, in any case, need to include not only forcing the Conwy well upstream and taking possession of Anglesey, but crossing from the island to the mainland at the very heart of the prince's citadel. Edward may well have recognized by the late summer of 1277 that he did not possess the resources to enable him to accomplish the combined movements which, in the event, he was to set in motion in the weeks following the death of Llywelyn.[174]

It is thus possible that the charter which Edward issued in favour of Dafydd ap Gruffudd on 10 October 1277 reflected his acknowledgement that he would not dislodge Llywelyn ap Gruffudd from Gwynedd Uwch Conwy, and that he no longer anticipated that he would be able to summon Owain ap Gruffudd and Dafydd ap Gruffudd to parliament, certainly not in respect of baronies west of the Conwy. Edward's decision may not have been dictated entirely by military, and hence financial, considerations. The document in which he set out his proposals for the disposition of Gwynedd Uwch Conwy during the summer had betrayed an underlying unease at the prospect of Dafydd securely entrenched in the heartland of Welsh resistance to royal authority. Dafydd's constant presence in the king's entourage in the following weeks may well have finally convinced the king that the displacement of Llywelyn by his brother – involving a major military commitment and a considerable outlay – would be a decidedly questionable advantage. For the present he would retain Rhos and Englefield for himself and he would proceed with the construction work at Rhuddlan and Flint; he would bestow the remainder of the Four Cantreds – Dyffryn Clwyd and Rhufoniog – upon Dafydd, and he would proceed no further with the work at Rhuthun. Dafydd might well be able to secure his portion of Gwynedd Uwch Conwy in the fullness of time, but that objective would not now be sought by the present campaign. Dafydd would have to reconcile himself to the fact it might be some time before he could secure lordship in the land beyond the Conwy.

---

[173] Below, pp. 526–7.

[174] Protections continued to be issued to those serving with Edward, some extending to the spring of 1278; this might suggest preparation for a lengthy campaign, but even then it might point to siege of Snowdonia rather than outright assault (*CPR, 1272–82*, 221–2). For some of the considerations which may have influenced Edward's decision to curtail the war, Prestwich, *Edward I*, 181–2.

Aberconwy

The main principles of the agreement that the king would be prepared to make with Llywelyn had possibly been agreed by the date of the grant to Dafydd. Two days later, 12 October, the chancery appears to have moved from Rhuddlan to Shrewsbury and documents were dated there until 2 November. The king's presence is more difficult to locate and it is possible that he was at Rhuddlan, or at least in Perfeddwlad, for part, if not the whole, of that period of twenty days.[175] The records suggest a still lower level of military activity in this period than before, and it is possible that by mid-October emissaries were empowered to discuss terms with the prince's proctors. Whatever the reason, after a period of exceptional quietude in the records, there was a sudden burst of activity from 2 November, and the chancellor hurried back to Rhuddlan.[176] On that day arrangements were made for the completion of peace negotiations conducted by the king's counsellors and those of Llywelyn at the Cistercian abbey of Aberconwy, exchanges in which Bishop Anian of St Asaph had played a mediating role.[177] Now Anthony Bek, Robert Tibetot and Brother William of Southampton, provincial of the Order of Preachers, were authorized to receive Llywelyn's oath and to confirm the agreements already made.[178] It is thus clear that Llywelyn ap Gruffudd's emissaries, his seneschal Tudur ab Ednyfed and Goronwy ap Heilin, had by then completed negotiations of some substance.[179] The sudden surge of activity now detectable in chancery records, registered in a new Welsh roll, may suggest that one side or the other had yielded upon a problem which had hitherto been difficult to resolve, or that both parties may have agreed upon a compromise on a fundamental issue. It may thus be significant that on 3

---

[175] Enrolments suggest that the chancery was at Shrewsbury 15–30 October (H. Gough, *Itinerary of Edward I 1272–1307* (Paisley, 1900); Morris, *WW*, 136). *Chancery Warrants* and *RG* indicate the king's presence at Rhuddlan, possibly continuously, 27 September–20 November (PRO, Itinerary of Edward I; *HKW*, i, 319, n. 6; Prestwich, *Edward I*, 180, n. 37). Carters moved the king's wardrobe during a period of seven days from 10 October and another of twelve days from 17 October (E101/3/15), but no details are recorded.

[176] On that day three documents were sealed with the king's privy seal before the arrival of the chancellor (*CWR*, 157). These orders were the first to be enrolled on the Welsh Roll (*Calendar of Chancery Rolls, Various*, 157–362 [*CWR*], with a full text to the end of 1281 in *RotWall*), another indication of renewed vigour in royal administration at that point.

[177] Anian's role, along with that of Prior William of Southampton and Anthony Bek, is noted in C47/27/2, a document of 1280 concerning the interpretation of the treaty considered later. Brother Ifor ap Gruffudd, prior of Rhuddlan, travelled to Aberconwy on the king's behalf (E101/3/15).

[178] *CWR*, 157; *LW*, 118–19. For Brother William, Provincial of the Dominican Order, Hinnebusch, *Early English Friars Preachers*, 479–81; idem, 'Diplomatic activities of the English Dominicans in the thirteenth century', *The Catholic Historical Review*, 28 (1942–3), 309–39; for Bek, C. M. Fraser, *A History of Antony Bek, Bishop of Durham 1283–1311* (Oxford, 1957), 14–15; *Throne of Scotland, passim*; for Tibetot, R. A. Griffiths, *PW*, i, 9.

[179] *LW*, 118. Tudur ab Ednyfed was Llywelyn's seneschal; Goronwy ap Heilin's importance in Llywelyn's entourage is reflected in his part in these negotiations, and in his activities, on behalf of prince and king, thereafter.

November, promptly upon that renewed activity to which the records bear witness, and a week before the final treaty was sealed, Edward issued a charter by which he announced important decisions that had been made by Llywelyn himself in regard to that part of Llywelyn's land to which Dafydd laid claim and which, in the king's estimation, belonged to Dafydd.[180] Once more, as in the discussion of the terms of the treaty of 1267, the position of Dafydd ap Gruffudd had required detailed consideration and the clauses which concerned him constitute a key feature of the new treaty. The problems reflected in those clauses are likely to have been prominent among the matters thrashed out by the negotiators during their prolonged exchanges, and the concessions on these matters yielded by king and prince, reflected in the brief document noticed more fully presently, enabled the emissaries to proceed to a speedy completion of the entire settlement.

If the treaty of Montgomery had reflected the king's wish to elevate the prince of Wales, the agreement negotiated by Tudur ap Ednyfed and Goronwy ap Heilin and the king's emissaries at Aberconwy had an altogether different purpose.[181] Llywelyn ap Gruffudd submitted himself entirely to the king's will and mercy; he promised that, when he had been absolved from excommunication and the interdict on his lands was removed, he would come before the king at Rhuddlan and swear fealty; he undertook to pay a substantial sum, as much as £50,000, to secure the king's peace and his grace. He was allowed to retain the title prince of Wales, but his principality was destroyed without even a mention, for the king did not find it necessary to revoke the treaty which had brought that principality into being. Nor did it proclaim, as the king of England had taken care to insist on several earlier occasions of triumph, that the homage of the lords of Wales now belonged to the king of England and to none other. It was the future of Gwynedd, rather than of Wales, which formed the substance of the discussions at the Cistercian abbey, and particularly the future of Gwynedd Uwch Conwy. The king's will had prevailed.[182] If those who formed the prince's entourage had any remembrance of the circumstances that had prevailed early in the century they would have appreciated the grim

---

[180] C47/27/1, no. 10.

[181] For the text of the treaty of Aberconwy (9 November), *LW*, 118–22; other documents which form part of the settlement are noted as necessary. Main clauses of the treaty summarized in French in *AnnOsney*, 272–4; in Latin in Cotton, *HistAng*, 155–6; Trevet, *Annales*, 297–8, among several contemporary notices.

[182] Llywelyn 'supponet se voluntati et misericordie dicti domini regis' (*LW*, 119). For an emphasis on the king's will (*voluntas, volente*) in letters to the king of France concerning Gaston de Béarn, written at Rhuddlan five days after his ratification of the treaty, *RG*, ii, 151, 161; J. B. Smith, 'Adversaries of Edward I: Gaston de Béarn and Llywelyn ap Gruffudd', 75–7.

fact that Llywelyn ap Gruffudd had accepted terms which, on several counts, were every bit as humiliating as those imposed on Llywelyn ap Iorwerth. And Llywelyn ap Iorwerth was thereafter able to enjoy long years of purposeful activity the like of which his grandson could have no realistic expectation.

Llywelyn had to yield the Four Cantreds in their entirety, as they had been in the time of Henry III, and in perpetuity. Dyffryn Clwyd and Rhufoniog would be ruled by Dafydd ap Gruffudd, Rhos and Tegeingl by the king.[183] The king would retain, too, every other territory taken in war, excepting only Anglesey; Llywelyn was left free to initiate legal action to establish his right to any land which had fallen to anyone other than the king, but with the exception of the Four Cantreds. This clause allowed him, in this one respect, to look beyond the confines of the territory conceded to him, and in a phraseology which proved to be of critical importance later, provision was made with regard to the law – Welsh law or marcher law – to be used in the event of legal proceedings being initiated.[184] This apart, the effect of the treaty was to contain Llywelyn within closely circumscribed bounds and, in a clause which represented the most cruel blow in the whole treaty, but one whose significance might easily be missed, his position within these bounds was grievously impaired. Once more the responsibility lay with Dafydd's persistence in pressing for his hereditary rights. A week before the treaty was agreed, as has been indicated already, the king issued a document by which he conveyed to Llywelyn, for the duration of his life, that part of Gwynedd which was due to Dafydd by hereditary right but which had hitherto been held by Llywelyn, along with Dafydd's portion of Anglesey.[185] This decision is reflected, in closely similar phraseology, in the terms of the treaty, and its relevance is obvious.[186] Llywelyn was allowed possession of the land judged to belong to Dafydd by hereditary right, and he was allowed to have it for his lifetime and no more. Dafydd would be given other land in lieu of that to which he had right in Gwynedd, but when either Dafydd or Llywelyn died that land would fall to the king. This clause laid down that Llywelyn's heir – if he were ever to be blessed with an heir – would receive no more than that part of Gwynedd Uwch Conwy which would remain after Dafydd's portion had been provided for him. Dafydd was determined, above all else, to secure that

---

[183] *LW*, 119. Llywelyn put his seal to a document to that effect the same day (*LW*, 116–17).

[184] *LW*, 119–20.

[185] C47/27/1, no. 10 (3 November); the king declares: 'concedimus et confirmavimus eidem Lewelino quod partem David fratris sui quam sibi debetur iure hereditario de terre quam idem Lewelinus nunc tenet, una cum parte sua de Engleseya, habeat et teneat ad vitam suam'.

[186] *LW*, 120. The clauses concerning Dafydd were afforded particular notice in the Peterborough chronicle (*ChronPetroburg*, 25–6), an interest relevant to matters discussed below, pp. 564–6.

patrimony and, if fulfilment of that ambition was postponed, it was not denied to him. And Dafydd, a younger man than Llywelyn, already had male heirs who would represent the hereditary claim in the next generation. The provision to be made for Dafydd had indeed been a key issue in the negotiations between the proctors of king and prince. The fact that Edward sealed the resulting document a few days before he completed the procedures for the peace as a whole strongly suggests that, by resolving the issue, the envoys of king and prince had been able to remove an obstacle which had previously greatly hindered the negotiations. Once that obstacle was removed final agreement was quickly reached. The treaty duly states that it was by the king's pure grace (*de mera gracia sua*) that the king gave Llywelyn possession of the land which belonged to Dafydd; already in the earlier document the king had said that he had acted in this way so as to establish peace between Llywelyn and himself. The king's words carry an implicit indication that he had compromised and he may thus have previously maintained that he would accept nothing less than unconditional submission on Llywelyn's part and insisted that the principle be accepted that the whole of Gwynedd was in his gift. Llywelyn would surely have maintained that he would yield nothing of his right to the land that he continued to defend. But the harshness of the condition embodied in the brief document and then in the final treaty suggests very strongly that the prince had had to acknowledge that he could no longer withstand the force of the principle to which the king rigidly adhered.[187]

Llywelyn had to agree to the same divisive principle when he agreed to provide for Rhodri ap Gruffudd that portion (*portio*) which was due to him, too, by hereditary right. The prince was allowed, however, to compensate his brother to the extent of 1,000 marks for quitclaiming that right, Edward, in effect, imposing upon Llywelyn an obligation to fulfil the terms of the agreement which he had made with Rhodri five years earlier.[188] The principle was not applied to Owain ap Gruffudd with the same degree of directness, but the arrangements made for this sad figure were noted in detail: after his release from prison he could choose either to arrange peace terms with his brother, by his free will and under the king's security, or he could be placed in the king's protection until justice were done to him in accordance with Welsh law, and if he secured his freedom he would be able to seek his inheritance if he so wished.[189] Owain ap Gruffudd could hardly be blamed if he were to feel that the second option was discomfortingly similar to the provision in the treaty of Gwerneigron which had meant no more than that his father, and he himself along with him, would be transferred from the prison of the prince of Gwynedd to that of the king of

---

[187] J. B. Smith, 'Dynastic succession', 223–4.
[188] *LW*, 121, with Llywelyn's new undertaking and that of 1272 in *LW*, 85–6, 117. Rhodri insisted in 1278 that he had received only 50 marks.
[189] *LW*, 119.

England. The terms of the new treaty did nothing to suggest that Edward intended to put Owain on the same footing as his brother Dafydd. The idea of inviting Owain and Dafydd to the gatherings of the magnates of England, solemnly declared only three months before, had been entirely set aside.

The territorial arrangements embodied in the treaty of Aberconwy were the product, not of any determined attempt to provide equitable settlements, but of political expediency. Owain did not present Edward with anything like the problem posed by Dafydd. Nor was Owain, as far as we know, ever any threat to Llywelyn nor of any great concern to him. After the long years languishing in prison he may well have wished for no more than the chance to spend his remaining time in unmolested tranquillity. The surviving evidence provides no inkling of the brothers' relationship in these last years. Owain was released by the end of November and Llywelyn appears to have made provision for him in Llŷn, and it is certain that he had died before his brothers Llywelyn and Dafydd met their death.[190] Little more may be said of him, except that he, too, along with the same two brothers, earned the poet's remembrance when the last princes of the lineage had finally yielded their patrimony to the king of England.[191]

If Owain and Llywelyn, after the pained relations of earlier years, managed to establish some kind of understanding with one another, the treaty of Aberconwy can hardly be said to have done anything to create confidence between Llywelyn and Dafydd. Llywelyn had managed to keep Dafydd out of Gwynedd Uwch Conwy, and, making provision for him in Perfeddwlad, Edward brought himself to accept an arrangement which Llywelyn may possibly have urged on Henry many years earlier. There is some irony in the fact that it was the humiliating treaty of 1277 which enabled Llywelyn to get his brother off his back. But even then he was hardly absolved from Dafydd's vexatious presence. The provision made for Dafydd was of a temporary nature, an arrangement which left him to covet that part of the patrimony to which he now had a formally recognized right. The treaty, as it provided Dafydd with no more than a life interest in Rhufoniog and Dyffryn Clwyd, made it imperative that he should persist in his quest for a permanent baronial estate for his lineage. Certainly, the treaty of Aberconwy threatened to perpetuate that jealousy and strife among brothers which had proved to be

---

[190] *BT* records that Owain was released about the feast of St Andrew (30 November) and received the *cantref* of Llŷn (*BT, Pen20*, 226; *Pen20Tr*, 119; *RBH*, 266–9). For the petitions of Thomas ap Rhodri c.1330, arising from Owain ap Gruffudd's possession of land in Llŷn, *CAP*, 229–31. It is stated in an editorial note, *CAP*, 230–1, following E. Owen, 'Owain Lawgoch', *THSC*, 1899–1900, 6–105, that Owain survived Llywelyn and Dafydd and lived until c.1310, but there does not appear to be evidence to support this view. Bleddyn Fardd's elegies to Owain, Llywelyn and Dafydd, cited later, indicate that Owain died before his brothers.

[191] Below, p. 581.

such a valuable asset to the English crown in the past. Whether the solution now achieved would prove advantageous to the crown in years to come was doubtful. Leaving the ambitions of the restive prince still unrequited, Edward might be sowing the seed of another even more momentous struggle. During the days of negotiation, the prince's envoys were struggling with the same essential problems as those with which the prince had contended in the period leading up to the battle of Bryn Derwin and the settlement left the prince sorely discomforted.[192] It would be easy, observing Llywelyn's rule in Snowdonia over the next five years, to lose sight of the extent to which the very foundation of his lordship in that territory had been undermined in the negotiations with the English crown. The fact that the discussions were protracted can be readily understood. Llywelyn had ultimately to concede that he had only a life interest in a part of Gwynedd Uwch Conwy which was now formally registered as Dafydd's portion of the patrimony, and he was invested with that interest only by the king's grace. It was by the same royal grace that he was allowed to re-establish his authority over Anglesey and, if he managed to ensure that the island should revert to the heirs of his body, he had to declare unequivocally that the land would be restored to the crown if he died without heirs.[193] He had to accept, too, that he was required to make an annual payment of 1,000 marks for Anglesey and, though he was acquitted of this obligation, as well as the sum of £50,000, the fact that he had had to accept the principle that payment should be made for the island made this one of the provisions which rankled most.[194] Besides, he was still left with the burden of having to pay 500 marks a year for Anglesey and for Dafydd's portion of the inheritance until the outstanding debt on the treaty of Montgomery was cleared. In his hour of humiliation he had to acknowledge a debt derived from his hour of triumph, and he did so in order to buy his possession of a portion of Gwynedd from the king of England.[195] Gwynedd

---

[192] Above, pp. 68–73, 86–7.

[193] *LW*, 119–21; Llywelyn's undertakings in respect of Anglesey and Dafydd's portion, *LW*, 117–18; *CWR*, 158. Whereas the treaty provided that Anglesey should be granted to Llywelyn and his legitimate heirs, Llywelyn granted on 16 November that Anglesey should fall to the king if Llywelyn died without heirs of his body (*LW*, 118, 120; *CWR*, 159).

[194] The annual 1,000 marks for Anglesey and the £50,000 to secure the king's grace were remitted 10–11 November (*CWR*, 157–8; *Foedera*, I, ii, 546–7). On 11 November, however, Llywelyn paid the king a sum of £2,000 'of the sum in which he is bound to the king' (*CWR*, 159), but it is not clear how that debt had been incurred, unless it were part of the £50,000 otherwise remitted on the same day.

[195] Llywelyn recognized his obligation, Edward acknowledging payments made in 1278, 1279 and 1280 (*LW*, 117–18; *CWR*, 157, 159, 169, 179, 186). During exchanges with Pecham in 1282 Llywelyn insisted that Edward had made financial demands upon him additional to those imposed by the treaty of Aberconwy. Even apart from these charges, difficult to verify, there is a marked difference between Edward's stern dealings with Llywelyn and the financial arrangements he made with his Gaston adversary Gaston de Béarn (J. B. Smith, 'Adversaries of Edward I', 77–8).

had come close to that fragmentation which had threatened before Llywelyn ap Gruffudd took the crucial decision to withstand his brother's demands, and the patrimony was now spared that fate only by the king's grace. Edward had not taken physical possession of Gwynedd Uwch Conwy, except for Anglesey, but Llywelyn had been unable to prevent the king from dictating terms for its disposition which were of unquestionable severity.

The transactions at Aberconwy were concerned almost entirely with Gwynedd alone and essentially with that part of the historic province which lay west of the Conwy. Even within these bounds there might yet be new uncertainties. The land conceded to Llywelyn included Meirionnydd, but Llywelyn would be well aware that he was likely to face litigation brought by Madog ap Llywelyn on the basis of that hereditary right for which Llywelyn had had no regard when he had driven Madog's father into exile in 1256.[196] A chancery record might indeed refer to Madog ap Llywelyn as 'lord of Meirionnydd' during the course of the conflict of 1277, and early in the next year he duly came before the king's justices and claimed the lordship.[197] Beyond the narrow bounds within which his power was confined by the new treaty Llywelyn was conceded only the homage of five lords, a concession linked, perhaps, with the king's readiness to tolerate his retention of the style 'prince of Wales'.[198] It was hardly a generous gesture. Of the five lords, Rhys Fychan ap Rhys ap Maelgwn had been entirely disinherited, and, whatever land he might hold it would not be for any part of his patrimony in Ceredigion that he would do homage to the prince.[199] The others were lords of Edeirnion: Dafydd ap Gruffudd ab Owain, Elise ap Iorwerth, and two sons of Owain ap Bleddyn. The homage of these, whose lands lay beyond the confines of the prince's territorial lordship as defined by the new treaty, might conceivably justify the retention of the style 'prince of Wales'. A contemporary chronicler in fact observed that a prince had need of some lords as his tenants.[200] How much Llywelyn gained by earning the service of these men is another matter, for two of them, Dafydd and Elise, had been imprisoned by Llywelyn during the war and were released under the terms of the treaty.[201] In the light of their political affiliation in 1277 the men of Edeirnion could prove to be anything but an asset to him and indeed be a means by which Edward could maintain surveillance upon the prince. The king certainly had other

---

[196] Above, p. 91.
[197] *WAR*, 237–8, 251.
[198] *LW*, 120.
[199] Rhys Fychan's flight to Gwynedd is noticed above, pp. 421–2.
[200] Trevet, *Annales*, 297–8.
[201] *LW*, 119; Dafydd had incurred Llywelyn's wrath (*CIM*, ii, 43). For these lords, A. D. Carr, 'The Barons of Edeyrnion, 1282–1485', *JMerHRS*, 4 (1961–4), 187–93, 289–301. In the event Dafydd ap Gruffudd and Elise ap Iorwerth were among those who rebelled in 1282, but they survived and found renewed royal favour (*WAR*, 352; *CWR*, 286).

potentially helpful adherents within Gwynedd Uwch Conwy. The treaty itself provided for the release of two such men in Rhys ap Gruffudd and Madog ab Einion. There were probably others in Gwynedd who had incurred Llywelyn's displeasure during the war and so would be wary of his doings thereafter, prepared perhaps to relay their grievances to the king.[202] Edward, however, still sought a formal means of securing Llywelyn's faithful adherence to the new engagements. He insisted that Llywelyn should hand over ten hostages from among the noblemen of his land as a security for the peace. Twenty men from each *cantref* were required to swear, in the presence of royal emissaries, that they would adhere to the terms of the treaty and ensure that their prince would do likewise.[203] If Llywelyn faltered and failed to make amends at once, they would be bound to abandon their fealty to the prince and transfer their loyalty to the crown. Llywelyn was bound in fidelity to the crown in a manner closely comparable to the means by which he had bound his tenant Gruffudd ap Gwenwynwyn when he was subjected to the prince's will in 1274. He was now worsted by a king who acted with a resolve which matched the determination with which King John had subjected Llywelyn ap Iorwerth to his authority in 1211. If the new agreement were to be literally fulfilled, the men of Gwynedd nominated to provide security would need to repeat their assurance year by year, and this would mean that royal officers would make their way to Gwynedd again and again to ensure that the prince was kept under observation.

Llywelyn sealed the main agreement at the abbey of Aberconwy on 9 November, as well as the related documents made out in his own name which conceded the Four Cantreds to the king and acknowledged his obligation to pay the 500 marks due to the royal coffers each year. The following day he crossed the Conwy in the company of Bishop Anian of St Asaph, Anthony Bek and Robert Tibetot and made his way to Rhuddlan. Even though his participation in the discussions may have facilitated the eventual agreement, Anian's presence may have been a saddening one for the prince, the more so since it fell to the bishop to release him from excommunication. Three miles from Rhuddlan they were met by Robert Burnell, bishop of Bath and Wells and chancellor, and Henry de Lacy, earl of Lincoln, and Llywelyn proceeded to the king to swear fealty.[204] Edward confirmed the treaty in his presence and cancelled the obligation by which Llywelyn would have had to pay £50,000 to the king and a further annual sum of 1,000 marks for Anglesey.[205] A date was set for him to go to the king to do homage, leaving Llywelyn to return to his

---

[202] *LW*, 119. For Madog's father, Einion ap Maredudd, above, p. 46.
[203] *LW*, 121.
[204] Statements based on provisions made in the treaty (*LW*, 121).
[205] *LW*, 157; *CWR*, 157–8 (10 November).

land to face the responsibility of establishing a relationship with the king of England in circumstances very different from those which had prevailed when he had come before King Henry at the ford of Montgomery just ten years before.

Llywelyn was summoned to London by Christmas, and he set out on one of the very few journeys which took him beyond the borders of Wales. He did homage, and the time that king and prince spent together may have given them an opportunity to ameliorate the relationship between them.[206] It certainly proved possible to deal with some practical issues which arose in implementing the terms of the treaty. Early in the new year, while Llywelyn was still at hand, a commission was appointed to go to Gwynedd to take the oaths of the twenty men in each *cantref*, to secure the release of hostages and prisoners, and to make recompense for injuries inflicted during the conflict. It meant that Llywelyn had to reconcile himself to the fact that a royal commission was put to work within his lordship, and the presence of the two Welsh Dominicans, Llywelyn ap Gruffudd and Ifor ap Gruffudd, may have done little to create confidence in the commission as a whole.[207] The addition of the name of Goronwy ap Heilin towards the end of 1278 may suggest that the original members had not found it easy to fulfil the tasks allotted to them.[208] This delegation was concerned with matters which largely belonged to the past, and more relevant to the future was another commission, appointed a few days later, to hear and determine legal actions in Wales and the marches.[209] Those named in the original commission were Ralph de Farningham, the chief justice, who was to serve only briefly in 1278, Walter de Hopton, who was to be chief justice thereafter, and Rhys ap Gruffudd, Goronwy ap Heilin and Hywel ap Meurig. They were to assemble at an early date and Llywelyn was told to appear before the justices in connection with any suits that he might wish to bring and to do and receive justice before them.

The prince's response to the creation of this judicial commission and its subsequent proceedings would be of some importance to Edward himself. Restricted to Snowdonia, Llywelyn was no longer in direct confrontation

---

[206] *CWR*, 160–1; *BT, Pen20*, 226; *Pen20Tr*, 119; *RBH*, 266–7; *ChronPetroburg*, 26; *Ann Winch*, 125; *ChronWykes*, 273; Rishanger, *Chronica*, 91. Wellcome Medical Historical Library MS 253 names some who were present, including Gruffudd ap Iorwerth and Madog ap Llywelyn.

[207] *CWR*, 162–3; the task was entrusted to Guncelin de Badlesmere, justice of Chester, Roger Lestrange and Brothers Llywelyn ap Gruffudd and Ifor ap Gruffudd; cf. J. C. Davies, in *WAR*, 39; comments in *WAR*, 42–3, on the loyalties of the friars need to be corrected.

[208] *CWR*, 177.

[209] *CWR*, 163. A new commission was issued in June (*CWR*, 167; J. C. Davies, in *WAR*, 97–121).

with the great powers of the march; he was no longer involved in that conflict with Clare and Bohun and Mortimer which had been so disturbing in years gone by and it was unlikely that he would be involved in further legal disputation with these men. Yet he was hardly likely to withdraw into his shell entirely, and the decision to prosecute an action, or not to do so, would not always lie with him. As soon as the justices held their first session Madog ap Llywelyn came and claimed Meirionnydd. Of much greater consequence, however, Llywelyn himself came before the justices to claim against Gruffudd ap Gwenwynwyn the lordship of Arwystli, thereby initiating much the most notable action of the next five years.[210] Edward did not see this initiative on Llywelyn's part as in any sense an ominous move; on the contrary, he took it to be an indication of Llywelyn's readiness to accept his lot and recognize the king's jurisdiction. When, in the very document which embodied the arrangements for the new judicial commission, the king instructed Llywelyn to prepare to appear before the judges he was almost certainly taking account of an intimation on the prince's part that he intended to initiate an action over Arwystli, and, no doubt, that he proposed to defend his interests against whomsoever might bring an action against him.[211] Edward's feelings are most clearly conveyed in a letter to Robert Burnell and Otto de Grandson, dispatched while they were proceeding on a journey which took them upon an embassy to the king of France and thence upon a difficult mission in Gascony. Conveying sentiments which could so easily be applied to the men of Wales, Edward expressed his concern that those of Gascony were proving refractory and were less than constant in their adherence to their agreements and promises. In Wales the whole aspect was now different. By God's grace not only were the kingdom of England and the marches well ordered, but Llywelyn with commendable goodwill was prepared to appear before royal judges to seek justice and take judgement both in actions in which he was the defendant and those in which he prosecuted his interests.[212] And, with Alexander of Scotland, too, having conveyed his readiness to do homage, Edward could count on several propitious indications. He expected that Alexander would come and fulfil his obligations in the autumn, and it is likely that the king had decided that he would at that time fulfil a promise that he had made to Llywelyn on a matter of great concern to him.

Not a single document makes any mention of the matter, but it is not unlikely that Edward and Llywelyn had been able to come to some

---

[210] J. C. Davies, in *WAR*, 131–2. Llywelyn's plea first appears on the roll in a session held on 22 July, but it had been initiated by mid-February and is mentioned in Edward's letter the next month (*CCR, 1272–79*, 493); the proceedings are examined in the next chapter.

[211] *CWR*, 163.

[212] *CCR, 1272–79*, 493; *Foedera*, I, ii, 554 (21 March 1278): 'coram justiciariis nostris comparens . . . benigne petit et recipit justiciam'.

Aberconwy

understanding with one another with regard to the prince's marriage to Eleanor de Montfort during the prince's stay in London. The documents relating to the agreement at Aberconwy make several references to what would or would not follow if Llywelyn had an heir or failed to have an heir, and there is an implicit assumption that Llywelyn's wife would be released from the king's custody. During Llywelyn's visit to London Goronwy ap Heilin was permitted to go to Eleanor on the prince's behalf, and was allowed to speak to her privately if he so wished.[213] The men whom Edward sent to Gwynedd were ordered to ascertain what arrangements Llywelyn had made for her dower, an indication that he was now dutifully assuming responsibility for his cousin's interests.[214] Llywelyn no doubt looked for her early release; she was already his wedded wife. But he was kept on probation for a little longer, a delay which he surely found irksome, and if the prospects had looked encouraging at the beginning of the year new anxieties began to gather by the summer of 1278.

By then the problems which were to reveal themselves in the great legal actions of the next years began to become apparent. Llywelyn gave warning of his displeasure, not that he was required to take justice in the king's courts, but that he was required to proceed in a manner which was not consonant with practice under Welsh law. The king was quick to insist that he was anxious to ensure that Llywelyn should be allowed to proceed in accordance with established custom, but it was already becoming clear that the provisions of the treaty of Aberconwy in this important respect were open to more than one interpretation. Edward was equally concerned to convince Llywelyn that he gave no credence to any tale which raised suspicion of the prince's motives, as long as he acted in complete good faith.[215] The tenor of the letters emanating from chancery reflect the indubitable fact that the conflict of recent years had left its legacy of difficulties, not least those which the bishop of Bangor felt need to report to the king. Close kinsmen of the bishop had fallen in the king's service, his churches burned and his properties plundered, and he sent the chancellor details of the manner in which Llywelyn had offended God and the church.[216] These were obviously matters to be brought to the king's notice. Edward, writing to Llywelyn, insisted that he had no wish to diminish the prince's liberties in any way but only to promote agreement between him and the bishop. His missives were set out in a request to Llywelyn and not in a peremptory manner. Yet, in urging Llywelyn to conduct himself in his relationship with the bishop in the courteous and seemly manner befitting a prince and deserving of divine approbation, Edward may have seemed

---

[213] *CWR*, 170; *Foedera*, I, ii, 549.
[214] *CWR*, 162–3; *Foedera*, I, ii, 548.
[215] *CWR*, 173–4; *Foedera*, I, ii, 557–8 (4 June 1278).
[216] *CAC*, 112–13.

exceedingly righteous.²¹⁷ Intimations of continuing royal surveillance, even a protestation of the king's unwillingness to give credence to sinister reports of Llywelyn's behaviour, were hardly reassuring. More and more of this could prove tiresome, and prolonged correspondence could become increasingly contentious. King and prince may well have been glad to arrange the meeting which took place at Rhuddlan in September.

Amongst much else, we can safely assume, the matter of Rhodri ap Gruffudd's recompense for his exclusion from the patrimony was finally resolved. Rhodri was present, as was Dafydd ap Gruffudd, who showed a readiness to facilitate agreement between the brothers.²¹⁸ Three of the sons of Gruffudd ap Llywelyn came together, if not the four, and this may have been the last occasion on which they were able to do so. The meeting led to the release, on account of Llywelyn's good faith, of hostages given upon the cessation of hostilities.²¹⁹ It was probably on this occasion, with a number of magnates of king and prince present together, that Edward held the feast for the Welsh at Rhuddlan which cost him a fair sum.²²⁰ All was not peace and goodwill at Rhuddlan by any means, and we shall need to take account again of one matter of some consequence which arose at this meeting upon which Llywelyn later laid great stress. But it was probably on this occasion, when confidence between Edward and Llywelyn had been to some degree restored once more, that arrangements were finally made for the consecration of the prince's marriage.

Llywelyn ap Gruffudd and Eleanor de Montfort were married in the cathedral church at Worcester on the Feast of St Edward, a festive occasion which brought together royalty and nobility, Edward and his queen, and Alexander of Scotland and his queen among them.²²¹ Edward gave the bride

---

²¹⁷ *CWR*, 174; *Foedera*, I, ii, 559–60 (14 July 1278).

²¹⁸ In response to Rhodri's claim to a share of the lands of Dafydd ap Llywelyn, on which he had brought a plea before the justices early in 1278, Llywelyn produced Rhodri's deed of 1272 (*LW*, 85–6). Rhodri acknowledged the deed, but said that he had received nothing of the promised 1,000 marks; Llywelyn said that he had paid 50 marks and agreed to pay the remainder upon Rhodri's renewal of the quitclaim, Dafydd giving security that the money could be raised on his English estates if there were need (*CCR, 1272–79*, 506–7). Rhodri married Beatrice, daughter of David of Malpas, and after her death married a second time. Thomas ap Rhodri, father of Owain ap Thomas (Owain Lawgoch), was a son of the second marriage (*DWB*, 690; Carr, *Owen of Wales*, 6).

²¹⁹ *CWR*, 169.

²²⁰ C62/57, m. 6; *Cheshire Pipe Rolls*, 123; on the same occasion arrangements were made for the restoration of the lands of the sons of Goronwy ab Ednyfed (*CWR*, 175); this may give some indication of who might have been present.

²²¹ *BT, Pen20*, 226; *Pen20Tr*, 119; *RBH*, 268–9; Trevet, *Annales*, 268–9; *Chron*Wykes, 277; *Ann*Worc, 476; Rishanger, *Chronica*, 94. For Llywelyn's reference to the occasion at Worcester as his wedding-day (*die disponsationis*), above, n. 30. Edward's giving of Eleanor in marriage, celebration of mass and prior dower provision reveal something of the liturgy of the celebration of marriage 'in the presence of the church' (*in facie ecclesie*).

in marriage, and it was thus by the king's hand that Eleanor became princess of Wales. Edward provided the feast, his generosity celebrating both the nuptials and a day which had a special place in the royal calendar. King and queen bestowed small gifts on the groom and his bride, a marker for Llywelyn's prayer-book, a kerchief for Eleanor.[222] They were a sign of the courtesies which were respected all too infrequently in relations between kings of England and princes of Wales.[223] Exchanges of gifts (Llywelyn had recently sent Edward a present of four hounds) were not of vast importance, nor could they of themselves determine relations between kingdoms and principalities. Yet they could reasonably be recognized as indications of a new normality in relations between the king and a vassal of royal lineage who by his marriage, and despite the deep antagonism which had inspired it, was brought into an affinity with the lineage of the king himself. Yet even this day was not without its blemish. Llywelyn was later to recall how on his very wedding day, before mass, the king had extorted from him his written consent to an adjustment to the agreement between them, by which, amongst other things, Llywelyn agreed that he would not hold any man in his land contrary to the king's will. He recounted later how, moved by the fear that can grip a steadfast man, he put his seal to the document, and he recorded the matter with more than a touch of soreness.[223] Precisely what was involved or what provoked the king's request is difficult to judge, nor can we tell whether the matter proved to be one of further concern, for, when Llywelyn eventually referred to it, England and Wales were once more at war. During the few years of peaceful interlude thereafter Eleanor was to recall the honour and kindliness which the king had shown to her and to her husband at Worcester. Yet she did so in a letter she felt bound to write so as to withstand the malevolence of those who wished to undermine the king's confidence in their fidelity. Sadly, there are only a few intimations of Eleanor's intercession on her husband's behalf.[224] It never fell to her, as it had fallen to Joan in the early years of the century, to intercede between her king and her prince in an hour of need. It would be too much to say that it was on Eleanor's account that war was waged between Wales and England in 1277, but it can hardly be doubted that the marriage arranged, and made, at that great distance three years before was a vital element in the making of the war which destroyed the principality of Wales. When she completed the journey which began at Montargis three years before, Eleanor, princess of Wales and lady of Snowdon, came to a much less extensive dominion than that from which the Dominicans had secretly travelled as

---

[222] Wellcome Medical Historical Library MS 253; C47/4/1, ff. 37, 46; J. C. Davies, in *WAR*, 43–4.

[223] *RPeck*, ii, 443; above, pp. 278–9.

[224] *CAC*, 75–6, four letters from Abereiddon, Llan-faes, Ystumanner and Nefyn; texts of three in *Foedera*, I, ii, 576, 584, 587.

envoys of their forceful, even vengeful, prince. Llywelyn's power was broken before the marriage was finally consecrated, but his wife, despite the animosity which had vitiated her husband's relations with the king and despite her own troubled inheritance, could yet bring something of great benefit from her nurturing in the conventions of the Christian nations. But her great responsibility, and her anxiety, as she set out on the morrow of her wedding feast upon the journey to her husband's court was the security of the lineage of Aberffraw.

CHAPTER 9

Contention and Conflict

D URING the early hours of Palm Sunday 1282 a force of Welshmen penetrated the defences of the castle of Hawarden while its constable, Roger Clifford, lay asleep.¹ Though little is known of the manner in which the attack was carried out it may be surmised that the initial action in the war of 1282 was taken, not with any strident proclamations, but by a stratagem accomplished by stealth deep in the night.² The constable's life was spared, but a number of his men were killed in a savage combat which revealed the fury of this sudden rising. Hawarden was not the only object of attack, for other groups of men struck at Flint and Rhuddlan, ransacking the boroughs and creating extensive damage.³ The dire news of the disaster at Hawarden on 22 March reached the king some three days later, and by then it was evident that the onslaught was not confined to a single area in north-east Wales. Even as royal authority in Ystrad Alun and Englefield was being challenged, the men of Penllyn and Edeirnion and Powys Fadog vented their anger by attacking the town of Oswestry.⁴ Still more striking was the coincident rising in south-west Wales. On the feast of St Mary at the Equinox, just three days after Palm Sunday, Aberystwyth castle fell in circumstances which bring a touch of mischief to the serious events of this Holy Week. Gruffudd ap

---

¹ The main chronicle entries are *BT, Pen20*, 227; *Pen20Tr*, 120; *RBH*, 268–9; *AnnWav*, 397; *AnnDunst*, 291–2; *AnnOsney*, 287–8; Trevet, *Annales*, 301 and the Hagnaby chronicle noticed later. The essence of their testimony, including the capture of Clifford, is confirmed in Edward's letter to his magnates, 25 March (*CWR*, 212–13). *AnnDunst* states that a relative of Clifford, Fulk Trigold, was among those killed; *BT* that Clifford and Payn Gamage were spared their lives and imprisoned. Clifford remained captive until 1283; for his connection with Hawarden, *HKW*, i, 329–30.

² *BT* gives the feast of St Bennett, 21 March; most sources attribute the attack to Palm Sunday, 22 March, and the action evidently took place on the night of 21–2 March. Bruce made a night attack on Berwick, 6 December 1312, frustrated by the barking of a dog (Barrow, *Bruce*, 274–5).

³ Several notices in *Flint Pleas*, 2 et seq.; e.g. the taking of livestock upon the crowing of the cock (*in gallicantu*).

⁴ *WAR*, 352–3.

Maredudd, acting in association with Rhys Fychan ap Rhys ap Maelgwn, came to the constable, and invited him to dinner. The constable could hardly have been aware of the happenings in the north-east and accepted the invitation, only to be taken captive by his host while a force of Gruffudd's men took possession of the castle. They paused a while, but in a day or two 'they burned the town and the castle and destroyed the rampart that was around the castle and the town', initiating a movement by which Gruffudd and Rhys Fychan carried rebellion far and wide over the commotes of Ceredigion.[5] On the day on which Aberystwyth castle was taken those of Llandovery and Carreg Cennen appear to have fallen to Rhys Wyndod and the men of Ystrad Tywi who raised rebellion in that area also.[6]

The evidence which we have is fragmentary, but it is enough to indicate the main course of events during this tumultuous week in the spring of 1282. To explain why disquiet in Welsh society burst forth in insurrection at this particular time is much more difficult. As far as we know the king had not had any reason to be concerned with the state of the land during the previous weeks and months, and the disturbances which occurred at these several strongholds cannot be seen to have been provoked by any specific action on his part. It would seem, however, that behind the various occurrences noticed by contemporary chroniclers there lay a single purpose and a co-ordinated plan, and there is reason to believe that the several sudden attacks witnessed over such a wide area were no fortuitous happenings. It is possible that anxieties borne of the scarcities of a long winter may explain the timing of the outbreaks, for the plundering of towns was a feature of several attacks, notably those at Flint and Oswestry.[7] Also relevant, perhaps, is that the building season was about to begin at several of the castles; if materials lay at hand and scaffolding was in place, those who might have set their minds on rebellion may have had good reason to strike at that particular time.[8] Among the nations of Christendom, even so, the days preceding Good Friday were regarded as days of peace and, according to the accepted conventions of war, a time for restraint from combat.[9] During the conflict of 1277 one of the king's officers had indicated a reluctance to engage his enemy during Christ's

---

[5] *AC*, 106; *BT, Pen20*, 227; *Pen20Tr*, 120; *RBH*, 268–71. *BT* attributes the attack on Llanbadarn Fawr or Aberystwyth to 25 March (the feast of Mary at the Equinox); Tibetot says 24 March (*CAC*, 44). For the damage to the castle, *HKW*, i, 304–5. In *AC* the attacks on Llanbadarn Fawr, Llandovery and Carreg Cennen are treated together and attributed to 26 March.

[6] *AC*, 106; *CAC*, 44 (letter, probably of Gilbert de Clare, attributing attacks on Llandovery and Carreg Cennen to Rhys Wyndod and Madog ab Arawdr).

[7] There may have been extensive plundering at Oswestry, with accusations of thieving and burning (*WAR*, 352–3).

[8] *HKW*, i, 312–15.

[9] J. W. Tyrer, *Historical Survey of Holy Week, its Services and Ceremonial* (Oxford, 1932), 45 *et seq.*

Passion. The same sensitivity is reflected in the remark of the Welsh chronicler who noted that those who attacked Aberystwyth in 1282 spared the defenders' lives because the days of the Passion were at hand.[10] But these qualms of conscience were not sufficiently strong to deter the attackers altogether. Their readiness to rise in armed conflict even during the days which in the Christian calendar were reserved for quiet devotion, served to confirm the image of the Welsh among the churchmen of England as barbarians entirely lacking the virtues of those possessed of the true Faith.[11] The sentiments to which they felt bound to give voice proved to be a means of underlining Edward's conviction that he had a divinely ordained duty to lead the recalcitrant nation back to the paths of Christian civility. Perfidious deeds had been done in Wales at that holy time of the year when Judas had betrayed his Lord.[12] For those who rose in rebellion the action taken in Holy Week may have been both a reflection of their wish to catch the authorities at an unsuspecting moment and a measure of the desperation which drove them into a war which, in the event, saw all Wales cast to the ground.

The anger which manifested itself so violently during Lent might not suggest an ordered movement with well-defined political aims. The action was characterized by destructive impulses, wreaking devastation upon the towns which had grown about the alien strongholds. The occurrences have some features of a peasant rising. Prosecutions brought against the men of Englefield after the war provide a detailed depiction of the damage inflicted upon the English inhabitants of the area, both in the main towns and in villages in the countryside.[13] The burgesses of Oswestry similarly complained of their grievous losses in goods and money and, in the opinion of one commentator, the whole purpose of the rebels was the destruction by the power of the sword of everything which belonged to the king and to the English.[14] We have an impression of a campaign of retribution on the part of ravaging hosts, with no clearer objective than indiscriminate pillage. There is, even so, evidence which takes us beyond such a portrayal of wilful devastation towards a comprehension of the duress endured by several communities who had lived under royal administration, and the experience of those of north-east Wales deserves particular notice.

---

[10] *CAC*, 71; *BT, Pen20*, 227; *Pen20Tr*, 120; *RBH*, 270–1.
[11] Pecham reproached Llywelyn with this charge in November 1282 (*RPeck*, ii, 436). Some chroniclers, e.g. *AnnDunst*, 294, convey that Dafydd incurred punishment for blasphemy by going to war during the Passion ('propter blasphemiam viscera eius incidenio sunt cremata'); others notice that the attack was made at that holy time, e.g. Guisborough, *Chronicle*, 218.
[12] *Foedera*, I, ii, 606.
[13] *Flint Pleas*, xii–xv, 2–10; apart from events at Hawarden, Flint and Rhuddlan, deaths were reported at hamlets such as Mertyn, Picton and Gronant, but the editor concludes that the emphasis of the evidence is laid 'not on slaughter, but on rapine'.
[14] *WAR*, 352–3; Guisborough, *Chronicle*, 218.

Since 1277 Rhos and Englefield, two of the Four Cantreds, had once more been ruled in the king's name and their communities brought under the direct administration of royal officials serving under the supervision of the justice of Chester, the office being entrusted for several years to Guncelin de Badlesmere.[15] The officers more immediately responsible for the two *cantrefi* were Welshmen. Rhos was administered by Goronwy ap Heilin and Englefield first by Hywel ap Gruffudd and then by Cynfrig ap Goronwy.[16] All three were kinsmen and drawn from a lineage distinguished for its services to the princes, but they were clearly men in whom Edward felt able to place his trust.[17] How effectively or with what measure of equity they fulfilled their functions is not easy to judge, for the material relating to the period after 1277 does not provide anything like the evidence of continuing friction between officials and communities which marked the previous period of royal administration three decades earlier. Yet towards the end of 1282, as part of the testimony presented to Archbishop Pecham, the communities of the two areas provided detailed accounts of their grievances against the king's officers.[18] They point to a sense of communal grievance which could clearly have a bearing upon the virulence of the opening encounters in the spring of 1282. Admittedly, it is impossible to prove the veracity of the charges made against Edward's officials. The recital of complaints no doubt embodies a measure of the mythology of oppression as well as an account of actual experience. We would do well to bear in mind that the testimony was presented as a means of demonstrating the injustice which had driven the communities to rebellion. The testimony embodied in the *gravamina* conveys, even so, a profound resentment against those who, before the outbreak of war, had been responsible for their administration. Oppression on the part of royal officers, heavy and arbitrary exactions, the undermining of indigenous rights, the deprivation endured by the Welsh as compared with the privileges accorded to English communities of the boroughs founded in the area, the advantages enjoyed by individual Englishmen who lived there: these are the mournful complaints of the inhabitants of the two areas. The men of Rhos insisted that they had been dealt with in a manner decidedly contrary to the law and

---

[15] Badlesmere held office October 1274–November 1281 (*CPR, 1272–81*, 60, 464; *CFR, 1272–1301*, 31).

[16] There are no records of appointments but there are references 1278–81 to Hywel ap Gruffudd and Cynfrig ap Goronwy in Englefield and Goronwy ap Heilin in Rhos (*CCR, 1272–79*, 476, 563–4; *CWR*, 168, 189, 198; *CIM*, i, no. 1149).

[17] Cynwrig and Goronwy were sons of Goronwy ap Cynfrig and Heilin ap Cynfrig, brothers of Ednyfed Fychan, and grandsons of Cynfrig ap Goronwy (Stephenson, *GG*, 102–4).

[18] *RPeck*, ii, 447–51, 454–8, 460–3.

custom of the land; those of Englefield likewise told that they were denied the law and custom of Wales, and each community backed up its charge with numerous specific instances of injustice.[19]

The complaints were concentrated particularly on the harsh and capricious rule of Reginald de Grey, who had been appointed justice of Chester only in November 1281.[20] Already before his coming there may have been some intensification of the administration of the area, for a royal instruction of the summer of that year suggests that the spheres of authority of Goronwy ap Heilin and Cynfrig ap Goronwy were being drawn more securely under the aegis of the justice of Chester.[21] The complaints made towards the end of the following year do indeed indicate that some of the wrongs endured by the communities were inflicted before Grey took office, and they make specific reference both to the injuries suffered and the attempts made to secure their correction.[22] But, in so far as the *gravamina* provide an understanding of the discontent in the two areas, it appears that the rigour of royal administration was greatly intensified following Grey's appointment. Goronwy ap Heilin was certainly removed from office, and Cynfrig ap Goronwy may also have been superseded as Grey introduced new officers – both Welsh and English – to implement his stringent rule.[23] Cynfrig Sais or Cynfrig Fychan incurred the wrath of the community no less than Hick Lemayn or Robert Crevequer, each of them identified as an agent of the ruthless justice.[24] Grey, it was averred, exercised a power which went far beyond the authority normally entrusted to a royal officer, a power tantamount to lordship. He had left the communities with a firm impression that he was nothing less than their 'true lord'.[25] Grey, according to the allegations made against him, exploited his

---

[19] Ibid. The men of Tegeingl held that they were denied the law of Wales which should have been available to them in the courts of Trefednyfed, Rhuddlan and Caerwys.

[20] Grey was appointed 14 November 1281; financial arrangements were made applicable from the previous Michaelmas (*CFR, 1272–1307*, 155; *CPR, 1272–81*, 464).

[21] *CWR*, 189 (9 June). Badlesmere and the abbot of Vale Royal, chamberlain of Chester, were to hold courts in the two *cantrefi*; bailiffs were instructed on the delivery of rents and other issues to the exchequer at Chester. For possible circumstances, below, p. 505.

[22] *RPeck*, ii, 447–51, 460–3.

[23] There is no direct evidence of Cynfrig's removal, but the complaints from Tegeingl say he was 'captured without cause' (ibid., 462); his grandsons held patrimonial lands in Brynffanugl and Twynnan in Rhos, 1334 (*SD*, 261, 297), and the lineage did not suffer permanent damage at the conquest. Goronwy's testimony, and his very different fate, are considered below.

[24] *RPeck*, ii, 449–50, 459, 461–2. Cynfrig Sais had received several payments from the king in 1277; cf. *Flint Pleas, sub nomine*, for later references. For Crevequer, below, n. 58.

[25] *RPeck*, ii, 450. Grey was given the territory at farm, it was alleged, 'ad tractandum homines predicte cantrede, prout sue placeret voluntati, qui compulsit nos jurare per manum suam cum deberemus jurare per manum domini regis et ubi crux domini regis levari deberet, quod crux predicti Reginaldi levaretur in signum quod ipse erat verus dominus'.

position to excess, exerting a tyrannical power over the community.[26] It was a matter of bitter complaint that he had prevented the men of the two areas from seeking justice at the king's court, threatening them that any messenger they ventured to send to the king would be beheaded. He held the entire community in fear and dread of his power.[27] Although his authority had been exercised for only a few brief months, discontent in Rhos and Englefield had evidently been greatly intensified and the area was brought to a state of ferment. The two communities maintained that they had been ruled in a manner entirely at variance with the assurances given upon their submission to the king's power, by virtue of which they had been promised remission for injuries previously inflicted upon the king and guaranteed government under the law and custom of the land.[28] The torment endured under Grey and his minions was so great that they felt themselves absolved from the oaths solemnly given to the king before God.[29] Reginald de Grey, on an objective appraisal of the evidence which is available to us, must bear a grave responsibility for the resort to armed resistance in the spring of 1282.

Grey's part in provoking conflict was not confined to his administration of the royal lands in Perfeddwlad, and this responsibility will be considered again. Yet he was by no means the sole source of injustice. The men of Ystrad Alun or Mold, the land where the castle of Hawarden stood, complained that they had been ruled by Roger Clifford in a manner contrary to justice and in derogation of their privileges and customs.[30] Those of Penllyn, a land under the prince's lordship, expressed their anger at the arrogant behaviour of the constable of Oswestry, and they specified the disabilities which they had endured when trading at the borough.[31] Part of the community of Powys Fadog had been under royal administration since 1277, for upon the death of

---

[26] It is not clear that Grey exercised his office on financial terms substantially different from earlier arrangements. When he exercised the office of justice, with authority over Chester alone, in 1270 the farm was set at 800 marks; upon his appointment in 1281 the farm for Chester with Tegeingl and Rhos was 1,000 marks, assigned to building works at Vale Royal. Upon his appointment in 1274 Badlesmere received an annual fee of 100 marks, with no responsibility for the Four Cantreds at that stage (*Cheshire Pipe Rolls*, 108; *CPR, 1272–81*, 464, 476; *CFR, 1272–1307*, 155). Adjustments made in view of Grey's responsibilities in the war are noted in *CCR, 1279–88*, 216–17.

[27] *RPeck*, ii, 451, 463.

[28] The two communities convey that Edward had promised them the justice and lordship, or the rights and privileges, which they had under Henry III (ibid., 447, 449–50, 460); those of Rhos also refer to an agreement between Edward and Llywelyn by which injuries committed by either side should be remitted (ibid., 449–50). The treaty of Aberconwy provided that the liberties and customs of the tenants of the Four Cantreds should be repected (*LW*, 120).

[29] For the Hagnaby chronicler's estimate of Grey's responsibility in provoking conflict, BL Cotton Vesp B. xi, f. 28v.

[30] *RPeck*, ii, 454–5; for Clifford, above, n. 1.

[31] *RPeck*, ii, 455–8. According to an inquisition taken at Oswestry men of Penllyn were among those who had attacked the town in Holy Week (*WAR*, 352–3).

Contention and Conflict

Madog ap Gruffudd, leaving two young sons, Maelor, or Bromfield, had come into the king's custody.[32] Difficulties were soon encountered there, and as early as 1279 Llywelyn ap Gruffudd felt bound to press the king to remove his officers and convey the land to his nephews Gruffudd ap Madog and Llywelyn ap Madog.[33] Clearly, in attempting to trace the origins of the war of 1282, particular account needs to be taken of the virulence of the initial conflict in those areas where a community was directly subject to the authority of royal officers, and attention has to be given to the documentary evidence which, though largely assembled to justify the resort to arms, provides detailed information for precisely the areas that saw fervid conflict. Going to war at this time the communities drew upon an experience closely comparable to that which had created the conditions for rebellion in Perfeddwlad in 1256, and enabled Llywelyn ap Gruffudd to extend his power over the whole of Gwynedd and create the impetus for an even greater extension of his influence. The situation in the two periods differed to the extent that those who rose in insurrection in 1282 did so, not so much after a prolonged period of friction, but mainly in violent reaction to a brief but intensive period of royal administration particularly associated with Reginald de Grey.

Yet it would be wrong to conclude that pillage and vengeance on the part of fraught communities were the sole characteristics of the rising of 1282. Behind the onslaught on particular castles and towns we may detect a unifying purpose which gave expression to the disillusion of the higher echelons of Welsh society as well as its peasantry. Whether their patrimony lay in moorland or lowland – in Pennardd or Gwynionydd, in Nanheudwy or Cynllàith, in Malláen or Caeo, in Rhufoniog or Ceinmeirch – prestigious individuals nurtured growing anger. For several of these princes their spirited response in 1282 marked a new resolve. Five years before, when Prince Llywelyn had need of their steadfast support, they had preferred, albeit with varying degrees of conviction or reluctance, to submit to the wishes of the king of England. Some had even gone to war against the prince; others had been quick to come to terms with the king. They were bound now in more committed resistance, though there were still conspicuous exceptions. Rhys ap Maredudd was to stand, alone among the princes of Deheubarth, in an allegiance to the king that remained firm even though he may have had some

---

[32] *CWR*, 161, 170, 180–1.
[33] *CAC*, 93–4. Roger Lestrange was put in charge of Powys Fadog (*CWR*, 160, 170; *WAR*, 247). Gruffudd ap Iorwerth was given custody of the lands of Madog's sons in December 1277; incurring displeasure by the way in which he exercised his office, he was removed in July 1279 (*CWR*, 161, 178). Llywelyn protested that the custody was given to a bailiff from England, and asked that the sons be allowed to appoint their own bailiffs. For the fate of the two young princes, below, p. 520.

qualms about the trend of events in Ystrad Tywi in the intervening years; Gruffudd ap Gwenwynwyn remained steadfast in the same fidelity in southern Powys.[34] Neither could convince himself that he naturally belonged to the fraternity of the princes of Wales in prosperity or in adversity, and they stood apart from the others in the spring of 1282. In marked contrast, Rhys ap Maredudd's kinsman, Rhys Wyndod, locked in a legal contest that threatened to deprive him of a valuable part of his inheritance in Ystrad Tywi, was among those who asserted the principle of his right to Welsh law in his attempt to withstand a plaintiff who made an unambiguous appeal to judgement by the common law of England.[35] In Deheubarth as a whole a more effective jurisdiction was certainly being exerted in the king's name as his officials, first Bogo de Knovill and then Robert de Tibetot, imposed a tighter royal control over the area.[36] These changes undoubtedly lay behind the complaints made by Gruffudd ap Maredudd and Cynan ap Maredudd of Ceredigion.[37] They might not be threatened with disinheritance, but these men were sorely troubled by the gradual undermining of their seigniorial authority by an increasingly intrusive royal jurisdiction. Whatever the precise reason for their resentment, they appealed to their inherent right to Welsh law, not as an appeal to an abstract issue of principle, but because they were impelled by an urgent necessity to withstand a dire threat to their hold upon their patrimony or to their authority within its bounds. In Powys Fadog, Llywelyn ap Gruffudd Fychan (or Llywelyn ap Gruffudd ap Madog), greatly irritated by the fact that he was denied recourse to Welsh legal procedures, was troubled also by the erosion of his seigniorial power in Nanheudwy and Cynllaith as royal officers in neighbouring territories disregarded his rights in his own land. He was aggrieved, too, by the men of the lordship of Oswestry who greedily took possession of his land at Lledrod and took timber from his woodland at Coed-gaer. He was brought to a point where he felt bound to forsake the loyalty to Edward that he had been so quick to declare even before the outbreak of the previous war. That early desertion had cost him dearly as his subsequent discomfiture at the hands of the men of Oswestry gave those whom he had forsaken some cause to 'rejoice in his vexation'. The poet Llygad Gŵr prophesied retaliation upon those who wronged Llywelyn, the threat to Ellesmere pointing to the part played in the prince's tribulation by Roger Lestrange, a key figure in the crown's administration of some lands of the dismembered lordships of Powys Fadog. Llywelyn is one of the princes of Wales whose disaffection can be readily established in the period preceding

[34] For indications that Rhys ap Maredudd was disconcerted by the proceedings before the justices, below, n. 155.
[35] *RPeck*, ii, 451–2; below, n. 148.
[36] R. A. Griffiths, *PW*, i, 20–1, 91; below, n. 150.
[37] *RPeck*, ii, 453–4.

the outbreak of war. A common experience in adversity eventually bound the wounds of earlier conflict.[38] On that momentous Palm Sunday Llywelyn ap Gruffudd Fychan and his brother Gruffudd Fychan took the whole power of their lands with them in an onslaught on Oswestry in which princes and peasantry released their pent-up anger. Their raid was closely co-ordinated with the attack on Hawarden and they repeated their assault with even greater force a few weeks later.[39]

Much of the substance of the grievances of the princes is preserved only in the material placed before the archbishop of Canterbury late in 1282, but signs of mounting disaffection may be read in the evidence of the period preceding their resort to arms, more particularly in the litigation examined later. Not all the participants of princely status were motivated by exactly the same considerations, nor did they necessarily act with the same degree of conviction, nor can it always be deduced whether their discontent had been of gradual gestation or whether their action was precipitated by a particular and recent adversity. In some instances, indeed, the troubles created by the previous conflict had never been put right. Several princes of the lineage of Deheubarth had, perforce perhaps, remained with the prince of Wales since 1277 or had found refuge in his land at some point in the intervening period: Rhys Fychan ap Rhys ap Maelgwn, Hywel ap Rhys Gryg, Llywelyn ap Rhys, Hywel ap Rhys.[40] Some had almost certainly abandoned all hope of enjoying any share in the patrimony long before the outbreak of war in 1282.[41] Dependent, in all probability, on the prince of Wales, Llywelyn ap Rhys and Hywel ap Rhys nevertheless joined their kinsmen in asserting the injustice they had endured; for they had been disinherited by a king who had denied them the laws and customs of Wales.[42] These expatriates may have helped to maintain a link between Llywelyn ap Gruffudd and those of their kinsmen, notably Rhys Wyndod, who retained a hold on their patrimonial lands, and

---

[38] *CAP*, 319-20; *WAR*, 262-3, 309, 317, 342, 352-3; *CAC*, 154-5; *GBF*, 28; P. Lynch, 'Llygad Gŵr: sylwebydd cyfoes', *Ysgrifau Beirniadol*, 16 (1990), 31-51. The responsibility exercised by Roger Lestrange, who may be the steward (*rhechdyr*) to whom the poet alludes, is noticed above, n. 33. Litigation in which Llywelyn ap Gruffudd Fychan was involved is considered later; his complaints in 1282 are in *RPeck*, ii, 463-5.

[39] *WAR*, 352-3; he fell alongside Prince Llywelyn in December 1282; below, p. 565.

[40] Rhys Fychan, Hywel ap Rhys Gryg, and Llywelyn ap Rhys, a brother of Rhys Wyndod, and perhaps another brother, Hywel ap Rhys, had gone to Gwynedd in 1277 (*BT, Pen20*, 224-5; *Pen20Tr*, 118-19; *RBH*, 264-7).

[41] Hywel ap Rhys Gryg was given the king's protection in 1278, but his presence with Llywelyn and his appeal to Burnell suggest exile from Deheubarth (*CWR*, 161; *CAC*, 123).

[42] *RPeck*, ii, 452-3. In November 1283 the commote of Is Cennen, held before the war by Llywelyn ap Rhys, or shared with his brother Hywel ap Rhys, was given to John Giffard, who already held Hirfryn and Perfedd in 1282 (*CWR*, 235, 283); Llywelyn may have lost possession of Is Cennen even before the conflict of 1282. Hywel ap Rhys, fugitive and outlaw, whose lands at Llanddarog were granted to another in 1281, may have been Llywelyn's brother (*CWR*, 185); below, p. 577, n. 227.

they are found together at Llywelyn's court on occasion.[43] Whether the presence of these disinherited or disenchanted princes can be interpreted as an indication that Llywelyn was deliberately gathering these men about him with a view to the resumption of armed conflict is by no means certain.[44] We certainly need to be wary of assuming that it was he who inspired the action on which the princes of Deheubarth and those of Powys Fadog embarked in Holy Week. More obviously relevant are the circumstances in which Dafydd ap Gruffudd found himself exposed to the same rigorous authority as that which troubled the communities of the lands adjacent to his own. His experience gave the volatile prince an identity of interest with those of peasant and princely stock who carried responsibility for the sudden and dramatic challenge to royal power in Wales.

In the period leading up to the war of 1277 Dafydd ap Gruffudd had made an early departure from the principality of Wales, to gain the protection once more of a king who would later recount how he 'had been received as an exile, nourished as an orphan and endowed with lands and placed among the great ones of the palace'.[45] Yet Dafydd was still to be counted among the most perfidious of Welshmen. Sensitive with regard to his interests, even as he contributed to his brother's downfall, and no doubt deeply frustrated by the eventual outcome of the conflict of 1277, Dafydd gave a singular indication of his resentment when, in the unequivocal statement of *Brut y Tywysogyon*, he 'took the castle of Hawarden'.[46] It is still difficult to fathom the precise reasons why Dafydd chose to abandon his allegiance to the crown and take the course which plunged him into rebellion and annihilation. His motives at several points in his career defy historical explanation. Our knowledge of Dafydd in the period between the wars is extremely meagre, and the really crucial evidence comes from the very last months before he rose in rebellion. It was at a late stage and, it seems, anticipated by no clear indications of gathering dissension, that Dafydd made an impressive statement of his right to judgement under the law of Wales.[47] It was not a statement of any originality, for the phraseology was closely similar to a pronouncement, to be considered presently, which Llywelyn ap Gruffudd had made some time

---

[43] Hywel ap Rhys Gryg and Llywelyn ap Rhys, with Rhys Wyndod, Gruffudd ap Maredudd and Cynan ap Maredudd, gave surety for the fidelity of Trahaearn ap Madog at Dolwyddelan, May 1278 (*LW*, 43; cf. above, p. 417, and below, p. 492, n. 157). The same expatriates, with Rhys Fychan ap Rhys ap Maelgwn, witnessed the prince's grant to Heilin ap Tudur ab Ednyfed at the castle, August 1281 (*RC*, 211).

[44] D. Stephenson, 'Llywelyn ap Gruffydd and the struggle for the principality of Wales, 1258–1282', *THSC*, 1983, 45–6 and R. R. Davies, *CCC*, 343, suggest that the gathering of these men in Gwynedd is one of several pieces of evidence which indicate that Llywelyn was preparing for a new offensive; for further comment, below, pp. 497–8.

[45] *CWR*, 281–2; *Foedera*, I, ii, 630.

[46] *BT, Pen20*, 227; *Pen20Tr*, 120; *RBH*, 268–9.

[47] *CAC*, 72–3.

Contention and Conflict

previously. Its importance lies in the vehemence and the suddenness with which Dafydd identified himself with the arguments of those of his peers who had been embroiled in litigation before royal justices during the previous years. The precise circumstances and the timing of Dafydd's declaration are thus relevant to our understanding of the call to arms.

We know that Dafydd was summoned to the county court of Chester late in 1281 to answer William de Venables, who claimed lands in Hope and Estyn which Edward had given to the prince in 1277.[48] This may not have been the first time he had been confronted with a legal action concerning these lands. In their submissions to the archbishop the men of Tegeingl alluded to the fact that in 'Dafydd's case' the decision of one justice of Chester had been overturned by another – namely Reginald de Grey – and this may suggest that Dafydd had successfully defended his right to the lands on an earlier occasion.[49] Writing to Edward when the case had been reopened, Dafydd certainly held that an inquisition previously taken by the justice of Chester had established what he regarded as the fundamental matter: the lands in question were in Wales and Welsh law, not English law, should apply to them.[50] In his ultimate recital of his grievances Dafydd inevitably gave prominence to this issue among those which had driven him to war.[51] But the depth of his feelings was revealed when he wrote to Edward before the outbreak of hostilities. There can be no doubt that it was Grey's appointment as justice of Chester which proved to be the turning point in his relations with the crown. In his later statement he saw the manner in which he was treated by Grey, and his failure to obtain redress, as a strange reward for his labours on the king's behalf in war. But his feelings are conveyed perfectly clearly in the period immediately before he resorted to war against the king. It appears that it was at a date subsequent to Grey's appointment, but on an occasion of which there is no other record, that Dafydd went to the county court – doing so out of reverence to the king – and raised his voice to declare that the land in dispute was in Wales and that he had no need to answer for it at the county

---

[48] *Calendar of County Court, City Court and Eyre Rolls of Chester, 1259–1297*, ed. R. Stewart-Brown (Manchester, Chetham Society, 84, 1925), 35. Venables, in the presence of Grey, proceeded against Dafydd on 6 December 1281. Dafydd did not appear, and by the king's mandate the plea was deferred to the next court. Records of 27 January and 17 March 1282 contain no reference to the case. As there is no complete series of court records it cannot be decided when Dafydd made the appearance in the county court or when the court made the judgement noticed in *CAC*, 72–3.

[49] *RPeck*, ii, 460.

[50] *CAC*, 73–4, one of two undated letters to Edward, attributed to '1278–March 1282'; the records of the county court, not used by the editor, suggest that both letters were written in 1281 or early 1282. The present letter precedes the other (*CAC*, 72–3).

[51] *RPeck*, ii, 445–7; Dafydd says that he was forewarned by someone at court of the effect of Grey's appointment, and his apprehension was fulfilled.

court.⁵² He placed the land in the peace of God and the king and withdrew, and later urged that the process in the county court, with the doomsmen's judgement that he was refusing to answer to the plea (though Dafydd never made any answer whatsoever), should be sent to the king. Echoing the argument already employed by his brother, Dafydd demanded that heed be taken of the principle that it was right, since the king was lord of several countries (*patrie*) whose several languages and several laws were administered and remained unchanged, that the laws of Wales should be left unchanged like the laws of other nations (*nationes*). No prince could argue more trenchantly, and the grievances which provoked these forthright assertions were closely comparable with those which troubled the princes of the other provinces. Dafydd had cause for complaint, too, of interference by royal officers in his lordship of Dyffryn Clwyd and Rhufoniog, his greater estates. He complained that three townships held in dower by Gwenllian de Lacy, which should have reverted to him upon her death, had been seized by the king, and Grey had taken his woods of Lleweni, scant rewards for his service to the crown and the dangers he had faced in war on his behalf.⁵³ His more acute problems may have arisen, however, from the legal proceedings which threatened his very hold on the lands of Hope and Estyn where, with Edward's help, he had built the castle of Caergwrle on the high ground overlooking the plains of Cheshire.⁵⁴ On both counts he could establish a bond of common experience with his fellow princes in Powys Fadog and Deheubarth. How long, in his case, the problems had been festering we cannot tell, but there can be no doubt that Dafydd's difficulties were greatly aggravated by the appointment of Grey as justice of Chester. Dafydd says so directly towards the end of 1282; still more helpfully, the evidence from the end of the previous year points unambiguously to a marked deterioration in relations between Dafydd and those who by then represented royal authority.

Yet even more relevant to the events of Holy Week than the experience which he shared with his fellow princes, Dafydd's relations with Grey gave him a bond with the communities of the neighbouring territories who, after what may have been a period of comparative quietude on the Chester front, were thrown into confrontation with a regime of unusual severity. Of the Four Cantreds, it was Rhos and Tegeingl which, as we have seen, experienced the full force of Reginald de Grey's administration; those of Rhufoniog and Dyffryn Clwyd were largely insulated from its rigours by reason of the

---

⁵² *CAC*, 72–3; *RPeck*, ii, 446.

⁵³ *RPeck*, ii, 445–6. Her lands had been granted to Grey upon his appointment as justice of Chester, with custody of Rhos and Englefield, in November 1281 (*CPR, 1272–79*, 464). For Gwenllian and the lands, *CRR*, xvi, no. 1596; J. E. Lloyd, 'Who was Gwenllian de Lacy?', *ArchCamb*, 6th ser., 19 (1919), 292–8.

⁵⁴ Above, p. 435.

lordship exercised by Dafydd ap Gruffudd. For one reason or another, Dafydd had the means suddenly, and perhaps unpredictably, in the spring of 1282, to bring all Four Cantreds into rebellion against the powers under which lord or community laboured. It is unquestionably in this quarter, and neither among the exiles gathered about Llywelyn ap Gruffudd nor among the princes discomforted by their experience in Powys or Deheubarth, that we need to look for the real impetus to war in 1282. Dafydd had dramatically pronounced that he placed the land about the castle of Caergwrle in the peace of God and the king. Edward, had he had the good sense to recall the circumstances in which, during the days of his youth, he had forfeited the Four Cantreds to the Welsh, might have pondered whether he was well advised to entrust the custody of two parts of that land to an aggressive administrator at a time when there were already signs of renewed tension. It proved to be a decision which saw the whole of Perfeddwlad and its environs suddenly removed both from the peace of God and the power of the king.

The interests of princes and the experience of communities at large are both important ingredients in the making of the war of 1282. Within those communities there were, of course, distinct gradations. If the destruction wrought upon the English during the early stages of the rising marks the anger of a desperate peasantry, neither the initiation of the conflict nor the durability of the resistance thereafter can be explained without taking account of the potent influence of those who, though not of princely rank, were powerful figures in the community. These, too, were men with material interests to safeguard and the fact that some of them exercised authority in the king's name did not necessarily bind them in indissoluble allegiance. Their very prominence left them so much more exposed to the vagaries of favour and disfavour dispensed at a higher level of authority. Several among them no doubt remained faithful to the crown, or quickly came to terms, but it would be wrong to dwell entirely on those who in 1282, as in 1277, served the king and neglect those who stuck to the rebellious princes. The complaints of the communities of Rhos and Englefield reflect the resentments of men well versed in the concordances of lord and community. They could recall that, before doing homage to Edward in 1277, each had been promised his right and jurisdiction, the liberties and privileges he had enjoyed under the lordship of King Henry, only to see them undermined by his rapacious officers. They had endured prosecutions for deeds done in time of war, even though the peace settlement had ensured them an amnesty. The presence of English settlers among them, creating a disturbing coincidence of burghal privilege and ethnic discrimination, sharpened the sensitivities of men acutely conscious of a status that was theirs by inherent right. These were men – *nobiles* or *optimates* – who spoke the language of *iura* and *iurisdictiones*, *libertates* and *privilegii*.⁵⁵ Particular and personal complaints could be sublimated into comprehensive charges that the men of the *cantrefi* had been deprived of the privileges of the *patria*, forced to take judgement by English law in courts where they should be judged by the law of Wales. What was done to them was done contrary to Welsh law and custom.

Their most conspicuous representative was undoubtedly Goronwy ap Heilin. He had served Llywelyn ap Gruffudd in the years of his supremacy and thereafter he had had an exceedingly difficult dual role as a servant of the crown – acting as a royal justice and serving in numerous other capacities – and as a representative of Llywelyn on important matters.⁵⁶ It would seem, even so, that he was placed in his most difficult predicament, not by his continued links with Llywelyn and his journeying to and fro between king and prince, but by his position of responsibility in Rhos. In the submissions of the men of that *cantref* (embodied in a document he may well have composed) he is said to have endured injuries affecting him personally, and his own complaints were set out at some length in a separate statement.⁵⁷ He was evidently at odds with Reginald de Grey and with his aide Robert Crevequer.⁵⁸ The document in Goronwy's name expands, however, not on matters of personal concern but on the manner in which his attempts to secure justice for others had been frustrated. His removal from office, almost certainly following Grey's appointment as justice, was itself a mark of the trend of events which precipitated the war of 1282. Yet, quite apart from any offices he had held under the crown, Goronwy ap Heilin was in his own right a man of standing in his community. The grievances which he and the men of Rhos and those of Tegeingl recounted in their submissions to Archbishop Pecham represent, more than the anger of disillusioned princes, the telling evidence that the *nobiles* of a community placed in what was historically a highly sensitive area were retaliating against the exceedingly harsh treatment meted out to them in the king's name. The testimony both of the community as a whole and its principal proctor are in close accord with one another. They cohere in a particularly significant manner in Goronwy's emphasis, less on his own disquiet, than on the king's failure, despite successive appeals, to correct

---

[55] *RPeck*, 447–51, 460–3.
[56] His service after 1277 is summarized by J. C. Davies, in *WAR*, 116–17.
[57] *RPeck*, ii, 458–60.
[58] Crevequer is alleged to have attempted to wrest Maenan, Penmaen and Llysfaen from Goronwy ap Heilin, who held the properties under lease; Grey then brought armed horsemen intending to capture Goronwy and have him decapitated (ibid., 449, 459). For Crevequer's estates in Prestatyn and in Grey's lordship of Dyffryn Clwyd after 1282, R. R. Davies, 'Colonial Wales', *Past and Present*, 65 (1974), 6; for later complaints against Grey's rule, *CAP*, 168–9.

the errors of his officers.[59] In what were clearly circumstances of acute tension, Goronwy ap Heilin found himself in direct confrontation with Grey and, facing the justice's armed force and fearing for his own safety, dared not go to the courts at Caerwys and Rhuddlan to which he had been summoned.[60] It was evidently at a time of great peril that Goronwy sent word to Edward telling him that he was in danger of losing the loyalty of the whole community. The shared experience of Dafydd ap Gruffudd and Goronwy ap Heilin became a vital axis in the stressful winter of 1281–2.[61]

So far, in tracing the origins of the war, very little has been said of Llywelyn ap Gruffudd himself. It is not easy to discern the relationship between the rebellion of 1282 and the political processes inextricably bound up with the personal endeavour of the prince of Wales. These broader issues, which will be considered more fully at a later stage, naturally impinge upon the more particular and exceedingly intriguing problem of whether Llywelyn was involved in the initiation of new conflict. Historical study may never satisfactorily resolve this matter, any more than it can solve the problems which arise in considering the manner in which he met his death. The narrative sources point to two different conclusions. Some writers harboured no doubts that the rebellion sprang from a new understanding between Llywelyn and Dafydd. 'And thus were Herod and Pilate reconciled' were the words of Walter of Guisborough, writing in the north of England some years after the event, and the notion of harmony and understanding between the brothers is conveyed in other sources, too.[62] Some went further. The Chester annalist, writing in fairly close proximity to the scenes of the very first assaults, though not perhaps at the time of the attacks, maintained that it was by Llywelyn's counsel that Dafydd attacked Hawarden. The chronicler of Dunstable, among others, refers to Llywelyn's presence at the siege of Flint and Rhuddlan, a comment which, if it could be confidently endorsed, would indicate that Llywelyn took the field at an early stage in the rising even if he

---

[59] *RPeck*, ii, 450, 459–60; both submissions recount the successive journeys which Goronwy made to the king. Among matters affecting him personally, a *nobilis* who had fostered Goronwy's son was killed, and when the kindred sought justice the killer was protected and the kindred denied their right.
[60] Ibid., 459.
[61] Ibid., 459–60: 'misit quendam nuncium deportantem duas litteras, unam ad dominum regem, et aliam ad fratrem Lewelinum, ad significandum domino regi quod amitteret totam patriam'. The significance of his sending a letter to 'brother Llywelyn' is unclear, but the wording suggests, not that a letter was sent to Dafydd's brother, but to Brother Llywelyn, the Dominican friar, clearly indicating Dafydd's anxiety to get a message to the king.
[62] Guisborough, *Chronicle*, 218; Langtoft, *Chronicle*, ii, 176. For these problems and the course of the war in Gwynedd, A. D. Carr, 'The last days of Gwynedd', *TCaernHS*, 43 (1982), 7–22.

were not present from the first.⁶³ Other chroniclers, in contrast, do not concur with the view that Llywelyn was present from the beginning. Works whose testimony normally carries some weight indicate that the first attack was launched without Llywelyn's knowledge. They suggest, too, that to postulate concord between the brothers is not tantamount to attributing to Llywelyn any part in the events of Palm Sunday nor indeed knowledge of the intention to go to war. Guisborough, though he speaks of fraternal concord, was convinced that the attack on Hawarden was launched by Dafydd in an attempt to convince his brother of his political conversion.⁶⁴ It is a view shared by several authors. Another possibility is broached by a writer who provides more detail than most. In the chronicle of the Premonstratensian house of Hagnaby in Lincolnshire, a source to which we shall need to turn again, we read of a meeting arranged between Dafydd and Llywelyn, on the one hand, and Reginald de Grey and Roger Clifford, on the other, to consider issues of contention between the Welsh and the alien officers.⁶⁵ The chronicler says that Dafydd himself aborted the discussion by attacking the two lords, and that Clifford withdrew to Hawarden castle where he remained until Palm Sunday. The account creates some difficulty, in that it implicitly conveys that the two lords might have been alerted to the possibility of an armed rising, whereas the evidence as a whole suggests that surprise was of the essence of the attack on Hawarden. But though he is the only author to mention it, the Hagnaby chronicler's account of a meeting deserves notice. Its testimony comes very close indeed to the thrust of the evidence of Goronwy ap Heilin and the men of Rhos, which decidedly points to repeated attempts to secure a dialogue between rulers and ruled.⁶⁶ Grey certainly occupied the key position of justice of Chester and there is, though late and partisan in nature, plenteous evidence of disaffection in the area under his authority. It is not inconceivable that a meeting between Grey and Dafydd, and indeed Llywelyn, might have been arranged. Besides, Dafydd vented his anger upon both Grey and Clifford, even though his measure of complaint against the custodian of Hawarden is less clear than those which explain his relations with Grey.⁶⁷ Altogether, the chronicle evidence tends to place the responsibility for starting the war of 1282 upon Dafydd. He, rather than Llywelyn, is seen to be the more obvious focus for the intense resentments which were engendered in Grey's sphere of activity in the months preceding the rebellion. This is the view indicated by several writers, including the Peterborough chronicler, who

⁶³ *AnnCestr*, 108 ('de consilio fratris sui Lewelini'); *AnnDunst*, 291–2.
⁶⁴ Guisborough, *Chronicle*, 218.
⁶⁵ Cotton Vesp. B xi, f. 27.
⁶⁶ *RPeck*, ii, 447–51, 458–60.
⁶⁷ The Bern document, noticed below, n. 70, mentioning that Dafydd made a gift of two salmon to Clifford as a sign of friendship, may point to some contact between them.

Contention and Conflict

is an important witness in relation to the war, Nicholas Trevet and the Hailes chronicler.[68] And, as we have seen, *Brut y Tywysogyon* attributes the attack on Hawarden to Dafydd.[69] A well-informed, though biased, account of the war, stridently written from the king's point of view sometime after the cessation of hostilities, again places the responsibility firmly on Dafydd.[70] All in all, the main body of contemporary commentators looks to Dafydd rather than to Llywelyn as the initiator of the war of 1282, and it was Dafydd who eventually incurred the most pungent expression of the king's wrath.

Regrettably, the evidence from the English chancery in the early weeks of the war, though full of condemnation of the rebels and informative in its account of the preparations for the king's campaign in Wales, provides very little help in identifying those initially responsible. Writing to Queen Margaret of France some two weeks after the outbreak of hostilities, Edward described the war 'which Llywelyn and his brother Dafydd' were waging against him in Wales. He wrote to Alphonso of Castile in the same terms at the same time.[71] These early references to Llywelyn may simply reflect an instinctive assumption at court that a new offensive in Wales was bound to be linked with Llywelyn. It is certainly noticeable that, after these early references, royal records do not make any specific mention of Llywelyn for

---

[68] *ChronPetroburg*, 55; Trevet, *Annales*, 301–2; M. N. Blount, 'A critical edition of the Annales of Hailes (MS Cotton Cleopatra D iii, ff. 33–59v) with an examination of their sources', MA thesis, University of Manchester, 1974, 84 (from f. 47v)

[69] Above, n. 1. The statement in *BT, Pen20*, 228; *Pen20Tr*, 120, that 'on Palm Sunday took place the breach between Llywelyn ap Gruffudd and Edward king of England' is the first entry, written in a new hand, in the continuation of the chronicle found in the Peniarth 20 text alone. For the continuation, ibid., xlv–xlix, lxxiii–lxxiv, 217; G. and T. M. Charles-Edwards, 'The continuation of *Brut y Tywysogion* in Peniarth MS 20', in T. Jones and E. B. Fryde (eds.), *Essays and Poems presented to Daniel Huws* (Aberystwyth, 1994), 293–305.

[70] Part of the text, from Canterbury Cathedral, Dean and Chapter MSS, Sede Vacante, III, ff. 169–70, is printed in *Report on Manuscripts in Various Collections*, i (HMC, 1901), 246–50. It is normally taken to have been written by someone in Pecham's service during or soon after the archbishop's negotiations with Llywelyn in November 1282. A complete text is in Burgerbibliothek Bern Cod. 69, among miscellaneous texts listed in H. Hagen, *Catalogus Codicum Bernensium* (Bern, 1875), 91–2. Written sometime after 1282–3, it gives a prominent place to Dafydd's part in the war, with details of his capture and sentencing. The author had detailed knowledge of the outbreak, knowing, for instance, of the presence of Payn de Gamage as well as Clifford at Hawarden. He attributes the initial actions to Dafydd, but says that Llywelyn was in league with him; Llywelyn is said to have been present at the siege of Rhuddlan and to have known from the beginning of the deeds committed in his name. Written after the war the work is less a factual account than a tract which chastizes the Welsh for their perfidy, and may be placed among the moral condemnations noticed later. I hope to be able to publish a text of this important composition.

[71] *CAC*, 56 (8 April); *Foedera*, I, ii, 606. A letter of the abbot of Bury St Edmunds giving an account of the prayers said for the army which went 'against Llywelyn' (*CAC*, 604), formerly attributed to 1282, has been shown to belong to 1277 (D. W. Burton, 'Requests for prayers and royal propaganda under Edward I', in P. R. Coss and S. D. Lloyd (eds.), *Thirteenth Century England*, 3 (Woodbridge, 1991), 25–35.

several weeks. Furthermore, neither the excommunication pronounced by the archbishop of Canterbury ten days after the outbreak, nor the second issued a month later, made any mention of either Llywelyn or Dafydd, in marked contrast to the process by which, in the months leading up to the war of 1277, Llywelyn was excommunicated by name (*nominatim*).[72] It is possible that we do not have a full record of the measures taken by the church in 1282, and it is obvious that in the circumstances created by sudden rebellion the church was not able to proceed with the deliberation that characterized the earlier excommunication. It is conceivable that neither secular nor church authorities wished to concede to Llywelyn, or Dafydd, any semblance of a political authority but preferred to castigate a body of unnamed rebels. Record evidence for the early weeks is exceedingly sparse, but what we have lends no certainty that Llywelyn was involved from the beginning, nor a definite indication that he was not involved. A record of subsequent judicial proceedings in Flint, which has been noticed already, reflects something of the beginnings of the conflict and indeed conveys that Llywelyn's influence was at work on Palm Sunday. The jurors verified the substance of charges levied against one who was alleged to have come to Northop on Palm Sunday to search for lead for the prince's use, and that he did so upon the instructions of the prince himself, delivering a good deal of it to Rhuddlan for the prince's engines when the castle was being besieged. Their testimony would appear to be corroborated by later evidence, but this serves, most of all, to underline the depth of the antipathy between the Welsh and the English in the aftermath of the struggle and to suggest that the line between criminal and politically motivated activity was not clearly drawn. It would be rash to place any weight on the allegation that Llywelyn was looking about for lead on Palm Sunday.[73] It is an exceedingly unlikely tale.

The material available to us, when every consideration has been given to personal interpretation on the part of chroniclers or to partisan pleadings by disaffected litigants, or for quick assumptions made at court on hearing bad news from Wales, suggests very strongly that the initiation of conflict in 1282 was due to a fusion of Dafydd ap Gruffudd's intense personal grievances with the disaffection of those communities in north-east Wales who lived under royal administration. It points, with a fair degree of probability, to an explosive reaction to the cumulative effect of the sequence of events which followed the appointment of Reginald de Grey as justice of Chester towards the end of 1281. There can be no doubt that Llywelyn would have been aware

[72] *RPeck*, i, 324–5, 352–3; *Councils*, i, 534–6; for the apparent absence of an excommunication *nominatim*, below, pp. 515–16.

[73] *Flint Pleas*, xviii–xx, 2–3; A. J. Taylor, 'The events of Palm Sunday, 1282: a further record', *JFlintHS*, 13 (1952–3), 51–2, where the relevant statement forms part of a record of proceedings containing assertions which need to be treated with reservation.

of the problems in Perfeddwlad, and we can be certain that he would have been sympathetic to the predicament of its communities. His concern for Perfeddwlad, and his fear that, left under royal government, they would continue to suffer injustice, stands out prominently among the concerns which he expressed during his exchanges with John Pecham. But that he initiated the action in the region or that he participated in the early movements is not indicated with any certainty in the evidence that survives. What remains available for consideration, despite its inconsistencies and contradictions, gives us no good reason to discount Llywelyn's depiction of the manner in which war began.[74] The matter will be considered more fully when we have examined the wider issues which arise in considering the prince's position, and especially his relations with the king in the period since his submission in 1277.

Shortly before his death Llywelyn ap Gruffudd set out an extensive statement of his grievances, some of them arising, not from issues of material interest, but from considerations of status, a matter on which he remained deeply sensitive for all his humiliation.[75] He did so in large part by reference to the clauses in the treaty of Aberconwy which, in his view, the king had disregarded. He was, indeed, able to describe an accumulation of difficulties of a more varied nature which show that, by the beginning of 1282, he had his own matters of concern, quite apart from those affecting his brother, or the other princes, or the communities of particular localities. Yet, most prominent among the matters recounted in his final statement was the fact, as he saw it, that he had been denied the law of Wales in direct contravention of the treaty he had made with Edward. Llywelyn referred specifically to the litigation over Arwystli, the *cause célèbre* of the years 1277–82, in which he was locked in contest with Gruffudd ap Gwenwynwyn and, as a consequence, in prolonged altercation with the king. The matter looms large in the evidence of the period, attracting extensive historical commentary.[76] The record

---

[74] J. G. Edwards, at first accepting that the Flintshire plea roll provided evidence of Llywelyn's early involvement, made no reference to the source in the important study he published in 1940 (*Flint Pleas*, xviii–xx; *LW*, lxiii–lviv). Although he was still of the view that Llywelyn had joined the rebellion soon after it erupted, he now judged that he had not been involved at the outset. See also Powicke, *Henry III*, ii, 675–6; Carr, 'Last days of Gwynedd', 9–11. Prestwich, *Edward I*, 182, accepts that the prince was present during the attacks on Flint and Rhuddlan.

[75] Llywelyn's statements are in *RPeck*, ii, 437–45; for his attitude in the period leading up to 1282, J. G. Edwards, in *LW*, lxii–lxiv and below, pp. 493–508.

[76] Among commentaries there are important contributions in J. E. Lloyd, 'Edward the First's commission of enquiry of 1280–81: an examination of its origin and purpose', *Y Cymmrodor*, 25 (1915), 1–20; 26 (1916), 252; A. J. Roderick, 'The dispute between Llywelyn ap Gruffydd and Gruffydd ap Gwenwynwyn (1278–82)', *B*, 8 (1935–7), 248–54; J. C. Davies, in *WAR*, 38 ff.; J. G. Edwards, in *LW*, lxiv–lxv; Powicke, *Henry III*, ii, 659–61, 666–76; idem, review of *WAR* in *EHR*, 56 (1941), 493–4; R. R. Davies, *CCC*, 344–7.

contains some of the most notable statements ever made in the course of thirteenth-century Anglo-Welsh relations and, besides, it embodies legal arguments with a direct bearing upon an understanding of the motives and predicaments of king and prince.

Llywelyn initiated the action over Arwystli and that part of Cyfeiliog which lay between the Dyfi and the Dulas very soon after the completion of the arrangements necessary under the terms of the treaty of Aberconwy. His purpose in bringing the action was evidently the repossession of the lands which, following the legal process in his court in 1274 already noticed, were forfeited by Gruffudd ap Gwenwynwyn and his son Owain on account of their unfaithfulness.[77] Gruffudd had recovered the lands during the war of 1277, but in Llywelyn's estimation the previous conviction still stood. In preparation for the legal proceedings to be examined presently he had a transcript of the process in his court prepared, and verified by the abbot of Aberconwy and the dean of Arllechwedd, to affirm that the conviction had in no way been erased or impaired.[78] It never came to matters of substance, however, and at the heart of the prolonged contention was the law to be used to resolve the case. Precisely what was at issue needs to be considered carefully. The argument might appear to have turned on the clause in the treaty of Aberconwy which provided that actions between Llywelyn and anyone else would be resolved according to the law of Wales if they arose in Wales and according to the law of the march if they arose in the march.[79] This proved to be a particularly important tenet of the treaty but it is unlikely that either Edward or Llywelyn would have wished to see the clause as a pronouncement of new policy. At the time the agreement was made each of them no doubt judged that the statement registered the practice which had previously been adopted in respect of such cases. Indeed, an inquiry made at the king's behest in 1278 confirmed what was, for Llywelyn certainly, the essence of the matter, namely that Welsh law was used in cases which arose between lords of Wales, but it might be noticed that the report made no distinction between the law of

---

[77] Lands in dispute are described in Owen, *Description of Penbrokeshire*, i, 221; iv, 599–60; J. E. Lloyd, *Y Cymmrodor*, 25 (1915), 4–6, 10–13; and 26 (1916), 252; J. G. Edwards, in *LW*, liii–liv; J. C. Davies, in *WAR*, 45–6; *BT, Pen20Tr*, 214. The process in 1274, above, pp. 370–1.

[78] *LW*, 110: 'non rasum nec abolitum nec in aliqua parte viciatum'; transcript prepared at Ardda 21 July 1278, probably in preparation for the proceedings before the justices at Oswestry the next day.

[79] *LW*, 120; above, p. 439.

Wales and the law of the march.[80] The point was put clearly: if an action arose between two of the magnates of Wales and the march, the plaintiff should put the matter to the king of England and he would be bound, if that were the plaintiff's wish, to resolve the matter in accordance with the law of Hywel Dda. In the light of this statement the distinction made in the treaty of Aberconwy between the law of Wales and the law of the march was not a meaningful one, and this was not the only document to indicate this view.

At precisely this time there are clear signs of an inclination on the part of the lords of the march to lay emphasis on their legal inheritance as lords of Wales. They argued that cases arising between them should be resolved in Wales and in accord with the practice of the law of Wales, and, in relation to matters of contention between neighbouring lordships, they gained the benefit of a formal decision of the king's council ceding the substance of their case.[81] But, more significant perhaps than any declaration of principle, the lords of the march, when pleading in particular cases, pressed that actions before the royal justices should proceed according to these means. Clare, and Mortimer, and Bohun: the great names in these cases are not unfamiliar. Llywelyn ap Gruffudd, in the years after 1277, found exceptionally clear indications that the magnates who had destroyed his power in the march were increasingly asserting their right to the law of their lordships as an integral part of their inheritance. And, as far as they were concerned, there was no need to distinguish between the law of the march and the law of Wales: they were lords of Wales, as their firm statements repeatedly declared, and the only meaningful distinction lay between the law of Wales and the law of the march on the one hand and the law of England on the other.[82] Roger Mortimer took this standpoint in an action between Gruffudd ap Gwenwynwyn and himself. Gruffudd insisted that the action should be resolved by the common law of England on the grounds that both plaintiff and defendant were barons of the king holding their lands by barony (*per baroniam*); Mortimer adhered to the view that the land was in Wales and that the case should be heard in accordance with the principles and practices of Welsh law, and his view

---

[80] *CIM*, i, no. 1109; J. C. Davies, in *WAR*, 36–8, 135–6; Powicke, *Henry III*, ii, 671. The inquisition, taken before Reginald de Grey and William de Hamilton at Oswestry, was specifically concerned with Gruffudd ap Gwenwynwyn's wish to establish a market and fair in his land. He claimed Welsh law, and the verdict was distinctly favourable to his argument on this issue, but ran counter to what he argued in the Arwystli case. For the action, *Select Cases concerning the Law Merchant*, iii, 140–2; inquisition, ibid., 170.

[81] Text of this important decision, *WAR*, 309; undated, it is written on a membrane containing a record of proceedings in December 1280.

[82] For the marchers' viewpoint, J. B. Smith, 'The legal position of Wales in the middle ages', 35–6. John Giffard was exceptional among marcher lords in seeking judgement by the common law of England in one set of actions, while taking judgement by Welsh law in another.

prevailed.[83] No prince of Wales could argue to better purpose than this, and the argument advanced by Mortimer was closely akin to that propounded by Llywelyn ap Gruffudd in the course of the proceedings which began when, by his own choice, he came before the justices to claim Arwystli against Gruffudd ap Gwenwynwyn. His initiative, as we have seen already, did not trouble Edward in the least but rather gave him reason to believe that, in an agreeable manner (*benigne*), the prince of Wales was coming to terms with his new situation after the treaty of Aberconwy and that he entirely respected the king's jurisdiction.[84] At no point in the course of the Arwystli plea was jurisdiction a matter at issue, and the prolonged and intense debate which ensued turned rather on the manner by which the plea should be resolved under the authority vested in the king's justices.[85]

Although there is no record on the roll of proceedings, Llywelyn probably initiated his plea on Arwystli at a session held before Ralph de Farningham at Montgomery on or about 16 February 1278. By then, at the very first session of the court at Oswestry a week earlier, a plea for the whole of Arwystli had been brought against Gruffudd ap Gwenwynwyn by one Adam of Montgomery, but there can be little doubt that the plea was brought in collusion with Gruffudd.[86] At the same session Gruffudd himself brought an action against Llywelyn in which, though he was secure in his possession of Arwystli, he claimed the whole of the land as well as the land on the confines of Powys and Meirionnydd. He also brought charges against the prince concerning the action taken against him by Llywelyn in 1274, as well as recounting other injuries both preceding and following his discomfiture in that year.[87] Gruffudd's plea was sent *coram rege* and there is no further record on the roll, whereas successive pleas brought by Adam recur in proceedings before the justices until the summer of 1281. On this evidence it might seem that Llywelyn's action on Arwystli was a counter-plea forced upon him by the other litigants, but it is much more likely that Gruffudd and Adam brought

---

[83] Gruffudd ap Gwenwynwyn first brought an action against the king over lands between the rivers Rhiw and Helyg (February 1278–December 1279), and Mortimer and Knovill, appearing for the king, pleaded Welsh law (*WAR*, 240–1, 285–6); later, after the king had conveyed the land to him, Mortimer (January–June 1281) took the same standpoint (*WAR*, 313–14). For the justices' judgement in Mortimer's favour, 15 June 1281, below, n. 137.

[84] *CCR, 1272–79*, 493; *Foedera*, I, ii, 554; above, p. 446.

[85] Below, pp. 486–7.

[86] Pleas by Adam and Gruffudd, *WAR*, 235. There is no record of proceedings on 16 February, but Adam was given a day at Montgomery on that date, and that was evidently the session before Farmingham at Montgomery to which Llywelyn referred in 1281 (*WAR*, 235, 334). The early proceedings and Farmingham's departure from the Welsh bench are noticed by J. C. Davies, in *WAR*, 97–100, 131–2; for his career in English justice, *The Early English Law Reports*, ed. P. A. Brand, 2 vols. (London, Selden Society, 1996), I, cxxxix–cxl. Adam's collusive pleas are noticed by J. C. Davies, in *WAR*, 125–30; below, n. 139.

[87] *WAR*, 241.

their pleas in anticipation of the action which, initiated before the justices entirely at his own volition, he was to pursue with dour determination over a period of four years. Llywelyn has to be regarded as the true begetter of the Arwystli litigation.

The first minute of the plea on the surviving roll, and the only entry relating to the case made upon the roll for the whole of the year, is a record made at Oswestry on 22 July. On that date, through his attorneys, Llywelyn claimed against Gruffudd ap Gwenwynwyn the whole of Arwystli and the land between the Dyfi and the Dulas.[88] Quite apart from subsequent indications that the plea had been brought early in the year, it emerges that, well before the hearing at Oswestry, Llywelyn had written to the king concerning the plea and that the key issue in the argument had already been broached. In successive communications Llywelyn was strenuously urging his view of what was implied by the provision in the treaty of Aberconwy which established his right to receive justice according to Welsh law in pleas which arose in Wales. It is obvious that issue was already joined, and early in June Llywelyn's representations elicited a letter, to be noticed again presently, which suggests that Edward already had a clear conception of what procedure by Welsh law meant in Llywelyn's mind.[89] There were already, indeed, some indications of tension for, while Edward felt bound to reassure the prince that he would not give credence to any sinister reports about him, he was at the same time impelled to express the hope that Llywelyn would match his words with deeds and maintain his fidelity. Edward, who in the spring had taken Llywelyn's initiation of the plea as a sign of his compliance with the new order in which he found himself, was now clearly concerned to seek a solution by agreement, for it was probably during the summer of 1278 that he tried to arrange a parley between Llywelyn and Gruffudd.[90] There is no indication that any bid to secure a negotiated settlement was in fact made and the argument continued. Further representations appear to have been made to Edward on the prince's behalf while he was at Gloucester on his way to Wales later that summer and, according to Llywelyn's subsequent account, he had had reason to believe that the king was favourably inclined to proposals that he had made concerning the procedures by which the plea should be resolved.[91] Whether or not he was justified in doing so, Llywelyn may have had hopeful expectations of Edward's stay at Rhuddlan in September 1278. Indeed, the association of Reginald de Grey and Roger Lestrange with the Welsh judicial bench, which on this occasion consisted of Walter de Hopton (now chief justice in

---

[88] *WAR*, 252.
[89] The substance may be gathered from Edward's replies, 4 June and 14 July (*CWR*, 173–4; *Foedera*, I, ii, 557–8), noticed further below, nn. 122, 126–7.
[90] Powicke, *Henry III*, 673, on the basis of a letter of Goronwy ap Heilin (*CAC*, 40).
[91] *RPeck*, ii, 440–1.

succession to Faringham), Hywel ap Meurig and Goronwy ap Heilin, suggests that the king was prepared for proceedings on weighty matters. But though the Arwystli case was examined at Rhuddlan there is no record of the fact on the roll of pleas heard there on 11 September and, with nothing to Llywelyn's advantage transpiring there, he ultimately recounted his bitterness at Edward's failure to adhere to what he held to have been his understanding of the king's intentions.[92] Most certainly by then, if not earlier, the precise significance of Llywelyn's claim to judgement by the law of Wales was made perfectly clear both to Edward and Gruffudd ap Gwenwynwyn.

At Oswestry, early in 1279, Llywelyn's arguments were set out before the justices in a clear exposition of his grounds for his expectation that the action would be resolved in accordance with Welsh law.[93] It was argued on his behalf that the land in question was in Wales, that both plaintiff and defendant were 'of Welsh condition' (*quia petens et defendens sunt condicionis Wallensice*) and that, by the terms of the treaty made between king and prince, it was agreed that actions concerning lands within the boundaries of Wales should be resolved according to Welsh law. The prince's argument was founded on a two-fold personal and territorial basis. Gruffudd ap Gwenwynwyn, in a highly significant answer, argued that he was a baron of the march holding Arwystli from the king by barony, and he maintained that he was prepared to defend his right to the land by the common law of England and not by the law of Wales. The choice now posed by Gruffudd lay, not between the law of Wales and the law of the march, but between the law of Wales and the common law of England.[94] In replication on Llywelyn's behalf his attorney continued to press the view that Arwystli was decidedly within the bounds of Wales and not in the march, an argument which, still reflecting the choice for which the treaty of Aberconwy had provided, failed to take account of the entirely new situation created by Gruffudd's declared preference for English law. Gruffudd cited precedents designed to show that the lords of Wales,

---

[92] Proceedings at Rhuddlan, *WAR*, 259–61; Llywelyn's later charges and an indication that the plea was heard at Rhuddlan are noticed below. The inquisition into Welsh law (*CIM*, i, no. 1109, above, n. 80) was set up on 18 October, a few weeks after the proceedings at Rhuddlan, and was entrusted to Grey, one of the justices then present, and William de Hamilton.

[93] The substance of the arguments before the justices, January 1279, is in *B*, 8 (1935–7), 252–4; *WAR*, 264–7; comment in Powicke, *Henry III*, ii, 667–70. The relevance of the arguments in political debate is noticed in M. Richter, 'Mittelalterlicher Nationalismus. Wales im 13 Jahrhundert', in H. Beumann and W. Schröder (eds.), *Nationes*, i, *Aspekte der Nationenbildung im Mittelalter* (Sigmaringen, 1978), 465–88; R. R. Davies, 'Law and national identity in thirteenth-century Wales', in R. R. Davies *et al.* (eds.), *Welsh Society and Nationhood* (Cardiff, 1984), 51–69; idem, 'The peoples of Britain and Ireland 1100–1400, III. Laws and Customs', *TRHS*, 6th ser., 6 (1996), 1–23; brief notice in Frame, *British Isles*, 154–6.

[94] *WAR*, 265.

princes and marchers alike, had long accepted the principle that he had now enunciated. They had on many occasions received judgement in the king's court according to English common law.[95] It was the king's right to hear pleas in his court between barons of Wales and the march by common law, and the crown would be dishonoured if this prerogative were not respected.

It was at this point that the prince entered a general proposition which sought to reconcile his view of the legal implications of Welsh nationality and his recognition of royal jurisdiction: since every province under the king's authority (*imperium*) had its lands and customs according to the practice of those parts, as had the Gascons in Gascony, the Scots in Scotland, the Irish in Ireland and the English in England, something which would tend to exalt the crown rather than diminish it, he asked that he might have his Welsh law and proceed according to it, especially as the king in the treaty of peace made between them had of his own will granted him and all the men of Wales their Welsh law. By common right, he declared, he ought to have his Welsh law and custom in the same way as the other nations (*nationes*) under the king's authority had their law and custom, each according to its language. He asked that by particular right and the king's particular concession, he might have this privilege. *Natio* and *imperium*: the prince raised the argument to a higher dialectical plane, but Gruffudd ap Gwenwynwyn had no wish to argue at that level. He was determined to stick to the proposition that the various nations should be governed in the king's court by a single common law and not by various and contradictory laws in one and the same court. Whether, in spurning the notion of diversity of laws under the king's jurisdiction, Gruffudd was merely speaking for himself or whether he was privy to the king's thoughts we cannot be sure. It would be rash to assume that he was reflecting a view which the king shared, still less a view that the king would wish to be bruited abroad. Certainly, the justices did not hesitate to correct him when, later that year, in response to an argument on the king's behalf that a land in dispute between them should be judged by Welsh law, Gruffudd ventured the opinion that the king proposed to annul Welsh law. The king might correct or annul certain of its features, but they had no reason to believe that he wished to annul Welsh law entirely.[96]

---

[95] *WAR*, 265–6. Cases cited included a plea brought *coram rege* against Gruffudd himself by Gruffudd ap Madog for Mochnant, Mechain and Deuddwr, resolved before the justices at Shrewsbury.

[96] *WAR*, 286. For the issue of diversity of law in the lordship of Ireland and a proposal that English law be more widely used, J. C. Otway-Ruthven, 'The request of the Irish for English law, 1277–80', *Irish Historical Studies*, 6 (1948–9), 261–9; A. Gwynn, 'Edward I and the proposed purchase of English law for the Irish, *c*.1276–80', *TRHS*, 5th ser., 10 (1960), 111–27. The analogy needs to be treated carefully as the issues raised in the Arwystli and cognate cases arose solely from pleas between magnates, though Pecham raised issues of a much broader nature in his denunciation of Welsh law.

Whereas Gruffudd's position is set out without any ambiguity, the highly evocative statement made on Llywelyn's behalf in response to the defendant's argument is liable to varied interpretation. His argument, envisaging an *imperium* comprehending the legal diversities of several *nationes*, could appear to be consonant with the inclinations of a king who was not altogether averse to an evocation of the inheritance of the Island of Britain. Certainly, Edward would have no compunction in availing himself of the notion of the broad supremacy over England, Wales and Scotland implicit in Geoffrey of Monmouth's legendary history when he came later in the century to establish his right to judge the succession to the throne of Scotland. Nor did he spurn the political language of *sovereign seignurie*.[97] But great care needs to be exercised in relation to the positions taken by king and prince alike in the Arwystli plea. This is especially so in relation to the question whether Llywelyn was taking issue over the nature of the jurisdiction appropriate to the examination of the case.[98] He would surely sense that Edward would stand firmly by the conception of a single realm and that he would be chary of making any admission that the problems posed by the prince of Wales raised broad issues of jurisdiction. Even at the height of his power Llywelyn had been regarded, as Edward put it clearly enough, as one of the greatest among the other magnates of his kingdom; and the prince's political power was now much reduced by comparison with the authority that he had exercised in the years following the crown's declaration of its wish, by the treaty of Montgomery, to honour his person. More particularly, however, we need to be careful not to assume that Llywelyn, in his intriguing reference to the *imperium* of the king of England, was intimating that he sought some extraordinary form of procedure appropriate to his status as a prince. This was not for him the crux of the matter. It was, quite simply, that under royal jurisdiction the procedures followed would be such as would allow the Arwystli case to be resolved by Welsh law. There is no doubt that he was no less sensitive to his status than he had been before his fall from power, but there is no reason to believe that it was this, nor any other qualms on matters of jurisdiction, which inspired his invocation of the idea of various *nationes*

---

[97] *Throne of Scotland*, ii, 298–300.

[98] The question whether Llywelyn was seeking a particular form of procedure appropriate to his status, a matter intimated by Powicke, *EHR*, 56 (1941), 493–4, is considered in J. B. Smith, 'England and Wales: the conflict of laws', in M. Prestwich, R. H. Britnell and R. Frame (eds.), *Thirteenth Century England*, 7 (Woodbridge, 1999), where it is suggested that this was not a point at issue and that there is no virtue in seeking analogy with, for instance, the arguments propounded by Robert Bruce in the Great Cause, that Edward should judge 'par dreit natural, par le quel reis regnent, et nule custume usee entre sujet et tenaunz de reame Descoce', and that he do so 'come son sovereyn et son empereur'.

existing under the king's *imperium*.⁹⁹ The issue was not one of jurisdiction but of law. The matter was put succinctly by Gruffudd ap Gwenwynwyn when he identified diversity of law as the matter at issue. Plaintiff and defendant concurred in their appreciation of the core of their problem.¹⁰⁰ There had been the possibility of a problem of law ever since the making of the treaty of Aberconwy, and Edward's realization that the principle then established would need to be reflected in practice was demonstrated in his appointment of Welsh justices – Rhys ap Gruffudd, Hywel ap Meurig and Goronwy ap Heilin – to join the chief justice on the Welsh and marcher bench.¹⁰¹ The roll of proceedings does not tell us who sat with Hopton at Oswestry during the momentous hearing at the beginning of 1279, but it is likely that the bench had a very clear understanding of the issues raised by Llywelyn's call for judgement by Welsh law.

The justices were not going to venture upon any interpretation of the vital clause of the treaty of 1277, let alone pronounce upon Llywelyn's more theoretical propositions, without the king's specific precept. These matters, as well as Gruffudd ap Gwenwynwyn's counter-proposal, were clearly issues to be reserved to king and council. It was, in fact, to be more than two and a half years before the justices were concerned with the Arwystli case again, apart from any involvement they might have had in the discussions in council.¹⁰² Edward, for his part, was not going to be drawn into a quick decision and there were successive adjournments at Westminster. In the summer of 1279 Llywelyn sent William de Merton, prior of the Franciscan house at Llan-faes, to press his arguments upon the king but, though he commended the friar's prudence, Edward was unable to promise a swift resolution. Llywelyn was told to send envoys properly informed in the case, and knowledgeable in the law of Hywel Dda as well as in the other customs used in the area, and to do so in time for the parliament which was to assemble in October 1279.¹⁰³ In a subsequent letter, not without a touch of tendentiousness, Llywelyn conveyed an impression that it was his assumption that the king intended to proceed

---

⁹⁹ Citations in *The Dictionary of Medieval Latin from British Sources* suggest that *imperium* in this context might be best translated as 'authority', certainly avoiding 'empire'.

¹⁰⁰ Jurisdiction is identified as a main issue in R. R. Davies, 'Law and national identity', 104–5; idem, *CCC*, 345; for the views put forward in this discussion, J. B. Smith, 'Conflict of laws'.

¹⁰¹ *CWR*, 163, 167.

¹⁰² There is a hiatus between the proceedings at Oswestry, January 1279, and the reopening of the case at Montgomery, October 1281 (*WAR*, 264–7, 333–4). Gruffudd's counter-plea on Arwystli has been noticed; for pleas, evidently collusive (*WAR*, 125–30), brought by Adam of Montgomery and his son Owain, descendants of Hywel ab Ieuaf of Arwystli, pleading by Welsh law, against Gruffudd ap Gwenwynwyn, *WAR*, 267, 270, 275–6, 280, 293, 323, 325; below, n. 139.

¹⁰³ *CAC*, 62.

according to the law of Hywel Dda.[104] The king was able to elicit from the envoys what the prince proposed but, finding that they were not empowered to act for him, the matter was deferred to the next parliament to be held in May 1280. Edward was anxious to make it absolutely clear that it was his wish that Llywelyn should send attorneys fully versed in the prince's law from whom the king could ascertain whether the court could proceed according to the law of Hywel Dda or according to the law by which Gruffudd ap Gwenwynwyn sought to have judgement.[105] It was an explicit indication that a choice was to be made between Llywelyn's insistence upon the law of Wales and Gruffudd's preference for the law of England. The prince's emissaries had now been summoned to be present on the occasion of what would prove to be crucial deliberations by the king's council in July: justice would be done according to God and right and the king's counsel.

In the first of his subsequent letters the king informed Llywelyn that a decision had been made in parliament, but he did not convey its substance. The prince's envoys, who were informed of council's decision, were left to provide an account of what had been resolved.[106] The substance of the decision was, however, embodied in a document drawn up at the insistence of the prince's envoys. Edward wished to adhere to the undertaking embodied in the treaty of Aberconwy, but he was not prepared to yield anything of the authority which his predecessors had exercised in Wales; actions arising in Wales would be determined in accordance with the practice of his predecessors, and the Welsh would be allowed those laws which were just and reasonable; the king would not act in any manner which might be damaging to the crown; he would abide by the promise made in his coronation oath that he would eradicate every bad custom, but he would respect customs which were consonant with justice.[107] One historian was firmly of the view that this was an outrageous case of special pleading which stemmed 'from a distorted legalistic mind', an argument 'too flagrant to deceive anyone', and that Edward was effectively taking Gruffudd ap Gwenwynwyn's position.[108] Yet, although the prince's envoys had been in attendance during the discussions of the matter in parliament, as Edward himself observes, Llywelyn was reluctant to concede that he understood the king's decision in any such unambiguous manner. In a letter written later that summer he asked Edward to declare his will in the matter, suggesting that a period of three years was time enough to interpret a single clause of the treaty of

[104] *CAC*, 87–8 (5 October 1279): the key words (from SC1/19, no. 35) are 'ad procendendum in presencia vestra secundum legem quod dicitur Howel Da'.

[105] Two letters, *CAC*, 58–9 (24–5 October 1279).

[106] *CAC*, 61–2 (May 1280).

[107] C47/27/2, no. 19 (19 May 1280); content summarized by J. C. Davies, in *WAR*, 59–60, 141–2.

[108] *WAR*, 142. Further comment by J. C. Davies on Edward's decisions in June 1282, below, n. 142.

Contention and Conflict

1277.[109] He was none the wiser after receiving another letter from the king, for Edward declined to be drawn into anything more than an affirmation of his resolve to adhere to the customs used in the time of his predecessors. Nor would he be hurried on a matter of such weight which required consultation with the prelates and magnates of the realm. These were men of prudence whose counsel would enable the king to decide, according to God and justice, what was consonant with reason. Llywelyn found himself instructed in the virtue of prudence, the primacy of reason.[110] More practically, he was told that determining the nature of the customs which prudence would commend as consistent with reason would be a matter for further inquiry: chancery records would be searched and a commission would be appointed to go to Wales to gather evidence concerning the practices of Welsh law.[111] In due course the results of the inquiry conducted in Wales came to hand, and the material constitutes a source which historians have found valuable for its information on several aspects of Welsh legal practices.[112] But neither this evidence, nor that which ensued from the searches among chancery records, provide any clear indication of what might be implied in the king's guarded words. More to the point, the statement which the king issued after the two inquiries had been completed, and after further consideration in council, was no clearer than those he had already made. In June 1281 Edward said again that the Arwystli case would be judged in accordance with the laws and customs used in the times of his predecessors and it could proceed according to them.[113] Even now, Llywelyn was none the wiser, or else he refused to acknowledge that he appreciated the meaning of the king's words, and he continued to press for elucidation.[114]

---

[109] *CAC*, 89–90 (6 July 1280); for the king's reply, *CAC*, 59–60 (18 July), and for an important letter from Pecham (8 August), below, pp. 480–1.

[110] A. Murray, *Reason and Society in the Middle Ages* (Oxford, 1978), 110–37, provides instructive discussion of prudence and reason.

[111] Edward's wish to have the records searched is indicated in C47/27/2, no. 19; *CAC*, 60. J. C. Davies, in *WAR*, 13–30, suggests that the results are reflected in the extensive material in KB26/159. The order for the inquiry in Wales was given on 4 December (*CWR*, 188), commission being given to Thomas Bek, bishop of St David's, Reginald de Grey and Walter de Hopton; the latter, a royal justice, would play a key role on the commission as well as the Welsh judicial bench appointed. Prestwich, *Edward I*, 186, confuses the composition of the commission of 1280–1 with the bench appointed in 1278, the remarks by J. C. Davies in *WAR*, 97 ff. applying to the bench and not the commission; for the bench, above, pp. 472–4, 477.

[112] *CWR*, 190–210; full text in *Rot Wall*, 23–36; *Leges Wallicae*, ed. W. Wotton (London, 1730), 518–31.

[113] *CWR*, 210; *Foedera*, I, ii, 593 (6 June 1281); critical commentary by J. C. Davies, in *WAR*, 68, 145–6; further comment by Powicke, *EHR*, 56 (1941), 494.

[114] *CAC*, 90–1, 99–100. The two letters belong to early 1281 or early 1282, and J. G. Edwards, in *CAC*, 99–100 and Powicke, *Henry III*, ii, 675, both favour the later date. This means that Llywelyn was still pressing for a clear answer even after he had been told of the decision of 6 June 1281, and this conclusion tends to be supported by what can be gathered of Llywelyn's attitude from Edward's letter 8 November 1281 (*CWR*, 210–11), considered presently.

He pressed John Pecham, too, and it was the archbishop's letter in August 1280 which provided the most explicit indication of what had been resolved in royal councils up to that point.[115] Pecham felt no compunction in undertaking to interpret the king's will (*rex respondit per organum vocis nostre*), and the first part of his missive was in accord with what Llywelyn had already been told in letters from chancery. The laws and customs to which the treaty of Aberconwy referred were those by which the king of England had ruled and resolved disputes, and those that were just and reasonable (*que juste sunt et rationabiles*). Pecham emphasized, as had Edward himself, that the king had an obligation to eradicate bad customs from his kingdom. The archbishop's letter differed in that he proceeded to urge the view that many of the laws of Wales were unacceptable. This was not the first time that he had expressed a view on the law of Hywel Dda for, calling Llywelyn to account for his failure to respect the privileges of the church of Bangor, he had the previous year made a critical reference to the prince's adherence to the law of Hywel Dda 'which is said to be at variance with several articles of the Decalogue'.[116] By now Pecham may well have examined the evidence for himself, for it is possible that Peniarth MS 28, a Latin text of Welsh law, came to the library at Canterbury at this time.[117] Llywelyn was delivered a sermon, under three heads, which opened up a much wider argument than anything necessary to resolve the specific question as to the law by which the Arwystli case should be determined. Welsh law was condemned by the Welsh themselves; a royal custom made a better law than the custom of any subject, for the king's will had the force of law; and, it was pressed again, the king had by his coronation oath sworn to eradicate all bad laws and remove all customs contrary to justice. Fundamental questions were thus raised in relation to the policy which the crown might reasonably pursue over Welsh law in general, suggesting that whatever decision might be made on the Arwystli case could have much wider implications. There could be debate, not only in cognate cases in which magnates were at issue over the possession of territory, but in other spheres also as the law as a whole would come to be scrutinized by the powers which laboured together under the dual impetus of the good (*utilitas*) of the earthly kingdom and the morality which the church was bound to safeguard. The problems confronting the king in Wales elicited from Pecham an emphasis on the consonance of secular and ecclesiastical authority somewhat at variance with the thrust of his earlier theoretical writings. Whatever their differences on other matters of a practical nature, the archbishop conveyed his conviction that Edward fully intended to adhere to the treaty of

---

[115] *RPeck*, i, 135–7.

[116] Ibid., 77–8. For Pecham's intervention to secure a composition between Llywelyn and the bishop of Bangor, ibid., 125–6.

[117] D. Huws, 'Leges Howelda at Canterbury', *NLWJ*, 19 (1975–6), 340–3.

Contention and Conflict

Aberconwy and urged Llywelyn to reciprocate in good faith.[118] The letter did nothing to assuage Llywelyn's unease during the summer of 1280, nor did it help to create confidence in the archbishop's intentions when he came to intercede between king and prince at the height of the conflict two years later.

As far as the surviving evidence indicates, Llywelyn did not rise to the bait offered in Pecham's letter and he was not drawn into a contentious argument over the merits of the law of Hywel Dda. He stuck to the central issue: were his wishes or those of Gruffudd ap Gwenwynwyn to prevail in the Arwystli case. He was to receive no further statement of the king's view than the repeated assertion of the king's determination to abide by the law used in the time of his predecessors. It is difficult to see that this necessarily implied a total rejection of Welsh legal procedures. In some cases heard before the justices in Edward's reign the propriety of Welsh law was acknowledged. Perhaps the most conspicuous instance was that, to which we have already referred, in which the appropriateness of Welsh law was argued by Roger Mortimer, but it would be hazardous to assume that the favourable decision made in this instance reflects any preferential treatment of a loyal confidant of the king. Apart from the cases in which the question as to whether Welsh law should be applied was the major issue in contention, there were numerous instances in which principles of Welsh law, or particular procedures of Welsh law, were admitted by the justices and served to influence the course of litigation. The evidence gathered from the *curia regis* rolls at Edward's behest, though it undoubtedly corroborated Gruffudd ap Gwenwynwyn's claim that Welsh litigants had pleaded by English common law, also established that Welsh procedures were admissible in litigation before royal judges at Westminster. This was certainly part of legal practice in the time of the king's immediate predecessor. It was particularly well illustrated in a case which had arisen in Powys Fadog in which a point of procedure was conceded, by which judgement was given to the plaintiff in a plea of land after the defendant's three successive defaults, and this practice would recur in litigation before the justices in the period between the wars.[119] Llywelyn may not have been in a position to cite precedents from proceedings in the king's court, but even as the Arwystli case lingered the justices, faced with numerous demands that particular principles and practices of Welsh law be respected, were in some cases prepared to acknowledge their admissibility and in others to deem the submissions to be of sufficient substance to warrant their consideration by king and council.[120]

---

[118] Pecham's views on secular and ecclesiastical authority are noticed below, p. 532.
[119] KB26/159, m. 2d; *WAR*, 326–9; above, p. 63.
[120] E.g. *WAR*, 242–3, 253–4, 256–8, 262–3, 323–4, 328–9, 352.

Edward's long delay in reaching a decision on the law to be used, and the guarded manner in which his statements are phrased, suggest that the problems presented by the Arwystli case were not entirely bound up with the particular status of the litigants nor a reflection of the pronounced antipathy between them. The matter may turn, rather, on the question of what precisely Edward was denying to Llywelyn and this raises the further question of what exactly Llywelyn was asking of the king. Certain pointers are given both in the course of the litigation and in exchanges between king and prince. When Llywelyn, amid the lofty arguments put before the justices in 1279 for judgement by Welsh law, demanded that Gruffudd ap Gwenwynwyn should attach himself by Welsh law and produce his hostages he was referring to a procedure which was part of the convention by which, as the lawbooks testify, an action for land was initiated under Welsh law. Hostages, 'in the form of living persons', were given for the duration of the plea as a pledge that the litigants would abide by the judgement of the court.[121] A wish on Llywelyn's part to adhere to a second feature of Welsh procedure is indicated in his demand, which can be deduced from Edward's reply to his letter in June 1278, that the action be heard, not at the places appointed by the royal justices, but rather, in accordance with Welsh right, within the boundaries of the land in dispute.[122] The point is confirmed in a letter that the prince addressed to the justice, Walter de Hopton, a month later. There he conveys his expectation that the case, concerned as it was with Welsh lands, would be resolved before him by Welsh law within the lands that were the subject of litigation (*que de iure tamen Walensico infra limites terrarum litigiosarum deberet decidi*).[123] This, too, is a practice which is described in the law texts.[124] These matters, the giving of hostages as pledges for the litigants and judgement on the land in dispute, were two features of a procedure in land actions, described in the texts of Welsh law which are of the Gwynedd tradition, in which pleadings were heard before a professional judge – the *ynad* or *iudex* – who then gave judgement.[125] There are thus very strong indications that the crux of

[121] *WAR*, 264–5; for hostages or pledges 'in the form of living persons' given upon the initiation of a plea and released upon its completion, *LlIor*, 45, 50; *LHD*, 85, 91; *LlCol*, 27, 30. Other instances of demands that hostages be given in accordance with Welsh procedure are in *WAR*, 253, 256–8.

[122] *CWR*, 173–4; *Foedera*, I, ii, 557–8 (4 June 1278).

[123] *WAR*, 252. The letter concerns the appointment of the prince's attorneys, Adam ap Maredudd and Gruffudd Fychan; the question whether Llywelyn also employed English serjeants, well practised in the procedures of the royal courts, is noticed in J. B. Smith, 'Conflict of laws'.

[124] *LlIor*, 45, 50; *LHD*, 84, 91; *LlCol*, 27, 30.

[125] A plea of land under Welsh law heard before the *ynad* is described in *LlIor*, 44–50; *LHD*, 83–91; *LlCol*, 26–30. For the functions of the *ynad*, particularly as revealed in post-conquest evidence, R. R. Davies, 'The administration of law in medieval Wales: the role of the *ynad cwmwd* (*iudex patrie*)', 258–73.

Contention and Conflict

Llywelyn's demand for Welsh law in the Arwystli case was that judgement should be given, upon the land in dispute, by one or more of these judges. This was probably clear to the king even by the summer of 1278 and explains his letter in which he deals with Llywelyn's complaint that, as it is recited in Edward's text, he was summoned to appear before the justices at Montgomery contrary to Welsh law.[126] This was in no way a refusal on Llywelyn's part, inspired by a sense of status or any other reason, to acknowledge the jurisdiction of the justices. It was rather an insistence on his expectation that, in accordance with Welsh law, the plea would be heard on the land in dispute. It elicited from Edward a statement of the view that, although a hearing of that nature might be admitted in the case of land held mediately of the king of England (*per medium*), land held immediately of the king should be judged at days and places appointed by the justices.[127] Edward was dealing with a request for an adjustment of the procedures that were normal under royal jurisdiction. Llywelyn was not to be daunted by the king's reply. In the evidence which he presented to Pecham in 1282 Llywelyn maintained that, prior to his coming to Rhuddlan in 1278, Edward had granted him that the case should be examined according to the laws and customs of Wales (*concessisset causam examinare secundum leges et consuetudines Wallie*). In accordance with this understanding advocates and *iudices* or *ynaid* were brought before the king at Rhuddlan so that they might make a judgement concerning the lands according to Welsh law (*ut judicarent de dictis terris secundum leges Wallicanas*). Llywelyn recounted that, by the king's intervention, the matter was not in fact brought to judgement and he insisted that thereafter he had been denied the judgement by Welsh law that was his right.[128]

The roll of proceedings has nothing of this and, though it is likely that the plea was heard at Rhuddlan, there is no other explicit indication at that stage of what exactly Llywelyn was insisting upon.[129] There can be no doubt, however, that the terms of reference of the commission of inquiry established by

---

[126] *CWR*, 173–4; *Foedera*, I, ii, 557–8.

[127] Ibid.: 'quod placita de terris et tenementis que de nobis et corona Anglie immediate tenentur in capite, seu teneri debent, in partibus marchie et Wallie etiam secundum consuetudines Wallicanas audiri et terminari consueverunt certis diebus et locis quos justiciarii ad huiusmodi placita audienda et terminanda assignati prefigere voluerunt; licet de terris aliis, que de nobis tenentur per medium, in locis in quibus huiusmodi terre litigiose consistunt multotiens consueverint placita audiri et ibidem justitia partibus exhiberi.' For actions on the writ of right in England, where the land is held of a lord other than the king and the lord would have jurisdiction, and Dr Paul Brand's comments upon Edward's letter, see J. B. Smith, 'Conflict of laws'.

[128] *RPeck*, ii, 440–1. Edward is said to have agreed to this means of proceeding when he was at Gloucester, 6–16 August, *en route* for Rhuddlan.

[129] *WAR*, 259–61 (11 September 1278), has a record of other pleas held at Rhuddlan; Rhirid ap Iorwerth, witness from the *cantref* of Rhos before the commission of 1281, testified that he had seen a plea between Llywelyn ap Gruffudd and Gruffudd ap Gwenwynwyn before the king at Rhuddlan (*CWR*, 198; above, n. 92).

Edward I in 1281 and the evidence then assembled indicate that the nature and function of the *ynaid* were among the key issues raised by Llywelyn ap Gruffudd's demand for Welsh law in the plea over Arwystli. The commissioners were charged with inquiring into pleas moved between Welsh barons and ascertaining before what judges the pleas were heard. They were concerned, not with establishing that the king had jurisdiction in pleas between magnates of Wales, but in eliciting how those pleas were heard: to establish before what judges or justices and in what court and where; to ascertain the place of question and answer, inquisition and assize; and to elicit whether a plea was adjudged 'according to the law called cyfraith', and that signified a hearing before the *ynad*.[130] Llywelyn himself evidently took the view that the commissioners would be concerned with Welsh judges and he referred directly to the areas in contention. He urged that they should enquire carefully as to whether there were in Arwystli and Cyfeiliog 'Welsh judges who held the office of judging the land and inhabitants there in accordance with Welsh law'; if the lands were not judged by Welsh law it would not be necessary for judges to be sworn and examined there. It was, he insisted, clearer than light that the sons of Cynyr ap Cadwgan were *ex officio* judges – *iudices, ynaid* – in Arwystli, and Iorwerth Fychan similarly in Cyfeiliog between the Dyfi and the Dulas.[131] It is thus evident that Llywelyn's claim to be judged by Welsh law was inextricably bound up with particular insistence that judgement be given by *ynaid*, and that they should give judgement within the boundaries of the lands in dispute. His statement of the position in Arwystli and Cyfeiliog is not, however, borne out by the testimony supplied by witnesses from the lands themselves who consistently stated that judgement was given there by the court and by recourse to the testimony of a jury. Two of the witnesses indeed declared that Iorwerth Fychan ap Iorwerth ap Rhys, far from fulfilling the role ascribed to him by Llywelyn, though he was called *ynad*, had never judged (*nunquam tamen judicavit*), but had acquired the name because he went to Gwynedd to learn the laws of Hywel Dda (*ad addiscendum leges Howel Da*).[132] When every allowance is made for the possibility that witnesses who appeared before the commissioners were subject to a certain degree of persuasion, the evidence drawn from Arwystli and Cyfeiliog still points assuredly to the conclusion that the *ynad* had no part in the administration of the law there. The testimony supplied in 1281 is credible, too, in the light of the fact that later evidence suggests very strongly

---

[130] *CWR*, 190–1; *RotWall*, 23. When Thomas Bek claimed his expenses for his travels he described the task as an inquiry 'de consuetudinibus, tenuriis et iudiciis Wallensium' (C47/3/48/7). R. R. Davies, *Domination and Conquest*, 104–4, offers a different emphasis on the purpose of the inquiry from that argued here.
[131] *CWR*, 195; *RotWall*, 26.
[132] *CWR*, 208–9; *RotWall*, 35.

that Arwystli and Cyfeiliog were among the areas where collective judgement was already well established by the late thirteenth century and, though earlier evidence is slight, that may have been the position for some time. [133]

No less relevant to the essential matter raised by Llywelyn was the evidence gathered from Perfeddwlad which provides a clear indication of the issue with which the enquiry was concerned and demonstrates the nature of the difficulty posed by Llywelyn's precise demand. In response to the commissioners' enquiries, witnesses consistently made a distinction between proceedings by 'the law called cyfraith', in which judgement (*iudicum*) was given by an *ynad* or *iudex,* and proceedings whereby a jury, by an *inquisitio per patriam,* produced a presentment (*veredictum*) upon which a judgement might be based.[134] The commissioners' keen concern with the distinction between *iudicum* and *veredictum* is highly significant. If Llywelyn was asking that the Arwystli case should be heard before an *ynad,* or before a bench of *ynaid,* he was effectively requiring that the power of judgement be deputed by royal justices to others besides themselves. The Arwystli case was not the only one in which the issue was raised, and the matters investigated by the commissioners in the course of their inquiry had in fact been broached in proceedings before the royal justices. Two cases which arose in Powys Fadog, in which, as we shall see again, litigants requested that recourse be made to an *ynad,* or to trustworthy persons of the land (*fidedigniores patrie*) in place of an *ynad,* reveal the unwillingness of the royal justices to delegate the power of judgement. They insisted on a clear distinction between a *veredictum,* which would obviously be admitted, and a *iudicum,* which could certainly not be tolerated.[135] It is highly likely that the issue raised in these cases, brought by lords of the lineage of Powys Fadog, was closely akin to that at the root of the Arwystli case without ever being explicitly set out in the surviving record of the litigation.

If, as appears likely, the precise implications of Llywelyn's demand that the Arwystli case be judged by Welsh law had become clear at Rhuddlan in the late summer of 1278, if not before, Gruffudd ap Gwenwynwyn's demand for the common law of England, made in proceedings before the justices five months later, is much more readily explained.[136] It may have taken the prince's advocates by surprise for, as we have seen, by persisting with an argument for the use of Welsh law rather than marcher law, they were hardly addressing the issue with which Gruffudd ap Gwenwynwyn now confronted them. Gruffudd's decision to claim judgement by the common law served his

---

[133] For early thirteenth-century judgements in Arwystli, *Charters of the Abbey of Ystrad Marchell,* nos. 63–5; above, pp. 202–3.
[134] *CWR,* 195–200; *RotWall,* 26–9.
[135] *WAR,* 246–8, 318.
[136] *WAR,* 265–6 (14 January 1279).

purposes very well, for it made an infinitely clearer distinction between two procedures by which the case might be resolved than the uncertain differentiation by which, as we have seen, the treaty of Aberconwy envisaged a choice between Welsh and marcher law. Still more crucial than Gruffudd ap Gwenwynwyn's reaction to Llywelyn's arguments was the response offered by Edward and those who shared in his decisions. The effect of Llywelyn's insistence on judgement by *ynaid,* and judgement on the land in dispute, was to deprive him of the opportunity to avail himself of those features of Welsh law which the justices were prepared to concede and which several litigants found advantageous. It might be noticed that in the summer of 1281 Edward, recently informed of the outcome of the inquiry in Wales and the search of the rolls, reaffirmed once more that the laws and customs to be used in cases arising in Wales were those used in the time of his predecessors, and just nine days later Roger Mortimer was given judgement by Welsh law in his dispute with Gruffudd ap Gwenwynwyn.[137] When circumstances indicated that recourse to Welsh law was to his benefit Gruffudd ap Gwenwynwyn, too, was prepared to argue the propriety of Welsh law and secured the justices' consent to have the matter at issue resolved in accordance with its procedures.[138] Llywelyn's tenacious resolve, not merely to establish the principle that Welsh law should be used, but to insist on a particular concession, which effectively meant that judgement would be taken away from the royal justices, made demands upon Edward that he could not possibly bring himself to allow and the prince's claim to a right inherent in Welsh nationhood itself was to be of no avail.

There can be no doubt that Llywelyn succeeded in placing Edward in an exceedingly difficult dilemma and, if his decision to initiate the legal action was inspired by purely political motives, he would have found some satisfaction in the discomfiture which surely lies behind the sententious pronouncements of the king's responsibility to secure adherence to good law. The difficulty lay in the sphere of law rather than that of jurisdiction, and this is an important distinction. It can hardly be said that Llywelyn challenged Edward's jurisdiction over Arwystli. It was Llywelyn who chose to bring the case before the king's justices in 1278 and, as we shall see, he came before the justices again three years later and revived the action even though it had long since faltered. Throughout the duration of the case he continued to press the king for a decision on how the case should be prosecuted, with a consistent

---

[137] *CWR*, 210; *WAR,* 313–14 (decision of 15 June 1281).

[138] For his claim to Welsh law in the action concerning his right to a market at Welshpool above, n. 80.

Contention and Conflict

implication that jurisdiction rested with the king.[139] At the same time he continued to seek the means whereby the judgement would, in effect, be made by other judges than the king's judges. When Edward, for his part, conveyed in cryptic terms the outcome of the deliberations in parliament in 1280, and insisted that he would not lessen the authority (*auctoritas*) exercised by his predecessors, Edward was indicating his response to the particular problem that Llywelyn had posed the previous year. He had to do so, and to continue to do so, in guarded phraseology. The Arwystli case placed the king in some considerable political difficulty, but his problem did not lie merely in a need to protect the interests of Gruffudd ap Gwenwynwyn in preference to those of Llywelyn though, as we shall see, a clear statement of his obligation to do right by Gruffudd would ultimately come from deliberations in council.[140] The main problem for Edward lay rather in the potentially perilous result of any clear pronouncement on the conflict of law. If he were to accede to Llywelyn's wishes he would in effect allow judgement to pass from his judges to the *ynaid* whom Llywelyn pressed upon him. If, on the other hand, the king were to declare his outright rejection of the prince's demand he would be liable to present Llywelyn with precisely the political advantage that he may well have sought from the outset. Edward's prognostication, and his constant adherence to a somewhat less than explicit form of words, is understandable, more so than historians have normally allowed. Any other response would have left him exposed to precisely the charges which Llywelyn would lay against him in the statement which he was to set out for Archbishop Pecham in 1282.[141] Llywelyn was by then in a position of great difficulty and he would have much preferred to have been able to level his charges against the king in more propitious political circumstances. This was exactly what Edward was determined to deny him.

When, in the summer of 1281, the king informed Llywelyn of the outcome of the inquiry in Wales and the search of the rolls he did nothing more than restate what he had said before: the laws and customs used in Wales would be

---

[139] This interpretation has a bearing on understanding of the significance of the pleas brought by Adam of Montgomery (above, n. 102). They were clearly collusive (J. C. Davies, in *WAR*, 125–30; Prestwich, *Edward I*, 184), but they were probably brought, not to prove that Edward's justices had jurisdiction over the Arwystli case, but to help establish the procedures appropriate in an action heard in accordance with Gruffudd's preference for the common law. Thus a plea brought in 1280 was probably intended to show that, as he held by marcher barony, Gruffudd had no need to answer without a writ, and the plea was opportunely sent *coram rege* by the time the Arwystli plea was considered by king and council in parliament.

[140] This is the difficulty noticed in Prestwich, *Edward I*, 186; for Edward's later indication of his concern for Gruffudd, below, nn. 197–8.

[141] *RPeck*, ii, 440–1.

those which had been used in the time of his predecessors.[142] The prince was told that he could prosecute his plea against Gruffudd ap Gwenwynwyn in accordance with those laws and customs, and the justices were ordered to provide a speedy solution. This could conceivably mean that Edward had decided that the plea should be determined by English law. But we have seen that, in response to earlier communications to exactly the same effect, Llywelyn had never admitted, certainly not in the letters addressed to Edward, that he saw the king's statements in such clear terms. Now, while appearing to indicate his wish for a quick resolution of the case, Edward continued to place his trust in a form of words which in fact ensured its further protraction, unless the prince were to be finally daunted. The king might have been greatly relieved if Llywelyn ap Gruffudd had decided there and then to abandon the Arwystli case altogether. Llywelyn did nothing of the kind. He decided to persevere with an action which had engaged his mind for a long time and, as yet, to no avail. On 6 October 1281 his attorney presented himself before the justices at Montgomery to claim for the prince of Wales the whole land of Arwystli and the whole land between the Dyfi and the Dulas.[143] He was now confronted with a new source of frustration. Gruffudd ap Gwenwynwyn maintained that, as each of them was a baron of the king, he had no need to answer without a writ. The prince's attorney maintained that when the plea was first brought before Ralph de Farningham, evidently at an early date in 1278, Llywelyn had indeed proceeded by the use of a writ. This was clearly a matter for further investigation. For his part, Llywelyn, who was probably present at Montgomery when this attempt was made on his behalf to reopen the plea, once more pressed the matter upon the king. He elicited a reply which proved to be the king's last statement on the Arwystli case.[144] Though courteous in its opening sentiments, the letter yielded nothing on the matters at issue. More forbiddingly, it embodied a warning that, while the king was anxious to accommodate Llywelyn's wishes, he would do so only if he could proceed without doing wrong to anyone else. More clearly than before, his obligations to Gruffudd ap Gwenwynwyn were a factor in the king's calculations. He reaffirmed his readiness to abide by the treaty of 1277 but he could not, he said a second time, omit to do to his barons

---

[142] *CWR*, 210 (6 June). J. C. Davies, in *WAR*, 68, 231–2, states that the king decided 'that the plea should be pleaded by English law and practice' and 'by the common law of England, before the king's justices, by writ'. Powicke, *EHR*, 56 (1941), 494, is not convinced that this understanding is justified.

[143] *WAR*, 333–4. The abandoning of Adam of Montgomery's collusive plea on 15 June 1281 (*WAR*, 323, 325), immediately after Edward's letter was sent to Llywelyn, may indicate an expectation that Llywelyn's case would now cease.

[144] *CWR*, 210–11; *RotWall*, 42 (8 November 1281); J. C. Davies, in *WAR*, 75, draws attention to the deficiencies in the calendar. The text, *WAR*, 334, does not prove that Llywelyn was present in person, but see below, n. 164.

that which he ought to do. He had been in consultation with his justices and council and they had considered Gruffudd's assertion before the justices that, unless the prince took out a writ, he would not be bound to answer for the lands in dispute. Search of exchequer records had confirmed that, without a writ, barons of Wales were not required to answer, nor had scrutiny of the writs brought any evidence that an original writ had been used to initiate the present action. In the absence of a writ there could be no further proceedings without doing harm to Gruffudd, and Llywelyn should not resent the king's decision. The king's last letter on the matter, by attending to the issue of the writ, embodied the first elaboration of his repeated declarations of his determination to decide the Arwystli case in accordance with the customs used in the times of his predecessors. His letter bears witness to a noticeable hardening in the king's attitude, marked in a pronounced concern for Gruffudd ap Gwenwynwyn's interests but by no means wholly attributable to that concern. It was at this time of heightened stress that Edward made his fateful decision to appoint Reginald de Grey as justice of Chester. The king's letter on the Arwystli case, written in early November 1281, is one to which we shall need to return.

Yet, despite the prominence of the Arwystli case in the period after 1277, and the attention which it has received from historians, we are still left to ask whether the arguments it provoked constituted the stuff of rebellion. More particularly we need to ask whether it had a bearing on the course of events leading to the rebellion which occurred in the spring of 1282. Llywelyn himself conveyed that Arwystli was, in material terms, of no great concern to him, and the *cantref* was not indeed a productive land. He was, he insisted, troubled by the disgrace (*opprobium*) to himself rather than by any concern for the gain that he might secure from possessing the land as he despaired at the king's inability to declare his will.[145] However, for several other princes, entrammelled in legal proceedings before the same justices in pleas which they did not bring upon themselves, much more was at stake. Of those mentioned already who may be counted among the early participants in the rising of 1282, Rhys Wyndod of Ystrad Tywi was one who had need to do his utmost to avoid losing part of his inheritance in Cantref Bychan to John Giffard, who brought an action before the royal justices. Giffard had, in fact, wrested part of the commote of Hirfryn from Rhys Wyndod during the war of 1277, thereby gaining a personal advantage from his participation in the advance by

---

[145] *CAC*, 90–1. For the indications, from the lay subsidy assessment of 1292–3 and later inquisitions, of the low value of Arwystli, A. D. Carr, 'A debateable land: Arwystli in the middle ages', *MontColl*, 80 (1992), 39–54.

which forces in royal pay had moved through the lordship of Brecon into Deheubarth.[146] Giffard sought to extend his holding in Cantref Bychan by a legal action before the justices in which he set out a mendacious claim to the commotes of Hirfryn and Perfedd.[147] Unlike Llywelyn, who had himself chosen to initiate his action against Gruffudd ap Gwenwynwyn over a land at some distance from his own and no part of his patrimony, Rhys Wyndod was defending his very own. With Giffard claiming the commote by the common law of England, Rhys Wyndod was constrained to insist that he should receive justice, not before the justices, but in the county court of Carmarthen and by the law of Wales.[148] It was an argument which might have been justified by reference to the assurances repeatedly given by the crown a generation earlier when the princes of Ystrad Tywi, in return for their acknowledgement that they were justiciable at the county court, had been told that they and their men could plead by Welsh law.[149] The need for successive reassurances may itself have been indicative of a tensive state of affairs, or at least a constant vigilance on the part of the princes, but the compatibility of royal jurisdiction and Welsh law was recognized on all sides. It became possible to restore that situation in Deheubarth upon the collapse of Prince Llywelyn's power in the war in 1277, but the appointment first of Bogo de Knovill and then Robert Tibetot augured the imposition of an increasingly vigorous royal administration and a shift away from earlier conventions.[150]

The renewed sensitivity of the Welsh princes to these new trends in the period 1277–82 is perhaps most clearly revealed in the complaints of Gruffudd ap Maredudd and Cynan ap Maredudd of Ceredigion. In their statement to Archbishop Pecham they declared how all Christians had their laws and customs in their own lands, indeed even the Jews among the English had their own laws. They, too, in their lands, and their ancestors before them, had their immutable laws and customs until the English after the last war had removed them.[151] Their appeal might end on a suitably oratorical note, but the substance of their submission, more particularly the indication that the jurisdiction of their courts was being undermined as their men were required to take justice before the royal officers, shows that the princes' material

---

[146] Above, pp. 416–17.

[147] *WAR*, 261–2, 268–70, 289–91, 310–11, 316–17, 320–1, 327–8, 338–40, are the main references. Giffard claimed by virtue of the right of Matilda his wife, whose ancestor, Walter de Clifford, was said to have held the land in the time of Henry III.

[148] *WAR*, 290; for his statement among the grievances presented to Pecham, *RPeck*, ii, 451–2. For judgement for Giffard by the law of Wales in a case against Rhys ap Maredudd, *WAR*, 328–9.

[149] J. B. Smith, 'The origins of the revolt of Rhys ap Maredudd', *B*, 21 (1964–6), 151–3.

[150] For changes made from November 1279, when Edward recovered the counties from Edmund, R. A. Griffiths, *PW*, i, 20–2, 91.

[151] *RPeck*, ii, 453–4.

interests were being adversely affected. The erosion of their jurisdiction was the key issue and, though their main statements were made in justification of insurgency, there are confirmatory indications from the years preceding the conflict.[152] In Ystrad Tywi the difficulties which arose from precisely these conditions were to be best reflected in the events which led, not to war in 1282, but to the dissension between Tibetot and Rhys ap Maredudd which culminated in rebellion in 1287. But there can be no doubt that, like their kinsmen in Ceredigion, Rhys ap Maredudd and Rhys Wyndod were exposed to more intrusive royal jurisdiction in the period leading up to the final conflict.[153] The latter's attempt to establish that he was justiciable, not before the specially appointed royal justices, but at the county court, is a measure of his desperation at what he could only regard as an even more pressing threat to his position. The bitterness of Rhys Wyndod's insistence, in his submission to Pecham, that Giffard had deprived him of his inheritance, and that he had been unable to secure justice by the law of his land and the law of the county of Carmarthen, can be readily understood.[154] Rhys ap Maredudd stood aside in the fateful conflict and secured some reward thereby but, during the course of the litigation over the commote of Perfedd, Rhys Wyndod was able to present Rhys ap Maredudd as his coparcenor in what can only be seen as a ruse to withstand Giffard's relentless thrusting towards a favourable judgement. Rhys ap Maredudd made no appearance before the justices and, with four successive defaults recorded against him, judgement went to Giffard and that, with a rare touch of irony, by the law of Wales. It was a judgement to which Rhys ap Maredudd reacted with physical resistance when his men went armed to the land and forcibly prevented Giffard's men from taking seisin.[155] For all his constancy in the king's service, even Rhys ap Maredudd may have been deeply troubled in the period leading up to 1282, and thoroughly tortured in the spring of that fateful year.

The argument used by Rhys Wyndod in the pleas concerning his lands in Cantref Bychan necessarily reflect the particular conditions which prevailed in that area. Yet he, too, made his appeal to the clause in the treaty of Aberconwy to which the prince of Wales consistently referred, and in so doing

---

[152] *RotParl*, i, 5.

[153] J. B. Smith, 'Rhys ap Maredudd', 157–9, 162–3. Decisions adversely affecting Rhys ap Maredudd were made in the summer of 1281 (*CWR*, 185).

[154] *RPeck*, ii, 451–2.

[155] He is named as a defendant and co-parcenor with Rhys Wyndod in proceedings which began at Montgomery, February 1281, when Giffard impleaded him for lands in Llandovery, Hirfryn and Perfedd. Judgement was given against him on the fourth successive default 'according to Welsh law' at St Michael's in Elfael, June 1281. The hindering of Giffard's taking of seisin, by Rhys's steward, Llywelyn ap Madog, his constable of Dryslwyn, Goronwy Goch, and others, is noted in the record of proceedings in July (*WAR*, 315–17, 320–1, 328–9, 332).

appropriated to his needs a clause which was strictly concerned with actions in which Llywelyn himself might be involved as litigant. For, though neither this clause nor any other in the treaty made any reference to the possible needs of others than the prince, Rhys sought to make its reference to Welsh law applicable to himself as one who was 'of Welsh condition', thereby adopting a phrase which Llywelyn had very recently employed.[156] There is every possibility that Llywelyn ap Gruffudd and the princes of Deheubarth had agreed upon the arguments which might be used before the royal justices. They could conceivably have considered matters among themselves at Dolwyddelan in the summer of 1278.[157] Though their needs were different, there was everything to be gained from an agreed course of action by which, quite apart from resort to conventional legal contrivances, they might argue the natural right of those who were 'of Welsh condition'. The clerks who kept a record of the proceedings before the justices appreciated that the notion of being 'of Welsh condition' was equivalent to being 'of the Welsh nation', and the reluctance of the justices to commit themselves to the veracity of the arguments made in this direction is not difficult to understand.[158] It was not for them to interpret the king's will in this respect, certainly not in the wake of the evocative submissions which the prince had made at Oswestry at the beginning of 1279. The political, as apart from the legal, implications of the argument may have been perfectly obvious even then. Although he was denied any authority outside Gwynedd Uwch Conwy, Llywelyn could become a focus for the new-found resolve of those whose anxieties engendered a consciousness of *natio* a good deal sharper than anything they had known during the years when, by the endeavour of the prince of Wales, the coherence of that nation had come the closest to being given meaningful political expression. Even so, Llywelyn was not placed in anything like the same predicament as some of the others. Rhys Wyndod had need of all the arguments he could muster to prevent the disintegration of his patrimony, and he was moved to use them not by any prompting on the part of Llywelyn but by dire necessity. The same may be said of Llywelyn ap Gruffudd Fychan who, defending his right to some of his lands in Powys Fadog in proceedings before the justices, became embroiled in an argument over the precise functions of the faithful men of the land –

[156] *WAR*, 269–70 (5 February 1279); Llywelyn had used the argument at Oswestry 14 January (*WAR*, 264–5).

[157] *LW*, 43. R. R. Davies, *CCC*, 343, suggests that this letter may be misdated and may belong to the early 1270s; but the case for accepting the date, which the author also prefers, is noted above, p. 417, n. 103.

[158] The justices referred the pleas *coram rege*, uncertain whether they should allow or deny the Welsh law granted to Welshmen in the treaty of peace, as they asserted, or whether they should decide otherwise concerning the king's seisin in pleadings in his court between man 'of whatever condition or nation they might be' (*cuiuscunque condicionis fuerint uel nacionis*, *WAR*, 269–70).

fidedigniores patrie – who stood in place of the *ynad.* Confronted with the justices' wish to make a clear differentiation between presentment (*veredictum*) and judgement (*iudicium*), Llywelyn revealed his anger in court in what was duly recorded as contumacious behaviour. The commotion before the justices was far from something inspired by Prince Llywelyn's concern with the same issue in another plea. It arose from a legal action which threatened Llywelyn's material interests.[159] And time was not on the side of Rhys Wyndod and Llywelyn ap Gruffudd Fychan. Llywelyn ap Gruffudd, on the other hand, chose to prosecute an action, persist with it for a period of some three years and then reopen it once more. He might be greatly irritated, but he was not deterred from continuing to prosecute the action. He did so for reasons other than material benefit, but there is nothing in the record of the later stages of the case, nor in his last exchanges with the king on the issue – though there were some inauspicious intimations in the king's last letter – to suggest impending violent conflict.[160]

During the autumn of 1281, immediately after the Arwystli plea was reactivated at Montgomery, Llywelyn ap Gruffudd made his way to a meeting at which he entered into an understanding with the most resolute of his old adversaries. Its precise significance is exceedingly difficult to understand but the agreement needs to be considered in any estimate of his intentions in the months immediately preceding the new outbreak of hostilities. Although the record provides no complete certainty that Llywelyn had been present during the proceedings at Montgomery, it is probable, as has been suggested already, that Llywelyn was close by when the plea was reopened. To reach Montgomery he would have traversed lands which had once formed part of his wider principality, passing through areas where he had seen strenuous conflict, and forded the Severn at precisely the place where he had won the king's formal recognition of the position that he had by then secured for himself. He then continued his journey southward. For at Radnor, just three days after the Arwystli plea was revived, a guest of Roger Mortimer at the castle that his men and the Montfort forces had battered during their joint offensive against their marcher opponents, Llywelyn entered into an agreement with his formidable

---

[159] *WAR*, 318. The key phrase in the account of the disturbance in court is misread and should read 'aliud non vult dicere seu proponere set sic contumaciter recessit in contemptum etc'.
[160] Below, pp. 495–8, 505–9.

antagonist.[161] They bound themselves in fidelity to one another, in peace and war, saving only their fealty to the king of England. It is certainly not easy to fathom the reasons why these two grandsons of Llywelyn the Great entered into their compact of 9 October 1281, nor to judge whether either of them felt threatened in any way, or whether they were moved by any common aspiration. Mortimer, getting older now, may perhaps have looked for some measure of assurance that his son's succession would be undisturbed. He had invested substantially in provision for the security of his marcher lands. Extensive building had been completed at Cefnllys, the castle above the River Ieithon which had been the focus of conflict in Maelienydd and had then aroused the prince's protestations at the extent of the new works.[162] More recently, probably since 1277, Mortimer had also built the new stronghold of Dinbod.[163] It stood on another elevated site above the same river, a few miles upstream and in a better position to dominate the approaches to the lordship from the north and west. Mortimer may have thought it prudent to seek further means of securing his marcher estate for, on the day on which he and the prince sealed their new agreement, Llywelyn drew up another charter by which he released to the lord of Wigmore all rights in Cefnyraelwyd in Gwerthrynion, a land whose boundaries he defined in detail.[164] This brief document may not seem to be of any vast significance, but it would be difficult to bring to mind any single place which better represents the long conflict between the two nations in the march of Wales. An act of valour at Cefnyraelwyd was among the deeds which the poet Cynddelw celebrated in his

---

[161] *LW*, 99–100. The two men placed themselves under the censure of the bishops of St Asaph and Hereford if either of them were to break faith. The possible significance of this concord in relation to heraldic material, especially St George's Roll, which contains the arms of Llywelyn, Dafydd and Amaury de Montfort, as well as Mortimer and several others closely linked with him, is noticed in N. Denholm-Young, *History and Heraldry, 1254–1310* (Oxford, 1965), 91–2, who places St George's Roll between the tournament at Kenilworth in 1279 and the agreement between Mortimer and Llywelyn in 1281. See also Siddons, *Welsh Heraldry*, i, 218–20 and n. 22; G. J. Brault, *The Rolls of Arms of Edward I* (Woodbridge, 1997), ii, 9.

[162] Above, pp. 361–2.

[163] There is nothing in the evidence before 1277 to suggest that Dinbod was a subject of controversy or conflict; building probably commenced later but was sufficiently advanced to make the castle operational by 1282 (E372/128; SC6/1209/1; P. M. Remfry, 'The native Welsh dynasties of Rhwng Gwy a Hafren 1066–1282', MA thesis, University of Wales, 1989, 185–9). For the structure, with polygonal ward and twin apsidal-tower gatehouse, *Inventory Radn*, 58; King, *CA*, 411–12. Various early forms of the name suggest that 'Dinbod' would be the appropriate modern form.

[164] Text in J. B. Smith, 'The middle march in the thirteenth century', *B*, 24 (1970–2), 90, from 'Liber Niger de Wigmore', BL, Harl. MS 1240, m.57-57v. The two documents were sealed at Radnor three days after the prince's attorney reopened the Arwystli case before the justices at Montgomery. Llywelyn and Mortimer were undoubtedly together at Radnor, and it is highly probable that Llywelyn had been present, or close at hand, when the attorney had entered the plea on his behalf at Montgomery (above, n. 144).

tribute to Cadwallon ap Madog. At one point the boundary of the land was marked by a dyke known as the place where Gwyn ap Cuhelyn had fallen.[165] The ridge of Cefnyraelwyd in fact straddled the frontier between Gwerthrynion and Arwystli.[166] If Llywelyn were ever to secure possession of Arwystli by legal process he would share a frontier with Mortimer once more. It might be an unlikely eventuality but Mortimer, who himself initiated a plea for possession of the southern parts of Arwystli, may have been anxious to ensure that his boundary at that point was clearly defined and that Cefnyraelwyd fell unequivocally on his side of it. The Cefnyraelwyd document, concerned with Mortimer's quest for security upon a frontier he might conceivably share with Llywelyn, may point to a broader search for security reflected in the more general agreement. Of course, Llywelyn's new pledge recalls an earlier undertaking to keep out of Mortimer's territory that he had failed to honour. But it is perfectly conceivable that he, too, older and no longer moved by the compulsive ambitions of earlier years, was genuinely committed to concord with the marcher. Whether one or the other, or both together, were motivated by any other particular considerations is difficult to judge. It would be still more difficult to justify the view that Llywelyn entered into his new agreement with Mortimer as part of an elaborate deception designed to conceal an intention to go to war once more.[167] Llywelyn may well have endeavoured to extend his influence in Powys Wenwynwyn in the period before 1277. His subsequent attempt to bind in allegiance to himself Gruffudd ap Gwên, known to have been the justice of Gruffudd ap Gwenwynwyn, may be an indication of a continued wish to further his interests in the area if opportunity arose.[168] It is, however, very unlikely that any initiative, certainly not a military attack on Gruffudd ap Gwenwynwyn, was intended at the time of the agreement with Mortimer. His attitude in relation to the Arwystli case would confirm this view. Far from abandoning the legal proceedings, and pursuing an alternative course of action, he revealed at precisely this time a stubborn, indeed a perverse, determination to persist with the litigation to the king's discomfiture

---

[165] *GCBM*, i, 21. 84. The boundary is traced, again noting the dyke where Gwyn ap Cuhelyn died, in Mortimer's charter to Cwm-hir in 1199 (Charles, 'An early charter of the abbey of Cwmhir', *TRadnS*, 40 (1970), 68–74).

[166] Cefnyraelwyd is marked at SO945786, and is placed in W. Rees, *South Wales and the Border in the Fourteenth Century*, NE sheet, just north of the boundary between Gwerthrynion and Arwystli, with the ridgeway named in the charter, Cefnffordd Cefnyraelwyd, traversing the boundary.

[167] Prestwich, *Edward I*, 187, understands the treaty as a sign that Llywelyn 'had finally lost patience with the legal proceedings in the Arwystli case and that he was intending to take military action against Gruffudd ap Gwenwynwyn whose lands lay between his own and Mortimer's'. The evidence on both counts appears to suggest a different conclusion, much in accord with the view of J. G. Edwards, in *LW*, lxii.

[168] Stephenson, 'Llywelyn ap Gruffudd and the struggle for the principality', *THSC*, 1983, 46; for another view of the agreement, above, p. 317.

and displeasure. However frustrated he might be on the main issue which had arisen in his relationship with the king since 1277, and on other matters to be considered presently, he was probably resolved to seek the security of his dynasty, and possibly the fulfilment of his enduring aspirations, not in any sudden rebellious challenge to the crown but by dint of continued application to the realistic political objectives to which he had never ceased to direct his mind even in the most aggressive phases in his career.

Llywelyn's decision to persevere with his plea over Arwystli points to a determination to avail himself of the political advantage which could still accrue to him if the king were ever to make an explicit statement of his unwillingness to concede what the prince demanded from him. Llywelyn had been unable to maintain the impetus created by the forthright arguments which he had employed in the earlier stages of the litigation, and those eloquent expositions had had to give way to more pragmatic exchanges. These reveal an underlying tension, and there is something to suggest a heightened stress in the winter of 1281–2, but we must be cautious in too readily envisaging a prince seething with ever increasing indignation in the months before the outbreak of hostilities, and especially wary of being led to believe that he was trumped in his resolve to lead his nation into a war of liberation only by the precipitate action of his brother. It may, of course, be too cosy a picture of Llywelyn which depicts him in the inter-war years as a prince who was 'master in his own house, on friendly terms with his lord the king, in touch with former vassals and bound in alliance with a very powerful marcher'.[169] It may reasonably be said none the less that he exercised lordship over a well-defined and compact territory, though it was a severely constricted land with troublous areas upon its borders and though, as we shall see, there was some concern for the integrity of his liberty even within its confines.[170] His financial obligations to the crown under the treaty, duties which he is known to have met to some degree at least, may have irritated him; he may have been subjected to other demands of which we have no knowledge or only an uncertain intimation. His relationship with the bishop of Bangor was not altogether cordial, and the difficulties between them opened the door to exactly the kind of royal interference in his lordship that the prince would be anxious to avoid.[171] He may have been on less than affable terms with the king, and some of their exchanges are painfully

---

[169] Powicke, *Henry III*, ii, 655.
[170] Below, p. 500.
[171] *CWR*, 174, a letter of Edward; *RPeck*, i, 125–6, a letter of Pecham, July 1280, after Llywelyn's composition with the bishop.

reminiscent of the tone of those of earlier years of confrontation. At the same time king and prince were able to be perfectly courteous to one another in their correspondence. Llywelyn could be reasonable in the manner in which he put his case to the king, and Edward could be accommodating in response to Llywelyn's wishes. A clutch of letters written by Eleanor, too, helps to suggest that historical judgement needs to be finely tuned to the temper of these years. Admittedly, each of the surviving letters has to do with a matter of difficulty, but the fact that Eleanor was able to raise these issues indicates some degree of confidence that her approach would not arouse the king's wrath anew. Her letter concerning the long delayed execution of her mother's will raised a vexed matter, and her plea that Nicholas de Waltham be allowed to execute the will may have touched a nerve at court for, long suspected of treacherous activity, he was eventually to be charged with surreptitious activity on behalf of Llywelyn and Amaury de Montfort.[172] Eleanor was not, however, constrained to let the matter rest, nor was she deterred from writing quite eloquently on behalf of Amaury, as well as urging the king to deal magnanimously with some of the smaller fry caught up in the ill-fated enterprise. More seriously, her letters convey an awareness that her husband enjoyed something less than the king's full confidence, and that there were some at work in an attempt to undermine the king's faith in the veracity of his submissions. The princess of Wales felt compelled to plead that Edward should not believe the sinister things said about Llywelyn and herself until she were able to tell the king directly.[173] Graciously, or diplomatically, she recalled the king's kindness towards them at Worcester; she was clearly anxious to create confidence between her husband and her kinsman, but it is difficult to deduce what exactly gave her cause for concern. The old animosities and suspicions had not been entirely removed, and there may have been some with access to the king whose interests lay in creating new difficulties, but there was at least some effort, on both sides, to maintain a civil dialogue.

Llywelyn's relations with those who had once been barons of the principality of Wales are not easy to establish. There was evidently some contact between them but it would be unwise to see these relations as necessarily conspiratorial. They were unlikely to spend a summer's day together, at Dolwyddelan or elsewhere, without there being something of common interest to discuss. Even so, Llywelyn's influence could well have tended to restraint rather than excitation.[174] The notion of intrigue, and the suspicion

---

[172] *CAC*, 75; *Foedera*, I, ii, 576 (Abereiddon, October 1279); for the charge against Waltham, above, p. 395.

[173] *CAC*, 75-6; *Foedera*, I, ii, 584, 587 (Ystumanner, October 1279-81; Llan-faes, 1279-82; Nefyn, February 1282).

[174] Above, p. 492.

that the prince was harmonizing the inclinations of his compatriots to rebellion, can easily be overdone. The surest signs of understanding are those which are reflected in the use which Rhys Wyndod, for instance, might make of the arguments used on Llywelyn's behalf during the proceedings before the justices, or in the manner in which the terms of the concessions made to Llywelyn in the treaty of 1277 were interpreted as though they applied to his fellow princes too. It would be well, as has been suggested already, to be wary of a supposition of conspiracy or deception in trying to understand the prince's agreement with Mortimer; it may be purely a reflection of a will on both sides to maintain a relationship of increased confidence. There is no evidence of any comparable transactions with other marchers, and he had little need of them. It would be easy to overlook the extent to which contentions with the marcher powers had subsided. Constricted within the confines of Gwynedd Uwch Conwy, Llywelyn was at least freed from vexatious confrontations with marcher barons. He did share a frontier with Gruffudd ap Gwenwynwyn, but their difficulties are not known to have been reflected in cross-border incidents. At no time was there any suggestion that Llywelyn was fomenting frontier incidents as a means of providing a pretext for intervention in the lands he sought by judicial process. The only frontier difficulties which Llywelyn, for his part, reported to the king, or recounted to the archbishop, were those which arose on the border which he shared with the king between Meirionnydd and Ceredigion and which are mentioned later.[175] The evidence of the years after 1277 is open to more than one emphasis. The prolonged argument over Arwystli certainly shows that Llywelyn had not withdrawn into a state of tranquil inertia, nor had he abandoned his resolve to safeguard and advance his interests. At the same time it would be foolish to interpret the evidence as though he was moving deliberately, still less being driven inexorably, to new confrontations with Edward. There is no doubt a consonance between the loftier pronouncements in the Arwystli business and those which he was to make during his exchanges with Archbishop Pecham in explanation of his commitment to the armed conflict. At each point there is explicit expression of the prince's sense of nationhood and its particular implications for himself, but to see these arguments as a force which drove him into rebellion is another matter altogether. None the less, when he presented his arguments to the archbishop he was able to cite a number of grievances, apart from the matter of Arwystli and Cyfeiliog. They are not issues of great moment in themselves, but they need to be taken into account, for the evidence which they bring forth may provide the surest way by which we can make an assessment of the temper of his relationship with the crown in the critical period before the war.

[175] Below, nn. 187–8.

Some of his grievances concerned the adversities endured by others, but several reflected matters of more personal concern.[176] They were submitted as part of an effort to justify the resort to arms, but they are not entirely a retrospective apologia for his part in resistance to Edward's authority. Several can be substantiated from the records of the period preceding the outbreak of war. Some concerned matters on which Edward was considered to have acted contrary to the treaty of Aberconwy and, as Llywelyn enumerated the charges, the relevant clauses were cited. Edward's denial to him of his right to Welsh law in the Arwystli case was the first. Llywelyn's complaint was urged with some force, now attributing to Edward a determination to deny him justice 'unless he was prepared to be judged according to the laws of England'.[177] Llywelyn had been careful not to say this explicitly when the argument was being waged, though he almost certainly interpreted Edward's standpoint in precisely this way. There was one matter which touched his jurisdiction. Under the terms of the settlement of 1277 Gruffudd Fychan had done homage to the king for Iâl and to Llywelyn for Edeirnion, and he alleged that in an action brought by Margaret, widow of Madog ap Gruffudd, for lands in Edeirnion, royal justices had asserted a jurisdiction which properly belonged to him. Llywelyn had tolerated the intrusion for the sake of peace.[178] It had not been quite like that. The problem lay rather in the fact that Margaret prosecuted her action, as Gruffudd Fychan complained, 'now before the king's justices and now before Llywelyn'. In response to representations from both Gruffudd and Llywelyn the king had transferred the hearing from his court to that of the prince. The matter was not readily or finally resolved there, but Llywelyn's problems arose, not from any wish on Edward's part to encroach upon Llywelyn's jurisdiction – rather the reverse – but from the inclination of the plaintiff to prosecute the action where it seemed best for her.[179] There were other difficulties. Llywelyn cited the treaty of Aberconwy to insist that, whereas it had been agreed that Rhys Fychan ap Rhys ap Maelgwn should do homage to Llywelyn 'with his land which he now holds', he had not been allowed to possess that land. He maintained that the commote of Genau'r Glyn was in Rhys Fychan's possession when the treaty

---

[176] The prince's broader arguments and his references to the grievances of others (*RPeck*, ii, 437–45) are considered below, pp. 532–4.

[177] *RPeck*, ii, 440–1.

[178] Ibid., 442; for his position under the treaty of 1277, *LW*, 120.

[179] When an assize was taken on her claim against Gruffudd Fychan for half of Glyndyfrdwy in November 1277 Margaret was told by the justices that, as Edeirnion was in the power and liberty of Llywelyn, she should seek justice in his court (*WAR*, 246). She probably sought justice again, for on 4 January 1278 Mortimer and Hopton were told to do justice to her (*CWR*, 171), and this may be the suit to which Llywelyn refers. The relevant letters can probably be dated thus: Gruffudd Fychan, *CAC*, 107: before December 1278; Llywelyn, *CAC*, 95–6: December 1278; and *CAC*, 85–6: October 1279.

was made and that it was subsequently taken from him, an assertion which is exceedingly difficult to substantiate as some of his kinsmen had certainly disputed his right to the lands he once held in Ceredigion in proceedings in the king's court.[180] Potentially more serious would be those matters which affected Llywelyn in his territorial lordship in Gwynedd, and there were some to relate. Quoting a clause which was more obviously relevant to cases such as that over Arwystli, Llywelyn held that royal justice had been intruded into Anglesey and his men had been judged contrary to Welsh law. The jury had been imposed upon them.[181] This could have been an important issue, though there appears to be no record of this problem during the period when it arose. The treaty had envisaged that royal officers would go the prince's lands and, if the treaty had been strictly applied, the king would have sent his emissaries each year to ensure that men from each *cantref* were bound in fealty to him and make certain that Llywelyn did not falter in his fidelity. This was quite apart from the requirement that Llywelyn provide ten hostages from among the *nobiles* of his land, another matter which probably necessitated the dispatch of royal officers to Gwynedd, and one which is not known to have created difficulty. The priors of Bangor and Rhuddlan and Goronwy ap Heilin are known to have travelled to Snowdonia on the king's behalf on at least four occasions.[182] Llywelyn is known, too, to have provided hostages from his land.[183] Dispensing judgement in the king's name within Llywelyn's liberty would be an altogether different matter, and it is a pity that we cannot establish the precise circumstances in which the *justiciarii* were employed.

Llywelyn, on these counts, quoted chapter and verse from the treaty of Aberconwy, but he also cited an important clause which appears only in the king's ratification of the treaty. In this clause Edward, at Llywelyn's request, provided an assurance that he would not impose his will (*voluntas*) in matters

---

[180] *RPeck*, ii, 441; for Rhys's position under the treaty of 1277, *LW*, 120 and above, p. 443. Gruffudd ap Maredudd and Cynan ap Maredudd claimed Genau'r Glyn and Perfedd against the king, asserting that they had been ousted by Llywelyn; Knovill, for the king, said that Rhys Fychan held the commotes when the king's army came; he did homage, then withdrew from the king's fealty, and forfeited them. He had been, by virtue of the treaty and 'by decision of the court of the king and the prince of Wales', judicially disinherited (*WAR*, 278–80; R. A. Griffiths, *PW*, i, 4–5). It is difficult to establish that 'the land he now holds' was the commote of Genau'r Glyn and that it was in Rhys's hands at any time after 1277.

[181] *RPeck*, ii, 442: 'vinetam ponendo super illos contra leges Wallie'.

[182] *LW*, 121; C62/57, mm.4–5. The emissaries travelled to fulfil tasks enjoined upon them by the king.

[183] Llywelyn in a letter to the king refers to the coming of Bartholemew de Sully and Guncelin de Badlesmere to him on the king's behalf 'to receive the hostages' (*CAC*, 90). The letter, probably February 1282, may refer to the orders of 4 and 11 January 1278, in which the same men are named (*CWR*, 162–3, 167).

Contention and Conflict

other than those embodied in the treaty.[184] Llywelyn had evidently sought, not only the king's confirmation of what had been agreed in his name and his promise that he would not act in a manner contrary to what had been agreed, but an assurance that no further conditions should be imposed upon him. In contravention of this *articulum,* the prince alleged, he had been required to contribute to the queen's gold (*exigebatur aurum ad opus regine*), a levy which had not been exacted from the Welsh either in the time of Henry III or in that of any other king of England. He had paid up for the good of the peace, but was then confronted with a demand for an aid for the elder queen, and this for the peace which had been made in the time of King Henry. The sum came to 2,500 marks and Llywelyn was placed under distraint in respect of it. It is astonishing that none of this emerges from the evidence of the previous years. Llywelyn had certainly been required, by the terms of the agreement in 1277, to pay off the debt which remained under the terms of the treaty of Montgomery, and he is known to have paid a sum of 500 marks in the following three years at least.[185] The allegations which the prince made in relation to the additional demands to which he refers are certainly puzzling. This is also true of another charge, expressed in quite forceful language, in which he insisted that the king had required him to agree that no man would be maintained in the prince's territory contrary to the king's wishes. It was, he insisted, an undertaking which was liable to be extended to all his men (*fideles*). He saw this as an unwarranted means of intrusion into his dominion, and he was particularly hurt by the fact that he had been called upon to agree to the king's demand on the very day of his wedding. Impelled by the fear to which a steadfast man can succumb – *compulsus per metum qui cadere potest in constantem virum* – Llywelyn had given the undertaking required of him, though it went well beyond what was provided in the agreement which he had made with the king.[186]

---

[184] In Llywelyn's submission to Pecham (*RPeck*, ii, 442) the clause reads: 'et licet idem princeps se nostre, ut dictum est, supposuerit voluntati, nos tamen concedimus et volumus quod voluntas nostra huiusmodi ultra dictos articulos se in aliquo modo non extendat'. This does not appear in the text of the king's confirmation in 'Liber A' (*LW*, 157; *Foedera*, I, ii, 546) but is included in the text on the Welsh Roll (C77/1, printed in *RotWall*, 4), only briefly noticed in *CWR*, 157–8.

[185] *LW*, 117–18; *CWR*, 157, 159, 169, 179, 186; above, p. 442. It seems impossible, from the surviving evidence, to verify Llywelyn's charges. The demand for the elder queen appears to be linked with the treaty of Montgomery, but if the payments imposed in 1277 had been diverted to the queen, without incurring extra charges, he had no cause for complaint. Material relating to queen's gold, examined in T. F. Tout, *Chapters in the Administrative History of Medieval England* (Manchester, 1920–33), ii, 42; v, 264–72; vi, 130, and later writers, is too fragmentary to allow any estimate of the veracity of the accusations.

[186] *RPeck*, ii, 443. The phrase 'compulsus per metum qui cadere potest in constantem virum', or a variant of it, recurs in Welsh documents at this time, among them a reference to the fear created among the men of Tegeingl by the actions of Reginald de Grey (ibid., 463). Of classical origin, it is also found in Scotland. For the problem of outlaws from Gwynedd harboured in England, see Edward's letter, 4 June 1278 (*CWR*, 173–4; *Foedera*, I, ii, 557–8).

Contention and Conflict

The intrusion of justices into his dominion; the exaction of queen's gold; the obligation not to maintain men in his land contrary to the king's wishes: each of these is, as yet, impossible to substantiate from the evidence of the period between the wars. On the other hand, the charges made in relation to the problems which arose in the Arwystli case, the problem of jurisdiction in Edeirnion, and Rhys Fychan's position in Genau'r Glyn, can be tested – though to vastly differing degrees – in the documentary sources of the period concerned. This is also true of two further matters which, though they were not related to specific clauses of the treaty, were seen by Llywelyn to be at variance with the tenor of the agreement. Difficulties encountered on the frontier between Meirionnydd and Ceredigion had arisen, he related, from a failure on the part of the king's officers to abide by the methods of redress which were normally employed when injuries were inflicted by men from one jurisdiction upon those of another. One incident had arisen when Llywelyn was hunting in the area, but this was not a matter of great concern itself and Llywelyn's account to the king, at the time it occurred, was set out in measured terms. More difficult problems arose from more serious infringement of the frontier conventions and elicited forceful expressions of the prince's concern, and these were the matters which Llywelyn subsequently recounted to Pecham.[187] He then asserted that Edward had inflicted injury upon him in this respect, but in his first response to Llywelyn's protestations Edward made an unequivocal statement that he had instructed Bogo de Knovill, his officer in south-west Wales, to ensure that amends were made for the trespasses inflicted upon the frontier in accordance with the custom of the area. Knovill appears to gave been reluctant to proceed 'at the accustomed places on the frontier', preferring that the matters be resolved before him at Llanbadarn Fawr. There may be more to this issue than Llywelyn's letters indicate; he himself conveyed that he sensed that the king was getting a different story from other sources, and the information which survives suggests that Edward experienced some difficulty in ensuring that his officers acted according to his wishes. It is not impossible that the king received from his officials an interpretation of events quite different from that retailed by Llywelyn. At the same time the king's declared wish that the frontier procedures should be followed has to be reconciled with his known reluctance to allow recourse to the arbitration procedures allowed by marcher custom where one of the territories concerned was royal land.[188]

An inability to ensure that the officers on the spot fulfilled his wishes appears at first to be the difficulty in another dispute, not a matter of vast

[187] *CAC*, 88–9; *RPeck*, ii, 444.
[188] *CAC*, 59–60, 88, 95. Frontier regulation is noticed above, pp. 132–3. For an indication that 'no one can have a march with the king', *CWR*, 336.

importance perhaps, but one which lingered for a long time and much to Llywelyn's annoyance. It concerned his right to the goods of ships wrecked upon the coasts of his territory. A merchant named Robert of Leicester claimed that, in an incident that had occurred before the war of 1277, his goods had been lost by wreck and, wrongly in Llywelyn's view, he was able to get the justice of Chester to proceed so as to compel the prince to make restitution. Llywelyn insisted that he was prepared to hold an inquiry and do justice in the matter; Edward concurred and Badlesmere was instructed to restore Llywelyn's distrained goods, and the merchant told to plead at Llywelyn's court and come to the king if he failed to obtain justice there.[189] Evidently not satisfied, either with the king's decision or with the manner in which the prince dealt with his case, the merchant persisted. Llywelyn was subject to new distraints by the justice of Chester.[190] The office was by then occupied by Reginald de Grey, but, looking at the evidence as it appears in the surviving record, he cannot be said to have acted in contravention of the king's mandate. On the contrary, Grey acted strictly in accordance with an instruction from the king which was very different from his earlier mandate.[191] Whether Llywelyn knew of this we cannot say; neither at the time nor in his subsequent submission did he place the responsibility upon the king. But he evidently suspected a change in the king's position, noticing that the new distraints were contrary to what the king had previously intimated to him and that they were either made unjustly by the justice or 'by somebody's instigation with the king's assent'. A letter written by Eleanor, touching on the same matter, similarly expressed her regret that credence should be given to those who complained against her husband before the matter could be discussed in the prince's land.[192] For whatever reason, Edward had taken a decision different from that which he had first conveyed to Llywelyn.

Now, as in the past, Llywelyn was revealing his sensitivity to the fact that Edward was susceptible to the persuasions of men who wished to inflict damage upon him. The case of the persistent merchant was not in itself a matter of great consequence, but the manner in which it was allowed to develop was something which the prince found disquieting. Llywelyn and

---

[189] *CAC*, 60, 89–90 (letters of Llywelyn and Edward, 6 and 18 July 1280); J. C. Davies, in *WAR*, 76–7.

[190] *CAC*, 90–1, Llywelyn to Edward, 2 February, the year uncertain; the editor suggests '1282 or possibly 1281', his preference for the later year justified by his dating of Eleanor's letter, *CAC*, 76–7.

[191] *CAC*, 78–9. Grey's letter to Edward states specifically that he was ordered by the king to seize Llywelyn's goods and asks for further instructions. The undated letter, attributed by the editor to November 1281–March 1282, was probably written shortly before Llywelyn's letter of 2 February 1282 (*CAC*, 90–1) The fact that Grey was, certainly on his testimony, acting in accordance with Edward's mandates at this time is important in relation to the complaints subsequently made against him by the men of the Four Cantreds.

[192] *CAC*, 76; cf. Powicke, *Henry III*, ii, 656–7.

Contention and Conflict

Eleanor both wrote to the king on the matter early in 1282 – the letters written at Nefyn are the last known communications to Edward on the part of the prince and princess of Wales – and their irritation was quite pronounced.[193] It seems that Llywelyn by then more than suspected that Reginald de Grey, who had by then aroused the wrath of many in Perfeddwlad, was acting in this connection, not simply with the king's support, but at his instruction. Llywelyn had no proper concern with relations between Grey and the communities east of the Conwy and, as far as we know, it was only after the outbreak of war that he expressed his concern at the way they were treated. Yet he was himself involved in a tussle with Grey on a matter which, while not of immense importance, still touched his regality in Gwynedd Uwch Conwy. By the beginning of 1282 Llywelyn's missives to the king had certainly revealed signs of increased tension. Brother William de Merton, of the Franciscan house of Llan-faes, felt compelled to write to the king.[194] The mendicant friar had previously been sent to the king on the Arwystli issue and that of Robert of Leicester, and Edward had commented on the prudence and honesty which he had shown in fulfilling his task on the prince's behalf.[195] William now took it upon himself to compose a letter in which, citing the two problems on which he had already been engaged, he impressed upon Edward how deeply aggrieved the prince felt on both counts. He wrote quite explicitly of his concern for the continuation of the peace between king and prince. Writing on the same two issues, Llywelyn conveyed his surprise at the turn for the worse in the matter of the merchant, his despair at the fact that the better prospect which appeared to have presented itself in the Arwystli business had still not materialized.[196] It is exceedingly difficult to judge on what grounds Llywelyn had come to believe that, as he insisted, things were going better for him over the Arwystli case. Nor can we estimate in what spirit he had decided to reopen the matter, whether he did so in a genuine expectation that he would finally win a decision in his favour, or whether, as has been intimated already, he did so out of an obdurate wish to keep the king locked in a quandary from which there was no release except by a decision which, be it favourable or unfavourable, would only accrue to the prince's advantage.

The consultations at Westminster in November 1281 may have been quite crucial. Beneath the courtesies of the king's last communication over this

---

[193] *CAC*, 76, 90.
[194] *CAC*, 99–100.
[195] *CAC*, 62, 89, 96. It is a reflection of the changed situation in Gwynedd that a member of the Franciscan house at Llan-faes should be Llywelyn's envoy rather than a Dominican of the house of Bangor. Brother Llywelyn ap Gruffudd, prior of the Dominican house, was among those who was appointed to act in Gwynedd on Edward's behalf after 1277 (e.g. *CWR*, 162, 167, 177).
[196] *CAC*, 90–1.

Contention and Conflict

vexed issue there were decidedly inauspicious indications.[197] The insistence that Llywelyn should obtain a writ so as to enable him to reopen the case was specifically linked with the king's wish not to do any wrong to Gruffudd ap Gwenwynwyn. And this was conveyed, as we have seen, as something that Llywelyn should not resent. More generally, and perhaps ominously, Edward's renewed assurance that he wished to observe the treaty of Aberconwy, as far as he could, was qualified by an admission of his resolve to do to his barons, and to others, that which he ought to do and which ought to be done. Edward may well have been bitterly dismayed that Llywelyn should wish to persist with the Arwystli case and his discussions with the justices concerned with the case and with other justices, and the deliberations in council, may have resulted in a marked hardening of the king's attitude. A new vigour borne of irritation is certainly indicated in his letter to Llywelyn. The favour shown to Gruffudd ap Gwenwynwyn on the very day that he wrote to the prince may be a small token of a major shift of emphasis in royal policy: the grant of the service of Maredudd ap Llywelyn of Mechain may not have been any great boon to the lord of Powys, but in the circumstances in which it was made it may have been a reflection of a commitment on Edward's part which did not augur well for the prince of Wales.[198]

Within a week Reginald de Grey had been appointed to the key position of justice of Chester, with the dire results already recounted. Llywelyn was, in one sense, only marginally affected by the change; for others, however, Grey's coming to Chester, with direct responsibility for the affairs of that part of Perfeddwlad which lay under royal lordship, had far more drastic consequences. Yet two things are reasonably clear and each has a bearing upon the course of events in the winter of 1281–2. The first is that Llywelyn was, as we have seen, directly affected by decisions which were taken by Grey in the pursuit of a policy in which the king was personally involved. The second is that the decision to appoint Grey may owe something to the king's irritation at the prince's continued prosecution of the Arwystli case. The appointment may, of course, owe more to what had emerged in Perfeddwlad when the king's commissioners, of whom Grey was one, had visited the area. The need for a sterner administration may well have been urged upon the king when the commissioners reported in June, and Grey may well have presented himself as just the man for the job that needed to be done.[199] Whatever the reasons, by mid-November, in the wake of discussions which may have centred on the resumption of the Arwystli case, Grey was appointed to this key position. His main confrontation was to be, not with Llywelyn but with

---

[197] *CWR*, 210–11; *RotWall*, 42.
[198] *CWR*, 211; *RotWall*, 42.
[199] Above, p. 455; for Grey's role on the commission, above, p. 479.

Contention and Conflict

Dafydd ap Gruffudd and the community of Perfeddwlad, and the evidence already recounted suggests that a highly tensive situation was created very soon after Grey's appointment. Dafydd ap Gruffudd evidently had reasons for his own forceful action, and he was able to make common cause with the communities of the areas in close proximity to his own. Whether Dafydd was also moved to avail himself of his brother's discomfiture, or whether he moved so that he might pre-empt an armed initiative on the part of his brother, is much more difficult to estimate. All in all, Dafydd ap Gruffudd may have concluded by the early spring of 1282 that it was time to strike.

The issues which concerned Llywelyn ap Gruffudd, and the matters on which he may have provoked the king, may thus have a bearing upon Edward's resolve to pursue the more vigorous policy which, in the event, led to war. At the same time the evidence which survives gives us no good reason to disregard Llywelyn's account of the manner in which the war began. In the letter which he wrote in response to Archbishop Pecham's first communication upon his intercession in the autumn of 1282, Llywelyn insisted that he knew nothing of the intentions of those who rose against the king until after they had taken action: *illud ignoravimus usque post factum*.[200] He stood by the actions of those who had gone to war and held that, moved by the injustice done not to himself alone but to the princes and communities who had endured the harshness of the king's rule, he had given his assent to those who had begun the war.[201] The whole tenor of the letters composed in response to Pecham's initiative – the only material available to us for the period following the outbreak of war – indicates that Llywelyn played no part in the initial action. We cannot, then, question the depth of the 'remorseless dilemma' in which Llywelyn ap Gruffudd was placed by his brother's forceful initiative at Hawarden: he had to choose between putting himself at the head of the rebellion and assisting Edward in suppressing it.[202] How soon he was able to resolve that dilemma is difficult to judge, and the conflicting evidence has already been examined. It is conceivable that it was not long – perhaps only a matter of a few days – before he gave his assent and brought his great influence to bear upon the course of events. But we cannot be sure of that, and it would be well to consider the possibility, already intimated in this discussion, that the prince took some time before he committed himself to the armed struggle for the last time. There is much to suggest that the issues which concerned him were matters that he would wish to pursue by continuing

---

[200] *RPeck*, ii, 438.
[201] Ibid., 444.
[202] J. G. Edwards, in *LW*, lxiii–lxix, provides a masterly and moving discussion of the prince's predicament.

disputation until, if resort were to be had to conflict at all, it would be at his decision and at a time of his own choice. A further matter may have been a crucial factor in his thinking in the winter of 1281–2 and perhaps had a bearing upon the calculations of his brother too.

Marriage had come to Llywelyn late in life but in that winter of heightened dissension his wife 'for whom he had for years longed' was with child. Llywelyn had reason to hope that Eleanor would give birth to the first of what could be for him a brood of children, just like that with which Dafydd ap Gruffudd was already blessed.[203] What feelings were aroused deep in Dafydd's heart by the knowledge that gave his brother hope is another matter altogether. Those words in the treaty of Aberconwy which may have proved most hurtful to Llywelyn were the very words which did most to raise Dafydd's hopes that, in the fullness of time, he would secure, not just that portion of Gwynedd Uwch Conwy of which he was assured by the terms of the treaty, but the portion which he might enjoy were his brother to die childless.[204] However difficult it might be to endure the oppressive actions of those who exercised authority on behalf of the king whom he had been so eager to serve in years gone by, Dafydd might have found it even more difficult to contemplate the consequences of the birth of a male heir of his brother's body. How these considerations relate to the events of the spring of 1282 is, even so, impossible to judge with any assurance, and it may be entirely erroneous to interpret Dafydd's motives even partially in dynastic terms, despite the havoc which those compulsions had caused in relations between the brothers over the previous thirty years. But the same considerations could make Llywelyn pause a while, even amidst a new political convulsion. In the position in which he was now placed, with his hopes for the future in Eleanor's womb, he had every reason to wait. If his hope that he might govern a wider principality and convey it to a successor had once been dashed, he now had a new hope that a broader dominion might yet be revived. It might be a distant hope, and there would be years of uncertainty ahead, but it was still conceivable that Llywelyn could convey to his heir an inheritance no less extensive than that which had first come to him. He could still provide a foundation for a new fulfilment of the fundamental aspirations of his lineage. Llywelyn ap Gruffudd's historical persona may be that of a forceful, even impetuous, prince. Yet time and again during his career Llywelyn had respected the need for patient restraint; in later years he may have regretted those occasions when he had failed to possess himself in patience. We cannot doubt that by the beginning of 1282, with tension perceptibly mounting, his patience with regard to those matters which concerned him directly may have

---

[203] For Dafydd's children, below, pp. 579–80.
[204] *LW*, 120.

been sorely tried. Nor can we doubt that Llywelyn felt impelled to intercede with the king – and with his officers – in the interests of those over whom he no longer exercised lordship but for whom he still felt a certain responsibility. It would be rash to assume, however, that this necessarily brought him to the point of initiating conflict, for this is a conclusion to which the historical evidence does not point with any certitude. Rather it suggests very strongly that we might hold back from assuming that the prince's combative instincts carried him into renewed conflict. We might reasonably consider whether his judgement caused him to pause at this most critical moment of his life when, as seems quite evident, Dafydd ap Gruffudd gave vent to his variously compounded frustrations with his fateful assault on Hawarden castle.

It is perhaps impossible to speak with complete certainty of Llywelyn's position upon the initiation of the final conflict, and we could speculate to excess. But divining his position is far from the only matter of interest which an examination of the war of 1282 brings to a study of his life's work. If he had contributed nothing towards the attack on Hawarden, nor to the subsequent movements in the first phase of the war, the course of events still needs to be considered in relation to the objectives which had dominated Welsh political endeavour in his time. It could be argued that, though he might have remained inactive at the outbreak of hostilities, and though he may not have sought to create the conditions for renewed conflict, his was the ultimate inspiration of the powerful forces unleashed in 1282. It is, sadly, only in the few weeks before the prince's death that we have anything in the nature of a statement of the compulsions which carried prince and compatriots into war. By then, at least, the documents are resonant with the language of the political forces which had seen the creation of a principality of Wales. There were doubtless men in Gwynedd who, from the early years of the prince's endeavour, were attuned to the needs of the *principatus,* who were able to employ the phraseology of princely authority and who were knowledgeable in its workings. At the same time, though the force of arms of the years of expansion points to the prince's capacity to mobilize large numbers of men, there is little to indicate that the nation as a whole had manifested a deep commitment to the polity which represented the prince's objectives. Yet by the end of 1282 eloquent declarations were made in the name of the Welsh people.[205] The documents convey an atmosphere different from anything which can be sensed before. The concord of lord and community, the unity of noble and peasant in the pangs of oppression, and the pride of a people in its inheritance and its freedom: these are the themes which pervade the evidence compiled in the last weeks of Llywelyn's life. We cannot tell precisely who was responsible for the compilation of the grievances placed before the

[205] *RPeck,* ii, 437–40, 469–71; below, pp. 532–4, 543–4.

archbishop or who prepared the statements made in the names of the principal princes, but these may be counted among the most exquisite expressions of the abiding aspirations of the Welsh nation. They speak of a principality possessed of greatness in times past, its lineage the custodian of an ancient and powerful political inheritance, recognized by the Christian church, fortified by the consonance of lord and community.[206] The various elements compounded in this synthesis suggest that Wales could draw upon those unifying influences which were to sustain the kingdom of Scotland in adversity and inspire the endeavour which brought the community of the realm from subjection to the king of England to its assured place among the nations of medieval Europe.[207]

In Wales the resonant declarations were made at a time when, whatever his dilemma in the spring of that year, the prince's leadership was unquestioned, even though his sphere of effective authority was already much diminished. His rule in the years of supremacy had created animosity, and after his death his misdeeds would be held against his memory as the communities he had governed came to terms with the new power to be exercised over them.[208] Yet there was little doubt, if only on the basis of the ferocity of the conflict to be examined later, that in 1282 Llywelyn represented something which transcended the recollection of extortion. He brought to the conflict a power which Dafydd ap Gruffudd, for all the ardour which flowed from his breach with authority, could hardly supply. Dafydd certainly had his impediments to overcome, for there may have been many who would have committed themselves to insurrection at his behest only with the greatest reluctance if they were not moved to insurrection on their own account. The opening assaults were spectacular, and the chroniclers of England reflect their impact, but to what extent the pressures upon the king were maintained in the weeks that followed is impossible to estimate. We have to rely entirely on the written record of the measures taken to counter the Welsh insurgents, and we see things through a glass no less darkly than before. It is, besides, some time before the account rolls of the king's armies tell us anything of the scale and the direction of the operations which were deemed to be necessary. From the month of June onward the accounts begin to provide a fuller picture, but specific references to Llywelyn ap Gruffudd do not appear for some time. Two English chroniclers report his appearance in south-west Wales in an entry which follows their account of a reverse suffered by the English army near Llandeilo Fawr on 16 June.[209] There is no certainty that his appearance in the area followed swiftly upon that event, but it would be reasonable to

---

[206] For the historical allusions, J. B. Smith, *SHMW*, 1, 14–15.
[207] Barrow, *Bruce*, 205ff.; idem, *Anglo-Norman Era*, 145–6.
[208] Above, pp. 255–60, 266–7.
[209] Trevet, *Annales*, 304; Rishanger, *Chronica*, 100; cf. below, pp. 520–1.

surmise that news of the damage inflicted upon the king's forces would have reached Llywelyn very shortly after he had suffered the loss of his wife in childbirth. The chronicle of Bury St Edmunds says that Eleanor died on 19 June.[210] The Welsh chronicler provides no precise date, only that Eleanor died in giving birth to a daughter who was called Gwenllian, and that the mother was borne to the monastery of the Barefooted Friars at Llan-faes in Anglesey.[211] Is it conceivable that, when he had accompanied her bier across the Menai Straits, in distress but with new-found resolve, Llywelyn ap Gruffudd entered into armed conflict for the last time? Is it possible that he went to war in the knowledge that, though at last he had a child of his body, his hopes for the future were finally shattered and that there was now nothing left for him but to put his weight behind the rebellion which his brother had begun? Llywelyn would have had no illusion as to what renewed conflict would bring. To rise in war against Edward I, after the experience of five years before, would need more than a capacity for valiant but impulsive action, more than an ability to inflict reverses upon the enemy and exacerbate his difficulties. Edward was unlikely, a second time, to draw back from the assault which would take his power to the furthermost fastnesses of Snowdonia. After the trauma of the last war any decision to enter into conflict once more, whenever it was taken, would have been taken in full realization of the magnitude of the power which had to be confronted. *Gŵr prudd megis Priaf*, the poet Bleddyn Fardd reflected in his elegy to Llywelyn ap Gruffudd, seeing in his prince the wisdom, perhaps the sadness, of Priam.[212] But, if it was to the legendary inheritance of Troy that the poet naturally turned, the allusion was not altogether apt. Priam, for all his anguish, had known the joy of male offspring. This was a felicity that Llywelyn never knew, for his fate was more that of the despondent progeny of Sisyphus.[213] Had Llywelyn waited in earnest hope, and then gone to war in utter despair?

---

[210] *ChronBury*, 74–6; the value of the chronicle in matters relating to Wales is noted later. Members of Eleanor's household were given safe-conduct to travel to England on 12 July (*CWR*, 234).

[211] *BT, Pen20*, 223; *Pen20Tr*, 117; *RBH*, 262–5. The chronicle brings together the information concerning Eleanor, apart from the notice of her marriage in 1278, in the entry for 1275.

[212] *GBF*, 50. 25.

[213] C. Davies, 'Marwnad Syr John Edward Lloyd a Fyrsil Aeneid VI', *Llên Cymru*, 12 (1972–3), 57–60; J. Rowlands, '"Marwnad Syr John Edward Lloyd" gan Saunders Lewis', in R. G. Gruffydd (ed.), *Bardos* (Cardiff, 1982), 111–27.

Chapter 10

Cilmeri

JUST three days before Eleanor's death, forces advancing from Chester under Reginald de Grey reached the castle of Caergwrle. Dafydd ap Gruffudd's stronghold stood in the lordship of Hope and it was, as he had so vehemently asserted, within the frontiers of Wales.[1] Even so, it stood very close to the border with Cheshire and it may be a measure of Dafydd's determined resistance, or conceivably a reflection of the fact that issue had hitherto not been joined in the field, that the castle fell only after war had been in progress for nearly three months. Even so, Edward, greatly surprised by the outbreak of rebellion in Wales, had reacted to the news with deliberate and purposeful directives.[2] He issued the first swift decisions of a military campaign upon which he was to concentrate his mind, to the exclusion of other matters to which he might otherwise have attended, until the subjugation of Wales had been completed. The problems of Castile or Sicily were of no concern beside the emergency which had arisen within his own kingdom.[3] During the following weeks and months his will was expressed in a host of orders sent out in his name. Edward remembered the Montfort rebellion, for as soon as he heard of the disturbances in north-east Wales he ordered a close watch on the Ely region, the last refuge of those who had once torn the realm apart.[4] He knew perfectly well that Llywelyn, no more than two years before, had sought to communicate with Amaury de Montfort and that the prince, no less than Eleanor and numerous other worthy persons, was anxious to see him released from captivity. The archbishop of Canterbury was exceedingly circumspect in this connection, and the powers of church and state alike took

---

[1] *AnnCestr*, 108 (16 June); *HKW*, i, 330–2.
[2] Several chroniclers say that Edward could hardly believe what he was told, e.g. *FloresHist*, iii, 56; *AnnDunst*, 292; Edward himself referred to 'the sudden rising of the Welsh' (*CAC*, 264).
[3] For Edward's concern with these lands, Powicke, *Thirteenth Century*, 241–5; Runciman, *Sicilian Vespers*, 183 *et passim;* Prestwich, *Edward I*, 318–20; for the priority given to the Welsh war, *Foedera*, I, ii, 606–7.
[4] *CWR*, 218.

a cautious view of Amaury's case before it was agreed that, though Wales was again at war, he could be released and allowed to leave the kingdom as long as he provided firm guarantees that he would be gone for ever.[5] Edward would maintain his vigilance over the remnants of the Montfortians, but his main concern was necessarily Wales itself. Within three days of the attack on Hawarden commanders were appointed to specified centres in north, central and south Wales, to be provided with forces supplied from the counties of England. The first contingents were required by mid-May, and by then it was agreed that the main force would be summoned to Rhuddlan by 2 August.[6] The morrow of the feast of St Peter in Chains was once more inscribed upon the king's calendar for a rendezvous with his Welsh adversaries. The taking of Caergwrle signalled the initiation of the advances preliminary to the main assault on the princes' positions.

In going to war in Wales again Edward had the benefit of his direct experience of warfare there and his investment in new fortifications which added to the number that he had inherited from his predecessors. His personal knowledge of Welsh topography, and particularly of the strategic and logistic problems to be surmounted in Gwynedd, were considerable assets. He could call, too, on military commanders of proven ability well acquainted with the terrain. Flint, Rhuddlan, Aberystwyth and Builth were accessions of strength which made the existing network of royal and marcher castles more effective than before.[7] Edward made sure of an adequate supply of ready cash by arranging loans from the bankers of Lucca, Florence and Siena.[8] He drew upon the resources of his wide dominions for men and horses, food and arms; his messengers made for Gascony and Ponthieu for wine and corn, fish and meat, while stringent measures were taken to prevent supplies from reaching his enemies. Men travelled to the Basque area to find the most resolute of horsemen, and Edward gathered about him a powerful army drawn from many lands.[9] The chronicler writing at Hagnaby held that no army like it had ever been seen before and there can be little doubt that the armies which advanced into Wales in 1282 were, in extent and the quality of their composition, among the most impressive in the history of medieval warfare to

[5] *RPeck*, i, 119; cf. above, pp. 399–401.
[6] Reginald de Grey, Roger Mortimer and Robert Tibetot were entrusted with military command in the northern, central and southern sectors (*CWR*, 212–13; *ParlWrits*, i, 222, 25 March).
[7] *HKW*, i, 293–327.
[8] Edward had secured the first of the loans advanced by the Riccardi and other societies, and by merchants of Cahors, by 14 April; further bonds were issued on 10 June (*CWR*, 215–16, 230–1). Sums lent appear as wardrobe receipts in E101/4/2; E101/351/10; see Kaeuper, *Bankers to the Crown*, 182–3; idem, 'The role of the Italian financiers in the Edwardian conquest of Wales', *WHR*, 6 (1972–3), 389ff.
[9] For e.g. the resources of Gascony and Ponthieu, *RG*, ii, nos. 698–707, 774, 807, 818; C47/3/17; *CWR*, 216; the embargo on trade, *CWR*, 254–5.

that date. The cavalry and infantry were augmented by large numbers of ancillaries, who included woodsmen and diggers, carriers and merchants. 'A king steeped in the methods of warfare' was one view of Edward at the time of his death. Possessor of a manual of warfare, already a participant in campaigns of a varied nature and a varied degree of success, he put into effect in Wales in 1282, more than before, that capacity for the management of war which he was to reveal again in later years.[10]

The flow of orders in the king's name from the spring of 1282 onward might thus appear to portray the inexorable manner by which, in accordance with masterly planning, the military might of England was gathered for the final conquest of Wales.[11] Yet the campaign was not without its difficulties, and Edward was not entirely able to overcome the problems which had hindered the efforts of his predecessors. The supersession of Robert Tibetot, the king's first choice for command in west Wales, by Gilbert de Clare, earl of Gloucester, appears to have been a response to the earl's ruffled sensitivities at the very outset of the preparations.[12] The reversal of Edward's initial decision to request paid baronial service, and his subsequent acceptance of unpaid service, may reflect a feeling among those of high baronial status that a war of conquest might prove more rewarding for the participants if they were not in receipt of royal pay. The nobility of England may not, however, have been of one accord in this for Humphrey de Bohun, earl of Hereford, was certainly concerned to secure the remuneration due to him as constable of England.[13] Whatever the reason, the reversal of the king's first preference suggests that this was a difficult issue and that the king might not enjoy the unfettered command that he would obviously prefer. Yet there can be no doubt that Edward relied heavily on paid service, including large numbers of paid cavalry. At Rhuddlan by early August, with the feudal host including 217 cavalry, he had 160 paid cavalry and the infantry on the same front amounted to over 6,500 men. Numbers fluctuated but there would be times,

---

[10] BL, Cotton Vesp. B xi, f. 21; W. W. Skeat, 'Elegy on the death of King Edward I', *Modern Language Review*, 7 (1912), 149–52; Edward's text of Vegetius has been noticed already.

[11] For early orders, see e.g. *CWR*, 212–22, 346–52; *HKW*, i, 330–1. Authorities on Edward's war organization are noticed above, p. 414, n. 85.

[12] Tibetot, appointed 25 March with Clare and the earl of Hereford and the lords of west Wales to provide support, was replaced on 10 April (*CWR*, 213; *ParlWrits*, i, 224).

[13] Morris, *WW*, 155–8; Prestwich, *WPF*, 71–2; idem, *Edward I*, 189. Hereford's claim is in *Foedera*, I, ii, 604. He was paid for thirty-six days' service 'in the king's army' in late 1282 and early 1283; he then appears to have withdrawn, his place taken by Hugh de Turberville, and his subsequent return coincided with a payment of £50 in settlement of his fee for the whole of the Welsh war (E101/4/1). By then the main territorial rewards had been distributed and, not among the beneficiaries, he may have insisted on a proper remuneration.

notably at the beginning of 1283, when very substantial numbers would be engaged.[14] Edward had to contend with the constant need to maintain good supplies for his soldiers; an insufficient supply of horses caused a particular difficulty, despite his care at an early stage in the campaign to seek all possible sources.[15] The king certainly had a good knowledge of Wales, but there were innumerable difficulties to overcome in what Archbishop Pecham had once termed 'your wild land of Wales' (*vostre terre sauvage de Gale*) in a letter to Edward written when the prelate had barely skirted the confines of Wales, and that in time of peace. 'When it is summer everywhere, it is winter in Wales' remarked Peter Langtoft, and Edward was well aware of the tribulations which might befall a king who would attempt the destruction of a resilient enemy in the heartland of Snowdonia.[16]

From one point of view, Edward's task was less forbidding now, for on the previous occasion he had to break the power of a prince who ruled a very extensive part of Wales; he had to destroy a political structure which, for all its inherent weaknesses, embraced seigniories whose lords held their position within a well-defined political authority. From another standpoint, and one which provides a more meaningful understanding of the new conflict, Edward had gone to war in 1277 knowing that he could choose his time and pursue his own method of dismembering the principality of Wales, and his success was to a large extent due to his ability to blend military and political arms in a purposeful manner. By now the Wales of the princes had no semblance of political unity, but the king faced rebellion over the length and breadth of the princes' lands. He was confronted with active resistance on the part of many who, nominally adherents of Llywelyn ap Gruffudd in 1277, had then been exceedingly quick to succumb to the king. He could not now be at all sure that he could, in an orderly manner, draw the strings about his opponents and confine them to their furthermost retreat. Besides, he knew that this time he had no choice but to force his way into that stronghold in Snowdonia. Our knowledge of activity on the part of the princes after the initial movements of Holy Week is extremely sparse. We cannot tell whether the momentum was maintained, or whether the offensive petered out in several weeks of phoney war. Nor do we know to what extent, after the first combined movements, the princes' endeavours were co-ordinated and, sadly, we cannot even tell who, if anyone, exercised the main influence among them in the first weeks of hostilities. What evidence we have, however, points to the conclusion that the English forces were constrained to maintain a constant defence over wide

---

[14] E101/3/30; E101/4/1, figures calculated by Dr R. F. Walker.

[15] *CAC*, 45–6; *CWR*, 252–3; *ParlWrits*, i, 226, notes the 'great lack in the realm of great horses at arms' (26 May, 22 June 1282).

[16] *RPeck*, i, 392g; *CAC*, 104 (Pecham may have entered Wales travelling north in 1280, writing to Llywelyn *en route*, *RPeck*, i, 125–6); Langtoft, *Chronicle*, ii, 176.

areas. Caergwrle fell only in early June, and even later it was considered necessary to maintain in that neighbourhood forces adequate for the protection of a sector only just within the bounds of Wales. During 1282, Edward, responding to the new crisis in Wales with alacrity but not initially on a massive scale, found that he was confronted with an altogether more forbidding and an infinitely more costly undertaking than he had embarked upon five years before. Military expenditure in the war is difficult to calculate accurately, but payments to cavalry, infantry and other forces came to £85,000 and costs of provisioning the army, and those incurred at the castles during the period of conflict, probably brought the costs of the war to a sum over £120,000. But, if financial considerations had been one influence upon Edward's decision to curtail the war of 1277, even the vastly greater expenditure incurred during the second conflict did not deter the king from seeking a decisive military solution of his problems in Wales.[17]

Neither the defenders nor those who pressed upon them were concerned only with material needs, though we know precious little of the princes' appeal to mind and spirit until the archbishop provided that brief and late intermission which, as we have seen already and will appreciate still more, proved so informative. As far as we know there was not now, as there had been before, any appeal to the papal court, and the predicament of churchmen and laymen alike at this time of supreme crisis remains virtually unrecorded. Our only measure of the strength of Welsh resistance is the effort to which the king was forced to resort in order to steel his kingdom for war. Edward sought ecclesiastical support at an early stage and called upon the archbishops of Canterbury and York and Dublin to excommunicate the

---

[17] Morris, *WW*, 196–7, calculated payments for cavalry, infantry and other forces from wardrobe accounts at £60,046 and costs at castles in the period of the war at £38,375, a total of £98,421. Further provisioning and transport costs, calculated from wardrobe accounts at about £2,500, provide a total of about £100,921. A roll of money received into the wardrobe specifically to meet war costs, E101/4/2 (March 1282–November 1284), gives a total of £101,621. The corresponding enrolled account, on the Pipe Roll, is E372/136, m. 31, and an abbreviated version of E101/4/2, entered on the Chancellor's Roll for 1291, is printed in *Chronica Johannis de Oxenedes*, ed. H. Ellis (RS, 1959), 326–36. Apart from these special war accounts the ordinary enrolled wardrobe accounts, E372/130, mm. 5, 5d, bring aggregate wardrobe receipts March 1282–November 1284 to about £204,500 (Tout, *Chapters*, ii, 113–15). Disbursements from the ordinary account included war expenses, but are difficult to calculate accurately. Prestwich, *WPF*, 170, estimated a war cost of £150,000, adjusted idem, *Edward I*, 200, to £120,000, the figure quoted in the text above. Campaign costs, excluding castle work but including supplies, transport and costs of forces at castles, come to a total in excess of that safely calculated by Morris; a sum at least four times the total comparable expenditure in 1277 can be estimated with some confidence. Publication of *Records of the Wardrobe and Household 1282–1284*, a volume of accounts and other material collected and prepared by A. J. Taylor, edited by R. F. Walker and Susan J. Davies, will greatly facilitate accurate calculation of costs and fuller study of the campaign in general.

rebels.[18] John Pecham, just ten days after the outbreak of hostilities, duly called upon his suffragans to issue sentence of excommunication, and the order was repeated a month later, though, as we have noticed already, no one was mentioned by name.[19] The archbishop won the assent of Bishop Anian of Bangor, and in the heart of Gwynedd church bells were rung and candles extinguished once more. Whether similar measures were taken in the see of St Asaph is less certain. Even as late as October, Pecham took Bishop Anian of St Asaph to task for his failure to do what was required of him, for the bishop was now as uncompromising in his resistance to the wishes of archbishop and king as he had stood in defiance of the prince in the period leading up to the previous conflict.[20] The origins of his changed attitude are not easy to trace. Anian had been favourably disposed towards Edward's plan for the removal of the see from St Asaph to Rhuddlan.[21] During 1281 he had written to Pope Martin acknowledging the disadvantages of a location exposed to insurgency and warfare, and the advantages of a site for which Edward's fortification provided greatly enhanced security.[22] But somewhat pointedly he entered the proviso that the liberties of the church should remain unaffected by the translation, a reference made more meaningful by the knowledge of his efforts, endorsed by the archbishop, to protect his episcopal jurisdiction against encroachment from royal justices.[23] Anian seems to have been somewhat troubled on his own account before the outbreak of war and, whatever his precise reasons, he proved at the very least dilatory in responding to the archbishop's call for sanctions against the rebels. And then, but only several weeks after Pecham's first call for excommunication, relations with archbishop and king alike became inflamed upon the burning of the cathedral church by English soldiers. It was hardly an accidental happening. The result of a raid by English forces on what was considered to be a sanctuary for rebel

---

[18] *CWR*, 246; *Councils*, i, 533–4 (18 March).

[19] *RPeck*, i, 323–5, 352–3; *Councils*, i, 534–6; *LibEpist*, no. 521 (1 April and 2 May). Neither Llywelyn nor Dafydd is named in either letter, nor in his call on Anian of St Asaph to pronounce sentence in October (*RPeck*, ii, 422–3). It has not proved possible to find any reference to their excommunication *nominatim* between the spring and autumn of 1282. In the précis of Pecham's letter in *Register of Bishop Godfrey Giffard, 1268–1301*, ed. J. W. Willis-Bund (Worcestershire Historical Society, 1898–1902), i, 150, Llywelyn is named, but a photographic copy of the original, consulted through the kindness of Dr Susan Davies, shows that there is no reference to Llywelyn in the text of the letter but his name is given in a marginal heading written, it seems, by the scribe who wrote the register. In calendaring, the reference to Llywelyn was incorporated as though it formed part of Pecham's letter. For the excommunications of 1277 and 1282, above, pp. 407–9, 412–14, 468; below, pp. 549–50.

[20] *RPeck*, ii, 422–3 (21 October).

[21] For the proposal and the difficulties which arose, A. J. Taylor, 'Rhuddlan cathedral: a "might have been" of Flintshire history', *JFlintHS*, 15 (1954–5), 43–51; G. Williams, *Welsh Church*, 12–13.

[22] *Councils*, i, 529.

[23] *RPeck*, i, 249–51; *Councils*, i, 531–2; G. Williams, *Welsh Church*, 12–13.

Cilmeri

forces, Pecham himself saw it as a consequence of legitimate conflict, an occurrence indeed characteristic of warfare in Wales (*justo prelio, secundum modum precipue preliandi in partibus Wallie*).[24] Concerned at Anian's threat to excommunicate, not the Welsh, but those among the English guilty of sacrilege, Pecham urged caution. Support for the measures being taken to secure peace in the realm was the overriding consideration which the bishop had need to respect. Anian was obviously distressed by the material damage done to his church at St Asaph and indeed elsewhere in his diocese. Damage was inflicted, sooner or later, on several other churches in his diocese, destruction to which the archbishop was to address himself with characteristic persistence after the war in demanding that the king make appropriate reparations.[25] Llandrillo, Llangwm, Clocaenog, Llanarmon, Gresford, Llansannan, Helygain, Ysgeifiog, Caerwys, Llanynys, Llanasa, Llandyrnog, Nannerch, Henllan: these were among the numerous churches in Perfeddwlad alone for which varying sums were paid from the royal exchequer in compensation.[26] Yet damage to the fabric of churches, even the extensive destruction at St Asaph, may have been only one among several considerations which left Anian deeply troubled. He had tarried over the imposition of spiritual sanctions for some time before the sacrilege of his church raised his temper. There is no firm evidence that he made any protestations on behalf of those who went to war, but his exile and the entrusting of his diocese to Robert Burnell may point to real concern on Pecham's part for what may well have been seen as, at the very least, solicitude for those in rebellion. When it was all over, and Pecham was anxious to get Anian back to his diocese and undertake the reform and reconstruction which were necessary, he found it necessary to tell Edward that he was convinced that Anian had not been implicated in the war and that the king would have no cause for concern if the bishop were to return.[27] Anian had, very clearly, been under suspicion.

The king's call for the excommunication of the insurgents, directed to the bishops of England as well as Wales, was one way of alerting the realm as a whole to the new peril. Edward, much more than ever before, had need to inspire in his subjects a commitment to the war effort that would enable him

---

[24] *RPeck*, i, 367–9.
[25] For letters of Pecham and Edward, July 1284, *LW*, 71, 107–8, 123, 162.
[26] Compensation in Perfeddwlad and elsewhere, *LW*, 59–76, 80–90, 93, 95–7, 127–30, 132–6, 174.
[27] Burnell was entrusted with the diocese 31 October 1282 (*RPeck*, ii, 426–7); in Anian's absence, September 1283, the bishop of Lichfield and the archdeacon of St Asaph were responsible for the arrangements for securing the peace in the diocese (*LW*, 154). Pecham urged Anian to exhort the Welsh to live in peace with the English and told Edward (3 July 1284), after inquiring into seditious activity in St Asaph and Bangor, that in Anian's case he had found nothing which, under canon law, gave any cause for concern (*RPeck*, ii, 737–43; iii, 773).

to secure the resources he needed to achieve his objectives. His efforts to do so constitute an important aspect of the conflict as the evident strength of the resistance drove him to increasingly strident exhortation. Predictably, the Welsh were portrayed as a deceitful nation, fickle and wayward, a people in dire need of repentance. Royal commands persistently urged the benefits which would come from the final destruction of the Welsh. The successive calls to arms, beginning with measured reference to the disturbing of the king's peace and the tranquillity of the realm, dwelt more and more on the need to ensure the security of the realm and the king's subjects.[28] The moral pressure came to a head late in 1282 when, in circumstances which shall be examined more closely, Edward urged his people to a supreme effort to ensure that the Welsh, from whose perfidy the kings of England and their people had long suffered, could never again threaten the realm and its people. The new endeavour had to be pursued for the common advantage, not by king and magnates alone, but by the will of the community of the realm.[29] Never before had the common interest of king and subjects been urged so forcibly. There were moral and spiritual purposes to be fulfilled. Edward, in explicit references after the war was over, portrayed his endeavour as a just war.[30] In close accord with the phraseology of royal documents, the archbishop's letters commended the quest for a permanent solution which would secure the peace of the kingdom and the historic task would be done in praise of God and in his honour.[31] When the war was over the archbishop held that if the king had been unable to fulfil his objectives in Wales the church of Rome itself would have gathered the forces for a crusade to fulfil a wholly necessary task.[32] When all care is taken to be attentive to the precise terminology of the documents it can reasonably be said that the war in Wales was seen as a political crusade. Edward ensured that his men advanced under a pennant with the arms of St George, and each soldier wore an armband depicting the cross of the saint. The main object of bearing the crosses was to make the troops distinctive, for there were pennants to distinguish the Welsh soldiers who came into the king's peace, but the crosses were also a symbol of that combination of physical and moral force with which the princes and their men

---

[28] *ParlWrits*, i, 10–11, 222–5.

[29] Ibid., 1, 10; *Select Charters,* ed. W. Stubbs (9th edn., ed. H. W. C. Davis, Oxford, 1913), 462. For the appeal to *necessitas* and *utilitas*, Harriss, *King, Parliament, and Public Finance,* 33–48.

[30] Edward invoked the notion of a just war in a letter from Baladeulyn concerning reparations to churches, June 1284 ('cum principibus liceat iustam gwerram exercere prout canonice permittunt sanctiones', *LW*, 107;· *Foedera*, I, ii, 642); for the theories, F. H. Russell, *The Just War in the Middle Ages* (Cambridge, 1975), 213–57.

[31] *RPeck*, ii, 435–7.

[32] Ibid., 741 (June 1284): 'Romana ecclesia, crucis si oporteret exercitu invocato, contra quos vires Wallie nihil possent.'

Cilmeri

had to contend.³³ That they had need to do so reflects the king's estimate of the extent of the task with which he was confronted. Edward had no choice but to move deliberately into what would prove to be a momentous struggle.

The princes would have little doubt that the main thrust of the English advance would be made from the Chester front, the traditional route being an even more obvious approach than before by virtue of king's prudent investment at Rhuddlan and Flint. Amadeus of Savoy was able to make an early advance to raise the siege of Rhuddlan.³⁴ More extensive movements were initiated in early June to coincide roughly with Edward's arrival at Chester.³⁵ If the attack on Hawarden had dramatically signalled the Welsh offensive, Dafydd ap Gruffudd's withdrawal from his castle at Caergwrle, in his lordship of Estyn or Hope, was a sign of the first major counter-offensive.³⁶ The security of Hawarden, Ewloe and Caergwrle could now be assured, though the need to maintain adequate forces in those areas, mainly concentrated at Hope, was acknowledged.³⁷ During the first half of June the princes of Powys Fadog faced English advances along the Dee and their successful outcome, or an expectation of their early completion, was indicated in the king's disposition of their lands. Those of Llywelyn ap Gruffudd Fychan in Nanheudwy, Cynllaith and Mochnant Is Rhaeadr – the future lordship of Chirk – were granted to the younger Roger Mortimer. Llywelyn ap Gruffudd Fychan, who had been among the princes who rose upon the first call to arms, remained in the princes' alliances and died with Llywelyn ap

---

³³ E101/3/29; E101/351/9.

³⁴ Rhuddlan was put under siege, according to the Chester annalist, on the day of the rising (*AnnCestr*, 108). Forces were sent to Chester under Amadeus, 8–30 April (E101/4/1; Taylor, *SCCB*, 49, n. 4). Amadeus refers, 9 May, to 'the time of the siege of Rhuddlan' (SC1/24/94; *CAC*, 129–30), the expedition, probably under his leadership, having left Chester about 21 April and returned four days later (C47/35/18). Taylor, *HKW*, i, 322–3, takes this to mean the raising of the siege, not the recovery of the castle, following Morris, *WW*, 153, 162, who held that there was 'conclusive evidence' that Rhuddlan had not fallen. Taylor also notes that Edward conveys (*CAC*, 56) that the castle had fallen and that extensive repairs were necessary on one of his castles in the area, but the meaning of the letter is not clear.

³⁵ For the military movements, Morris, *WW*, 149 ff. remains indispensible, though his account needs to be modified and amplified at several points; these unprinted accounts are particularly valuable: C47/2/4, an account of the army in south Wales, including details of the advance to Castell y Bere; E101/3/29; E101/351/9, a substantial 'necessaries' account for the period April 1282–October 1284; E101/4/1, cavalry roll; E101/3/30, infantry roll.

³⁶ When Grey reached the castle he found it had been slighted by the defenders before departing (*AnnCestr*, 108); account of John of Lincoln includes costs of repairs (C47/2/3).

³⁷ In early July, when Edward visited Hope, there were forty-five Cheshire cavalry there and a large body of archers; Grey, 28 July, still found it prudent to retain at Hope a body of men summoned for Rhuddlan (*CWR*, 233; C47/2/3; A. J. Taylor, 'The Hope castle account of 1282', *JFlintHS*, 33 (1992), 21–53, from C47/2/3).

Gruffudd on the fateful day in December, but even by the early summer he had failed to withstand the pressure exerted by the king's forces upon his lordship.[38] A little later Maelor and Iâl – the future lordship of Bromfield and Yale – were lost to the princes, and, for the present, entrusted to Reginald de Grey.[39] The young heirs to the inheritance, Gruffudd ap Madog and Llywelyn ap Madog, sons of Madog ap Gruffudd, had evidently died but in circumstances still unknown.[40] Owain ap Gruffudd forfeited his part of Cynllaith, and Gruffudd Fychan yielded his land of Glyndyfrdwy to which he was, by the king's grace, eventually restored. Gruffudd was the one lord of Powys Fadog to survive the débâcle of 1282.[41]

Powys Fadog, Hope and Ystrad Alun or Mold had now fallen to the king, but it had taken Edward's forces a good three months to reassert his authority in the region, and in some areas his control remained uncertain for some time yet. The advance into the interior of the Four Cantreds was still to be undertaken. Whether the delay was due to the ferocity of the combat or to the fact that adequate forces had not yet been committed to the task is difficult to judge. Although the major concentration of forces was scheduled for the beginning of August it is likely that Edward was looking now, as in 1277, for an early completion of the operations in Perfeddwlad in anticipation of a coordinated assault on Gwynedd Uwch Conwy once the great army had assembled. Our knowledge of the course of events in Perfeddwlad is very slight and the main engagement of which there is record in this period occurred, not in the northern sector, but in Deheubarth where Welsh forces inflicted a reverse upon their opponents noticed by several English

---

[38] *CWR*, 223 (2 June); *CAC*, 108; for Llywelyn's death, below, n. 188. The advance along the Dee valley was made by Grey, who also took Ellesmere, not Ewloe as stated by Morris, *WW*, 161 from E101/4/1. Ewloe does appear to have been a focus of resistance in this war any more than in 1277.

[39] *CWR*, 226 (15 June); they were granted to John de Warenne, earl of Surrey, in October; below, p. 529.

[40] The sons appear to have died between the outbreak of war in 1282 and the autumn, for on 7 October John de Warenne was granted the land of Maelor (Bromfield) said to have been held by the named sons of Madog ap Gruffudd at the beginning of the war (*CWR*, 240). T. Pennant, *Tours in Wales* (London, 1784), i, 217, states that the sons of Madog were drowned in the Dee at Holt bridge by Warenne and Roger Mortimer the younger, their guardians, citing a MS communicated by the Revd Mr Price, Keeper of the Bodleian Library. Cf. J. Y. W. Lloyd, *History of the Princes, the Lords Marchers and the Ancient Nobility of Powys Fadog* (London, 1881–7), i, 178, the statement there said to be drawn from the continuation of the Welsh chronicle, but there is no supporting testimony in the Peniarth MS 20 text of *BT*. D. Powel, *Historie of Cambria* (1584), 212–13, refers to the 'destruction' of the two princes, whose guardians, Warenne and Mortimer, 'so garded their wardes with so small regard, that they neuer returned to their possessions. And shortlie after the said guardians did obtaine the same lands to themselves by charters of the king.'

[41] Owain ap Gruffudd, who held Cynllaith, was 'in the king's faith' on 15 June but later described as a rebel (*CWR*, 226, 266, 271–2; *CCR, 1279–88*, 229, 231; J. E. Lloyd, *Owen Glendower* (Oxford, 1931), 9–10).

chroniclers. An army under Gloucester's command was engaged in Ystrad Tywi early in June, probably deployed in two divisions which advanced from Carmarthen and Brecon.[42] With a garrison maintaining a secure hold on Dinefwr the army's immediate tasks were the recovery of Llandovery and Carreg Cennen and these were successfully completed. But on 16 June part of Gloucester's army came under vigorous attack in the neighbourhood of Llandeilo Fawr. The chroniclers suggest that the force attacked was returning from a plundering raid, but the circumstances are far from clear. Nor is the extent of the reverse easy to assess.[43] Five knights were among the fatal casualties, however, and they included William de Valence, son of the lord of Pembroke, who was buried at the Franciscan friary of Carmarthen.[44] The reverse, which occurred on the day that English forces took possession of Caergwrle, was certainly sufficiently serious to terminate Gloucester's command. The earl, so anxious at the outset of the campaign to be entrusted with the leadership of royal forces in the area, could no longer maintain his position and command was given to William de Valence, lord of Pembroke, with Robert Tibetot, the king's justice in west Wales, also given a specific military role alongside him.[45] The reverse may not have been on a scale comparable with the disaster at Cymerau exactly twenty-five years earlier, but it prompted the king's council into a similar revision of their strategy. Although progress was at last being made in north-east Wales, it was acknowledged that it was not advisable to concentrate on that area to the extent that had been intended. Edward was dealing with a determined and elusive enemy, and there was no knowing where the next blow would fall. The princes' forces had demonstrated, not least to themselves, their capability to inflict a reverse upon their adversaries and their success could well be repeated elsewhere. Some forces originally intended for Rhuddlan were now directed to Montgomery, Oswestry and Builth, and the contingents available to the king's commanders in south-west Wales were increased. Roger Mortimer and those, such as Roger Springhose, associated with him in the defence of the march from Oswestry to Builth, would need the means of dealing with unpredictable challenges, made perhaps with considerable force, and the king had to rely on the resourcefulness of his commanders in the area.[46] The elderly Mortimer maintained garrisons at his own strongholds at Radnor, Cefnllys,

---

[42] C47/2/4. Operations in south-west Wales are described in R. F. Walker, 'William de Valence and the army of west Wales, 1282–1283', *WHR*, 18 (1996–7), 407–29.

[43] *AC*, 106; Trevet, *Annales*, 304; *AnnDunst*, 292; *AnnOsney*, 288–9; Rishanger, *Chronica*, 100. Morris, *WW*, 166, suggests that the force was on its way back to Dinefwr from Carreg Cennen.

[44] His death is noticed by the chroniclers; for his burial and tomb, T. James, 'Excavations at Carmarthen Greyfriars 1983–90', *Medieval Archaeology*, 41 (1997).

[45] *CWR*, 229–30 (6 July). Tibetot was to take command if Valence did not wish to do so.

[46] *CWR*, 222, 253–5.

Dinbod and Dolforwyn but, with much wider responsibilities to bear, he had to display once more the qualities which Edward had commended when, in his first response to the new crisis, he paid tribute to his proven loyalty and judgement.[47] More generally, it was for the marchers, in implementing royal command or exercising authority in their own lordships, to judge when they needed to exert force and when it was prudent to admit Welsh communities into the king's peace.[48] If, after the violence of the initial uprisings in Wales, there had been something of a remission, by the middle of June conflict was being waged in earnest in several theatres. In some areas, notably in Powys Fadog, the English commanders could be credited with important advances, but they knew that everywhere they remained exposed to the possibility that they would see continuing recrudescence of conflict in areas seemingly under their control. In Deheubarth effective royal control was still to be imposed.

Precisely when Llywelyn ap Gruffudd committed himself to the rebellion is, as we have seen, a matter that may never be resolved with certainty, but, with the account rolls of the king's army providing by the summer of 1282 a fuller record than before, it is clear that the field commanders came to recognize Llywelyn as their adversary. On occasion his presence is mentioned at unexpected places: a marcher lord recalled his being near Crughywel, a royal clerk explained the considerable expense incurred in providing soldiers to guard money being taken to Carmarthen by the fact that Llywelyn was with his army in the vicinity of Neath and Swansea.[49] Particularly relevant, as these are dated references, are the notes of payments made at Carmarthen and Cardigan early in August to soldiers ordered to attack Llywelyn (*ad occurrendum Lewelinum*).[50] These occur at the time of a new offensive launched by Valence and Tibetot when English forces had been regrouped and reinforced after their reverse at Llandeilo Fawr. It is possible that Llywelyn had hastened south after that triumph, just as he had done after Cymerau in 1257, to exercise his influence at what was likely to be a time of greatly heightened confrontation. But there is no certainty that Llywelyn intervened in south-west Wales then nor at any time during the war, and reports of his presence may represent no more than rumours nourished in apprehension. The English chroniclers' statements, which might seem to suggest his intervention at that stage, are not substantiated in the military accounts, nor do they suggest that

---

[47] For Mortimer's concern for his own strongholds, with particular care for Dolforwyn, SC6/1209/1; E372/128 (Stafford); Edward's letter is in *CWR*, 212.

[48] E.g. *CWR*, 221–2, 228, 232–3, 235.

[49] *CAC*, 116–17; C47/2/4: four *satellites* with four barded horses and 400 infantry guarded the money 'quia Lewelinus erat tunc temporis in exercitu suo ex alia parte aque'.

[50] C47/2/4.

the Welsh success was followed by further pressure against their adversaries.[51] For their part the king's forces in Deheubarth were to be strengthened. Despite an earlier summons to Rhuddlan, the feudal tenants already serving were to remain there and were to be augmented by forces from the counties of south-west England now ordered to Carmarthen so as to be engaged, like those at Rhuddlan, on 2 August, the morrow of St Peter's.[52] But well before that date substantial forces were raised in the lordships of south Wales. They included a contingent from Abergavenny but the greater part was drawn from the lordships which encircled Deheubarth, more particularly Gower, Cydweli, Emlyn and Cemais.[53] Throughout July those of Valence's forces which were based at Cardigan may have fulfilled a largely defensive role, with occasional forays such as that which took an infantry force into the lands of Gruffudd ap Maredudd and Cynan ap Maredudd. Early in August, however, Valence's main army set out from Carmarthen and made for Ystrad Tywi. In 1277 Payn de Chaworth had made a similar advance into Cantref Mawr and had been able to link up with forces brought into Cantref Bychan from Brecon by Henry de Bray and John Giffard. Now, in precisely the same way, Valence's advance was co-ordinated with the efforts of Giffard, again in all probability operating from bases in Builth and Brecon, to establish himself in the commotes of Hirfryn and Perfedd.[54] The objectives of the royal forces in Ystrad Tywi in 1282, first under Gloucester and then Valence, were closely similar to those of the earlier conflict, and the central figure in their calculations was again the lord of Dryslwyn.

Valence's advance was said to be intended 'to attack Llywelyn', but its main objective in Cantref Mawr was to provide relief and support for Rhys ap Maredudd. On 28 July, a few days before the army set out, Rhys was formally granted the lands of his kinsmen who had gone to war, Edward explicitly acknowledging that he alone among the princes of Deheubarth had remained faithful to him.[55] Rhys Wyndod, whose attacks on the royal strongholds in Ystrad Tywi had been a feature of the initial movements in Holy Week, appears to have held his own in his commotes. But now, in anticipation of an early advance into the area, Malláen and Caeo were conferred on Rhys ap

---

[51] Statements in Trivet, *Annales*, 304; Rishanger, *Chronica*, 100; *AnnOsney*, 286, were taken by Morris, *WW*, 166, to indicate Llywelyn's presence immediately after the English reverse at Llandeilo Fawr, but the sequence of the chroniclers' statements (conflict at Llandeilo, Llywelyn's presence, and then his death) does not necessarily indicate that one event followed another in quick succession.

[52] *CWR*, 253–4; *ParlWrits*, i, 227 (2 July); Morris, *WW*, 166–8.

[53] C47/2/4, with precise figures for each contingent; Morris, *WW*, 168–9; R. F. Walker, 'William de Valence', 412–14.

[54] Giffard's movements are not recorded, but he was empowered 16 August to receive the men of Hirfryn and Perfedd into the king's peace; Llandovery had first been committed to him, possibly in anticipation of its recovery, on 14 April (*CWR*, 213–14, 222, 235).

[55] *LW*, 165–6; *CWR*, 233–4, 236–7.

Maredudd. At the same time Gwynionydd and Mabwynion in Ceredigion, lands which belonged to Gruffudd ap Maredudd and Cynan ap Maredudd, were also granted to Rhys. He thus secured four commotes in a grant which went some way towards requiting the territorial ambitions which he had inherited from his father, Maredudd ap Rhys Gryg, ambitions which he had himself pursued with some determination during the last war. He may have been discomforted by several decisions made by Edward, or in his name, in 1277 and afterwards, and we cannot tell whether his loyalty was tested in the spring of 1282.[56] Nor can we do more than wonder whether he was perturbed anew by the determined manner in which John Giffard now secured his hold on those commotes of Hirfryn and Perfedd which his father had sought from Henry III, lands he would need to secure, along with Is Cennen, before he could truly be lord of Ystrad Tywi. He won rather less than he would have wished but his adherence to the king was reciprocated with a tangible and unconditional expression of the king's favour. Edward was evidently persuaded that a concession of this nature, and the provision of adequate military protection for Rhys, was essential to the success of his endeavours in Ystrad Tywi. Llywelyn ap Gruffudd's efforts there, if he had intervened in the province at this stage, would have been dictated by the need, if Rhys could not be persuaded to adhere to the princes, to put him under the greatest possible duress. By the middle of August Valence's forces, largely consisting of soldiers drawn from Gower and Cydweli, had made their way through Cantref Mawr to Dinefwr and Llangadog, their progress evidently facilitated by good work on the part of Rhys ap Meredudd's men who were duly rewarded.[57] It is clear that, quite apart from the fact that the king's forces were largely drawn from the Welsh communities of the marcher lordships on the fringes of Deheubarth, loyalties within Ystrad Tywi itself were divided.[58] Communities might transfer their allegiance from the one side to the other, yet rifts were created which were not to be easily repaired. After exercising dominion over a large part of Ystrad Tywi for five years Rhys ap Maredudd himself was to rise in rebellion, giving vent to a frustration not dissimilar to that which had driven his kinsmen to war in 1282.[59] He was then to reap the fruits of the accumulated animosities of two divisive conflicts, as men of some consequence in Ystrad Tywi, who had been steadfast in their support of their

---

[56] Above, pp. 420–1, 491.

[57] At Llangadog, 17 August, Valence made a gift to Rhys's foot-soldiers for their commendable service on that day; Rhys was given £10 the next day (C47/2/4). Rhys, the son of Isabella Marshal, was a second cousin of Valence's wife Joan (R. F. Walker, 'William de Valence', 415–16, 428).

[58] E.g. men of Is Cennen came to the king's peace and were promptly taken into royal pay (C47/2/4).

[59] J. B. Smith, 'The origins of the revolt of Rhys ap Maredudd', *B*, 21 (1964–6), 151–63; R. A. Griffiths, *Conquerors and Conquered in Medieval Wales* (Stroud, 1994), 67–83.

princes in 1272 and 1282, gave no heed to his call upon their loyalty in his hour of singular desperation. Madog ab Arawdr was one who had been a constant adherent of the princes, and named as a person associated with Rhys Wyndod in the attacks on Carreg Cennen and Llandovery, but one who was to stand aside in 1287. His sons were among those who eventually pursued Rhys ap Maredudd to his last refuge in Malláen.[60] For the present Rhys found satisfaction in an explicit recognition of the king's gratitude for his constancy and Valence's acknowledgement of his aid in the field. He got, too, the protection he needed. Valence's forces then turned westward, moving through Rhys's dominions in Cantref Mawr, and entered Ceredigion. The forces based at Cardigan had now secured the southern commotes of Gwynionydd and Mabwynion. With his southern flank made safe, Valence was able to move northwards to Llanbadarn Fawr where he arrived at the beginning of September.[61] Over a period of four weeks the power of the princes in Ystrad Tywi had been shattered.

Even then, though the effect of the advance from Dinefwr to Llanbadarn Fawr was never undone, the king's commanders could by no means be sure that resistance had been finally extinguished. The situation in Ceredigion, in particular, remained uncertain for some time. Intelligence reports during September forced Valence and Tibetot to take a substantial contingent from Cardigan to the commote of Anhuniog to attack the castle of Gruffudd ap Maredudd at Trefilan.[62] The earlier operations had evidently not permanently dislodged Gruffudd and his brother Cynan ap Maredudd, but Gwynionydd and Mabwynion had by now been granted to Rhys ap Maredudd, and his influence there, and their proximity to the royal stronghold at Cardigan, ensured that these commotes were finally ceded. In the valley of the Aeron, on the other hand, the brothers were still capable of resistance and, though they escaped from their encounter with the king's forces only with some difficulty, they were still able to cause some discomfiture to their opponents. Resistance would be raised again in Ceredigion, for before the end of 1282 and again early in the new year Valence would be forced to take further action in the area. But Cynan and Gruffudd, like Rhys Wyndod, never again secured effective control over their patrimonies. Llywelyn ap Gruffudd's adherents in Deheubarth had not succeeded in stemming the advance of their opponents' forces. Despite the dissimilarities between the conditions in which the two wars were fought,

---

[60] For Madog ab Arawdr's association with Rhys Wyndod in the attacks on the castles, *CAC*, 44; J. B. Smith, 'Rhys ap Maredudd', 160–1.

[61] C47/2/4; payments are recorded at Dinefwr, Llangadog, Lampeter, Tregaron (Caron), Lledrod, Llanrhystud and, on 2 September, Llanbadarn Fawr.

[62] *CAC*, 131–2; the editor suggests a date in late August–early September; C47/2/4 shows that Trefilan was attacked on 20 September, and payments for loss of horses in Dyffryn Aeron (*LW*, 192) point to an engagement at this time.

Cilmeri

events in Deheubarth in 1282 had taken a course which, in political as well as military terms, closely paralleled the process by which Welsh power had been undermined five years before. The prince could do no more than provide a refuge for the disinherited in Gwynedd, a land which was itself soon to be subject to very considerable military pressure. Edward would still need to disperse his forces, to a greater degree than he would wish, so as to contain further disturbances which might occur anywhere in the land of the princes or even in the march. But the advances first into Powys Fadog and then into Deheubarth enabled him to concentrate his mind and his main resources on the final resolution of the conflict in Snowdonia.

Throughout the summer of 1282 preparations for the decisive encounter proceeded and were concentrated on two main objectives. The first was the capture of Anglesey. The campaign was launched by an amphibious assault in the second half of July and by the middle of the next month at the latest the island was garrisoned by a substantial force under the command of Luke de Tany. Llywelyn ap Gruffudd found that Llan-faes, where his wife had so recently been laid to rest, was now the centre of an extensive encampment which became the base for military operations on the island.[63] As in 1277 the invaders came to Anglesey in time to deprive the tillers of the soil of the benefit of their harvest and, once more, the reapers followed the advancing soldiers. This time, however, the occupation of Anglesey had a further purpose. It emerges at an early stage in the preparations for the campaign that plans were laid for the construction of a bridge of boats which would enable the king's forces to cross the Menai Straits and establish a bridgehead on the mainland.[64] The advantages of a construction of this kind were commended by Vegetius, for a bridge made of boats lashed together had, for a brief while, the solidity of a bridge of stone.[65] And it is possible, as has been suggested already, that

---

[63] *CWR*, 235; for Llan-faes as a centre for operations below, n. 114. Complete accounts of the operations in Anglesey have not survived, but Ralph de Broughton answered for expenditure of £3,540, with a further £590 for the protection of ships, not including the wages of the sailors of the Cinque Ports (E101/3/30).

[64] Naval forces were alerted on 10 April for service on 24 June (*CWR*, 247). Sailors of the Cinque Ports had completed their fifteen days' unpaid service when they came into royal pay for the period 25 July–15 September, and a force of crossbowmen serving in the ships was paid 14–23 July; two royal galleys were deployed 23 July–15 September (E101/3/26; E101/3/30; *CWR*, 235–47). Operations were probably completed by 18 August (*CWR*, 235). For the bridge, *HKW*, i, 354–7, incorporating Edward's letter, *CAC*, 109, but suggesting a date before 28 May; on the site, below pp. 538–42.

[65] *Vegetius*, Lib. III, 7, recommends a bridge of boats hollowed out of one piece of timber and lashed together: 'paulo latiores scafulas ex singulis trabibus excauatas, pro genere ligni et subtilitate leuissimas, carpentis secum portet exercitus tabulatis pariter et clauis ferreis praeparatis'.

Cilmeri

Edward had realized in 1277 that an assault on the mainland from Anglesey would need to be an essential part of any plan for the conquest of Gwynedd Uwch Conwy. Whatever the inspiration may have been, it was certainly a key feature of Edward's operational plan in Wales in 1282–3 and it would be a stratagem to which Edward would have recourse again during his Scottish campaigns.[66] Discussions with the men of the Cinque Ports summoned to court as early as April 1282 may have covered, not only the provision of ships, but the provision of the flat-bottomed boats to which records subsequently refer. Shortly afterwards orders were given that forty boats be brought to Chester, but, in view of the difficulty of transporting boats of the required size, the king was advised to summon men from the Cinque Ports to build them at Chester.[67] Stephen of Pencester was required to find the carpenters with the necessary skills and get them to Chester by 23 June. Pontoons were then built to be linked together to form a deck over which a body of troops and horsemen could cross. The constructions were then taken to Rhuddlan and on to Anglesey. There was more work to be done and the men of the Cinque Ports in Tany's service were ordered 'to make a bridge there'. It is likely that by late September, or shortly afterwards, the carpenters had done their work and the bridge was completed.[68] Tany, and the several senior officers with him, awaited their orders for the assault upon the mainland. The conception and the building of the bridge of boats speaks, more eloquently than any verbal declaration of intent, of Edward's resolve to penetrate the very heart of Gwynedd.

It was surely an essential part of the king's strategy that no assault should be made from Anglesey until the forces on the mainland were in a position to force the Conwy. That was the second main objective. It was preferable to do so, not at the estuary, but well upstream and this made it essential that the army penetrate and secure the Four Cantreds completely before any co-ordinated attack on Gwynedd Uwch Conwy was launched. The chronology of the princes' ceding of Perfeddwlad is not easy to establish.[69] Apart from the important advance along the Dee into Powys Fadog in June, already noticed, the efforts of the forces concentrated on the Chester front appear to have been

---

[66] Guisborough, *Chronicle*, 219: 'super naves multas adinuicem coniunctas compositis lignis et coniunctis tabulis super ipsos naves ita quod in fronte vna transire possent lx armati' (the capacity of the bridge probably exaggerated); *BS*, 258–9, a bridge built 'with boats' (*o ysgraffav*). For the bridge over the Forth, Barrow, *Bruce*, 178; *HKW*, i, 416–17.

[67] *CAC*, 109.

[68] *CWR*, 235 (18 August); *HKW*, i, 354–7; E101/3/26, an account of payment to soldiers and sailors in Anglesey. Taylor, 'Master Bertram', 300, n. 58, suggests (from E101/3/31) that Bertram may have been the engineer in charge of the construction.

[69] The English army's movements and the chronology may be deduced from the accounts. Even so, direction and dates of cavalry and infantry movements are difficult to establish, the accounts providing more on movement of supplies and equipment than on troop advances. Dates are normally those on which payments are authorized, not those on which expenditure was incurred.

directed to the consolidation of the areas about the strongholds of Flint, Rhuddlan and Caergwrle and on securing lines of communication. Major movements beyond these secure but confined areas may have been delayed until the arrival of the main army at Chester, but during August the Welsh forces defending Dyffryn Clwyd faced the advance of the feudal host which, with over 10,500 infantry engaged and perhaps as many as 450 cavalry, made significant progress. From Rhuddlan the army moved along the Clwyd through Llandyrnog to Rhuthun by 28 August.[70] There they were met by forces brought along a more southerly approach by Reginald de Grey and, with a further advance to Derwen Llanerch and Pentrefoelas, Dyffryn Clwyd was secured for the crown.[71] Penetration beyond these areas, and particularly into Penllyn, may have been considerably delayed. Moreover, despite the great strength of the forces deployed during the summer, no appreciable progress appears to have been made for some time in Rhufoniog. By the middle of September, however, an advance was made into Rhos Is Dulas and a base established at Llangernyw. It is likely that it was from Llangernyw, taking a westerly approach to Rhufoniog, that a new offensive was launched some time later. This was possibly accompanied by another advance from the southern parts of Dyffryn Clwyd and the two movements forced a Welsh withdrawal from the *cantref*.[72] Rhufoniog would now become the base for further advances through Rhos Uwch Dulas to the Conwy in the neighbourhood of Llanrwst and Betws.[73] Somewhat surprising, in view of the relatively early advance along the Clwyd, is the late date for which there is firm evidence for the taking of Denbigh, where Henry de Lacy, earl of Lincoln, would establish the centre of a lordship formed out of five commotes of the *cantrefi* of Rhos and Rhufoniog: Is Dulas, Uwch Dulas, Is Aled, Uwch Aled and Ceinmeirch. Specific references to operations at Denbigh are difficult to establish before mid-October, and the surge of activity there from then onwards suggests very strongly that the king's forces had not reached the locality very much earlier.[74] There is much to suggest that Denbigh was

---

[70] E101/3/29; E101/3/30; E101/4/1, figures calculated by Dr Walker.

[71] *CWR*, 237–8 (Rhuthun, 8 September; Derwen Llannerch ('Addernewyn'), 12 September). Edward came to Derwen Llannerch again in the war of 1294–5, when it appears to have been a base for operations in Penllyn (R. F. Walker in *Book of Prests of the King's Wardrobe for 1294–5*, ed. E. B. Fryde (Oxford, 1962), xxx, 58 *et passim*.

[72] E101/3/30; Morris, *WW*, 178. Letters dated Llangernyw from 18 September, Denbigh from 22 October (*CWR*, 239, 243). Pentrefoelas was reached in August but the area may not have been held until later.

[73] E101/359/9 reveals activity in the Llanrwst and Betws area only from January 1283. Accounts suggest little military movement in November and the first twenty days of December; for subsequent intense activity, below, p. 573 *et seq*.

[74] E101/3/29 has evidence of activity at Denbigh from 21 October; cf. *HKW*, i, 333–4. Edward was at Denbigh by 23 October (*CWR*, 243).

Dafydd ap Gruffudd's main strongpoint in his defence of the land east of the Conwy, and the works promptly initiated there on the king's behalf may have been taken on a site already fortified by the prince.[75] The dating of royal documents first at Llangernyw and then at Denbigh suggests that English control over Rhos and Rhufoniog was reasonably secure by mid-October, but not much earlier, and tracts of the moorland interior may still have been only incompletely controlled.

Progress had been slow, marked in the account rolls by the details of the trundling of siege-engines and the carrying of supplies for the soldiers whose positions were probably slightly further forward than the places named.[76] How costly the campaign had been in casualties is impossible to tell, though the king acknowledged that the military cemetery at Rhuddlan was full to capacity.[77] Conflict upon what was in some areas a difficult terrain, with determined opponents who knew that they were defending the threshold of their main citadel, may well have been fierce. Of the extent of the losses on the Welsh side we have no evidence whatsoever nor can we detect where the main lines of defence were drawn. The conflict for Perfeddwlad had already been long, and possibly costly in casualties on both sides, and it was not yet over. Even so, for the leading English commanders, it was time to share the spoils. Important decisions were now made. John de Warenne, earl of Surrey, was granted Maelor and Iâl; Lacy was given Rhos and Rhufoniog, and Grey received Dyffryn Clwyd.[78] The final stage in the English advance could now be launched and spies were sent into Snowdonia to watch the movements of Llywelyn and Dafydd. The forces in Anglesey were still awaiting the order to advance, but the recent return of Luke de Tany to the island, accompanied by Roger Clifford the younger, William Audley and other knights, was perhaps an indication that preparations for the combined advance upon Gwynedd Uwch Conwy were nearing completion, and that the launch of the final assault was imminent.[79] Resistance elsewhere in Wales appeared to be quelled and Llywelyn and Dafydd now faced the full force of the resources gathered by the king for their defeat in the land which formed the core of their

---

[75] *HKW*, i, 333; for Denbigh under the princes above, pp. 225–6.

[76] E.g. the siege-engines 'Pyceyns' and 'Howans' were taken from Chester to Rhuthun and thence to Derwen Llannerch 22–3 August; there were other engines named 'Hath' and 'Tribul' (E101/359/9). For named engines in Edward's Scottish campaigns, notably the siege of Stirling, e.g. *Documents Illustrative of the History of Scotland, 1286–1306*, ed. J. Stevenson (Edinburgh, 1870), ii, no. 4656. The precise object of the deployment of siege-engines at locations in Perfeddwlad where no major fortifications are known to have stood is puzzling.

[77] *CCW*, i, 7; *Councils*, i, 540 (Denbigh, 27 October).

[78] *CWR*, 240–1, 243: to Warenne at Rhuddlan, 7 October; to Lacy at Rhuddlan, 16 October; to Grey at Denbigh, 23 October.

[79] E101/3/29 (nine spies sent into Snowdonia 'ad Lewelinum et David fratrem suum insidiandum'); E101/4/1.

patrimony. Then, at Denbigh on 25 October, with the magnates of the realm gathered about him, Edward made a decision which meant that the final thrust had to be delayed a little longer.

It is not difficult to believe that, with autumn drawing to a close and fearful of the prospect of a winter in Snowdonia, Edward found it difficult to countenance John Pecham's wish to intercede in his conflict with Llywelyn.[80] The archbishop certainly maintained that it was contrary to the king's wishes that he intervened in Wales and, apart from the military and financial problems raised by a further delay in making an advance into Gwynedd Uwch Conwy, the king may have harboured grave doubts about the advantages of the enterprise. It is unlikely that Edward was greatly troubled that Pecham might compromise his position, for the archbishop's previous pronouncements did nothing to suggest that he would be sympathetic to the prince in his present predicament. Edward may indeed have suspected that the archbishop's earlier tirades would make his task extremely difficult. Spiritual pastor pledged to the ideals of St Francis though he might be, his forceful condemnations of the morals of the Welsh people placed him securely among those who voiced the attitudes cultivated among erudite members of a powerful nation when they confronted a society which, in their estimation, held values and followed a code of behaviour distinctly different from their own.[81] Pecham was by no means alone in expressing his views, but his strictures carried the authority of his position as provincial and, among those he addressed, they inevitably aroused the anxieties bound up with the historical relationship between Canterbury and the English crown.[82] Even as he travelled to Wales he dwelt on the transgressions of its people, and throughout his mission he conveys an underlying conviction that he was dealing with a rebellious nation in dire need of correction. Setting out to bring the Welsh back to the unity of the catholic church, he came close to his subsequent depiction of the conquest of Wales as a political and spiritual crusade.[83]

[80] For Pecham's mission, D. L. Douie, *Archbishop Pecham* (Oxford, 1952), 236–405, 247–51.

[81] The tract in Bern Burgerbibliothek Cod. 69 (above, p. 467, n. 69), though not a product of the time of the negotiations with Llywelyn, is an important text in this connection and contributes to an appreciation of the mental attitudes examined in W. R. Jones, 'The image of the barbarian in medieval Europe', *Comparative Studies in Society and History*, 13 (1971), 376–407; idem, 'England against the Celtic Fringe', *Journal of World History*, 13 (1971), 155–71; Bartlett, *Gerald of Wales*, 158–77.

[82] Pecham's later comments on the barbarous and untamed Welsh and their dire need of reform are in *RPeck*, iii, 776–8, 991–2; for his observations on Welsh law, above, pp. 480–1.

[83] He told Anian of St Asaph that the action of the Welsh in going to war incurred their excommunication, and informed Burnell that he was going to Wales for the spiritual good of its people 'eosque ad unitatem revocare catholicam' (*RPeck*, ii, 422–3, 426).

Cilmeri

Even so, it would be folly to discount his intervention or to question the earnestness with which he sought to bring the hostilities to an end, nor can we doubt that he was confronted with deep animosity between king and prince. It is the evidence relating to Pecham's initiative which provides the fullest indication of that enmity, for there is no record whatsoever of any exchanges between Edward and Llywelyn after the outbreak of war. We have nothing to compare with the arguments of the period leading up to the previous war in the successive exchanges of letters and the statements made to the papal court. Only at this late stage does Llywelyn emerge as the person whom Edward recognized as the leader of the rebellion. It is not inconceivable that Edward's reluctance to allow Pecham to interfere was in part due to his fear, in which he may have been justified, that the prelate's discussions would serve to give the rebellion a political dimension that he would wish to deny to it. The intervention was liable, in particular, to afford Llywelyn ap Gruffudd a position of centrality of which he had been divested by the king's efforts in the war of 1277, a position which the prince could re-establish, in the king's estimation, only by unjustified force. But if the archbishop was sincere in seeking out the issues on which reason could be brought to bear, Llywelyn, too, is likely to have been earnest in his hope that, once presented with a statement of his viewpoint, Pecham would be able to bring some influence to bear upon the king. Prince and archbishop may each have been anxious to secure a sensible dialogue.

Pecham initiated the exchanges before he met the king in Wales, for he had already sent as an emissary to the prince his distinguished fellow Franciscan moralist and theologian John of Wales.[84] Llywelyn thereby received a compatriot whose scholarly writings included a discourse on the qualities of a prince, in the course of which he had discussed the circumstances in which a prince could be justified in waging war and the manner in which a war should be waged.[85] John of Wales could certainly have engaged the prince in purposeful discussion on his own account, but he took with him a document listing seventeen articles which the archbishop wished to be considered.[86]

---

[84] Pecham's safe-conduct was given to John of Wales, 21 October, that of Edward, noting that the king had not hitherto granted any safe-conduct to anyone to go to Llywelyn, three days later (*RPeck*, ii, 421–2; *CCW*, i, 7). For the chronology of Pecham's discussions with Edward and Llywelyn, below, n. 100.

[85] J. Swanson, *John of Wales: A Study of the Work and Ideas of a Thirteenth-Century Friar* (Cambridge, 1989), examines the 'Breviloquium de Virtutibus Antiquorum Principum et Philosophorum' and the 'Communiloquium', each of which gives prominence to a discussion of the qualities of a prince. See also B. Smalley, *English Friars and Antiquity in the Early Fourteenth Century* (Oxford, 1960), 51–5; W. A. Pantin, 'John of Wales and medieval humanism', in J. A. Watt (ed.), *Medieval Studies presented to Aubrey Gwynn, S.J.* (Dublin, 1961), 297–319; *DWB*, 439. For the virtues of *prudentia* and *justitia*, above, p. 479.

[86] *RPeck*, ii, 435–7; another text in *RegPontissara*, ii. 636–8. The headings are phrased differently, but each text indicates that the document contains the articles conveyed to the Welsh on the archbishop's behalf.

Insisting that he undertook his mission against the king's will and at the risk of incurring his grave displeasure, he begged the Welsh, by the blood of Christ, to come to unity with the English people and to the king's peace. He urged them to respond positively and swiftly, for there was no one else to plead their cause and if they rejected his efforts he would be bound to report their obstinacy to the papal court. England enjoyed the special protection of the apostolic see, more so than other kingdoms, and the papal court would not tolerate anything which would be damaging to the state (*status*) of the kingdom of England.[87] Besides, royal power increased day by day and its ultimate triumph was inevitable. Pecham stressed his deep Christian concern, but he was firm in his condemnation of the action taken by those who opposed the king. The arguments now uppermost in his mind carried a very different emphasis from those which he had broached in the distinctly Franciscan propositions of his theoretical writings on the relationship of secular and ecclesiastical powers, perceptions which had informed his very recent arguments with Edward I.[88] Whereas he had only the previous year stressed the subordination of the secular power to the spiritual, in the present contingency he placed the whole weight of his argument upon the rightful and exalted secular authority to which the Welsh should show obedience. In terms hardly appropriate at the initiation of a sensitive mediation he dwelt on the cruel excesses of the Welsh, condemned them for violating the sanctity of the most holy time of the Christian year with treacherous rebellion, and held that they were in some respects worse than Saracens.[89] Whereas Saracens ransomed prisoners the Welsh disposed of them, sometimes even after taking ransoms. If they felt that their laws were discounted or if treaties had not been respected, they should provide him with the detail, and indicate how they would wish to see a durable concord established. But their sedition called for unqualified repentance, and if they continued to resist they would incur severe secular and ecclesiastical censure.

Llywelyn's initial response to the document transmitted to him was both courteous and discreet, though with a touch of irony.[90] He graciously acknowledged Pecham's labours on behalf of himself and his nation (*natio*),

---

[87] *RPeck,* ii, 436: 'quod regnum Anglie est sub speciali protectione sedis apostolice et quod Romana curia plus inter regna cetera diligere consuevit . . . quod eadem curia nullomodo volet statum regni Anglie vacillare, quod sibi specialibus obsequiis est devotum'.

[88] J. Coleman, 'The Dominican political theory of John of Paris in its context', in D. Wood (ed.), *The Church and Sovereignty c.590–1918* (Studies in Church History, 9, London, 1991), 191–202. His position was set out with characteristic force in a letter to Edward in November 1281 in which an appeal to history included reference to the pristine liberties of the British church ('sicut patet de parte illius ecclesie quae hactenus mansit in partibus Wallie, quae contra libertates huiusmodi non dedicit conculari', *RPeck,* i, 239–44).

[89] *RPeck*, ii, 436.

[90] Ibid., 437–40; *RegPontissara,* ii, 638–40.

the more so since the archbishop was acting contrary to the king's wishes. In the first part of his reply he gave a full and dignified statement of the broad issues. He declared his readiness to come to the king's peace, provided that the king would be pledged to a real and proper peace with the prince and his men. The king had no need to wage war against them, for they were ready to serve him if their rights and laws were guaranteed. The realm of England might be specially beloved by the papal court, but the pope was yet to learn of the violation of treaties and the atrocities committed by the English. Churches had been wasted and burned and priests, and even women with children at their breasts and in the womb, had been slaughtered. Details of sacrilege and crimes too horrible to be envisaged even among heathens could be recounted, and these matters would be set out in the documents which, at the archbishop's invitation, they would prepare for him. Llywelyn insisted that he knew nothing of the intention of those who went to war, and he expressed his regret that conflict had begun at that holy time, but it had been a clear choice between war and servitude. With regard to those things which were done against God they would, as true Christians, repent. Nor did they wish to prolong the war but, if they were to withstand disinheritance and death, they had to defend themselves to the best of their ability. Touching on the great issues of the morality of war, the prince held that they were fighting for their rights and the freedom of their territory.[91] They had to defend themselves against subjection to slavery, for they were treated as though they were Saracens or Jews. They endured the excesses of royal officers and were unable to secure redress for mounting oppression. The prince recommended that the wrongs which had been endured should be put right before greater military might be summoned and the priesthood moved against them. And he urged the archbishop not to believe all that was said in defamation of their opponents by those who were the real oppressors, and to examine the evidence for himself. Llywelyn may not have been present at the outbreak of war, but he gave the archbishop no reason to believe that he did not condone the action of those who had begun the war.

In the second part of his reply he provided a more specific statement of the matters which troubled him and those on which he felt injustice had been done to others. These were, as we have seen, partly matters on which Edward had acted contrary to the treaty of Aberconwy: the denial of Welsh law in the Arwystli case; the intrusion of royal justice into Edeirnion and even into Anglesey; the injustice to Rhys Fychan ap Rhys ap Maelgwn. They were partly matters on which Edward, contrary to his undertaking, had gone further than the treaty allowed: the levying of queen's gold, and the exaction of a promise that the prince would not harbour, not only outlaws, but his

---

[91] For Edward's invocation of the notion of a just war, above, n. 30.

faithful men.[92] Citing the treaty again, but concerned with matters which affected others than himself, he drew Pecham's attention to the acute problems which had arisen in Perfeddwlad. The treaty had laid down that men of that area should hold their lands as they had been held before the war and that they should be ensured of their laws and customs, but Reginald de Grey had acted in a manner contrary to the terms of the agreement.[93] Again, contrary to what had been agreed, Grey, promptly upon his appointment, had prosecuted men of the Four Cantreds for wrongs done before the war.[94] Llywelyn's statement reaffirms the testimony already considered which suggests very strongly that much of the difficulty in the area where conflict erupted was due to Grey's stern administration in the months immediately preceding the resort to arms. The grievances which he recited, particularly those which concerned himself, are difficult to evaluate and it has been suggested that, where verification is possible by reference to documents from the period before the war, his complaints cannot always be substantiated.[95] They remain important, even so, as an indication of what Llywelyn chose to contribute to that sense of communal grievance which had led, not to a short-lived insurrection, but to a sustained conflict which, more than any other in the previous history of medieval Wales, merits the name of a war of independence. They were, rightly or wrongly, the specific grievances which were sublimated in the broader arguments propounded both in anticipation of Pecham's arrival and after his final withdrawal.

Llywelyn's submissions were part of that substantial body of evidence, already considered in dealing with the outbreak of war, which were set out in rolls for transmission to the archbishop in explanation of the concerted rebellion: the undermining of native law and the disregard of established customs, the avarice and capriciousness of those in authority, the iniquitous denial of inherent rights. The *gravamina* constituted a justification of insurrection. But Pecham was sufficiently impressed by the evidence to recommend to Edward, at the first of two meetings, that the complaints be examined and that wrongs be corrected where that was appropriate.[96] Edward would have none of it: the damage inflicted by the Welsh was unforgivable; he had always been ready to do justice to those who wished to complain but the time for that

---

[92] *RPeck*, ii, 440–5; above, pp. 499–501.
[93] *LW*, 120; *RPeck*, ii, 441 (art. 4).
[94] *LW*, 119; *RPeck*, ii, 441 (art. 2).
[95] Above, p. 502.
[96] *RPeck*, ii, 465. Pecham had evidently seen the submissions when he met the king for the first of two discussions of the Welsh issues and the chronology appears to be as follows: he had sent John of Wales to Llywelyn on or shortly after 21 October; Edward, at Denbigh 27 October, expected to see Pecham there; their meeting took place at Rhuddlan soon afterwards, for there on 31 October Pecham appointed Burnell as his vicar should anything untoward happen to him in Gwynedd (*Councils*, i, 540; *RPeck*, ii, 426).

Cilmeri

had evidently long passed. Despite the king's manifest unwillingness to relent, Pecham urged him again to allow the aggrieved to set out their complaints before him, but the king refused. He was always ready to do justice to those who complained, but the time for the submission of grievances was over and, implicitly, the Welsh were at fault for not doing so in good time. He would not grant them the right to come and go.[97] During the course of what may well have been an exceedingly difficult interview Pecham came to appreciate the full extent of the king's displeasure. The archbishop was resolved to make his way into Snowdonia, but he set out in no way encouraged by the king's initial reaction to his proposals.

Pecham's record of his meeting with Llywelyn ap Gruffudd is quite brief.[98] After a broad discussion, the prince responded to the archbishop's plea by declaring his readiness to submit to the king's will upon two conditions: that respect should be had to his conscience with regard to the people for whom he was responsible, and that his status be respected. Llywelyn's standpoint can be gathered more fully from the documents which he prepared for Pecham at a later stage in the transactions. But the archbishop was able to give Edward a full account at a second interview promptly upon his return from Llywelyn's court.[99] The essence of the matter was that Llywelyn was convinced that unconditional submission to the king's will would be tantamount to his extinction and the irretrievable damage of his people. The substance of Edward's standpoint could be expressed equally briefly: he had no wish for any transactions concerning peace with Llywelyn or his subjects other than their complete submission to his will. The surviving record reveals, more clearly than at any other time in their turbulent relationship, the determination and intransigence of king and prince alike, and their deep mutual suspicion. Archbishop Pecham now knew the full extent of the difficulties confronting him, and he deserves credit for his persistence. Knowing that the Welsh would not submit except upon terms acceptable to them, by the king's consent he entered into discussions with the magnates who were present. A set of proposals was prepared for transmission to Llywelyn in writing by the hand of John of Wales. They embodied the recommendations which the magnates would make to the king if Llywelyn ap Gruffudd were to agree to make the submission on which the king insisted. Before they were delivered to Llywelyn, and quite possibly before Pecham had been able to hold his discussions with king and magnates, the English forces suffered a disaster which undoubtedly served to harden the king's conviction that only by

---

[97] *RPeck*, ii, 465.
[98] Ibid., 465–6.
[99] Ibid., 466.

Cilmeri

unqualified submission on the prince's part could the vexatious problem of Wales be finally resolved.

Pecham had made his way into Gwynedd in the first week in November and probably conducted his negotiations with Llywelyn between the first and the fifth of the month.[100] Precisely where they met is not certain, for the only indication of the prince's whereabouts comes from a letter which he wrote a few days after Pecham's return to Rhuddlan. He was then at Garthcelyn, a site not yet identified with certainty but probably that of a hall close by the prince's manor of Aber.[101] There is much to suggest that Aber was an important court and it is quite conceivable that Llywelyn received the archbishop there or nearby. The possible place and the likely date of the meeting are both relevant to an appreciation of the impact of the disaster which befell the king's forces on the Menai Straits, not perhaps during the course of the discussions between prince and archbishop but almost certainly during the subsequent discussions at the king's court. The event is noticed by several chroniclers, some in detailed accounts, and there can be no doubt of its effect on the sensibilities of king and kingdom. For some time already the army in Anglesey, under the command of Luke de Tany, had been poised for the crossing to the mainland and awaited the king's instructions. The order would be given, it is reasonable to conclude, when the king was ready to force the Conwy and initiate the co-ordinated movements which would break Welsh resistance in Gwynedd Uwch Conwy. Delayed first by the gradual manner by which Perfeddwlad was secured and then, perhaps, by Pecham's mission, the order for the crossing was not forthcoming. But on 6 November, which may have been the day before that on which Pecham gave Edward an account of his transactions with Llywelyn, English cavalry and infantry launched their attack upon the mainland by the bridge of boats.[102]

Walter of Guisborough provides the fullest account of the events of St Leonard's Day and, though written some time after the event, it deserves

---

[100] The itinerary in *Register of John Pecham, Archbishop of Canterbury 1279–1292*, i, ed. F. N. Davis (London, Canterbury and York Society, 1969), xii, needs to be corrected. Pecham was not at Garthcelyn on 11 November but at Rhuddlan; Garthcelyn was the place where Llywelyn dated a letter to him on that day (*RPeck*, ii, 432–3, 468–9). On 3–6 November Pecham is said to be at 'Rhuddlan and Aber', the reference to Aber probably deduced from the fact that Llywelyn is likely to have been at Aber or Garthcelyn. Dateable documents place the archbishop at Rhuddlan up to 31 October; there is then a hiatus of several days until 6 November, when three documents were issued at Rhuddlan (*RPeck*, ii, 426–9; iii, 1072; *Register of John Pecham*, ii, 179). Pecham would appear to have been in Gwynedd Uwch Conwy within the period 1–5 November.

[101] *RPeck*, ii, 468–71; for Aber and Garthcelyn, above, pp. 221, 233–5.

[102] For possible reasons for the precipitate assault, Prestwich, *Edward I*, 192.

Cilmeri

careful notice.[103] He relates that, when the king was still not ready to order a crossing, English knights and armed men crossed the bridge at low tide eager for glory and renown.

When they had reached the foot of the mountain and, after a time, came to a place at some distance from the bridge, the tide came in with a great flow, so that they were unable to get back to the bridge for the depth of the water. The Welsh came from the high mountains and attacked them, and in fear and trepidation, for the great number of the enemy, our men preferred to face the sea than the enemy. They went into the sea but, heavily laden with arms, they were instantly drowned.[104]

While the author of *Brenhinedd y Saesson* also writes of a bridge breaking 'with the flow of the tide' (*gan ffrwd y llanw*), the continuation of *Brut y Tywysogyon* in Peniarth MS 20 has a slightly different emphasis, with the bridge breaking under an excessive load, a view shared with several English chroniclers.[105] Some commentators speculate on the attackers' motives, maintaining that the assault was made with the deliberate intention of undermining the negotiations which the archbishop was conducting, or to secure a territorial advantage in advance of a settlement. Other matters are left unclear, notably the question whether Tany was attempting to set up a bridgehead, or whether the crossing was conceived as a raid from which the soldiers would return. But whatever Tany's motives or his objectives may have been, there can be no doubt of the profound effect of the outcome, the response in the kingdom of England being comparable with that later provoked by the disaster at Stirling Bridge. Though the contretemps on the Menai Straits was not altogether a military defeat inflicted entirely by a triumphant enemy, the psychological effect of such a major reverse cannot be questioned. Many of those engaged had close associations with the king's circle. Luke de Tany himself and the young Roger

---

[103] Chroniclers give the date as St Leonard's Day, 6 November. Pecham had probably returned to Rhuddlan by then; Edward's letters were dated at Denbigh on 6 November, and at Rhuddlan on the following day. Pecham's second meeting with the king was at Rhuddlan, probably on 7 November. Consultations in council, the composition of the proposals and their transmission to Llywelyn and the composition of Llywelyn's reply had all been completed by 11 November (*RPeck*, ii, 468–71).

[104] Guisborough, *Chronicle*, 219; cf. Morris, *WW*, 179–80; *HKW*, i, 356–7.

[105] *BS*, 258–9; *BT, Pen20*, 228; *Pen20Tr*, 120. The continuation starts with a record of the events of Palm Sunday, the king's coming to Rhuddlan and the taking of Anglesey by English forces and continues: 'And they desired to gain possession of Arfon. And then was made a bridge over the Menai; but the bridge broke under an excessive load, and countless numbers of the English were drowned and others were slain.' This is followed by two further important entries considered later, the betrayal of Llywelyn in the belfry of Bangor and his departure from Gwynedd. Main English notices are: *AnnDunst*, 292; *AnnOsney*, 289–90; Rishanger, *Chronica*, 101–2; Langtoft, *Chronicle*, ii, 176–8; *FloresHist*, iii, 57.

Clifford were among those who lost their lives, and Otto de Grandson was said to have escaped drowning only with difficulty.[106] Philip Burnell and William Burnell, nephews or perhaps sons of the chancellor Robert Burnell, were also among the fatal casualties.[107] William Audley's shattered body, subsequently buried in the Cistercian abbey of Hulton, testifies to the ferocity of the combat.[108] The death of Hywel ap Gruffudd ab Ednyfed indicates that one prominent Welsh adversary of the princes participated in the ill-fated enterprise and may suggest that there were Welsh casualties among the large numbers of infantry who perished.[109] For the English this was a calamity, but on both sides the effect of the disaster was to heighten the determination to forge ahead with the struggle. It is an English writer who says that the Welsh saw the catastrophe which befell the English as a new inspiration to vigorous resistance, and he may well be right in his estimate of the Welsh response.[110] On the English side there was certainly a new determination borne of an acknowledgement that there was no alternative to an uncompromising struggle which could take them through the winter. The effect of the military reverse was underlined by the realization that the discussions between archbishop and prince had proved abortive. There is no doubt that the documents compiled in the days following the disaster are marked, on all sides, by steadfast adherence to intransigent positions.

Traditionally the disaster which befell the English on St Leonard's Day has been remembered as 'the battle of Moel-y-don', a place on the Anglesey shore at the point where the Menai Straits are narrow and where there was for centuries a ferry to the mainland.[111] Tradition recounts that Agricola, too,

---

[106] *AnnCestr*, 110–12, names sixteen knights who died and says that many esquires and 300 infantry perished. The Hagnaby chronicler places the blame for the enterprise on Roger Clifford's wish to release his father from captivity (Cotton Vesp. B xi, f. 38).

[107] Rishanger, *Chronica*, 101–2, describes them as the 'germani' of Robert Burnell; for a letter of commiseration with Burnell written by his clerk, *CAC*, 126.

[108] Audley was summoned to join Mortimer in March 1282 and received the submission of Owain ap Gruffudd ap Madog in June; he commanded 500 men at Rhuddlan 7–29 October, and, like Luke de Tany, was among those sent to Anglesey to lead the assault on the mainland. He took four knights and six esquires, but his main forces were taken to Anglesey on 6 November, the day of his death (*CWR*, 212, 228; C47/3/18; E101/3/26; E101/4/1; E101/3/30). For the skeleton, with the marks of a body slashed by a sword, at the Cistercian abbey of Hulton, of which the Audleys were founders and patrons, see the bone analysis by S. Browne in P. Wise (ed.), *Hulton Abbey: A Century of Excavation* (Stoke-on-Trent, Staffordshire Archaeological Studies, 2 (1985), 8–10, 17, 93–6). I am grateful to Dylan Adams who brought the discovery to my notice and W. D. Klemperer who provided information concerning it. The writ for the inquisition *post mortem* on Audley was issued on 25 December (*CIPM*, ii, no. 476).

[109] *AnnCestr*, 110; compensation to his widow Gwenhwyfar, *LW*, 122–3; Taylor, *SCCB*, 203; below, n. 151.

[110] *FloresHist*, iii, 57.

[111] H. R. Davies, *The Conway and Menai Ferries* (Cardiff, 1942), 63–71; *Inventory Angles*, clxxviii–clxxx.

Cilmeri

had crossed the water by a bridge of boats at the same spot when he had invaded Anglesey.[112] On the other hand, like the chroniclers, the account rolls which provide the details of the construction of the bridge refer to 'the bridge near Bangor', and the earliest references to 'the battle of Moel-y-don' appear to be those of sixteenth-century historians.[113] The traditional accounts need to be re-examined, particularly in the light of the strategy for the subjugation of Gwynedd which, partly revealed in the military operations already completed, would be demonstrated more fully in the movements initiated at the very end of 1282. Taken together these suggest that a crossing at a point further north than Moel-y-don, either at Bangor or still further north, would have better served Edward's purposes. English naval and military activity in Anglesey appear to have been concentrated on the north-east coast of the island in the vicinity of Llan-faes, close to the site later chosen for the castle of Beaumaris, and it is likely that that quarter of the island was chosen for the initial amphibious operation. Troops and supplies for the Anglesey campaign, dispatched from Rhuddlan and bases further afield, were directed to Llan-faes, where a major encampment was set up.[114] The land on either side of the water at this point, an important crossing point throughout the ages, mattered greatly in the calculations of both sides at this crucial stage in the war. Before Llan-faes, extending to the mainland at Aber across the greatly broadened Menai Straits, lay the expanse of the sandbank of Traeth Lafan over which the tide ebbed and flowed. Aber was itself a key point on an ancient route westwards from Perfeddwlad leading from the lowest short crossing of the Conwy at Tal-y-cafn, through the pass of Bwlch y Ddeufaen, to descend to the coast for the crossing to Anglesey. Clear traces of the Roman road which ran from Caerhun on the west bank of the Conwy through the pass to Aber, the way that Pecham is likely to have taken for his meeting with Llywelyn, are part of the historical record of the importance of this route. The crossing from Aber to Llan-faes was a much frequented route at successive periods in history as travellers traversed the sandbank at low water to be ferried across the remaining narrow channel. There is good reason to believe that it was from Aber, not many months before, that Eleanor de

---

[112] D. Powel, *Historie of Cambria* (1584), 372: 'they made a bridge of boates and plankes ouer the water where before Iulius Agricola did the like, when he subdued the Ile to the Romans'. *Cornelii Taciti De Vita Agricolae*, ed. R. M. Ogilvie (Oxford, 1967), 104–5, records an unplaced crossing by men who had to swim across the Straits.

[113] The earliest references to Moel-y-don as the place where the bridge was built appear to be those of Humphrey Llwyd and David Powel (NLW, Llanstephan MS, 177, f. 212a; D. Powel, *Historie of Cambria* (1584), 371–2). Moel-y-don is derived from Bon-y-dom, a name given in *HGK*, 2; *MPW*, 55, as the site of a castle built by the Danish King Olaf (*Inventory Caern*, III, cxxxix; A. H. A. Hogg, *ArchCamb*, 111 (1962), 56–8). *HKW*, i, 354–7, cites the documentary evidence for the bridge, including the detailed accounts E101/4/6; C47/3/48, m. 34.

[114] For Llan-faes in the military operations see e.g. E101/4/6.

Montfort – like Joan, princess of Llywelyn Fawr, in whose honour the house was founded – had been borne to her final resting-place at the Franciscan friary at Llan-faes.[115] This was now a strategic quarter of great importance to Llywelyn and Edward alike. With the heights of Penmaen-mawr and Foel Las, Penmaen-bach and Graig Lwyd, which dropped steeply to the sea, effectively barring his opponent's advance from the Conwy along the north coast, Llywelyn would need to concentrate on blocking Edward's approach from the river to Bwlch y Ddeufaen.[116] Equally he had to be prepared to withstand the invasion from Anglesey that Edward's occupation of the island threatened. The synchronized offensive which the king launched by the beginning of 1283 could already be anticipated: the forcing of the Conwy upstream to make an advance both along the west bank of the river to Aberconwy and along the Lledr valley to Dolwyddelan, and the making of a bridgehead behind the prince's natural defences by means of a crossing from Anglesey. A bridgehead on the coast somewhere between Bangor and Aber would serve Edward very well. Along with the advance from the southerly direction already planned, the appropriation of Gwynedd by military means could finally be accomplished.

When Edward's forces, at the second attempt, achieved a successful crossing at the end of 1282 a bridgehead was established 'near Bangor'. The precise location of the bridge is not indicated, nor can we be certain that the two attempts were made at the same place. But two possible positions might be considered. One is certainly a site close to Bangor itself, where the Menai Straits are still narrow, a second further north, close to Llan-faes where, as we have seen, the Straits are broader. A location here, for all the historic importance of the crossing between Llan-faes and Aber, might seem an unlikely choice for the perilous task confronting the English army. But it is just conceivable that the bridge was designed, not as a means of crossing the Menai Straits from shore to shore at a narrow point, but as a way of crossing the channel which remained to be negotiated at low water at a broader point. Indeed, a bridge from shore to shore, placed in position, would hardly have been left alone by the defenders. A construction at Llan-faes, more difficult for the defenders to disturb, would enable an army ordered to advance at low water to cross the channel, which through the ages ran close to the Anglesey shore, and then traverse the sandbank that lay on the mainland side of the

---

[115] For the road and the crossing, *Inventory Caern*, I, lxxiii–lxxvi; *Inventory Angles*, clxxii– clxxiii; Davies, *Ferries*, 111, 115, 231–2, 234.

[116] Edward was to suffer some discomfiture, possibly the loss of a supply train, during an advance west of Conwy in 1294 (Morris, *WW*, 255: R. F. Walker, in *Book of Prests*, xxxii–xxxiv). Exactly where the incident occurred is not clear; Morris assumes the king advanced by Penmaen-mawr, but the route through Bwlch y Ddeufaen is also possible. See Trevet, *Annales*, 335; Guisborough, *Chronicle*, 251–2.

Cilmeri

Straits. This would have been an exceedingly hazardous undertaking, and before the attackers, rising steeply from the coast, were the heights of Fridd Ddu, from which the encampments at Llan-faes may well have been visible. These could be imagined to be the very heights from which, in Guisborough's account, the Welsh descended upon their enemies. If he had brought off a successful attack at this point, Luke de Tany would have delivered a stunning blow at the very heart of Llywelyn's dominion.

Both Guisborough's account and the brief notice in *Brenhinedd y Saesson* call for a place susceptible to the ebb and flow of the tides. Specialist knowledge of tidal flow in the Menai Straits and meticulous calculation, by the calendar and the phases of the moon, made available by the great kindness of John Simpson, has provided a valuable estimate of the conditions which would have prevailed on the Menai Straits on St Leonard's Day 1282.[117] The range of the tide and currents would have been relatively large, though not exceptional, and the largest tides in the cycle would have occurred three days earlier. The currents would have varied in strength between the vicinity of Bangor on the one hand and Llan-faes on the other. On the day in question, when high water was at 1.00 p.m. the current at Bangor on the ebb would have been fairly large, up to 2.5 knots, reaching a maximum thirty minutes later. At Llan-faes the currents would have been considerably smaller, at less that 1.5 knots. A bridge placed at Llan-faes would have been less exposed to the potentially damaging effect of tidal flow. Nevertheless forces crossing by a bridge at Llan-faes faced the further considerable hazard of the crossing of Traeth Lafan, already described, particularly the peril of failure to complete the operation at low water, and doing so in the face of the determined resistance of the defenders. It is possible that, on the fateful day, as several chroniclers suggest, the English army was forced back to a bridge which failed to withstand the weight of horses and men to which it was subjected at a time of high tidal flow. It is not difficult to envisage the distress of an army driven in some disarray across Traeth Lafan at an inopportune hour of the day. At the same time, while there would be fewer complications at the site of a short crossing near Bangor, the tidal flow would have been even more severe than at Llan-faes and a catastrophic outcome at that point can be envisaged equally well. The fact that a fortified bridgehead was established 'near Bangor' on the second attempt may suggest, though we cannot be sure that

---

[117] I owe the information on tidal conditions in the Menai Straits entirely to the kindness of Professor J. H. Simpson, Professor of Physical Oceanography at University of Wales, Bangor, who, in generous response to my inquiry, made careful calculations from modern tidal predictions, taking account of Julian and Gregorian calendars and accounting for leap years. A prediction of the new moon before Easter 1282 proved to be consistent with the recorded date. Calculations made at Bangor were kindly confirmed by colleagues at the Proudman Oceanographic Laboratory at Bidston. I am deeply grateful to Professor Simpson and his colleagues at Bangor and Bidston.

the two attempts were made at the same place, that the first assault was attempted and the second accomplished at the narrow crossing-point close to Bangor. A position close to the site of the modern pier is one clear possibility, another a few hundred yards to the north where, though the Straits begin to broaden, a rocky outcrop, clearly visible at low water, protrudes for some distance into the Straits from the mainland.[118] Sadly, the evidence known to be available for historical study does not permit any firm conclusion concerning the precise location of the calamity which so caught the attention of the chroniclers of both nations.

Llywelyn ap Gruffudd was in no position to judge on whose authority the decision to cross the Menai Straits was made; he was not to know whether the order was given by an impulsive field commander or by the king himself. He might reasonably have concluded that it was intended, if not to abort the discussions, to provide a stern military reaction to any conciliatory moves on his own part or that of the archbishop. Their discussions had almost certainly been completed before Luke de Tany's forces struck, and it is possible that Edward knew of the reverse he had suffered on the Menai Straits when Pecham gave him an account of those discussions.[119] On the day following the disaster Edward moved from Denbigh, where he had been for several days, to Rhuddlan, his mind soon to be occupied less with the results of the negotiations than with the military and political implications of what may have been a precipitate action on the part of his officers in Anglesey. The outcome of the enterprise may have brought joy to the defenders, but the fact that the assault had been attempted could only confirm Llywelyn in his conviction that submission to Edward was in no way consonant with his duty before God and his responsibility for his people. Edward could only be confirmed in his resolve to seek nothing less than the unconditional surrender of his adversary. Pecham could do no more in the tense circumstances which prevailed at Rhuddlan upon his return than secure the assent of his magnates to those proposals which, it has been intimated already, they would commend to the king if Llywelyn were to accept the need to surrender unconditionally. The archbishop did not venture into the wild country for further deliberations and John of Wales was sent with a set of proposals, some to be considered by

---

[118] In *TC*, 364–5, I favoured an attempted crossing at Llan-faes in November; further consideration has served to underline the difficulty in making a decision between the two proposed locations and to suggest that the evidence for the bridgehead established by the end of 1282 points to a second, successful, crossing near Bangor. But the evidence strongly suggests that Moel-y don has to be eliminated.

[119] *RPeck*, ii, 466; the chronology established already (above, n. 100) suggests that the conclusion that Pecham's stay at Aber 'coincided with Tany's action' (Douie, *Pecham*, 243) is not correct.

prince and council, others for the personal consideration of Llywelyn and Dafydd.[120] The open document offered nothing of substance: Edward would not discuss either Anglesey or the Four Cantreds, nor would he offer their inhabitants anything other than the assurance that he would deal with them mercifully as would befit a king; Llywelyn was offered nothing except the promise that the same mercy would be extended to him if he submitted unconditionally. Dafydd was not mentioned. Secretly, the magnates conveyed that, if Llywelyn were to surrender his territory, the king was likely to agree to offer him honourable maintenance in England. He would in fact be offered an earldom and appropriate financial support, and the provision would benefit his heir if he were to marry again and have a male child; the daughter to whom Eleanor had given birth would be provided for in an appropriate manner.[121] Choosing to make no distinction between the open and secret documents, and preferring to consider the two together with his council, Llywelyn rejected the proposals made to him. The answer which he wrote to the archbishop at Garthcelyn on 11 November 1282 stands among the truly inspired declarations in the history of the nation.

Writing in courteous and considered terms, Llywelyn declared his readiness to submit to the king's grace if he were able to do so in trust and with honour (*sub forma tamen nobis secura et honesta*).[122] However, he found the proposals conveyed to him unacceptable, for they promised the destruction of his people and himself rather than their honour and security. He faced insurmountable difficulties, not least the king's refusal to negotiate over the future of Anglesey and the Four Cantreds. The king's intransigence brought forth a vivid expression of Llywelyn's consciousness of an ancient inheritance bound up with the legendary history of his people and their distant forebears. In a reference unique among the documents which emanate from his court, Llywelyn saw himself as the lineal descendant of Camber son of Brutus, one of the three sons of the Trojan founder of the lineage who had shared the rule of Britain after their father's death. It is significant that in this singular appeal to the testimony of the *Historia Regum Britanniae* Llywelyn should call upon the passage which depicts an island of Britain in which authority was shared among three rulers, two of whom acknowledged the primacy of the third, who was vested with the territory of England. Still more revealing of the care with which this document was composed is the fact that, at two points in the text,

---

[120] *RPeck*, ii, 466–8.

[121] It appears that in 1296 Edward offered John Balliol an English earldom if he agreed to surrender all claim to Scotland. E. L. G. Stones and M. N. Blount, 'The surrender of King John of Scotland to Edward I in 1296: some new evidence', *BIHR*, 48 (1975), 94–106; *Throne of Scotland*, ii, 120–1.

[122] Llywelyn's reply is in two parts, a letter to Pecham, dated at Garthcelyn, 11 November, and a further statement of his argument (*RPeck*, ii, 468–71).

Cilmeri

the allusion to the legendary history is closely and deliberately linked with the strictly historical record of the circumstances in which, by the intercession of the Holy See in 1267, the political relationship between Wales and England implicit in the legendary history was made real. Legend and history were bound together at the behest of political necessity. The sense of history deepened the prince's awareness of the supreme responsibility which he now carried.[123] It was his duty to ensure that his inheritance remained unimpaired. It would not be right for him to cede an inheritance which his ancestors had possessed since the times of Brutus, and confirmed to him by papal mediation, and take lands in a country where he would be unaccustomed to the language and the law and customs, amidst his old enemies who would seek to deprive him of his land. He could give no credence to the word of magnates who maintained that the king would allow him to possess lands in England, especially when it was remembered that his own lands were barren and the lands of England so fruitful. Deeply suspicious of the promises of the very men who sought to disinherit him in Wales, Llywelyn was sceptical of the prospect that the king would allow him to have land in England, where he had no right, after striving to deprive him of his inheritance. He did not speak for himself alone, nor was the question of a refuge in England the matter which troubled him most. The men of Perfeddwlad, for whose well-being he remained resolutely concerned, were agreed that they dare not submit themselves to a king who had kept neither covenant nor pledge and allowed his men to impose their tyranny in abuse of the community by ruthless exercise of power. In Snowdonia, where his authority stood firm, there was a steadfast resolve between prince and people. He would never yield Snowdonia, a land which was part of the principality of Wales which he held by ancient inheritance. His council would never allow him to renounce his right to that land, nor would his people ever do homage to a stranger.

There would be no submission on Llywelyn's part, to leave his people exposed to destruction and extinction. He may have hesitated on the outbreak of conflict, perhaps for rather longer than has sometimes been allowed. Faced by that remorseless dilemma, confronted with a choice between leading the rebellion and suppressing the endeavours of men of his own nation, he had made his decision and brought to the rebellion an authority to which no one else could aspire. The document which proved to be his last message to the king of England could be none other than a declaration of his resolve to defend the stronghold of the principality of Wales which he held by right of

---

[123] J. B. Smith, *SHMW*, 14–15. For the passage on which Llywelyn drew, see *Historia Regum Britanniae*, 253 (II, i); *Brut Dingestow,* 21; Geoffrey of Monmouth, *History of the Kings of Britain*, 75. Edward used the same passage from the *Historia* during his attempt to establish his authority in Scotland, though with an emendation calculated to emphasize his superior lordship (*Throne of Scotland*, ii, 298–300).

ancient inheritance, but whose existence in its finite form had been entirely due to his vision and determination.[124]

His brother, too, received a secret communication and the propositions put to Dafydd ap Gruffudd suggest that, if Llywelyn was the one whom Edward acknowledged to be the focus of Welsh resistance, Dafydd was the prime object of the king's anger. Unacceptable though the terms offered to Llywelyn may have been in his estimation, Edward appears to have been prepared to allow him the sanctuary of his kingdom. Dafydd was offered nothing but exile, simply that he should leave for the Holy Land, and stay there unless he were recalled by the king.[125] This proposal, and the stern warning of the secular and ecclesiastical censure that he would incur if he continued to resist, elicited a predictably trenchant reaction.[126] When Dafydd went to the Holy Land he would do so of his own free will, for God and not for man. He had gone to war, and the others with him, not to invade other men's lands, but to defend their patrimony, their right, and their liberties; the king's men waged war out of inveterate hatred and a wish to secure Welsh lands. He sincerely believed that he was fighting a just war, and trusted that God would bring his judgement upon those who devastated churches and killed priests, infants and the infirm.[127] He told the archbishop directly to turn his denunciations upon those who perpetrated these enormities and bring remedy to those who endured. It was indeed, as Pecham had intimated to him, hard to live in war and danger, but it was harder to suffer destruction and extinction. And these were Christians who sought nothing except to defend their right, men who were driven to these measures by necessity and the greed of their enemies. Dafydd stood by his action and declared his readiness to answer before God for what he had done in the name of justice. For many years the brothers had had a troubled relationship and, during the course of the conflict, Edward may have harboured the hope that their new-found amity would not last. He may even have hoped that he might be able to draw Llywelyn away from Dafydd, and he may have countenanced Pecham's intervention partly on this account. He knew that they could not be separated now.

Pecham, too, acknowledged that further effort would be futile, and before leaving Rhuddlan he paused and composed a valedictory epistle which made its own appeal to the legendary history of the men of Troy so as to stress the

---

[124] The phraseology of this paragraph reflects an indebtedness to J. Goronwy Edwards, who wrote a moving and memorable account of the prince's predicament, *LW*, lxi–lxix.

[125] *RPeck*, ii, 467–8. In 1286 Edward and Philip of France agreed that Gaston de Béarn should go to the Holy Land and remain there unless he were recalled by the king of England (S. D. Lloyd, *English Society and the Crusade*, 95, from C47/29/2 no. 2; J. B. Smith 'Adversaries of Edward I: Gaston de Béarn and Llywelyn ap Gruffudd', 80).

[126] *RPeck*, ii, 471–3.

[127] Ibid., 471: 'credimus in hoc justam gwerram nos fovere'; Edward's appeal to the notion of a just war has been cited above (n. 30).

pristine immorality of those from whom the Welsh claimed descent. Theirs was a waywardness to which the very law they cherished bore clear witness, and he spelled out the inherent incapacity of this nation to adhere to the moral code that he was under solemn duty to maintain.[128] He enlarged on these themes later, deeply troubled then by the addiction of the Welsh to prophecy, but still vexed by the iniquity of those for whom he prayed and laboured.[129] The archbishop had said enough already. For the present he took his leave of a nation whose conquest by the English would be pure again, a nation so utterly depraved in its sorry existence in isolation upon the furthermost frontiers of Europe, so sadly deprived of the benefits of civilized life. He left his emissary, the Dominican friar Adam of Nannau, in Gwynedd and departed.[130] And we cannot tell by what mysterious ways this irate arbiter was brought to the Herefordshire border by the day on which Llywelyn was slain.[131]

If Goronwy ap Heilin had been among those who gathered for the discussions with the archbishop he may have found good cause to reflect on the course of events since he and Tudur ab Ednyfed had put the prince's seal to the agreement they negotiated at Aberconwy. Despite his humiliation and his constriction within a narrow territory, and for all the uncertainties for the future, Llywelyn had been left in possession of a well-defined territory in Gwynedd Uwch Conwy. Yet Goronwy ap Heilin knew that the years since the death of Llywelyn ap Iorwerth had shown how difficult it was to separate the lands east and west of the Conwy and treat Is Conwy and Uwch Conwy as entirely distinct territories. Llywelyn ap Gruffudd, even had he preferred to do so, could not escape from the enduring influence of his predecessors, nor cast off their troublous legacy. The prince's insistence that the Four Cantreds, equally with Snowdonia, was part of his principality (*principatum*) was not an entirely fictive concept to be summoned up in political extremity. By asserting the unity of the two territories he was, of course, discounting the terms of the

---

[128] *RPeck*, ii, 473–7.
[129] Ibid., 737–43; for his concern with prophecy after 1282, J. B. Smith, *SHMW*, 15–16.
[130] *RPeck*, ii, 488. Pecham's charge to Adam is indicated in his letter to the friar dated at Sugwas, west of Hereford, 11 December 1282, noticed later. Douie, *Pecham*, 253, notes the 'curious coincidence' by which Adam was recalled on the day of Llywelyn's death. Adam was a beneficiary of the will of Bishop Anian of St Asaph, receiving the bishop's Bible, and was an executor. The text of the will (above, p. 210, n. 109) twice refers to 'brother Adam' rather than to 'his brother Adam' and the calendar version in *ArchCamb*, 6th ser., 19 (1919), 186–7, needs to be corrected in this respect. There is every possibility, in fact, that the two Dominican friars from Nannau were brothers.
[131] For Pecham's visitation, made between Richard de Swinfield's election and consecration, and the resistance offered by dean and chapter, including an appeal to Pope Martin, *Charters and Records of Hereford Cathedral*, ed. W. W. Capes (Hereford, 1908), 144–6.

treaty on which he founded so many of his complaints against Edward. But even in defeat Llywelyn had secured an assurance that the men of Perfeddwlad should hold their lands, with their liberties and customs, as they had held them before the war under the prince's lordship, and the experience of the communities to the east of the Conwy had long been closely bound up with that of their counterparts to the west. Beyond this, the arguments which Llywelyn had propounded in his exchanges with Pecham conveyed a conception of a still broader community, for he had on occasion dwelt upon his responsibility for nothing less than his nation. Edward's appeal to his nation for aid in resolving the problems posed by the foreign nation beyond his western frontier is itself an implicit recognition of the sense of common purpose among his opponents which, fleetingly during the course of 1282, transcended the political fragmentation of the recent past. One of the wonders of this conflict is the spontaneous rising of communities in diverse and sometimes unexpected localities. In Ellesmere, for instance, upon the further confines of the territory occupied by communities of the Welsh nation, there was a spirited rising which led to the disinheritance of many, and, as it happened, the consequent enrichment of a few who were intimately bound up with the events in which Llywelyn ap Gruffudd lost his life.[132] However localized the disaffection might be, a community in adversity would tend to interpret its grievances in terms of oppression by an alien nation. These indications would be particularly pronounced in those territories which had historically formed part of the patrimonial inheritance of the princes of Gwynedd.

In Perfeddwlad, in particular, potent influences were blended together. The years spent under royal administration had seen a community which had historically formed an integral part of Gwynedd suffer for lack of justice, certainly in the period immediately preceding the rebellion. Goronwy ap Heilin inevitably represented in this community, not just the memory of a vanished supremacy, but the urgent needs of a people under stress. While the prince of Wales lived a society with a sense of persecution could turn to one who could provide both strenuous leadership and a link with the political tradition that he personified. In reality relations between prince and society had probably been far from wholly harmonious, but more recent tribulations which could be laid at the door of alien rulers would tend to efface the more ambivalent attitudes of earlier years. How responsive Llywelyn had been to the initial movements in Perfeddwlad remains uncertain; he may have respected the genuine discomfitures endured within the land, yet remained resentful perhaps of the manner in which they may have been manipulated by

---

[132] *CPR, 1281–92*, 120–1; *CWR*, 285; a beneficiary of the forfeitures, Robert Body, is noticed later. At least one Welshman who lived in England was moved to return to his native land to fight in Llywelyn's army (*CFR, 1272–1307*, 169).

men who had not been conspicuous for their constancy in earlier years. Yet, in the last resort, the fundamental identity of interest upon which his power had once been founded was bound to tell. In Goronwy ap Heilin the men of Rhos found one capable of interpreting their experience in a manner which, taking full account of their present predicament, was consonant with the political ethos which had been cultivated during the prince's supremacy. Goronwy had been well placed to win royal favour; in no sense was he a desperado with nothing to lose.[133] Although he had his own discontent to contend with, it was by choice that he identified his personal experience with that of the people among whom he lived, and he stood firm to the very end in the company of those disinherited princes who maintained their die-hard resistance in the months following Llywelyn's death. Even as they formulated their grievances for the archbishop's consideration, or argued their case in his presence, or drew upon the historical inheritance of their nation in their final declarations, those who shared the prince's innermost counsels knew the magnitude of the crisis in which they found themselves. They matched that realization with a resolve to stand firm, and it was to be a resolve reciprocated in a manner entirely without precedent by Edward I.

Still at Rhuddlan, Edward made his preparations for the next stage in the conflict, resolved that the community of the realm should be committed to greater and more purposeful endeavour than had ever been accomplished hitherto. Within days of the disaster on the Menai Straits he took steps to secure the men and materials necessary, not simply to continue with the war effort through the winter, but to wage the conflict with greatly increased force.[134] Edward sensed that Llywelyn might now try to broaden the field of combat, and new contingents were summoned not only to Rhuddlan but to Carmarthen as well, the summons prompted perhaps by knowledge of renewed resistance in Ceredigion.[135] The king's greatly increased military and financial needs inspired a noticeably heightened appeal to the common purpose of king and community of the realm. Writs issued on 24 November summoning representatives to the assemblies arranged for Northampton and York recounted the troubles which Llywelyn ap Gruffudd and his antecedents in rebellion had created for the king and his predecessors. They amounted to a summons to arms for a final solution of the problem of Wales. It was better that king and people should, for the common good (*pro communi utilitate*),

---

[133] Service to the crown has been noticed already; conscientious inclinations are reflected in *CAC*, 40.

[134] E.g. *CWR*, 259.

[135] Orders, 12 November, addressed to thirty-eight tenants-in-chief and sheriffs of four counties summoning forces to Carmarthen by 12 December to serve with Valence (*CWR*, 258); Dr Walker notes that Walter of Nottingham's payroll has no trace of their arrival. Deployment of forces in Ceredigion in mid-November is noticed below, n. 169.

Cilmeri

endure the labour and expense necessary to secure peace once and for all than that the disturbances created by the Welsh should continue to burden generations to come. This was a task to which king and magnates and the community at large would be committed together, recognizing their common need at a time of emergency and their common advantage in its permanent resolution.[136] Pecham had himself proclaimed his conviction of the righteousness of the king's cause and, in the aftermath of the events of that bleak St Leonard's Day, he warned the Welsh that the Old Testament provided proof enough that, though the chosen people might suffer their reverses, their final triumph was not denied them.[137] Pecham and the archbishop of York were assured of the king's renewed resolve and each was urged to ensure that the clergy were present along with the laity at the assemblies summoned so as to deliver the means whereby the king could secure an objective that would not only reflect the magnificence of the king and secure the perpetual peace of the realm but would be in praise and honour of God.[138]

Now, more clearly than at any other stage in the 1282 conflict, and itself perhaps an indication of the king's wish to concentrate the mind of the nation on the difficult task in hand, Llywelyn was recognized as the main adversary with whom they had to contend. References to Llywelyn in royal documents had hitherto been exceedingly sparse, and much the same may be said of those emanating from Canterbury. In marked contrast to the period leading up to the war of 1277, the surviving records of the present conflict do not show that Llywelyn was excommunicated by name (*nominatim*) either upon the first excommunication of the Welsh nor on the second pronouncement a month later. Similarly in the autumn, writing to Anian of St Asaph, Pecham took the bishop to task for failing to excommunicate the Welsh who had risen in rebellion, but again without naming the prince.[139] The archbishop, despite the vehemence with which he denounced those in rebellion, may have taken care to ensure that negotiations with Llywelyn should not be jeopardized by the use of ecclesiastical censure specifically directed to the prince at that stage.[140] On the failure of those negotiations, however, he informed Llywelyn that he had given no sufficient reason why he should be spared from sentence of excommunication and, though no document appears to have survived, it is

---

[136] *ParlWrits*, i, 10; *Select Charters*, 457–8; *CWR*, 275–6. The writs and subsequent deliberations are considered in Mitchell, *Taxation*, 225–6; Harriss, *King, Parliament, and Public Finance*, 39–41.

[137] *RPeck*, ii, 476–7 (14 November).

[138] *ParlWrits*, i, 10; *Select Charters*, 459. Pecham's response to Edward's call is indicated in *RPeck*, ii, 486–8; *Councils and Synods*, II, ii, 821–2; *RegPontissara*, i, 241–3, 396–8 (10 December).

[139] *RPeck*, ii, 422–3; above, n. 19.

[140] *RPeck*, ii, 422; John of Wales was told not to impose any ecclesiastical censure.

likely that Llywelyn was thereupon excommunicated by name.[141] Llywelyn had now failed to respond to the plea solemnly made to him in the name of the Christian church. Edward called on the material and spiritual resources of his kingdom to put down a rebellion which, in the view of state and church alike, was directed and sustained by the personal authority of Llywelyn ap Gruffudd. One of the main effects of Pecham's intervention was to establish Llywelyn, more clearly than before, as the power which had to be destroyed. Llywelyn's person would be rather more than an object of vigilance for the forces expensively gathered for the winter campaign.

Edward's suspicion that Llywelyn ap Gruffudd would now make every effort to broaden the field of resistance was borne out, as we shall see, by a new outbreak of activity in the lands of Gruffudd ap Maredudd and Cynan ap Maredudd in Ceredigion. Renewed resistance in the area reflected the prince's capacity to create a diversion from Gwynedd Uwch Conwy of some of the forces arrayed against the defenders. Why Llywelyn himelf should decide to leave Gwynedd is much more difficult to explain. It could be argued, as historians have tended to argue in the past, that the prince's overwhelming responsibility was to ensure the steadfast defence of the natural bastion of Snowdonia. The true heartland of Welsh independence was in Gwynedd Uwch Conwy and this was the territory which now had to be defended and the prince's personal responsibility lay there.[142] Yet Llywelyn ventured out of Gwynedd and, for the last time, made for the march of Wales. 'And then', says the continuation of the Welsh chronicle, 'Llywelyn ap Gruffudd left his brother Dafydd guarding Gwynedd and he himself took his host and went to gain possession of Powys and Builth'.[143] The entry is brief and there lies behind these few words more than we can possibly fathom. We need, even so, to ask: why did the prince choose to leave his patrimony at such a critical time?

In attempting to understand the compulsions which took Llywelyn on his last journey historical inquiry has tended to concentrate on the possibility of deceit and treachery. He died in the vicinity of Builth, and in some earlier studies the men of Builth have come under close scrutiny. Yet the traditional

---

[141] *RPeck*, ii, 477. There does not appear to be any record of Llywelyn's excommunication *nominatim*, but some chroniclers (e.g. Trevet, *Annales*, 303; *AnnOsney*, 290) say that Pecham excommunicated him after departing from Snowdonia. This is likely as, after the prince's death, Pecham said that he could not absolve (*assouther*) Llywelyn unless it could be shown that he had repented before his death (*RPeck*, ii, 488–9, 759). Pecham's undated excommunication of Dafydd (*RPeck*, ii, 483–4) does not belong to the autumn of 1282, as suggested in *Councils*, i, 538–9, but was given at Sugwas 2–7 January 1283.

[142] Morris, *WW*, 113.

accounts need to be used with caution. Men of Builth had been burdened with the charge of treachery long before the death of Llywelyn, placed 'beyond the law of all Wales' for killing their lord, Owain ap Maxen, and it is possible that traditions became confused.[144] Treachery may be sensed, however, in the evidence of the late thirteenth century itself, though suspicion does not at that stage fall on the men of the locality where he died. It falls rather upon the marcher lords. Intimations of treachery, of breach of faith, are so often conveyed darkly, and no chronicle, nor any other source, provides the unequivocal testimony which might enable us to unravel the threads in the various accounts of the tragic happening in the neighbourhood of Builth. It was alleged at the time, or shortly afterwards, in the most explicit statement we have, that the prince's decision to venture into the area was influenced by one of the sons of his old adversary Roger Mortimer. The Hagnaby chronicler, an important source for the events of the day on which Llywelyn died, was quite definite: Roger Mortimer, he says, but, more correctly, his brother Edmund Mortimer, drew the prince there by beseeching him to come to the neighbourhood of Builth to take his homage and that of his men. Along with other lords he hatched a plot to corner Llywelyn and kill him.[145] Others, too, notably the Dunstable annalist, allege that Edmund Mortimer pretended friendship with the prince, and treachery to the king, to draw Llywelyn to his death.[146] Edmund's relations with the king at this time, noticed presently, may indeed have lent credibility to a ruse of this nature. There is undoubtedly

---

[143] *BT, Pen20*, 228; *Pen20Tr*, 120.

[144] *Red Book of the Exchequer*, ed. H. Hall (RS, 1896), ii, 762. For the historical tradition incriminating the men of Builth see Humphrey Llwyd's references in NLW, Llanstephan 177, f. 224, and in T. Twyne, *The Breviary of Britayne* (London, 1573), 59, to the belief that Llywelyn was 'betrayed by the men of Buellt' and D. Powel, *Historie of Cambria* (1584), 374, 'beetraied by the men of Buelht'. Men of Builth are not charged with betrayal in any medieval chronicle. Of late fifteenth-century poets' references, *Gwaith Lewys Môn*, ed. E. I. Rowlands (Cardiff, 1975), 112, refers to Llywelyn's betrayal without reference to Buellt; *Gwaith Dafydd Llwyd o Fathafarn*, ed. L. Richards (Cardiff, 1964), 65: 'Llywelyn a'r llu aelaw / Amwyll drud ym Muellt draw', does not pin responsibility for what occurred in Buellt on men of the locality. For the tradition, E. Phillimore, 'The traitors of Builth', *Western Mail*, 7 May 1924.

[145] BL, Cotton Vesp. B xi, f. 28; text with trans. in Rh. Griffiths, *1282: A Collection of Documents* (Aberystwyth, 1986), 16–17. Mortimer sent to Llywelyn 'ut ueniret et acciperet homagium de se et hominibus suis et assignauit locum. Prouiderat enim dominus Rogerus et alii magnates Anglie quod dominum Leulinum dolo caperent et occiderent'. The chronicle twice names Roger Mortimer rather than Edmund; it was the latter who inherited Maelienydd and Gwerthrynion, lands close by the lordship of Builth. For the Hagnaby text, below, n. 181.

[146] *AnnDunst*, 292: Llywelyn came 'de Snoudone in terris que fuerunt Rogeri de Mortimer, ad capiendum homagium hominum illorum, sicut per filios dicti Rogeri fraudeliter fuerat evocatus'; *AnnOsney*, 290–1; the Hailes chronicle (BL, Cotton Cleopatra D iii, f. 48) states that the prince was killed by Edmund Mortimer's army; 'Register and chronicle of the abbey of Aberconway', ed. H. Ellis, *Camden Miscellany*, i (London, Camden Society, 39, 1846), 12, attributes the capture, killing and beheading of Llywelyn to Edmund Mortimer.

some documentary evidence which tends to support the view that the Mortimers, Edmund and Roger, were implicated in the death of Llywelyn. Their servants hovered about the prince when he fell, for Edmund heard from them that Llywelyn had asked for a priest as he lay wounded. Archbishop Pecham, in an important letter which he sent to Edward I six days after Llywelyn was killed, revealed that Edmund Mortimer had in his possession two things from among those found on Llywelyn's person by those who were at his death. These were his privy seal and a treasonable letter disguised by false names (*une lettre de guisee par faus nuns de traysun*). The letter would evidently prove discomforting for certain men and, passing the contents of the letter to Robert Burnell, the archbishop insisted that his main concern was that no one should be troubled on account of it.[147] Deception on the part of magnates, committed in the vicinity of Builth but not by the men of Builth, has clearly to be postulated in seeking an elucidation of the circumstances in which Llywelyn died.

This is not, however, the only element of treachery suggested in the historical remembrance of the events leading to his death. In its notices of the death of kings and princes the Welsh chronicler time and again takes up the theme of treachery. It was by the treachery of his own men that Gruffudd ap Llywelyn, head and shield of all the Britons, had fallen two centuries earlier, and Bleddyn ap Cynfyn, too, had fallen by treachery. Dafydd ap Gruffudd and Rhys ap Maredudd would be taken by the treachery of their men before they suffered the horrid fate of those charged with treason.[148] Treachery looms large in Welsh historical as in legendary awareness, recent memories recalling the devastating effect of the perfidy of Vortigern or Medrod for, it was later recalled, 'it was by their deceit and treachery that the finest of princes were destroyed'.[149] The chroniclers' entries are not entirely the reflection of a convention in historical writing upon which they drew instinctively, for their attributions are, upon occasion at least, supported by other testimony. The Welsh chronicler, indeed, makes no mention of treachery in his account of the events which occurred in the neighbourhood of Builth. But, between his account of the disaster which befell the English in the Menai Straits and his notice of Llywelyn's departure from Gwynedd, he provides an entry fraught with difficulties but with a compelling interest: 'and then was done the betrayal of Llywelyn in the belfry of Bangor by his own men'.[150] It is neither easy to postulate who might have been in the belfry nor safe to speculate upon what exactly they might have set out to achieve. We know that Llywelyn was not assured of the unfailing loyalty of all his men in

[147] Letters to Edward and Burnell, 17 December (*RPeck*, ii, 489–92, 759–60).
[148] *AC*, 25–6; *BT, Pen20*, 19, 21, 229; *Pen20Tr*, 15–16, 121; *RBH*, 26–9.
[149] J. B. Smith, *SHMW*, 11–12.
[150] *BT, Pen20*, 228; *Pen20Tr*, 120.

this war any more than he had been in 1277. There had been a number of seceders during the earlier conflict, as we have seen, and we would need to start with some of the same names if we were to try to estimate the degree to which he was deserted during 1282. Those of the lineage of Ednyfed Fychan would be prominent among them. The chronicle notes that Hywel ap Gruffudd ab Ednyfed was 'leader at their head' as Edward's forces overran Anglesey and, as we have seen, he lost his life in the attempt to force the Menai Straits on St Leonard's Day. His brother Rhys ap Gruffudd was, once more, of the same allegiance, and he might well have been among those who escaped from the chilly waters. A third brother, the Dominican friar Llywelyn ap Gruffudd, was certainly in Edward's service very soon after the cessation of hostilities.[151] The names of those in receipt of royal favour in the course of the conflict are not, perhaps, as numerous as they had been in 1277 but this may be due to a disparity in the documentation, particularly the absence of rolls recording the king's gifts comparable to those which survive for the earlier war. Many of the names may reflect, moreover, no more than submissions made upon the advance of the English armies, evidence of an ultimate yielding to superior force rather than a defection which undermined the capacity of the princes to resist. In later years descendants of some of the powerful figures of this generation insisted that their forebears had accepted the pardon offered by Edward I to those prepared to submit to his authority, but the chronology and hence the effect of these desertions – even whether Llywelyn or Dafydd was the one to suffer – is impossible to establish.[152] This would, in any case, be an indication of surrender; treachery is an altogether different matter.

The treachery to which the chronicler alludes was alleged to have occurred in the church of St Deiniol itself. It preceded Llywelyn's departure for the march and, whatever was involved, it occurred at a time of immense importance in the resistance to the king's forces. The location points to the involvement, among 'his own men', of churchmen and possibly of members of religious orders. These were not altogether a breed apart. Even though it is only infrequently that the familial affinities of those in holy orders can be ascertained, it is likely that many of those in authority in church and friary were closely related to men of substance in the lay community, and these

---

[151] *BT, Pen20*, 228; *Pen20Tr*, 120; petition of Gruffudd Llwyd, his son, *CAP*, 265, states that Hywel died 'at the bridge of Anglesey' in the company of Grandson; cf. above, n. 109: He is probably the 'Sir Howele' or 'Hywel the Welshman', who served as a knight on the mainland and was sent to Anglesey, probably in mid-October (E101/3/31; E101/4/1). Rhys was in royal service, and Friar Llywelyn ap Gruffudd would be employed from July 1283 in making extents of the conquered lands (above, p. 191, n. 21).

[152] *RC*, 151, 167–8, 210–11. *CWR*, 240, names some who deserted the prince, 6 October 1282.

connections may have mattered immensely at this time of crisis.[153] The prior of Bangor, Llywelyn ap Gruffudd, may have been only the most conspicuous among a whole number of ordained men whose lay associations proved quite crucial. Indeed, he was perhaps too conspicuous an adherent of the king to have played a direct role in influencing the course of events in Llywelyn's dominion in 1282 and others may have played a more active role. Likely culprits are not easily recognized. It would be hazardous, and possibly unfair, to impute to Iorwerth Foel or Madog ap Cynfrig, well-favoured though they were in the period following the annexation of Gwynedd, anything more than timely secession, though we can never be sure.[154] Pecham, promptly upon Llywelyn's death, was concerned for the safety of clergymen in Snowdonia, and there might be two good reasons for his anxiety. He may, of course, have been concerned that clergymen who had been involved in rebellion might be subjected to retaliation by invading forces. He was later to provide protection for Madog Fychan 'an instigator of war' (*incentor guerre*), when due expiation had been made in accordance with canon law. On the other hand, Iorwerth of Llan-faes, likewise *incentor guerre*, was also charged with betraying Dafydd ap Gruffudd. It may thus be that Pecham, immediately after the prince's death, was concerned for the safety of clergymen who might have been instrumental in undermining the prince's position, or something worse. He certainly identified Iorwerth of Llan-faes as one who had betrayed Dafydd.[155] His reference to the clerks whom he had taken into Gwynedd is intriguing, as is his suggestion that some might be advised to withdraw to France. His concern may, of course, point not to any surreptitious or perfidious activity but only to the rigours to which the clergy were inevitably exposed in a time of bitter conflict, especially if they were striving to mitigate the severity of the hostility about them. The most tantalizing question is the precise purpose which Pecham had in mind when he left Brother Adam of Nannau in Gwynedd. Adam was required to fulfil certain duties with regard to Llywelyn and the magnates of the land 'for the benefit of the state' (*pro utilitate rei publice*). We have no indication of what was involved, but the words have distinctly ominous overtones. And we can only ponder the significance of the fact that, on the very day on which Llywelyn died, John Pecham was inspired to order Brother Adam to return to the archbishop without delay. Then at Sugwas, west of Hereford, Pecham wrote a noticeably

[153] For the loyalties of Scottish churchmen, Barrow, *Kingdom of the Scots*, 233–57.

[154] Stephenson, *GG*, 36–7, 224, carefully considers the evidence concerning Master Gervase, who served the prince and then the king; ibid., 237 for Madog ap Cynfrig, archdeacon of Anglesey, given the office of *offeiriad teulu* (priest of the household) in 1284, who is probably the Matthew, archdeacon of Anglesey, engaged with Friar Llywelyn ap Gruffudd in making extents in 1283 (*CWR*, 284; E101/351/9). For Huw ab Ithel, below, n. 244.

[155] *RPeck*, ii, 489–92, 759–60; iii, 780–1.

Cilmeri

edgy letter, and it provokes at least a cautious surmise as to what onerous public service the Dominican friar had been commissioned to undertake in Gwynedd. Only the previous day Pecham had commended to the bishops of his province the king's call for strenuous effort on the part of the churchmen of the realm 'for the common good' (*pro communi utilitate*), and for their presence at an assembly called to transact what was necessary 'for the state' (*pro re publica*).[156] Pecham's anxiety, particularly for Brother Adam, may not necessarily reflect a knowledge that men in holy orders had been placed in peril by disloyalty to the prince. Yet, betraying some considerable agitation, and written on that particular day, his letter remains an intriguing composition. The precise identification of who might have been up to no good in the belfry is quite impossible, and it may be rather less relevant to our inquiry than the other and equally difficult matter of what purpose a conspiratorial group might have sought to fulfil in that brief period – if the chronicler's sequence of events is accurate – between the shambles on the Menai Straits and the death of Llywelyn.

The question has a bearing on the matter of the motives which led Llywelyn to set out from Gwynedd to the march: on the one hand we have, on the testimony of the chronicler, rumour of treachery in Gwynedd; on the other hand there is a suspicion of a stratagem in the vicinity of Builth. Was there a link between the two? Did the ruse by which he may have met his death have its origin in a conspiracy involving some of his confidants in his patrimonial land and some of the magnates of the march? It would be easy to weave a plethora of hypotheses, but there are some personal connections which may have a bearing on this matter. The link between Roger Lestrange and Rhys ap Gruffudd was evidently relevant to the defection which was engineered for Rhys in 1277, and the association between Ellesmere and Tregarnedd may have had its part in the period of intensified animosity which followed the English disaster on St Leonard's Day.[157] Rhys's relations with Llywelyn had been anything but easy for some time, and there happens to be a record of a rift between them towards the end of the previous year.[158] Known adherents of the king though they might be, Rhys ap Gruffudd and his Dominican brother may still have had the means of infiltrating the prince's innermost councils. Treachery may equally have played its part in influencing the prince's decisions and in gathering intelligence upon his intentions, and the key to the meaning of the betrayal in the belfry might be sought in one or other, or both, of these possibilities. If Edmund Mortimer had conspired to

---

[156] *RPeck*, ii, 486–8.

[157] *CWR*, 285.

[158] On 8 December 1281 Rhys ap Gruffudd entered into an obligation by which he might secure the prince's grace for disobedience and contempt at Aberffraw (*LW*, 31).

draw Llywelyn to the march, any intimation transmitted to the prince is likely to have been considered in the prince's immediate entourage and Llywelyn might have been misled with regard to the veracity of the missive even within that restricted circle. The 'treachery' alleged to have occurred in the belfry may well have been related, possibly by the provision of false evidence, to the considerations which lured Llywelyn from Gwynedd and took him to the neighbourhood of Builth. He could have been the victim of false information, quite apart from the possibility that knowledge of the prince's intentions were relayed to the king's commanders. For, whatever might explain his decision to go to the march, his subsequent movements would have been of great interest to his opponents. The spies, the *insidiatores* of the king's pay rolls, no doubt played their part, but his commanders may have had infinitely better sources of intelligence than these.

After the death of the elder Mortimer the direction of the king's operations in the march was entrusted to Roger Lestrange, and, whatever may have been the information or the instinct which brought him to do so, he had gathered a mighty force in the vicinity of Builth by the time the prince arrived there. In two letters written to Edward, Lestrange reveals a detailed knowledge of the whereabouts of Llywelyn's forces and of the prince himself. He was able to trace his movements to 'the land of Gruffudd', presumably to Powys Wenwynwyn, and thence to the marches of Builth and Elfael.[159] This may be no more than good evidence of the competence of a field commander, but Lestrange had something of the inner knowledge of the Welsh nation, witness his ability to seek out some of Llywelyn's possessions after his death.[160] Certainly, there can be no doubt of the key role that he played in the death of the prince. Lestrange had good reason to look to Edward for some reward after the conquest – Penllyn and Edeirnion or Maelor Saesneg he thought – and the king's failure to provide for him from the spoils of war is astonishing.[161] The key co-ordinator of military activity in the march after the failure of the archbishop's negotiations, Lestrange may have benefited a good deal from his access to knowledge of what was happening on the Welsh side. Additionally, as suggested already, decisions taken by Llywelyn and his confidants may have been influenced by what was fed to them, with or without the king's knowledge, by those magnates of the march who had useful associations with laymen and churchmen in close attendance on the prince. The problems which had arisen in Edmund Mortimer's lordship in the march, noticed presently, would almost certainly have been known to Llywelyn and might, even of themselves, have brought him to the march.

---

[159] *CAC*, 84; SC1/23/180.
[160] *ExtMer*, 185; Lestrange was responsible for securing some of the prince's possessions at Cymer and Abereiddon.
[161] *CAC*, 124.

Knowledge of those difficulties might certainly have inclined the prince to give credence to whatever overtures Edmund Mortimer may have made to him.

The themes of treachery and subterfuge are exceedingly difficult to pursue when the evidence is so slight. Yet the intensification of the conflict in the last weeks of 1282, and the ideological appeal made in church and state in England for an irresistible drive for a permanent solution, point to a sense of compelling necessity to resort to whatever means would bring the struggle to an early conclusion. It would not be in any way invidious to conclude that, to some at least of the principal figures involved in the war, the central objective was now the death of Llywelyn. Undoubtedly the person mainly responsible for the deployment of the forces which confronted Llywelyn before Builth, one with close links with the soldiers most directly involved in the action in which the prince was killed, and the person who sent the king the crucial communiqué from the battlefield, Roger Lestrange may have brought to his task more than the qualities of an astute military commander. His role in the prince's death was well known in the immediate aftermath of the event. It is to him, even perhaps more than Edmund Mortimer, that we need to look most closely in any estimate of the influences which might have brought Llywelyn to meet his death in the march of Wales.[162]

Such an interpretation would, of course, mean that Llywelyn ap Gruffudd fell prey, not simply to a stratagem conceived by those who confronted him upon his coming to the march, but that he was drawn to his death from Gwynedd Uwch Conwy. There are, however, other considerations which have to be weighed, namely those strictly military needs which could, by themselves, explain his journey to the march, if not the trap into which he finally fell. It would be foolish to assume that Llywelyn possessed in his hereditary land an unassailable fortress and that it was, for whatever reason, an error of judgement on his part to leave Gwynedd on an altogether risky enterprise. An enemy force had indeed come to grief in the Menai Straits, yet Llywelyn would have known very well that his adversary had not been foiled indefinitely and that in a little while he would surely make another bid to execute the plan which had not succeeded on that first, precipitate, attempt. For the moment Edward had been frustrated, but he was to complete that key

---

[162] A letter written by a royal clerk at Rome, Stephen of St George, shows that, immediately after the event, Lestrange was credited with the means whereby Llywelyn's death was accomplished. The writer thought that it was fitting that 'a knight estranged by name yet close in loyalty should have exacted the extreme penalty from the rebel and traitor Llywelyn who, by the error of his infidelity, is estranged indeed' (Taylor, *SCCB*, 229–31, for the letter with valuable commentary; Lestrange's letter to the king on Llywelyn's death, below, n. 186).

manœuvre before the year was out.[163] Llywelyn may well have judged that the king would soon make a second attempt to establish a bridgehead on the mainland, a movement coupled with advances into Snowdonia from other directions. He would have appreciated the imperative need to open a second front. The question why he ventured to the march could be answered purely in terms of military necessity. This would also explain why Llywelyn went to the area in person, rather than send Dafydd, or another, in his place. He may have taken a large force with him – the 'host' to which the chronicler refers – but he may have set out, not so much on a campaign by which he would impose his power, but on a mission calculated to raise support in the areas he traversed. He was the one person with the capacity to do so. He had come to Brecon in 1263 at the request of the men of that lordship, as the chronicler tells us in a statement amply borne out by the support which the prince is known to have evoked there and in neighbouring areas.[164] Towards the end of November 1282, after the collapse of his negotiations with the archbishop, he could have set out for the march to win precisely that kind of adherence.

He may have been encouraged to do so by considerations other than the duplicity of the marchers. Humphrey de Bohun is known to have been confronted with resistance among his tenants in Brecon during the course of 1282. More relevant still was the situation in the lands which Roger Mortimer had held until his death in late October and, partly arising from that situation, the king's relations with his sons. In a letter which Edward wrote to the younger Roger a few days after his father died he recalled the father's valour and fidelity and expressed the hope that, by his good service, the king would to some extent recover in the son what he had lost in the father.[165] Yet, despite these seemingly generous sentiments, and the unwonted meditation upon life and afterlife induced by the old man's death, Edward's letter has a decidedly peremptory tone. It may have been written to ensure that the young Roger Mortimer appreciated his duty to serve under a command which the king had entrusted to Roger Lestrange, perhaps to Mortimer's displeasure.[166] Yet more intriguing, and more pertinent to a consideration of the circumstances which prevailed in that sector of the march to which Llywelyn came, no comparable letter of condolence is known to have been written to Edmund Mortimer. The king's treatment of Edmund in the weeks following his father's death is not

---

[163] Activity in Anglesey was resumed before the end of November and the bridgehead on the mainland established before the end of the year (E101/351/9; below, n. 217).

[164] Above, pp. 149–51.

[165] *CWR*, 257.

[166] In a letter noticed later (*CAC*, 84), Lestrange asked the king to order Warenne, Roger Mortimer and Edmund Mortimer to do what Lestrange considered necessary to ensure that Llywelyn was denied supplies from their lordships. This could be normal protocol, but it might suggest that his command needed royal imprimatur when he dealt with major figures such as these.

Cilmeri

easy to understand. Inheriting, along with the family's estate at Wigmore, the marcher lordships of Radnor, Clun, Maelienydd and Gwerthrynion, Edmund faced a major responsibility in a key strategic area. Strangely, however, he was not allowed to assume lordship immediately. Edward retained possession of the Mortimer lands for well over a month after the father's death. Edmund may not have found the king favourably disposed towards him. Edward's wish to deny him speedy access to his patrimony, even in the perilous conditions which prevailed in the march at this time, is made even more remarkable by the king's contrasting generosity to the younger brother, Roger, who had received a major part of Powys Fadog to become his lordship of Chirk. The Osney chronicler, attributing Llywelyn's coming to the area to the influence of Edmund Mortimer, may make a perceptive observation in his remark that he did so 'to win the king's heart'.[167] Whatever impelled the king to retain the father's lands, it is evident that royal officials faced difficulty in imposing their authority there. The problems were enough to cause Roger Springhose, placed in charge of the lands, to write to Robert Burnell to say that, though he had done what he could to persuade the inhabitants into the king's peace, they remained fickle and haughty. The difficulties arose from the fact that the tenants had 'no definite lord', and Springhose feared that they would not remain in peace if their liege lord did not come to them. He urged that the king be persuaded to allow Edmund possession of the inheritance.[168] The need for the personal presence of the lord was clear, and if he knew the circumstances in the area, as well he might, Llywelyn would have judged that he could turn the situation to his advantage if he were able to establish his personal presence there. Historically this was an area where allegiances fluctuated. Apart from a Mortimer ruse, even apart from the particular problems which had arisen in the Mortimer lordships, there were good reasons why the prince should make a bid to create a major diversion of royal resources to this area. The problems in the Mortimer lands, and the possibility that Edmund Mortimer was genuinely discomforted by the imprudent delay in investing him with his estates, would undoubtedly have enhanced the credibility of whatever entreaties may have been conveyed to Llywelyn ap Gruffudd.

Part of a broader effort, calculated at the very least to divide the enemy forces, perhaps an effort with much more far-reaching objectives, there was a marked resuscitation of conflict in Deheubarth. There is some suggestion that

---

[167] *AnnOsney*, 290–1: 'ut regis animum complacaret'.

[168] The lands were taken into the king's hands 29 October, three days after Mortimer's death (*CWR*, 256; *CFR, 1272–1307*, 171). Springhose wrote two letters to Burnell before 24 November, when seisin was given to Edmund (*CAC*, 130–1; *CFR, 1272–1307*, 171, 174): the first conveys that the Welsh tenants were well disposed towards the king, though he had encountered problems in Clun; the second suggests a more general problem in the area.

Llywelyn went to the march by way of Ceredigion and Ystrad Tywi, but this may rather be a reflection of the extensive nature of the renewed Welsh activity. The disturbed conditions particularly evident in Ceredigion were probably due to new efforts on the part of Gruffudd ap Maredudd and Cynan ap Maredudd. William de Valence was forced to wage a new campaign in their lands by the middle of November, a close watch was kept on Welsh movements in Ceredigion during the weeks immediately preceding the prince's death, and arrangements were put in hand to summon a substantial force to be deployed there again before the year was out.[169] Lestrange, too, was vigilant in the wide marcher sector with which he was entrusted. In the first of two letters written at the end of November or early December he reported to Edward that enemy forces were concentrated not only beyond the Berwyn, which might be expected, but beyond Pumlumon, too, a further possible indication of Welsh military deployments in Ceredigion.[170] They were in mountains difficult to penetrate and his forces would be put at risk if he were to attempt to engage the enemy. Lestrange felt that the best which could be done for the present would be to ensure that the march was properly guarded so that supplies could not pass to the Welsh, and he urged that Roger Mortimer should provide adequate guard in Powys Fadog and that Edmund Mortimer and the bailiffs of Builth and Brecon should do likewise. Then, as though suddenly on the night the letter was written, Lestrange gathered that Llywelyn had come down to 'the land of Gruffudd'. He proposed to go there directly, a response which strongly suggests that the land in question was not that of Gruffudd ap Maredudd but Gruffudd ap Gwenwynwyn. It is not unlikely, even so, that Llywelyn's forces had crossed from Ceredigion or that forces from Ceredigion had joined an army moving southward and advanced into Powys Wenwynwyn. When he next wrote, Lestrange was able to supply

[169] Forces from Cydweli summoned to Cardigan to attack the lands of Gruffudd ap Maredudd and Cynan ap Maredudd were engaged 17–19 November and searches were made in various parts of Ceredigion 26 November–9 December, in advance of the muster at Carmarthen scheduled for 12 December. Patrick de Chaworth brought a force from Cydweli to Rhuddlan Teifi on 16 December. Further contingents of about 1,500 troops were summoned to Cardigan and advanced to Llanbadarn Fawr early in 1283 (C47/2/4).

[170] *CAC*, 84. Welsh concentrations were reported beyond the Berwyn and 'Morugge' ('Moor Ridge'). E. A. Lewis, 'The development of industry and commerce in Wales during the middle ages', *TRHS*, 3rd ser., 17 (1907), 145, quoting E101/485/20, places 'Morugge' in the Pumlumon range, at the western end of Cwmwd Deuddwr; similarly W. Rees, *South Wales and the Border*, NE sheet. The main medieval authority is *GirCamb Op*, 119, 170 (*Itin.* II, iv; *Descr.* I, v), who refers to the mountains of 'Moruge', the English equivalent of Elenid, and clearly indicates Pumlumon. For Elenid, 'the mountain land where the river Elan rises', R. J. Thomas, *Enwau Afonydd a Nentydd Cymru* (Cardiff, 1938), 65–6; *PKM*, 259; *BT, Pen20Tr*, 207. Lestrange's letter, alerting the bailiff of Builth among others, is consistent with concern for the land beyond Pumlumon. Forces were deployed in the area of 'Mourugg' in May 1283 (below, n. 221).

Cilmeri

the news that Llywelyn was 'in the marches of Builth and Elfael'.[171] These words describe quite accurately the position which Llywelyn is known to have reached by 11 December. The intelligence gathered in Ceredigion and in the march suggests a major Welsh initiative in the second half of November, even a sense of impending crisis. It might be rash to discount altogether the view of one chronicler that Llywelyn would have won the support of the country anew had he only lived a few days longer.[172] Whatever brought him to the area, and from whatever lands he mustered support, Llywelyn appears to have led a large army to the lordship of Builth. And, whatever brought them to the area – good intelligence on the part of the king's commanders or something much more intriguing – there to meet him were substantial forces led by a number of Edward's most important military leaders: Roger Lestrange, Edmund Mortimer, Roger Mortimer, Gruffudd ap Gwenwynwyn, Peter Corbet, Reginald FitzPeter, as well as the constable of Builth, John Giffard.[173] The military might of the whole march from Oswestry to Hereford gathered together at the place where Llywelyn was to fall.

The majority of the chroniclers reveal an interest in the events of the day, though there are uncertainties and inconsistencies which make a reconstruction difficult.[174] Repetition of details in a number of sources may reflect only the interrelationships of texts. By comparison with the English sources, the information from Welsh texts is slight, but the poetry conveys the authors' deep sense of tragedy, with some intimation of the circumstances, and the chronicle testimony is instructive. *Brut y Tywysogyon*, in the text in Peniarth MS 20 which forms the continuation of the chronicle from 1282, certainly helps trace Llywelyn's movements and the disposition of forces on either side. It relates that Llywelyn took his host to Powys and Builth, that he proceeded as far as Llanganten and sent men to take the homage of the men of

---

[171] *CAC*, 84; SC1/23/180. The second letter, addressed to Burnell, is not in *CAC* and I am indebted to Dr Arnold Taylor for the text. It is only partly legible but the words 'ke Lewelin esteit en la marche de Buelt et de Elvayl' can be read clearly. Lestrange refers to a message brought to him by Robert de Scarborough, a chancery clerk, and payments authorized 7–16 November (E101/3/29) refer to his journey to Lestrange on war business (*pro negociis guerre*). Lestrange thus wrote after Scarborough's journey, excusing himself from going to a meeting at Shrewsbury to which he had been summoned. Clearly, too much was happening in this sector of the march for the commander to be away, even in response to a royal order.

[172] Hailes chronicle, Bodley MS Laud Misc. 529, f. 7: 'quod Wallica lingua convertetur ad ipsum si per duos dies ultra supervixisset'.

[173] *ChronPetroburg*, 57, provides a list.

[174] The evidence is examined carefully in Llinos B. Smith, 'The death of Llywelyn ap Gruffydd: the narratives reconsidered', *WHR*, 11 (1982–3), 200–13, and references are here confined to the main sources. From among earlier discussions see J. E. Lloyd, 'The death of Llywelyn ap Gruffydd', *B*, 5 (1929–31), 349–53; Taylor, *SCCB*, 229–31. For some key texts, Rh. Griffiths, *1282*, above, n. 145.

Cilmeri

Brycheiniog. It suggests therefore that Llywelyn's forces, with the highland behind them to the west and north-west, occupied the slopes of the land which extended as a promontory between the Wye and the Irfon, its furthermost point at the confluence of the rivers close by the town of Builth.[175] On this basis we can envisage Llywelyn's army on the one side, the king's army on the other, separated by the Wye and the Irfon, a position which accords with Lestrange's report that Llywelyn had come to the 'marches of Builth and Elfael'.[176] We can visualize a prince at the very front of conflict, facing one of the strongholds of the march. But if *Brut y Tywysogyon* helps to establish the probable location of the two armies, the course of the conflict has to be deduced, to the extent that is possible, from English narrative sources. Among the several varying accounts there are two which, in view of their detail, call for particular notice.

The fullest account, and the one on which historical understanding has traditionally been based, is that of Walter of Guisborough.[177] It describes the prince's descent from the mountains, with one servant (*armiger*) in attendance upon him, to ascertain whether the men of the land were still loyal to him, leaving the main part of his army on the slopes above the Wye with a contingent guarding a bridge across the Irfon. The English considered how they might force the Irfon and, seeing that it would prove impossible to cross the bridge, they were urged to resort to a ford upstream where a detachment could cross and attack the defenders at the bridge from the flank. The remainder of the army could then cross the bridge and attack the Welsh forces on the ground above the river. The bridge was taken and the main body of the army made its assault upon the Welsh positions. Llywelyn heard the noise of combat and hurried to join his army, but was pursued by an English soldier

---

[175] *BT, Pen20*, 228; *Pen20Tr*, 120. A. Edwards, *Appointment at Aberedwy: The Death of Llywelyn ap Gruffudd, Prince of Wales* (Pen-y-groes, 1992), 37–48, urges that more notice be taken of the tradition which links the death of Llywelyn with Aberedwy, in the lordship of Elfael. The earliest evidence for the tradition appears to date from the late sixteenth century and there is nothing in the material of the late thirteenth century which lends credence to it. For an example of the traditional material, verses from NLW, 872D, a memorial for the slaying of Llywelyn spoken by the ghost of Goronwy ab Ednyfed Fychan, Rh. Griffiths, *1282*, 25.

[176] SC1/23/180. *ChronPetroburg*, 57, states that Llywelyn came to Roger Mortimer's land of Gwerthrynion (*Woryemon*) between Cwm-hir and the *villa* called *Ynlanmake*, possibly Llanfair, that is Builth. After 1277 the king's officers in Builth had ditches dug at three points, with the evident purpose of regulating movement into the lordship; one, at Cefn-y-bedd, was in the area occupied by Llywelyn's forces in December 1282 and those at *Coedely* and *Retheresger* (probably Coedelai and Rhydyresgair, but as yet unidentified) were also likely to have been placed so as to control the approaches from north and west (E372/124, m. 24). For Cefn-y-bedd, below, n. 206.

[177] Guisborough, *Chronicle*, 220–1; for previous acceptance of this account, Morris, *WW*, 182–3; J. E. Lloyd, 'Death of Llywelyn', 350; D. Stephenson, *The Last Prince of Wales* (Buckingham, 1983), 59–62, 75–8.

Cilmeri

who, without recognizing him, struck him a blow and left him wounded. The Welsh forces remained on the slopes awaiting their prince, but suffered a bloody slaughter before the determined onslaught of the enemy horsemen and foot-soldiers. After the battle the soldier returned to the person whom he had struck down earlier in the day; he now recognized him as the prince of Wales and drew his sword. Llywelyn's head was struck off and sent to the king as a gruesome sign of triumph.

Walter of Guisborough's narrative was written in the north of England perhaps a quarter of a century after the event, but it may embody some authentic material. Writing at the house of the Austin canons at Guisborough, the author was well placed to avail himself of whatever information might be derived from Welshmen who passed through the area on their way to serve the king of England in Scotland. A magnate from the area, William Latimer, had survived the catastrophe in the Menai Straits and, though he is unlikely to have been present at Builth a month later, he could have proved to be a good source for the major events of the campaign as a whole. Yet there are important considerations which serve to raise serious doubts about the veracity of what has often been taken to be an authoritative account of the prince's death. There is a disturbing similarity between Guisborough's account of the conflict at the bridge on the Irfon and his depiction of the battle of Stirling Bridge in 1297. At Stirling Bridge, as in the case of the encounter near Builth, the defenders had an advantage in that their forces were positioned across a river which had to be forced by a heavily defended bridge; at Stirling, and on the Irfon, it was pointed out to the English that there was a ford nearby where the river could be negotiated and the defenders attacked from the flank or the rear. The account of the two battles have important elements in common, and though Guisborough's description of the conflict of 1282 has certain features which command attention, the fact that he alone describes a conflict on a bridge after forces had crossed a river by a ford, and that this is one of several features which it shares with the conflict of 1297 at Stirling – nearer to the time of writing and a battle for which he would have had access to good information – makes it imperative that his account of the earlier encounter be treated with great caution.[178] Guisborough is the author who makes most of the location of the battle on the banks of the Irfon, but that is a perfectly credible location consistent with what is found in other sources of evidence, including that of

---

[178] Prestwich, *Edward I*, 193, accepts that the accuracy of Guisborough's account needs to be questioned; he is not convinced that the accounts of the battles of Irfon Bridge and Stirling Bridge are 'conflated'; conflation is not suggested, but rather that suspicion must fall on the chronicler's use of such similar elements in the two accounts. The similarity of the two accounts, along with the probable date of composition, makes a compelling case for great caution with regard, at least, to the account of the earlier battle. For reliance placed on Guisborough for Stirling Bridge, Barrow, *Bruce*, 123–6.

Cilmeri

Brut y Tywysogyon, which provide testimony on which we may reasonably rely. The bridge on the Irfon is an altogether different proposition.

No other chronicler provides an account of the death of the prince as full as that of Guisborough, but there is another source which offers a very different interpretation deserving careful notice. The chronicle written at the Premonstratensian house of Hagnaby typifies the interest shown by a group of commentators from eastern England in Edward's activities in Wales. The texts reveal a broad interest in the affairs of Wales but an intense concern with the life and death of the prince of Wales. There may be one particular reason for this. After her father's death Gwenllian was taken to the Gilbertian nunnery at Sempringham, and historians writing in the area may have been keenly interested in the circumstances which brought her from the mountains of Snowdonia to the Fenlands.[179] The chronicle of Bury St Edmunds, the Peterborough chronicle and that of Robert Manning of Bourne all bring testimony to bear upon the events of 1282 and especially the death of Llywelyn.[180] The Hagnaby chronicle is particularly valuable, and differs substantially from that of Guisborough.[181] It states, as we have seen already, that Llywelyn came to Builth at the instance of Mortimer, invited there so that he might take his homage and that of his men. Mortimer conspired with others to capture Llywelyn and put him to death. When the prince came to the place agreed on the appointed time, virtually unarmed, he was attacked. There was a long and fierce battle, with heavy losses on both sides until the prince's army was thrown into confusion and virtually destroyed, leaving Llywelyn alone with only one servant. As they left the battlefield two of their enemies came upon them and pursued them to a wood. They were found and surrounded and after a strenuous fight the prince fell, calling out and revealing his identity.[182]

---

[179] Events and associations which might have excited the chroniclers' interest are fully considered in Ll. B. Smith, 'Death of Llywelyn', 200–13.

[180] *ChronBury*, 74–6; *ChronPetroburg*, 55–8, and, for Robert Manning, *The Works of Thomas Hearne* (London, 1810), iv, 242–3. Texts of Peterborough and Manning in Rh. Griffiths, *1282*, 9–10, 14–15. The chronicle of Sempringham itself, Archivio Segreto Vaticano, Barb. Lat. 3528, f. 57v. carries only a brief notice of the rebellion of Llywelyn and Dafydd and their deaths. I am most grateful to Father Leonard E. Boyle, Prefect of the Vatican Library, and Mgr Charles Burns, for their great kindness in consulting this text.

[181] Cotton Vesp. B xi, f. 28; Rh. Griffiths, *1282*, 16–17. For the value of this text as a source for the war of 1294–5, M. Prestwich, 'A new account of the Welsh campaign of 1294–5', *WHR*, 6 (1972–3), 89–94; R. F. Walker, 'The Hagnaby chronicle and the battle of Maes Moydog', *WHR*, 8 (1976–7), 125–38.

[182] Cotton Vesp. B. xi, f. 29; Rh. Griffiths, *1282*, 16–17: 'ingruente bello et per longum durante ceciderunt ex utraque parte quam plurimi. Tandem confusi sunt Wallici et fere omnes exstructi, ita ut nullus remaneret nisi dominus Leulinus et armiger eius. Cum vero reuersi essent de prelio indentes duos ex aduerso latitantes prosecuti sunt eos usque ad siluam. Tandem inuenti et ab hostibus congressi per longum dimicauerunt sed ad extremum princeps Wallie qui se in omnibus strenue agebat cecidit, clamans et confitens nomen suum. Cognoscentes eum adversarii eius decollauerunt eum offerentes caput eius domino regi, quod iussit Londoti deferri'.

Cilmeri

This account has no reference to river or bridge or ford, nor does it recount a sudden attack upon Llywelyn and his wounding before battle commenced. It describes a fierce encounter, with the prince participating until, after the defeat of his army, he himself was put to death. The greatly differing Guisborough and Hagnaby versions are difficult to evaluate, yet they have some common features which may be considered alongside the account of other commentators. Each provides an impression of a prince somehow or other separated from the main body of his army, and a conflict on a major scale. Each element is attested by other writers, though their explanations differ. *Brut y Tywysogyon* tells that the prince's host came to Llanganten and that Llywelyn sent his steward and his men to take the homage of the men of Brycheiniog, leaving him 'with but a few men with him' until the king's host came upon them without warning.[183] The chronicles of Chester and Osney gathered the same impression that the prince was left with only a small band about him.[184] Gruffudd ab yr Ynad Coch, in his elegy, bewailed the 'killing of the eighteen'.[185] Others speak of great armies and bitter conflict. Roger Lestrange provided an early account in a dispatch from the battlefield 'in the neighbourhood of Builth' (*en le pays de Buellt*) in which he informed the king of the prince's death, the defeat of his forces and the death of 'the flower of his troops'.[186] The Peterborough chronicle tells of Llywelyn's coming with a great army and a battle in which the Welsh suffered heavy losses and, according to this account, Llywelyn was killed late in the day.[187] Three men of substance fell with their prince in battle, one of them being Llywelyn ap Gruffudd Fychan (Llywelyn ap Gruffudd ap Madog) of Powys Fadog.[188] We may never know exactly what occurred on the day the prince of Wales died: was it a

---

[183] *BT, Pen20*, 228; *Pen20Tr*, 120.

[184] *AnnCestr*, 108; *AnnOsney*, 291.

[185] The elegy is noticed presently; 'the eighteen' would presumably have formed, or formed part of, his bodyguard.

[186] *CAC*, 83–4; full text *EHR*, 14 (1899), 507; Rh. Griffiths, *1282*, 11.

[187] *ChronPetroburg*, 57–8: Llywelyn was killed 'about the hour of vespers' (*hora quasi vespertina*); *AnnDunst*, 292: 'after sunset' (*post solis occasum*).

[188] *ChronPetroburg*, 57–8. The three named are Llywelyn Fychan, 'who was lord of Bromfield', Rhys ap Gruffudd, 'who was steward of all the prince's lands', and 'Almafan', described as lord of 'Lampadervar'. Llywelyn ap Gruffudd Fychan (or Llywelyn ap Gruffudd ap Madog) of Powys Fadog, has been noticed several times; reference to his death in 1282 in *CAP*, 441. The second is probably the man who served as Llywelyn's steward in the marcher lordships in his possession before 1277 (*CAC*, 53–4; above, pp. 315, 404, n. 57). The third cannot be identified: 'lord of Llanbadarn Fawr' might suggest a man of Ceredigion, but there was a Llanbadarn Fawr in Maelienydd, and 'Almafan' could be another person from the marcher area. The name itself presents some difficulty, though the reading in the MS is accurately reproduced in the printed text. A Melwyn de Buellt is named in 1271 (*LW*, 40–1), but there is no certainty that he was the man killed in 1282. *AnnDunst*, 292, notes that three of his magnates were killed with Llywelyn but gives no names. See Ll. B. Smith, 'Death of Llywelyn', 208–10.

sudden, even accidental, happening, or the result of a long-conceived plot; was he a lone fugitive or a prince who fell with his men in fierce combat? The possibility that the prince of Wales was drawn to the vicinity of Builth by a stratagem in which Edmund Mortimer played a particularly important role is strongly suggested by the evidence not only of the chroniclers but in the archbishop's intriguing reference to that treasonable letter disguised by false names which was then in Edmund Mortimer's possession along with the prince's privy seal.[189] The further possibility that Llywelyn was somehow separated from the main body of his army by a ruse which may or may not have been part of a wider stratagem is more difficult to establish, but it is a possibility which cannot be discounted. There are endless difficulties, yet some things are clear. Of the princes of the dynasty of Gwynedd, he was the first for several generations to die in battle. 'A man who did not wish to flee the nearest way', said the poet Bleddyn Fardd in his elegy, and it may be fair to envisage the last prince of Wales as one who met his death, as he had lived, at the head of the defenders of his nation.

No mention has yet been made of Stephen de Frankton, the man who, according to the often accepted version of events, was responsible for the prince's death. He is the soldier named by Guisborough and other chroniclers as the one who struck the blow which felled the prince, and what is known of his associations tends to lend credence to the narrative accounts that he was indeed the one who drew his sword upon Llywelyn.[190] He was a man of Shropshire, and had close personal ties with Roger Lestrange, whose estates lay in the county and in its environs. He had served as Lestrange's esquire (*valletus*) some years before. The forces employed on the day of Llywelyn's death were under Lestrange's command, as he himself noted in his letter to the king, and Frankton was probably among those in his immediate service.[191] Frankton's credentials would make him a strong candidate for the responsibility of striking the fatal blow. But another man is named by Robert Manning of Bourne, one of the chroniclers of eastern England, writing early in the fourteenth century. His work invites careful attention because he had associations with Sempringham, and his work contains details of the life of Gwenllian and of her death, and the death of her cousin Gwladus, who was a daughter of Dafydd ap Gruffudd.[192] Manning names Robert Body as the person who killed Llywelyn. After describing how Lestrange had found

---

[189] *RPeck*, ii, 489–90, 759–60; above, n. 147.

[190] Guisborough, *Cronica*, 220–1; comment on Frankton's role in e.g. Morris, *WW*, 183–4; *HW*, ii, 763; J. E. Lloyd, 'Death of Llywelyn', 351; Taylor, *SCCB*, 231.

[191] Frankton served with Lestrange in co. York 1274–5 (C62/51); a pardon for abjuring the realm was ratified at the instance of Lestrange (*CPR, 1272–81*, 104); he led the men of Ellesmere in Lestrange's contingent in 1287 and had been killed by 1295 (Morris, *WW*, 184, 210; *CPR, 1292–1301*, 158).

[192] Hearne, *Works*, iv, 243.

Cilmeri

Llywelyn in a wood he relates that 'Sir Robert Body, a knight whose sword cut best of all, promptly dismounted and cut off Llywelyn's head'.[193] The known details of Body, too, lead to an association with Lestrange. His land lay in Shropshire, and Lestrange bestowed upon him after the conquest additional properties forfeited by those in his lordship of Ellesmere who had risen in rebellion.[194] More directly relevant is the fact that he was in Lestrange's entourage during the siege of Castell y Bere in the spring of 1283; he could very well have been among those who served with Lestrange at Builth four months earlier.[195] Stephen de Frankton or Robert Body? We cannot decide between them, and we can only conclude that, probably somewhere near Llanganten, above the Irfon in Buellt, on the feast of St Damasus in the heart of winter Llywelyn ap Gruffudd died by the hand of a soldier serving the king of England.

'Glory to God in the highest, peace on earth to men of good will, a triumph to the English, victory to king Edward, honour to the church, rejoicing to the Christian faith . . . and to the Welsh everlasting extermination.'[196] It was thus that a clerk in Edward I's service, writing from Orvieto early in 1283, celebrated the joyful news that the old serpent Llywelyn, once prince of Wales, father of treachery, child of rebellion, son of iniquity, author of sedition, patron of ingratitude, convict of perjury and head of all evil had been vanquished on the field of battle. Stephen of St George's words express, in vivid phraseology, the ethos of the conquest of Wales and the glorification of impending victory which was shared among the English upon hearing of Llywelyn's death. The clerk was quite sure that the prince was utterly undeserving of Christian burial, and we cannot be entirely certain of the fate of Llywelyn's body. After the battle Maud Longespée, who could claim affinity with Llywelyn – for she was a grand-daughter of Llywelyn ap Iorwerth – and whose estate of Cantref Selyf was not far from the place where he was killed, quickly wrote to Archbishop Pecham. She asked that the prince be absolved so that he might be buried in consecrated ground. Maud was told that nothing could be done unless it were proved that the prince had shown signs

---

[193] 'Sir Roberd Body, a knyght his suerd best bote, Doun sone he he light and Leulyn hede of smote' (Hearne, *Works*, iv, 243; Rh. Griffiths, *1282*, 15).

[194] *Feudal Aids*, iv, 226; *CPR, 1281–92*, 120–1; *CWR*, 285; Ll. B. Smith, 'Death of Llywelyn', 211.

[195] He was a leader of the Ellesmere and Knockin contingents; as a scutifer of Lestrange he took hostages to the king from Montgomery in July 1283 (C47/2/4; E101/351/9).

[196] The letter, probably written at Orvieto upon news reaching the papal court on 22 January 1283, little more than five weeks after the event, is printed with translation and commentary in Taylor, *SCCB*, 229–31.

Cilmeri

of true repentance before he died.[197] Pecham, making a visitation of the diocese of Hereford, had been in its western reaches since early December and he may well have been close to the scene of the crucial encounter shortly afterwards.[198] On his own testimony, he had within a week of the prince's death seen the small things discovered on the most secret part of his body, including that treasonable letter disguised by false names.[199] Yet he did not know all he wished to know, or he chose to give that impression, for he was concerned to know whether Llywelyn had been buried in the abbey of Cwm-hir. He wrote two letters on the matter but we do not know whether he was able to elicit a reply. Though there may be no certainty there are good grounds to believe that the chronicler of Bury St Edmunds, another writing in eastern England who provides valuable evidence on the affairs of Wales, was not amiss when he noted that Llywelyn found his last resting-place in the consecrated ground of the Cistercian abbey of Cwm-hir.[200] It would be the very last irony if he was put to rest in Maelienydd, a land where he fought so fiercely in the early years of his supremacy and to whose vicinity he came again in his last days. Each time he came there he came to grips with a lineage which, closely related though it was to his own, had contributed a great deal to the troubles of his lifetime and to his ultimate degradation. But it was a broken body which was buried in the abbey of Cwm-hir. The prince's head was taken to the king at Rhuddlan and then sent, perhaps, to be shown to the soldiers in Anglesey before it was taken to London.[201] With an iron spike thrust through it, the severed head was raised on the Tower of London, displayed for the derision of the crowd and adorned with a crown of ivy in mocking fulfilment of a prophecy which said, so the English were led to

---

[197] *RPeck*, ii, 488–9, 759. Maud, widow of William de Longspée, was the daughter and heiress of Walter de Clifford and Margaret, daughter of Llywelyn ap Iorwerth, and was thus a second cousin of Llywelyn ap Gruffudd. She had married John Giffard and brought him the lordship of Cantref Selyf, above, p. 356.

[198] Letters of Pecham are dated at Sugwas on 11 December, Pembridge from 17 December (*Register of John Pecham*, ii (1969), xii); Pecham may have gone to Builth or thereabouts between 11 and 17 December.

[199] It was at Pembridge, 17 December, that he wrote the letters to the king and Burnell which gave an account of the things found on the prince's person, including that treasonable letter 'which we have seen' (*RPeck*, ii, 489–92, 759–60; above, n. 147). He had not been sent a copy of the letter, he had seen the original, and his fretful concern suggests his presence at or close by the scene of the action within a very few days.

[200] *ChronBury*, 76. This statement and Pecham's keen inquiries, for a second letter was sent to the archdeacon of Brecon, 28 December (*Register of John Pecham*, ii, 185), are probably enough to resolve the doubts expressed in R. Morris, 'The burial of Llywelyn ap Gruffydd', *ArchCamb*, 6th ser. 11 (1911), 26–42; cf. J. E. Lloyd, 'Death of Llywelyn', 354.

[201] *ChronBury*, 75–6; *ChronPetroburg*, 58; *AnnDunst*, 293; *FloresHist*, iii, 57.

believe, that one of the Britons would be crowned in London.[202] Scorn and barbaric exultation at the death of the prince in the triumphant nation. And in the nation cast into despondency, expressed with dignity in the poetry of an erudite tradition redolent with the civilized values of a Christian society, a profound sense of loss. Bleddyn Fardd drew upon the mythological remembrance of another whose severed head had been carried to London, though Bendigeidfran's head was taken there by his compatriots for honourable burial in the White Mount in accordance with his wishes.[203] Bleddyn's cerebral and sensitive work stands among the most noble of elegiac compositions as he mourns the death of a man of great valour who was slain for his nation, and beseeches that Christ, who himself endured tortured torment, would bear his lord to share God's great mercy.

> Gŵr a las drosom, gŵr oedd drosaf,
> Gŵr oedd dros Gymru, hy y'i henwaf:
> Gwrawl Lywelyn, gwraf o Gymro,
> Gŵr ni garai ffoi i'r ffordd nesaf.
> Y Gŵr a gymyrth engyrth ingaf
> Angau dros bymoes (drymloes dromaf)
> A gymero rhwyf rhywiocaf – fonedd
> Yn rhan drugaredd, fawredd fwyaf.[204]

And the cosmic images invoked by Gruffudd ab yr Ynad Coch, as he pondered upon the severing of the prince's head, bring forth the majesty of

---

[202] *Chronicles of the Reigns of Edward I and Edward II*, ed. W. Stubbs (RS, 1882–3), i, 90; Cotton, *HistAng*, 162–3; *FloresHist*, iii, 58–9; Guisborough, *Cronica*, 221; 'Register and chronicle of the abbey of Aberconway', 12. For the decapitation, F. Suppe, 'The cultural significance of decapitation in high medieval Wales and the marches', *B*, 36 (1989), 147–69, which also notices the decapitation of Gruffudd ap Llywelyn and the sending of his head to Earl Harold and King Edward, and the use made of the metaphor of the head (*pen*) by poets and chroniclers in reference to Welsh princes. For the use of the metaphor by Gruffudd ab yr Ynad Coch see below.

[203] *GBF*, 51; elegiac stanzas also published, with trans. by R. Geraint Gruffydd, in Rh. Griffiths, *1282*, 26–7; see especially ll. 5–8: 'Llas Bendigeidfran gydfryd, – a chymri / A chymraw oedd hefyd, / Llas Llywelyn llafn greulyd, / Llas Arthur benadur byd.' (He of the same mind as Bendigeidfran has been killed, and it was terror, / It was affliction, Llywelyn of the blood-stained blade has been killed, / Arthur has been killed, chieftain of the world.) For Bendigeidfran's burial, PKM, 19; *Mabinogion*, 40.

[204] *GBF*, 50, quoting ll. 17–20, 37–40; text of elegy, and trans. J. P. Clancy, in Rh. Griffiths, *1282*, 28–9; also trans. in J. P. Clancy, *The Earliest Welsh Poetry* (London, 1970), 168–9: 'A man was slain for us, a man of might, / A man for Wales was bold, I name him, / Manly Llywelyn, best man of Welshmen, / Man who loved not the nearest way out. / The Man who bore, dread, most straitened, / Death for five epochs, tortured torment, / May He bear my ruler, most nobly bred, / To share the most majestic mercy.' Trans. also in A. Conran, *The Penguin Book of Welsh Verse* (London, 1967), 132–3.

Cilmeri

the prince's endeavour, the agony of his loss, and the tragic consequences for the nation for which he had laboured.

> Poni welwch chwi hynt y gwynt a'r glaw?
> Poni welwch chwi'r deri yn ymdaraw?
> Poni welwch chwi'r mor yn merwinaw – 'r tir?
> Poni welwch chwi'r Gwir yn ymgyweiraw?
> Poni welwch chwi'r haul yn hwylaw – 'r awyr?
> Poni welwch chwi'r sŷr wedi'r syrthiaw?
> Pani chredwch chwi i Dduw, ddyniaddon ynfyd?
> Pani welwch chwi'r byd wedi'r bydiaw?
> Och hyd atat Ti, Dduw, na ddaw – môr tros dir!
> Pa beth y'n gedir i ohiriaw?
> Nid oes le y cyrcher rhag carchar braw,
> Nid oes le y trigier: och o'r trigiaw!
> Nid oes na chyngor na chlo nac egor,
> Unffordd i esgor brwyn gyngor braw.
>
> Pen pan las, ni bu gas gymraw,
> Pen pan las, oedd lesach peidiaw;
> Pen milwr, pen moliant rhag llaw,
> Pen dragon, pen draig oedd arnaw,
> Pen Llywelyn deg: dygn a fraw – i'r byd
> Bod pawl haearn trwyddaw;
> Pen f'arglwydd, poen dygngwydd a'm daw,
> Pen f'enaid heb fanag arnaw,
> Pen a fu berchen ar barch naw – canwlad
> A naw canwledd iddaw;
> Pen tëyrn, hëyrn hëid o'i law,
> Pen tëyrnwalch balch, bwlch edeifnaw,
> Pen tëyrnaidd, flaidd flaengar, ganthaw:
> Pen tëyrnedd nef, Ei nawdd arnaw![205]

---

[205] *GBF*, 36; *Oxford Book of Welsh Verse*, 45–9; Rh. Griffiths, *1282*, 31–2, quoting ll. 63–76, 87–100; trans. in Conran, *Penguin Book of Welsh Verse*, 128–31; Clancy, *Earliest Welsh Poetry*, 171–3; *Oxford Book of Welsh Verse in English*, 31–3; revised trans. by Clancy in Gwyn Thomas (ed.), *Llywelyn 1282* (Gregynog, 1982); Rh. Griffiths, *1282*, 32–4: 'See you not the rush of wind and rain? / See you not the oaks thrashing each other? / See you not that the sea is lashing the shore? / See you not that the truth is portending? / See you not that the sun is hurtling the sky? / See you not that the stars have fallen? / Do you not believe in God, foolish men? / See you not that the world is ending? / Ah, God, that the sea would cover the land! / What is left us that we should linger? / No place of escape from terror's prison, / No place to live: wretched is living! / No counsel, no clasp, not a single path / Open to be saved from fear's sad strife. / Head cut off, no hate so dreadful, / Head cut off, thing better not done, / Head of a soldier, head of praise, / Head of a warlord, dragon's head, / Head of fair Llywelyn: ḥarsh fear strikes the world, / An iron spike through it. / Head of my prince – harsh pain for me – Head of my soul rendered speechless./ Head that owned

Cilmeri

It would be fitting, on many counts, to bring this study to a close with the terminal event in the neighbourhood of Builth, at the place long known as Cefn-y-bedd but now named Cilmeri.[206] The chroniclers of both nations saw the death of Llywelyn as a disaster which broke the willpower of those in rebellion, and Edward was in due course to proceed to complete the final subjugation of Wales. For some months, however, resistance was maintained under the leadership of Dafydd ap Gruffudd. The king had every need of the financial resources to which he laid claim in a most demanding manner shortly before Llywelyn's death. Dafydd ap Gruffudd assumed the style of prince of Wales and lord of Snowdon, determined to maintain the unifying and stabilizing influences bound up with the notion of a principality.[207] He was the first in the history of his nation to secure a succession to the title, and some English commentators gained the impression that he was indeed able to maintain the activities and formalities appropriate to a principality. We seem to have something to substantiate this impression in a group of documents of the early summer of 1283. Reflecting, perhaps, some of the impulses which may have taken Llywelyn upon his fateful journey to Builth, Dafydd ap Gruffudd, prince of Wales and lord of Snowdon, authorized his emissary John ap Dafydd to call the men of Builth, Brecon and Maelienydd, Elfael, Gwerthrynion and Ceri to his allegiance. The document, dated at Llanberis on 2 May, seems to bear the imprint of a well-ordered princely administration. Similarly, on that same day, Dafydd issued a charter granting the *cantref* of Penweddig in northern Ceredigion to Rhys Fychan ap Rhys ap Maelgwn and this document, too, conforms to normal diplomatic practice. The prince of Wales and lord of Snowdon granted the *cantref* on terms which were binding on their respective heirs. Graciously yielding possession of Penweddig to Rhys Fychan, Gruffudd ap Maredudd ensured that the heirs to the patrimony of Maredudd ab Owain were certain of their right to the remainder of Ceredigion.[208] Each document

honour in nine hundred lands, / Nine hundred feasts were his. / Head of a king, his hand hurled iron, / Head of a king's hawk, forcing a gap./ Head of a kingly wolf out-thrusting, / Head of heaven's kings, be his haven!'

[206] The place traditionally linked with the death of Llywelyn was Cefn-y-bedd ('the ridge of the grave'), a name which gave rise to a supposition that his body was buried there, perhaps temporarily, but J. E. Lloyd, 'Death of Llywelyn', 352, showed that Cefn-y-bedd occurred in a document of 1277 (E101/485/21) and that the name had nothing to do with the prince's death. It would have been reasonable, even so, to retain Cefn-y-bedd as the name of place where the prince fell, but it has more recently become usual to refer to Cilmeri. This was originally the name of a nearby estate but, with the coming of the railway, Cilmeri, first applied to the station, came to supplant Cefn-y-bedd as the name of the village. It might be well to accept Cilmeri, a name well established in broader awareness of the significance of 1282 and the place where the prince's memorial stands.

[207] Langtoft, *Chronicle*, ii, 180–1, describes a gathering (*parlement*) at Christmas, where it was resolved to maintain resistance; Edward states that Dafydd assumed the name 'prince' ('sibi nomine principis verbaliter usurpato', *LibEpist*, no. 68).

[208] *LW*, 74–5, 77, 133.

571

made provision for generations yet to come, and taken together they could be taken as an illustration of the manner by which the interests of the barons of the principality could be reconciled under the aegis of a stable authority. There to witness the documents, precisely as they had been present, and given their assent to important transactions, in the period of Llywelyn ap Gruffudd, were those who represented the political community of the principality: Hywel ap Rhys Gryg, Rhys Wyndod, Llywelyn ap Rhys, Morgan ap Maredudd, and the prince's steward, Goronwy ap Heilin. Taken out of context the documents could convey an impression of ordered government, but even a careful reading of the documents themselves, apart from any other consideration, reveals the reality of the situation confronting these men. The grants which the prince of Wales made to Rhys Fychan were conditional upon his readiness to come to Dafydd with all his strength, whenever he was required to do so before a specified date. Dafydd's charter was dictated by his hope that Rhys Fychan might be brought to his allegiance, not from a position of neutrality, but from active service to the king. Rhys Fychan was at that very time in royal pay; he and Cynan ap Maredudd had adhered to the king after William de Valence had driven through Ceredigion with a force raised in south-west Wales early in the year.[209] By the summer Rhys Fychan was being employed to guard for the king the very area which Dafydd formally granted to him and he was being paid to hunt down the grantor himself. The little group still identified with Dafydd ap Gruffudd was by then in a desperate plight.

Cooped up in their last redoubt in Snowdonia their situation could reasonably be regarded as the inevitable result of the relentless advance which Edward had put in hand before Llywelyn's death and completed in accordance with a carefully laid strategy. As soon as negotiations with Llywelyn had been terminated Edward, as we have seen, called upon the community of the realm for a new effort to complete his task in Wales and, easing nothing of the pressure upon his opponents nor his demands on his subjects, he pressed on to achieve his purpose. At assemblies held in England early in 1283 to consider the king's request for aid the laity obliged and, though the clergy pleaded that the demand was made to finance a war in which Christian blood would be

---

[209] Valence led a force of some 1,600 men drawn from south-west Wales in an advance from Carmarthen and Cardigan to Aberystwyth by mid-January (C47/2/4). Rhys and Cynan, who submitted to Valence then or soon afterwards, were in the king's service, probably continuously, from March to July, each on occasion supplied with a contingent deployed for the security of the area around Llanbadarn Fawr or to search for Dafydd, Gruffudd ap Maredudd and Rhys Wyndod. Subsequently defecting, they were captured and in August taken to Bridgnorth to begin a long confinement (E101/351/9; *CAC*, 46; N. Fryde, *List of Welsh Entries in the Memoranda Rolls 1282–1343* (Cardiff, 1974), 4, 7). They were eventually admitted to the king's service, appearing in Flanders, 1297 (E101/6/28; BL, Add. MS 37655, f. 10v; Cotton Nero C viii, f. 43v, and references in chancery enrolments).

shed, they, too, agreed to contribute a reduced amount.[210] Military forces were summoned anew. The troops deployed included a contingent of sturdy warriors from Gascony and the Basque country. If Gaston de Béarn had not come in person, as he had intimated he might, he was represented by barons and soldiers, largely crossbowmen, of a breed not always inclined to peaceful ways in their own parts. Their contingents included as many as 47 knights, 121 mounted crossbowmen and 1,430 foot crossbowmen.[211] They formed part of the large force of mounted crossbowmen (the serjeants-at-arms) and foot crossbowmen whose lethal weapons could be used to telling effect. The quest for food and equipment, and for the means to pay the wages, went on relentlessly. There were new supplies of tents to provide protection against winter weather, and, probably doing more for the infantryman than the cross of St George which he carried on his arm, there were white clothing and boots to provide camouflage and warmth as he trudged through a terrain more *sauvage* than anything his lord archbishop had known.[212] It may have proved to be a ruthless conflict, with English troops able to claim by the king's gift one shilling a head for the heads of Welshmen brought back from combat, and contingents sent out to search for booty explicitly at the king's command.[213] It was an expensive enterprise, too, but Edward would see it through and, within a month of Llywelyn's death, the king's plans began to take effect in Gwynedd Uwch Conwy, though the time it took to bring them to completion reflects the resilience of the defenders.

By the beginning of 1283, but not very long before, Llanrwst and Betws became bases for English operations in the upper Conwy valley, and it seems that a crossing of the river had been forced by then.[214] The Welsh forces faced an advance made in two directions. One army moved upstream along the Conwy and Lledr valleys to Dolwyddelan, a key position in the defensive

---

[210] *AnnDunst*, 295–6; H. S. Deighton, 'Clerical taxation by consent, 1279–1301', *EHR*, 68 (1953), 161–91.

[211] Gaston declared his willingness to fight in Wales, though indicating that he might do more in the king's interest were he to serve him south of the Pyrenees (*Foedera*, I, ii, 611; J. B. Smith, 'Adversaries of Edward I: Gaston de Béarn and Llywelyn ap Gruffudd', 79). Chroniclers notice the arrival of the Gascons and Basques and account rolls give details of their service (e.g. Langtoft, *Chronicle*, ii, 180–1; E101/3/27; E101/14/4 (the Gascons' payroll and account of their horses), E101/351/9; cf. Morris, *WW*, 187–91; Trabut-Cussac, *L'Administration anglaise de Gascogne*, 69–70). The force was available for service from December 1282, reaching its greatest strength in January and February 1283, with 45 knights, 121 mounted crossbowmen and 1,373 foot crossbowmen. Details in E101/3/27 do not include Gaston's contingent, which may have served in Anglesey, but 1,000 of his men sailed from Dover on 14 February (E101/351/9).

[212] E101/351/9; *HKW*, i, 336, n. 2.

[213] Taylor, 'Hope castle account', 38–9, 41–3 (C47/2/3); E101/3/30 (troops sent out in the vicinity of Dolwyddelan 'per preceptum regis ad querendum predam').

[214] Morris, *WW*, 190–1; *HKW*, i, 336–7; E101/3/29 and E101/351/9 remain informative sources for this phase of the conflict.

Cilmeri

preparations of the princes. By 18 January the castle was in the king's possession and it is difficult to judge with what degree of resolve it had been defended. It is certainly possible that Edward had negotiated its surrender even before his forces set out upon their advance along the Lledr valley, for the fidelity of its constable, Gruffudd ap Tudur, is open to question.[215] Masons and carpenters were immediately put to work and the castle was munitioned as a base for further advance. Less well recorded in its progress, but an exceedingly important advance, another army moved down the Conwy valley to Aberconwy. By early March 1283 the encampment became Edward's main centre of operations.[216] The king had by then accomplished the two movements which were almost certainly intended to be co-ordinated with the crossing of the Menai Straits from Anglesey. Arrangements on the island were entrusted to Otto de Grandson and the bridge of boats refurbished for a new assault. This time the English army was not to be repelled and, almost certainly before the end of 1282, Grandson established a bridgehead in the vicinity of Bangor.[217] Supplied directly from Rhuddlan and Chester, the army was able to consolidate its position and begin the advance which would enable it to link up with the forces from Aberconwy and gradually take the king's power southward to Caernarfon and Cricieth.[218] By the end of March forces were penetrating even to Ardudwy and Penllyn. William de Valence had finally secured Ceredigion by a campaign waged in early January and, though he maintained a close watch on the area from a base at Llanbadarn Fawr, he was confident enough to entrust some of the responsibility to Cynan ap Maredudd and Rhys Fychan ap Rhys ap Maelgwn. In early April he moved northward into Meirionnydd, gathering for the last time the contingents from south-west Wales which he had summoned to his aid for successive campaigns against his

---

[215] E101/359/9 provides the date. Payments are made to one named Tudur ap Gruffudd, constable of Dolwyddelan, at court for twelve days from 5 December 1282 (E101/4/1); Prestwich, *Edward I*, 194–5, noting that he received double the wages to which his rank entitled him, rightly suggests that a deal was made between the defenders and the English commanders. The name given in E101/3/20 is Gruffudd ap Tudur; he was constable of Dolwyddelan from 4 July 1283 and was granted the castle for life on 22 August 1284 (E101/4/1; *CWR*, 288), and the scribe of E101/351/9 has probably given the name wrongly. He can be identified as Gruffudd ap Tudur ap Madog, a son of the Tudur ap Madog who has been noticed as an early adherent of Llywelyn (Stephenson, *GG*, 132; above, pp 44–5, 263). For substantial intake of supplies (suggesting that the castle had not been prepared for a long siege, as Dr Walker notes), and the works undertaken from the day of the capture, *HKW*, i, 336–7.

[216] E101/351/9; references to Aberconwy abound from early March and the king's letters are dated there from 13 March.

[217] Ibid.; E101/4/1; shipments from Rhuddlan and Chester to Bangor are recorded in payments authorized 28 December–3 January and constantly thereafter. It is likely that a bridgehead had been established by the end of 1282 or the very first days of 1283; cf. *CAC*, 203; *HKW*, i, 357.

[218] E101/3/30.

Cilmeri

resourceful opponents. Roger Lestrange, with the marches now finally secured, was more willing than he had been before to advance into the Berwyn range to combine with the forces advancing from the south. He may have brought a force similar to that which he had under his command at Builth at the end of the previous year.[219] Valence and Lestrange converged on Castell y Bere, completing the movements which Llywelyn had probably anticipated. The king's commanders had a formidable force at their service, and the facilities for a siege, but the custodian, Cynfrig ap Madog, and those with him, accepted the terms that were offered to them provided they were to surrender the castle by a stated date. Castell y Bere and Dolwyddelan had fallen without any resistance. Dafydd may well have intended to make a stand at Castell y Bere, but he was not there when Valence and Lestrange received its submission on 25 April.[220] Dafydd was a fugitive now, with the king's soldiers, guided by Welshmen recruited for the purpose, pursuing him into the most remote retreats. He took some finding, for the king's commanders were forced into expensive searches by successive contingents, not only in Gwynedd – where Ardudwy, Meirionnydd and Penllyn were carefully combed – but far and wide as they sought the elusive prince in Mawddwy and Powys and in the marches beyond, and in the lands of Gruffudd ap Maredudd in Ceredigion and Rhys Wyndod in Ystrad Tywi.[221] Even at this stage the king's men could not be certain that they had contained their adversary, but the search was increasingly concentrated on Ardudwy and Penllyn and Snowdonia.[222] In extremity

---

[219] Forces were mustered for an advance into Meirionnydd on 2 May by orders of 14 and 21 March (*CWR*, 278–81). Valence, acting earlier than he was called upon, took about 700 men, later increased, from Aberystwyth, 13 April, and reached Castell y Bere on 15 April. Lestrange reached the castle on 21 April, bringing forces raised mainly in Ellesmere, Knockin, Whittington, Caus, Powys and Montgomery (E372/128; C47/2/4; E101/3/30).

[220] For the siege of Castell y Bere, where more than 3,000 men gathered, *HKW*, i, 367; Master Bertram's engineering skills were available (Taylor, 'Master Bertram', 310, 314), but may not have been called upon. The castle was yielded on terms offered by Valence and Lestrange on 22 April, by which the defenders would be given £80 if the castle were surrendered within a week (*LW*, 189–90); it was yielded three days later and payment of £53 6s. 8d. is recorded in C47/2/4. Each document names Gruffudd ap Madog among the defenders; this was the name of the poet Gruffudd ab yr Ynad Coch, and the presence of a person of this name at Bere is noticed in view of the suggestion made by Tomos Roberts, based on the references to the names Nantcaw and Nancol (places close by the castle) in the elegy to Llywelyn, that the poem was composed at Castell y Bere (*GBF*, 36, background note p. 414; for the places, above, p. 228, n. 192). The identification of the poet with the person at Castell y Bere is uncertain, however, and it would be prudent to reserve judgement.

[221] Payments for searches or custody of particular areas, sometimes involving several contingents, are noted in E101/3/30; E101/351/9; C47/2/4: e.g. the sons of Gruffudd ap Gwenwynwyn took their men to the mountains of Mawddwy and 'Mourreg'. Welshmen were often employed to guide soldiers along remote passes and ridges.

[222] Resistance was maintained in some areas, e.g. Penllyn, where Elias the Chaplain went 'on the king's business' in April but where Llywelyn ap Gruffudd ap Gogan was still engaged 'to spy on wrongdoers' in July (E101/351/9).

Cilmeri

Dafydd may even have made an attempt to secure the king's mercy, for the Hagnaby chronicler says that he sent his wife and Roger Clifford to the king. Edward would have none of it, for his anger towards Dafydd, so clearly revealed upon his capture, was not to be assuaged. Dafydd had to be pursued.[223] It was in Snowdonia, at Llanberis and right at the foot of Snowdon itself, that we have the last glimpse of the last cohort of the princes of the principality of Wales. Dafydd was probably captured in this area, finally betrayed, we are told, by his own men.[224] Some of his adherents held out even longer, but there was now a general collapse of Welsh resistance, as not only known partisans of the crown such as Gruffudd ap Iorwerth led contingents of men in royal service, but others, such as Tudur ap Goronwy, who may well have abandoned the princes' ranks only recently, also served in the king's forces.[225] Early in July formal submissions were made on behalf of the communities of Gwynedd Uwch Conwy by which six of the most responsible men of each *cantref* bound themselves under ecclesiastical censure to ensure that the peace was kept in their localities.[226]

The months following the death of Llywelyn had indeed revealed the manner in which Edward's preparation and persistence confined his opponents to their last redoubts and pursued them even there, but this last phase in Welsh resistance cannot be altogether understood without taking account of the internal factors which mattered to Dafydd as they had mattered to Llywelyn. The last months were not entirely a phase apart, for the defenders' anxieties were mounting before the death of Llywelyn. On the other hand, those gathered about Dafydd may not have seen their predicament entirely in terms of military desperation until almost the very end. Even in their final extremity the memory of their political objectives remained. Hywel ap Rhys

---

[223] Cotton Vesp. B xi, f. 29v: 'destinavit nuncios ad regem Anglie, Rogerum videlicet de Clifford, quem dudum ceperat, et uxorem suam exorans ut ei pacem concederat in terram suam'; there is a further statement that Dafydd's wife, who was a sister of Robert de Ferrers, returned without success.

[224] *CWR*, 281–2; *Foedera*, I, ii, 630; also *RPeck*, iii, 780, quoting a charge that a cleric, Iorwerth of Llan-faes, had betrayed Dafydd. Among chroniclers' comments: *BT, Pen20*, 228; *Pen20Tr*, 121; *AnnDunst*, 293, 298; *AnnOsney*, 292; *ChronWykes*, 292; Trevet, *Annales*, 307.

[225] E101/3/30.

[226] Documents for the *cantrefi* of Gwynedd Uwch Conwy, except Anglesey, drawn up before the bishop of Bangor, 9 July 1283, and for Tegeingl, before the bishop of Chester and Lichfield and the archdeacon of St Asaph (in the absence of the bishop), 25 September, *LW*, 151–2, 154–7. Similar transactions were completed in the *cantrefi* of Rhos and Rhufoniog at the instance of the earl of Lincoln, 26 July (DL25/2063; summary of content and names of those who put their seals to the document in F. Jones, 'Welsh bonds for keeping the peace, 1283 and 1295', *B*, 13 (1948–50), 142–4). For further transactions by the bishop of Bangor and the communities of Gwynedd Uwch Conwy, 2 August, registering the complaints against the late prince, Llinos B. Smith, 'The *gravamina* of the community of Gwynedd against Llywelyn ap Gruffudd', *B*, 31 (1984–5), 158–76; above, pp. 193, 255–60, 266–7, 271–2.

Cilmeri

Gryg was one who had been through adversity and triumph and adversity again. In his youth, after disinheritance and exile, he had known the camaraderie of those who stood defiant in the mountain retreats of Gwynedd and inspired the chronicler to compare them with the Maccabees in their standfast valour. In his mature years Hywel had seen their hopes of better days come to fulfilment as Llywelyn ap Gruffudd brought the benefit of political processes as well as military effort. He had then seen the disintegration of the political community and we can only guess what his true feelings had been when he, who had been unwavering in his fidelity, found those who had been so quick to secede so eager to rise in new rebellion.[227] But he stood by Dafydd ap Gruffudd to the very end, and so did Goronwy ap Heilin. We may perhaps detect his influence in the last pronouncements made in the name of the prince of Wales in response to the archbishop's initiative, and we can only wonder whether he truly believed that those elevated and courageous sentiments could be reflected in political reality thereafter. His own statements and those made in the name of the community of Rhos are, as we have seen, eloquent testimony to the experience which had brought many men into rebellion, but he, too, may have been bemused by the new-found bravery of disillusioned princes, sceptical as to whether the sense of oppression in the community at large was enough to sustain the momentous struggle in which they became locked, even with Llywelyn ap Gruffudd to give the endeavour coherence and direction. The last months saw inward disintegration as well as submission to superior force. Nevertheless, Goronwy had committed himself to the struggle and died in rebellion, alongside the disinherited princes who stood with Dafydd ap Gruffudd in the last springtime of the principality of Wales, diehards who knew that theirs was not the heroism of a new beginning but the ultimate stand of the very last cohort clutching the last figment of the political order that they had once been privileged to know.[228]

---

[227] He was at Castell y Bere in 1286 (C47/4/3; *LW*, 187). Of the other princes in Dafydd's company in May, Rhys Wyndod and his brother Hywel ap Rhys were captured and taken from Caernarfon to the Tower of London about the end of July (E101/351/9; Cotton Vesp. B xi, f. 28; Trevet, *Annales*, 307–8; *AnnDunst*, 293). Rhys died in the Tower 1302, but Llywelyn ap Rhys, also captured, was still detained there, in unsatisfactory conditions, several years later (Fryde, *Welsh Entries in the Memoranda Rolls*, 4; *CAC*, 98–9, 261–2, with further references). Hywel ap Rhys may be the 'Hywel o Landingat' whose elegy was composed by Trahaearn Brydydd Mawr (*Gwaith Gruffudd ap Dafydd ap Tudur, Gwilym Ddu o Arfon, Trahaearn Brydydd Mawr ac Iorwerth Beli*, ed. N. G. Costigan (Bosco) *et al.* (Aberystwyth, 1995), no. 11).

[228] *SD*, 297, records that Goronwy ap Heilin ap Cynfrig had died against the peace and his lands had escheated. His son, Llywelyn, endured long imprisonment in Chester castle, along with Trahaearn, son of Hywel ap Rhys (*Accounts of the Chamberlains of the County of Chester 1301–1360*, ed. R. Stewart-Brown (Lancashire and Cheshire Records Society, 59, 1910), 11, 26, 45, 79, 86).

Cilmeri

At another time, in different circumstances, Dafydd ap Gruffudd might well have been capable of maintaining the political order which his remaining adherents still represented to some degree. He had always been a restive one, but just as Edward I gave vent to his anger towards him in these last months, so had Henry III recognized the qualities in his nature which made him a dangerous person to be allowed to succeed to Llywelyn's princedom.[229] The responsibilities of authority might have served to bring stability. He had much to his advantage, not least the fact that he had two sons, Owain and Llywelyn, who gave him a stake in the future, unlike Llywelyn ap Gruffudd.[230] Up to the spring of 1282 this was still something which mattered immensely, and it was Dafydd himself, whatever moved him, who cast those prospects aside. By the last week in June 1283, probably on the 22nd, Dafydd had at last been captured.[231] On 28 June Edward proclaimed in exultant language that the last of the treacherous lineage, princes of the turbulent nation which had so disturbed the realm of England, was in his grasp, captured by men of his own nation (*per homines lingue sue*).[232] The magnates of England and representatives of the shires and boroughs were gathered together in Shrewsbury on the morrow of Michaelmas in response to a summons whose phrasing reflects the king's deep felt anger towards Dafydd, the last survivor of a family of traitors.[233] He was tried and sentenced to death for treason, and judgement was executed, in a barbaric manner, on 2 October.[234] Dragged to the scaffold at the horse's tail for betraying the king, he was hanged alive for homicide, he was disembowelled and his entrails burned for his sacrilege in committing his crimes in the week of Christ's Passion, and his body, quartered for plotting the king's death, was dispatched

---

[229] Above, pp. 137–8.

[230] He had married after 1265 Elizabeth, daughter of Robert Ferrers, earl of Derby, and widow of William Marshal, and thereby gained possession of the manor of Folesham, co. Norfolk, then exchanged with John Marshal for the manor of Norton, co. Northampton (*LW*, 139–40, 142–3). He also held by the king's grant for life in September 1278 the manor of Frodsham, co. Chester, previously held at will (*CCR, 1272–79*, 317; *CPR, 1272–81*, 279).

[231] The Hagnaby chronicler states that Dafydd and one son were captured on 21 or 22 June (his use of the Christian and Roman calendars giving a discrepancy of one day), and that the other son was taken on 29 June. Dafydd, seriously wounded (*graviter vulneratus*), was taken to the king the same night (Cotton Vesp. B xi, f. 30). *AnnDunst*, 293, gives the date of Dafydd's capture as 22 June; the London chronicler notes that Dafydd's wife, two sons and seven daughters were also taken (*Chronicles Edward I and Edward II*, i, 90). Dafydd was taken to Rhuddlan and later escorted to Chester and Shrewsbury.

[232] *CWR*, 281–2; *Foedera*, I, ii, 630; *RegSwinfield*, 79–80; *RegPontissara*, ii, 631–2.

[233] The king's anger towards Dafydd is again vehemently expressed in a letter ordering the return to the original depositaries of the tax of one-tenth collected for the Holy Land (*LibEpist*, no. 68).

[234] J. G. Bellamy, *The Law of Treason in England in the Later Middle Ages* (Cambridge, 1970), 24–9, examines the trial in relation to the development of the law of treason. There is no full record of the trial and chronicle evidence is used to elucidate the role of king, magnates and justices in the conviction.

to the four corners of the kingdom.²³⁵ His head was displayed beside the head of Llywelyn on the Tower of London, his cruel death deeply lamented by Bleddyn Fardd.²³⁶

Nor were Dafydd's sons to escape the king's wrath, for they were heirs to a lineage condemned to extinction. After the father's capture the search for Llywelyn ap Dafydd, the *primogenitus* of the captive prince, had continued until he, too, was found.²³⁷ Llywelyn and his brother Owain were taken away under adequate escort and confined at Bristol.²³⁸ Llywelyn ap Dafydd died in 1287 and was buried in the Dominican church; Owain ap Dafydd endured prolonged imprisonment. At one time he was compelled to spend his nights in a timber cage bound with iron to ensure that there was no escape. Languishing in Bristol castle, short of food and clothing, a child seeking permission to play within the walls of his prison: it is the last chilling evidence we have of Owain ap Dafydd, who might have been a prince of the lineage of Llywelyn ap Gruffudd and Llywelyn ap Iorwerth and Owain Gwynedd.²³⁹ Edward took good care, too, to ensure that his adversaries' daughters would do no harm in years to come. Shortly after Dafydd's execution he wrote to the prior and prioress of the Gilbertine house of Alvingham in Lincolnshire and recalled the perfidy of Dafydd and Llywelyn. He conveyed his wish that, remembering their gender and tender age, and anxious that the innocent and the unwitting should not be seen to atone for the iniquity of the wicked, one or more of the prince's daughters be admitted to the Order at the priory. Dafydd's daughters were in fact sent to the security of the priory at Sixhills,

---

[235] Geoffrey of Shrewsbury was paid 20s. for executing, on 2 October, the judgement on Dafydd (E101/351/9). It was a gruesome task, its results noticed in several chronicles noted in Bellamy, *Treason*, 293–4, including *FloresHist*, iii, 58–9, and *AnnDunst*, 293–4; Hagnaby (Cotton Vesp. B xi, f. 29v); *Le Livere de Reis de Brittanie*, 322, may be added. For comment upon a sentence 'comprehensive and savage, if not unprecedented in its viciousness', Prestwich, *Edward I*, 202.

[236] *GBF*, 52, 53, an *awdl* and a sequence of *englynion*. The poet mourns the loss of a man of great valour, the sixth of the princes he had known, Llywelyn ap Iorwerth, his sons and three of his four grandsons

[237] E101/3/30; the son captured with Dafydd would have been Owain. Gruffudd ap Iorwerth was among those engaged in the task of seeking Llywelyn ('ad querendum filium David primogenitum').

[238] A force of cavalry and infantry was deployed to escort Llywelyn and Owain from Gwynedd through Acton Burnell to Bristol before the end of July 1283 and the two were detained there (*Accounts of Bristol Castle*, 17, 26–7). Gruffudd ap Dafydd Goch, whose stone effigy, c.1385, is in the church of Betws y Coed, is said in genealogical sources to have been a son of Dafydd Goch, illegitimate son of Dafydd ap Gruffudd (Bartrum, *WG*, i, 447; Gresham, *Medieval Stone Carving*, 194–6; Siddons, *Welsh Heraldry*, i, 193, 235–6; ii, 189).

[239] *Accounts of Bristol Castle*, xxx, 17, 26–7; *CPR, 1281–92*, 71; *CPR, 1307–13*, 452; *CCR, 1318–23*, 267; *CCR, 1323–27*, 400, and, for the petition, *CAP*, 521–2. For the cage, *HKW*, ii, 580, and for Edward's decision, about the same time, to put some women of the kindred of Robert Bruce in cages, Barrow, *Bruce*, 230–1.

Cilmeri

another Gilbertine house in the same neighbourhood.[240] It stood some way to the north of Sempringham, the nunnery of the same Order chosen for their cousin Gwenllian, daughter of Llywelyn, one in whose veins ran all the honour and anguish of the lineages of Gwynedd and Montfort. She would remain there until the day of her death more than fifty years later.[241] We know nothing of the distress which she may have felt as she came to years, only that the chronicler who wrote that she was taken into captivity upon her father's death also tells us that before coming of age she was made a nun against her will.[242]

The progeny of Llywelyn and Dafydd spent their years in captivity and exile, and in Wales, by word and deed, the nation bore testimony to the realization that the tragedy on the day of Pope Damasus had seen 'all Wales cast to the ground'.[243] In a truly concluding formality the sacred relic of the Croes Naid was handed over to Edward at Aberconwy.[244] It was, the chancery clerk solemnly records, part of the most holy wood of the True Cross which

[240] Letter, given by the king's privy seal at Ludlow, 11 November 1283 (*MonAng*, VI, ii, 959, from the cartulary of Alvingham, Bodley Laud Misc. 642, f. 42a). E101/351/9 notes provision made for the needs of Dafydd's daughters. Robert Manning (Hearne, *Works*, iv, 243), himself a canon of Sempringham and then of Sixhills, states that Gwladus was placed at Sixhills and that she died a year before her cousin Gwenllian. The arrangements made for the others, whose names are not known, do not appear to be recorded. The choice of nunneries is not readily explained, but the houses were far enough from Wales, and Sempringham was a major house with accommodation for as many as 200 nuns.

[241] Robert Manning, ibid., records that she was brought to Sempringham, by the king's command, 'in hir credill'. Gwenllian was one of a number of ladies of noble birth at Sempringham (*CPapL*, ii, 185, 273; *Foedera*, II, i, 313; III, 606; B. Golding, *Gilbert of Sempringham and the Gilbertine Order c.1130–c.1300* (Oxford, 1995), 153). The houses of Sixhills and Walton were later chosen for Bruce's sister and daughter (Barrow, *Bruce*, 230–1). For the Gilbertine houses generally, R. Graham, *St Gilbert of Sempringham and the Gilbertines* (London, 1901); Golding, *Gilbert of Sempringham* and earlier works cited. By an undated petition Gwenllian, 'daughter of Llywelyn formerly prince of Wales', sought financial maintenance consistent with the promise made to her by Edward I (*CAP*, 458, and, for payments of £20 a year, *Calendar of Memoranda Rolls, 1326–7*, no. 2160; *CCR, 1327–30*, 65, 175, 273, 322, 438). For Manning's notice of her coming to Sempringham and her death, see also below, p. 586.

[242] *BT, Pen20*, 223; *Pen20Tr*, 117; *RBH*, 264–5. An inquiry in 1289 concerning the custody of the daughters of Llywelyn and Dafydd (*CPR, 1281–92*, 321; *Foedera*, i, ii, 712) notes that they had by then taken the veil of the order of Sempringham.

[243] *BS*, 258–9, a reflection which concludes a factual account in close accord with what appears in the Peniarth 20 text.

[244] *CWR*, 273–4, gives the names of those who handed over the Croes Naid in June 1283; their exemption from military service outside the Four Cantreds was authorized by a warrant which stated that the relic of the True Cross had been passed from prince to prince from the first time it had come to England down to the time of Dafydd ap Gruffudd (C81/1685/25; Taylor, *SCCB*, 283–4). Dr Taylor, printing an entry from an Alms Roll for 1283 which records that Edward provided support at Oxford for a Welsh cleric, Huw ab Ithel, who had brought the Croes Naid to Edward, suggests that this was the unnamed secretary of Prince Dafydd who, according to Rishanger, *Chronica*, 104, brought the relic to the king; cf. Trevet, *Annales*, 307.

Cilmeri

Llywelyn ap Gruffudd, prince of Wales, and his ancestors, princes of Wales, had possessed. Edward, out of reverence for Him who had suffered death on that wood for the redemption of mankind, granted the laymen who had brought it to him exemption from military service outside Perfeddwlad, and for the cleric Huw ab Ithel he provided support for his studies at Oxford. The handing over to the king of England of the Croes Naid was an acknowledgement that the dynasty which had cared for it, and gained its protection, through the ages had been irretrievably destroyed. It fell to Bleddyn Fardd to compose the final commemoration in elegies to Owain and Llywelyn and Dafydd, each in turn, and then to the three of them together. The rifts between the brothers had gone deep, and the nation shared a searing anguish. For lowly and noble alike the wrath visited upon their leader brought their utter undoing. Unlike Dafydd Benfras, who had once commemorated three princes of the dynasty when all three were laid to rest together at a sacred spot, Bleddyn Fardd had neither place nor occasion to inspire his verse.[245] He was left only with a compelling need to affirm that the blow which had felled the prince was a truly fatal blow, and to beseech God's blessing on his soul.

---

[245] For the elegy to the three brothers, *GBF*, 54; trans. Clancy, *Earliest Welsh Poetry*, 169–70. Dafydd Benfras's elegy to Llywelyn ap Iorwerth, Gruffudd ap Llywelyn and Dafydd ap Llywelyn is noticed above, pp. 64–5.

CHAPTER 11
Epilogue

THE elegies composed by Bleddyn Fardd and Gruffudd ab yr Ynad Coch upon the death of Llywelyn ap Gruffudd, the one an erudite composition of rare sensitivity, the other a personal and passionate effusion of anguish, convey the sense of a tragedy with dire consequences for their nation. They stand among the most moving commemorations of a medieval ruler ever written, and in these last pages we shall consider the extent to which these estimations of Llywelyn were to be replicated down the ages.[1] How were the prince and the principality that he had created remembered after the death of the prince and the destruction of the principality? In the ordinances by which Edward I provided for the government of the lands brought under his authority he made no mention of the principality of Wales, let alone its prince. In a preamble which declared that a change was now made in the status of Wales, it was not the principality but the land of Wales (*terra Wallie*), previously subject to the king by feudal right (*iure feodali*), which was now united to the crown of England.[2] It might seem that prince and principality alike were destined to be consigned to the memory of those now made subject to the new order. In the years following the conquest, quite apart from any profound sense of history, the material needs of some among the king's subjects indeed induced them to cite Llywelyn's name when they wished to justify to the new authorities a claim to a privilege derived from his time or to resist an imposition claimed to be at variance with the practice which had obtained under his rule.[3] More significant is the fact that, in times of heightened stress, the notion of a princedom might suggest itself as a focus for a political initiative taken in violent reaction to the crown's authority.

---

[1] Above, pp. 569–70. This brief epilogue is largely based, by generous permission, on Llinos B. Smith, 'Llywelyn ap Gruffydd and the Welsh historical consciousness', *WHR*, 12 (1984–5), 1–28, which provides an extensive documentation only partially reflected in this chapter.
[2] *Statutes of the Realm*, i, 55.
[3] E.g. *RC*, 220; *CAP*, 27 *et passim*.

Epilogue

Madog ap Llywelyn assumed the style 'prince of Wales' when he rose in rebellion in 1294.[4] A member of the princely lineage of Gwynedd, though not the illegitimate son of Llywelyn ap Gruffudd that an English chronicler, and several later historians, believed him to be, Madog and those about him sought to raise the prospect of a resurgent principality. Two generations later a lone survivor of the lineage, Owain ap Thomas ap Rhodri (Owain Lawgoch), laid claim to his inheritance in Wales though without, according to the surviving record of his eloquent proclamation, evoking the memory of a principality.[5] But, in the early fifteenth century, Owain Glyndŵr styled himself 'prince of Wales' from the very outbreak of his rebellion and concentrated his strenuous efforts on the creation of a principality of Wales. In his references to his predecessors, though none are named, he seems to have had in mind his historic forebears quite apart from the distant legendary figures whom he certainly recalled in his evocation of the past.[6] By then, however, for a hundred years, a principality of Wales had been closely identified with the political authority that Owain sought to overthrow.

Although no reference was made to a principality of Wales in the ordinances of 1284 the arrangements which Edward made for the crown lands, keeping the new shires apart from the government of those of England in important respects, facilitated the creation of the principality of Wales upon which Edward was resolved by 1301. The shires granted to Edward of Caernarfon, along with the marcher lordships in north-east Wales whose lords were required to do him homage, constituted a territory which approximated closely to the principality of Llywelyn ap Gruffudd.[7] Edward I's charter in that year in fact said nothing of prince or 'principality', but his heir became known as prince of Wales and the term 'principality' came to be used to describe the territories which formed his estate. For the second creation of 1343 the record is fuller than it is for the earlier occasion, and the heir to Edward III's throne, summoned to parliament as one whom the king had created prince of Wales and granted the principality of Wales, is known to have received formal investiture 'according to custom'.[8] There are thus good grounds for the conclusion that the principality created in 1301 'was

---

[4] J. G. Edwards, 'Madog ap Llywelyn, the Welsh leader in 1294–5', *B*, 13 (1948–50), 207–10; G. Roberts, 'Madog ap Llywelyn', *B*, 17 (1956–8), 40–1; *RC*, 220; DL 25/3569.

[5] Carr, *Owen of Wales*, 27–8; proclamation (1372) in translation in E. Owen, 'Owain Lawgoch', *THSC*, 1899–1900, 61–2.

[6] R. R. Davies, *The Revolt of Owain Glyn Dŵr* (Oxford, 1995), 102, 158–60; texts of important documents in *Welsh Records in Paris*, ed. T. Matthews (Carmarthen, 1910), 23–54.

[7] *CChR*, iii, 5; *CPR, 1343–45*, 227–34; J. G. Edwards, *Principality of Wales*, 9–15, 31–4.

[8] *CChR*, v, 14; texts and commentary in Sir Matthew Hale's *The Prerogatives of the King*, ed. D. E. C. Yale (London, Selden Society, 1976), 23–5. For fourteenth-century investiture, F. Jones, *Princes and Principality of Wales*, 119–24.

Epilogue

regarded as being institutionally continuous with Llywelyn's principality of 1267'.[9] Edward I's evident wish to preserve the coronet – or crown – that he secured upon the death of Llywelyn, and his concern to take good care of the Croes Naid, point to a desire to conserve the symbols and relics of a princely inheritance which, though it might be regarded as a compendium of rights that had been wrested from the kings of England in years gone by, was in recent memory identified with the prince of Wales whom he had vanquished.[10] When a further stage in the incorporation of Wales within the realm of England was completed in 1536 the preamble to the enactment refers to 'the dominion, principality and land of Wales' and, subsequently provided with a judicature which remained separate from the Westminster courts, the greatly extended principality remained a distinct jurisdictional entity for another three centuries.[11] The principality which had its origins in the achievement formally registered in the treaty which Llywelyn ap Gruffudd negotiated with the crown in 1267 endured for a very long time. But to what extent, and by what means, was the memory of its progenitor sustained among those of his own nation in the centuries following his death?

The elegies to Llywelyn undoubtedly reflect the trauma in the minds of those who represented the distinguished eulogistic tradition that had been sustained by the kings and princes of the Welsh dynasties over many generations. Yet the tenor of these inspired threnodies would not be recaptured in the poetry of the next two centuries. The poetic tradition was itself to see a marked reorientation in the changed circumstances in which royal and marcher power came to be consolidated in the era of conquest. The poets remained among the remembrancers of the historical inheritance, but their work reflects the adjustment to new political conditions made by the patrons, no longer of princely rank, upon whom they depended. There were indeed times of restiveness in Welsh society, apart from those of overt rebellion, but disaffection

---

[9] J. G. Edwards, *Principality of Wales*, 10–11, 15–16.

[10] The cost of work done by the king's goldsmith, William de Farndon, on Llywelyn's crown and its gilding (*pro factura et auro apposito super coronam Leulini*) is noted in E101/372/11, m.1, a reference I owe to Susan Davies. The text indicates crown rather than the coronet or *talaith* noticed above, pp. 332–3; similarly English chronicles refer to a crown and make it the crown of Arthur (*FloresHist*, iii, 59: 'Corona quondam famosi regis Britonum Arthuri regi Anglie cum aliis jocalibus reddebatur;' cf. Rishanger, *Chronica*, 101; *AnnWav*, 378–9). Allusion to the crown as that of Arthur is a feature of English writing rather than Welsh (J. B. Smith, *SHMW*, 9); contemporary Arthurian predilections are considered in R. S. Loomis, 'Edward I, Arthurian enthusiast', *Speculum*, 28 (1953), 114–27. The Croes Naid, is noticed above, pp. 333, 580–1.

[11] 27 Henry VIII, 26; 35 & 35 Henry VIII, c. 26; J. G. Edwards, *Principality of Wales*, 21–8; J. B. Smith, 'The legal position of Wales in the middle ages', 21–2. For seventeenth-century legal commentary, John Vaughan, *Reports and Arguments* (London, 1677), 399–405.

Epilogue

with the ruling order was only occasionally reflected in any invocation of the memory of the princes. Certainly, the prospect that Owain ap Thomas ap Rhodri might come to his country to seek his inheritance inspired the poet Gruffudd ap Maredudd ap Dafydd to recall the historical experience set in train on the battlefield of Bryn Derwin. Then the prevailing circumstances lent credibility to a composition distinguished by a consonance in style and imagery and sentiments with the work of the poet's predecessors in the period of the princes.[12] Moreover, the death of Goronwy ap Tudur, descendant of the prince's seneschal Goronwy ab Ednyfed, and a member of a lineage which may well have had some knowledge of Owain's ambitions, moved Llywelyn Goch ap Meurig Hen to recall the death of the prince exactly a hundred years before.[13] During the remainder of the medieval period occasional allusions to Llywelyn certainly occur, sometimes in a prophetic context. There was evidently an impression of his greatness and there was a memory of betrayal at Builth, but it is difficult to judge the extent to which the often enigmatic invocations of Llywelyn's name reflect a meaningful grasp of the prince's significance in the history of the nation.[14] The references are not numerous and the poets, custodians of an indigenous inheritance though they undoubtedly were, tended to evoke the figures of a distant legendary era more readily than they remembered those of the historical memory of more recent experience.[15]

The poets shared their remembrance with others, for the genealogists were kindred keepers of the nation's memory. Llywelyn had left no heir to help sustain his memory in their parchments. Of the two great princes of the thirteenth century, it was Llywelyn ap Iorwerth who was the better remembered. This was partly because the Mortimer family, who had a conspicuous presence in fourteenth-century Wales duly marked in poetic celebration, could include the elder prince in their pedigree. They could trace their

---

[12] *Poetry in the Red Book of Hergest*, cols. 1313–14; Carr, *Owen of Wales*, 81–2. A *cywydd* to Owain by an unidentified poet includes a reference to the death of his uncles, that is Llywelyn and Dafydd (*Cywyddau Iolo Goch ac Eraill*, ed. H. Lewis, T. Roberts and I. Williams (Cardiff, 1937), no. xxx; *Gwaith Iolo Goch*, ed. D. R. Johnston (Cardiff, 1988), xxv–xxvii).

[13] *Poetry in the Red Book of Hergest*, col. 1307. 23–8; with a possible reference to Llywelyn's death by Gruffudd ap Maredudd ap Dafydd, prompted by the same circumstances, ibid., col. 1231. 2–3. References are examined in D. R. Johnston, 'Tri chyfeiriad at Lywelyn ap Gruffudd', *B*, 36 (1989), 97–101.

[14] Ll. B. Smith, 'Historical consciousness', 10; there is a valuable anthology in *Llywelyn y Beirdd*, 109–50. Important references are Ieuan Deulwyn's comparison of the death of William Herbert (1469) with that of Llywelyn, Dafydd Llwyd's reference (in a prophecy addressed to Henry Tudor) to the treachery at Builth, and a further reference by Lewys Môn to the prince's betrayal (ibid., nos. xvii, xx; *Casgliad o Waith Ieuan Deulwyn*, ed. I. Williams (Bangor, 1909), no. xxxv; *Gwaith Dafydd Llwyd*, 23; *Gwaith Lewys Môn*, 112; above, p. 551, n. 144).

[15] Studies of the legendary history are noticed below, nn. 27, 29.

Epilogue

ancestry to Gwladus Ddu, daughter of Llywelyn the Great, and thereby fashion a claim to princely inheritance.[16] The poet Iolo Goch, in whose work the conflicting impulses in post-conquest society are graphically reflected, was able to celebrate the family connection with Aberffraw that the Mortimers were themselves careful to record in their baronial archive.[17] Llywelyn ap Gruffudd had left only Gwenllian, who was to spend her years in the seclusion of the nunnery at Sempringham. Her presence there, and then her death, were to be noticed by chroniclers of that distant land rather than by those of her own country. She died on 7 June 1337 and Robert Manning, a canon of the house when Gwenllian was brought to Sempringham in her cradle fifty-four years before, wrote of her courtesy and the esteem in which she was held, and reflected that in more propitious circumstances she could have been her father's solace and pride in his old age.[18] But bereft of heirs in his own land Llywelyn's memory suffered accordingly, and the genealogists of the later medieval centuries were even unsure of his mother's identity. It is a measure of the inexorably receding memory that there even proved to be uncertainty over the identity of the woman who had given birth to one who would be prince of Wales.[19]

The indications in the poetry and in genealogy suggest continuing neglect, but it would be well to consider whether, in the immediate aftermath of conquest, there were influences at work which, for all the anguish of those who composed the great elegies, might tend to diminish, if not erase, the memory of the last prince. We might remember that those who came to Nancall in the summer of 1283, proctors on behalf of the communities that had lived under the prince's rule in Gwynedd, came together not to praise Llywelyn but to dwell upon his oppressive rule.[20] We have seen, too, that after his death, quite apart from the elegies, the prince was commemorated in two sets of verses of a more informal style, the one said to be the work of a Welsh rhymester, the other of an English counterpart. The one extolled the prince as the law and light of his people, a model for the future; the other portrayed him as the epitome of evil, an oppressor of men.[21] The nature of the business done at Nancall might suggest that the verses attributed to the English rhymester

---

[16] M. E. Giffin, 'Cadwalader, Arthur and Brutus in the Wigmore manuscript', *Speculum*, 16 (1941), 19–20. The pedigree of Roger Mortimer (d. 1398) is traced through Gwladus Ddu in *The Chronicle of Adam of Usk 1377–1421*, ed. C. Given-Wilson (Oxford, 1997), 40–3.

[17] Gwaith Iolo Goch, no. xx.

[18] Hearne, *Works*, iv, 243; other commentators noticed above, p. 564. For Manning's association with Sempringham and Sixhills, Golding, *Gilbert of Sempringham*, 153.

[19] Above, pp. 37–9. For the commemoration of Llywelyn's death in the Welsh ecclesiastical calendar, see e.g. Bodleian Library, Jesus College MS 7.

[20] Above, pp. 255–60, 266–7.

[21] Above, p. 273.

Epilogue

might be more likely to strike a chord with the prince's former subjects than those which were attributed to one of their own countrymen. Does historical remembrance offer any indication of resentful rejection rather than neglect?

We know of no scholarly study of Llywelyn ap Gruffudd. The secular biography was not unknown in medieval Wales for, as we have seen already, we have in the *History of Gruffudd ap Cynan* a composition in which classical and indigenous influences are skilfully blended.[22] There is a seventeenth-century reference to a life of Llywelyn ap Iorwerth and Dafydd ap Llywelyn, possibly 'the lives of a troublesome prince or two' to which Nicholas Robinson, bishop of Bangor, referred. But we do not know that any William of Poitiers devoted his talents to a commemoration of the life of Llywelyn ap Gruffudd, and it would be several centuries before Llywelyn became the subject of a study specifically devoted to him, even in a brief essay.[23] We can harbour no expectation of any extended prose commemoration at the end of the thirteenth century, and attention needs to be concentrated on the historical writing represented by *Brut y Tywysogyon* on which this study has depended for much of the inner knowledge of the prince's fortunes. What can be discerned of the manner by which the Chronicle of the Princes was composed would not suggest any dismissive rejection of the prince upon his death. Rather, the following years appear to have seen the writing of a Latin chronicle which traced the history of the kings and princes of Wales from the death of Cadwaladr the Blessed to the death of Llywelyn. It seems that a substantial Latin chronicle was already in hand before the prince's death. But the last years of the thirteenth century certainly saw the composition of a work extending from the last of the kings of Britain to the last of the princes of Wales and envisaged as a continuation of Geoffrey of Monmouth's *Historia Regum Britanniae*.[24] The death of Llywelyn was evidently seen as the end of an era which deserved appropriate historical memorial. Its author may have shared the inspiration which brought the monks at the *scriptorium* of Ystrad Fflur to put together the magnificent compendium of the poetry of the princes known

---

[22] *HGK*; *MPW*.

[23] Ll. B. Smith, 'Historical consciousness', 3. In NLW Peniarth 120, f. 423, a list by Edward Lhuyd from a note-book of Robert Vaughan includes a reference to 'a life of Llywelyn ap Iorwerth and David his sonne' at St Bennet's College, Cambridge; the work has not been traced. For William of Poiters, R. H. C. Davis, 'William of Poitiers and his history of William the Conqueror', in R. H. C. Davis and J. M. Wallace-Hadrill (eds.), *The Writing of History in the Middle Ages: Essays presented to Richard William Southern* (Oxford, 1981), 71–100.

[24] *Pen 20Tr*, xxv–xliv; J. B. Smith, *SHMW*, 7–8, 15–17. For a garbled recollection of Llywelyn by a Brabancon chronicler, see Th. M. Chotzen, 'Welsh history in the continuation of the "Spiegel Historiael" by Lodewijk van Veltham', *B*, 7 (1933–5), 42–54.

Epilogue

as *Llawysgrif Hendregadredd*.[25] Historical interest in the era of the princes was sufficiently sustained to ensure that the Latin chronicle was translated into Welsh in the two versions of *Brut y Tywysogyon*. It would form part of a trilogy tracing the history of the Welsh people and their earliest Trojan forebears down to the death of the last of the princes: Dares Phrygius, the History of the Kings of Britain and the Chronicle of the Princes.[26] Neither of the surviving Welsh texts of *Brut y Tywysogyon* contains an encomium of Llywelyn comparable with those of Owain Gwynedd or Rhys ap Gruffudd, and it is possible that the text on which they were based was incomplete. But it seems clear that the death of the last of the princes was deemed to mark a historic event comparable with the death of the king by whose demise the British lost the sovereignty of Britain.

Thereafter, however, interest in the kings and princes of Wales was to wane. Not a single manuscript of the Latin original of *Brut y Tywysogyon* is known to have survived the medieval period, and Welsh texts are not numerous. In marked contrast, the period saw a fixation with the legendary history of Britain. Geoffrey's *Historia Regum Britanniae* had come into vogue in the thirteenth century, with Welsh texts appearing in the form of *Brut y Brenhinedd*.[27] Llywelyn himself, as we have seen, endeavoured to draw political advantage from the concept, enshrined in the *Historia*, of an early Britain consisting of three kingdoms. John Pecham remarked upon the Welsh obsession with the Trojan inheritance of Britain and feared its prophetic connotations, and the nation's interest in its early history was sustained for a very long time to come.[28] For, despite the creative impulses which in the wake of conquest gave birth to *Brut y Tywysogyon*, it was the legendary history which prevailed in Welsh awareness. Texts of Geoffrey of Monmouth's work multiplied and its figures loomed large in the allusions of the poets.[29] The loss

---

[25] D. Huws, 'Llawysgrif Hendregadredd', *NLWJ*, 22 (1981–2), 1–26. Other productions of the period of the conquest and its immediate aftermath may include material of a genealogical nature added to a text of the *Historia Regum Britanniae* (NLW, Mostyn MS 117) and the prophetic matter of the *Book of Taliesin* (M. Haycock, 'Llyfr Taliesin', *NLWJ*, 25 (1987–8), 357–86; J. B. Smith, *SHMW*, 10–11).

[26] *BT, Pen20Tr*, xliv–lix; *RBH*, xx–xxxviii; T. Jones, 'Historical writing in medieval Welsh', *Scottish Studies*, 12 (1968), 15–27; J. B. Smith, *SHMW*, 7–8.

[27] *HRB*; for the Welsh texts and the theme of loss of sovereignty, *Brut y Brenhinedd*, ed. B. F. Roberts (Dublin, 1971), xxiv–xxxvi; B. F. Roberts, 'Geoffrey of Monmouth and Welsh historical tradition', *Nottingham Medieval Studies*, 20 (1976), 29–40 (repr. in idem, *Studies in Middle Welsh Literature* (Lampeter, 1992), 25–40); idem, 'The Red Book of Hergest version of *Brut y Brenhinedd*', *SC*, 12–13 (1977–8), 147–86; idem, 'Testunau hanes Cymraeg canol', *Y Traddodiad Rhyddiaith yn yr Oesau Canol*, ed. G. Bowen (Llandysul, 1974), 274–302.

[28] *RPeck*, ii, 469–70, 473–7, 741–2.

[29] E. Reiss, 'The Welsh versions of Geoffrey of Monmouth's *Historia*', *WHR*, 4 (1968–9), 97–113; B. F. Roberts, 'Ymagweddau at *Brut y Brenhinedd* hyd 1890', *B*, 24 (1970–2), 122–38.

Epilogue

of the sovereignty of Britain was a theme enshrined in historical awareness while the loss of the governance of Wales, which might have provided a complementary theme with a more direct bearing upon the nation's perplexities, was sorely neglected.[30]

Thus, while the period following the conquest of Wales saw a very considerable achievement in the preservation and transmission of the nation's writings, the breach with the indigenous political tradition had a profound effect upon historical activity. Unlike so many other European nations whose monarchical institutions remained intact, Wales was left without a political stimulus to continued commemoration of the deeds of those who had ruled in the historic past. It was the grandeur of a distant legendary past that retained the attentions of the nation's remembrancers. In Scotland it was different, and the continued vigour of political activity centred on the monarchy enabled its historians to dispel the legendary inheritance and adhere to an authentic account of its historic rulers. The difference was due to the fact, of which historians of Scotland were well aware, that Wales had been thoroughly conquered by Edward I.[31] In Wales historical activity lapsed and the kings and princes of historic times slipped more deeply into oblivion. A sense of the breach with the historical memory was conveyed very clearly by the sixteenth-century author of the 'Three Antiquities of Britain' (*Tri Chof Ynys Brydain*):

> After the dissolutione of the aunciant Bruttish government of Cambria ... in Edward the First's time, whoe not respectinge the honor nor the dignitie of the Bruttayne natione, lawe, antiquitie or rights but endevored by all meanes hee and all his successors could ... to destroy and extinguish both them, there honor and antiquities ... And the prydyddion at this time likewise are of noe estimation, for divers reasones neyther dyd the bards write any continuance of the aforsayd History at all sythence the Lawe was extinguished by the death of the princes whos acts they were bound to preserve, soe that there is noe History written by the Bards sythence the death of Llywelyn ap Gruffyth ap Llywelyn, the last prince of Cambria, for they had noe princes of their owne to sett foorth there acts.[32]

---

[30] Exceptions include an epitome of British history in a Latin text in NLW, Peniarth 32 and BL, Cotton Titus D xxii (the latter printed in *Lives of the Cambro-British Saints*, ed. W. J. Rees (Llandovery, 1853), 278–86), where the death of Llywelyn and the handing over of the Croes Naid are noticed. Historical uncertainty is indicated in the total confusion between Llywelyn ap Iorwerth and Llywelyn ap Gruffudd in the chronicle of Elis Gruffudd (NLW, Mostyn MS, 158, ff. 108–11).

[31] J. B. Smith, *SHMW*, 18; John Major, *A History of Greater Britain*, ed. A. Constable (Edinburgh, Scottish History Society, 1892), Lib. I. ix; IV. ix–xviii, notices that the Welsh were forced into absolute submission by Edward I.

[32] G. J. Williams, 'Tri Chof Ynys Brydain', *Llên Cymru*, 3 (1954–5), 234–9.

Epilogue

Historians of Wales retained for a long time a residual allegiance to the legendary history, but fortuitously the work of Humphrey Llwyd and David Powel ensured that something of the memory of the nation's historical past was salvaged for the generations to come. Their work, drawn from *Brut y Tywysogyon* and the texts of English chroniclers, placed Llywelyn ap Gruffudd in an authentic historical context. Llwyd, in the manuscripts in which his work survives, traced the prince's achievement to its climax with the sealing of the treaty of Montgomery. Powel in turn, with the publication of *The Historie of Cambria* (1584), completed the account of 'the last prince of Brytaine's blood who bore dominion and rule in Wales', embodying in his narrative translated texts of Llywelyn's exchanges with Pecham and the complaints submitted to the archbishop by the princes and communities of Wales.[33] Between them Llwyd and Powel established a new tradition in Welsh scholarship in which the historical rather than the legendary eras were accorded the attention they deserved.

Yet Llywelyn ap Gruffudd's place in historical consciousness was far from assured. Already, by the end of the sixteenth century, Owain Glyndŵr was set fair to capture the imagination of a broad public in a way that neither Llywelyn nor any of his forebears could match. The interest in the rebellion revealed by sixteenth-century English historians, notably Ralph Holinshed, and the influence of William Shakespeare's characterization, enabled Owain Glyndŵr to survive the critical appraisal of those, David Powel and George Owen among them, who had some reservations over the truly heroic quality of Owain's rule. In the eighteenth century Thomas Pennant, with access to new historical sources, established Owain's fame on secure foundations.[34] It was Owain rather than Llywelyn who was destined to be, like William Wallace among the Scots, the hero of popular imagination. The kings and princes of earlier ages were not entirely neglected by any means. In the seventeenth century Robert Vaughan explored the history of the period between Rhodri Mawr and Llywelyn ap Gruffudd in a manner of great benefit to later inquirers.[35] Theophilus Evans, though his discussion in *Drych y Prif Oesoedd* (1716) was largely devoted to the legendary origins of Wales, commended the *Historie of Cambria* to readers who wished to pursue the history of the princes, and ended his historical discussion with a brief reference to Llywelyn ap Gruffudd as 'the last prince of pure British blood to

---

[33] NLW, Llansteffan, 177; D. Powel, *Historie of Cambria* (1584), 314–75, the translations by Thomas Yale, chancellor to Matthew Parker, archbishop of Canterbury. For the work of Llwyd and Powel, I. M. Williams, 'Ysgolheictod hanesyddol yr unfed ganrif ar bymtheg', *Llên Cymru*, 2 (1952–3), 111–24, 209–23. Professor Williams is preparing a critical edition of Llwyd's 'Cronica Walliae', which will be the first published version of this important work.

[34] J. E. Lloyd, *Owen Glendower*, 1–7; R. R. Davies, *Revolt of Owain Glyn Dŵr*, 325–32.

[35] R. Vaughan, *British Antiquities Revived* (London, 1662), noticed later.

Epilogue

govern Wales', with quotations from the elegies of Bleddyn Fardd and Gruffudd ab yr Ynad Coch.[36] William Williams, Llandygái, in *Prydnawngwaith y Cymry* (published posthumously in 1822), endeavoured to continue the study that Evans had begun, a task he found necessary 'since the common Welshman has hardly heard a word of the princes who ruled in Wales'. Evan Evans commemorated Llywelyn among the great men of his nation, and warned those who studied its history to be wary of the English historians who failed to do justice to the valour of the princes. Yet even then it was not Llywelyn, nor any other authenticated figure among the princes of his dynasty, who attracted those in eighteenth-century Wales who took an inventive interest in the nation's historical inheritance. It was the mythical Madog ab Owain Gwynedd whose quest for a distant shore took precedence over the deeds of the prince who had struggled to defend his native land.[37] In a firmer tradition of historical enquiry, B. B. Woodward, William Warrington, Thomas Price and Gweirydd ap Rhys (R. J. Pryse) each included extended discussions of Llywelyn in accounts founded upon an increasingly substantial documentation.[38]

Some of the themes broached by these historians will be noticed presently, and it might be said that their hopes that the history of the princes would become better known in the nation at large was to some degree realized. During the nineteenth century Llywelyn ap Gruffudd – increasingly known as Llywelyn ein Llyw Olaf, Llywelyn the Last – came to be commemorated in a variety of written forms and in music, too. He was featured in epic poetry and in patriotic verses set to music, and in cantatas destined for stage productions. The investiture of the prince of Wales in 1911 inspired compositions in several

---

[36] Th. Evans, *Drych y Prif Oesoedd yn ôl yr Argraffiad Cyntaf: 1716*, ed. G. H. Hughes (Cardiff, 1961), 100–2; W. Williams, *Prydnawngwaith y Cymry* (Trefriw, 1822), iii–iv, 85–123; Evan Evans, *The Love of our Country, a poem with historical notes addressed to Sir Watkin Williams Wynn of Wynnstay* (Carmarthen, 1772); cf. G. H. Jenkins, *The Foundations of Modern Wales: Wales, 1642–1780* (Cardiff, 1987), 407–8. For work in English, W. J. Hughes, *Wales and the Welsh in English Literature* (Wrexham, 1924).

[37] G. A. Williams, *Madoc: The Making of a Myth* (London, 1979). The myth is placed in the context of eighteenth-century thought in P. Morgan, *The Eighteenth Century Renaissance* (Llandybïe, 1981), 101–35.

[38] B. B. Woodward, *The History of Wales from the Earliest Times to its Final Incorporation with the Kingdom of England* (London, 1853–9); W. Warrington, *The History of Wales* (London, 1786); T. Price (Carnhuanawc), *Hanes Cymru a Chenedl y Cymry o'r Cynoesoedd hyd at Farwolaeth Llywelyn ap Gruffydd* (Crughywel, 1842); Gweirydd ap Rhys [R. J. Pryse], *Hanes y Brytaniaid a'r Cymry* (London, 1872–4). Even so Llywelyn did not enjoy a posthumous career comparable with that of, among others, Edward I, for which see e.g. G. Templeman, 'Edward I and the historians', *Cambridge Historical Journal*, 10 (1950–2), 16–35; F. M. Powicke, 'King Edward I in fact and fiction', in D. J. Gordon (ed.), *Fritz Saxl (1890–1948). Knowledge and Learning: A Volume of Memorial Essays* (London and Edinburgh, 1957), 120–35.

Epilogue

forms.[39] Artistic depictions were not numerous, though an effigy of Llywelyn, in armour and with sword in hand, appeared early in the eighteenth century. Illustrations of Llywelyn at court or his death on the field of battle appeared in historical works. A marble group on the death of Llywelyn by the sculptor Henry Watkins was exhibited at the Great Exhibition in 1851, and a statue of Llywelyn by Henry Pegram was duly included among the historic sculptures, eleven in number, placed in the Cardiff City Hall in 1916.[40] Public awareness of the last of the princes was clearly sharpened, and political figures might make references to Llywelyn in the rhetoric of their addresses.[41] Yet efforts to raise by public subscription a monument in his memory, a subject of successive initiatives, came to naught, despite the earnest efforts of men and women representing a broad spectrum of Welsh society, supported by academic and political figures of some eminence. The spot where Llywelyn was believed to have met his death was eventually marked by the generosity of Stanley Bligh, squire of Cilmeri and an Englishman, who in 1902 built at his own cost an obelisk suitably inscribed in Welsh and in English.[42] It stood for half a century until a massive stone, hewn from the rock of Snowdonia, was

---

[39] Ll. B. Smith, 'Historical consciousness', 4–8, with extensive references, which include valuable discussion in H. T. Edwards, *Gŵyl Gwalia: Yr Eisteddfod Genedlaethol yn Oes Aur Victoria 1858–1868* (Llandysul, 1980); idem, *Codi'r Hen Wlad yn ei Hôl 1850–1914* (Llandysul, 1989), 212–34. A reference in 'Cywydd Coffa hen Ddefodau y Cymry', R. Davies, *Diliau Barddas* (Denbigh, 1827), 70, to 'Llywelyn Lyw Olaf' is an early instance of 'Llywelyn the Last Prince'. Compositions in music include *Llywelyn, a Dramatic Cantata* by Pencerdd Gwalia, with libretto in Welsh by Talhaiarn and English by Thomas Oliphant (1863); *Llywelyn ein Llyw Olaf, Drama Gantata* by Alaw Ddu with words by Beriah Gwynfe Evans (1883), and the patriotic songs *Cymru fy Ngwlad*, by D. Pughe Evans with words by J. Gwili Jenkins (1895) and *Baner ein Gwlad*, by Joseph Parry with words by Mynyddog (1877). Publications in 1911 included W. Jenkyn Thomas, 'Llywelyn the Last, a Sketch', *Wales*, 1 (1911), 108–11; J. Russ, 'The Eighteen of Pont Orewyn', *Wales*, 1 (1911), 133. Folklore, much of it linked with the neighbourhood of Builth (e.g. Theophilus Jones, *A History of the County of Brecknock*, 2 vols. (Brecon, 1805–9), i, 138–43), is not considered in this study, but an early instance is the memory in *Chronicle of Adam of Usk*, 116–17, that a spring near Builth where Llywelyn's head was washed 'flowed with pure blood throughout one whole day'.

[40] J. L., A Cambro-Briton, *A True (tho' a short) Account of the Antient Britons . . . with the Effigies of Llewelyn ab Gruffyth, the last Prince of Wales of the British Blood* (London, 1716); Gweirydd ap Rhys, *Hanes y Brytaniaid a'r Cymry*, ii, 107, 136 (by George Cattermole, who also illustrated works by William Scott and Charles Dickens); *Catalogue of the Great Exhibition, 1851* (London, 1851); for the historic sculptures, J. R. Wilson, *Memorializing History: Public Sculpture in Industrial South Wales* (Aberystwyth, 1996), 12–14. For other illustrations, and a painting by William Roos and medal by W. Goscombe-John, Ll. B. Smith, 'Historical consciousness', 24–5. David Jones, 'Cara Wallia Derelicta', is a notable composition in calligraphy

[41] T. E. Ellis, *Addresses and Speeches* (Wrexham, 1912), 12–14; *Llanelli Labour News*, 1 August, 1925.

[42] Ll. B. Smith, 'Historical consciousness', 25–7; Edwards, *Codi'r hen Wlad yn ei Hôl*, 196–200. For Bligh, G. Evans, 'The squire of Cilmery', *Brycheiniog*, 15 (1971), 57–61; a note on the obelisk, with photograph, *Brycheiniog*, 2 (1956), 153–5.

Epilogue

raised at the same place in 1956, to become increasingly a place of pilgrimage.[43]

The dubious quality of much of the writing in which the prince was remembered, indeed the frivolity of some of the material, and the difficulty encountered in the efforts to secure a suitable memorial, raise questions as to the extent to which there was in nineteenth-century Wales a meaningful appreciation of the political objectives of the last prince of Wales. The infinitely more reflective tenor of writing in the twentieth century, in prose and poetry, testifies both to deepening concern for the nation's destiny and to a growth in informed historical study.[44] Understanding was certainly furthered by the work of English historians, of whom William Stubbs is a representative figure, even though their references to the princes might be largely confined to the occasions when their troublesome presence on the western confines impinged upon the tranquillity of the realm. Much was owed, too, to those who wrote on Wales itself, sometimes in substantial volumes. The works of Warrington, writing in English, and Gweirydd ap Rhys in Welsh, were among the precursors to the consummate narrative of the history of Wales to its conquest by Edward I which came with the publication of John Edward Lloyd's work in 1911. Some of the themes struck in these writings, each of which finds its inspiration in the historical record of the thirteenth century, will be noticed briefly.

Pen milwr, pen draig oedd arno: 'finest of warriors, his was a dragon's head'. Writers who had recourse to thirteenth-century sources, in poetry and prose, could find much to corroborate the image of a prince well versed in the practices of war which is conveyed by Gruffudd ab yr Ynad Coch. Matthew Paris provided a spirited commentary on the prince's military achievements and his capacity to gird his people into action to ensure their nation's liberty, his exhortations embodied in an oration composed in the manner of the ancients.[45] Other chroniclers of England, as well as *Brut y Tywysogyon* and the poets, enhanced the prince's military persona. The image of Llywelyn came to be, and to an excessive degree, that of the warrior prince. Heroic endeavour in arms under the leadership of a man of great valour committed

---

[43] Reports on the unveiling ceremony, *Brycheiniog*, 11 (1956), 154–68; for Cilmeri as a place of pilgrimage see e.g. *Y Ddraig Goch*, 26 (1954), a reference I owe to Robert Smith.

[44] Twentieth-century writings are represented in T. Gwynn Jones, *Y Dwymyn* (1944); D. Gwenallt Jones, *Gwreiddiau* (1959); David Jones, *In Parenthesis* (1961); idem, *Epoch and Artist* (1959); Harri Webb, *Collected Poems* (1995); Marion Eames, *Y Gaeaf Sydd Unig* (1982); Gerallt Lloyd Owen, *Cilmeri a Cherddi Eraill* (1991), the poem 'Cilmeri' also included in *Llywelyn y Beirdd*, 153–85, an anthology of contemporary poetry commemorating Llywelyn.

[45] Above, pp. 100–1.

Epilogue

to the defence of his country is a theme in the work of Warrington, who saw Llywelyn's stand in Snowdonia in 1282 in the image of Leonidas in the straits of Thermopylae.[46] Gweirydd ap Rhys wrote of the prince's 'brave and glorious defence of his country, its laws, its rights and its independence'.[47] Some might, even so, feel bound to justify the prince's military reputation as a virtue made necessary by the predicament in which he was placed. Moved to compensate for the nation's neglect of its kings and princes, William Williams envisaged a prince whose inclinations were towards peace, recognizing the destruction wrought by war, but one who was forced to resort to conflict to save his subjects from oppression.[48] Similarly J. H. Parry, including Llywelyn among the figures selected for his *Cambrian Plutarch*, and assuring his readers that 'the courageous resistance of the Welsh was associated with circumstances which have peculiar claim upon our sympathy', portrayed him as a prince who sought to cultivate peace and the tranquillity of his dominion as long as he could do so 'without compromising his own honour or the national independence'.[49] In the estimation of R. W. Morgan, Llywelyn's military abilities present 'a study unparalleled for its staunchness and nobility of principle', but he was one among others who felt bound to reconcile the prince's commitment to the needs of the Welsh nation with their own identification with the cause of imperial Britain.[50] The warrior prince was deeply ingrained upon the scholarly pages of Lloyd's work, and the relationship between resort to armed force and search for political solutions called for scrupulous historical assessment of the years in which Llywelyn sought to establish a supremacy and secure its recognition.

Cynechrau doniau dinam fawredd: 'source of blessings perfect in their splendour'. The prince's concern for the well-being of his people and his responsibility as their protector against oppression is another theme that historians could identify in the work of their thirteenth-century antecedents, Matthew Paris again and *Brut y Tywysogyon* among them. David Powel, aware that Llywelyn had not succeeded by hereditary right, insisted that he assumed authority by the will of his subjects, and the documents relating to Pecham's intervention in 1282 that he embodied in his narrative, both Llywelyn's letters and the complaints submitted to the archbishop,

---

[46] Warrington, *History of Wales*, 253–4.
[47] Gweirydd ap Rhys, *Hanes y Brytaniaid a'r Cymry*, ii, 136.
[48] Williams, *Prydnawngwaith y Cymry*, 93–6.
[49] J. H. Parry, *The Cambrian Plutarch* (London, 1834), 173–208. William Owen, *Hanes Owain Glandwr, Blaenor y Cymry mewn Rhyfel* (Caernarfon, 1833), stressed the duty of the nation's leaders to defend their people 'from falling prey to foreign plunderers' and meditated on the fate of the Welsh left to survive 'like badgers in the mountains'.
[50] R. W. Morgan, *The British Kymry or the Britons of Cambria* (Caernarfon, 1857), 173–4, 258. Imperial inclinations may be detected in e.g. O. M. Edwards, *Wales* (London, 1901), 403.

Epilogue

substantiated the notion of the continuing common interest of prince and community. He included the documents, he wrote, 'to set downe for the laieing open of the truth to the view of all men which heretofore was either malicioslie concealed or negligentlie omitted'.[51] Successive writers had recourse to the *gravamina* of that year to demonstrate the prince's wish to be at one with his people. William Williams saw him as a ruler who strove, more than anything, to relieve his people 'of thraldom and oppression'.[52] Not all commentators saw the prince in these generous terms. Woodward had no sympathy with these sentiments and portrayed Llywelyn as one among the princes who were concerned only with 'the enhancement of their own personal dignity'.[53] Warrington offered a more sympathetic appraisal, insisting that 'it was not in the nature of Llywelyn when the dearest concerns of his people were mingled with his own to entertain any idea of interest exclusive of theirs'.[54] And, following Powel, he, too, provided a text of the *gravamina* of 1282. Gweirydd ap Rhys felt that Llywelyn was a prince who considered that 'his people's welfare and his own were intertwined and who in his last crisis would not consider any terms that the king might offer if they did not ensure the safety of his people'.[55] The notion of a concordance between prince and people is an enduring theme, though it was not to commend itself in popular estimation to the same extent as Owain Glyndŵr's programme, elicited though it might be from somewhat meagre historical testimony, was deemed to be attuned to nineteenth-century social and political aspiration.[56]

More difficult to discern is any perceptive appreciation of the thrust of the prince's objectives beyond the need to provide sturdy defence of his people's liberties and protect them against oppression. *Aur dalaith oedd deilwng iddo*: 'he was deserving of a gold coronet', pronounced Gruffudd ab yr Ynad Coch. The coronet was a symbol of a political status attained by the common purpose of prince and subjects in war and peace. Llygad Gŵr captured the essence of the political process by which the prince's broad objectives were pursued in his appreciation of Llywelyn's success in concentrating in his own

---

[51] D. Powel, *Historie of Cambria* (1584), 317.

[52] W. Williams, *Prydnawngwaith y Cymry*, 110.

[53] Woodward, *History of Wales*, 464; the author had no regard for the *gravamina* of 1282 which he saw as 'mere pretexts for the indulgence of habits of turbulence and brigandage' (ibid., 499).

[54] Warrington, *History of Wales*, 472, 496.

[55] Gweirydd ap Rhys, *Hanes y Brytaniaid a'r Cymry*, ii, 131.

[56] The essential document is Owain's letter to the king of France, dated at Pennal, 1406 (*Welsh Records in Paris*, 42–54; R. R. Davies, *Revolt of Owain Glyn Dŵr*, 169–72, with nineteenth-century aspirations noticed ibid., 331–2). For the inclination to associate contemporary aspirations with Glyndŵr rather than the earlier princes, Edwards, *Wales*, ix–x; Owen Rhoscomyl [Arthur Owen Vaughan], *Flame-Bearers of Welsh History* (Merthyr Tydfil, 1905), 202–19; and for a late instance of the preference, F. P. Jones, 'Pam Llywelyn', *Y Genhinen*, 19 (1968–9), 244–7.

Epilogue

person the status signified by the coronets of Aberffraw, Dinefwr and Mathrafal.[57] In due course Humphrey Llwyd and David Powel perceived the significance of the fact that, becoming the liege lord of the princes of Wales by the treaty of Montgomery, the prince's status came to be recognized by the crown.[58] Robert Vaughan set out the essence of the matter in *British Antiquities Revived* (1662) when, turning to the lawbooks' account of the tribute due to the court of Aberffraw from the other courts of Wales, he wrote that its princes 'had the soveraignty over all Wales'.[59] His discussion takes the form of an answer to George Owen's contribution to a debate, not perhaps excessively serious in intent, on whether the sovereignty of Wales had belonged to Deheubarth or Gwynedd. Vaughan does not make extensive reference to the prince who came nearest to making that 'sovereignty' meaningful in practical terms, but his discourse, which takes account of the fact that the thirteenth-century princes of Gwynedd took the fealty of the princes of Deheubarth and Powys, is a harbinger of the discussion of the political structure of medieval Wales which was to engage historians in the twentieth century. It was, as Vaughan implicitly conveyed, this change of great moment in political history which gave the final conquest of Wales its true significance.

The way in which this change unfolded was given its most authoritative exposition in the work of John Edward Lloyd.[60] Yet in his narrative the structural change in Welsh political relations, and the consequent change in the nature of the relationship with England, remains strangely elusive. His opening remarks upon the period of Llywelyn ap Gruffudd convey his view of the period as one in which the interest is peculiarly personal. Llywelyn is the single force who secures an unquestioned dominance only to meet, through his lack of prudence, a sadly ruinous end, so that the narrative closed 'in a vein of dignified tragedy, as who would tell the vain struggle of weak human will against the resistless forces of nature'. It is the warrior prince who emerges most clearly in the narrative, one whose star was now 'fairly in the ascendant', now bringing upon his country the 'dull pallor of nightfall'. His

---

[57] Above, p. 336.

[58] D. Powel, *Historie of Cambria* (1584), 326–7; ibid., 315, for the prince of Gwynedd as 'the superiour prince of all Wales, to whom the other princes of Southwales and Powys did paie a certeine tribute yearelie'.

[59] Vaughan, *British Antiquities Revived*, 3–7, 17–23, 39–40. Owen's tract, noticed in B. G. Charles, *George Owen of Henllys: A Welsh Elizabethan* (Aberystwyth, 1973), 140–3, from College of Arms, Prothero MS (Box 36/xx), argues that the sovereignty of Wales was ceded upon the death of Rhys ap Tewdwr, that everyone who rose against the king thereafter was a rebel and traitor, and that Edward I 'did not take that he conquered a prince of Wales, but subdued one that rebelled against him, for when the head of the said Llewelin was sent unto the king . . . he sent the same to London, and caused the same to be put upon the highest turret of the Tower of London as the heads of other traitors were used'.

[60] *HW*, 716, *et seq.*

Epilogue

work had a scholarly quality that no historian of Wales had hitherto attained, and it remains for those who have come after him a narrative enriched with a great wealth of informed and perceptive observation. His view of Llywelyn was, even so, affected by an evident reluctance to address the years of supremacy in other than descriptive terms and by the fact, suggested at the beginning of this study, that his account of Llywelyn was in effect cut short at 1277. Perhaps hurrying to complete a work on which he had been engaged for many years, Lloyd divested himself of the opportunity to consider the extensive documentation of the prince's last years which does so much to inform a study of his life's work as a whole.

The publication by John Goronwy Edwards of *Littere Wallie* (1940), a volume of documents of the thirteenth century with a historical introduction, opened a new era in historical interpretation of the period.[61] Edwards generously attributed to his precursor 'a notable modification of emphasis' in the study of the period of the princes. He felt that, although Lloyd's *History of Wales* ended with the death of Llywelyn in the manner of the older historians, the work was different in that, concentrating not on the prince's downfall but on his rise to power, he was able to show how Llywelyn reconciled 'the legal equality of the Welsh princes as royal persons with the political need of subordinating them to some single central authority in Wales'. Placing his emphasis upon Llywelyn as the first prince of Wales rather than as 'the Last Prince', Lloyd had 'heightened not only the dramatic irony but also the historical significance of his life'. But Edwards's estimation of Lloyd's work was undoubtedly infused with his own perception of the meaning of the prince's achievement.[62] His essay on Llywelyn ap Gruffudd formed part of a contribution which, including seminal studies of the law of Wales and of the march of Wales, made a significant breach with earlier conventions in historical writing on medieval Wales.[63] He saw the policies pursued by Llywelyn as an attempt to overcome problems of a structural nature, specifically the 'chronic decentralization' which was characteristic of government in thirteenth-century Wales. In a discussion illustrated by the documents from 'Liber A' that he presented in the volume, many published for the first time, he considered the course of action that Llywelyn pursued in dealing with the dynastic problems that confronted him in Gwynedd and in establishing contractual relationships with the princes of Powys and

---

[61] *LW*, xxxvi–lxix.

[62] J. G. Edwards, 'John Edward Lloyd', *PBA*, 41 (1956), 319–27, is both a notable tribute to Lloyd and an important statement of the author's view of the period.

[63] J. G. Edwards, *Hywel Dda and the Welsh Lawbooks* (Bangor, 1929), repr. in D. Jenkins (ed.) *Celtic Law Papers Introductory to Welsh Medieval Law and Government* (Brussels, 1973), 135–60; J. G. Edwards, 'The Normans and the Welsh march', *PBA*, 42 (1957); cf. *WHR*, 8 (1976–7), 466–77.

Epilogue

Deheubarth, initatives by which he was able 'to cut across the established order in Wales'. It was on the basis of these achievements that, achieving a measure of coalescence not hitherto characteristic of Welsh society, he was able by 1267 to negotiate with the crown, for himself and his heirs, 'a position which legally was as near independence as they could hope to attain'. His estimate of the prince's conduct in the sequence of events that led to two major conflicts, an account in which rigorous critical judgement was joined with a sensitive appreciation of the predicament in which the prince was placed at successive crises in the last decade of his life, was made so much more telling by his evaluation of the political achievement now put at risk. He was later to return to the same themes in his essay *The Principality of Wales 1267–1967* (1969).[64] Edwards had laid the foundations for a consideration of Llywelyn ap Gruffudd as one who, for all his aggressive initatives in armed conflict, stood to be judged in history for his resolve in fashioning his country's political institutions. His labours would be best examined, not simply as a triumphant assertion of native power nor a stalwart defence against oppression, but as an effort to reconcile the disparate ambitions of the princely lineages in an increasingly fragmented society by the creation of a unifying political framework.

The persuasive influence of Edwards's essay was first reflected in a generous and perceptive chapter on Wales which F. M. Powicke included in *King Henry III and the Lord Edward* (1948), and his work has informed subsequent writing.[65] The work of scholars concerned with historical problems in which Llywelyn ap Gruffudd is a central figure has in recent decades been facilitated, and yet made more arduous, by the development of studies in spheres other than political history. The important work by J. E. Morris, *The Welsh Wars of Edward I* (1901), has been followed by studies of military organization which, though necessarily concentrating on the evidence for English arrangements which the documents provide, nevertheless demonstrate the factors with which the prince had to contend. Similarly, clearer awareness of the financial resources available to Edward, and the crucial importance of this factor in Anglo-Welsh relations in the latter part of the thirteenth century, has deepened our appreciation of the predicament in which the prince was placed and quickened our estimate of the judgement he revealed in resolving it. Knowledge of the architecture of the castles of Llywelyn's dominion and their building history has been advanced, and archaeological investigation of the courts that he is known to have visited, sites so elusive for so long, has been initiated with informative results. The lawbooks have been afforded a textual study of a thoroughness unknown to

---

[64] J. G. Edwards, *Principality of Wales*, 5–9.
[65] Powicke, *Henry III*, ii, 618–85; see further, below, n. 71.

Epilogue

earlier investigators, and their relationships and the chronology of their redaction more firmly established. Critical editions of the whole corpus of the poetry of the princes has eased the study of a source long respected but exceedingly difficult to comprehend. The methods by which the economic resources of the prince's lands were exploited, and the landscape that he would have viewed upon his circuit of his courts, fields of study explored by T. Jones Pierce and Glanville Jones, are now more clearly envisaged than before. And inquiry into new sources of evidence, and reappraisal of sources long known, has enabled historians to probe, not only the prince's dealings with kings and princes and marcher lords, but his relationship with those whom he governed and upon whom he depended in the pursuit of his political objectives. Even though no statistical evidence survives, consideration of the resources at his disposal, along with an estimate of the calls made upon them, raises crucial questions concerning relations between prince and community and affords the study of the period a dimension of great value.

The greatly extended range of recent investigations of thirteenth-century Wales induces its own constraints upon historical assessment of the prince. The confident assertions of earlier generations of historians – assured exaltations and pungent condemnations alike – are no longer the province of historical discourse. Restraint is underlined by the need to acknowledge that Llywelyn remains an exceedingly elusive person, the surviving evidence betraying little of his personal characteristics. The eulogy and elegy of the poets portray a man of honour and dignity but the *awdlau*, in no sense intimate profiles of the prince, are essentially memorials to the admiration inspired by his valour or the anguish aroused by his death. Contemporary commentators convey little of the man behind the political figure and the letters in his name were composed at the imperatives of diplomacy and political calculation.[66] We do not know whether he was prone to be moved to violent anger or deep resentment which might have influenced his course of action, though there are occasions when the phraseology or the tenor of his letters suggest a person moved to express himself with conviction, even with passion, and he reveals an acute sensitivity concerning his dignity and status. In the light of historical writings of earlier years it would be well to consider whether, in the record of the period following the formal recognition of his

---

[66] The poets afford little indication of his appearance, except that he was handsome and manly. There is nothing comparable to Trevet's description of Edward I (Trevet, *Annales*, 281–2), which was used at some length in Powicke, *Henry III*, ii, 686–7; but it might be remembered that Trevet wrote some time after Edward's death (R. J. Dean, 'Nicholas Trevet, Historian', in J. G. G. Alexander and M. T. Gibson (eds.), *Medieval Learning and Literature: Essays presented to Richard William Hunt* (Oxford, 1976), 328–52).

Epilogue

hegemony, a change may be discerned in the quality of his political judgement. The early years were characterized, as Matthew Paris perceptively observed, not by aggression alone but by a marked restraint as he sought a consolidation of his achievements in a negotiated settlement with the king.[67] Yet his conduct in the period after 1267 has raised questions concerning his discretion during the course of events by which the credibility of that settlement was undermined and then its whole authority revoked in renewed conflict. While the more strident pronouncements of earlier historians hardly commend themselves in commentary upon the complexities of these years it is not easy to dispel entirely the view that his judgement was affected by the conspicuous successes registered during his assertion of supremacy, that he manifestly failed to appreciate that circumstances in England were not conducive to a return to the trauma of the era of baronial disaffection, and that he was gravely mistaken if he imagined that he might stir the fires of old animosities in the realm.

These questions, noticed presently, are necessarily raised by the devastating outcome of the war of 1277 and this in turn raises the issue of the prince's role in the defence of his dominions. The venerable image of a warrior prince, with its uninhibited depiction of Llywelyn as a valiant and capable commander, is one which can to a large extent be salvaged from the earlier histories as a fair reflection of the sterling qualities that he revealed during the years in which he established his ascendancy. Reverses were undoubtedly suffered even at the height of the expansive campaigning, but the efficacy of his military initiatives cannot be seriously questioned.[68] Capability in the defence of his country and the protection of his people in adversity, a virtue so highly esteemed among the theorists of the authority of a medieval prince, is much more difficult to measure. Far more than his offensive movements, a prince's competence in defence calls for a searching estimate of the respective roles of military prescience and material resources. Castle-building in stone was already part of the defensive provision for his patrimony before his time, for he inherited Dolbadarn and Dolwyddelan, Criccieth and Castell y Bere, and he was able to determine the deployment of the forces available to him as the immediate lord of the territory. But the defences of mainland Gwynedd Uwch Conwy were never tested while he lived: a negotiated settlement was achieved before conflict began there in 1277, and in the final conflict he was dead before their custodians yielded Dolwyddelan and Castell y Bere and thereby eased their opponents' entry into the very redoubts that they were meant to fortify. The

---

[67] Above, p. 118.

[68] Reverses at Abergavenny and Clun are noticed in discussion; there may have been others unknown to the historical record, but the offensives of the years in which Llywelyn achieved his supremacy appear to have been conducted without exposure to major set-piece battles.

Epilogue

limitations placed on Llywelyn's capacity to organize the defence of his wider dominion have been recounted, and they have a particular bearing on any estimate of the effectiveness of the prince's protective measures in 1277 when, at the beginning of hostilities, his political authority was intact over the principality as a whole.[69] By then Llywelyn had built two castles anew. Ewloe, just beyond the frontier of Perfeddwlad, cannot be shown to have impeded the advance of the king's army. Dolforwyn, testimony to the prince's appreciation of the strategic importance of the frontier in the vicinity of Montgomery, was yielded after a siege of only some fifteen days, but the English army had taken a very long time to advance the short distance from the Severn to the environs of the castle. This may be an indication of prolonged engagement, perhaps an instance of thirteenth-century trench warfare, which may owe a good deal to preparations made by Llywelyn during the time that he is known to have spent on the front on the eve of conflict, if not to his continued presence. Elsewhere beyond the confines of Gwynedd his capability as a strategist in defensive role has to be estimated in the knowledge that his command was inhibited by the seigniorial authority exercised by the lords of Deheubarth and Powys Fadog over the military resources of their territories. In the several lordships of Deheubarth the castles were the preserves of their seigneurs, the service of the communities at their call, and we have seen that their defensive responsibilities were hardly discharged with great resolve. At the same time dynastic dissension in Powys Fadog, and a crucial secession to the king on the part of one of the princes, vitiated the defence of that vital sector. It was only as lord of Gwynedd that Llywelyn had effective military command, and his withdrawal from Perfeddwlad upon the English advance had many a precedent in the annals of his dynasty. The part that he played in the conflict of 1282 remains uncertain and, while his former vassals demonstrated a willpower that they had not shown before, it would have been even more difficult now than in the previous encounter to impose a coherent defensive strategy upon the lands of the former principality. The surviving records provide no certainty that Llywelyn intervened in the lands outside Gwynedd before the expedition to the march on which he met his death. A campaign waged in a direction determined by the prince, at a time of his choosing and for a duration that served his purposes could be managed to telling effect. The defence of the wider territory, over much of which he exercised only indirect lordship, against an opponent able to dictate the strategy and the timing that his massive forces would follow was an altogether more taxing charge.

The marked imbalance in the resources that king and prince could command in major conflict certainly underscores the questions, posed as we have seen by historians of earlier years, that have particular relevance to

---

[69] Above pp. 292–4, 414–25.

Epilogue

Llywelyn's discretion in the critical years before the first conflict. It bears upon the question whether the unequal contest between Wales and England could have been averted if Llywelyn had displayed more political sagacity. His questionable judgement in intervening in Glamorgan has been noticed in this volume, a prolonged and taxing diversion during years when his attention might have been better concentrated on the consolidation of his authority within his frontiers.[70] In the event the lesser of the two conflicts, the war of 1277 was none the less one which could reasonably have been foreseen as an encounter in which Llywelyn's prodigious achievements in creating a broad dominion under his authority could be imperilled. Unlike the precipitate outbreak of the later conflict the issues which led to war were the subject of protracted exchanges between king and prince which could conceivably have led an agreed settlement that might have been sufficient to leave Llywelyn with his authority over an extensive principality still intact. Of this we cannot by any means be certain, but it is reasonable even so that historical inquiry should raise the question why Llywelyn, who so eloquently declared his concern for the well-being of his subjects shortly before his death, should have left them exposed, five years before, to a conflict waged on issues whose bearing upon their needs is far from clear. It might equally fairly be asked why Llywelyn, whose forceful pursuit of his objectives had carried his people with him to achieve a political cohesion never known before, was not able to avert a calamity in which his ascendancy was terminated.

Answers to questions such as these are best sought, not in ponderous reflection upon a political process that might appear to be doomed to end in the nemesis of conquest, but rather in more deliberate examination of the exigencies in which decisions were made and in some assessment of the fundamental concerns that may have governed the prince's thinking. The prince's decisions in his dealings with Edward after his return to the kingdom in 1274, and the course of events in the king's absence which affected those decisions, are obviously of crucial relevance. That Llywelyn found himself, in his dealings with Edward, in a predicament not by any means entirely of his own making is clear, and the exigencies in which he found himself are by now likely to induce a more sympathetic historical hearing than he might have been afforded in years gone by. Llywelyn ap Gruffudd could well emerge as a beneficiary of modern reappraisal of the eulogistic estimations of Edward I that were for so long, certainly to the time of the highly prestigious works of Powicke, part of the tradition of English historical writing.[71] The more critical

---

[70] Above, pp. 339–55.

[71] For a recent review, M. T. Clanchy, 'Inventing thirteenth-century England: Stubbs, Tout, Powicke – now what?', in P. R. Coss and S. D. Lloyd (eds.), *Thirteenth Century England*, 5 (Woodbridge, 1995), 1–20; the remarks in Prestwich, *Edward I*, 558–66, provide a summary assessment which reflects the balanced judgements of the volume as a whole.

estimates of recent years indeed owe something to historians' enhanced comprehension of Edward's relations with Wales and, more particularly, with Scotland, quite apart from new evaluation of his government of the realm of England.[72] The person with whom Llywelyn dealt is better understood, the prince's situation perhaps better appreciated. The righteous tenor of the king's letters, the tendency to admonish, the compulsion to corrective censure, may have been hard to bear. Yet there was no release from the reality that, in extremity, the king's strictures could be put to effect with decidedly superior force. It is clear, moreover, that Llywelyn's disadvantage was by no means entirely a matter of limited resources. It was equally a matter of the limiting nature of his relationships both with the barons of his principality and the communities of his patrimonial lordships, in each case custodians of deeply entrenched interests. Llywelyn was not among those rulers who might, for instance, establish new relationships with emergent urban communities which could bring both an accession of commercial wealth and political alliance with a new 'estate' within the the polity. Pursuing his wider ambitions within these severe constraints would mean that demands he might make to meet new needs would be tolerated only to the extent that he fulfilled his obligations with unfailing rectitude. This in turn left Llywelyn exposed to the threatening possibility that the disenchanted among those subject to his power, and not those of baronial status alone, could have resort to an alternative source of protection. The haven offered by the realm of England stood in perilous proximity to the principality of Wales, and Dafydd ap Gruffudd and Gruffudd ap Gwenwynwyn were only the most conspicuous among those who were able to turn to the king at a time of need. Never in the history of the Welsh nation had the vulnerability of its rulers on this account been more clearly stated. Much of Llywelyn's difficulty in the critical years, and perhaps the key to the unyielding intransigence with which he stands charged, may stem from the manner in which his efforts to secure his position by stern measures exacerbated the very problems that he was seeking to address. The course of events can in part be seen as the outcome of successive exigencies. Yet the key to understanding Llywelyn's conduct may lie in his own realization of the fragility of his position. His early experience, in the years following the death of Llywelyn ap Iorwerth, would have left an enduring memory of the devastating effect of royal and marcher intervention. He would remain tormented by the fear of intrusion into the marcher areas accredited to him by a treaty that he had secured only by prolonged perseverance on his part even though political circumstances had been unusually propitious for his initiative. Llywelyn remained fearful of royal intervention in the provinces of Powys and Deheubarth that had been conceded to him

---

[72] Barrow, *Bruce*, 43–7, 69–71, 83–6, 102–3; Prestwich, *Edward I*, 356–75.

Epilogue

only against the grain of Anglo-Welsh political relations over a very long time. He remembered that his assertion of power within his own dynasty had been made not only in defiance of his kinsmen but in contravention of the king's preferences for the future of the patrimony. His sensitivities in the period after 1267 are understandable, and close attention to the chronology of his relations with the crown suggests how, more especially in the period of Edward's absence from the realm, his fears may have taken him from a position of steadfast resolution to one of unyielding obduracy. That Llywelyn should stand charged with bringing the war of 1277 upon himself, and upon those for whose destiny he bore responsibility, can hardly be altogether disclaimed on the evidence that survives. Even so we cannot be certain that we have finite knowledge of the grounds on which Llywelyn came to the decisions that mark the road that took him to political ruin. It would be reasonable to conclude that his argument with Edward over his obligations as a vassal, far from being an issue which touched his dignity alone, was in his mind inseparable from his concern to ensure that the political order registered by the treaty of Montgomery, so fundamentally different from the settlement that the crown had once striven to impose upon Wales and would wish to impose again, should remain inviolate.[73]

Detached assessment might support the view that, while faltering political judgement at a critical phase in the story may have adversely affected his efforts to realize 'the potentialities of normal political growth' in thirteenth-century Wales, Llywelyn ap Gruffudd may be counted among the state-builders of medieval Europe.[74] It was in his time alone that, giving reality to intimations that may be noticed in the time of Owain Gwynedd and Llywelyn ap Iorwerth, parallels with processes at work in contemporary Europe can justifiably be made in broad terms. In the language of political discourse threads may be traced to the experience of other lands in ideas of *natio* and *patria*, and in a sense of a political order in which *justitia* and *potestas* are exercised under a stable authority. Thirteenth-century Wales provides a cameo of the way in which a sense of history and law, nourished in a people bound by language and territory, could be joined with purposeful political action to create a cohesive dominion.[75] Precise comparisons are not easy to find even so. Meaningful comparison with the great powers of France or

---

[73] For recent perceptive comment on the critical years between 1267 and 1277, Carr, *Llywelyn ap Gruffydd*, 53–63; R. R. Davies, *CCC*, 320–30. For comparative commentary with reference to the same period, J. F. Lydon, 'Lordship and crown: Llywelyn ap Wales and O'Connor of Connacht', in R. R. Davies (ed.), *The British Isles 1100–1500: Comparisons, Contrasts and Connections* (Edinburgh, 1988), 48–63.

[74] The phrase belongs to T. Jones Pierce, *MWS*, 19, in an essay which explores the relationship between social and political themes in thirteenth-century Wales.

[75] For the fusion of ideas and political action, S. Reynolds, 'Medieval *origines gentium* and the community of the realm', *History*, 68 (1983), 375–90.

Epilogue

England is precluded, not entirely because of the disparity in the scale of the material resources in totality, but on account of the widening divergencies created by the manner in which the economic potential of the greater lands was realized in methods of taxation and government finance which enhanced their capabilities still further. The Anglo-Welsh wars of the time of Llywelyn ap Gruffudd were an early signal of an enormously significant change. Parallels with Wales need to be sought among lands where the ingredients of medieval nationhood are found in association with resources on a lesser scale, more especially perhaps within the frontiers or France or Spain,.or within the frontiers of Germany and upon their northern and eastern fringes. Even then the resources of a ruler of Burgundy or Catalonia or Bohemia would prove to be vastly greater than those of a prince of Wales, the time to fashion the institutions of enduring nationhood so much more generous.

In making an estimate of Llywelyn ap Gruffudd's achievement, more than the extent of the resources at his disposal or even the time that he was given, it is the the quality of the prince's relationships, varied and often strained, that commend themselves most pressingly upon historical inquiry. The prince has need to be understood, and no doubt judged, not merely in his relations with those beyond his frontiers, kings of England and marcher lords, who may have opposed his initiatives, but in his dealings with many others. His relations with members of his own dynasty and with princes of other dynasties who, for all the fragmentation of their once royal inheritances, might prove themselves anything but readily amenable to the prince's overtures, were crucial issues from his very first assertion of power to the last crises of his life. The fears and compulsions of those in thirteenth-century society who may not have been prominent participants in the events of which we have knowledge, and who have barely left their mark in the historical record, remain a factor in the prince's calculations which the historian needs to ponder. Whoever ventures to comprehend the triumphs and tribulations of Llywelyn ap Gruffudd is aware of the wide range of resources available for study, ever widening even as the writing proceeds, and of the increasingly onerous nature of the task to be faced in offering an interpretation of the period. Not least among those challenges is the realization that the historical record of the age of Llywelyn ap Gruffudd provides, to a greater extent than any other over a period of many centuries, an opportunity to consider the means by which the law of Wales, the intellectual inheritance enshrined in its literary tradition, and the sense of history nurtured among its people, each an ingredient of the nation's enduring identity, were engaged in the task of fortifying a sustained endeavour to create the political institutions by whose cohering influence its destiny might be determined.

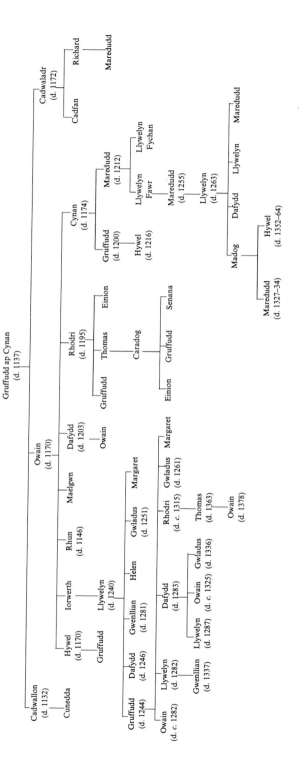

Gwynedd

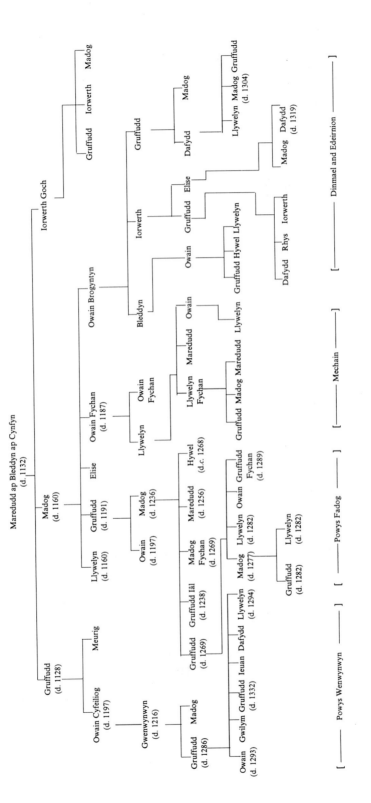

Powys

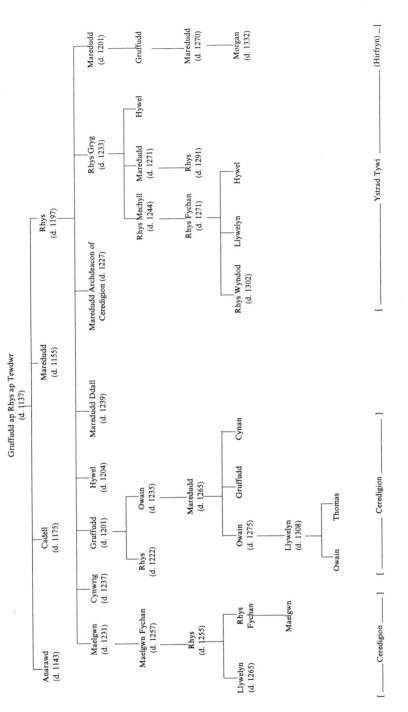

Deheubarth

Wales

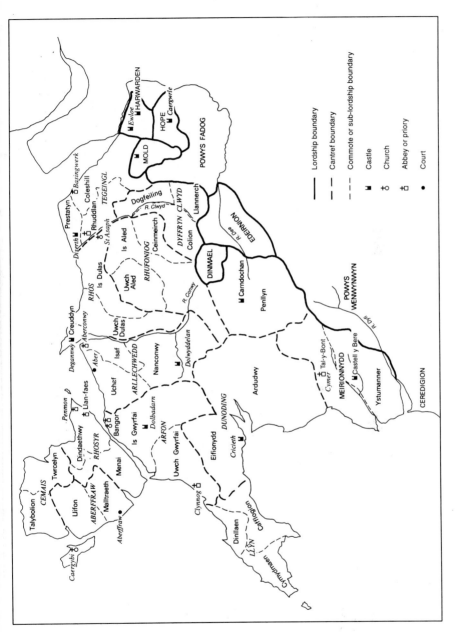

Powys

Deheubarth

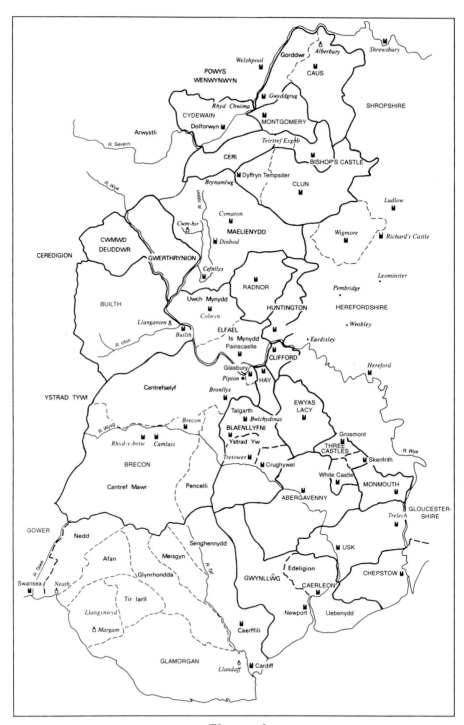

The march

Bibliography

Original Sources: Unpublished

Public Record Office, London: Chancery: Miscellanea (C47); Charter Rolls (C53); Liberate Rolls (C62); Patent Rolls (C66); Welsh Rolls (C77). Exchequer: Books (E36); Various Accounts (E101); Miscellanea (E163); Miscellaneous Books (E164); Augmentations Miscellaneous Books (E315); Pipe Rolls (E372). Records of the King's Bench: Curia Regis Rolls (KB26); Coram Rege Rolls (KB27). Special Collections: Ancient Correspondence (SC1); Ministers' Accounts (SC6); Papal Bulls (SC7); Ancient Petitions (SC8). Duchy of Lancaster: Account Rolls (DL29); Deeds (DL25)
National Library of Wales, Aberystwyth: NLW MSS; Peniarth MSS; Church in Wales Records
British Library, London: Additional MSS; Cotton MSS; Harleian MSS
Bern Burgerbibliothek MSS
Bodleian Library, Oxford, Bodley MSS; Laud MSS; All Souls MSS; Jesus College MSS
Canterbury Cathedral Archives, Dean and Chapter MSS
Longleat, Marquess of Bath MSS
Society of Antiquaries, London, MSS
University of Wales, Bangor, John Edward Lloyd Papers
Vatican Library, Rome, MSS
Wellcome Medical Historical Library, London, MSS
Worcester Record Office, Diocese of Worcester MSS

Original Sources: Published Works

Accounts of the Chamberlains of the County of Chester, 1301–1360, ed. R. Stewart-Brown (Lancashire and Cheshire Records Society, 59, 1910).
Accounts of the Constables of Bristol Castle in the Thirteenth and Early Fourteenth Centuries, ed. M. Sharp (Bristol Records Society, 34, 1982).
Ancient Laws and Institutes of Wales, ed. A. Owen. 2 vols. (Record Commission, 1841).
Anglo-Scottish Relations 1174–1328, ed. E. L . G. Stones (Oxford, 1970).
Annales Cambriae, ed. J. Williams ab Ithel (RS, 1860).
Annales Cestrienses, Chronicle of the Abbey of St Werburg at Chester, ed. R. C. Christie (Lancashire and Cheshire Records Society, 14, 1886).
'Annales Monasterii Burtonensis', *Annales Monastici*, i, ed. H. R. Luard (RS, 1864).
'Annales Monasterii de Oseneia', *Annales Monastici*, iv, ed. H. R. Luard (RS, 1869).
'Annales Monasterii de Theokesberia', *Annales Monastici*, i, ed. H. R. Luard (RS, 1864).

Bibliography

'Annales Monasterii de Waverleia', *Annales Monasterii*, ii, ed. H. R. Luard (RS, 1865).
'Annales Monasterii de Wintonia', *Annales Monastici*, ii, ed. H. R. Luard (RS, 1865).
'Annales Prioratus de Dunstaplia', *Annales Monastici*, iii, ed. H. R. Luard (RS, 1866).
'Annales Prioratus de Wigornia', *Annales Monastici*, iv, ed. H. R. Luard (RS, 1869).
Annals of Connacht A.D. 1224–1544, ed. A. Martin Freeman (Dublin, 1944).
Aquinas, *Selected Political Writings*, ed. A. P. D'Entreves (Oxford, 1959).
Bartholemaei de Cotton Historia Anglicana, ed. H. R. Luard (RS, 1859).
Book of Prests of the King's Wardrobe for 1294–5, ed. E. B. Fryde (Oxford, 1962).
Bracton on the Laws and Customs of England, ed. E. Thorne. 4 vols. (Cambridge, Mass., 1968–77).
Brenhinedd y Saesson or The Kings of the Saxons, ed. T. Jones (Cardiff, 1971).
Breudwyt Ronabwy, ed. M. Richards (Cardiff, 1948).
Brut Dingestow, ed. H. Lewis (Cardiff, 1942).
Brut y Brenhinedd, ed. B. F. Roberts (Dublin, 1971).
Brut y Tywysogyon, Peniarth MS 20, ed. T. Jones (Cardiff, 1941).
Brut y Tywysogyon, or The Chronicle of the Princes, Peniarth MS 20 Version, Translation and Notes, ed. T. Jones (Cardiff, 1952).
Brut y Tywysogyon or The Chronicle of the Princes, Red Book of Hergest Version, ed. T. Jones (Cardiff, 1955).
Calendar of Ancient Correspondence concerning Wales, ed. J. G. Edwards (Cardiff, 1935).
Calendar of Ancient Petitions relating to Wales, ed. W. Rees (Cardiff, 1975).
Calendar of Chancery Rolls, Various (London, 1912).
Calendar of Chancery Warrants, 1244–1326 (London, 1927).
Calendar of Charter Rolls (London, 1903–).
Calendar of Close Rolls (London, 1900–).
Calendar of County Court, City Court and Eyre Rolls of Chester, 1259–1297, ed. R. Stewart-Brown (Manchester, Chetham Society, 84, 1925).
Calendar of Documents relating to Ireland, ed. H. S. Sweetman. 5 vols. (London, 1875–86).
Calendar of Documents relating to Scotland, ed. J. Bain. 4 vols. (London, 1881–8).
Calendar of Fine Rolls (London, 1911–).
Calendar of Inquisitions Post Mortem (London, 1904–).
Calendar of Liberate Rolls (London, 1917–).
Calendar of Memoranda Rolls 1326–27 (London, 1969).
Calendar of Miscellaneous Inquisitions (London, 1916–).
Calendar of Papal Letters (London, 1894–).
Calendar of Patent Rolls (London, 1901–).
'Calendar of Welsh Rolls', *Calendar of Chancery Rolls, Various* (London, 1912).
Canterbury Professions, ed. M. Richter (London, Canterbury and York Society, 67, 1973).
Cartae et Alia Munimenta quae ad Dominium de Glamorgancia pertinent, ed. G. T. Clark. 6 vols. (Cardiff, 1910).
The Cartulary of Shrewsbury Abbey, ed. Una Rees. 2 vols. (Aberystwyth, 1975).
Casgliad o Waith Ieuan Deulwyn, ed. I. Williams (Bangor, 1909).
Catalogue of Manuscripts relating to Wales in the British Museum, ed. E. Owen. 4 vols. (London, Cymmrodorion Record Series, 4, 1900–22).
Charters of the Abbey of Ystrad Marchell, ed. G. C. G. Thomas (Aberystwyth, 1997).
Charters of the Honour of Mowbray 1107–1191, ed. D. E. Greenway (London, 1972).
Charters and Records of Hereford Cathedral, ed. W. W. Capes (Hereford, Cantilupe Society, 1908).
Cheshire in the Pipe Rolls, 1158–1301, ed. R. Stewart-Brown (Lancashire and Cheshire Records Society, 92, 1938).

Bibliography

Chronica Johannis de Oxenedes, ed. H. Ellis (RS, 1859).
Chronica Maiorum et Vicecomitum Londoniarum de Antiquis Legibus Liber, ed. T. Stapleton (London, Camden Society, 34, 1846).
Chronica Rogeri de Hovedone, ed. W. Stubbs. 4 vols. (RS, 1868–71).
The Chronicle of Adam of Usk, ed. C. Given-Wilson (Oxford, 1997).
The Chronicle of Bury St Edmunds, 1212–1301, ed. A. Gransden (London, 1964).
Chronicle of the Kings of Mann and the Isles, ed. G. Broderick and B. Stowell (Edinburgh, 1973).
The Chronicle of Melrose, ed. A. O. Anderson and M. O. Anderson (London, 1936).
Chronicle of Pierre de Langtoft, ed. T. Wright. 2 vols. (RS, 1866–8).
'Chronicle of the thirteenth century, MS Exchequer Domesday', *ArchCamb*, 3rd ser. 8 (1862), 272–83.
The Chronicle of Walter of Guisborough, ed. H. Rothwell (London, Camden Society, 89, 1957).
Chronicles of the Reigns of Edward I and Edward II, ed. W. Stubbs. 2 vols. (RS, 1882–3).
Chronicon Petroburgense, ed. T. Stapleton (London, Camden Society, 47, 1849).
'Chronicon Thomae Wykes', *Annales Monastici*, iv, ed. H. R. Luard (RS, 1869).
Close Rolls (London, 1902–).
Cornelii Taciti De Vita Agricolae, ed. R. M. Ogilvie (Oxford, 1967).
Councils and Ecclesiastical Documents relating to Great Britain and Ireland, ed. A. W. Haddan and W. Stubbs. 3 vols. (Oxford, 1869–71).
Councils and Synods with Other Documents relating to the English Church, II, ed. F. M. Powicke and C. R. Cheney. 2 vols. (Oxford, 1964).
Crith Gablach, ed. D. A. Binchy (Dublin, 1941).
' "Cronica de Wallia" and other documents from Exeter Cathedral Library MS 3514', ed. T. Jones, *B*, 12 (1946–8), 27–44.
Curia Regis Rolls (London, 1923–).
Cywyddau Iolo Goch ac Eraill, ed. H. Lewis, T. Roberts and I. Williams (Cardiff, 1937).
Damweiniau Colan. Llyfr y Damweiniau yn ôl Llawysgrif Peniarth 30, ed. D. Jenkins (Aberystwyth, 1973).
Diplomatic Documents, i, *1101–1272*, ed. P. Chaplais (London, 1964).
Documents Illustrative of the History of Scotland 1286–1306, ed. J. Stevenson. 2 vols. (Edinburgh, 1870).
Documents of the Baronial Movement of Reform and Rebellion 1258–1267, ed. I. J. Sanders (Oxford, 1973).
Earldom of Gloucester Charters, ed. R. B. Patterson (Oxford, 1973).
The Earliest English Law Reports, ed. P. A. Brand. 2 vols. (London, Selden Society, 1996).
Early Welsh Genealogical Tracts, ed. P. C. Bartrum (Cardiff, 1966).
Edward I and the Throne of Scotland, 1290–1296, ed. E. L. G. Stones and G. G. Simpson. 2 vols. (Oxford, 1978).
Episcopal Acts and Cognate Documents relating to Welsh Dioceses 1066–1272, ed. J. C. Davies. 2 vols. (Cardiff, Historical Society of the Church in Wales, 1946–8).
English Historical Documents, iii, *1189–1327*, ed. H. Rothwell (London, 1975).
Excerpta e Rotulis Finium in Turri Londinensi Asservati, 1216–1272, ed. C. Roberts. 2 vols. (Record Commission, 1835–6).
'The Extent of Anglesey', in F. Seebohm, *The Tribal System in Wales* (2nd edn. London, 1904), App. Aa, 3–25.
The Extent of Chirkland, 1391–1393, ed. G. P. Jones (Liverpool, 1933).
'Extent of Merionethshire *temp.* Edward I', *ArchCamb*, 3rd ser., 13 (1867), 184–92.

Bibliography

Facsimile of the Chirk Codex of the Welsh Laws, ed. J. G. Evans (Llanbedrog, 1909).
Feudal Aids. 6 vols. (London, 1899–1921).
The First Extent of Bromfield and Yale A.D. 1315, ed. T. P. Ellis (London, Cymmrodorion Record Series, 11, 1924).
Flavius Vegetius Renatus: Epitoma Rei Militaris, ed. L. F. Stelten (New York, 1995).
Flint Pleas, 1283–1285, ed. J. G. Edwards (Flintshire Historical Society Publications, 8, 1922).
Flintshire Ministers' Accounts, 1301–1328, ed. A. Jones (Flintshire Historical Society Publications, 3, 1913).
Florentii Wigornensis Chronicon ex Chronicis, ed. B. Thorpe. 2 vols. (London, English Historical Society, 1848–9).
Flores Historiarum, ed. H. R. Luard. 3 vols. (RS, 1890).
Foedera, Conventiones, Litterae, et Acta Publica, ed. T. Rymer. 4 vols. (Record Commission, 1816–69).
Fordun, John de, *Chronica Gentis Scotorum*, ed. W. F. Skene. 2 vols. (Edinburgh, 1871–2).
Fouke le fitz Warin, ed. E. J. Hathaway (Oxford, Anglo-Norman Text Society, 1975).
Gascon Register A, ed. G. P. Cuttino. 3 vols. (London, 1975–6).
Geoffrey of Monmouth, *The History of the Kings of Britain*, trans. L. Thorpe (London, 1966).
Gervase of Canterbury, *The Chronicles of the Reigns of Stephen, Henry II and Richard I*, ed. W. Stubbs. 2 vols. (RS, 1879–80).
Gesta Regis Henrici Secundi Benedicti Abbatis, ed. W. Stubbs. 2 vols. (RS, 1867).
Giraldi Cambrensis Opera, vi, *Itinerarium Kambriae et Descriptio Kambriae*, ed. J. F. Dimock (RS, 1868); viii, *De Principis Instructione Liber*, ed. G. F. Warner (RS, 1891).
Gramadegau'r Penceirddiaid, ed. G. J. Williams and E. J. Jones (Cardiff, 1934).
The Great Roll of the Pipe for the Fourteenth Year of the Reign of King John, ed. P. M. Barnes (London, Pipe Roll Society, NS, 30, 1954).
Guillaume de Poitiers, *Histoire de Guillaume le Conquerant*, ed. R. Foreville (Paris, 1952).
Gwaith Bleddyn Fardd a Beirdd Eraill Ail Hanner y Drydedd Ganrif ar Ddeg, ed. Rhian M. Andrews *et al.* (Cardiff, 1996).
Gwaith Cynddelw Brydydd Mawr, ed. Nerys Ann Jones and Ann Parry Owen. 2 vols. (Cardiff, 1991–5).
Gwaith Dafydd Benfras ac Eraill o Feirdd Hanner Cyntaf y Drydedd Ganrif ar Ddeg, ed. N. G. Costigan (Bosco) *et al.* (Cardiff, 1995).
Gwaith Dafydd Llwyd o Fathafarn, ed. L. Richards (Cardiff, 1964).
Gwaith Gruffudd ap Dafydd ap Tudur, Gwilym Ddu o Arfon, Trahaearn Brydydd Mawr ac Iorwerth Beli, ed. N. G. Costigan (Bosco) *et al.* (Aberystwyth, 1995).
Gwaith Iolo Goch, ed. D. R. Johnston (Cardiff, 1989).
Gwaith Lewys Môn, ed. E. I. Rowlands (Cardiff, 1975).
Gwaith Llywarch ap Llywelyn 'Prydydd y Moch', ed. Elin M. Jones (Cardiff, 1991).
Gwaith Llywelyn Fardd I ac Eraill o Feirdd y Ddeuddegfed Ganrif, ed. Kathleen A. Bramley *et al.* (Cardiff, 1994).
Gwaith Meilyr Brydydd a'i Ddisgynyddion, ed. J. E. Caerwyn Williams (Cardiff, 1994).
Hale, Sir Matthew, *The Prerogatives of the King*, ed. D. E. C. Yale (London, Selden Society, 1976).
Handlist of the Acts of the Native Welsh Rulers 1132–1283, ed. K. L. Maund (Cardiff, 1996).
Hearne, Thomas, *The Works of Thomas Hearne.* 4 vols. (London, 1810).
Historia Gruffud vab Kenan, ed. D. S. Evans (Cardiff, 1977).

Bibliography

The Historia Regum Britanniae of Geoffrey of Monmouth, ed. A. Griscom (London, 1929).
Historical Papers and Letters from the Northern Registers, ed. J. Raine (RS, 1873).
Issues of the Exchequer, Henry III–Henry IV, ed. F. Devon (Record Commission, 1847).
The Latin Texts of the Welsh Laws, ed. H. D. Emanuel (Cardiff, 1967).
'The Laws of Hywel Dda: The Black Book of Chirk, Peniarth MS 29', ed. T. Lewis, *Zeitschrift für Celtische Philologie*, 20 (1936), 30–96.
The Laws of Hywel Dda: Law Texts from Medieval Wales, trans. and ed. D. Jenkins (Llandysul, 1986).
Leges Wallicae, ed. W. Wotton (London, 1730).
Leland, John, *The Itinerary in Wales in or about the years 1536–9*, ed. L. Toulmin Smith (London, 1906).
The Letters of John of Salisbury: The Early Letters (1153–61), ed. W. J. Millor, S. J. and H. E. Butler and C. N. L. Brooke (Edinburgh, 1955).
Lettres de rois, reines et autres personnages de cours de France et d'Angleterre tirées des archives de Londres par Brequiny, ed. J. J. Champollion-Figeac. 2 vols. (Paris, 1839–47).
The Liber Epistolaris of Richard de Bury, ed. N. Denholm-Young (London, Roxburghe Club, 1950).
List of Welsh Entries in the Memoranda Rolls 1282–1343, ed. N. Fryde (Cardiff, 1974).
Littere Wallie preserved in Liber A in the Public Record Office, ed. J. G. Edwards (Cardiff, 1940).
Le Livere de Reis de Brittanie e le Livere de Engleterre, ed. J. Glover (RS, !865).
Lives of the Cambro-British Saints, ed. W. J. Rees (Llandovery, 1853).
Llawysgrif Hendregadredd, ed. J. Morris-Jones and T. H. Parry-Williams (Cardiff, 1933).
Llyfr Blegywryd, ed. S. J. Williams and J. E. Powell (Cardiff, 1942).
Llyfr Colan, ed. D. Jenkins (Cardiff, 1963).
Llyfr Du Caerfyrddin, ed. A. O. H. Jarman (Cardiff, 1982).
Llyfr Iorwerth, ed. A. R. Wiliam (Cardiff, 1960).
Llywelyn, 1282, ed. G. Thomas (Gregynog, 1982).
Llywelyn y Beirdd, ed. J. E. C.Williams, E. Rolant and A. Llwyd (Swansea, 1984).
The Mabinogion, trans. G. Jones and T. Jones (London, 1949).
Marwnadau Llywelyn ap Gruffudd, ed. R. G. Gruffydd and T. Roberts (Pen-y-garn, 1982).
Materials for the History of Thomas Becket, ed. J. C. Robertson. 7 vols. (RS, 1875–85).
Matthaei Parisiensis Monachi Sancti Albani Chronica Majora, ed. R. Luard. 7 vols. (RS, 1872–84).
Matthaei Parisiensis Historia Anglorum sive Historia Minor, ed. F. Madden. 3 vols. (RS, 1866–9).
A Medieval Prince of Wales: The Life of Gruffudd ap Cynan, ed. D. S. Evans (Lampeter, 1990).
The Merioneth Lay Subsidy Roll, 1292–3, ed. K. Williams-Jones (Cardiff, 1976).
Monasticon Anglicanum, ed. W. Dugdale. 6 vols. (London, 1830–49).
Monumenta Franciscana, ed. J. S. Brewer and R. Howlett. 2 vols. (RS, 1858–82).
Ockham, Wilhelm von, *Breviloquium de Principatu Tyrannico*, ed. R. Scholz (Stuttgart, 1952).
Ordericus Vitalis Historia Ecclesiastica, ed. M. Chibnall. 6 vols. (Oxford, 1969–80).
Owen, George, *The Description of Penbrokeshire*, ed. H. Owen. 4 vols. (London, Cymmrodorion Record Series, 1902–36).
The Oxford Book of Welsh Verse, ed. T. Parry (Oxford, 1962).

Bibliography

The Oxford Book of Welsh Verse in English, ed. G. Jones (Oxford, 1977).
Oxford City Documents, 1268–1665, ed. J. E. T. Rogers (Oxford Historical Society, 1891).
Parliamentary Writs and Writs of Military Summons, ed. F. Palgrave. 2 vols. (Record Commission, 1827–34).
Patent Rolls 1216–32 (London, 1901–3).
Pedeir Keinc y Mabinogi, ed. I. Williams (Cardiff, 1931).
The Poetry in the Red Book of Hergest, ed. J. G. Evans (Llanbedrog, 1911).
Poitiers, William de, *Gesta Guillelmi Ducis Normannorum et Regis Anglorum*, ed. R. Foreville (Paris, 1952).
Red Book of the Exchequer, ed. H. Hall. 3 vols. (RS, 1897).
Regesta Honorii Papae, ed. P. Pressutti. 2 vols. (Rome, 1888–95).
Regesta Regum Scottorum: The Acts of Malcolm IV, 1153–65, ed. G. W. S. Barrow (Edinburgh, 1960).
Regesta Regum Scottorum: The Acts of William I, 1165–1214, ed. G. W. S. Barrow and W. W. Scott (Edinburgh, 1971).
'Register and chronicle of the abbey of Aberconway', ed. H. Ellis, *Camden Miscellany*, i (London, Camden Society, 39, 1846).
Register of Bishop Godfrey Giffard, 1268–1301, ed J. W. Willis-Bund. 2 vols. (Worcestershire Historical Society, 1898–1902).
The Register of John Pecham, Archbishop of Canterbury, 1279–1292. 2 vols., i, ed. F. N. Davis; ii, ed. Decima Douie (London, Canterbury and York Society, 1968–9).
The Register of Walter Giffard, Lord Archbishop of York, 1266–1279, ed. W. Brown (London, Surtees Society, 109, 1904).
Registres des papes (École française de Rome, 1884–): *Innocent IV, 1243–1254*, ed. E. Berger; *Urban IV, 1261–1264*, ed. J. Guiraud; *Clement IV, 1265–1268*, ed. E. Jordan; *Gregoire X, 1271–1276 et Jean XXI, 1276–1277*, ed. J. Guiraud and E. Cadier; *Nicholas III, 1277–1280*, ed. J. Gay; *Martin IV, 1281–1285*, ed. F. Olivier Martin.
Registrum Epistolarum Fratris Johannis Peckham Archiepiscopi Cantuariensis, ed. C. T. Martin. 3 vols. (RS, 1882–86).
Registrum Johannis de Pontissara Episcopi Wintoniensis, 1282–1304, ed. C. Deedes. 2 vols. (London, Canterbury and York Society, 1915).
Registrum Ricardi de Swinfield Episcopi Herefordensis, 1293–1317, ed. W. W. Capes (London, Canterbury and York Society, 1909).
Registrum Thome de Cantilupo Episcopi Herefordensis, 1275–1282, ed. R. G. Griffiths and W. W. Capes (London, Canterbury and York Society, 1897).
Registrum Vulgariter Nuncupatum: The Record of Caernarvon, ed. H. Ellis (Record Commission, 1838).
Report on Manuscripts in Various Collections, i (Historical Manuscripts Commission, 1901).
Report on MSS in the Welsh Language, ed. J. G. Evans. 2 vols. (Historical Manuscripts Commission, 1898–1910).
Rishanger, William, *Chronica et Annales*, ed. H. T. Riley (RS, 1865).
Rishanger, William, 'Chronicon de duobus bellis apud Lewes et Evesham commissis', *Ypodigma Neustriae*, ed. H. T. Riley (RS, 1876).
Rôles Gascons, ed. Francisque-Michel and C. Bémont. 3 vols. (Paris, 1885–1906).
The Roll of the Shropshire Eyre of 1256, ed. A. Harding (London, Selden Society, 1981).
Rotuli Hundredorum, ed. W. Illingworth and J. Caley. 2 vols. (Record Commission, 1812–18).
Rotuli Litterarum Clausarum, ed. T. D. Hardy. 2 vols. (Record Commission, 1833–44).
Rotuli Litterarum Patentium, ed. T. D. Hardy (Record Commission, 1835).

Bibliography

Rotuli Parliamentorum. 7 vols. (Record Commission, 1783–1832).
Rotulus Walliae, ed. T. Phillips (Cheltenham, 1865).
Royal and Other Historical Letters Illustrative of the Reign of Henry III, ed. W. W. Shirley. 2 vols. (RS, 1862–6).
Select Cases in the Court of King's Bench, ed. G. O. Sayles. 7 vols. (London, Selden Society, 1936–71).
Select Cases concerning the Law Merchant, ed. H. Hall. 3 vols. (London, Selden Society, 1908–32).
Select Charters, ed. W. Stubbs (9th edn., revised H. W. C. Davis, Oxford, 1913).
Statutes of the Realm. 11 vols. (Record Commission, 1810–28).
Survey of the Honour of Denbigh, 1334, ed. P. Vinogradoff and F. Morgan (London, British Academy Records of Social and Economic History, 1, 1914).
The Treatise on the Laws and Customs of the Realm of England commonly called Glanvill, ed. G. D. G. Hall (London, 1965).
Treaty Rolls, i, *1234–1325,* ed. P. Chaplais (London, 1955).
Trevet, Nicholas, *Annales Sex Regum Anglie, 1135–1307,* ed. T. Hog (London, English Historical Society, 1845).
The Valuation of Norwich, ed. W. E. Lunt (Oxford, 1926).
The Welsh Assize Roll 1277–84, ed. J. C. Davies (Cardiff, 1940).
Welsh Medieval Law, ed. A. W. Wade-Evans (Oxford, 1909).
Welsh Records in Paris, ed. T. Matthews (Carmarthen, 1910).
Willelmi Malmesburiensis Monachi, De Gestis Regum Anglorum, ed. W. Stubbs. 2 vols. (RS, 1887–9).
Wynn, Sir John, *The History of the Gwydir Family and Memoirs,* ed. J. G. Jones (Llandysul, 1990).

Secondary Sources

Arnold, C. J. and Huggett, J. W., 'Excavations at Mathrafal, Powys, 1989', *MontColl,* 83 (1995), 61–5.
Alcock, L., 'Excavations at Deganwy Castle, Caernarvonshire, 1961–6', *Archaeological Journal,* 124 (1967), 190–201.
Alcock, L., King, D. J. C., Putnam, W. C. and Spurgeon, C. J., 'Excavations at Castell Bryn Amlwg', *MontColl,* 60 (1967–8), 8–27.
Altschul, M., *A Baronial Family in Medieval England: The Clares 1217–1314* (Baltimore, 1965).
Andrews, Rhian, 'Rhai agweddau ar sofraniaeth yng ngherddi'r Gogynfeirdd', *B,* 27 (1976–8), 23–30.
Anglo, S., 'The *British History* in early Tudor propaganda', *Bulletin of the John Rylands Library,* 44 (1961), 17–48.
Arnold, C. J., and Huggett, J. W., 'Excavations at Mathrafal, Powys, 1989', *MontColl,* 83 (1995), 59–74.
Avent, R., *Cestyll Tywysogion Gwynedd: Castles of the Princes of Gwynedd* (Cardiff, 1983).
— 'Castles of the Welsh princes', *Chateau Gaillard,* 16 (1994), 11–20.
— *Dolwyddelan Castle. Dolbadarn Castle* (Cardiff, 1994).
— 'The early development of three coastal castles', *Sir Gâr, Studies in Carmarthenshire History,* ed. H. James (Carmarthen, 1991), 167–88.
Baldwin, J. F., 'The household administration of Henry de Lacy and Thomas of Lancaster', *EHR,* 42 (1927), 180–200.
Balon, J., 'L'Organisation judicaire des marches féodales', *Annales de la Société Archéologique de Namur,* 46 (1951), 5–72.

Bibliography

Bannerman, J. W. M., 'The king's poet and the inauguration of Alexander III', *Scottish Historical Review*, 69 (1989), 120–49.
Barker, P., and Higham, R., *Hen Domen, Montgomery* (London, Royal Archaeological Institute, 1982).
Barrell, A. D., and Davies, R. R., 'Land, lineage and revolt in north-east Wales 1243–1441: a case-study', *CMCS*, 29 (1995), 27–51.
Barrow, G. W. S., *The Anglo-Norman Era in Scottish History* (Oxford, 1980).
— *The Kingdom of the Scots* (London, 1973).
— *Robert Bruce and the Community of the Realm of Scotland* (London, 1965).
— *Scotland and her Neighbours in the Middle Ages* (London, 1992).
Bartlett, R., *Gerald of Wales 1146–1223* (Oxford, 1982).
— *The Making of Europe: Conquest, Colonization and Cultural Change, 950–1350* (London, 1993).
— 'Technique militaire et pouvoir politique, 900–1300', *Annales: Economies, Societies, Civilizations*, 41 (1986), 1135–59.
Bartrum, P., 'Hen lwythau Gwynedd a'r Mars', *NLWJ*, 12 (1961–2), 201–35.
— *Welsh Genealogies, AD 300–1400* (Cardiff, 1974).
Baugh, G. C., 'The franchises', *Victoria County History: A History of Shropshire*, iii, ed. G. C. Baugh (Oxford, 1979), 34–42.
Bellamy, J. G., *The Law of Treason in England in the Later Middle Ages* (Cambridge, 1970).
Bémont, C., *Simon de Montfort, Comte de Leicester* (Paris, 1884).
— *Simon de Montfort, Earl of Leicester, 1208–1265* (Oxford, 1930).
Besly, E., 'Short-cross and other medieval coins from Llanfaes, Anglesey', *British Numismatic Journal*, 65 (1995), 46–82.
Binchy, D. A., *Celtic and Anglo-Saxon Kingship* (Oxford, 1970).
— 'Irish history and Irish law', *Studia Hibernica*, 15 (1975), 7–36; 16 (1976), 7–45.
— 'Some Celtic legal terms', *Celtica*, 3 (1956), 221–31.
Blount, Margaret N., 'A critical edition of the Annals of Hailes (MS Cotton Cleopatra D. iii, ff. 33–59v.) with an examination of their sources', MA thesis, University of Manchester, 1974.
Boon, G. C., *Welsh Hoards, 1979–1981* (Cardiff, 1986).
Boutruche, R., *Seigneurie et Féodalité*. 2 vols. (Paris, 1959–70).
Bowen, D. J., 'Dafydd ap Gwilym a Morgannwg', *Llên Cymru*, 5 (1958–9), 164–73.
Boyle, L. E., '*E Cathena et carcere*: the imprisonment of Amaury de Montfort, 1276', in *Medieval Learning and Literature: Essays presented to Richard William Hunt*, ed. J. J. G. Alexander and M. T. Gibson (Oxford, 1976), 379–97; repr. L. E. Boyle, *Pastoral Care, Clerical Education and Canon Law, 1200–1400* (London, 1981).
Brault, G. J., *The Rolls of Arms of Edward I*. 2 vols. (Woodbridge, 1997).
Broderick, C., 'Irish and Welsh strands in the genealogy of Godred Crovan', *Journal of the Manx Museum*, 8 (1980), 32–8.
Bromwich, R., *Trioedd Ynys Prydein* (Cardiff, 1961).
Brown, A. E., 'The castle, borough and park of Cefnllys', *TRadnS*, 42 (1972), 11–22.
Brown, R. A., Colvin, H. M., and Taylor, A. J., *The History of the King's Works: The Middle Ages*. 2 vols. (London, 1963).
Brundage, J. A., *Law, Sex and Christian Society in Medieval Europe* (Chicago and London, 1987).
Burton, D. W., 'Requests for prayers and royal propaganda under Edward I', *Thirteenth Century England*, 3, ed. P. R. Coss and S. D. Lloyd (Woodbridge, 1991), 25–35.
Butler, L. A. S., 'Dolforwyn castle, Montgomery, Powys, first report: the excavations, 1981–1986', *ArchCamb*, 138 (1989), 78–89.

Bibliography

— 'Dolforwyn castle, Montgomery, Powys, second report: the excavations 1987–1994', *ArchCamb*, 144 (1995), 133–203.
— 'Medieval finds from Castell-y-Bere, Merioneth', *ArchCamb*, 123 (1974), 78–112.
Caenegem, R. C. van, *Royal Writs in England from the Conquest to Glanvill* (London, Selden Society, 1959).
Carpenter, D. A., *The Battles of Lewes and Evesham, 1264–65* (Keele, 1987).
— *The Minority of Henry III* (London, 1990).
— *The Reign of Henry III* (London, 1996).
Carr, A. D., 'An aristocracy in decline: the native Welsh lords after the Edwardian conquest', *WHR*, 5 (1970–1), 103–29.
— 'Anglo-Welsh relations, 1066–1282', *England and her Neighbours, 1066–1453: Essays in Honour of Pierre Chaplais*, ed. M. Jones and M. Vale (London, 1989), 121–38.
— 'The barons of Edeyrnion, 1282–1485', *JMerHRS*, 4 (1961–4), 187–93, 289–301.
— 'A debateable land: Arwystli in the middle ages', *MontColl*, 80 (1992), 39–54.
— 'The extent of Anglesey, 1352', *TAngAS*, 1971–2, 150–272.
— 'The last days of Gwynedd', *TCaernHS*, 43 (1982), 7–22.
— *Llywelyn ap Gruffydd* (Cardiff, 1982).
— *Medieval Anglesey* (Llangefni, 1982).
— 'Medieval Dinmael', *TDenbH*, 13 (1964), 9–21.
— *Owen of Wales: The End of the House of Gwynedd* (Cardiff, 1991).
Chandler, Helen, 'The will in medieval Wales to 1540', M.Phil. thesis, University of Wales, 1991.
Chaplais, P., *English Medieval Diplomatic Practice*. 2 vols. (London, 1982).
— *Essays in Medieval Diplomacy and Administration* (London, 1981).
Charles, B. G., 'An early charter of the abbey of Cwmhir', *TRadnS*, 40 (1970), 68–74.
— *George Owen of Henllys: A Welsh Elizabethan* (Aberystwyth, 1973).
Charles-Edwards, G. and T. M., 'The continuation of *Brut y Tywysogion* in Peniarth MS 20', *Essays and Poems presented to Daniel Huws*, ed. T. Jones and E. B. Fryde (Aberystwyth, 1994), 293–305.
Charles-Edwards, T. M., '*Cynghawsedd*: counting and pleading in medieval Welsh law', *B*, 33 (1986), 188–98.
— *Early Irish and Welsh Kinship* (Oxford, 1993).
— *The Welsh Laws* (Cardiff, 1989).
Charles-Edwards, T. M., Owen, M. E. and Russell, P. (eds.), *The Welsh King and his Court* (in preparation).
Cheney, C. R., 'The alleged deposition of King John', *Studies in Medieval History presented to Frederick Maurice Powicke*, ed. R. W. Hunt, W. A. Pantin and R. W. Southern (Oxford, 1948), 100–16.
— *Notaries Public in England in the Thirteenth and Fourteenth Centuries* (Oxford, 1972).
Chotzen, Th. M., 'Welsh history in the continuation of the "Spiegel Historiael" by Lodewijk van Velthem', *B*, 7 (1933–5), 42–54.
Clanchy, M. T., 'Did Henry III have a policy?', *History*, 53 (1968), 203–16.
— *From Memory to Written Record: England 1066–1307* (London, 1979).
— 'Inventing thirteenth-century England: Stubbs, Tout, Powicke – now what?', *Thirteenth Century England*, 5, ed. P. R. Coss and S. D. Lloyd (Woodbridge, 1992), 1–20.
Clancy, J. P., *The Earliest Welsh Poetry* (London, 1970).
Coleman, J., 'The Dominican political theory of John of Paris in its context', *The Church and Sovereignty c.590–1918*, ed. D. Wood (Studies in Church History, 9, London, 1991), 191–202.

Bibliography

Contamine, P., *War in the Middle Ages* (Oxford, 1984).
Cosgrove, A. (ed.), *Medieval Ireland, 1169–1534* (Oxford, 1987).
Coss, P. R., 'Sir Geoffrey de Langley and the crisis of the knightly class in thirteenth-century England', *Past and Present*, 68 (1975), 3–37.
Cowan, E. J., 'Myth and identity in early medieval Scotland', *Scottish Historical Review*, 63 (1984), 111–35.
Cowley, F. G., *The Monastic Order in South Wales, 1066–1349* (Cardiff, 1977).
Cox, D. C., 'The battle of Evesham in the Evesham chronicle', *Historical Research*, 62 (1989), 337–45.
Crew, P. and Crew, S., 'Medieval bloomeries in north-west Wales', *The Importance of Ironmaking: Technical Innovation and Social Change*, ed. G. Magnusson (Stockholm, 1995), 43–50.
Crouch, D., 'The last adventure of Richard Siward', *Morgannwg*, 35 (1991), 7–30.
Cuttino, G. P., *English Diplomatic Administration, 1259–1339* (Oxford, 1940).
Dauvillier, J., *Le Mariage dans le droit classique de l'église* (Paris, 1933).
Davies, C., 'Marwnad Syr John Edward Lloyd a Fyrsil Aenid VI', *Llên Cymru*, 12 (1972–3), 57–60.
Davies, E., 'Hendre and hafod in Caernarfonshire', *TCaernHS*, 40 (1979), 17–46.
— 'Hendre and hafod in Denbighshire', *TDenbHS*, 26 (1977), 49–72.
— 'Hendre and hafod in Merioneth', *TMerHRS*, 7 (1973–6), 13–27.
— 'Hafod and lluest: the summering of cattle and upland settlement in Wales', *Folk Life*, 23 (1984–5), 77–96.
Davies, H. R., *The Conway and Menai Ferries* (Cardiff, 1942).
Davies, J. C., 'A grant by David ap Gruffydd', *NLWJ*, 3 (1943–4), 29–32.
— 'A grant by Llywelyn ap Gruffydd', *NLWJ*, 3 (1943–4) 158–62.
Davies, R. R., 'The administration of law in medieval Wales: the role of the *ynad cwmwd* (*iudex patrie*)', *Lawyers and Laymen*, ed. T. M. Charles-Edwards, M. E. Owen and D. B. Walters (Cardiff, 1986), 258–73.
— 'Colonial Wales', *Past and Present*, 65 (1974), 3–23.
— *Conquest, Coexistence and Change: Wales 1063–1415* (Oxford, 1987).
— *Domination and Conquest: The Experience of Ireland, Scotland and Wales 1100–1300* (Cambridge, 1990).
— 'Frontier arrangements in fragmented societies: Ireland and Wales', *Medieval Frontier Societies*, ed. R. Bartlett and A. Mackay (Oxford, 1989), 77–100.
— 'Kings, lords and liberties in the march of Wales, 1066–1272', *TRHS*, 5th ser., 29 (1979), 41–61.
— 'Law and national identity in thirteenth-century Wales', *Welsh Society and Nationhood: Historical Essays presented to Glanmor Williams*, ed. R. R. Davies, R. A. Griffiths, I. G. Jones and K. O. Morgan (Cardiff, 1984), 51–69.
— *Lordship and Society in the March of Wales 1282–1400* (Oxford, 1978).
— 'The peoples of Britain and Ireland, 1100–1400, *TRHS*, 6th ser., 4 (1994), 1–20; 5 (1995), 1–20; 6 (1996), 1–24.
— *The Revolt of Owain Glyn Dŵr* (Oxford, 1995).
Davies, Wendy, '*Braint Teilo*', *B*, 26 (1974–6), 123–37.
Davis, R. H. C., 'William of Poitiers and his history of William the Conqueror', *The Writing of History in the Middle Ages: Essays presented to Richard William Southern*, ed. R. H. C. Davis and J. M. Wallace-Hadrill (Oxford, 1981), 71–100.
Dean, R. J., 'Nicholas Trevet, historian', *Medieval Learning and Literature: Essays presented to Richard William Hunt*, ed. J. J. G. Alexander and M. T. Gibson (Oxford, 1976), 328–52.
Deighton, H. S., 'Clerical taxation by consent, 1279–1301', *EHR*, 68 (1953), 161–91.
Denholm-Young, N., *History and Heraldry, 1254 to 1310* (Oxford, 1965).

Bibliography

— *Richard of Cornwall* (Oxford, 1947).
Donkin, R. A., *The Cistercians: Studies in the Geography of Medieval England and Wales* (Toronto, 1978).
Douie, D. L., *Archbishop Pecham* (Oxford, 1952).
Du Boulay, F. R. H., *The Lordship of Canterbury* (London, 1966).
Dumville, D., 'The aetheling, a study in Anglo-Saxon constitutional history', *Anglo-Saxon England*, 8 (1979), 1–33.
Dunbabin, J., 'The Maccabees as exemplars in the tenth and eleventh centuries', *The Bible in the Medieval World*, ed. K. Walsh and D. Loud (Oxford, 1985), 31–41.
Duncan, A. A. M., *Scotland: the Making of the Kingdom* (Edinburgh, 1975).
Dwnn, L., *Heraldic Visitations of Wales*, ed. S. R. Meyricke. 2 vols. (Llandovery, 1846).
Easterling, R. C., 'Anian of Nanneu', *JFlintHS*, 5 (1914–15), 9–30.
Edwards, A., *Appointment at Aberedwy: The Death of Llywelyn ap Gruffudd, Prince of Wales* (Pen-y-groes, 1992).
Edwards, H. T., *Codi'r Hen Wlad yn ei Hôl 1850–1914* (Llandysul, 1989).
— *Gŵyl Gwalia: Yr Eisteddfod Genedlaethol yn Oes Aur Victoria 1858–1868* (Llandysul, 1980).
Edwards, J. G., 'The building of Flint', *JFlintHS*, 12 (1951), 5–20.
— 'The early history of the counties of Carmarthen and Cardigan', *EHR*, 31 (1916), 90–8.
— *Hywel Dda and the Welsh Lawbooks* (Bangor, 1929); repr. *Celtic Law Papers Introductory to Medieval Welsh Law and Government*, ed. D. Jenkins (Brussels, 1973), 135–60.
— 'Madog ap Llywelyn, the Welsh leader in 1294–5', *B*, 13 (1948–50), 207–10.
— 'The Normans and the Welsh march', *PBA*, 42 (1957), 155–77.
— *The Principality of Wales, 1267–1967: A Study in Constitutional History* (Caernarfon, 1969).
— 'Sir John Edward Lloyd, 1861–1947', *PBA*, 41 (1956), 319–27.
Edwards, O. M., *Wales* (London, 1901).
Ellis, T. E., *Addresses and Speeches* (Wrexham, 1912).
Ellis, T. P., *Welsh Tribal Law and Custom in the Middle Ages*. 2 vols. (Oxford, 1926).
Esmein, A., *Le Mariage en droit canonique*. 2 vols. (2nd edn. Paris, 1929–35).
Evans, D. L., 'Llyfr Coch Asaph', *NLWJ*, 4 (1945–6), 177–83.
— 'Some notes on the history of the principality of Wales in the time of the Black Prince (1343–1376)', *THSC*, 1925–6, 25–110.
Evans, G., 'The squire of Cilmery', *Brycheiniog*, 15 (1971), 57–61.
Evans, E., *The Love of our Country: A Poem with Historical Notes Addressed to Sir Watkin Williams Wynn* (Carmarthen, 1972).
Evans, Theophilus, *Drych y Prif Oesoedd yn ôl yr Argraffiad Cyntaf: 1716*, ed. G. H. Hughes (Cardiff, 1961).
Eyton, R. W., *Antiquities of Shropshire*. 12 vols. (London, 1854–60).
Farmer, D. L., 'Some grain price movements in thirteenth-century England', *EcHR*, 2nd ser., 10 (1957–8), 207–20.
— 'Some livestock price movements in thirteenth-century England', *EcHR*, 2nd ser., 22 (1969), 1–16.
Fisher, J., 'Three Welsh wills', *ArchCamb*, 6th ser., 19 (1919), 186–7.
Frame, R., *The Political Development of the British Isles 1100–1400* (Oxford, 1990).
Francis, E. A., 'The background of *Fulk fitz Warin*', *Studies in Medieval French presented to Alfred Ewert*, ed. E. A. Francis (Oxford, 1961), 322–7.
Fraser, C. M., *A History of Antony Bek, Bishop of Durham, 1283–1311* (Oxford, 1957).
Fryde, E. B., *Studies in Medieval Trade and Finance* (London, 1983).

— and Fryde, M. M., 'Public credit, with special reference to north-west Europe', *Cambridge Economic History of Europe*, 3 (1963), 430–553.
Ganshof, F. L., *Feudalism* (London, 1952).
Gatto, L., *Il pontificato di Gregorio X, 1271–1276* (Rome, 1959).
Genicot, L., *L'Économie rurale namuroise au bas moyen âge*. 2 vols. (Louvain, 1943–60).
Giffin, M. E., 'Cadwalader, Arthur and Brutus in the Wigmore manuscript', *Speculum*, 16 (1941), 109–20.
Giuseppi, M. S., *A Guide to the Manuscripts preserved in the Public Record Office*. 2 vols. (London, 1923–4).
Given, J., *State and Society in Medieval Europe: Gwynedd and Languedoc under Outside Rule* (Ithaca and London, 1990).
The Glamorgan County History, ed. G. Williams, iii, *The Middle Ages*, ed. T. B. Pugh (Cardiff, 1971).
Golding, B, *Gilbert of Sempringham and the Gilbertine Order c.1130–c.1300* (Oxford, 1995).
Goetinck, G., *Peredur: A Study of Welsh Tradition in the Grail Legends* (Cardiff, 1975).
Gough, H., *Itinerary of Edward I, 1272–1307* (Paisley, 1900).
Graham, R., 'Letters of Cardinal Ottoboni, 1265–68', *EHR*, 15 (1900), 87–120.
— *St Gilbert of Sempringham and the Gilbertines* (London, 1901).
Green, M. A. E., *Lives of the Princesses of England*. 6 vols. (London, 1849–55).
Gresham, C. A., 'The Aberconwy charter', *ArchCamb*, 94 (1939), 123–62.
— 'The Aberconwy charter: further consideration', *B*, 30 (1982–3), 311–47.
— 'The commotal centre of Arllechwedd Isaf', *TCaernHS*, 40 (1979), 11–16.
— *Eifionydd: A Study in Landownership from the Medieval Period to the Present Day* (Cardiff, 1973).
— *Medieval Stone Carving in North Wales* (Cardiff, 1968).
— 'Ystumgwern and Prysor: medieval administrative districts of Ardudwy', *JMerHRS*, 10 (1985–9), 100–18, 221–6.
Gresham, C.A., and Hemp, W. J., 'Castell Prysor', *ArchCamb*, 100 (1949), 312–13.
Griffith, M. O., 'Abereiddon and Esgaireiddon', *JMerHRS*, 9 (1981–4), 367–89.
Griffiths, J., 'Early accounts relating to North Wales temp. Edward I', *B*, 14 (1950–2), 235–41, 302–12; 15 (1952–4), 126–56; 16 (1954–6), 109–33.
— 'Two early ministers' accounts for North Wales', *B*, 9 (1937–9), 50–70.
Griffiths, R. A., *Conquerors and Conquered in Medieval Wales* (Stroud, 1994).
— *The Principality of Wales in the Later Middle Ages: The Structure and Personnel of Government*, i, *South Wales, 1277–1536* (Cardiff, 1972).
— (ed.), *Boroughs of Mediaeval Wales* (Cardiff, 1978).
Griffiths, Rh., *1282: A Collection of Documents* (Aberystwyth, 1986).
Gweirydd ap Rhys [R. J. Pryse], *Hanes y Brytaniaid a'r Cymry*. 2 vols. (London, 1872–4).
Gwynn, A., 'Edward I and the proposed purchase of English law for the Irish c.1276–80', *TRHS*, 5th ser., 10 (1960), 111–27.
Hagen, H., *Catalogus Codicum Bernensium* (Bern, 1875).
Handbook of British Chronology, ed. E. B. Fryde, D. E. Greenway, S. Porter and I. Roy. 3rd edn. (London, 1986).
Harriss, G. L., *King, Parliament, and Public Finance in Medieval England to 1369* (Oxford, 1975).
Harvey, P. D. A., 'The English inflation of 1180–1220', *Past and Present*, 61 (1973), 3–30.
— 'The Pipe Rolls and the adoption of demesne farming in England', *EcHR*, 2nd ser., 27 (1974), 345–59.

Bibliography

Haycock, M., 'Llyfr Taliesin', *NLWJ*, 25 (1987–8), 357–86.
Hemp, W. J., 'The castle of Ewloe and the Welsh castle plan', *Y Cymmrodor*, 39 (1928), 4–19.
Herlihy, D., *The Social History of Italy and Western Europe 700–1500* (London, 1978).
Hill, C.F., *Treasure Trove in Law and Practice* (Oxford, 1936).
Hinnebusch, W. A., 'Diplomatic activities of the English Dominicans in the thirteenth century', *Catholic Historical Review*, 28 (1942–3), 309–39.
— *The Early English Friars Preachers* (Rome, 1951).
A History of Carmarthenshire, ed. J. E. Lloyd. 2 vols. (London, 1936).
Hogg, A. H. A., 'Castell Carndochan', *JMerHRS*, 2 (1953–6), 178–80.
Holmes, G. A., *The Estates of the Higher Nobility in Fourteenth-Century England* (Cambridge 1957).
Holt, J. C., *Magna Carta* (2nd edn., Cambridge, 1992).
— 'Politics and property in early medieval England', *Past and Present*, 57 (1972), 3–52.
Hooke, D., 'The Ardudwy landscape', *JMerHRS*, 9 (1981–4), 245–60.
— 'Llanaber, a study in landscape development', *JMerHRS*, 7 (1973–6), 221–30.
Hopewell, D., *Ty'n Tŵr, Bethesda: Archaeological Excavation* (Bangor, Gwynedd Archaeological Trust, Report No. 96, 1993).
Howell, M., 'Regalian right in Wales and the march: the relation of theory to practice', *WHR*, 7 (1974–5), 269–88.
Howells, D., 'The four exclusive possessions of a man', *Studia Celtica*, 8–9 (1973–4), 48–67.
Hughes, K., *Celtic Britain in the Early Middle Ages* (Woodbridge, 1980).
Hughes, R. E. *et al.*, ' A review of the density and ratios of sheep and cattle in medieval Gwynedd', *JMerHRS*, 7 (1973–6), 373–83.
Hughes, W. J., *Wales and the Welsh in English Literature* (Wrexham, 1924).
Huws, D., 'Leges Howelda at Canterbury', *NLWJ*, 19 (1975–6), 340–3.
— 'Llawysgrif Hendregadredd', *NLWJ*, 22 (1981–2), 1–26.
— 'Llyfrau Cymraeg 1250–1400', *NLWJ*, 28 (1993–4), 1–21.
An Inventory of the Ancient Monuments in Anglesey (London, The Royal Commission on Ancient and Historical Monuments in Wales, 1937).
An Inventory of the Ancient Monuments in Caernarvonshire. 3 vols. (London, The Royal Commission on Ancient and Historical Monuments in Wales, 1956–64).
An Inventory of the Ancient Monuments in Carmarthenshire (London, The Royal Commission on Ancient and Historical Monuments in Wales, 1917).
An Inventory of the Ancient Monuments in Glamorgan, iii, *Medieval Secular Monuments*: 2 vols.: Part 1a, *The Early Castles* (London, The Royal Commission on Ancient and Historical Monuments in Wales, 1991); Part 1b, *The Later Castles* (Aberystwyth, The Royal Commission on Ancient and Historical Monuments in Wales, 1999).
An Inventory of the Ancient Monuments in Radnorshire (London, The Royal Commission on Ancient and Historical Monuments in Wales, 1913).
Jack, R. I., 'The lordship of Dyffryn Clwyd in 1324', *TDenbHS*, 17 (1968), 7–53.
— *Medieval Wales: The Sources of History* (London, 1972).
James, T., 'Excavations at Carmarthen Greyfriars, 1983–90', *Medieval Archaeology*, 41 (1997).
Jarman, A. O. H., 'Brwydr y Cymerau ac oed Llyfr Du Caerfyrddin', *B*, 14 (1950–2), 179–85.
Jenkins, D., '*Cynghellor* and chancellor', *B*, 27 (1976–8), 115–18.
— 'A family of medieval Welsh lawyers', *Celtic Law Papers Introductory to Welsh Medieval Law and Government*, ed. D. Jenkins (Brussels, 1973), 121–33.

Bibliography

— 'Kings, lords and princes: the nomenclature of authority in thirteenth-century Wales', *B*, 26 (1974–6), 451–62.
— 'The lawbooks of medieval Wales', *The Political Context of Law*, ed. R. Eales and D. Sullivan (London, 1987), 1–15.
— 'Property interests in the classical Welsh law of women', *The Welsh Law of Women*, ed. D. Jenkins and M. E. Owen (Cardiff, 1980), 69–92.
Jenkins, G. H., *The Foundations of Modern Wales: Wales 1642–1780* (Cardiff, 1987).
— (ed.), *The Welsh Language before the Industrial Revolution* (Cardiff, 1997).
Johns, C. N., *Caerphilly Castle* (Cardiff, 1978).
— 'The Celtic monasteries of north Wales', *TCaernHS*, 21 (1960), 14–43.
Johnstone, N., 'An investigation into the location of the royal courts of thirteenth-century Gwynedd', *Landscape and Settlement in Medieval Wales*, ed. N. Edwards (Oxford, 1997), 149–87.
— *Llys and Maerdref: An Investigation into the Location of the Royal Courts of the Princes of Gwynedd* (Bangor, Gwynedd Archaeological Trust, Report no. 167, 1995).
— *Ty'n y Mwd, Aber: Archaeological Excavation* (Bangor, Gwynedd Archaeological Trust, Report no. 86, 1994).
Jolliffe, J. E. A., *Angevin Kingship* (London, 1955).
— 'Northumbrian institutions', *EHR*, 41 (1926), 1–42.
Jones, D., *Epoch and Artist* (London, 1959).
Jones, F., *The Princes and Principality of Wales* (Cardiff, 1969).
— 'Welsh bonds for keeping the peace, 1283 and 1295', *B*, 13 (1948–50), 142–4.
Jones, F. P., 'Pam Llywelyn?', *Y Genhinen*, 19 (1968–9), 244–7.
Jones, G. R. J., 'The defences of Gwynedd in the thirteenth century', *TCaernHS*, 30 (1969), 29–43.
— 'The distribution of bond settlements in north-west Wales', *WHR*, 2 (1964–5), 19–36.
— 'The distribution of medieval settlement in Anglesey', *TAngAS*, 1955, 29–96.
— 'Die Entwicklung de landlichen Besiedlung in Wales', *Zeitschrift für Agrargesichte und Agrarsoziologie*, 10 (Frankfurt am Main, 1962), 174–94.
— 'Field systems of north Wales', *Studies of Field Systems in the British Isles*, ed. A. R. H. Baker and R. A. Butlin (Cambridge, 1973), 430–79.
— 'Forms and patterns of medieval settlement in Welsh Wales', *Medieval Villages*, ed. D. Hooke (Oxford University Committee for Archaeology, 1985), 155–69.
— 'Hereditary land: its effect on the evolution of field systems and settlement patterns in the Vale of Clwyd', *Man, Culture and Settlement*, ed. R. C. Eidt, K. N. Singh and R. P. B. Singh (New Delhi, 1977), 82–96.
— 'The impact of state policy on the rural landscape of Gwynedd in the thirteenth century', *The Medieval and Early Modern Rural Landscape of Europe under the Impact of the Commercial Economy*, ed. H.-J. Nitz (Göttingen, 1987), 11–24.
— 'The models for organisation in Llyfr Iorwerth and Llyfr Cyfnerth', *B*, 39 (1992), 95–118.
— 'Multiple estates and early settlement', *Medieval Settlement: Continuity and Change*, ed. P. H. Sawyer (London, 1976), 15–40.
— 'The multiple estate: a model for tracing the inter-relationships of society, economy and habitat', *Archaeological Approaches to Medieval Europe*, ed. K. Biddick (Kalamazoo, 1984), 9–41.
— 'The pattern of medieval settlement in the commote of Rhos Is Dulas and its antecedents', *Genetische Ansätze in der Kulturlandschaftforschung*, ed. W. Pinkwart (Würzburg, 1983), 41–50.
— 'The portrayal of land settlement in Domesday Book', *Domesday Studies*, ed. J. C. Holt (Woodbridge, 1986), 183–200.

Bibliography

— 'Post-Roman Wales', *The Agrarian History of England and Wales*, I, ii, ed. H. P. R. Finberg (Cambridge, 1972), 281–382.
— 'Rural settlement in Anglesey', *Geography as Human Ecology*, ed. G. R. J. Jones and S. J. Eyre (London, 1966), 199–230.
— 'The tribal system in Wales: a re-assessment in the light of settlement studies', *WHR*, 1 (1960–3), 111–32.
Jones, Owen E., 'Llyfr Coch Asaph: a textual and historical study', MA thesis, University of Wales, 1968.
Jones, T., 'Historical writing in medieval Welsh', *Scottish Studies*, 12 (1968), 15–27.
Jones, Theophilus, *A History of the County of Brecknock*. 2 vols. (Brecon, 1805–9).
Jones, W. H., 'Llywelyn ap Gruffudd', *Y Beirniad*, 1 (1911), 123–7.
Jones, W. R., 'England against the Celtic fringe', *Journal of World History*, 13 (1971), 155–71.
— 'The image of the barbarian in medieval Europe', *Comparative Studies in Society and History*, 13 (1971), 376–407.
Kaeuper, R. W., *Bankers to the Crown: The Riccardi of Lucca and Edward I* (Princeton, 1973).
— 'The role of the Italian financiers in the Edwardian conquest of Wales', *WHR*, 6 (1972–3), 387–403.
— *War, Justice and Public Order: England and France in the Later Middle Ages* (Oxford, 1988).
Keen, M. H., *Chivalry* (London, 1984).
Kelly, F., *A Guide to Early Irish Law* (Dublin, 1988).
Kelly, R. S., 'The excavation of a medieval farmstead at Cefn Graeanog, Clynnog, Gwynedd', *B*, 29 (1980–2), 859–87.
Kendrick, T. D., *British Antiquity* (London, 1950).
Ker, N. R., *Medieval Libraries of Great Britain* (2nd edn. London 1964; suppl. 1987).
King, D. J. C., 'Camlais and Sennybridge castles', *Brycheiniog*, 21 (1984–5), 9–11.
— *Castellorum Anglicanum*. 2 vols. (London, 1983).
— 'The castles of Breconshire', *Brycheiniog*, 7 (1961), 71–94.
— 'A castle of Llywelyn ap Gruffydd in Brycheiniog', *Brycheiniog*, 11 (1965), 151–3.
— 'Two castles in northern Powys: Dinas Brân and Caergwrle', *ArchCamb*, 123 (1974), 113–39.
Kingsford, C. L., 'Sir Otho de Grandison (1238–1328)', *TRHS*, 3rd ser., 3 (1909), 125–95.
Knowles, C. H., 'The resettlement of England after the Barons' War, 1264–67', *TRHS*, 5th ser., 32 (1982), 25–41.
L., J., A Cambro-Briton, *A True (tho' a short) Account of the Antient Britons... with the Effigies of Llewelyn ab Gruffydd, the last Prince of Wales of the British Blood* (London, 1716).
Labarge, M. W., *Simon de Montfort* (London, 1962).
Lambourne, L., and Hamilton, J., *British Watercolours in the Victoria and Albert Museum* (London, 1980).
Latimer, P., 'Henry II's campaign against the Welsh in 1165', *WHR*, 14 (1988–9), 523–52.
Lawrence, C. H., *St Edmund of Abingdon* (Oxford, 1960).
Legge, M. D., *Anglo-Norman Literature and its Background* (Oxford, 1963).
— 'The inauguration of Alexander III', *Proceedings of the Society of Antiquaries of Scotland*, 80 (1945–6), 73–82.
— 'The Lord Edward's Vegetius', *Scriptorium*, 7 (1953), 262–5.
Lemarignier, J.-F., *Recherches sur l'hommage en marche et les frontières féodales* (Lille, 1945).

Bibliography

Lennard, R., *Rural England, 1086–1135* (Oxford, 1959).
Le Patourel, J., 'The king and the princes in fourteenth-century France', *Europe in the Late Middle Ages*, ed. J. R. Hale, J. R. L. Highfield and B. Smalley (London, 1965), 155–83.
Lestrange, H., *Le Strange Records, 1100–1310* (London, 1916).
Lewis, Alun, 'The English activities of Cardinal Ottobuono, legate of the Holy See', MA thesis, University of Manchester, 1937.
— 'Roger Leyburn and the pacification of England, 1265–7', *EHR*, 54 (1939), 193–214.
Lewis, A. W., 'Anticipatory association of the heir in early Capetian France', *American Historical Review*, 83 (1978), 906–27.
— *Royal Succession in Capetian France: Studies on Familial Order and the State* (Cambridge, Mass., 1981).
Lewis, C. W., 'The treaty of Woodstock, 1247: its background and significance', *WHR*, 2 (1964–5), 37–65.
Lewis, E. A., 'The development of industry and commerce in Wales during the middle ages', *TRHS*, 3rd ser., 17 (1907), 121–73.
— *The Mediaeval Boroughs of Snowdonia* (London, 1912).
Lewis, F. R., 'William de Valence, c.1230–1296', *Aberystwyth Studies*, 13 (1934), 11–35; 14 (1936), 69–92.
Lewis, P. S., 'Of Breton *alliances* and other matters', *War, Literature and Politics in the Late Middle Ages*, ed. C. T. Allmand (Liverpool, 1976), 122–43.
Lloyd, J. E., 'The age of the native princes (400–1282 A.D.)', *A History of Carmarthenshire*, ed. J. E. Lloyd. 2 vols. (London, 1935–9), i, 113–200.
— 'Border notes', *B*, 11 (1941–4), 48–54.
— 'The death of Llywelyn ap Gruffydd', *B*, 5 (1929–31), 349–53.
— 'Dolforwyn', *B*, 10 (1939–41), 306–9.
— 'Edward the First's commission of enquiry of 1280–1: an examination of its origin and purpose', *Y Cymmrodor*, 25 (1915), 1–20; 26 (1916), 252.
— 'Ewloe', *Y Cymmrodor*, 39 (1928), 1–3.
— *A History of Wales from the Earliest Times to the Edwardian Conquest* (London, 1911).
— *A History of Wales* (London, 1930).
— 'Llywelyn ap Gruffydd and the lordship of Glamorgan', *ArchCamb*, 6th ser., 13 (1913), 56–64.
— 'Medieval Eifionydd', *ArchCamb*, 6th ser., 5 (1905), 296–9.
— 'The mountains in history and legend', *The Mountains of Snowdonia*, ed. R. C. Carr and G. A. Lister (London, 1948), 3–34.
— *Owen Glendower* (Oxford, 1931).
— 'Wales 1066 to 1485', *The Cambridge Medieval History*, vii (Cambridge, 1932), 508–26.
— 'Who was Gwenllian de Lacy?', *ArchCamb*, 6th ser., 19 (1919), 292–8.
Lloyd, J. Y. W., *History of the Princes, the Lords Marcher and the Ancient Nobility of Powys Fadog*. 6 vols. (London, 1881–7).
Lloyd, S. D., *English Society and the Crusade, 1216–1307* (Oxford, 1988).
— 'Gilbert de Clare, Richard of Cornwall and the Lord Edward's crusade', *Nottingham Medieval Studies*, 30 (1986), 46–66.
— 'The Lord Edward's crusade, 1270–72, its setting and significance', *War and Government in the Middle Ages*, ed. J. B. Gillingham and J. C. Holt (Woodbridge, 1984), 120–33.
Lloyd-Jones, J., 'The court poets of the Welsh princes', *PBA*, 34 (1948), 167–97.
Llwyd, H., *Britannicae Descriptionis Commentariolum* (London, 1731).
Loomis, R. S., 'Edward I, Arthurian enthusiast', *Speculum*, 28 (1953), 114–27.

Bibliography

Lowe, W. Bezant, *The Heart of Northern Wales*. 2 vols. (Llanfairfechan, 1912–27).
Luchaire, A., *Histoire des institutions monarchiques de la France sous les premiers Capétiens (987–1180)*. 2 vols. (2nd edn. Paris, 1891).
Lunt, W. E., *Financial Relations of the Papacy with England to 1327* (Cambridge, Mass., 1939).
Lydon, J. F., 'Lordship and crown: Llywelyn of Wales and O'Connor of Connacht', *The British Isles 1100–1500: Comparisons, Contrasts and Connections*, ed. R. R. Davies (Edinburgh, 1988), 48–63.
— 'Three Exchequer documents from the reign of Henry III', *Proceedings of the Royal Irish Academy*, 65 (1966–7), Section C, 1–27.
Lynch, P., 'Llygad Gŵr: sylwebydd cyfoes', *Ysgrifau Beirniadol*, 16 (1990), 31–51.
McFarlane, K. B., 'An indenture of agreement between two English knights for mutual aid and counsel in peace and war, 5 December 1298', *BIHR*, 38 (1965), 200–210.
— *The Nobility of Later Medieval England* (Oxford, 1973).
McKenna, C. A., 'The theme of sovereignty in *Pwyll*', *B*, 29 (1980–2), 35–52.
Macneill, C., 'Harris: Collectanea de Rebus Hibernicis', *Analecta Hibernica*, 6 (1934), 248–450.
MacNeill, E., *Celtic Ireland* (Dublin, 1921).
Mac Niocaill, G., 'The "heir-designate" in early medieval Ireland', *The Irish Jurist*, NS, 3 (1968), 326–9.
Maddicott, J. R., *The English Peasantry and the Demands of the Crown, 1294–1341* (Past and Present Supplement, 1, Oxford, 1975).
— *Simon de Montfort* (Cambridge, 1994).
Major, John, *A History of Greater Britain (1521)*, ed. A. Constable (Edinburgh, Scottish History Society, 1892).
Martin, C.T., *Catalogue of the Archives of All Souls College* (London, 1877).
Mason, M. A., 'Llywelyn's Hall, Conwy', *TCaernHS*, 56 (1995), 11–35.
Maud, R., 'David, the last prince of Wales', *THSC*, 1968, 43–62.
Miller, E., 'England in the twelfth and thirteenth centuries: an economic contrast?', *EcHR*, 2nd ser., 24 (1971), 1–14.
— 'Farming in northern England during the twelfth and thirteenth centuries', *Northern History*, 11 (1975), 1–16.
— 'War, taxation and the English economy in the late thirteenth and early fourteenth centuries', *War and Economic Development*, ed. J. M. Winter (Cambridge, 1975).
Mills, M., 'Exchequer agenda and estimates of revenue, Easter Term 1284', *EHR*, 40 (1925), 229–34.
Mitchell, S. K., *Studies in Taxation under John and Henry III* (New Haven, 1914).
Morgan, P., *The Eighteenth Century Renaissance* (Llandybie, 1981).
Morgan, R., 'The barony of Powys, 1275–1360', *WHR*, 10 (1980–1), 1–42.
— 'The territorial divisions of medieval Montgomeryshire', *MontColl*, 69 (1981), 9–44; 70 (1982), 11–39.
Morgan, R. W., *The British Kymry or Britons of Cambria* (Caernarfon, 1857).
Morris, J. E., *The Welsh Wars of Edward I* (Oxford, 1901).
Morris, R., 'The burial of Llywelyn ap Gruffydd', *ArchCamb*, 6th ser., 11 (1911), 26–42.
Murray, A., *Reason and Society in the Middle Ages* (Oxford, 1978).
Neaverson, E., *Mediaeval Castles in North Wales* (London, 1947).
Nicholls, K., 'Anglo-French Ireland and after', *Peritia*, 1 (1982), 370–403.
Nicholson, R., 'The Franco-Scottish and Franco-Norwegian treaties of 1295', *Scottish Historical Review*, 38 (1959), 114–32.

Bibliography

O'Corrain, D., 'Irish regnal succession, a reappraisal', *Studia Hibernica*, 11 (1971), 7–39.
— 'Nationality and kingship in pre-Norman Ireland', *Nationality and the Pursuit of National Independence*, Historical Studies, 12, ed. T. W. Moody (Belfast, 1978), 1–35.
Orpen, G. H., *Ireland under the Normans 1169–1333*. 4 vols. (Oxford, 1911–20).
Otway-Ruthven, J. C., 'The constitutional position of the great lordships of south Wales', *TRHS*, 5th ser., 8 (1958), 1–20.
— 'The request of the Irish for English law, 1277–80', *Irish Historical Studies*, 6 (1948–9), 261–9.
Owen, D. Huw, 'The lordship of Denbigh 1282–1425', Ph.D. thesis, University of Wales, 1967.
— 'Tenurial and economic developments in north Wales in the twelfth and thirteenth centuries', *WHR*, 6 (1972–3), 117–42.
— 'Treth and ardreth: some aspects of commutation in north Wales in the thirteenth century', *B*, 25 (1972–4), 446–53.
Owen, E., 'The Croes Nawdd', *Y Cymmrodor*, 43 (1932), 1–18.
— 'Owain Lawgoch', *THSC*, 1899–1900, 6–105.
Owen, H. and Blakeway, J. B., *A History of Shrewsbury*. 2 vols. (Shrewsbury, 1825).
Owen, H. J., 'The romance of the chalice and paten of Cymer abbey', *JMerHRS*, 2 (1953–6), 181–90.
Owen, M. E., 'Literary convention and historical reality: the court in the Welsh poetry of the twelfth and thirteenth centuries', *Études Celtiques*, 22 (1992), 69–85.
Owen, William, *Hanes Owen Glandwr. Blaenor y Cymry mewn Rhyfel* (Caernarfon, 1833).
Owen Rhoscomyl [Arthur Owen Vaughan], *Flame Bearers of Welsh History* (Merthyr Tydfil, 1905).
Painter, S., *Studies in the History of the English Feudal Barony* (Baltimore, 1943).
Palmer, A. N., 'The portionary churches of medieval north Wales', *ArchCamb*, 5th ser., 3 (1886), 175–209.
Pantin, W. A., 'John of Wales and medieval humanism', *Medieval Studies presented to Aubrey Gwynn, S.J.*, ed. J. A. Watt (Dublin, 1961), 297–319.
Parry, J. H., *The Cambrian Plutarch* (London, 1834).
Parry-Williams, T. H., 'Croes Naid', *Y Llinyn Arian* (Aberystwyth, 1947), 91–4.
Peers, C.R., 'Harlech Castle', *THSC*, 1921–2, 63–82.
Pennant, T., *Tours in Wales*. 3 vols. (London, 1784).
Phillimore, E., 'The traitors of Builth', *Western Mail*, 7 May 1924.
Phillips, J. R. S., *Aymer de Valence, Earl of Pembroke, 1307–1324: Baronial Politics in the Reign of Edward II* (Oxford, 1972).
Pierce, T. Jones, 'Aber Gwyn Gregin', *TCaernHS*, 23 (1962), 37–43.
— 'Einion ab Ynyr (Anian II), bishop of St. Asaph', *JFlintHS*, 17 (1957), 16–33.
— 'Lleyn ministers' acounts, 1350–51', *B*, 6 (1931–3), 255–75.
— 'Llywelyn ap Gruffydd', *DWB*, 597–8.
— *Medieval Welsh Society: Selected Essays*, ed. J. B. Smith (Cardiff, 1972).
— 'The old borough of Nefyn, 1355–1882', *TCaernHS*, 18 (1957), 36–53.
— 'Two early Caernarvonshire accounts', *B*, 5 (1929–31), 142–55.
— 'Wales, History. The Emergence of Wales; From the Normans to the Union with England', *Encyclopaedia Britannica* (1979 edn.), xxiii, 155–8.
— 'Wales, History: Llywelyn ap Gruffudd, The Age of the Two Llywelyns', *Chambers's Encyclopaedia* (London, 1966), viii, 62–9; xiv, 384–5.
Pierce, T. Jones and Griffiths, J., 'Documents relating to the early history of the borough of Caernarvon', *B*, 9 (1937–9), 236–46.
Pollock, F., and Maitland, F. W., *The History of English Law*. 2 vols. (Cambridge, 1911; reissued, 1968).
Post, G., *Studies in Medieval Legal Thought* (Princeton, 1964).

Bibliography

Postan, M. M., *Essays on Medieval Agriculture and General Problems of the Medieval Economy* (Cambridge, 1973).
Powel, D., *The Historie of Cambria* (London, 1584, repr. Amsterdam and New York, 1969).
Powicke, F. M., 'King Edward I in fact and fiction', *Fritz Saxl (1890–1948). Knowledge and Learning: A Volume of Memorial Essays,* ed. D. J. Gordon (London and Edinburgh, 1957), 120–35.
— *King Henry III and the Lord Edward: The Community of the Realm in the Thirteenth Century.* 2 vols. (Oxford, 1947).
— *The Thirteenth Century 1216–1307* (Oxford, 1953).
— *Ways of Medieval Life and Thought* (London, 1949).
— Review: *Littere Wallie*, ed. J. G. Edwards; *The Welsh Assize Roll 1277–84*, ed. J. C. Davies, *EHR*, 56 (1941), 491–4.
Powicke, M. R., *Military Obligation in Medieval England* (Oxford, 1962).
Prestwich, M., *Edward I* (London, 1988).
— 'A new account of the Welsh campaign of 1294–5', *WHR*, 6 (1972–3), 89–94.
— *War, Politics and Finance under Edward I* (London, 1972).
Price, Thomas (Carnhuanawc), *Hanes Cymru a Chenedl y Cymry o'r Cynoesoedd hyd at Farwolaeth Llywelyn ap Gruffydd* (Crughywel, 1842).
Pryce, H., 'Ecclesiastical sanctuary in thirteenth-century Welsh law', *Journal of Legal History*, 5/3 (1984), 1–13.
— *Native Law and the Church in Medieval Wales* (Oxford, 1993).
— 'Owain Gwynedd and Louis VII: the Franco-Welsh diplomacy of the first prince of Wales', *WHR*, 19 (1998–9), 1–28.
— (ed.), *Literacy in Medieval Celtic Societies* (Cambridge, 1998).
Rees, W., *Caerphilly Castle and its Place in the Annals of Glamorgan* (Caerphilly, 1974).
— *A History of the Order of St John of Jerusalem in Wales and the Welsh Border* (Cardiff, 1947).
— *South Wales and the Border in the Fourteenth Century* (Cardiff, 1932) [map in four sheets].
— 'Survivals of ancient Celtic custom in medieval England', *Angles and Britons, O'Donnell Lectures* (Cardiff, 1963), 148–68.
Reiss, E., 'The Welsh versions of Geoffrey of Monmouth's *Historia*', *WHR*, 4 (1968–9), 97–113.
Remfry, P. M., 'The native Welsh dynasties of Rhwng Gwy a Hafren 1066–1282', MA thesis, University of Wales, 1989.
Renn, D., and Avent, R., *Flint Castle. Ewloe Castle* (Cardiff, 1995).
Reynolds, S., *Fiefs and Vassals* (Oxford, 1994).
— *Kingdoms and Communities in Western Europe 900–1300* (Oxford, 1984).
— 'Law and communities in Western Christendom, c.900–1140', *American Journal of Legal History*, 25 (1981), 205–24.
— 'Medieval *origines gentium* and the community of the realm', *History*, 68 (1983), 375–90.
Richardson, H. G., 'The coronation of Edward I', *BIHR*, 15 (1937–8), 94–9.
Richter, M., 'David ap Llywelyn, the first prince of Wales', *WHR*, 5 (1970–1), 205–19.
— 'Mittelalterlicher Nationalismus. Wales im 13 Jahrhundert', *Nationes*, 1, *Aspekte der Nationenbildung im Mittelalter,* ed. H. Beumann and W. Schroder (Sigmaringen, 1978), 465–88.
— 'The political and institutional background to national consciousness in medieval Wales', *Nationality and the Pursuit of National Independence*, Historical Studies, 11, ed. T. W. Moody (Belfast, 1978), 37–56.

Bibliography

Ridgeway, H. W., 'Foreign favourites and Henry III's problems of patronage, 1247–58', *EHR*, 104 (1989), 590–610.
— 'King Henry III's grievances against the council in 1261: a new version and a letter describing political events', *Historical Research*, 61 (1988), 227–42.
— 'The Lord Edward and the Provisions of Oxford (1258): a study in faction', *Thirteenth Century England*, 1, ed. P. R. Coss and S. D. Lloyd (Woodbridge, 1986), 89–99.
Roberts, B. F., 'Dwy awdl Hywel Foel ap Griffri', *Bardos*, ed. R. G. Gruffydd (Cardiff, 1982), 60–75.
— 'Geoffrey of Monmouth and Welsh historical tradition', *Nottingham Medieval Studies*, 20 (1976), 29–40.
— *Gerald of Wales* (Cardiff, 1982).
— 'The Red Book of Hergest version of *Brut y Brenhinedd*', *SC*, 12–13 (1977–8), 147–86.
— *Studies in Middle Welsh Literature* (Lampeter, 1992).
— 'Testunau hanes Cymraeg canol', *Y Traddodiad Rhyddiaith yn yr Oesau Canol*, ed. G. Bowen (Llandysul, 1974), 274–302.
— 'Ymagweddau at *Brut y Brenhinedd* hyd 1890', *B*, 24 (1970–2), 122–38.
Roberts, G., *Aspects of Welsh History* (Cardiff, 1969).
Roderick, A. J., 'The dispute between Llywelyn ap Gruffydd and Gruffydd ap Gwenwynwyn (1278–82)', *B*, 8 (1935–7), 248–54.
— 'The Four Cantreds: a study in administration, *B*, 10 (1939–41), 246–56.
Roderick, A. J., and Rees, W., 'Ministers' accounts for the lordships of Abergavenny, Grosmont and White Castle, 1256–57', *South Wales and Monmouthshire Record Society*, 2 (1950), 67–125; 3 (1954), 21–47; 4 (1957), 5–29.
Rogers, Michael, 'The Welsh marcher lordship of Bromfield and Yale, 1282–1485', Ph.D. thesis, University of Wales, 1992.
Röhricht, R., 'La Croisade du prince Edouard D'Angleterre, 1270–1274', *Archives de l'Orient latin*, i (1881), 617–32.
Rowland, J., *Early Welsh Saga Poetry* (Cambridge, 1990).
Rowlands, J., ' "Marwnad Syr John Edward Lloyd" gan Saunders Lewis', *Bardos*, ed. R. G. Gruffydd (Cardiff, 1982), 111–27.
Runciman, S., *The Sicilian Vespers* (Cambridge, 1958).
Russell, F. H., *The Just War in the Middle Ages* (Cambridge,1975).
Russell, P., 'Scribal (in)competence in thirteenth-century north Wales: the orthography of the Black Book of Chirk (Peniarth MS 29)', *NLWJ*, 29 (1995–6), 129–76.
Sanders, I. J., *English Baronies* (Oxford, 1960).
Sawyer, P. H., and Thacker, A. T., 'Domesday survey', *Victoria County History: A History of the County of Chester*, i, ed. B. E. Harries (Oxford, 1987), 293–370.
Seebohm, F., *The Tribal System in Wales* (2nd edn. London, 1904).
Sheehan, M. M., *The Will in Medieval England* (Toronto, 1963).
Siddons, M. P., *The Development of Welsh Heraldry*. 3 vols. (Aberystwyth, 1991–3).
— 'Welsh equestrian seals', *NLWJ*, 23 (1983–4), 292–318.
— 'Welsh seals in Paris', *B*, 29 (1980–2), 531–44.
Simms, K., 'The O Hanlons, the O Neills and the Anglo-Normans in thirteenth-century Armagh', *Seanchas ArdMhacha*, 9 (1978–9), 70–94.
Skeat, W. W., 'Elegy on the death of King Edward I', *Modern Language Review*, 7 (1912), 149–52.
Smalley, B., *English Friars and Antiquity in the Early Fourteenth Century* (Oxford, 1960).
— *Historians in the Middle Ages* (London, 1974).
Smith, J. B., 'Adversaries of Edward I: Gaston de Béarn and Llywelyn ap Gruffudd', *Recognitions: Essays in Honour of Edmund Fryde* (Aberystwyth, 1996), 55–88.

Bibliography

— 'The "Cronica de Wallia" and the dynasty of Dinefwr', *B*, 20 (1962–4), 261–82.
— 'Crown and community in the principality of north Wales in the reign of Henry Tudor', *WHR*, 3 (1966–7), 145–71.
— 'Cydfodau o'r bymthegfed ganrif', *B*, 21 (1964–6), 309–24; 25 (1972–4), 128–34.
— 'Dower in thirteenth-century Wales: a grant of the commote of Anhuniog, 1273', *B*, 30 (1982–3), 348–55.
— 'Dynastic succession in medieval Wales', *B*, 33 (1986), 199–232.
— 'Edward II and the allegiance of Wales', *WHR*, 8 (1976–7), 139–71.
— 'England and Wales: the conflict of laws', *Thirteenth Century England*, 7, ed. M. Prestwick, R. H. Britnell and R. Frame (Woodbridge, 1999).
— 'Gwlad ac arglwydd', *Beirdd a Thywysogion: Barddoniaeth Llys yng Nghymru, Iwerddon a'r Alban*, ed. M. E. Owen and B. F. Roberts (Cardiff, 1996), 237–57.
— 'Land endowments of the period of Llywelyn ap Gruffudd', *B*, 34 (1987), 150–64.
— 'The lordship of Glamorgan', *Morgannwg*, 2 (1958), 28–34.
— 'The legal position of Wales in the middle ages', *Law-making and Law-makers in British History*, ed. A. Harding (London, Royal Historical Society, 1980), 21–53.
— 'Llywelyn ap Gruffudd and the march of Wales', *Brycheiniog*, 20 (1982–3), 9–22.
— *Llywelyn ap Gruffudd, Tywysog Cymru* (Cardiff, 1986).
— 'Magna Carta and the charters of the Welsh princes', *EHR*, 99 (1984), 344–62.
— 'Marcher regality: *quo warranto* proceedings relating to Cantrefselyf in the lordship of Brecon, 1349', *B*, 28 (1978–80), 267–88.
— 'The middle march in the thirteenth century', *B*, 24 (1970–2), 77–93.
— 'Offra principis Wallie domino regi', *B*, 21 (1964–6), 362–7.
— 'The origins of the revolt of Rhys ap Maredudd', *B*, 21 (1964–6), 151–63.
— 'Owain Gwynedd', *TCaernHS*, 32 (1971), 8–17.
— 'The regulation of the frontier of Meirionnydd in the fifteenth century', *JMerHRS*, 5 (1965–6), 105–11.
— *The Sense of History in Medieval Wales* (Aberystwyth, 1989).
— 'The succession to Welsh princely inheritance: the evidence reconsidered', *The British Isles, 1150–1500: Comparisons, Contrasts and Connections*, ed. R. R. Davies (Edinburgh, 1988), 64–81.
— 'The treaty of Lambeth, 1217', *EHR*, 94 (1979), 562–79.
— 'Treftadaeth Deheubarth', *Yr Arglwydd Rhys*, ed. N. A. Jones and H. Pryce (Cardiff, 1996), 18–52.
— 'Welsh Dominicans and the crisis of 1277', *B*, 22 (1966–8), 353–7.
Smith, Llinos B., 'The Arundel charters to the lordship of Chirk in the fourteenth century', *B*, 23 (1968–70), 153–66.
— 'The death of Llywelyn ap Gruffydd: the narratives reconsidered', *WHR*, 11 (1982–3), 200–13.
— 'Disputes and settlements in medieval Wales: the role of arbitration', *EHR*, 106 (1991), 835–60.
— 'The gage and the land market in late medieval Wales', *EcHR*, 2nd ser., 29 (1976), 537–50.
— 'The *gravamina* of the community of Gwynedd against Llywelyn ap Gruffudd', *B*, 31 (1984–5), 158–76.
— 'Inkhorn and spectacles: the impact of literacy in late medieval Wales', *Literacy in Medieval Celtic Societies*, ed. H. Pryce (Cambridge, 1998), 202–22.
— 'Llywelyn ap Gruffydd and the Welsh historical consciousness', *WHR*, 12 (1984–6), 1–28.
— 'The Welsh language before 1536', in *The Welsh Language before the Industrial Revolution*, ed. G. H. Jenkins (Cardiff, 1997), 15–44.

Bibliography

Smith, Ll. O. W., 'The lordships of Chirk and Oswestry, 1282–1415', Ph.D. thesis, University of London, 1970.
Sommer-Seckendorff, E. M. F., *Studies in the Life of Robert Kilwardby, OP* (Rome, 1937).
Spufford, P. J., *Money and its Uses in Medieval Europe* (Cambridge, 1988).
Spurgeon, C. J., 'Builth castle', *Brycheiniog*, 18 (1978–9), 47–59.
— 'Dolbadarn: the castle', *Dolbadarn: Studies on a Theme*, ed. P. Joyner (Aberystwyth, 1990), 65–82.
— 'Gwyddgrug castle (Forden) and the Gorddwr dispute in the thirteenth century', *MontColl*, 57 (1961–2), 125–36.
Stenton, F. M., *The First Century of English Feudalism 1066–1166* (Oxford, 1961).
Stephenson, D., *The Governance of Gwynedd* (Cardiff, 1984).
— *The Last Prince of Wales* (Buckingham, 1983).
— 'Llywelyn ap Gruffydd and the struggle for the principality of Wales, 1258–1282', *THSC*, 1983, 36–47.
— 'The politics of Powys Wenwynwyn in the thirteenth century', *CMCS*, 7 (1984), 39–61.
— *Thirteenth Century Welsh Law Courts* (Pamphlets on Welsh Law, Aberystwyth, 1980).
Stones, E. L. G., and Blount, M. N., 'The surrender of King John of Scotland to Edward I in 1296: some new evidence', *BIHR*, 48 (1975), 94–106.
Stringer, K. J., *Earl David of Huntingdon* (Edinburgh, 1985).
Stubbs, W., *The Constitutional History of England*. 3 vols. (4th edn. Oxford, 1896).
Studd, J. R., 'The Lord Edward and King Henry III', *BIHR*, 50 (1977), 4–19.
— 'The Lord Edward's lordship of Chester, 1254–72', *Transactions of the Historic Society of Lancashire and Cheshire*, 128 (1979), 1–25.
— 'The marriage of Henry of Almain and Constance of Béarn', *Thirteenth Century England*, 3, ed. P. R. Coss and S. D. Lloyd (Woodbridge, 1989), 161–79.
Suppe, F. C., 'The cultural significance of decapitation in high medieval Wales and the marches', *B*, 36 (1989), 147–69.
— *Military Institutions on the Welsh Marches: Shropshire AD 1066–1300* (Woodbridge, 1994).
Swanson, J., *John of Wales: A Study of the Work and Ideas of a Thirteenth-Century Friar* (Cambridge, 1989).
Taylor, Arnold J., 'The events of Palm Sunday, 1282: a further record', *JFlintHS*, 13 (1952–3), 51–2.
— 'The Hope castle account of 1282', *JFlintHS*, 33 (1992), 21–53.
— 'Master Bertram, *ingeniator regis*', *Studies in Medieval History presented to R. Allen Brown*, ed. C. Harper-Bill, C. J. Holdsworth and J. L. Nelson (London, 1989), 289–315.
— 'Rhuddlan cathedral: a "might have been" of Flintshire history', *JFlintHS*, 15 (1954–5), 43–51.
— *Studies in Castles and Castle-Building* (London, 1985).
— *The Welsh Castles of Edward I* (London, 1986).
— 'White Castle in the thirteenth century: a reconsideration', *Medieval Archaeology*, 5 (1961), 169–75.
Templeman, G., 'Edward I and the historians', *Cambridge Historical Journal*, 10 (1950–2), 16–35.
Tennant, W. Coombe, 'Croes Naid', *NLWJ*, 7 (1951–2), 102–15.
Thomas, C., 'Livestock numbers in medieval Gwynedd', *JMerHRS*, 7 (1973–6), 113–17.
— 'Peasant agriculture in medieval Gwynedd', *Folk Life*, 13 (1975), 24–37.
— 'Thirteenth-century farm economies in north Wales', *Agricultural History Review*, 16 (1968), 1–14.

Bibliography

Thomas, R. J., *Enwau Afonydd a Nentydd Cymru* (Cardiff, 1938).
Thomas, W. J., 'Llywelyn the Last, a sketch', *Wales,* 1 (1911), 108-11.
Thornton, D. E., 'A neglected genealogy of Llywelyn ap Gruffudd', *CMCS,* 23 (1992), 9-23.
Thorpe, L., 'Mastre Richard, a thirteenth-century translator of the "De Re Militari" of Vegetius', *Scriptorium,* 6 (1952), 39-50; 7 (1953), 120-1.
Tout, T. F., *Chapters in the Administrative History of Medieval England.* 6 vols. (Manchester, 1920-33).
— *The Collected Papers.* 3 vols. (Manchester, 1932-4).
— *Edward the First* (London, 1906).
— *The History of England, 1216-1377* (London, 1905).
— 'Llywelyn ap Gruffydd', *DNB,* 12 (1909), 13-21.
— Review: Lloyd, *History of Wales: EHR,* 27 (1912), 131-5.
Trabut-Cussac, J. P., *L'Administration anglaise en Gascogne sous Henry III et Edouard I de 1254 à 1307* (Geneva, 1972).
— 'Le Financement de la croisade anglaise de 1270', *Bibliothèque de l'école de chartes,* 119 (1961), 113-40.
Treharne, R. F., *The Baronial Plan of Reform, 1258-1263* (Manchester, 1932; repr. 1971).
— 'The Franco-Welsh treaty of alliance in 1212', *B,* 18 (1958-60), 60-75.
— *Simon de Montfort and Baronial Reform,* ed. E. B. Fryde (London, 1986).
Tupling, G. H., *The Economic History of Rossendale* (Manchester, 1923).
Tyrer, J. W., *Historical Survey of Holy Week, its Services and Ceremonial* (Oxford, 1932).
Twyne, T., *The Breviary of Britayne* (London, 1573).
Vaughan, John, *Reports and Arguments* (London, 1677).
Vaughan, Richard, *Matthew Paris* (Cambridge, 1958).
Vaughan, Robert, *British Antiquities Revived* (Oxford, 1662).
Walker, D., 'The lordship of Builth in the middle ages', *Brycheiniog,* 20 (1982-3), 23-33.
Walker, R. F., 'Edward I and the organization of war', *WHR,* 7 (1974-5), 357-65.
— 'The Hagnaby chronicle and the battle of Maes Moydog', *WHR,* 8 (1976-7), 125-38.
— 'Hubert de Burgh and Wales, 1218-1232', *EHR,* 87 (1972), 465-94.
— 'The supporters of Richard Marshal, earl of Pembroke, in the rebellion of 1233-34', *WHR,* 17 (1994-5), 41-65.
— 'William de Valence and the army of west Wales, 1282-1283', *WHR,* 18 (1996-7), 407-29.
Walters, D. B., 'The renunciation of exceptions: Romano-canonical devices for limiting possible defences in thirteenth-century Welsh law suits', *B,* 38 (1991), 119-28.
— 'Roman and Romano-canonical law and procedure in Wales', *Receuil de mémoires et travaux publié par la société d'histoire du droit et des institutions des ancient pays de droit écrit,* 15 (Montpellier, 1991), 67-102.
Warren, W. L., *Henry II* (London, 1973).
— *King John* (London, 1961).
Warrington, W., *The History of Wales.* 2 vols. (London, 1786).
Waters, W. H., 'Account of the sheriff of Caernarvon for 1303-1304', *B,* 7 (1933-5), 143-53.
Watt, D. E. R., 'The minority of Alexander III of Scotland', *TRHS,* 5th ser., 21 (1971), 1-23.
Waugh, S. C., 'Tenure to contract: lordship and clientage in thirteenth-century England', *EHR,* 101 (1986), 812-39.

Bibliography

Wharton, H., *De Episcopis Londoniensis et Assavensis* (London, 1695).
Wickham, C., 'Pastoralism and underdevelopment in the early middle ages', *Settimane di studio del Centro italiano di studis sull'Alto medioevo*, 31 (1985), 401–51.
Willard, J. F., *Parliamentary Taxation on Personal Property 1290–1334* (Cambridge, Mass., 1934).
Williams, G., *The Welsh Church from Conquest to Reformation* (Cardiff, 1962).
Williams, G. A., *Madoc: The Making of a Myth* (London, 1979).
— 'The succession to Gwynedd, 1238–47', *B*, 20 (1962–4), 393–413.
Williams, G. J., *Agweddau ar Hanes Dysg Gymraeg*, ed. A. Lewis (Cardiff, 1969).
— 'Tri Chof Ynys Brydain', *Llên Cymru*, 3 (1954–5), 234–9.
Williams, I. M., 'Ysgolheictod hanesyddol yr unfed ganrif ar bymtheg', *Llên Cymru*, 2 (1952–3), 11–24, 209–23.
Williams, I., 'Eryri', *B*, 4 (1927–9), 137–41.
Williams, J. E. C., *The Court Poet in Medieval Wales* (Lampeter, 1997).
— *The Poets of the Welsh Princes* (Cardiff, 1994).
Williams, S. W., *The Cistercian Abbey of Strata Florida* (London, 1889).
Williams, W., *Prydnawngwaith y Cymry* (Trefriw, 1822).
— 'A survey of the ancient and present state of the county of Caernarvon', *TCaernHS*, 33 (1972), 190–210; 34 (1973), 112–60
Williams-Jones, K., 'Caernarvon', *Boroughs of Mediaeval Wales*, ed. R. A. Griffiths (Cardiff, 1978), 73–101.
— 'Llywelyn's charter to Cymer abbey in 1209', *JMerHRS*, 3 (1957–60), 45–78.
Wilson, J. R., *Memorializing History: Public Sculpture in Industrial South Wales* (Aberystwyth, 1996).
Winchester, A. J. L., *Landscape and Society in Medieval Cumbria* (Edinburgh, 1987).
Wise, P., (ed.), *Hulton Abbey: A Century of Excavation* (Staffordshire Archaeological Studies, 2, Stoke-on-Trent, 1985).
Wolfram, H., *Intitulatio*. 2 vols. (Mitteilungen des Instituts für Österreichische Geschichtsforschung, 21, 24 (1967–73).
— 'The shaping of the early medieval kingdom', *Viator, Medieval and Renaissance Studies,* 1 (1970), 1–20.
— 'The shaping of the early medieval principality', *Viator, Medieval and Renaissance Studies*, 2 (1971), 35–51.
Woodward, B. B., *The History of Wales from the Earliest Times to its Final Incorporation with the Kingdom of England.* 2 vols. (London, 1853–9).
Wormald, P., 'Celtic and Anglo-Saxon kingship: some further thoughts', *Sources of Anglo-Saxon Culture*, ed. P. E. Szarmach (Kalamazoo, 1986), 151–83.
Yates, W. N., 'Bishop Peter de Aquablanca, 1240–1268, a reconsideration', *Journal of Ecclesiastical History*, 22 (1971), 303–17.
Young, A., 'The political role of Walter Comyn, earl of Menteith, during the minority of Alexander III of Scotland', *Essays on the Nobility of Medieval Scotland*, ed. K. J. Stringer (Edinburgh, 1985), 131–49.
— 'Noble families and political factions in the reign of Alexander III, 1249–1286', *Scotland in the Reign of Alexander III, 1249–1286*, ed. N. H. Reid (Edinburgh, 1990), 1–30.

Index

Abbreviations

abp.	archbishop	cmt.	commote
Aug.	Augustinian	co.	county
b.	bishop	dép.	*département*
Ben.	Benedictine	dioc.	diocese
bor.	borough	Dom.	Dominican
btl.	battle	e.	earl
cas.	castle	Gilb.	Gilbertine
Cist.	Cistercian	k.	king
ct.	court	lsp.	lordship
ctf.	cantref	p.	pope

Aber, 55, 221, 223–5, 243–4, 429, 536, 539–40
Aberconwy, advance to (1283), 540, 574
   Edward receives Croes Naid at, 580–1
   Cist. abbey, 12, 64, 205, 235, 291, 437–8, 444
      abbot, 52, 64, 129–30, 136, 290, 322, 470; *see also* Anian; Maredudd
      grange, 221
      see also Ardda; Hafod y Llan; Llanfair Rhyd Castell
   treaty of (1277), 314, 438–44, 447, 469–70, 477, 499–502, 507, 533–4, 546–7
      clause concerning legal process, 470–1, 473–5, 477–81, 486, 491–2
      other clauses, *see* Llywelyn ap Gruffudd
Aberdaron, church of, 208
   canons of, 68
Abereiddon, Cist. grange, 214, 220–1, 383–5
Aberffraw, ct. and *maerdref*, 17–20, 66, 138, 199, 221–4, 239, 247, 333, 596
   ctf. 66
   coronet of, 595–6
   crowned ruler of, 336
   lineage of, 17, 19, 38, 43, 450
   province of, 123
   supremacy of, 117, 285–6
   tribute (*mechdeyrn ddyled*) to, 286–6, 295
Abergavenny, cas. & lsp., 131, 149–52, 171, 416, 523
Abergwili, 121
Abertawe, 24; *see also* Swansea
Aberystwyth, 451, 453, 512; *see also* Llanbadarn Fawr
Acre (Israel), 368

Adam of Montgomery, 472, 487 n.139
Adam of Nannau, Dom. friar, 546, 554–5
Adrian V, p., 400, 401, 411; *see* Ottobuono
Agricola, 538–9
Aguillon, Robert, 178
Albanactus, son of Brutus, 278, 335
   see Historia Regum Britanniae
Alberbury, Grandmontine priory, 160–1
Alexander II, k. of Scots, 22
Alexander III, k. of Scots, 110–11, 115, 118, 137, 165, 274–9, 332, 367, 446, 448
Almain, Henry of, 125, 178, 391–2
Alphonso X, k. of Castile, 104, 137, 148, 281, 407, 467
Alvingham (Lincs.), Gilb. priory, 579
Amadeus, count of Savoy, 519
Amiens (*dép.* Somme), 137, 161
Aneurin, 90
Angharad, wife of Owain ap Maredudd, of Ceredigion, 304
Anglesey, 54, 66–7, 102, 104–5, 188–9, 191, 194, 198, 219–24, 233, 425, 432, 439, 442–5, 500, 510, 533, 543, 568, 574
   conflict in, 428, 435–6, 526–7, 529, 536–42, 553
   cts. and demesnes in, *see* Gwynedd
   fiscal obligations in, 237–8, 243–4
   co. 248
Anhuniog, cmt., 304–5, 416, 421, 525
Anian, abbot of Aberconwy, 119, 322
Anian, b. of Bangor (1267–1305/6), 255, 272, 413, 516
   disputes over jurisdiction, 164, 209, 480
   emissary of Llywelyn ap Gruffudd, 312, 322–3

Index

guarantees agreement between Llywelyn and Dafydd ap Gruffudd, 374–5, 377–8, 382
grievances against Llywelyn registered before him, 193, 255–60, 267, 271–2
pledge of loyalty to king before him, 267–8
Anian, b. of St Asaph (1249–66) [Anian I], see Einion, b. of St Asaph
Anian, b. of St Asaph (1268–93) [Anian II], 328 n.205, 377, 428–9, 437, 444
counsellor and emissary of Llywelyn ap Gruffudd, 312, 322, 354
disputes over jurisdiction, 210–15, 255–8, 377–84, 408–9
dispute with abbot of Valle Crucis, 379–81
guarantees agreement between Llywelyn and Dafydd ap Gruffudd, 374–5, 377–8, 382
learning and will, 328
position at time of Llywelyn's excommunication (1276–7), 407–9, 413
position during war of 1282–3, 516–17, 549
Aquinas, 281, 295–6
Archwedlog, 231
Ardda, Cist. grange, 322
Ardudwy, cmt., 7, 14, 67, 194, 221, 227–9, 237, 239, 241–2, 574–5
Arfon, ctf., 7, 72–3, 194, 255
Breintiau Arfon (Privileges of Arfon), 269–70
Arfon Is Gwyrfai, cmt., 67–8, 221, 227, 229–30
Arfon Uwch Gwyrfai, cmt., 66, 221, 227
Arllechwedd, ctf., 7, 67, 256
dean of, 470
Arllechwedd Isaf, cmt., 67, 234–5
Arllechwedd Uchaf, cmt., 67, 233–5
Arwystli, ctf., 95, 159, 301–2, 371, 416, 423, 446, 470, 489, 495
legal practice in, 202–3, 484–5
litigation over, 202, 371, 469–89, 493–6, 498–9, 500, 502, 504–5, 533
Aston, 160, 405
Audley, James, 120–2, 129, 133–4, 137, 142, 144, 161, 163
Audley, William, 529, 538
Augustinian Canons, *see* Bardsey; Dunstable; Guisborough; Penmon; Ynys Lannog

Badlesmere, Guncelin de, justice of Chester, 454, 503
Bagod, William, 368
Bala, ct. and *maerdref*, 229
Baladeulyn, 230 n.204, 518 n.30
Bangor, 44, 67, 233, 539–42, 574
dioc., 43, 57, 413, 480, 516
b. of, 44, 59, 67, 164–5, 206, 287, 290–1, 325, 372, 374–5, 377, 381–2, 447–8, 496; *see also* Richard; Anian; Robinson, Nicholas
cathedral church of St Deiniol, 413
treachery in belfry, 552–3
clergy, 323
courts and jurisdiction, 204, 208–10
dean, 325, 369–70, 373, 403
Dom. friary, 206, 432
prior, 500
see also Llywelyn ap Gruffudd (ab Ednyfed Fychan), Dom. friar
Bardsey, Aug. priory, 206, 208
canons, 68
Barefooted Friars, The, *see* Franciscan Order
Basingwerk, Cist. abbey, 67, 96, 426–7
Basque country, 512, 573
Bassett, Philip, 144, 147–8, 350
Bauzan, Stephen, 84, 92–3, 95, 97–8, 106–7
Béarn, Gaston de, 55, 80, 247, 280, 334, 366–7, 545 n.125, 573
Beauchamp, William, e. of Warwick (d.1298), 414, 423–5, 428, 435
Beaumaris, cas., 539
Becket, Thomas, abp. of Canterbury (1162–70), 283–4
Beckley, Hugh de, 231
Bek, Anthony, 437, 444
Bendigeidfran, 569; *see also* Four Branches of the Mabinogi
Berriew, 94
Bersted, Stephen, bp. of Chichester (1262–87), 392
Bertheos, 230
Bertram, Master, 418, 575 n.220
Berwyn, mountains, 560, 575
Betws, 528, 573
Bigod, Roger, e. of Norfolk (d.1306), 406
Bishop's Castle, lsp. (including Teirtref Esgob), 156, 160, 184, 405
Blaenau Morgannwg, 113, 176, 339–40, 342, 355; *see also* Meisgyn; Senghennydd
Blaenllyfni, lsp., 150, 356
Bleddfa, 147
Bleddyn ap Cynfyn (d. 1075), 552
Bleddyn Fardd, 38, 74–5, 199, 265, 313, 433, 510, 566, 569, 579, 582–2, 591
Bleiddiog, 227
Bligh, Stanley, 592
Blorenge, mountain, 152
Bodafon, 223
Bodfel, 239–40
Bodunod, 223, 263
Body, Robert, 566–7
Bodyddon, 99
Bodynog, 223
Bohemia, 605
Bohun, Humphrey de, e. of Hereford (d.1275), 95, 102, 120–2, 129, 142, 144, 147–51

640

Index

Bohun, Humphrey de (d. 1265), 162, 172, 175
Bohun, Humphrey de, e. of Hereford (d. 1298), 250, 329, 339, 350, 355–8, 362, 366, 387, 446, 471, 513, 558
Bourne, *see* Manning, Robert
'Bracton', 287, 291
Braose, family, 140–1
Braose, Isabel de, wife of Dafydd ap Llywelyn, 35
Braose, William de (d.1230), 25, 141
Bray, Henry de, 523
Brecon,
  cas. & bor., 151, 162, 196
  lsp., 126, 131, 142, 150–2, 162, 175, 182–3, 340–2, 355–9, 366, 404, 416–19, 429, 490, 521, 523, 357, 558, 560, 571
Brenhinedd y Saesson, 537, 541
Bret, Philip le, 127, 132, 144, 153
Breuddwyd Rhonabwy, 10
Brian, family, 253
Brian, Guy de, 142, 419
Bristol, 171, 396, 399
Britain, Island of, 18, 476
  legendary history of, *see* Historia Regum Britanniae
  sovereignty of, 588–9
  imperial, 594
Bromfield, cmt., *see* Maelor
Bromfield and Yale, lsp., 192, 520
Bronllys, cas., 356
Bron yr Erw, btl., 7
Bruce, Robert (Robert I), k. of Scots, 297, 331
Brutus, 37, 189, 335–6, 543–4: *see* Historia Regum Britanniae
Brut y Brenhinedd, 588
Brut y Tywysogyon, 6, 100, 102, 109, 139, 150, 176, 265, 282–3, 286, 310, 341, 370, 373, 386–8, 397, 427–8, 460, 467, 537, 550, 552, 558, 561–2, 564–5, 580, 587–8, 590, 593–4
Brycheiniog, 562, 565; *see also* Brecon, lsp.
Bryncelyn, 264
Bryn-coch, 229
Bryn Derwin, btl., 8, 44, 60, 66, 72–7, 86–9, 94, 97, 284, 312, 374, 411, 442, 585
Brynhalog, 230
Bryn-tyrch, 230
Buan, 227
Buchan, e. of, *see* Comyn, Alexander, e. of Buchan
Buellt, 567; *see also* Builth, lsp.
Builth, cas. & town, 125–7, 133, 315, 512, 521, 550–1, 555–7, 562–3, 567, 571, 575, 585
  lsp., 95, 125–7, 182–3, 196, 357, 418, 429, 523, 550–1, 556, 560–2, 564, 571, 585
  marches of, 556, 561–2
Burgundy, 282, 605
Burnell, Philip, 538

Burnell, Robert, b. of Bath and Wells (1275–92), 349–50, 358–9, 365, 444, 446, 517, 538, 552, 559
Burnell, William, 538
Bury St Edmunds (Suffolk), Ben. abbey, chronicle, 510, 564, 568
Bwlch y Ddeufaen, 429, 233–4, 539–40
Bwlch-y-groes, 230

Cadwaladr (d. 1172) ap Gruffudd ap Cynan, 11, 57
Cadwaladr the Blessed (Cadwaladr Fendigaid), 587
Cadwallon (d.1197) ap Madog, 19, 494–5
Cadwgan, foster-son of Cynan ap Maredudd, 318–19
Cáeluisce (co. Fermanagh), 116
Caeo, cmt., 421, 457, 523
Caereinion, cmt., 159, 371, 424
Caerffili, cas., 253, 351–3
Caergwrle, cas., 435, 462–3, 511–12, 515, 519, 521, 528
Caergybi, 266
Caerhun, 539
Cae-hwsni, 240
Caerleon, lsp., 28, 171, 345–6, 352
Caernarfon, ct. and *maerdref*, 68, 221, 230, 574
  co., 192, 231, 248
Caerwys, 52, 465, 517
Cafflogion, cmt., 66, 227, 239–40, 244, 264
Caledan, 226
Camber, son of Brutus, 37, 278, 326, 335, 543; *see* Historia Regum Britanniae
Camville, family, 253
Camville, William de, 419
Canterbury,
  abp., 53, 128, 214, 291, 369, 383–4, 387, 406, 459, 515–16, 530, 549–50
    see also Becket; Langton; Edmund; Kilwardby; Pecham
  archdeacon, 406
  cathedral church, library, 480
  province, 114, 214, 378, 413
  clergy of, 412
  court of, 379–81
Cantref Bychan, ctf., 421, 489–91, 523
Cantref Mawr, ctf., 420–1, 523–5
Cantref Selyf, lsp., 142, 167, 344, 356, 567
Caradog ap Thomas ap Rhodri ab Owain, 45
Cardiff, 102
Cardigan, cas. and bor., 22–3, 62, 97–8, 106, 108, 404, 522–3, 525
Carew, Richard de, 95
Carmarthen, 22–4, 55, 62, 98, 106, 108, 420, 521–3, 548
  county court, law of, 490–1
  Franc. friary, 521
Carndochan, cas., 252
Carn Fadrun, 241

Index

Carnwyllion, cmt., 95
Carreg Cennen, cas., 421, 452, 521, 525
Castell Dinas Brân, cas., 30–1, 308, 423–4
Castell y Bere, cas., 227–8, 252, 567, 575, 600
Castile, 280–1, 511
   k. of, *see* Alphonso X
Castle Wright, *see* Chestroke
Caswallon, 21; *see* Four Branches of the Mabinogi
Catalonia, 605
Catheiniog, cmt., 421
Caus, lsp., 157, 160, 184
Cefnllys, cas., 139–41, 143–5, 147, 149, 182–3, 253, 361–2, 494, 521
Cefnteilo, 228
Cefn-y-bedd, 571
Cefnyraelwyd, 494–5
Cegidog, 225
Ceinmeirch, cmt., 154, 225–6, 231, 457
Cemais, ct. and *maerdref* (Anglesey), 223–4
Cemais, lsp. (Dyfed), 95, 99, 102, 108, 119, 135, 142, 523
Ceredigion, 55, 93, 106, 304, 306, 316, 420–2, 443, 452, 498, 500, 502, 524–5, 548, 550, 560–1, 571–2, 574
   lords of, 292, 305, 458, 491
Ceri, lsp., 28, 60, 155, 183, 371, 418, 571
Champagne (France), 282
Chaworth, Patrick de, 95, 106, 108, 121, 142, 420
Chaworth, Payn de, 142, 403, 405, 414, 417, 419–22, 523
Cheshire, *see* Chester, co.
Chester, 32, 49–50, 53, 56, 71, 78, 102, 104, 118, 128–9, 142, 345, 385–8, 393, 402, 414, 423, 425–8, 430, 432, 462, 511–12, 519–20, 527–8, 574
   Ben. abbey of St Werbergh, abbot of, 124
      annalist at, 164, 465, 565
   co., 83, 172–3, 190, 462
      frontier of, 78, 90, 132, 511
      court, 461–2
   earldom of, 80, 164, 386
   e. of, *see* Hugh of Avranches
   justice of, 59, 65, 70, 73, 77, 96, 136, 144, 454–5, 461, 503; *see also* Badlesmere, Guncelin de; Grey, John de; Grey, Reginald de; Lestrange, John de; Orreby, Thomas de; Talbot, Gilbert
Chestroke, 160, 405
Chillon (Vaud, Switzerland), 361
Chirk, lsp., 192, 519, 559
Chishull, John de, 178
Chronicle of the Princes, *see* Brut y Tywysogyon
Cilan, 240
Cilcennis, 225
Cilgerran, 108
Cilmeri, 571
Cinque Ports (Kent), 527

Cistercian Order, abbeys, *see* Aberconwy; Basingwerk; Cwm-hir; Cymer; Dore; Hulton; Margam; Strata Florida; Strata Marcella; Whitland
   abbots, 115, 312, 379, 381; *see also* Llywelyn; Madog
   granges, 220, 296; *see also* Abereiddon; Ardda; Dinas Teleri; Gwern-y-go; Hafod-y-llan; Llanfair Rhyd Castell
Clare, Gilbert de, e. of Gloucester (d. 1295), 329–30, 354–55, 358, 362, 366, 387, 406, 411, 471
   relations with Montfort and Montfortians, 166, 171, 174–6, 250
   relations with Mortimer, 341–2, 350–2
   relations with Edward I, 345–8, 352
   conflict over Senghennydd and Caerleon, 339–48, 341–8, 350–5
   command in Deheubarth, 513, 521
Clare, Richard de, e. of Gloucester (d. 1262), 63, 102–6, 119–20, 125–9, 142, 144, 148, 342
Clement IV, p., 164, 173, 178, 389
Clifford, Roger, the elder (d. 1286), 125, 142, 156, 166, 174, 451, 456, 466, 576
Clifford, Roger, the younger (d. 1282), 529, 537–8
Clifford, Walter, 34
Clocaenog, 221, 226, 517
Clun, lsp., 142, 155–6, 158, 160, 184, 252, 362, 372 n.118, 559
Clynnog Fawr, 206
Coed-gaer, 458
Coed Llathen, btl., 98–9
Coed-mawr, 230
Coleshiłł, cmt., 221
Colion, cmt., 226
Colwyn, cas., 140–1
Comyn, family, 110–11
Comyn, Alexander, e. of Buchan (d. 1290), 110
Comyn, Walter, e. of Menteith (d. 1258), 110
Conwy, bor., 'hall of Llywelyn' at, 235
   see also Aberconwy
Corbet, family, 157
Corbet, Peter, 184, 416, 561
Corbet, Thomas, 157–8, 160
Cornwall, e. of, *see* Edmund; Richard
Coventry and Lichfield, b. of, 129, 144
Creuddyn, cmt., 78, 123
Crevequer, Robert, 455, 464
Cricieth, cas., 32, 35, 221, 252, 574, 600
Croes Naid, the, 199, 333–5, 580–1, 584
Crogen, 229
Crughywel, lsp., 150, 356, 522
Cunedda ap Cadwallon, 11
Cwmclored, 230
Cwm-hir, Cist. abbey, 19, 568
Cwmllannerch, 67, 263
Cydewain, lsp., 155, 183, 202, 360, 371, 375, 418; lord of, *see* Maredudd ap Robert

642

Index

Cydweli, cas. and lsp., 23, 95, 108, 142, 253, 419, 523–4
Cyfeiliog, cmt., 159, 301–2, 371, 423–4, 470
  legal practice in, 484–5
  litigation over part of, 371, 469–89, 493–6, 498–9; *see also* Arwystli
Cyfraith Hywel, *see* Wales, law of
Cymaron, cas., 19, 140–1
Cymer, Cist. abbey, 12, 205–6, 220, 291
  abbot, 52, 64; *see* Llywelyn
Cymerau, btl., 98–9, 102, 105, 107, 293, 403, 420, 521–2
Cymydmaen, cmt., 66, 69, 208, 227, 239, 244
Cynan ap Maredudd (ab Owain), of Ceredigion, 318–19, 422, 458, 490–1, 523–5, 550, 560, 572, 574
  foster-son of, *see* Cadwgan
Cynddelw ap Iarddur, 263
Cynddelw Brydydd Mawr, 6, 10, 19, 268–70, 494–5
Cynfrig ap Goronwy, 454–5
Cynfrig Fychan, 455
Cynfrig Sais, 46, 50, 433, 455
Cynllaith, cmt., 424, 457–8, 519–20
Cynyr ap Cadwgan, jurist, 203;
  sons of, 484

Dafydd, dean of Arllechwedd, 322
Dafydd ab Einion, 178–80, 314
Dafydd (d. 1203) ab Owain Gwynedd, 11, 21 n.69
Dafydd (d. 1283) ap Gruffudd (ap Llywelyn), 104, 152, 251, 311, 399, 433, 437, 448, 468, 507, 509, 553, 558
  parents and youth, 14, 55, 37–9, 68–9
  hostage in king's hands, 39
  lord of Cymydmaen, 66, 68–9, 208
  hereditary right and fealty to Henry III, 60, 69–72, 81, 83, 86–7
  relations with Owain and Llywelyn, 68–9, 71–2, 86–7
  defeat at Bryn Derwin (1255) and imprisonment, 72–4
  release and lordship in Perfeddwlad, 85–7, 194, 216, 249, 251
  in Llywelyn's service, 108, 111, 122, 132
  Henry III attempts to win allegiance, 104
  Henry denies his right in Wales, 137–8, 578
  defection and grant by Edward of lordship in Perfeddwlad, 154, 157, 374
  provision under treaty of Montgomery (1267), 180–1, 374
  agreement with Llywelyn (1269), 374–5
  service to Llywelyn, 311, 353–4
  conspiracy to kill Llywelyn (1274), 301, 369–76, 382, 386
  defection and refuge in England, 372–4, 383, 386, 394, 603
  attacks on Llywelyn, 383, 404–5, 411
  command of royal forces (1277), 423, 425–6, 429
  territorial provision in Gwynedd Uwch Conwy and Hope (August, 1277), and in Perfeddwlad (October), 425–6, 434–6
  hereditary right acknowledged by Llywelyn, 438–40
  provision under treaty of Aberconwy (1277), 439–40
  litigation in court of Chester and claim to Welsh law, 460–2
  contention with Grey, grievances and motives for rebellion, 461–2, 468, 505–8
  attack on Hawarden (1282) and responsibility for war, 460–3, 465–8
  resistance, 511, 519, 528–9; *see also* Caergwrle
  proposals to conveyed by Pecham and rejected, 542–3, 545
  Edward's anger towards, 545, 578
  continued resistance, 571–7
  'prince of Wales and lord of Snowdon', 189, 571
  excommunication, 549 n.141
  betrayal and capture, 552, 554, 576, 578
  trial, execution and display of head, 578–9
  wife, 576, 578 n.230
  sons and daughters, 371, 566, 578–80; *see* Llywelyn ap Dafydd; Owain ap Dafydd; Gwladus
  seal, 332
  elegies, 581
Dafydd ap Gruffudd ab Owain, 443
Dafydd (d. 1246) ap Llywelyn, 57, 60, 63–4, 69, 237, 287, 313–14, 587
  heir to Gwynedd, 12–14, 25–6, 28–9, 31–2
  submission to Henry III (1240), 29–32; (1241), 32–5, 39, 43–4, 56–7, 61
  wears coronet (*talaith*), 29, 322–3
  relations with Gruffudd ap Llywelyn, 14, 31–2, 39–40, 48–9, 50–1, 76
  relations with Llywelyn ap Gruffudd, 49–51, 54–5
  relations with Welsh princes, 28–31, 48, 55
  support in Gwynedd, 44–5, 54–5, 114
  resistance to Henry III, 40, 48–55, 62, 92, 103
  seeks to hold dominion as papal fief, 52–3
  'prince of Wales', 53
  illness, 50–1
  marriage, 25
  death and elegy, 49, 54–5, 233
  contemporary estimate of, 54–5
Dafydd Benfras, 45–8, 54, 64, 90, 265, 276–7, 313, 581
D'Aigueblanche, Peter, bp. of Hereford (1240–68), 124, 149
Dares Phrygius, 588
David I, k. of Scots, 275
Defynnog, 416
Degannwy, cas., 50, 53–5, 59, 78, 83, 91, 103–5, 109, 123, 131, 154, 427–8, 435

643

Index

Deheubarth, 3, 127, 272, 284, 306, 309, 316, 318, 330, 334, 358, 376, 426–7, 430, 463, 499–500, 596–8, 601
  political fortunes:
    succession to Rhys ap Gruffudd and partition (1216), 10–11, 18
    supremacy of Llywelyn ap Iorwerth, 14–17, 20, 23–5, 285
    royal authority (1246–55), 62–3, 82
    supremacy of Llywelyn ap Gruffudd, 90–3, 95, 97–103, 182, 184, 286–301, 304–5, 309, 313, 333
    intervention by Henry III (1257), 102–8
    conflict (1276–7), 403–5, 414, 416–22
    royal authority (1277–82), 457–8
    conflict (1282–3), 451–3, 457–60, 513, 520–6, 550, 559–60, 574–5
  crowned prince of, 333, 336
  law and legal practice in, 203, 301, 303
  lords of:
    association with Llywelyn ap Iorwerth, 22–5; *see also* Rhys Gryg
    association with Dafydd ap Llywelyn, 28–9, 31, 34, 48, 55–6, 62
    association with Llywelyn ap Gruffudd, 68, 85, 91–3, 95, 99–100, 103–9, 112–13, 121–2, 151–2, 209, 346; *see also* Hywel ap Rhys Gryg; Maredudd ab Owain; Maredudd ap Rhys Gryg; Rhys Fychan; Rhys Wyndod
    association with Dafydd ap Gruffudd, 571–2
    grievances (1277–82), 457–60, 489–92
  principal court of, *see* Dinefwr
Denbigh, 528, 530, 542; *see also* Dinbych
  lsp., 192, 231, 249, 528–9
Derwen Llannerch, 528
Deuddwr, cmt., 159, 371, 416
Dinan, 223
Dinas Teleri, Cist. grange, 220–1
Dinbod, cas., 253, 494, 521
Dinbych, 221, 225–6
Dindaethwy, cmt., 66, 221, 224, 237–8, 243–4, 256, 263
Dinefwr, ct. & cas., 17, 23–4, 92–3, 98, 106, 138, 420–1, 521, 524
  coronet of, 595–6
  lord of, *see* Rhys (d.1197) ap Gruffudd; Rhys Gryg; Rhys Mechyll; Rhys Fychan; Rhys Wyndod
  province of, 123; *see also* Deheubarth; Ystrad Tywi
Dinllaen, cmt., 66, 221, 227, 239, 244
Dinllwydan, 222
Dinmael, lsp., 113
Dinorben, 221, 360
Dinorben Fawr, 225–6
Dinorben Fychan, 225
Dinorwig, 217, 230, 266
Dinsylwy Rys, 266
Diserth, cas., 59, 78, 83, 91, 104, 123, 131, 154

Disinherited, the, 174–6, 341
Dolbadarn, cas., 67, 74 n.149, 229–30, 252, 500
  manerium, 230–1
Dolbenmaen, 227, 235
Dolforwyn, cas., 252, 360–2, 375, 393, 415–18, 420, 423, 521–2, 601
  legal process at (1274), 370–1, 379
Dolgynwal, Hospital of Knights of St John, 206
Dominican Order, 206, 265, 393
  friaries, *see* Bangor; Montargis; Rhuddlan
  friars, 93, 397, 403–4, 430–2, 445, 449–50; *see also* Adam of Nannau; Anian, b. of St Asaph; Ifor ap Gruffudd; Llywelyn ap Gruffudd (ab Ednyfed Fychan)
  provincial, *see* Southampton, William of
Dore, Cist. abbey, abbot of, 360
Dover, 148
Dryslwyn, cas., 92, 100, 349, 421
  lord of, *see* Maredudd ap Rhys Gryg; Rhys ap Maredudd (ap Rhys Gryg)
Dublin, abp., 515–16
Dunoding, ctf., 194
Dunstable, Aug. priory, chronicle, 82, 90, 100, 465–6, 551
Dyfed, 90, 121, 292
  army of, 55, 93
Dyffryn Clwyd, ctf., 7, 40–1, 43–4, 46, 50, 78–9, 190, 194, 226, 249, 428, 528
  lsp. of Dafydd ap Gruffudd, 154, 194, 249, 434, 436, 439, 441, 462–3
  lsp. of marcher lord, 192, 249, 529
  deanery, 43–4
Dyffryn Tefeidiad (Tempsiter, Shropshire), 156, 160, 184, 362, 405, 418

Eardisley (Heref.), 149
Ederirnion, cmt., 34 n.115, 93, 113, 220, 242, 246, 311, 443, 451, 499, 502, 533, 556
Edeligion, cmt., 345, 352
Edmund of Abingdon, abp. of Canterbury (1233–40), 26–7
Edmund, e. of Cornwall (d. 1300), 406, 411
Edmund, e. of Lancaster (d. 1296), 178, 422
Ednyfed Fychan, 45, 51, 204, 217, 261, 265, 313
  lineage of, 265, 314, 316, 430, 553
Edryd ap Marchudd, 191, 217, 261, 263, 266
Edward I, k. of England, 16, 58, 62, 64, 116, 134–5, 181, 187, 220, 235, 254, 266, 274, 281, 292, 306, 309, 369, 379, 391, 408, 445, 461, 476, 510
  The Lord Edward, 123, 126, 144, 169, 172, 194
  lordship in Perfeddwlad (1254–6), 77, 81–9, 123
  in Gwent, 103
  responsibility in Wales and the march (1256–7), 92–101, 105–7; (1259–60)

125, 128–32; (1263–5) 153–7, 161–3, 166, 171
reaction to loss of Builth (1260), 128–30
relations with Roger Mortimer (1263), 153–4
grant to Dafydd ap Gruffudd of lordship in Perfeddwlad (1263), 154
participant in negotiations leading to treaty of Montgomery (1267), 178–9, 185, 359
relations with Llywelyn ap Gruffudd (1267–70), 338–48
their meeting at Rhyd Chwima (1269), 344–5
homage of Maredudd ap Gruffudd (1269), 345–7, 351–2
homage of Maredudd ap Rhys Gryg (1270), 348–9
relations with Gilbert de Clare, 347–8, 351–2
departure for the Holy Land (1270), 339, 348–50
situation in his absence, 350–63
accession, 338, 354, 359, 363
stay in Savoy and Gascony, 361, 366–7
return to the kingdom and coronation, 367–8
relations with Llywelyn (1274–7), 338–9, 366–414
call upon Llywelyn to do homage at Shrewsbury (1274), 367–9, 373, 382–3; Chester (1275), 385–7, 427; Westminster and Winchester (1275–6), 387;
demand for payment of indemnity under the treaty of 1267, 363–6
provides refuge for Dafydd ap Gruffudd and Gruffudd ap Gwenwynwyn, 373–4, 383, 386–7
reaction to Llywelyn's marriage to Eleanor de Montfort, 390–9:
concern at danger to the realm, 390–7
surveillance and detention of Amaury de Montfort, 391–3, 399–401
detention of Eleanor, 390, 401–2, 411–12
letters to papal court, 326, 401–2
Llywelyn's intransigence and infidelity, 401–2
estimate of the status of the prince of Wales, 279–81, 335, 401–2, 476
proposed campaign in 1276, 402–4
condemnation of Llywelyn (1276), 402, 406–7
receives Llywelyn's submissions (1276–7), 409–12
letter to Alphonso of Castile, 407
war in Wales (1277), 414–36:
the march and Powys Wenwynwyn, 415–18
Deheubarth, 418–22

Powys Fadog, 423–4
Perfeddwlad, 425–33
Anglesey, 219–20, 427–9
proposed annexation of Gwynedd Uwch Conwy, with provision for Owain ap Gruffudd and Dafydd ap Gruffudd, 425–6
annexation withheld and provision for Dafydd in Perfeddwlad, 434–6
negotiations with Llywelyn and recognition of Dafydd's hereditary right in Gwynedd Uwch Conwy, 437–8
treaty of Aberconwy (1277), 438–45
receives Llywelyn's fealty (Rhuddlan) and homage (London), 444–5
arrangements with Llywelyn for implementation of the settlement, 445–8:
meets Llywelyn at Rhuddlan and gives feast for the Welsh (1278), 448
gives Eleanor in marriage at Worcester, 448–9
pleas on Arwystli and Cyfeiliog:
initial reaction to Llywelyn's plea, 446, 472–4, 483
exchanges with Llywelyn and session at Rhuddlan (1278), 473–4
deliberations in council (1279–81), 477–9, 481–3, 486–8
statement of his position, 202, 478–9, 486–8
commission of inquiry (1281), 202, 204, 274, 319, 479, 483–7
search of the rolls, 479, 487–8
the king's dilemma, 486–7
irritation at Llywelyn's persistence, 504–5
situation on the eve of war:
grievances of Llywelyn and Dafydd, 461–3, 496–506
grievances of communities in Perfeddwlad, 454–6, 463–5
war in Wales, 1282–3, 451–69, 511–79:
the king's response, 451–69, 511–19
vigilance of the Montfortians, 511–12
military measures, 511–15
financial provision and war costs, 512, 515
seeks ecclesiastical support, 515–17
seeks broad support in the realm, 331, 517–18
grants to Rhys ap Maredudd and English barons, 523–4, 529
campaign in Perfeddwlad and Anglesey, 526–9
reaction to archbishop's intercession, 530–1
refuses to consider Welsh grievances and insists on unconditional surrender, 534–5, 542–5
prepared to offer Llywelyn an estate in England, 543

Index

resumption of conflict for a permanent solution of the Welsh problem, 548–9, 571–3
estimate of Roger Mortimer and relations with Edmund, 521–2, 558–9
informed of Llywelyn's death, 565
receives the severed head, 568
his victory celebrated by Stephen of St George, 567
campaign against Dafydd, 572–7
takes Dolwyddelan and Castell y Bere, 231, 573–5
announces Dafydd's capture and arranges trial at Shrewsbury, 578–9
denounces Dafydd's perfidy, 460, 578
aftermath of war:
pledge of loyalty by communities of Gwynedd, 267–8
provision for Gwenllian and Dafydd's daughters at Gilbertine houses, 577–80
receives the Croes Naid at Aberconwy, 332–5, 580–1
Edward III, son of, *see* Edward, the Black Prince
Edward of Caernarfon, prince of Wales (cr. 1301), 182, 583
Edward, the Black Prince, prince of Wales (cr. 1343), 282, 583
Edward the Confessor, k. of England, 345
Edwards, John Goronwy, 385, 597–8
Eifionydd, cmt., 7, 66, 72–3, 194, 227, 256
Einion, b. of St Asaph (1249–66) [Anian I], 114–15, 209, 287, 290–1
Einion ab Ynyr, *see* Anian, b. of St Asaph (1268–93) [Anian II]
Einion ap Caradog, 45, 113, 178–80, 314, 384
Einion ap Gwalchmai, 314
Einion ap Madog, 429–30
Einion ap Maredudd, 40, 46
Einion ap Rhys, 357, 417
Einion Fychan, 45, 114, 314, 327–8
Eleanor of Castile, wife of Edward I, 501
Eleanor of Provence, wife of Henry III, 83–4, 123, 501
Elfael, lsp., 140–1, 150, 183, 357, 404, 418, 429, 571
marches of, 556, 561–2
Elfael Is Mynydd, lsp, 130, 141, 168, 183, 315, 340
Elfael Uwch Mynydd, lsp., 130, 141, 183
Elise ap Iorwerth, 113, 443
Ellesmere, lsp., 168, 183, 458, 547, 555, 567
Ely, Isle of (Cambs.), 511
Emlyn, lsp., 523
Emma, wife of Gruffudd (d.1269) ap Madog, 305
England, kingdom of, 1–3, 57, 76, 101, 104, 142, 147, 156, 166, 195, 232, 254, 265, 315, 325, 342, 365, 393, 407, 424, 426, 446, 449, 475, 601–2, 604–5

bishops of, 387, 403–4, 407–9, 411–14, 515–17; *see* Kilwardby, Robert; Pecham, John
chancery of, 323–5
chronicles of eastern counties of, 564–7, 586
constable of, 513; *see* Bohun, Humphrey de, e. of Hereford (d. 1298)
kings of, 77, 109, 114, 216, 264, 298, 312, 329, 386, 430; *see also* Henry II; John; Henry III; Edward I;
princes' obligations to, 245; *see also* Llywelyn ap Iorwerth; Llywelyn ap Gruffudd
princes' relations with, *see* Llywelyn ap Iorwerth; Dafydd ap Llywelyn; Llywelyn ap Gruffudd; Dafydd ap Gruffudd
princes' treaties with, *see* Worcester (1218); Gloucester (1240); Gwerneigron (1241); Woodstock (1247); Montgomery (1267); Aberconwy (1277)
tribute due to, from king of Aberffraw, 17–18, 285
law of, 82, 304, 306–7, 458, 471–2, 474–5, 478–9, 489–90
magnates of,
proposals to Llywelyn and Dafydd, 535–6, 542–3
gathered at Shrewsbury for judgement on Dafydd ap Gruffudd, 578
parliament of, 118–20, 274, 402–4, 425–6, 436, 477–9
realm of,
disturbance and conflict in, and effect on Welsh political aspirations, 116–34, 148–52, 155–66, 171, 390–7, 401–2
held in special favour at the papal court, 532
support for war in Wales (1282–3), 572–3, 578
Englefield, cmt, *see* Tegeingl
Erddreiniog, 217
Estyn, *see* Hope
Europe, 251, 270, 365
Evans, Evan, 591
Evans, Theophilus, 590–1
Evesham (Worcs.), btl., 166, 171–3, 175
Ewloe, cas., 172–3, 252, 388, 519, 601
manor, 226, 249

Farningham, Ralph de, 445, 472, 474, 488
Feidiog, Y, 229
Fenlands, the, 427, 564
Ffridd Ddu, 541
FitzAlan, John, 94, 102, 122, 142, 144, 148, 155–7, 160, 178, 362
FitzMartin, Nicholas, 55, 95, 121, 135, 142
FitzPeter, Reginald, 150 n.39, 356–7, 561
FitzWarin, Fulk, 160 n.80, 168 n.115

Index

Flanders, 282
Flint, cas. and bor., 426–8, 436, 451–2, 465, 468, 512, 519, 528
  co., 192, 249
Florence, 512
Foel Las, 540
Four Branches of the Mabinogi, 21, 194; *see also* Bendigeidfran; Caswallon; Lleu Llaw Gyffes; Math fab Mathonwy; Manawydan
Four Cantreds, the, *see* Perfeddwlad
France, 9, 27, 124, 137, 254, 282, 345, 348, 354, 390, 554
  k. of, 161, 177, 280, 324–5, 367, 411, 446, 604–5; *see also* Philip Augustus, Louis IX, Philip III
  qu. of, *see* Margaret of France, wife of Louis IX
Franciscan Order, 206, 233, 504
  friaries, *see* Carmarthen; Llan-faes
  friars, *see* Merton, William de; Wales, John of
Frankton, Stephen de, 566–7

Galchefed, 231
Garthcelyn, 233–4, 536, 543
Gascony, 55, 60, 69, 80–1, 83, 134, 148, 165, 177, 278, 280, 282, 324, 446, 475, 512, 573
Genau'r Glyn, cmt., 251, 422, 499–500, 502
Geoffrey of Monmouth, *see Historia Regum Britanniae*
Germany, 605
Gervase, Master, *see*, Iorwerth, Master
Giffard, Godfrey, 178
Giffard, John, 156, 175, 356, 419, 489–90, 523–4, 561
Giffard, Walter, abp. of York (1266–79), 350, 358, 365
Gilbertine Order, priories, *see* Alvingham; Sempringham; Sixhills
Giraldus Cambrensis, 15, 17, 101, 103, 281–2
Glamorgan, lsp., 56, 63, 99, 102–3, 127, 142, 144, 148, 171, 176, 184, 311, 330, 334, 339–48, 350–5, 363, 366, 377, 602
'Glanvill', 304
Glasynys, 229
Gloucester, 171, 473
  treaty of (1240), 29–32, 168
Gloucester, e. of, *see* Clare, Gilbert de; Clare, Richard de
Godred, son of the k. of Man, 38
Gorddinan, 230
Gorddwr, lsp., 157–6, 160, 184, 371, 416
Goronwy ab Ednyfed Fychan, 114, 122, 151, 169–70, 179, 204, 265, 313–14, 316, 432, 585
  sons of, *see* Goronwy Fychan; Hywel ap Goronwy (ab Ednyfed Fychan)
Goronwy ab Einion, of Cyfeiliog, 317

Goronwy ap Heilin, 194, 328, 437–8, 445, 447, 454–5, 464–6, 500, 546–8, 571, 577
  grievances as bailiff of Rhos, 464–5, 466
  member of judicial bench, 474, 477
Goronwy ap Tudur (d. 1382), 585
Goronwy Fychan (ap Goronwy ab Ednyfed), 316
Gower, lsp., 23, 96, 99, 102, 523–4
Graig Lwyd, 540
Grandson, Otto de, 416–18, 446, 538, 574
Gregory X, p., 280–1, 375, 379–81, 387, 389, 392, 408, 411
Gresford, 132, 345, 350, 388, 517
Grey, John de, 149–53
  justice of Chester, 58, 79
Grey, Reginald de, 473–4, 511, 520, 528–9
  justice of Chester, 455–7, 461–2, 464–6, 468–9, 489, 503–6, 534
Gronant, 233, 235
Grosmont, cas. & lsp., 150
Gruffudd ab Ednyfed Fychan, 45–6, 265, 313, 430
Gruffudd ab yr Ynad Coch, 199, 332, 433, 565, 569–70, 582, 591, 593, 595
Gruffudd (d. 1137) ap Cynan, 6–7, 11, 33, 35
Gruffudd ap Gwên, 287–8, 317
  justice of Gruffudd ap Gwenwynwyn, 317, 495
Gruffudd (d. 1286) ap Gwenwynwyn, of Powys Wenwynwyn, 25, 30, 138, 184, 286, 399, 411, 495, 498, 560–1
  possession of Powys Wenwynwyn, 29–30
  service to the crown, 34, 48, 53, 55, 71, 94, 112
  attack on Gorddwr and agreement with Llywelyn (1263), 115, 157–60, 287– 90, 293–4, 299–300, 302, 327
  service to Llywelyn, 169, 181, 311, 353–4
  conspiracy to kill Llywelyn (1274), 184, 369–76, 386, 423
  legal process against, 300–2, 317, 325, 370–1, 379, 382, 444, 470
  flight and refuge in England, 373, 383, 386, 394, 411, 603
  attacks on Llywelyn, 383–4
  possession of patrimony and custody of Dolforwyn (1277), 317, 416, 418, 423, 457–8, 470
  pleas on Arwystli and part of Cyfeiliog (1278–81), 469–90, 496, 504–5
  preference for the common law of England, 471, 474–5, 477–8, 485–6, 488
  provision for the succession, 306–7
  justice of, *see* Gruffudd ap Gwên
  wife of, *see* Lestrange, Hawise
  son of, *see* Owain ap Gruffudd (ap Gwenwynwyn)
Gruffudd ap Iorwerth, 113, 266–7, 432–3, 457 n.33, 576, 579 n.237
Gruffudd (d. 1063) ap Llywelyn, 552

647

Index

Gruffudd (d. 1244) ap Llywelyn,
  exclusion from succession to Gwynedd, 12–14
  imprisonment by John and Llywelyn ap Iorwerth, 13–14
  challenge to Dafydd ap Llywelyn's succession, 28–9, 31–2
  imprisonment by Dafydd, 32
  hereditary right recognized by Henry III (1241), 32–4, 48–9, 69
  imprisonment by Henry, 35–6, 39
  relations with Dafydd, 39–40, 48–9, 76
  attempt to escape from Tower of London and death (1244), 39–40, 47–8
  burial and elegy, 54, 64
  personal qualities, 14, 276
  wife of, *see* Senana
  sons and daughters, 56, 59–60, 73–5, 110, 448; *see also* Owain ap Gruffudd (ap Llywelyn); Llywelyn ap Gruffudd; Dafydd ap Gruffudd (ap Llywelyn); Rhodri ap Gruffudd (ap Llywelyn); Gwladus; Margaret
Gruffudd (d. 1269) ap Madog, of Powys Fadog, 30–1, 34, 48, 53, 60, 63, 68, 70–1, 73, 93–4, 105, 111, 122, 138, 157, 164, 169, 181, 286, 288–9, 294, 305–6, 308, 327, 423
  sons of, *see* Madog (d. 1277) ap Gruffudd ap Madog; Llywelyn ap Gruffudd Fychan; Owain ap Gruffudd (ap Madog); Gruffudd Fychan ap Gruffudd ap Madog
Gruffudd (d. 1282) ap Madog (d. 1277) ap Gruffudd, of Powys Fadog, 457, 520
Gruffudd ap Maredudd (ab Owain), of Ceredigion, 420–2, 451–2, 458, 490–1, 523–5, 550, 560, 571, 575
Gruffudd ap Maredudd ap Dafydd, 585
Gruffudd ap Maredudd ap Iorwerth, 76
Gruffudd (d. 1201) ap Rhys, of Deheubarth, 11
Gruffudd ap Rhys, of Senghennydd, 339, 342–3, 347, 354, 359
Gruffudd ap Tudur, 574
Gruffudd Budr ei Hosan, 317
Gruffudd Fychan (ap Gruffudd (d. 1269) ap Madog, of Powys Fadog, 458, 499, 520
Gruffudd Gryg, 46, 50
Guala, papal legate, 185
Guisborough (Yorks.), Aug. priory, 563
Guisborough, Walter of, 465–6, 536–7, 541, 562–6
Gwalchmai ap Meilyr, 6, 314
Gweirydd ap Rhys (R. J. Pryse), 591, 593–4
Gwenllian, daughter of Llywelyn ap Gruffudd, 510, 566, 579–80, 586
Gwent, 148, 151, 346, 352
Gwenwynwyn (d. 1216) ab Owain Cyfeiliog, of Powys Wenwynwyn, 18, 30, 157, 286

Gwerneigron, treaty of (1241), 33–5, 39–40, 52, 168, 440
Gwern-y-go, Cist. grange, 95
Gwerthrynion, lsp., 19, 25, 30, 41–3, 94, 130, 140–1, 182–3, 196, 362, 404, 418, 429–30, 494–5, 559, 571
Gwidigada, cmt., 23, 106
Gwilym ap Gwrwared, 121
Gwladus, daughter of Gruffudd (d. 1244) ap Llywelyn, wife of Rhys Fychan (d.1271), 14, 38, 42
Gwladus, daughter of Dafydd (d. 1283) ap Gruffudd, 566, 579–80
Gwladus Ddu, daughter of Llywelyn (d. 1240) ap Iorwerth, wife of Ralph Mortimer (d. 1246), 586
Gwredog, 217
Gwyddgrug (Gorddwr), cas., 158
Gwydir, 230
Gwyn ab Ednywain, 204
Gwyn ap Cuhelyn, 495
Gwyn ap Madog, 95
Gwynedd
  kingship and lordship
    patrimony and political inheritance, 4–8, 187–92
    succession to the patrimony, 8–14, 28–36, 48–9, 52–3, 56–60, 65–77; *see also* political aspiration: policies of the princes
    lineage and supremacy of the court of Aberffraw, 17–20, 117, 285–6; *see also* Aberffraw
    military, seigniorial and regalian authority, 197–201, 246–7
  administration of the patrimony:
    the historical record, 191–2, 248
    divisions of the territory (*gwlad, regnum*): *cantref* and commote, 12, 190, 193–6, 267–8;
    officers of the localities: *rhaglaw* and *rhingyll*, *maer* and *cynghellor*, 194–7, 268–71
  officers of the court:
    distain and *justiciarius*, 204–5, 303–4, 312–15; *see* Ednyfed Fychan, Goronwy ab Ednyfed; Tudur ab Ednyfed
    offeiriad teulu, chancellor, 319–23
    penteulu, 69, 197, 204, 312–13
    ministerial servants, 113–14, 287, 314–15
  law and administration of justice:
    law and lawbooks, 201–5, 301, 303, 320; *see also Llyfr Colan, Llyfr Iorwerth*; Wales, law of
    legal practice, 201–5, 302–3, 482–6
    ynad (iudex), 201–5, 301–3, 319–20, 482–6
    ynad llys (iudex curie), 204–5, 303–4, 312
  court and council, 204–5, 309–16

Index

muniments, 323–7
jurisdiction:
  ecclesiastical delegation, 205–14
  monastic orders: Cistercians, 12, 205–6, 291–2; *see also* Aberconwy; Cymer
  mendicant orders: Franciscans and Dominicans, 206; *see also* Bangor; Llan-faes; Rhuddlan
  secular church:
    regnum and *sacerdotium,* 206–8
    church of Bangor, 164, 208–9, 214–15, 381–2, 480; *see also* Anian of Bangor; Richard of Bangor
    church of St Asaph, 210–15, 377–82
    see also Anian of St Asaph
  lay delegation:
    baronial estates, 215–17, 289, 374–7, 382; *see also* Dafydd ap Gruffudd; Hywel ap Gruffudd
    patrimonial estates, 217–19; *see also* Wyrion Ednyfed
  economic foundation of authority
    courts and demesne lands, 219–36:
      economic resources, 219–20
      the princes' itinerary, 220–1
      demesnes: *maerdrefi* and *tir cyfrif,* 221–36, 243–4; 262–6
      vaccaria and *hafodydd,* 228–34, 240–1
    proprietors' fiscal obligations, 197–201, 237–47:
      procuration dues (*cylch, porthiant*), 197–9, 237–9
      animal and crop husbandry, 219–20, 239–41
      commutation and retention of renders in kind, 178, 241–6
      commercial development, 243–4
    income and expenditure, 248–54:
      estimated income, 248–50
      expenditure, 250–4:
      indemnity under treaty of Montgomery, 250–1, 363–6
      castle-building and war costs, 252–4, 292, 600–1; *see also* Carndochan; Castell y Bere; Cricieth; Dolbadarn; Dolforwyn; Dolwyddelan; Ewloe
  relations of lord and community, 255–73
    complaints of exacting lordship, 193, 255–60, 267, 271–3:
    conflicting interests of hereditable estate and lord's demesne, 260–4
    patronage and political allegiance, 264–7, 430–3
    precedents in relations: *Breintiau Gwŷr Powys* (Privileges of the Men of Powys) and *Breintiau Arfon* (Privileges of Arfon), 268–70
    the quality of the prince's government, 271–3
  political aspiration:
    policies of the princes: *see* Owain

Gwynedd; Llywelyn ap Iorwerth; Dafydd ap Llywelyn; Owain ap Gruffudd; Llywelyn ap Gruffudd; Dafydd ap Gruffudd
  the princes' style, 15–17, 25, 53, 109–10, 145–6, 188–9, 282–5, 571
  see also Gwynedd Uwch Conwy; Perfeddwlad; Wales, principality of
Gwynedd Is Conwy, 16 n.52
  see also Perfeddwlad
Gwynedd Uwch Conwy, 44, 154, 191, 221, 316, 331
  area, 52, 188
  courts and demesnes, 221, 226–35
  jurisdiction, economy and social organization, *see* Gwynedd
  political fortunes:
    Llywelyn ap Iorwerth confined to (1211), 16
    Owain ap Gruffudd and Llywelyn ap Gruffudd maintain resistance and confined to (1246–7), 56–60
    partition between the princes and shared lordship (1247–55), 65–8
    assertion of hereditary right by Dafydd ap Gruffudd and reintegration by Llywelyn (1252–5), 68–77
    related problems of Gwynedd Uwch Conwy and Perfeddwlad, 83–9
    placed under siege (1277), 429–30, 434–6
    annexation proposed by Edward I and reconsidered, 425–6, 434–6
    Dafydd's hereditary right recognized, 154, 438–43, 507
    Llywelyn confined to by treaty of Aberconwy (1277), 438–43
    placed under siege (1282), 526–30, 548–9
    Llywelyn entrusts defence to Dafydd, 550
    conflict (1282–3), 520, 526–30, 536–42, 571–7,
  sequel to conquest:
    communities bound to keep the peace, 194, 576
    communities register grievances against Llywelyn, 193, 255–9, 586
    see also Anglesey; Gwynedd; Snowdonia
Gwynionydd, cmt., 105–6, 421, 457, 524–5
Gwynllŵg, lsp., 142, 171, 345–6

Hafod-boeth, 230
Hafodelwy, 231
Hafod-lom, 231
Hafod-y-llan, Cist. grange, 221
Hagnaby (Lincs.), Premonstratensian abbey, chronicle, 466, 512, 551, 564–5, 576
Hailes (Glouc.), Cist. abbey, chronicle, 467
Harlech, cas., 228
Haughmond (Shropshire), Aug. abbey, abbot of, 360

Index

Hawarden, cas. and lsp., 164, 168, 172–3, 183–4, 451, 456, 458, 460, 465–6, 506, 508, 512, 519
Hay, cas. and lsp., 131, 142, 162–3, 171–2, 355
Heilin ap Tudur, 265, 313
Helygain, 517
Henllan, 517
Henry II, k. of England, 15, 21, 140, 283–4
Henry III, k. of England, 16, 74, 94, 96–8, 110, 124, 139, 161–3, 166, 171, 274–5, 278, 305, 327, 348, 391, 439, 463, 501
   agreement with Llywelyn ap Iorwerth (1218), 19, 21–2
   recognition of Dafydd ap Llywelyn as heir, 25–6
   avoids discussion of peace treaty, 26–7
   receives Dafydd's homage (1240), 29–30, 332–3
   provision for Gruffudd ap Llywelyn and submission of Dafydd (1241), 32–4, 37
   annexation of Tegeingl, 41–3, 268
   relations with the princes (1237–44), 28–30, 39–40
   conflict in Wales (1244–6), 48–55
   reaction to Dafydd's appeal to papal court, 52–3
   treaty of Woodstock (1247) and settlement of Wales, 58–64
   recognition of Dafydd's hereditary right, 69–70, 86–8
   government of Perfeddwlad, 78–81, 85–8, 190
   conflict and truce with Llywelyn, 96–7
   campaign in Wales (1257), 101–5, 157
   agreement with Maredudd ap Rhys Gryg, 103–8, 420
   relations with Llywelyn (1258–9), 116–25
   reaction to offensives in Builth (1260), 125–31
   maintenance of state of truce (1258–62), 119–20, 131–7
   reaction to rumour of Llywelyn's illness (1262), 137–8
   response to offensives in the march (1262–3), 144–53
   entrusts reponsibility in the march to Edward, 148, 153–5
   agreement with Llywelyn while in Montfort's power (1265), 166–70
   negotiations and sealing of treaty of Montgomery (1267), 173–4, 177–86, 335
   grants Llywelyn the title 'prince of Wales'and the principality of Wales, and the homage of the Welsh lords of Wales, 180–1
   receives Llywelyn's homage, 1–2, 179–80, 341, 389, 445
   reaction to Llywelyn's intervention in Glamorgan, 341–3
   commends Llywelyn's discussions with Edward at Rhyd Chwima (1269), 345
   grants Llywelyn the homage of Maredudd ap Rhys Gryg (1270), 348–9
   communications with Llywelyn after Edward's departure from the realm (1270), 348, 350–4
   death, 338, 354, 359, 386
Hereford, 148–9, 153–4, 163, 166–7, 170–2, 554
   co., 142, 416, 546
   dioc., 568
   b. of, 149, 156, 160, 388; *see* D'Aigueblanche, Peter de
   estates of, *see* Bishop's Castle
Hirdref, 227
Hirdre-faig, 223
Hirfryn, cmt., 289, 346, 421, 489–90, 523–4
Historia Regum Britanniae, 278, 335–6, 543–4, 587–9; *see also* Albanactus; Brutus; Camber; Locrinus
Historie of Cambria, The, see Powel, David
History of Gruffudd ap Cynan, The, 6–8, 587
Holinshed, Ralph, 590
Holy Land, 354, 391
Honorius III, p., 25–6
Hope, lsp., 249, 426, 435, 461–2, 511, 519–20; *see also* Caergwrle
Hopton, Walter de, 445, 473–4, 477, 482
Hugh of Avranches, e. of Chester (d. 1101), 7
Hulton (Staffs.), Cist. abbey, 538
Huntington, lsp., 142, 162, 355
Huw ab Ithel, 580–1
Hwfa ap Cynddelw, 217–18, 222, 261, 266, 432
Hywel ab Ednyfed, b. of St. Asaph (c.1240–7), 44
Hywel (d. 1171) ab Owain Gwynedd, 11, 187
Hywel ap Goronwy (ab Ednyfed Fychan), 316, 432–3
Hywel ap Goronwy of Penmynydd (d. 1366), 217
Hywel (d. 1216) ap Gruffudd (ap Cynan), 12, 216, 289
Hywel (d. 1282) ap Gruffudd (ab Ednyfed Fychan), 432–3, 454, 538, 553
Hywel (d. c.1268) ap Madog (ap Gruffudd), of Powys Fadog, 112, 132, 138, 169, 179, 181
Hywel ap Maredudd, of Meisgyn, 56, 63, 113, 169, 311, 342
Hywel ap Meurig, 132, 147, 372 n.118, 417–18, 429, 445, 474, 477
Hywel ap Rhys (Fychan), of Ystrad Tywi, 459
Hywel ap Rhys Gryg, of Ystrad Tywi, 112, 115, 169, 287, 289–90, 311, 318–19, 326, 422, 459, 572, 576–7
Hywel Dda (d. 949/50), law of, 211, 257; *see* Wales, law of

650

Index

Hywel Foel ap Griffri, 75–6
Hywel Fychan, of the march, 132
Hywel Fychan, possibly of Ceredigion, 318, 324

Iâl, cmt., 499, 520
Ieuan ap Gruffudd, of Tregarnedd, 217
Ifor ap Gruffudd, of Elfael, 315, 429
Ifor ap Gruffudd, Dom. friar, 445
Innocent III, p., 17 n.53, 278
Innocent IV, p., 52–3, 278
Innocent V, p., 411
Instructus, Master, 320
Iolo Goch, 586
Iorwerth, Master (Gervase), 323, 409, 554 n.154
Iorwerth ap Goronwy, of Cyfeiliog, 317
Iorwerth ap Gwrgunan, 44, 66, 67, 113, 263, 327–8
Iorwerth ap Llywelyn, of Builth, 357
Iorwerth ap Madog, jurist, 269–70, 319
Iorwerth of Llan-faes, 554
Iorwerth Foel, of Aberffraw, 433
Iorwerth Foel, priest, 554
Iorwerth Fychan (ap Iorwerth ap Rhys), 484
Ireland, 92, 98, 103–6, 116, 163, 173, 250, 278, 475
   justice of, 53;
   law in, 9–10, 475 n.96;
   lords of, 53, 165
Irvine, Alan of, 111, 134
Isaf, cmt., *see* Arllechwedd Isaf
Is Aled, cmt., *see* Rhufoniog Is Aled
Is Cennen, cmt., 421, 524
Is Dulas, cmt., *see* Rhos Is Dulas
Is Gwyrfai, cmt., *see* Arfon Is Gwyrfai
Italy, 391–2
   bankers of, 426

Jews, 533
Joan (d. 1237), wife of Llywelyn ap Iorwerth, 12, 16, 233, 449, 539–40
John, k. of England, 11–13, 16–18, 25, 32–4, 117, 444
John XXI, p., 397, 400, 411–12
John ap Dafydd, 571
Jones, Glanville, 599
Judas Maccabeus, *see* Maccabees

Kempsey (Worcs.), 172
Kenilworth (War.), 175
   Dictum of, 175
Kilkenny (Ireland), 339
Kilwardby, Robert, abp. of Canterbury (1273–8), 325, 380–1, 383–4, 393, 395, 397, 402–5, 407–9, 412–13, 428–9, 431
Kinnerley (Shropshire), 25, 94
Knighton, 147
Knovill, Bogo de, 405–6, 416, 458, 490, 502
Knucklas, 147

Lacy, Gwenllian de (d.1281), 41 n.16, 462
Lacy, Henry de, e. of Lincoln (d. 1311), 231, 250, 411, 415–18, 420, 424, 444, 528–9
Lambeth, treaty of (1217), 21–2
Langley, Geoffrey de, 82–4
Langtoft, Peter, 514
Langton, Stephen, abp. of Canterbury (1207–28), 18, 117, 121
Larchdeacon, Thomas, 396
Latimer, William, 563
Laugharne, cas. and lsp., 102, 142, 253, 419
Leicester, Robert of, 503–4
Lemayn, Hick, 455
Leonidas, 593–4
Lestrange, Hamo, 102, 125, 142, 144, 148, 158, 161, 173, 178, 184 n.174
Lestrange, Hawise, wife of Gruffudd ap Gwenwynwyn, 157
Lestrange, John (d. 1269), 87–8
   justice of Chester, 49, 53, 60–1
Lestrange, John (d. 1275), 94, 104, 136, 155
Lestrange, Roger, 432, 445 n.207, 457 n.33, 458, 473–4, 555–6, 566–7, 575
   command in march, 556–8, 560–2, 565–7
Lewes (Sussex), btl., 162–3, 165, 169
Leyburn, Roger, 125, 156, 174–5
'Liber A', 597
Lincoln, canon of, *see* Waltham, Nicholas de
Lincoln, co., 466
Lincoln, e. of, *see* Lacy, Henry de
Lingayn, John de, 132
Llanaber, 228, 241
Llanarmon (yn Iâl), 517
Llanasa, 517
Llanbadarn Fawr, 93, 422, 502, 525; *see also* Aberystwyth
Llanbeblig, 230
Llanberis, 571, 576
Llanbleddian, cas., 102
Llandaff, dioc., 63
Llanddwywe, 228
Llandeilo Fawr, 98, 509, 521–2
Llandovery, cas., 421, 452, 521, 525
Llandrillo (yn Rhos), 517
Llandyrnog, 517, 528
Llanegryn, 221, 227
Llanengan, 228
Llan-faes, ct. and *maerdref*, 221, 224, 233, 243–4, 412–13, 540–1
   military base, 526, 539–41
   Franc. friary, 206, 233, 477, 504, 510, 539–40
Llanfair Prysgol, 230
Llanfair Rhyd Castell, Cist. grange, 220
Llanfihangel Crucornau, 150–2
Llanfor, 372
Llangadog, 524
Llanganten, 561, 565, 567
Llangernyw, 528–9
Llangïan, 239–41

Index

Llangollen, 379
Llangwm, 517
Llangynwyd, cas., 102
Llannerch, cmt., 40, 43–4, 46, 190
Llannerch Hudol, cmt., 159, 371, 416
Llanrwst, 528, 573
Llansannan, 517
Llansteffan, cas. and lsp., 102, 253, 419
Llanynys, 517
Llawysgrif Hendregadredd, 588
Llebenydd, cmt., 345, 352
Llechtalhaearn, 226
Lledrod (cmt. Cynllaith), 458
Lleu Llaw Gyffes, 194; *see also* Four Branches of the Mabinogi
Lleweni, 462
Llifon, cmt., 66, 222, 237
Lloyd, John Edward, 2–3, 593, 596–7
Llwyd, Humphrey, 590, 596
Llwynoron, 230
Llyfr Coch Asaph, 325
Llyfr Colan, 207, 212–13, 320
Llyfr Iorwerth, 202, 207, 210, 212, 214, 323
Llygad Gŵr, 5, 47, 72, 90, 182, 197, 199, 276, 333, 336–7, 458, 595–6
Llŷn, ctf., 7, 57, 66, 69, 188, 194, 227, 239–40, 256, 425, 441
Llysdulas, 223
Llywarch ap Llywelyn, Prydydd y Moch, 23, 216
Llywelyn, abbot of Cymer, 312
Llywelyn ab Owain (ap Maredudd), of Ceredigion, 422
Llywelyn (d. 1287) ap Dafydd (ap Gruffudd), 578–9
Llywelyn ap Goronwy Fychan, of Trecastell, 217
Llywelyn ap Gruffudd (ab Ednyfed Fychan), Dom. friar, 191–2 nn.21–2, 265, 430–2, 445, 553–5
Llywelyn (d.1282) ap Gruffudd, political action:
  inheritance, 6–27
  parents, 14, 35, 37–9; *see* Gruffudd ap Llywelyn; Senana
  birth, 39
  brothers and sisters, 14; *see* Owain ap Gruffudd; Dafydd ap Gruffudd; Rhodri ap Gruffudd; Gwladus; Margaret
  early political initiatives (*c.* 1241–3), 39–47:
    lordship in Dyffryn Clwyd, 40–1
    agreement with Ralph Mortimer (1241), 41–3
    political relationships, 44–7
    adherence to Dafydd ap Llywelyn (1244–6), 49–55
    resistance to Henry III (1245–7), 49–50, 53–5
  lordship in Gwynedd Uwch Conwy:
    shared lordship with Owain (1246–55), 56, 66–8, 85
    agreement with Henry III at Woodstock (1247), 58–62
    Dafydd's assertion of hereditary right, 68–72, 312, 597–8
    negotiations with Henry, 71–2
  supremacy in Gwynedd Uwch Conwy (1255), 72–7; *see also* Bryn Derwin
    imprisonment of Owain, 74–7
    relations with Dafydd, 71–4, 216
  annexation of Perfeddwlad, 77, 81, 84–5, 88–9, 457
  supremacy in Wales, 30, 48, 90–108, 313
    authority in Meirionydd, Deheubarth and Powys, 91–5, 108–16, 216
    relations with Maredudd ap Rhys Gryg (1251–61), 67–8, 85, 91–3, 97–101, 103–8, 115, 121–2, 289, 292–3, 297–300
    homage of the lords of Wales (1258), 109–13
    ecclesiastical support, 114–15
    style 'prince of Wales' (1258), 109–10, 145
    treaty with magnates of Scotland, 110–11
  search for settlement with Henry (1258–82):
    proposals for a peace treaty, 20–1, 96–7, 110, 117–25, 134–7, 145–7, 152–3, 330
    situation under terms of truce, 131–2
    offensives in the march (1260, 1262–3), 125–31, 139–40, 144–5, 148–57:
      Builth (1260), 125–6
      Maelienydd (1262–3), 139–41, 143, 147–9
      Brecon and Abergavenny (1263), 149–53
      Montgomery and Clun (1263), 155–7
    alliance with Gruffudd ap Gwenwynwyn (1263), 115, 157–60, 287–90, 293–4, 299–302
    illness and Henry's reaction (1262), 137–8
    style 'prince of Wales and lord of Snowdon', 145
    relations with Simon de Montfort, e. of Leicester (1263–5):
      military collaboration in the march (1264–5), 139–40, 154–5, 161–5
      agreement (1265), 165–70
      relations with Montfort after the agreement, 170–2
  the treaty of Montgomery:
    defence of the frontier with Chester (1265), 172–3
    initiatives of the papal legate Ottobuono, 173–8, 584
    negotiations at Shrewsbury (1267), 177–80

Index

the treaty of Montgomery:
his person honoured by Henry III, 180, 275, 476
granted title 'prince of Wales' and the principality of Wales, and the homage of the Welsh lords of Wales, 180
provision to be made for Dafydd, 180–1, 374–5
indemnity, 181
territorial provisions, 182–5
treaty sealed at Montgomery, 29 September, 1267, 179–80
homage to Henry at Rhyd Chwima, 1–2, 179
see also, Montgomery, treaty of
the principality of Wales, 1267–77:
intervention in Glamorgan and Caerleon (1266–72), 171, 339–48, 350–5
homage of Gruffudd ap Rhys, of Senghennydd, 342–3
homage of Maredudd ap Gruffudd, of Caerleon, 345–7
relations with the Lord Edward (1267–70), 338–9, 348–50
homage of Maredudd ap Rhys Gryg (1270), 348–50, 364–5
effect of Edward's departure from the realm, 350–1
position in relation to Humphrey de Bohun, lords and communities in the lordship of Brecon, 355–60, 418
relations with Roger Mortimer, 358–63
the building of Dolforwyn (1273), 360
Mortimer building at Cefnllys (1273), 361–2
failure to swear fealty to Edward I (1273), 359–60, 363–4, 387
the indemnity under the treaty of Montgomery, 245, 247, 250–1, 295, 363–6, 390
position on Edward's return to England (1274), 363–7
conspiracy on his life (1274), 369–74
process against Gruffudd ap Gwenwynwyn, 302, 369–77, 470
initiation of process against Dafydd ap Gruffudd, 374–7
relations with Anian, bishop of St Asaph, 210–15, 377–84
relations with Edward (1274–7), 367–414
summons to do homage at Shrewsbury (1274), 382–3; Chester (1275), 385–8; Westminster and Winchester (1275–6), 387, 402
letters to Gregory X (1274–5), 280, 387–8, 394
letters to clergy of England (1275), 214–15, 387
marriage to Eleanor de Montfort (1275), 165, 279, 390–402

marriage *per verba de presenti*, 397–9
complaint to Edward over her imprisonment, 398–9
reaction of Edward to Llywelyn's intransigence, *see* Edward I
political judgement (1267–77), 338, 385, 390, 599–604
political crisis (1276–7):
proposals to the king (1276–7), 406, 409–12
condemnation in council (1276), 402, 406–7
excommunication *nominatim* (1276–7), 407–8, 412
charter to the church of St Asaph, 212–15, 407–9
war in Wales (1277), 414–36:
position destroyed in march and Powys Wenwynwyn, 415–18; in Deheubarth, 418–22; in Powys Fadog, 423–4
resistance in Gwynedd, 425–34
defection of religious and lay members of the community, 430–3
the treaty of Aberconwy (1277), 437–45:
submission to the king's will and fine, 438
yields Perfeddwlad and Anglesey, 439
recognizes Dafydd's hereditary right in Gwynedd Uwch Conwy, 438–41
provision for Owain and Rhodri, 440–1
fine remitted and Anglesey restored, 442
retains style 'prince of Wales' and homage of five lords, 443
gives hostages and concedes measures to secure his adherence to treaty, 444
provision for Welsh or marcher law in legal actions, 439
fealty at Rhuddlan and excommunication removed, 444
homage in London and implementation of the treaty, 445
relations with Edward after the treaty:
exchanges with the king, 445–9
meeting at Rhuddlan (1278), 448
marriage to Eleanor at Worcester, 398, 446–50, 507–8
plea over Arwystli and part of Cyfeiliog (1278–81), 446, 469–89, 493–6:
origins and initiation of plea, 370–1, 446, 472–3
acknowledgement of royal jurisdiction, 472, 475–7, 483, 486–7
insistence on process and judgement by Welsh law, 277–8, 473–4, 477–9
precise implications of demand, 476–7, 482–6; *see also under* Gwynedd, law and administration of justice, *ynad (iudex)*
insistence on legal practice in Arwystli and Cyfeiliog, 301–2, 484
presses for decision on procedure, 477–81

653

denies material interest in Arwystli, 489
persistence with the plea (1281), 488–9, 504–5
later claim that he was denied Welsh law, 469, 483, 487, 499
position on the eve of conflict (1282), 465–9, 496–504, 506–10:
  agreement with Roger Mortimer (1281), 478, 493–6, 498
  intercession on behalf of Amaury de Montfort, 400, 511
  grievances and anxieties expressed in letters to Edward, 496–504; *see also* Leicester, Robert of; Grey, Reginald de
  relations with princes of Deheubarth and Powys Fadog, 459–60, 491–3, 497–8
  birth of daughter, Gwenllian, and death of Eleanor, 510; *see* Montfort, Eleanor de; Gwenllian
  his position at the outbreak of war: chronicle and record testimony, 465–9
  his 'remorseless dilemma', 506–9;
  commitment to conflict, 509–10, 522–3, 577
armed conflict:
  resistance in Gwynedd Uwch Conwy, 526–30
  response to Archbishop Pecham's intercession, 530–4
  conveys *gravamina* of princes and communities, 534–5
  discussion with the archbishop, 535
  receives and rejects proposals conveyed by the archbishop, 542–5:
  appeal to history, 543–4
  concern for his people, 296, 334, 468–9, 544, 546–7, 594–5, 602
  refusal to yield Snowdonia, 544
  receives the archbishop's valedictory denunciation of the Welsh nation, 545–6
  excommunication, 549–50
  recognized as main adversary, 549–50, 557
the death of the prince of Wales, 550–67
  entrusts defence of Gwynedd Uwch Conwy to Dafydd and goes to the march, 550
  military considerations, 557–9
  ruse on the part of the marchers, 550–2, 556–61, 558–61
  situation in the lands of Edmund Mortimer and his part in Llywelyn's death, 556, 558–9
  betrayal in the belfry at Bangor, 552–5
  his movements monitored and convergence of forces on the marches of Builth and Elfael, 559–61
  evidence for the circumstances of his death, 551–2, 561–7

'treasonable letter' and privy seal found on his body, 552, 566, 568
burial at Cwm-hir, 567–8
the severed head taken to Edward and displayed at the Tower of London, 568–9
celebration of his death by Stephen of St George, 567
mourned by Bleddyn Fardd and Gruffudd ab yr Ynad Coch, 569–70, 581
resistance maintained after his death, 571–7
provision made at Sempringham for Gwenllian, 579–80
the Croes Naid presented to Edward at Aberconwy, 580–1
government:
inheritance, 4–27
the lordship of Gwynedd, 187–273: *see* Gwynedd
the principality of Wales, 274–337; *see* Wales, principality of
character and renown:
contemporary estimates:
  eulogy and elegy, 5, 75–6, 90–1, 276–7, 333, 336–7, 433, 510, 569–70, 581–2, 584: *see also* Bleddyn Fardd; Dafydd Benfras; Gruffudd ab yr Ynad Coch; Hywel Foel ap Griffri; Llygad Gŵr
chroniclers' estimates, *see* Brut y Tywysogyon; Paris, Matthew; Dunstable chronicle; Trevet, Nicholas
commemorative verses, 273, 586
celebration of his death by Stephen of St George, 567
historical assessment, 2–3, 385, 582–606; *see also* political judgement; quality of his lordship
literary and artistic commemoration, 591–2
monument in the prince's memory, 592–3
personal relations:
  brothers, *see* Owain ap Gruffudd; Dafydd ap Gruffudd; Rhodri ap Gruffudd
  princes of Wales, *see* Gruffudd ap Gwenwynwyn; Gruffudd ap Madog; Hywel ap Rhys Gryg; Llywelyn ap Gruffudd Fychan; Maredudd ab Owain; Maredudd ap Rhys Gryg; Rhys Wyndod
  bishops of Wales, *see* Anian of Bangor; Anian of St Asaph; Richard of Bangor
  monastic and religious orders, *see* Cistercian Order; Dominican Order; Franciscan Order
  the community of his patrimony, 255–73; *see also* Goronwy ab Ednyfed; Goronwy ap Heilin; Gruffudd ap Iorwerth; Rhys ap Gruffudd (ab Ednyfed)

Index

kings of England, *see* Henry III;
    Edward I
lords of the march, *see* Bohun,
    Humphrey de, e. of Hereford (d. 1298);
    Clare, Gilbert de, e. of Gloucester;
    Mortimer, Roger (d. 1282)
political judgement, 338–9, 354–5, 385–9,
    406–14, 506–10, 543–5, 593–605
quality of his lordship, 255–9, 266–7,
    271–3, 586
concern for his people, 296, 334, 468–9,
    544, 546–8, 602
harshness of his rule, 255–9, 266–7,
    271–3, 586
capacity for generosity, 257, 271–2
sense of history, 543–4, 488; *see also*
    Historia Regum Britanniae
Llywelyn ap Gruffudd ap Madog, *see*
    Llywelyn (d. 1282) ap Gruffudd Fychan
Llywelyn (d. 1282) ap Gruffudd Fychan, of
    Powys Fadog, 308, 410 n.76, 411,
    423–4, 433, 458–9, 492–3, 519–20, 565
Llywelyn (d. 1240) ap Iorwerth, 162, 196,
    202, 204, 209, 214, 237, 271, 277,
    279–80, 289, 302, 313–14, 316, 319–21,
    330, 334, 587
political action: lordship over Gwynedd,
    11–14
submission to John (1211), 12–13,
    16–17, 28, 35, 245, 438–9, 444
supremacy, 2, 14–29, 141, 180, 182, 185,
    285–6, 342
letter to king of France (1212), 17, 310,
    322, 334
succession to, 12–14, 25–6, 28–9, 31–4
relations with: Gruffudd ap Llywelyn,
    12–14, 28
lords of Wales, 17–25, 28–30, 285–6
marcher lords, 19–20, 23–7, 141, 356
Henry III, 21–9, 274–5, 285–6
castle-building, 252
charters of, 12, 205–7, 216–18, 261, 263
conception of principality and *status
    Wallie*, 281, 290, 292, 333
historical estimation of, 2–3, 271, 585–6
life of, 587
lineage of, 579, 586
style, 188, 221, 284
death, 29–30, 168, 178, 546, 603
wife, *see* Joan
sons, *see* Gruffudd ap Llywelyn; Dafydd
    ap Llywelyn
daughter, *see* Gwladus Ddu
grandsons, *see* Owain ap Gruffudd;
    Llywelyn ap Gruffudd; Dafydd ap
    Gruffudd; Rhodri ap Gruffudd;
    Mortimer, Roger
granddaughters, *see* Gwladus; Longespée,
    Maud; Margaret
see also Gwynedd; Wales
Llywelyn (d. 1282) ap Madog, son of

Madog (d.1277) ap Gruffudd, of Powys
    Fadog, 457, 520
Llywelyn (d.1160) ap Madog (ap
    Maredudd), of Powys, 10
Llywelyn (d. 1263) ap Maredudd, of
    Meirionnydd, 55, 59, 91, 155–6, 216,
    443
Llywelyn ap Rhys (Fychan), of Ystrad
    Tywi, 422, 459, 572
Llywelyn ap Rhys (ap Maelgwn Fychan), of
    Ceredigion, 112, 306
Llywelyn Fychan (ap Llywelyn ab Owain),
    of Mechain, 113
Llywelyn Goch ap Meurig Hen, 585
Locrinus, son of Brutus, 278, 335; *see
    Historia Regum Britanniae*
London, 35, 176, 341, 345, 387–8, 445, 447
    crown of, 54
    kingship of, 18
    Tower of, 35, 41, 47–8, 568, 579
    White Mount in, 569
Longespée, Maud, 356 n.65, 567–8
Louis IX, k. of France, 347
Lucca (Italy), 512
Ludlow (Shropshire), 154, 163, 166
Lynde, John de la, 178
Lyons, Council of (1274), 380–1

Mabelfyw, cmt., 112, 287, 289
Mabudrud, cmt., 421
Mabwynion, cmt., 106, 421, 524–5
Maccabees, 7, 56, 81, 282, 577
Machen, 345
Madog, abbot of Valle Crucis, 312, 379–80
Madog ab Arawdr, 318, 357 n.67, 525
Madog ab Einion (ap Maredudd), 46 n.33,
    444
Madog ab Owain ap Maredudd, of Elfael,
    127
Madog ab Owain Gwynedd, 591
Madog ap Cynfrig, 554
Madog (d. 1236) ap Gruffudd, of Powys
    Fadog, 31 n.104, 70
Madog (d. 1277) ap Gruffudd (ap Madog),
    of Powys Fadog, 308, 423–4
    wife of, *see* Margaret, sister of Llywelyn
        ap Gruffudd
Madog ap Gwenwynwyn, 112, 307
Madog ap Llywelyn, 191, 425–6, 433, 443,
    446, 583
Madog ap Magister, 323
Madog (d. 1160) ap Maredudd, of Powys,
    10
Madog ap Philip, 119
Madog Fychan (ap Madog ap Gruffudd), of
    Powys Fadog, 93, 111, 169
Madog Fychan, priest, 554
Maelgwn (d. 1231) ap Rhys, of Ceredigion
    11, 112
Maelgwn Fychan (d. 1257 ap Maelgwn ap
    Rhys), of Ceredigion, 34, 55–6, 112

655

Maelienydd, lsp., 19–20, 25, 30, 42–3, 130, 139–41, 147, 149–50, 152, 182–3, 342, 361–2, 418, 429, 494, 559, 568, 571
Maelor (Bromfield), cmt., 424, 457, 520, 529
Maelor Saesneg, cmt., 305, 556
Maenan, 235
Maenordeifi, 108
Maenordeilo, cmt., 421
Malláen, cmt., 421, 457, 523, 525
Malltraeth, cmt., 66, 222, 237, 239
Man, k. of, 37–8, 52
Manawydan, 21; *see* Four Branches of the Mabinogi
Manning, Robert, of Bourne, 564, 566–7, 586
Mar, e. of, *see* William, e. of Mar
March, *see* Wales, march of
Marchros, 239–40
Maredudd, abbot of Aberconwy, 322
Maredudd (d. 1265) ab Owain, of Ceredigion, 55, 93–5, 98, 106–8, 112, 125, 151, 286, 289, 292, 294, 305–6, 311, 421, 571
Maredudd (d. 1212) ap Cynan, of Meirionnydd, 216
Maredudd (d. 1270) ap Gruffudd, of Caerleon, 289, 345–8, 351–2
Maredudd ap Iorwerth, 76
Maredudd ap Llywelyn, of Mechain, 113, 505
Maredudd (d. 1201) ap Rhys ap Gruffudd, of Deheubarth, 346
Maredudd (d.1271) ap Rhys Gryg, of Ystrad Tywi, 24, 31, 55, 97–8, 103–8, 138, 151, 286, 306, 419–21
 relations with Llywelyn, 68, 85, 91–4, 97–8, 100, 103, 105–8, 112, 115, 121–2, 145, 288–90, 292–3, 297–300, 311, 319, 324, 327, 372, 419–20
 homage (1267–70), 180–2, 348–50, 364–5
Maredudd ap Richard (ap Cadwaladr), 57–8, 61, 65
Maredudd (d. 1244) ap Robert, of Cydewain, 34, 113, 202
Margam, Cist. abbey, 102
Margaret, sister of Llywelyn ap Gruffudd, wife of Madog (d.1277) ap Gruffudd, 14, 38, 308 n.119, 423, 499
Margaret of France, wife of Louis IX, 400, 467
Marshal, family, 142
Marshal, Gilbert, e. of Pembroke (d. 1241), 62
Marshal, Richard, e. of Pembroke (d. 1234), 26
Marshal, William, e. of Pembroke (d. 1231), 25
Martin IV, p., 400, 516
Math fab Mathonwy, 194; *see* Four Branches of the Mabinogi
Mathafarn Eithaf, 223

Mathafarn Wion, 223
Mathrafal, ct., 17, 138, 333
 coronet of, 595
 crowned ruler of, 327
 province of, 123
Matthew, Master, 134
Mawddwy, cmt., 159, 307, 371, 424, 575
Mechain, ctf., lsp., 113, 424, 505
Medrod, 552
Mefennydd, cmt., 421
Meifod (cmt. Rhos Is Dulas), 225
Meilyr Brydydd, 6, 314
Meirionnydd, ctf., lsp., 7, 12, 14, 55, 59–60, 91, 155, 194, 198, 216, 228, 251, 289, 443, 446, 472, 498, 502, 574–5
 lord of, *see* Hywel ap Gruffudd; Llywelyn ap Maredudd
Meisgyn, cmt., 63, 342, 344
Mellington, *see* Muleton
Menai, cmt., 66, 223, 237, 239
Menai Straits, 233, 429, 510, 548, 574
 bridge over and crossing, 526, 536–42, 548, 552–3, 555, 557, 563
Menteith, e. of, *see* Comyn, Walter, e. of Menteith
Merioneth, co., 191–2, 219, 242, 248
Merton, Walter de, 178, 358–9
Merton, William de, Franc. friar, 477, 504
Meurig ap Gruffudd, of Elfael, 357
Meurig ap Llywelyn, of Brecon, 357, 429
Middleton, William, archdeacon of Canterbury, 404
Mochdre (cmt. Rhos Uwch Dulas), 226
Mochnant Is Rhaeadr, cmt., 519
Mochnant Uwch Rhaeadr, cmt., 159, 371
Moel-y-don, 538–9
Mold, lsp., 361, 451, 456, 520
Mold, Roger of, 34, 122, 124, 183
Molis, Nicholas de, 55–6, 93, 103, 105–6
Môn, 7; *see also* Anglesey
Monmouth, 171
Monmouth, Geoffrey of, 476; *see also* Historia Regum Britanniae
Montargis (*dép.* Loiret), Dom. friary, 390–1, 394, 397, 399, 449
Montfort, family, 279, 580
 banner of, 390, 397, 399
 adherents (Montfortians), 174–7, 511–12; *see also* the Disinherited
Montfort, Amaury de, 390–5
 alleged conspiracy with Llywelyn ap Gruffudd, 394–7, 401–2, 497
 capture and imprisonment, 390, 395, 399–401
 intercession by Llywelyn, 511
 intercession by churchmen and release, 399–401, 512
 writings, 399
Eleanor de (d. 1275), widow of Simon de Montfort, e. of Leicester (d.1265), 390–1, 395

656

Index

Montfort, Eleanor de (d. 1282), princess of Wales, wife of Llywelyn ap Gruffudd, 165, 389, 400, 449, 511
  at Montargis, 390–1
  arrangements for marriage with Llywelyn, 390, 393–7
  marriage *per verba de presenti*, 397–8
  capture and imprisonment, 390, 393, 395–7, 401–3, 430
  Llywelyn seeks her release, 410–11
  marriage at Worcester (1278), 447–9
  'princess of Wales and lady of Snowdon', 189, 398, 448–9
  letters to Edward, 279, 449, 497, 503–4
  birth of daughter, 507, 510, 543; *see* Gwenllian
  death and burial at Llan-faes, 233, 510–11, 539–40
  seal, 332
Montfort, Guy de, 391–3, 395
Montfort, Henry de, 162, 164
Montfort, Peter de, 149–53, 167, 169
Montfort, Simon de, e. of Leicester (d. 1265); 80–1, 119, 125, 127–8, 340
  return to England and conflict in the march, 139, 154, 156, 161–5, 493
  agreement with Llywelyn ap Gruffudd (1265), 166–9, 311
  last movements in the march and death, 170–2
  wife, *see* Eleanor (d. 1275); sons, *see* Amaury; Guy; Henry; Simon
  daughter, *see* Eleanor (d. 1282), princess of Wales, wife of Llywelyn ap Gruffudd
Montfort, Simon de (d. 1271), 171, 391–2
Montgomery, cas. and lsp., 25, 113, 155, 160, 168, 183–4, 350, 382–3
  centre of military command, 102, 142, 414, 424, 414–18, 521
  conflict on frontier at, 94–5, 97, 160, 163, 404–5, 414–18, 431, 601
  Llywelyn ap Gruffudd offers to do homage at, 406, 410
  parliamenta or negotiations at ford of, *see* Rhyd Chwima
  proceedings before royal justices at, 472, 483, 488, 493
  treaty of (1267), 314, 329, 331, 335, 338–9, 341, 343–4, 381, 389, 407, 584
    Henry III initiates negotiations, 177
    negotiations conducted by Ottobuono, 178–80, 335, 381, 401, 543–4
    person of Llywelyn honoured, 180, 275, 476
    Llywelyn and his heirs granted title 'prince of Wales' and principality, 180, 394–5
    homage of the lords of Wales, 180–2, 348–9
    provision for Dafydd ap Gruffudd, 180–1, 438

  indemnity, 181, 247, 250–1, 295, 338, 363–6, 442, 501
  territorial provisions, 182–5, 341–2, 356
  Llywelyn's homage to Henry and sealing, 1–2, 179–80, 336
  Ottobuono's estimate of treaty, 185–6
  status of principality under, 181–2
  interpretation of treaty, 342–3, 354–5, 358–9, 361–3, 600, 603–4
  historical estimation, 584, 590, 596, 598
Morfa Mawr, 93
Morgan ap Maredudd, 346 n.28, 572
Morgan, R. W., 594
Morgannwg, *see* Blaenau Morgannwg; Glamorgan
Morlaàs, Béarn (*dép.* Pyr. Atl.), 247
Morris, J. E., 598
Mortimer, family, 19–20, 132, 585–6
Mortimer, Edmund (d.1304), 560–1
  his part in death of Llywelyn ap Gruffudd, 551–2, 555–7, 559, 564, 566
  difficulties in his lordships, 556–9
  'treasonable letter' and prince's seal in his possession, 566
Mortimer, Hugh (d. 1227), 20, 141
Mortimer, Ralph (d. 1246), 30, 32, 34, 41–3, 94, 141
Mortimer, Roger (d.1214), 19
Mortimer, Roger (d. 1282), 95, 136, 143–4, 174, 329–30, 339, 341, 343, 387, 429, 446
  yields Gwerthrynion (1257), 94
  influence and fidelity in the march, 120–2, 129, 133–5, 138–43, 152–3, 157, 160–1
  custodian of Builth (1260), 125–6, 130, 135
  yields Maelienydd and Cefnllys (1262–3), 139–41, 147–50
  relations with Edward, 153–4
  resistance to Montfort (1263–5), 161–6
  attitude to Montfortians, 174–6
  influence in realm and march (1270–4), 339, 341–2, 350–2, 358–63, 366, 404, 411
  Dolforwyn and Cefnllys (1273), 253, 360–2
  command (1277), 404–5, 414–20, 424, 431–2
  Welsh and marcher law, 329, 471–2, 481, 486
  agreement with Llywelyn (1281), 493–6, 498
  command (1282), 521
  death and Edward 's estimate of, 521–2, 556, 558
  sons, *see* Edmund; Roger (d. 1326)
Mortimer, Roger (d. 1326), 519, 520 n.40, 551–2, 558–9, 561
'Morugge', mountain, 560 n.170, 575 n.221
Muleton, 160, 405
Mynydd Hiraethog, 226

Index

Nancall, Cist. grange, 193, 255, 258–9, 267, 269, 271, 586
Nancaw, 228, 575 n.220
Nancol, 229, 575 n.220
Nanconwy, cmt., 67, 229–30, 263, 322
Nanheudwy, cmt., 424, 457–8, 519
Nanhwynan, Cist. grange, 232
Nannau, 377
Nannerch, 517
Nantcriba, 158
Narberth, lsp., 102
Neath, 522
Nefyn, ct. and *maerdref*, 221, 227, 244, 504
Neigwl, c. and *maerdref*, 227
Netherwent, 126
Newport, 171
New Temple (London), 400, 413
Nicholas III, p., 400
Norfolk, e. of, *see* Bigod, Roger, e. of Norfolk
Normandy, 143
Northop, 468
Norway, 280, 324
Norwich, b. of, 144

Occam, William of, 282
O'Neill, Brian, 116
Ordericus Vitalis, 143
Orléanais, the, 394
Orreby, Thomas de, justice of Chester, 129
Orthez, Béarn (*dép.* Pyr. Atl.), 366
Orvieto (Umbria, Italy), 392, 567
Osney (Oxon.), Aug. abbey, annals, 559, 565
Oswestry, cas., bor. and lsp., 126, 142, 153, 232, 405–6, 410, 415, 451–3, 456, 458–9, 521
   proceedings before royal justices at, 472–4, 477, 492
Otto, papal legate, 185
Ottobuono, papal legate, 1, 173–5, 177–80, 185–6, 335, 345, 379, 381, 389, 392, 401; *see also* Adrian V
Owain ap Bleddyn, of Edeirnion, 113, 169, 181, 311, 443
Owain ap Dafydd (ap Gruffudd), 578–9
Owain (d. *c.* 1282) ap Gruffudd (ap Llywelyn), 14, 32, 35, 38–9, 49, 56–8, 104, 288, 327, 425, 436,
   agreement with Henry III (1247), 58–62
   lordship in Gwynedd Uwch Conwy, 64–8, 85–6, 92, 288, 327
   position regarding Dafydd's hereditary right, 68–71
   defeat and imprisonment, 72–6
   provision under treaty of Aberconwy (1277), 440–1
   death and elegies, 441, 581
Owain ap Gruffudd (ap Gwenwynwyn), 307, 369–74, 382, 470
Owain ap Gruffudd (ap Madog), of Powys Fadog, 308, 520

Owain ap Llywelyn ab Owain, of Mechain, 113
Owain (d.1275) ap Maredudd (ab Owain), of Ceredigion, 304–5, 318–19
Owain (d. 1261) ap Maredudd (ap Robert), of Cydewain, 113; *see also* Cydewain
Owain (d. *c.*1260–7) ap Maredudd, of Elfael, 127, 130, 141, 340 n.8
Owain ap Maxen, 551
Owain (d. 1378) ap Thomas ap Rhodri (Owain Lawgoch), 448 n.218, 583, 585
Owain Cyfeiliog (d. 1197), 10
Owain Glyndŵr (d. *c.* 1415), 191, 583, 590, 595
Owain Gwynedd (d. 1170), 10–11, 15–16, 283–4, 588, 604
   lineage, 314, 579
Owain Lawgoch, *see* Owain ap Thomas ap Rhodri
Owen, George, 596
Oxford, 21, 117–21
   parliament at (1258), 117–20, 123
   Provisions of (1258), 119–20, 131, 175, 392
   e. of, *see* Vere, Robert de, e. of Oxford

Padua, 392
Pandulf, papal legate, 185
Paris, 366, 391
   parlement of, 280
   treaty of (1259), 124
Paris, Matthew, 31–2, 47, 49, 52–3, 74, 80, 82, 94, 96, 100–1, 106, 117–18, 120, 593–4, 600
Parry, J. H., 594
Passelowe, Simon, 129
Pecham, John, abp. of Canterbury (1279–92), 323, 334, 514
   privileges of the church of Bangor, 211, 480
   intestacy, 258–9
   law of Wales, 480–1
   release of Amaury de Montfort, 400, 511–12
   war of 1282:
      support for Edward and excommunication of rebels, 468, 516, 518–19, 532, 549–50
      burning of church of St Asaph, 516–17
      resistance from Bishop Anian, 516–17, 549
      intercession in conflict:
      exchanges with Llywelyn, 189–90, 469, 498, 506, 530–4, 590, 594
      receives grievances of the Welsh, 232, 454–6, 459, 461, 464, 487, 490, 502, 534–5, 590, 594
      discussions with Edward, 534–5, 536
      meeting with Llywelyn, 535–6
      discussion with barons and formulation of proposals, 311, 535–6

Index

proposals to Llywelyn and Dafydd, 542–5
denunciation of the depravity of the Welsh nation, 4, 545–6
the Trojan inheritance, 545–6, 588
excommunication of Llywelyn, 549–50
the death of Llywelyn
  visitation of diocese of Hereford, 546, 568
  concern for Adam of Nannau and clergy in Gwynedd, 323, 554–5
  letter on Llywelyn's death, 552, 566, 568
  burial of Llywelyn, 567–8
register of, 325
Pegram, Henry, 592
Pembroke, lsp., 25, 55, 108
  lord of, *see* Valence, William de
Pembroke, e. of, *see* Marshal, Gilbert; Marshal, Richard; Marshal, William
Penamnen, 230
Pencester, Stephen of, 368 n.105, 527
Penllyn, cmt., 67, 188, 220, 227, 229, 232, 237, 239, 242, 372, 425, 428, 451, 456, 528, 556, 574–5
Penllyn Is Meloch, 239
Penmaen, 229
Penmaen-bach, 540
Penmaen-mawr, 540
Penmon, Aug. priory, 206–7
Penmynydd, 217
Pennal, 221, 227
Pennant, Thomas, 590
Pennardd, cmt., 457
Pen-rhiw, 230
Penrhos, ct. and *maerdref*, 221, 223–4
Pentraeth, btl., 11
Pentrefoelas, 528
Penweddig, ctf., 571
Penwynllys, 263
Perfedd, cmt., Ceredigion, 93, 105, 422
Perfedd, cmt., Ystrad Tywi, 421, 490–1, 523–4
Perfeddwlad (Gwynedd Is Conwy, the Four Cantreds), 44, 46, 90–1, 93–4, 96–7, 102, 196, 233, 316, 378, 437, 505, 539, 581, 601
  area, *cantrefi* and relationship with Gwynedd Uwch Conwy, 7, 189–91, 543–4, 546–7; *see also* Dyffryn Clwyd; Rhos; Rhufoniog; Tegeingl (Englefield)
  boroughs, *see* Flint, Rhuddlan
  castles, *see* Degannwy; Diserth; Flint; Rhuddlan
  courts and demesnes, and tenants' fiscal obligations, *see* Gwynedd
  legal practices recorded by commission of inquiry (1281), 203, 272, 485
  political fortunes:
    ceded by Llywelyn ap Iorwerth (1211) and recovered, 16–17
    Tegeingl ceded and Dyffryn Clwyd, Rhos and Rhufoniog retained by Dafydd ap Llywelyn (1241), 40–1, 61
    lordship established in Dyffryn Clwyd by Llywelyn ap Gruffudd, 40–1, 50, 113–14
    Owain ap Gruffudd and Llywelyn cede possession (1247), 58–9
    administration as 'the king's new conquest in Wales' (1247–56), 59–85
    grievances of communities, 62–85
    annexation by Llywelyn (1256), 81–5, 96–7, 172
    relationship between problems of Gwynedd Uwch Conwy and Perfeddwlad, 85–9
    campaign by Henry III (1257), 102, 104–5
    granted to Llywelyn by treaty of Montgomery (1267), 182
    campaign by Edward I (1277), 425–8
    ceded by Llywelyn by treaty of Aberconwy (1277), 439, 444
    royal administration of Tegeingl and Rhos, and lordship of Dafydd ap Gruffudd in Rhufoniog and Dyffryn Clwyd (1277–82), 194, 216, 434–6, 439, 441
    grievances of communities under royal lordship (1277–82), 453–7, 462–5, 468–9, 504
    conflict (1282), 451–3, 511–12, 516–17, 519–20, 527–30, 536
    concern for communities expressed by Llywelyn, 534, 543–4, 546–7
  see also Gwynedd; Snowdonia
Peryf ap Cedifor, 11
Peterborough (Northt.), Ben. abbey, chronicle, 466–7, 564–5
Peuliniog, cmt., 119
Philip Augustus, k. of France, 17, 310, 322
Philip III, k. of France, 281
Philip IV, k. of France, 407 n.65, 411
Philip, count of Savoy, 361
Pichard, Roger, 150 n.39, 356
Pierce, T. Jones, 241–2, 599
Pipton, 167, 169–70
Poitiers, William of, 587
Ponthieu, 512
Postyn, 226
Powel, David, 590, 594–6
Powicke, F. M., 287–8, 598, 602
Powys, 3, 15–17, 20, 90–1, 93–5, 99, 113, 157, 160, 182–4, 284, 287, 289, 295, 297, 300, 309, 313, 316, 330, 376, 426, 430, 472, 550, 561, 575, 603–4
  kings and lords of, 28–9, 53, 91, 209, 272, 285, 305, 309, 334, 463, 596–8
  succession in, 10–11, 306–8
  legal practice in, 203, 301–2, 305–6
  principal court of, *see* Mathrafal

Breintiau Gwŷr Powys (Privileges of the Men of Powys), 268–70
northern Powys, *see* Powys Fadog; southern Powys, *see* Powys Wenwynwyn
Powys Fadog, 25, 30–1, 34, 48, 60, 68, 70–1, 73, 93–4, 111–12, 138, 157, 198, 237, 241, 405, 458
lords of, 30–1, 105, 111–12, 458–60, 462–3, 485, 519–20; *see also* Madog (d.1236) ap Gruffudd; Gruffudd (d.1269) ap Madog; Madog (d.1277) ap Gruffudd; Llywelyn (d. 1282) ap Gruffudd Fychan; Owain ap Gruffudd (ap Madog), Gruffudd Fychan (ap Gruffudd ap Madog); Llywelyn (d.1282) ap Madog; Gruffudd (d. 1282) ap Madog
conflict in (1276–7), 404–5, 418, 423–5, 431; (1282), 451, 456–7, 458–60, 519–20, 522, 526–7, 560
lands granted to English barons, 192, 519–20; *see* Chirk; Bromfield and Yale
legal practice in, 305, 481, 485
succession in, 308, 423–4
Powys Wenwynwyn, 18, 25, 29–30, 155, 157–60, 302, 316–17, 375, 383, 418, 431, 458, 495, 556, 560
lords of, *see* Gwenwynwyn ab Owain Cyfeiliog; Gruffudd ap Gwenwynwyn
lands of, seized by Llywelyn, 94
held of Llywelyn, 158–60, 302
forfeited to Llywelyn and restored with exception of Arwystli and part of Cyfeiliog, 370–1
recovered by Gruffudd ap Gwenwynwyn, 416, 418, 423, 470
lands subject to litigation (1278–81), *see* Arwystli; Cyfeiliog
succession to, 306–7
Preachers, Order of, *see* Dominican Order
Premonstratensian Order, abbeys of, *see* Hagnaby; Talyllychau
Prestatyn, cmt., 123
Presteigne, 147
Priam, 510
Price, Thomas, 591
Priestholm, *see* Ynys Lannog
Prior, 226
Prydydd Bychan, y, 74, 112
Pryse, R. J., *see* Gweirydd ap Rhys
Prysor, 229, 237, 239–40
Pumlumon, 560; *see also* 'Morugge'
Pwllheli, ct. and *maerdref*, 227
Pyrenees, 241, 270, 366

Radnor, cas. and lsp., 140–1, 153, 161–3, 429, 493, 529, 559
Rhinog, 229, 241
Rhirid ap Madog, 232
Rhiw, 226

Rhiw and Helyg, land between, 159, 371
Rhodri (d. c.1315) ap Gruffudd (ap Llywelyn), 14, 35, 38–9, 73–4, 86–7, 322, 440, 448
Rhodri (d.1195) ab Owain Gwynedd, 11
Rhodri Mawr (d. 878), 590
Rhos, ctf., Dyfed, 99, 102, 108
Rhos, ctf., Perfeddwlad, 7, 34, 40–1, 50, 53, 78–9, 190–2, 198, 224–6, 238, 242, 249, 360, 436, 439
grievances of communities (1282), 454–6, 462–4, 466, 577
marcher lsp. (part of), 528–9; *see also* Denbigh, lsp.
Rhos Is Dulas, cmt., 5, 221, 225, 528
Rhosmor, 222
Rhosmynach, 223
Rhos Uwch Dulas, 190, 226, 528
Rhosyr, ct. and *maerdref*, 223–4
Rhuddlan, cas. and bor., 34–5, 78, 427–8, 436–8, 444, 516, 536, 542, 545
court of, 372, 465
Edward and Llywelyn meet at, 448
Arwystli plea heard at, 473–4, 483, 485
attack and siege (1282), 451, 465, 468, 519
military centre (1282), 512–13, 519, 521, 523, 527–9, 539, 548, 568, 574
Dom. friary, 206
prior, 500; *see also* Ifor ap Gruffudd, friar
Rhufoniog, ctf., 40–1, 50, 78–9, 190–2, 198, 224–5, 238–9, 242, 249
lsp. of Dafydd ap Gruffudd, 154, 194, 434, 436, 439, 441, 462–3, 528–9
marcher lsp. (part of), 192, 224–5, 249, 528; *see also* Denbigh, lsp.
Rhufoniog Is Aled, cmt., 221, 225–6, 231, 263
Rhufoniog Uwch Aled, cmt., 225–6, 231
Rhunallt, daughter of k. of Man, 37–8
Rhuthun, 428, 436, 528
Rhyd Chwima (the ford of Montgomery), 121–2, 126, 129, 132–3, 144, 147, 161, 177, 311, 343–5, 353–4, 360–1, 367, 387–8
Llywelyn does homage at, 1–2, 179, 185–6, 277, 336, 389
Llywelyn called to swear fealty at, 359–60, 363, 445
Llywelyn and Edward meet at, 345, 348, 351
Rhyd-y-briw, cas., 252, 416–17
Rhys ab Ednyfed, 318, 344
Rhys ap Gruffudd, the Lord Rhys (d. 1197), of Deheubarth, 10–11, 21 n.69, 23, 140, 588
Rhys ap Gruffudd, bailiff of Builth, 315, 565 n.188
Rhys ap Gruffudd (ab Ednyfed Fychan), 247, 265–6, 430–3, 444–5, 477, 553, 555

660

Index

Rhys (d.1255) ap Maelgwn Fychan, of Ceredigion, 112
Rhys (d.1292) ap Maredudd (ap Rhys Gryg), of Ystrad Tywi, 24, 107–8, 410, 419–22, 457–8, 491, 523–5, 552
Rhys Fychan (d. 1302) ap Rhys ap Maelgwn Fychan, of Ceredigion, 112, 422, 443, 452, 459, 499–500, 502, 533, 571–2, 574
Rhys Fychan (d. 1271 ap Rhys Mechyll), of Ystrad Tywi, 68, 92–3, 97–100, 105–8, 112, 122, 127, 151, 169, 288, 293, 306, 311
Rhys Gryg (d. 1233), of Ystrad Tywi, 23–4, 31, 92, 420
Rhys Mechyll (d. 1244), of Ystrad Tywi, 55, 92
Rhys Wyndod (d. 1302), of Ystrad Tywi, 421–2, 452, 459–60, 489, 523, 525, 572, 575
   litigation before royal justices, 458, 489–93, 498
   grievances submitted to archbishop, 491
Riccardi of Lucca, 426–7
Richard, b. of Bangor (1236–67), 41, 43–4, 56–7, 180, 413
   agreement with Llywelyn, 208–10, 214–15, 381–2
   envoy to Henry III, 126–30, 290, 312, 322
   imprimatur on agreements between Llywelyn and the princes 114–15, 290–1
   residence at St Albans, 57
Richard, e. of Cornwall (d. 1272), 83, 87, 89, 96–7, 123, 161, 180, 347–8, 350–1, 353
Richard's Castle (Heref.), 163
Robert I, k. of Scots, *see* Bruce, Robert
Robinson, Nicholas, b. of Bangor (1566–85), 587
Rome, 173
   papal court, 52–3, 278, 280–1, 365, 379–80, 389; *see also* Lyons, Council of
   emissaries to, 312, 401
   letters to, 312, 326, 387–8
   see also Innocent III, Honorius III, Innocent IV, Clement IV, Gregory X, Adrian V, John XXI, Martin IV
   papal legates' mediation, 173–5, 177–8, 185–6, 335; *see also* Guala; Pandulf; Otto; Ottobuono
Rug, 230

Saillon (Valais, Switzerland), cas., 361
St Albans (Herts), Ben. abbey, 57, 101
St Asaph, dioc., 210–15, 516–17
   courts and jurisdiction, 204, 208, 210–15; *see also* Anian, b.
   b., 44, 114–15, 209–10, 287, 290–1, 325, 374, 403; *see also* Hywel ab Ednyfed; Einion; Anian
   dean and chapter, 210–15, 326–7
St Clears, cas. and lsp., 24

St David's, dioc., 290
   clergy, 115
St Deiniol, church of, *see* Bangor, cathedral church
St Edward, shrine of, Westminster, 332
St Georges d'Espéranche (*dép*. Isère), 361
St George, Stephen of, 567
St George, cross of, 573
St John, Order of Knights of, *see* Dolgynwal; Ysbyty Ifan
Salies, Béarn (*dép*. Pyr. Atl.), 366
Saracens, 407, 532–3
Sauveterre, Béarn (*dép*. Pyr. Atl,), 366
Savoy, county of, 361, 366; *see also* Amadeus; Philip
Scilly, Isles of, 396
Scota, daughter of Pharaoh, 336; *see also* Scotland, sense of history in
Scotland, 27, 173, 195, 280, 297, 324, 332, 475, 509, 527
   kingdom of, 274–9
   k. of 165, 274–80; *see also* David I; Alexander II; Alexander III; Robert I
   magnates of, 110–11, 115, 284, 310
   sense of history in, 335–6, 589
Segrwyd, 226
Sempringham (Lincs.), Gilb. priory, 564, 566, 580, 586
Senana, wife of Gruffudd (d. 1244) ap Llywelyn, 34, 37–9, 41, 69, 73
   agreement with Henry III (1241), 32–3, 35, 37, 41–2, 57
   lineage of, 45
Senghennydd, lsp., 176, 339–44, 347, 351–5
Senghennydd Is Caeach, cmt., 343–4, 351–3
   see also Caerffili
Senghennydd Uwch Caeach, cmt., 344
Sennybridge, cas., *see* Rhyd-y-briw
Shakespeare, William, 590
Shrewsbury, 32, 34–5, 128, 177–8, 180, 373–4, 383
   treaty negotiated at (1267), 1, 177–85, 314, 342
   Llywelyn called to do homage at (1274), 367–9, 382
   Ben. abbey, abbot of, 177
Shropshire, 142, 165, 184, 374, 383, 416, 566–7
Sicily, 101, 511
Siena, 512
Simpson, John, 541
Sisyphus, 510
Siward, Richard, 63
Sixhills (Lincs.), Gilb. priory, 579–80
Skenfrith, cas. and lsp., 150
Snowdon, 188, 576
   lord of, 25, 145–6, 188–9, 219
   lordship of, 187–273; *see also* Snowdonia
Snowdonia, 16, 50, 55, 59, 67, 76, 104, 113, 342, 387–8, 399, 417, 425–6, 430, 434–6, 442, 445, 500, 510, 526, 529–30, 554, 564, 575–6, 592–4

661

extent, 187–8
surveys and accounts, 191–2, 248
see also Gwynedd; Gwynedd Uwch Conwy; Perfeddwlad
Southampton, William of, Provincial of the Dominican Order, 437
Spain, 605
Springhose, Roger, 521, 559
Stirling Bridge, btl., 537, 563
Strata Florida (Ystrad Fflur), Cist. abbey, 28, 56, 95, 379, 381, 587
chronicle, *see* Brut y Tywysogyon
Strata Marcella, Cist. abbey, abbot of, 290
Stubbs, William, 140, 593
Sugwas (Heref.), 554
Surrey, e. of, *see* Warenne, John de
Swansea (Abertawe), cas. and bor., 24, 95, 102, 522
Sychdyn, 221, 226, 388

Talbot, Gilbert, justice of Chester, 82
Talgarth, lsp., 150
Talybolion, cmt., 66, 223
Tal-y-bont, cmt., 150, 220–1, 227–8, 243–4
Tal-y-cafn, 539
Talyllychau, Premonstratensian abbey, abbot of, 379–80
Tangwystl, mother of Gruffudd (d.1244) ap Llywelyn, 12–13
Tany, Luke de, 526–7, 529, 536–7, 541–2
Tedaldo Visconti, *see* Gregory X
Tegeingl (Englefield), ctf., 7, 34, 40, 50, 53, 61, 77–9, 190, 192, 194, 226, 249, 268, 427, 436, 439, 451, 453–4, 462–3,
grievances of community of (1282), 454–6, 461, 463–4
Teirswydd, 159, 371
Teirtref Esgob, 160, 184, 405
see also Aston; Bishop's Castle; Castle Wright; Mellington
Tempsiter (Shropshire), *see* Dyffryn Tefeidiad
Tewkesbury (Glouc.), Ben. abbey, chronicle, 29, 332
Thermopylae, 593–4
'Three Antiquities of Britain', *see* Tri Chof Ynys Brydain
Three Cantreds, the, 79–80
Three Castles of Gwent, the, 150; *see also* Grosmont; Skenfrith; White Castle
Tibetot, Robert, 437, 444, 458, 490, 513, 521–6
Tir Iarll, 102
Tony, family, 150 n.39, 130
Tony, Roger de, 168 n.115, 183, 340 n.8
Traeth Lafan, 539, 541
Trahaearn ap Hywel, 121
Trahaearn ap Madog, 417, 460 n.43
Treberfedd, 222
Trecastell, 217, 222
Treferwydd, 223

Tref Feibion Meurig, 222,
Trefgored, 227
Trefilan, 525
Trefioseth, 223
Trefriw, 229
Tregarnedd, 217, 266, 555
Tretower, lsp., 356; *see also* Ystrad Yw
Treuddyn, 388–9
Trevet, Nicholas, 393–4, 467
Tri Chof Ynys Brydain, 589
Troy, 335–6
men of, 101, 190, 545–6
legendary history of, 510, 588–9; *see also* Historia Regum Britanniae
Tudur ab Ednyfed, 45, 132, 179, 181, 265, 287, 327–8, 384, 437–8, 546
distain, justice of Wales, 204, 313–14, 328
Tudur ap Goronwy (ab Ednyfed Fychan), 265, 432 n.160, 576
Tudur ap Goronwy, of Cyfeiliog, 317
Tudur ap Gruffudd, 433
Tudur ap Madog, 44, 51, 113, 263
Tudur Fychan, 433
Turberville, Hugh de, 356–7, 513 n.13
Twrcelyn, cmt., 66, 221, 223, 237
Twrgarw, 263

Uchaf, cmt., *see* Arllechwedd Uchaf
Usk, cas., 171
Uwch Aled, cmt., *see* Rhufoniog Uwch Aled
Uwch Dulas, cmt., *see* Rhos Uwch Dulas
Uwch Gwyrfai, cmt., *see* Arfon Uwch Gwyrfai

Valence, William de (d. 1296), 95, 119, 141–2, 166 n.103, 521–6, 560, 572, 574–5
Valence, William de, the younger (d. 1282), 521
Valle Crucis, Cist. abbey, 379–80
abbot of, 326–7, 379–81, 384; *see* Madog
Vaughan, Robert, 377 n.134, 383 n.155, 590, 596
Vegetius, 414, 419, 434, 513, 526
Venables, William de, 461–2
Vere, Robert de, e. of Oxford (d. 1296), 174
Viennois (*dép.* Isère), 361
Viterbo (Latium, Italy), 391–2
Vortigern, 552

Walerand, Robert, 178
Wales, barons of, *see* lords
bishops of, 128–9
professions of obedience, 114–15
relations with princes: *see* Anian, b. of Bangor; Anian, b. of St Asaph; Einion, b. of St Asaph; Hywel ab Ednyfed, b. of St Asaph; Richard, b. of Bangor
conquest of, 511–81
ethos of, 331, 517–19, 530, 567
historical writing after the conquest, 587–90

Index

kingdoms of, princes' inheritance from, 5–20, 187–201
law of,
  law texts, 5, 8–9, 201–5, 269–71, 320, 482–3; *see also Llyfr Colan; Llyfr Iorwerth*
  law in political discourse:
  custom of Wales and partition of baronies, 32–4, 59–60, 69–70
  provision under treaty of Woodstock (1247), 61
  claimed by lords of Deheubarth (1247–56), 48, 62–4
  claimed by communities of Perfeddwlad (1247–56), 79–80, 82–3
  provision under treaty of Aberconwy (1277), 439, 470–1, 473–7
  claimed (1277–82) by Llywelyn ap Gruffudd, 470–89, 504–6; Dafydd ap Gruffudd, 461–2; lords of Deheubarth and Powys Fadog, 458–9, 485, 489–93; communities of Rhos and Tegeingl, 454–5, 463–4
  marcher lords' view of, 471–2
  Edward I's alleged view of, 475
  Archbishop Pecham's critical appraisal of, 480–1
  examined by king and council (1278–81), 477–9, 482–9
  inquiry by Edward I (1281), 202, 204, 479, 483–5
  Edward I's denial of Welsh law alleged by Llywelyn, 487, 533
  practice of:
  arbitration, 201–3
  collective judgement, 203, 301
  dower provision, 305
  dynastic succession, 8–11
  function of *ynad llys (iudex curie)*, 204, 319
  hostages as pledges, 482
  judgement on land in dispute, 482
  judgement by the *ynad (iudex)*, 201, 301–2, 319–20, 482–5
  judgement upon four successive defaults in plea of land, 491
  legendary history of, 278, 543–4; *see also Historia Regum Britanniae*
lords of, allegiance of, sought by Llywelyn ap Iorwerth, 17–22, 26–9
  retained by crown, 19, 21–2, 29–31, 34, 59
  sought by Llywelyn ap Gruffudd, 108–10, 114–38, 152–5, 167–70;
  retained by crown and (1267) conceded, 137–8, 178–86
  contested by prince and king (1277), 418–24; (1282–3), 451–2, 457–63, 514–15; 519–26, 550, 571–2, 574–7
  grievances of (1277–82), 489–93
march of, conflict in, 17–20, 94–7, 102–3, 121–2, 125–34, 136–7, 139–41, 144–52, 155–68, 172–3, 176, 339–48, 350–9, 362–3, 383, 386–7, 411, 415–18, 424–5; *see also* Brecon; Builth; Glamorgan; Gwerthrynion; Maelienydd
  disputes resolved by arbitration, 130–4, 343–5; *see also* Rhyd Chwima
  Wepre forces from march engaged in war in Gwynedd (1277), 429–30
  law, liberties and regality of, 63, 329–30, 354–5, 439, 470–2
  lords' relations with princes, *see* Bohun, Humphrey de, e. of Hereford (d. 1298); Clare, Gilbert de, e. of Gloucester; Llywelyn ap Iorwerth; Llywelyn ap Gruffudd; Mortimer, Roger
nation (*natio, gens, lingua Wallensica*), 116, 123–4, 131–2
  nation and language, 331
  nation and law, 474–7
  nation and principality, 331–7, 492, 604–5
prince of,
  heraldic arms, 494 n.161
  seal, 332, 552
  status, 274–81
  style, 1, 53, 110, 145–6, 180, 283–5, 334, 571
  terms *princeps, tywysog,* 281–5
  see Dafydd ap Llywelyn; Llywelyn ap Gruffudd; Dafydd ap Gruffudd
princess of, *see* Montfort, Eleanor de;
principality of, *acta,* 319–29
  barons or magnates of, *see* lords of
  creation and destruction of,
  origin of the notion, 17–22, 26–9, 281–6, 295
  as conceived by Llywelyn ap Gruffudd, 188–9, 543–4
  as political objective, 17–22, 26–9, 108–10, 114–38, 152–5, 167–70
  conceded by Montfort (1265), Henry III (1267), 1, 166–9, 178–86
  put at risk, 385–9, 406–8
  dismembered and destroyed (1277), 414–45
  as conceived after the conquest, 582–4
  historical awareness, 587–99
  see also Llywelyn ap Iorwerth; Llywelyn ap Gruffudd
  functionaries and institutions of:
  court and council, 298–301, 303–4, 309–19, 370–1
  distain or *justiciarius,* 204–5, 328; *see also* Tudur ab Ednyfed
  ministerial servants, 312–16
insignia and relics of:
  coronet (*talaith*), 332–3
  Croes Naid, 199, 333–5, 580–1, 584
  seal, 332, 552
political community, 333–4, 386

status
  constitutional status, 274–85
  iura, status, 123–4, 292, 333, 360
  principality and marcher regality, 329–30
  status reflected in Statute of Wales (1284), 181–2
  structure and organization:
  contractual obligations of prince and lords, 285–92
  financial organization, 294–7
  jurisdictional organization, 297–304
  military organization, 292–4
  Statute of (1284), 181–2, 188, 582–3
  Union, with England (1536), 584
Wales, John of, Franc. friar, 531, 535, 542
Wallace, William, 590
Waltham, Nicholas de, canon of Lincoln, 395, 497
Warenne, John de, e. of Surrey (d. 1304), 125, 166 n.103, 250, 406, 411, 520 n.40, 529
Warrington, William, 591, 593–5
Warwick, e. of, *see* Beauchamp, William, e. of
Watkins, Henry, 592
Welshpool, cas., 94, 160, 294, 371 n.119, 373, 416
Wenlock (Shropshire), Cluniac priory, prior of, 129, 360
Weobley (Heref.), cas., 149
Wepre, 124–5, 132
Westminster, 28, 49–50, 80, 129–30, 144, 347, 352, 365, 367, 504, 584
  chronicle, 332
  church, 345
  parliament at, 274
  pleas at, 477–9, 481
White Castle, cas. and lsp., 150
Whitland, Cist. abbey, 349, 420
Whittington, lsp., 168, 183–4
Wig, 234
Wigmore, cas. and lsp., 19–20, 140–1, 147–9, 161, 166, 175, 559
  lineage of, 41–3
  lord of, *see* Mortimer, Edmund; Mortimer, Ralph; Mortimer, Roger (d. 1282)
William ap Daniel, 323

William, e. of Mar (d. 1281), 110
Williams, William, Llandygái, 591, 594–5
Williams-Jones, Keith, 251
Winchester, 402
  b. of, 406
Windsor, cas., 56–7, 129, 161, 401
Woodstock, 64, 102, 105
  treaty of (1247), 58–60, 70, 78–9, 86, 168
Woodward, B. B., 591, 595
Worcester, 28, 163, 406, 422
  agreement at (1218), 21–2, 24–5
  cathedral church, marriage of Llywelyn at, 398, 448–9, 497
  chronicle, 398
Wrexham, 379
Wriothesley, Thomas, 274–5
Wynn, John, of Gwydir, 40, 45, 50
Wyrion Ednyfed, 217, 261, 263

Ynys Lannog (Priestholm), Aug. priory, 66, 69, 206
York, province of, 413
  abp., 387, 412, 515–16, 549
Ysbyty Ifan, Hospital of St John, 206
Ysgeifiog, 517
Ystrad Alun, *see* Mold
Ystrad Fflur, *see* Strata Florida
Ystrad Geirch, 239
Ystrad Marchell, cmt., 159, 371, 416
  Cist. abbey, abbot of, *see* Strata Marcella
Ystrad Owain, 225
Ystrad Tywi, 23–5, 31, 55, 68, 92–3, 97–101, 105–8, 112, 306, 316, 318, 346, 418–21, 452, 458, 489, 491
  conflict in (1277), 418–21; (1282) 521–5, 560, 575
  lords of, 288, 327, 490; *see also* Maredudd ap Rhys Gryg; Rhys ap Maredudd; Rhys Fychan; Rhys Gryg; Rhys Mechyll; Rhys Wyndod
Ystrad Yw, lsp., 150; *see also* Tretower
Ystumanner, cmt., 159, 221, 227–8, 242–3, 370
Ystumgwern, 221, 228, 237
Yverdon (Vaud, Switzerland), cas., 361

Zusche, Alan la, justice of Chester, 71, 78–83